CW00750709

Who's Who
in the Age of
Alexander and his Successors

Who's Who

in the Age of

Alexander and his Successors

From Chaironeia to Ipsos
(338–301 BC)

WALDEMAR HECKEL

GREENHILL BOOKS

CASEMATE

Who's Who in the Age of Alexander
First published in 2021 by
Greenhill Books,
c/o Pen & Sword Books Ltd,
47 Church Street, Barnsley,
S. Yorkshire, S70 2AS

www.greenhillbooks.com
contact@greenhillbooks.com

ISBN: 978–1–78438–648–1

_____

Published in the United States of America in 2021 by
CASEMATE PUBLISHERS
1950 Lawrence Road, Havertown, PA 19083, USA

Hardcover edition: 9-781-61200-983-4
Digital edition: 9-781-61200-984-1

_____

CIP data records for this title are available from the British Library

Designed and typeset by Donald Sommerville

Printed and bound in the UK by TJ Books Ltd, Padstow

Typeset in 10.2/11.8 pt Garamond Premier Pro

Cover illustrations: By courtesy of the British Library – Digital Store 012631.l.7.

For Sabine Müller

Contents

Foreword

Waldemar Heckel has created a triumph of scholarship in his *Who's Who in the Age of Alexander and his Successors* that will hold its place as the standard reference far into the future. This is not the work of a diligent pedant but an act of heartfelt communion with countless ghosts of an age rarely equaled in its daring and drama.

This communion the Greeks called *nekyia* or *nekya* (νέκυια ἡ νέκυα), the summoning of ghosts to ask them of the future. We find it first in Homer's *Odyssey*. In Chapter 11 Odysseus relates the rite:

> I took the victims, over the trench I cut their throats
> and the dark blood flowed in—and up out of Erebus they came,
> flocking toward me now, the ghosts of the dead and gone . . .
> Brides and unwed youths and old men who had suffered much
> and girls with their tender hearts freshly scarred by sorrow
> and great armies of battle dead, stabbed by bronze spears,
> men of war still wrapped in bloody armor—thousands
> swarming around the trench from every side—[1]

Heckel may not have been seeking to know the future or have been as fearful as Odysseus was at this moment, but in the preparation of this work, the ghosts of Macedonians, Greeks, Persians, Egyptians, Sogdians, Indians surely swarmed around him whispering, "Do not forget me!" "Remember my deeds." "No, this did not happen this way." "I held the shield over Alexander when he was wounded in the Mallian fort."

This writer experienced much the same thing when editing the first edition of what would become *The Greenhill Book of Military Quotations*. I was an Army intelligence analyst burning the candle at both ends during the Gulf War in the early months of 1991. At night I would put in another shift typing in the thousands of quotations. I felt the presence of the men and women I quoted. When asked at her trial how she got the French soldiers to perform such prodigious acts of valor, Joan of Arc, replied, "I tell them to go boldly in among the English and then go boldly in myself." She was there, too, in my reveries. Think how much more Alexander would have loved her, rather than the Sogdian Roxanne.

This book is a significant clarification and expansion of its first edition, *Who's Who in the Age of Alexander the Great: Prosopography of Alexander's Empire* (2006). The number of entries in the new edition increases by 43 percent to almost 1,200. In this current edition the entries are helpfully numbered. As someone of Greek origin, I was delighted that he put the names into their Greek forms rather than their latinized ones, for example, Demetrios rather than Demetrius. The exceptions are the names so commonly imbedded in the public's mind in their anglicized forms such as Alexander instead of Alexandros; Philip instead of Philippos; Ptolemy instead of Ptolemaios.

---

1. Homer, *The Odyssey*, tr. Robert Fagles (New York: Penguin, 1996), p. 250.

Darius on the other hand retains his hellenized name of Dareios. Each entry begins with the name in Greek or the hellenized forms for non-Macedonians/Greeks. Happily, there is a Concordance at the end of the book which tells those who have used or own the previous edition, where the entries dedicated to individuals (under Latin headings) in that volume can now be found. Hence, it includes only those 820 or so individuals that were in the original *Who's Who*.

In addition to numbering the entries, Heckel has organized them to make them more user friendly. Each entry begins with the nationality and patronymic where possible. The use of the patronymic in the genitive case is still a feature of modern Greek names, as the middle name. This is a vital feature considering how many names were common among Macedonians and Greeks. In this book there are 15 Alexanders, 22 Philips, 21 Demetrios's, 14 Amyntas's, and 9 Ptolemies and Nikanors. Aside from The Invincible One, Aniketos himself, the patronymic is often vital to understanding who is who.

References are peppered throughout each entry such as the following for Alexander's decision to end his expedition in India: (Arr. 5.25.1-29.1; Curt. 9.2.1–3.19; Diod. 17.93.2–95.2; 62; Metz Epit. 68–9; Justin 12.8.9–17). Abbreviations for classical sources are, for the most part, those used by the *Oxford Classical Dictionary*.

Heckel's parents were German refugees from the Soviet occupation of Eastern Europe: his mother was deported from the Sudetenland and his father from West Prussia. They were settled in Bad Königshofen, Unterfranken (northern Bavaria), where Waldemar was born in 1949. The family emigrated in 1953 to Canada, initially to Dawson Creek, British Columbia, the beginning of the Alaska Highway. He spent most of his young life on Vancouver Island.

Heckel gained his master's degree in 1973 from McMaster University in Hamilton, Ontario, and his doctorate in 1978 at the University of British Columbia in Vancouver, BC. He taught as a professor of ancient history at the University of Calgary from July 1977 until his retirement in December 2013. He is recognized internationally as a distinguished researcher and author on Alexander the Great.

When asked by this writer what led him to classical history, he remarked, "When I was an undergraduate, I met fellow students who were carrying around volumes in the Penguin Classics series. I started reading some of these: Homer, Herodotus, Thucydides and became hooked on the ancient world. It was one of my greatest pleasures to produce (along with John Yardley) the Penguin of Q. Curtius Rufus in 1984." He and Pat Wheatley provided the commentary on J. C. Yardley's new translation of Justin: *Epitome of the Philippic History of Pompeius Trogus*: Volume II: *Books 13–15: The Successors to Alexander the Great* (Clarendon Ancient History Series), 2011.

His first major book, based on his dissertation, was *Alexander's Marshals: A Study of the Makedonian Aristocracy and the Politics of Military Leadership*, 1993 & 2016. Other works include: *Macedonian Warrior: Alexander's Elite Infantryman*, 2006; *The Conquests of Alexander the Great* (Key Conflicts of Classical Antiquity), 2007; *The Wars of Alexander the Great*, 2002 & 2020; *In the Path of Conquest: Resistance to Alexander the Great*, 2020. Additionally, he has co-authored a number of other books. He has written a vast number of articles; the bibliography of this work cites fifty of his articles and another nine he co-authored.

Who's Who in the Age of Alexander and his Successors is the culmination of a half century of loving and skilled scholarship by a distinguished historian. I have no doubt it will quickly establish itself as a reference masterpiece of that long-ago age that still echoes with the tramp of armies and the *pothos* of the invincible Alexander. I cannot praise it too highly.

Peter G. Tsouras
Lt. Col., USAR (ret.)

Preface

The core of this volume appeared in 2006 under the title *Who's Who in the Age of Alexander the Great: Prosopography of Alexander's Empire* and treated (with a few exceptions) individuals who made their first appearance in the historical accounts before 323, the year of the Conqueror's death. Some 820 persons were included in that volume. The unnumbered entries were headed by names in their Latin forms (see the Concordance at the end of this edition) and the method of referencing ancient sources was idiosyncratic and not always clear. Nevertheless the book quickly replaced Helmut Berve's *Das Alexanderreich auf prosopographischer Grundlage* (Munich, 1926)—or, more precisely, the second volume of Berve's study—as a primary resource for Alexander scholars and enthusiasts, in large part because it was written in English. Like all prosopographies, it was not without its errors and omissions. Nor, despite my greatest efforts, do I believe the current volume will be entirely satisfactory. What I have attempted to do is to enlarge the scope of the work (to call it a second edition would thus be only half correct), adding roughly 350 new individuals and presenting them in a way that can be more easily cited by users. Entries are numbered consecutively; names are given in their Greek forms (except where they have been named exclusively by Latin authors); citations of ancient works employ (for the most part) the abbreviations listed in the *Oxford Classical Dictionary*. It should, however, be clear that Aesch. stands for Aeschines and not Aeschylus. This prosopography covers the period 338–301, but includes events after 301 when they involve leading individuals—in the case of Pyrrhos down to his death in 272—or members of the most prominent families (as reflected in the stemmata at the end of the volume).

I have excluded from my catalogue those people who appear only in the history of Agathokles of Sicily, in the Italian or Sicilian campaigns of Pyrrhos, and those whose careers belonged solely to the period 300–272. Leading individuals from Greek city-states, particularly Athens and Sparta, are discussed only if their careers had a direct bearing on the activities of the Diadochoi. The mere appearance of an individual on an inscription dating to this period is not sufficient in itself to warrant inclusion; archons, elected officials, proposers of decrees, religious functionaries, are all omitted if they are not otherwise engaged with the leading personalities of this period. With only a few exceptions, I have also excluded individuals about whom the record shows only that they received grants of land or were sent as envoys to shrines. I have tried as much as possible to avoid being dragged into the quagmire of Athenian politics, a subject treated in depth by scholars more familiar with this material than I am. Inconsistency is both unavoidable and necessary.

It also seemed to me that the majority of readers who turn to this volume will be interested in sorting out the large and confusing cast of characters in the historical literature; for I believe that the conventional way of approaching the history of the age is through the Greek and Latin texts. This is particularly true now that readers can consult the excellent English translation of Diodorus, Books 16–20, by Robin Waterfield in the

Oxford World's Classics series, and J. C. Yardley's translation of the relevant books of Justin in the Clarendon Ancient Histories series (which include commentaries by myself and P. V. Wheatley). Once the historical narratives have begun to dry up, we are confronted with the anecdotal evidence in biographers and writers such as Athenaeus, Polyaenus, and Frontinus, the geographers and antiquarians; and this information is supplemented but rarely complemented by epigraphic and numismatic evidence. Hence, individuals appear virtually in isolation or with often imprecise reference to leading figures and events, and to add them without detailed discussion of context would have only limited value. They have, indeed, been discussed in other volumes in the kind of depth that could not be attempted here. But, where my treatment of individuals and events disappoints, the reader will find other more certain guides in the scholarly literature. I have, therefore, not mined the corpus of inscriptions, a collection that grows steadily, always fraught with problems of text and context. Instead, I have begun with the literary texts, which provide a convenient introduction to the world of Alexander and his Successors, and supplemented the information found in them with the fruits of epigraphic research, relying to a great extent, though not exclusively, on the judgment of other scholars. Without the expertise of epigraphers, my task would have been even more difficult. Indeed, as I was finishing my work during six months of Covid-19 isolation, many published collections of inscriptions were inaccessible on account of library closures. My debt to the fine work of Pascalis Paschidis is thus even greater and will become evident in the pages that follow.

Whether one likes to admit it or not, the publisher has the ultimate power to shape the scope, length, and content of a book. In this case, I am grateful to Michael Leventhal for allowing me to exceed the original word limit by 20 percent.

This brings me to the pleasant task of thanking the many people who have supported me in this endeavor (and others as well). I express my gratitude and affection for a long list of friends, colleagues, and students: Lindsay Adams, Sheila Ager, John Atkinson, Elizabeth Baynham, Richard Billows, Gene Borza, Pierre Briant, Beth Carney, Christopher Collom, Monica D'Agostini, Erin Garvin, Bill Greenwalt, Franca Landucci Gattinoni, Alexander Meeus, Daniel Ogden, Marek Olbrycht, Jeanne Reames, Yossi Roisman, Gordon Shrimpton, Carol Thomas, Carolyn Willekes, and Graham Wrightson. The late Miguel Alonso-Nuñez urged me to publish the earlier version of this prosopography, Al Bertrand of Wiley-Blackwell made that a reality, and both Peter Green and Brian Bosworth used their unrivaled authority to persuade prospective readers of that book's merits. I am most grateful to Michael Leventhal of Greenhill Books for his willingness, on the recommendation of Peter Tsouras, to publish this new version. I thank Donald Sommerville for his diligent attention to my typescript and for his skill and care in bringing this volume into print. My longtime friend, Stan Burstein, saved me from numerous errors and helped persuade me to set Ipsos as my lower limit. The impressive new biography of Demetrios by Pat Wheatley and Charlotte Dunn (*Demetrius the Besieger,* Oxford, 2020) arrived just as I was finishing my work, and I wish that I had been able to make more extensive use of it. Yuri Kuzmin kindly kept me up to date on recent publications in the field, as did Maxim Kholod. I am similarly indebted to Hans Hauben and David Whitehead, who promptly heeded my call for help and sent me materials and much needed advice. Ed Anson, Johannes Heinrichs, Timothy Howe, Fred Naiden, Frances Pownall, and Larry Tritle have been a source of support and encouragement in the good and the bad times. My friend John Vanderspoel converted my crude stemmata into the polished versions found at the end of this volume, while Konrad Kinzl kept me amused via Skype and gave me the generous gift of those volumes of Niese and Berve that had once belonged to Fritz Schachermeyr's personal library. Most of all, I thank Sabine Müller, to whom this book is dedicated, for encouragement, support, and inspiration. My sister, Anneli Purchase, has once again helped with all the difficult tasks of proofreading and copy-editing. Finally, to Lois, to Julia, Kevin and Alexander, to Darren and Sarah, my love and appreciation. I conclude on a sad note, to give paws to those who read the Preface to the 2006 version: Subedei has gone to the Happy Mouse-Hunting Ground.

Waldemar Heckel

Abbreviations

Major Works

Anson   E. M. Anson. *Eumenes of Cardia. A Greek among Macedonians*. Leiden. 2004.

Anspach I–III   A. E. Anspach. *De Alexandri Magni expeditione Indica*. Leipzig. 1903.

Aulbach   Anika Aulbach. *Die Frauen der Diadochendynastien. Eine prosopographische Studie zur weiblichen Entourage Alexanders des Großen und seiner Nachfolger*. Munich. 2014.

Bagnall   R. Bagnall. *The Administration of Ptolemaic Possessions outside Egypt*. Leiden. 1976.

Baumbach   A. Baumbach. *Kleinasien unter Alexander dem Grossen*. Diss., Jena, publ. Weida i. Th. 1911.

Bayliss   A. Bayliss. *After Demosthenes. The Politics of Early Hellenistic Athens*. London. 2011.

Berthold   Richard M. Berthold. *Rhodes in the Hellenistic Age*. Ithaca and London. 1984.

Bevan, *Ptolemaic Dynasty*   E. R. Bevan. *A History of Egypt under the Ptolemaic Dynasty*. London. 1927.

Bevan, *Seleucus*   E. R. Bevan. *The House of Seleucus*. Vol. 1. London. 1902.

Bouché-Leclercq, *Lagides* I   A. Bouché-Leclercq. *Histoire des Lagides*. Vol. 1. Paris. 1903.

Bouché-Leclercq, *Séleucides*   A. Bouché-Leclercq. *Histoire des Séleucides*. Paris. 1913–14.

Briant   P. Briant. *From Cyrus to Alexander. A History of the Persian Empire*. Translated by Peter T. Daniels. Winona Lake. 2002.

Brosius   Maria Brosius. *Women in Ancient Persia (559–331 BC)*. Oxford. 1996.

Brown, *Onesicritus*   T. S. Brown. *Onesicritus. A Study in Hellenistic Historiography*. Berkeley and Los Angeles. 1949.

Buraselis   Kostas Buraselis. *Das hellenistische Makedonien und die Ägäis. Forschungen zur Politik des Kassandros und der drei ersten Antigoniden im Ägäischen Meer und in Westkleinasien*. Munich. 1982.

Burstein, *Outpost*   S. M. Burstein. *Outpost of Hellenism. The Emergence of Heraclea on the Black Sea*. Berkeley and Los Angeles. 1976.

Droysen   J. G. Droysen. *Geschichte des Hellenismus*. 3rd edn, Darmstadt. 1980.

Eggermont   P. H. L. Eggermont. *Alexander's Campaign in Sind and Baluchistan and the Siege of the Brahmin Town of Harmatelia*. Leuven. 1975.

Ferguson   W. S. Ferguson. *Hellenistic Athens: An Historical Essay*. London. 1911.

Fraser   P. M. Fraser. *Cities of Alexander the Great*. Oxford. 1996.

Fuller   J. F. C. Fuller. *The Generalship of Alexander the Great*. New York. 1960.

Garoufalias   P. Garoufalias. *Pyrrhus. King of Epirus*. London. 1979.

Giannantoni I–II   Gabriele Giannantoni. *Socraticorum Reliquiae*. Vols. I–II. Rome. 1983.

Goukowsky I–II   P. Goukowsky. *Essai sur les origins du mythe d'Alexandre*. 2 vols. Nancy. 1981.

Habicht[2]   Chr. Habicht. *Gottmenschentum und griechische Städte*. 2nd edition. Munich. 1970.

Habicht, *Pausanias*   Chr. Habicht. *Pausanias' Guide to Ancient Greece*. Berkeley and Los Angeles. 1985; reprinted with a new preface in 1998 .

Hatzopoulos I–II   M. B. Hatzopoulos. *Macedonian Institutions under the Kings*. 2 volumes. Athens. 1996.

Heckel   Waldemar Heckel. *In the Path of Conquest. Resistance to Alexander the Great*. Oxford. 2020.

Heinen   H. Heinen. *Untersuchungen zur hellenistischen Geschichte des 3. Jahrhunderts v. Chr.: Zur Geschichte der Zeit des Ptolemaios Keraunos und zum Chremonideischen Krieg.* Wiesbaden. 1972.

Herzfeld   E. Herzfeld. *The Persian Empire. Studies in Geography and Ethnography of the Ancient Near East.* Wiesbaden. 1968.

Hill I   G. Hill. *A History of Cyprus.* Vol. 1. Cambridge. 1949.

HMac II   N. G. L. Hammond and G. T. Griffith. *History of Macedonia.* Vol. 2. Oxford. 1979.

HMac III   N. G. L. Hammond and F. W. Walbank. *History of Macedonia.* Vol. 3. Oxford. 1988.

Hornblower, *Hieronymus*   J. Hornblower. *Hieronymus of Cardia.* Oxford. 1981.

Hornblower, *Mausolus*   S. Hornblower. *Mausolus.* Oxford. 1982.

Jacobs   B. Jacobs. *Die Satrapienverwaltung im Perserreich zur Zeit Dareios' III.* Wiesbaden. 1994.

Judeich   W. Judeich. *Kleinasiatische Studien.* Marburg. 1892.

Julien   P. Julien. *Zur Verwaltung der Satrapien unter Alexander dem Grossen.* Weida. 1914.

Kaerst I³–II³   J. Kaerst. *Geschichte des Hellenismus.* 3rd edn. Leipzig and Berlin. 1926–7.

Karttunen   K. Karttunen. *India in the Hellenistic World.* Helsinki. 1997.

Krumbholz   P. Krumbholz. *De Asiae Minoris Satrapis Persicis.* Diss. Leipzig. 1883.

Landucci, *Lisimaco*   F. Landucci Gattinoni. *Lisimaco di Tracia: Un sovrano nella prospettiva del primo ellenismo.* Milan. 1992.

Lane Fox   R. Lane Fox. *Alexander the Great.* London. 1973.

Lassen I–IV²   Chr. Lassen. *Indische Altertumskunde.* 4 vols. 2nd edition. Leipzig. 1861–74.

Lund   Helen S. Lund. *Lysimachos. A Study in Early Hellenistic Kingship.* London. 1992.

McCrindle   J. W. McCrindle. *The Invasion of India by Alexander the Great.* London. 1896.

Niese   B. Niese. *Geschichte der griechischen und makedonischen Staaten seit der Schlacht bei Chaironeia.* Gotha. 1893.

Olmstead   A. T. Olmstead. *History of the Persian Empire.* Chicago. 1948.

Ormerod   Henry A. Ormerod. *Piracy in the Ancient World.* Liverpool. 1924 [repr. Baltimore. 1997].

Pearson   L. Pearson. *The Lost Histories of Alexander the Great.* Philadelphia. 1960.

Rawlinson   G. Rawlinson. *Phoenicia. History of a Civilization.* London. 1889.

Schachermeyr   F. Schachermeyr. *Alexander der Große. Das Problem seiner Persönlichkeit und seines Wirkens.* Vienna. 1973.

Schaefer   A. Schaefer. *Demosthenes und seine Zeit.* Vol. 3. 3rd edn, Leipzig. 1887.

Stewart   Andrew Stewart. *Faces of Power. Alexander's Image and Hellenistic Politics.* Berkeley and Los Angeles. 1993.

Tarn I–II   W. W. Tarn. *Alexander the Great.* 2 vols. Cambridge. 1948.

Tarn, *AG*   W. W. Tarn. *Antigonos Gonatas.* Oxford. 1913.

Weiskopf   M. Weiskopf. *The So-called "Great Satraps' Revolt," 366–30 BC. Concerning Local Instability in the Achaemenid Far West.* Wiesbaden. 1989.

Welles   C. Bradford Welles. *Diodorus of Sicily.* Vol. VIII. Loeb Classical Library. Cambridge, MA. 1963.

Werner   R. Werner. "Die Dynastie der Spartokiden." *Historia* 4:412–44. 1955.

Wheatley and Dunn   P. V. Wheatley and C. Dunn. *Demetrius the Besieger.* Oxford. 2020.

Prosopographies or Works that include Major Prosopographical or Onomastic Studies

Beloch III²–IV²   K. J. Beloch. *Griechische Geschichte.* 2nd edn, Vols. 3–4. Leipzig. 1927.

Bengtson I–II   H. Bengtson. *Die Strategie in der hellenistischen Zeit.* Darmstadt. 1937–52.

Berve I–II   H. Berve. *Das Alexanderreich auf prosopographischer Grundlage.* 2 vols. Munich. 1926.

Berve, *Tyrannis I–II*   H. Berve. *Die Tyrannis bei den Griechen.* 2 volumes. Munich. 1967.
Billows   R. A. Billows. *Antigonos the One-Eyed and the Creation of the Hellenistic State.* Berkeley and Los Angeles. 1990.
Bradford   A. S. Bradford. *Prosopography of Lakedaimonians from the Death of Alexander the Great, 323 BC, to the Sack of Sparta by Alaric, A.D. 396.* Munich. 1977.
Carney   E. D. Carney. *Women and Monarchy in Macedonia.* Norman. 2000.
Davies   J. K. Davies. *Athenian Propertied Families 600–300 BC.* Oxford. 1971.
Develin   R. Develin. *Athenian Officials 684–321 BC.* Cambridge. 1989.
Grainger, *APS*   J. D. Grainger. *Aitolian Prosopographic Studies.* Leiden. 2000.
Grainger, *SPG*   J. D. Grainger. *A Seleukid Prosopography and Gazetteer.* Leiden. 1997.
Gude   M. Gude. *A History of Olynthus with a Prosopographia and Testimonia.* Baltimore. 1933.
Hammond, *Epirus*   N. G. L. Hammond. *Epirus.* Oxford. 1967.
Hauben   H. Hauben. *Het Vlootbevelhebberschap in de vroege Diadochentijd (323–301 v. C.). Een prosopografisch en institutioneel onderzoek.* Brussels. 1975.
Heckel, *Marshals*[2]   Waldemar Heckel. *Alexander's Marshals. The Makedonian Aristocracy and the Politics of Military Leadership.* London and New York. 2016.
Hoffmann   O. Hoffmann. *Die Makedonen, ihre Sprache und ihr Volkstum.* Göttingen. 1906.
Hofstetter   J. Hofstetter. *Die Griechen in Persien: Prosopographie der Griechen im Persischen Reich vor Alexander.* Archäologische Mitteilungen aus Iran. Ergänzungsband 5. Berlin. 1978.
Justi   F. Justi. *Iranisches Namenbuch.* Marburg. 1895.
Kirchner   J. Kirchner. *Prosopographia Attika.* 1901–1903.
Launey   M. Launey. *Recherches sur les armées hellénistiques.* 2 vols. Paris. 1949–50.
Lehmann-Haupt   C. F. Lehmann-Haupt. "Satrap." *RE* IIA (1923) 82–188.
LGPN   *Lexicon of Greek Personal Names.* Oxford. 1987– .
Macurdy   Grace Macurdy. *Hellenistic Queens. A Study of Woman-power in Macedonia, Seleukid Syria and Ptolemaic Egypt.* Baltimore. 1932.
O'Connor   J. B. O'Connor. *Chapters in the History of Actors and Acting in Ancient Greece together with a Prosopographia Histrionum Graecorum.* Chicago. 1908.
Ogden   D. Ogden. *Prostitutes, Polygamy and Death. The Hellenistic Dynasties.* London. 1999.
Olshausen   E. Olshausen. *Prosopographie der hellenistischen Königsgesandten. Vol. 1. Von Triparadeisos bis Pydna.* Leuven. 1974.
Osborne   M. J. Osborne. *Naturalization in Athens.* 3 vols. Brussels. 1981–83.
PAA   J. Traill (ed.). *Persons of Ancient Athens.* Toronto. 1994– .
Pape-Benseler   W. Pape and G. Benseler. *Griechische Eigennamen.* Braunschweig. 1911.
Paschidis   Pascalis Paschidis. *Between City and King. Prosopographical Studies on the Intermediaries between the Cities of the Greek Mainland and the Aegean and the Royal Courts in the Hellenistic Period (322–190 BC).* Meletemata 59. Athens. 2008.
Pollitt   J. J. Pollitt. *The art of Ancient Greece. Sources and Documents.* Cambridge. 1990.
Poralla   P. Poralla. *Prosopographie der Lakedaimonier bis auf die Zeit Alexanders des Großen.* Breslau. 1913.
Rathmann   M. Rathmann. *Perdikkas zwischen 323 und 320. Nachlassverwalter des Alexanderreiches oder Autokrat?* Vienna. 2005.
Sandberger   F. Sandberger. *Prosopographie zur Geschichte des Pyrrhos.* Stuttgart. 1970.
Shayegan   M. Rahim Shayegan. "Prosopographical Notes: The Iranian Nobility during and after the Macedonian Conquest." *Bulletin of the Asia Institute* n.s., 21 (2007) 97–126.
Sherwin-White   Sherwin-White. *Ancient Cos.* Hypomnemata, Heft 51. Göttingen. 1978.

ABBREVIATIONS

Tataki   A. B. Tataki. *Macedonians Abroad. A Contribution to the Prosopography of Ancient Macedonia*. Athens. 1998.

Tataki, *PB*   A. B. Tataki. *Ancient Beroia: Prosopography and Society*. Athens. 1988.

Translations and Commentaries

Atkinson I–II   J. E. Atkinson. *A Commentary on Q. Curtius Rufus'* Historiae Alexandri Magni. 2 vols. Amsterdam. 1980, 1994.

Atkinson and Yardley   *Curtius Rufus: Histories of Alexander the Great, Book 10*. Commentary by J. E. Atkinson; translation by J. C. Yardley. Oxford. 2009.

Auberger   J. Auberger. *Historiens d'Alexandre*. Paris. 2001.

Austin²   M. M. Austin. *The Hellenistic World from Alexander the Great to the Roman Conquest*. 2nd edition. Cambridge. 2006.

Bosworth I–II   A. B. Bosworth. *A Historical Commentary on Arrian's* History of Alexander. 2 vols. Oxford. 1980, 1995.

Brunt I–II   P. A. Brunt. *Arrian. The History of Alexander and Indica*. Loeb Classical Library. 2 vols. Cambridge, MA. 1976, 1983.

Burstein   S. M. Burstein. *The Hellenistic Age from the Battle of Ipsos to the Death of Kleopatra VII*. Translated Documents of Greece and Rome, Vol. 3. Cambridge. 1985.

Gow, *Machon*   A. S. F. Gow. *Machon*. Cambridge. 1965.

Hamilton   J. R. Hamilton. *Plutarch,* Alexander: *A Commentary*. Oxford. 1969.

Harding   P. Harding. *From the end of the Peloponnesian War to the Battle of Ipsos*. Translated Documents of Greece and Rome, Vol. 2. Cambridge. 1985.

Heisserer   A. J. Heisserer. *Alexander and the Greeks: The Epigraphic Evidence*. Norman. 1980.

Long and Sedley I–II   A. A. Long and D. N. Sedley. *The Hellenistic Philosophers*. 2 vols. Cambridge. 1987.

Nederlof   A. B. Nederlof. *Plutarchus' Leven van Pyrrhus. Historische Commentaar*. Paris. 1940.

R&O   P. J. Rhodes and Robin Osborne (eds.). *Greek Historical Inscriptions 404–323 BC*. Oxford. 2003.

Roisman and Worthington   *Lives of the Attic Orators. Texts from Pseudo-Plutarch, Photius, and the* Suda. Introduction and Commentary by J. Roisman and Ian Worthington; translation by Robin Waterfield. Oxford. 2015.

Stronk   Jan P. Stronk. *Semiramis' Legacy. The History of Persia According to Diodorus of Sicily*. Edinburgh. 2017.

Walbank, *HCP*   F. W. Walbank. *A Historical Commentary on Polybius*. 3 vols. Oxford. 1957–79.

Waterfield   R. Waterfield (tr.). *Diodorus of Sicily. The Library, Book 16–20. Philip II, Alexander the Great, and the Successors*. OWC. Oxford. 2019.

Welles   C. Bradford Welles (tr.). *Diodorus of Sicily. Library of History*. Vol. VIII. Books 16.66–17. Cambridge, MA. 1963.

Welles, *RC*   C. Bradford Welles. *Royal Correspondence in the Hellenistic Period*. New Haven. 1934.

Worthington   I. Worthington. *A Historical Commentary on Dinarchus. Rhetoric and Conspiracy in Later Fourth-Century Athens*. Ann Arbor. 1992.

Yardley   J. C. Yardley (tr.). *Q. Curtius Rufus. The History of Alexander*. Penguin. Harmondsworth. 1984.

Yardley and Heckel   *Justin. Epitome of the* Philippic History *of Pompeius Trogus*. Volume 1: *Alexander the Great*. Translated by J. C. Yardley; Commentary by Waldemar Heckel. Oxford. 1996.

Yardley–Wheatley–Heckel   *Justin. Epitome of the* Philippic History *of Pompeius Trogus.*
Volume 2: *The Successors to Alexander the Great.* Translated by J. C. Yardley; Commentary
by Pat Wheatley and Waldemar Heckel. Oxford. 2011.

Collections of Inscriptions and Fragments, Dictionaries and Encyclopaedias

Arnim, *SVF*   H. von Arnim. *Stoicorum Veterum Fragmenta.* 1903–.

Barr. Atl.   *The Barrington Atlas of the Greek and Roman World.* R. J. A. Talbert (ed.).
Princeton. 2000.

BNJ   *Brill's New Jacoby.* I. Worthington ed. Online.

BNP   *Brill's New Pauly.*

CAH²   *The Cambridge Ancient History.* Second edition.

DNP   *Der Neue Pauly.*

FGrH   F. Jacoby, *Die Fragmente der griechischen Historiker.* Berlin-Leiden. 1923– .

FHG   C. Müller. *Fragmenta Historicorum Graecorum.*

I.Cret   M. Guarducci. *Inscriptiones Creticae.* 4 vols. Rome. 1935–50.

I.Délos   *Inscriptions de Délos.*

I. di Cos   M. Ségre. *Inscrizioni di Cos.* Rome. 1993.

I.Didyma   A. Rehm. *Die Inschriften. Milet.* Vol. 3. Berlin. 1914.

I.Ephesos   H. Wankel et al. *Die Inschriften von Ephesos.* 7 vols. Bonn. 1979–81.

IG   *Inscriptiones Graecae.* 2nd edn, Berlin. 1913– .

I.Ilion   P. Frisch. *Die Inschriften von Ilion.* Bonn. 1975.

I.Orop.   Basileios Ch. Petrakos. Οἱ ἐπιγραφὲς τοῦ Ὠρωποῦ. Athens. 1997.

I.Rhamn.   Basileios Ch. Petrakos. Ὁ δῆμος τοῦ Ραμνοῦντος. Σύνοψη τῶν ἀνασκαφῶν καὶ
τῶν ἐρευνῶν (1813–1998). Athens. 1999.

Kl. Pauly   *Der Kleine Pauly.*

LexAM   W. Heckel, J. Heinrichs, S. Müller, and F. Pownall (eds.). *Lexicon of Argead
Macedonia.* Berlin. 2020.

Michel, *RIG*   C. Michel. *Recueil d'inscriptions grecques.* Brussels. 1900.

Moretti, *ISE*   L. Moretti. *Iscrizione storiche ellenistiche.* 2 vols. Florence. 1965, 1970.

OGIS   W. Dittenberger. *Orientis Graeci Inscriptiones Selectae.* Leipzig. 1903–5.

PCG   R. Kassel and C. Austin. *Poetae Comici Graeci.* 2 vols. 1983, 1991.

RE   A. Pauly, G. Wissowa and W. Kroll (eds.). *Paulys Real-Encyclopädie der classischen
Altertumswissenschaft.* Stuttgart. 1894–1980.

Robert, *Coll. Froehner*   L. Robert. *Collection Froehner I: Inscriptions grecques.* Paris. 1936.

Schwenk   Cynthia J. Schwenk. *Athens in the Age of Alexander. The Dated Laws and Decrees
of the Lykourgan Era 338–322 BC.* Chicago. 1985. .

Schmitt, *Staatsvertr.* III   H. H. Schmitt. *Die Staatsverträge des Altertums,* vol. 3. Munich.
1969.

SEG   *Supplementum Epigraphicum Graecum.*

SH   H. Lloyd-Jones and P. Parsons (eds.). *Supplementum Hellenisticum.* Berlin. 1983.

Syll³   W. Dittenberger. *Sylloge Inscriptionum Graecarum.* 3rd edition. Leipzig. 1915–24.
Often cited in other works as *SIG³·*

Tod I–II   M. N. Tod (ed.). *Greek Historical Inscriptions.* 2 vols. 1946.

A

1 ABDALONYMOS

(Ἀβδαλώνυμος. Diod. 17.46.6 has Βαλ[λ]ώνυμος, Pollux 6.105: Ἀβδελλώνυμος; the form Abdalonymus appears in Curt. 4.1.19, 21, 23, 26; Justin 11.10.8; reasonably restored by Cobet from ἀραλυνομος in Plut. *Mor.* 340d). Abd-elonim = "servant of the gods" (Eissfeldt 1940–41; see also Peters 1941). An impoverished scion of the Sidonian royal house (Curt. 4.1.19: *longa quidem cognatione stirpi regiae adnexum*; Plut. *Mor.* 340c–d wrongly makes him one of the Kinyradai and removes him to Paphos on Kypros; Diod. 17.46.6 mistakenly places him in Tyre), A. was appointed king of Sidon in December 333 or January 332 in place of the deposed Straton (Abd-astart), the successor of Tennes (cf. also Berve no. 728; Straton no. 1084), who although he submitted to Alexander was considered loyal to Dareios III (Diod. 17.47.1; somewhat different in Curt. 4.1.16: *sed quia deditionem magis popularium quam sua sponte fecerat, regno visus indignus . . .*; Plut. *Mor.* 340c says A.'s predecessor ruled unjustly and wickedly: ἀδίκου καὶ πονηροῦ φανέντος). The selection of A. by Hephaistion (no. 513) is found only in Curtius and Diodorus: two "hosts" (*hospites*; a singular *xenos* in Diod. 17.47.2) of Hephaistion recommended A. for the kingship because of his exceptional nature and lifestyle, although he was constrained by poverty to work as a gardener; the man was found at his work, unperturbed by the war going on around him (Justin 11.10.9; Diod. 17.47.1–6; Curt. 4.1.17–26; for the motif, cf. Cincinnatus in Livy 3.26, but the story has Near Eastern antecedents: Drews 1974; Bosworth 2003a, 182–3; Burstein 2007). Despite its dramatic and cynic touches (Niese I 78 n.5), the Vulgate does give us some insight into the factional strife in Sidon, which was bound to accompany the defeat of Dareios and the arrival of foreign troops. A. was favored by the popular party (Diod. 17.47.6), which may indeed have played some part in securing the deposition of Straton (cf. Curt. 4.1.16); but opposition to the appointment came from the wealthy, who sought to influence Alexander's decision by lobbying his Companions (Curt. 4.1.19, 24). Alexander confirmed the selection of A., giving him some of the Persian booty captured at Issos and enlarging his territory (Curt. 4.1.26; cf. Briant 1015, with additional literature). According to Plut. *Mor.* 340d, A. was enrolled in Alexander's *hetairoi* (cf. Diod. 17.47.6: φίλος γενόμενος Ἀλεξάνδρῳ, a privilege which he appears to have extended to at least some of the kings of Kypros as well: cf. Arr. *Ind.* 18.8).

Of his activities during Alexander's lifetime, we hear only that A. sent Alexander a gift of perfume from henna and lilies (Pollux 6.105), Sidon being famed in antiquity for the former (Athen. 15.688f). A bilingual inscription from Kos (*SEG* XXXVI 758: [. . .]τιμος Ἀβδαλωνύμου [Σιδ]ῶνος βασιλέως) shows that Abd-elonim's name was not Graecized into Apollodoros and that he was thus not the father of Philokles as was previously thought (Merker 1970; cf. Atkinson I 281). A. had a son whose name survives only partially: a plausible restoration is [Dio]timos (no. 397). The accession of Philokles son of Apollodoros does, however, signal the end of A.'s line (see Grainger 1991, 63 and Billows 444–5 no. 129). Seibert 1970, 337 suggested that A. was supported by Ptolemy son of Lagos when he took over Syria from Laomedon in 319 but deposed by Antigonos Monophthalmos in 311 and replaced by Philokles (cf. Billows 444–5). The evidence for this is weak; nor is there anything to support the view of Graeve 1970 that A. died fighting for Demetrios in the battle of Gaza in 312. The theory that he was the occupant of the so-called Alexander Sarcophagus, as was suggested by Studniczka 1894 (cf. Schefold 1968), despite its inherent implausibilities, retains an unshakeable hold on art historians and those who accept their conclusions unquestioningly (Stewart 1993, 294–306, and 2014, 258; Queyrel 2011; Palagia 2017, 182; cf. the more cautious comments of Hauben 2004, 31–2 n.25). But the occupant appears to have been a Persian and to have fought in two major battles against Alexander. Neither of which suits A. See Heckel 2006 and below s.v. Mazaios (no. 685). J. Kaerst, *RE* I.1 (1893) 22; G. Wirth, *Kl. Pauly* I 6; Berve II 3 no. 1; Billows 444–5 no. 129.

2 ABISARES

(Ἀβισάρης). Aelian Ἀποσειράρης, Diod. 17.87.2 Ἐμβίσαρος, 17.90.4 Σασαβισάρης and Σαβαρσάνης. Dynast of Abhisara. Ruler of the Indians of the hill-country (ὄρειοι Ἰνδοί) bounded by the Indos or the Hydaspes on the west (that is, Kashmir; Arr. 5.8.3; Curt. 8.12.13; cf. Metz Epit. 53; see also Arr. *Ind.* 4.12). Cf. Jacobs 236–7, Abb. 1–2; 241–2; his realm was north of that of Taxiles but between the Hydaspes and the Akesines, according to Smith 1914, 59 n.1. The location of Abhisara is debated. Smith 1914, 59 n.1 follows Stein, who in 1910 located the kingdom between the Jhelum and the Chenab; but Stein 1929, 123 equates Abhisara with Hazara, which bordered on the Indos (see also Bosworth II 177; Eggermont 1970, 113–14). This area has, however, been equated with Urasa (thus Berve II 81 no. 147). Jacobs 236–7, Abb. 1–2, and 241–2, places A. in Kashmir and argues that Arsakes' kingdom must have been on the Akesines: "Einziger Anhaltspunkt dafür ist das Zusammentreffen des Arsakes mit Alexander den Großen am Akesines." But, since the Indians in the vicinity of Aornos fled to A. (Arr. 4.30.7) and since Arsakes' subordination to A. was confirmed by Alexander near the Akesines (Arr. 5.29.4), I would place Arsakes in Hazara, which is immediately adjacent to Kashmir. Megasthenes (*FGrH* 715 F9 = Arr. *Ind.* 4.12) mentions the Abissarians, mountain dwellers in whose territory the Soanos, a tributary of the Indos, rises (Tomaschek, *RE* I (1894) 101 s.v. "Abisareis"; cf. Pliny, *HN* 6.23.77, where *Abi Suri* should be emended to *Abisari*; they are the Abhisāras of the Mahābhārata, thus Karttunen 1997, 33).

According to Indian custom, he took his name from the territory he ruled. A. had known of Alexander's advance since at least winter 327/6: he sent troops to Ora ('Udegram') in a futile attempt to bolster its defenses (Arr. 4.27.7). After the fall of Aornos in 326, natives from the region between Dyrta and the Indos fled to him (Arr. 4.30.7), and he renewed his alliance with Poros (he was thus an enemy of Taxiles), with whom he had earlier conducted a rather ineffectual expedition against the Oxydrakai (Arr. 5.22.2). Although somewhat inferior in authority to Poros (Curt. 8.12.13), A. could muster an army of comparable size (Diod. 17.87.2); hence Alexander planned to attack the latter before A. could join forces with him (Diod. 17.87.3). A. did not, in fact, act in time to aid his ally (Curt. 8.14.1). Instead, he made (token?) submission to Alexander, content to await the outcome of events (Curt. 8.13.1; Arr. 5.8.3; Metz Epit. 55). After Poros' defeat, he sent a second delegation to Alexander (Curt. 9.1.7; Diod. 17.90.4; Arr. 5.20.5, who says he sent his own brother (**A84**) with some other envoys, bringing money and 40 elephants as gifts).

A. ignored Alexander's demand that he come in person (Curt. 9.1.7–8; Arr. 5.20.6; cf. Metz Epit. 65): instead he sent his brother, in concert with Arsakes, who ruled Hazara, and the envoys whom Alexander had sent to Abhisara (Metz Epit. 55 names a certain Nikokles, no. 795), bringing a further 30 elephants (Arr. 5.29.4) and offering the excuse that A. himself was too ill to present himself, a fact verified by Alexander's own agents. The King allowed A. to retain his kingdom and included in his administrative sphere Hazara, the hyparchy of Arsakes (Arr. 5.29.5). A. was, however, assessed an annual tribute (Arr. 5.29.5), which was probably due to the satrap of India between the Hydaspes and the Indos, Philip son of Machatas. Although A. is referred to as "satrap" by Arrian (5.29.5), his son doubtless followed an independent course of action after Alexander's return to the West. Unlike Poros and Taxiles, there is no reference to an Abisares in the satrapal allotments of 323 or 320 (cf. Brunt II 474). In 325, Alexander received word that the elder A. had died of illness, and he approved the accession of his son, who also took the dynastic name (Curt. 10.1.20–1).

Onesikritos (*FGrH* 134 F16b = Ael. *NA* 16.39) claimed that A. kept two snakes measuring 140 and 80 cubits respectively, and that Alexander was anxious to see them. Onesikritos had seen neither the snakes nor A. personally but took his information from A.'s ambassadors (*FGrH* 134 F16a = Strabo 15.1.28 C698; cf. Brown, *Onesicritus* 76, 95). Cf. also *FGrH* 134 F16c = Tzetz. *Chil.* 3.940–9. Kaerst, *RE* I.1 (1893) 101; Berve II 3–4 no. 2; Anspach II 5 n.132.

3 ABISARES

('Αβισάρης). Indian dynast of Abhisara (Kashmir); son of the former ally of Poros. The father's death from illness was reported in a letter from Poros and Taxiles (who also reported the death of Philip (no. 908) son of Machatas: Curt. 10.1.20) to Alexander in Karmania in 325. The son inherited the father's kingdom—apparently with Alexander's approval; for he was scarcely in a strong position to deny it—and the royal name of Abisares (Curt. 10.1.21). He appears to have pursued an independent policy after Alexander's departure from the East and into the time of the Diadochoi. Nothing else is known about him (cf. Karttunen 1997, 254 n.8). Berve II 4–5 no. 3.

ABISTAMENES. Curt. 3.4.1; Shayegan 97 no. 1. See **SABIKTAS**.

4 ABOULITES

('Αβουλίτης. Plut. *Alex.* 68: Ἀβουλήτης, Diod. 17.65.5: Ἀβουλεύτης). A high-ranking Persian. Ps.-Call. 2.22.1 mentions a certain Adoulites (*sic*), an uncle of Dareios; Pseudo–Callisthenes is, at any rate, speaking of Persia, not Sousiana. The Aboulites mentioned in Ktesias' *Persika* (Phot. *Bibl.* 72 p. 44b = *FGrH* 688 F30) as living in the reign of Artaxerxes II may have been a relative, possibly even his father. The name is Babylonian (hardly surprising since both Dareios II and his sister-wife Parysatis were allegedly children of Babylonian concubines): see Briant 870; cf. 723–5. Born no later than the 370s; the fact that his son, Oxathres (no. 830), was old enough to command the Ouxians and Sousianoi at Gaugamela (Arr. 3.8.5) may indicate that A. was considerably older. As satrap of Sousiana under Dareios III, A. surrendered the city of Sousa and himself to Philoxenos (Arr. 3.16.6, possibly an error for Xenophilos: Heckel 2002), whom Alexander had sent to him after the battle of Gaugamela. Sending his son (A102) ahead to confirm the arrangement (Arr. 3.16.6; Curt. 5.2.8–9 calls the son a *iuvenis*, which may mean that he was a son other than Oxathres, whom Plut. *Alex.* 68.7 calls "one of Aboulites' sons": τῶν Ἀβουλήτου παίδων ἕνα), A. made his official surrender in person to Alexander on his arrival (Curt. 5.2.9–10; cf. Arr. 3.16.7). His gifts included dromedaries and twelve elephants sent to Dareios from India; Diod. 17.65.5 and Curt. 5.2.8 claim that A. surrendered in order to buy time for the Great King to mobilize another army by placing distractions in Alexander's path. He was allowed to retain his satrapy (Curt. 5.2.17), which he later enlarged at the expense of Madates (Curt. 5.3.16, giving him authority over the Ouxians of the mountains); Alexander, nevertheless, established a military garrison in the city (Arr. 3.16.9; Curt. 5.2.17). There is little agreement in the sources about the commanders of this garrison. Arr. 3.16.9 names Mazaros (no. 687), one of the *hetairoi*, as *phrourarchos* ([καταλιπὼν] φρούραρχον δὲ ἐν τῇ ἄκρᾳ τῶν Σούσων Μάζαρον τῶν ἑταίρων) and Archelaos (no. 159) son of Theodoros as *strategos*. Curtius entrusts the city to Archelaos, the citadel to Xenophilos (no. 1165), and the treasury to Kallikrates (no. 563; Curt. 5.2.16–17). Bosworth I 319, may be correct in identifying Mazaros with the Persian commandant, whom Xenophilos replaced. A. fell into disfavor when he failed to send Alexander supplies requisitioned during the Gedrosian campaign (Plut. *Alex.* 68.7), and, when Alexander returned to Sousa, he sought to buy his forgiveness with three thousand talents but was executed along with this son, Oxathres (Arr. 7.4.1; cf. Plut. *Alex.* 68.7: Alexander ran Oxathres through with his sarissa). Plutarch's anecdote about Alexander throwing the coins to the horses suggests that A. may have sent money instead of supplies. But Arr. 7.4.1 says that A. was guilty of mismanaging *the affairs of Sousa* (ὅτι κακῶς ἐπεμελεῖτο τῶν Σουσίων); Badian 1961, 21 sees A. as a scapegoat for the Gedrosian disaster. Kaerst, *RE* I.1 (1893) 125; Berve II 5 no. 5; Shayegan 97–8 no. 2.

5 ACHILLEUS

(Ἀχιλλεύς). Athenian of unknown family. A. and Diophantos (no. 394) were sent by the Athenians to Alexander to negotiate the release of their countrymen, who had been captured at the Granikos and sentenced to hard labor in Macedonia. They met Alexander near Tyre as he returned from Egypt in 331 and achieved their purpose (Arr. 3.6.2; cf. Curt. 4.8.12–13). Berve II 98 no. 192; Kirchner 2796; Develin 388.

6 ACHILLEUS

(Ἀχιλλεύς). From Megara in Atintania. According to Plutarch (*Pyrrh.* 2.8), A. was the first man to take the infant Pyrrhos in his arms and ferry him across the river to safety when he was being rescued from Epeiros in 316. The fact that in mythology Achilles was the father of Pyrrhos casts doubt on the historicity of the event, the account of which appears to derive from Proxenos (Schubert 1894, 27; cf. Sandberger 13; also Garoufalias 217 n.6; see also Pownall, *LexAM* 37–8). Hammond, *Epirus* 800 (inaccurate); Sandberger no. 1. Molossian claims to descent from Neoptolemos and Andromache: Schubert 1894, 89, and Heckel 1981d.

7 ADA

(Ἄδα). Daughter of the Karian dynast Hekatomnos (Arr. 1.23.7; Strabo 14.2.17 C656; Tod no. 161B) and possibly Aba (Hornblower, *Mausolus* 36 and 37 n.9); A. was both sister and widow of Idrieus (Hidrieus in Arr. 1.23.7), and also the sister of Mausolos and his sister-wife, Artemisia (Diod. 16.45.7, 69.2; cf. Hornblower, *Mausolus* 366, M7), and of Pixodaros (no. 963). A. was presumably born in the 390s—the *terminus ante quem* is 377, the year of Hekatomnos' death and the beginning of Mausolos' reign—since it is likely that she died of old age no later than 324 (perhaps before 326: see Philoxenos no. 947; cf. Baumbach 63 with n.1 against Niese I 88). Berve II 11 calls A. the fourth child of Hekatomnos, but this is far from certain. She was clearly not older than either Mausolos or Artemisia, who as the eldest children formed the first ruling couple, but we have no way of knowing her position in the birth order. All that is certain is that Pixodaros was the youngest of the three sons (Diod. 16.74.2; implied also by Strabo 14.2.17 C656). The use of the word *gynaion* (Diod. 17.24.2), in this case a term of endearment (cf. Hamilton 57), may also suggest that in 334 A. was an elderly lady (Stronk 287 n.60). She appears to have ruled jointly with Idrieus between 351/0 and 344/3: a Milesian dedication of statues of the pair at Delphi (Tod no. 161B; cf. 161A) probably dates to the last years of their reign (certainly after the end of the Sacred War in 346: thus Tod II 181). An inscription at Tegea (Tod no. 161A) identifies Zeus, flanked by Ada and Idrieus, shown in relief below the inscribed names. The relief depicts the two rulers worshipping Zeus Stratios of Labraunda (photo in Roscher, *Lexikon* IV 1548; Cook II 503); see also R&O 267–9.

After Idrieus' death she ruled alone (Arr. 1.23.7; cf. Diod. 17.24.2) for a period of four years (from 344/3 to 340/39: Diod. 16.69.2), until she was ousted by Pixodaros (Diod. 16.74.2; cf. Krumbholz 1883, 83). By the time Alexander arrived in Asia Minor, Pixodaros had died (Diod. 16.74.2; cf. Strabo 14.2.17 C657), leaving Orontobates (his son-in-law: Arr. 1.23.8) in charge of Karia and the elder A. living in Alinda (Strabo 14.2.17). A. met Alexander as he marched into Karia (Diod. 17.24.2–3), seeking reinstatement and promising to help him win over those areas of the satrapy that continued to resist. Alexander's troops confined Orontobates to the citadel of Halikarnassos, and Asandros (no. 232) and Polemaios (no. 967) captured it in 333 (Arr. 2.5.7 calls Polemaios Ptolemy). Although A. recovered the satrapy of Karia, the adjacent territory of Lykia, which had been under Hekatomnid control (Keen 1998, 172–4), was detached and given to Nearchos (no. 765) to administer. Alexander allowed himself to be adopted by A. (Arr. 1.23.8), which certainly strengthened his own claims to Karia (Sears 2014 sees this as an attempt to display his "Greekness" to the Hellenes of Asia Minor). The story goes that his adoptive mother sent him delicacies and even a cook for his meals, though Alexander declined the latter, preferring to adhere to a more "Spartan" regimen imposed upon him early in life by his tutor Leonidas (Plut. *Alex.* 22.7–10; cf. Plut. *Mor.* 180a, 127b, 1099c). Abramenko's argument (1992) that the mother of the King who warned him to beware of Alexander Lynkestes (no. 45; Diod. 17.32.1) was A. and not Olympias is not compelling. (For possible Macedonian connections with Karia dating to the early fifth century see Hdt. 8.136). Nothing further is known about A.'s life or reign in Karia. She must have died no later than 324/3; for in 323 we find a certain Philoxenos in Babylonia with troops from his satrapy of Karia (Arr. 7.23.1, 24.1; cf. [Aristotle], *Oecon.* 2.31.1531). Tests intended to identify the physical remains of the queen exhumed in Halikarnassos with Ada have been inconclusive (Özet 1994). For the Hekatomnid dynasty see Beloch III² 2.141–5; Hornblower, *Mausolus* 34–51; Ruzicka 1992. Ada's life and career: Judeich, *RE* I.1 (1893) 339; Badian, *BNP* I 130–1; Berve II 11–12 no. 20; Baumbach 63; Lehmann-Haupt 140–1; Abramenko 1992; Carney 2005; Sears 2014; Howe 2021; cf. Judeich 251–5.

8 ADA

(Ἄδα). Eldest daughter (Plut. *Alex.* 10.1) of Pixodaros (no. 963) and Aphneis, a woman from Kappadokia (Strabo 14.2.17 C656–7). Ada II was apparently the bride offered to Arrhidaios in spring 336, though these plans were disrupted by the intervention of Alexander (Plut. *Alex.* 10.1–2). Soon thereafter Pixodaros reverted to a pro-Persian policy and arranged her marriage to Orontobates (Strabo 14.2.17; cf. Arr. 1.23.8: Brunt I 99 translates γαμβρός as "brother-in-law," but the word refers simply to someone related by marriage and should here be translated as "son-in-law"; see also Judeich 254 n.1). This marriage took place very soon after Pixodaros' failure to gain an alliance with Philip II, and Orontobates appears to have ruled Karia jointly with his father-in-law (Krumbholz 1883, 83; Judeich 251; *contra* Ruzicka 1992, 132). The arrival of Pixodaros' messenger (Aristokritos) in Macedonia occurred after the crossing of Parmenion, Attalos, and Amyntas into Asia in the spring of 336 (Heckel 1981c, 55; cf. Olmstead 490). When A.'s father died, some time before the summer of 335 (Diod. 16.74.2), she may have ruled Karia briefly with her husband (cf. Hornblower, *Mausolus* 49–50) until her aunt, Ada I, was reinstated by Alexander in the summer of 334. How she was dealt with by her potentially vindictive aunt—if, indeed, she came into her power—and what became of her, we do not know. Berve II 12 no. 21; Hornblower, *Mausolus* 49–50; Ruzicka 1992, 131–2; 2010.

9 ADAIOS

(Ἀδδαῖος, probably Ἀδαῖος). Macedonian of unknown family background (Tataki 220 no. 18; the name was widespread in Macedonia: Hoffmann 190 n.102): a relationship to Adaios Alektryon ("the Cock"), a mercenary captain of Philip II who died fighting Chares in 353 (Athen. 12.532e = Theopompos, *FGrH* 115 F249), is remotely possible. A. appears as a chiliarch—apparently of hypaspists (cf. Berve II 12)—during the siege of Halikarnassos in 334. Here he served under the command of Ptolemy (no. 1006) the *somatophylax basilikos*, along with Timandros (no. 1137; Arr. 1.22.4), and was killed in a skirmish with enemy troops who sallied forth from the Tripylon (Arr. 1.22.7). Kirchner, *RE* I.1 (1893) 349 no. 1; Berve II 12 no. 22; Heckel 1992, 303; Tataki 220 no. 18.

10 ADEA

(Ἀδέα). Hoffmann 216, followed by Berve II 12, reads Hadea: Ἀδέα = Ἡδεῖα, i.e., "Sweetness"; I prefer Adea; cf. *Syll*³ 1.373 ("Adeia," "fearless" or "without concern"; Pape-Benseler I 17 explain the masc. "Adeas" as "Ohnesorge"). Daughter of Kynnane (no. 634) (Kynna)—who trained her in the Macedonian art of war (Douris, *FGrH* 76 F52 = Athen. 13.560f; cf. Polyaenus 8.60, also from Douris; Heckel 1983–84)—and Amyntas Perdikka (no. 76; Arr. *Succ.* 1.23; Ael. *VH* 13.36 wrongly calls her the daughter of Philip II). Born not later than 335, for Amyntas Perdikka was known to have been dead by the spring of that year (Arr. 1.5.4). She was of marriageable age in 322/1, when her mother led her to Asia to arrange a union with Philip III Arrhidaios, a plan that was fulfilled only after the death of Kynnane on the orders of Alketas (Polyaenus 8.60; Arr. *Succ.* 1.22–3). Upon marrying the King, A. was renamed Eurydike (Arr. *Succ.* 1.23), by which she is known in all subsequent references. For the dynastic significance of the name see Heckel 1983; Ogden 22–3. For the view that A. had a sister named Kynnane, who married Kassandros son of Antipatros see Palagia 2008 (unconvincing: see Heckel 2013b; also Kuzmin 2013).

After the death of Perdikkas son of Orontes in Egypt, A. began to agitate for greater political power in the name of her husband: hence she wreaked havoc upon the elected guardians of the "Kings," Arrhidaios (no. 214) and Peithon (Diod. 18.39.2; Arr. *Succ.* 1.30–1), who resigned at Triparadeisos. In the turbulent events that followed, her ambitions were further inflamed by the arrival of Attalos son of Andromenes, and she was aided by the *grammateus* Asklepiodoros (no. 240; Arr. *Succ.* 1.33). But when Amyntas departed, Antipatros, to whom the *epimeleia* was entrusted, managed to subdue the strong-willed queen (Diod. 18.39.3–4). Once back in Europe, A., threatened by Polyperchon's proposal that Olympias assume the *epimeleia* of her grandson Alexander IV, formed an alliance with Kassandros (Justin 14.5.1–4) and brought an armed force against Olympias and Aiakides of Epeiros at Euia (Douris *ap.* Athen. 13.560f; Diod. 19.11.1–2). Here her troops defected to the old Queen Mother (Diod. 19.11.1–3; Justin 14.5.8–10) and A. was captured as she fled towards Amphipolis with her adviser Polykles (no. 982) (Diod. 19.11.3). Upon the death of her husband, and after tending to his body, she committed suicide, shunning the instruments of death (dagger, rope, poison) sent to her by the vindictive Olympias in favor of her girdle (Diod. 19.11.6–7; but Ael. *VH* 13.36 says she used the rope; cf. Diod. 19.35.1, news of her death reaches Kassandros). Her body, along with that of Philip III Arrhidaios, and her mother Kynnane, was buried by Kassandros in 315 (Diod. 19.52.5; Diyllos, *FGrH* 73 F1 = Athen. 4.155a). The question of whether A. and her husband were the occupants of Tomb II at Vergina has been much discussed (see most recently Borza and Palagia 2007; *contra* Lane Fox 2011a). Pape-Benseler I 17; Hoffmann 216; Berve II 12–13 no. 23; Kaerst, *RE* VI 1326 no. 13; Tataki 221 no. 23; Heckel 1983 and 1983–84; Carney 132–7; Carney 1987a; Borza and Palagia 2007; Landucci 2010; Lane Fox 2011a. **Stemma I.**

11 ADEIA

(Ἀδεία). Wife of Autodikos (no. 270), brother of Lysimachos, known only from the inscription on the base of a statue, dedicated by the king for his sister-in-law in the Amphiaraion of Oropos (*Syll*³ 373). Beloch IV² 2.130; Tataki 221 no. 24.

12 ADEIMANTOS

(Ἀδείμαντος). For the name see Pape-Benseler I 17. Son of Androsthenes, from Lampsakos. Courtier (hence also *kolax* or *parasitos* in the opinion of hostile observers), ambassador, and *strategos* of Demetrios and Antigonos (Strabo 13.1.19 C589; Athen. 6.255c; Petrakos 1993, 7); he was particularly active in the years 304–302 (thus Billows 363). According to Strabo, A. was one of Lampsakos' four most important natives. He and his followers erected statues at Thria to "Aphrodite Phila," establishing also the *Philaion* in honor of Demetrios' wife (Dionyios Tryphonos, *Onomastikon*, Bk 10 *ap.* Athen. 6.255c; cf. Athen. 6.254a). Demetrios was allegedly disgusted by such flatteries—the paeans sung to him by flattering Athenians—and commented that there were no decent Athenians left (Demochares, *FGrH* 75 F1 = Athen. 6.252f–253a). Diog. Laert. 5.57 says A. was friend of Theophrastos (no. 1114) and received one of three copies of his testament. Decrees were moved in his honor in Eretria and Athens (*IG* XII.9 198; cf. Paschidis 450–1, with 451 n.1;

Moretti, *ISE* no. 9). The Eretrians granted him citizenship and a statue for service to the community; he was nominated by Demetrios to be one of the *proedroi* of the new League of Korinth that the Antigonids had established (cf. Daux, *Delphes* 351 no. 2). On this, and a new (only partially published) inscription (*SEG* XLIII 27; Petrakos 1993, 7, showing that he held a two-year generalship under Demetrios during the Four Years War (307–304), see Wallace 2013). Some of our information about A. comes from Demochares son of Laches, the nephew of Demosthenes; hence we must treat this with caution, since Demochares was an enemy of Demetrios Poliorketes. Despite his importance at Demetrios' court, we know nothing about A. from Diodorus or other sources based on Hieronymos of Kardia. Toepffer, *RE* I.1 (1893) 355 no. 8; Badian-Martin 1985; Billows 362–4 no. 1; Habicht² 55–8; Robert, *Hellenica* II 15–33; Wehrli 1968, 123–5; Paschidis 450–1; Wallace 2013.

13 ADMETOS

(Ἄδμητος). Macedonian officer (Tataki 221 no. 26), perhaps commander of the *agema* of the hypaspists, and a man of great bodily strength (Diod. 17.45.6), A. commanded the ship carrying the hypaspists in the naval assault on Tyre (Arr. 2.23.2). He displayed great courage, fighting as he did in full view of Alexander, and, although he was the first to scale the wall, he was killed by a spear (Arr. 2.23.5) or perhaps by an axe (Diod. 17.45.6). Kirchner, *RE* I.1 (1893) 380 no. 4; Berve II 13 no. 24; Heckel 1992, 253.

14 ADRASTOS

(Ἄδραστος). Lydian who fought in the Lamian War, though the Lydians officially remained aloof. He perished in the battle near Lamia in 322, fighting on the Greek side against the forces of Leonnatos, as we know from the inscription of the base of a statue erected in front of the sanctuary of Persian Artemis by the Lydians (Paus. 7.6.6). A. may have been a resident of Lydia who happened to be in Greece when the Lamian War broke out. Cauer, *RE* I.1 (1893) 416 no. 4.

15 AËROPOS

(Ἀέροπος). Macedonian (Tataki 223 no. 38) commander (*hegemon*) in the army of Philip II at the time of the battle of Chaironeia (338). A., together with another officer, Damasippos, was banished from Macedonia for bringing a female harpist, whom they had hired at a local inn, into the camp (Polyaenus 4.2.3). The punishment is clearly too harsh for the crime, and one suspects that Philip regarded the actions of A. as a deliberate flouting of his authority. Hence it may be that the incident became a pretext for removing from Macedonia a political rival. If A. can be identified as a member of the Lynkestian royal house, perhaps even the father of Arrhabaios and Heromenes, the Lynkestian involvement in the murder of Philip takes on a new dimension. Damasippos may have been a close friend of A. This identification of A. is speculative but ought not to be dismissed out of hand. Hoffmann 206; Kirchner, *RE* I.1 (1893) 679 no. 6.

16 AGAROS

(Ἄγαρος). King of the Skythians. In 310 A. gave refuge to Pairisades (no. 838), the rightful heir to the Kimmerian Bosporos, who fled his uncle Eumelos (Diod. 20.24.3). He is otherwise unattested, but App. *Mithr.* 88 mentions a Skythian tribe called the Agaroi (*Barr. Atl.* 84 B2; cf. W. Sontheimer, *Kl. Pauly* I 114 s.v.).

17 AGATHOKLES

(Ἀγαθοκλῆς). Samian *taxiarches* in Alexander's army (presumably a commander of allied infantry, perhaps mercenaries), A. had been held in high esteem by the King, but he narrowly missed being exposed to a lion because he wept when passing Hephaistion's (no. 513) grave, thereby regarding him as dead rather than divine. The story, found only in Lucian, *Cal.* 18, continues that A. was saved through the intervention of Perdikkas (no. 871), who observed that A. wept not because he considered Hephaistion dead but because he remembered his former friendship. The story itself is suspect, and there may be some confusion of the popular, but equally fictitious, report that Lysimachos (son of Agathokles!) was exposed to a lion because he pitied Kallisthenes and gave him poison (Justin 15.3.6–8). For the cults of Hephaistion and Alexander see Habicht[2] 30–6, who clearly gives no credence to the story of Agathokles. Berve II 6 no. 7.

18 AGATHOKLES

(Ἀγαθοκλῆς). Macedonian (Tataki 148 no. 2). Son of Lysimachos and Nikaia (no. 775; Beloch IV[2] 2.132; Niese I 402 thinks his mother was Odrysian, perhaps confusing him with Alexander no. 52), hence also brother of Arsinoë I (the wife of Ptolemy II Philadelphos and mother of Ptolemy III Euergetes); he was named after his paternal grandfather (cf. Arr. 6.28.4). Born *c.*320/19, nothing is known of his earlier career. He was captured in the Getic campaign against Dromichaites and ransomed by his father (Paus. 1.9.6); the Getai claimed that they hoped to regain through humanity what Lysimachos had seized of their kingdom (Diod. 21.11). According to another version of the story, it was Lysimachos who was captured and ransomed by his son. At some point, his father awarded him an estate in Sermylia (*Barr. Atl.* 51 B4), bordering on that of Limnaios son of Harpalos (Hatzopoulos II 45–6 no. 22). A. married Lysandra (no. 668), the daughter of Ptolemy I Soter and Eurydike (Paus. 1.9.6, 10.3; cf. Plut. *Demetr.* 31.5), and the widow of Alexander V, whom Demetrios Poliorketes had murdered in 294 (Paus. 9.7.3; Diod. 21.7; Justin 16.1.8; Plut. *Demetr.* 36). Hence the marriage can be dated, in all likelihood, to 294 or 293. In 286/5 (for the date: Lund 186; Wheatley and Dunn 451), when Demetrios threatened Lysimachos' possessions in Asia Minor, A. was sent against him with an army and drove him eastward, bottling him up in Kilikia, and thus sealing his fate (Plut. *Demetr.* 46.7–47.3).

Most of what we know about A. concerns his death and its circumstances. Indeed, Justin 17.1.1–3 reports that an earthquake, which destroyed Lysimacheia, was an omen of the ill that would befall Lysimachos' kingdom. A. appears to have been the victim of the machinations of his jealous stepmother, Arsinoë (no. 221; the daughter of Ptolemy I and Berenike), whom Lysimachos married *c.*300/299 (Seibert 1967, 74). That this was a consequence of amphimetric strife at a court that practiced polygamy (or else serial monogamy) is clear enough. A.'s death in 283/2 (Heinen 94) was plotted and accomplished by Arsinoë (Justin 17.1.4, she poisoned him at Lysimachos' urging), who feared lest her children fall into A.'s hands when Lysimachos died. Justin 17.1.6 says that Lysimachos killed many of his own people because they were sympathetic to A. One version, with Phaedra-like dramatics, says A. rejected Arsinoë's love—she was not much younger than he—and she plotted against him. Lysimachos, who was old and bereft of friends, was powerless to stop Arsinoë (Paus. 1.10.3–4). App. *Syr.* 64 claims that Lysimachos himself killed his own son (cf. Strabo 13.4.1 C623), but others attribute the act to a certain Ptolemy, thought to be Arsinoë's half-brother, Keraunos (Memnon 5.6); but Heinen 3–17 has presented cogent arguments that the murderer was actually Arsinoë's eldest son, also named Ptolemy. Keraunos clearly had nothing to gain from A.'s death, which strengthened the position of Arsinoë and her sons in Macedonia and Thrake and did nothing to improve his own chances (which were slim to begin with) of recovering his perceived birthright in Egypt. See the discussion s.v. Ptolemy (no. 1011). A.'s widow, Lysandra, and their children, fled to the court of Seleukos. Wilcken, *RE* I.1 (1893) 757 no. 18; Landucci, *Lisimaco* 209–14; Lund 186–98; Ogden 59–62; Heinen 3–17; Müller 2009, 38–40; Carney 2013, 44–7. **Stemma IX.**

19 AGATHOKLES

('Ἀγαθοκλῆς). Tyrant of Syracuse. Born in 361, A. lived for 72 years and ruled for twenty-eight (Diod. 21.16.5). Son of Karkinos of Rhegion and a girl from Therma, the daughter of a certain Agathokles (Diod. 19.2.2, 5). A. had at least three wives (Beloch IV² 2.254–6): the widow of Damas (Diod. 19.3.2), a source of great wealth and mother of Archagathos (or Agatharchos); Alkia (Diod. 20.33.5), mother of Agathokles and Lanassa; and Theoxene (no. 1117), a daughter of Ptolemy I (Justin 23.2.6), who had young children at the time of A.'s death. For his rise from obscure origins see Diod. 19.2–9. In his early years, it is alleged that A. was trained by his father to be a potter (Diod. 19.2.7; Justin 22.1.1–15 gives a list of A.'s vices: he was of low birth, a potter by trade, and a male prostitute, who later debauched women; he was guilty of larceny and piracy. "He had neither property to lose nor honor to tarnish": Justin 22.1.7, Yardley tr.). But Meister 385 argues that the family may have been in the pottery business, employing others, and that the low status of potter would have prevented A. from attaining high military command. A. overthrew the oligarchs in Syracuse and established a tyranny in 316/15 (*Marm. Par.* B§14; Diod. 19.9; cf. Polyb. 15.35.1–6; for the confused chronology see Beloch IV² 2.249–54). His struggle against Carthaginian forces in Sicily prompted him to make a daring attempt on Africa, though this ultimately failed. In 304 he took the title of king in imitation of the Diadochoi (Demetrios mocked him as *nesiarch* or "ruler of the islands": Plut. *Demetr.* 25.7, *Mor.* 823c–d; the derogatory comment refers, in the opinion of Hauben 1974, 113 to A.'s failed African venture, which left him merely as ruler of Sicily). He may have played a role in securing Pyrrhos' return to Epeiros from Egypt; for he was married to a daughter (or stepdaughter) of Ptolemy I, Theoxene (Justin 23.2). But A. was also careful to check the growth of "Macedonian" power in the west, as is clear from his seizure of Kerkyra in 299/8 (Diod. 21.2.1). Nevertheless, he married his daughter Lanassa (no. 640) to Pyrrhos, with Kerkyra as her dowry, and this points to a certain degree of political cooperation. That Lanassa's separation from Pyrrhos—Plut. *Pyrrh.* 10.7 attributes this to her anger over her husband's preference for his Illyrian and Paionian wives—and her withdrawal to Kerkyra marks a political break between Pyrrhos and A., and likewise a shift from alliance with Ptolemy to Demetrios Poliorketes, is possible but difficult to prove. His downfall is attributed by Diodorus, in part, to his relationship with Menon the Egestaian, whom he captured and sexually abused (Diod. 21.16.2 describes Menon as διὰ δὲ τὴν τῆς πατρίδος συμφορὰν καὶ τὴν περὶ αὑτὸν ὕβριν ὑπούλως ἔχων πρὸς τὸν δυνάστην). Menon killed A. by poisoning the quill with which he was accustomed to clean his teeth (Diod. 21.16.4). But Justin 23.2.4–12 says A. died of a lingering (unspecified) illness. Diod. 21.16.5

adds that Oxythemis (no. 836), the *philos* of Demetrios Poliorketes, who was at A.'s court placed him on a pyre and burned his body while A. was still alive but unable to utter a sound. The story smacks of sensationalism and depicts A.'s end as a fitting punishment for his past atrocities (πρέπουσαν παρέσχε τῇ παρανομίᾳ τὴν τοῦ βίου καταστροφήν). Sandberger no. 4; Niese, *RE* I.1 (1893) 748–57 no. 15. Full account of his life and career, see especially Berve 1953; Berve, *Tyrannis* I 441–57, II 728–31 (with sources and earlier literature); Meister, *CAH* VII[2] 1, 384–411; for the source tradition, Pearson 1987, 225–55.

20 AGATHOKLES

(Ἀγαθοκλῆς). Son of Agathokles the tyrant and his second wife Alkia (cf. Beloch IV[2] 2.255; Berve, *Tyrannis* I 455; Diod. 21.15; 21.16.3); hence probably also the full brother of Lanassa (no. 640), who married Pyrrhos. Around 290, A. was sent by his father to arrange a peace with Demetrios Poliorketes. He was favorably received by Demetrios and returned to his father accompanied by Oxythemis (no. 836; Diod. 21.15), whose real purpose may have been to spy on the Sicilians. The elder Agathokles wanted to leave A. as heir to the kingdom and sent him to the army encamped at Etna (presumably to take over the military force bound for Libya). There, the king's grandson Archagathos, who induced Menon of Egesta to murder his grandfather (see above), invited A. to a feast, and having made him drunk, murdered him during the night. A.'s body was thrown into the sea but eventually recovered and conveyed to Syracuse (Diod. 21.16.3). Niese, *RE* I.1 (1893) 757 no. 16; Beloch IV[2] 2.255; Berve, *Tyrannis* I 455.

21 AGATHON

(Ἀγάθων). Son of Tyrimmas (Arr. 3.12.4), apparently of Macedonian origin (Tataki 218 no. 7). Commander of the Thrakian cavalry between 334 and 330. Including the Paionians, the Thrakian horse numbered 900 (Diod. 17.17.4). Hammond 1980, 83 estimates that A.'s squadron numbered about 150, assuming that the Thrakians were divided into six squadrons of 150. Of the remaining units, the Paionian *prodromoi* (150 strong) were commanded by Ariston and four squadrons of Lancers were under the lead of Amyntas son of Arrhabaios (no. 78). But Berve I 134 thinks that the Thrakians were heavily armed horsemen (or at least "mittelschwer gerüstet"), and that some 700 were under A.'s command, the majority of them Odrysians. Marsden 1964, 71–3, thinks the Odrysian cavalry unit was formed only after Asklepiodoros son of Eunikos brought 500 Thrakians as reinforcements to Memphis; Marsden also thinks they were 342 strong, counting 171 as the strength of a squadron. A. is attested at the Granikos (Arr. 1.14.3) and Gaugamela (Arr. 3.12.4; he was stationed on the left wing with Sitalkes and Koiranos). Although in the latter case A.'s troops are described as "Odrysians," he will have been the commander of the entire Thrakian cavalry (so Berve II 6; cf. Brunt I 263 n.7). In mid-330, he remained behind at Ekbatana, with his cavalry unit and in the company of Parmenion, Kleandros, Herakon, and Sitalkes (Arr. 3.19.7). He soon played a role in the elimination of Parmenion (Curt. 10.1.1). But in 325/4, A. was charged with maladministration when Alexander returned from India. Together with Herakon, Kleandros, and Sitalkes, he met the King in Karmania, where he was arrested and presumably executed together with the 600 troops who were the instruments of their crimes (Curt. 10.1.1–8; cf. Arr. 6.27.3–4). Kaerst, *RE* I.1 (1893) 760 no. 7; Berve II 6–7 no. 8; Heckel 1992, 361; Marsden 1964, 71–3.

22 AGATHON

(Ἀγάθων). Prominent Macedonian from Pydna, though his family background is unknown. A. first appears as the commander of 700 Macedonian troops garrisoning the citadel of Babylon (Diod. 17.64.5; Curt. 5.1.43 gives him an additional 300 mercenaries; his appointment is not mentioned by Arr. 3.16.4). Nothing else is known about him. Kaerst, *RE* I.1 (1893) 760 no. 8; Berve II 7 no. 9; Tataki 169 no. 1.

23 AGATHON

(Ἀγάθων). Macedonian from Beroia (Tataki 73 no. 2). Brother of Asandros (no. 233), hence also son of Agathon (Diod. 19.75.2; for Asandros' patronymic see *Syll*³ 272 and 320, lines 12–13). In winter 313/12, he was given as a hostage to Antigonos Monophthalmos for the good conduct of his brother. Asandros soon secured his escape and rebelled against Antigonos (Diod. 19.75.2). Both may have taken refuge with Ptolemy when Antigonos overran Karia (Diod. 19.75.3–6), but neither is heard of again. Kaerst, *RE* I.1 (1893) 760 no. 9; Tataki 73 no. 2; Billows 120–1.

24 AGESILAOS

(Ἀγησίλαος). A member of the Eurypontid house of Sparta, A. was the son of Archidamos III and brother of Agis III and Eudamidas I (Plut. *Agis* 3.3). In 333/2, Agis sent to A. ten triremes, which he had secured from Autophradates at Siphnos; these ships and thirty talents of silver were conveyed to Tainaron by Hippias (no. 534), with instructions that he should pay the wages of the crews and sail to Krete to set affairs in order there (Arr. 2.13.6), that is, to secure Krete as a base for the Persian fleet (cf. Bosworth I 224). Nothing else is known about A. Bosworth believes that he may have died before the battle of Megalopolis, since after Agis' death Eudamidas succeeded to the kingship (Plut. *Agis* 3.3); Berve may be correct in assuming that A. was the youngest of the brothers. Plutarch speaks of only two sons of Archidamos, but he is merely recounting the lineage of Agis IV and may have overlooked A. because he did not rule. Niese, *RE* I.1 (1893) 804 no. 5; Welwei, *BNP* I 337 no. 3; Berve II 7 no. 11; Poralla 9 no. 11; Clauss 1983, 126. **Stemma XVIIIb.**

25 AGESILAOS

(Ἀγησίλαος). Greek. Sent by Antigonos Monophthalmos in 315 to win over the allegiance of the kings of Kypros. He was successful in bringing Pymiathon of Kition (no. 1015), Stasioikos II of Marion (no. 1077), Praxippos of Lapethos (no. 992), Androkles of Amathos (no. 99) and an unnamed ruler of Keryneia (A103) into alliance with Antigonos (Diod. 19.57.4, 59.1). Although he appears to have been a man of some importance, he is otherwise unattested, and neither his background nor his fate is known. Billows 364 no. 3; Olshausen no. 62; Beloch IV² 2.331–3; Seibert 1969, 143–4; Hill I 158 with n.3.

26 AGESIMENES

(Ἀγησιμένης). Son of Hermesideios, hence grandson of Hermos, who shared the tyranny of Eresos in the 340s with his brothers Heraios and Apollodoros. A. was banished after the fall of the tyrants (cf. s.v. Herodas no. 527); in 332 he joined Alexander and sought restitution. The King left the matter to the Eresians, who voted to uphold the banishment of the tyrants and their descendants (Heisserer 38–9; Harding no. 112; *OGIS* I 8, II). Berve II 7 no. 12; Berve, *Tyrannis* I 337–8; Heisserer 27–78; Lott 1996; Wallace 2016.

AGESIPOLIS. Berve II 8 no. 13 (cf. Poralla 9–10 no. 15). See **603 KLEOMENES**.

27 AGIS

(Ἆγις). Agis III of Sparta. A member of the Eurypontid house, A. was the eldest son of Archidamos III (Plut. *Agis* 3.3; Paus. 3.10.5) and brother of Eudamidas and Agesilaos (Arr. 2.13.6). Succeeded to the Spartan throne upon the death of his father, who was killed in Italy on the very day of the battle of Chaironeia (Diod. 16.63.2, 88.3–4). Diod. 16.88.4 says that Agis ruled for nine years; the fifteen years attributed to him at 16.63.2 can be explained by the fact that Archidamos' death is reported (incorrectly) under the events of 346/5. From 338 to 331/0 he ruled in Sparta, which rejected the Macedonian alliance and failed to join the League of Korinth (Arr. 1.1.2, 7.4), and spearheaded the anti-Macedonian movement in the Peloponnese. An early attempt at rebellion was suppressed in 336/5 by the speedy action of Alexander (Diod. 17.3.5, confusing the activities of the Arkadians and Lakedaimonians; cf. Justin 11.2.7, with Yardley and Heckel 86), but we know nothing of A.'s involvement. In late 333, A. sailed with a single trireme from Tainaron to Siphnos, where he met Pharnabazos and Autophradates and requested money and ships (Arr. 2.13.5); this coincided with the arrival of news of Dareios' defeat at Issos. Autophradates gave him 30 talents of silver and ten triremes, which A. sent to his brother Agesilaos at Tainaron through the agency of a certain Hippias (no. 534) (Arr. 2.13.6), ordering the former to pay the wages of the crews and sail to Krete to set affairs in order there, that is, to secure Krete as a base for the Persian fleet (cf. Bosworth I 224). Diod. 17.48.1 and Curt. 4.1.39 record that after Issos 8,000 Greek mercenaries took service with A. He himself remained briefly at Siphnos and then joined Autophradates at Halikarnassos (Arr. 2.13.6), but nothing further is known of his activities in Asia Minor.

On his return to Greece, A. fashioned a dangerous uprising against Macedonian authority in 332/1 (Aesch. 3.165, 167; Din. 1.34; [Dem.] 17.15; Diod. 17.62.6–63.4; Curt. 6.1.1–20). His cause was hampered by the failure of the Athenians to participate in a general rebellion. A. had the support of Sparta's traditional Peloponnesian allies (excluding the Messenians), the Eleans, the Arkadians except for the Megalopolitans, and all Achaia except Pellene (cf. Din. 1.34; Curt. 6.1.20; Paus. 7.27.7; [Dem.] 17.7.10; for the background see McQueen 1978). Justin's claim that virtually all of Greece joined in the uprising is a gross exaggeration (12.1.6, with Yardley and Heckel 187). In an early campaign he defeated the Macedonian *strategos* Korrhagos. But he was eventually defeated and killed in the battle of Megalopolis in summer 331 (Diod. 17.63; Curt. 6.1.1–16, 21; Justin 12.1.4–11; cf. Paus. 1.13.6; Plut. *Agis* 3.3). A saying of his, extolling Spartan bravery and military efficiency is preserved in Plut. *Lyc.* 19 and *Mor.* 191e. Niese, *RE* I.1 (1893) 819 no.3; Welwei, *BNP* I 341 no. 3; Clauss 1983, 126; Badian 1967a and 1994; Berve II 8–9 no. 15; Brunt II 480–5; Hofstetter 5–6 no. 5; Poralla 13 no. 27; Wirth 1971, 617–20. **Stemma XVIIIb**.

28 AGIS

(Ἆγις). Greek from Argos, A. was an epic poet and flatterer of Alexander (Curt. 8.5.8; Arr. 4.9.9), found in the King's entourage in 328/7. Plut. *Mor.* 60b gives a splendid example of how A. resorted to flattery in his condemnation of flatterers with whom he was clearly vying for the King's favor (cf. Plut. *Mor.* 65d, where Ἀγησίαις should be corrected to read Ἅγισι). Whether he wrote an epic poem about Alexander himself (Berve II 9), as did Choirilos, who alone surpassed him in the writing of bad verse, is uncertain. Wissowa, *RE* I.1 (1893) 821 no. 8; Berve II 9 no. 16 = II 7 no. 10 "Agesias."

29 AGIS

(Ἆγις). Greek commander in the service of Ptolemy I Soter. In 313, Ptolemy sent him as *strategos* of the land forces (see s.v. Epainetos no. 414 for the fleet) to suppress the revolt at Kyrene. A. took the city by storm and sent the ringleaders of the sedition in chains to Alexandria, whither he himself returned, after disarming the populace and setting Kyrenean affairs in order (Diod. 19.79.2–3). Kirchner, *RE* I.1 (1893) 821 no. 5.

30 AGONIPPOS

(Ἀγώνιππος). Greek from Eresos, patronymic unknown. Installed, along with Eurysilaos (no. 459), as tyrant when Memnon recaptured most of Lesbos in 333 (Arr. 2.1.1; Diod. 17.29.2). The previous tyranny of Apollodoros and his brothers, in power since 338 and friendly to Philip II, had been driven out in 334 (thus Lott 1996; confirmed by Wallace 2016; but see R&O 417), probably through the efforts of Alkimachos son of Agathokles, whom Alexander had sent to establish democracies in the area (Arr. 1.18.1–2; cf. [Dem.] 17.7). A. and Eurysilaos exercised the tyranny in a most cruel fashion (*OGIS* 8a). Hegelochos' "liberation" of Lesbos in 332 led to the overthrow of the tyrants, who were handed over to the Macedonian admiral (Arr. 3.2.5) and, in turn, to Alexander in Egypt (winter 332/1: Arr. 3.2.7; cf. *OGIS* 8a, 13–15). A. and Eurysilaos were sent back to Eresos to stand trial, sentenced to death (by an overwhelming majority), and executed (*OGIS* 8b, lines 60–9; cf. Curt. 4.8.11). Kirchner, *RE* I.1 (1893) 869 no. 1; Baumbach 33 n. 1; Berve II 10–11 no. 19; Berve, *Tyrannis* I 338, II 691; Habicht² 14ff.; Heisserer 27–78; Hofstetter 6–7 no. 6; Harding no. 112 B and F; Lott 1996; Wallace 2016; R&O no. 83.

31 AIAKIDES

(Αἰακίδης). The name reflects the claims of the Molossian royal house to be descended from the mythical Aiakos (Plut. *Alex.* 2.1; Paus.1.11.2; cf. Heckel 1981d, 80–2). Son of Arybbas and Troas (Plut. *Pyrrh.* 1.5; Diod. 16.72.1; Paus. 1.11.1; cf. Justin 7.6.11 for the marriage of Arybbas and Troas, thus also a nephew of Alexander I of Epeiros (cf. Justin 17.3.16). Born perhaps as early as 357 (Sandberger 17); Alketas II was apparently his half-brother. A. married Phthia (no. 960), the daughter of Menon of Pharsalos (Plut. *Pyrrh.* 1.6; the Aiakidai appear to have had a bond of *xenia* with Menon's family; cf. Xen. *Anab.* 2.6.28; Brown 1986), no later than the outbreak of the Lamian War; the couple produced three children: Pyrrhos (Paus. 3.6.3; Diod. 16.72.1; Plut. *Pyrrh.* 1.7), Deidameia and the younger Troas (Plut. *Pyrrh.* 1.7; Justin 14.6.3; Diod. 19.35.5). A. may have ascended the Molossian throne as early as 331, when Alexander I was killed in Italy (Justin 17.2.16; cf. Paus. 1.11.3); that he shared the kingship, at any point in his career, with a son of Alexander (thus Hammond, *Epirus* 561) is unlikely, as is the view that his father Arybbas returned to the throne in 323, and that he was succeeded by A. soon afterwards. This is based on the uncertain evidence of Diod. 18.11.1 (rightly rejected by Reuss 1881, 161–2; see discussion s.v. Aryptaios no. 230). In 317/16 he supported Polyperchon and Olympias against Adea-Eurydike and Philip III Arrhidaios (Diod. 19.11.2), thereby alienating many of his followers (Paus. 1.11.3–4; Justin 14.5.9, 17.3.16) and incurring the enmity of Kassandros (Plut. *Pyrrh.* 3.2). His attempt to relieve Olympias, who was besieged in Pydna, was foiled by Kassandros' general Atarrhias (no. 251), who held the passes between Epeiros and Macedonia against him (Diod. 19.36.2). Distrustful of his army, he allowed those who did not support him to leave, thus weakening his forces and dooming himself to failure. He was expelled in 316 by the Molossians, who made an alliance with Kassandros (Diod. 19.36.2–4; cf. Plut. *Pyrrh.* 2.1, with discussion s.v. Neoptolemos no. 773); his son Pyrrhos was taken to safety in Illyria by A.'s supporters (Plut. *Pyrrh.* 2; Justin 17.3.16–20). Upon Olympias' defeat by Kassandros, A. accompanied Polyperchon to Aitolia (Diod. 19.52.6). He was eventually forgiven by the Epeirots (Paus.1.11.4) but opposed by Philip, the brother of Kassandros, who had marched on Aitolia in 313 only to find A. re-entrenched in Epeiros (Diod. 19.74.3). In a battle at Oiniadai, A. was wounded; he died shortly afterwards (Paus.1.11.4; Diod. 19.74.4–5 says he died in the battle). His successor was Alketas II (Diod. 19.88.1; Paus. 1.11.5). Sandberger no. 5; Kaerst, *RE* I.1 (1893) 922 no. 4; Zahrnt, *BNP* I 164 no. 2; Reuss 1881; Cross 43–7; Hammond, *Epirus* 561–2, 567; Nederlof 10–17; Kienast, *RE* XXIV (1963) 1208–65 s.v. "Pyrrhos" no. 13; Heckel 2021. **Stemma IIb.**

AIGOBARES (Αἰγοβάρης). Shayegan 98 no. 3. See **AUTOBARES**.

32 AIMATHE

(Αἰμάθη). Virgin, sacrificed by the priest Amphion when Antioch was founded (Malalas 8.13 = 255 Dindorf). Grainger, *SPG* 132.

33 AISCHETADES

(Αἰσχητάδης). Athenian (Kirchner 322). General in charge of Salamis in 318/17. Sentenced to death by the Athenians for treachery in the war with Kassandros, in which he surrendered to the Macedonians (Paus. 1.35.2; cf. Polyaenus 4.11.1). Ferguson 117, with n.2; Niese I 244 n.4, 247 n.1.

34 AISCHINES

(Αἰσχίνης). Athenian orator from the deme Kothodikai. Born *c.*390/89 (Aesch. 1.49; cf. Harris 1988). Known for his political opposition to Demosthenes. Son of Atrometos, who had been exiled in the time of the Thirty, and Glaukothea ([Plut.] *Mor.* 840a). Many details of his family—which was, admittedly, undistinguished—were invented and distorted by political enemies (see Davies 544–7 and Roisman and Worthington 175–7). Demosthenes (18.312–15) compares his own career with that of A., with many unflattering revelations about the latter: he says that A.'s mother conducted Phrygian Dionysiac rites, and that A. joined in the Dionysiac march and gave out the Bacchic cry! Demosthenes also accused A. of having worked as an actor (cf. Quint. 2.17.12; for details of his career as an actor see O'Connor 74–7 no. 15, with *testimonia*) and then as assistant to his father who was a schoolteacher, *grammatodidaskalos*, both indications of servile origins. See [Plut.] *Mor.* 840a–b; Strabo 10.3.18 C471 and also Dem. 19.199, 249, 281. He had two brothers, Aphobetos and Philochares (Dem. 19.237), of whom the former was a commissioner of the Theoric Fund. A. himself was a supporter of Aristophon and Euboulos. He appears to have come to oratory and a public career late, and it is doubtful that he actually studied with Isokrates, Plato, and others ([Plut.] *Mor.* 840b). What we know of his military career comes from A. himself: he fought at Nemea, Mantinea, and twice on Euboia (Aesch. 2.168–70). In the period leading up 346, A. supported Euboulos' attempts to bring about a Common Peace as a means of pre-empting the expansion of Macedon under Philip II. He was sent on two embassies to Philip, which resulted in the conclusion of the Peace of Philokrates, which represented the failure of Euboulos' initiative. Nevertheless, A. came to accept the fact of Macedonian hegemony and his pro-Macedonian stance was attacked by Demosthenes, especially in his speeches *On the Peace* and *On the False Legation*. A. is most famous for his indictment of Ktesiphon for proposing illegal honors for Demosthenes (Aesch. 3 = *Against Ctesiphon*, answered by Dem. 18 = *De Corona*). The charge was made originally in 336, before the death of Philip II, but was postponed until 330, no doubt in part because of the changing political climate (Harris 140; cf. Will 1983, 28). A. failed to gain a conviction—or even one-fifth of the vote—and was forced into exile, going perhaps to Ephesos ([Plut.] *Mor.* 840c–d) and then to Rhodes (Plut. *Dem.* 24.2–3; cf. Quint. 11.3.7; 12.10.19; Pliny, *HN* 7.110), where he set up a school. Eventually he moved to Samos, where he died soon after Alexander's death ([Plut.] *Mor.* 840d–e). Three speeches of his have survived: 1. *Against Timarchos*, 2. *On the Embassy*, and 3. *Against Ctesiphon*. A brief life is given by [Plutarch] *Lives of the Ten Orators* 7 = [Plut.] *Mor.* 840a–841a. See also the introduction in C. D. Adams' Loeb edition of *The Speeches of Aeschines no.* 106. On A. as an orator see Quint. 10.1.77; 11.3.168;12.10.19, 23. Thalheim, *RE* I.1 (1893) 1050–62 no. 15; Engels and Weißenberger, *DNP* I 347–9 no. 2; Berve II 15–16 no. 33; Kirchner 354; cf. Davies 544–7; Harris 1988; Cawkwell, *OCD*[3] 25–6; Roisman and Worthington 175–89; Pownall, *LexAM* 44–7.

35 AISCHRION

(Αἰσχρίων). Cf. Pape-Benseler 41. Mytilenean (Tzetz. *Chil.* 8.398). An epic poet who, on the recommendation of his friend, Aristotle, accompanied Alexander in order to commemorate his achievements (Nikandros *ap. Suda* s.v. Αἰσχρίων). Nothing else is known about him. Knaak, *RE* I.1, 1063, identifies him with Aischrion of Samos (on whom see Athen. 7.296f, 8.335c–d), which appears to be ruled out by his Mytilenean origin. Knaak, *RE* I.1 (1893) 1063–4 no. 7; Berve II 16 no. 34.

36 AISCHYLOS

(Αἰσχύλος). Rhodian (Curt. 4.8.4) in Alexander's entourage in Egypt in 332/1. At Memphis, Alexander appointed him and Ephippos (son of Chalkideus, or "the Chalkidean"; Brunt I 234 n.3; but cf. Bosworth I 276) as *episkopoi* of the mercenaries left behind in Egypt (Arr. 3.5.3; Curt. 4.8.4, omitting Ephippos). He is apparently identical with the admiral of 319, who was conveying 600 talents of silver to Macedonia from Kilikia (Diod. 18.52.7)—hence a supporter of Polyperchon. A.'s cargo was confiscated by Antigonos, who claimed he needed it to pay his mercenaries, and A. himself appears to have entered Antigonos' service at that time. He is next attested as an agent of Antigonos, sent with Demarchos, to negotiate first with Kassandros and then with Ptolemy (cf. Olshausen 88 no. 63). The result of these negotiations was the "Peace of the Dynasts" (*OGIS* 5.5, 48 = Welles, *RC* 1). Billows 365 suggests, on the basis of *IG* II[2] 569, that A. the Rhodian may have been the Antigonid commander of Lemnos between 310 and 307. Ps.-Call. 2.21 names A. as the man who established the temple of Alexander and served as Alexander's first priest (see Ausfeld, *Alexanderroman* 166). Kroll's text of Pseudo-Callisthenes A, however, gives the name as Moschylus (Μόσχυλος). Berve II 17 no. 35; Kaerst, *RE* I.1 (1893) 1065 no. 12; Billows 364–5 no. 4; Hauben 7–9 no. 1; Schoch, *RE* Supplbd. IV no. 12a–b; Olshausen no. 63.

37 AKIOS

("Ακιος). Perhaps Macedonian (Tataki 226 no. 52). Emissary of Antigonos I, sent to Skepsis with a copy of the treaty of 311; he was authorized by Antigonos to discuss its provisions with the Skepsians (*OGIS* 5, line 70 = Welles *RC* 1), who praised him for this service (*OGIS* 6). A. was, in comparison with others, a relatively minor player at Antigonos' court. He is otherwise unknown. Billows 365–6 no. 5; Michel 1919; Olshausen no. 64; Schoch, *RE* Supplbd IV (1924) no. 12.

38 AKOUPHIS

("Ακουφις). For the name see Justi 12; McCrindle 79 n.3 suggests the Sanskrit form "Akubhi"; Eggermont links the name with OP Akaufaciya (= mountaineers). Indian dynast. The foremost (Plut. *Alex.* 58.7 says "eldest") of the 30 ambassadors sent by the Nysaians to Alexander to ask for peace and independence (Arr. 5.1.3). The Nysaians inhabited what is identified as Dionysopolis or *Nagarahara*, near Jalalabad: thus Eggermont 178; cf. McCrindle 338; cf. also Strabo 15.1.27 C698; Pliny, *HN* 6.79; Diod. 1.19.7; Arr. *Ind.* 5.9. Alexander demanded 300 horsemen to serve with him in India (Arr. 5.2.2, 4; cf. 6.2.3 for their return) and entrusted A. with the rule of Nysa (as *hyparchos*, though no doubt he would have been responsible to Nikanor (no. 783), satrap of Gandhara), which had previously been ruled by 300 leading citizens. The story goes that, when Alexander appointed him as ruler and demanded one hundred of his best men as hostages, A. replied that he would serve him better by taking 200 of the worst (Arr. 5.2.3; Metz Epit. 37–8; cf. Plut. *Alex.* 58.9). Although the King relented on the demand for 100 hostages, he did take the son and grandson (A70–1) of A. instead (Arr. 5.2.4). Curt. 8.10.7–18 and Justin 12.7.6–8 describe Alexander's dealings with Nysa without reference to A. Anspach I 20ff.; Berve II 17 no. 36; Bosworth II 203; Yardley and Heckel 238–40.

39 AKROTATOS

(Ἀκρότατος). Spartan (Bradford 22 no. 1), A. was the son of Kleomenes II of Sparta (*regn.* 370–309: Diod. 20.29.1) and the older brother of Kleonymos (Paus. 1.13.5) and thus of the Agiad line. Born *c.*350, he died before the end of his father's reign (Plut. *Agis* 3.6), but the throne passed to his son, Areus I, despite the rival claim of Kleonymos (Paus. 1.13.5; 3.6.2–4). A. appears to have had a gift for making himself disliked (Diod. 19.70.4–5, 71.1–5; Plut. *Mor* 240e–f, but the story may be apocryphal). In 331, after the Spartan defeat at Megalopolis and the death of Agis III, A. is said to have opposed a decree exonerating the surviving Spartans (*tresantes*) from shame; hence, it is clear that he himself had not participated in the battle. This no doubt reflects political tensions between the Eurypontid and Agiad royal houses. For this stance, he became the victim of abuse and intrigue at home (Diod. 19.70.4–5), and thus he accepted an invitation from the Syracusan exiles in Akragas to lead them in the war against Agathokles in 314. Leaving without the ephors' permission, he set sail for Sicily but landed near Apollonia, where he persuaded the Illyrian king Glaukias, who was besieging the city, to come to terms with the inhabitants

(Diod. 19.70.6–7). From here he sailed to Tarentum and requisitioned twenty ships for his enterprise (Diod. 19.70.8). His leadership in Akragas soon disappointed high expectations, and A.'s luxurious lifestyle—out of character with his upbringing (though his son and grandson followed his example: Athen. 4.142b)—alienated those who had summoned him (Diod. 19.71.1–3). After murdering the popular Syracusan exile, Sosistratos, A. was deposed and almost stoned to death. He fled back to Lakonia before the twenty ships from Tarentum arrived (Diod. 19.71.5–6). A. died sometime before 309, apparently on Krete (Plut. *Mor.* 240f), but the date and circumstances of his death are confused (Paus. 8.27.11, 30.7 says he died at Megalopolis, thus confusing him with his grandson). Niese, *RE* I.1 (1893) 1207 no. 1; Volkmann, *Kl. Pauly* I 223 no. 1; Launey 1119; Beloch IV² 2.157–8. **Stemma XVIIIb.**

40 ALEXANDER

('Αλέξανδρος). [References in **boldface** are to Plutarch's *Life of Alexander.*] Alexander III ("the Great") of Macedon (356–323; *regn.* 336–323). Son of Philip II and Olympias; born on the 6th day of Hecatombaeon = July 20, 356 (**3.5**), it may be that his birthdate was deliberately misrepresented to make it coincide with Philip's chariot victory at Olympia. Kleopatra was his full-blooded sister, born *c.*353. A precocious youth, he was educated by Lysimachos of Akarnania and Leonidas the Epeirot, a kinsman of Olympias. Stories of his questioning of Persian ambassadors and his breaking of Boukephalas (**5–6**) illustrate the intelligence, daring, and disregard for physical dangers that were to become his trademark. A. was educated by Aristotle between 343 and 340 (**7–8**) and would remain in correspondence with him until the end of his life, though their relationship had doubtless suffered as a result of the disgrace and execution of Kallisthenes. At the age of sixteen he was left by Philip as regent, though under the watchful eye of Antipatros. A. campaigned against the Maidians and founded a city named Alexandropolis (**9.1**); such practice was the prerogative of kings. Two years later, he commanded the Macedonian left at Chaironeia, destroying the vaunted Sacred Band (**9.2–3**), an accomplishment somewhat diminished by the fact that he was surrounded by Philip's most notable generals (Diod. 16.86.1: παρακαταστήσας αὐτῷ τῶν ἡγεμόνων τοὺς ἀξιολογωτάτους). Despite the father's admiration for his young son (**9.4**: Φίλιππος ὑπερηγάπα τὸν υἱόν), their relationship soured when Philip married Kleopatra (no. 607) in 337 (Köhler 1890). The quarrel between father and son was precipitated by the drunken toast of Attalos, guardian of the bride, who prayed for *legitimate* heirs from the new union and thus insulted A. by challenging his right to the throne (**9.7–10**; Satyros *ap.* Athen. 13.557d; cf. Justin 9.7.3–4). A. fled first to Epeiros, where he deposited his mother with her brother, Alexander I, and then to Illyria (**9.11**; Justin 9.7.5). Summoned back to Macedonia, through the agency of Demaratos of Korinth, A. returned but viewed his father's actions with suspicion. Whether he participated in Philip's punitive campaign against the Illyrian king Pleurias (Diod. 16.93.6) in the winter of 337/6 is unknown. But he did misinterpret Philip's plan to marry Arrhidaios (A.'s mentally deficient half-brother) to Ada, the daughter of Pixodaros of Karia. Encouraged by his mother and his *hetairoi* (Harpalos, Erigyios, Laomedon, Ptolemy, and Nearchos) to regard this as a threat to his inheritance, A. sent Thessalos to Pixodaros, informing him of Arrhidaios' mental state and offering himself instead as a groom. Philip responded by banishing these *hetairoi* from Macedonia for the remainder of his reign (**10.1–5**; Arr. 3.6.5).

In October 336, after celebrating the wedding of his daughter Kleopatra to Alexander I of Epeiros, Philip was murdered by one of the hypaspist guard as he entered the theater at Aigai (Vergina), where he had witnessed his own statue carried in procession behind those of the twelve Olympian gods. A.'s role in the murder was the subject of speculation in antiquity (see esp. Justin 9.7.1–6), just as it is today. Those who see him as a regicide undermine their arguments by emphasizing the weakness of A.'s own position (Hamilton 1965; Badian 1963; Green 1991, 108–10). Olympias too has been singled out as a plausible candidate (Develin 1981; Heckel 1981c), but the case against her cannot be proved either. Nor does it necessarily follow that he who benefited most was behind the murder; for many who stood to gain were caught entirely off guard by the act. The assassin himself, Pausanias of Orestis, was quickly dispatched—some say too quickly—and a number of political rivals were eliminated on the mere suspicion of favoring and instigating the murder (cf. Bosworth 1971a; Ellis 1971; Fears 1975). Hence, the new King, who gained the throne with the help of Antipatros and Alexander the Lynkestian, purged the court and the army of dissidents: Heromenes and Arrhabaios (Arr. 1.25.1), Attalos (Diod. 17.2.3–6), and Amyntas IV (Arr. 1.5.4). Secure at home, he turned his attention to the kingdom's borders and established his right to succeed Philip as *archon* of Thessaly, *hegemon* of the League of Korinth (Diod. 17.4.1–2; Justin 11.3.1–2; Westlake 1935, 217–20), and director of Greek affairs. In conjunction with this he inherited the expedition against Persia, which was destined to bring him undying fame, but at predictable cost.

The year 336/5 saw A. preoccupied with pre-emptive expeditions, putting to rest any thoughts the Greeks might have of throwing off the Macedonian yoke, and securing the borderlands of the northeast and northwest (**11.1–6**). First A. confronted the so-called autonomous Thrakians and the Triballians in a campaign that took him over Mount Haimos and to the Danube, where he also made a brief demonstration against the Getai who lived beyond the river; at Pellion he displayed his power by overcoming Glaukias and Kleitos, while his ally Langaros dealt with the Autariatai (Arr. 1.1–6; Fuller 219–26). But a more dangerous uprising occurred when the Thebans, incited by their Athenian "allies," besieged the Macedonian garrison on the Kadmeia and called upon their fellow Greeks to join forces with the Great King and end the "tyranny" of Macedon (Diod. 17.9.5). Encouraged by promises of Athenian aid and rumors of A.'s death in Illyria, the Thebans found themselves suddenly confronted by a Macedonian army 30,000 strong. The Athenians melted away and A.'s army made short work of the Thebans, who paid the ultimate price: their men were slaughtered, their women and children sold into slavery, and their city razed to the ground (Arr. 1.7–9; Diod. 17.8.2–14.4; **11.6–13.5**; Justin 11.3.6–4.8). At the time it was an effective lesson to any others who contemplated rebellion, but it appears that as the campaign progressed, A. had reason to regret his harsh measures (see s.vv. Dionysodoros, Thessaliskos). A.'s provisions for the restoration of Thebes in the forged *Last Days and Testament* (*LM* 109) may indicate that he had actually considered the idea in his lifetime.

In 334, he was free to launch the Persian expedition, moving via Amphipolis to the Hellespont and crossing to Asian soil, which he claimed as "Spear-won Land" (Diod. 17.17.2; Justin 11.5.10; cf. Arr. 1.11.7). His army at this point comprised 32,000 infantry and 5,100 cavalry (Diod. 17.17.3–4; cf. **15.1**, between 34,000 and 48,000 in total; Front. 4.2.4: 40,000). A. also exploited the full arsenal of panhellenic propaganda, linking himself and the Greco-Macedonian forces with the heroes of the Trojan War. At Troy he is said to have crowned the tomb of Achilles, his mythical ancestor and childhood hero, but the stories of his emulation of Achilles (and, by extension, Hephaistion's role as a second Patroklos) were all later inventions inspired by the early deaths of the king and his dearest friend (Diod. 17.17.3; **15.8–9**; Arr. 1.12.1–2; Ael. *VH* 12.7; Perrin 1895; Heckel 2015, distinguishing between literary fiction and A.'s own self-image; cf. Moloney 2015 for Herakles and the Argeads). Having dispensed with the formalities of propagandizing, A. confronted a coalition of satraps at the Granikos River. Their army contained a large body of Greek mercenaries, led by Memnon of Rhodes, but the deployment of the Persian troops and the overall battle plan were defective, at least in retrospect (McCoy 1989; but see Harle 1997, 307–12). The Persian cavalry and lightly armed were quickly routed, the Greek mercenaries left to the mercy of the victors, who enslaved those who survived the butchery (Arr. 1.13–16; Diod. 17.19–21; **16**; Justin 11.6.8–13). Again, Alexander played the panhellenism card, calling the Greek mercenaries who fought for pay against their countrymen traitors and sentencing them to hard labor in Macedonia. In the aftermath of the Granikos battle, Sardis was surrendered by its Persian garrison commander Mithrenes (Arr. 1.17.3; Curt. 3.12.6; Diod. 17.21.7; **17.1**), and various Greek cities welcomed A. as liberator. The belief that they showed genuine enthusiasm for the contrived war of vengeance is naïve; for the strengthening of Persian power under Memnon a few months later brought the liberated back into the fold of their oppressors, arguing then, as they would later when A. repeated the conquest, that they had no choice but to yield to overwhelming force. Miletos (Arr. 1.19; Diod. 17.22.1–23.3; **17.2**) and Halikarnassos were defended by Memnon, Orontobates, and those loyal to Dareios, but fell to the Macedonian war-machine. A. established Ada as ruler of Karia, strengthening and legitimizing his (as well as her own) claims to the area by becoming her adopted son (Arr. 1.23.8). Winter 334/3 saw A. in Lykia and Pamphylia.

In a move designed to boost the morale of his troops, spread the word of his successes in Asia, and garner new recruits, A. sent those who had recently married (*neogamoi*) back to Macedonia to spend the winter with their wives (Arr. 1.24.1, 29.4). In their absence, A. received disturbing news that Alexander the Lynkestian, who since the promotion of Kalas to the satrapy of Hellespontine Phrygia, commanded the Thessalian cavalry, was implicated in a plot to murder him. The negotiations between the Lynkestian and Dareios came to light when the messenger, Sisines, was captured and interrogated by Parmenion and then sent to the King at Phaselis. A. sent Amphoteros, brother of Krateros, to arrest the Lynkestian (Arr. 1.25; cf. Diod. 17.32.1–2, in a different context; Justin 11.7.1–2), who was kept in chains until he was finally executed in 330 in the aftermath of the Philotas affair (Curt. 7.1.5–10, 8.8.6; Diod. 17. 80.2). The spring saw the reuniting of the armies, the return of the *neogamoi* with reinforcements, and the capture of Kelainai; soon afterwards A. defied the problem of the Gordian knot and claimed the prophecy of mastery over Asia as his reward (Arr. 2.3; Curt. 3.1.14–18; **18.2–3**; Justin 11.7.2–16; Strabo 12.5.3 C568). Some believed he had cheated by cutting the knot with his sword. When the army pushed on to Kilikia, which he entered after frightening the defenders to abandon an unassailable position, A. was stricken with illness as he bathed in the frigid waters of the Kydnos River near Tarsos (Curt. 3.6.1–17; Diod. 17.31; **19.4–10**; Justin 11.8.3–9; Val. Max. 3.8 ext. 6). Possibly, it was a severe bout of malaria (Engels 1978b); Dareios himself mistook the delay for cowardice—or so he told his troops (Curt 3.8.10–11). This induced him to enter Kilikia from the northeast and to abandon the spacious plains of Mesopotamia near Sochoi. In the event, this was a miscalculation, and so it was presented to him by his advisers; the result was a crushing defeat at Issos in November 333 (Arr. 2.8–11; Curt 3.9–11; Diod. 17.33–4; **20.5–10**; Justin 11.9.1–10; *FGrH* 148). Victorious on the battlefield, A. captured the Persian camp (and with it the family of Dareios: Curt. 3.11.24–12.26) and also the Persian treasures which had been deposited before the battle at Damaskos. The latter were taken by Parmenion (Curt. 3.13; Arr. 2.15.1; Athen. 13.607f–608a; cf. Justin 11.10.2; **21.8**).

The stunning success at Issos and the temporary confusion of Dareios' affairs allowed A. to turn his attention to the Phoinikian coast. Some cities—Arados, Marathos, Byblos, and Sidon—surrendered at his approach, but Tyre held out against the enemy, confident in its seemingly impregnable position and the King's lack of naval power. But the latter was quickly remedied, when the ships of the newly surrendered Phoinikian towns, and those of the Greeks of Kypros, defected from the Persian fleet. After a siege of seven months (January–August 332), in which the causeway, which remains a feature of the topography today, was built to link the island to the mainland, Tyre fell (paradoxically) to troops attacking the weaker walls from the sea (Arr. 2.16.10–24.5; Curt. 4.2–4; Diod. 17.40.2–46.5; **24–25**; Justin 11.10.10–14; Polyaenus 4.3.3–4; 4.13). From Tyre A. advanced to Gaza, which he also captured, after a siege of two months (see s.v. Batis). After securing the Levantine coast, A. entered Egypt, where he met with no resistance: the Egyptian satrap, Sabakes (no. 1029), had been killed at Issos. His replacement, Mazakes, had recently defeated a mercenary force led by Amyntas son of Antiochos. Whether A. was crowned "Pharaoh" in Memphis has been debated; in 332/1 he marched to the Oasis of Siwah, where he was greeted by the high priest as son of Amun, which A. and his followers would have taken to mean "son of Zeus." Probably on his return from Siwah, A. founded Alexandria at the Canopic mouth of the Nile (for the Egyptian sojourn see Arr. 3.4–5; Curt. 4.7.8–8.9; Diod. 17.49.2–52.7; *Itiner. Al.* 48–50; **26.3–27.11**; Justin 11.11.1–13; Strabo 17.1.43 C814).

A.'s return from Egypt in 331 took him back through Phoinikia; he crossed the Euphrates at Thapsakos and proceeded to cross the Tigris before confronting Dareios' army, this time at Gaugamela. Greatly outnumbered and on terrain that favored the enemy, A. nevertheless put Dareios to flight a second time and won an overwhelming victory (Arr. 3.11–15; Curt. 4.13–16; Diod. 17.57–61; **31.6–33.11**; Justin 11.13.1–14.7; Polyaenus 4.3.6, 17; Marsden 1964). As a consequence, Babylon was surrendered to him by Mazaios, and Sousa by its satrap Aboulites. Next, A. dealt with the Ouxians, a hill-tribe that had retained a measure of independence under the Achaimenids, charging payment for safe passage through their territory. In the event, it was the Ouxians who paid. On the route to Persepolis, A.'s advance stalled briefly at the Persian Gates, but he was able to circumvent the position held by the satrap of Persis (Arr. 3.18.1–9; Curt. 5.3.16–4.34; Diod. 17.68; **37.1–2**; Polyaenus 4.3.27; Speck 2002; Moritani 2014; Howe 2015b; see s.v. Ariobarzanes no.182). The clearing of the Persian Gates left the road open to Persepolis, which was surrendered by Tiridates; the palace was burned as a symbolic gesture: A. was after all still leader of the panhellenic war of vengeance (for the capture of the Persian capitals see Arr. 3.16.3–18.12; Curt. 5.1.17–7.11; Diod. 17.64.3–72.6; **35–38**; Justin 11.14.7–12). In May 330, the pursuit of Dareios continued; for the Great King had been in Ekbatana awaiting reinforcements from the Upper Satrapies. Forced to flee again, Dareios was finally arrested and killed by his own subordinates; his corpse was found by the roadside by A., just to the east of the Caspian Gates (for details see s.v. Dareios).

The death of Dareios saw a stream of defections from the Persian army, and A. received the prominent Persians with clemency, even retaining them in office. One of these, Satibarzanes, repaid the King's kindness by further betrayal, killing the Macedonian forces under Anaxippos who accompanied him back to his satrapy. A. was thus diverted from the direct route to Baktria via the Merv Oasis (Margiana) and forced to march into Aria. At Phrada (modern Farah) he dealt with the conspiracy of Demetrios the Bodyguard, exposed somewhat unwittingly by a certain Dimnos, which raised doubts about the loyalty of Philotas (Arr. 3.16; Diod. 17.79–80; Curt. 6.7–7.2; **48.1–49.13**; Strabo 15.2.10 C724; Justin 12.5.1–8). Philotas and his father Parmenion were executed as a consequence, justly it seems in the case of the son. A. followed the Helmand River valley upstream, founding Alexandria in Arachosia (Kandahar), and then crossing the Hindu Kush near Kunduz he made his way to Baktra (Balkh). Under the pressure of A.'s pursuit, Bessos fled across the Oxos River (Amu-Darya), but was arrested by his colleagues, most notably Spitamenes, and surrendered to A. The punishment of the regicide did not end the resistance in Baktria and Sogdiana (see esp. Holt 2005). When the King proceeded to the Iaxartes River (Syr-Darya), a smaller force left behind at Marakanda (Samarcand) was attacked; troops lured out from their defensive position were massacred at the Polytimetos River (see s.vv. Menedemos, Pharnouches). It was only the capture of two mountain fortresses—the Rocks of Sogdiana (Ariamazes) and Chorienes (Sisimithres)—and the political marriage of A. and Rhoxane that brought peace to the region.

In 327, A. proceeded to India through the Swat and Buner regions, defeating en route the Aspasians and Assakenians (see s.vv. Assakenos, Cleophis), and eventually reaching the Indos (Arr. 4.22.3–30.7; Curt 8.9.1–12.3), which had been bridged by an advance force under Hephaistion and Perdikkas (Arr. 4.30.9; Curt. 8.12.4). From there he marched into the kingdom of Taxiles, who had submitted voluntarily while the King was still in Gandhara (Curt. 8.12; Metz Epit. 49–54), and by May 326 he had reached the Hydaspes (Jhelum). Defeating the rajah Poros in a difficult struggle at the Hydaspes (Arr. 4.8.4–18.5; Curt. 8.13–14; Diod. 17.87–8; Justin 12.8.1–8; **60**; Polyaenus 4.3.9, 22; Front. 1.4.9; Metz Epit. 58–60), he founded cities on each side of the river (Boukephala and Nikaia). As a clear sign of the limits he placed on his conquests, A. reached an agreement with Poros and began a shipbuilding program on Hydaspes for the purpose of conveying the army to the Ocean that lay to the south. His eastward advance to the Hyphasis (Beas) was an attempt to create a buffer zone on the edge of his empire. It is doubtful that he really expected his troops to show enthusiasm for an expedition to the Ganges (Arr. 5.25.1–29.1; Curt. 9.2.1–3.19; Diod 17.93.2–95.2; **62**; Metz Epit. 68–9; Justin 12.8.9–17). The scene that played out at the Hyphasis, or perhaps only the accounts of what was alleged to have happened, was nothing more than an exercise in image–building. The King, whose urge for conquest was depicted as insatiable, was deprived further glory in the East by tired and homesick troops, who forced him to turn back. At the Hydaspes, he found the preparations for the voyage south well in hand.

During the descent of the Indos River system, A. received a near fatal wound in the town of the Mallians (near modern Multan; Arr. 6.6–11; Curt. 9.4.15–5.21; Diod. 17.98–9; Justin 12.9.1–10.1; **63**, Plut. *Mor.* 327b, 341c, 343d–e, 344c–d), but he was rescued by his bodyguard and nursed back to health by the skilled physician Kritoboulos. Sind was conquered, the Indos Delta (and the island of Patala) secured, and after sacrificing in the Indian Ocean, A. made his return to the West. On the return march, A.'s need to maintain contact with the Ocean fleet (led by Nearchos) took the land army through inhospitable terrain. Particularly difficult was the Gedrosian march (Arr. 6.22–3; Curt. 9.10.5–18; Diod. 17.104.4–106.1; **66.4–7**; Justin 12.10.7). If A. had requested supplies in advance, they did not materialize, and the governors of surrounding satrapies were held responsible and punished for the debacle. Whether he needed scapegoats or not, A. found a disturbing pattern of malfeasance in these areas; for it appears that few expected him to return from India (Badian 1961; Higgins 1980). In Karmania, A. was reunited with Krateros, who had taken the road through Drangiana, and visited by Nearchos, who informed him of the progress of the fleet. A period of rest and relaxation followed before the army continued on to Persia and Sousiana. At Sousa the King took further steps to integrate the conquered: military reforms and mass intermarriage. But the attempt was marred by mutiny at Opis. Once this was contained and 10,000 veterans selected for demobilization, A. continued to Ekbatana, where he suffered the loss of his oldest and dearest friend, Hephaistion, in October 324 (Arr. 7.14; Diod. 17.110.8; **72**; Justin 12.12.11–12). A brutal campaign against the Kossaians over the winter of 324/3 served as an outlet for A.'s rage. But it was an embittered King who returned to Babylon to contemplate future campaigns.

Like his father, Philip II, A. blended military success with diplomacy and propaganda—but often this created dissension among his own troops. Although he exploited panhellenic symbols and ideology in his dealings with the Greeks (for example, the sacrifices at Ilion and the punishment of the mercenaries who fought for the Great King), he soon forged alliances with the defeated Persians: he kept Mithrenes in his entourage and later appointed him satrap of Armenia; he allowed Ada to recover her kingdom and was pleased to recognize her as his adoptive mother (Arr. 1.23.8); he treated the captive members of the royal family with respect (Arr. 2.12.6–7; Curt. 3.12.15–26; Diod. 17.37.5–6, 114.2; **21**; *Itiner. Al.* 37); and he accepted the surrender of prominent Persians in Egypt (see s.vv. Amminapes, Mazakes). After Gaugamela, he accelerated this program of "inclusion," allowing Mazaios to rule in Babylon and retaining Aboulites and Oxathres in Sousa and Paraitakene; Tiridates' surrender of Persepolis was rewarded, and large numbers of leading Persians entered his entourage at the time of Dareios' arrest and death (notably the family of Artabazos). In Sogdiana he married Rhoxane, the daughter of Oxyartes, and encouraged his *hetairoi* to follow his example. Not all experiments with "orientalism" were successful: the army objected to his adoption of Persian dress, even in a scaled-down form (**45.1–4**; Metz Epit. 2; Curt. 6.6.2–10; Arr. 4.7.4; Val. Max. 9.5 ext. 1), rejected the introduction of *proskynesis* (Arr. 4.9.7ff.; Curt. 8.5.5–22; **54.3–6**), and grumbled about the integration of barbarians into the army. But the King persisted and, at Sousa, conducted a mass marriage of 10,000 average Macedonians to their common–law barbarian "wives" and wedded almost a hundred prominent *hetairoi* to the daughters of Iranian nobles (Arr. 7.4.4–8; Diod. 17.107.6; **70**; Plut. *Eum.* 1.6–7; Athen. 12.538b–539a; Ael. *VH* 8.7; cf. Curt. 10.3.11–12; Bosworth 1980). This was followed by the infiltration of large numbers of barbarian troops into the Royal Army (Arr. 7.23.1–4). The reaction to this was strongly negative, as one might expect, but although the implementation of the program was suspended by the King's sudden death in 323, his Successors had their share of foreign troops and could scarcely have survived without them.

In matters of religion, A. showed great tolerance, with the result that the conquered had little cause for complaint, at least on that score. Uprisings came instead from members of the Persian aristocracy—in some cases descendants of the Seven (in the case of Orxines it is difficult to determine if he was villain or victim)—who had been equally perfidious under Achaimenid rule, or from Greek mercenaries who found themselves planted in military colonies far from home (Curt. 9.7.1–11; Diod. 17.99.5; 18.7), and conspiracies arose from internal conflicts that touched in many cases on Alexander's enlightened views. His acceptance of Zeus-Amun as his divine father was, undoubtedly, for political advantage and there are numerous indicators that he was not taken in by his new status (at least not in the early years; see s.vv. Anaxarchos, Dioxippos), but the King's divine pretensions did not sit well with the *hetairoi* for whom the Macedonian King had always been *primus inter pares*. This only helped to fuel existing political rivalries among the Macedonian factions: those whose support for A. had been lukewarm in 336 were now more open in their criticisms, and the great confrontations with Philotas (Arr. 3.26; Curt. 6.7–72; Diod. 17.79–80; Justin 12.5.1–8; 48–49; Strabo 15.2.10 C724), Kleitos (Arr. 4.8.1–9.6; Curt. 8.1.9–2.12; 50.1–52.2; *Mor.* 71c; Justin 12.6.1–18), and the Pages (see s.v. Hermolaos) all had resentment of the King's aloofness and orientalisms as a unifying theme. On two significant occasions, at the Hyphasis in 326 and at Opis in 324 (Curt. 10.2.8–4.3; Diod. 17.108–10; 70–2; Justin 12.11.4–12.6), the army voiced its displeasure, but these were objections to policy rather than to the person of the King. Though these episodes, which often required brutal countermeasures, stained A.'s reputation, one must remember that, in comparison with other rulers who enjoyed less success but wielded similar power, A. remained relatively safe in his own camp and continued to be adored by the common soldier (for opposing views see Badian 2000a; Heckel 2003a and 2009). They had followed him to the ends of the earth, and the possibility that he would not be present to lead them home constituted one of their greatest fears.

In the course of the expedition A. founded numerous cities, most of them named Alexandria. Plut. *Mor.* 328e speaks of seventy, which is perhaps no exaggeration if one takes military foundations and the resettlement of older towns into account; Steph. Byz. Ἀλεξάνδρεια names eighteen famous Alexandrias, and Ps.-Call. 3.35 mentions nine; Justin 12.5.12–13 names Alexandria-on-the-Tanais and twelve cities in Baktria and Sogdiana alone (Strabo 11.11.4, only eight). Not only did many of these survive to become influential centers in the Hellenistic age, but also the program of military settlements and synoecisms was imitated by the Successors and their descendants (full discussion in Tarn II 232–59; Fraser 1996).

A.'s true appearance is another matter of uncertainty. He appears to have been of average, or slightly less than average, height: his friend Hephaistion is said to have been physically more imposing (Curt. 3.12.16–17); his feet did not reach to the footstool when he seated himself on the Persian throne at Sousa (Diod. 17.66.3); and the Amazon Queen thought that his physical appearance did not do justice to his reputation (Curt. 6.5.29). But the claim of the *Alexander Romance* that he was less than three cubits in height (Ps.-Call. 3.4) must be dismissed as absurd, as is the claim that he had eyes of different colors. Portraits of the King were certainly stylized, emphasizing the tilt of the head, his flowing locks, and the upward turn of the eyes; for he permitted only certain artists to represent him in the various media (4; see s.vv. Apelles, Lysippos, Pyrgoteles); coin portraits too are idealized (for a full account see Stewart, with images and *testimonia*). His sexual appetites seem not to have been very strong: his parents are alleged to have introduced him to a courtesan in the hope of stimulating his interest in women (Athen. 10.435a; see s.v.

Kallixeina), and despite the now popular view that he and Hephaistion had a homoerotic relationship (**39.8**; Ael. *VH* 7.8, 12.7; Val. Max. 4.7 ext. 2; Arr. 7.14.4; Reames-Zimmerman 1999; cf. Müller 2011), a number of liaisons with women are attested (Ael. *VH* 12.34; Justin 11.10.2–3; see s.vv. Barsine, Pankaste)—one must leave aside the fictitious encounter with the Amazon Queen and the doubtful story about the Assakenian Cleophis. His rejection of boys (**22.1–3**), if not a deliberate attempt to counter rumors about his relationship with Bagoas, may reflect a lack of enthusiasm for pederasty, which had had dire consequences for his father (see s.v. Pausanias). In the case of Bagoas, it ought to be stressed that those writers who depicted him as "vile" were reacting to the fact that he was a eunuch (and an eastern one at that), and they were not finding fault with him as A.'s *eromenos*. Attempts to see Olympias as the cause of A.'s alleged sexual insecurities have met with only limited success, but the modern scholar will interpret these personal details in accordance with his or her own predilections (and social milieu), and the reader will believe whatever he or she chooses, often with little regard for cultural context. A. is known to have fathered three children (the illegitimate Herakles, son of Barsine; a child by Rhoxane who died in India; and Alexander IV, who would be the legitimate king of Macedon, though he never exercised any power). Whether his Persian brides conceived is unknown: Rhoxane was clearly taking no chances; for she had Stateira murdered after A.'s death (**77.6**), and Parysatis may have met a similar fate.

The combined effects of campaigning and the hard Macedonian lifestyle took their toll on the King's body. He suffered wounds from clubs and arrows against the Illyrians, a blow to the head and a grazing scalp wound at the Granikos, a thigh injury at Issos, an arrow to the ankle and a blow to the shoulder at Gaza, three more arrow wounds in India, including a near fatal one to the chest at the town of the Mallians (Plut. *Mor.* 327a–b); at the Iaxartes an arrow broke his tibia (**45.5–6**); and he suffered from a variety of diseases during the course of the expedition. To this we may add a penchant for drinking which, despite the hostility of the sources (e.g. Ephippos of Olynthos), cannot be dismissed or explained away. Perhaps his drinking accounted for his relatively low sex drive; and certainly the argument with Kleitos that led A. to murder him was fueled by alcohol (but see also Tritle 2003); at worst, it may even have caused his own death (O'Brien 1992).

He died in Babylon on June 11, 323 (Depuydt 1997), after a lengthy illness, the exact nature of which cannot be determined, although there is no shortage of speculation (often by writers with no medical training). Typhus, malaria, alcoholism, pancreatitis, perforated bowel, even West Nile virus and bereavement have all been suggested. Rumors of poisoning were fabricated by the party hostile to Antipatros, Antigonos, and their adherents, and it appears that the pamphlet on the *Last Days and Testament of Alexander* was published in the early years of the Successors: 321 (Ausfeld 1895, 1901; Merkelbach 1954, 1977), 318/17 (Tarn 1921; Heckel 1988); and 308 (Bosworth 2000) have all been proposed as dates for its publication with Perdikkas, Polyperchon, and Ptolemy respectively regarded as the instigators of the propaganda (a date soon after 315 is also possible); though one recent book actually argues that Ptolemy was the "assassin" (Doherty 2004, 141–86). After a brief period of indecision regarding the succession, it was agreed that Arrhidaios would be recognized as king and renamed Philip (III), and that a share of the kingdom be reserved for Rhoxane's child in the event that it was a boy (see s.v. Alexander IV no. 41). The arrangements were neither unanimous nor enforceable. Instead they triggered a series of coalitions and wars that ended in the extermination of the male members of the Argead house, the assumption of the royal title by some of A.'s former marshals, and the eventual formation of the Hellenistic kingdoms. Relatives of A.'s generals ruled in the East until the death of Kleopatra VII of Egypt in 30 BC. For the impact of Alexander's conquests see Green 1990; Erskine 2003; and for his image in Rome, Spencer 2002.

Contemporary sources are lost or survive only in second-hand fragments. The most important of the writers who accompanied the expedition and knew the King personally deserve mention: Eumenes of Kardia and Diodotos of Erythrai were said to have been the authors of the Royal Journals or *Ephemerides*, but the authenticity and nature of this work are hotly debated. Chares of Mytilene was the court chamberlain and an eyewitness source for some of what went on behind the scenes. Kallisthenes of Olynthos accompanied A. as the "official historian" and sent reports back to Greece at the end of each campaigning season, serving thus as both propagandist and war correspondent (Heckel 2020). Both Onesikritos and Nearchos described the progress of the fleet from the Hydaspes to the Tigris and their fragments deal primarily with India; the former may have written a work closely modeled on Xenophon's *Cyropaedia* (Brown, *Onesicritus*; cf. Winiarczyk 2007). Ptolemy and Aristoboulos, who were regarded by Arrian of Nicomedia as the most reliable (perhaps because the least critical) sources, still enjoy inflated reputations (Strasburger 1934; Kornemann 1935; but see Errington 1969; Roisman 1984). Others in A.'s entourage wrote memoirs and scurrilous gossip (Medeios of Larisa, Polykleitos, and Ephippos), while the bematists measured the miles and provided a foundation for the expedition's itinerary. Marsyas of Pella, a *syntrophos* of the King and a half-brother of Antigonos the One-Eyed, contributed little to the history of events after 333; for he remained with Antigonos in Phrygia. Kleitarchos of Alexandria appears not to have participated in the expedition, though he did have access to written work and eyewitness reports (Schachermeyr 658–62; Prandi 1996). His date of writing has recently been challenged on the basis of a papyrus fragment of questionable value (discussion in Prandi 2012).

The fragments of the lost Alexander historians are collected in volume IIB of Jacoby, *Die Fragmente der griechischen Historiker*; English translations in Robinson 1953; cf. Auberger (French); discussion in Pearson 1960 and numerous works by Truesdell S. Brown; cf. Pédech 1984. Extant sources are cited throughout this work. Kaerst, *RE* I.1 (1893) 1412–34 no. 10; Müller, *LexAM* 63–8. Modern literature on Alexander is immense. Tarn I–II and Badian 2012 (his *Collected Papers*) present dogmatic and diametrically opposed views that form the basis of many important scholarly debates; Schachermeyr 1973, Bosworth 1988a, and Müller 2019, insightful and sound; Lane Fox; Green 1991, and Cartledge 2004, popular and well written; MacLean Rogers 2004, a no-nonsense, minimalist view. Fuller 1960 (military history); cf. Heckel 2008; Heckel (resistance to A.'s conquests). See also Bieber 1964; Schwarzenberg 1967 and 1976; and Stewart, for Alexander in Art.

41 ALEXANDER

(Ἀλέξανδρος). Alexander IV of Macedon (*regn.* 323/2–310). Son of Alexander and Rhoxane (Paus. 9.7.2), A. was born no later than September 323 (Rhoxane was six or eight months pregnant when Alexander died at the beginning of June; cf. Arr. *Succ.* 1.1, 1.8; App. *Syr.* 52.261, referring to Rhoxane as ἡ κύουσα). Upon his birth he was recognized (by pre-arrangement) as *symbasileus* with Philip III Arrhidaios (Arr. *Succ.* 1.1, 1.8; Justin

13.4.3; but *P.Eleph.* 1 calls 311 the "seventh" year of his reign, clearly dating from the year of Arrhidaios' death). His birth provided Perdikkas with the opportunity to usurp the *prostasia*, since Krateros did not exercise his claim, which at any rate pertained only to Philip III Arrhidaios (cf. Diod. 18.23.2). Perdikkas took A. with him to Kappadokia and Pisidia (Justin 13.6.10), and eventually to Egypt (Paus. 1.6.3), whence he came to Triparadeisos in northern Syria. There the Kings were entrusted to Antigonos the One-Eyed (Arr. *Succ* 1.38; cf. Justin 16.1.13). But when Kassandros became suspicious of Antigonos' intentions, A. and Philip III were taken by Antipatros to Macedonia (Arr. *Succ* 1.42, 44; Heid. Epit. 3.2). After Antipatros' death, Polyperchon assumed the guardianship of A. and summoned Olympias to Macedonia to exercise the *epimeleia* and see to the boy's upbringing (Diod. 18.49.4; cf. 19.23.2). It was, no doubt, Olympias who arranged the betrothal of A. to Deidameia, the daughter of Aiakides and sister of Pyrrhos (Plut. *Pyrrh.* 4.3). A. was in the company of Olympias when she was besieged at Pydna by Kassandros' forces (Diod. 19.35.5; Justin 14.6.2, confusing A. and Herakles), and eventually he and his mother were sent to Amphipolis, where they were kept under guard (Diod. 19.52.4; Justin 14.6.13; 15.1.3). Although an agreement made with Antigonos, Ptolemy, and Lysimachos spelled out that Kassandros should be *strategos* of Europe until A. came of age (Diod. 19.105.1), a certain Glaukias, who commanded the guard over A., murdered him and his mother Rhoxane in 310 and concealed their bodies (Diod. 19.105.2; Justin 15.2.5, cf. 16.1.15; Heid. Epit. 2.3; Paus.9.7.2 says A. was poisoned). His death (along with that of Barsine's son, Herakles) put an end to the Argead dynasty and cleared the way for the leading Successors to make their claims to kingship (App. *Syr.* 54.275; cf. 52.261). Schroder 1982 absurdly identifies one of the figures—obviously female—on the Boscoreale Murals as Alexander IV. It may relate to the family of Demetrios and Antigonos Gonatas; but see the sensible analysis of Landucci 2003, 89–93 and 2009, 271–5, with additional bibliography. Kaerst, *RE* I.1 (1893) 1434–5 no. 11; Tataki 227 no. 57; G. Wirth, *Kl. Pauly* I 250 no. 7; Badian, *BNP* I 475 no. 5); Müller, *LexAM* 71. **Stemma I.**

42 ALEXANDER

('Αλέξανδρος). Macedonian (Tataki 229–30 no. 71). Alexander V of Macedon (*regn.* 295–294). Youngest son of Kassandros and Thessalonike (Plut. *Pyrrh.* 6.3; Justin 16.1.2; Paus. 9.7.3; Porphyr. Tyr. *FGrH* 260 F3 §5). Born no earlier than 313 (the oldest son, Philip, can have been born no earlier than 315). Expelled from Macedonia by his elder brother, Antipatros, who also killed their mother Thessalonike for favoring A. (Plut. *Pyrrh.* 6.3; Justin 16.1.1–4; Plut. *Demetr.* 36.1). Married to Lysandra, daughter of Ptolemy I Soter (Porphyr. Tyr. *FGrH* 260 F3 §5); the betrothal may have taken place before Kassandros' death, but in light of A.'s age in 297 it appears that the marriage occurred in the time of Thessalonike's regency. A. sought vengeance by summoning both Pyrrhos from Epeiros and Demetrios Poliorketes from the Peloponnese (Plut. *Demetr.* 36.1; Justin 16.1.5–6, the latter mentioning only Demetrios). Pyrrhos arrived first and made it clear that he had designs on Macedonia, taking a portion for himself (Plut. *Demetr.* 36.2). Aware of the dangers of accepting outside help, A. met Demetrios at Dion and told him that he no longer needed his support, but feigning friendship, the young man appears to have plotted against Demetrios' life at a banquet (Plut. *Demetr.* 36.3–4). Demetrios foiled the plot (Plut. *Demetr.* 36.6), if it was, in fact, real and not invented to excuse Poliorketes' later actions. On the following day, Demetrios pretended to be called away by urgent affairs in

Thessaly and allowed A. to accompany him as far as Larisa, where he ordered his guards to murder him (Plut. *Demetr.* 36.7–12). According to another version, when it appeared that the rival brothers were about to be reconciled, at the urging of Lysimachos (Justin 16.1.7), Demetrios murdered him and stole his kingdom (Paus. 9.7.3; Diod. 21.7.1; Justin 16.1.8–10, 16; Porphyr. Tyr. *FGrH* 260 F3 §5). Sandberger no. 6; Kaerst, *RE* I.1 (1893) 1435–6 no. 14; Levêque 126ff.; Seibert 1967, 75–6. **Stemma V.**

43 ALEXANDER

(Ἀλέξανδρος). Alexander I of Epeiros. Son of Neoptolemos I (cf. Head, *HN*² 322; brother of Olympias and Troas; nephew of Arybbas (Justin 8.6.5; cf. 7.6.10–11; 12.2.1; Livy 8.3.7). Born *c.*362 (Justin 8.6.7), A. came to the Macedonian court at some point after 357 and remained there until 342; the charge that he was Philip II's catamite was doubtless fabricated (Justin 8.6.6, 8). In 342, Philip II deposed Arybbas and placed the twenty-year-old A. on the throne (Justin 8.6.7–8, 17.3.14–15; Trogus, *Prol.* 8; Diod. 16.72.1; [Dem.] 7.32; cf. Errington 1975a). Front. 2.5.10 reports a stratagem against the Illyrians that must date to the early years of A.'s reign, and it appears that A. aided Philip in the establishment of a garrison in Ambrakia (Diod. 17.3.3; cf. Theopompos, *FGrH* 115 F229). In 336, in the aftermath of the family quarrel that accompanied his marriage to Kleopatra-Eurydike and the flight of Olympias to her brother's court, Philip II arranged the marriage of A. to his daughter, Kleopatra, the bridegroom's niece (Justin 9.6.1, 7.7; cf. 13.6.4; Diod. 16.91.4–93.2). A. and Kleopatra *may* have produced two children, but this is based on the assumption that Kadmeia (no. 557), who is attested by Plutarch (*Pyrrh.* 5.11) as the sister of Neoptolemos II (known to be a son of a certain Alexander), was born in 335 and named to commemorate the sack of Thebes by her uncle, Alexander the Great (Plut. *Pyrrh.* 5.11). Furthermore, Plutarch maintains that "the sons of Neoptolemos" (which many scholars take to be a reference to Neoptolemos II himself), ruled Epeiros after the expulsion of Pyrrhos (Plut. *Pyrrh.* 5). This is highly speculative and fails to stand up to vigorous scrutiny (see s.v. Neoptolemos no. 773). A. accepted the invitation of Tarentum to act as its champion against the Lucanians of southern Italy (Strabo 6.3.4 C280). His departure is generally synchronized with that of his namesake for the East (Gell. *NA* 17.21.33; Justin 12.2.1–15). It is likely to have occurred in 334/3, if not in the spring of 334 (Oxyrhynchos Chronicle = *P. Oxy.* 12, *FGrH* 255 F1 §6). Certainly, Tauriskos, who had fled with Harpalos before the battle of Issos (late 333), was sent by him to Alexander I and found him in Italy (Arr. 3.6.7). After several victories against the Bruttians and Lucanians, A. took Heraclea, Sipontum, Consentia, and Terina, as well as other towns of the Messapians and Lucanians; he sent 300 nobles as hostages to Epeiros (Livy 8.24.4). A. had also attempted unsuccessfully to transfer the national festival of the southern Greeks (*panegyris*) from Heraclea to Thourioi, to a fortified place on the Acalander River (*Barr. Atl.* 45 E4), and thus earned their enmity (Strabo 6.3.4 C280). He was fated to die in Lucania (Livy 9.17.17; cf. Paus. 1.11.3, 7; according to Pliny, *HN* 3.11.98 = Theopompos, *FGrH* 115 F318, he died in the Lucanian town of Mardonia or Mandonia, possibly a corruption of Pandosia). For his campaign and death see Justin 12.2.1–15. His death in winter 331/0 (Aesch. 3.242; cf. Bosworth I 284) is said to have been foreshadowed by the oracle of Dodona (Livy 8.24.1–3; Justin 12.2.3–4; Strabo 6.1.5 C256). It was during the campaign near Pandosia, where he was attended by some two hundred Lucanian exiles, that he was cut off by the enemy and in danger of being handed over to the Lucanians by these exiles, who asked in return to be restored to their homes. A. broke away, killed the Lucanian general in hand-to-hand combat, but finally was killed by a javelin hurled by an unnamed Lucanian exile (Livy 8.24.5–13; cf. Plut. *Mor.* 326b). His body was mutilated and cut into two parts; half the body was buried by a woman in Consentia who sent the bones to Kleopatra and Olympias in Epeiros, hoping to gain the release of her husband and children who had been captured by the enemy (Livy 8.24.14–17). His death is described at length by Livy, who dates it in the same year as the foundation of Alexandria in Egypt (8.24.1, but Livy misdates both events to 326; cf. 8.3.6 where he misdates Alexander's crossing into Italy to 340). If there is any truth that Bruttian, Lucanian, and Etruscan envoys came to Babylon in 323 (Arr. 7.15.4), it may be on account of Alexander I's activities in Italy. Kaerst, *RE* I (1894) 1409–10 no. 6; Badian, *BNP* I 475 no. 6; Berve II 19–21 no. 38; Werner 1987. **Stemma IIa–b.**

44 ALEXANDER

(Ἀλέξανδρος). Son of Alketas II (Diod. 19.88.3), a son of Arybbas, who claimed the Molossian throne after the expulsion of Aiakides. Brother of Teukros, Nisos, and Esioneus. When Lykiskos (no. 661) invaded Epeiros and encamped at Kassope, Alketas set out to meet him with the forces at his disposal, but he sent A. and Teukros to the Epeirot cities to levy more troops and rejoin him (Diod. 19.88.3). A. thus came to his father's aid when the latter was besieged at Eurymenai by Lykiskos. But, despite some initial success (cf. Mikythos no. 733, Lysandros no. 669), A., Teukros, and Alketas were defeated in a second battle at Eurymenai, when Deinias (no. 346) brought Lykiskos reinforcements. A., with his father and brother, retreated to an unnamed fortress, leaving Lykiskos to plunder and destroy Eurymenai (Diod. 19.88.5–6). He may have been the father of Kadmeia (no. 557) and Neoptolemos II (no. 773), who won the Molossian throne in 302 when Pyrrhos was expelled. Nothing else is known about either A. or his brother Teukros. Kaerst, *RE* I.1 (1893) 1437 no. 19; Hammond, *Epirus* 567–8; Heckel 2021. **Stemma IIa.**

45 ALEXANDER

(Ἀλέξανδρος). A son of Aëropos (Arr. 1.7.6, 17.8) of Lynkestis (Diod. 17.32.1, 80.2; Curt. 7.1.5; 8.8.6; Justin 11.2.2, 7.1) and brother of Heromenes and Arrhabaios (Arr. 1.25.1); A. married a daughter of Antipatros (Curt. 7.1.7; Justin 11.7.1; 12.14.1; Diod. 17.80.2 wrongly calls his father-in-law Antigonos; cf. Habicht 1977a; Heckel 1989, 32–3, 37). A. was probably a member of the Lynkestian royal house. Although his brothers were executed for complicity in the murder of Philip (Arr. 1.25.1; Justin 11.2.1–2; cf. Diod. 17.2.1; Plut. *Alex.* 10.8), A. was spared on account of his connections with Antipatros and because he was the first to hail his namesake as "King" (Arr. 1.25.2; Justin 11.2.2). He was promptly appointed *strategos* of Thrake (Arr. 1.25.2): in 335 it was rumored in Thebes that the approaching Macedonian army was led by Alexander Lynkestes, coming from Thrake; for certain politicians had encouraged a false report that Alexander the Great was dead (Arr. 1.7.6). In 334, A. accompanied the King, who clearly did not trust him with the *strategia* of Thrake in his absence. He succeeded Kalas as commander of the Thessalian cavalry, when the son of Harpalos was appointed satrap of Hellespontine Phrygia (Arr. 1.25.2). The King's *consilium* may have expressed doubts about A.'s suitability at the time, but Arr. 1.25.5 could refer to a retrospective judgment. A. was hipparch for only a few months, in which time he helped Kalas establish himself in the Troad (Arr. 1.17.8; cf.

Polyaenus 4.3.15). In 334/3 Parmenion informed the King that a Persian named Sisenes had been arrested, bearing a letter from Dareios III to A. that offered him 1,000 talents of gold if he assassinated his King (Arr. 1.25.3; the offer may have come from Nabarzanes, Curt. 3.7.12). The Lynkestian was arrested, through the agency of Amphoteros, whom Alexander sent from Phaselis to Parmenion's camp (Arr. 1.25.9–10; Diod. 17.32.1–2 places the arrest shortly before Issos; Badian 2000a, 56–60 implausibly argues that Sisenes' evidence was contrived; see Heckel 2003a, 210–13). Deposed from office and kept under guard until 330, A. was eliminated in the aftermath of the Philotas affair (Curt. 7.1.5–9; Diod. 17.80.2; Justin 12.14.1). His execution has been treated by many as an afterthought, as if it were a simple housekeeping matter, but this obscures the fact that A. would have been a serious candidate for the kingship, if the conspirators at Phrada had been able to assassinate Alexander the Great. Curt. 7.1.6 speaks of two informants against A., gives a radically different version of the arrest of Sisenes (no. 1050; Curt. 3.7.11–15; cf. Atkinson I 183ff.), and appears to have discussed him in the lost second book of his *History* (cf. Heckel 1991, 125). But Curt. 7.1.6 follows a primary source that dates the arrest of A. to autumn 333 (i.e., not long before Issos); in this context, most sources describe Parmenion's suspicions that Philip of Akarnania had been bribed by Dareios to poison Alexander (Curt. 3.6.1–17; Plut. *Alex.* 19.4–10; Val. Max. 3.8 ext. 6; Ps.-Call. 2.8.4–11; Jul. Valer. 2.24; Sen. *de Ira* 2.23.2; also Arr. 2.4.8–11). Kaerst, *RE* I.1 (1893) 1435 no. 12; Badian, *BNP* I 476 no. 7; Beloch III² 2.77, and *passim*; Berve II 17–19 no. 37; Bosworth 1971a; Carney 1980; Heckel, *Marshals*² 22–31; Tataki 201 no. 2; Badian 2000a, 56–60; Heckel 2003a, 210–13. **Stemma XV.**

46 ALEXANDER

(Ἀλέξανδρος). Macedonian from Tymphaia (Tataki 211 no. 1), son of Polyperchon (Diod. 18.65.3; 19.53.1, 54.3, 61.1, 63.2, 66.2, 67.1; Arr. *Succ.* 1.38). A. was born before 334 and, in the light of his appointment as Somatophylax of Philip III at Triparadeisos in 320 (Arr. *Succ.* 1.38), most likely in the 340s. His appointment as Somatophylax was undoubtedly intended to give Polyperchon some input into the management of affairs. Conversely, it may be seen as a way for Antipatros the Regent to keep at his court the relatives of prominent men, who might serve as hostages. At some point he married Kratesipolis (no. 626; Diod. 19.67.1; cf. Plut. *Demetr.* 9.5), a Macedonian woman who was to prove herself a formidable force in the struggles of the Successors (see Macurdy 1929). A. arrived with an army in Attika in 318 to back up demands for the liberation of Athens, but he was soon persuaded by Phokion and others of the pro-Macedonian party to retain Mounychia and Peiraieus for himself; hence A. conferred in secret with Nikanor (Diod. 18.65.3–5). The party that favored Polyperchon was deposed and they, including Phokion, took refuge with A., who sent favorable letters on their behalf to his father (Diod. 18.66.1). His negotiations with Nikanor came to naught, and soon Kassandros sailed into Peiraieus to relieve the city. Polyperchon took the bulk of the army to the Peloponnese, leaving the remainder with A. in Attika (Diod. 18.68.3). What he did in the interval, we are not told, but it appears that A. was either near or in the Peloponnese when Kassandros directed his attentions to Macedonia in 317 (Diod. 19.35.1). In 316, Aristonous, in control of Amphipolis, looked in vain for relief from Polyperchon and his son (Diod. 19.50.8). After the collapse of the Polyperchon-Olympias faction in Macedonia, Kassandros returned to the Peloponnese and A. (Diod. 19.53.1), who now occupied the Isthmus, stood idly by when Kassandros ferried his troops to the Argolid and began to recapture the Peloponnesian cities (Diod. 19.54.3–4). In 315, when Ptolemy, Lysimachos, and Kassandros had formed a dangerous alliance against him, Antigonos sent Aristodemos of Miletos to attempt to win A. and his father to his side (Diod. 19.57.5). This met with initial success, with Polyperchon supporting Antigonos' cause in the Peloponnese, while A. sailed to Asia to meet Antigonos (Diod. 19.60.1), with whom he established a pact (Diod. 19.61.1). Antigonos sent him back to Greece with 500 talents and high expectations (Diod. 19.61.5). Ptolemy responded by sending Polykleitos with 50 ships to the Peloponnese to attack A. who, along with his father, was now cooperating with Aristodemos (Diod. 19.62.5). A. wasted an opportunity to seize Argos in the absence of Kassandros' general Apollonides (no. 151; Diod. 19.63.2). Kassandros himself turned his attentions to Korinth and captured A.'s garrisons there (Diod. 19.63.4–5) before directing his army to Orchomenos. This action Kassandros followed up by sending Prepelaos to A. and persuading him to desert Antigonos (and Polyperchon) by accepting the position of *strategos* of the Peloponnese (Diod. 19.64.2–5; cf. 19.66.2). As Kassandros' lieutenant, A. suppressed an uprising by the Dymaians, only to lose the city soon after his departure (Diod. 19.66.5–6). Setting out from Sikyon in 314 he was murdered by Alexion (no. 56), a Sikyonian who had pretended friendship (19.67.1). A.'s wife Kratesipolis was successful at keeping the army together and retaining some control over the Peloponnese (Diod. 19.67.1, 74.2). Berve II 21 no. 39; Kaerst, *RE* I.1 (1893) 1435 no. 13; Heckel 1992, 283; Wirth, *Kl. Pauly* I 250 no. 9; Badian, *BNP* I 476 no. 8. **Stemma XII.**

47 ALEXANDER

(Ἀλέξανδρος). Macedonian. Namesake of the King (Aristoboulos, *FGrH* 139 F2b = Plut. *Mor.* 259e; cf. *Mor.* 1093c). The leader of a band of Thrakians (ἦρχε δὲ Θρᾳκίου τινὸς ἴλης suggests that he was a cavalry officer) who burst into the home of Timokleia (no. 1140) during the sack of Thebes (335). He raped the woman but was fatally deceived by her. Timokleia pretended to have hidden gold and silver in a well, into which she pushed A. to his death (Plut. *Alex.* 12). According to Polyaenus 8.40, he went into the well looking for plunder, and Timokleia threw rocks down upon him and killed him. It is tempting to see in the name Alexander a personification of the excess that led to the "rape of Thebes" by the Macedonians. But it is unlikely that Aristoboulos, who was an apologist for the King, would have been the source of such an unflattering depiction. Lane Fox 146 perversely identifies him with Alexander the Lynkestian, which is impossible. Griffith, *HMac* II 433 n.4.

48 ALEXANDER

(Ἀλέξανδρος). Macedonian (Tataki 228 no. 63). A member of Alexander's cohort (*sua cohors*: Curt. 8.11.9–10) but apparently not a Page. Together with Charus (no. 325), A. led a band of 30 young men selected from the Royal Hypaspists for the assault on Aornos. A. and Charus were killed in a valiant attack (Curt. 8.11.15). Curtius' description of their deaths recalls Virgil's account of Nisos and Euryalos (*Aeneid* 9.176ff.), but the historicity of the event (cf. Plut. *Alex.* 58.5) and of A. and Charus themselves need not be questioned. Berve II 21 no. 40; Heckel 295–6.

49 ALEXANDER

(Ἀλέξανδρος). Allegedly a son of Alexander the Great and the Assakenian queen, Cleophis (no. 332). His existence is questionable, and certainly his paternity may be doubted. Perhaps, Cleophis named a son Alexander after the Macedonian conqueror (Curt. 8.10.36; Justin 12.7.9–10), though in some accounts she is depicted as a grandmother. Seel 1972, 181.

ALEXANDER. Diod. 17.17.6. Textual error. See s.v. **ARISTANDROS**.

50 ALEXANDER

(Ἀλέξανδρος). Aitolian general in 321/0 (presumably *strategos* of the Aitolian League; cf. Grainger, *APS* 73). Commanded 12,000 infantry and 400 horse who invaded Lokris and Thessaly in accordance with the pact made between the Aitolians and Perdikkas against Antipatros (Diod. 18.38.1). When Antipatros and Krateros left Europe, the Aitolians *en route* to Thessaly attacked the city of the Amphissan Lokrians, overrunning the countryside and capturing neighboring settlements. They defeated Antipatros' general Polykles (no. 981), killing him and many of his soldiers; of the remainder, some were sold into slavery and others ransomed (Diod. 18.38.1–2). A. then entered Thessaly and persuaded the inhabitants to rebel against Antipatros. Thus, he gathered a force of 25,000 infantry and 1,500 horse (Diod. 18.38.3), including the numbers he brought with him. But his attention was diverted by news of an Akarnanian invasion of Aitolia, which forced him to abandon Thessaly, leaving his non-citizen troops there under Menon of Pharsalos and returning home with his Aitolians (Diod. 18.38.4–5). Of A. himself nothing else is recorded. Grainger, *APS* 89 no. 1.

51 ALEXANDER

(Ἀλέξανδρος). Macedonian (Tataki 227 no. 60), *philos* of Demetrios Poliorketes. Sent by Demetrios into Rhodes to a certain mercenary captain, Athenagoras (no. 253) the Milesian, who had promised to betray the city (his men guarded the trench that the Rhodians had built to counter the work of Demetrios' sappers) but proved instead to be a double agent. This man reported the plan to the Rhodians and betrayed A. who was captured (Diod. 20.94.5). What became of him is unknown, though the Berlin Papyrus 11632 (*FGrH* 533 F2) suggests that he may have been freed when Demetrios sent a herald to the city. Nothing else is known about him. Billows 366 no. 6; Olshausen no. 73; Kaerst, *RE* I.2 (1894) no. 21; Launey 303, 1171.

52 ALEXANDER

(Ἀλέξανδρος). Macedonian (Tataki 148 no. 7). Son of Lysimachos by an Odrysian woman (**A99**; Paus. 1.10.5; though Polyaenus 6.12 makes him the son of Amastris (no. 67), which is unlikely, since Lysimachos did not make a claim to Herakleia on his son's behalf after Amastris' death). After the death of his half-brother, Agathokles (no. 18), A. fled to the court of Seleukos (App. *Syr.* 64), whom he urged to wage war on Lysimachos (Paus. 1.10.4). When Lysimachos was killed at Koroupedion in 281, A. recovered his father's body (though the vengeful Lysandra was reluctant to give it up) and buried it in the Thrakian Chersonnese (Paus. 1.10.5). Appian (*Syr.* 64.340) reports that some writers claimed that Thorax (no. 1130) the Thessalian buried Lysimachos' body, but others said A. found it partly decomposed. His capture of Kotiaion in Phrygia by trickery (Polyaenus 6.12) probably dates to before his flight from Lysimacheia (*contra* Melber in the Teubner edition). Kaerst, *RE* I.1 (1893) 1436–7 no. 17; Lund 202, 206; Grainger, *SPG* 637 no. 3. **Stemma IX.**

53 ALEXANDER

(Ἀλέξανδρος). Son of Demetrios Poliorketes by Deidameia (no. 343). Born *c.*302/1, he accompanied his mother when she joined Demetrios in Kilikia in 299 (Plut. *Demetr.* 32.5). After his mother's death, he appears to have gone to Alexandria as a hostage along with his uncle Pyrrhos (thus Webster 1922, 358, who considers him the Alexander of *P. Lond. Inv.* 2087). According to Plut. *Demetr.* 53.8 he spent most of his life in Egypt. Kaerst, *RE* I (1894) 1437 no. 20; Tataki 227 no. 59; Webster 1922. **Stemma IIb.**

54 ALEXANDER

(Ἀλέξανδρος). Alexander II of Epeiros. Son of Pyrrhos and Lanassa (no. 640; Plut. *Pyrrh.*9.3), hence grandson of Agathokles of Syracuse. A. was born in all likelihood in 294/3 (Justin 18.1.3 makes him younger than his brother Ptolemy (no. 1014), who was 15 in 280) and ruled the Molossians after the death of his father (Phylarchos *ap.* Athen. 3.73b). He accompanied his father and brother Helenos (no. 511) to Italy in 280 (Justin 18.1.3) and, in 278, Pyrrhos took A. with him to Sicily, leaving Helenos in Tarentum; for the Syracusans welcomed Pyrrhos because of his marriage to Lanassa, A.'s mother (Diod. 22.8.2; cf. Justin 23.3.3, confusing A. with Helenos). Pyrrhos allegedly marked out Sicily as A.'s future realm; Italy was reserved for Helenos (Justin 23.3.3). After Pyrrhos' failure to win over the Sicilians, A. returned with his father to Italy, and then to Epeiros. In 272, his father's ashes were given to Helenos by Antigonos Gonatas to return to A. (Val. Max. 5.1 ext. 4). Since Ptolemy had been killed in the campaign against Sparta, Pyrrhos' death left A. as king of Epeiros. He ruled from 272 until 255. Frontinus preserves one of his stratagems from the mid-260s (*Strat.* 3.4.5). Aeneas Tacticus *ap.* Ael. *Tactica* 1.2 claimed that A., like his father, wrote a work on tactics. Sandberger no. 7; Kaerst, *RE* I.1 (1893) 1410–11 no. 7; G. Wirth, *Kl. Pauly* I 249–50 no. 6. **Stemma IIb.**

55 ALEXARCHOS

(Ἀλέξαρχος). Macedonian (Tataki 231 no. 80). Son of Antipatros (Strabo 7 C331 frg. 35; Athen. 3.98d; Plin. *HN* 4.37; Clem. Al. *protr.* 54). Brother of Kassandros (Athen. 3.98d), built the city of Uranopolis on Mt. Athos—the circuit of its walls was 30 stades (Strabo 7, frg. 35)—at some point between 316 and 300; for coin issues inscribed ΟΥΡΑΝΙΔΩΝ ΠΟΛΕΩΣ or ΟΥΡΑΝΙΔΩΝ see Mørkholm 1991, 60. The city, and perhaps A. himself, did not endure long after Kassandros' death in 297. Like Dionysios of Syracuse, A. had a reputation for using elaborate names for simple objects (Athen. 3.98e–f = Herakleides Lembos, *FHG* III 169 frg. 5). Kaerst, *RE* I.2 (1894) 1463 no. 3; Hoffmann 266–8; Berve II 21 no. 41; Grainger 2019, 157, 205. **Stemma V.**

56 ALEXION

(Ἀλεξίων). Prominent Sikyonian (cf. Skalet no. 23), A. had pretended friendship with Alexander (no. 46) son of Polyperchon but, in 314, he and some unnamed accomplices murdered him on his return from Dymai (Diod. 19.67.1). They may have resented Alexander's alliance with Kassandros (cf. Griffin 1982, 77). What became of him is unknown. Alexander's widow arrested and crucifed thirty rebel leaders (Diod. 19.67.2); A. may have been among them. Skalet 79 no 23; Paschidis 229–30 B10.

57 ALEXIPPOS

(Ἀλέξιππος). Physician who treated Peukestas (no. 882) when he was wounded in a bear hunt (Plut. *Alex.* 41.4); A. received a letter of thanks from Alexander (Plut. *Alex.* 41.6). Berve II 22 suggests that the incident occurred after Peukestas assumed the satrapy of Persis in 325/4. This is rendered more likely by the fact of Alexander's letter, which implies that Peukestas and A. were not in the King's camp. A. is otherwise unknown. Wellmann, *RE* I (1894) no. 6; Berve II 21–2 no. 43.

58 ALEXIS

(Ἄλεξις). Tarentine rhapsode; performed at the mass marriage ceremony in Sousa in 324 (Chares of Mytilene, in the tenth book of his *History of Alexander*, *FGrH* 125 F4 = Athen. 12.538e). Nothing else is known about him. Kirchner, *RE* I (1894) no. 8; Berve II 22 no. 44.

59 ALKAIOS

(Ἀλκαῖος). Son of Heraios, from Ainos. Served Demetrios Poliorketes in the last decade of the fourth century. A. is honored as a benefactor by both the Athenians, in one of many decrees moved by Stratokles (*IG* II² 495 = Moretti, *ISE* no. 6: citizenship for A. and his descendants), and the Epidaurians (*IG* IV² 58). In the latter case this may be due, as Billows 366 suspects, to his involvement in Demetrios Peloponnesian campaign of 303. Nothing else is known about him. Billows 366 no. 7; Schoch, *RE* Supplbd. IV (1924) no. 8a; Osborne, *Naturalization* no. D60.

60 ALKENOR

(Ἀλκήνωρ). Greek. Hunchback (κυρτός) at the court of Ptolemy I in 308 (Athen. 6.244d). Identification with the comic poet and Lenaian victor in the 330s (*IG* II² 2325, III col. IV) is unlikely.

61 ALKETAS

(Ἀλκέτας). Younger brother of Perdikkas (Justin 13.6.15; Diod. 18.29.2; Arr. *Succ.* 1.21), hence probably also a son of Orontes of Orestes (cf. Arr. 3.11.9; 6.28.4; *Ind.* 18.5); his sister was Atalante (cf. Diod. 18.37.2). Possibly of Argead descent, unless Curt. 10.7.8 (calling Perdikkas *stirpe regia genitus*) refers to the Orestian royal house. Born *c.*355, he succeeded his brother as general of the phalanx of Lynkestians and Orestians, perhaps as early as 331/0 (when Perdikkas assumed the post of Somatophylax vacated by Menes: Arr. 3.15.9), though Perdikkas retained nominal command (cf. Arr. 3.18.5). In 327 A. campaigned with Krateros, Polyperchon and Attalos in Paraitakene (Arr. 4.22.1; cf. Curt. 8.5.2), receiving by letter news of the abortive attempt to introduce *proskynesis* and the conspiracy of Hermolaos (Plut. *Alex.* 55.6; cf. Hamilton 155; Heckel 1978b). During the Swat campaign of 327, A., Attalos, and Demetrios the hipparch attacked the town of Ora, while Koinos besieged Bazeira (Arr. 4.27.5). Arrian speaks of οἱ ἀμφὶ Ἀλκέταν (4.27.6), as if to suggest that A. was the commander-in-chief, but attributes the actual capture of the city to

Alexander (4.27.9; Curt. 8.11.1 gives the honor to Polyperchon). At the Hydaspes, A. was stationed with Attalos and Meleagros halfway between the main camp and the eventual crossing-point of the river (Arr. 5.11.3 refers to mercenaries, who must have supplemented three phalanx battalions). Nothing else is known of his career under Alexander.

In 321, A. urged his brother to marry Nikaia and remain on friendly terms with Antipatros, although Eumenes favored a union with Kleopatra (Arr. *Succ.* 1.21). A.'s advice won out temporarily, though Perdikkas' negotiations with Kleopatra raised suspicions amongst his political enemies. A. was sent north to prevent Kynnane and Adea from reaching Pisidia, but his extreme measures—putting the defiant Kynnane to death—caused a mutiny in the army, which insisted that Adea be taken to Perdikkas and that her mother's wish that she marry Philip III Arrhidaios be fulfilled (Arr. *Succ.* 1.22–3; Polyaenus 8.60; cf. Diod. 19.52.5). A. disobeyed Perdikkas' instructions that he take orders from Eumenes (Diod. 18.29.2; Justin 13.6.15; Plut. *Eum.* 5.2), claiming that his Macedonian troops would not fight against Antipatros and were favorably disposed towards Krateros (Plut. *Eum.* 5.3). Although the enmity between A. and Eumenes is reported only in the accounts of the Successors, the two may have been on bad terms already during Alexander's reign. In 320, after Perdikkas and his sister Atalante were killed near Memphis, A. and some fifty other leaders of the Perdikkan faction were outlawed by the Macedonian assembly and condemned to death (Diod. 18.37.2; cf. 18.39.7; Justin 13.8.10; Arr. *Succ.* 1.30, 39). At the time, A. was in contact with Eumenes in Phrygia (Plut. *Eum.* 8.7–8 implies that they were both at Kelainai), but the two would not settle their differences (Arr. *Succ.* 1.41; Plut. *Eum.* 8.8) and A., aided by Dokimos and Polemon son of Andromenes, moved south into Karia, where he was joined by Attalos and by Laomedon, who had been ousted from Koile-Syria by Ptolemy's general Nikanor (App. *Syr.* 52.265). In Karia, A. and Attalos defeated the satrap Asandros (Arr. *Succ.* 1.41).

Late in 319, A. was in Pisidia, supported by a substantial native force, whose friendship and loyalty he cultivated through military honors (Diod. 18.46.2). Antigonos, to whom the task of dealing with the outlaws had been entrusted (Diod. 18.39.7; cf. Arr. *Succ.* 1.43), hurried south from Kappadokia, covering 2,500 stades in seven days (Diod. 18.44.2) with an army of 40,000 infantry, 7,000 cavalry and an unspecified number of elephants (Diod. 18.45.1). A. and his officers took up a position in the so-called Pisidic Aulon (in the vicinity of Kretopolis; for the battle see Diod. 18.44–5, 50.1; cf. Polyaenus 4.6.7 and Engel 1972; Ramsay 1923, for the topography; Bean 1960, 52–3 locates Kretopolis on the plain of Bucak; but Mitchell 1994, 132 puts it "further to the south-west between the north end of Bozova and the entrance to the Climax pass"; see *Barr. Atl.* 65 D3). A. was surprised by the speed of Antigonos' march. Just how well informed A. was about Antigonos' movements is difficult to say. Antigonos, for his part, was betrayed by the noise of his elephants, and A. rushed to seize the foothills overlooking the Aulon with his cavalry. From this position, it would have been possible to attack the enemy's flank, but A.'s forces were vastly inferior in numbers—16,000 infantry and 900 horse—and Antigonos, engaging him with his right wing, managed to cut off his retreat to the phalanx with 6,000 horse. Hemmed in by the advancing elephants and the cavalry in all sides, A. escaped from the battlefield with his hypaspists and the Pisidians, reaching Termessos in safety (Diod. 18.45.2–3; for troop numbers see Heckel, *Marshals*² 188 n.209). Here, A. fell victim to the treachery of the city's elders and committed suicide; his body was handed over to Antigonos, who maltreated it for three days and then left it unburied (Diod. 18.47.3).

The younger Pisidians recovered the body and buried it with appropriate honors. (Diod. 18.47.3). Berve II 22–3 no. 45; Kaerst, *RE* I.2 (1894) 1514 no. 5; Badian, *BNP* I 442 no. 4; Heckel 1992, 171–5 and *Marshals*² 184–8; Tataki 204 no. 2. For what appears to be A.'s tomb, see Kleiner 1963, 71ff.; Picard 1964, 298ff.; Rice 1993, 234–5; Pekridou 1986; Fedak 1990, 94–6. **Stemma XII.**

62 ALKETAS

(Ἀλκέτας). Alketas II of Epeiros (*regn.* 317–306). Son of Arybbas (Paus. 1.11.5; Diod. 19.88.1). His mother was probably an earlier wife of Arybbas and it appears that he was born in the mid-360s (Cross 1932 47 n.1; *contra* Sandberger 9). Father of Alexander and Teukros (who were both old enough to lead armies in 313) and two younger sons named Nisos and Esioneus (Diod. 19.88–9). A. was banished by his father, at some point before 342 (Diod. 19.88.1; Paus. 1.11.5, allegedly for his lack of restraint, but perhaps on account of concerns over the succession). In 316/15, Aiakides was driven out of Epeiros, in the aftermath of Olympias' cruel victory at Euia, and Epeiros was soon ruled by an *epimeletes* named Lykiskos, installed by Kassandros. It was against him that A. attempted to assert his claims to the Molossian throne. In 313/12, after the death of Aiakides (in the battle of Oiniadai: Paus. 1.11.4; Diod. 19.74.4–5), who had briefly regained the Molossian throne, the Epeirots promoted A. to the kingship (Diod. 19.88.1). Lykiskos brought an army against him and caused many of the Epeirots to defect, causing A. to take refuge in Eurymenai (Diod. 19.88.2–4). Alexander and Teukros then arrived with reinforcements and defeated Lykiskos (no. 661; Diod. 19.88.4: see also s.vv. Lysandros no. 669, Mikythos no. 733), but when they in turn were defeated by another force under Deinias, A. and his sons were forced to flee (Diod. 19.88.6). Nevertheless, Kassandros made peace and allowed A. to remain on the throne (19.89.1). Diod. 19.89.3 has led scholars to assume that his reign was of very short duration (χρόνον μέν τινα διέμενον is vague), but it appears that he reigned until 307, when Glaukias restored Pyrrhos to his homeland (Plut. *Pyrrh.* 3.5; Beloch IV² 2.153, though I see no evidence for joint rule with Neoptolemos II). A. and his two youngest sons (still children: παῖδας ὄντας) were killed by the Epeirots who found his rule oppressive (Diod. 19.89.3; Paus. 1.11.5). He may have been the grandfather of Neoptolemos II (Cross 1932, 56 and App. III 106–8). Hammond's case for Neoptolemos as son of Alexander I (1967, 561–8 for a history of events from 323 to 296) is weak, though it has won considerable support. Kaerst, *RE* I.2 (1894) 1514 no. 4; Cross 1932, 47–8; Heckel 2021. **Stemma IIa.**

63 ALKIA

(Ἀλκία). Sicilian Greek. Wife of Agathokles of Syracuse and, hence, stepmother of Archagathos, who, according to rumor, was having adulterous relations with her (Diod. 20.33.5, 68.3). A. appears to have been the mother of the younger Agathokles and Lanassa (Berve, *Tyrannis* I 455), who married Pyrrhos I of Epeiros in 295/4. In light of the relative ages of Agatharchos (last son of the first wife) and Lanassa, we may date the marriage to the time between 316 and 310 (cf. Beloch IV² 2.255). Berve, *Tyrannis* I 455; Beloch IV² 2.255. **Stemma IIb.**

64 ALKIAS

(Ἀλκίας). Greek from Elis. A. brought 150 cavalrymen from his homeland to Alexander at Gordion (Arr. 1.29.4). Presumably he remained with them and shared in Alexander's conquests until at least 330. He is not mentioned again by the sources. Kirchner, *RE* I.2 (1894) 1515 no. 1; Berve II 23 no. 46.

65 ALKIMACHOS

(Ἀλκίμαχος). Son of Agathokles, A. is generally identified as a brother of Lysimachos, Philip and Autodikos (Beloch IV² 2.131 adds a word of caution). This may be correct, but there is no explicit evidence to support the identification beyond the patronymic and the existence of a certain Philip son of Alkimachos (Hoffmann 224: *IG* VII 316.2). After the battle of Chaironeia, A. and Antipatros were sent by Philip II to Athens, where they were granted *proxenia* (Hypereides, frg. B 19.2 Burtt = 77 Jensen; Anaximenes, *FGrH* 72 F16 = Harpocration s.v. Ἀλκίμαχος). It is far from certain that *IG* II² 239 (= Tod no. 180 = Schwenk no. 4) honors the son of Agathokles and, if so, whether the Athenians granted him *proxenia* or citizenship (see the discussion in Schwenk 29). *IG* II² 391 records honors for Alkimachos son of Alkimachos of Apollonia, granting him similar honors to those held by his father. If this is the grandson of Agathokles, then our A. may have been granted property in Apollonia by Philip II (cf. similar grants to Polemokrates, father of Koinos, and the sons of Larichos and Androtimos). A. may also have been the father of Lys[ip]pos who is honored as *proxenos* at Ios (*IG* XII.5, 1001); the decree refers to the *eunoia* of his father toward the state. This may very well refer to the son and grandson of Agathokles. A. served in Asia Minor with Alexander in 334 and was sent to establish democracies in the Aiolian and Ionian cities (Arr. 1.18.1–2). He is almost certainly the Alkimachos named in the *Second Letter to the Chians* (*SEG* XXII. 506; cf. Heisserer 96–116). Alexander asks that A. not prosecute an unnamed individual (there is a *lacuna* in the text), whom he describes as a "friend" and who was thought to have acted with good intentions; clearly the King sought to put an end to civil strife and retributions in the time preceding Memnon's recapture of Chios. Forrest's contention (1969b, 204–5) that the text reads Ἀλκίμαχον and refers to a different individual also named Alkimachos is, I believe, rightly rejected by Heisserer (but see also Bosworth I 134; R&O no. 84, with commentary). Kirchner, *RE* I.2 (1894) 1540 no. 5; Berve II 23 no. 47; Lenschau 1940, 201; Wilhelm 1943; cf. Tod II p. 267; Tataki 148–9 no. 8. See Tataki 66; Osborne II 102–3 (Alkimachos son of Alkimachos); Tataki 360 (Lysippos). Forrest 1969b, 204–5; Bosworth I 134; Heisserer 96–111.

66 ALKIMOS

(Ἄλκιμος). An Epeirot officer in the service of Demetrios Poliorketes. During the siege of Rhodes, Demetrios gave a suit of armor manufactured by Zoilos the Kyprian (no. 1173) to A. because he had both great strength and a very warlike spirit. He alone wore armor of two talents' weight, double the normal weight. But these suits of armor, of virtually impenetrable iron, made by Zoilos weighed only forty minae (Plut. *Demetr.* 21.6). A. and some of his men, along with Mantias, had forced their way inside the walls of Rhodes (Diod. 20.98.8) but in the heavy fighting near the theater both A. and Mantias were killed after receiving many wounds (Diod. 20.98.9; cf. Plut. *Demetr.* 21.6). That he was the man honored in an Athenian decree (*IG* II² 773), of which very little remains, is speculation at best. Billows 366–7 no. 8; Kirchner, *RE* I.2 (1894) 1642 no. 11; Habicht 1977a; Launey 408, 1204.

AMADAS. Justin 12.12.8. See **DAMIS.**

AMASTRINE. Arr. 7.4.5. See **AMASTRIS.**

67 AMASTRIS

(Ἄμαστρις. Ἀμαστρίνη Arrian; Ἄμηστρις Memnon, *FGrH* 434 F1 §4.4; Strabo 12.3.10 C544; Polyaenus 6.12; Diod. 20.107; 20.109.7; Arr. 7.4.5; Steph. Byz. s.v. Ἄμαστρις; Scymn. 964). Persian princess, daughter of Oxyathres (Arr. 7.4.5; Diod. 20.109.7; Strabo 12.3.10 C544; Memnon, *FGrH* 434 F1 §4.4; Steph. Byz.) and thus niece of Dareios III. A. and her cousin Stateira were of similar age and raised together (Memnon 4.4); she accompanied the royal family westward during the Issos campaign and was captured at Damaskos after the battle (Curt. 3.13.13). Hence, she too accompanied Alexander's army as far as Sousa, where she remained from 331 until 324, when she married Krateros in the mass marriage ceremony (Arr. 7.4.5; Memnon 4.4; Diod. 20.109.7). In 322/1, she was given in marriage to Dionysios of Herakleia Pontika (Strabo 12.3.10 C544; Steph. Byz.), with Krateros' consent, and bore him three children: two sons, Klearchos and Oxyathres and a daughter, also named Amastris (Memnon 4.8). After Dionysios' death in 305, A. ruled as regent for her underaged children, supported by Antigonos the One-Eyed. The endless debate about whether the Macedonians repudiated or retained their barbarian wives is based on two examples: Amastris who was repudiated in favor of Phila (no. 897), and Apama (no. 138), whose blood ran through the Seleukid line. See Berve 1938; Bosworth 1980; Hamilton 1988; Müller 2013. But in 302/1 A. married Lysimachos, with whom she resided as queen in Sardis (Diod. 20.109.7; Memnon 4.9; Polyaenus 6.12). Polyaenus wrongly makes her the mother of Alexander, who was in all probability the son of an Odrysian concubine (**A99**; Paus. 1.10.5). A. is accepted as Alexander's mother by Wilcken, *RE* I.2 (1894) 1750; Brosius 78 n.70. Burstein 1976, 141–2 n.17 believes that Lysimachos could have had more than one son named Alexander; but it is surely significant that Lysimachos did not pursue any claims to Herakleia Pontika on the basis of Alexander's maternity. The marriage was, however, terminated amicably in 300 or 299 when Lysimachos married Arsinoë, the daughter of Ptolemy I Soter (Memnon 4.9, incorrectly identifying Arsinoë as the daughter of Philadelphos). A. founded a city east of the Parthenios River in Paphlagonia (*Barr. Atl.* 86 C2) that bore her name, synoecizing the four settlements of Sesamos, Kytoron, Kromma and Tieon, though the last revolted from the united city (Strabo 12.3.10; Memnon 4.9; see also Steph. Byz. s.v.; Scymnus 962ff.; scholia to Apollonius, *Argonautica* 2.941–2; Demosthenes Bithynus, *FHG* III 385, *Bithynika* 9 claims that the city was founded by Amastris the Amazon). She may have taken up residence in her city, where she minted coins proclaiming herself "Queen Amastris" (ΑΜΑΣΤΡΙΟΣ ΒΑΣΙΛΙΣΣΗΣ: Head, *HN*² 505–6; Mørkholm 1991, 95–6). A. was murdered (by drowning) by her own sons (*c.*284; thus Burstein 1976, 85, cf. 93–4) and her death was avenged by Lysimachos to his own political advantage (Memnon 5.2–3). Wilcken, *RE* I (1894) 1750 no. 7; Badian, *BNP* I 562 no. 3; Berve II 24 no. 50; Burstein

1976, 75–86; Lund 75, 82, 88, 188; Brosius 18, 78; Mørkholm 1991, 95–6; Shayegan 98 no. 4. **Stemma III.**

68 AMASTRIS

(Ἄμαστρις). Daughter of Amastris (no. 67) and Dionysios of Herakleia Pontika (Memnon 4.8). Nothing is known about her life or whether her mother or her brothers arranged a suitable (politically advantageous) marriage for her.

69 AMEDINES

The name occurs only in Latin authors. Secretary of Dareios III (*scriba regis*), A. had presumably surrendered to Alexander after the Great King's death; he was appointed satrap of the Ariaspians (or Euergetai; on whom see Strabo 15.2.10 C724; Arr. 3.27.4; Diod. 17.81.1–2) in autumn 330 (Curt. 7.3.4). The appointment is difficult to reconcile with two other notices: Arr. 3.27.5 says that Ariaspians remained free (but this may simply refer to an extension of the grant of *ateleia*; cf. Diod. 17.81.1; Bosworth I 366 notes that their autonomy could only have been nominal), and Diodorus 17.81.2 says that Tiridates was appointed satrap of the Gedrosians and the Euergetai. Berve's suggestion (II 25) that A. was a native of the region points to a possible solution, but the same ought to apply to Tiridates, if he was A.'s successor. Berve II 24–5 no. 51; Shayegan 98 no.5.

70 AMMINAIS

The name appears only in the Metz Epitome and is probably corrupt. Brother of the Indian dynast Assakenos (no. 244) and (possibly) a son of Cleophis (Metz Epit. 39), A. brought into the city of Massaga 9,000 mercenaries (Metz Epit. 39), who were later treacherously massacred by Alexander (Diod. 17.84; Metz Epit. 43–4; Polyaenus 4.3.20; Arr. 4.27.2–4 is apologetic). He may have been in charge of the operations against the Macedonians, since his brother had recently died and Cleophis herself ruled the kingdom (Curt. 8.10.22; cf. Metz Epit. 39). Perhaps he was the *hegemon* of the place, whose death precipitated the surrender of the Assakenians (Arr. 4.27.2: Arrian does not record the names of any of Assakenos' relatives). Berve II 26, however, thinks that A. is that brother of Assakenos who opposed Alexander in the Buner region after the fall of Aornos (Arr. 4.30.5); Eggermont 183 identifies this "brother" with Aphrikes (Diod. 17.86.2; Erices in Curt. 8.12.1, thus Anspach I 32 n.92, emends Diodorus to Αἰρίκης). But Bosworth II 194 rightly notes that Arr. 4.30.5 cannot easily be reconciled with the accounts of Curtius and Diodorus. Furthermore, Diodorus speaks of Ἀφρίκης τις Ἰνδός (cf. Curt. 8.12.1: *Erico quodam*), which is not the kind of designation one would expect for a brother of Assakenos. It is possible that after the surrender of Massaga, A. moved to the vicinity of Dyrta and subsequently abandoned his position and fled across the Indos to Abisares; but it is more likely that this individual was an unnamed brother of Assakenos. In either case, Aphrikes/Erices (no. 143) may have been the commander of his forces. Berve II 25–6 no. 54; Eggermont 183–4.

71 AMMINAPES

(Ἀμμινάπης, Manapis). Prominent Parthian who had come to the court of Philip II as an exile during the reign of Artaxerxes III Ochos (Curt. 6.4.25) and later, together with Mazakes, surrendered Egypt to Alexander (Arr. 3.22.1). A. remained with Alexander until

330 (Curt. 6.4.23; Arr. 3.23.4), when he was appointed satrap of Hyrkania and Parthyaia (Arr. 3.22.1; cf. Curt. 6.4.25, naming only Hyrkania). Alexander left Tlepolemos as *episkopos* to keep an eye on A.'s activities. Although the satrapies were later returned to Phrataphernes (Arr. 3.28.2; 5.20.7; cf. Curt. 8.3.17), there is no indication of A.'s death or misconduct on his part. What became of him is unknown. Berve II 26 no. 55; Shayegan 98 no. 6; Heckel 2018b, 98–9.

72 AMPHIMACHOS

(Ἀμφίμαχος). Arr. *Succ.* 1.35 calls A. "the king's brother" (τῷ τοῦ βασιλέως ἀδελφῷ); hence Berve II 32 (cf. Bosworth 2002, 113 with n.60; Carney 276, with n.45) identifies him as a son of Philine of Larisa from an earlier union. He is probably the brother of Arrhidaios the satrap of Hellespontine Phrygia (thus Jacoby, *FGrH* IID, *Kommentar* 583, following Beloch IV² 2.316; but Meeus 2013, 91–2 has methodological doubts), who was sometimes confused with Philip III Arrhidaios (cf. Justin 13.4.6: *Arridaeus rex*), and perhaps the son of a certain Alexander (cf. Billows 1993). Satrap of Mesopotamia and Arbelitis in the settlement of Triparadeisos in 320 (Arr. *Succ.* 1.35; Diod. 18.39.6). In 317, he supported Eumenes against Antigonos the One-Eyed at Paraitakene, bringing 600 horsemen who were stationed between the troops of Stasandros and Kephalon (Diod. 19.27.4). Thereafter, he is not heard of again. He may have been killed at Gabiene, executed afterwards (cf. Diod. 19.44.1), or simply deposed. His successor in the satrapy was Blitor (no. 303). Kaerst, *RE* I.2 (1894) 1942 no. 9; Berve II 32 no. 66; Tataki 239 no. 133.

73 AMPHION

(Ἀμφίον). Priest of Seleukos I; sacrificed a virgin named Aimathe when Antioch in Syria was founded (Malalas 8.200). Grainger, *SPG* 76, 138.

74 AMPHISTRATOS

(Ἀμφίστρατος). Sculptor. A. produced a statue of the historian Kallisthenes of Olynthos (Pliny, *HN* 36.36; Tatian. *adv. Gr.* p.34, 12). The date of this work is uncertain, as is whether A. had any personal connection with Alexander. Robert, *RE* I.2 (1894) 1958 no. 3; Berve II 32 no. 67.

75 AMPHOTEROS

(Ἀμφοτερός). Macedonian from Orestis (Tataki 204 no. 3; cf. Arr. *Ind.* 18.5), A. was the son of Alexander (Arr. 1.25.9; cf. Arr. *Ind.* 18.5) and, perhaps, Aristopatra (cf. Strabo 15.1.35 C702 = *FGrH* 153 F2), and the brother of Krateros (Arr. 1.25.9). The generally accepted view that A. was the younger brother (Berve II 32) is not compelling. Krateros' achievements outshine those of his brother, but do not impute seniority. The fact that Alexander used A. for some rather delicate missions (Arr. 1.25.9–10; 3.6.3; Curt. 4.8.15; cf. Bosworth 1975), and even appointed him *nauarchos* of the Aegean fleet (Curt. 3.1.19), suggests that he was a man of some experience. During the winter of 334/3 he was sent by Alexander from Phaselis to Parmenion in Gordion with orders to arrest Alexander Lynkestes on a charge of treason (Arr. 1.25.9–10). A. travelled in native dress, accompanied by guides from Perge, in order to avoid recognition (Arr. 1.25.9). From there, in the spring of 333, he proceeded to the coast to share the command of the reconstituted Aegean fleet with Hegelochos (Curt. 3.1.19; cf. Arr. 2.2.3). Together they secured control of Tenedos, Chios, and Mytilene (Arr.

3.2.3–5; Curt. 4.5.14–22), and A. captured Kos with a separate force of 60 ships (Arr. 3.2.6). Both appear to have rejoined Alexander in Egypt (Arr. 3.2.3; cf. Bosworth 1975, 31 n.20), whence A. was sent to the Peloponnese in 331 to aid those who remained loyal to Macedon at the time of Agis' revolt (Arr. 3.6.3); Curt. 4.8.15, however, claims that A. was sent to liberate Krete and that he left not from Egypt but when Alexander made his return visit to Tyre. Although the departure point is confused, both authors may refer to an expedition against Krete, since Strabo 10.4.1 C474 includes Krete in the Peloponnese (cf. Bosworth 1975, 34–5). What became of A. is unknown, but since Alexander had moved rapidly into the heart of the Persian Empire in 331 it appears that, unless some mishap occurred at sea, he remained in the West under the authority of Antipatros. Whether Plutarch's clever tale about Ἑκατερός and Ἀμφοτερός refers to A. and his brother Krateros (cf. Atkinson I 92) is unclear. If so, it paints a less than flattering picture of A. Kaerst, *RE* I.2 (1894) 1977 no. 4; Berve II 32–3 no. 68; Bosworth 1975; Hauben 1972a, 57 and 1976, 82–7; Heckel 1992, 107–8 n.231.

76 AMYNTAS

(Ἀμύντας). Macedonian (Tataki 237 no. 117). Son of Perdikkas III (Arr. *Succ.* 1.22), and thus nephew of Philip II. A. was born *c.*365, the rightful heir to the kingdom at the time of his father's death (360/59). But, on account of his youth, he yielded the throne to Philip II, who served either as regent (Justin 7.5.9–10; Satryus *ap.* Athen. 13.557b) or as king (Diod. 16.1.3, 2.1). I do not see why the evidence of Diodorus, which represents little more than a brief notice, should be preferred to the combined testimony of Justin-Trogus and Satyros. Furthermore, regencies in Macedonia were frequent (Ptolemy of Aloros had been regent for Perdikkas III, just as Antigonos Doson would be for Philip V, though it is significant that in both cases the regent died and thus allowed the legitimate king to ascend the throne). A. grew up at the court of his uncle and could claim several important members of the Macedonian aristocracy as his *syntrophoi* (cf. Curt. 6.9.17, 10.24). Philip later married him to his daughter Kynnane; their daughter Adea in turn married Philip III Arrhidaios (Arr. *Succ.* 1.22; cf. Polyaenus 8.60). The honors for Amyntas Perdikka at Lebedeia (*IG* VII 3055, 9) and Oropos (*Syll³* 258; R&O no. 75), the former calling him *basileus*, may belong to the turmoil after the death of Philip II, but it must be stressed that by spring 335 A. had been executed by his cousin (Justin 12.6.14), Alexander; for Arr. 1.5.4 makes it clear that Kynnane was a widow at that time and was offered as bride to Langaros, king of the Agrianes. Clearly there was a faction in Macedonia that favored him over Alexander (Plut. *Mor.* 327c), whether he himself sought the kingship or not. Kaerst, *RE* I.2 (1894) 2007 no. 15; Berve II 30–1 no. 61. Ellis 1971; Prestianni-Giallombardo 1973–4; Errington 1974; Prandi 1998; Worthington 2003; Heckel, *Marshals²* 287–90; Müller, *LexAM* 88. **Stemma I.**

77 AMYNTAS

(Ἀμύντας). Macedonian (Tataki 236 no. 109). Son of Antiochos (Arr. 1.17.9; *Syll³* 258, 2, 4; R&O no. 75). He and Amyntas son of Perdikkas were awarded proxenies by the Oropians at some point before 338 (cf. Ellis 1971). After the death of Philip II, and the murder of Amyntas Perdikka, A. fled from Macedonia (Diod. 17.48.2; Curt. 3.11.18) and is found in 334, probably as commander of mercenaries, at Ephesos, which he and its Greek garrison deserted after the news of Alexander's victory at the Granikos (Arr.

1.17.9). A. appears to have joined Dareios at Sochoi, shortly before the battle of Issos, in the company of Thymondas (cf. Curt. 3.8.1; certainly he was there advising the Persian king not to abandon that position: Plut. *Alex.* 20.1–4; Arr. 2.6.3; cf. Curt. 3.8.2). At some point in 334, he appears to have acted as the agent of Alexander Lynkestes in his treasonous dealings with the Persians (Arr. 1.25.3). A. fought at Issos (Arr. 2.13.2; Diod. 17.48.2; Curt. 3.11.18), whence he fled to Egypt, via Tripolis in Phoinikia, with 4,000 mercenaries (Diod. 17.48.2). At Tripolis he took enough ships to transport his troops and, burning the remaining ships, he sailed to Kypros. Here he augmented his forces and fleet and continued to Pelousion, which he seized, claiming that Dareios had sent him there as *strategos* in place of Sabakes (no. 1029), the satrap who had fallen at Issos. At first A. was greeted with some enthusiasm (Curt. 4.7.1–2), but, in an attack on Memphis, he and his troops were slaughtered after they had turned to careless plundering (Diod. 17.48.3–5; Curt. 4.1.27–33; Arr. 2.13.2–3; Heckel 116–17). Kaerst, *RE* I (1894) 2007 no. 16; Badian, *BNP* I 625 no. 5; Berve II 28–9 no. 58; Ellis 1971; Hofstetter 13–14 no. 15.

78 AMYNTAS

(Ἀμύντας). Macedonian (Tataki 201 no. 4). Son of Arrhabaios (Arr. 1.12.7, 14.1, 6; 1.28.4), brother of the defector Neoptolemos (Arr. 1.20.10; cf. Diod. 17.25.5 putting Neoptolemos on the Macedonian side) and thus probably a member of the Lynkestian royal house. Born no later than the 360s, he was probably the grandson of Aëropos and nephew of Alexander Lynkestes. Berve II 29 identifies him tentatively with the envoy sent (with Klearchos) by Philip to Thebes in 338 (Marsyas, *FGrH* 135/6 F20 = Plut. *Dem.* 18.1–2). Given the frequency of the name in Macedonia, this is far from certain. He may have been one of the commanders of the advance force in Asia Minor in 336–334 (Justin 9.5.8), along with Parmenion and Attalos. In 334, he led the scouting party (*skopoi*)—four *ilai* of *hippeis prodromoi* (i.e. *sarissophoroi*), and the squadron of Sokrates son of Sathon— from Hermotos towards the Granikos (Arr. 1.12.7), and in the battle, his squadrons (*sarissophoroi* and Paionians: Arr. 1.14.1) were deployed on the right wing and initiated the assault on the Persians on the opposite riverbank (Arr. 1.14.6–15.1; cf. 1.16.1). In winter 334/3, in the absence of Parmenion, A. commanded the entire left at Sagalassos (Arr. 1.28.4; *Barr. Atl.* 65 E2). All three attested commands show that the son of Arrhabaios was an officer of high standing, militarily competent and trusted by the King. This makes his disappearance from history all the more intriguing, as Berve II 29–30 rightly notes. Had he died—in battle or from illness—in the first year of the campaign, the sources would almost certainly have recorded the fact. The battle of Sagalassos occurred after the arrest of Lynkestian Alexander (cf. Arr. 1.25), unless Diodorus' claim that Alexander was arrested shortly before the battle of Issos (Diod. 17.32.1–2; cf. Curt. 7.1.6) is to be taken seriously. The arrest was, however, conducted in secret (Arr. 1.25.9–10), and probably not revealed to Alexander's troops until all detachments reunited at Gordion. With the apparent treason of Alexander, A.'s presence became dangerous and his removal a necessity (cf. Heckel, *Marshals*[2] 32). Probably, his disappearance is a consequence of the arrest of his uncle. His successor appears to have been Protomachos. Identification with Amyntas Lynkestes (Curt. 5.2.5), the infantry commander, is impossible given the ranks of the two individuals (cf. Heckel 1992, 247 n.32, for the obscurity of the commanders appointed in Sittakene). Berve II 29–30 no. 59; Bosworth I 109; Heckel, *Marshals*[2] 31–2. **Stemma XV.**

79 AMYNTAS

(Ἀμύντας). Macedonian (Tataki 211–12 no. 2). Eldest of four attested sons of Andromenes (Arr. 1.8.2, 14.2; Diod. 17.45.7); one of Alexander's *hetairoi* (*philoi*, Diod. 17.45.7). A. was born perhaps soon after 365 and brought up at the court of Philip II as a *syntrophos* of Amyntas son of Perdikkas (no. 76), probably along with Philotas (no. 940) son of Parmenion (cf. Curt. 7.1.11). He first appears as a phalanx commander in the Theban campaign (335), where his unit was teamed with that of Perdikkas, whom they followed in the assault on the city (Arr. 1.8.2). Of his role at the Granikos, we know only that he was stationed to the right of center (Arr. 1.14.2). After the battle he was sent to occupy Sardis, which its commandant Mithrenes had surrendered to Alexander (Arr. 1.17.4; cf. Diod. 17.64.6); he remained there until Pausanias was installed as *phrourarchos* (Arr. 1.17.7). Perhaps his was one of the three battalions assigned to Philotas at Miletos (Arr. 1.19.8); he reappears in the unsuccessful attack on Myndos, together with the Companion Cavalry and the battalions of Perdikkas and Koinos (Arr. 1.20.5–7). At Issos, A.'s battalion is found beside that of Ptolemy son of Seleukos (Arr. 2.8.4; Curt. 3.9.7). Diod. 17.45.7 says that he shared Alexander's determination not to break off the siege of Tyre (although the Greek is ambiguous). After the capture of Gaza (late 332), Alexander sent A. to Macedonia with ten triremes for the purpose of enlisting reinforcements (Diod. 17.49.1); he rejoined the King near Sittakene in late 331, bringing 6,000 Macedonian infantry and 500 cavalry, 3,500 Thrakian foot and 600 horse, 4,000 mercenary infantry and 380 cavalry from the Peloponnese, as well as fifty *paides basilikoi* (Curt. 5.1.42; cf. Diod. 17.65.1). Diod. 17.65.1 speaks of Trallians and numbers the Peloponnesian horse at just under a thousand. Upon his return, A. resumed the command of his battalion, which formed part of the contingent sent to bridge the Araxes River while Alexander dealt with Ariobarzanes at the Persian Gates (Arr. 3.18.6; Curt. 5.4.20, 30). In the Mardian campaign, his battalion and Koinos' accompanied the King (Arr. 3.24.1); the same force was led by Alexander against Satibarzanes at Artakoana (Arr. 3.25.6).

The loyalty of the sons of Andromenes was called into question when Philotas was implicated in the conspiracy of Demetrios (no. 358) the Bodyguard (Arr. 3.27.1). Curt. 6.7.15 names a certain Amyntas in Dimnos' list of conspirators but this is either a mistake or refers to an otherwise unknown man of that name (Badian 1960, 334 n.30; Heckel 1975, 394–5). The case against the son of Andromenes did not amount to much: he had been arrogant in his dealings with Antiphanes, the *scriba equitum* (Curt. 7.1.15); during a recruiting mission to Macedonia, he had pressed into service some young men from Olympias' court (Curt. 7.1.37–8; cf. Diod. 17.65.1), and indeed Olympias had written damaging letters about him and his brothers to her son (Curt. 7.1.12); but, most of all, he had close ties of friendship with Philotas (Curt. 7.1.11; cf. Arr. 3.27.1); like Philotas, he must have been on friendly terms with Amyntas son of Perdikkas and Amyntas son of Antiochos. He had powerful connections: fully one-third of the Macedonian infantry could be expected to stand by him (his own battalion and that of Polyperchon), and his brother Attalos had been raised at the court with Alexander himself. A. was acquitted after a vigorous defense (Arr. 3.27.2), but not long afterwards he was killed during the siege of a small town (Arr. 3.27.3). Kaerst, *RE* I (1894) 2007 no. 17; Badian, *BNP* I 625 no. 6; Berve II 26–7 no. 57; Heckel, *Marshals*[2] 189–91. **Stemma XII.**

80 AMYNTAS

(Ἀμύντας). Arr. 1.7.1 describes A. as a member of the occupying force on the Kadmeia in Thebes in 335. He and Timolaos (no. 1143) were murdered by a group of Theban exiles who had slipped into the city during the night, and the action was followed by the rebellion of the Thebans. There is a strong likelihood that A. is identical with Anemoitas, whom Demosthenes in the *de Corona* names as a traitor to the Theban cause, along with Timolaos and Theogeiton (Dem. 18.295; cf. Schaefer III² 107 n.2). Hence A. and Timolaos were not garrison troops but rather leaders of the pro-Macedonian party; for their own security, they doubtless resided on the Kadmeia. Bosworth I 74 rejects the identification with Anemoitas and accepts Arrian's claim that A. and Timolaos were "two members of the Macedonian garrison, captured in the lower city during the outbreak of the revolt." Arr. 1.7.1–2, however, indicates that the incitement to rebellion occurred after the murder, and it appears that the victims were deliberately chosen because of their importance; one wonders how Arrian's source would have known, or why he might have preserved, the names of two insignificant members of the garrison who had the misfortune of being caught off guard. One recalls the liberation of Thebes in 379/8, when the leaders of the pro-Spartan party were deliberately targeted. Berve II 31 no. 62; Beloch III² 1.615 n.2.

81 AMYNTAS

(Ἀμύντας). Macedonian (Tataki 235 no. 107) of unknown origin. In the contest of valor in Sittakene, A. was awarded fourth place and appointed *chiliarches* or *pentakosiarches* (presumably the latter) of the hypaspists or of some battalion of light infantry (Curt. 5.2.5; see literature s.v. Atarrhias no. 250). Bosworth I 148–9, suggests that Curtius has confused matters somewhat and that the victors in this contest did not become chiliarchs but rather pentakosiarchs. Heckel 1992, 305; Atkinson II 233; Heckel and Jones 2006, 43–4.

82 AMYNTAS

(Ἀμύντας). Macedonian (Tataki 201 no. 2). An infantry commander of Lynkestian origin, A. finished sixth in the contest of valor in Sittakene and was appointed *chiliarches* or *pentakosiarches* (presumably the latter) of the hypaspists (Curt. 5.2.5; see literature s.v. Atarrhias no. 250). The relatively low social status of the hypaspists and their commanders, who were chosen by merit, rules out identification with the son of Arrhabaios. Berve II 31 no. 63; Heckel 1992, 305; Atkinson II 233; Heckel and Jones 2006, 43–4.

83 AMYNTAS

(Ἀμύντας). Macedonian (Tataki 235 no. 106). An officer (*regius praetor*) who gave a speech attacking Philotas in 330 (Curt. 6.9.28). Not the son of Andromenes, as I suggested in Heckel 1975 and 1994a, 69–70. Atkinson II 233 believes he may have been one of the hypaspist commanders promoted at Sittakene (Curt. 5.2.5; see nos. 53 and 54 above), but the term *regius praetor* suggests that the troops he led were also designated *regii* or *basilikoi*. He may have belonged to the *hypaspistai basilikoi*, although we do not know the size of this unit or its command structure. Berve II 31–2 no. 65.

84 AMYNTAS

(Ἀμύντας). Macedonian (Tataki 235 no. 105). Curt. 6.7.15 lists him amongst the conspirators who had joined with Dimnos (no. 377) against Alexander; he was executed with the other conspirators (Curt. 6.11.38). The name is too common to make identification with any known Amyntas certain. But, since he is mentioned together with Demetrios the Somatophylax (no. 358), A.'s inclusion in the list may have been influenced by the subsequent trial of Amyntas son of Andromenes (Heckel 1975, 394–5; cf. Badian 1960, 334 n.30, rejected by Bosworth I 360). Berve II 31 no. 64.

85 AMYNTAS

(Ἀμύντας). Macedonian (Tataki 44 no. 1). Son of Nikolaos (Arr. 4.17.3); perhaps the brother of Pantauchos (no. 843), and thus from Aloros (Arr. *Ind.* 18.6). When Artabazos asked to be excused from his satrapy of Baktria on account of old age (summer 328), Alexander at first designated Black Kleitos as his replacement (Curt. 8.1.19); but after the latter's death, the satrapy was given to A. (Curt. 8.2.14; Arr. 4.17.3; *Itiner. Alex.* 103), who appears to have taken office in the autumn of 328. Because of the unrest in the satrapy, Alexander left the battalions of Koinos and Meleagros, 400 Companions and all the *hippakontistai*, as well as the loyal native troops, with A. at Baktra, all under Koinos' command (Arr. 4.17.3). These were presumably the troops that defeated, after a stubborn fight, the 2,500 Baktrian rebels who had left Xenippa at Alexander's approach (Curt. 8.2.15)—they lost some 700 men, while the Macedonian casualties numbered 80 dead and 350 wounded (Curt. 8.2.16–17). When Alexander departed for India (spring/summer 327), he left 3,500 cavalry and 10,000 infantry with A. in Baktria (Arr. 4.22.3), most of these were Greeks, who rebelled in 325 on the false report that Alexander had died in India (Curt. 9 7.1–11; Diod. 17.99.5–6; cf. Diod. 18.7.1). It appears that A. was killed during this uprising, for in 323 the satrap of Baktria and Sogdiana is Philip (Diod. 18.3.3; Dexippos, *FGrH* 100 F8 §6), who (as is implied by Curt. 10.10.4) was the ruler at the time of the King's death. Justin 13.4.23 assigns the satrapy to A. in error. Berve II 30 no. 60; Kaerst, *RE* I (1894) 2007 no. 18; Julien 43; Lehmann-Haupt 147 §120; cf. Beloch III² 2.243 §110; Holt 1988, 81ff.; Klinkott 2000, 22, with nn.58, 62.

86 AMYNTAS

(Ἀμύντας). Bematist or, at least, author of a work on the *Stages* (*Stathmoi*) of Alexander's expedition (eight fragments of his work survive: *FGrH* 122). Whether he was contemporary with the events he describes and a participant in the expedition is unknown. His presence in Alexander's camp cannot, however, be ruled out. Nothing is known about his origins or his life. Schwartz, *RE* I.2 (1894) 2008 no. 22; Berve Abschn. II no. 4; Jacoby, *FGrH* 122; Karttunen, *BNP* I 625–6 no. 7.

87 AMYNTAS

(Ἀμύντας). (Tataki 123 no. 2). Son of Alexander of Mieza (cf. Arr. *Ind.* 18.6), A. was the brother of the Royal Hypaspist and Somatophylax Peukestas and was himself appointed Somatophylax of Philip III Arrhidaios at Triparadeisos in 320 (Arr. *Succ.* 1.38). Otherwise nothing is known about him unless he can be identified with the hipparch of Perdikkas' expedition against Kypros in 321/0 (Arr. *Succ.* 24.6, lines 26–7). If this is the case, then the entire force will have gone over to Antigonos and received favorable treatment from Antipatros: Medeios of Larisa, the *xenagos* of this expedition, is found in the camp of Antigonos. Antipatros may have found Peukestas a useful ally in the east, to keep both Eumenes and Antigonos in check; for it is perhaps significant that Antipatros did not appoint Peithon's brother Eudamos (or another, if one existed) in place of A. son of Alexander. The appointment of the latter suggests that Antipatros trusted Peukestas more than he did Peithon. Berve II 26 no. 56; Kaerst, *RE* I (1894) 2007 no. 20; Heckel 1992, 282–3.

88 AMYNTAS

(Ἀμύντας). Macedonian *strategos*, probably in the service of Antigonos Monophthalmos (thus Kirchner). In Kappadokia, he confronted Ariarathes II, who had been supplied with an army by Ardoates (no. 170) of Armenia. He was, however, defeated and killed. (Bengtson II 77–8 dates this battle to 260, but Diod. 31.19.5 clearly places it during Monophthalmos' lifetime; cf. Ballesteros Pastor 2013, 185 and 195 n.17). As a result of the engagement, the Macedonians were driven out of Kappadokia and Ariarathes II recovered his kingdom (Diod. 31.19.5). Since we know that Peukestas was later in Antigonos' service, it is possible that the *strategos* Amyntas is the son of Alexander (see above). Kirchner, *RE* I.2 (1894) 2006 no. 6; Ballesteros Pastor 2013.

89 AMYNTAS

(Ἀμύντας). Rhodian navarch during the famous siege of the city by Demetrios Poliorketes in 305–304 (Diod. 20.93.5). Captured the pirate chief (*archipeirates*) Timokles (no. 1142), who was serving Demetrios at the time, off the coast of Karia (Diod. 20.97.5–6; Berlin Papyrus 11632 = *FGrH* 533 F2). Hauben 9–11 no. 2; Kirchner, *RE* I.2 (1894) 2006 no. 8; Berthold 73, 75; Ormerod 123.

90 ANANIAS

(Ἀνανίας). Rhodian *strategos*, killed during the siege of the city (Diod. 20.97.7). He is otherwise unknown. Kirchner, *RE* I.2 (1984) 1818 s.v. "Ameinias" no. 14; Berthold 75 (Ananias).

91 ANAXAGORAS

(Ἀναξάγορας). Ephesian, son of Echeanax. Together with his brothers Kodros (no. 609) and Diodoros (no. 378), he murdered the tyrant of Ephesos, Hegesias. Philoxenos forced the Ephesians to surrender Anaxagoras and his brothers and imprisoned them for a long time (ἐπὶ μακρόν) in Sardis. From here A. and Kodros escaped to Athens, but Diodoros was injured in the escape, recaptured and sent to Alexander in Babylon. After the King's death, when Perdikkas sent Diodoros back to Ephesos to be tried, A. and Kodros intervened to save him (Polyaenus 6.49). The events appear to have spanned the years 325/4–323. Berve II 33 no. 69.

92 ANAXARCHOS

(Ἀνάξαρχος). Abderite philosopher of the school of Democritus, born *c*.380 (Diog. Laert. 9.58 gives his *floruit* as the 110th Olympiad, 340–337); a student of Diogenes of Smyrna. A. accompanied Alexander on his campaigns. He alienated Nikokreon (no. 797) of

Salamis by saying to Alexander at a feast, that all that was missing was the head of some satrap (*sic*), meaning Nikokreon (Diog. Laert. 9.58; cf. Plut. *Alex.* 28.4). A. is depicted as a flatterer of Alexander (Athen. 6.250f–251a)—especially in the aftermath of the Kleitos affair (Plut. *Alex.* 52.4–7; cf. *Mor.* 449e)—and an opponent of Kallisthenes of Olynthos (Arr. 4.10.5–11.9; Plut. *Alex.* 52.8–9), but several of the anecdotes concerning A. are elsewhere told of other individuals or reported in different ways. Alexander was supposed to have ordered his financial officer to give A. as much money as he asked for: he demanded and received 100 talents (Plut. *Mor.* 179f; but in other versions, Alexander's monetary rewards go to Xenokrates, with A. receiving only honor: Plut. *Alex.* 8.5; Plut. *Mor.* 331e, though perhaps the text is corrupt, cf. Diog. Laert. 9.60; cf. Plut. *Mor.* 181e). A.'s comment that Alexander's blood was the "ichor of the blessed gods" (Diog. Laert. 9.59) is told elsewhere of Dioxippos (Aristoboulos, *FGrH* 139 F47 = Athen. 6.251a; cf. Plut. *Alex.* 28.3 for the story in general). On the other hand, A. is said to have mocked Alexander's pretensions to divinity (Ael. *VH* 9.37). According to Val. Max. 8.14 ext. 2 (cf. Plut. *Mor.* 466d), Alexander, hearing from A. that the philosophers believed in numerous worlds, lamented that he had not yet conquered one. In another account he is critical of excessive luxury (Plut. *Alex.* 28.5). Hence there is little that can be considered certain. He was said to have consulted and annotated the so-called Casket Copy of the *Iliad*, which Alexander carried with him (Strabo 13.1.27 C594). In 323, he persuaded Alexander to ignore the warnings of the Chaldaians (who predicted Alexander's death) and enter the city of Babylon (Justin 12.13.5; Diod. 17.112.4–5). According to Klearchos (*ap.* Athen. 548b–c), A. accumulated great wealth and lived in luxury. After Alexander's death, he was driven ashore on Kypros and captured by Nikokreon who ordered him put to death. When he made light of his sentence, Nikokreon ordered his tongue to be cut out, but A., it was said, bit it off and spat it out (Diog. Laert. 9.59; Val. Max. 3.3 ext. 4). Kaerst, *RE* I.2 (1894) 2080 no. 1; Berve II 33–5 no. 70; Borza 1981; Bernard 1984; Dorandi, *BNP* I 658–9.

93 ANAXIMENES

(Ἀναξιμένης). Son of Aristokles (*Suda* A 1989; cf. Ps.-Call. 1.13; Jul. Valer. 1.7), he was a famous orator and sophist from Lampsakos (Strabo 13.1.19 C589; Diod. 15.76.4 shows that Ephoros considered A. one of the leading lights of his era) and an enemy of Theopompos of Chios. A. was said to have authored a pamphlet abusing the Athenians, Spartans, and Thebans, which he wrote in the style of Theopompos and published under his name. Although the truth became known, the publication created great hostility towards Theopompos (Paus. 6.18.5; *Suda* A 1989). A. was a student of Diogenes the Cynic and Zoïlos (Diog. Laert. 3.57; *Suda*); that he was a teacher of Alexander is, however, chronologically impossible and derives from the *Alexander Romance* (cf. Berve II 35). The author of a history that included the exploits of Philip II and Alexander, A. accompanied the latter on his Asiatic expedition and saved the Lampsakenes, who had supported the Persian cause, from condign punishment by means of a simplistic trick (Paus. 8.18.2–4; Val. Max. 7.3 ext. 4; *Suda*). The Lampsakenes had sent an envoy to A. asking him to intervene on their behalf with Alexander. The King replied that he would do the opposite of what A. asked him. Hence A. requested that the women and children of Lampsakos be enslaved, their city razed and the sanctuaries of the gods burned. That Alexander allowed himself to be fooled by such a transparent ploy is hard to believe. The story also suggests that A. was the benefactor of his state just as Aristotle persuaded Philip II to refound Stageira.

Nothing certain is known about A.'s relationship with Alexander, and various anecdotes confuse him with others at the King's court (Choirilos, Anaxarchos). A. published a work τὰ περὶ Ἀλέξανδρον, which seems to have formed the last of a trilogy of historical studies that began with the *Hellenica* (Diod. 15.89.3) and *Philippica*. For his historical works see Jacoby, *FGrH* 72; Pearson 243–5. Brzoska, *RE* I.2 (1894) 2086–98 no. 3. Also Weißenberger, *BNP* I 662–3 no. 2; Berve II 35–7 no. 71.

94 ANAXIPOLIS

(Ἀναξίπολις). Rhodian. Son of Timaratos from the deme of Physkos (Lindos: Berthold 42). *Prytanis* in 305. Led an embassy to Ptolemy I during the early stages of the siege of Rhodes by Demetrios (*Lindos* II 2 D 95–115; esp. 114–15). Paschidis 354–5 D2.

95 ANAXIPPOS

(Ἀνάξιππος). Macedonian (Tataki 240 no. 138); family background unknown. A. is described as one of Alexander's *hetairoi* (Arr. 3.25.2). In 330, he was sent with 40 *hippakontistai* from Susia (Tus, near modern Meshed) in Aria to accompany the reinstated satrap, Satibarzanes (no. 1037), back to his capital and prevent the plundering of Aria (Arr. 3.25.2). A.'s position is hardly clear: Arrian claims that he was to establish a guard in advance of the Macedonian army to prevent it from plundering Aria as it passed through, but the number of men assigned for this alleged purpose is ridiculously small (cf. Bosworth I 355, who suspects "a lacuna either in the text or in Arrian's excerpting"). Berve II 37 n.3 suggests that A. was to be the Macedonian *episkopos* (cf. Neiloxenos, Arr. 3.28.4). Soon after Alexander's departure from the satrapy, Satibarzanes murdered A. and his men (Arr. 3.25.5). Kirchner, *RE* I.2 (1894) 2098 no. 2; Berve II 37 no. 72; Heckel 1992, 361.

96 ANDROBAZOS

(Ἀνδρόβαζος). For the name see Justi 16 ("erobernden Arm habend"). Prominent Persian, sent in 317 by Oxyartes, satrap of Parapamisadai, with a contingent of 1,200 infantry and 400 cavalry, to Eumenes in his fight against Antigonos (Diod. 19.14.6). A. presumably fought at Paraitakene and Gabiene. If he survived the latter battle, he may have been executed along with Antigenes, Eudamos, and Kephalon (Diod. 19.44.1; the fact that Antigonos took no action against Oxyartes, who was absent, does not mean that he extended the same courtesy to his subordinate, A.: Diod. 19.48.2).

97 ANDROKLEIDES

(Ἀνδροκλείδης). Epeirot (Molossian, Hammond, *Epirus* 797), apparently a higher ranking official at the court of Aiakides. When the latter was driven out by his political enemies, A. and Angelos fled from Epeiros, taking with them the infant Pyrrhos, some servants and a nurse (Plut. *Pyrrh.* 2.1). Because the servants and the nurse slowed their escape, A. and Angelos handed P. over to Androkleion, Hippias, and Neandros who hurried on to Megara in Macedonia while A. and Angelos held off the enemy, by force and by entreaty, eventually putting the enemy to flight. Then they rejoined the party with Pyrrhos (Plut. *Pyrrh.* 2.2; for a full and dramatic account of the escape see Plut. *Pyrrh.* 2.3–8). Sandberger no. 11.

98 ANDROKLEION

(Ἀνδροκλείων). Epeirot (Molossian, Hammond, *Epirus* 797), supporter of Aiakides and his family. When Aiakides was driven from the throne, A., Hippias, and Neandros led the group that fled with the young prince, Pyrrhos, to Megara in Macedonia, while Androkleides and Angelos (see s. vv.) held off and finally routed the pursuers (Plut. *Pyrrh.* 2.2; for a full and dramatic account of the escape see Plut. *Pyrrh.* 2.3–8). The party came eventually to the court of the Illyrian king, Glaukias, whose wife was Aiakid by blood (Justin 17.3.18–19, see s.v. Beroa no. 294). Sandberger no. 12.

99 ANDROKLES

(Ἀνδροκλῆς). The ruler of Amathos on Kypros (Diod. 19.62.6: δυνάστης, perhaps used only for variation), he appears to have joined the other Kypriot and Phoinikian kings, who sailed with the Aegean fleet of Pharnabazos and Autophradates in 334 but defected after the battle of Issos and joined Alexander at Sidon in 332 (Arr. 2.20.3). Thereafter, he took part in the final assault on Tyre, though his own quinquereme was destroyed (along with those of Pnytagoras of Salamis and Pasikrates of Kourion) by a Tyrian attack as it lay at anchor in the harbor (Arr. 2.22.2). He remained in control of Amathos, and in 321/0 he joined Nikokreon (no. 797), Pasikrates (no. 852) and Nikokles (no. 794) in allying himself with Ptolemy against Perdikkas, who sent Aristonous and Sosigenes against the Kypriot cities (Arr. *Succ.* 24.6). We have no details of this campaign, though Antigonos appears to have come to the aid of the Kyprians (see discussion in Billows 66–7). From that point on, A. appears to have taken a pro-Antigonid stance until 315, when he was forced by Seleukos into giving a guarantee of neutrality (?), or of cooperation with the Ptolemaic forces (Diod. 19.62.6, where the dynast is apparently still A.). A Delian inscription (*IG* XI 2. 135) names Ἀνδροκλῆς Ἀμαθουσῶν βασιλεύς as the dedicator of a gold crown *c.*313, which may mean that A. did not assume the kingship until after 315 (Hill I 149 n.6). Berve II 37 no. 73; Hill, *Catalogue of Gr. Coins, Cyprus* (1904), p. xxv; Kirchner, *RE* I (1894) 2148 no. 8.

100 ANDROKYDES

(Ἀνδροκύδης). Greek physician who was supposed to have written to Alexander urging him to be more moderate in his drinking (Pliny, *HN* 14.58); Theophrastos, *Hist. Plant.* 4.16.6 says that A. recommended the use of cabbage to counteract the effects of wine (cf. Pliny, *HN* 17.240). Klearchos *ap.* Athen. 6.258b cites A. for the etymology of the word *kolax* ("flatterer"), which may suggest that he had some experience of Alexander's court. Wellmann, *RE* I.2 (1894) 2149 no. 1; Berve II 37–8 no. 74.

101 ANDROMACHOS

(Ἀνδρόμαχος). Macedonian (Tataki 242 no. 149). Son of Hieron, first attested commanding the mercenary horse at Gaugamela (Arr. 3.12.5). In 330 he remained briefly in Ekbatana, rejoining the King in Aria in the company of Philip son of Menelaos (Arr. 3.25.4). In 329, A. led 60 Companions—in the company of Karanos (who commanded 800 mercenary horse; Arr. 4.3.7), Pharnouches and Menedemos—at the Polytimetos (Zeravshan) River, where the Macedonian forces were ambushed by Spitamenes (Arr. 4.3.7; 4.5.5–6.2). Arr. 4.6.2 says that forty cavalrymen and 300 infantry escaped the slaughter. If A. had been among them we should expect Arrian to have mentioned the fact. Curtius' account of the Polytimetos disaster omits A. entirely (7.6.24, 7.7.31–9). Kaerst, *RE* I.2 (1894) 2152 no. 6; Berve II 38 no. 75; Heckel 1992, 364.

102 ANDROMACHOS

(Ἀνδρόμαχος). Macedonian (Tataki 241 no. 146). Possibly identical with Alexander's *nauarchos* at Tyre (see below). In 332, presumably on Alexander's instructions, Parmenion left him in charge of Koile-Syria (Curt. 4.5.9), apparently as the *strategos* assigned to Sanballat (no. 1034) in Samaria (he was not satrap of southern Syria, as Bosworth 1974, 50–1 suggests). A. was killed during a local uprising (Curt. 4.8.9). Kaerst, *RE* I.2 (1894) 2153 no. 7; Berve II 38–9 no. 76; Bosworth 1974.

103 ANDROMACHOS

(Ἀνδρόμαχος). Macedonian (Tataki 241 no. 145). *Nauarchos* at the siege of Tyre in 332, where he commanded the Kypriot contingent which blockaded the northern harbor (Arr. 2.20.10). There is a strong temptation to identify him with the officer assigned to Sanballat in Samaria (see above), but the Macedonian origin of the *nauarchos* is far from certain (cf. Tataki 241 no. 145). Identification with the son of Hieron is much less likely. Kaerst, *RE* I.2 (1894) 2152 no. 5; Berve II 39 no. 77.

ANDRON (Arr. *Ind.* 18.7 = Nearchos, *FGrH* 133 F1). See s.v. **HAGNON**.

104 ANDRONIKOS

(Ἀνδρόνικος). Noble Macedonian (Tataki 129 no. 5, identifying him with the adviser of Demetrios), son of Agerros (Arr. 3.23.9). Father of Proteas (and perhaps also Theodoros: Berve II 176 no. 362; cf. Carney 1981, 152, with n.10) and in all likelihood the husband of Lanike, daughter of Dropidas and sister of Black Kleitos. If this identification is correct, then A. may have been the father of the two unnamed sons of Lanike who died at Miletos in 334 (Curt. 8.2.8; cf. Arr. 4.9.4; A24–5). A. is first attested in 330 as the officer sent by Alexander (in accordance with their request) to the 1,500 Greek mercenaries who had served with Dareios III. These, after the Great King's death, were prepared to surrender to Alexander (Arr. 3.23.9; Artabazos went with him, presumably as a guide). He returned with these men and interceded on their behalf with the King, who spared their lives and installed A. as their commander (Arr. 3.24.5). Not long afterwards, Alexander sent A., along with Karanos, Erigyios, and Artabazos against the rebel Satibarzanes (Curt. 7.3.2; Arr. 3.28.2–3 does not mention him, perhaps because he was subordinate to Erigyios and Karanos). Carney 1981, 157 suggests that he commanded 1,500 mercenaries sent against Spitamenes in 329, but their commander was clearly Menedemos. Andromachos commanded 60 Companions, Karanos the 800 mercenary cavalry; Pharnouches (a Lykian) led the expedition (Arr. 4.3.7). That leaves Menedemos in charge of the infantry, a point which may explain his prominence in the Vulgate (Curt. 7.6.24; 7.7.31, 34–9; 7.9.21; cf. Metz Epit. 13). I do not see how Menedemos could be an error for A.; but Curtius (7.6.24) does give Menedemos 3,000 infantry, in addition to 800 cavalry, and it is remotely possible that A. served under him. Carney 157–8, furthermore, argues that the poem (composed by Pranichos or Pierion) which angered Kleitos and provoked the quarrel with Alexander (Plut. *Alex.* 50.8) dealt with the Polytimetos engagement, in which Kleitos' brother-in-law was (by her theory) killed. Certainly the identification of Proteas as "son of Lanike" creates the impression that his father was already dead in the final years of Alexander's life (Athen. 4.129a; Ael. *VH* 12.26). That Proteas forgave Alexander for his murder of Kleitos is not unreasonable; despite the apologetic tone of most sources, there is no reason to suppose that Alexander faked his grief. But, it is less likely that Proteas would have remained on intimate terms with a King who condoned the ridiculing of his father; and, indeed, it was not Kleitos but other older Macedonians who first found the poem objectionable. If A. son of Agerros did perish in the Polytimetos (Zeravshan) fiasco, this episode will not have been the subject of Pranichos' (Pierion's) composition. Berve II 39 no. 78; Carney 1981; Heckel 1992, 341–2.

105 ANDRONIKOS

(Ἀνδρόνικος). Macedonian from Olynthos (Gude 39 no. 4; Tataki 129 no. 5), A. had accompanied Alexander on the entire expedition (πᾶσαν τὴν στράτειαν, Diod. 19.69.1)—though nothing is known of his activities before 314, when he conducted the siege of Tyre briefly in Antigonos' absence (Diod. 19.59.2)—and was already πρεσβύτερος in 314, when he became an adviser of the young Demetrios Poliorketes (Diod. 19.69.1). Hence we may date his birth to *c.*370. Billows 167 no. 9 (followed by Tataki) identifies him implausibly with the son of Agerros (above). He commanded 1,500 cavalry on the right wing in the battle of Gaza (Diod. 19.82.4). Antigonos left him as *phrourarchos* of Tyre, in which capacity he refused to surrender the city to Ptolemy, to whom he responded in abusive terms. But, when his troops mutinied and expelled him from Tyre, A. fell into Ptolemy's hands, only to receive kind treatment from him; he appears to have ended his career as one of Ptolemy's *philoi* (Diod. 19.86.1–2). But Paschidis 2013, 124 believes that a fragmentary inscription from the Athenian Agora (*Agora* XVI 107, lines 10–12) honors Andronikos Olynthios, who was installed in some office by Demetrios (Ἀνδρόν[ικος Ὀλύνθιος (?) καθεστηκὼ]ς ὑπὸ Δη[μητρίου). The restoration of the name of the honorand is fairly secure but his ethnic, as Paschidis' reconstruction shows, is pure conjecture and difficult to reconcile with the evidence of Diodorus (but see Billows 368 and Paschidis 2013, 136 n.9). Berve II 39–40 no. 79; Badian, *BNP* I 687 no. 1; Billows 367–8 no. 9; Wilcken, *RE* I 2162 no. 11; Launey 301–4, 1170; Paschidis 2013.

106 ANDROSTHENES

(Ἀνδροσθένης). Son of Kallistratos (Arr. *Ind.* 18.4 = Nearchos, *FGrH* 133 F1). Greek from Thasos (Strabo 16.3.2 C766) who had been settled in Amphipolis and presumably had received Macedonian citizenship (Arr. *Ind.* 18.4, 6). A. is named as one of Alexander's trierarchs of the Hydaspes fleet in 326 (Arr. *Ind.* 18.4); later he accompanied Nearchos on his ocean voyage (Strabo 16.3.2 C766). Of this voyage, A. also wrote his own account (Strabo *ibid.,* citing Eratosthenes; Athen. 3.93b), which included also his Arabian expedition and appeared soon after Alexander's death (it was used by Theophrastos, *HP* 2.5.5). In 324/3, Alexander sent A. down the Euphrates to explore the Arabian coast (see also, Archias no. 166, Hieron no. 529); he skirted the coast of Arabia in a triakontor, sailing farther than Archias, who had reached Tylos (Manamah), but not as far as Hieron (Arr. 7.20.7). Nothing else is known about him. Berger, *RE* I.2 (1894) 2172–3 no. 9; Berve II 40 no. 80; Papastavru 1936, 60–81 no. 8; Potts 1990, II 5–6, 179.

107 ANGELOS

(Ἄγγελος). Epeirot (Molossian, Hammond, *Epirus* 796), apparently a high-ranking official at the court of Aiakides. When Aiakides was driven from the throne in 316, A. and Androkleides contrived to rescue the infant prince, Pyrrhos. (For his role in the dramatic escape see Plut. *Pyrrh.* 2.1–2; 2.3–8). His allies in the cause included also Androkleion, Hippias, and Neandros, who hurried to Megara in Macedonia, while A. and Androkleides delayed the pursuers (Plut. *Pyrrh.* 2.2). Ultimately, the party made its way to the court of the Illyrian Glaukias, whose wife Beroa was an Aiakid (Justin 17.3.18–19, see no. 294). Sandberger no. 13.

108 ANTENOR

(Ἀντήνωρ). Pankratiast. Apparently the son of Xenareus of Miletos and an honorary Athenian citizen (cf. Kirchner 970). He was undefeated in all three weight classes; his victory at Olympia in 308 is recorded (Africanus *ap.* Euseb. 1.206 Schoene; *IG* V 2.549; cf. *Mem. Ac. Linc.*[8] 8.131), as is a Lenean victory (*IG* V 2.549). He was also the lover of Mania (no. 681), who was at the time involved in a full-time relationship with another pankratiast, Leontiskos. When A. complained about her "infidelity" (Machon refers to the incident as "adultery," although Mania herself was a prostitute), she replied that she had wanted two Olympic athletes in one night, in order to size them up "blow for blow" (Athen.13.578f, Machon fr. 15 Gow); A.'s strength is alluded to by Athen. 4.135d, who speaks of an eel of such size and weight that even A. and a certain Astyanax could not lift it. Kirchner I.2 (1894) 2353 no. 4; Gow, *Machon* 102; Ogden 234.

ANTIBELOS. See BROCHUBELUS.

109 ANTIGENES

(Ἀντιγένης). Macedonian (Tataki 149–50 no. 15) officer of uncertain origin, though possibly from Pellene (or Pella). A. was born sometime around 380; for he was among the veterans discharged at Opis in 324 (Justin 12.12.8; cf. Plut. *Eum.* 16.7, who claims that none of the Argyraspids, whom A. commanded, was younger than sixty). In late 331 in the military contest held in Sittakene he received second prize and, with it, the rank of chiliarch of the hypaspists (Curt. 5.2.5; see literature s.v. Atarrhias no. 250). Since this was a reward for previous military valor, we may assume he came to Asia with Alexander in 334. A. reappears in the accounts of the Hydaspes battle in 326, where he (together with Tauron and Seleukos) commands infantrymen who are clearly not *pezhetairoi* (Arr. 5.16.3; cf. Curt. 8.14.15), hence probably his own chiliarchy (and perhaps another) of regular hypaspists, which crossed the Hydaspes with Alexander. A. is next found in conjunction with Krateros and the *apomachoi*, patrolling Drangiana and Arachosia and rejoining Alexander in Karmania (Arr. 6.17.3). Sent home to Macedonia from Opis, in the company of Krateros, Polyperchon, Gorgias, Polydamas, White Kleitos, and 10,000 veterans (12.12.8; cf. Arr. 7.12.4; Curt. 10.10.15), A. was nevertheless still in Kilikia in late 323 and appears to have remained there when Krateros was summoned to aid Antipatros in the Lamian War (Diod. 18.12.1, 16.4–5). Schachermeyr 1970, 14 n.10 suggests that Krateros left A. and the 3,000 Argyraspids in Kilikia and, after his death, Antipatros picked them up and led them to Syria, whence they were sent in due course to Sousiana (320). But A.

was already in Perdikkas' camp when he invaded Egypt (Diod. 18.37.1; but see 18.33.1, with Hornblower, *Hieronymus* 51; cf. Errington 1970, 55 n.127). Full discusssion in Heckel, *Marshals²* 309–11. In Egypt, he was one of the generals who murdered Perdikkas (Arr. *Succ.* 1.35; Diod. 18.39.6; Nepos, *Eum.* 5.1, adding Seleukos; cf. Diod. 18.36.5 for Peithon's role). A. was at that time already commander of the Silver Shields (Arr. *Succ.* 1.35: Ἀντιγένει . . . τῶν ἀργυρασπίδων Μακεδόνων ἡγουμένῳ) a unit of superannuated hypaspists, formed in India in 326/5 (cf. Curt. 8.5.4; Heckel 2013a; *contra* Lock 1977).

Awarded the satrapy of Sousiana at Triparadeisos (replacing the otherwise unknown Koinos: Dexippos, *FGrH* 100 F8 §6; cf. *LM* 121; Justin 13.4.14), A. appears to have seen Sousa on only two occasions between 320 and his death in 316/315: first in 320, when he conveyed some of the treasure from there to Kyinda (Quinda) in Kilikia, and again in 317, when he accompanied Eumenes to the East. Xenophilos may have administered Sousiana in Antigenes' absence (Curt. 5.2.16; cf. Diod. 19.17.3, 18.1, 48.6). A.'s satrapal rank may be reflected by the fact that, in the battle of Paraitakene, Antigenes and Peukestas shared an *agema* of 300 horse (Diod. 19. 28. 3), i.e., two *agemata* of 150 horsemen (cf. Diod. 19.27.2, where Eudamos has an *agema* of 150 cavalry, which Devine1985a, 76 terms "his satrapal *agema*"). The death of Antipatros and the ensuing wars between Antigonos and Eumenes in Asia and Kassandros and Polyperchon in Europe forced A. to choose sides. Letters from Polyperchon "and the kings" calling upon the Argyraspids to support their cause and serve with Eumenes had their desired effect (Diod. 18.58.1, 59.3; Plut. *Eum.* 13.3). A. welcomed the outlawed Greek, though not without some suspicion and resentment (Nepos, *Eum.* 7.1). A compromise saw the theoretical command of their forces retained by the spirit of Alexander, in whose tent the commanders met to decide policy (Diod. 18.60.1–61.3; Plut. *Eum.* 13.7–8; Polyaenus 4.8.2; Nepos, *Eum.* 7.1–2). Entreaties and bribes from both Ptolemy (Diod. 18.62.1–2) and Antigonos' agents (Philotas and thirty others: Diod. 18.62.3–63.6) were rejected—though A. found his colleague Teutamos (no. 1102) wavering in his loyalty (Diod. 18.62.5–6). The royalists soon moved eastward through A.'s satrapy (Diod. 19.15.5–6), which had been entrusted to Xenophilos (Diod. 19.17.3), the *phrourarchos* of Sousa since 331/0 (Curt. 5.2.16; cf. Arr. 3.16.9, naming Mazaros (no. 687), perhaps the Persian whom Xenophilos replaced). Though he resisted Antigonos, the satrapy itself was annexed and assigned to Seleukos (Diod. 19.18.1). For A., hope of recovering Sousiana lay in the defeat of Antigonos and his allies Peithon and Seleukos; to the Argyraspids, these barred a return to Macedonia which had been pre-empted by the outbreak of the Lamian War. The forces from the Upper Satrapies now joined the cause of Eumenes led by the orientalizing Peukestas (Diod. 19.14.2–8), a man of no mean ambition. And their presence, together with Peukestas' rivalry with Eumenes, served rather to bolster the support of the Argyraspids for the latter; A., who served Eumenes on the written orders of the kings, was not disposed to support Peukestas, and instead asserted the right of the Makedones to select a leader (Diod. 19.15.1–2). A. appears, as the army moved towards the Tigris, to have exercised some kind of joint command with Eumenes (cf. Diod. 19.17.4). When it was learned that Antigonos was in Media, A. and Eumenes shared the opinion that the army should move back to the coast. But this was rejected by the satraps of central Asia (Diod. 19.21.1). With Antigonos' forces threatening and the oriental element inclining towards Peukestas, the Macedonians opted for Eumenes, calling out for him in the Macedonian tongue (Plut. *Eum.* 14.8–11). The story is only partially told by Diod. 19.24.4ff. During Eumenes' illness, A. and Peukestas jointly led the army on its march (19.24.6).

At Paraitakene, A.'s subordinate role is clearly spelled out: together with Teutamos, he leads the Argyraspids and the hypaspists (6,000 men in all), and he shares an *agema* (300 horse) with Peukestas (Diod. 19.28.1, 3); Eumenes has an *agema* of 300 to himself. But the setback in Paraitakene put Eumenes' supreme command in jeopardy. Teutamos plotted with other prominent officers to remove the Greek once he served his purpose in the upcoming battle. Plutarch (*Eum.* 16.2) includes A. in this plot, but this is inconsistent with the other evidence and can be ascribed either to the tendency to lump the commanders of the Argyraspids together or to a source hostile to A. himself. At Gabiene, distressed because their baggage and the camp followers had fallen into Antigonos' hands, the Silver Shields delivered up Eumenes to the enemy (Diod. 19.43.7–9; Plut. *Eum.* 17; cf. Nepos, *Eum.* 10.1–2). Antigonos handed some 1,000 of them to Sibyrtios (no. 1044), satrap of Arachosia, ordering him to wear them out and destroy them (Diod. 19.48.3; Plut. *Eum.* 19.3; Polyaenus 4.6.15), but A. himself was thrown into a pit and burned alive (Diod. 19.44.1). A. had remained loyal to Eumenes to the end. Plutarch (*Eumenes* 17.1–2) makes it clear that Teutamos (οἱ περὶ Τεύταμον) led the betrayal. Antigonos rewarded Eumenes' captors with gifts (Polyaenus 4.6.15), though he punished a large number of the Silver Shields. The evidence thus shows that the Argyraspids and their commanders were divided on the matter of Eumenes. Although A. was executed, there is no mention of Teutamos, who was doubtless among those rewarded by Antigonos. Despite his negative image, A. appears to have been a committed royalist, a supporter of the concept of *Reichseinheit*. His participation in the plot against Perdikkas was motivated not by hope of personal gain but disillusionment: Perdikkas was a self-seeking individual with no sense of humanity and little regard for the sufferings of his troops (cf. Justin 13.8.2; Diod. 18.33.3, 5; 18.36.1). A. was consistently loyal to Eumenes, willingly obeying the orders of Polyperchon (Diod. 18.58.1), allying himself with Eumenes (18.59.3), and rebuffing embassies from Ptolemy (18.62.1–2), Antigonos (through the agency of Philotas, 18.62.4–7), Seleukos and Peithon (19.12.2–3, 13.1). Hieronymos is unlikely to have praised him (Diod. 18.62.6), had he regarded A. as a traitor. Berve II 41–2, nos. 83–4; Kaerst, *RE* I.2 (1894) 2399 no. 9; Launey 1172; Badian, *BNP* I 744 no. 2; Heckel, *Marshals*² 308–14; Anson 147–90; Schäfer 2002, 123–66. See also Anson 1988b; Lock 1977; Heckel 2013a and 1985; Hammond 1984 and 1989, 64–5; Roisman 2010 and 2012, 177–236.

110 ANTIGENES

(Ἀντιγένης). Macedonian (Tataki 149–50 no. 15) officer of uncertain origin, though possibly from Pellene (or Pella). Plutarch (*Alex.* 70.4–6 and *Mor.* 339b) speaks of a certain one-eyed man named Antigenes in the time that preceded the demobilization of the troops in Sousiana. But the information is of limited value, since it attributes to A. actions and intentions reported elsewhere about Atarrhias (another hypaspist commander) and Eurylochos. A. is said to have lost an eye during the siege of Perinthos (Plut. *Alex.* 70.4–6) when he was young (νέος). Billows 27–9 sees possible confusion with Antigonos the One-Eyed, which presents two difficulties: (1) Antigonos was never in Alexander's camp after 333 and (2) neither the hypaspist commander nor Monophthalmos (they were, in fact, coeval) could be described as "young" at the time of Philip's siege of Perinthos (340). It is futile to attempt to sort out the inconsistencies of these stories. There remains, however, the remote possibility that this A. is to be distinguished from the Argyraspid commander. Berve II 41 no. 84.

111 ANTIGENIDAS

(Ἀντιγενίδας). Son of Simulos. One of twenty-four cavalrymen from Orchomenos, who served with Alexander's allied cavalry until the expedition reached Ekbatana in 330. There he and his compatriots were discharged. On their return (*c.*329), they made a dedication to Zeus Soter in Orchomenos (*IG* VII 3206). Berve II 42 no. 85.

112 ANTIGONE

(Ἀντιγόνη, Ἀντιγόνα). Macedonian (Tataki 1550 no. 16). A good-looking woman, Pydnaian (Plut. *Alex.* 48.4) or Pellaian (Plut. *Mor.* 339e) by birth, A. had been captured, after sailing to Samothrake to celebrate the mysteries, by the Persian admiral Autophradates (Plut. *Mor.* 339d–f). The year of her capture is uncertain, but Hamilton 133, rightly rejects Burn's suggestion (1947, 180 = 1973, 133) that she was sold into slavery after Philip's capture of Pydna in 356. Nevertheless, Hamilton's suggestion that she was captured earlier in 333 leaves little time for her to have found her way to Damaskos, where she was taken by Parmenion late in that year. Berve's (II 42) observation that she was captured at sea goes beyond the evidence of Plut. *Mor.* 339e. The use of the word *gynaion* in both Plutarchean passages implies that she was of low birth. She soon became Philotas' mistress (though Müller 2020 rightly rejects the notion of romantic attachment) and the sounding board for his complaints about the King. During the Egyptian campaign, Philotas' comments were related by A., innocently we may assume, to her friends, and eventually the gossip came to the attention of Krateros, who secretly took her to the King so that she could repeat what she had heard; Alexander encouraged her to continue informing against her lover (Plut. *Alex.* 48–9). How much her reports affected the King's view of Philotas cannot be known, but the fact that almost three years intervened between her meeting with Alexander and Philotas' arrest suggests that she provided no truly damning information. What became of her we do not know. Wilcken, *RE* I.2 (1894) 2404 no.7; Berve II 42 no. 86; Hofstetter 16–17 no. 19a; Müller 2020.

113 ANTIGONE

(Ἀντιγόνη, Ἀντιγόνα). Macedonian (Tataki 245 no. 168). Daughter of Kassandros (no. 478), a brother of Antipatros. Wife of Magas (Schol. Theocr. 17.34, where Λάγου should be emended to Μάγα; cf. Hoffmann 222–3; Beloch IV² 2.602) and mother of Berenike (Schol. Theocr. 17.61), who named her children Antigone and Magas. Accepting the reading Λάγου (which makes A. the wife of Lagos, father of Ptolemy I), Wilcken 1894, 2404 (cf. Tataki 245 no. 168) regards Berenike as both "Schwester und Gemahlin" of Soter, which is almost certainly incorrect. Nothing else is known about her life. Wilcken, *RE* I.2 (1894) 2404 no. 5; Beloch IV² 2.180, 601–2; Heckel 1989, 33–4; Ogden 70; Carney 2013, 20; Grainger 2019, 53–4. **Stemma V.**

114 ANTIGONE

(Ἀντιγόνη, Ἀντιγόνα). Macedonian (Tataki 244 no. 165). Daughter of Berenike by her first husband, the obscure Philip (no. 919; Plut. *Pyrrh.* 4.7); born in the mid-to-late 320s, i.e., before Berenike's departure for Egypt with her cousin, Eurydike (*c.*321). Sister of

Magas, who ruled Kyrene from 300 to 250 (see s.v.). Justin calls her "daughter of Ptolemy," referring to her adoptive father (Justin 17.2.14–15; cf. Paus. 1.11.5). No doubt she had inherited some of the charm and intelligence of her mother, and Plutarch's comment that she had many suitors may be more than mere flattery or ascribable to political motives alone (Plut. *Pyrrh.* 4.7). On the other hand, the preferment of Pyrrhos as a son-in-law had more to do with his claims to Epeiros than to his charm or Berenike's influence. Ptolemy Soter thus gained a powerful ally against Kassandros, while detaching the young man from the influence of Demetrios. The betrothal and marriage occurred in Egypt (*c.*298/7; Plut. *Pyrrh.* 4.7; Paus 1.11.5), where Pyrrhos had been detained as a hostage after the battle of Ipsos in 301 (at that time, Pyrrhos' sister Deidameia was wife of Demetrios Poliorketes). The marriage appears to have been happy, and one that enhanced Pyrrhos' reputation (Plut. *Pyrrh.* 5.1). A. bore an heir, Ptolemy, named in honor of A.'s stepfather (Plut. *Pyrrh.* 6.1; 9.3; Justin 18.1.3 puts his birth in 296/5). Whether she was also the mother of Olympias (no. 809; Justin 28.1.1) remains uncertain (assumed by Sandberger 32; Beloch IV² 2.148; *contra* Corradi 1912, 194). Otherwise, little is known about her: Plut. *Pyrrh.* 5.13 tells the story of a certain Phainarete who revealed to A. a plot to poison Pyrrhos. A. appears to have died no later than 295, certainly before Pyrrhos' marriage to Lanassa (cf. Sandberger 32; Pyrrhos remarried μετὰ τὴν Ἀντιγόνης τελευτήν); Pyrrhos thereafter contracted several political marriages (Plut. *Pyrrh.* 9.1). Antigoneia on the Aous river was apparently named in her honor, either by Pyrrhos himself or by Ptolemy (Steph. Byz. s.v. Ἀντιγόνεια, Polyb. 2.5; Ptol. 3.13.5; Sandberger 33; but see Tarn, *AG* 312 and H. Treidler, *Kl. Pauly* I 380 s.v. "Antigoneia (4)," who consider the town a foundation of Antigonos Gonatas). Pyrrhos also founded a city in the Epeirot Chersonese (near modern Preveza; see also Hammond 1967, 578–9, who thinks it was intended to commemorate Pyrrhos' landing place in 297, when he recovered his kingdom) which he named for A.'s mother, Berenike (Plut. *Pyrrh.* 6.1). Beloch IV² 2.148; Sandberger no. 14; Seibert 1967, 76–7, 100; Wilcken, *RE* I.2 (1894) 2404 no. 6. **Stemmata IIb and V.**

115 ANTIGONOS

(Ἀντίγονος). Nicknamed "the One-Eyed": *Monophthalmos, Heterophthalmos* or *Kyklops* (Ael. *VH* 12.43; Plut. *Ser.* 1.8; Pliny, *HN* 35.90; Polyb. 5.67.6; cf. Plut. *Mor.* 633c). Macedonian (Tataki 245 no. 169). A. was born not long after 386/5 (Hieronymos *ap.* [Lucian], *Macrob.* 11 = *FGrH* 154 F8; App. *Syr.* 55.279; cf. Plut. *Demetr.* 19.4, who says that in 306 he was "a little short of 80 years old"; Porphyry of Tyre, *FGrH* 260 F32 says he was 86 at the time of his death!), the son of a certain Philip (Arr. 1.29.3; *Syll³* 278, 5; Strabo 12.4.7 C565; Justin 13.4.14; Ael. *VH* 12.43; Plut. *Demetr.* 2.1; Hieronymos *ap.* [Lucian], *Macrob.* 11 = *FGrH* 154 F8). The name of his mother is not recorded, but we do know that she remarried at some point after the birth of A. and his brothers, this time to Periandros (otherwise unknown), to whom she bore a son named Marsyas (*Suda* M 227. See below no. 683). Since Marsyas was born *c.*356—he was a *syntrophos* of Alexander the Great (*Suda*)—we may assume that the mother was still very young when she bore A., Demetrios and, apparently, a third son of Philip, Polemaios (father of A.'s nephew of the same name who was active in the early age of the Successors). Dioskourides is also named as a nephew of A., but the name of his father is unknown. That A. began his career as a common laborer is hostile propaganda, characteristic of the Diadochic period (cf. Ael. *VH* 12.43; *Suda* M 227; cf. Diod. 21.1 ἐξ ἰδιώτου γενόμενος δυνάστης). Philip V's later claim of kinship with Philip II and Alexander (Polyb. 5.10.10), if not outright invention, suggests that Stratonike, the daughter of Korrhagos and wife of A., may have been related to Philip II (the name is attested in the Argead house; cf. Thuc 2.101.6). Their children were Demetrios and Philip (Plut. *Demetr.* 2.1–2, *Pyrrh.* 4.3).

An *hetairos* of Alexander (Ael. *VH* 14.47a; cf. Justin 16.1.12), in 334, A. commanded 7,000 allied Greek hoplites, when the expedition crossed into Asia (Diod. 17.17.3; Briant 1973, 27–41; Billows 36–41). At some time before August 334 he was sent to secure the loyalty of Priene: the initial arrangements were confirmed, in terms favorable to the city, by Alexander himself (cf. Tod nos. 184–5). Priene, appreciative of A.'s efforts (Tod II 245–46), honored him, bestowing *proxenia,* citizenship, and exemption from taxation (*Syll*[3] 278 = *I.Priene* no. 2 = Tod no. 186; Harding no. 103). A. seems to have remained with Alexander until early spring 333, when he was appointed satrap of Phrygia (capital: Kelainai; Arr. 1.29.3; Curt. 4.1.35 wrongly says "Lydia"; cf. 4.5.13, linking him with Lykaonia), which he ruled until his death in 301. Balakros son of Amyntas replaced him as commander of the Greek infantry (Arr. 1.29.3). Kelainai had not yet surrendered to the Macedonians, though its inhabitants promised to do so at the end of the second month, if no help arrived from Dareios III (Arr. 1.29.2; Curt. 3.1.8). The garrison of 1,000 Karians probably continued to serve A. after the surrender; the 100 Greek mercenaries may, however, have been handed over to Alexander or shipped to Macedonia for punishment. As satrap of Phrygia, controlling the main lines of communication in Asia Minor, A. dealt with the remnants of Persian resistance in the area (see Anson 1988, 471). After Issos (November 333), a substantial force, loyal to the Persian king, escaped from the battlefield and prepared a counterstrike with troops from Kappadokia and Paphlagonia (Curt. 4.1.35). These forces were crushed in three separate battles in 332: A. himself was victorious in Lykaonia, as was Kalas in Paphlagonia; Balakros expelled the Persians from Miletos (Curt. 4.5.13). Curt. 4.5.13 merely elucidates the more compressed observation at 4.1.35 (for these events see Heckel 121–3). I do not believe that A. won three successive battles before his victory in Lykaonia. Nor am I inclined to accept the view that "Lydia" in Curt. 4.1.35 is anything more than an error on Curtius' part. That A. assumed "overall command in Asia Minor," as Billows 44 n.80 suggests, can neither be proved nor disproved. After Nearchos' departure in 331/0, A. assumed control of Pamphylia and Lykia (cf. Diod. 18.3.1; Curt. 10.10.2; cf. Baumbach 57). Confirmed as satrap of Greater Phrygia in 323 (Diod. 18.3.1, 39.6; Arr. *Succ.* 1.6; Dexippos, *FGrH* 100 F8 §2; Curt. 10.10.2; Justin 13.4.14), he was ordered by Perdikkas to aid Eumenes in the conquest of Kappadokia, and his refusal to obey these instructions placed him in jeopardy when Perdikkas called him to account (Plut. *Eum.* 3.4–5; Diod. 18.23.3–4; cf. Arr. *Succ.* 1.20; Diod. 18.23.4). A. fled to Europe, bringing with him reports of Perdikkas' duplicity and aspirations (Diod. 18.23.3–4; Arr. *Succ.* 1.20, 24). He gave damning evidence that Perdikkas intended to send Nikaia back to her father and marry Alexander's sister instead (Arr. *Succ.* 1.26). Reports of this hastened the invasion from the north by Krateros and Antipatros, who persuaded White Kleitos to abandon the Perdikkan cause and allow their entry into Asia (Arr. *Succ.* 1.26). He himself crossed the Aegean with ten Athenian ships and 3,000 troops, landing in Karia, where he was welcomed by his kinsman, the satrap Asandros (Arr. *Succ.* 25.1). It was undoubtedly A.'s purpose to gain a foothold in Asia Minor and rally the disaffected satraps until Krateros and Antipatros could cross the Hellespont. Menandros immediately went over to A., angered by the high-handedness of Perdikkas, who had left him in charge of the satrapal forces but placed him under the authority of Kleopatra (Arr. *Succ.* 25.2).

A., in the meantime, moved inland, intending to catch Eumenes in an ambush. But his troop movements were reported to Kleopatra at Sardis, and Eumenes managed to escape to Phrygia (Arr. *Succ.* 25.6–8). It was presumably soon afterwards that A. joined Krateros and Antipatros near the Hellespont where a council of war was held. Krateros, it was decided, would deal with Eumenes, while Antipatros pushed on to Kilikia; A. meanwhile was sent to Kypros to engage the forces under the command of Aristonous (thus Arr. *Succ.* 1.30; cf. 24.6); he was perhaps accompanied by Dionysios of Herakleia Pontika (Memnon, *FGrH* 434 F2 §§3–6). Whether A. won a clear victory there is debatable (*pace* Billows 68): nothing is recorded about the campaign except his participation in it. It appears that he came to terms with Aristonous' forces once news of Perdikkas' death became known. Of the enemy commanders there, at least one, Medeios of Larisa, joined him. From Kypros, A. was summoned to northern Syria, where, at Triparadeisos, he was recognized as a virtual equal partner with Antipatros, whom he had saved from the rampaging mob that had once been Perdikkas' Royal Army (Arr. *Succ.* 1.32–3; Polyaenus 4.6.4). A. was now confirmed as satrap of Phrygia (Diod. 18.39.6; Arr. *Succ.* 1.37), with control of Greater Phrygia, Lykaonia, Pamphylia and Lykia, and appointed *hegemon* of the Royal Army; his task was to wage war on Eumenes and the outlawed party (Diod. 18.39.7; Arr. *Succ.* 1.38; cf. App. *Syr.* 53.266; Justin 13.8.10, 14.1.1; Plut. *Eum.* 8.4). Presumably he was recognized as *strategos* of Asia Minor (cf. Diod. 18.50.1). In theory, he was second only to Antipatros in the hierarchy of Alexander's orphaned empire. Perhaps, Antipatros sensed that his own end was near and regarded A. as the most worthy to exercise the supreme authority. But the decision to leave the Kings with A. and his chiliarch, Kassandros, suggests that Antipatros was content to rule Macedonia and Europe and to leave the problems of Asia and the misfit Kings to another (Arr. *Succ.* 1.38; Justin 16.1.13). A. and Kassandros soon fell out, however, and Antipatros, acting on his son's advice, took the Kings to Europe (Arr. *Succ.* 1.42–5). He had thus taken back the symbolic authority over the empire as a whole, but in fact left Asia to A., who lacked neither the ambition nor the resources to gain supremacy. It was later said that A. exercised his power unjustly (Diod. 21.1.1), and this was apparent already in the first years after Alexander's death. After an unsuccessful attempt (through letters) to detach Eumenes' troops from their commander (Justin 14.1.9–14), A. brought his foe to battle at Orkynia (Justin 14.2.1; Plut. *Eum.* 9.3–12) and then besieged him in the fortress of Nora (*Barr. Atl.* 63 E4; Diod. 18.53.1, 4, 5; Justin 14.2.–4; Nepos, *Eum.* 5.2–3; Plut. *Eum.* 10.2, 11.1; for discussion of the location, see Yardley–Wheatley–Heckel 173, with earlier literature). He could not, however, bring Eumenes to terms (Plut. *Eum.* 10.3–7, including a personal meeting between A. and Eumenes) and he eventually eluded his grasp (Diod. 18.53; Nepos, *Eum.* 5.7; for the oath demanded by A. and Eumenes' trickery see Plut. *Eum.* 12.1–4). A.'s attempt to reinstitute the siege failed (Plut. *Eum.* 12.7). A. turned south in the direction of Pisidia and caught the forces of Alketas and Attalos off guard by the speed of his march. At Kretopolis, he won a resounding victory, and, although Alketas escaped, he was finally killed by the Pisidians and his body maltreated by Monophthalmos (Polyaenus 4.6.6–7; Diod. 18.44–7). On his return from Kretopolis, A. learned from Aristodemos that Antipatros had died and that the regency in Macedon was now held by Polyperchon (Diod. 19.47.4). Not too much later he would learn that Polyperchon and Kassandros were engaged in a struggle for power.

A. moved against Arrhidaios (no. 214) in Hellespontine Phrygia (Diod. 18.52), while Kassandros, for his part, sailed to Asia to beg for A.'s support, to which he agreed (Diod. 18.54.3), though his real motive was to surround Polyperchon with enemies (Diod. 18.54.4; cf. 18.64.1; for A.'s support of Kassandros and his open rebellion against the Kings see Diod. 18.55.2–3). Indeed, Eumenes would not take orders from A., since it was clear that he was seeking royal power (Diod. 18.58.4: ἔκρινεν Ἀντίγονῳ μὲν μὴ προσέχειν ἐξιδιαζομένῳ τὴν βασιλείαν). A. sent Menandros (no. 706) against Eumenes in Kappadokia (Diod. 18.59.1), and he recognized that Polyperchon's support of Eumenes was jeopardizing his own position (Diod. 18.62.3). Eumenes persuaded Antigenes that it was better for Eumenes than for A. to remain alive (Diod. 18.62.6). A. wrote a letter to the Silver Shields (carried by Philotas no. 942), accusing Eumenes and ordering the Silver Shields to arrest him and put him to death (Diod. 18.63.2), although they were in a quandary (Diod. 18.63.3), they rejected Philotas and opted to support Eumenes (Diod. 18.63.6). A. gave material aid to Kassandros, sending him thirty-five warships and 4,000 troops, with which he sailed to Peiraieus (Diod. 18.68.1; possibly the same warships that joined Nikanor's force at the Hellespont, 18.72.3). At the Hellespont, Nikanor suffered an initial setback, but A. brought up his light-armed troops, slingers and archers, and fell upon Kleitos' men who had encamped for the night (Diod. 18.72.5–6), leading to the destruction of the remainder of the fleet by Nikanor (Diod. 18.72.7–9; see Kleitos no. 596). The victory emboldened A., who now set out to make himself master on land and sea; he moved with 20,000 lightly armed infantry and 4,000 cavalry to bring the war to Eumenes in Kilikia (Diod. 18.73.1–2).

Eumenes attempted to detach Seleukos and Peithon from their support of A. (Diod. 19.12.1), but without success. A. soon received an appeal for help from Seleukos who was hardpressed by Eumenes in Mesopotamia (Diod. 19.13.5); A. brought his forces into Mesopotamia while Eumenes was in Sousiana (Diod. 19.15.6; cf. 19.16.1, and also 19.15.3 for Eumenes' fear that divisions in his army would only help A.). From Mesopotamia, A. moved to Babylon where he made an alliance with Seleukos and Peithon and received additional forces from them (Diod. 19.17.2). A. assigned the satrapy of Sousiana to Seleukos and placed the citadel of Sousa under siege, since Xenophilos (no. 1165), the *phrourarchos*, held out against him (Diod. 19.18.1), having been instructed to have no dealings with A. (Diod. 19.17.3), while he himself advanced to the Koprates River. There his men suffered a major setback in their attempt to cross the river (Diod. 19.18.2–7). A.'s advance firmed up Peukestas' support for Eumenes; for he feared that A. would deprive him of his satrapy (Diod. 19.17.5). A. next proceeded to Badake, on the Eulaios River, and then into Media and Ekbatana (Diod. 19.19.1–2). On the way he was confronted by the Kossaians, against whom he sent light-armed troops under Nearchos (Diod. 19.19.2–5); nevertheless, the army was mauled by the Kossaians, and A. regretted not heeding Peithon's advice to purchase safe passage (Diod. 19.19.6–8). Thus, in Media, A.'s troops became unruly and he had difficulty winning back their loyalty (Diod. 19.20). Eumenes spread false rumors that Polyperchon had crossed into Asia to lend assistance (Diod. 19.23.2). A., meanwhile, moved into Persia (Diod. 19.24.4), but his attempts to lure the satraps away from their support of Eumenes met with no success (Diod 19.25.2–7).

The first major confrontation with Eumenes was at Paraitakene (Diod. 19.27–31 and 19.25–6 for the preliminaries; cf. Devine 1985a). The importance of the battle and extent of Eumenes' "victory" are doubtless exaggerated by pro-Eumenid propaganda

(Devine 1985a, 86; but see Anson 180–1 n.97). Plut. *Eum.* 15.1–3 deals with the battle only briefly (cf. Nepos, *Eum.* 8.1); Justin does not discuss it at all. For the aftermath of Paraitakene see Diod. 19.32.1, 5; 19.34.8: 19. 37–8. But the battle of Gabene or Gabiene (Plut. *Eum.* 16; Nepos, *Eum.* 10.1–2; Justin 14.3.1–3, compressing the events of 317/16; Diod. 19.40.1–43.6, and 19.39 for the preliminary skirmishing; cf. Plut. *Eum.* 15; Nepos, *Eum.* 8.4–10.1: he was out-generaled by Eumenes) proved decisive (Justin 14.4.19). In this battle, A. captured the baggage (and the families) of the Argyraspids, who sought to win back what they had lost by surrendering Eumenes to the victor (Plut. *Eum.* 16.11–18.5; Diod. 19.43.7–9; Justin 14.3.3–4.16; Nepos, *Eum.* 10.2, 13.1 calls the battle a victory for Eumenes, adding that his capture was the result of Macedonian betrayal: *captus non Antigoni virtute sed Macedonum periurio*). A. kept Eumenes under guard for a while (Nepos, *Eum.* 11.3–5)—he allegedly wished to spare him and have him as an ally against the other Successors (Nepos, *Eum.* 10.3–4; Plut. *Comp. Sertorius and Eumenes* 2; cf. Plut. *Eum.* 18.7 for his kindness to Eumenes)—but, realizing that no meaningful agreement could be reached and fearing his popularity with the troops, he had him put to death (Plut. *Eum.* 19.1; Diod. 19.44.1; Nepos, *Eum.* 12 says he referred the matter to a council, who resolved to let Eumenes die of starvation, though in the end he was strangled, implausibly, without A.'s knowledge (*insciente Antigono*)—two forms of exculpation; Justin 14.4.21 does not report his death in context; see also Yardley–Wheatley–Heckel 189–91; App. *Syr.* 53.267). A. sent Eumenes' ashes to his wife and children in Kappadokia (Nepos, *Eum.* 13.4). Although some of Eumenes' officers were taken into his entourage (Diod. 19.44.3: Hieronymos no. 531), A.'s treatment of enemy leaders was generally harsh: he had Antigenes (no. 109) thrown into a pit and burned alive, and he killed Eudamos (no. 434) and Kephalon (no. 582; Diod. 19.44.1: for the identification of the latter, called Kelbanos by Diodorus, Heckel 1980c). Although he took some of the Argyraspids into his army, he assigned most of them to Sibyrtios and told him to wear them out with service in his satrapy (Plut. *Eum.* 19.3; Diod. 19.48.4; Polyaenus 4.6.15; cf. Justin 14.4.20). After his victory at Gabiene, A. wintered in Media, distributing his troops throughout the region, while he himself stayed at Rhagai (Diod. 19.44.4). Suspicious of Peithon's ambitions, he deceived him with promises and then arrested and executed him (Diod. 19.46.1–4); this was followed by a successful operation against the remaining supporters of Peithon under Meleagros (no. 697) and Okranes (no. 807; Diod. 19.47). A. now reorganized the East, placing new satraps in Karmania, Baktria, and Aria (Diod. 19.48.1–2), but he was forced to leave others in power since further campaigning in Central Asia was not feasible (19.48.2). Handing over the most unruly of the Silver Shields to Sibyrtios (Diod. 19.48.3–4; they were clearly divided between the supporters of Antigenes and those of Teutamos: see s.vv.), A. now turned his attention to Peukestas, whose supporter, Thespios (no. 1120), he put to death (Diod. 19.48.5); Xenophilos, on orders from Seleukos, came over to A. and made the treasures of Sousa available to him, some twenty-five thousand talents (Diod. 19.48.6–8). A. pretended friendship, fearing that Xenophilos might change his mind (Diod. 19.48.6), but the man's disappearance from the historical accounts is doubtless no coincidence. He appointed Aspeisas (no. 242) satrap of Sousiana (Diod. 19.55.1) and then set out for Babylon, where he expelled Seleukos on what appears to have been a trumped up charge (Diod. 19.55.2–4; cf. App. *Syr.* 53.267–8). Seleukos fled to Egypt, where he was taken in by Ptolemy (Diod. 19.55.5); that flight gave rise to an *ex post facto* "prophecy" of the

Chaldaians that A. would lose his life in battle with Seleukos, a reference to Ipsos (Diod. 19.55.6–9). For his part in allowing Seleukos to escape, Blitor (no. 303) was deposed by A. (App. *Syr.* 53.269), who extended his own authority over Babylonia and Mesopotamia.

If A. received a letter from Adea-Eurydike appealing for aid (Justin 14.5.3), it either arrived too late or at a time when there was little that he could do to support her. A. now found himself confronted by an alliance of Ptolemy, Seleukos (who exposed A.'s ambitions and the magnitude of his resources: Diod. 19.56.1–3), Lysimachos, and Kassandros, despite his attempts to prevent this (Diod. 19.56.3–4), and he responded by excoriating Kassandros for his treatment of Olympias and the royal family (Justin 15.1.2–3). Before moving back to the West, he assigned Babylon to Peithon son of Agenor (no. 868; Diod. 19.56.4). In Kilikia he seized the treasures at Kyinda (Diod. 19.56.5) and then moved to Upper Syria in 315, where he was met by envoys of the coalition. These threatened him with war if he did not share the spoils (Diod. 19.85.3; Justin 15.1.9) and give Kappadokia and Lykia to Kassandros, Hellespontine Phrygia to Lysimachos, Syria to Ptolemy, and Babylonia to Seleukos, a proposal he rejected (Diod. 19.57.1–2; App. *Syr.* 53.270; Justin 15.1.1–3). A. countered by sending Agesilaos to Kypros, while Idomeneus and Moschion went to Rhodes; Polemaios was ordered to drive Kassandros' forces out of Kappadokia (Diod. 19.57.3–4); Aristodemos he sent to the Peloponnese to forge an alliance with Alexander and Polyperchon, and to recruit mercenaries with whom to confront Kassandros in Greece (his activities: Diod. 19.66–7); a chain of fire-signals was used to expedite communications (Diod. 19.57.5). A. himself prepared to secure Phoinikia and besiege Tyre, sending out also a force of 8,000 men to cut and transport timber for the building of a fleet (Diod. 19.58.1–4); for Seleukos had been sent from Egypt with a fleet of 100 ships, which were now in control of the seas (Diod. 19.58.5) and A. proposed to equip 500 of his own (Diod. 19.58.6). Learning that Ptolemy was winning over the kings of Kypros, he himself left 3,000 men under Aristonikos to besiege Tyre and took the army to capture Joppa and Gaza before returning to the siege (Diod. 19.59.1–3). Aristodemos (no. 191), in Greece, won over Polyperchon and Alexander (Diod. 19.60.1, 61.1) but Polemaios' force in Asia Minor had more limited success (Diod. 19.60.2–4), and A. now launched a propaganda campaign, accusing Kassandros of crimes against the royal house and of illegally re-establishing the city of Thebes, and he proclaimed the "Freedom of the Greeks" in the hope of winning their allegiance as well as the support of the eastern satraps, who had joined Eumenes in their support of the royal house (Diod. 19.61.1–4). Then he turned back to the siege of Tyre which held out for a year and three months (Diod. 19.59.2, 61.5). A conference with Ptolemy, who met him at Ekregma, solved nothing (Diod. 19.64.8). For the activities of A.'s generals in Karia see Diod. 19.68.2–7. A. left his son Demetrios in Syria, with some trusted advisers (Diod. 19.69.1) and moved back to Kelainai, losing many men in a treacherous winter crossing of the Tauros range (Diod. 19.69.2). After distributing his men to winter quarters in Phrygia (winter 314/13), he summoned Medeios and the fleet from Phoinikia (Diod. 19.69.3). In 313 he sent forces to aid the Kallatians against Lysimachos (Diod. 19.73.6); Telesphoros (no. 1100), another nephew of A. was dispatched to the Peloponnese (Diod. 19.74.1, 75.7). Meanwhile, in Karia, A. came to terms with Asandros, who agreed to transfer his troops to him and gave his brother Agathon as a hostage; but Asandros soon regretted the move and, after securing Agathon's escape, sent envoys to Ptolemy and Seleukos (Diod. 19.75.1–2). A. retaliated by bringing Miletos, Tralles, Kaunos, and Iasos over to his side (Diod. 19.75.3–6) and by making an alliance with the Aitolians and Boiotians (19.75.6; cf. the further activities of his generals in Greece: Diod. 19.77.2–7, 78.2–5; 87). Negotiations with Pymiathon, king of Kition (Diod. 19.57.4, 59.1), ended with Ptolemy putting the king to death (Diod. 19.79.4 calls him Pygmalion); nor did support of the Antigonids turn out well for the rulers of Marion, Lapethos, and Keryneia. Not much later, Ptolemy defeated Demetrios at Gaza, and recovered Antigonid territory in Syria and Phoinikia (Diod. 19.80–86; cf. Justin 15.1.6).

In the aftermath of Ptolemy's victory, Seleukos made a dash with smaller forces to recover his satrapy (Diod. 19.90.1), leaving the Antigonid supporters to seek refuge in the citadel commanded by Diphilos (Diod. 19.91.3). When the citadel was taken by storm, those whom A. had imprisoned there were freed (Diod. 19.91.4); later A.'s earlier conduct induced many Persians serving with Nikanor to defect after the death of their own commander Euagros (Diod. 19.92.4). A. himself was at Kelainai when he learned of Demetrios' two battles in Syria, and he moved his army south of the Tauros. Ptolemy withdrew to Egypt (Diod. 19.93.4–5). A.'s next move was to deal with the Nabataians (Diod. 19.94.1) but the efforts of his general Athenaios (no. 254) proved inadequate (Diod. 19.95–6) and were followed by a new expedition led by Demetrios (Diod. 19.96.4; Wheatley and Dunn 76–83). Only then did A. turn his attention to Babylonia; for he received a letter from Nikanor detailing his setbacks in Media (Diod. 19.100.3). He promptly dispatched Demetrios to Babylonia with 5,000 Macedonians, 10,000 mercenaries and 4,000 cavalry, ordering him to recover the territory and return to the sea (Diod. 19.100.4). The outcome was less than satisfactory (see s.v. Demetrios no. 360; Wheatley and Dunn 98–101). In 311, A. made the so-called Peace of the Dynasts (also the "Peace of 311") with Kassandros, Ptolemy, and Lysimachos, which granted him first place in Asia (Diod. 19.105.1: Ἀντίγονον δὲ ἀφηγεῖσθαι τῆς Ἀσίας πάσης), which only inspired further regal ambitions (Diod. 19.105.3–4).

More than the other Successors, Antigonos relied on relatives to execute his military/ political objectives, and this led to rivalry and disaffection. His nephew Polemaios, who was operating in the Peloponnese in 310, complained of insufficient honors and defected to Kassandros, encouraging also his friend Phoinix to take an anti-Antigonid stance in Hellespontine Phrygia (Diod. 20.19.2; cf. 20.27.3). A. sent his younger son Philip to deal with Phoinix, while Demetrios set out to combat Leonides in Kilikia, where Ptolemy was now attempting to limit Antigonid power (Diod. 20.19.3–5). Demetrios' actions appear to have been successful, but Ptolemy seized Xanthos in Lykia, which had been protected by an Antigonid garrison (309 BC: Diod. 20.27.1). A move by Nikokles of Paphos to align himself with A. against Ptolemy had dire consequences for the Kypriot king (Diod. 20.21). In the following year, A. instructed the governor (*epimeletes*) of Sardis to prevent Kleopatra, the sister of Alexander the Great, from traveling to meet and marry Ptolemy; not content with detaining her, A. ordered her murder at the hands of those who attended upon her (Diod. 20.37.3–6; Carney 123–8). After Demetrios had captured Peiraieus (Diod. 20.45) and won Athens for the Antigonids, statues of father and son were erected in Athens on a decree of Stratokles (Diod. 20.46.2); learning of this from Athenian envoys, A. supplied the city with grain and timber and set in motion a plan to organize the Greek states (20.46.4–5), allegedly, to their advantage (κελεύων τῶν μὲν συμμαχίδων πόλεων συνέδρους συστήσασθαι τοὺς βουλευσομένους κοινῇ περὶ τῶν τῇ Ἑλλάδι συμφερόντων).

Enmity arose between the Rhodians and A. when the former refused Demetrios' demand that they wage war on Ptolemy (Diod. 20.46.6). A., meanwhile, was in Syria and founded the city of Antigoneia on the Orontes (Diod. 20.47.5), believing the city well suited for keeping an eye on Babylonia and the Upper Satrapies (εὐφυὴς γὰρ ἦν ὁ τόπος ἐφεδρεῦσαι τῇ τε Βαβυλῶνι καὶ ταῖς ἄνω σατραπείαις). But the city was soon dismantled and replaced by Seleukos' settlement of Antiocheia (Diod. 20.47.6). After Demetrios' victory at Salamis in 306, A. and his son were hailed as "Kings" (Justin 15.2.10; App. *Syr.* 54.275; Plut. *Demetr.* 17.2–6; Diod. 20.53.2). A., after the death of his son Philip, summoned Demetrios from Kypros and prepared to invade Egypt, using Antigoneia as his base (Diod. 20.73.1–2); A. commanded the land forces and ordered Demetrios to bring the fleet along the Levantine coast. The campaign (Diod. 20.73–6) ended in utter failure, however, because of the difficulties of the land route beyond Gaza (Diod. 20.73.3), the adverse conditions that prevented the fleet from advancing up the Nile (Diod. 20.74), and Ptolemy's attempts to suborne the mercenaries in the Antigonid army (Diod 20.75.1–2). A. then turned his attentions towards the Rhodians (Diod. 20.81.1), whom he tried to detach from their support of Ptolemy, and he assigned the war against them to Demetrios (Diod. 20.82–8, 91–9), but although Demetrios won great fame for his siege of Rhodes, the campaign ended in a hollow victory, which left the Rhodians independent and allied to A., as long as this alliance did not require them to wage war on Ptolemy (Diod. 20.99.2–3). For details of the campaigns of Salamis, Egypt, and Rhodes see s.v. Demetrios (no. 360). A.'s victories were due, in part, to his opponents' lack of cooperation (Justin 15.2.15) and led to a strengthened coalition of Kassandros, Lysimachos, and Ptolemy (Justin 15.2.16–17; cf. Diod. 20.2.3; 21.1.2), who were supported by Seleukos (Justin 15.4.1, 21). In the end, these four, in a unified effort, brought A.'s power and his life to an end.

Peace negotiations with Kassandros fell apart in 302 (Diod. 20.106.2–3) and Kassandros made a pact with Lysimachos, Ptolemy, and Seleukos to attack A. (Diod. 20.106.3–5). In Asia Minor, Lysimachos persuaded Dokimos to defect from A. (Diod. 20.107.4), and followed this up by capturing all of Sardis, except the acropolis; for although A.'s general Phoinix deserted him, Philip the *phrourarchos* of Sardis remained loyal (Diod 20.107.5). News of these events forced A. to cancel games and festivities, on which he had lavished some 200 talents, in Antigoneia and lead his forces north through Kilikia, Kappadokia, and into Phrygia-Lykaonia, where he dealt with those who had deserted (Diod. 20.108.1–3). Lysimachos did not face him in battle but rather took up a defensive position, waiting for the arrival of Seleukos' army; but when A. began to endanger his food supply Lysimachos withdrew to Dorylaion, which he fortified with a triple palisade (Diod. 20.108.4–7). But A. followed and besieged him, forcing Lysimachos to abandon his position yet again (Diod. 20.109.1–2). A. now prepared to winter his army but sent messengers to summon Demetrios from Greece (Diod. 20.109.4–5); these found him in Thessaly (20.111.1), where he had 1,500 cavalry and 56,000 infantry (20.110.40). Meanwhile in Asia A. welcomed defectors from Lysimachos' camp—2,000 Autariatai, as well as 800 Lykians and Pamphylians (Diod. 20.113.3). In the end, their respective armies met at Ipsos in Asia Minor in 301 (Diod. 21.1.2), where A. continued to exercise command, despite his advanced age (App. *Syr.* 55.279). A. was pierced by javelins and died on the battlefield; he was later buried with royal honors (App. *Syr.* 55.279–80; Plut. *Demetr.* 29.7–8; Justin 15.4.22; Diod. 21.1.2, 4b). His death was allegedly predicted by the Chaldaians in Babylon, who also foretold Seleukid domination in Asia (Diod. 19.55.7;

21.1.3; cf. Arr. 7.18.5, a similar prophecy by Peithagoras of Amphipolis). His kingdom was partitioned after his death (Diod. 21.1.5).

A towering man, larger than his own son Demetrios (Plut. *Demetr.* 2.2), who was himself reputedly tall (Diod. 19.81.4; 20.92.3), A. became exceedingly corpulent late in life—to the extent that this rather than old age hampered his performance on the battlefield (Plut. *Demetr.* 19.4; cf. Plut. *Mor.* 791e). Jovial (Plut. *Demetr.* 28.8), witty (Plut. *Demetr.* 14.3–4; *Mor.* 182d–e; cf. 633c), and sometimes restrained (Plut. *Mor.* 182a–b, 182c–d), he could nevertheless be loud and boastful (Plut. *Eum.* 15.3; *Demetr.* 28.8), and his humility was doubtless insincere (Plut. *Mor.* 182a, 182b–c). Though affectionate at home (Plut. *Demetr.* 3) and clearly devoted to his wife Stratonike, he was driven by *philotimia* and *philarchia* to the extent that he alarmed Alexander the Great (Ael. *VH* 12.16; 14.47a) and alienated many others (Diod. 18.50.1; 21.1.1; Plut. *Demetr.* 28.8). Stories of an affair with the courtesan Demo (Herakleides Lembos *ap.* Athen. 13.578a–b) appear to confuse him with his grandson Gonatas (but see Ogden 177 and 231). In some areas of his personal life he was less tolerant of criticism: he allegedly executed Theokritos (no. 1112) for a tactless remark about his eyes (cf. Teodorsson 1990, 380–2), though he had himself once joked that the characters of a letter were large enough for a blind man to read (Plut. *Mor.* 633c). With his own troops he could be a strict disciplinarian (Plut. *Mor.* 182a). In his dealings with political and military foes, he could be ruthless: Alketas' body was denied burial (Diod. 18.47.3); and, of the officers taken captive at Kretopolis, only Dokimos managed to save himself (and this was through treachery; Diod. 18.45.3; 19.16; cf. Simpson 1957); White Kleitos and Arrhidaios were driven from their satrapies (Diod. 18.52.3–6); Peukestas was deposed (Diod. 19.48.5), Peithon eliminated through treachery (Diod. 19.46.1–4), and Antigenes burned alive in a pit (Diod. 19.44.1). The claim that Eumenes was murdered by his guards without A.'s permission is feeble and transparent *apologia* (Nepos, *Eum.* 12.4). In one case, his own son Demetrios was forced to betray his father's trust to secure the escape of his friend Mithridates (Plut. *Demetr.* 4, *Mor.* 183a). Plut. *Phoc.* 29.2 suggests that he was less oppressive towards his subjects than those who followed him (Plut. *Phoc.* 30.9 confuses A. with Perdikkas). Plut. *Mor.* 791e contributes little to our knowledge of his life or his kingship.

Oikonomides 1989b suggests that the bust of an old one-eyed man in the Ny Carlsberg Glyptothek, I. N. 212 may be Antigonos the One-Eyed. Billows 8 follows Charbonneaux 1952, 219ff., in identifying A. with one of the horsemen, shown (significantly?) in profile (cf. Pliny, *HN* 35.90; Pollitt 161), on the Alexander Sarcophagus. Apart from the fact that the sarcophagus could be as early as the mid-320s (Heckel 2006), it should be noted that the battle scene depicts the battle of Issos or, in my view, Gaugamela; A. participated in neither of these. A. was also painted by Protogenes (Pliny, *HN* 35.106; Pollitt 173). Smith 1988 cautiously avoids identifying any surviving portrait as Antigonos I. Kaerst, *RE* I (1894) 2406–13 no. 3; Badian, *BNP* I 748–9 no. 1; Berve II 42–4 no. 87; Müller 1973; Briant 1973; Anson 1988; Engel 1976; Billows 1–80; Heckel 1992, 50–6; Grainger, *SPG* 637–8; Hauben 11–13 no. 3; Champion 2014; Billows, *LexAM* 89–90. **Stemma VI.**

116 ANTIGONOS

(Ἀντίγονος). Macedonian (Tataki 245 no. 170). Son of Demetrios Poliorketes and Phila, A. was the brother of Stratonike (Plut. *Demetr.* 53.8; Porphyr. Tyr. below); A. was also a half-brother of the younger Krateros (no. 623; for their relationship see Plut. *Mor.* 486a),

Antipatros (no. 130) son of Balakros, and possibly of Balagros and Thraseas (Reger 1991, with stemma on p. 154). He appears to have been called Gonatas after Thessalian Gonnoi (Steph. Byz. s.v. Γόννοι; Porphyr. Tyr., *FGrH* 260 F3 §12), where he was born *c.*319 (thus [Lucian] *Macrob.* 11, who says he died at the age of 80 in 240/39, having ruled Macedon for 44 years; Porphy. Tyr. F3 §12 gives him a 43-year reign over the Macedonians and states, incorrectly, that he died at the age of 83). A. was a student of Euphantos, who wrote a treatise *On Kingship* for him (Diog. Laert. 2.110), and of Zenon, though probably later in life (cf. Gabbert 1997, 5). He may have spent some of his younger years in Kelainai, where his grandfather Monophthalmos had been satrap since 333. If, like Pyrrhos of Epeiros, who was roughly coeval, he served at Ipsos, this is unrecorded; he may have been in Athens in the last years of the fourth century (cf. Gabbert 1997, 6–7). A. may have been with his parents when his sister Stratonike was given in marriage to Seleukos (Plut. *Demetr.* 31.5; 32.2–3). He appears for the first time in 291, when Demetrios entrusted him with the siege of Thebes, while he himself dealt with Pyrrhos' invasion of Thessaly (Plut. *Demetr.* 40.1). In 288 A. was left in charge of Greece (where Ptolemy was attempting to foment rebellion) while his father moved north to deal with Macedonia, which had been invaded by both Lysimachos and Pyrrhos (Plut. *Demetr.* 44.4). But, although A. held Peiraieus, he could not prevent revolution in Athens, incited by the arrival of Ptolemy's fleet under Zenon, which resulted in the expulsion of the partisans of Demetrios and the re-establishment of Athenian independence (Tarn, *AG* 92–3). When his father left for Asia in 286, never to return, protection of Antigonid power in Europe became A.'s responsibility (Plut. *Demetr.* 51.1; cf. Plut. *Pyrrh.* 12.6 for Pyrrhos' visit to Athens to prevent the resurgence of Antigonid power). After his capture by Seleukos, Demetrios issued instructions that A. should not trust letters bearing his seal but should treat him "as if he were dead" (ὥσπερ τεθνηκότος), bitter news for the young prince, who petitioned Seleukos and offered to cede his territory and to serve as a hostage in return for his father's release, all to no avail (Plut. *Demetr.* 51.2–4; *Mor.* 183c); if he hoped that his sister Stratonike would intervene on the father's behalf, he was sorely disappointed. The rise of Lysimachos in the north threatened both Pyrrhos and A., who appear to have formed an alliance in 286/5, but were defeated by Lysimachos (Paus. 1.10.2). A.'s grudging respect for Pyrrhos can be seen in the anecdote that, when asked who was the best general, A. replied: "Pyrrhos, if he reaches old age" (Plut. *Pyrrh.* 8.4), a comment Plutarch reports in the aftermath of Pyrrhos' victory over Pantauchos (see s.v.). In 283, after his father's death, A. took the title of king (Porphyr. Tyr., *FGrH* 260 F3 §12; [Lucian] *Macrob.* 11), though his territorial base was restricted; he sought to win control over the Greek states, countering the ambitions of Ptolemy and Pyrrhos. After the deaths of Lysimachos (at Koroupedion) and Seleukos (at the hands of Ptolemy Keraunos), A. made an unsuccessful bid for the crown of Macedon but was defeated by Keraunos and forced to withdraw to Boiotia (Memnon 8.4–6). Shortly before this (Justin 24.1.8) A., Keraunos, and Antiochos, though they were on hostile terms, provided aid to Pyrrhos, who was about to cross into Italy, thinking his departure to be mutually beneficial: A. for his part provided ships to ferry the Epeirot army across the Ionian Sea (Justin 17.2.13). The incursion of the Gauls into Macedonia, which resulted in the death of Keraunos and a succession of ephemeral kings, presented a new opportunity for A. to recover his ancestral kingdom. Before that, A. won Nikomedes of Bithynia as an ally and waged war on Antiochos I in Asia Minor. These hostilities ended with the marriage of A. to Antiochos' daughter (A.'s own niece) Phila. For his career as king of

Macedon see Tarn, *AG*; Gabbert 1997. Kaerst, *RE* I.2 (1894) 2413–14 no. 4; Billows 368–9 no. 10; Sandberger 34–48 no. 15; Edson 1934; M. Chambers 1954. **Stemma VI.**

117 ANTIGONOS

(Ἀντίγονος). Macedonian. Son of Kallas, apparently from Amphipolis (cf. Bosworth I 59). A winner in athletic contests at Tyre in 332, his achievements are commemorated on an inscription now in the Amphipolis museum (Moretti no. 113). Nothing else is known about him.

118 ANTIGONOS

(Ἀντίγονος). Apparently Macedonian (Tataki 246 no. 175). In late 331, A. was awarded fifth place in a contest of valor in Sittakene and thus became a *pentakosiarches* of the hypaspists (Curt. 5.2.5; see literature s.v. Atarrhias no. 250). Ps.-Call. 3.19 mentions a hypaspist (μέγιστον ὑπερασπιστήν: Ps.-Call. λ) named Antigonos in the (fictitious) Kandake episode (see Berve II 415 no. 9). Heckel 1992, 305.

119 ANTIGONOS

(Ἀντίγονος). Macedonian (Diod. 20.98.1; Tataki 245 no. 172). A. was sent by Ptolemy I Soter to Rhodes (which he supplied with grain and other necessities) as commander of a force of 1,500 soldiers in 304. Nothing else is known about him. Kirchner, *RE* I.2 (1894) 2420 no. 10; Launey 303, 497 n.4, 1172; *PP* VI no. 15178.

120 ANTIKLES

(Ἀντικλῆς). Macedonian (Tataki 248 no. 186). Son of Theokritos. One of the *paides basilikoi*, A. was persuaded by Hermolaos and Sostratos to join the so-called conspiracy of the Pages in 327 (Arr. 4.13.4; Curt. 8.6.9). He was later arrested, tortured, and executed (Arr. 4.13.7, 14.3; Curt. 8.8.20; cf. Plut. *Alex.* 55.7; Justin 12.7.2). Berve, *RE* Supplbd. IV (1924) 32 no. 8; Berve II 44 no. 88; Heckel 1992, 289; Hoffmann 180.

121 ANTIKYRA

(Ἀντικύρα). Prostitute (Harpocration s.v.), lover of Demetrios Poliorketes (*Demetr.* 24.1). According to Aristophanes of Byzantion in his work *On Courtesans*, her real name was Oia and she became the mistress of the physician Nikostratos, who predeceased her and left her nothing but helebore (Athen. 13.586f, though this A. may be a different woman). She was named (along with Chrysis, Korone, Ischas, and Nannarion) by Menander in his *Kolax* as one of a number of well-known courtesans (Athen. 13.587d–e). Aulbach §8.2.2.1.

122 ANTIMENES

(Ἀντιμένης). Rhodian. In 324 A. succeeded Harpalos as the chief financial officer of the empire. He saw to it that royal storehouses were provisioned for troops on the march, instituted an insurance plan for slave-owners, which guaranteed the recovery of runaways or compensated owners for their loss, and revived an old Babylonian tithe that brought money into the imperial treasury ([Aristotle], *Oecon.* 2.34 p.1352b; 2.38 p.1353a; the meaning of ἡμιόδιος γενόμενος is unclear. Berve II 44 n.2 assumes that it is the title of Antimenes' position as Harpalos' successor). Otherwise, nothing is known about him. Thalheim, *RE* I.2 (1894) no. 4; Berve II 44–5 no. 89; Garlan 1988, 194–5.

123 ANTIOCHOS

(Ἀντίοχος). Probably Macedonian (Tataki 249 no. 195). Commander of Macedonian archers (Arr. 3.5.6), at Issos he was stationed on the right, next to the Paionians (Arr. 2.9.2; cf. Curt. 3.9.9); the Kretan archers were on the left (Curt. 2.9.3). A. appears to have succeeded Kleandros or possibly Klearchos in 334/3. In 332/1, A. died of unknown causes—perhaps in Egypt, possibly in earlier campaigning. Alexander replaced him with the Kretan Ombrion (no. 812; Arr. 3.5.6). Kirchner, *RE* I.2 (1894) 2450 no. 13; Berve II 45 no. 91; Heckel 1992, 337.

124 ANTIOCHOS

(Ἀντίοχος). Macedonian of unknown family background (Tataki 249 no. 194), A. first appears in 327 as a chiliarch of the hypaspists. Alexander sent him, with his chiliarchy and two others, from Dyrta on a reconnaissance mission (Arr. 4.30.5–6). A. appears to have been subordinate to Nearchos (wrongly called a chiliarch of the hypaspists), who took with him also the Agrianes and the light infantry (*psiloi*). Nothing else is known about him. Badian 1975, 150–1; Berve II 45 no. 90; Heckel 1992, 303.

125 ANTIOCHOS

(Ἀντίοχος). Macedonian (Tataki 249 no. 196). Antiochos I Soter (*regn.* 281–262), son of Seleukos I Nikator and his Iranian wife, Apama (Plut. *Demetr.* 31.5; Strabo 12.8.15 C578, wrongly calling her the daughter of Artabazos). A.'s siblings were apparently numerous (Justin 15.4.9 mentions *filii* of Seleukos; *OGIS* 213, lines 3, 26 calls him the oldest of Seleukos' sons), but no brother is mentioned by name (Beloch IV² 2.204–5 supposed that Achaios was a younger brother; but see Grainger, *SPG* 5 no. 2; cf. Wilcken, *RE* I.1 (1893) 206 no. 3; Ogden 120). Malalas 8.198, 202–3 refers to two sisters, Apama and Laodike (see s.vv.). Phila, the daughter of Stratonike and Seleukos, was both his half-sister and stepdaughter. A. was born *c.*323, assuming that the birth occurred soon after the Sousan marriage (324) was consummated (Arr. 7.4.6). He was thus about eight years old when his father was driven from Babylon in 315; A. spent the next few years in Egypt, and was probably not recalled until Seleukos had settled affairs in the satrapy, probably after the "Peace of 311." His first attested military role comes at Ipsos in 301, when he commands the cavalry contingent that was opposite the forces of Demetrios (Plut. *Demetr.* 29.4), who made a tactical error in pursuing him before the battle was won (Plut. *Demetr.* 29.5–8). Grainger, *SPG* 9 calls A.'s retreat "decoying Demetrios." It certainly turned out that way, but it puts a good face on A.'s defeat, which must have been due in part to his own inexperience. In 299/8, not long after Ipsos, Seleukos made an alliance with Demetrios, sealed by the marriage of the latter's daughter, Stratonike, to Seleukos (Plut. *Demetr.* 31.5; 32.3; 38.1). But A. fell in love with his stepmother who was, indeed, younger than he was; he did not reveal his passion but resolved to die of lovesickness. Concerned about his son's health, Seleukos sent to his side the physician Erasistratos, who correctly diagnosed the nature of his illness. Hence, upon learning this, Seleukos agreed to give his bride to A. in order to save his son (Plut. *Demetr.* 38; App. *Syr.* 59–61; Diod. 21.20; Breebaart 1967; Broderson 1985; Ogden 2017, 207–46). By giving Stratonike, who had produced only a daughter, Phila (no. 899), to his son, Seleukos avoided creating the dynastic chaos; for a son by a Macedonian bride might have threatened A.'s right of succession (Ogden 211–12). In addition to the marriage, A. was given the eastern part of the empire (beyond the Euphrates) to rule. Appian (*Syr.* 59.308) says Seleukos made him "King of Upper Asia." This constituted a sharing of the kingdom, as well as an attempt to accustom the subjects to the rule of Seleukos' heir, not a formal division of territory. Evidence for A.'s administration of the eastern realm rarely specifies which things were done during his joint rule and which ones belonged to the period 281–261. A. sent his general Demodamas to cross the Tanais (i.e. the Iaxartes) and erect altars to Apollo Didymaios (Pliny, *HN* 6.18.49), and founded Antiocheia in Margiana (Strabo 11.10.2 C516, adding that the circuit of its was walls was 1,500 stades). Exploration of the Indian marches and the Kaspian Sea appears to have been conducted in Seleukos' lifetime (Pliny, *HN* 2.67.167; cf. 6.21.58, see s.v. Patrokles no. 854). The town of Artakabene was given new fortification walls by A. (Pliny, *HN* 6.25.93), perhaps also at this time, but the transfer of the inhabitants of Kelainai to Apamea (Strabo 12.8.15 C577–8) appears to belong to the period after his father's death. The joint rule is also attested at Lemnos, where the Athenians of the island were freed from Lysimachos' rule by Seleukos and temples were erected for both father and son (Phylarchos, *FGrH* 81 F29 = Athen. 6.254f–255a).

When Demetrios was captured by Seleukid forces and kept in detention, Seleukos wrote to A., who was in Media, telling him how to deal with Demetrios, namely, to set him free as an act of kindness to his father-in-law (Diod. 21.20). This, of course, never came about (Plut. *Demetr.* 51.4). There is no evidence of A.'s participation in the battle of Koroupedion—affairs in the East demanded his attention (*OGIS* 219 = *I.Ilion* 32; Burstein no. 15)—but when his father was killed in Europe by Ptolemy Keraunos (no. 1011), A. received Seleukos' ashes from Philetairos of Pergamon and buried them at Seleukeia, the seaport of Antioch, and erected a temple to his father, surrounding it with a precinct known as the Nikatoreion (App. *Syr.* 63.336). Keraunos' crime invited vengeance, and the perpetrator hastened to win Gonatas and Philadelphos to his side (Justin 17.2.9–10). Anxious to limit the number of potential enemies, A. contributed money to fund Pyrrhos' Italian venture (Justin 17.2.13). Hostilities between A. and Keraunos were at best desultory, since both were beset by problems in their realms: A. faced opposition from Bithynia (for hostility already in Seleukos' time see Memnon 6.3; against A.: Memnon 10.2) and the Pontic cities (Herakleia had sent ships to support Antigonos Gonatas: Memnon 8.4). The Gallic invasion solved the problem of Keraunos, and both A. and Antigonos, who had made a truce earlier (Justin 25.1.1), contributed 500 men each toward the defense of Thermopylai (Paus. 10.20.5). Nevertheless, A. and Gonatas were soon at war with each other (A.'s support of the Kassandreian tyrant Apollodoros belongs to this time: Polyaenus 6.7.2). Hostilities between A. and Gonatas were ended by the marriage of Antiochos' stepdaughter, Phila, to Gonatas (*Vita Arati* 53, 60, Westermann). A. gained the epithet *Soter* ("Savior") after his victory over the Gauls who had invaded Asia Minor (App. *Syr.* 65.343; cf. *Suda* s.v. Σιμωνίδης, *FGrH* 163 T1, with a textual problem). A. died in 262/1 (Euseb. 1.249, the claim that he was 64 cannot be correct, since this would put his birth *before* Seleukos' marriage to Apama in 324, though the figure is accepted by both Bouché-Leclercq, *Séleucides* 75 and Bevan, *Seleucus* I, 168 without question). For the First Syrian War and the remainder of A.'s life, see Bevan, *Seleucus* I, 147–70; Grainger 2014, 142–71; Bouché-Leclercq, *Séleucides* 66–75.

According to Steph. Byz. s.v. Ἀντιόχεια, A. founded a city, which he named after a wife named Nysa. Perhaps she was a relative of Sandrokottos (Chandragupta); for

App. *Syr.* 55.282 says that Seleukos established friendship with him and connection by marriage (κῆδος) with the Indian ruler (Mehl 173–6; Ogden 120 with n.16; cf. Strabo 15.2.9 C724: ἐπιγαμία). Macurdy 77 speaks of "a marriage of Seleucus with a daughter of the Hindoo king Sandracottus in 303": the deal may have been sealed by a union of Sandrokottos' daughter with Seleukos' son. By Stratonike, A. had four children (cf. Diod. 21.20): Seleukos, Antiochos II (Theos), Stratonike and Apama. Seleukos had been elevated to co-ruler (Burstein no. 19; Wörrle 1975) but was put to death on a charge of treason (Trogus, *Prol.* 26; John of Antioch, Müller, *FHG* IV, 558 F55); Antiochos II (*regn.* 261–246) married first Laodike and, late in his life, Berenike, the daughter of Ptolemy II, which soon triggered the so-called Laodikeian War. Stratonike married Demetrios II (Justin 28.1.1); Apama became the wife of Magas of Kyrene (see s.v. Demetrios the Fair no. 362). Wilcken, *RE* I.2 (1894) 2450–5 no. 21; Sandberger 48–9 no. 16; Grainger, *SPG* 9–13. **Stemma XI.**

126 ANTIPATRIDES

(Ἀντιπατρίδης). *Hetairos* of Alexander, apparently Macedonian. A. is attested in the period 336–323 only in an anecdote illustrating Alexander's restraint in sexual matters. A. was said to have brought to dinner a beautiful harp player who aroused the King's interest. But, upon learning that A. was in love with her, Alexander refrained from touching her (Plut. *Mor.* 180f; *Mor.* 760c–d). Identification with the Antipatrides of Polyaenus (5.35), who was a *palaios philos* of Nearchos, is remotely possible but depends in part on the date of Nearchos' capture of Telmessos (probably after Alexander's death, when Nearchos was in the service of Antigonos). Kirchner, *RE* I.2 (1894) 2501; Berve II 45 no. 92.

127 ANTIPATROS

(Ἀντίπατρος). Macedonian (Tataki 146 no. 1). Son of Iolaos, from Palioura. Born in 399/8 (*Suda* A 2704; cf. [Lucian] *Macrob.* 11; *Marm. Par.* = *FGrH* 239 B12). Beloch's view (IV² 2.125) that he was coeval with Philip II is unconvincing. A. would scarcely have been described in a letter of Demades as "an old and rotten thread" (Arr. *Succ.* 1.14; Plut. *Dem.* 31.5; Plut. *Phoc.* 30.9) if he had not been well advanced in age in 323/2. At least ten children are attested: four daughters and six sons, of whom the names of all but one *anonyma* (the wife of Alexander Lynkestes) are known (**Stemma V**). Kassandros, named for Antipatros' brother (Schol. Theocr. 17.61), is by far the most important. Phila, Nikaia, and Eurydike all played important roles in sealing political alliances in the years before and after Triparadeisos. Philip, Alexarchos, Iolaos, Pleistarchos, and Nikanor are identified as either sons of A. or brothers of Kassandros (see also Landucci 2021). Militarily active and possibly influential at the Court during the reign of Perdikkas III (365–360/59), A. was almost forty at the time of Philip's accession and belonged to the most powerful of Philip's *hetairoi* (Plut. *Mor.* 179b; Athen. 10.435d). A. and Parmenion were involved in the peace negotiations in the spring of 346 (Dem. 19.69; Aesch. 3.72; Din. 1.28). About A.'s diplomatic efforts in Athens little is known. It was at this time that he made the acquaintance of Isokrates; his friendship with Phokion may belong to the period after Chaironeia (see Plut. *Phoc.* 26.4–6; 30.3; Plut. *Mor.* 142c–d; cf. 64c; 188f; 533d; Plut. *Agis* 2.2). In summer 342 A. represented Philip II as *theoros* at the Pythian games (Dem. 9.32, disparagingly τοὺς δούλους ἀγωνοθετήσοντας πέμπει; cf. Libanius 23.311) and as regent of Macedonia in the King's absence (Isoc. *Ep.* 4). In 340, when his services were needed in Thrake, A. turned over the affairs of the state to Alexander, now sixteen (Plut. *Alex.* 9.1), and campaigned at Perinthos (Diod. 16.76.3; Front. 1.4.13; cf. Polyaenus 4.2.8, clumsy doublet) and, later, against the Tetrachoritai (Theopompos, *FGrH* 115 F217). After Chaironeia (338), he was sent to Athens to negotiate a peace and awarded a proxeny (Justin 9.4.5; Harpocration s.v. Ἀλκίμαχος = Hyper. frag. 19.2).

It was undoubtedly at his urging that Alexander Lynkestes was the first to hail his namesake as "King" (Arr. 1.25.2; Curt. 7.1.6–7; cf. Ps.-Call. 1.26; Justin 11.2.2). A. acted as regent whenever Alexander was absent from Macedonia, apparently sending an embassy to the Isthmus in an attempt to prevent the Arkadians from aiding Thebes in 335 (Din. 1.18). Rumor at Thebes held that Alexander had been killed in the north and A. himself was coming to deal with their uprising (Arr. 1.7.6; cf. Justin 11.2.8). Polyaenus 4.3.12 claims that A. played a significant role in the capture of Thebes. This is contradicted by the Alexander historians and inherently improbable: the Theban demand that the Macedonians surrender A. was not meant to be taken seriously (Plut. *Alex.* 11.8; cf. Hamilton 30). When he set out for Asia in 334, Alexander left A. firmly in charge of European affairs (Arr. 1.11.3; Curt. 4.1.39; Justin 11.7.1; Diod. 18.12.1; cf. 17.118.1; *Itiner. Al.* 17) with 12,000 infantry and 1,500 horse, having ignored his advice to produce an heir to the throne before his departure (Diod. 17.16.2).

By the time of Agis' war, A.'s resources had been significantly depleted by the flow of reinforcements to Alexander in Asia. In response to the threat from Memnon the Rhodian A. commissioned a fleet, commanded by Proteas, who defeated the Persian admiral, Datames (no. 341), at Siphnos (Arr. 2.2.4–5). In 331 Agis rallied the Peloponnesians—the Spartan alliance now included Elis, Achaia (except for Pellene) and all the Arkadians except Megalopolis (Aesch. 3.165; Din 1.34; cf. Curt. 6.1.20; cf. also [Dem] 17.7.10; Paus. 7.27.7; see also McQueen 1978)—and easily defeated A.'s general, Korrhagos (no. 619). Agis then besieged Megalopolis (Aesch. 3.165) with a force of 20,000 infantry—to which we might add as many as 8,000 mercenaries who had escaped from Issos (Curt. 6.1.39; Diod. 17.48.1–2; but cf. Brunt I 481–2)—and 2,000 cavalry (Diod. 17.62.7). A. received news of the uprising just as he was dealing with the rebellion in Thrake (Diod. 17.62.5ff. Polyaenus 4.4.1 may refer to this campaign but it appears to belong to 347/6; cf. Steph. Byz. s.v. Τετραχωρῖται). Concluding hostilities as best he could under the circumstances, he gathered a force of 40,000 (Diod. 17.63.1)—greatly augmented by his Greek allies— and invaded the Peloponnese. At Megalopolis he was victorious, and Agis was killed in the battle (Plut. *Agis* 3; Diod. 17.63.4; Curt. 6.1.1–15; Justin 12.1.6–11); Alexander, however, disparaged the engagement as "a battle of mice" (μυομαχία, Plut. *Ages.* 15.6). Order was restored to Greece in consultation with the League of Korinth (Curt. 6.1.19– 20). The Spartans, for their part, were forced to send ambassadors to Alexander to beg his forgiveness (Aesch. 3.133; Diod. 17.73.5–6; Curt. 6.1.20), and it is clear that A. was not prepared to make a decision on their future without Alexander's approval. For Spartan measures after the battle see also Diod. 19.70.5. The oligarchy that was established in Megalopolis by A. must date from this time (Diod. 18.68.3, 69.3–4).

There were claims that A. had regal aspirations (Curt. 10.10.14; cf. Plut. *Mor.* 180e), that he negotiated in secret with the Aitolians (Plut. *Alex.* 49.14–15) and he quarreled with Olympias (Plut. *Alex.* 39.13; Plut. *Mor.* 180d; Diod. 17.118.1; cf. 19.11.9). Alexander's decision to replace him as regent of Macedon with Krateros (Arr. 7.12.4; Justin 12.12.9) aroused the suspicions of both ancient and modern writers (Curt. 10.10.15). And, not surprisingly, stories circulated that A. and his sons conspired with several of the King's *hetairoi* to murder him (see Heckel 1988, with *testimonia*). After Alexander's death, a compromise was proposed that saw Europe jointly administered by Krateros and A. (Curt. 10.7.9; cf. Arr. *Succ.* 1.7); this was soon abandoned and A. recognized as *strategos autokrator* of Macedonia and Greece (Justin 13.4.5; Diod. 18.3.2; cf. 18.12.1; Arr. *Succ.* 1.3); the lands of the Thrakians, Illyrians, Triballians and Agrianes, as well as Epeiros, were added to his sphere (Arr. *Succ.* 1.7; Dexippos, *FGrH* 100 F8 §3; see Kanatsulis 1968, 121, for the view that A. was *archon* of Thessaly). Lysimachos, the *strategos* of Thrake, was clearly subject to Antipatros' authority. A. nevertheless attempted to secure the cooperation of the leading marshals through marriage alliances: Nikaia was promised to Perdikkas; Phila to Krateros and Eurydike to Ptolemy. Nikaia was betrothed to Perdikkas, to whose camp she was escorted by Iollas and Archias (Arr. *Succ.* 1.21); later Nikaia married Lysimachos (Strabo 12.4.7 C565); Phila married Krateros, who rejected Amastris in her favor (Memnon *FGrH* 434 F4 §4).

In Greece, news of Alexander's death ignited the Hellenic ("Lamian") War (cf. Diod. 18.8). Leosthenes had gathered mercenaries, ostensibly for some private undertaking, in an attempt to deceive A. (Diod. 18.9.2–3). The Athenians now openly supported Leosthenes, defraying his expenses with Harpalos' money; they allied themselves also with the Aitolians (Diod. 18.9.4–5). A fleet of 40 quadriremes and 200 triremes was commissioned (Diod. 18.10.2; cf. Justin 13.5.8) and eventually much of Greece joined the Hellenic war against Macedon. For the members of the anti-Macedonian alliance see Diod. 18.11.1–2; Paus. 1.25.3–4; Arkadia remained neutral: Paus. 8.6.2; 8.27.10. A. summoned Krateros (no. 622) and Leonnatos (no. 654) from Kilikia and Hellespontine Phrygia respectively (Diod. 18.12.1 reads "Philotas"; Diod. 18.16.4), promising Leonnatos the hand of one of his daughters in marriage. Leaving Sippas in charge of Macedonia, he moved into Thessaly with 13,000 Macedonians and 600 cavalry. Antipatros also had a fleet of 110 ships, which had conveyed monies from Asia to Macedonia (Diod. 18.12.2). But the desertion of the Thessalians to the Greek cause (Diod. 18.12.3) proved to be a major setback, and Antipatros found it necessary to take refuge in Lamia and await reinforcements from Asia (Diod. 18.12.4; Plut. *Dem.* 27.1; Plut. *Phoc.* 23.5; also [Plut.] *Mor.* 846d–e; Hyper. 6.12; Justin 13.5.8 has Antipatros shut up in Herakleia). Leosthenes invested the city (Diod. 18.13.1–3), but at one point was struck by a stone or javelin (Justin 13.5.12) and killed (Diod. 18.13.5; cf. Plut. *Phoc.* 24.1; see also Hyper. 6; cf. [Plut.] *Mor.* 849f); Antiphilos replaced him (Diod. 18.13.6; Plut. *Phoc.* 24.1). The Athenians abandoned the siege of Lamia, when Leonnatos answered A.'s call for help (Diod. 18.14.4–5; cf. Plut. *Eum.* 3.6), and moved against him before he could join forces with A. (Diod. 18.15.1). In numbers of infantry the armies were roughly equal—the Athenians had some 22,000, for the Aitolians had left previously to deal with some local matter (18.13.4) and were still absent—but in cavalry the Greeks excelled: 2,000 of their total 3,500 were Thessalians under the command of Menon (Diod. 18.15.2, 4). In the ensuing battle, Leonnatos was killed (Diod. 18.15.3); his infantry retreated to higher ground, where on the following day they were joined by A. (Diod. 18.15.4–5; on the engagement and its location see Sprawski 2008). The engagement had freed A. from Lamia, rid him of a dangerous rival and augmented his forces (Justin 13.5.15. Arr. *Succ.* 1.9). Nevertheless, A. chose to avoid giving battle on the plain, owing to his inferiority in cavalry; instead he withdrew over more rugged ground towards the Peneus (Diod. 18.15.6–7; cf. 18.16.5; less accurately Justin 13.5.16). Krateros soon entered

Thessaly with an additional 10,000 foot, 3,000 slingers and archers, and 1,500 cavalry, bringing to about 48,000 the entire Macedonian force (Diod. 18.16.5; the Greeks had 25,000 infantry and 3,500 cavalry: Diod. 18.17.2), with which he and A. confronted the Greeks near Krannon (Diod. 18.17; Plut. *Phoc.* 26; Plut. *Dem.* 28.1; Plut. *Cam.* 19; Paus. 10.3.4; cf. Arr. *Succ.* 1.12) on 5 August, 322 (7 Metageitnion: Plut. *Cam.* 19.8; Plut. *Dem.* 28.1). Once the Macedonian cavalry had engaged its Greek counterpart, A. led the phalanx forward and drove the enemy infantry to the high ground. Seeing this, the Greek cavalry disengaged, conceding victory to the Macedonians, and leaving more than 500 Greek and 130 Macedonian dead on the battlefield (Diod. 18.17.4–5; Paus. 7.10.5 says 200 of the Greek dead were Athenian). Menon and Antiphilos now sued for peace, but A. refused to deal with the Greeks collectively, demanding instead separate peace terms with each state. The Thessalian towns were taken by siege or storm and offered easy peace terms (Diod. 18.17.7; cf. [Plut.] *Mor.* 846e, for the capture of Pharsalos), leaving the Athenians and Aitolians to face Macedon alone. In the Peloponnese, A. installed pro-Macedonian oligarchies, often headed by personal friends and supported by garrisons (Diod. 18.18.8, 55.2, 57.1, 69.3).

The Athenians, in consternation, sent a deputation led by Phokion and Demades to A.; they met him at the Kadmeia in Thebes (Diod. 18.18; Plut. *Phoc.* 26; Paus. 7.10.4; Nepos, *Phoc.* 2). Mindful of Leosthenes' hard line at Lamia, A. demanded the unconditional surrender of the city (Diod. 18.18.1–3), but treated the Athenians with leniency, though he insisted on establishing a garrison on Mounychia (Plut. *Phoc.* 27–8, 30; Plut. *Dem.* 28.1; Diod. 18.18.5; Plut. *Mor.* 188f; cf. Paus. 7.10.1; Diod. 20.46.3; see s.v. Menyllos no. 727). The leading anti-Macedonian politicians were hunted down by Archias of Thourioi and put to death (Demosthenes; Hypereides; Himeraios, the brother of Demetrios of Phaleron; and Aristonikos: Arr. *Succ.* 1.13; Plut. *Phoc.* 27ff.; Plut. *Dem.* 28–9; [Plut.] *Mor.* 849b–c; Paus. 1.8.3; 1.25.5; *Suda* A 2704, Δ 456; Nepos, *Phoc.* 2.2; cf. Plut. *Dem.* 29–30; [Plut.] *Mor.* 846e– 847b; Athen. 12.542e; Cooper 1993). Making peace with Athens, A. and Krateros turned on the Aitolians (Diod. 18.24–5), only to be forced by the situation in Asia to come to terms with them (Diod. 18. 25. 5; cf. Arr. *Succ.* 1.24; Justin 13.6.9 wrongly speaks of peace with the Athenians). A.'s decision was hastened by the arrival of Antigonos and news of Perdikkas' duplicity (Diod. 18.23.4–24.1; 18.25.3; Arr. *Succ.* 1.21, 24; cf. Justin 13.6.5–6). Advancing to the Thrakian Chersonese, Antipatros sent envoys to secure the defection of White Kleitos and his own safe crossing of the Hellespont (Arr. *Succ.* 1.26). Friendship with Ptolemy in Egypt was renewed (Diod. 18.14.2, 25.4).

In Asia, A. and Krateros were joined by Neoptolemos (no. 772), a recent defector from Eumenes; he promised easy victory (Arr. *Succ.* 1.26; cf. Diod. 18.29.4–5). Leaving Krateros to deal with Eumenes, A. moved in the direction of Kilikia (Diod. 18.29.6; Plut. *Eum.* 6.4); he was joined en route by the remnants of Krateros' and Neoptolemos' army after their defeat by Eumenes (Arr. *Succ.* 1.28; Diod. 18.33.1). In Kilikia, he learned of Perdikkas' defeat at Kamelon Teichos and was given a favorable reception by Philoxenos. At Triparadeisos, he met Peithon, Arrhidaios and the remnants of the Perdikkan army. These men were embroiled in a bitter dispute with the queen, Adea-Eurydike, who had usurped the prerogatives of her half-witted husband and was supported by the troops, who demanded their pay (Arr. *Succ.* 1.31–2; cf. Diod. 18.39.1–2). Attalos son of Andromenes heightened tensions by journeying inland from Tyre in the hope of winning the army back to the Perdikkan cause (Arr. *Succ.* 1.33, 39). Hence A. was greeted, on his arrival, by an angry mob, which might have lynched him, had it not been for the efforts of Seleukos and Antigonos (Arr. *Succ.* 1.33; cf. Polyaenus 4.6.4; Diod. 18.39.3–4). In due course, A. frightened Eurydike into submission (Diod. 18.39.4) and, as *prostates*, reassigned the satrapies (App. *Syr.* 52.263; Diod. 18.39.5–7) and entrusted the war against the Perdikkans to Antigonos, with whom he left the "Kings," Philip III and Alexander IV (Arr. *Succ.* 1.34–8), some 8,000 additional infantry (Diod. 19.29.3), and Kassandros as "chiliarch of the cavalry" (Arr. *Succ.* 1.38; Diod. 18.39.7). Then he marched back to Macedonia. At Sardis, he and Kleopatra exchanged recriminations (Arr. *Succ.* 1.40), though she remained unharmed in the city. Asandros was dispatched to engage the forces of Attalos and Alketas, only to be worsted (Arr. *Succ.* 1.41). Kassandros fell out with Antigonos, whom he suspected of harboring designs on a grander scale, and A. decided to take the "Kings" back to Europe (Arr. *Succ.* 1.42–4). Nevertheless, by making Antigonos *strategos* of Asia, A. had all but recognized him as an equal partner. He died of illness in autumn 319 (Diod. 18.48), assigning European affairs to Polyperchon and appointing Kassandros *chiliarchos*. Demades' embassy, requesting the removal of Menyllos' garrison from Mounychia, helps to date A.'s death. The old man was mortally ill when Demades reached him, but the latter did not leave Athens before the end of June 319 (as is clear from *IG* II² 383b); cf. Plut. *Phoc.* 30. 4–6; Plut. *Dem.* 31.4–6. Aristodemos brought news of his death to Antigonos in the vicinity of Kretopolis (Diod. 18.47.4). Kaerst, *RE* I.2 (1894) 2501–8 no. 12; Badian, *BNP* I 770–1 no. 1; Berve II 46–51 no. 94; Kanatsulis 1958/59 and 1968; Griffith 1965; Heckel, *Marshals*² 33–43 and *LexAM* 90–4; Grainger 2019, 3–128. **Stemma V.**

128 ANTIPATROS

(Ἀντίπατρος). Macedonian (Tataki 253 no. 218). Born *c.* 313; son of Kassandros (Justin 16.1.1–4); son-in-law of Lysimachos (Justin 16.1.7, 19; 16.2.4–6; Porphyr. Tyr. *FGrH* 260 F3 §5; Droysen, *Hellenismus* II² 263: the wife was apparently Eurydike, daughter of Nikaia). Elder of the two surviving sons of Kassandros and Thessalonike after the death of Philip IV. In 294, A. killed his mother and drove out his brother, Alexander (Justin 16.1.1–4; Plut. *Pyrrh.* 6.3; cf. Diod. 21.7.1: τὸν μητραλοίαν "the matricide"), whom she allegedly favored (Paus. 9.7.3; cf. Diod. 21.7; Porphyr. Tyr. *FGrH* 260 F3 §5). When Alexander summoned aid from Pyrrhos and Demetrios, A. took refuge with Lysimachos, who appears to have made some effort to win Pyrrhos over to A.'s side (Plut. *Pyrrh.* 6), but eventually (in 287) murdered him (Porphyr. Tyr. *FGrH* 260 F3 §5; Justin 16.1.19 says only that Lysimachos ceded A.'s portion of the kingdom to Demetrios). Diod. 21.7 incorrectly says that Demetrios killed A. Kaerst, *RE* I.2 (1894) 2508–9 no. 13; Badian, *BNP* I, 771–2 no. 2. **Stemma V.**

129 ANTIPATROS

(Ἀντίπατρος). Macedonian (Tataki 253 no. 220). Son of Philip, the brother of Kassandros (Porphyr. Tyr. *FGrH* 260 F3 §10), and thus a grandson of the famous regent. After the death of Ptolemy Keraunos and the brief reign of Meleagros (no. 698), A. ruled Macedonia for 45 days and was thus given the nickname "Etesias" (Diod. 22.4; since this was the length of time that the Etesian (yearly) winds blew; cf. Porphyr. Tyr. *FGrH* 260 F3 §§10–11). Sidelined in favor of Sosthenes, A. reappears in 278/7 (cf. Tarn, *AG* 167) when he opposed, without success, Antigonos Gonatas' attempts to secure his claims to Macedonia (Polyaenus 4.6.17, without a precise historical context). Kaerst, *RE* I.2 (1894) 2509 no. 14; Tarn, *AG* 37, 139, 147, 159, 170; *PP* 16101. **Stemma V.**

130 ANTIPATROS

(Ἀντίπατρος). Macedonian (Tataki 252 no. 217). Son of Balagros. Dedicated a golden wreath at Delos at some point before 279 (*IG* XI 2, 161B, l. 85 and 287B, l. 57). Probably the son of Phila (no. 897), who is identified by Antonius Diogenes *ap*. Phot. *Bibl.* 166, p.111a–b as the wife of Balagros. The father was clearly Balakros (no. 283) son of Nikanor, a former Somatophylax of Alexander, and the mother a daughter of Antipatros the regent and the later wife of Krateros and then Demetrios Poliorketes. Although nothing else is known about Balagros himself, Reger 1991 has plausibly identified him as the brother of another Balagros (no. 281) and Thraseas (no. 1132). As stepsons of Demetrios, they were clearly in the Antigonid camp. Heckel 1987; Reger 1991; Paschidis 438 n.3.

131 ANTIPATROS

(Ἀντίπατρος). Macedonian (Tataki 252 no. 216). Son of Asklepiodoros the satrap of Syria (Arr. 4.13.4; cf. Curt. 8.6.9). Curtius writes Antipatros and Asklepiodoros (*Antipatrum Asclepiodorumque*) instead of Antipatros son of Asklepiodoros. A. was one of the *paides basilikoi* (Pages). Persuaded by Hermolaos and Sostratos to join their conspiracy in 327, he was later arrested, tortured, and executed for his involvement (Curt. 8.8.20; Arr. 4.13.7, 14.3; Plut. *Alex.* 55.6–7; Justin 12.7.2). For full details see Hermolaos (no. 526). Kaerst, *RE* I.2 (1894) 2509 no. 15; Berve II 45–6 no. 93; Hoffmann 179–80; Heckel 1992, 289.

132 ANTIPATROS

(Ἀντίπατρος). Macedonian officer (Tataki 252 no. 214), unknown family background. He appears in 317 as one of those who had been captured by Antigonos (presumably at Kretopolis, Diod. 18.45.3: he was one of τῶν ἀξιολόγων ἡγεμόνων), along with Attalos, Polemon and Dokimos, and held in a strong fortress in Phrygia (Diod. 19.16.1). Hence, he had probably served under Alexander and was a member of the Perdikkan group that resisted Antigonos and Antipatros the regent after their leader's death. An escape attempt was foiled and, after holding out in a fortified position for one year and four months, A. and his accomplices (excluding Dokimos, who secured his own escape) were recaptured (Diod. 19.16). What became of him is unknown, but Billows 383 may be correct in assuming that he and his accomplices were killed. Simpson 1957.

133 ANTIPHANES

(Ἀντιφάνης). Apparently Macedonian (Tataki 253 no, 222). *Scriba equitum*, according to Curt. 7.1.15, apparently the *grammateus* of the Companion Cavalry. In late 330, very shortly before the Philotas affair, A. had attempted to commandeer a number of horses from Amyntas son of Andromenes, who refused to surrender them and rebuffed A. with abusive language that included, allegedly, some discourteous remarks about Alexander himself (Curt. 7.1.15–17). A. testified to this at the trial of Amyntas, who was suspected of complicity in the conspiracy of Demetrios the Bodyguard, but Amyntas defended himself arguing that he had already surrendered eight of his ten horses and was reluctant to give up the remaining two, lest he should be compelled to fight on foot (Curt. 7.1.32–4). Amyntas' apology to A. and Alexander gives some credence to A.'s charge of insolence, but not of complicity in the Philotas "conspiracy" (Curt. 7.1.35). But we cannot be entirely certain of the historicity of either the charge or of A. himself. He is not mentioned elsewhere. Berve II 51 no. 95.

134 ANTIPHANES

(Ἀντιφάνης). Comic poet. Athen. 13.555a says that Alexander did not particularly like one of his plays. If A. can be identified with the prodigious poet of Middle Comedy, who was said to have been born *c.*407 and to have lived 74 years, it may be that the so-called *Philothebaios* was the play in question and that their meeting occurred in Greece, before Alexander's departure for Asia. A reference to "King Seleukos" in *Parekdidomene* appears to be a later interpolation. Kaibel, *RE* I.2 (1894) 2521 no. 15.

135 ANTIPHILOS

(Ἀντίφιλος). Greek painter from Egypt (Pliny, *HN* 35.114); student of Ktesidemos (cf. Pliny, *HN* 35.140; Berve II 52 calls him Kleitodemos) and contemporary of Apelles and Protogenes (Quint. 12.10.6; Theo. prog. 1.3; Varro, *RR* 2.2). Painted Philip II and young Alexander, as well as Philip, Alexander and Athena (Pliny, *HN* 35.114), the latter perhaps after the victory at Chaironeia (Berve II 52). Late in life, in Alexandria, he painted a scene of Ptolemy I hunting (Pliny, *HN* 35.138), and he was allegedly a rival of Apelles for that king's favor (see Pollitt 163). Berve II 52 no. 96; Rossbach, *RE* I.2 (1894) 2525 no. 6.

136 ANTIPHILOS

(Ἀντίφιλος). Athenian (Kirchner 1264). A man of military skill and courage (Diod. 18.13.6), A. was chosen by the Athenian assembly as commander-in-chief of the Lamian War to replace the recently killed Leosthenes (Plut. *Phoc.* 24.1). He commanded the infantry in Thessaly when the Greeks defeated and killed Leonnatos before Antipatros could join him (Diod. 18.15.7; Plut. *Phoc.* 25.5). When Krateros returned from Asia to reinforce Antipatros, A. and his fellow general, Menon of Pharsalos (no. 725), were defeated at Krannon (Diod. 18.17.1–5; cf. Plut. *Phoc.* 26.1; Paus. 7.10.5; Plut. *Cam.* 19.5). After considering whether to await the return of some of their allies, who had withdrawn after the victory over Leonnatos, A. and Menon decided to ask Antipatros for terms (Diod. 18.17.6). Judeich, *RE* I.2 (1894) 2524–5 no. 2; Engels, *BNP* I 777–8 no. 1.

137 ANTISTHENES

(Ἀντισθένης). Admiral (*nauarchos*) in the service of Demetrios Poliorketes, in 307/6 A. was left with ten quinqueremes (*penteres*) to prevent the Salaminian fleet from sailing out to join Ptolemy's forces; for the narrow entrance to the city's harbor was easily blockaded (Diod. 20.50.1; cf. Plut. *Demetr.* 16.1). Ptolemy's brother Menelaos manned sixty ships and placed them under the command of Menoitios, who broke the blockade but arrived too late to have an impact on the battle of Salamis, where Demetrios was victorious (Diod. 20.52.5). Billows 369 no. 11; Kirchner, *RE* I.2 (1894) 2537 no. 2; Hauben 13 no. 4, 114.

APAMA (Plut. *Eum.* 1.7); Shayegan 99 no. 9. See **ARTAKAMA**.

138 APAMA

(Ἀπάμα, Ἀπάμη). Daughter of Spitamenes, A. married Seleukos at Sousa in 324 (Arr. 7.4.6; Arr. *ap.* Phot. *Bibl.* 68b; Plut. *Demetr.* 31.5; Malalas 8.198, where her father is called

Pithamenes and described as Parthian; Strabo 12.8.15 C578 confuses her with the daughter of Artabazos; Livy 38.13.5, wrongly calls her Seleukos' sister). She was born probably *c.*340. According to Malalas (8.198) she bore Seleukos two daughters, Laodike and Apama (cf. Ogden 2017, 170). Her son was Antiochos (Strabo 12.8.15 C578; Plut. *Demetr.* 31.5; born in 324/323, since he died in 261 at the age of 64), later known as Soter, who named the city of Apamea in Phrygia—to which he transferred the population of Kelainai—for her (Strabo 12.8.15 C578; cf. Livy 38.13.5), as he did Apamea near the Tigris (Plin. *HN* 6.132); App. *Syr.* 57 says that Seleukos Nikator named three cities after her (cf. Steph. Byz. s.v. Ἀπαμεία, who mistakenly calls her the "mother of Seleukos"). Strabo C749; Euseb. *Chron.* 1.261 Schoene. Malalas' statement that she had died before Seleukos married Stratonike in 299 need not be correct. The endless debate about whether the Macedonians repudiated or retained their barbarian wives is based on two examples: Amastris (no. 67) who was repudiated in favor of Phila (no. 897), and Apama, whose blood ran through the Seleukid line. See Berve 1938; Bosworth 1980; Hamilton 1988; Müller 2013; Harders 2016; Engels and Erickson 2016; Ramsey 2016. Berve II 52 no. 98; Wilcken, *RE* I.2 (1894) 2662 no. 1; Meier, *BNP* I 816 no. 1; Grainger, *SPG* 38 no. 3; Macurdy 77–8; Ogden 119–21; Shayegan 99 no. 10; Aulbach §7.1.1.1. **Stemma XI.**

139 APAMA

(Ἀπάμα, Ἀπάμη). Daughter of Seleukos I Nikator and Apama; sister of Antiochos Soter and Laodike (Malalas 8.198, 203). Her existence has been questioned (Beloch IV² 2.198; Grainger, *SPG* does not include her in his prosopography; Wilcken, *RE* I.2 (1894) 2662 believes Malalas has confused her with the daughter of Antiochos), but although there is no corroborating evidence she may nevertheless be historical. **Stemma XI.**

140 APAMA

(Ἀπάμα, Ἀπάμη). Daughter of Antiochos I and Stratonike (Euseb. 1.249), and thus a sister of Antiochos II Theos (*regn.* 262–246), Seleukos, and Stratonike, who married Demetrios II. Born not much before 291; her parents married in 293. At some point between 279 and 274, A. was married to Magas of Kyrene (Paus. 1.7.3; Porphyr. Tyr. *FGrH* 260 F 32.6; Euseb. *Chron.* 1.40.5. Justin 26.3 calls her Arsinoë), though it is not certain whether Magas sought Seleukid support against his half-brother Philadelphos (Paus. 1.7.3) or, as Bevan 147 suggests, "it may well be that Apama carried with her to Cyrene the instigations to revolt." When Magas died in 250, A. summoned Demetrios the Fair, a son of the Besieger, to Kyrene to marry her daughter, Berenike, even though Magas had betrothed her to Philadelphos' son Ptolemy, later known as Euergetes (Justin 26.3.2–3). Soon after Demetrios' arrival, A. became infatuated with him and became his lover, thus arousing the suspicions of her daughter and the ill will of the Kyreneans (Justin 26.3.4–5). Berenike arranged for assassins to come to A.'s bedroom, with instructions to spare the mother but murder Demetrios (Justin 26.3.6–8). Pompeius Trogus seems to have been fond of such stories (cf. the adultery of Eurydike with her son-in-law Ptolemy of Aloros: Justin 7.4.7). Apart from this salacious story (on which see McAuley 2016), little else is known about A.'s personal life. Wilcken, *RE* I.2 (1894) 2662–3 no. 3; Grainger, *SPG* 38 no. 1.

141 APELLES

(Ἀπέλλης). Son of Pytheas, from Kolophon (*Suda* A 3008) and, later, Ephesos (Strabo 14.1.25 C642; Ael. *NA* 4.50). Born *c.*370 (Pliny, *HN* 35.79, who says he was from Kos). Perhaps the greatest of the Greek painters (although he was suitably impressed by Protogenes' painting of *Ialysos*: Plut. *Demetr.* 22.6), Apelles was a student of Ephoros of Ephesos and Pamphilos of Sikyon. Among his many paintings were numerous depictions of Philip II (Pliny, *HN* 35.93) and Alexander. Alexander was allegedly so impressed by his work that he allowed no one else to paint him (Cicero, *Ad Fam.* 15.12.7; Horace, *Epistles* 2.1.239–40; Val. Max. 8.11 ext. 2; Pliny, *HN* 7.125; cf. Stewart 1993, TT51–8). His painting of Alexander with thunderbolt, which was set up in the temple of Artemis in Ephesos, although it depicted his complexion as too swarthy, so impressed the King that he awarded the painter 20 talents (Cic. *Verr.* 6.60; Pliny, *HN* 35.92; cf. Plut. *Alex.* 4.3–4). The popular story that he fell in love with Alexander's favorite mistress (*paelix*), Pankaste, who posed nude for Apelles' Aphrodite Anadyomene, and received her as a gift from Alexander (Pliny, *HN* 35.86–7; Lucian *Imagines* 7) is probably fictitious. In addition to Alexander, he painted several of his generals: Menandros and Kleitos (Pliny, *HN* 35.93) and Neoptolemos on horseback, Antigonos walking beside his horse, and Archelaos with wife and daughter (Pliny, *HN* 35.96). Whether it was Apelles or Mikon (a painter of the fifth century) who was faulted for painting lower eyelashes on horses was unclear to Aelian (*NA* 4.50). He was on good terms with Antigonos the One-Eyed, managing to conceal his defect with his art, but he fell out with Ptolemy during Alexander's lifetime and had the misfortune of being carried to Alexandria by a storm later when Ptolemy had become king, although he impressed him with his talents upon his arrival (Pliny, *HN* 35.89–90). Apelles appears to have lived into the early 3rd century. For the charges brought against him by Antiphilos and the chronological problems see Pollitt 163. Rossbach, *RE* I.2 (1894) 2689–92 no. 13; Hoesch, *BNP* I 821–2 no. 4; Berve II 53–5 no. 99; Pollitt 158–63; Stewart 1993, 33–5.

142 APHOBETOS

(Ἀφόβητος). Macedonian (Tataki 276 no. 335). Conspired with Dimnos (and thus Demetrios the Bodyguard) in 330 to murder Alexander; Philotas too was implicated in this plot. A.'s name was given to Nikomachos (Curt. 6.7.15) and, in turn, to Kebalinos, who brought the matter to Alexander's attention. He and the other conspirators were found guilty and stoned to death by the Macedonian army (Curt. 6.11.38). Berve II 97 no. 190.

143 APHRIKES

(Ἀφρίκης. Curt.: Erices). Eggermont 184, arguing for a linguistic connection between the name Aphrikes and the territory Udyana (also called Aurdayana), sees Aphrikes as the tribal chieftain named by the Greek historians for the place he ruled (but see further Goukowsky II 241–2; Benveniste 1966; Litvinsky 1968, 134–5). Perhaps a brother of Assakenos and Amminais (Metz Epit. 39); thus also a son of Cleophis, together with whom he is found at Massaga in autumn/winter 327 (Metz Epit. 42). A. attempted, after the capture of Aornos, to oppose the Macedonians in one of the passes of the Buner region (near Embolima) with a force of 20,000 Indians (Curt. 8.12.1; Diod. 17.86.2, giving him also 15 elephants); he was killed by his own troops, who sent his head to Alexander in order to win his pardon (Diod. 17.86.2; Curt. 8.12.3: the suggestion that the troops may have acted out of hatred is pure speculation). Eggermont 183–4 sees Assakenos as ruler of the western Swat basin and A. as chief of the eastern Swat (or Udyana); Berve II 26 identifies the unnamed brother of Assakenos (Arr. 4.30.5) with Amminais (see above s.v.) and distinguishes him from Aphrikes. Metz Epit. 42 says Cleophis consulted *araplicem* and her other friends, but there is no need to emend this corruption to read "Ariplex" and, by a further stretch of the imagination, identify him with Aphrikes. Hence, there is no good reason to believe that A. was in Massaga before the city fell. If Arr. 4.30.5, speaking of a "brother of Assakenos," who had taken refuge in the vicinity of Dyrta and possessed elephants that Alexander was eager to obtain, has any connection to the story of A., then we must assume that A. was the leader of his forces and that Assakenos' unnamed brother fled with many of his people across the Indos to the kingdom of Abisares (Arr. 4.30.7). Berve II 97–8 no. 191; Eggermont 183–4.

144 APHTHONIOS

(Ἀφθόνιος). Elaptonius (Curt. 8.6.9. Hedicke emends the name to Aphtonius; "der ... Name ist sicher verderbt," Hoffmann 180). A member of the "conspiracy of the Pages," A. was arrested, tortured, and executed (Curt. 8.8.20; cf. Arr. 4.13.7, 14.2, who does not name either Elaptonius or A.; Plut. *Alex.* 55.6; Justin 12.7.2). Berve II 149 no. 296; Heckel 1992, 289–90.

145 APOLLODOROS

(Ἀπολλόδωρος). Greek from Eresos on Lesbos; brother of Hermon and Heraios, together with whom he exercised the tyranny in the city (*OGIS* 1, 8 = Tod no. 191). Lott 1996 (cf. Wallace 2016) has argued convincingly, on the basis of [Dem.] 17, that A. and his brothers held the tyranny (Berve, *Tyrannis* I 337) from 338 to 334. Baumbach 32–4; Berve, *Tyrannis* I 337–8; II 691. Hofstetter 18–19 no. 23.

146 APOLLODOROS

(Ἀπολλόδωρος). Macedonian from Amphipolis (Arr. 3.16.4; 7.18.1; Diod. 17.64.5; Tataki 47 no. 14). In late 331, when Alexander made Mazaios satrap of Babylon, he appointed A. *strategos* of the troops left there (Arr. 3.16.4; cf. 7.18.1). Curt. 5.1.43, gives him 2,000 troops and 1,000 talents with which to hire more mercenaries, but he says that A. and Menes were to govern Babylonia and Kilikia (perhaps the text here should read *regioni Babyloniae ac Cilici<a tenus Mesopotami>ae*; Shackleton-Bailey 1981, 176; cf. Diod. 17.64.5). A.'s *strategia* is almost certainly restricted to Babylonia, and the Vulgate has conflated his office with the later appointment of Menes as *hyparchos* of Syria, Phoinikia and Kilikia (Arr. 3.16.9–10; for further discussion see s.v. Menes). He appears to have retained this office until the King's death (Arr. 7.18.1); his brother, Peithagoras, also resided in Babylon (Arr. 7.18). A. feared Alexander, perhaps because of the purge the King had conducted after his return from India, and he was told by his brother, the seer Peithagoras, that Hephaistion and Alexander would soon be dead (Arr. 7.18 = Aristoboulos, *FGrH* 139 F54; Plut. *Alex.* 73.3; cf. App. *B Civ.* 2.21.152). The prophecies are clearly inventions after the fact but A.'s concerns will have been real. Berve II 55–6 no. 101; Kaerst, *RE* I.2 (1894) 2851 no. 42.

147 APOLLODOROS

(Ἀπολλόδωρος). Son of Telestes. One of twenty-four cavalrymen from Orchomenos, who served with Alexander's allied cavalry until the expedition reached Ekbatana in 330. There he and his compatriots were discharged. On their return (c.329), they made a dedication to Zeus Soter in Orchomenos (*IG* VII 3206). Berve II 55 no. 100.

148 APOLLONIDES

(Ἀπολλωνίδης). Chian of the pro-Persian party (Curt. 4.5.15; *Syll*[3] 283), whose supporters were Athenagoras, Phesinos, and Megareus. All four were captured in 333/2 by Hegelochos and Amphoteros and taken to Alexander in Egypt (Curt. 4.5.17; Arr. 3.2.5). He sent them to Elephantine under a strong guard (Arr. 3.2.7), probably a precaution after the escape of Pharnabazos. What became of him is unknown. He appears to have left behind a son named Angeliskos (*Syll*[3] 402, 2). Kaerst, *RE* II.1 (1895) 119 no. 20; Berve II 56 no. 102; Hofstetter 20 no. 26; Heisserer 79–95.

149 APOLLONIDES

(Ἀπολλωνίδης). A Greek or Macedonian of unknown background, A. was a cavalry officer in the army of Eumenes, hence perhaps already an officer in Perdikkas' Royal Army and that of Alexander the Great (thus Berve II 56). Before the battle of Orkynia in Kappadokia, Antigonos, whose army was vastly inferior in numbers (10,000 infantry, 2,000 cavalry and 30 elephants to Eumenes' 20,000 foot and 5,000 horse: Diod. 18.40.7), suborned A. (Diod. 18.40.5) to desert in the midst of the battle, thus turning the tide against Eumenes, who lost 8,000 men in the defeat (Diod. 18.40.8; cf. Plut. *Eum.* 9.3). A. appears to have remained in Antigonos' service, although we hear nothing more about him. Engel 1971, 229–30 believes that Diodorus and Plutarch disagree on the fate of A., the former claiming that he made good his escape to Antigonos, the latter saying that Eumenes, although he had turned in flight, arrested and crucified the traitor (Plut. *Eum.* 9.3). But Plutarch, as Bosworth 1992, 87 n.119 recognizes, clearly refers to an earlier incident, in which a certain Perdikkas had betrayed Eumenes, only to be captured by Phoinix of Tenedos and executed in Eumenes' camp (Diod. 18.40.2–4). Nevertheless, the words ἡττηθεὶς ὑπ' Ἀντιγόνου διὰ προδοσίαν καὶ διωκόμενος show that Plutarch too has conflated the Perdikkas and Apollonides episodes. Kirchner, *RE* II.1 (1895) 118–19 no. 10; Berve II 56 no. 103; Engel 1971; cf. Kaerst *RE* II 118 no. 10; Hofstetter 20 no. 26.

150 APOLLONIDES

(Ἀπολλωνίδης). Son of Charops, probably from Kyzikos. Apollonides was honored by the Athenians, on a motion by Stratokles, at the time when Demetrios Poliorketes controlled the city (307–301). He is praised for the help given to Athenian survivors at the time of Kleitos' victory over Nikanor at the Hellespont (322)—apparently from his home base of Kyzikos—and awarded a golden crown for his goodwill towards the "Kings" (Antigonos and Demetrios) and the reinstated democracy (*IG* II[2] 492; cf. Habicht[2] 57 n.9). He was also awarded citizenship by the Ephesians for bringing good news to the city (*Syll*[3] 352, lines 11ff., which Billows 370 believes may have involved the report of the victory at Salamis and the assumption of the kingship by Antigonos and his son). Although a friend of Demetrios Poliorketes, he was later found at the court of Seleukos. When Demetrios was prepared to surrender, Seleukos sent Apollonides to him to assure him that he would be well looked after (Plut. *Demetr.* 50.3, 6). But Apollonides' assurances proved to be false, since Seleukos had become alarmed at Demetrios' popularity and decided instead to send his rival to the Syrian Chersonese (Plut. *Demetr.* 50.6–7). Billows 369–70 no. 12; Olshausen nos. 65, 74; Kirchner, *RE* II.1 (1895) 119 no. 11; Wehrli 1968, 125 n.147; Grainger, *SPG* 79.

151 APOLLONIDES

(Ἀπολλωνίδης). Macedonian of unknown family (Tataki 257 no. 240), appointed by Kassandros as *strategos* of Argos. In 315/14 he anticipated an attempt by a hostile faction to betray the city to Alexander (no. 46) son of Polyperchon in his absence. A., learning of this, returned and locked 500 of his opponents in the city hall and burned them alive (Diod. 19.63.1–2). Kirchner, *RE* II (1895) 119 no. 12.

152 APOLLONIOS

(Ἀπολλώνιος). Son of Charinos, apparently Greek. Appointed in 331 as governor of the region west of the Nile Delta (Arr. 3.5.4; Curt. 4.8.5); whether, in financial matters, he was responsible to Kleomenes of Naukratis (thus Curt. 4.8.5; cf. Atkinson I 367), who, in addition to governing the "Arabian" area east of the Delta, was the chief financial officer (Arr. 3.5.4 speaks only of the nomarchs of Egypt as subject to Kleomenes; cf. Bosworth I 277), is uncertain. We do not know how long he remained in office or what became of him. Kaerst, *RE* II.1 (1895) no. 49; Atkinson I 367; Berve II 56 no. 104; Bosworth I 275–7.

153 APOLLONIOS

(Ἀπολλώνιος). Brother of Glaukippos (no. 476) and Hippodamas (no. 536), son of Dionysios, from Antigoneia. Honored along with his two brothers by the Eretrians for favors to their compatriots serving with Demetrios' fleet (*IG* XII.9, 210 = *Syll*³ 348; cf. Wilhelm 1892, 119–25). Glaukippos and A. served Demetrios in Greece in 304–302. Cf. Diod. 20.110.2. Launey 1263; Billows 370 no. 13.

154 APOLLONIOS

(Ἀπολλώνιος). Family and ethnic unknown. Garrison commander at Rhamnous, appointed by Asklepiades (no. 236). A. was honored in a decree moved by Archedemos son of Euphron, probably in 303/2, for his good service to the king (Demetrios), his general, and the Athenians (*I.Rhamn.* 2). A. is otherwise unknown. Paschidis 112–13 A37.

155 APOLLOPHANES

(Ἀπολλοφάνης). Prominent Macedonian. In 325 A. was appointed satrap of the Oreitai (that is, of Gedrosia cf. Arr. *Ind.* 23.5). He was left in Ora with Leonnatos and sufficient troops to deal with hostilities there and ensure safe passage of the coast for Nearchos (Arr. 6.22.2–3), but in the military engagement that followed, although the Macedonians enjoyed an overwhelming victory, A. was killed (Arr. *Ind.* 23.5; cf. Arr. 7.5.5 and Curt. 9.10.19 for the battle). Arr. 6.27.1 claims that A. was deposed when Alexander reached Pura, the capital of Gedrosia, for neglect of his duties. It appears that Arrian has confused A. with Astaspes of Karmania who was subsequently deposed for this very reason. A.'s successor was Thoas. It is hard to imagine how A., who had been left behind in Ora, could have been deposed at Pura. Those who were charged with neglect of duty had failed to supply the King during his Gedrosian march (for example, Astaspes, Aboulites and Oxyathres). Arr. 6.27.1 appears to have garbled the account of the appointment of Thoas as satrap of Gedrosia, to replace the deceased A., and the subsequent removal of Astaspes from Karmania (cf. Curt. 9.10.21, 29). I do not see how Badian 1961, 17, with n.6, can have A. both "deposed" and "killed in action," but this seems also to be the view of Seibert 1985, 177: "Möglicherweise haben sich beide Vorfälle zeitlich überlagert." His satrapy was added to that of Sibyrtios, who subsequently ruled Arachosia and Gedrosia (see Heckel 2017a). Kaerst, *RE* II.1 (1895) 165 no. 8; Berve II 57 no. 105; Heckel 2017a.

156 ARBOUPALES

(Ἀρβουπάλης). Justi 21. Son of that Dareios who was son of Artaxerxes II; he was thus born no later than 362 (for Dareios' death see Briant 681), and it may have been on account of his youth that he survived the purge that accompanied the accession of Artaxerxes III (Ochos) in 359/8. Arboupales was among the dead commanders (*hegemones*) at the Granikos battle (Arr. 1.16.3). Cauer, *RE* II.1 (1895) 421; Justi 21; Berve II 57 no. 106; Shayegan 99 no. 11.

157 ARCHEDIKOS

(Ἀρχέδικος). Athenian (Kirchner 2336; cf. *LGPN* II 68 no. 3, with references to inscription evidence). Son of Naukritos of Lamptrai. A. proposed a decree regarding benefactions for the city from the friends of the King and of Antipatros (*SEG* XLII (1992) 91). The decree was originally dated to the time immediately after Chaironeia but the prevailing opinion is that it belongs to the aftermath of the Athenian defeat at Krannon (Bosworth 1993, 420–1; Poddighe 2002, 32). What survives of the inscription provides little specific evidence of what measures were to be taken. A. is probably identical with the writer of comedy (*PCG* II 533–6, FF1–3; Polyb. 12.13.3 calls him an obscure comic writer) who was a friend of Antipatros and enemy of Demochares (Polyb. 12.13.7–8; Habicht 1993). Paschidis 37–9 A1.

158 ARCHELAOS

(Ἀρχέλαος). Son of Androkles. Macedonian (Tataki 269 no. 304) and one of the *hetairoi*. Appointed *phrourarchos* of the Baktrian rock known as Aornos (Arr. 3.29.1). What became of him we do not know. Berve II 85 speculates that he may have been killed in the mercenary uprising in Baktria in 326/5. Kaerst, *RE* II.1 (1895) 448 no. 11; Berve II 85 no. 157.

159 ARCHELAOS

(Ἀρχέλαος). Macedonian (Tataki 269 no. 305). Son of Theodoros. He had probably accompanied Alexander from the beginning of the campaign. In 331, he was appointed *strategos* of Sousa (Arr. 3.16.9; cf. Curt. 5.2.16) with 3,000 troops to keep an eye on the satrap Aboulites. Apelles is said to have painted him, together with his wife and daughter, probably soon after 331 (Pliny, *HN* 35.96). Identification with the *philos* of Demetrios Poliorketes (Diod. 19.100.7) is possible. It is much less likely that he is the *phrourarchos* of Tyre attested in 320 (Diod. 18.37.4). Kaerst, *RE* II.1 (1895) 448 no. 10; Berve II 85 no. 158.

160 ARCHELAOS

(Ἀρχέλαος). Macedonian (Tataki 269 no. 299), family background unknown. *Phrourarchos* of Tyre. He may have been appointed to that position by Alexander as a successor to Philotas (no. 943; Curt. 4.5.9), unless Perdikkas, when he moved to attack Egypt, had doubts about Philotas' loyalty and replaced him with Archelaos. Perdikkas gave him 800 talents for safekeeping. When news of Perdikkas' death reached Attalos at Pelousion, he sailed to Tyre where Archelaos turned affairs of the city and the 800 talents over to him (Diod. 18.37.4, emphasizing his trustworthiness: χρήματα δεδομένα ὑπὸ Περδίκκου φυλάττειν, τότε δὲ δικαίως ἀποδεδομένα). Identification with the *philos* of Demetrios (Diod. 19.100; cf. Kirchner, *RE* no. 20) is not compelling. Kirchner, *RE* II.1 (1895) no. 19; Berve II 85 no. 159: Launey 1174.

161 ARCHELAOS

(Ἀρχέλαος). Macedonian (Tataki 269 no. 300). One of the *philoi* of Demetrios Poliorketes; when he made his attempt on Babylon (312) Demetrios took one of the citadels but had to besiege the other; he was forced to return to Antigonos and therefore left A. to continue the siege with 5,000 infantry and 1,000 cavalry (Diod. 19.100.7). Billows 371 no. 14 identifies him with the *phrourarchos* of Tyre (but see above). Kirchner, *RE* II.1 (1895) 452 no. 20; Billows 371 no. 14; Grainger, *SPG* 639.

162 ARCHEPHON

(Ἀρχεφῶν). Parasite of Ptolemy I Soter. He appears to have accompanied Ptolemy on his expedition to Greece in 308 (Athen. 6.244b–d).

163 ARCHEPOLIS

(Ἀρχέπολις). Macedonian of unknown origin (Tataki 270 no. 308). One of the fellow conspirators of Dimnos in autumn 330 (Curt. 6.7.15); his name was given by Dimnos to Nikomachos and was eventually reported to Alexander. He was arrested and executed by stoning at Phrada for his part in the plot (Curt. 6.11.38). Berve II 86 no. 161.

164 ARCHESTRATOS

(Ἀρχέστρατος). Athenian (Kirchner 2407), otherwise unknown. In 318 he proposed a decree, supported by Hagnonides, denouncing Phokion to Polyperchon (Plut. *Phoc.* 33.6). His actions will have contributed ultimately to Phokion's death. Kirchner, *RE* II.1 (1895) 458 no. 5.

165 ARCHESTRATOS

(Ἀρχέστρατος). Macedonian (Tataki 270 no. 309). Son of Nikon (*OGIS* 9; Tataki 270 no. 309). *Strategos* of Demetrios Poliorketes, A. with his naval force was based at Klazomenai. He was probably sent to Ionia in 302, when Kassandros' general Prepelaos briefly gained control of Ephesos (for its "liberation" see Diod. 20.111.3). For his service to the city, the Ephesians honored A. with citizenship and other benefits, including exemptions from taxes. Hauben 14–18 no. 5; Billows 371 no. 15; Kaerst, *RE* II.1 (1895) 459 no. 11; Launey 304, 644, 1174; Bengtson I 190–3, 196.

166 ARCHIAS

(Ἀρχίας). Prominent Macedonian from Pella (Tataki 151 no. 23); son of Anaxidotos. Archias was one of the trierarchs of the Hydaspes fleet in 326 (Arr. *Ind.* 18.3) and also accompanied Nearchos on the voyage from the Indos delta to the Persian Gulf as a trusted officer and colleague. Archias acted as Nearchos' second-in-command in the capture of an unnamed coastal town (Arr. *Ind.* 27.8–28.9; perhaps in the Gwatar bay: thus Brunt II 387 n.5) and was one of a small group of Macedonians who marched inland to meet Alexander in Karmania; his meeting with Alexander hints at Archias' rank and intimacy with the King (Arr. *Ind.* 34–5). In 324/3 Alexander sent Archias to circumnavigate Arabia in a *triakontor*, but Archias went as far as the island of Tylos before turning back (Arr. 7.20.7; cf. Arr. *Ind.* 43.8). Androsthenes and Hieron of Soloi also made unsuccessful attempts at rounding Arabia. Nothing else is known about him. Kirchner, *RE* II.1 (1895) no. 17; Berve II 86 no. 162.

167 ARCHIAS

(Ἀρχίας). Macedonian (Tataki 271 no. 311). Together with Iolaos son of Antipatros he brought Nikaia from Macedonia for Perdikkas to marry (Arr *Succ* 1.21). It is possible that Archias was a son of Antipatros, but this is not required by the circumstances. Identification with Archias of Thourioi seems impossible.

168 ARCHIAS

(Ἀρχίας). Greek from Thourioi (Paus. 1.8.3; Arr. *Succ.* 1.14) in southern Italy. A. was originally an actor ([Plut.] *Mor.* 849b; cf. Plut. *Dem.* 29.2–3, 6; Lenaian victor in 329: *IG* II 977 u(z)), studied rhetoric with Anaximenes ([Plut.] *Mor.* 846f) and Lakritos. A. was himself the teacher of Polos of Aigina (Plut. *Dem.* 28.3). In 322, he became Antipatros' agent and hunted down the Athenian politicians who had gone into exile, thus gaining the name φυγαδοθήρας ("exile hunter"). A. captured Hypereides, Aristonikos, and Himeraios (Arr. *Succ.* 1.13) and forced Demosthenes to commit suicide (Plut. *Dem.* 28–30; [Plut.] *Mor.* 846f, 849b; Strabo 8.6.14 C374; Paus. 1.8.3; Luc. *Encom. Dem.* 27–50; Roisman and Worthington 234–5). He later died in poverty and disgrace (Arr. *Succ.* 1.14) in a way that recalls the fate of Kallixenos (Xen. *HG* 1.7.35). Judeich, *RE* II.1 (1895) no. 10; O'Connor no. 87; Volkmann, *BNP* I 985 no. 5.

169 ARCHON

(Ἄρχων). Macedonian from Pella (Tataki 151 no. 24). Son of Kleinias (Arr. *Ind.* 18.3) and Synesis; brother of Isokrates; honored at Delphi in 333/2; Archon's horses had been victorious at the Pythian and Isthmian games (R&O no. 92, block a §ii). In 326 he served as a trierarch of the Hydaspes fleet (Arr. *Ind.* 18.3). Archon appears to have succeeded Stamenes (Ditamenes) as satrap of Babylon in the last year of Alexander's life. He was confirmed as satrap in 323 (Diod. 18.3.3; Justin 13.4.23). In 321, he may have colluded with Arrhidaios and Ptolemy in the diversion of Alexander's funeral carriage to Egypt (cf. Schober 39). Perdikkas did not trust him and sent Dokimos to assume control of Babylon and to kill Archon, who put up a gallant fight, enlisting even some of the native population, but later succumbed to his wounds (Arr. *Succ.* 24.3–5). Kaerst, *RE* II.1 (1895) 564 no. 5; Badian, *BNP* I 1027 no. 1; Berve II 86–7 no. 163; cf. R&O 466–71 no. 92.

170 ARDOATES

(Ἀρδοάτης, Justi 21 no. 1). King of Armenia, A. occupied the throne from at least 322 to 301, for according to Diodorus (31.19.5) it was to him that Ariarathes II fled after the death of his adoptive father Ariarathes I in 322, and it was with A.'s help that he recovered his kingdom—at about the time that Antigonos and Seleukos were waging war at Ipsos—by defeating the Macedonian *strategos* Amyntas. About A. himself nothing further is recorded. Beloch IV² 2.361 and Bengtson II 77–8 dates these events to 260, Diodorus clearly believed that they occurred before the battle of Ipsos.

171 ARETES

(Ἀρέτης). Macedonian (Tataki 260 no. 258). Named only in the accounts of Gaugamela, where he commanded the *sarissophoroi* or *hippeis prodromoi* (Curt. 4.15.13), having replaced, at some point between 333 and 331, Protomachos. He was stationed on the right wing (Arr. 3.12.3; cf. Bosworth I 303), next to the ilarch Ariston, commander of the Paionians (cf. Curt. 4.9.24). During the engagement, Aretes was sent to relieve the cavalry of Menidas, who were under heavy attack from the Skythian horse (Arr. 3.13.3, 14.1, 3; Curt. 4.15.13, 18). Nothing else is known about Aretes, who may, however, be identical with Aretis (no. 172), Alexander's *anaboleus* at the Granikos (Arr. 1.15.6). Kaerst, *RE* II.1 (1895) 678 no. 1; Berve II 58 no. 109; Bosworth I 303, 305–6; cf. I 122; Heckel 1992, 354.

172 ARETIS

(Ἀρέτις). Macedonian (Tataki 260 no. 259). Termed *anaboleus* by Arr. 1.15.6, he fought at the Granikos River but was unable to hand Alexander a lance since his, like that of the King, had been broken in the engagement. Possibly (*pace* Hoffmann 179) he is to be identified with the commander of the *hippeis prodromoi* at Gaugamela (Arr. 3.12.3; Curt. 4.15.13). Krüger, followed by Roos/Wirth in the Teubner edition, reads Ἀρέτην instead of Ἀρέτιν in Arr. 1.15.6. In non-combat situations, it was the task of the *paides basilikoi* to help the King mount his horse (Arr. 4.13.1), but Aretis/-es was probably a member of the *ile basilike* assigned the task of helping Alexander remount if he was unhorsed or his mount was killed or wounded under him. Thus he fought in the immediate vicinity of the King. If Aretes, who commanded a special unit at Gaugamela, was the same man, he was no longer the King's *anaboleus*. See Aretes (no. 171). Berve, *RE* Supplbd. IV (1924) 46; Berve II 58 no. 110; Hoffmann 179; Heckel 1992, 290.

173 AREUS

(Ἄρευς). Spartan (Bradford 43–4 no. 1) king (*regn.* 309–265), son of Akrotatos (Diod. 20.29.1; Paus. 1.13.5; 3.6.2, 4; 6.12.5; Plut. *Pyrrh.* 26.18, *Agis* 3.6; *IG* I³ 433) and grandson of Kleomenes II, A. ascended the throne in 309/8 and ruled for 45 years (Diod. 20.29.1). Since the father predeceased Kleomenes II, a power struggle resulted at Kleomenes' death in 309/8 between the supports of Kleonymos, Akrotatos' younger brother, and A. The *gerousia* chose A. (Paus. 3.6.2; cf. Plut. *Pyrrh.* 26.16); the fact that Kleonymos led the army suggests that the new king was relatively young. Areus' reign lasted 45 years (Diod. 20.29.1), during which time he appears to have campaigned in Sicily (Plut. *Mor.* 217f). In 281 he conducted a campaign against the Aitolians (Scholten 2000, 20 n.83 with additional literature), the allies of Antigonos Gonatas, but his forces, after initial success, were dispersed by the enemy and further attempts to lead a Greek war of "liberation" against Macedonian supremacy were rebuffed by his erstwhile allies, who suspected the Spartans of seeking domination (Justin 24.1.5–7; Tarn, *AG* 132–3). Indeed, it appears that, during the last fifteen years (at least) of A.'s reign, he was intent upon restoring Spartan power, though perhaps unrealistically (Cartledge 1989, 37; cf. Walbank, *CAH* VII² 1.252). When Pyrrhos attacked Sparta in 273/2, A. was absent, making war on behalf of the Gortynians in Krete (Plut. *Pyrrh.* 27.2) but he returned with 2,000 soldiers in time to participate in the successful resistance (Plut. *Pyrrh.* 29.11); as decisive for the outcome was the arrival of forces under Ameinias. When Pyrrhos decided instead to move against Argos, A. set an ambush for his forces, in which Pyrrhos' son Ptolemy was killed (Plut. *Pyrrh.* 30.4–6); after this he brought a force of Kretans, Spartans, and Gauls to the aid in the defense of Argos (Plut. *Pyrrh.* 32.4) A. appears to have conducted three campaigns (267, 266, 265) against Antigonos Gonatas during the Chremonidean War (for his relationship with Ptolemy II see *IG* I³ 433; doubted by Sandberger 50) and died in the final one (Paus. 3.6.4; Tarn, *AG* 301 dates A.'s death to 274, but see Heinen 103–5 and 173–5); he was killed in battle at Korinth (Trogus *Prol.* 26; Plut. *Agis* 3.7, his successor was Akrotatos II; cf. Will 2003, 226); but Paus. 3.6.6 says A. marched home, not wishing to risk his life recklessly. Two statues of A. were erected at Olympia (Paus. 6.12.5–6; 6.15.9). His remark that women should not be the subject of conversation (Plut. *Mor.* 217f) is of no historical value, though it illuminates his character. Athen. 4.142b (= Phylarchos, *FGrH* 81 F44) comments on A.'s extravagance, not that he was nevertheless outdone by many other Spartans in this respect. The claim that Areus made diplomatic contact with the Jews, may be true (thus Forrest 1969a, 142), but cannot be established with certainty (Josephus, *AJ* 12.225–7, 13.167; 1 Maccabees 12.1–23, the latter quoting a letter in the royal style; Bickerman 1988, 144–5 believes it is "a Hasmonean forgery"). Sandberger 49–52 no. 17; Niese, *RE* II 682–3 no. 1; Lévêque 1957, *passim*; Paschidis 256–60 B17. **Stemma XVIIIa.**

ARGAIOS (Ἀργαῖος). Dexippos, *FGrH* 100 F8 §6; cf. Metz, *LM* 121. See **OROPIOS.**

174 ARGAIOS

(Ἀργαῖος). Possibly Macedonian (Tataki 260 no. 254). A Friend of Ptolemy Soter, who sent him, along with Kallikrates (no. 564), to Menelaos, the *strategos* of Kypros, to secure the elimination of Nikokles, king of Paphos, because he had formed an alliance with Antigonos (Diod. 20.21.1). Nikokles killed himself, and his entire family followed suit (against the incorrect but persistent view that Nikokles is an error for Nikokreon see Gesche 1974). Kirchner, *RE* II.1 (1895) 685 no. 7.

175 ARGAIOS

(Ἀργαῖος). Son of Ptolemy I and (probably) Eurydike (see Beloch IV² 2.179, 186; Ager 2018, 39, 42). Hence probably born before the end of the fourth century. Brother of Ptolemy II, who murdered him on the charge of plotting against him (Paus. 1.7.1). *PP* 144.

176 ARGILIAS

(Ἀργιλίας). Son of Laonikos. One of twenty-four cavalrymen from Orchomenos, who served with Alexander's allied cavalry until the expedition reached Ekbatana in 330. There he and his compatriots were discharged. On their return (*c.*329), they made a dedication to Zeus Soter in Orchomenos (*IG* VII 3206). Berve II 57 no. 108.

177 ARIAKES

(Ἀριάκης). Commander of the Kappadokian forces at Gaugamela (Arr. 3.8.5). Ἀριάκης may be a corruption of the name Ἀριαράθης (Meyer 1879, 28; Bosworth, I 291). Berve (II 58) rejects that identification as "nicht zu beweisen" and "wenig glaublich," arguing that Ariakes was the successor of Mithrobouzanes, who fell at the Granikos, and that he fled to Dareios. But Mithrobouzanes' troops, in all likelihood, dispersed to their homes after their leader's death; certainly, it is doubtful that they remained together as a unit beyond the battle of Issos (late 333). The Kappadokians at Gaugamela must be from Kappadokia-Pontos, and their leader was Ariarathes. See below s.v. Ariarathes (no. 179). Berve II 58 no. 111; Shayegan 99 no. 12.

178 ARIAMAZES

(Ἀριαμάζης, Ἀριμάζης). Sogdianian dynast. Commander of the so-called Rock of Sogdiana (Curt. 7.11.1–29; Metz Epit. 15–18; Strabo 11.11.4 C517). Trusting in the fortress, which he regarded as impregnable, he refused to surrender to Alexander, arguing that the Macedonians would need men with wings in order to take his fortress; Curt. 7.11.1 says, implausibly, that he had a force of 30,000 and supplies to maintain them for two years. When Alexander sent climbers to occupy the heights above Ariamazes' position, the latter surrendered (Polyaenus 4.3.29). He was, however, scourged and crucified for his arrogance (Curt. 7.11.28; but Metz Epit. 18 says he was murdered by his own men). Arrian, who does not mention Ariamazes by name, says that it was here, at the Rock of Sogdiana, that Alexander captured and married Rhoxane (Arr. 4.18.4, 19.5). This is, however, contradicted by all other sources, and Strabo clearly distinguishes between the Rock of Sogdiana and the place of Rhoxane's capture. Bosworth II 131 attempts to reconcile the two versions and suggests that Rhoxane "may have been in Alexander's entourage for several months before the King noticed and married her." But Curt. 7.11.28–9 makes it clear that the leaders associated with Ariamazes (which ought to have included Oxyartes, if his daughter was being kept on the Rock of Sogdiana) were whipped and executed, adding that the captives were sold into slavery. Oxyartes later acted as a liaison between Alexander and Sisimithres and he may have been induced to do so because his family had taken refuge on Sisimithres' rock. Berve II 59 no. 112; cf. Tomaschek, *RE* II.1 (1895) 812–13 s.v. Ἀριαμάζου πέτρα; Badian, *BNP* I 1078; Vacante 2012; Shayegan 99 no. 13.

179 ARIARATHES

(Ἀριαράθης). Ariarathes I of Kappadokia. Born in 404/3 ([Lucian] *Macrob.* 13 = Hieronymos, *FGrH* 154 F4 says he lived to be 82), Ariarathes was the son of Ariaramnes (Diod. 31.19.2 has Ariamnes) and brother of Orophernes (no. 823; Diod. Ὀλοφέρνης), of whom he was exceedingly fond. The first to be called the "King of the Kappadokians," he annexed Kataonia, which had previously been a separate nation (Strabo 12.1.2 C534). Ruled Kappadokia in Pontos (from Gazioura in the Lykos valley: *Barr. Atl.* 87 B4; Bevan, *Seleucus* I 80; Ballesteros Pastor 2013, 185; cf. Strabo 12.3.15 C547) already in the time of Artaxerxes III Ochos; for he sent his brother to serve with the Persian king against the Egyptian rebels (Diod. 31.19.3). Whether he is the leader of the Kappadokians at

Gaugamela, whom Arr. 3.8.5 calls Ariakes, is uncertain. A. held out successfully against Alexander, but in 323 Eumenes was instructed to win the satrapy away from him (Curt. 10.10.3; cf. Plut. *Eum.* 3.4). Perdikkas invaded Kappadokia in 322 or 321, defeated Ariarathes in two battles (Arr. *Succ.* 1.11), and captured and impaled him along with his prominent followers (Diod. 18.16.1–3; cf. Diod. 18.22.1; Justin 13.6.1; App. *Mithr.* 8 = *FGrH* 154 F3); but according to Diod. 31 (frag. 19.3–5 Dindorf) Ariarathes fell in battle— his adopted son Ariarathes, the natural son of Orophernes (Diod. 31.19.4), escaped and later recovered the throne (Diod. 31.19.5). The remainder of A.'s subjects were granted immunity and placed under the rule of Eumenes of Kardia (Plut. *Eum.* 3.13; App. *Mithr.* 8). Berve II 59–60 no. 113; Niese, *RE* II.1 (1895) 815–16 no. 1; Meyer 1879, 28–9; Shayegan 99–100 no. 14.

180 ARIARATHES

(Ἀριαράθης). Ariarathes II of Kappadokia. Son of Orophernes and brother of Aryses (Diod. 31.19.3); nephew of Ariarathes I. After his father's death in the 330s, he was adopted by his uncle. When his adoptive father was killed by Perdikkas in 322, A. fled to Armenia. At some point before 301, with the aid of the Armenian king Ardoates (no. 170), A. defeated Antigonos' general, Amyntas (no. 88), and drove the Makedonians out of Kappadokia, thus recovering his kingdom (Diod. 31.19.5; Ballesteros Pastor 2013, 185). Father of three sons, the eldest of whom, Ariamnes, succeeded him. His grandson was Ariarathes III, who married Stratonike, the daughter of Antiochos II Theos (Bevan, *Seleucus* I 172, 194). McGing, *OCD*[3] 156; Niese, *RE* II 816 no. 2; Shayegan 100 no. 15.

ARIMMAS. See MENON.

181 ARIOBARZANES

(Ἀριοβαρζάνης). Son of Dareios III by an earlier wife. He was probably a nephew of Pharnakes and brother-in-law of Mithridates, both of whom were killed at the Granikos (Arr. 1.15.7, 16.3; Diod. 17.21.3; cf. Plut. *Mor.* 326f). According to Aretades of Knidos (*FGrH* 285 F1 = Plut. *Mor.* 308c), A. plotted with Alexander to betray his father but Dareios, learning of this, had him beheaded. Berve II 61 assumes that the cause of his grievance may have been the eclipse of his status by Dareios' new family, especially Ochos, who may have had a stronger claim to the throne. The deaths of two prominent kinsmen must have contributed to A.'s isolation. Judeich, *RE* II.1 (1895) 833 no. 3; Berve II 61 no. 116; Shayegan 100 no. 17. **Stemma III.**

182 ARIOBARZANES

(Ἀριοβαρζάνης). Persian noble of unknown family—possibly he belonged to one of the aristocratic families that ruled Kappadokia-Pontos or Hellespontine Phrygia (he was perhaps also the father of Mithridates, Diod. 19.40.2). A. was satrap of Persis since at least 331 (Arr. 3.18.2). Identification with the son of Artabazos who later surrendered to Alexander (Arr. 3.23.7) appears to be ruled out by Curtius' claim (5.4.34), which need not be taken at face value; (see Shayegan 100 no. 16) that the satrap of Persis died before Alexander's capture of Persepolis (cf. Bosworth I 325, against Berve II 60). At Gaugamela, he commanded the Persians and, presumably, the neighboring Mardians (Curt. 4.12.7; cf. Arr. 3.8.5, "those bordering on the Persian Gulf"), though under the direction of

Orxines. After the Persian defeat, he withdrew to his satrapy and, in late 331, he attempted to block Alexander's passage at the so-called Persian, or Sousian, Gates with a force of 25,000 infantry (Curt. 5.3.17; Diod. 17.68.1, adding 300 cavalry; Arr. 3.18.2: 40,000 and 700, exaggerated). Although he managed to stymie the initial (frontal) attack, A. soon found his position circumvented by Alexander and fled with but a few horsemen (Arr. 3.18.9; cf. Curt. 5.4.33; for the battle see Arr. 3.18.2–9; Curt. 5.3.17–4.34; Diod. 17.68, badly confused; Polyaenus 4.3.27; cf. Plut. *Alex.* 37.1–2; Fuller 226–34). Returning to Persepolis, he found himself barred from the city and is said to have perished in a desperate battle with the Macedonians near the Araxes River (Curt. 5.4.34). If he was not, in fact, killed at that time, he could be identical with the son of Artabazos (no. 183). Berve II 60–1 no. 115; Bosworth I 324 –5; Howe 2015b; Heckel 145–8; Speck 2002.

183 ARIOBARZANES

(Ἀριοβαρζάνης). Son of Artabazos, born before 350. According to Diod. 16.52.4, Artabazos came to the court of Philip II (*c.*349/8; though the date is disputed) with eleven sons and ten daughters. Together with his father and his brothers, Arsames and Kophen, he surrendered to Alexander in Hyrkania (Arr. 3.23.7; cf. Curt. 6.5.4, who says that Artabazos surrendered along with nine sons). Nothing else is known about him, unless he was the satrap of Persis and Curt. 5.4.23 is wrong in claiming that he died in a skirmish before Persepolis. If this is the case, Alexander did not reward him for his bravery at the Persian Gates (see Heckel 2018b, 97). Kaerst, *RE* II.1 (1895) 833 no. 4 (identifying him with the satrap of Persis); Bosworth I 325, against Berve II 60–1 no. 115; cf. also Hofstetter 34 no. 57 s.v. "Astyanax"; Kuhrt/Sherwin-White, *BNP* I 1082–3 no. 2. **Stemma IV.**

184 ARIPHARNES

(Ἀριφάρνης). King of the Sirakes; (Diod. 20.22.4 MS Θρᾳκῶν "Thrakians," emended to Σιρακῶν; Tomaschek dismisses Θατέων on the grounds that they could not field an army such as that which A. led). It appears that the Sirakes and the Thateans both lived along or near the Kuban (Hypanis) River (*Barr. Atl.* 84 C3), which flows into the Kimmerian Bosporos via the Apatourian Gulf (cf. Hind, *CAH*[2] 501). Whichever people A. ruled, they and their allies came from this region. A.'s capital was said to be on an otherwise unknown river named the Thates (Diod. 20.22.3, 23.1; see Niese I 413 n.5), clearly an alternative name for another river, probably the Kuban or a tributary of it (Cunliffe 2019, 258 speaks of them as different rivers, without further comment). This would also explain how it was that Satyros' corpse was conveyed from the camp (Gargaza) not far from A.'s capital by river (διὰ τοῦ ποταμοῦ) or through the strait (διὰ τοῦ πορθμοῦ) to Pantikapaion (Diod. 20.23.8). A. entered into an alliance with Eumelos (no. 442) son of Pairisades (no. 837) in his bid for the throne of the Kimmerian Bosporos (Diod. 20.22.4). Together with Eumelos, A. fought against the legitimate ruler, Satyros, beyond the so-called Thates River. Diod. 20.22.4 says A. had 20,000 horse and 20,000 infantry. In the battle, A., fighting in the centre with his cavalry, was routed by Satyros and fled the battlefield (Diod. 20.22.5); he appears to have been spared further embarrassment (and possible capture or death) when Satyros was forced to turn his attentions to the right wing, where Eumelos' forces were getting the upper hand. Accompanied by Eumelos, A. now returned to his capital on the Thates (Diod. 20.23.1), where he conducted a gallant defense against Satyros' besieging army, using the devastating power of his archers (Diod.

20.23.3). A. escaped danger when Satyros died of a wound to the upper arm and the siege was abandoned. Whether A.'s troops were the barbarians that Eumelos used (Diod. 20.24.1) to win the kingdom against Prytanis (no. 1003) is unknown. Nothing else is known about him. Tomaschek, *RE* II.1 (1895) 845.

ARIPLEX. See **APHRIKES**.

185 ARISTANDROS

(Ἀρίστανδρος). Greek from Telmessos (Telmissos) (Arr. 1.11.2, 25.8; 3.2.2; Lucian, *Philop.* 22), A. accompanied Alexander as a seer of great renown (Curt. 4.2.14, 6.12; cf. 5.4.2; Diod. 17.17.6, where the text ὁ μὲν θύτης Ἀλέξανδρος should read either ὁ μὲν θύτης Ἀρίστανδρος or Ἀλεξάνδρου). Born perhaps *c.*380 (thus Berve II 62), A. was already in Philip's entourage in 357/6, when he correctly interpreted one of the King's dreams as revealing Olympias' pregnancy (Plut. *Alex.* 2.5). During Alexander's campaigns he interpreted various omens for the King: the sweating of the statue of Orpheus (Arr. 1.11.2; Plut. *Alex.* 14.8–9; cf. Ps.-Call. 1.42; Jul. Valer. 1.46); the toppling of the statue of Ariobarzanes (Diod. 17.17.6); the actions of birds at Halikarnassos (Arr. 1.25.6–8, relating to the plot of Lynkestian Alexander) and at Gaza (Arr. 2.26.4, 27.1; Curt. 4.6.10–12) and at the founding of Alexandria in Egypt (Arr. 3.2.1–2; cf. Curt. 4.8.6); bleeding bread (Curt. 4.2.14) or dreams about Herakles (Arr. 2.18.1) at Tyre; and oil at the Oxos (Arr. 4.15.8). A.'s services were also sought before and at Gaugamela (Arr. 3.7.6; Curt. 4.13.15, 15.27; Plut. *Alex.* 31.9; cf. Arr. 3.15.7); the Persian Gates (Curt. 5.4.1–3), at the Iaxartes (Arr. 4.4.3, 9; Curt. 7.7.8, 22–9). It is also said that A. and Kleomenes were instructed by Alexander to sacrifice on behalf of Kleitos' safety in the light of an unfavorable omen (Plut. *Alex.* 50.3–5). Two other references to A. are almost certainly unhistorical: thirty days after Alexander's death A. was supposed to have predicted that the land that became home to his body would enjoy great prosperity, thus causing Ptolemy to bring it to Egypt (Ael. *VH* 12.64); A. was also supposed to have predicted Lysimachos' kingship (App. *Syr.* 64.338). Fraenkel 1883 and Robinson 1929 believed that A. was a feature of Kallisthenes' history and they attribute his disappearance after 328/7 to the historian's demise. It is more likely, however, that A. simply died of illness or old age during the campaign. Kaerst, *RE* II.1 (1895) 859–60 no. 6; Berve II 62–3 no. 117; Robinson 1929; Greenwalt 1982; Badian, *BNP* I 1089 no. 1.

186 ARISTARCHOS

(Ἀρίσταρχος). A leading Ambrakiot, A. persuaded his fellow citizens to expel the city's Macedonian garrison immediately after Philip II's death and establish a democracy (Diod. 17.3.3). Since Alexander allowed the Ambrakiots their freedom (Diod. 17.4.3), it would appear that A. went unpunished for his role. Nothing else is known about him. Kirchner, *RE* II.1 (1895) 861 no. 6; Schaefer III² 91; Berve II 63 no. 118.

187 ARISTEIDES

(Ἀριστείδης). Theban painter, son of Nikomachos (Pliny, *HN* 35.98); Aristeides the elder was apparently his grandfather (cf. Pliny, *HN* 35.75, 108). A. was a contemporary of Apelles (Pliny, *HN* 35.98) and reportedly the first to depict human emotions. During the sack of Thebes, Alexander saw A.'s painting of a dying mother with child, which so impressed him that he had it taken to Pella (Pliny, *HN* 35.98; Sil. 9.41ff.; Anth. Pal. 7.623). Another painting, depicting a battle with the Persians and containing 100 human figures, appears to have been inspired by one of Alexander's campaigns against Dareios (Pliny, *HN* 35.99). The painting was said to have been sold for 10 minae per human figure to Mnason, the tyrant of Elateia. See Pollitt 168–9. Rossbach, *RE* II.1 (1895) 897 no. 30; Berve II 63 no. 119; Hoesch, *BNP* I 1101 no. 6.

188 ARISTION

(Ἀριστίων). Son of Aristoboulos, whom Aesch. 3.162 identifies as an apothecary (φαρμακοπώλης). Young man of Plataian (Marsyas, *FGrH* 135/6 F2) or Samian (Diyllos, *FGrH* 73 F2) origin, sent by Demosthenes to Hephaistion, asking him to intercede with Alexander on Demosthenes' behalf. A.'s presence at Alexander's court is dated to 331 by an Athenian embassy which found him there (Aesch. 3.162). Kirchner, *RE* II.1 (1895) 900 no. 12; Schaefer III² 195 n.5; Berve II 63 no. 120.

189 ARISTOBOULOS

(Ἀριστόβουλος). Son of Aristoboulos (Arr. 6.28.2), from Kassandreia (Plut. *Dem.* 23.6; [Lucian] *Macrob.* 22). Since Kassandreia was not founded until 316, it may be that A. came from somewhere in Chalkidike, possibly Potidaia, though he may have come from any part of the Greek world (for the view that he may have been Phokian see Pearson 151–52; cf. *Fouilles de Delphes* III 3, 207, which mentions a certain Sophokles son of Aristoboulos, "a Phokian living in Kassandreia"). His birthdate is uncertain: he is said to have surpassed the age of ninety and did not begin writing his *History* until he was 84 ([Lucian] *Macrob.* 22; Tarn II 42–3 believes he wrote between 294 and 288). A. seems to have accompanied Alexander from the beginning of the Asiatic campaign and remained with the King until his death (Arr. *proem.* 2; cf. Strabo 15.1.17 C691, 15.1.45 C706); his account of the Timokleia story does not prove that he was with the King at the sack of Thebes (*FGrH* 139 F2a–b = Plut. *Mor.* 1093c, 259d–260d). He appears to have joined the expedition in what we would call the engineering corps. In fact, he was entrusted with the task of restoring the tomb of Kyros the Great at Pasargadai after it had been plundered by thieves (Strabo 15.3.7 C730; Arr. 6.29.4–10). After Alexander's death he returned to Europe, perhaps in the company of Antipatros in 320 (cf. Jacoby IID 508), and after the regent's death he may have become a supporter of Kassandros and one of Kassandreia's first citizens (but Pownall, *LexAM* 104 believes he did not publish his *History* until after the death of Kassandros, who was hostile to Alexander). His *History* was used by Arrian, alongside that of Ptolemy son of Lagos, because of its favorable treatment of Alexander. He was noted for his flattering style (*FGrH* 139 T5 = Walz, *Rhetores Graeci* III 610) and was not encumbered by the truth but a blatant apologist for the King. Lucian (*How to Write History* 12) claims that A. depicted Alexander in hand-to-hand combat with Poros and that, when he read the account to the King as they sailed down the Hydaspes, Alexander grabbed the text and threw it overboard, saying that A. deserved the same treatment. *FGrH* 139 F62 (= Arr. 7.29.4) asserts that Alexander drank to be sociable rather than for love of wine. A. also placed the blame for Kleitos' death on the victim himself (F29 = Arr. 4.8.9) and claimed that the Pages themselves asserted that Kallisthenes had instigated the Hermolaos conspiracy (F31 = Arr. 4.14.1), adding also that Kallisthenes died a natural death, albeit in chains (F33 = Arr. 4.14.3). For the scope and nature of his *History*, of which some 62 genuine fragments survive, see Jacoby, *FGrH* 139 and Pearson 150–87. Schwartz, *RE* II.1 (1895) 912–18 no. 14; Berve II 64–6 no. 121; Badian, *BNP* I 1105–6 no. 7. For his work see Pearson *LHA* chap. 6, 150–87; Jacoby *FGrH* 139; Schwartz *RE* II 914ff.; Pownall, *LexAM* 103–5.

190 ARISTOBOULOS

(Ἀριστόβουλος). Ambassador of Ptolemy I, A. was sent to Antigonos to receive the oath from him to abide by the terms of the Peace of 311 (*RC* 1, line 50 = *OGIS* 5, l. 50; on the peace see Will 2003, 61–5). Identification with Aristoboulos of Kassandreia is impossible. It appears that A. continued to serve Ptolemy in Karia (Bagnall 91 suggests that he may have been the Ptolemaic governor), where a Iasian inscription (*I.Iasos* 3, lines 1–18) preserves the details of negotiations between the city and the king, asking for confirmation of its status as an autonomous ally, in a time after 305. Asklepiodotos, named in a second letter (*I.Iasos* 3, lines 19–28) that renews at the Iasians request the oath sworn by A., may have been his successor, but his appointment probably occurred after Ipsos (hence his omission from this compilation). Olshausen 25 no. 9; Schoch, *RE* Supplbd IV (1924) 47 no. 4a; *PP* no. 14749; Bagnall 90–1.

191 ARISTODEMOS

(Ἀριστόδημος). Greek from Miletos. Son of Parthenios. A. was rumored to be the son of a cook (Plut. *Mor.* 182d), but nevertheless one of Antigonos' *philoi* (Plut. *Demetr.* 9.2; at 17.2, Plutarch calls him the foremost of Antigonos' flatterers, an unduly harsh judgment; cf. Eutropion (no. 464) for the combination of cook and military man, though possibly Plutarch has confused the two men). Their relationship appears to go back to Antigonos' early years in Asia Minor: A. may have been with Antigonos when he was satrap of Phrygia (thus Billows 372; whether he joined him when he fled to Antipatros in 321 is a matter of speculation). After Antigonos had defeated Alketas in Pisidia, he came to Kretopolis, where A. brought news of Antipatros' death and Polyperchon's appointment as guardian of the Kings (Diod. 18.47.4). But this need not imply that A. himself was in Macedonia when these events occurred. In 314, when Antigonos found that Ptolemy, Lysimachos, and Kassandros had formed a coalition against him, he sent A. to the Peloponnese with 1,000 talents and orders to reach an agreement with Polyperchon and his son Alexander and recruit an army to fight Kassandros (Diod. 19.57.5). A. fulfilled this mission, recruiting some 8,000 mercenaries (with the permission of the Spartan authorities; cf. Griffith 1935, 52), appointing Polyperchon *strategos* of the Peloponnese, and urging Alexander to sail to Antigonos in Asia (Diod. 19.60.1). As a consequence of A.'s activities, Ptolemy responded by sending a force under Polykleitos to the Peloponnese (Diod. 19.62.5) and Kassandros, after failing to detach Polyperchon from Antigonos, mobilized his forces in central Greece and moved south of the Isthmus (Diod. 19.63.3–5). Together with Alexander, A. set out to remove the garrisons that Kassandros had installed in the Peloponnesian cities (Diod. 19.64.2), but his work was temporarily undone by the perfidy of his ally, who now joined Kassandros, abandoning also his own father (Diod. 19.64.4). In response to Alexander's defection, A. persuaded the assembly of the Aitolians to support Antigonos; with a force of Aitolian mercenaries he sailed to Kyllene, which was besieged by Alexander and the Eleans. Raising the siege, he moved on to Patrai, Aigion, and Dyme, and through a series of victories strengthened Antigonos' position in southern Greece (Diod. 19.66). In

312, A. received help from Telesphoros and Ptolemy, nephews of Antigonos, though the latter was now given supreme command (cf. Diod. 19.77.2). Hence, Antigonid control of Greece (with the exception of Athens) was secured. For the negotiations between Antigonos and Kassandros, and the subsequent peace of 311, see *OGIS* 5. As part of the negotiations, A. was sent with Aischylos and Hegesias to Ptolemy in Egypt (*OGIS* 5, 48). A. accompanied Demetrios, first to Athens, where he negotiated the surrender of Kassandros' representative, Demetrios of Phaleron (Plut. *Demetr.* 9.2–3), for which he was honored by the Athenians (*IG* II² 459; Habicht 1977b, 39 n.3), and then to Salamis. After Demetrios' naval victory, he brought the news to Antigonos (Plut. *Demetr.* 17.2) who was then at Antigoneia-on-the-Orontes, addressing him as "King Antigonos" (Plut. *Demetr.* 17.3–6). He is last attested in his homeland, holding the rank of *stephanephoros* in Miletos in 306/5 (Rehm, *Milet* I 123, line 11) and aiding the Ephesians in their bid for freedom from taxation (Knibbe and Iplikcioglu 1982, 130–2), also after 306. Launey 1209; Billows 371–4 no. 16; Kirchner, *RE* II.1 (1895) 923–4 no. 16; Schoch, *RE* Supplbd IV (1924) no. 8a (wrongly "Gesandter des Ptolemaios I. zu Antigonos"); Olshausen 1974, nos. 66, 75; Habicht, 1977b, 39 n.3.

192 ARISTOGEITON

(Ἀριστογείτων). Athenian (Kirchner 1775). Son of Kydimachos (who had been condemned to death by the Athenians but went into exile in Eretria: [Dem.] 25.54, 65, 77; Din. 2.8). Berve II 66 calls him "one of the most shameless demagogues and sycophants of his time," thus reflecting the judgment of his political opponents (cf. Dem. 27, 28); Plut. *Phoc.* 10.3 says he was in the front ranks of those urging the *demos* to declare war but the first to shirk military service. Deinarchos alleged that he spent more time in prison than out of it (2.2), that he neglected his father when he was in exile (2.8), and that he had been fined the maximum amount for bringing false charges against the priestess of Artemis at Brauron and her family (2.12). In 324 he was charged with accepting bribes from Harpalos (Din 2.1 says he took twenty minae), a charge supported by the findings of the Areiopagos. Deinarchos' speech, *Against Aristogeiton*, survives in an incomplete form and relies heavily on rhetorical topoi (see Worthington 287–312 for analysis and commentary). Despite his alleged history of abuses, Aristogeiton was acquitted (Dem. *Ep.* 3.37–8, 43; Goldstein 1968, 143, 231–2). Thalheim, *RE* II.1 (1895) 931–2 no. 2; Berve II 66 no. 122; Schaefer, *passim*; Sealy 1960; Worthington 287–312.

193 ARISTOGEITON

(Ἀριστογείτων). An Athenian of unknown family background (Kirchner 1774), A. was sent as ambassador to Dareios in 333/2 and was captured by Parmenion at Damaskos (Curt. 3.13.15, adding Iphikrates and Dropides). Arr. 3.24.4, however, records the capture of Dropides in 330, in a context where Curtius (6.5.6–9) names Demokrates, perhaps a mercenary captain (so, plausibly, Bosworth I 234). An Athenian embassy of three men was normal practice, and 333/2 makes eminently good sense. Berve II 66 no. 123; Hofstetter 27 no. 42; Atkinson I 464–5; Bosworth I 233–4; Develin 385, 392.

194 ARISTOKRATES

(Ἀριστοκράτης). Theban harpist who performed at the Sousan marriage festival (see also Herakleitos of Tarentum) in 324 (Chares, *FGrH* 125 F4 = Athen. 12. 538f). He is otherwise unknown. Crusius, *RE* II.1 (1895) 941 no. 24; Berve II 67 no. 124.

195 ARISTOKRITOS

(Ἀριστόκριτος). A tragic actor of unknown origin, A. served as envoy of the Karian prince Pixodaros, who sought a marriage alliance with Philip II in spring 336 (Plut. *Alex.* 10.1; for the date see Olmstead 490). He apparently returned with Philip's proposal that Pixodaros' daughter should marry Arrhidaios. Alexander subsequently undermined these negotiations by sending another actor, Thessalos (no. 1123), to the Karian dynast. A. reappears (along with Thessalos and Athenodoros) in Sousa, where he performed at the marriage festival in 324 (Chares, *FGrH* 125 F4 = Athen. 12.538f). Thereafter he is not heard of again. Kirchner, *RE* II.1 (1895) 942 no. 1; Berve II 67 no. 125; O'Connor no. 65.

196 ARISTOMEDES

(Ἀριστομήδης). Thessalian from Pherai (Arr. 2.13.2; cf. Curt. 3.9.3). As Westlake 1935, 225–26 suggests, A. was probably one of many Thessalians who chose Persian service over Macedonian domination. A. had joined the generals of the Great King in 341/0 in opposing Philip II, who mentioned him in a letter to the Athenians (Theopompos, *FGrH* 115 F222; Westlake 1935, 206). He later served Dareios at Issos (333), where he commanded 20,000 barbarian infantry stationed on the left wing (Curt. 3.9.3): whether these were Kardakes (on whom see Cook 1983, 55; Sekunda 1992, 51–3; Briant 1999, 120–4; Cook 1983, 55; Briant 1036–7; Charles 2012; cf. Atkinson I 102), as Berve II 67 suggests, is not clear; from Arrian's description (2.8.6–7), it appears that the 60,000 Kardakes (see Heckel 95, with n.18) were positioned on either side of the Greek mercenaries but that an additional 20,000 troops (A.'s force) were placed to their left. After the battle, A. managed to escape, along with Amyntas (no. 77) son of Antiochos and Bianor (no. 296) the Akarnanian, first to Tripolis in Phoinikia, where they had left the ships which brought them from Lesbos, and thence to Kypros (Arr. 2.13.2–3, with 8,000 troops; Curt. 4.1.27 and Diod. 17.48.2–3, only 4,000). Diod. 17.48.4 says that the troops who continued on to Egypt perished to a man, but names no other officer except Amyntas. Bianor, Thymondas (no. 1136) and A. may have parted ways with Amyntas on Kypros (Anaximenes, *FGrH* 72 F17 mentions only his flight to Kypros), perhaps taking some of the mercenaries to Krete, which would account for the discrepancy in the numbers of mercenaries and failure of any source to mention deaths of the other three commanders (see Bosworth I 222–3). Kirchner, *RE* II.1 (1895) 946 no. 2; Berve II 67 no. 128; Westlake 1935, 206, 225–6; Hofstetter 27–8 no. 44.

197 ARISTOMENES

(Ἀριστομένης). Greek of unknown background. A. commanded a fleet of unknown size in the Hellespontine region. He was defeated by Hegelochos (no. 496), perhaps early in 322 (Curt. 4.1.36). That "Aristomenes" is an error for "Autophradates" seems unlikely (Atkinson I 289). What became of him is unknown. Berve II 67 no. 126; Seibt 107; Hofstetter 28 no. 45; Berve, *RE* Supplbd. IV (1924) 48.

198 ARISTON

(Ἀρίστων). Nothing is known about the family and background of A., who appears to have been a Macedonian of high standing (Tataki 264 no. 275). He is first attested at Gaugamela, where his squadron of Companions was stationed between those of Glaukias and Sopolis on the right wing (Arr. 3.11.8); he may have been an ilarch since at least the beginning of Alexander's reign. Otherwise, nothing is known about the man. Berve (II 74) and Billows (375 no. 17) identify him tentatively with the man who brought the remains of Krateros to his widow, Phila (Diod. 19.59.3). Ariston of Pharsalos (no. 199) must be a different individual since it is doubtful that a Thessalian commanded a squadron of the Companion Cavalry (Heckel 1988, 43). Berve II 75 no. 139; Kirchner, *RE* II.1 (1895) 951 no. 28; Billows 375 no. 17; Heckel 1992, 348.

199 ARISTON

(Ἀρίστων). Pharsalian (Ps.-Call. 3.31.8), apparently a Thessalian *hetairos* of Alexander and a friend of Medeios of Larisa, whose dinner party he attended on 16 Daisios 323. A. is named by the author of the Pamphlet on *The Last Days and Testament of Alexander the Great* as one of those who conspired to poison the King (Ps.-Call. 3.31.8); *LM* 97 mentions in this context "Polydoros," which may be a textual corruption or, what is remotely possible, the name of A.'s father. The Pamphlet was a propaganda work of the early age of the Successors (the date is disputed: see Ausfeld 1895, 1901; Heckel 1988; Bosworth 2000) that attacked the party of Antipatros/Kassandros and Antigonos the One-Eyed. A., as a friend of Medeios, belonged to that group. It is tempting to see in A. the man who brought the remains of Krateros to his widow, Phila, at that time the wife of Demetrios Poliorketes (Diod. 19.59.3), though Berve and Billows identify that man with the former ilarch of Alexander (no. 198). Berve II 75 no. 139; Heckel 1988, 43–4.

200 ARISTON

(Ἀρίστων). An officer in the service of Eumenes; after that general's defeat, he brought the remains of Krateros to his widow, Phila, who was now married to Demetrios Poliorketes (Diod. 19.59.3). Possibly identical with either the ilarch of Alexander or with Ariston of Pharsalos.

201 ARISTON

(Ἀρίστων). Presumably a member of the Paionian royal house, possibly even the brother of Patraos (Berve II 307 no. 611) and father of the later King Audoleon (for the apparent grandson, Ariston son of Audoleon, see Polyaenus 4.12.3; cf. Merker 1965, 45). His service with Alexander, like that of Sitalkes the Thrakian and others, helped to ensure the loyalty of his nation to Macedon in the King's absence (Front. 2.11.3; cf. Justin 11.5.3). From the beginning of the expedition, he commanded the single *ile* of Paionians, who occupied a position on the right at the Granikos (Arr. 1.14.1) and at Issos (Arr. 2.9.2). In 331 the Paionians fell in with some 1,000 cavalrymen left by Mazaios in the vicinity of the Tigris (Curt. 4.9.24–5) and routed them; A. slew in single-combat their leader Satropates (Atropates?) and brought his head to Alexander (Curt. 4.9.25; Plut. *Alex.* 39.2; Merker 1965, 44–5 argues persuasively that the incident is commemorated on the coinage of Patraos; cf. Marsden 1964, 31 n.4. Atkinson I 384 suggests that Curtius may have misplaced the episode. Unless there really was an earlier engagement at the Tigris, A.'s *aristeia* may have occurred about 3 days later, when the Macedonian army encountered some 1,000 stragglers (Curt. 4.10.9–11; cf. Arr. 3.7.7–8.2). Certainly, it is more likely that Alexander should send a single *ile* of Paionians against them than against a cavalry force of 1,000. It does, however, make A.'s victory somewhat less heroic. Marsden 1964, 31 goes further and suggests that "he was hauled over the coals by Alexander afterwards" for killing Satropates, who might have given the Macedonians valuable information about enemy numbers and deployments. At Gaugamela, A. and his Paionians were again stationed on the right wing, together with the *prodromoi*, immediately behind Menidas' mercenary horse (Arr. 3.12.3; cf. Bosworth I 303; Marsden 1964, 48) and concealing from enemy view the Agrianes, archers, and *archaioi xenoi*. In the initial engagement, Ariston brought the Paionians up to aid Menidas, who was hard-pressed by the Skythian and Baktrian cavalry and, supported by the *prodromoi* and Kleandros' mercenaries, succeeded in breaking the enemy formation (Arr. 3.13.3–4). Nothing else is known about him. Kirchner, *RE* II.1 (1895) 951–2 no. 32; Berve II 74–5 no. 138; Atkinson I 384–5; Heckel 1992, 354–5; Tataki 207 no. 4; Marsden 1964, 31, 48, 50; Merker 1965, 44–6.

202 ARISTON

(Ἀρίστων). A comic actor, A. performed at the mass marriage ceremonies at Sousa in 324 (Chares, *FGrH* 125 F4 = Athen. 12.539a). He is otherwise unknown. v. Jan, *RE* II.1 (1895) 952 no. 40; Berve II 75 no. 140; Ghiron-Bistagne, p. 314; O'Connor no. 74.

203 ARISTONIKOS

(Ἀριστόνικος). Greek of unknown family background, but presumably Methymnaian. In late 333, as a consequence of Memnon's recapture of Lesbos (Arr. 2.1.1), he was installed by the Persians as tyrant of Methymna (Arr. 3.2.4; Curt. 4.5.19, 8.11); whether he had any personal connections with his predecessor Aristonymos (cf. Polyaenus 5.44.3), who had been expelled in 334, we do not know. A.'s tyranny appears to have been of short duration, for, coming to the aid of Pharnabazos in 332, he sailed into the harbor of Chios with five pirate ships (Arr. 3.2.4; cf. Curt. 4.5.19), unaware that it was in Macedonian hands. Captured by Alexander's admirals, Amphoteros and Hegelochos (Curt. 4.5.19–21; Arr. 3.2.4–5, Hegelochos only), A. was brought (along with Apollonides, Phesinos, and Magareus; Curt. 4.5.15, 17 names also a certain Athenagoras) to the King in Egypt, who sent him back to Methymna to be punished by his own citizens (Arr. 3.2.5, 7); these put him to death by torture in 331 (Curt. 4.8.11). Kaerst, *RE* II.1 (1895) 961 no. 13; Badian, *BNP* I 1121 no. 2; Berve II 68 no. 131, Berve, *Tyrannis* I 337; Ormerod 120–1; Hofstetter 29 no. 48; Atkinson I 330.

204 ARISTONIKOS

(Ἀριστόνικος). Greek from Karystos, probably the son of Aristodemos. A. was a ballplayer (*sphairistes*) in Alexander's entourage. According to Athen. 1.19a, A. was granted Athenian citizenship at an unspecified time and had a statue erected to him, although Athenaeus says this was on account of his skill (διὰ τὴν τέχνην); cf. *IG* II² 385(b) (cf. *SEG* XXI 341), which awards citizenship and other honors, including *sitesis* (limited to those who rendered the highest service: Dow 1963, 82–3), to A. son of Aristodemos (the ethnic Καρύστιος is a plausible restoration in line 8). The award of citizenship probably belongs to 307–301 (thus Paschidis 457). It was apparently the same A. who was honored by the Eretrians (*IG* XII.9, 207, line 41), towards the end of the 290s, possibly as a result of his services in the entourage of Demetrios Poliorketes (though Paschidis 458 believes he was dead by 301 and assumes he was somehow involved in the expulsion of Kassandros' forces in 304). The Karystian festival known as the Aristonikeia (*IG* XII 9, 207, l. 41) appears to have been instituted in his honor (Paschidis 458, with some reservations). Kaerst, *RE* II.1 (1895) 961 no. 5; Berve II 68 no. 129; Billows 445 no. 130; Osborne, *Naturalization* D49; Paschidis 457–8.

205 ARISTONIKOS

(Ἀριστόνικος). Athenian politician from Marathon (Kirchner 2028). Little is known about his background, but he was an Athenian trierarch and is thus described by Schaefer III² 136 n.1 as "ein wohlhabender Mann." Follower of Demosthenes and Hypereides, A. was prosecuted in 324 in the Harpalos case (Dion. Hal. *Din.* 10 [654] Pal. Anth. 2.62, on which see Worthington 54, 79–80; Din. frag. 10A [Burtt]). He was exiled from Athens and fled to Aigina with Demosthenes, Hypereides, and Himeraios, the brother of Demetrios of Phaleron (Arr. *Succ.* 1.13). A. was condemned to death *in absentia* on the proposal of Demades. This decree was executed by Antipatros, who sent Archias of Thourioi to capture him and send him to Kleonai, where he was executed (Arr. *Succ.* 1.13–14; Plut. *Dem.* 28.4; Luc. *Encom. Dem.* 31; cf. Schaefer III² 392–3). Kaerst, *RE* s.v. no. 1; Berve II 68 no. 130; Thalheim, *RE* II.1 (1895) 960–1 no. 1; Schaefer III² 135–6, 392.

206 ARISTONIKOS

(Ἀριστόνικος). Harpist (*kitharoidos*) from Olynthos (Gude 40 no. 18; Polyaenus 5.44.1, in the service of Memnon; Theopompos, *FGrH* 115 F236, says he was in Philip II's entourage after Chaironeia), A. may have accompanied Alexander since 334. In 328, he was left behind at Zariaspa with the wounded and the non-military personnel. Forced to take up arms against the Massagetai, he fell in battle (Arr. 4.16.6; not in Alexander's defense, as Plut. *Mor.* 334e says). Alexander ordered that a statue be erected at Delphi, depicting him with lyre in one hand and thrusting spear in the other (Plut. *Mor.* 334e–f). Kirchner, *RE* II.1 (1895) 961 no. 4; Berve II 68 no. 132.

207 ARISTONOUS

(Ἀριστόνους). The son of Peisaios (Arr. 6.28.4; *Succ.* 1.2), A. is described as both Πελλαῖος (Arr. 6. 28. 4) and of Eordaian origin (Arr. *Ind.* 18. 5), which must mean that he was from Eordaia but raised at the Court in Pella (cf. Leonnatos). Until his name appears in Arrian's list of the Somatophylakes (Arr. 6.28.4 = Aristoboulos, *FGrH* 139 F51), he is unknown in the *Anabasis*. He may have been appointed to that office before 336 (Heckel 1978d), though the first hint of his role as Somatophylax comes in 328. Plutarch names a certain Aristophanes, termed σωματοφύλαξ, in the Kleitos affair (*Alex.* 51.5–6), almost certainly a corruption of the name Aristonous (Hamilton 143; Ziegler 1935; *contra* Berve II 74 no. 136). In 326, A. assumed a trierarchy at the Hydaspes (*Ind.* 18.5 = Nearchos, *FGrH* 133 F1), as did the other six Somatophylakes. His wounding in the town of the Mallians (Curt. 9.6.15ff.) is not reported by Arrian (Ptolemy), perhaps because, after Alexander's death, A. was a loyal supporter of Perdikkas (Curt. 10.6.16; cf. Errington 1969, 235–6); the golden crown awarded him at Sousa in 324 (Arr. 7.5.6) supports Curtius' claim. In 323, A.

espoused the Perdikkan cause (Curt. 10.6.16) and in 321/0 served as the commander-in-chief of the expedition against the Kypriot kings who had allied themselves with Ptolemy (Arr. *Succ.* 24.6). A. was apparently forced to surrender to Ptolemy's ally Antigonos. Antipatros, it appears, pardoned him and allowed him to return to Macedonia, perhaps on the understanding that he would retire to private life (cf. the case of Holkias, Polyaenus 4.6.6). In 319/8, A. joined Polyperchon, who had allied himself with Eumenes and the remnants of the Perdikkan party. Nothing is known of his role in the early stages of the war between Polyperchon and Kassandros, but in 316, when Olympias was forced to seek refuge in Pydna, A., on the Queen Mother's orders, took control of those troops who were still loyal to Alexander's house (Diod. 19.35.4). A. appears to have accomplished little: once Kassandros had prevailed over Aiakides of Epeiros and Polyperchon, both of whose armies were weakened by defections, A. thought it prudent to fall back on Amphipolis. This town he defended until early 315 (Diod. 19.50.3)—indeed, he had actually defeated Kassandros' general Krateuas at Bedyndia (19.50.7–8). He was induced by a letter of Olympias to surrender Amphipolis. Kassandros, although he pledged A. his safety (Diod. 19.50.8), feared him on account of his popularity, which he derived from his high position in Alexander's lifetime, and had him killed through the agency of some of the relatives of Krateuas (Diod. 19.51.1), though it is not clear if these represent the family of A.'s fellow Somatophylax Peithon son of Krateuas. Paschidis 448–9 plausibly identifies A. with the honorand of *IG* XII 9, 221 (cf. Knoepfler 2001, 185–95), who was awarded *proxenia*, and (less plausibly) as the *theorodokos* for the Nemaia between 321 and 317 (Paschidis 449 n.1). Berve II 69 no. 133; Kaerst, *RE* II.1 (1895) 967 no. 8; Badian, *BNP* I 1124 no. 3; Heckel 1992, 275–6; Heckel 1978d; Ziegler 1935, 379–80; Errington 1969, 235–6 and 240–1; Paschidis 448–9.

208 ARISTONYMOS

(Ἀριστώνυμος). An Athenian (Kirchner 2186) harp soloist who performed at the mass marriage festival in Sousa in 324 (Chares, *FGrH* 125 F4 = Athen. 12.538e). Apart from Klearchos' (*ap.* Athen. 10.452f) comment that A. was fond of riddles, nothing else is known about him. Kirchner, *RE* II.1 (1895) 968 no. 4; Berve II 75 no. 141.

ARISTOPHANES. See ARISTONOUS.

209 ARISTOTELES

(Ἀριστοτέλης). Athenian (Kirchner 2054). In 314, at the urging of Kassandros, Demetrios of Phaleron and Dionysios (who was in command of Mounychia) sent A. to Lemnos with twenty ships (Diod. 19.68.3). A. summoned Seleukos there and attempted to persuade the Lemnians to abandon their allegiance to Antigonos. When they refused, he put them under siege, but when Seleukos sailed away, A. was defeated, with the loss of most of his ships, by Dioskourides (no. 395; Diod. 19.68.4). A. himself appears to have escaped but he is not heard of again. Hauben 18–19 no. 6; Kirchner, *RE* II (1895) 1011 no. 7.

210 ARISTOTLE

(Ἀριστοτέλης). [All references in **boldface** are to Diogenes Laertius.] Eminent Greek philosopher, born in Stageira in Chalkidike. Son of Nikomachos and Phaistis. According to Timaios (codd. Timotheos), A. had a son by Herpyllis, his concubine, whose name was

Nikomachos (**5.1**; Athen. 13.589c). Aristotle was also a kinsman of Kallisthenes; both were honored with crowns at Delphi at some point between 337 and 327 (*Syll³* 275; R&O no. 80). The father had been a physician of Amyntas III, father of Philip II, and it appears that A. became familiar with the slightly younger prince during his stay in Pella. In 367, at the age of 17, A. left Macedonia for Athens and became a student of Plato, but he did not succeed his teacher as head of the Academy, the position going to Plato's kinsman Speusippos. A. and Xenokrates went to Asia Minor in 347 at the invitation of Hermeias, tyrant of Assos and Atraneus. Whether his departure from Athens was due to anti-Macedonian feeling there or bitterness over the appointment of Speusippos is unclear. Against the view that A.'s failure to secure the position was caused by his philosophical disagreements with Plato see Guthrie 1981, 24–6. The claim (**5.2**) that he left the Academy before Plato's death and was absent as an Athenian ambassador at Philip's Court when Xenokrates became its head may be an attempt to explain away A.'s "failure." **5.3** makes it clear that there was some bitterness over Xenokrates' appointment. In the Troad, A. married Pythias, the adopted daughter of Hermias (Strabo 13.1.57 C610, she was the daughter of Hermias' brother; cf. **5.4**). In 343 he was invited to Pella by Philip II to become, for the next two years, the tutor of Alexander (Plut. *Mor.* 327e, 604d; Plut. *Alex.* 7–8; Justin 12.16; Pliny, *HN* 8.44; Athen. 9.398e; Ael. *VH* 4.19; Quint 1.1.23; Dio Chrys. 49.4). Although Strabo 13.1.57 C610 claims that A. and Xenokrates escaped from the area when Memnon of Rhodes captured Hermias of Atarneus and sent him to the Great King to be executed, Hermeias' death did not occur until 341. The relationship between the great philosopher (though at the time A. had not yet earned that reputation) and the future world conqueror has captured the imagination of historians and philosophers since antiquity, but it appears that Alexander was not excessively influenced by his teacher's views and it is doubtful that A. considered his pupil an intellectual prodigy. A. later successfully petitioned Alexander to restore Stageira, which Philip had destroyed (Diod. 16.52.9), and drew up a law code for the city (**5.4**). According to Diogenes Laertius Aristotle made the appeal in Pella, and Hamilton 17 suggests plausibly that Alexander may have "interceded with Philip" on A.'s behalf. Plut. *Alex.* 7.3 says that the restoration of Stageira was Philip's payment for the education of Alexander. For the various accounts of the restoration see Plut. *Mor.* 1097b, 1126f; Ael. *VH* 3.17, 12.54; Dio Chrys. 2.79; 47.9; Val. Max. 5.6 ext. 5; Pliny, *HN* 7.109; Tzetz. *Chil.* 7.140, 441–5. A. inspired in Alexander a lifelong interest in literature and science (Plut. *Alex.* 8.1); and he is said to have produced an edition of the *Iliad* for him, later to become known as the "casket copy" (Plut. *Alex.* 8.2 = Onesikritos, *FGrH* 134 F38; Strabo 13.1.27 C594; cf. Plut. *Alex.* 26.2). He presented his nephew Kallisthenes (no. 570) to Alexander before his departure to Athens (Val. Max. 7.2 ext. 11; cf. *Suda* K 240). The execution of Kallisthenes by Alexander in 327 gave rise to later rumors that A. had been involved in a plot to poison the King (Plut. *Alex.* 77.3; Arr. 7.27.1); Plut. *Alex.* 55.7 says that in a letter to Antipatros, Alexander threatened to punish Aristotle for his connections with Kallisthenes and for recommending him (**5.10**). A friendship between A. and Antipatros is attested (Paus. 6.4.8; **5.11**, who says that, in the absence of Nikanor, Antipatros was to be executor of Aristotle's will; cf. Plut. *Alex.* 74.5) and it is possible that their relationship became closer as that between A. and Alexander deteriorated. **5.27** mentions nine books of letters to Antipatros. There are also letters to Hephaistion and Olympias from A., but only one book each. In 334 he returned to Athens, where he taught at the Lyceum, the walkway of which was the perfect place for teaching philosophy, whence he derived the name "Peripatetic" (**5.2**). He taught Phanias and Theophrastos of Eresos (cf. Strabo 13.2.4 C618) and Neleus, leaving his school and library to Theophrastos; Theophrastos in turn left the library to Neleus (Strabo 13.1.54 C608); Neleus later sold the library to Ptolemy II Philadelphos (Athen. 1.3a–b). In 322 he made his way to Chalkis on Euboia, where he ended his days (Strabo 10.1.11 C448). Eurymedon the hierophant (or Demophilos, according to Favorinus) charged him with *asebeia* (**5.5**). The impiety was that he wrote a hymn for Hermias and an inscription for his statue at Delphi. He died at Chalkis at the age of 70, drinking aconite (so Eumelos, in the fifth book of his history, cited by **5.6**), but Diogenes corrects this and says that A. died at age 63 and came to be Plato's student at seventeen (**5.6**). **5.1** gives a brief physical description of him: he spoke with a lisp, he had skinny legs and small eyes; he was conspicuous by his clothes and his rings, and his hair was cut short. Gercke, *RE* II.1 (1895) 1012–54 no. 18; Frede, *BNP* I 1136–46 no. 6; Berve II 70–4 no. 135; Squillace, *LexAM* 105–6. For a life of Aristotle see Diogenes Laertius 5.1– 35; the basic biographical information, from all ancient sources, is collected and discussed in Düring 1957 (see pp. 284–99 for Aristotle and Alexander). See also Chroust 1973 and Guthrie 1981 for his life and philosophy. See also *OCD*³ 165–9, with bibliography on 169.

211 ARKESILAOS

(Ἀρκεσίλαος). Macedonian, probably the father of Alkanor of Oropos (*IG* VII 4257, 10; Tataki 232 no. 84; cf. Hoffmann 202). A. received the satrapy of Mesopotamia in the settlement of 323 (Diod. 18.3.3; Justin 13.4.23; Dexippos = *FGrH* 100 F8 §6 calls him Archelaos). There is no mention of the satrapy during Alexander's lifetime (cf. Julien 27), but Leuze 1935, 460–2 may be right in assuming that it was detached from Babylonia when Mazaios was placed in charge of the latter. Hence A. may have administered Mesopotamia since 331/0. A. was perhaps deposed or forced to flee: in the Triparadeisos settlement (320), the satrapy was awarded to Amphimachos (Arr. *Succ.* 1.35; Diod. 18.39.6). His disappearance may be attributed to his support for Perdikkas. On the other hand, he may, like Archon in Babylon, have been removed by Dokimos (Arr. *Succ.* 24.3–5). Berve II 75 no. 142; Tataki 265 nos. 278–9; Julien 27; Kaerst, *RE* II (1896) 1164 no. 14.

212 ARKESILAOS

(Ἀρκεσίλαος). Painted portrait of Leosthenes and his sons. This was situated in the precinct of Zeus and Athena in the Peiraieus, or at least in a long portico near a marketplace for those who live by the sea (Paus. 1.1.3).

213 ARRHABAIOS

(Ἀρραβαῖος). Lynkestian. Son of Aëropos and brother of Heromenes and Alexander (Arr. 1.25). Apparently, the father of Amyntas (Arr. 1.12.7; rejected by Kaerst 1895, 1224) and Neoptolemos (Arr. 1.20.10; Bosworth I 109, 145 does not believe Neoptolemos was his son), and thus born no later than *c*.380. Executed, along with Heromenes, for their alleged complicity in the murder of Philip II (cf. Diod. 17.2.1; Justin 11.2.1–2). If there is any truth to the charge that they conspired against Philip, then it is most likely that they espoused the cause of Amyntas (IV), the son of Perdikkas III (Plut. *Mor.* 327c). Polyaenus 4.2.3 speaks of a commander (*hegemon*) in Philip's army named Aëropos who was banished for bringing a female harpist into camp during the Theban campaign (338). If it were possible to identify him with the father of A. and Heromenes, then we might have a motive for their enmity towards Philip and Alexander. Kaerst, *RE* II.1 (1895) 1224 no. 2; Berve II 80 no. 144; Bosworth 1971a. **Stemma XV.**

ARRHIDAIOS. See PHILIP.

214 ARRHIDAIOS

(Ἀρριδαῖος). Prominent Macedonian (Tataki 266 no. 282), possibly son of Alexander (*IG* XII.9 212) and perhaps the brother of Amphimachos (Arr. *Succ.* 1.35). He was present in Babylon when Alexander died, but we have no indication of whether he accompanied the King from the beginning of the campaign or joined the expedition in progress. A. was given the responsibility of conveying the King's corpse to Egypt (Diod. 18.3.5, 26.1; Justin 13.4.6), a task which he completed with the aid of Ptolemy (Diod. 18.28.2) despite Perdikkas' plan to bring the funeral carriage to Aigai (Paus. 1.6.3; Arr. *Succ.* 1.25), resisting the forces of Polemon and Attalos, who had been sent against him by Perdikkas (Arr. *Succ.* 1.25; 24.1). After the death of Perdikkas, A. and Peithon son of Krateuas were chosen *epimeletai* of the "Kings" by the army, primarily through the influence of Ptolemy (Diod. 18.36.6–7). But, after taking the remnants of the Perdikkan army to Triparadeisos in Syria (Diod. 18.39.1) and experiencing difficulties with Adea-Eurydike, they resigned their offices and Macedonians elected Antipatros in their place (Diod. 18.39.2). In the division of the satrapies at Triparadeisos, A. received Hellespontine Phrygia (Diod. 18.39.6; Arr. *Succ.* 1.37), in place of Leonnatos, who had died in the Lamian War. After the death of Antipatros in 319, A. feared the expansionist designs of Antigonos and sought to strengthen his satrapy and garrison its cities (Diod. 18.51.1). In the process he launched an attack on Kyzikos (*Marm. Par.* B12 = *FGrH* 239; cf. Athen. 11.509a), which resisted and gave Antigonos an excuse for interfering; when A. refused to withdraw from his satrapy, Antigonos sent forces against him (Diod. 18.51–2). A. took refuge with Kleitos of Lydia, who assumed control of some of his forces (Diod. 18.72.2–3), but after Kleitos' defeat and death in 317, A. may have come to terms with Antigonos. An Eretrian inscription honors an Arrhidaios son of Alexander in 303/2, a man who had served Antigonos and Demetrios (*IG* XII.9 212; cf. Billows 1993). But the identification is tenuous at best. Whether he is the Arrhidaios honored with citizenship in Ephesos in 316 (*I.Ephesos* 5 no. 1451) is unclear. Nor is it possible to determine if the "Arribbaios" of Polyaenus 7.30 refers to A. or what is the name of the city defended by Mempsis. Nothing else is known about him. Kaerst, *RE* II.1 (1895) 1249–50 no. 5; Berve II 80 no. 145; Billows 375 no. 18 and Billows 1993; Hoffmann 264–6.

215 ARSAKES

(Ἀρσάκης). Persian. In 330, Alexander appointed A. satrap of Aria after the defection of Satibarzanes (Arr. 3.25.7); how he came to be in Alexander's entourage is unclear. Drangiana was not placed under his authority (*pace* Julien 38–9; Jacobs 75); that office went to Arsames (no. 218 below). His performance was unsatisfactory, and Alexander had him arrested for shirking his responsibilities (ἐθελοκακεῖν, on which see Bosworth 1981, 20–1). Stasanor of Soloi, who was appointed in his place, brought A. in chains to Alexander at Baktra (Arr. 4.7.1; Mendoza Sanahuja 2017, 47). Berve II 80–1 no. 146; Shayegan 100–1 no. 18.

216 ARSAKES

(Ἀρσάκης). Indian hyparch, ruler of Hazara (= Urasa, the territory east of the Indos and directly north of the kingdom of Taxiles). The name appears to derive from the district he ruled, but Karttunen 35 n.81 cautions that it could be Iranian. A. appears to have been under the control of Abisares, king of the Kashmir (Abhisara), who lent support to the natives of Ora ('Ude-gram) and took in the refugees from the Swat and Buner regions (Arr. 4.27.7, 30.7; these fled directly across the river into Hazara). Bosworth II 359 considers A. "an independent princeling." Nothing is known of A. himself until he appears in Alexander's camp with Abisares' brother and other ambassadors from the Kashmir (Arr. 5.29.4). His territory was included by Alexander in the administrative sphere of Abisares (Arr. 5.29.5). Along with the kingdom of Kashmir, Urasa appears to have freed itself of Macedonian control soon after Alexander's return to the West. A. does not reappear in our sources. Meyer, *RE* II.1 (1895) 1269–70 no. 8; Berve II 81 no. 147.

217 ARSAMES

(Ἀρσάμης, Ἀρσαμένης. Pers. Arshama). Noble Persian, family background unknown. Satrap of Kilikia in 334/3. Diod. 17.19.4 calls him *satrapes* and Curt. 3.4.3 writes: *Arsames, qui Ciliciae praeerat*. But Leuze 1935, 248–9 argues that Diodorus' usage is imprecise, and that *satrapes = hyparchos* (cf. Mithrenes, the *phrourarchos* of Sardis, called *satrapes* by Diod. 17.21.7); A. was thus a lieutenant of Mazaios, who had been satrap of Kilikia under Artaxerxes III and to whose territories Syria was later added. A. fought with his cavalry on the left wing at the Granikos, along with Memnon the Rhodian (Diod. 17.19.4), and escaped from the battle to Kilikia, where he was unable to prevent the satrapy or the capital, Tarsos, from falling into Macedonian hands (Curt. 3.4.3–5 suggests that A.'s scorched earth policy caused the native defenders of the Kilikian gates to abandon their posts because A. was destroying the very territory they were defending). Arrian claims that A. had planned to put Tarsos to the torch but was prevented from doing so by the speedy arrival of the Macedonian troops (2.4.5–6; cf. Curt. 3.4.14). A. fled to Dareios (Arr. 2.4.6), who was at this time in Syria. He died on the battlefield of Issos (Arr. 2.11.8). Berve II 81–2 no. 149; Leuze 1935, 244ff.; Justi 29 "Arsames (7)"; Shayegan 101 no. 20.

218 ARSAMES

(Ἀρσάμης. Pers. Arshama; Justi 29). One of at least eleven sons of Artabazos, A. accompanied his father, his brothers, and ten sisters into exile in 349/8, finding refuge at the Court of Philip II (Diod. 16.52.4). Faithful to Dareios III, Artabazos and his sons joined him in flight after the battle of Gaugamela (331) but surrendered to Alexander (along with Autophradates) after the Great King's death in 330 (Arr. 3.23.7, naming three sons: A., Kophen, and Ariobarzanes; Curt. 6.5.4 gives no names but says there were nine in all). In 330/29, A. appears to have joined his father in the campaign against Satibarzanes (cf. Arr. 3.28.2). At that time, he was installed as satrap of Drangiana (Curt. 8.3.17; cf. 7.3.1, corrupt: the name is restored by Hedicke). Nothing is known about his activities as satrap, but his replacement by Stasanor of Soloi (Arr. 4.18.3; Curt. 8.3.17) was probably part of the removal of Artabazos' family from Central Asia to the West (Heckel 2018b). What became of him is unknown. Berve II 81 no. 148; Shayegan 101 no. 19.

219 ARSIMAS

(Ἀρσίμας. Justi 31). A Persian of unknown origin (perhaps one of the King's *syngeneis*, cf. Curt. 4.11.1); in early 332, while Alexander was at Marathos, A. and a certain Meniskos (who most likely acted as translator) delivered a letter from Dareios III to Alexander, asking for the return of his family (Arr. 2.14.1–3; cf. Curt. 4.1.8–10; Diod. 17.39.1–2; Plut. *Alex.* 29.7). A. and Meniskos were sent back to Dareios along with Thersippos, Alexander's *epistoleus*, their mission unfulfilled (Arr. 2.14.3–4; cf. Curt. 4.1.14). Nothing else is known about him. Berve II 82 no. 150. For the letter of Dareios to Alexander see Griffith 1968; Kaiser 1956; Bosworth I 227ff.; Shayegan 101 no. 21.

220 ARSINOË

(Ἀρσινόη). Daughter of Lysimachos (Paus. 1.7.3; Schol. Theocr. 17.128), though it is not certain by which wife. Nikaia appears the most likely mother (cf. Beloch IV² 2.130), if Arsinoë was not the daughter of a concubine (for example, the unnamed Odrysian who was mother of Alexander). The suggestion that she was the daughter of Arsinoë (Rohde 1914, 81) has been convincingly rejected (Macurdy 109; Bennett 2003, 65; Müller 2009, 91). Married Ptolemy II (before he became Philadelphos and perhaps at the beginning of his co-rule with Soter in 285, thus Beloch IV² 2.182 and Lund 104; Müller 2009, 90; but cf. Seibert 1967, 79 n.24: "Ebenso es kommt auch das Jahr 283 in Frage") and bore him three children: Lysimachos (cf. Polyb. 15.25.2, with Walbank, *HCP* 481), Berenike, and Ptolemy, the later Euergetes (Schol. Theocr. 17.128). Bennett (64) rightly calls her "the least visible of Ptolemaic queens." At some point before 275/4, Arsinoë was apprehended plotting with a certain Amyntas and Chrysippos, a Rhodian physician, against the life of the king. She was banished to Koptos. Whether there is any connection between the conspiracy (real or alleged) and Ptolemy's decision to marry his sister, Arsinoë II, cannot be determined (but see Carney 2013, 67–70). She is not heard of again. It is perhaps superfluous to note that Arsinoë, whom Justin 26.3.3, 7 names as the mother of Berenike of Kyrene, is a mistake by Pompeius Trogus or his epitomator (but see the lengthy discussion in Bennett 2003, 66–8). Beloch IV² 2.130, 182; *RE* II 1281–2 no. 25; Macurdy 109–11; Bennett 2003; Carney 2013, 67–70; Aulbach §6.3.1.1. **Stemmata IX and X.**

221 ARSINOË

(Ἀρσινόη). Macedonian (Tataki 267 no. 289). Daughter of Ptolemy I Soter and his mistress/wife Berenike (no. 293), she later married her full-blooded brother Ptolemy II (Paus. 1.7.1; cf. 1.8.6). Born *c.*316/15, she married Lysimachos soon after the battle of Ipsos (for marriageable age see Greenwalt 1988). Hence she became the stepmother of Agathokles (Justin 17.1.4–6) and Lysimachos' other children, including Arsinoë I, whom she later replaced as queen in Alexandria (Rohde 1914, 81 implausibly makes her A.'s daughter; see Macurdy 109; Bennett 2003, 65; Müller 2009, 91). Half-sister of Ptolemy Keraunos and Lysandra. A. was the mother of three sons by Lysimachos (Justin 17.2.6–8): Ptolemy, Lysimachos, and Philip. Anecdotal evidence suggests that she was not popular at the Thrakian court; Lund 16 and Carney 2013, 39 suggest that Demetrios' remark that a whore at his own court was more chaste than Lysimachos' "Penelope" is a reference to A. (Phylarchos, *FGrH* 81 F12 = Athen. 14.615a), but it is more likely that it was a reference to Nikaia (for Penelope was a "long suffering" wife, whereas Arsinoë was a relatively new bride;; see Bosworth 2002, 272–3; Rose 2015, 232). A certain Telesphoros was mutilated and caged by Lysimachos for making a joke at her expense (Athen. 14.616c; cf. Sen. *De Ira* 3.17.3–4, not specifying the nature of his offense). Soon after her marriage to Lysimachos, she was said to have resented her husband's relationship with Amastris and (according to Memnon 4.9, 5.3, whose view of A. is unfavorable) caused her to leave him. After Amastris' death (and Lysimachos' revenge upon her murderous sons; Memnon 5.2–3), she gained control of the city, which she ruled through her agent Herakleides of Kyme (Memnon 5.4–5; cf. Burstein, *Outpost* 86–7). In 283/2, fearing for her own children (the story that she acted out of vengeance when Agathokles rejected her sexual advances (Paus. 1.10.3) is nonsense), she contrived to murder Lysimachos' oldest son and heir apparent, Agathokles. Lysimachos was said to be either a party to this plan or powerless to stop the murder (Paus. 1.10.3–4), but it is hard to imagine that such an act could have been undertaken (publicly or in secret) without the father's assent. The actual murder was the work of a man named Ptolemy, probably A.'s own son (thus Heinen 3–17). The claim that Ptolemy Keraunos was the murderer (thus Memnon 5.6, who says that Lysimachos had failed to kill him with poison and therefore threw him into a prison where he was killed) is almost certainly wrong (see no. 1011). The catastrophic events in Lysimacheia led eventually to a confrontation between her husband and Seleukos, to whom Agathokles' widow had fled. While matters were being decided on the battlefield of Koroupedion (Feb. 281; the chronology see Heinen 94), A. was residing in Ephesos. Upon her husband's death, men were sent to kill the widow, but A. escaped by using a familiar stratagem: she dressed one of her attendants in royal robes and surrounded her with hypaspists, while she herself escaped in disguise to the harbor and fled home by sea (Polyaenus 8.57), apparently taking refuge in Kassandreia (Justin 24.2.1). The imposter was killed by the troops of Menekrates, but A. will hardly have been troubled by this loss of an innocent life. Seleukos did not enjoy his victory for long: in August or September 281, Keraunos murdered him and seized the Macedonian throne, portraying himself as Lysimachos' avenger (Justin 17.2.6). But, by seizing the throne, he usurped the rights of A.'s son Ptolemy, who remained hostile and sought help elsewhere. Over the winter 281/0, Keraunos prevailed upon his half-sister to marry him, swearing an oath on the altar of Zeus that was witnessed by A.'s agent, Dion, that he would recognize only her sons as his own, thus acknowledging their right to succeed (Justin 24.2.6–9). Justin's account is uniformly hostile to Keraunos and depicts A. as a victim (Hazzard 1999, 83), duped by her half-brother, who gained access to Kassandreia through the marriage and promptly murdered her two younger sons, Lysimachos and Philip (Justin 24.3.1–8). Although Justin creates the impression that the children were killed immediately after the wedding ceremony, this probably occurred much later, when it became clear to Keraunos that A.'s son Ptolemy was not going to become a pawn in his bid for power. Hence, there would have been a short period in which A. and Keraunos made a dedication to Delos (a golden shield bearing a thunderbolt: *I.Delos* 1417); Heinen 83–4 thinks the Ptolemy in question is Philadelphos, and indeed the thunderbolt alone does not prove the argument for Keraunos. After the murder of her sons, A. went into exile on Samothrake (Justin 24.3.9). In due course (perhaps as early as 279/8; though possibly as late as 276/5), A. came to the Egyptian court of her brother, Philadelphos, whom she married after her namesake (a daughter of Lysimachos and Nikaia) had been banished from the court (Schol. Theocr. 17.128; see above). The precise relationship of these events is unclear: we do not know if

Philadelphos banished his queen before or after A.'s arrival; nor do we know if A. was the cause of the rift between her brother and his first wife. The marriage was incestuous, but the union produced no children and, despite Sotades' scandalous remark (Athen. 624a; cf. Plut. *Mor.* 11a), which cost him his life, we may assume that it was a purely political affair, unaccompanied by sexual delights. A. adopted Ptolemy's children by his first wife (Schol. Theocr. 17.128) but she died not much later. Her only surviving son by Lysimachos was with her briefly in Egypt (no. 1013). Wilcken, *RE* II.1 (1895) 1282–7 no. 26; Bengtson 1975, 111–38; Burstein 1982a; Carney 2013; Longega 1968; Grainger, *SPG* 641; Hazzard 1999, 82–90; Ager 2005, 4–5; Dmitriev 2007; Müller 2009; Aulbach §6.3.1.2. **Stemmata IX and X.**

222 ARSITES

(Ἀρσίτης). Satrap of Hellespontine Phrygia (Arr. 1.12.8; *hyparchos = satrapes*, see Bosworth I 112) since at least 340 (Paus. 1.29.10, he sent an Athenian named Apollodoros with a mercenary force to defend Perinthos against Philip, perhaps on instructions from Artaxerxes III, thus Griffith, *HMac* II 563 n.2; Hofstetter 18 no. 23); father of Mithropastes (Nearchos, *FGrH* 133 F28 = Strabo 16.3.7 C767). A.'s territory included Paphlagonia, as is clear from his command of the Paphlagonian horse and from Curt. 3.1.22–4. A. took part in the war–council at Zeleia (Arr. 1.12.8) where he was foremost in opposing Memnon's scorched earth policy (Arr. 1.12.10), probably because the confrontation with the Macedonians occurred in his satrapy. At the Granikos, he commanded the Paphlagonian cavalry, stationed on the left wing, just to the right of Arsames and Memnon (Diod. 17.19.4). He fled from the battlefield at the Granikos but committed suicide soon afterwards because the blame for the disaster seemed to fall on his shoulders (Arr. 1.16.3), since the defeat occurred in his territory. I can find no support for the view of Cook 1983, 226 that "he may have been responsible for the failure to throw the Greek mercenary corps into the fight." His successor in the satrapy was Kalas son of Harpalos. Kaerst, *RE* II.1 (1895) 1290; Berve II 82 no. 151; Shayegan 101 no. 22.

223 ARTABAZOS

(Ἀρτάβαζος). Son of Pharnabazos (the famous satrap of Hellespontine Phrygia) and the Achaimenid princess Apama (Plut. *Artox.* 27.4; Xen. *HG* 5.1.28, Xen. *Ages.* 3.3; cf. Plut. *Alex.* 21.9; *IG* II² 356 = Tod II 199 = R&O no. 98; see Curt. 3.13.13; 5.9.1; and Arr. 3.23.7 for his importance at the Persian court). Born *c.*387, or possibly as early as *c.*391 (thus Brunt 1975, 24 n.3; Curt. 6.5.3 claims that A. was 94 years old in 330. This is rightly rejected by Berve II 82). The history of the so-called Great Satraps' Revolt is fraught with problems, which cannot be discussed here (see Hornblower 1982 and Weiskopf, *passim*; cf. Krumbholz 73–5; Judeich 204ff.). About A. himself, we can say that he was initially a supporter of his grandfather Artaxerxes II, who sent him as *strategos* against the rebel Datames in Kappadokia (Diod. 15.91, with Stylianou 1998, 541–3; the campaign is dated by Diodorus to 362/1 but probably belongs to 359) and installed him as satrap in Daskyleion, in place of Ariobarzanes. A. did, however, rebel against royal authority, supported first by Chares (356/5) and then Pammenes the Theban (353/2); in 352 he fled to the court of Philip (Diod. 16.52.3–4, under the year 349/8; cf. Curt 5.9.1; 6.5.2), where he remained an exile until perhaps the mid-to-late 340s. He had fathered eleven sons and ten daughters by the same woman (Diod. 16.52.4; cf. Curt. 6.5.4, who mentions nine sons by the same mother who were with A. in 330; see **A2–8, 9–14**). The woman captured in Damaskos (**A37**), along with her young son Ilioneus (Curt. 3.13.13), was (*pace* Berve II 83) probably not the Rhodian wife. A. was a staunch supporter of Dareios (Curt. 5.9.1) and in 330 attempted to defuse the tension between the king and Nabarzanes and Bessos (Curt. 5.9.12–13, 17; 5.10.10–11). But although he remained vigilant in his defense of Dareios (Curt. 5.12.7–8), he could not prevent Bessos from arresting the king and chose instead to abandon the camp with his followers and seek refuge in the Elburz mountains (Curt. 5.12.18; Arr. 3.21.4). He surrendered to Alexander in Hyrkania (Curt. 6.5.2–6; Arr. 3.23.7), along with nine of his sons (Curt. 6.5.3–4; Arr. 3.23.7 names only three of them). He no doubt expected a favorable reception at Alexander's hands, since his daughter Barsine was at this point the King's mistress. A. was soon sent with Erigyios, Karanos, and Andronikos against the rebel Satibarzanes in Aria (Arr. 3.28.2; Curt. 7.3.2). In 329 he was appointed satrap of Baktria (Arr. 3.29.1). Curt. 7.11.29 says that A. was left in charge of the captured Rock of Ariamazes, thus extending his administrative area into Sogdiana. In 328, when Alexander divided his mobile troops and conducted a sweep of Baktria-Sogdiana, A. was attached to Hephaistion's third of the army (Curt. 8.1.10; cf. 8.1.1); Arr. 4.16.2–3 says there were five sections and that A. joined Koinos, moving against the Skythians who had given refuge to Spitamenes. A year later he asked to be excused from this office on account of old age (Curt. 8.1.19; Arr. 4.17.3). Alexander replaced him with Kleitos (Curt. 8.1.19), and after Kleitos' death with Amyntas son of Nikolaos (Arr. 4.17.3). A. is not heard of again. Judeich, *RE* II.1 (1895) 1299–1300 no. 3; Berve II 82–4 no. 152; Weiskopf 54–64; Krumbholz 1883, 73–5; Briant 2008, 151–5; Shayegan 101–2 no. 23; Heckel 2018b. **Stemma IV**.

224 ARTAKAMA

(Ἀρτακάμα). Daughter of Artabazos (Arr. 7.4.6; cf. Arr. *ap.* Phot. *Bibl.* 68b; Plut. *Eum.* 1.7 calls her Apama; Strabo 12.8.15 C578 confuses her with the daughter of Spitamenes). Tarn 1921, 26 assumes that Artakama is the correct form—observing that "presumably Ptolemy knew his wife's name"—and that the form Apama was mistakenly given by Douris of Samos (whom Tarn regards as the source of Plut. *Eum.* 1.7). Aristoboulos (*FGrH* 139 F52) appears to have been the source of the information for the marriage of Alexander to Parysatis, but it appears that the list of brides and bridegrooms was probably recorded by both of Arrian's primary sources (Kornemann 1935, 90; Brunt II 212–13 n.4; Hammond 1993, 284 n.14). Brosius 185 believes that Apama may have been her official name. It is, however, typical of Aristoboulos to supply alternative forms of both personal and place names. A. was one of ten girls born to the sister of Mentor and Memnon the Rhodians (Diod. 16.52.4; cf. Dem. 23.154, 157). Since Artabazos and his family sought refuge at the court of Philip II at some time after 353/2, and certainly before 344 (thus Griffith, *HMac* II 484 n.5), A.'s birth occurred, in all likelihood, between 355 and 345, since she will scarcely have been much older than thirty when she married in 324. Soon after 341, she returned to Asia with her family, and it may be that, in late 333, she was captured by Parmenion at Damaskos, where the families of the noble Persians had been sent for safety (cf. Curt. 3.13.12–14, naming her sister Barsine, her stepmother, and her half-brother, Ilioneus; cf. also Arr. 2.11.9; Diod. 17.32.3). If she and her sister Artonis were among the captives, they may have been taken by the Macedonians as far as Sousa (cf. Diod. 17.67.1), where, in 324, she married Ptolemy son of Lagos (Plut. *Eum.* 1.7; Arr. 7.4.6). It is assumed that Ptolemy repudiated her after Alexander's death (cf. Bouché-

Leclercq, *Lagides* 1.7 n.1), but there is no direct evidence to this effect. On the other hand, it is difficult to see what advantages Ptolemy would have gained from retaining a Persian bride in a land that resented Persian rule (Müller 2013, 203–6). What became of her is unknown. Judeich, *RE* II.1 (1895) 1303; Wilcken, *RE* I 2662 no. 2 "Apame"; Berve II 52 no. 97 "Apame"; Brosius 78, 185; Müller 2013; Van Oppen 2014, 30–1; Shayegan 99 no. 9; Aulbach §6.2.1.3 "Apama." **Stemma IV.**

225 ARTEMIOS

(Ἀρτέμιος). A Greek of unknown family, from Kolophon. In summer or autumn 328, he was present at the banquet in Marakanda at which Kleitos was murdered by the King (Plut. *Alex.* 51.4). Schubert may be right in suggesting that either Artemios or Xenodochos (no. 1159) was the eyewitness source from which Chares (if he was not himself present) drew his information. Berve's rejection of Schubert's view (1898, 109), that Artemios and Xenodochos may have arrived recently from the west with the caravan that brought also fresh fruit from the Mediterranean, as "grotesk" (followed by Hamilton 142) strikes me as less so. Berve II 84 no. 153; Schubert 1898, 99ff.

226 ARTIBOLES

(Ἀρτιβόλης). Son of Mazaios and, apparently, a Babylonian wife. Alexander enrolled him in the Companion Cavalry in 324 (Arr. 7.6.4), along with his brother Hydarnes. The view that he is identical with the son who surrendered to Alexander in 330 (Arr. 3.21.1: Ἀντίβηλος. Curt. 5.1.17: *Brochubelus*) is remotely possible, but would force us to postulate a series of textual errors. Berve II 84 no. 154; Bosworth I 341; Shayegan 102 no. 24.

227 ARTONIS

(Ἀρτῶνις, Ἀρτώνη). Arr. *ap.* Phot. *Bibl.* cod. 91, p. 68b; for the name see Justi 40. The daughter of Artabazos (Arr. 7.4.6; Plut. *Eum.* 1.7), A. was one of ten girls born to the sister of Mentor and Memnon the Rhodians (Diod. 16.52.4; cf. Dem. 23.154, 157). Since Artabazos and his family sought refuge at the court of Philip II at some time after 353/2, and certainly before 344 (for the date see s.v. Artakama no. 224), her birth must have occurred between 355 and 345; for she will scarcely have been much older than thirty when she married in 324. Soon after 341, she returned to Asia with her family, and it may be that, in late 333, she was captured by Parmenion at Damaskos, where the families of the noble Persians had been sent for safety (cf. Curt. 3.13.12–14, naming her sister Barsine, her stepmother, and her half-brother, Ilioneus; cf. also Arr. 2.11.9; Diod. 17.32.3). If she and her sister Artakama were among the captives, they may have been taken by the Macedonians as far as Sousa (cf. Diod. 17.67.1), where, in 324, she married Eumenes (Plut. *Eum.* 1.7; Arr. 7.4.6; Phot. *Bibl.* 68b). The remains of Eumenes' body were given to his wife and children, apparently, A. and her children (Plut. *Eum* 19.2), though, given the age of Eumenes, this could refer to the family Eumenes left behind when he went to Asia in 334. Judeich, *RE* II.2 (1896) 1460; Berve II 84–5 no. 155; Brosius 78; Shayegan 102 no. 25. **Stemma IV.**

228 ARYBBAS

(Ἀρύββας, Diod. 16.72.1: Ἀρύμβας). Member of the Molossian royal house. Born in the 390s at the latest, A. was a son of Alketas I (Plut. *Pyrrh.* 1; Paus. 1.11.1), perhaps by an earlier wife than the one who bore his brother Neoptolemos. A. bears the name (in a slightly different form) of his paternal grandfather Tharyps (Tharypas), which suggests that he was older than Neoptolemos, who was named Alketas' successor. A. challenged his brother's right to the throne and received a share of the kingdom (Paus. 1.11.3). The brothers ruled jointly until some point before 357, in which year he gave Neoptolemos' daughter to Philip II in marriage (Justin 7.6.10–11; cf. Plut. *Alex.* 2.2), a clear indication that Neoptolemos was no longer alive. A. married his brother's daughter Troas (sister of Olympias and Alexander I of Epeiros), thus consolidating his claim to the throne (Paus. 1.11.3; Justin 7.6.11; Plut. *Pyrrh.* 1). A. banished his son by an earlier wife, Alketas II, on account of his uncontrollable temper (Diod. 19.88.1; cf. Paus. 1.11.5), though perhaps in the interest of securing the succession for Aiakides, his only attested child by Troas. Aiakides himself was the father of Pyrrhos (Plut. *Pyrrh.* 1.5; Diod. 16.72.1). A. was sole ruler until 342—a reference to an Illyrian campaign (Front. *Strat.* 2.5.19) cannot be dated—when he was driven into exile by Philip II, who placed Alexander I on the throne (Justin 7.6.12; 8.6.7; Diod. 16.72.1 confuses his exile with his death, saying he ruled for only ten years; *IG* II² 226 = Tod II 173 = R&O no. 70; the date of his exile is challenged by Errington 1975a; cf. also Heskel 1988). How long A. lived after 342/1 is difficult to say (Justin 7.6.12 says *in exilio consenuit*). An attempt to identify him with Aryptaios (Diod. 18.11.1), who joined the Hellenic cause in the Lamian War (Μολοττῶν οἱ περὶ Ἀρυπταῖον), is unlikely (suggested by Reuss 1881, 172; cf. Hammond, *Epirus* 561; the idea was rejected by Schubert 1894, 108; cf. Errington 1975a, 46; see below s.v. no. 230). Kaerst, *RE* II.2 (1896) 1495–7 no. 1; Reuss 1881; Errington 1975a; Heskel 1988; Heckel 2021. **Stemma IIa.**

229 ARYBBAS

(Ἀρύββας). For the name see Hoffmann 177. Probably of Epeirot origin (hence, not listed in Tataki) and, to judge from his high standing at the Macedonian court, a member of the Molossian royal house (i.e., a relative of Olympias, and thus also related to the *archihypaspistes* Neoptolemos). A. was one of the seven Somatophylakes, possibly appointed to that office by Philip II, who may have sought some type of regional representation. He died of illness in Egypt in the winter of 332/1 and was replaced as Somatophylax by Leonnatos (Arr. 3.5.5). Kaerst, *RE* II.2 (1896) 1497 no. 2; Berve II 85 no. 156; Heckel 1992, 261; Hoffmann 176–7.

230 ARYPTAIOS

(Ἀρυπταῖος). Leader of a Molossian contingent that fought against Antipatros in the Lamian War but soon went over to the Macedonian side (Diod. 18.11.1). He has been identified, implausibly, with Arybbas (the Molossian king who was exiled by Philip II in 342 and took refuge in Athens: *IG* II² 226; thus Reuss 1881, 172; followed by Hammond, *Epirus* 561; rejected by Schubert 1894, 108; Errington 1975a, 46). Despite Hammond's claim (561), the name is not "a *common* variant of the name Arybbas" (this is the only occurrence of the name), and the theory (based on Diod. 18.11.1) that the Molossians recalled Arybbas in 323 is tenuous at best and creates more historical problems than it solves. If Aryptaios was indeed identical with Arybbas, he must have led a disaffected group of Molossians (οἱ περὶ Ἀρυπταῖον could simply mean "those who were of the Arybbas faction," i.e. supporters of his branch of the family) but gained nothing from his betrayal of the Epeirots. It is more likely that Aryptaios was a different individual, possibly a scion of the royal house. What became of him is unknown. Reuss 1881; Schubert 1894, 108; Kaerst, *RE* II.2 (1896) 1498; Errington 1975a; Hammond, *Epirus* 561; Heckel 2021.

231 ARYSES

('Ἀρύσης). Brother of Ariarathes II (Diod. 31.19.3–5), who gained the kingdom of Kappadokia in 301. He survived the death of his father, Orophernes, which occurred shortly before Alexander's conquest of the Persian Empire. If he lived to see Kappadokia annexed by Perdikkas in 322, he may have accompanied his brother into exile in Armenia (see Ardoastes and Ariarathes). Nothing else is known about him.

232 ASANDROS

("Ασανδρος). Macedonian (Tataki 271–2 no. 313). Son of Philotas (Arr. 1.17.7). Berve II 87, followed by Badian 1960, 329 (and consequently many others; e.g. Cartledge 2004, 97), identifies Asandros son of Philotas as the brother of the great general, Parmenion (Welles 1970, 39, calling him Parmenion's cousin, could be closer to the truth; for arguments against the identification see Heckel 1977a and 1992, 385; cf. Bosworth I 130). Asandros was appointed satrap of Lydia (Arr. 1.17.7) and, later, together with Ptolemy (Polemaios, a brother of Antigonos the One-Eyed by Billows 425–6 no. 99), defeated Orontobates (Arr. 2.5.7, with Bosworth I 195–6). In 331, he was replaced as satrap by Menandros (Arr. 3.6.7) and rejoined Alexander in the Upper Satrapies (Curt. 7.10.12, wrongly stating that he came from "Lykia"). He may be identical with the Κάσανδρος of Diod. 17.17.4 (almost certainly an error for Ἀσανδρος), if this man is not the son of Agathon. Adams 1984 argues that this cavalry commander is Kassandros son of Antipatros, but such an appointment would be inconsistent with the rest of that man's career. What became of Asandros son of Philotas is unknown. Kaerst, *RE* II (1896) 1515 no. 2; Berve II 87 no. 165; Bosworth I 130; Heckel 1992, 385.

233 ASANDROS

("Ασανδρος). Son of Agathon, Macedonian from Beroia (Tataki 76 no. 16); he had some family relationship with Antigonos the One-Eyed (Arr. *Succ.* 25.1); Kaerst's suggestion (*RE* 1896, 1516) that he may have been a relative of Parmenion is highly unlikely. Brother of Agathon. Satrap of Karia in 323 (Arr. *Succ.* 1.6; Dexippos, *FGrH* 100 F8 §2; Curt. 10.10.2; Diod. 18.3.1; but the reading of the MSS is consistently Κάσανδρος; *Syll*³ 311.2–3; cf. *LM* 117). Asandros is also attested in inscriptions in Asia Minor: *SEG* XXVI (1976/77) 1228; *SEG* XXXIII (1983) 872; *Syll*³ 272. Attended the dinner party of Medeios but was ignorant of the plot against Alexander (Metz, *LM* 97–8); awarded Karia in the forged *Testamentum Alexandri* (Metz, *LM* 117). In 321/0 he received Antigonos on his return from Europe, thus defecting from the Perdikkan cause (Arr. *Succ.* 25.1), but nothing further is known of his actions in the First Diadoch War. He was confirmed in his satrapy at Triparadeisos in 320 (Arr. *Succ.* 1. 37; Diod. 18. 39. 6, text has Καρίαν δ' Κασάνδρῳ), but he fared poorly in an indecisive battle against Alketas and Attalos in the winter of 320/19 (Arr. *Succ.* 1.41; Wheatley 1995, 437; cf. Justin 13.6.14). Intimidated by the growing power of Antigonos, he joined Ptolemy in 315 (Diod. 19.62.2), who sent Myrmidon (no. 759) with mercenaries to give him aid against Antigonos' rebellious nephew Polemaios (Diod. 19.62.5); those forces appear to have accomplished little. Asandros crossed to Athens and was honored by a decree of Thrasykles son of Nausikrates for providing ships and soldiers

(*Syll*³ 320, lines 12–13; O'Sullivan 1997, speculative). With the aid of Kassandros, who sent his general Prepelaos (no. 993) back to Asia Minor with him (Diod. 19.68.5), he attempted to overcome the Antigonid forces by sending Eupolemos (no. 449) against Polemaios (winter 313/12). But Eupolemos was captured by Polemaios, who fell unexpectedly on his camp (Diod. 19.68.5–7). Asandros was thus forced to make peace with Antigonos: he surrendered his troops to Antigonos, relinquished his claims to the Greek cities of Karia and surrendered his brother Agathon as a hostage to his new overlord (Diod. 19.75.1–2). Regretting this decision, he secured Agathon's escape and turned to Ptolemy and Seleukos for help (Diod. 19.75.2). They appear to have been unable (or unwilling) to do much on his behalf: Antigonos invaded his territory, and Asandros is not heard of again. Berve II 87 no. 164; Kaerst, *RE* II.2 (1896) 1515–16 no. 3; O'Sullivan 1997.

234 ASKLEPIADES

(Ἀσκληπιάδης). Athenian (Kirchner 2590). Son of Hipparchos. Allegedly the first to bring the news of Alexander the Great's death to the Athenians (Plut. *Phoc.* 22.5–6). Berve II 87 no. 166 and *RE* Supplbd IV (1924) 50.

235 ASKLEPIADES

(Ἀσκληπιάδης). Of Byzantion. Clearly a supporter of Demetrios and Antigonos (τοὺς βασιλεῖς), A. was honored by the Athenians with a statue (to be set up in his native city) but not citizenship in the period 307/6–304/3 (*IG* II² 555). Billows 375–6 no. 19.

236 ASKLEPIADES

(Ἀσκληπιάδης). Greek or possibly Macedonian of unknown family. Served as either a general of Demetrios Poliorketes in Attika c.303/2 or as an elected *strategos* of the Athenians. A. appointed a certain Apollonios (no. 154) garrison commander in Rhamnous. Unless he is identical with A. of Byzantion (no. 235), he is otherwise unknown. Paschidis 112, with n.4.

237 ASKLEPIODOROS

(Ἀσκληπιόδωρος). Son of Eunikos. Prominent Macedonian (Tataki 273 no. 318), apparently from Pella. Father of the Page Antipatros (Arr. 4.13.4; Curt. 8.6.9 mistakenly writes *Antipatrum Asclepiodorumque*). Asklepiodoros first joined Alexander in 331, when he brought 500 Thrakian cavalry to the King at Memphis. He was later appointed satrap of Syria (Arr. 4.13.4), probably replacing Menon son of Kerdimmas (Arr. 3.6.8 speaks of "Arimmas"). In 329 he relinquished this position to bring 4,000 infantry and 500 cavalry to the King in Zariaspa (Baktra; Arr. 4.7.2; Curt. 7.10.12). In early 327, Asklepiodoros' son Antipatros became involved in the conspiracy of the pages (Arr. 4.13.4; cf. Curt. 8.6.9). The disgrace does not appear to have affected Asklepiodoros' career: he reappears as a trierarch of the Hydaspes fleet in 326 (Arr. *Ind.* 18.3). Arr. *Ind.* 18.3 = Nearchos, *FGrH* 133 F1 should perhaps read: Λεοννάτος ὁ <Ἀντέου καὶ Ἀσκληπιόδωρος ὁ> Εὐν<ίκ>ου (thus Jacoby *FGrH* IIB 681, IID "Kommentar," 450). This solves the problem of Leonnatos' incorrect patronymic (Εὔνου); cf. Heckel 1992, 371. What became of him we do not know. Kaerst, *RE* II.2 (1896) 1636 no. 5; Berve II 88 no. 167.

238 ASKLEPIODOROS

(Ἀσκληπιόδωρος). Son of Timandros, a Macedonian from Pella (Tataki 152 no. 26), trierarch of the Hydaspes fleet in 326 (Arr. *Ind.* 18.3). Identification of his father with the hypaspist commander who distinguished himself at Halikarnassos (Arr. 1.22.7) is improbable, since hypaspist commanders were generally men of lower rank and the trierarchs were clearly men of means. If there is indeed a textual corruption involving Asklepiodoros son of Eunikos, it may also have affected the reading Ἀσκληπιόδωρος ὁ Τιμάνδρου. Timandros may be a corruption of Timanthes, which appears in the following line, or the name of Timandros' son (whatever it was) may have dropped out of the text. Identification of the general of Kassandros (thus Berve II 88) and also the man sent as an ambassador to the Phokians, honored in *IG* II² 367 with the son of Timandros is a remote possibility at best. Kaerst, *RE* II.2 (1896) 1636 no. 7; Berve II 88 no. 168; Jacoby, *FGH* IIB, 681; IID, 450.

239 ASKLEPIODOROS

(Ἀσκληπιόδωρος). Son of Philon (Arr. 3.16.4), place of origin unknown. Possibly Macedonian (Tataki 273 no. 319); perhaps Greek. Left behind in Babylon in late 331 and placed in charge of collecting tribute (Arr. 3.16.4). Billows 376 identifies him with the man whom Antigonos established as satrap of Persis (316/5), in the face of Persian opposition (see s.v. Thespios no. 1120), in place of the popular Peukestas (Diod. 19.48.5). Asklepiodoros is otherwise unattested. What became of him after Seleukos' recovery of Babylonia is unknown. Berve II 88 no. 169; Kaerst, *RE* II.2 (1896) 1636 no. 6 (cf. no. 9); Billows 376 no. 20.

240 ASKLEPIODOROS

(Ἀσκληπιόδωρος). Macedonian (Tataki 272 no. 317). Arrian calls him *grammateus*, hence probably secretary of the "Royal Army" that withdrew to Triparadeisos after the death of Perdikkas. In the turmoil that followed the resignation of the *epimeletai*, Peithon and Arrhidaios, he supported Eurydike, who incited the army against the newly appointed guardian, Antipatros. In this she was aided also by Attalos son of Andromenes (Arr *Succ* 1.33). A.'s fate is uncertain: if he reached an accommodation with Antipatros, he may be the later general of Kassandros (see below); otherwise, since the rioting initiated by A. placed Antipatros' very life in peril (cf. Polyaenus 4.6.4), he may have been executed, if he did not escape from the camp. Kaerst, *RE* II.2 (1896) 1636 no. 8.

241 ASKLEPIODOROS

(Ἀσκληπιόδωρος). General of Kassandros. In 315 he besieged Amisos (*Barr. Atl.* 87 B3). It was relieved by Polemaios (no. 968), the general and nephew of Antigonos, who recovered the satrapy of Kappadokia and dismissed A. under truce (Diod. 19.60.2). Kaerst, *RE* II.2 (1896) 1636 no. 10 (wrongly "Strateg des Asandros").

242 ASPEISAS

(Ἀσπείσας. Ἀσπίσας: Diodorus). A native of Sousiana (perhaps Elamite, thus Billows 376–7; cf. Hornblower, *Hieronymus* 116). In the archonship of Praxiboulos (315/14), Antigonos left Aspeisas as satrap of Sousiana (Diod. 19.55.1), the satrapy assigned at Triparadeisos to

Antigenes. Billows 376 notes that "Diodorus' report … is confirmed by the finding of Asiatic posthumous Alexander coins bearing on the reverse the legend ΑΣΠΕΙΣΟΥ." He was doubtless deposed after Seleukos' recovery of Babylonia, and possibly executed. Nothing else is known about him. Billows 376–7 no. 21.

243 ASSAGETES

(Ἀσσαγέτης, Ashvajit). A local chieftain of the Assakenians; probably hyparch of a small region south of Aornos (Pir-sar) and along the western banks of the Indos River (Arr. 4.28.6). Together with Kophaios, A. accompanied Alexander to Aornos, though we know of no role that he played in the campaign (Arr. 4.28.6). He is most likely to have been the hyparch of the Assakenians, whose assassination by his own people was reported by Sisikottos to Alexander at some point after the battle of the Hydaspes (Arr. 5.20.7). Berve II 89 suggests this identification. But elsewhere (II 276) he identifies the hyparch of the Assakenians with Nikanor (no. 783). For discussion see Bosworth II 321–2. Berve II 89 no. 171.

244 ASSAKENOS

(Ἀσσακηνός). Indian dynast; leader of the Assakenians, whose kingdom centered on the area between the Panjkora (Gouraios) and Swat rivers; see also Karttunen 33. Caroe 1962: 52, locates Massaga (Mazaga; Mesoga) in "the Katgala Pass between the valleys of Talash and Adinzai, about eight miles north of Chakdarra on the present road to Dir"; cf. Eggermont 178. Massaga thus lies on the road leading to Bir-Kot (Bazeira) and ʻUde-gram (Ora). The Assakenians were identified with the Aspasians (cf. Lassen II² 145 n.2; *CHIndia* I 316 n.1), and Berve II 89 assumes that the *hyparchos* of the Aspasians, who opposed the Macedonians at a certain river (there is a lacuna in the text of Arr. 4.24.1, and we know the name of neither the river nor the city referred to), is A. (Curt. 8.10.22 says that he had died shortly before Alexander's arrival at Massaga; hence he cannot have been the *hegemon* of the troops at Massaga, Arr. 4.27.2). But Arrian makes a distinction between the Aspasians (4.24.1), the Gouraians (4.25.7) and the Assakenians (4.25.5; 4.26), and it seems far from certain that the leader of the Aspasians, who was killed in hand-to-hand combat with Ptolemy son of Lagos was A. (Arr. 4.24.3–5). When Alexander attacked Massaga, the capital of the Assakenians (so Curt. 8.10.22; Strabo 15.1.27 C698 (Masoga); Arr. 4.26.1 calls it the greatest city of that region), A. was already dead, and the kingdom was governed by his mother Cleophis (Curt. 8.10.22; Metz Epit. 39, she was aided by his brother Amminais). Cleophis and her granddaughter (Metz Epit. 39, 45, grandson) were captured along with the city (Arr. 4.27.4; Curt. 8.10.33–5 is somewhat different, and the child is Cleophis' *own son*; cf. Metz Epit. 39, 45). Berve II 89 no. 172; Eggermont 178, 183–5; cf. Tomaschek, *RE* II.2 (1896) 1740–1 s.v. "Assakenoi."

245 ASTASPES

(Ἀστάσπης). Prominent Persian, satrap of Karmania. A. was probably satrap under Dareios III and was confirmed by Alexander in 330; for the King did not visit the area until his return from India. In early 324 he was suspected of plotting rebellion, and executed (Curt. 9.10.21, 29). For the turmoil following his execution see Arr. *Ind.* 36.8. His successor was Tlepolemos. Berve II 89 no. 173; Badian 2000a: 90–1; cf. Heckel 2017a; Shayegan 102 no. 26.

246 ASTIS

(Ἄστις). The name appears thus in the MSS of Arrian; Astes (Berve no. 691) is the emendation of B. Vulcanius (1575); Sanskrit "Hasti" (Smith[3] 50); but Rapson, *CHIndia* 318, suggests that the name "is short for Ashtakaraja, king of the Ashtakas," which is more likely, if Astis, like Taxiles and Assakenos, was a dynastic name. Hyparch of Peukelaotis (Peukolaitis, Strabo 15.1.27 C698, that is, the territory of Gandhara, of which Pushkalavati was the capital) ruler of the Astakenians; he resisted the Macedonian advance party under the command of Hephaistion and Perdikkas and held out in an unnamed city in his territory, which fell to the Macedonians after a siege of thirty days. This was probably his own capital (modern Charsadda, thus Rapson, *CHIndia* I 318: Pushkalavati). Berve II 90, following Anspach I 90 n.36, and Droysen I[2] 2.114 assumes that Orobatis (Arr. 4.28.5) is the city at which A. was killed. Anspach points out that Alexander himself captured Peukelaotis, but Arr. 4.28.6 probably refers to the formal surrender to Alexander of the city already subdued by Hephaistion and Perdikkas (cf. Eggermont 1970, 71–4, identifying Orobatis with Shahbazgarhi). For Peukelaotis as the site of A.'s defeat, see now Badian 1987. Pushkalavati (Charsadda) had replaced Peshawar as the capital of Gandhara (Caroe 1962, 48). A. himself perished in the defense and his territory was handed over to Sangaios (apparently a local noble), who had rebelled from his authority (Arr. 4.22.8). Peukelaotis, upon formal surrender to Alexander, was garrisoned by Macedonians under the command of Philip (Arr. 4.28.6). Anspach (I 13; cf. Berve II 90) supposes that A. was originally among the hyparchs who submitted to Alexander along with Taxiles (Arr. 4.22.6), but it appears that Taxiles was accompanied by Sangaios, a rival of A. who sought, with Taxiles' aid, to win Macedonian backing for his cause. Hence A.'s opposition to the forces of Hephaistion and Perdikkas (cf. Brunt I 415 n.7). Berve II 89–90 no. 174; Anspach I 13–14; Lassen II[2] 135; Eggermont 1970, 68–75; Badian 1987.

247 ASTYKRATIDAS

(Ἀστυκρατίδας). Prominent Spartan (Poralla no. 168). Lived at the time of Agis III's death at Megalopolis in 331 (whether he participated in the battle is not clear). One saying of his is preserved by Plut. *Mor.* 219b, expressing the Spartans' determination to die rather than be enslaved by Macedon. Berve II 90 no. 175.

248 ASTYLOS

(Ἀστύλος). Arkadian *strategos*. The Thebans, unable to persuade the Arkadians to abandon their alliance with Alexander, hoped to gain their help by bribing Astylos (according to Din. 1.20, the orator Stratokles had also commented on A.'s susceptibility to bribes, but this is a rhetorical *topos*), who demanded ten talents. This money the Thebans did not have, and Din. 1.20 claims that Demosthenes, who had the money from Persia, would not part with it (Din. 1.20; cf. Aesch. 3.240 who mentions nine talents). Nothing else is known about him. Berve II 90 no. 176; Schaefer III[2] 133; Worthington 163–4.

249 ATALANTE

(Ἀταλάντα, Ἀταλάντη). Macedonian (Tataki 204–5 no. 6). Daughter of Orontes from Orestis; sister of Perdikkas and Alketas. A. married Attalos son of Andromenes in 323 and appears to have borne him two daughters (Diod. 19.35.5; **A90–1**). The marriage was most likely arranged in Babylon to seal a political friendship between Perdikkas and Attalos (Heckel 1992, 381–4). A. accompanied her brother on his expedition against Ptolemy in 321/0, only to be murdered along with him (Diod. 18.37.2). Her death was a savage and, almost certainly, spontaneous act by the Macedonian soldiery and not, as Granier 1931, 72 suggests, the result of a decision by the army assembly. Berve II 90 no. 177; Heckel 1992, 381–4; Kaerst, *RE* II.2 (1896) 1894–5 no. 5. **Stemma XII**.

250 ATARRHIAS

(Ἀταρρίας). Son of Deinomenes (Plut. *Mor.* 339b). The only commander of regular hypaspists (excluding the *archihypaspistes* Nikanor) whose patronymic is attested. Fought with distinction at Halikarnassos in 334 (Curt. 8.1.36; cf. Arr. 1.21.5), and later placed first in the military contest in Sittakene which determined the chiliarchs and pentakosiarchs of the hypaspists (Curt. 5.2.5; on these appointments and reforms see Atkinson II 57–62 and 1987; Daniel 1992; Hatzopoulos I 444–52; Heckel, *Marshals*² 271, with n.44). As the foremost hypaspist officer, after Neoptolemos, A. appears in charge of the "police force" that arrested Philotas at Phrada (Curt. 6.8.19–22), and he took an active role in demanding the execution of Alexander Lynkestes (Curt. 7.1.5). Nothing further is recorded about A., except that he was heavily in debt by the end of the campaign and attempted to defraud the King (Plut. *Mor.* 339b: "Tarrhias"; cf. Ael. *VH* 14.47a: Alexander regarded him as undisciplined). Identification with the homonymous officer of Kassandros, who appears in 317 (Diod. 19.36.2), is remotely possible (thus Berve) but probably rightly rejected by Kaerst. He is referred to as old (*senex*) already at the time of the Kleitos affair in 328 (Curt. 8.1.36). Berve II 90–100 no. 178; Hoffmann 203–4; cf. Kaerst, *RE* II.2 (1896) 1898; Heckel 1992, 304.

251 ATARRHIAS

(Ἀταρρίας). Macedonian. Background unknown. In 316/15, he appears as a general of Kassandros, assigned to block the passes leading from Epeiros to Macedonia (Diod. 19.36.2–3). This was intended to keep Olympias' nephew and ally, Aiakides, from bringing aid when she was besieged at Pydna. Atarrhias' actions not only sealed Olympias' fate but prompted an already unwilling Epeirot army to mutiny against Aiakides. It is likely that the majority of Kassandros' generals had served Antipatros during Alexander's Asiatic campaign. Hoffmann 203; Kaerst, *RE* II.2 (1896) 1898.

252 ATHENAGORAS

(Ἀθηναγόρας). Chian. Family background unknown. A member of the pro-Persian oligarchy which was toppled by the democratic faction in 334 (Curt. 4.5.15). But, he regained control of Chios, after the Persian counter-revolution in 334/3, along with Apollonides and other oligarchs supported by Memnon (Curt. 4.5.15). The city was taken by Hegelochos (Curt. 4.5.17), who exploited divisions within the city. In 332/1, A. was brought in chains to Alexander in Egypt (Arr. 3.2.5, 7 mentions only Apollonides, Phesinos and Megareus) and, presumably, sent to Elephantine. See also *Syll*³ 283. Berve II 13–14 no. 26; Hofstetter 35 no. 60a; Berve, *Tyrannis* I 339.

253 ATHENAGORAS

('Ἀθηναγόρας). Milesian, sent by Ptolemy Soter as mercenary captain to Rhodes, where he intrigued with Demetrios, promising to betray the city to him but rather played him false (see s.v. Alexander) and received a golden crown and five talents of silver from the Rhodians (Diod. 20.94.3–5; Berlin Papyrus = *FGrH* 533 F2). Launey 1209; Kirchner, *RE* II.2 (1896) 2020 no. 3.

254 ATHENAIOS

('Ἀθηναῖος). Officer (and *philos*) in the service of Antigonos Monophthalmos, who sent him in 311 against the Nabataians with a force of 4,000 light infantry and 600 cavalry and with orders to seize their livestock (Diod. 19.94.1). Since, the Arabs were attending a regional festival (on which see Bosworth 2002, 198–9) and had left their wives, children, and elderly at home, A. made a surprise attack on them at "the Rock" (Petra). He killed many and captured considerable booty, including myrrh, frankincense, and some 500 talents of silver, but he was careless in his retreat and all his men, except about 50 of the cavalrymen were killed (Diod. 19.95.2–7). The attack, which led down the main road from Gaza to Petra via Elousa and Eboda (*Barr. Atl.* 70 F3–4), had probably been planned to coincide with the festival. But A. was unprepared for the speed of the Nabataian counterattack. Whether A. himself escaped is uncertain, but since Diodorus does not specifically mention his death, he may have survived. At 19.96.1–2 we hear only of A.'s party and not A. himself. The campaign was followed by a punitive attack by Demetrios, which is reported differently by Diod. 19.96.4–98.1 and Plut. *Demetr.* 7.1–2. Billows 377 no. 22; Kirchner, *RE* II.2 (1896) 2023 no. 1; Bosworth 2002, 198–202.

255 ATHENODOROS

('Ἀθηνόδωρος). Athenian (Tod II no. 149, 3–4; Dem. 23.12; Kirchner 280), nicknamed "Imbrios," perhaps because he came from a cleruch family on Imbros (Berve II 14; Hofstetter 35). Born *c*.385, he was a mercenary leader in Persian service in 360 (Aen. Tact. 24.10; *Suda* A 734 calls him στρατιώτης); around this time he was voted honors and a bronze statue by Kios on the Bithynian coast for his good service (*euergesia*) to the city (Tod II no.149). A. served the Thrakian dynast Berisades to whom he was related by marriage, and after Berisades' death (356) came to the aid of his sons in their struggle against Amodokos (Dem. 23.10); for his activities in Thrake (Dem. 23.170–80; cf. Isoc. 8.24, A. founded a city in Thrake). After fighting with the Persians against Phokion at Atarneus (Polyaenus, *Strat.* 5.21), A. eventually entered the service of Dareios III and was captured at Sardis in 334, but released from prison—along with Echekratides the sophist, and Demaratos and Sparton the Rhodians—through the efforts of Phokion (Plut. *Phoc.* 18.6; Ael. *VH* 1.25). Judeich, *RE* II.2 (1896) 2043 no. 2; Berve II 14 no. 27; Hofstetter 35–6 no. 61; Olmstead 421.

256 ATHENODOROS

('Ἀθηνόδωρος). Native of Teos, harpist. According to Chares of Mytilene, in the tenth book of his *History of Alexander*, A. (along with Kratinos of Methymna and Aristonymos of Athens) entertained at the mass wedding ceremony in Sousa in 324 (Chares, *FGrH*

125 F4 = Athen. 12.538e). Nothing else is known about him. Kaerst, *RE* II.2 (1896) 2044 no. 10; Berve II 14 no. 28.

257 ATHENODOROS

(Ἀθηνόδωρος). A Greek mercenary (perhaps an officer) of unknown origin, A. had been left with the garrison at Baktra in 327/6. In 325, when it was rumored that Alexander had died in India, he led his fellow mercenaries in seizing the citadel of Baktra, putting to death those of his comrades who did not support him (Curt. 9.7.1–2). Although he allegedly took the title of king (though not claiming Macedonian or Achaimenid kingship; cf. Iliakis 2013, 188–9; but see Boxos no. 310), his chief aim was to lead the Greeks back to the coast (Curt. 9.7.3), a plan which was pre-empted by the treachery of Biton and Boxos, who murdered him at a banquet, alleging that he had plotted against Biton's life (Curt. 9.7.4–5). Kaerst, *RE* II.2 (1896) 2044 no. 11; Berve II 14 no. 29; Holt 1988, 82–6; Iliakis 2013, 187–90.

258 ATHENODOROS

(Ἀθηνόδωρος). A tragic actor of unknown origin, A. was a victor at the Dionysia in 342 (also a Lenaian victor in that year?) and 329 (O'Connor 73–4). A. appears to have been among the prominent artists who joined Alexander in Egypt in 332/1 (Arr. 3.1.4; cf. Bosworth I 262); he performed at Tyre (331), with Pasikrates of Soloi acting as *choregos,* and was victorious over Thessalos, whom Nikokreon of Salamis supported and Alexander himself favored (Plut. *Alex.* 29.3–4; Plut. *Mor.* 334e). Soon afterwards he returned to the Greek mainland, as his Dionysiac victory of 329 shows. At some point, however, A. was fined by the Athenians for failing to appear at the festival, and he asked Alexander to intercede in writing on his behalf; the King instead paid his fine (Plut. *Alex.* 29.5). In 324 A. reappears at the Sousan wedding festival, along with Aristokritos and Thessalos (Chares, *FGrH* 125 F4 = Athen. 12.538f). Kaerst, *RE* II.2 (1896) 2044 no. 9; Berve II 14–15 no. 30; Hamilton 76; O'Connor no. 13.

259 ATHENOPHANES

(Ἀθηνοφάνης). Athenian of unknown family (Kirchner 285). A. attended Alexander when he bathed (Plut. *Alex.* 35.5). The only story told of him, that he smeared naphtha on the face of a homely youth named Stephanos and nearly killed him when it ignited (Plut. *Alex.* 35.5–9), smacks of sadism. Strabo 16.1.15 C743 attributes this act of cruelty to Alexander himself. Berve II 15 no. 31.

260 ATIZYES

(Ἀτιζύης also Ἀτιξύης, Ἀντιξύης). Prominent Persian; satrap of Phrygia in 334 (Arr. 1.25.3; it was to A. that Sisines claimed to be going when he carried the letter from Dareios to Alexander Lynkestes). Baumbach 56 n.1, rejects the suggestion of Buchholz 58, that A. became satrap of Phrygia only after the death of Spithridates, who administered Lydia, Ionia, and Phrygia. Although he is not named in the war council at Zeleia or in actual description of the battle at the Granikos (Diod. 17.21.3 wrongly says he died in that battle), Arrian 2.11.8 is undoubtedly correct in naming him as one of the cavalry leaders (presumably of the Phrygian contingent) in that battle. After the battle, he appears to have returned to Phrygia, whence he fled at Alexander's approach, leaving in Kelainai a garrison of 1,000 Karians and 100 Greek mercenaries (Arr. 1.29.1; cf. Curt. 3.1.6–8). A. himself joined Dareios to fight again at Issos, where he perished (Arr. 2.11.8; Curt. 3.11.10; Diod. 17.34.5). His successor in Phrygia was Antigonos son of Philip (Arr. 1.29.3). Berve II 91 no. 179; Krumbholz 71; Baumbach 56; Beloch III² 2.153; Bosworth I 111, 216; Atkinson I 231; Shayegan 102–3 no. 27.

261 ATROPATES

(Ἀτροπάτης, Athenaeus: Σατραβάτης). Iranian (Justi 49). A. was satrap of the Medes, whom he commanded at Gaugamela in 331 (Arr. 3.8.4). He appears to have remained with Dareios until his arrest and death, whereafter he surrendered to Alexander. By that time, his satrapy had been awarded to Oxydates (Arr. 3.20.3; Curt. 6.2.11). He appears to have remained in Alexander's entourage until 328/7, when Oxydates was arrested for failure to perform his duties, and A. was reinstated in his old satrapy (Arr. 4.18.3; Curt. 8.3.17, wrongly calling him *Arsakes*). He rejoined the King in 324 at Pasargadai, bringing Baryaxes and other rebels to Alexander for punishment (Arr. 6.29.3). From Sousa he was sent back to his satrapy (Arr. 7.4.1), a clear indication that the King was satisfied with his performance. One of his daughters (unnamed) married Perdikkas in the mass marriages at Sousa (Arr. 7.4.5; cf. Justin 13.4.13, calling him Atropatos). When Alexander arrived in Ekbatana in October 324, Atropates was said to have entertained him (Athen. 12.538a = Ephippos, *FGrH* 126 F5: Satrabates) and presented him with 100 women on horseback, dressed as Amazons (Arr. 7.13.2–6), something which may have contributed to the later fiction that Alexander encountered the Amazon queen Thalestris. In 323, after Alexander's death, he was appointed satrap of Lesser Media (Justin 13.4.13; Diod. 18.3.3; cf. Herzfeld 302; Briant 737), a demotion that allowed Peithon son of Krateuas to assume control of Media (Diod. 18.3.1; cf. Berve II 92). A. appears to have made himself independent of the Macedonians in the early age of the Successors, taking the title of king (Strabo 11.13.1 C523), possibly after the battle of Gabiene and the replacement of Peithon from Greater Media by Orontobates the Mede (Diod. 19.46.5). His territory became known as Media Atropatene (Steph. Byz. s.v. Ἀτροπατία, Strabo 11.13.1; for the location see Strabo 11.13.2). Kaerst, *RE* II.2 (1896) 2150; Berve II 91–2 no. 180; Hyland 2013; Heckel 2018b; Shayegan 103 no. 28.

262 ATTALOS

(Ἄτταλος). Prominent Macedonian (Tataki 273–4 no. 322), patronymic unknown, A. was born *c.*390. Uncle of Hippostratos (Satyros *ap.* Athen. 13.557d), and thus apparently the brother of Amyntas (Marsyas of Pella, *FGrH* 135/6 F17; cf. Heckel 1980d, 456); both had died by the late summer or autumn of 337. Hence it was A. who acted as guardian for the young Kleopatra (no. 607), who was, as fate would have it, the last wife of Philip II (Plut. *Alex.* 9.7; Satyros *ap.* Athen. 13.557d; Paus. 8.7.7; wrongly Kleopatra's brother, Diod. 17.2.3; Justin 9.5.9; Ps.-Call. 1.20.1; or nephew, Diod. 16.93.9). Nothing is known of A.'s career until late summer 337, by which time he was an influential man at the Court (Diod. 16.93.7). A.'s prayer at the wedding feast, that Kleopatra might produce legitimate heirs to the Macedonian throne (Satyros, frg. 5; Plut. *Alex.* 9.7ff.; cf. Justin 9.7.3. Ps.-Call. (L) 1.20.1 calls him Lysias; but Ps.-Call. (A) 1.21.1 and Jul. Valer. 1.13–14 distinguish between A. and Lysias (see Berve II 424 no. 47), was both tactless and fatal: Alexander was driven from the court (Justin 9.7.3–8; Plut. *Alex.* 9.7–11) and, although reconciled with his father, he never forgave A. and considered him a threat to his life (Curt. 8.8.7; cf. 6.9.17). According to the popular account, A. was a friend of the younger Pausanias, who had confided to him the details of the insults uttered by Pausanias of Orestis and his own plans for a glorious death (Diod. 16.93.5). The latter occurred in a battle with the Illyrians of King Pleurias, probably in early 336. Soon thereafter A. avenged his friend's death by plying Pausanias of Orestis with wine at a dinner party and handing him over to his muleteers to be sexually abused (Diod. 16.93.7; Justin 9.6.5–6, alleging that he was abused by A. himself. For this episode and the sources see Fears 1975). There is no need to identify Pleurias with Pleuratos (Marsyas of Pella, *FGrH* 135/6 F17) or to date the campaign to 344/3. Hatzopoulos 2005 is pure fantasy; see Heckel, *Marshals*² 10–11. For the date of Pausanias' death see Heckel 1981c, 56. By the time of Pausanias' complaint, A. had been designated general of the advance force that was to cross into Asia (Diod. 16.93.8–9); for this reason, and because of their relationship (cf. 16.93.8), Philip was unwilling to reprimand A. for his crime against Pausanias, who in turn vented his rage on the king. A. had crossed the Hellespont at the beginning of spring 336 (Justin 9.5.8; cf. Diod. 16.91.2; Trogus, *Prol.* 9), sharing the command with Parmenion (Diod. 17.2.4; cf. Justin 9.5.8–9), whose daughter (**A26**) he had married (Curt. 6.9.17; she was presumably the same woman who married Koinos in 334; cf. Curt. 6.9.30). Their force of 10,000 advanced as far as Magnesia on Sipylos (Heckel 15–16; cf. Buckler 2003, 520 n.31; not Magnesia-on-the-Maiandros, as generally thought), where they were defeated by Memnon the Rhodian, and thus forced to seek refuge in the city (Polyaenus 5.44.4). On the news of Philip's death, A., trusting in his popularity with the troops, plotted rebellion and communicated with the anti-Macedonian party in Athens (Diod. 17.2.4, 5.1; 17.3.2, naming Demosthenes; cf. Judeich 304). Whether he was in fact guilty is a moot point, since Alexander may have used these charges to justify his murder (Diod. 17.5.1; at 17.2.3 he is called a rival for the throne, though he scarcely had any legal claims to it). Judeich's suggestion (304–5), that the Macedonian retreat from Magnesia to the Hellespont can be explained by A.'s rebellion against Alexander, is unlikely. Hekataios was sent to secure his execution (Diod. 17.2.5–6), which he could not have brought about without Parmenion's complicity (Diod. 17.5.2; Curt. 7.1.3; see also Curt. 8.1.42; cf. 8.1.52; and 8.7.4–5; Justin 12.6.14). Justin's claim (11.5.1) that Alexander, before his departure for Asia, killed all Kleopatra's relatives is a rhetorical exaggeration: only A. is meant. Kaerst, *RE* II.2 (1896) 2158 no. 4; Berve II 94 no. 182; Bosworth 1971a, 102ff.; Heckel, *Marshals*² 7–12; Judeich 302, 304–5; Schachermeyr 97; also Heckel, Howe, and Müller 2017; Müller, *LexAM* 129. **Stemmata I and XIV.**

263 ATTALOS

(Ἄτταλος). Macedonian (Tataki 274 no. 323), commander of the Agrianes at Issos (Arr. 2.9.2) and, perhaps, since at least the beginning of the Asiatic campaign. At Gaugamela, as at Issos, he was positioned on the right wing, this time with half the Agrianes and adjacent to Kleitos' *ile basilike* (Arr. 3.12.2; cf. Curt. 4.13.31). When Alexander rushed ahead in pursuit of Bessos, who had by this time arrested Dareios III, he ordered A. and the Agrianes, as well as the hypaspists under Nikanor, to follow as lightly equipped as possible; the rest of the infantry were to continue at their normal pace (Arr. 3.21.8). This is our last reference to A., although he may have retained his command until at least the end of the expedition. Certainly there is no record of his replacement by another officer. Kaerst, *RE* II.2 (1896) 2158 no. 6; Berve II 94–5 no. 183; Heckel 1992, 332–3.

264 ATTALOS

(Ἄτταλος). If not a literary fiction, A. was a Macedonian of unknown origin. Born probably in the mid-350s, he resembled Alexander and impersonated him at the Hydaspes River in order to divert Poros and his troops from the fact that the real Alexander had marched upriver to attempt another crossing (Curt. 8.13.21; Metz Epit. 58). Two points appear to rule out identification with the son of Andromenes (as suggested by Berve II 93): the latter was stationed upstream from Alexander's camp during the manoeuvres against Poros (Arr. 5.12.1) and the Vulgate calls him *Attalos quidam* (Metz Epit. 58), which suggests an otherwise unknown figure rather than a prominent phalanx commander. The name Attalos is, furthermore, far too common to allow automatic identification with a well-known figure. Nothing else is known about him. Heckel 1978c, 378 n.8.

265 ATTALOS

(Ἄτταλος). Macedonian (Tataki 212 no. 4). Son of the Tymphaian Andromenes and thus brother of Amyntas, Polemon, and Simmias. A *somatophylax* (Royal Hypaspist) of Philip II in 336 (Diod. 16.94.4), A. had undoubtedly been one of that king's Pages and a *syntrophos* of the prince, Alexander. Hence a birthdate *c.*356 is consistent with the evidence for A.'s career before and after Alexander's reign. Nothing is known of his career between 336 and 330, but two years after the family's brief disgrace at Phrada, A. is found at the head of Amyntas' brigade (Arr. 4.16.1). The curious fact that A. alone attained high office after 330 is ascribed by some scholars to the influence of Perdikkas, but it is not at all certain that the two were related by marriage at that time. Berve (II 325–6 no. 654, following Hoffmann 156 n.59) assumed that Polyperchon, son of a certain Simmias, and Andromenes (both of Tymphaian origin) were related. If this is so, then Polyperchon may have supported the latter's sons at the time of the Philotas affair. The younger Simmias may have died, or perhaps left the army, while Polemon's youth and disgraceful flight from Alexander's camp will account for his failure to attain higher office before 323. As for A., he is first mentioned as leader of an infantry brigade in Baktria in 328; here he appears with Krateros, Gorgias, Polyperchon, and Meleagros (Arr. 4.16.1). In the following spring, he campaigned in Sogdiana with Krateros, Polyperchon, and Alketas (Arr. 4.22.1), where he received by letter the news of the Pages' conspiracy in Baktria (Plut. *Alex.* 55.6). During the Swat campaign, A. and his brigade served with Koinos, against the Aspasians (Arr. 4.24.1), and then later, along with Balakros, under the command of Leonnatos (Arr. 4.24.10; cf. 4.25.3, though their contribution is eclipsed by that of Ptolemy, who enhanced his own actions). Together with Alketas, A. conducted the siege of Ora (Arr. 4.27.5). Curtius (8.13.21), in his account of the Hydaspes campaign, describes a certain A. as *aequalem sibi* [sc. *Alexandro*] *et haud disparem habitu oris et corporis,* which appears to suit the son of Andromenes. This man remained in the main camp, opposite Poros' forces, disguised as Alexander, who, in the meantime, took a portion of the army upstream in an effort to cross the river undetected. But the identification must be resisted (*pace* Berve II 93). Arrian (5.12.1) tells us that A., Gorgias, and Meleagros were stationed halfway between the main camp and Alexander's crossing-point (cf. Schubert 1901, 467–8). Furthermore, the description of him in Metz Epit. 58 as *Attalos quidam* suggests that we are not dealing with the well-known taxiarch. In 325, the son of Andromenes accompanied Krateros, Meleagros, Antigenes, and (possibly) Polyperchon westward to Karmania via Arachosia and Drangiana (Arr. 6.17.3). In the eastern satrapies, A. had served with Alketas, the brother of Perdikkas, on two attested missions, but more often he is associated with the more conservative leaders of the phalanx: Krateros, Koinos, Polyperchon, Meleagros. (A.'s commands between 328 and 325: with Alketas, Arr. 4.27.5; with Koinos, Arr. 4.24.1; Meleagros, Arr. 4.16.1; 5.12.1; 6.17.3; Krateros, Arr. 4.16.1. implied by 4.17.1; 4.22.1; 5.12.1; 6.17.3; Polyperchon, Arr. 4.16.1; 4.22.1; implied by Justin 12.10.1). Hence it is not surprising to find him closely linked with Meleagros in the days that followed Alexander's death. Koinos had died at the Hydaspes in 326; Krateros and Polyperchon were in Kilikia, bound for Macedonia. That left A. and Meleagros as natural allies, and the spokesmen of the infantry (cf. Justin 13.3.2, 7–8). But their joint opposition to the *principes* in Babylon came to naught and A. was easily induced to abandon his colleague by the prospect of marriage to Perdikkas' sister Atalante (Diod. 18.37.2; Heckel 1992, 381–4). This new alliance isolated Meleagros, who, despite his appointment as Perdikkas' *hyparchos,* fell victim to the purge that followed the reconciliation of cavalry and infantry. For A., and indeed for the bride, it was a fateful union. First attested in Perdikkas' service during the winter of 321/0, A. attempted, with his brother Polemon, to recover Alexander's funeral carriage. This had been diverted from its westerly route at Damaskos by Arrhidaios, who was taking it to Egypt against the expressed orders of Perdikkas (Arr. *Succ.* 24.1, line 3; cf. Arr. *Succ.* 1.25, naming Polemon alone). Furthermore, Ptolemy had come with an army to escort the King's body to his own satrapy (Diod. 18.28.3); A.'s efforts were thwarted and he rejoined Perdikkas, who had now invaded Kilikia and deposed Philotas. Here Perdikkas equipped two fleets. One, led by Aristonous, the former Somatophylax, was to suppress the Ptolemaic faction on the island of Kypros. The other was entrusted to A., who skirted the coast of Phoinikia and secured the Pelousiac mouth of the Nile, where he remained, guarding the entrance to the Delta against the naval forces of Antigonos and Antipatros. A. was near Pelousion in May 320 when he received word that Perdikkas had been assassinated and Atalante murdered by the raging army (Diod. 18.37.3). From Pelousion, he took the fleet to Tyre, where the Macedonian garrison commander Archelaos received him into the city and handed back 800 talents, which Perdikkas deposited there for safekeeping. There too A. received those troops who had remained loyal to the Perdikkan cause and had fled from the army near Memphis (Diod. 18.37.3–4). There were further defections at Triparadeisos, where A. appeared in person (Arr. *Succ.* 1.33, 39) to incite the army, which now rejected the leadership of Peithon and Arrhidaios (cf. Errington 1970, 67 n.131; Briant 278 n.6; Billows 68; Kaerst, *RE* II.2 (1896) 2158–9 no. 7, followed by Berve II 95 no. 184, treats this Attalos as a different individual). A. thus gathered a force of 10,000 infantry and 800 cavalry, with which he set sail for Karia, intending to attack Knidos, Kaunos, and Rhodes (Arr. *Succ.* 1.39). Arrian's account does not say that A. and his fleet actually attacked the Kaunians and Knidians. Either these states joined forces with the Rhodians, with the credit for the victory going to Rhodes and Demaratos, or A.'s strike against them was pre-empted by the Rhodian victory. Berthold 1984, 60 treats them as separate battles. Hauben 21 speaks of "een aanval op Rhodos en de tegenover gelegen steden Knidos en Kaunos," as if referring to a single engagement. But the Rhodians, led by their navarch Demaratos, defeated him, and A. soon rejoined that portion of the Perdikkan army under Alketas, which had only recently separated from Eumenes in Phrygia (Plut. *Eum.* 8.8). Alketas' supporters were Polemon and Dokimos. Plutarch's failure to mention A. may be an oversight, but it appears more likely that A. did not rejoin Alketas until the latter had moved into Karia. Reunited, Alketas and A. successfully repulsed an attack from the Karian satrap Asandros, acting on Antipatros' orders (Arr. *Succ.* 1.41). Nevertheless, they now withdrew into Pisidia, where in the following year, they were defeated near Kretopolis by Antigonos. Diod. 18.44–5; 18.50.1. Diod. 18.41.7 says that Antigonos set out against Alketas and A., "who commanded the entire fleet" (τὸν τοῦ στόλου παντὸς κυριεύοντος). What had become of A.'s fleet, or what remained of it after its defeat by the Rhodians, we do not know. Hauben 22–3 thinks A.'s fleet might have been at anchor in Lykia or Pamphylia. A. was captured, together with his brother Polemon, Dokimos, and two otherwise unattested commanders named Antipatros and Philotas (Diod. 18.45.3; 19.16.1). They were imprisoned in a secure fortress which, although unnamed, appears to have been in Greater Phrygia; for Stratonike, Antigonos' wife, who resided in Kelainai, was said to have been nearby (Diod. 19.16.4; Ramsay 1920, 107 identifies it as Afiom-Kara-Hissar = Leontos-Kephalai). In 317, when Antigonos had moved to the East to campaign against Eumenes, the captives overpowered their guards and planned to escape, but A.'s health was failing and the Antigonid forces from neighboring garrisons arrived quickly to lay siege to the place. Dokimos, who had planned the whole affair, escaped by a secret route and betrayed his former comrades. The fortress was recaptured after a siege of one year and four months. Diod. 19.16 for the full account. For A.'s poor health, caused by incarceration, see 19.16.3. The length of the siege: 19.16.5. Diodorus does not say what became of the prisoners, but it is likely that they were executed. If A. lived to see its capture, he did not outlive it by much. The "daughters of Attalos," who were in the company of Olympias when she fled to Pydna in 317 (Diod. 19.35.5) with the royal entourage, were clearly those of a high-ranking official or officer, probably the son of Andromenes. These daughters appear to have been his children by Atalante. Berve II 92–3 no. 181 (cf. no. 184); Kaerst, *RE* II (1896) 2158 no. 5 (cf. no. 7); Schubert 1901, 467–8; Simpson 1957; Schachermeyr 1970, 125; Heckel 1992, 180–3; Hauben 19–24 no. 7; *PP* VI no. 16061. **Stemma XII.**

266 ATTINAS

(Ἀττινᾶς). Macedonian (Hoffmann 194; Tataki 275 no. 330) of unknown family background, A. had been appointed *phrourarchos* of an unnamed fort in Baktria (probably in 329/8). This place was attacked by Spitamenes and a force of Massagetai, who lured A. and his 300 cavalrymen into an ambush and slaughtered them (Curt. 8.1.3–5). The details of the incident as described by Arr. 4.16.4–5 are somewhat different and the name of the *phrourarchos* is not given, but there can be little doubt that we are dealing with the same person. Curt. 8.1.5 says A. was killed in the engagement; Arr. 4.16.5 has him taken prisoner, in which case A. was probably executed afterwards. Bosworth II 114–15 believes that Arrian and Curtius describe two different episodes, pointing out that in Arr. 4.16.4 the Macedonians are taken by surprise whereas in Curt. 8.1.3–4 they made a deliberate sortie. But the element of surprise can be found in both accounts: Curtius calls A. *insidiarum, quae parabantur, ignarus*. Furthermore, although the expression *praefectus regionis eius* is often used to designate a satrap or hyparch (Curt. 5.2.8; 5.3.4; 5.8.4; 10.1.20), it cannot mean that in this instance, since the satrap of Baktria-Sogdiana was Artabazos (not Attinas), and the term *praefectus* is also used of those in charge of smaller places (for example, the prefect of Damaskos, Curt. 3.13.10 or Gobares the prefect of Pasargadai). Hence I see no reason to believe that A. was not a *phrourarchos*. The different accounts will be attributable to the primary sources. Berve II 95 no. 185. Hoffmann 194; Bosworth II 114–16.

267 AUDATA

(Αὐδάτα). Daughter of an Illyrian chieftain (Athen. 13.557c), presumably Bardylis, whom Philip II defeated in 359/8 (Diod. 16.4.3–7). First or possibly second wife of Philip II, A. must have sealed the "glorious peace" (ἔνδοξον εἰρήνην) that he had forged with the Illyrians (Diod. 16.8.1). The fact that her name was changed to Eurydike (Arr. *Succ.* 1.22) may have some dynastic significance: for a brief period, she was Philip's "official" queen. Philip's mother, Eurydike, was herself partially Illyrian, and Carney suggests that Audata may have been related to her. The mother of Kynnane, A. was the grandmother of Adea, who also took the name Eurydike (Arr. *Succ.* 1.22–3; Heckel 1983). The assignment of the name Eurydike to Kleopatra, the niece of Attalos, in 337/6 may suggest that A. was no longer alive or at the court at that time, but Alexander will certainly have encountered her in Pella as a child. Kaerst, *RE* II.2 (1896) 2277; Heckel 1983; Carney 57–8; Ogden 22–4.

268 AUDOLEON

(Αὐδολέων, thus Diodorus; Plutarch writes Αὐτολέων). King of the Paionians, son of Patraos (*IG* II² 654 l.37) and father of Ariston (Polyaenus 4.12.3), who had a distinguished career under Alexander the Great. In 310, he was hard-pressed by the Autariatai and aided by Kassandros, who settled these peoples (some 20,000 in number) near Mt. Orbelos (Diod. 20.19.1; cf. Justin 15.2.1). A.'s (unnamed) daughter (A93; Sandberger no. 19) married Pyrrhos, at some point after the death of Antigone (*c*.296/5), but appears not to have borne him children (Plut. *Pyrrh.* 9.2). In 288, in the archonship of Diotimos, he was awarded various honors by the Athenians, including citizenship, for past services and *eunoia* toward the state (*IG* II² 654). Kaerst, *RE* II.2 (186) 2279; Seibert 1967, 101.

AUSTANES. Shayegan 103 no. 29. See **HAUSTANES**.

269 AUTOBARES

(Αὐτοβάρης, Wata-para; the form Αἰγοβάρης is a corruption, Justi 208). Prominent Persian, brother of Mithrobaios: their father is not named. Both were enrolled in the *agema* of the cavalry at Sousa in 324 (Arr 7.6.5). Berve II 15 no. 32 ("Aigobares"); Shayegan 98 no. 3.

270 AUTODIKOS

(Αὐτόδικος). Brother of Lysimachos, Philip, and Alkimachos. Apparently the youngest of the sons of Agathokles, A. was born in the early-to-mid 340s and appointed one of the four Somatophylakes of Philip III Arrhidaios at Triparadeisos (Arr. *Succ.* 1.38). He appears later in an inscription as the husband of a certain Adeia (*Syll*³ 373). Berve II 95 no. 187; id., *RE* Supplbd. IV 57; Beloch IV² 2.130; Wilcken, *RE* II 2602 no. 7. (Αὐτόλυκος).

271 AUTOPHRADATES

(Αὐτοφραδάτης, Wata-fradata). A Persian of unknown family background; possibly a relative of that Autophradates who participated in Satraps' Revolt of the 360s (Diod. 15.90.3; Polyaenus 7.27; cf. Weiskopf 38ff.). Commanded the Persian fleet in the Aegean in 333, under the supreme command of Memnon (cf. Arr. 2.1.3); perhaps he was active in 337/6 against the pro-Macedonian party at Ephesos (Polyaenus 7.27.2). Together with Memnon's successor, Pharnabazos, A. conducted the siege of Mytilene, which was later taken and occupied (Arr. 2.1.3–5). While Pharnabazos turned his attention to Lykia, A. campaigned in the islands, but the Persians soon dispatched Datames to deal with the Kyklades, and A. joined Pharnabazos in bringing Tenedos back under Persian domination (Arr. 2.2.1–3), garrisoning Chios (cf. Arr. 3.2.3–5) and attacking Siphnos (Arr. 2.13.4). He gave Agis 10 triremes and 30 talents (Arr. 2.13.6). But after Alexander's victory at Issos and his advance into Syria and Phoinikia, A.'s fleet began to disintegrate (Arr. 2.20.1, 6: defection of Phoinikians). Berve II 96 suggests that A. may have gone with his remaining ships to Krete, to which island Alexander soon sent Amphoteros (Arr. 3.6.3). The *hetaira* Antigone (no. 112), who was captured by A. near Samothrake, was probably taken in the period immediately before Alexander's crossing into Asia (Plut. *Mor.* 339e); but see Berve II 96 n.3 for a plausible scenario in 334. Kaerst, *RE* II.2 (1896) 2607 no. 1; Berve II 96 no. 188; Baumbach 29ff., 50ff.; Shayegan 103 no. 30; Weiskopf.

272 AUTOPHRADATES

(Αὐτοφραδάτης, Wata-fradata; Curt. Phradates). Persian. Dareios III's satrap of the Tapourians who dwelt near the Caspian Sea (Arr. 3.23.7); he led the Caspian contingent at Gaugamela, positioned on the right wing (Curt. 4.12.9). Berve II 96 conjectures that A. served under Phratapernes; but Phradates could as easily be an error for Phratapernes. Curtius' account is extremely confused. At 4.12.7 he speaks of the Persians, Mardians, and Sogdianoi. The last are probably the Sousianoi (for the confusion of Sogdiana and Sousiana cf. Dexippos, *FGrH* 100 F8). The Mardians ought to have been brigaded with the Tapourians, and the Caspians are perhaps the Hyrkanians subject to Phratapernes: Arrian (3.8.4, 11.4) mentions Topeiri, Hyrkanians, and Parthians under his command. In 330, A. surrendered voluntarily to Alexander in 330 (Arr. 3.23.7; followed by Julien 37); Curt. 6.4.23–4 says he was brought to Alexander by Krateros and Erigyios (cf. Arr. 3.23.2 for Krateros' and Erigyios' activities in the area). Alexander allowed him to keep his satrapy (Arr. 3.23.7; Curt. 6.4.25), which was soon enlarged to include the Mardians or Amardians (Arr. 3.24.3; Curt. 6.5.21). But in 328/7 he was arrested and replaced by Phratapernes, whose satrapy was thus enlarged (Arr. 4.18.2; Curt. 8.3.17). On his return from India in 325/4, Alexander had A. executed, allegedly for aspiring to the kingship (Curt. 10.1.39). Kaerst, *RE* II.2 (1896) 2608 no. 2; Berve II 96–7 no. 189; Julien 36–7; Badian 2000a, 91–2; Shayegan 103–4 no. 31.

273 AXIOTHEA

(Ἀξιοθέα). Wife of Nikokles of Paphos, who had made an alliance with Antigonos. When Argaios (no. 174) and Kallikrates (no. 564) brought instructions from Ptolemy to Menelaos, the *strategos* and brother of Ptolemy, to force Nikokles to commit suicide, Axiothea killed her virgin daughters and persuaded the other royal women to commit suicide. She then killed herself as well (Diod. 20.21.2). Polyaenus 8.48 (where Ptolemy is anachronistically designated as *basileus*) depicts Axiothea and other women hurling themselves into the flames of the burning palace; but Diodorus, who claims that Ptolemy had intended the women no harm, says that the fire was set by Nikokles' brothers after the suicide of the women (20.21.1–3 for the whole story). Mistakenly identified as the wife of Nikokreon by Athenaeus (8.349e, where the MS reads Βιοθέα). For the confusion of Nikokreon and Nikokles (summed up by Hill I 161 n.1 but with the wrong conclusion) see Gesche 1974.

274 AZEMILKOS

(Ἀζέμιλκος, Ozmilk; Abdimilkutti in Assyrian inscriptions). Ruler of Tyre (?–332). Born before 370, since his son (whose name is unknown) was in 333/2 old enough to rule in his absence while A. served with the Persian fleet of Autophradates (Arr. 2.15.7). But Berve II 13 rightly suggests that the siege of Tyre will have summoned him back to Phoinikia before the general defection of Phoinikian and Kypriot commanders (Arr. 2.20.1–3). When the city was captured A. and many other prominent Tyrians fled to the temple of Melqart. Although he was pardoned (Arr. 2.24.5), he appears to have been deposed (but see Grainger 1991, 36–8, 59; Elayi 2013, 301: "Alexandre . . . laisse Ozmilk sur le trône"). Kaerst, *RE* II.2 (1896) 2641; Rawlinson 216–36; Berve II 13 no. 25; Elayi 298–301.

B

275 BAGISTHANES

(Βαγισθάνης). A Babylonian noble (Arr. 3.21.1; but Ps.-Call. 2.19.7 calls him a eunuch), in 330, at the time of Alexander's pursuit of Dareios, B. fled from the Persian camp, which was not far from Alexander's (cf. Arr. 3.21.3), together with Antibelos son of Mazaios (Brochubelus, Curt. 5.13.2: at Tabai, in the remotest part of Paraitakene) and reported Dareios' arrest at the hands of Bessos and Nabarzanes (Arr. 3.21.1; but Curt. 5.13.3 claims that the king had not yet been harmed but was in danger of being murdered or put in chains). Nothing else is known about him. Kaerst, *RE* II.2 (1896) 2771 s.v. "Bagistanes"; Berve II 98 no. 193; Justi 59; Shayegan 104 no. 32.

276 BAGOAS

(Βαγώας, Bagoses, Josephus, *AJ* 11.300–1). Eunuch, apparently of Egyptian origin (Ael. *VH* 6.8; *Suda* Λ 3), who rose to be the most powerful of Artaxerxes III's courtiers (Diod. 16.47.3, 50.8; for the power of eunuchs in the Near East see Grayson 1995). Despite his physical condition he was a man of great daring (Diod. 16.47.4; 17.5.3) and acted as a military commander (cf. Josephus, *AJ* 11.300: *strategos*) at Sidon and in Egypt (350/49) where he cooperated with Mentor the Rhodian (Diod. 16.47.3, 49.4–6, 50.1–7). Having administered the Upper Satrapies (cf. Briant 746), he became chiliarch of Artaxerxes III (Ochos) and engineered that king's death, as well as that of his successor Arses (Diod. 17.5.3–4; Strabo 15.3.24 C736; for his role as king-maker see also Plut. *Mor.* 337e; cf. 340c–d, in which Plutarch confuses Oarses (Arses) and Dareios). B. was alleged to have hated Ochos because he killed the Apis calf; hence he had Artaxerxes' body dismembered and eaten; he then made knife handles out of his thigh bones (Ael. *VH* 6.8; cf. *Suda* Λ 3). Alexander was later to charge Dareios with seizing the throne illegally from Arses through the agency of B. (Arr. 2.14.5; cf. Curt. 6.3.12, 4.10; Diod. 17.5.5; Grayson 1975, 24–37). B. was, however, forced to drink his own poison when he plotted against Dareios (Diod. 17.5.6). The garden of Bagoas in Babylon and the house in Sousa, which Alexander gave to Parmenion, may have been his (Pliny, *HN* 13.41; Theophrastos, *HP* 2.6.7; Plut. *Alex.* 39.10). The name Bagoas became synonymous with eunuchs (Pliny, *HN* 13.41; *Judith* 12:11; Ovid, *Amores* 2.2.1), a type unworthy of respect or artistic representation (Quint. 5.12.21). Cauer, *RE* II.2 (1896) 2771–2 no.1; Briant 769–80.

277 BAGOAS

(Βαγώας). A good-looking eunuch of Dareios III, with whom he had been sexually intimate, B. surrendered to Alexander after the Great King's death in 330, along with Nabarzanes the regicide, whose life he saved through his persuasive charms (Curt. 6.5.23). B. appears to have been of Lykian descent, the son of Pharnouches (Arr. *Ind.* 18.8). The identification is rejected by Berve II 98 but Cauer, in his *RE* entry, does not dismiss the idea (for Persians in Lykia see Goukowsky 220; Mosley 1971). B. soon became a favorite and a flatterer of Alexander (Athen. 13.603b; Plut. *Mor.* 65d). It was perhaps through his influence that Pharnouches was appointed one of the leaders of the force sent against Spitamenes, and probably also it was because of their resentment of the eunuch that the historians blamed Pharnouches (no. 891) for the Polytimetos disaster. Clearly, B. had accumulated a measure of wealth, as had his namesake (above); both had been granted estates by the Great King, the former near Babylon (Ael. *VH* 3.23), the latter in Sousa. B. was wealthy enough to serve as a trierarch of the Hydaspes fleet (Arr. *Ind.* 18.8). Dikaiarchos (*ap.* Athen. 13.603a–b) claims that Alexander too became infatuated with the youth and, in Pura, the Gedrosian capital, he was overcome by B.'s performance and fondled and kissed him in the theater to the shouts and applause of the audience (Plut. *Alex.* 67.7–8; cf. Curt. 10.1.26, for the charge that Alexander was intimate with B.). Curt. 10.1.22–38, 42 claims that B. engineered the destruction of Orxines (no. 828; also Orsines), descended from the Seven, because he would not pay court to "one of Alexander's whores" (that is, to B.), alleging that Orxines had plundered the tomb of Kyros the Great at Pasargadai. Cauer, *RE* II.2 (1896) 2772 no. 2; Berve II 98–9, nos. 194–5; Justi 60, nos. 3–4; Badian 1958; Shayegan 104 no. 33.

278 BAGODARAS

(Βαγωδάρας, Cobares, Gobares). For the name see Justi 60 (cf. Briant 740 for the rarity of Medes in the Alexander historians). A Mede—possibly a magos (Curt. 7.4.8)—who remained with Bessos after he usurped the kingship (330/29). At a banquet, he advised Bessos to surrender to Alexander and seek his mercy, but Bessos became angry with B., who escaped from the camp and joined Alexander. His favorable reception induced others to follow his example and contributed to the downfall of Bessos (Curt. 7.4.8–19; Diod. 17.83.7–8). Kaerst, *RE* II.2 (1896) 2772; Berve II 99 no. 196; Shayegan 104 no. 34.

279 BAGOPHANES

(Βαγοφάνης). Commander of the Persian garrison and the treasures at Babylon in 330; hence possibly a eunuch. B. surrendered to Alexander on his arrival (Curt. 5.1.20)—apparently induced by the actions of Mazaios, who had taken refuge in the city (Curt. 5.1.17–20)—and welcomed the Macedonian King with pomp and circumstance (cf. 5.1.20–3). Despite B.'s gesture of good faith, Alexander appointed Agathon (Diod. 17.64.5; cf. Arr. 3.16.4 for different arrangements and no mention of Agathon) commander of the Babylonian citadel and kept B. in his entourage (Curt. 5.1.43–4). What became of him, we do not know. Kaerst, *RE* II.2 (1896) 2772–3; Berve II 99 no. 197; Justi 60; Shayegan 104 no. 35.

280 BAITON

(Βαίτων). Bematist (Athen. 10.442b; Pliny, *HN* 6.61). Baiton's work appears to have been titled *Asiatic Stages* (so Strabo 15.2.8 C723) or *The Stages of Alexander's Journey* (Athen. 10.442b: Σταθμοὶ τῆς Ἀλεξάνδρου πορείας). Eight fragments of his work survive, but nothing is known about his origins or his life beyond that the fact that he accompanied Alexander and wrote the *Stages* (*Stathmoi*). Schwartz, *RE* II.2 (1896) 2779; Berve II 99–100 no. 198; Jacoby, *FGrH* IIB 119; on the bematists in general see Pearson 261.

281 BALAGROS

(Βάλαγρος, Βάλακρος). Son of Balakros (no. 283) son of Nikanor and Phila. Brother of Antipatros (no. 130) and Thraseas (no. 1132). He and his brothers were clearly politically aligned with their stepfather, Demetrios Poliorketes. Attested at Delos (*IG* XI 2, 154 A 41) in 296. Reger 1991, 153–4 believes B. was on his way to Asia, bringing news of Lachares' coup in Athens, when he stopped at Delos. Otherwise nothing is known of his life and career. Reger 1991; Paschidis 484 n.3.

282 BALAKROS

(Βάλακρος). Prominent Macedonian (Tataki 279 no. 15), son of Amyntas (Arr. 1.29.3; 3.5.5). He appears to have accompanied Alexander's expedition from the beginning and replaced Antigonos the One-Eyed at Kelainai (spring 333) as commander (*strategos*) of the allied infantry (Arr. 1.29.3), in which capacity he fought at Issos, Tyre, and Gaza. Early in 331, B. was left, along with Peukestas (no. 881) son of Makartatos, as *strategos* of the army in Egypt (Arr. 3.5.5); the command of the allied infantry was transferred to Koiranos (Arr. 3.5.6, perhaps Karanos?). Nothing further is known about him. Kaerst, *RE* II.2 (1896) 2816 no. 2; Berve II 100 no. 199; Heckel 1992, 335; Hoffmann 176 n.82.

283 BALAKROS

(Βάλακρος). Macedonian (Tataki 279 no. 20). The epigraphic form Balagros has the support of Antonius Diogenes (*ap.* Phot. *Bibl.* 111a–b) and Curt. 4.13.28 where *Phaligrus* appears to be a corruption of *Philippus Balagri*. Son of Nikanor (Arr. 2.12.2; Diod. 18.22.1), also father of another Nikanor (no. 778; *Suda* N 376, Harpocration), possibly the later governor of Alexandria in Parapamisadai (Arr. 4.22.5; Berve II 275–6 no. 556; though Bosworth 1994 identifies him tentatively with Kassandros' lieutenant in Peiraieus), and possibly of Philip (no. 906; Berve II 383–4 no. 778; Curt. 4.13.28; Diod. 17.57.3). Born, in all likelihood, in the 380s, he appears to have been politically allied with Antipatros, whose daughter he married (Antonius Diogenes *ap.* Phot. *Bibl.* 166, p. 111a–b), perhaps just before the Asiatic campaign. Antipatros son of Balagros (Balakros) who appears in the Delian inscriptions, *IG* XI.2.287b, 57; and 161, 85, was probably their son (Heckel 1987, 161–2; cf. Badian 1988); Reger 1991 completes the family tree by proposing (plausibly) that B. had two other sons, another Balagros (*IG* XI 2, 154 A41; cf. Paschidis 438 n.3) and Thraseas (*IG* XI 4, 585; cf. Paschidis 438 s.v. Tharsynon D80). As sons of Phila, they were solidly in the camp of Demetrios Poliorketes. B. had apparently been a Somatophylax of Philip II, unless he was appointed at the time of Alexander's accession and served Alexander in that capacity until shortly after the battle of Issos, when he was named satrap of Kilikia (Arr. 2.12.2; cf. Diod. 18.22.1). He is almost certainly the Balakros of Curt. 4.5.13 (not Berve's no. 203), who in 332 joined with Antigonos (satrap of Phrygia) and Kalas (Hellespontine Phrygia) in completing the conquest of Asia Minor (Schachermeyr 212; cf. also Briant 70; Bosworth I 219; Bosworth 1974, 58–9; and Billows 44–5; I see no reason to assume that B. was killed in this campaign). As satrap he also controlled finances and minted coins bearing at first his own name, later merely the letter B (Aulock); perhaps, as Bosworth 1988, 232 suggests, he was "primarily responsible for the payment of the army during the long siege of Tyre" (hence also the reference to Tyre in Antonius Diogenes *ap.* Phot. p. 111a–b). Late in Alexander's reign—shortly before

Harpalos' arrival at Tarsos—B. was killed in an attempt to quell an insurrection by the Isaurians and Larandians (Diod. 18.22.1; for this view, cf. Higgins 1980, 150; Bosworth I 219 argues for an earlier date, perhaps "associated with Antigonos' campaigns in Lykaonia during 332 [Curt. 4.5.13]"). Kaerst, *RE* II.2 (1896) 2816 no. 1; Aulock 1964; Badian 1988; Baumbach 45, 65, 69; Berve II 100–1 no. 200, and II 101–2 no. 203; Heckel 1992, 260–1. **Stemma V.**

284 BALAKROS

(Βάλακρος). A Macedonian (Tataki 278 no. 13) of unknown family origin, B. commanded the javelin-men, perhaps since the beginning of the expedition. At Gaugamela, these were stationed on the right, where they effectively negated the threat of the Persian scythe-chariots (Arr. 3.12.3, 13.5; Marsden 1964, 66–7, estimates that B.'s men numbered about 1,000). This same B. is undoubtedly the commander of *psiloi* who campaigned against the Skythians north of the Iaxartes (Syr-Darya) in 329 (Arr. 4.4.6) and among the Aspasians in 327/6. On the latter occasion, his troops, along with Attalos' battalion of *pezhetairoi*, belonged to Leonnatos' third of the army (Arr. 4.24.10; Kaerst, *RE* II.2, 2816 no. 4, implausibly identifies this man with the son of Amyntas). B. led a detachment of men to reconnoiter Aornos and discovered that the Indians there had fled from the rock (Curt. 8.11.22). Thereafter he is not heard of again. It is highly doubtful that he is identical with the Balakros who defeated Hydarnes and recaptured Miletos (Curt. 4.5.13); that man was probably the son of Nikanor, a former Somatophylax and satrap of Kilikia. Kaerst, *RE* II.2 (1896) no. 3; Berve II 101 nos. 201–2; Bosworth 1973, 252–3; Heckel 1992, 332.

285 BARDYLIS

(Βάρδυλις). Illyrian chieftain, father of Birkenna (no. 299), whom he gave in marriage to Pyrrhos (Plut. *Pyrrh.* 9.2). B. may have been the son of Kleitos and thus a grandson of the famous Bardylis (Arr. 1.5.1; Kaerst, *RE* 1897, 12 no. 1), who defeated Perdikkas III in 360/59. Kaerst, *RE* III.1 (1897) 12 no. 2.

286 BARSAENTES

(Βαρσαέντης). A noble Persian. Satrap of Arachosia (and Drangiana, Arr. 3.21.1; cf. Curt. 6.6.36) under Dareios III, B. commanded his regional troops and the so-called Mountain Indians at Gaugamela (Arr. 3.8.4; located on the left wing, 3.11.3). After this battle, he fled with Dareios towards the Upper Satrapies and soon joined Bessos and Nabarzanes in arresting the king (Arr. 3.21.1; cf. Justin 11.15.1) and later putting him to death (Arr. 3.25.8; Curt. 6.6.36; Diod. 17.74.1, "Barxaes"). In 329, B. fled to his own satrapy. On the approach of the Macedonians and the appointment of Menon, with a force of 4,600, he took refuge with the dynast of the neighboring Indians, Samaxos (Sambos; see Eggermont 18–19; cf Vogelsang 1985, 78), who harbored the regicide until 326 but then turned him over to Alexander (Curt. 8.13.3–4; Arr. 3.25.8, anticipating events some three years later; cf. also Metz Epit. 3, where Ariobarzanes should be corrected to Barsaentes), presumably to win the King's favor. Alexander had B. executed (Arr. 3.25.8). Kaerst, *RE* III.1 (1897) 26–7; Berve II 102 no. 205; Vogelsang 1985; Shayegan 104–5 no. 36.

287 BARSINE

(Βαρσίνη). Daughter of Artabazos (Plut. *Eum.* 1.7; Euseb. *Chron.* 1.231–32 and Porphyr. Tyr. *ap.* Syncell. 504 = *FGrH* 260 F3 §2 wrongly make her the daughter of Pharnabazos) and a Rhodian woman (whose name is not recorded), the sister of Mentor and Memnon (Diod. 16.52.4; Dem. 23.154, cf. 23.157). B. was one of twenty-one children (eleven brothers, including Pharnabazos, Ariobarzanes, Arsames, Kophen and, possibly, Ilioneus; nine sisters, of whom we know only the names of Artonis, whom Plut. *Eum.* 1.7 wrongly calls "Barsine," and Artakama or Apama). Ilioneus may have been a half-brother by a younger wife of Artabazos. B.'s birthdate depends on when she married Mentor, assuming that she married him at puberty or soon afterwards. She was still with her parents when they fled to Macedonia: any time between 352 and 344/3. She was married first to her uncle Mentor (she is not the wife mentioned by Klearchos of Soloi *ap.* Athen. 6.256d), whom she may have borne three daughters (Curt. 3.13.14); but only one of these daughters of Mentor, Nearchos' bride at Sousa in 324, can be identified with certainty as B.'s child (Arr. 7.4.6; Arr. *ap.* Phot. *Bibl.* cod. 68b). After Mentor's death she married Memnon, by whom she had a son (**A43**), born no later than 334 (Curt. 3.13.14). They were left at Damaskos with the other women and children of noble Persians (Arr. 2.11.9; Diod. 17.32.3; cf. Curt. 3.8.12) and captured in late 333 by Parmenion (Curt. 3.13.14; Justin 11.10.2; cf. Arr. 2.11.10). Thus she came to the attention of Alexander, who was captivated by her beauty (Justin 11.10.2–3); she was reputedly the only woman with whom Alexander had consorted before his marriage to Rhoxane (Plut. *Alex.* 21.7–9, who adds that Parmenion urged Alexander to marry her). B. received a Greek education (Plut. *Alex.* 21.9), perhaps in connexion with the family's stay in Macedonia (Diod. 16.52.3–4), where she may have met Alexander for the first time. In 327/6 (Diod. 20.20.1; or 325/4, according to Justin 15.2.3), B. bore the King a son named Herakles (Justin 11.10.3; Plut. *Eum.* 1.7; cf. Justin 13.2.7; 15.2.3; Paus. 9.7.2; Curt. 10.6.11, 13; Diod. 20.20.1; 20.28.1; for doubts concerning his identity see Müller 2019, 110). After Alexander's death, Nearchos proposed, without success, that this son be recognized as king (Curt. 10.6.10–12; cf. also Justin 13.2.7). B. herself had withdrawn to the West, probably at the time of Alexander's union with Rhoxane. We know that she was resident in Pergamon in mid-323 (Justin 13.2.7). In 309, Kassandros persuaded Polyperchon to abandon Herakles and his mother; it appears that the mother was killed along with the son (Justin 15.2.3; Paus. 9.7.2, who says Herakles was killed by poison, says nothing about the mother; cf. Diod. 20.28.1; Brosius 78 locates the actual murder in Pergamon). Kaerst, *RE* III.1 (1897) 29 no. 2; Berve II 102–4 no. 206; Hofstetter 36–7 no. 63; Tarn 1921; Brunt 1975; Shayegan 105 no. 37; Aulbach §4.3.2; Carney 100–5, 149–50; Müller 2021. **Stemma IV.**

BARSINE. (Aristoboulos, *FGrH* 139 F52 = Arr. 7.4.4). See s.v. **STATEIRA**.

288 BARYAXES

(Βαρυάξης). A Mede who assumed the upright tiara and the title of king, probably after the replacement of Oxydates by Atropates (cf. Arr. 4.18.3; cf. Curt. 8.3.17). He and his followers were, however, defeated and arrested by Alexander's satrap of Media, Atropates, who brought them in early 324 to the King at Pasargadai, where they were executed (Arr. 6.29.3). Confusion of B. and Oxydates is highly unlikely. The former is called a

Mede, whereas Oxydates is specifically identified as a Persian (Arr. 3.20.3). Furthermore, the charge against Oxydates was that he was deliberately shirking battle (Arr. 4.18.3: ἐθελοκακεῖν), not aspiring to the throne. Arr. 6.29.3 says that he was calling himself "king of the Persians and Medes." Badian 2000a, 93 suggests that he was descended "from the old Median kings." Briant 740 notes that only three men are specifically identified as Medes in the Alexander historians (see also Atropates and Gobares) but rightly observes that the scarcity of Medes in aristocratic circles may not indicate a decline of their power as much as it reflects the incomplete and uneven nature of the source evidence. Kaerst, *RE* III.1 (1897) 35; Berve II 104 no. 207; Justi, p. 65; Badian 2000a, 93 no. 3; Briant 740; Shayegan 105 no. 39.

289 BARZANES

(Βαρζάνης, Βραζάνης). Persian supporter of Bessos, who in 330/29 left him in charge of Parthia. Alexander, however, reinstated Dareios' satrap, Phrataphernes, who arrested B. and brought him to the King in Zariaspa (Baktra) for punishment (Arr. 4.7.1; cf. 4.18.1). He was presumably executed. B. is otherwise unknown and the name looks sadly in need of a prefix. Barzanes may be a corruption of the name Nabarzanes (no. 762). Kaerst, *RE* III.1 (1897) 36; Berve II 102 no. 204; Heckel 1981e and 2018b; Shayegan 105 no. 38.

290 BAS

(Βᾶς). Son of Boteiras. Bithynian dynast, born in 398/7. Ruled for 50 years until his death in 328/7. Alexander had apparently sent his satrap of Hellespontine Phrygia, Kalas (no. 559) son of Harpalos, to subdue Bithynia, but the latter was defeated by B. and forced to recognize his independence (Memnon, *FGrH* 434 F1 12.4; I see no good evidence for the view that Kalas was killed in the battle: Billows 45, with n.85). His son and successor was Zipoites. Meyer, *RE* II.1 (1897) 36; Berve II 104 no. 208.

291 BATIS

(Βάτις, Betis. Babemesis Josephus, *AJ* 11.320). Eunuch—according to Hegesias (*FGrH* 142 F5) he was corpulent and black—and *phrourarchos* of Gaza in the reign of Dareios III (Arr. 2.25.4; *Itiner. Al.* [19] 45 Tabacco; cf. Curt. 4.6.7), if not earlier. In September–October 332, he conducted a stubborn, two-month defense of Gaza (Diod. 17.48.7; 10,000 Persians and Arabs were said to have died in the siege: Curt. 4.6.30; cf. Plut. *Alex.* 25.4). When the city fell, he was taken by Leonnatos and Philotas son of Parmenion to Alexander (Hegesias, *FGrH* 142 F5; cf. Curt. 4.6.26), who is said to have dragged him (alive) behind his chariot, thus imitating in a rather gruesome way Achilles' treatment of Hektor (Curt. 4.6.29). The imitation of Achilles may be part of the later tradition concerning Alexander, but we have no good reason for doubting that B. was killed in a most barbaric fashion. Kaerst, *RE* III.1 (1897) 140; Berve II 104–5 no. 209; Tarn II 265–70; Shayegan 105 no. 40; Heckel 114–16.

292 BELEPHANTES

(Βελεφάντης). Leader of the Chaldaians who spoke to Nearchos in 323 (not 324, as Berve II 105 claims; Alexander had just returned from his winter campaign against the Kossaians: Diod. 17.112.1) and urged him to dissuade Alexander from entering Babylon, since this would bring about his death (Diod. 17.112.3). The Chaldaians also urged Alexander to avert the danger to himself by rebuilding the tomb of Belus (Bel-Marduk; on which see Stronk 374 n.190), which the Persians had destroyed. Baumstark, *RE* III.1 (1897) 201–2; Berve II 105 no. 210.

293 BERENIKE

(Βερενίκη). Macedonian (Tataki 280 no. 26). Daughter of Antigone (no. 113), who was herself a daughter of Kassandros and niece of Antipatros (Theocr. 17.61), and a certain Magas (schol. Theocr. 17.34 reads Βάγα, which is more sensibly emended to Μάγα than to Λάγου; the latter is accepted by Tataki 280). Berve II 105 dates her birth to "spätestens um 340" and places her first marriage to an otherwise unknown and low-born Philip (no. 919) around 325. From this marriage, B. produced a son Magas (Paus. 1.7.1; *PP* no. 14533), a daughter Antigone (no. 114), who married Pyrrhos (Plut. *Pyrrh.* 4.7; cf. Paus. 1.11.5), and possibly also a second daughter, Theoxene (no. 1117), who later married the Sicilian tyrant, Agathokles (Justin 23.2.6; cf. F. Geyer, *RE* V 2255, s.v. "Theoxene"; Ogden 70). Given the relatively low station of her husband, it is not unusual that B.'s son should bear the name of the maternal grandfather (another argument in favor of the aforementioned emendation). What became of Philip, we cannot be sure, but B. seems to have been widowed already when she accompanied her cousin, Eurydike, to Egypt in 319 (Paus. 1.6.8); she became the mistress of Ptolemy I *c.*317 (Ogden 215 flirts with the idea that B. may have been a courtesan, which seems impossible), to whom she bore Arsinoë II (in 316) and Ptolemy II (in spring 308 on the island of Kos; schol. Theocrit. 17.60; *Marm. Par.* a.309/8; Callimachus, *Hymn to Delos* 160ff.) and Philotera (birthdate unknown, cf. Strabo 16.4.5 C769). Sandberger 58 believes that Ptolemy married B. in 317/6 and elevated her to the position of βασίλισσα in the period between 294 and 290, and he points out that *c.*300 three of Berenike's children (two from her previous marriage) had important standing, which suggests that their mother was not merely Ptolemy's mistress at that time. How much we can make of this is uncertain: Eirene, the daughter of Ptolemy by the courtesan Thaïs became the bride of the Kypriot king, Eunostos—though it may be argued that Agathokles of Syracuse and Lysimachos, who married Theoxene and Arsinoë respectively, were considerably more important than Eunostos. Berve II 105 no. 211; U. Wilcken, *RE* III.1 (1897) 282–3 no. 9; H. Volkmann, *Kl. Pauly* I 863–4 no. 1; Beloch IV² 2.180–1; Sandberger 55–61 no. 2; Macurdy 104–9; Carney 203, 16–30; Ogden 68–73; Aulbach §6.2.1.4; Ager 2018. **Stemma X.**

294 BEROA

(Βερόα). Possibly Beroia. Epeirot woman of the royal house (one of the Aiakidai). Wife of Glaukias the Illyrian king. B. cared for Pyrrhos when he was a child in exile (Justin 17.3.18–19; cf. Plut. *Pyrrh.* 3). Glaukias adopted him, probably after the death of his father in 313. B. raised him along with her own sons, whose names are not preserved. Sandberger 61–2 no. 22; Kaerst, *RE* III.1 (1897) 304 no. 6 s.v. "Beroe."

295 BESSOS

(Βῆσσος). Prominent Persian, kinsman of Dareios III (Arr. 3.21.5). Satrap of Baktria (Arr. 3.8.3; Curt. 4.6.2; Diod. 17.73.2). Dareios summoned him from Central Asia after the battle of Issos and the failure of diplomatic negotiations (Curt. 4.6.2, foreshadowing B.'s betrayal of the king). At Gaugamela he commanded the Baktrian cavalry on the Persian left (Arr. 3.8.3; Curt. 4.12.6), with the aim of blunting Alexander's attack on that side (Curt. 4.15.2; Arr. 3.13.3–4). Nothing else is recorded of his participation in the battle. After the defeat he joined Dareios in flight to Media with 3,300 cavalry (Curt. 5.8.4; cf. Arr. 3.16.1). Curtius says that these were mainly Parthians but Arrian speaks of Baktrians. *Parthienorum* in the text of Curt. 5.8.4 should probably be emended to *Bactrianorum* (Atkinson II 137). In Curt. 4.12.11 the Parthians are named last of the contingents on the left wing, i.e., closest to the center, and this would agree with Arr. 3.16.1 where Dareios is accompanied by those who were deployed close to him in battle. But Arrian calls these cavalrymen Baktrians. In Arr. 3.11.4 the Parthians are located on the Persian right. B. was joined by Nabarzanes, Barsaentes and other prominent Persians in the plot to remove Dareios. Nabarzanes bases B.'s claim to the leadership on his position as satrap of Baktria, the region into which the Persian forces were fleeing (Curt. 5.9.8; cf. Arr. 3.21.4–5) but B.'s authority must have been based largely on kinship; for Nabarzanes himself, as chiliarch, must have wielded considerable power. Together they arrested Dareios (Curt. 5.9–12; Arr. 3.21.1, 4; Diod. 17.73.2) and considered handing him over to Alexander in order to win his favor (Arr. 3.21.5; Curt. 5.9.2, 10.5). Ultimately, they chose to kill the king (Curt. 5.13.15–25; Arr. 3.21.10; Diod. 17.73.2) and fled towards Baktria (Diod. 17.74.1) where B. assumed the military leadership and the title of king (Diod. 17.74.2; Curt. 6.6.13; Arr. 3.25.3; Metz Epit. 3; Khalili Archive IA 21; Mairs 2014, 43). Satibarzanes, who had at first come to terms with Alexander, threw in his lot with B. and appealed for help (Diod. 17.78.1–2; Curt. 6.6.13, 20; Arr. 3.25.5) but was defeated and killed before B. could be of aid. B. was, however, soon abandoned by his fellow conspirators—some perhaps out of resentment, but others influenced by Alexander's lenient treatment of Nabarzanes and others who had surrendered. Diod. 17.83.7–8 and Curt. 7.4.8–18 mention a certain Gobares (Gobryas; Diodorus calls him Bagodaras) who escaped from B.'s camp and received a warm reception from Alexander. This prompted others to expect lenient treatment from the King. But it also appears that the conspirators were convinced that Alexander would not pursue them into Baktria but turn instead to the warmer and richer lands of India. When their hopes were proved false, many dispersed and B., with whatever followers remained, crossed the Oxos River into Sogdiana and proceeded towards the Iaxartes (Curt. 7.4.20–21; Arr. 3.28.8–10). B. was finally arrested by Spitamenes, Dataphernes, and Katanes and handed over to Alexander (Arr. 3.29.6–30.5; Curt. 7.5.19–26, 36–8; Metz Epit. 5–6). There are two versions of B.'s extradition (Heckel 2018a, 9–10). One based on Ptolemy himself (Arr. 3.29.7–30.5) claims that B. was abandoned by the road by Spitamenes and his fellow conspirators for Ptolemy to bring to Alexander; the second, recorded also by Aristoboulos (Arr. 3.30.5) relates that Spitamenes himself handed B. over to the King (cf. Curt. 7.5.36–7). He was tortured briefly by some of those who had arrested him (Curt. 7.5.40–2; Arr. 3.30.5), and then sent on to Ekbatana to be punished by the Persians as a regicide (Curt. 7.5.43; Arr. 4.7.3). Arr. 3.30.5 has him sent to Baktra (Zariaspa) for execution, but at 4.7.3 Arrian reports that he was mutilated here (his nose and earlobes were cut off) before he was sent to Ekbatana for execution. Plut. *Alex.* 43.6 has B. executed—he was torn apart by recoiling trees—on the spot where he was handed over to Alexander; Diod. 17.83.9 also has B. mutilated and executed on the spot. Metz Epit. 14 has him killed in Baktria (presumably at Baktra). For a discussion of these accounts and Curtius' attempts to reconcile two primary sources see Heckel 1994a, 70. Kaerst, *RE* III.1 (1897) 331; Berve II 105–8 no. 212; Shayegan 105–7 no. 41; Müller, *LexAM* 141–4.

296 BIANOR

(Βιάνωρ). Akarnanian of unknown family, B. fought as a commander of Greek mercenaries in the Persian army at Issos in late 333 (Arr. 2.13.2). After Dareios' defeat there, B. joined Amyntas son of Antiochos (no. 77), Thymondas (no. 1136) and Aristomedes (no. 196) in flight to Tripolis in Phoinikia. From there he appears to have accompanied Amyntas as far as Kypros (Diod. 17.48.3; Arr. 2.13.2–3), but since we know only of Amyntas' death in Egypt, and no mention is made of the other officers, it may well be that they did not continue on with him to Egypt; perhaps B. went instead to Krete (cf. Bosworth I 222–3). Nothing else is known about him. Whether he is identical with the B. who was related by marriage to Amadokos of Thrake (Dem. 23.10, 17, 180) is impossible to determine. Bosworth I 222 believes he may have belonged to that faction in Akarnania exiled after Chaironeia (Tod II no. 178; Diod. 17.3.3). Kaerst, *RE* III.1 (1897) 381 no. 5; Berve II 109 no. 214; Hofstetter 38 no. 67.

297 BIANOR

([Βιάν]ωρ). Honored in an Athenian decree moved by Stratokles in 304/3. Bianor (if his name is correctly restored; Theanor and Euenor are also possibilities) appears to have been an officer or envoy of Demetrios (*SEG* XVI 58 = *Hesperia* 7 (1938) 297 no. 22). Billows 377 no. 23.

298 BION

(Βίων). Greek mercenary in the service of Dareios III; he defected to the Macedonians on the eve of the battle of Gaugamela and revealed to Alexander the locations of traps set on the battlefield for the Macedonian cavalry by the Persians (Curt. 4.13.36–7). This episode is mentioned only by Curtius. Both the details of the story and B. himself may well be fictitious. Berve II 109–10 no. 217; Berve, *RE* Supplbd IV (1924) s.v. "Bion (3a)"; Hofstetter 38–9 no. 68; Marsden 1964, 41.

299 BIRKENNA

(Βιρκέννα). Illyrian, daughter of Bardylis. After Antigone's death Pyrrhos married a daughter of Autoleon the Paionian, then Birkenna, and then Lanassa the daughter of Agathokles of Syracuse (thus Plut. *Pyrrh.* 9.2, but the actual order of the marriages is probably reversed). B. was the mother of Helenos (no. 511), Pyrrhos' youngest son (Plut. *Pyrrh.* 9.3; cf. Justin 18.1.3; see s.v. Helenos). The relationship between B. and her husband appears to have been congenial; we are told that Lanassa quarrelled with Pyrrhos because he preferred his barbarian wives (Plut. *Pyrrh.* 10.7). Sandberger 62–3 no. 23; Kaerst, *RE* III.1 (1897) 491; Seibert 1967, 101–2; Hammond 1966, 239ff. **Stemma IIb.**

300 BISTHANES

(Βισθάνης). Son of Artaxerxes III (Ochos), perhaps, as Bosworth I 335 suggests, by one of his concubines; Diod. 17.5.4–5 says that Arses was the only son to survive Bagoas' initial purge of Ochos' family and that, after Arses' death, there was no successor to the throne. B. encountered Alexander when he was three days' march from Ekbatana in Media (Arr. 3.19.4) and reported that Dareios had fled from the city four days earlier with 7,000 talents from the treasury, 3,000 cavalrymen, and 6,000 infantry (Arr. 3.19.5; cf. Curt. 5.13.1, without naming B.). Whether he had accompanied Dareios in flight from Gaugamela (thus Berve II 109) or whether he had been in residence at Ekbatana is not clear. Nothing else is known about him, but we may assume that he remained in Alexander's entourage. Kaerst, *RE* III.1 (1897) 504 s.v. "Bistanes"; Berve II 109 no. 215; Shayegan 107 no. 42.

301 BITHYS

(Βίθυς). Son of Kleon, from Lysimacheia (*IG* II² 808, line 15). Lund 181 believes he may have been Thrakian. B. had great influence with Lysimachos and, in the literary sources, is treated as one of the king's courtiers, one of his most influential *philoi* according to Phylarchos, *FGrH* 81 F12 (*ap.* Athen. 14.614f), but referred to as *parasitos* by Aristodemos (*ap.* Athen. 6.246e). His disyllabic name, as well as that of Paris (and, presumably, also Mithres) prompted Demetrios Poliorketes to comment that the Thrakian king's court was like the comic stage (Athen. 14.614f). Aristodemos (*FHG* III 310 *ap.* Athen. 6.246e) tells how Lysimachos put a wooden scorpion down the cloak of B. He was terrified, but when he learned the truth, B. is said to have tried to scare Lysimachos, who was particularly stingy, by asking him for a talent (Ath 6.246e; Plut. *Mor.* 633b). Although these stories may belong to the 290s, B. was doubtless at Lysimachos' court already in the fourth century. Lysimachos granted B. land, adjacent to the properties of Limnaios son of Harpalos and the king's own son, Agathokles: *SEG* 38 (1988) 619; Hatzopoulos II 45–6 no. 22. The record of this land grant, which provides the father's name, has strengthened the view that *IG* II² 808 (dated by Burstein 1980, 45 to "the second half of the 280s") refers to him. Nothing else is known about his career. Hatzopoulos II 45–6 no. 22; Burstein 1980; Lund 181; Landucci, *Lisimaco* 70, 206–7.

302 BITON

(Βίτων). A Greek mercenary leader of unknown origin, B. was left behind with the garrison at Baktra in 327/6. When Athenodoros (no. 257) led an uprising of Greeks and seized the citadel of Baktra in 325—for it was rumored that Alexander had died in India (Diod. 17.99.5–6; cf. Curt. 9.7.1; also Diod. 18.7)—B. induced a certain Baktrian named Boxus (no. 310) to invite Athenodoros to dinner and there to murder him (Curt. 9.7.4). B. then called a meeting of the Greek rebels and announced that Athenodoros had plotted against him and narrowly missed a lynching at the hands of Athenodoros' supporters. But those officers who had appealed to the mob to save B. were also betrayed by him, and, although he was sentenced to be tortured, he escaped even this punishment and returned safely to Greece with some followers (Curt. 9.7.5–11). Kaerst, *RE* III.1 (1897) 545 no. 3; Berve II 109 no. 216; Iliakis 2013, 187–90.

303 BLITOR

(Βλίτωρ). Macedonian (Hoffmann 205; Tataki 282 no. 37). Satrap of Mesopotamia 317 (his position is defined by Appian only as *hegemon*). It is likely that Antigonos sent him to Mesopotamia after the battle of Gabiene to replace Eumenes' supporter Amphimachos (no. 72), who was either killed in battle, executed after the defeat, or removed from office. Antigonos deposed B. in 315, when Seleukos fled to Ptolemy, charging that B. had allowed him to escape (App. *Syr.* 53.269). He is not heard of again. Kaerst, *RE* III.1 (1897) 570; Schober 1981, 88, 95 n.1; Mehl 64–5; Billows 377–8 no. 24.

304 BOIOTOS

(Βοιωτός). A longtime friend of Antigonos and privy to his secrets (Diod. 19.85.2). Possibly Macedonian (Tataki 282 no. 39). Perhaps his relationship with Antigonos goes back to the time before Alexander's death (possibly to Antigonos' time as satrap of Phrygia). B. died at the battle of Gaza (Diod. 19.85.2). Nothing else is known about him. Billows 378 no. 25; Kirchner, *RE* III (1897) 666 no. 8.

305 BOLON

The name occurs only in Curtius. A common Macedonian (Tataki 283 no. 41), a man of no refinement who had risen from the ranks to some lower military office (Curt. 6.11.1), B. gave a speech at Phrada in 330 denouncing the arrogance of Philotas and thereby incited hatred against him and contributed to his fall (Curt. 6.11.2–8). He is, however, mentioned only by Curtius, who may have invented the individual and the sentiments expressed for dramatic effect. Berve II 110 no. 218; Hoffmann 222.

306 BOUBAKES

(Βουβάκης). Although the name may be a corruption of Boubares/Boupares, identification with the Babylonian commander at Gaugamela is impossible (Arr. 3.8.5). Prominent Persian of unknown family. B. was killed in the battle of Issos in late 333 (Arr. 2.11.8). Berve II 110 rightly dismisses the idea that he was the local dynast of Boubakene in Central Asia (*Barr. Atl.* 99 D1; cf. Curt. 8.5.2), even though dynasts of the Indian frontier took official regional names. There were no representatives of these regions in the Persian force at Issos. Berve II 110 no. 220; Justi 71; Shayegan 107 no. 44.

307 BOUBAKES

(Βουβάκης). A faithful eunuch who remained with Dareios III to the end of the king's life. He may have acted as an interpreter (Curt. 5.11.4; but his role in this episode may simply have been that of intermediary), although we know that the king had an official interpreter in Melon (no. 700; Curt. 5.13.7). Whether B. is historical or merely inserted into Curtius' account for dramatic effect cannot be determined. In a touching scene, B. is praised by Dareios for his loyalty and urged to save himself (Curt. 5.12.10–11). Possibly he surrendered to Alexander soon afterwards. Berve II 110 no. 221; Shayegan 107 no. 45.

308 BOUPARES

(Βουπάρης). Prominent Persian. B. is attested only once in the Alexander historians: Arr. 3.8.5 says he led the Babylonian contingent at Gaugamela. He may have been satrap of Babylonia, but his subsequent disappearance must then be explained. Berve II 110, following Lehmann-Haupt 115, 142, accepts him as satrap. But it is odd that none of the sources, when describing Mazaios' surrender of Babylon, mentions B., whether he had fled, died, or been deposed. Bosworth I 291 accepts Leuze's view (1935, 410–12) that B. was merely acting on behalf of the Babylonian satrap, who may have been unfit to lead the army. But this again fails to explain why there is no mention of Dareios' satrap in the account of the city's surrender. One possibility is that he was killed at Gaugamela and replaced after the battle by Mazaios (thus Briant 849). Berve II 110 no. 222. Lehmann-Haupt 115, 142; Leuze 1935, 410–12; Bosworth I 291; Briant 849.

309 BOURICHOS

(Βούριχος). Probably Greek. Officer in the service of Demetrios Poliorketes (307/6). After the defeat of the Ptolemaic forces in the battle of Salamis, B. and Neon were given the transport ships and ordered to pursue and pick up the survivors (Diod. 20.52.4). The use of the word διώκειν ("to pursue"; cf. Habicht[2] 56: "Verfolgung des fliehenden Feindes") suggests that Demetrios was primarily concerned with collecting prisoners. Although nothing further is known of Neon, B. was clearly an influential member of Demetrios' entourage. He is referred to as one of his parasites, and allegedly received shrines and had libations poured to him by the flattering Athenians; even paeans sung to him, to the extent that Demetrios found it disgraceful and said that there were no decent Athenians left (Athen. 6.252f–253a = Demochares, *FHG* II 449; *FGrH* 75 F1). It was probably Demetrios' esteem for B. rather than the latter's service to Athens that motivated those who voted him honors, and perhaps for that reason they were regarded as excessive. Wilcken, *RE* III.1 (1897) 1067; Habicht[2] 55–8, Hauben 114–15; Billows 378 no. 26.

310 BOXOS

(Βόξος). For the name see also Strabo 16.4.20 C779, citing Ktesias, *FGrH* 688 F66. A Baktrian of unknown family; supporter of the mercenary leader Biton (no. 302), who induced him to murder Athenodoros (no. 257) at a dinner party (Curt. 9.7.4). The Greeks decided that B. should be executed and Biton subjected to torture. Although turmoil ensued and Biton escaped in the confusion, it appears that B.'s execution was carried out immediately. It is tempting to speculate that Curt. 9.7.3 is mistaken when he says that Athenodoros claimed the kingship—such a move makes little sense for a mercenary leader—and that B. was a native usurper who attracted Greek mercenaries to his cause. When this uprising failed to gather sufficient support, B. was arrested and killed. (Curt. 9.7.7–8; cf. Holt 1988, 85). Berve II 110 no. 219; Shayegan 107 no. 43; Iliakis 2013, 187–90.

BRISON (Βρίσων. Arr. 3.12.2). See **OMBRION**.

311 BROCHUBELUS

The name is attested only in Curtius. According to Curt. 5.13.11, a son of Mazaios, perhaps by a Babylonian wife (Brochubelus is a legitimate Babylonian name; cf. Briant 724; Atkinson II 160). Berve II 40 identifies him with Antibelos, but Bosworth I 341 thinks that Arrian (or presumably his source) confused Antibelos and Artiboles, since "the two names ... seem to be derived from the Babylonian Ardu-bel, and it is highly probable that they are alternative Hellenizations of the same original." B. deserted soon after the arrest of Dareios by Bessos and Nabarzanes, surrendering to Alexander somewhere between Rhagai and Thara (Curt. 5.13.11). Arr. 3.21.1 places the surrender of Antibelos earlier (at Khar) and in conjunction with that of Bagisthanes (see Bosworth I 340–1). That we are dealing with two different sons of Mazaios seems unlikely. What became of him we do not know. Perhaps he is the son of Mazaios whose territory was enlarged by Alexander (Plut. *Alex.* 39.9, with Hamilton 104–5), though we are not told what that territory was. Curt. 5.13.11 reads: *Brochubelus, Mazaei filius, Syriae praetor*. This is usually emended to read *praetor<is>* to make it refer to Mazaios. But if the text is correct, B. may have exercised some administrative role (a *hyparchos* of sorts) in Syria. Berve II 40 no. 82 Ἀντίβηλος); Bosworth I 340–1; Hamilton 105.

312 BRYAXIS

(Βρύαξις). Sculptor. Apparently Karian. B. was one of the artists (along with Skopas, Timotheos, and Leochares) who worked on the sculptures of the Mausoleum (Pliny, *HN* 36.30–1); he also sculpted Seleukos I (Pliny, *HN* 34.73). Pollitt 91–2 and 1986, 277–80; Robert, *RE* III.1 (1897) 916–20; Grainger, *SPG* 643.

C

313 CALIS

Possibly Kalas (Tataki 334 no. 4); the name is attested only in its Latin form in Curtius. A young Macedonian, apparently of high standing, C.'s role in the conspiracy of Demetrios the Bodyguard (autumn 330) was exposed at the trial of Philotas. C. confessed that he and Demetrios had planned the conspiracy against Alexander (Curt. 6.11.36–7). He was, presumably, put to death together with those conspirators named by Dimnos and Nikomachos (Curt. 6.11.38; cf. 6.7.15). He appears only in Curtius' heavily dramatized version of the Philotas affair, and this raises some doubts about both the historicity of the individual and his involvement in the conspiracy. Berve II 189 no. 398 and *RE* Supplbd. IV (1924) 855.

314 CARTHASIS

The name appears only in its Latin form (Curt. 7.7.1; Metz Epit. 8). C. was the brother of the king of the Skythians who lived beyond the Iaxartes (Syr-Darya) River and was sent by him to destroy the newly founded Alexandria Eschate, which threatened the Skythians' mobility and livelihood (Curt. 7.7.1; cf. Holt 1988, 56–60). His force was, however, attacked north of the Iaxartes (Curt. 7.8–9, Metz Epit. 10–12, and Arr. 4.4.2–8 for the battle; cf. Fuller 238–41) and defeated with heavy casualties (Curt. 7.9.16; cf. Metz Epit. 12). Arr. 4.4.8 speaks of 1,000 Skythian dead, including one of their commanders, whom he calls Satrakes, and 150 captured. Unless C. is identical with Arrian's Satrakes (Bosworth II 31), we do not know what became of him. Berve II 201 no. 413; Shayegan 108 no. 46.

315 CHAIREAS

(Χαιρέας). Greek. Sculptor. Produced statues of Philip II and Alexander (Pliny, *HN* 34.75 = Stewart 1993, T101). Nothing else is known about him or his work, unless he can be identified with Chares of Lindos (thus Stewart 106, following Schreiber 1903, 268–72); Berve II 403 rejects this identification on chronological grounds. Robert, *RE* III.2 (1899) 2023–4 no. 9; Berve II 403 no. 817.

316 CHAIRON

(Χαίρων). Greek from Megalopolis. Philip II sent him to Delphi in 356 to inquire about dreams he had had concerning Olympias. Ch. returned with the response that Philip should revere the god Amun, and the prediction that he would lose the eye with which he watched the god in the form of a snake through a crack in Olympias' door (Plut. *Alex.* 3.1–2). The story is almost certainly a fiction, although Ch. himself may be historical. If he is not historical, perhaps the name Chairon was suggested by that of Sokrates' emissary to Delphi, Chairephon (Plato, *Apology* 21). But this is no more than speculation.

317 CHAIRON

(Χαίρων). Wrestler who was twice victorious at the Isthmian games and a four-time Olympic champion, installed by Alexander as tyrant of Pellene (Paus. 7.27.7). Student of Plato and Xenokrates (Athen. 11.509b). Antipatros' general Korrhagos may have installed him as tyrant of Pellene (in Alexander's name) at some point before 331 ([Dem.] 17.10; Paus. 7.7.1 says Pellene was the only Achaian city to have been subjected to a tyranny). Ch. remained loyal to Macedon during Agis' war (Aesch. 3.165; cf. Din. 1.34 for the timing of the war) and this will account in no small way for the negative comments concerning his rule. Athen. 11.509b, for example, claims that Ch. gave the property and wives of his enemies to their slaves (cf. [Dem.] 17.10). Nothing else is known about him, but Berve, *Tyrannis* II 677 observes: "Da Phainias ihn vermutlich in seiner Schrift über Beseitigung von Tyrannen aus Rache (vgl. fr. 14ff. Wehrli) erwähnte, dürfte er umgebracht worden sein." Kroll, *RE* III.2 (1899) 2032–3 no. 4; Berve II 403 no. 818; Berve, *Tyrannis* I 307–8 and II 677.

318 CHARES

(Χάρης). Athenian of the deme Angele (Kirchner 15292). Son of Theochares. Davies 568 comments: "Our ignorance of Chares' family remains complete." The father is otherwise unknown, and Ch.'s birthdate, on the assumption that he was at least 30 when he was first elected to the *strategia* in 367/6 (Xen. *HG* 7.2.18–23, 4.1; Diod. 15.75.3; cf. Develin 256), could not have been much later than 400. Ch. is attested as *strategos* on at least sixteen further occasions, the last time in 338 at Chaironeia ([Plut.] *Mor.* 843d; Polyaenus 4.2.8; Diod. 16.85.2). Ch. was elected *strategos* in 367/6–366/5; 361/0; 358/7–353/2; 349/8–347/6; 341/0–338/7 (ancient sources collected in Develin under each year). He appears to have been a man of physical strength but of poor judgment (Plut. *Mor.* 788d–e), and he had a turbulent relationship with the Athenians (Theopompos, *FGrH* 115 F105 = Athen. 12.532a–b). For his activities between 356 and 338, during which time he served as *strategos* in the Social War (Diod. 16.21; cf. Isoc. 1.50), then as a mercenary commander for Artabazos (Diod. 16.22.1; cf. Dem. 4.24) and later seized Lampsakos and Sigeion (cf. Dem. 2.28), see Cawkwell, *OCD*[3] 317 s.v. "Chares (1)," and the more extensive discussion by Hofstetter 40–1 and Kirchner *RE* 1899, with references. As an opponent of Macedon, he is listed amongst those whom Alexander demanded the Athenians to deliver after the sack of Thebes in 335 (Arr. 1.10.4; *Suda* A 2704; not named in Plut. *Dem.* 23.4); Bosworth I 94 may be correct in assuming that Ch. left Athens and retired to Sigeion (*Barr. Atl.* 57 E2) soon after Chaironeia in order to escape prosecution (cf. the fate of Lysikles: Diod. 16.88.1–2; [Plut.] *Mor.* 843d). Certainly, he is attested in Sigeion in 334 (Arr. 1.12.1); for he greeted Alexander with a golden crown at Ilion at that time. Ch. nevertheless soon took up service with Persia. In 332, he occupied Mytilene, which had been recovered by the Persian fleet, with 2,000 mercenaries, but he later handed the city over to Hegelochos on the understanding that he himself could leave unharmed (Curt. 4.5.22; Arr. 3.2.6). [Plut.] *Mor.* 848e says he commanded a mercenary force at Tainaron in 324, at which time he must have been at least in his mid-seventies. He died in 324/3 [Dem.] *Ep.* 3.31; cf. Davies 369). Kirchner, *RE* III.2 (1899) 2125–8 no. 3; Davies 568–9; Berve II 403–4 no. 819; Hofstetter 40–2 no. 73.

319 CHARES

(Χάρης). Chares of Mytilene (*FGrH* 125 T1, 3a). Accompanied Alexander from the beginning of the Asiatic expedition and held a high position at the court. Perhaps he was recommended to the King by the prominent Mytileneans, Laomedon and Erigyios. After the King's adoption of Persian court ceremonial, Ch. became the Royal Usher (*eisangeleus*: Plut. *Alex.* 46.2); he was thus knowledgeable about everyday occurrences at the court and an eyewitness to events like the murder of Kleitos (Plut. *Alex.* 50–2, thought to be based primarily on Ch.: Hamilton 139), the introduction of *proskynesis* (Plut. *Alex.* 54.4–6; cf. Arr. 4.12.3–5), the death of Kallisthenes (Plut. Alex. 55.9), and the mass marriages in Sousa (Athen. 12.538b–539a). Whether he had a personal dislike for Alexander's tutor, Lysimachos, is unclear (Berve II 241; *contra* Pearson 56–7). Author of a *History of Alexander*, of which some 19 fragments survive. The work is of greater interest to the social and cultural historian and presents little of value on politics or the military. Schwartz, *RE* III.2 (1899) 2129 no. 13; Berve II 405–6 no. 820; Jacoby *FGrH* 125; Pearson 50–61; Müller, *LexAM* 161–3.

320 CHARIAS

(Χαρίας). Origins unknown. Student of Polyeidos of Thessaly (Athen. Mech 10; Vitr 10.13.3). Engineer in Alexander's entourage (Athen. Mech. 5, 10; cf. Whitehead and Blyth 71). He wrote a book on siege machinery (Vitruv. 7 *praef.* 14; 10.19.3). See also Diades (no. 375). Hultsch, *RE* III.2 (1899) 2133 no. 11; Berve II 406 no. 821; Marsden 1977; Whitehead and Blyth 71–2, 85–6; Stronk 308 n.131.

321 CHARIDEMOS

(Χαρίδημος). Son of Philoxenos, from Oreos on Euboia ([Arist.] *Oecon.* 2.1351b 19; Ael. *VH* 2.41; Theopompos *ap.* Athen. 10.436b–c; *IG* II² 32, 36; cf. Davies 570). Born in the 390s, Ch. first saw military action as a *psilos* when Chabrias attacked Oreos between 378 and 376 (cf. Diod. 15.30.5). In the period 368/7–365, he fought with Iphikrates as a mercenary captain (*xenagos*) at Amphipolis (Dem. 23.148–9). After the removal of Iphikrates from command, Ch. delivered the Amphipolitan hostages back to their home rather than conveying them to Athens (Dem. 23.149). Ch. spent some time with Kotys of Thrake and was later captured en route to Amphipolis. He took up service with Timotheos (Dem. 23.149–50). In 362 he went to Asia Minor to serve under Mentor and Memnon the Rhodians, waging war in Aiolia and taking control of Skepsis, Kebren, and Ilion (Dem. 23.154ff.; Aen. Tact. 24.3; Plut. *Ser.* 1; Polyaenus 3.14; for his further activities there see Dem. 23.155–6, [Aristotle] *Oecon.* 2.30.1351b 19ff.; *Syll³* 188). He returned to Thrake where he served Kotys and his son Kersobleptes and acted as an agent in Thrakian dealings with Athens, whereupon he earned Athenian citizenship (Kirchner 15380; Dem. 23.141, 203; cf. Parke 1928, 170; Davies 571; Kelly 1990; Hamel 1998, 18) and was enrolled in the deme Acharnai (*Syll³* 962, 322). Ch. reported the death of Philip II in 336 (Aesch. 3.77). After the sack of Thebes, he was exiled on Alexander's orders and took refuge with Dareios III (Arr. 1.10.4, 6; cf. Plut. *Phoc.* 17.2, Plut. *Dem.* 23.4; *Suda* A 2704; Din. 1.32–4). Shortly before the battle of Issos, he advised Dareios to split his forces and entrust a portion of them to him (Diod. 17.30.2–3), but he was suspected of planning to betray the Persians and was put to death (Diod. 17.30.4–5); Curt. 3.2.10–19 gives an account strongly reminiscent of the Demaratos episode in Hdt. 7.101–5 (see Blänsdorff 1971, but the resemblance was already noted by Rüegg 1906, 44–5; Kaerst I³ 361 n.1; Parke 1933, 183 n.5). Ch. had three sons by a sister of Kersobleptes (Dem. 23.129; cf. Davies 571): Eurymedon, Phylakos, and Troilos (*IG* II² 1627, 207–16, 217–22): the sons paid a debt owed by their father for a trierarchy before 336 (cf. Dem. 23.136, 138). Kirchner, *RE* III.2 (1899) 2135–8; Schaefer III² 143–4; Berve II 406–7 no. 823; Blänsdorf 1971; Seibt 108–9; Atkinson I 462–3; Hofstetter 42–3 no 74; Kelly 1990; Parke 1928, 170; cf. Parke 1933, 100, 125–32, 146–8, 183; Bengtson, *Staatsv* II no. 324; Judeich; Hornblower, *Mausolus* 213ff., 261, 279; Buckler 374–6, 431.

322 CHARIKLES

(Χαρικλῆς). Son of Menandros (Arr. 4.13.7), most likely the satrap of Lydia (no. 706); but Bosworth II 97 suggests, less plausibly, that the father "was the Companion later executed for leaving the command to which he was assigned." Perhaps one of the King's Pages in 327. Though not party to the Hermolaos conspiracy, he was informed of it by his lover Epimenes (no. 423) and brought the matter to the attention of the latter's brother, Eurylochos (thus Arr. 4.13.7; Curt. 8.6.20 omits Ch. entirely), who revealed the plot to Alexander, through the agency of Ptolemy and Leonnatos. The conspirators themselves were arrested, tortured, and executed, but Ch. and Epimenes were spared (cf. Curt. 8.6.26). Nothing further is known about him. Berve II 407 no. 824; Heckel 1992, 290; Hoffmann 180.

323 CHARIKLES

(Χαρικλῆς). Athenian of unknown background. Ch. must have come from a prominent family, since he was deemed worthy to marry a daughter of Phokion (Plut. *Phoc.* 21.5), though Phokion may have had some reservations about the man's character (Plut. *Phoc.* 22.4). His connections with Harpalos and Pythionike (no. 1020) may go back to the time of Harpalos' first flight (cf. Arr. 3.6.4–7), but Plut. *Phoc.* 21.5, if taken literally, indicates that Harpalos befriended Ch. in 324 (see also Tritle 1988, 119). Ch. accepted 30 talents for the construction of a funeral monument to Pythionike, and this excessive amount may have included a substantial bribe (Plut. *Phoc.* 22.1–2); certainly he was brought up on bribery charges in connection with the Harpalos case (Plut. *Phoc.* 22.4). When Phokion and his associates were attacked by Hagnonides in 318, Ch. and Kallimedon (no. 568) fled the city (Plut. *Phoc.* 33.4). Ch. was condemned to death *in absentia* (Plut. *Phoc.* 35.5). He was the guardian of the daughter (A89) of Harpalos and Pythionike (Plut. *Phoc.* 22.1, 3). Kirchner, *RE* III.2 (1899) 2140 no. 2; Kirchner 15403; Berve II 408 no. 825.

324 CHARON

(Χάρων). Greek from Chalkis in Alexander's entourage at an unspecified time. At a drinking party in the quarters of Krateros, Alexander praised the young boy who was the *eromenos* of Ch. When the latter urged the boy to kiss Alexander, the King declined the offer on account of the pain it would cause Ch. (Karystios *ap.* Athen. 13.603b). Nothing else is known about him. Berve II 408 no. 827.

325 CHARUS

Named only by Curtius. Macedonian (Tataki 458 no. 5). A member of Alexander's cohort (Curt. 8.11.9–10) but apparently not a Page; hence a member of the "Royal Hypaspists." Ch. commanded (together with a certain Alexander no. 48) a troop of thirty hypaspists in an assault on Aornos, where he was killed in battle and fell upon the corpse of his friend Alexander (Curt. 8.11.15–16). Curtius' description of their deaths recalls Virgil's account of Nisos and Euryalos (*Aeneid* 9.176–445; Minissale 1983, 89), but the historicity of the event (cf. Plut. *Alex.* 58.5, naming Alexander) and of Ch. and Alexander themselves need not be questioned. Berve, *RE* Supplbd. IV (1924) 215; Berve II 408 no. 826; Heckel 1992, 296.

CHEIROKRATES (Berve II 408 no. 828). See **DEINOKRATES**.

326 CHILON

(Χίλων). Son of Chilon. An Achaian wrestler from Patrai, who died in battle against the Macedonians in the Lamian War (Paus. 6.4.6–7; 7.6.5). Since Pausanias twice notes that he was the only Achaian to fight in the Lamian war, his uncertainty about whether Ch. died at Chaironeia or later is pointless (6.4.7). Ch. was buried by Achaians at state expense (Paus. 6.4.6). As an athlete he won two victories at Olympia, one at Delphi, four at the Isthmian and three at the Nemean games, as we learn from an inscription at Olympia and a statue of him attributed to Lysippos (Paus. 6.4.6–7).

327 CHIONIDES

(Χιωνίδης). Athenian from Thria (Kirchner 15558). Third member of an embassy to Antigonos in 305 (*IG* II² 1492B; details s.vv. Kleainetos no. 487, Xenokles no. 1160). Also proposed a decree in honor of Nikomedes son of Aristandros from Kos (see Paschidis 87 with nn.3–4; cf. Billows 411). Otherwise unknown. Paschidis 109 A32.

328 CHOIRILOS

(Χοίριλος). Execrable epic poet (Constantine Porphyrogenitus on Horace, *Ars Poetica* 5.357 calls him *poeta pessimus*) from Iasos (Hesychius; *Suda*; Steph. Byz. s.v. Ἴασος), Ch. accompanied Alexander to Asia (Curt. 8.5.8) and wrote a poem in which Alexander appeared as Achilleus. Alexander is supposed to have remarked that he would rather be Thersites in Homer's *Iliad* than Ch.'s Achilleus. The work was generally derided and condemned. Crusius, *RE* III.1 (1899) 2361–2 no. 5; Berve II 408–9 no. 829.

CHORIENES. See **SISIMITHRES**.

329 CHRYSIPPOS

(Χρύσιππος). Greek dancer of unknown origin. Alexander mentioned him in a letter to his financial officer Philoxenos (Athen. 1.22d). Cf. also Theodoros no. 1108. Berve II 409 no. 830.

330 CHRYSIS

(Χρύσις). A prostitute, apparently resident in Athens, who had relations with Demetrios Poliorketes (Plut. *Demetr.* 24.1). Aulbach §8.2.2.2.

331 CLEADAS

The name is attested only in its Latin form. A Theban who was captured when the city was sacked in 335 (Justin 11.4.1), C. spoke in defense of the Theban uprising, alleging that Thebes had rebelled only on the false rumor of the King's death (Justin 11.4.1–6). His remarks fell on deaf ears. About the historicity of C. and his appeal (cf. Hegesias, *FGrH* 142 FF6–20) we cannot be certain. Berve II 204 no. 421.

332 CLEOPHIS

The name is found in Latin sources only and may have been invented in the Augustan Age as a play on the name Kleopatra (cf. Gutschmid 1882, 553–4; Seel 1972, 181–2). Mother of Assakenos (Curt. 8.10.22; Metz Epit. 39; cf. Arr. 4.27.4, who does not name her), the Indian dynast of the Assakenians of the Swat and Panjkora region. She conducted the defense of Massaga (a fortress in the Katgala Pass; cf. Caroe 1962, 51–3), the capital city of the Assakenians, since her son had died only shortly before the advent of Alexander (Curt. 8.10.22); the actual operations appear to have been managed by Assakenos' brother (another son of C. ?), known in Metz Epit. 39 as Amminais, and 9,000 mercenaries (Curt. 8.10.23 says the city was garrisoned by 38,000 infantrymen, which may include the above-mentioned mercenaries, though Curtius, oddly, says nothing about their fate). After a valiant defense (Curt. 8.10.27–33), in which the *hegemon* of the place was killed (Arr. 4.27.2), the Assakenians sent a herald to Alexander to discuss terms of surrender. Arrian (4.27.3–4) differs from the Vulgate in the details of this proposed capitulation, claiming that Alexander slaughtered the mercenaries because they planned to desert and took the city by force, capturing in the process the mother and *daughter* of Assakenos. Curtius writes that C. and the noble women came in person to surrender to Alexander (cf. Metz Epit. 45), that she placed *her own son* (Assakenos' son in Metz Epit. 39, 45) on the King's knee and thereby won his pardon and retained her position as queen (Curt. 8.10.34–5). C. subsequently bore a son, named Alexander (Curt. 8.10.36; Justin 12.7.10 claims that Alexander himself was the father, cf. Oros. 3.19.1–2). Justin gives a scandalous account of the queen's behavior, claiming that she retained her kingdom through sexual favors and was thus called *scortum regium* (12.7.9–11; Pliny, *HN* 9.119 calls Kleopatra VII *regina meretrix*; cf. Propertius 3.11.39). Berve II 214 thinks that the romantic elements of this episode found their way into the Kandake story of the Alexander Romance (Ps.-Call. 3.18). Kroll, *RE* XI.1 (1921) 791–2; Berve II 214 no. 435.

D

333 DAMIS

(Δάμις). Spartan of unknown family. In 324, upon hearing that Alexander was requesting divine honors, D. is supposed to have remarked, "Let's agree that Alexander be called a god, if he so wishes" (Plut. *Mor.* 219e; cf. Ael. *VH* 2.19). Schaefer III² 313 n.4 suggests that "Damis" may be a corruption of "Eudamidas"; Berve's observation (II 115) that the sources fail to designate the speaker as a king is not compelling. Nothing else is known about him. Niese, *RE* IV.2 (1901) 2056 no. 2; Berve II 115 no. 239; Poralla no. 216.

334 DAMIS

(Δάμις). Probably a Megalopolitan. D. served with Alexander in Asia—presumably in an allied contingent or as a mercenary; if he had belonged to the allied contingent he must have re-enlisted in 330—where he gained experience in the use of elephants in warfare (Diod. 18.71.2). This knowledge he used to good effect in the successful defense of Megalopolis against Polyperchon in 318 (Diod. 18.71). He appears to have been installed as the city's governor (*epimeletes*) by Antipatros, perhaps after the Lamian War, and was confirmed in this position by Kassandros in 315 (Diod. 19.64.1). The MSS of Curt. 10.8.15 mention a certain *Amissus* of Megalopolis (which Hedicke imaginatively emends to *Damyllus*) as one of the agents who negotiated a settlement between the cavalry and infantry factions in Babylon after Alexander's death. This appears to be a corruption of the name Damis. Since Diod. 19.74.2 says that in 313/12 Telesphoros (no. 1100) liberated all the cities of the Peloponnese, except Korinth and Sikyon, we may assume that Damis was deposed at that time. Berve II 115 no. 240; cf. no. 53 "Amissos"; Niese I 245 n.3; cf. Heckel 1981e, 63; see also Kirchner, *RE* IV (1901) 2056 no. 1; Paschidis 275–6 B32.

335 DAMON

(Δάμων). Macedonian (thus Tataki 290 no. 9) common soldier under the command of Parmenion (apparently in Syria, as the context of Plutarch's account suggests). D. and Timotheos (no. 1145) were charged with seducing the "wives" (γύναια) of certain Greek mercenaries. Alexander instructed Parmenion to investigate and execute them if they were found guilty (Plut. *Alex.* 22.4). The outcome of the proceedings is unknown. Berve II 115 no. 241.

336 DAMOPHILOS

(Δαμόφιλος). Rhodian *nauarchos*. During the height of the siege by Demetrios Poliorketes, when the Rhodians were already dismantling buildings in order to build a second wall, D. and two other commanders (of whom only Menedemos is named) sailed out and did great damage to Demetrios' fleet. Royal robes belonging to Demetrios and captured by

Menedemos were sent on D.'s authority to Egypt (Diod. 20.93). Willrich, *RE* IV (1901) 2076 no. 5; Hauben 24–6 no. 8.

337 DAMOSTHENES

(Δαμοσθένης). Son of Pyrrhinos. One of twenty-four cavalrymen from Orchomenos, who served with Alexander's allied cavalry until the expedition reached Ekbatana in 330. There he and his compatriots were discharged. On their return (*c*.329), they made a dedication to Zeus Soter in Orchomenos (*IG* VII 3206). Berve II 116 no. 242.

338 DAMOTELES

(Δαμοτέλης). Rhodian *prytanis* (one of the city officials), killed during a hard-fought battle against the forces of Demetrios Poliorketes during the siege of Rhodes (Diod. 20.98.9). Willrich, *RE* IV.2 (1901) 2081 no. 4.

339 DANDAMIS

(Δάνδαμις). Mandanis: Strabo 15.1.64 C715, 15.1.69 C718. Indian philosopher. The oldest of the so-called Gymnosophists. Plut. *Alex.* 64–5 fails to distinguish between the Brahmans and the Gymnosophists; Metz Epit. 71–4, 78–84 locates them among the Mallians. See the comments of Hamilton 178–9; for the difference between Brahmans (who were the highest caste and served as political advisers) and philosophers (see Nearchos, *FGrH* 133 F23 = Strabo 15.1.66 C716; also Stoneman 1994, 1995). At Taxila D. was summoned by Alexander through the agency of Onesikritos (*FGrH* 134 F17a = Strabo 15.1.63–5; cf. F17b = Plut. *Alex.* 65.3), but D. refused to present himself, denying the King's divine paternity and giving in to neither promises of gifts or threats of punishment (Arr. 7.2.2–4; cf. also Plut. *Alex.* 8.5, showing that Alexander respected his independence). There appears to have developed a tradition that deliberately contrasted D. and Kalanos, depicting the former as a man of integrity and the latter as a parasite (Megasthenes, *FGrH* 715 F34a = Strabo 15.1.68 C718). Kaerst, *RE* IV.2 (1901) 2099; Berve II 116 no. 243; Stoneman 2019, 289–319.

340 DAREIOS

(Δαρεῖος). (*c*.380–330; *regn.* 336–330). Son of Arsanes and grandson of Ostanes, who had been a brother of Artaxerxes II (Diod. 17.5.5; for the family see Sisygambis no. 1052). His mother was Sisygambis, apparently a sister of Arsanes. D. clearly belonged to a cadet branch of the royal house, though certain hostile accounts depicted him a slave and courier (Plut. *Mor.* 326e; cf. *Suda* A3906; Ael. *VH* 12.43; Strabo 15.3.24 C736). Allegedly known as Codomannus before his accession (Justin 10.3.3). During the reign of Artaxerxes III Ochos, D. volunteered to fight the champion of the Kadousians in single combat and, after defeating and killing him, was honored greatly by the king, who made him satrap of Armenia (Justin 10.3.3–4; Diod. 17.6.1). Before Philip's death (Diod. 17.7.1), D. himself gained the throne through the machinations of the eunuch chiliarch, Bagoas, who had poisoned Ochos, his son and successor Arses, and all the latter's brothers and children, thus eliminating the direct line of Ochos (Diod. 17.5.3–6; Plut. *Mor.* 337e; cf. Arr. 2.14.5). But D. soon learned of Bagoas' plot against him and forced the eunuch to drink his own poison (Diod. 17.5.6). Born *c*.380—he was about fifty at the time of his death in 330 (Arr. 3.22.2, 6)—D. is described as the most handsome of men (Plut. *Alex.* 21.6), just as his second wife, his sister Stateira (Plut. *Alex.* 30.3; Arr. 2.11.9; Justin

11.9.12; Gell. *NA* 7.8.3; her name is given only by Plut. *Alex.* 30.5, 8), was the most beautiful woman in Asia (Arr. 4.19.6; Plut. *Alex.* 21.6; Plut. *Mor.* 338e). By her D. had at least three children: two daughters, Stateira and Drypetis, and a son named Ochos (**Stemma III**). He had also been married to a sister of Pharnakes (Arr. 1.16.3; Diod. 17.21.3), apparently a member of the Kappadokian-Pontic nobility (thus Berve II 117), who bore him a son named Ariobarzanes (Aretades of Knidos, *FGrH* 285 F1) and a daughter, who married Mithridates (Arr. 1.15.7, 16.3; Diod. 17.20.2, wrongly "Spithrodates").

Although D. was not present in the west in 334/3, it is clear that he kept himself informed about Alexander's progress and took measures to deal with him. D. had allegedly not taken Alexander seriously, on account of his youth (Diod. 17.7.1), and entrusted the defense of the Aegean littoral to Memnon of Rhodes (Diod. 17.7.2). In the first year of Alexander's expedition, it may be true that D. despised his opponent, especially since the advance force under Parmenion had made little headway in 336–335. But D. appears also to have been preoccupied with the revolt of Khababash and its aftermath (Nylander 1993, 148; Burstein 2000). Badian 2000b, 254 objects that "if Dareios III had begun his reign with an outstanding success, which his predecessors had taken generations to achieve, completing the reconquest of Egypt in a few months, it is inconceivable that none of the Alexander sources would have seized on this opportunity of enhancing the stature of Dareios for the greater glory of Alexander." Briant 820, 860, 1017–18 treats the chronology with caution, but Badian's is an argument from silence and it is pointless to speculate about how the Alexander historians might have treated D.'s achievement. It is, of course, conceivable that they did not know—indeed, did not care—about the recent events in Egypt. But this too is idle speculation. The first concerted action against the Macedonians was taken by a coalition of satraps, who distrusted Memnon and the Greek mercenaries. After the disaster at the Granikos, D. gave greater authority to Memnon (Arr. 1.20.3; cf. 2.1.1), who had sent him his wife, Barsine, and children as hostages (Diod. 17.23.5–6; cf. Curt. 3.13.14; Justin 11.10.2; Plut. *Alex.* 21.7–9). The Great King sent him funds with which to prosecute the war (Diod. 17.29.1); but Memnon died soon afterwards of illness (Diod. 17.29.4), and the command was handed to Pharnabazos. By the summer of 333, D. had assembled an army (Diod. 17.31.1–2) and moved it to Sochoi in northern Mesopotamia (Arr. 2.6.1). Curt. 3.1.10 says that in the spring D. had not yet crossed the Euphrates; in fact, Curt. 3.2.1 claims that he did not plan to take the field in person until he received news of Memnon's death, at which time he was still in Babylon. His exact movements are hard to determine, but Curt. 3.7.1–2 says that when he learned of Alexander's illness in Kilikia he "advanced to the Euphrates" and that he crossed this on pontoon bridges in five days, by which time Alexander had already moved on to Soloi in Kilikia. The account of his display and enumeration of forces, in the style of Xerxes, is probably nothing more than embellishment, modeled on the Herodotean account (see Blänsdorf 1971). He did not act in time to send help to Kelainai (cf. Curt. 3.1.8). In his service was the Athenian exile, Charidemos (no. 321). Charidemos and Amyntas son of Antiochos appear to have come with the mercenaries led by Thymondas (Curt. 3.3.1, 8.2–11; cf. Arr. 2.2.1), who numbered about 30,000 (Arr. 2.8.6; Diod. 17.31.2; Curt. 3.2.9, 9.2). But he was advised by his courtiers that Charidemos was plotting treachery and had him arrested and executed (Diod. 17.30.2–5; Curt. 3.2.10–19). While there are good reasons for rejecting some of the Charidemos story as literary fiction, the reference to distrust of Greek advisers may be historical. Although there may be some truth to the claim that D.

repented this action, there is none to the stories of the Great King haunted by dreams of Alexander and Macedonian fighting qualities (Diod. 17.30.6–7); for there is no way that such information could have been brought to the attention of Greek historians. Curtius cleverly reworks this information and casts Charidemos in the role of Demaratos, the Spartan adviser of Xerxes (see Blänsdorf 1971). Note that the advice of Charidemos was given while D. was in Babylon, not at Sochoi. In other versions it is at Sochoi and the advice is given by Amyntas son of Antiochos (Plut. *Alex.* 20.1–4; Arr. 2.6.3). The alleged bribery of Philip of Akarnania (Curt. 3.5.14–15, 3.6.4–13), appears to be a doublet for the negotiations conducted by Lynkestian Alexander with the Persian king through the agency of Sisines (no. 1050). From Sochoi, D. sent his money and a great number of the non-combatants in his army to Damaskos (Diod. 17.32.3; Curt. 3.8.12; Arr. 2.11.9–10) under the command of Kophen son of Artabazos (Arr. 2.15.1).

The size of D.'s army is grossly exaggerated: 600,000 men (Arr. 2.8.8; Plut. *Alex.* 18.6; *P.Oxy.* 1798, col. 4 = *FGrH* 148); 400,000 infantry and 100,000 cavalry (Justin 11.9.1; Diod. 17.31.2; cf. Diod. 17.39.4 says that the roughly one million troops raised in 332 were about double the number he had at Issos); Curt. 3.2.4–9 has a little over 300,000. The Persian dead at the end of the battle are given as 100,000 infantry and 10,000 cavalry (Curt. 3.11.27; Diod. 17.36.6; but Arr. 2.11.8 says the 100,000 included 10,000 cavalry); 61,000 infantry dead, 40,000 infantry captured, 10,000 cavalry killed (Justin 11.9.10); 53,000 dead (*P.Oxy.* 1798, col. 4). Ptolemy (*FGrH* 138 F6 = Arr. 2.11.8) claimed that D. and his pursuers could cross a ravine filled in by the bodies of the dead.

Whatever its true size, D. unwisely took the numerically superior army away from the plains and moved into Kilikia via the Amanic Gates (Arr. 2.7.1; Curt. 3.8.13; Kallisthenes *ap.* Polyb. 12.17.2; Josephus, *AJ* 11.314 wrongly says he crossed the Tauros), thinking that Alexander was deliberately avoiding battle (Curt. 3.7.1, 8.10). It turned out to be a near-fatal miscalculation. The first major battle between D. and Alexander thus took place at Issos (Curt. 3.9–11; Diod. 17.33–4; Arr. 2.8–11) in November 333 (Arr. 2.11.10 for the date); Alexander set out to attack him directly during the battle (Diod. 17.33.5); but he was valiantly defended by his brother Oxyathres (Diod. 17.34.2–4). Chares of Mytilene (*FGrH* 125 F6 = Plut. *Alex.* 20.9; cf. Plut. *Mor.* 341b) says that D. wounded Alexander on the thigh with his sword. Justin 11.9.9 claims that both kings were wounded in the engagement but does not mention single combat. Cf. also Kallisthenes *ap.* Polyb. 12.22. D.'s horses were wounded in battle (Diod. 17.34.6), and after changing to another chariot he was seized with fear and led the flight from the battlefield (Diod. 17.34.7–9; Curt. 3.11.11), D. mounted a horse that had followed the chariot precisely for this purpose (Arr. 2.11.4–7; Plut. *Arr.* 20.10), abandoning his family and possessions to the enemy (Diod. 17.35.1–4; cf. 17.31.2, 36.2–4; Arr. 2.11.9, 12.3–7; Curt. 3.11.20–6, 12.4–16; Plut. *Alex.* 21.1–6; Justin 11.9.11–16; Josephus, *AJ* 11.316; Ael. *NA* 6.48 says it was a mare that had recently foaled; Plut. *Alex.* 33.8 tells the same story about Gaugamela). At D.'s own tent, the Macedonian Pages welcomed their victorious King (Diod. 17.36.5; Plut. *Alex.* 20.12–13; cf. Curt. 3.12.1–3), who had broken off pursuit after some 200 stades (Diod. 17.37.2), while D. himself changed horses frequently and hurried to the heart of his empire (Diod. 17.37.1). Amongst the captive Persians the rumor spread that D. had been killed (Diod. 17.37.3), but this was dispelled by Leonnatos, who had been sent by Alexander himself.

D. fled through the night with some 4,000 followers and crossed the Euphrates at Thapsakos (Arr. 2.13.1): together with those who had accompanied him from Issos, he reached Babylon, where he wrote to Alexander about the ransoming of his family and the conclusion of a peace treaty that conceded Asia west of the Halys to Macedon (Diod. 17.39.1; Justin 11.12.1), a proposal rejected by Alexander (Diod. 17.39.2; Justin 11.12.2). D. now prepared for an even greater engagement (Diod. 17.39.3–4). Apart from the failed diplomatic negotiations (cf. Bernhardt 1988; Bloedow 1995), we learn little of D.'s activities between the time of his defeat at Issos and the preliminaries of Gaugamela. The defense of Tyre may have been an attempt by the Tyrians to prove their goodwill towards D. (cf. the case of Straton of Sidon who was deposed for his stubborn adherence to Persia, Diod. 17.47.1) and likewise give him an opportunity to regroup his forces (Diod. 17.40.3), but the king appears to have done little on his part to aid the Tyrians, except perhaps by supplying ships, money and mercenaries to Agis III (cf. Diod. 17.48.1–2). Furthermore, he took no precautions to protect Egypt, whose satrap Sauakes had been killed at Issos, and instead allowed it to be disrupted by the mercenaries under Amyntas son of Antiochos (Diod. 17.49.2–4). But, at least by the time Alexander returned to Syria in 331, D. had assembled another and more powerful army (Diod. 17.53.1), which he had equipped in a manner more suitable for fighting the Macedonians (on which see Badian 1999, 80–1; Heckel 2017b), adding also some two hundred scythe-bearing chariots. From Babylon he marched, with an army of some 800,000 infantry and 200,000 cavalry, in a northwesterly direction, keeping the Tigris on his right at first; but later he crossed the river and established a camp at Arbela (Diod. 17.53.3–4). Despite his numerical advantage and the opportunity of choosing favorable terrain, D. launched another peace initiative, this time offering all territory west of the Euphrates, 30,000 talents and the hand of one of his daughters in marriage, an offer that was once again rejected (Diod. 17.54.1–6; Justin 11.12.9–16). At about this time, his wife Stateira died (Diod. 17.54.7). Diodorus does not describe the arrival of the news of Stateira's death in D.'s camp. Plut. *Alex.* 30 says she died after the embassy, but Curt. 4.10.18–34 and Justin 11.12.6–7 place it before. The suggestion that she may have died in childbirth or of complications associated with pregnancy is exploited by the authors who based their account on Kleitarchos. D. suffers extreme anxiety, believing that his wife has been violated by her captor, but Alexander himself is depicted as a man of great restraint.

Attempts to delay Alexander's progress were futile, and D. finally met his opponent on the battlefield of Gaugamela (Curt. 4.12–16; Diod. 17.56–61; Arr. 3.8–15; Plut. *Alex.* 31.6–33.11; cf. Polyaenus 4.3.5, 17; Justin 11.13.1–14.7; Oros. 3.17.1–4); for the date of the battle, see Arr. 3.15.7, who gives the month as Pyanepsion (October/November), but Plut. *Cam.* 19.3 dates it to 26 Boedromion (1 October) 331. Despite his greater numbers, he was again soundly defeated and forced to flee (Diod. 17.60.1–4; Plut. *Alex.* 33.8; Justin 11.14.3; Curt. 4.15.30–3; Arr. 3.14.3). Whereas at Issos, D.'s flight is said to have caused the collapse of Persian opposition, there is a tradition that D. did not flee from Gaugamela until his troops were beginning to abandon him. Curt. 4.15.30 says he actually contemplated an honorable death by suicide. See Nylander 1993: 159 n.86, comparing the accounts of D.'s flight at Issos and at Gaugamela. Furthermore, D. refused to destroy the bridge over the Lykos (Justin 11.14.4, wrongly calling it the Kydnos) because the act, while delaying the enemy, would also doom many of his men to death or capture (Curt. 4.16.8–9). At any rate, the description of D. as lacking spirit and common sense (Arr. 3.22.1) is probably unfair. Immediately he escaped in the direction of Arbela, which he reached in the middle of the night (Curt. 4.16.8–9; 5.1.3; D. did not stop in Arbela; he left his treasure and equipment, which he stored there before the battle, behind for Alexander to capture: Arr. 3.15.5; Curt. 5.1.10), and he now abandoned the centers of Babylon, Sousa, and Persepolis and went instead directly to Ekbatana (Diod. 17.64.1; Arr. 3.16.1; Curt. 5.1.9, 8.1; cf. Strabo 2.1.24 C79); he gathered and rearmed stragglers (Arr. 3.16.2; cf. Curt. 5.8.3–5) as he went, and hoped to rebuild his army (Arr. 3.19.1–2).

But those generals and courtiers who remained with him were divided in their loyalties to the man and their strategies for saving the empire. To make matters worse, the base of his future military power was the region governed by his most dangerous enemy, Bessos, a man with some Achaimenid blood and, hence, at least marginal claims to the kingship. That D. wrote to Aboulites in Sousa, telling him to turn the city and its riches over to Alexander in the hope of delaying his progress (Diod. 17.65.5), makes a virtue of necessity. By contrast, the efforts of Madates, ruler of the Ouxians and a kinsman of the king, to impede Alexander's progress (Diod. 17.67.4) appear to have been a matter of policy, though they met with little success.

During Alexander's advance from Babylon to Persepolis, D. had remained at Ekbatana, summoning troops from the Upper Satrapies. But these failed to materialize by the time Alexander set out for Media, and D. began his flight towards Baktra (Diod. 17.32.1; Curt. 5.8.1) with a force of 30,000 Persians and mercenaries (Diod. 17.73.2; Curt. 5.8.3–4 says 30,000 native infantry and 4,000 mercenaries; 4,000 slingers and archers, and 3,300 cavalry. Arr. 3.19.5 gives radically different numbers: 3,000 cavalry and 6,000 infantry; he adds that D. took 7,000 talents from the treasury at Ekbatana; cf. Strabo 15.3.9 C731: 8,000 talents). When Alexander was three days away from Ekbatana, he was met by Bisthanes, who reported that D. had fled from there four days earlier (Arr. 3.19.4–5). As Alexander gained ground in his pursuit (Arr. 3.20–1), D. was arrested (Curt. 5.10–12, for a highly dramatized account; Arr. 3.21.1, 4–5) and murdered by Bessos (Diod. 17.73.2; Justin 11.15.1–14; Curt. 5.13.15–25; Arr. 3.21.10). Arr. 3.21.10 says that D. was killed by *Satibarzanes* and Barsaentes. The former may be an error for Nabarzanes (cf. Bosworth I 344–5). Alexander found him already dead and covered him with his cloak (Plut. *Mor.* 332f; Plut. *Alex.* 43.5); he also gave him an extravagant burial (Diod. 17.73.3; Arr. 3.22.1 says his body was sent to Persepolis to be entombed; cf. Arr. 3.22.6; Plut. *Mor.* 343b; Pliny, *HN* 36.132; Justin 11.15.15; Plut. *Alex.* 43.7 says his body was sent to his mother). There was however a tradition that Alexander found the dying D., who begged him to avenge his death (Diod. 17.73.4; Ps.-Call. 2.20). Swoboda, *RE* IV.2 (1901) 2205–11 no. 3; Berve II 116–29 no. 244; Seibert 1987; Nylander 1993; Badian 2000b; Briant 2015. **Stemma III.**

341 DATAMES

(Δατάμης). Justi 81 s.v. no. 6. Persian noble, perhaps a relative or descendant of the famous Kappadokian satrap Datames. An officer in the Aegean fleet of Pharnabazos and Autophradates, he was given an independent command of ten Phoinikian ships (cf. Arr. 2.2.4) in 333 to subdue the Kyklades (Arr. 2.2.2). He was, however, attacked at dawn, as he was anchored at Siphnos, by the Macedonian admiral Proteas, who captured eight of his ships. D. himself escaped with the remaining two (Arr. 2.2.4–5) and rejoined the main Persian fleet. Nothing else is known about him. Berve II 129 no. 245; Shayegan 108 no. 47.

342 DATAPHERNES

(Δαταφέρνης. Justi 81). Data-farnah. Prominent Persian or Baktrian noble. D. conspired with Katanes and Spitamenes in arresting the regicide Bessos (Curt. 7.5.21; Arr. 3.29.6–7; Metz Epit. 5) and handing him over to Ptolemy, who had been sent out by Alexander (Arr. 3.30.1, 5). Spitamenes and D. continued to resist Alexander and, after the former's death in 328/7, D. was arrested by the Dahai and turned over to Alexander (Curt. 8.3.16; Metz Epit. 23). Kaerst, *RE* IV.2 (1901) 2226; Berve II 129 no. 246; Shayegan 108 no. 48.

343 DEIDAMEIA

(Δειδάμεια). Epeirot princess. Daughter of Aiakides and Phthia; sister of Troas and Pyrrhos (Plut. *Pyrrh.* 1.7; cf. Diod. 19.35.5). Her name, like those of other members of the family, reflects the Molossian royal house's claim to descent from Achilles. D. was born, in all likelihood around 321 (cf. Reuss 1881, 172; Sandberger 68). At an early age she was betrothed to Alexander IV, the son of Alexander the Great and Rhoxane (Plut. *Pyrrh.* 4.3; Seibert 1967, 29), and in 317 she was among those members of Olympias' family who were besieged in Pydna by Kassandros (Diod. 19.35.5; Justin 14.6.3). It is unclear who took custody of D. after the city was taken (Diod. 19.50.5–6), but at some point (perhaps at the time of Pyrrhos' restoration to the throne in 307) she must have returned to the court in Epeiros. In 303 she married Demetrios Poliorketes in a public ceremony at the festival of Hera (mid-to-late July) at Argos (Plut. *Demetr.* 25.2; cf. *Pyrrh.* 4.3). The marriage sealed an alliance between Pyrrhos and Demetrios (see Schubert 1894, 119; Garoufalias 20). D. soon bore him a son, named Alexander (no. 53; Plut. *Demetr.* 53.8). When her new husband crossed to Asia, where he and his father, Antigonos, were destined to be defeated at Ipsos, she was left behind in Athens (Plut. *Demetr.* 30.3). After the defeat at Ipsos, the Athenians refused to let Demetrios back into the city and sent D. to Megara with proper honors (Plut. *Demetr.* 30.4: μετὰ τιμῆς καὶ πομπῆς πρεπούσης). Whether she joined Demetrios briefly in Korinth, as Macurdy 64, maintains is uncertain. In 299 she joined Demetrios in Kilikia, but she died of illness a short time later (Plut. *Demetr.* 32.5; cf. *Pyrrh.* 7.3). Her death will have cleared the way for an alliance with Ptolemy, sealed by Demetrios' marriage to Ptolemais, the daughter of Eurydike (Plut. *Demetr.* 32.6; cf. Sandberger 70 for the chronology). Sandberger 68–70 no. 27; Kaerst, *RE* IV.2 (1901) 2383 no. 5; Macurdy 63–4; Seibert 1967, 28ff.; Carney 166; Aulbach §8.2.1.3. **Stemma IIb**.

344 DEINARCHOS

(Δείναρχος). Son of Sostratos, from Korinth. Born *c.*360 and died not long after 292/1. [Plut.] *Mor.* 850c says he was still young when, during the time of Alexander's expedition, he came to Athens to study under Theophrastos; but it may be that D. arrived at the beginning of Alexander's reign (cf. Worthington 5). He wrote speeches for pay, but as a metic was not allowed to participate personally in the law courts. Some 87 speeches were attributed to D. in antiquity, of which about 60 are authentic; his three surviving speeches—*Against Demosthenes, Against Aristogeiton, Against Philocles*—pertained to the Harpalos case in Athens ([Plut.] *Mor.* 850c–d). He was an imitator of Demosthenes and some speeches in the Demosthenic corpus have been, rightly or wrongly, attributed to him (Worthington 12; Cawkwell, *OCD*³ 469). A supporter of Antipatros and Kassandros, D. was particularly influential in Athens in the time of Demetrios of Phaleron (317–307) but exiled when the city was "liberated" by Demetrios Poliorketes. He returned as an old man, with failing eyesight, in 292 ([Plut.] *Mor.* 850d speaks of 15 years of exile) and prosecuted Proxenos, thus making his only appearance in the Athenian courts ([Plut.] *Mor.* 850e). He had no personal contact with Alexander. Biographical information, late and somewhat unreliable, can be found in Ps.-Plutarch's *Lives of the Ten Orators* (= [Plut.] *Mor.* 850c–e); cf. Photius; Dion. Hal. *On Dinarchus*; and *Suda* Δ 333, although there seems to be some confusion with Deinarchos (no. 345) below. Berve II 130 no. 247; Thalheim, *RE* IV.2 (1901) 2386 no. 1; Worthington 3–12; Shoemaker 1968.

345 DEINARCHOS

(Δείναρχος). Korinthian of unknown family. He is perhaps identical with the Deinarchos who served with Timoleon in Sicily (Plut. *Tim.* 21.3, 24.4). Demaratos, who is associated with D. in Sicily, appears to have been a *xenos* of Philip II. Pro-Macedonian politician during the reigns of Philip and Alexander, and thus included by Demosthenes in a long list of Greeks who betrayed their fellow citizens (Dem. 18.295). The *Suda* (Δ 333) claims that Antipatros made him *epimeletes* of the Peloponnese (cf. [Dem.] *Ep.* 6 for his pro-Antipatrid stance). He accompanied Phokion on his final embassy to Polyperchon (though D. fell ill on the way, Plut. *Phoc.* 33.6), whom they encountered near Pharygai in Phokis. D. was, however, seized by Polyperchon's men, tortured, and executed (Plut. *Phoc.* 33.8); for he was believed to be a supporter of Kassandros. D. had known Polyperchon as a lieutenant of Antipatros and wrongly believed that he had some influence with him (Plut. *Phoc.* 33.5). Berve II 130 no. 248.

346 DEINIAS

(Δεινίας). General of Kassandros. Occupied Tempe against Olympias in 317/16 (Diod. 19.35.3). In 312 he brought reinforcements to Lykiskos in Epeiros and thus helped him overcome the forces of Alexander (no. 44) and Teukros (no. 1101), the sons of Alketas II, in a second battle of Eurymenai (Diod. 19.88.6). Kirchner, *RE* IV.2 (1902) 2389 no. 1.

DEINOCHARES. See DEINOKRATES.

347 DEINOKRATES

(Δεινοκράτης). Architect from Rhodes (Pliny, *HN* 5.62: "Deinochares"; Ps.-Call. 1.31–2; Jul. Valer. 1.25), but Vitruv. 2 praef. 2 calls him *architectus Macedo*. It appears that the Alexander sources have confused the name of the architect, noted for his outrageous projects, and referred to him as Diokles, Cheirokrates and Stasikrates. Diokles is said to have been from Rhegion and Stasikrates is listed as Bithynian, but the projects are the same. Stewart 1993, 28, opts for Stasikrates as the correct name, since the forms Deinokrates ("Marvel Master") and Cheirokrates ("Hand Master") are "overtly programmatic," but I see no way of deciding the matter. All are named as the proposers of a plan to convert Mount Athos into a giant statue of Alexander (Vitruv. 2 praef. 3; Strabo 14.1.23 C641; Plut. *Mor.* 335c–f; Plut. *Alex.* 72.5–8; see also Eusthatius on Homer's *Iliad* 14.229 and Tzetz. *Chil.* 8.199, lines 408–15; also Lucian, *Imagines* 9 and *How to Write History* 12) and restorers of the temple of Artemis in Ephesos (Strabo 14.1.23 C641; Solinus 40.5); only the layout of Alexandria in Egypt is attributed consistently to D. or the variant Deinochares (Val. Max. 1.4 ext. 1; Ps.-Call. 1.31–2; Jul. Valer. 1.25; Solinus 32.41; Pliny, *HN* 5.62; cf.

Curt. 4.8.6). Plut. *Alex.* 72.5 says that Alexander longed for Stasikrates when he needed someone to build Hephaistion's tomb (cf. Diod. 17.115). Fabricius, *RE* IV.2 (1901) 2392–3 no. 6; Berve II 130 no. 249; Stewart 1993, 28–9, 41.

348 DELIOS

(Δήλιος). Ephesian of unknown family, companion of Plato. Sent by the Asiatic Greeks to Alexander (perhaps at Korinth in 336) to encourage him to campaign against Persia (Plut. *Mor.* 1126d). Berve II 131 no. 251.

349 DEMADES

(Δημάδης). Athenian orator (Kirchner 3263), son of Demeas ([Demades] *On the Twelve Years* 7; Ael. *VH* 12.43 says that, in spite of D.'s prominence in Athens, his father's name was not a matter of common knowledge), reputedly a sailor (*Suda* Δ 415). Like Demosthenes, he was from the deme Paiania. Born before 380, perhaps as early as 390 (Davies 100): Antipatros at some point in the 320s referred to him as an old man of whom little else remained except tongue and guts (Plut. *Phoc.* 1.3; cf. Plut. *Mor.* 183f). He was amongst the captives at Chaironeia and rebuked Philip for, in his drunken state, "acting like Thersites when fortune had cast him in the role of Agamemnon" (Diod. 16.87.1–2). Philip was won over by Demades' charm and released the Athenian prisoners (Diod. 16.87.3). He advocated Athenian participation in the common peace, i.e. membership in the League of Korinth (Plut. *Phoc.* 16.5). In 336, when the Greeks threatened to rebel against Macedonian authority, D. worked to secure peace between Athens and Alexander. And, when in 335, after the sack of Thebes, Alexander demanded the extradition of certain politicians, including Demosthenes, D. first proposed that ambassadors be sent to him, congratulating him on his safe return from Illyria and his suppression of the Theban revolt (Arr. 1.10.3; [Demades] *On the Twelve Years* 17). Although the first mission accomplished little, a second embassy, led by Phokion (Plut. *Phoc.* 17.6; Arr. 1.10.6; Plut. *Dem.* 23) and including D. (Diod. 17.15.3), persuaded the King to relent. That Demosthenes paid D. five talents to intercede with the King is certainly a fabrication (Diod. 17.15.3). Din. 1.104 claims that D. admitted without shame that he had regularly accepted bribes (but see Williams 1989; cf. also Plut. *Mor.* 188f for D.'s alleged venality, and Plut. *Phoc.* 20.6, 30.4–5 for his extravagance). The extent of D.'s contribution can be seen from the honors, including a statue, that the Athenians conferred upon him (Din. 1.101; Plut. *Mor.* 802f). He was pro-Macedonian in his politics (Plut. *Phoc.* 1.1) and opposed Athenian cooperation with Agis in 331/0 (Plut. *Mor.* 818e; Plut. *Cleom.* 27.1; cf. Plut. *Mor.* 191e). He proposed that Alexander be recognized as a god, only to be fined 10 talents (Athen. 6.251b; Ael. *VH* 5.12, wrongly 100 talents; cf. Val. Max. 7.2 ext. 13). Convicted of accepting bribes from Harpalos, he did not fight the charge and was fined (Din. 1.104; 2.15) and deprived of his citizenship (Plut. *Phoc.* 26.3; Diod. 18.18.1–2, adding that he had been convicted of introducing illegal measures three times in the past; *Suda* Δ 415, twice; Plut. *Phoc.* 26.3, seven times), though he remained in Athens. D.'s alleged remark that the Macedonian army after the death of Alexander was "like the Cyclops with his one eye put out" (Plut. *Mor.* 181f; cf. Plut. *Galba* 1.4 but Plut. *Mor.* 336f, more plausibly, attributes the remark to Leosthenes) suggests a hostility towards Alexander, as does his famous remark that if Alexander were really dead the world would be filled with the stench of his corpse (Plut. *Phoc.* 22.5). But he was, after all, a politician and his utterances were intended to please or amuse his audience. Demades proposed honors, proxenies and citizenship for various Macedonians: Antipatros and Alkimachos (Harpocration s.v. Ἀλκίμαχος = Hyper. frag. 19.2 [Burtt]; Schwenk no. 4), a son of a certain Andromenes (Schwenk no.7; even if not the father of Amyntas, Simmias, Attalos, and Polemon, then certainly a prominent *hetairos* of Philip II); Amyntor son of Demetrios, perhaps the father of Hephaistion (*IG* II² 405 = Schwenk no. 24; cf. Heckel 1991); as well as a certain Thessalian from Larisa (*IG* II² 353 = Schwenk no. 51); and a certain Nikostratos of Philippoi (*Agora* 16.100; cf. Paschidis 48 n.2).

After the Lamian War he was reinstated and regarded as responsible for "betraying" Athens to Antipatros (Nepos, *Phoc.* 2.2; Paus. 7.10.4 calls him one of the traitors at Athens, προδοτῶν): it was his decree that called for the deaths of anti-Macedonian leaders, including Demosthenes (Plut. *Dem.* 28.2; Nepos, *Phoc.* 2.2; Arr. *Succ.* 1.13). He fell out with Phokion (cf. Plut. *Mor.* 811a) but developed a reputation for dealing well with Macedon on Athens' behalf (Diod. 18.48.1; for possible involvement in the decision concerning the Samian exiles see Paschidis 44). In 319, as Antipatros neared death and D. came to Macedonia to request the removal of the garrison from Mounychia (Diod. 18.48.1), he was put to death by Kassandros and Antipatros, not only because of the accusations of Deinarchos of Korinth (Arr. *Succ.* 1.15; Diod. 18.48.2), but also because letters found amongst the royal papers showed that he had written to Perdikkas to come and save Greece from an old and rotten thread which was binding it, meaning Antipatros (Arr. *Succ.* 1.14). He was executed after first witnessing the slaughter of his son Demeas (Arr. *Succ.* 1.14; Diod. 18.48.3–4; Plut. *Phoc.* 30.8–9; Plut. *Dem.* 31.4–6). In the end, the Athenians felt great hatred towards him and are said to have melted down his statues to make chamber pots ([Plut.] *Mor.* 820f). Slanders against him are common enough: Athen. 2.44f called D. a drunkard. Though clearly a man of wit, Demades' alleged reference to Aigina as "the eyesore of Peiraieus" (Athen. 3.99d) was originally attributed to Perikles. Berve II 131–2 no. 252; Davies 99–101; Williams 1989; Worthington 271–2; Paschidis 40–9.

350 DEMARATOS

(Δημάρατος). Korinthian. Born *c*.400 (Plut. *Alex.* 56.2 says he died of old age in 328/7). D., who campaigned with Timoleon in Sicily in 345 (Plut. *Tim.* 21, 24, 27), was prominent among the pro-Macedonians in his city (Dem. 18.295). As a *xenos* of Philip II, he brought Boukephalas as a gift to the young Alexander (Diod. 17.76.6; but Plut. *Alex.* 6.1 says that it was Philoneikos (no. 934) of Thessaly who brought the horse), and in 337/6 he urged Philip to reconcile with his son, who had fled to Illyria (Plut. *Alex.* 9.12–14; Plut. *Mor.* 70b–c, 179c). D. was almost certainly present in Aigai when Philip was assassinated in 336 (Diod. 16.91.4–6), and in 334 he accompanied Alexander on the Asiatic expedition as one of his *hetairoi*, fighting though well advanced in years. At the Granikos he gave his spear to Alexander, when the King's own spear had broken (Arr. 1.15.6). D. is said to have wept with joy to see Alexander seated on Dareios' throne at Sousa (Plut. *Mor.* 329d; Plut. *Alex.* 37.7, 56.1; Plut. *Ages.* 15.4). He died shortly before the Indian campaign, and the army built a funeral mound for him that was 80 cubits high; his ashes were conveyed to the coast, for transport to Korinth, in a magnificent four-horse carriage (Plut. *Alex.* 56.2). Kirchner, *RE* IV.2 (1901) 2705–6 no 4; Berve II 133 no. 253.

351 DEMARATOS

(Δημάρατος). Rhodian, patronymic unknown, brother of Sparton. D. and his brother were arrested at Sardis by Alexander but freed through the efforts of Phokion (Plut. *Phoc.* 18.6; Ael. *VH* 1.25). The reason for his arrest is unknown; nor do we know anything about his personal or political connections with Phokion. Possibly identical with the *nauarchos* Demaratos (below; Arr. *Succ.* 1.39). Willrich, *RE* IV.2 (1901) 2706 no. 5; Berve II 133 no. 254; Hofstetter 46 no. 78.

352 DEMARATOS

(Δαμάρατος). Rhodian *nauarchos*—the first such attested official in Rhodes—defeated Attalos son of Andromenes and his fleet in 320 (Arr. *Succ.* 1.39; cf. Berthold 60). Possibly identical with Demaratos the brother of Sparton. Hauben 26–7 no. 9; Willrich, *RE* IV (1901) 2706 no. 5.

353 DEMARCHOS

(Δήμαρχος). Greek or, possibly, Macedonian (Tataki 292 no. 17). D. was satrap of Hellespontine Phrygia briefly from the death of Kalas until 323. Of his activities nothing is known. After Alexander's death, he was replaced by Leonnatos (Arr. *Succ.* 1.6; Dexippos = *FGrH* 100 F8 §2; Diod. 18.3.1; Curt. 10.10.2; Justin 13.4.16). Willrich, *RE* IV.2 (1901) 2712 no. 5; Berve II 133–4 no. 255; Billows 45 n.85.

354 DEMARCHOS

(Δήμαρχος). Son of Taron, Lykian. D. was the leader of Phila's bodyguard (*Syll*³ 333), perhaps in Lykia, and probably at the time when Demetrios was besieging Rhodes (though Paschidis 387–8 places it any time between 305 and 295, specifically in 299; the identity of *basilissa* Phila is not entirely certain). He is honored both for his connections with the Antigonids and his earlier service to Samians in exile. Possibly, he is identical with the D. who conducted negotiations between Antigonos and Kassandros in 311 (*OGIS* 5 = Welles, *RC* 1). But a Lykian seems more likely to have been a mercenary captain than an ambassador. Kirchner, *RE* IV.2 (1901) 2712 no. 3; Launey 1220; Billows 379 no. 28; Paschidis 387–9.

355 DEMARCHOS

([Δήμα]ρχος). Envoy sent by Antigonos to Kassandros in 311 in the negotiations that led to the so-called Peace of 311 (*OGIS* 5 = Welles, *RC* 1). Olshausen no. 67; Welles, *RC* p. 9, identifying him tentatively with the son of Tauron, but wrongly calling him a "Lydian"; Billows 379 no. 28; Schoch, *RE* Supplbd IV (1924) 219 no. 6.

356 DEMEAS

(Δημέας). Athenian (Kirchner 3322). Son of Demades of the deme Paiania (Diod. 18.48.3; Plut. *Phoc.* 30.10). Born *c.*355. Athen. 13.591f claimed that D. was Demades' son by a flute girl, a charge that he attributes to Hypereides. But the uncorroborated allegations of orators need not be taken seriously. An orator, like his father, he nevertheless had only a short number of years in public life (two speeches by Hypereides against Demeas are attested: fragments 26 and 33; cf. Pollux 10.15). Plutarch (*Phoc.* 30.3) claims that Demades told his son that he was paying for his wedding with the money of kings and dynasts (βασιλεῖς καὶ δυνάσται). This may indicate the lavishness of the family's lifestyle or be nothing more than an attack on the father's integrity. In 319, he accompanied Demades on an embassy to Macedon and was executed (in front of his father) by Antipatros, who was now suffering from a fatal illness. The father's execution followed that of the son (Diod. 18.48.3–4; Plut. *Phoc.* 30.10, *Dem.* 31.6; Plutarch's account depicts Demades' clothes spattered with the blood of his son). Paschidis 68 A2.

357 DEMETRIOS

(Δημήτριος). Macedonian (Tataki 293–4 no. 30). Son of Althaimenes (Arr. 3.11.8), D. is the only one of eight ilarchs named at Gaugamela who attained prominence in the latter half of the campaign. First attested in the battle order at Gaugamela, where he was stationed between Herakleides and Meleagros (Arr. 3.11.8), D. may have held the rank of ilarch since 334, if not earlier. He reappears during the Swat campaign of 327/6, now with the rank of hipparch, with Attalos son of Andromenes and Alketas son of Orontes at the town of Ora (Arr. 4.27.5), which was captured after Alexander's arrival (Arr. 4.27.9). In the Hydaspes battle, D.'s hipparchy crossed the river with Alexander and was deployed on the right with that of Koinos (Arr. 5.16.3). D.'s last recorded command was in the Mallian campaign (326/5): he and Peithon the taxiarch, along with some lightly armed troops, were sent to subdue those Mallians who had taken refuge in the woods near the river (Arr. 6.8.2–3, presumably the Hydraotes; cf. Arr. 6.7.1). D. vanishes from our records at this point. His prominence may be due to family connections. If Amyntor, the father of Hephaistion, can be identified with Amyntor son of Demetrios (*IG* II² 405 = Schwenk no. 24, the mover of the decree was Demades), then there may have been a relationship between Hephaistion (no. 513) and D.: Althaimenes may have been the brother (or possibly brother-in-law) of Amyntor, making Hephaistion and D. first cousins. Kirchner, *RE* IV.2 (1901) 2768–9 no. 25; Berve II 134 no. 256; Hoffmann 183; Heckel 1992, 345–6.

358 DEMETRIOS

(Δημήτριος). Macedonian (Tataki 293 no. 26). Somatophylax of Alexander. D.'s family background is unknown, but the temptation to identify him with the brother of Antigonos Monophthalmos (Plut. *Demetr.* 2.1) must be resisted. Arrian (3.27.5) claims that Alexander deposed D. from office in the land of the Ariaspians, "suspecting that he had a share in Philotas' conspiracy." Curtius includes his name in the list of conspirators given by Dimnos to his lover Nikomachos (6.7.15). Despite his vigorous defense (Curt. 6.11.35), he was convicted by the testimony of a second witness (Calis: Curt. 6.11.37) and executed along with the others (Curt. 6.11.38). It is suspicious, however, that D. (the most notable individual to be linked to the conspiracy) is given very little attention by Alexander or by the sources. That D. was removed from office, as Arrian says, on a mere suspicion, and that his only crime was friendship with Philotas, is inherently implausible, given his high rank. Curtius' introduction of Calis (not named in 6.7.15) as D.'s accomplice, suggests contamination from a second source. The conspiracy, of which Dimnos had detailed knowledge and which Philotas failed to report to the King, was probably organized by D. and some other prominent individuals (the ones named are, for the most part, otherwise unknown, but that does not justify calling them nonentities) in response to Alexander's Orientalizing policies (full discussion in Heckel, *Marshals*² 55–9). Ptolemy son of Lagos replaced him as Somatophylax. Berve II 135 no. 260; Kirchner, *RE* IV.2 (1901) 2768 no. 24; Bosworth I 366–7; Heckel 1992, 261–2; Heckel 203–8.

359 DEMETRIOS

(Δημήτριος). One of Alexander's *hetairoi*—hence probably Macedonian (Tataki 294 no. 34), but possibly Greek—son of Pythonax (Arr. 4.12.5) and nicknamed *Pheidon* (Plut. *Alex.* 54.6). Although he is described as a flatterer (*kolax*) of Alexander (Plut. *Mor.* 65c), this does not rule out a military role in the campaign. In 327, when the King attempted to introduce *proskynesis*, D. is alleged to have alerted Alexander to Kallisthenes' failure to fulfill a promise to do obeisance (Plut. *Alex.* 54.6 = Chares, *FGrH* 125 F14; Arr. 4.12.5). D. may have remained with Alexander until the end of the King's life, but the evidence of Ps.-Call. 3.17 (cf. Jul. Valer. 3.15–16), which appears to mention Pheidon, is all but worthless. Berve II 134–5 no. 258; Ribbeck, *RE* s.v. "Kolax (85)".

360 DEMETRIOS

(Δημήτριος). [All references in **boldface** are to Plutarch's *Life of Demetrius*.] Macedonian (Tataki 292 no. 20). Demetrios Poliorketes. Son of Antigonos the One-Eyed and Stratonike (no. 1085), although Plutarch reports a variant which makes him the son of Antigonos' brother, Demetrios, who had been Stratonike's first husband (**2.1**). The story is not entirely implausible but, although it is more common for the first son to take the name of the paternal grandfather, D. may have been named in honor of his recently deceased uncle. Born in 335 or 334—he was twenty-two at the time of the battle of Gaza (**5.2**; Diod. 19.69.1; App. *Syr.* 54.272)—D. came to Phrygia as a small child and was raised at his father's satrapal residence in Kelainai (cf. Wheatley 1999); it was here in all likelihood that the younger brother, Philip (**2.2**), was born. He fled to Europe with his father, when Perdikkas was bringing charges against Antigonos (Diod. 18.23.4). In 320/19 at the latest, he married Phila (see no. 897), the daughter of Antipatros and widow of Krateros (Diod. 19.59.3–6), a union with a much older woman that was clearly arranged by his father (see also Wheatley and Dunn 29–34). The marriage is discussed by Plutarch in a chapter on D.'s love life, which thus downplays its political importance (**14.2–4**).

He accompanied his father in the campaigns against Eumenes, although he was still in his mid-teens, commanding troops for the first time (Diod. 19.29.4, 40.1 says he was in charge of the right wing (at Paraitakene and Gabiene); but this must have been a nominal command under the supervision of more experienced officers), and it is said that, when Eumenes was captured by Antigonos after the battle of Gabiene, D. and Nearchos tried in vain to save his life (Plut. *Eum.* 18.6). Not much else is known of his life before 312, except for anecdotes illustrating his character and his family relationships (see below). At the age of twenty-two he was sent with an army to oppose Ptolemy in Koile-Syria, with Peithon son of Agenor, Andronikos of Olynthos, Nearchos, and Philip as his advisors (Diod. 19.69.1). There he was defeated by Ptolemy's forces (**5.3**; Justin 15.1. 6, the MSS read *Galama*; cf. Trogus, *Prol.* 15; Diod. 19.80.5–84.8; for the battle see **5–6**, also Oros. 3.23.35; Paus. 1.6.5; Joseph. *Contra Ap.* 1.184–6 = Castor of Rhodes, *FGrH* 250 F12; *Marm. Par.* = *FGrH* 239B §16; Porphyry of Tyre, *FGrH* 260 F32.4; Syncellus, *Chron.* 321; Libanius, *Or.* 11.82; Devine 1984; Wheatley and Dunn 63–72; and Yardley-Wheatley-Heckel 225–9, with further literature) and D. fled some 270 stades to Azotos, leaving 500 dead on the battlefield and 8,000 who were captured by Ptolemy (Diod. 19.85.1–3). Ptolemy showed clemency and released D.'s friends, along with their property, giving them other gifts in addition, and restoring D.s property and slaves (Justin 15.1.7–8; Diod. 19.85.3). According to Appian (*Syr.* 54.272), after he was defeated by Ptolemy, D. marched north to Tripolis in Phoinikia and summoned reinforcements from Kilikia (Diod. 19.85.5). Whether a second battle occurred in Phoinikia (τὴν ἄνω Συρίαν) early in 311, this time between D. and the Ptolemaic commander Killes (no. 585), after which D. was able to repay Ptolemy's generosity (6.2–5; Diod. 19.93.1–2), is open to doubt, although it has generally been accepted as factual (cf. Hornblower, *Hieronymus* 228; Billows 129; Niese II 300; Elkeles 9; Seibert 1969, 150; Anson 2014, 146). It nevertheless strikes the reader as an attempt to salvage the young man's reputation; even if a victory was achieved, the impact may not have been as great as some have believed (Paus. 1.6.5: τινας τῶν Αἰγυπτίων λοχήσας διέφθειρεν οὐ πολλούς), and Ptolemy abandoned Syria in the face of Antigonos' move southward. Plutarch maintains that D. was sent soon afterwards against the Nabataians, in which campaign he gave a good account of himself (7.1). But Diodorus gives a full account of the campaign, clearly deriving from Hieronymos of Kardia (Hornblower, *Hieronymus* 144–51), and shows that the undertaking against the Nabataians had been assigned to Athenaios (no. 254; Diod. 19.94.1), who, on his return from plundering Petra, was surprised in his encampment on his way back to Antigonos and heavily defeated (Diod. 19.95.1–96.2). At that point, Antigonos sent D. with a second force—equal in the number of light-armed infantry but vastly superior in cavalry numbers (more than 4,000, compared with the six hundred of Athenaios: Diod. 19.96.4). For the campaign (including a digression on the Nabataians and their territory) see Diod. 19.98–100. Antigonos was displeased that D. had settled affairs through negotiations (Diod. 19.97.6; discussion in Bosworth 2002, 199–207; Wheatley and Dunn 79–83, esp. 83: "a time-wasting distraction from far more vital matters").

Not much later, D. led an offensive against Babylon, which Seleukos had recovered in the wake of the Ptolemaic victory at Gaza (Diod. 19.90.1). D. captured one of the city's two citadels and installed a force of 7,200 men, but since he was summoned back to the coast by his father, he left Archelaos (no. 161) with a force of 5,000 infantry and 1,000 cavalry to besiege the other (Diod. 19.100.7). The campaign proved ultimately to be a failure (7.2–4; Diod. 19.100.4–7; cf. also the so-called *Diadochoi Chronicle*: BM 36313 + 34660; Smith 1924, 124–49; Grayson 1975, 115–19). Nevertheless, with Seleukos preoccupied with recovering and enlarging his power in the East, D. and his father turned their attentions back to Ptolemy, and to a lesser extent, Kassandros, who was still being challenged in Greece by Polyperchon. The Peace of 311 (Diod. 19.105.1; cf. *RC* 1; Harding no. 132; cf. Diod. 20.19.3), far from settling affairs, merely gave the signatories greater opportunity to make accusations against their rivals. D. campaigned and won control of the cities in Kilikia that Ptolemy had occupied (Diod. 20.19.5). D. lifted the siege of Halikarnassos by Ptolemy's forces (7.5), and the Antigonids now posed as guarantors of the "Freedom of the Greeks" (8.1).

In 307, D. sailed with a considerable force from Ephesos to Athens (Diod. 20.45.1), where he gained access to Peiraieus when its defenders mistook his fleet for that of Ptolemy (8.5). Proclaiming that he was coming to liberate the city, D. ultimately forced the commandant of Peiraieus to flee to Mounychia, while Demetrios of Phaleron withdrew to the city. The latter soon entered into negotiations that saw him withdraw to Thebes (Diod. 20.45.2–5). Dionysios' (no. 389) garrison in Mounychia, under heavy siege, surrendered and their commander was taken into custody by D. (20.45.7). Freed from the control of Kassandros and Demetrios of Phaleron, Athens recovered its ancestral constitution (**8.7**; Diod. 20.46.1–3), but its dependence on the Antigonids became clear in actions incited or initiated by Stratokles (no. 1082) and men such as Dromokleides (**13**). For these sycophantic measures see (**10–13**; Diod. 20.46.2). Even D.'s marriage to Euthydike (no. 461), a woman of the distinguished family of Militiades and the widow of Ophellas (no. 817), was treated as a compliment by his supporters in Athens and their flock (**14.1**). But this, and most of D.'s outrageous behavior—for the endless flattery and debasement of the Athenians had in Plutarch's opinion a deleterious effect on the man—occurred in the period after the campaigns against Kypros, Rhodes, and Egypt (of which only the first was a success), when the Besieger spent an extended period in the city (see the discussion of D.'s personal life, below). Between his capture of Peiraieus and the taking of Mounychia, D. spent about a month reducing Megara (Diod. 20.46.3; **9.8–10**), though before attacking the city, he nearly fell into an ambush when he sailed to Patrai and planned a liaison with Kratesipolis, the widow of Alexander (no. 46) son of Polyperchon (**9.5–7**). The episode is doubtless sensationalized (though we need not reject the idea of D.'s romantic inclinations); the worldly Kratesipolis may, in fact, have planned to recover some of her own power or else set a trap for him (for the problems of geography and chronology associated with Plutarch's account, see Wheatley 2004, reiterated in Wheatley and Dunn 122–5; Rose 2015, 159–60; discussion s.v. Kratesipolis no. 626). D. was soon called away from Greece by his father, who ordered him to sail to Kypros and wage war on Ptolemy (Diod. 20.46.5–6), whose brother Menelaos now controlled the island. En route he attempted to lure the Rhodians away from their support of Ptolemy; their rejection marked them as future targets of the Antigonids (Diod. 20.46.6).

D. was able to reverse his humiliation at Gaza and pay back Ptolemy (in 306) with defeat and kindness at the battle of Salamis (Justin 15.2.6–8); among the prisoners returned to Ptolemy were his brother Menelaos (no. 710) and his son Leontiskos (no. 656), along with other members of their entourage (Justin 15.2.7); the courtesan Lamia (no. 639) was also captured but not returned (**16.5**), perhaps in accordance with her own wishes. Thereupon Antigonos and D. were proclaimed "Kings" by their troops (Justin 15.2.10; Diod. 20.53.2; App. *Syr.* 54.275–7; Heid. Epit. 5.1; Nepos, *Eum.* 13.2–3; *1 Macc.* 1.7.9; Oros. 3.23.40; **18.1**; for the dramatics of Aristodemos see **17.2–6**); for the two sons of Alexander the Great (Alexander IV and Herakles) had been dead for some time and there was no recognized king within the disintegrating empire. Summoned to Syria by his father, D. was placed in charge of the fleet that accompanied the Antigonid army as it moved south to invade Egypt in 306/5. The campaign proved to be a dismal failure (**19.1–3**; Paus. 1.6.6) and Antigonos was forced to turn back (Diod. 20.73–6). This bitter failure was followed by retribution against Rhodes, which had earlier declined to support him against Ptolemy (Diod. 20.46.6, 82.1–2; Paus. 1.6.6). These three campaigns deserve closer attention.

(a) The Salamis campaign (306). D. crossed to Kypros from Kilikia, where he had gathered additional troops, with a fleet of 110 triremes, fifty-three heavier ships that were used to carry troops, and other transports, sufficient to convey an army of 15,000 infantry and 400 cavalry (Diod. 20.47.1; **15.2–4** for preliminaries). Landing at Karpasia, he set up camp and brought both Ourania and Karpasia (*Barr. Atl.* 72 E1) under his control before marching on Salamis, where Menelaos awaited him with 12,000 infantry and 800 horse. In the first engagement with the Ptolemaic foe, D. killed about 1,000 and took 3,000

prisoners; his attempt to enrol them in his own army failed because many defected and, in the end, he sent them to detention in Syria (Diod. 20.47.2–4). D. now turned to besiege Salamis, prompting Menelaos to send to Ptolemy for help (Diod 20.47.7–8). D. prosecuted the siege with his usual vigor (Diod. 20.48). Reinforcements from Egypt (140 warships, Diod. 20.49.2; **16.1** 150; on fleet strengths see Hauben 1976) made it clear that the issue would be decided at sea, and D. placed bolt-catapults and stone throwers (καταπέλτας ὀξυβελεῖς καὶ λιθοβόλους) on board some of his ships (Diod. 20.49.4). Leaving ten ships under Antisthenes to blockade the harbor of Salamis (despite the small number of ships, the blockade held long enough to prevent the Ptolemaic commander Menoitios (no. 721) from participating in the main battle: Diod.20.52.5; **16.1–2**), D. advanced to battle with 108 ships (**16.2**: 180), including quinqueremes and septiremes (Diod. 20.50.1–2; for Hellenistic siege and naval warfare see Tarn 1930, 101–52; Murray 2012, 171–85; Grainger 2011, 27–53), deploying the various units under the supreme command of Medeios (no. 690; Diod. 20.50.3: Μηδίου τοῦ ναυάρχου τὴν ἡγεμονίαν ἔχοντος) on the left, Themison (no. 1106) and Marsyas (no. 683) in the middle, and Pleistias (no. 965) and Hegesippos (no. 503) on the right (Diod. 20.50.4). The battle (Diod. 20.51.1–52.3; **16**), initiated at daybreak (Diod. 20.50.5), was a hard-fought affair and, although Ptolemy enjoyed some success against those opposite him (undoubtedly pro-Ptolemaic propaganda), D. destroyed his right wing and sent his opponent fleeing to Kition (Diod. 20.52.3; cf. **16.3** says he had only eight ships with him). It was left to Bourichos (no. 309) and Neon (no. 769) to pick up survivors and capture those of the enemy (Diod. 20.52.4). Ptolemaic casualties were heavy, both in terms of ships and men (including some 8,000 captive soldiers); by comparison D. suffered the loss of only twenty ships, disabled in the battle (Diod. 20.52.6). Menelaos surrendered Salamis, along with what remained of the fleet and an army of 12,000 infantry and 1,200 horse (**16.7**). From the spoils D. bought the favor of the Athenians, sending them 1,200 panoplies (**17.1**). The outcome of the battle was the mastery of Kypros (Diod. 20.53.1) and the Antigonid claims to kingship that were soon followed by those of their rivals (**18.1–4**; Justin 15.2.11–12; cf. Gruen 1985). Ancient accounts: Diod. 20.46.5–47.4; 20.47.7–52; Polyaenus 4.7.7; App. *Syr.* 54.275; Paus. 1.6.6; **15–16**; Justin 15.2.6–9; *Marm. Par.* (*FGrH* 239 B21); Athen. 6.254a. Modern discussions of the battle can be found in Seibert 1969, 190–206; cf. Billows 151–5; Niese I 318–21; Hill I 166–71; Murray 2012, 105–11; Champion 2014, 116–23; Wheatley and Dunn, 151–8.

(b) The Egyptian campaign (Oct.–Dec. 306). It was at this time that D.'s brother Philip (no. 918) died (Diod. 20.73.1). Not long after, Antigonos summoned D. from Kypros and prepared to invade Egypt (Wheatley 2014b, 93 calls it an attempt "to follow up their stunning victory and deliver the knockout blow"), using Antigoneia as his base (Diod. 20.73.1–2); while his father commanded the land forces, D. brought the fleet along the Levantine coast. The campaign (Diod. 20.73–6) ended in utter failure, however, because of the difficulties of the land route beyond Gaza (Diod. 20.73.3), the adverse conditions that prevented the fleet—the storm struck near Raphia (20.74.1), but D. brought his ships to Kasion (20.74.2–5)—from advancing up the Nile (on the difficulties see Kahn and Tammuz 2009), and Ptolemy's attempts to suborn the mercenaries in the Antigonid army (Diod 20.75.1–2). In fact, even with the naval force, severe measures had been taken to prevent defection (Diod. 20.75.3). The entire campaign is summed up by Plutarch in one short paragraph (**19.1–3**). Full discussion in Wheatley 2014b; Wheatley and Dunn 171–7; cf. Hauben 1975–6.

(c) The Siege of Rhodes (305–304). Certainly, the best known of D.'s campaigns was his spectacular but unsuccessful siege of Rhodes. This began in August 305 and concluded almost a year later (Wheatley and Dunn 149). D. was sent by his father with a fleet and siege engines to wage war on the Rhodians and, although they were willing to submit on reasonable terms, D. demanded that they give up one hundred of their leading citizens as hostages and admit his fleet to their harbors (Diod. 20.82.1–3). These terms were unacceptable and the hostilities began in earnest. Using Loryma in Karia as his base (*Barr. Atl.* 61 G4), D. sailed across to the island with a fleet of 200 warships and 170 transports, the sight of which was designed to frighten the defenders (Diod. 20.82.4–83.1). Landing near the city, he constructed a mole, in order to create a harbor for his ships, and built a camp secured by palisades (Diod. 20.83). The Rhodians for their part took what measures they could: they sent ambassadors to Lysimachos, Kassandros, and Ptolemy; expelled from the city any foreigners who were not prepared to help with the defense; and they purchased the freedom of able-bodied slaves who could serve as soldiers (Diod. 20.84.1–3). D. concentrated on the harbor, and the Rhodians devised countermeasures, including the use of fire-ships (Diod. 20.86.3–4), just as the Tyrians had done against Alexander. Eight days of assaulting the city began to bear fruit but the Rhodians successfully attacked the attackers, killing some, driving off the rest, and burning their ships (Diod. 20.87.1–2); a full-scale attack on the walls was also repulsed and D. was forced to spend seven days regrouping and repairing his siege equipment (Diod. 20.87.3–88.1). A force under Exekestos (no. 466) was sent to attack those of D.'s ships equipped with siege engines, achieving some success, even though the admiral was wounded and captured (Diod. 20.88.6); reinforcements also came from Knossos, as well as mercenaries from Ptolemy (20.88.9; cf. 20.98.1 for additional troops from Ptolemy, ironically under the leadership of a certain Antigonos no. 119). D. had failed to take the city in the initial stages and the siege soon became a prolonged affair, with the action shifting from the sea to land (Diod. 20.91.1–93.1; 20.94–8). During this stage of the siege, the Rhodian Menedemos captured a quadrireme carrying royal effects sent by Phila to her husband (20.93.4; **22.1**). The siege was marked by a succession of setbacks for D. and his forces and the heroic actions of men like Athenagoras (no. 253; 20.94.3–5), Amyntas (no. 89; 20.97.5), and Ananias (no. 90; 20.97.7); of D.'s men, Mantias (no. 682) and Alkimos (no. 66) distinguished themselves in battle (20.98.9; **21.6**). Furthermore, the valiant defense was bolstered by shipments of grain from Ptolemy (20.96.1, 98.1), as well as Kassandros and Lysimachos (20.96.3) A story is told with different variations that D. spared the famous painting of *Ialysos* by Protogenes (**22.4–6**; Gell. 25.31; Pliny, *HN* 7.126, 35.105; Plut. *Mor.* 183a–b; see no. 1000). In the end, after much loss of life and equipment, and through the agency of the Athenians (**22.8**) or the Aitolian Confederacy (Diod. 20.99.3), D. was told by his father to settle the dispute, achieving what could have been accomplished through negotiation at the very start: the Rhodians would agree to friendship with the Antigonids but would not go to war with Ptolemy. Full discussion of the siege in Wheatley and Dunn, 184–201; Champion 2014, 130–42; Niese I 326–33; Murray 2012, 111–17.

The final years leading up to Ipsos saw D. embroiled once again in the affairs of European Greece and in conflict with Kassandros. D. sailed from Rhodes to Aulis in Boiotia. He ousted the Boiotian garrison in Chalkis and formed an alliance with the Aitolians, intent on waging war with Kassandros and Polyperchon (Diod. 20.100.5–6). In the Peloponnese, Sikyon was taken, as the defenders were alarmed by the sight of his siege engines. Here he demolished a portion of the city near the harbor and transferred the population to a more defensible position; the citizens in gratitude renamed the place Demetrias (Diod. 20.102.2–3). D. next turned his attention to Korinth, gaining access by treachery and forcing the garrison to retreat to Akrokorinth; but this too surrendered at the sight of the siege engines (20.103.1–3); Plutarch says that much of his success in Sikyon, Argos, and Korinth was due to bribery (**25.1**). D. advanced into Achaia, capturing Boura and Skyros (*Barr. Atl.* 58 C1), but Orchomenos proved more difficult under its commander Strombichos (no. 1089; Diod. 20.103.4–5). After storming the place he crucified Strombichos and about eighty of his supporters, enrolling the other mercenaries in his own army (20.103.6). All of Arkadia except Mantineia came over to him (**25.1**). Having secured the friendship of the Aitolians, D. made an alliance with Pyrrhos, who since his restoration to the throne in 307 had reached a *détente* with Kassandros. The bond was sealed by political marriage, and D. married Pyrrhos' sister Deidameia (no. 343) in Argos in July 303 (**25.2**; cf. *Pyrrh.* 4.3); the move backfired on Pyrrhos, who was deprived of his kingship by the pro-Kassandros party when he went to Illyria to attend the wedding of one of Glaukias' sons (Plut. *Pyrrh.* 4.1). D. had effectively cleared Kassandros and Polyperchon out of Greece, and Kassandros now sent out peace feelers only to be rudely rebuffed by Antigonos (Diod. 20.106.2–3). The end result was an alliance against the Antigonids that brought Lysimachos and Kassandros' generals to Asia Minor, encouraged the defection of Antigonid generals and officials, and set the stage for a military confrontation at Ipsos (Diod. 20.106.4–109.2). Demetrios made a brief stop in Athens, attending the mysteries of Eleusis, despite his ineligibility to participate (**26**; Diod. 20.110.1; Wheatley and Dunn 222–6), and then moved into Central Greece and Thessaly, ferrying his troops around Thermopylai (which Kassandros guarded) by ship (Diod. 20.110.2). With a vastly superior force that included 56,000 infantrymen, D. wrested Pherai from Kassandros and found himself well prepared to advance on Macedonia (20.110.3–5). But the situation in Asia Minor had forced Antigonos to summon his son home (20.109.5) and his envoys reached D. in Thessaly (20.111.1). Gathering transport ships, D. sailed with his entire army to Ephesos, winning back the city which Prepelaos had won only some months before (20.111.3). He was able to rejoin his father before the coalition forces were sufficiently prepared. But the outcome of the battle at Ipsos in 301 was disastrous: Antigonos was killed on the battlefield, waiting in vain for his son—who had gone in pursuit of the enemy cavalry (**29.4–6**)—to save him from the collapse of the forces under his immediate command (**29.3–8**; for his death see also Thorax no. 1130); D. himself was left with little of his former kingdom except the navy and a few strongholds. According to Diod. 21.1.4[b], D. and his mother Stratonike, who had remained in Kilikia with all their valuables, sailed to Salamis in Kypros, which was an Antigonid possession. But Plutarch says D. fled to Ephesos with 5,000 infantry and 4,000 cavalry with the intention of going to Athens (**30.2**) He had pinned his hopes on the Athenians, who had striven to outdo one another when D. was all powerful. But they quickly abandoned him, escorting Deidameia to Megara (**30.4**).

The remainder of D.'s career, from Ipsos until his death in late winter 282, must be treated in cursory fashion (Wheatley and Dunn 253–436 is now the authoritative discussion of this period of the Besieger's life). Despite the mass defections that followed Ipsos, D. managed to maintain a naval force and to reassert himself in Greece and Macedonia. His fortunes were improved by the mutual suspicions of Lysimachos, Kassandros, Ptolemy, and Seleukos. Since Ptolemy and Lysimachos had bound themselves to an alliance sealed by the marriage of Lysimachos to Arsinoë II (no. 221), Seleukos agreed to an alliance by marrying D.'s daughter Stratonike (no. 1086; 31.5–32.3, 38.1). Although the alliance brought D. little in the way of overt support, it did dampen the enthusiasm of his rivals to challenge him unnecessarily. And his prospects in Europe were improved by the death of Kassandros in 297 and, months later, of his son Philip IV (36.1). Athens, which had abandoned him, soon found itself under the thumb of the tyrant, Lachares (see Ferguson 130–5; Habicht 1997, 82–7), whom D. expelled in 295. With no alternative and in fear of punishment, the Athenians welcomed D. as their liberator and voted to hand over to him Peiraieus and Mounychia; as a precaution D. seized the Mouseion Hill as well (33–34). Possession of Athens gave him a base from which to meddle in the affairs of Boiotia. But it was his good fortune that the younger sons of Kassandros, Antipatros (no. 128), and Alexander (no. 42) were not content to share the Macedonian kingdom and turned upon each other. Even though events drew D. away from his campaign against Sparta (294), he answered the appeal of Alexander, whom he treacherously murdered, seizing the kingdom for himself (Plut. *Pyrrh.* 7.1–2; 36–7; Justin 16.1.8–18). Thereafter he overcame two rebellions in Boiotia (293/2 and 292/1; 39) and gained Kerkyra by marrying Agathokles' daughter, Lanassa (no. 640), who had left her first husband Pyrrhos (Plut. *Pyrrh.* 10.7). The death of Deidameia in 300 (or soon afterward) had strained the relationship between D. and Pyrrhos—it did not help that the latter regained his kingdom with the help of Ptolemy—and the liaison with Lanassa and the loss of Kerkyra served only to drive them farther apart. Pyrrhos had won territorial concessions (Plut. *Pyrrh.* 6.4) from Alexander when he came to his aid while D. was delayed by other business but he had withdrawn to his own kingdom after brokering a peace between the brothers (Plut. *Pyrrh.* 6.8–9; cf. Justin 16.1.7). D.'s murder of Alexander and seizure of the kingdom, as well as his attacks on Epeiros in 290/89, led Pyrrhos to challenge D. for control of Macedon. In 287, D. was ousted from Macedonia (43–4) and lost the support of the Athenians as well. D. fled to Kassandreia, where his first wife Phila committed suicide by drinking poison (45.1). He crossed back into Asia in 286, hoping to restore the land where he had grown up to Antigonid control. At that time he also took his last wife, Ptolemais (46.5), daughter of Eurydike, whom Ptolemy had abandoned in favor of Berenike. Held in check by the forces of Lysimachos' son Agathokles (46.8–47.2), D. was finally cornered in the Amanus mountains in winter 286/5. He was forced to surrender and live in honorable detention in the Syria Chersonese (47–52), where (disappointed in his hopes that his daughter Stratonike, now married to Antiochos I, would intervene on his behalf: 50.9) he gave himself over to heavy drinking and died in early 282 at the age of 54 (52.5).

His appearance, character and personal life. D. was not as large as his father though he was *megas*, but he was extremely good-looking; words or portraits could scarcely do justice to his appearance (2.2). The harmony, love and trust in the house of Antigonos—and especially between father and son—is emphasized by Plutarch (3). Antigonos could allow his son to sit next to him, fresh from the hunt and in his hunting clothes, carrying his javelins (3.2). His concern for friends was demonstrated by his warning to Mithridates son of Ariobarzanes to flee from danger at the court (4.1–4). D. had a passion for Athenian *hetairai*: including Lamia and Leaina (Athen. 13.577c–d; on Lamia especially Athen. 3.1013, 4.128a–b), Mania (Athen. 13.578a, from Ptolemy son of Agesarchos, *FGrH* 161 F4; cf. Machon *ap.* Athen. 13.579a), and Myrrhine (Nikolaos of Damaskos *ap.* Athen. 13.593a).

But Herakleides Lembos (*FHG* III 168–9 frag. 4 = Athen. 13.578a–b) is probably mistaken about Demo (no. 364). Even free women and boys were not protected against his sexual advances, and it is alleged that a beautiful boy named Demokles (no. 366) chose to throw himself into a cauldron of boiling water in order to avoid being seduced by him (24.3–5). D. had compared Lysimachos' court with the comic stage since his courtiers had disyllabic names (Bithys, Paris), but Lysimachos countered by saying he had not previously seen a whore on the tragic stage. D., for his part, remarked that a whore at his court was more chaste than the Penelope at the court of Lysimachos (Athen. 14.614f–615a; thought to be a reference to Arsinoë II, but probably referring to Nikaia: Bosworth 2002, 272–3; Rose 2015, 232). D.'s flatterers would not address the other successors as kings but called Seleukos "master of the elephants" (ἐλεφαντάρχης), Lysimachos "the treasurer" (γαζοφύλαξ), Ptolemy "the admiral" (ναύαρχος) and Agathokles "lord of the islands" (νησιάρχης) (Plut. *Mor* 823c–d; Phylarchos *ap.* Athen. 6.261b; Hauben 1974). This may well have been in return for the epithet *Poliorketes*, which was applied (no doubt disparagingly; Gell. *NA* 15.31.1 takes it seriously; see also the vigorous defense by Wheatley 2020) to D. after his failed siege of Rhodes (cf. Heckel 1984; Berthold 1984, 79; see Wheatley and Dunn, 150 n.24). Much of what we know about D.'s revelries comes from Lynkeus (no. 667) of Samos (Athen. 3.101e; 4.128a–b), the brother of the historian Douris (no. 403). For his love of luxury and extravagance see Athen. 12.535f–536a; also 6.253c–255c. According to the twentieth book of Demochares' *History* (*FHG* II 449), D. did not approve of the flattery of the Athenians: disgraceful were the temples to Aphrodite Leaina and Lamia; shrines and libations to his parasites Bourichos, Adeimantos, and Oxythemis (Athen. 6.252f–253a). Polemon in *On the Painted Porch in Sikyon* says the Thebans flattered D. by establishing a temple of Aphrodite Lamia (Athen. 6.253b).

His wives and children. Unlike his father, who appears to have been monogamous, D. took numerous wives and fathered many children. Phila, the widow of Krateros, was the first and produced Antigonos (surnamed Gonatas) and Stratonike (**Stemmata V-VI**); Euthydike, the widow of Ophellas, gave him a son named Korrhagos after his maternal grandfather. By Deidameia he had a son named Alexander (**Stemma IIb**); both Ptolemais and an Illyrian woman (**A98**) gave him sons named Demetrios, distinguished by the epithets *Kalos* (**Stemma X**) and *Leptos* respectively (**53.8–9**). To these we may add his notorious mistress Lamia, the mother of a daughter named Phila (no. 898). Kaerst, *RE* IV.2 (1901) 2769–92 no. 33 Sandberger 72–89 no. 30; Billows 379–80 no. 29; Wheatley, *LexAM* 195–6. His life, well documented in the ancient sources (esp. Plutarch's *Life of Demetrius*, and Diod. 19–20), has not received proper scholarly treatment, an anomaly in the scholarship of the Successors, until now: see Wheatley and Dunn; also Wheatley 1997b, 1999, 2001, 2003, 2004, and 2014b; Rose 2015; Wehrli 1968; Sandberger 72–89 no. 30; Bengtson 1975, 64–90. **Stemma VI**.

361 DEMETRIOS

(Δημήτριος). Macedonian (Tataki 292–3 no. 23). One of two sons of Demetrios Poliorketes named after the father. This man, nicknamed *Leptos* (λεπτός, "the Thin") was the son of an Illyrian woman whose name has not been handed down to us (Plut. *Demetr.* 53.8). Nothing else is known about him. Kaerst, *RE* IV.2 (1901) 2794 no. 36.

362 DEMETRIOS

(Δημήτριος). Macedonian (Tataki 292 no. 21). Son of Demetrios Poliorketes and Ptolemais, the daughter of Ptolemy I and Eurydike (Justin 26.3.3), known by the epithet ὁ καλός ("the Fair"; cf. Justin 26.3.4, for his good looks). Born in 285 (his father married Ptolemais in 286 and soon left to campaign, never to return). Kaerst 2793 believes that the Demetrios who defeated Alexander II of Epeiros and drove him out of his kingdom (Justin 26.2.9–11) was D. the Fair and not Antigonos Gonatas' son (rightly rejected by Tarn, *AG* 304 n.83). The description of D. as "a mere boy" (*puer admodum*) is hardly applicable to the Besieger's son, who was now in his early twenties, whereas Gonatas' son was anywhere from five to ten years younger. Justin distinguishes the two men by calling one *filius* [sc. *Antigoni*] (26.2.11) and the other *fratrem regis Antigoni* (26.3.3). In the mid-260s, D. married Olympias, daughter of Polykleitos of Larisa (presumably of the Aleuadai), who bore him a son, Antigonos (later known as Doson, *regn.* 229–221; Kaerst, *RE* I.2 (1894) 2418–19 no. 5) in 264/3 (Euseb. 1.243). He later ruled Kyrene (Plut. *Demetr.* 53.8), though only briefly. Summoned by Apama, after the death of her husband Magas (his death now appears to date to 250; Will 2003, 243–6), with the promise of marriage to Berenike, he was rumored to have had a relationship with Apama herself. At the instigation of Berenike, D. was killed by those who favored the marriage of Berenike to Ptolemy III. For the sordid tale of his relations with Apama and his death see Justin 26.3.3–8 (where the queen is incorrectly called "Arsinoë"). Kaerst, *RE* IV.2 (1901) 2793–4 no. 35; Beloch IV² 2.139; Clayman 2014, 34–8; also Macurdy 131–4; Seibert 1967, 81; Ogden 80–1; Carney 171. **Stemma X.**

363 DEMETRIOS

(Δημήτριος). Athenian. Son of Phanostratos, from Phaleron (Kirchner 3455, with references), brother of Himeraios (no. 532). According to scandal, he had once been a household slave of Timotheos and Konon (Aelian, *VH* 12.43). Born *c.*350, or slightly earlier: Diog. Laert. 5.85 says that he made his political debut at the time of Harpalos' arrival in Athens in 324. A peripatetic philosopher who studied with Theophrastos (Strabo 9.1.20 C398; Diog. Laert. 5.39, 75), D. was pro-Macedonian but certainly disillusioned when his brother Himeraios was murdered on Antipatros' order (Arr. *Succ.* 1.13). At that time, D. went to live with Nikanor (Athen. 13.542e). Together with Phokion, D. led the aristocratic faction at Athens, which favored Kassandros against Polyperchon, whom the democrats supported (Nepos *Phocion* 3.1); when Polyperchon expelled Kassandros from Macedonia (319/8), the popular party gained the upper hand in Athens and outlawed the leaders of the aristocratic faction (Nepos, *Phoc.* 3.2); Phokion was executed, D. condemned to death *in absentia* (Plut. *Phoc.* 35.5). But when Kassandros gained control of Athens, he installed D. as governor (*prostates* or *epistates*) of the city (Diod. 18.74.3; 19.78.3), which he ruled for ten years (317–307) until his expulsion by his namesake, the Besieger. In his first years he reformed the Athenian constitution on an oligarchic basis, though Diod. 18.18.4–5 says such reforms were begun already by Antipatros in 322 (Strabo 9.1.20 curiously remarks that he not only did not destroy the democracy but actually improved it, and then comments upon the hostility the Athenians felt for the oligarchy; Plut. *Demetr.* 10.2 says that D. exercised a virtual monarchy). He acted on Kassandros' orders and sent twenty ships to Lemnos under the command of Aristoteles (no. 209), but this failed to accomplish its mission of holding the island against Ptolemy (Diod. 19.68.3–5). When Demetrios Poliorketes gained access to Athens (Polyaenus 4.7.6), D. made his way first to Boiotia (Plut. *Mor.* 69c) and then, after the death of Kassandros (Diog. Laert. 5.78; cf. Ferguson 125 n.1), to Egypt (Diod. 20.45.2–5; cf. Plut. *Demetr.* 8.4; 9.2–3; Strabo 9.1.20 C398), where he was influential with Ptolemy I Soter (Plut. *Mor.* 189d) and became the librarian in Alexandria. Nevertheless, he incurred the enmity of Philadelphos by urging Soter to bestow his kingdom on his children by Eurydike and, after Soter's death, came to an unhappy end; he died some time before or around 280 (Diog. Laert. 5.78, says he was bitten by an asp). Three hundred statues of D. in Athens were taken down, according to Plut. *Mor.* 820e–f. By his political enemies he was attacked for his personal habits: Douris of Samos (*FGrH* 76 F10 = Athen. 12.542b–e) commented on his extravagance, debauchery, and vanity (cf. Athen. 12.542f). For his reforms in Athens see Ferguson 1911, 38–94; Habicht 1997, 53–87; for the philosopher politician see Gehrke 1978. Kirchner 3455; Berve II 135 no. 259; Martini, *RE* IV.2 (1901) 2817 no. 85; Bosworth, *OCD*³ 448 no. 3; O'Sullivan 2009; Worthington 2021, 29–51.

364 DEMO

(Δημώ). Athenian prostitute. Mistress of Antigonos Gonatas and mother of Halkyoneus (no. 492; Ptolemy son of Agesarchos *ap.* Athen. 13.577f–578a = *FGrH* 161 F4). Herakleides Lembos (*FHG* III 168–9 frag. 4 = Athen. 13.578a–b) said, mistakenly, that Demetrios' father (*sic*) had fallen in love with Demo and put to death Oxythemis (no. 836) because he had tortured and killed Demo's maid-servants. If there is any truth to the story, it will have involved Gonatas and not Monophthalmos (cf. Billows 414). The date of Demo's liaison with Gonatas is uncertain, but it must have begun before the death of Poliorketes, since their son, Halkyoneus, was old enough to conduct affairs against Pyrrhos in 272. Plutarch's conflation of Demo and Mania (*Demetr.* 27.9) is incorrect, unless he is speaking of a different Demo, which was not an uncommon name for a prostitute (Gow, *Machon* 98; Ogden 247–8, somewhat convoluted). Kirchner, *RE* IV.2 (1901) 2863 no. 5; Ogden 178; Tarn, *AG* 247–8 n.92.

365 DEMOCHARES

(Δημοχάρης). Athenian (Kirchner 3716: ΔΗΜΟΧΑΡΗΣ ΛΑΧΗΤΟΣ ΛΕΥΚΟΝΟΕΥΣ). Son of Laches and Demosthenes' sister, hence the orator's nephew ([Plut.] *Vit. X Or.* 847c; Cic. *Brut.* 286, *de Orat.* 2.95; Polyb. 12.13.4; Dem. 27.4: Demosthenes was two years older than D.'s mother, who was thus born in 382). Since D. makes his first appearance in 322 (unless he was an ambassador to Philip in 338/7) and died in 271, it is assumed that he was born between 355 and 350 (cf. Swoboda 2864). Athen. 13.610f, 6. 253b–d wrongly calls him a cousin (ἀνεψιός) of Demosthenes. D. was noted for his excellence in war and on the *bema* ([Plut.] *Mor.* 847c) and belonged to the democratic, anti-Macedonian party. He was said to have been sent with others to Philip II, whom he offended by saying that if he wanted to please the Athenians he should "hang himself" (Sen. *de Ira* 3.23.2–3, calling him *Parrhesiastes* or "outspoken"; Polyb. 12.13 claims that Timaios said many false and scurrilous things about D.). If there is any truth to the story, his birth must have occurred in the 360s, in which case he was in his nineties when he died. Kirchner's suggestion (p.252) that the king in question is Philip IV, the son of Kassandros, is unconvincing. Paschidis 153 n.2 suggests Philip III, but Polyperchon and Philip III were at the time supporting the democrats and so unlikely to have earned Demochares' disdain. The story is most likely fictitious reflecting Demochares' known anti-Macedonian views and those of his more celebrated uncle. D. did speak against the surrender of the orators demanded by Antipatros at the end of the Lamian War ([Plut.] 847d: a statue of D. in the Prytaneion wearing a sword, as he did when he addressed the *ekklesia* on this matter). Unsuccessful in his opposition to Antipatros, D. went into exile and did not return until the reign of Demetrios of Phaleron ended. During the early years of the reinstated democracy, D. was a political leader, along with Stratokles (but not such a fawning supporter of Demetrios Poliorketes). Inscriptional evidence shows that he worked for the defense and welfare of the state (*IG* II² 463, 468; *Syll*³ 334; [Plut.] *Mor.* 851d). Less to his credit is his support in 306 or 305 of Sophokles' motion that put the philosophical schools under state control, a move that, in effect, drove the philosophers from the city (Diog. Laert. 5.38; Athen. 11.508f, 13.610f; cf. Habicht 1997, 73–4; Ferguson 106–7). D., who wrote *Historiai* (*FGrH* 75, five fragments attested with certainty), recorded in the 20th book that Demetrios Poliorketes did not like the flattery of the Athenians: particularly such disgraceful acts as altars to Aphrodite Leaina and Lamia, shrines and libations to Demetrios' *kolakes* Bourichos, Adeimantos, Oxythemis (Athen. 6.252f–253a); nevertheless, he became an enemy of the Besieger and Stratokles and was exiled 303 (Plut. *Demetr.* 24.10–11). What is known of the remainder of his career comes from a petition to the *boule* and the *demos* by his son Laches in 271/0, recorded by [Plut.] *Mor.* 851d–f: he was recalled from exile in 288/7 (in the archonship of Diokles) and introduced economic measures to limit the cost of government. D. was sent as an envoy to Lysimachos, from whom he gained 130 talents of silver; later he received another twenty from Antipatros of Macedon. An embassy to Egypt, which D. proposed (though clearly did not participate in) secured 50 additional talents. As a fitting summary of D.'s career, the Laches decree notes: "he held no office after the democracy had been overthrown, and he was the only Athenian of those who were engaged in public life in his time who never plotted to alter the government of the country by changing it to a form other than democracy" ([Plut.] *Mor.* 851f, Fowler tr.). Swoboda, *RE* IV.2 (1901) 2863–7 no. 6; Paschidis 153–9 A49; Müller, *LexAM* 196–7.

366 DEMOKLES

(Δημοκλῆς). Handsome young man from Athens (Kirchner 3489), nicknamed "the beautiful" (ὁ καλός), who resisted the sexual advances of Demetrios Poliorketes and threw himself into a cauldron of boiling water to avoid being seduced by him (Plut. *Demetr.* 24.2–5).

367 DEMOKRATES

(Δημοκράτης). Athenian (Kirchner 3513), named by Curtius but otherwise unattested. D. was apparently sent as an ambassador to Dareios before Gaugamela and, after the king's defeat, attached himself to the Greek mercenaries in the Persian army (Bosworth I 234 suggests, plausibly, that he was a mercenary leader and that his name was confused by Arrian 3.24.4 with that of Dropides). When these surrendered to Alexander, through the agency of Artabazos, in 330, D. despaired of obtaining mercy from Alexander because of his strong anti-Macedonian views and committed suicide (Curt. 6.5.9). Identification with the anti-Macedonian Demo*chares* (Seneca, *de Ira* 3.23.2–3; thus Schaefer II² 381 n.1) is at best a remote possibility. But Kirchner 3716, regards this man as the nephew of Demosthenes, in which case the identification must be ruled out, since that Demochares was still alive in the time of Demetrios Poliorketes (Plut. *Demetr.* 24.10–11; see no. 365). Kirchner, *RE* V.1 (1903) 134 no. 6; Berve II 135 no. 261; Hofstetter 47–8 no. 81.

368 DEMON

(Δήμων). Athenian (Kirchner 3736) from the deme Paiania. Son of Demomeles, and a nephew or cousin (ἀνεψιός can mean either) of Demosthenes (Plut. *Dem.* 27.6; [Plut.] *Mor.* 846d; cf. Dem. 32.31). A member of the anti-Macedonian faction in Athens, he is named by Plutarch as one of those politicians whose extradition was demanded by Alexander after the sack of Thebes in 335 (Plut. *Dem.* 23.4). This information is not corroborated by the three other lists, and Bosworth I 94 notes that "his is the only name in Plutarch which is at all suspicious." Perhaps his name has been confused with that of Diotimos who appears in both Arr. 1.10.4 and the *Suda*. It is also interesting that the comic poet Timokles, in his play *Delos*, mentions D. in connection with Kallisthenes, who is also unique to the list of Plut. *Dem.* 23.4. In 324 he was charged with accepting money from Harpalos, but he appears not to have been convicted (cf. Timokles *ap.* Athen. 8.341f). In the following year he secured the recall of Demosthenes, on the condition that Demosthenes use the 30 talents he owed to adorn the temple of Zeus the Savior in Peiraieus ([Plut.] *Mor.* 846d; Plut. *Dem.* 27.6). Probably not identical with the Atthidographer (*FGrH* 327; Kirchner 3733), who may nevertheless have been a member of the family. Kirchner, *RE* V.1 (1903) 141–2 no. 3; Berve II 142 no. 266; Davies 116–18; Roisman and Worthington 213.

369 DEMONIKOS

(Δημόνικος). Son of Athenaios. Macedonian from Pella (Tataki 153 no. 35), D. was presumably one of Alexander's *hetairoi* and served in 326 as a trierarch of the Hydaspes fleet (Arr. *Ind.* 18.3). Nothing else is known about him. Berve II 136 no. 262.

370 DEMOPHILOS

(Δημόφιλος). Athenian (Kirchner 3675). Grandson of Euxitheos and nephew of Sostratos and Lysikles, if Kirchner is correct in identifying him as the son of Demophilos I (3674). D. was active in the 320s. He allegedly was induced by the hierophant Eurymedon to bring charges of impiety against Aristotle in 323, on the grounds that his poem to Hermias of Atarneus was a paean and thus not fit for a mortal (Athen. 15.696b; Diog. Laert. 5.5). In 318 he was one of Phokion's accusers, along with Epikouros. D. was hunted down and apparently killed by Phokion's son (Plut. *Phoc.* 38.2).

371 DEMOPHON

(Δημοφῶν). Seer, apparently of Greek origin, in Alexander's entourage. The King ignored D.'s prediction of danger before the attack on the Mallian town in India (Diod. 17.98.3–4; Curt. 9.4.27–9). He was among those who were said to have slept in the temple of Serapis in Babylon shortly before Alexander's death (Arr. 7.26.2), and may have been, along with Kleomenes (no. 601), the King's leading seer after the death of Aristandros (no. 185). Nothing else is known about him. Berve II 141 no. 264.

372 DEMOPHON

(Δημοφῶν). Perhaps Greek. One of Alexander's butlers (*trapezokomos* or *trapezopoios*), whose only claim to fame was that he felt cold in the sunshine but warm in the shade (Diog. Laert. 9.80; cf. Sextus Empiricus, *Outlines of Pyrrhonism* 1.82). Berve II 141–2 no. 265.

373 DEMOSTHENES

(Δημοσθένης) [All references in **boldface** are to Plutarch's *Life of Demosthenes*.] Athenian. Son of Demosthenes (**4.1**), from the deme Paiania (**20.3**; [Plut.] *Mor.* 844a; see Kirchner 3597; Davies 113); Aischines' assertions about the foreign and disreputable background of Demosthenes' mother, Kleoboule the daughter of Gylon (Aesch. 3.171–2; cf. **4.2**), are for the most part slanderous (but see Roisman and Worthington 213). Despite their political differences, it appears that D. and Aischines may have had family connections (Badian 2000c, 14–15. Aischines had an uncle named Kleoboulos, Aesch. 2.78). On the other hand, it is difficult to imagine these orators casting aspersions on relatives that they had in common. Cf. D.'s portrayal of Aischines' mother: Strabo 10.3.18 C471; Dem. 18.130, 259. Athen. 13.593a alleges that both D. and his wife had sexual relations with a boy named Cnosion. Demochares the historian was a nephew of D. (Athen. 6. 252f–253a), as was Demon (no. 368).

Born in 385/4 or 384/3 (Dem. 21.154; cf. Davies 126 §XII; Roisman and Worthington 213), D. lost his father at the age of seven—his sister was only five at the time ([Plut.] *Mor.* 844b)—and, although he inherited a considerable estate, much of this was squandered by his guardians. His speeches against Aphobos and Onetor, whom he prosecuted when he was 21, have been published with a commentary by Pearson 1972. Of an estate valued at about 14 talents, D. received only a little over 7,000 drachmas when, in 366, he reached the age of 18 (see the figures in Davies 126–8). He was reportedly a student of Isokrates or of the latter's student, Isaios of Chalkis; others stated erroneously that he was a student of Plato ([Plut.] *Mor.* 844b). His love of oratory was the result of having heard Kallistratos of Aphidna in the *ekklesia* ([Plut.] *Mor.* 844b–c, for this and other influences on D.'s craft; stories of his training: [Plut.] *Mor.* 844d–f and 845a–c). In the archonship of Timokrates (364/3; Develin 261), he prosecuted the guardians who had squandered his inheritance: Aphobos, Therippides, and Demophon or Demeas ([Plut.] *Mor.* 844c–d).

Beginning his career as a speech writer, D. soon took an active role in Athenian politics and is best known for his outspoken opposition to Philip II ([Plut.] *Mor.* 844f–845a, 845c–846a), and there is a story that he treated the news of Philip's death as a cause for celebration (**22.1–3**; [Plut.] *Mor.* 847b; Aesch. 3.77, cf. 3.160). But his anti-Macedonian utterances, which continued into the reign of Alexander, were soon muted by Alexander's presence in Central Greece and his demand for D.'s extradition. After Philip's death D. aroused the Athenians against Alexander, whom he derided as a child and a "Margites" (Aesch. 3.161; Marsyas of Pella, *FGrH* 135/6 F3; Plut. *Alex.* 11.6; **23.2**; cf. Aesch. 1.166–8), and communicated with Attalos (Diod. 17.3.2; **23.2**), who later turned D.'s letter over to Alexander in order to save himself (Diod. 17.5.1). In 336, when Alexander made his first entry into Greece, D. was among the envoys sent to the King, but he went no further than Mount Kithairon and returned to Athens (Diod. 17.4.7; **23.3**; Aesch. 3.161; cf. Din. 1.82). Either he feared punishment for his anti-Macedonian policies or he had been in collusion with the Persian King, who had given him a large sum of money to oppose Macedon (Diod. 17.4.7–8; Aesch. 3.238–40; Din. 1.10, 18; cf. Justin 11.2.7), evidence for which was supposed to have been found by Alexander in Sardis in 334 (**20.5**). The amount of 300 talents is attested only by the orators Aischines and Deinarchos. Although the Persian king may have considered distributing such sums to the Greek states in general, there is certainly no possibility that D. himself received such a sum. Equally questionable is the claim that Arkadia (see Astylos no. 248) did not send help to the Thebans in 335 because D. withheld the promised funds (Aes 3.240; Din. 1.18–21; see also the discussion in Worthington 139–43, 160–4). D. and Hypereides opposed Alexander's request for Athenian ships ([Plut.] *Mor.* 847c, 848e), probably for the Danubian campaign; for it would be hard to imagine such defiance in 334 when both orators had narrowly escaped Alexander's wrath. In 335, D. encouraged false rumors that Alexander had been killed fighting the Triballians (Justin 11.2.8) and incited the Thebans to rebel, going so far as to send them military equipment (Diod. 17.8.5); and although he persuaded the Athenians to support the Thebans, no help ever materialized (Diod. 17.8.6; Aesch. 3.156 holds D. responsible for Thebes' fate). After the destruction of the city, Alexander demanded the extradition of Athens' leading politicians and generals, including D. (**23.4**; Arr. 1.10.4; Plut. *Phoc.* 17.2; *Suda* A 2704); it was also falsely stated that D. paid Demades five talents to intercede with Alexander (Diod. 17.15.3). Although it was said that he hoped that Alexander would be defeated and killed by Dareios (Aesch. 3.164), after Issos D. recognized the futility of such hopes and sent a certain Plataian named Aristion to Hephaistion in 332/1 for the sake of securing immunity and reconciliation (Aesch. 3.162; Marsyas of Pella, *FGrH* 135/6 F2). Significantly, he did nothing to help Agis III at the time of his uprising against Macedon (**24.1**; Aesch. 3.165; Din. 1.34–5). Aischines' prosecution of Ktesiphon for illegally proposing a crown for D. occurred in 330, and although the speeches given by the two parties are rich in information about the careers and politics of the two orators they belong primarily to the world of Athenian politics (see Aesch. 3, *Against Ctesiphon*, and Dem 18, *On the Crown*; cf. Pliny, *HN* 3.110). D. was also a political rival of both Demades (Athen. 2.44e–f.) and Phokion; in 322, the former proposed the decree that condemned him to death and the latter did nothing to help him. Phokion owed his success to D., who supported him against Chares; he defended him against several capital charges and yet it was Phokion who betrayed him and had him exiled (Nepos, *Phoc.* 2.2–3). Cf. Plut. *Mor.* 188a; Plut. *Phoc.* 9.8, 16.3, 17.1–3 for their rivalry. Polyeuktos was said to have remarked that D. was the best orator but Phokion was the most effective speaker, and D. himself allegedly remarked that Phokion was the "cleaver (*kopis*) of my speeches" (Plut. *Phoc.* 5.5, 9). Plut. *Phoc.* 7.5 treats D. as one of those whose contribution was solely in the political/oratorical sphere (and not that of a general).

Of D.'s activities vis-à-vis Macedon and Alexander in the years from 330–325, little is known. He was sent to Olympia in late summer 324 as *architheoros* and probably communicated with Nikanor of Stageira concerning the implementation of the Exiles' Decree (cf. Diod. 17.109.1; Curt. 10.2.4; Justin 13.5.3–4); his failure to oppose divine honors for Alexander (Din. 1.94; Hyper. 5, col. 31[Burtt]) was doubtless an attempt to retain the goodwill of Alexander in the hope of mitigating the terms of the Exiles' Decree. At the games he publicly humiliated Lamachos, who delivered encomia on Philip and Alexander (**9.1**; [Plut.] *Mor.* 845c). But on his return to Athens D. became embroiled in the Harpalos fiasco, the complexities of which belong to the world of the Athenian courts and politics, and are not discussed here (see Schaefer III² 293–350; Berve II 138–41; Will 113–27; Jaschinski; Worthington 41–77; Blackwell 1999, 133–44; Worthington 1994 and 2000, 101–8). Suffice it to say that after recommending that Harpalos be imprisoned and his money confiscated, D. was soon charged with having accepted bribes from Alexander's fleeing treasurer (Diod. 17.108.8). An investigation by the Areiopagos appears to have established his guilt, and although he claimed he would submit to the death penalty if found guilty (Din 1.8, 40, 61, 108), this was pure bluster. He was exiled from Athens, and resided in the Megarid (Justin 13.5.9; Diod. 18.13.6; Arr. *Succ.* 1.13); D. was forced to retire to Kalauria, an island off Troizen (Paus. 1.8.2). But he was recalled and banished again after the Lamian War (Paus. 1.8.2; Plut. *Phoc.* 26.2, 27.5); he went to Kalauria on his second exile, committed suicide by taking poison (Plut. *Phoc.* 29.1); he was the only Greek fugitive whom Archias did not bring back to Antipatros and the Macedonians (Paus. 1.8.3). There was a statue of D. in Athens near the eponymoi and the sanctuary of Ares (Paus. 1.8.2–4). Kineas the Thessalian, an adviser of Pyrrhos, was said to have been a student of D. (Plut. *Pyrrh.* 14.1). For ancient accounts of his life see Plut. *Dem.* and [Plut.] *Mor.* 844a–848d. Berve II 136–141 no. 263; Cawkwell, *OCD³* 456–8 no. 2; Roisman and Worthington 211–46; Worthington, *LexAM* 197–202; full discussion of Demosthenes and his family in Davies 113–39; see also Schaefer I–III²; Sealey; Worthington (ed.) 2000.

374 DERDAS

(Δέρδας). Apparently a relative of Alexander's treasurer Harpalos, possibly a son of the elder Derdas, who was the brother of Phila (no. 895), Philip II's Eleimiot wife (Satyros *ap.* Athen. 13.557), or of the elder Harpalos and thus perhaps a brother of Kalas. D. was sent as an ambassador to the so-called European Skythians (παρὰ τῶν ἐκ τῆς Εὐρώπης Σκυθῶν) north of the Iaxartes River in 329 (Curt. 7.6.12; cf. Arr. 4.1.1–2). The embassy was in fact an intelligence gathering mission. Curtius speaks of Skythians "beyond the Bosporos," which reflects the mistaken geography of Alexander and his historians, who believed that the Iaxartes was the Tanais (i.e. the Don), which flowed into the Sea of Azov and separated Europe from Asia. See Brunt I 524–5. He returned with a Skythian delegation in 328 (Curt. 8.1.7; cf. Arr. 4.15.1). Berve II 131 no. 250; Hoffmann 201–2; Tataki 195 no. 9.

375 DIADES

(Διάδης). Thessalian engineer. Student of Polyeidos of Thessaly (Athen. Mech. 10.10–11; Vitruv. 10.13.3), possibly from Lykia (Whitehead 2015, 82–3). D. (along with Charias) was entrusted with the siegework at Tyre (*Laterculi Alexandrini* col. 8, 12–15) and other cities, and author of a work on siegecraft (Vitruv. 7 *praef.* 14; 10.13.3–8; Athen. Mech. 10.10–11, cf. 5.13). He claims to have invented movable towers, the borer and the climbing machine, on which besiegers could be brought level with the top of the enemy's walls (Vitruv. 10.13.3). Fabricius, *RE* V.1 (1903) 305 no. 2, with Kroll, *RE* Supplbd VI (1935) 25–7 no. 2; Berve II 142 no. 267; Marsden 1977, 220–1; Whitehead and Blyth 85–108, 176–87; Whitehead 2015; Stronk 308 n.131.

376 DIDYMEIA

(Διδυμεία). Sister of Seleukos Nikator, and thus daughter of Laodike and Antiochos. By an unnamed husband she bore two sons, Nikanor and Nikomedes (Malalas 8.198). The source of this otherwise uncorroborated information is late, and it may be that the name Didymeia is associated with Seleukid mythology, pertaining to Laodike's alleged sexual liaison with Apollo and to the allegation that the oracle of the Branchidai greeted Seleukos as "King" in 312 (Diod. 19.90.4; cf. Hadley 1974, 53, 58–9; Grainger 1990a, 3–4). Willrich, *RE* V.1 (1903) 442; Berve II 142; Beloch IV² 2.198 is sceptical; perhaps rightly omitted by Grainger, *SPG*; Ogden 2017, 58.

377 DIMNOS

(Δίμνος, Λίμνος in Plutarch). Macedonian (Tataki 98 no. 1) *hetairos* (Diod. 17.79.1) from Chalaistra (Plut. *Alex.* 49.3). In autumn 330, he joined the conspiracy of Demetrios (no. 358) to murder Alexander (Diod. 17.79.1; Plut. *Alex.* 49.3 calls it Dimnos' conspiracy; Curt. 6.7.6 suggests he joined a conspiracy but was not the instigator). D. enlisted his *eromenos* Nikomachos (Diod. 17.79.2; Curt. 6.7.2–14; Plut. *Alex.* 49.3) and revealed to him the names of the conspirators (Curt. 6.7.15: Demetrios, Peukolaos, Nikanor, Aphobetos, Iolaos, Dioxenos, Archepolis, Amyntas). But the plot was divulged by Kebalinos, who learned of the details from his brother, Nikomachos. D. was thus arrested and later committed suicide (Diod. 17.79.6; Curt. 6.7.29–30; Plut. *Alex.* 49.7 says he was killed resisting arrest), indicating by his death the gravity of his crime (Curt. 6.7.34). The resulting trial led to the execution of those whose names D. had given to Nikomachos, as well as that of Philotas, who had failed to bring the matter to the King's attention, and the murder of his father, Parmenion. Kirchner, *RE* V.1 (1903) 648; Berve II 142–3 no. 269. For the whole affair see Badian 1960 and 2000a; Rubinsohn 1977; Heckel 1977b and 2003a; Adams 2003; Reames 2008.

378 DIODOROS

(Διόδωρος). Brother of Anaxagoras (no. 91) and Kodros (no. 609), all sons of Echeanax; they slew Hegesias (no. 498), tyrant of Ephesos, in 325 or 324; D. himself was probably also Ephesian. Philoxenos then satrap of Ionia demanded the extradition of the assassins, but the Ephesians refused. Philoxenos marched in and arrested the sons of Echeanax and imprisoned them for a lengthy period (ἐπὶ μακρόν) in Sardis (Polyaenus 6.49). The brothers made a daring escape attempt, in which D. fell and was lamed in both feet (χωλωθεὶς ἄμφω τὼ πόδε). He was recaptured and sent to Alexander (Berve II 144 thinks Menandros took him to the King in 323). But Alexander died before he could deal with D. and Perdikkas sent him back to Ephesos to be tried. When word of this reached Anaxagoras and Kodros, who had escaped to Athens, they returned and saved their brother (Polyaenus 6.49). He appears to have shifted his allegiance to Antigonos the One-Eyed and served as Demetrios Poliorketes' mercenary captain, during the capture of Sikyon in 303 (Polyaenus 4.7.3; cf. Skalet 1928, 81)—though one would have to assume that the damage to his legs had caused only temporary physical impairment. In 301, Demetrios, sailing off against Karia, left D. as *phrourarchos* of Ephesos. When D. made a pact to betray the city to Lysimachos for fifty talents, Demetrios got wind of the plan and sailed back. He left his ships at anchor in one place and sailed into the harbor with only one boat (and in the company of Nikanor) and he hid himself in the boat; Nikanor summoned D. aboard his boat, pretending that he wished to discuss the handing over of soldiers—presumably those in the garrison. When D. felt safe and came near in a small boat, Demetrios jumped out of hiding and sank the boat. Some of the crew met their deaths by drowning, others were captured, but D.'s fate is unknown (Polyaenus 4.7.4). Kirchner, *RE* V.1 (1903) 659 no. 20; Berve II 144 no 273; Billows 380 no. 30.

379 DIODOROS

(Διόδωρος). Son of Telesarchos. One of twenty-four cavalrymen from Orchomenos, who served with Alexander's allied cavalry until the expedition reached Ekbatana in 330. There he and his compatriots were discharged. On their return (*c.*329), they made a dedication to Zeus Soter in Orchomenos (*IG* VII 3206). Berve II 144 no. 274.

380 DIODOTOS

(Διόδοτος). Greek from Erythrai. D. is identified as one of the authors of Alexander's *Ephemerides* (Athen. 10.434b = *FGrH* 117 T1), working under the direction of Eumenes of Kardia (who is identified as *archigrammateus*). Nothing else is known about him. It is possible that Diodotos was a pseudonym for Eumenes himself (cf. Xenophon's attribution of the *Anabasis* to Themistogenes of Syracuse, Xen. *HG* 3.1.2) or that D. was responsible for a later reworking of the *Ephemerides* and not a member of Alexander's expedition. Berve II 143–4 no. 272.

381 DIOGENES

(Διογένης). Son of Hikesios; philosopher from Sinope (Diog. Laert. 6.20), better known as "the Cynic." D. spent a portion of his life in exile, in Athens and Korinth, and it is in the latter city that Alexander was said to have met him. In the famous, but almost certainly fictitious, tale of their meeting Alexander asked the philosopher if there was anything he could do for him. D. replied that the King might move aside, since he was blocking D.'s enjoyment of the sun (Plut. *Alex.* 14.2–5; Plut. *Mor.* 331e–f, also 605d, 782a; Val. Max. 4.3 ext. 4a; Arr. 7.2.1; Diog. Laert. 6.38); Alexander, for his part, remarked that, if he were not Alexander, he would be Diogenes. That D. died on the same day as Alexander is also false (Diog. Laert. 6.79), although it is true that he was an old man during the 113th Olympiad (324–321); references to being summoned by Perdikkas (Diog. Laert. 6.44) and Krateros (Diog. Laert. 6.57), if they have any value, would appear to belong to this time. For his career see Diog. Laert. 6.20–81. Natorp, *RE* V.1 (1903) 765–73 no. 44; Berve II 417–18 no. 22.

382 DIOGENES

(Διογένης). Greek from Mytilene, D. was a leader of the pro-Persian oligarchy. Although he was driven out when the Macedonians captured Lesbos in 334, he was installed as tyrant of Mytilene by Pharnabazos and Autophradates in the following year (Arr. 2.1.5). In 332, Chares (no. 318) had come to the defense of Mytilene (Arr. 3.2.6; Curt. 4.5.22), but he surrendered the city in return for his safety. In 332/1, Hegelochos brought D. to Egypt, where Alexander returned him to face the judgment of the Mytileneans, who in all likelihood had him executed (Arr. 3.2.7). Kirchner, *RE* V.1 (1903) 736 no. 14; Berve II 143 no. 270; Berve, *Tyrannis* I 336–7, II 690; Olmstead 502; Hofstetter 51 no. 86.

383 DIOGNETOS

(Διόγνητος). Bematist, apparently from Erythrai (Pliny, *HN* 6.61; Hyginus, *Poetica astronomica* 2.30). Nothing is known about his life beyond his participation in Alexander's expedition and his authorship of a work along the lines of Baiton's *Stages*. Two fragments of which survive (*FGrH* 120). Berger, *RE* V.1 (1903) 785 no. 16; Berve II 143 no. 271.

384 DIOGNIS

(Δίογνις). A favorite of Demetrios of Phaleron (Athen. 12.542f–543a). Nothing else is known about him.

385 DIOKLES

(Διοκλῆς). Greek from Rhegion in southern Italy. According to Eusthathius on *Iliad* 14.229 (see Stewart T138), D. proposed to turn Mount Athos into a giant statue of Alexander, a plan that is otherwise ascribed to Stasikrates or Deinokrates or Cheirikrates. Diokles may be a corruption of the name Deinokrates, but his homeland suggests that he was someone else. Berve II 144 considers it possible that D. was a historical person in Alexander's entourage. Berve II 144 no. 275; Fabricius, *RE* V.1 (1903) 814 no. 57; Stewart 1993, 41.

386 DIONYSIOS

(Διονύσιος). Son of Klearchos and nephew of Satyros (Memnon *FGrH* 434). Klearchos gained the tyranny of Herakleia Pontika (*Barr. Atl.* 86 B2) in 364/3 and ruled for 12 years (Diod. 15.81.5; 16.36.3); he was succeeded by D.'s brother Timotheos, who in turn ruled for 15 more (Diod. 16.36.3, 88.5), until his death in 338/7 brought D. to power (Diod. 16.88.5). D., born in 360/59, was co-ruler with Timotheos, at least, in the last years of the latter's life—Memnon 3.1 says "since the beginning" (αὐτίκα); the joint rule is attested on coinage bearing the legend ΤΙΜΟΘΕΟΥ ΔΙΟΝΥΣΙΟΥ (thus Beloch III² 1.139 n.2)— and ruled from 338/7 to 305 (cf. *Syll³* 304, 36ff.). D. expanded his territory as a result of Persian weakness caused by Alexander's invasion in 334, but he was later threatened by those who had been exiled by the Herakleiot tyranny, who asked Alexander to restore them. For this reason, D. made contact with Kleopatra, the King's sister, who appears to have interceded with Alexander on D.'s behalf—although she may have done little more than delay the restoration of the exiles (Memnon, *FGrH* 434 F1 4.1; cf. Burstein, *Outpost* 74). But upon Alexander's death (which D. celebrated by erecting a statue to *Euthymia*, according to Memnon 4.2), these exiles turned to Perdikkas, only to have their hopes dashed when Perdikkas was murdered in 320 (Memnon 4.3). He was a supporter of Antigonos. Married Amastris (no. 67) the daughter of Oxyathres (brother of Dareios III) after she was repudiated by Krateros (Memnon 4.4; Strabo 12.3.10 C544). They had three children: Amastris (no. 68), Klearchos (no. 593) and Oxathres (no. 831; Memnon 4.8). The elder Amastris may be responsible for the development of closer ties between Dionysios and Antigonos; for Demetrios son of Antigonos had now married Krateros' widow, Phila, whom Amastris must have known since her arrival in Kilikia in late 324. As a result of his new marriage and his wealth, he became ostentatious in his lifestyle, purchasing the royal equipment of Dionysios of Syracuse (Memnon 4.5); but his rule was also mild, earning him the epithet Χρηστός, "the Good" (Memnon 4.8). The bond with Antigonos was strengthened when in 314 a daughter (**A92**) of D. by an earlier wife married Polemaios (no. 968), Antigonos' nephew (Memnon 4.6; Diod. 19.61.5). The text of Memnon 4.6 (as preserved by Photios) says D. aided Antigonos in this siege of Kypros. But this is probably a reference to the siege of Tyre: Κύπρον should probably be emended to read Τύρον (Droysen II³ 218 n.89). Late in his life, after Antigonos and Demetrios had been proclaimed "kings," D. also took the title for himself (Memnon 4.6). By this time, he had become extremely obese and ugly (Memnon 4.7; Ael. *VH* 9.13; Nymphis, *FGrH* 432 F10 = Athen. 12.549a). He died in 305 at the age of 55, having ruled for thirty-two years (Diod. 16.88.5; 20.77.1; Memnon 4.8, who says he ruled for 30 years; Nymphis [above] 33 years) and was succeeded by his sons who ruled for seventeen years (Diod. 20.77.1). For D.'s coinage, showing his portrait on the obverse and Herakles erecting a trophy accompanied by the legend ΔΙΟΝΥΣΙΟ on the reverse see, e.g. Mørkholm 1991, 95 and fig. 275. Kaerst, *RE* V.1 (1903) 912–13 no. 66; Berve II 144–5 no. 276; Beloch III² 2.94–6; Burstein, *Outpost* 72–80; Billows 380–1 no. 32; Berve, *Tyrannis* I 320–2.

387 DIONYSIOS

(Διονύσιος). Herakleiot flutist. Performed at the mass marriage ceremony in Sousa in 324 (Chares, *FGrH* 125 F4 = Athen. 12.538f). Berve II 145 no. 277.

388 DIONYSIOS

(Διονύσιος). A native of Messene (that is, of Charakene in the Tigris region, rather than Messenia in Greece: see Abramenko 2000, 366). The name Dionysios is therefore suspect. During Alexander's final stay in Babylon, when the King had removed his robes to play ball, this man arrived unnoticed and, putting on the King's mantle and diadem, seated himself upon the throne. When this was discovered, he claimed that he had been imprisoned for some crime and brought to Babylon, but there had been freed by the god Serapis and told to do what he had done (Plut. *Alex.* 73.7–9; Diod. 17.116.2–5, making no mention of Serapis). Diodorus goes on to say that the man was executed. What occurred was, in fact, no accident but the enactment of the Near Eastern "Substitute King" ritual, in which a substitute for the King is placed on the throne and later put to death to "fulfill" and deflect from the real King a portended death (see Bottéro 1992, 138–55). Dio Chrys. 4.66 describes a practice during the feast known as the Sakaia in which a prisoner destined to be executed plays out the role of King for a day; Berossus, *FGrH* 680 F2 = Athen. 14.639c (cf. Ktesias, *FGrH* 688 F4) depicts this as a Babylonian feast in which for a period of five days servants exchange roles with their masters. Abramenko 2000 sees the Dionysios episode as part of a genuine conspiracy against Alexander, which is questionable. Berve II 145 no. 278; Abramenko 2000.

389 DIONYSIOS

(Διονύσιος). Macedonian (Tataki 300 no. 68). D. commanded the garrison in Mounychia, perhaps since Kassandros gained control of Athens and assassinated Nikanor in 317 (cf. Diod. 18.75.1). Kassandros wrote to D. in 314, and to Demetrios of Phaleron, telling them to send 20 ships to Lemnos against Antigonos' forces; they sent the ships under the command of Aristoteles. (Diod. 19.68.3; for the fate of this expedition see s.v. Aristoteles). In 307 Demetrios attacked the city and entered via Peiraieus; when the Antigonid forces breached the walls and admitted additional troops, D. sought refuge in Mounychia (Diod. 20.45.2–3). Demetrios, however, assaulted Mounychia with his forces and siege equipment and captured the fortress, taking D. alive (Diod. 20.45.6–7; cf. Plut. *Demetr.* 10.1). According to *Suda* Δ 431, Demetrios had D. put to death. Kirchner, *RE* V.1 (1903) 911 no. 48.

390 DIONYSIOS

(Διονύσιος). Official of Demetrios Poliorketes and Antigonos, honored, together with another person whose name is lost, in a decree of Stratokles between 307 and 301 (*IG* II² 560). Billows 380 no. 31 identifies him with D. of Amphipolis, honored with a proxeny on Samos for his benefactions (Habicht 1957, 171 no. 4), but Habicht 1996b, 85 tentatively identifies him with Dionysios of Sinope. But the actions of that man appear to be limited to his homeland. If he is to be identified with either, Billows' suggestion strikes me as more likely to be correct. Billows 380 no. 31.

391 DIONYSIOS

(Διονύσιος). From Sinope. An Antigonid official. Honored for his service as an intermediary between his state and an unspecified queen who made benefactions to the city (*I. di Cos* ED 20). The latter is thought to be either Phila, the wife of Demetrios, or her granddaughter, the wife of Gonatas; though Stratonike, the wife of Antigonos, is also a possibility (see discussion in Paschidis 366–8, with scholarly literature). Hence, the date is far from certain. Identification of D. with the honorand of *IG* II² 560 (Billows 380 no. 31, suggested by Habicht 1996b, 85) of Amphipolis, is regarded by Paschidis 366 as "plausible but not at all certain." See above. Paschidis 365–8 D9.

392 DIONYSODOROS

(Διονυσόδωρος). Theban, Olympic victor. Ambassador to the Persian King; captured at Damaskos in late 333 (Arr. 2.15.2). Alexander released him and his fellow Theban Thessaliskos (no. 1121) because of the former's Olympic victory and because he recognized that their attempts to win restoration of their city were understandable (Arr. 2.15.3–4); presumably Alexander had cause to regret the severity of the punishment meted out to Thebes (Plut. *Mor.* 181b). Kirchner, *RE* s.v. "Dionysodoros (12)"; Berve II 145 no. 279; Hofstetter 52 no. 89.

393 DIOPHANTOS

(Διόφαντος). Greek flutist. Performed at the mass marriage ceremony in Sousa in 324 (Chares, *FGrH* 125 F4 = Athen. 12.538f). Berve, *RE* Supplbd IV (1924) 227; Berve II 146 no. 282.

394 DIOPHANTOS

(Διόφαντος). Athenian (Kirchner 4421). D. was sent along with Achilleus on the Athenian state galley, Paralos, to Alexander to negotiate the release of their countrymen, who had been captured at the Granikos River in 334 and sentenced to hard labor in Macedonia (cf. Arr. 1.29.5). They met Alexander at Tyre as he returned from Egypt in 331, where they congratulated the King on his victories (apparently offering him a crown: *IG* II² 1496, col. III 56–7) and achieved their purpose (Arr. 3.6.2; cf. Curt. 4.8.12). Attempts to identify him with any of the other known Athenians are fruitless, given the frequent occurrence of the name. Schoch, *RE* Supplbd IV (1924) 227 "Diophantes" no. 2; Berve II 146 no. 283.

395 DIOSKOURIDES

(Διοσκουρίδης). Macedonian (Tataki 302 no. 77) Nephew of Antigonos the One-Eyed (Diod. 19.62.9); Tataki 302, following Billows 381, suggests he may have been a son of Polemaios. He could easily have been the son of a sister of Antigonos; but this could only be confirmed if we knew his patronymic. In 315/14, having collected eighty ships from the Hellespont and Rhodes, he joined Antigonos at Tyre (Diod. 19.62.7); Themison had brought an additional forty ships, and Antigonos appears to have given him ten more, sending him to the Peloponnese, while D. remained in the Aegean with 190 ships, looking after Antigonid interests there (Diod. 19.62.9). His role was to protect those islands that were in alliance with the Antigonids and to win over others (Diod. 19.62.9); thus he played a key role in the formation of the Nesiotic League (cf. Buraselis 41–4; and esp. 60–87). In 314/13, D. drove Aristoteles out of Lemnos, capturing twenty of his ships (Diod. 19.68.4). Nothing is known about his life after this point. It is idle to speculate what became of him. Billows 381–2 no. 33; Kirchner, *RE* V.1 (1903) 1125 no. 1; Buraselis 41–4; Hauben 27–30.

396 DIOTIMOS

(Διότιμος). Athenian (Kirchner 4384) from the deme Euonymon, from a wealthy family that had mining interests at Laureion. Son of Diopeithes. Born *c.*375, he made his first political appearance in 349/8 (Dem. 21.208). D. held various generalships (338/7, 337/6, 335/4, 334/3) and trierarchies, dedicated shields after Chaironeia (Dem. 18.114, 116; *IG* II² 1496, 22–5) and, in 335/4, conducted a naval expedition to suppress piracy (*IG* II² 1623, 276–85), for which he was honored in a decree moved by Lykourgos ([Plut.] *Mor.* 844a). He belonged to the anti-Macedonian party: as such he is associated with Demosthenes, Nausikles, Hypereides, and Polyeuktos ([Plut.] *Mor.* 845a), and was one of the orators/politicians whose extradition was demanded by Alexander in 335 (Arr. 1.10.4; *Suda* A 2704; but Plut. *Dem.* 23.4 appears to have substituted Demon for Diotimos). Alexander relented in the case of D. and some others, but D. appears to have died at some point before 325/4 (cf. *IG* II² 1629). He has no other direct connections with Alexander. Kirchner, *RE* V.1 (1903) 1148 no. 8; Berve II 146 no. 281; Lauffer 289ff.; Davies 163–5; Develin 343, 346, 373, 379.

397 DIOTIMOS

([Διό]τιμος). Son of the Sidonian king, Abdalonymos (no. 1). D. made a dedication to Aphrodite–Astarte on Kos (*SEG* XXXVI (1986) 758), but his activities, as Hauben 2004, 32 notes, involved Sidonian maritime affairs. His political loyalties (whether pro-Antigonid or pro-Ptolemaic) are a matter of speculation. Although it appears to belong to the fourth century, the inscription cannot be dated with any certainty (Hauben 2004, 34).

398 DIOXIPPOS

(Διώξιππος). Athenian pankratiast and Olympic champion (Pliny, *HN* 35.139 and Aristoboulos, *FGrH* 139 F47 = Athen. 6.251a call him a pankratiast; Curt. 9.7.16 is alone in referring to him as a boxer; Diod. 17.100.2, Hyper. 2.5–6, and Ael. *VH* 12.58 are vague; cf. Diog. Laert. 6.43) in the entourage of Alexander. At some point around 333 he attended the wedding of his sister, then a widow, to Charippos (Hyper. 2.5–6). Hence, we know he did not accompany Alexander from the beginning of the campaign. Certainly, he was present in 326/5, when he was challenged to single combat by the Macedonian Korrhagos (no. 620), whom D. defeated with relative ease (Ael. *VH* 10.22 wrongly says that D. killed his opponent). But it is alleged that subsequently he was falsely accused of theft by agents of Alexander and driven to suicide (Diod. 17.100–1; Curt. 9.7.16–26). D. was regarded as one of Alexander's flatterers (*kolakes*) and was said to have likened the King's blood to the ichor of the immortal gods (Aristoboulos, *FGrH* 139 F47 = Athen. 6.251a; for the anecdote see also Plut. *Alex.* 28.3, *Mor.* 341b, 190e; Diog. Laert. 9.60; Sen. *Ep.* 6.7.12; Dio Chrys. 44). His portrait was painted by Alkimachos (Pliny, *HN* 35.139). Kirchner, *RE* V.1 (1903) 1151 no. 2; Berve II 146–7 no. 284.

399 DIPHILOS

(Δίφιλος). In charge of the citadel of Babylon (315–311) under Antigonos Monophthalmos. Resisted Seleukos but was captured after a siege. His fate is not recorded (Diod. 19.91.3–5). Grainger, *SPG* 647; Kirchner, *RE* V.1 (1903) 1152 no. 8; Billows 383 no. 34.

DITAMENES. See STAMENES.

400 DOKIMOS

(Δόκιμος). Macedonian (Tataki 304 no. 84), unattested in the Alexander historians. There is nothing to commend the view that D. was the Tarentine commander demoted by Philip II for bathing in warm water (Polyaenus 4.2.1; Griffith 1935, 247 with n.1). D. served Perdikkas, Antigonos, and Lysimachos in succession (Lund 72 calls him "ambitious and flexible"), but he most likely participated in Alexander's campaigns. As a supporter of Perdikkas, he captured Babylon and deposed Archon (no. 169), who had collaborated with Arrhidaios in diverting Alexander's corpse to Egypt (Arr. *Succ.* 24.3–5). After the failure of Perdikkas' expedition he joined Alketas and Eumenes but was reluctant to serve the latter (Plut. *Eum.* 8.8). He served with Alketas in Karia (cf. Arr. *Succ.* 1.41) and at Kretopolis (Diod. 18.44–5; Polyaenus 4.6.7), where he was captured (Diod. 18.45.3), along with Attalos (no. 265), Polemon (no. 971) and some other important officers. Imprisoned in Greater Phrygia, he planned an escape, eventually betraying his comrades to Antigonos' forces (Diod. 19.16; cf. Simpson 1957). Antigonos took him into his service, and in 313 D. and Medeios (no. 690) captured Miletos; D. commanded the army and Medeios the fleet (Diod. 19.75.3–4). At some point, he was appointed *strategos* of Phrygia, or at least a portion of Phrygia around Synnada (cf. Diod. 20.107.4; Tarn, *CAH* VI 503 suggests "very possibly both Phrygias and the Dardanelles were in his charge"; this is unlikely and Billows 272–8 is probably correct in accepting, in general, Köhler's view (1898) that smaller parts of Antigonos' realm were administered by officials called *strategoi* or some similar term), where he founded the city of Dokimeion (cf. Strabo 12.8.14 C577: it is hard to imagine that Antigonos allowed an eponymous foundation; cf. Lund 197). In 302/1, D. went over to Lysimachos and helped him to gain control of Synnada, together with its wealth (Diod. 20.107.4). With him he brought Philetairos (no. 900), possibly the treasurer of Synnada, who later was installed by Lysimachos as *gazophylax* of Pergamon (Paus. 1.8.1). What his role was at Ipsos and what became of him are not known. Berve II 147 no. 285; Billows

382–3 no. 35; Schober 38–41; Simpson 1957; Hornblower, *Hieronymus* 125–6; Launey 1176; Kaerst *RE* V.1 (1903) 1274 nos. 4–5; Bengtson I 199–201; Grainger, *SPG* 647–8.

401 DOLOASPIS

(Δολόασπις). Arrian says he was Egyptian, though the Iranian name suggests otherwise. In 331, Alexander left D. and Petisis (another Egyptian) as nomarchs of Egypt; they must have been overseers of the lesser nomarchs of Upper and Lower Egypt, although we cannot say which of the two regions was assigned to D. Petisis soon relinquished his position and the offices were combined under D. (Arr. 3.5.2). Berve II 147 no. 286.

402 DORKEIDAS

(Δορκείδας). Son of Melambichos. One of twenty-four cavalrymen from Orchomenos, who served with Alexander's allied cavalry until the expedition reached Ekbatana in 330. There he and his compatriots were discharged. On their return (*c.*329), they made a dedication to Zeus Soter in Orchomenos (*IG* VII 3206). Berve II 147 no. 288.

403 DOURIS

(Δοῦρις). Lived *c.*340–*c.*260. Son of Kaios. He succeeded his father as tyrant of Samos. The view that he was once a disciple of Theophrastos has been demonstrated to be based on a faulty textual emendation of Athen. 4.128a; though his brother Lynkeus (no. 667) certainly was the philosopher's student. D. was an accomplished historian: his *Makedonika* spanned the period from 370 to the battle of Koroupedion in 281 in at least twenty-three books (Jacoby, *FGrH* 76; cf. Kebric 1977). He also wrote a *History of Samos* and a *Life of Agathokles*. Of his entire corpus 96 fragments survive, a disproportionate number of which come from Athenaeus and Plutarch's *Moralia*. Hence, it is difficult to characterize his work. He appears to have been critical of ostentation and extravagance and was clearly more sensational than his contemporary, Hieronymos of Kardia. Attempts to establish bias, for or against any of the Diadochoi, have met with limited success. See Pownall 2013. D. was an important source for Plutarch and, apparently, also for Diodorus of Sicily (cf. Landucci 1997). Paschidis 391–2 D34; Pownall, *LexAM* 210–11; *BNJ* 76.

404 DOXARES

(Δοξάρης). Indian dynast (*nomarches*, on which see Bosworth II 261) of the upper Indos region; sent envoys to offer his submission to Alexander in 326 (Arr. 5.8.3). He is otherwise unattested. Berve II 147 no. 287.

405 DRAKON

(Δράκων). Koan doctor, son of Hippokrates. Personal physician of Rhoxane (*Suda* Δ 1497). His son, Hippokrates (no. 537), succeeded him in this capacity and was killed along with Rhoxane and Alexander IV in 310. Berve II 147 no. 289; Sherwin-White no. 104.

406 DRAKON

(Δράκων). Son of Straton from Kos. Greek in the service of Antigonos I. Honored by the Samians (*IG* XII 6, 29), on a motion by [Theod]ektes son of Hyblesios, for helping their ambassadors to the king (hence after 306). Billows 384 no. 36; Paschidis 386 s.v. Theodektes D27.

407 DROMOKLEIDES

(Δρομοκλείδης). Athenian (Kirchner 4568) from Sphettos, orator and flatterer of Demetrios Poliorketes. After Athens' "liberation" in 307, he proposed that the Athenians seek an oracle *from* Demetrios concerning a dedication to Delphi (Plut. *Demetr.* 13), and in 294 he proposed that Peiraieus and Mounychia be handed over to him (Plut. *Demetr.* 34.6). Plutarch criticizes D., Stratokles, and their followers who used public affairs for personal profit. In fact, they used to joke about the orator's platform, calling it the "golden harvest" (Plut. *Mor* 798e–f). Paschidis 129–31 A42.

408 DROPIDES

(Δρωπίδης). Athenian (Kirchner 4575) ambassador to Dareios III. D. was captured, according to Curt. 3.13.15, at Damaskos by Parmenion in 333/2. Arr. 2.15.2 mentions only Iphikrates but he places the capture of D. in 330, after the death of Dareios (Arr. 3.24.4). If D., Aristogeiton (no. 193) and Iphikrates (no. 554) were all part of an Athenian embassy (for the use of three ambassadors see Mosley 1973, 55ff.), their fates are difficult to explain. Perhaps, D. escaped capture at Damaskos and rejoined Dareios. But the fact that Arrian also reports the capture of the Lakedaimonian envoys in Hyrkania, whereas Curtius says that they too were taken at Damaskos, raises further questions concerning what is an inexplicable confusion in the sources. Perhaps the Athenian ambassadors remained with Alexander until the demobilization of the Greek troops, at which time they too were sent home. Neither Arrian nor Curtius mentions what became of them. Hofstetter 55 dismisses Curtius' evidence off hand as "Irrtum." Berve II 148 no. 291; Hofstetter 55 no. 95; Atkinson I 261; Bosworth I 233–4.

409 DRYPETIS

(Δρύπετις). Younger of the known daughters of Dareios III and Stateira (no. 1078); sister of the younger Stateira (no. 1079) and Ochos (no. 806); granddaughter of Sisygambis (cf. Curt 3.11.25; 4.10.19, 21). Drypetis was born between 350 and 345. She accompanied her father to Issos in late 333, where she was captured along with her mother, siblings, and grandmother by the Macedonian troops (Curt. 3.11.25; Diod. 17.36.2; Arr. 2.11.9; Justin 11.9.12; Plut. *Alex.* 21.1). She was treated with respect by Alexander (Curt. 3.12.21; 4.11.3), who came in person to the captive family of Dareios (Curt. 3.12.13–26) and said he would surpass Dareios in providing doweries for D. and Stateira (Diod. 17.38.1, 3; cf. 17.37.3–6; Curt. 3.12.3–26 for events associated with her capture). She remained with Alexander's expedition until the end of 331 (Curt. 4.10.19, 21 gives a dramatic story of her mother Stateira dying in her arms, and of D. consoling Sisygambis), despite repeated attempts by Dareios to ransom his family (cf. Diod. 17.39.1, 54.2; Curt. 4.11.5–6, 12–15; Justin 11.12.1–3; Plut. *Alex.* 29.7) and Parmenion's alleged advice that Alexander accept the offer (Curt. 4.11.12–14). D. was left behind at Sousa with her sister and grandmother (Curt. 5.2.17; Diod. 17.67.1) and given instruction in the Greek language (Diod. 17.67.1; Curt. 5.2.18–22 has an implausible story about "wool-making"). Here she remained until 324, when she was given as a bride to Hephaistion (no. 513; Arr. 7.4.5; Diod. 17.107.6; cf. Brosius 77–8), who soon left her a widow (Curt. 10.5.20; cf. Arr. 7.14; Plut. *Alex.* 72). Soon after Alexander's death, she and her sister were murdered by Rhoxane and Perdikkas (Plut. *Alex.* 77.6). Stähelin, *RE* Supplbd IV (1924) s.v. "Drypetis"; Berve II 148 no. 290; Justi 86; Shayegan 108 no. 49. **Stemma III.**

E

410 ECHEKRATIDAS

(Ἐχεκρατίδας). Methymnaian, peripatetic philosopher, friend of Aristotle (Steph. Byz. s.v. "Methymna"). Phokion interceded with Alexander to obtain the release of E. from prison in Sardis (Plut. *Phoc.* 18.6; Ael. *VH* 1.25). The exact date of his imprisonment or release is not known. Perhaps he was arrested in connection with the political upheavals on Lesbos (334/3). Berve II 162 no. 333; Hofstetter 55 no. 96.

411 ECHMON

(Ἤχμων). Son of Echmon. One of twenty-four cavalrymen from Orchomenos, who served with Alexander's allied cavalry until the expedition reached Ekbatana in 330. There he and his compatriots were discharged. On their return (*c.*329), they made a dedication to Zeus Soter in Orchomenos (*IG* VII 3206). Berve II 175 no. 358.

412 EIRENE

(Εἰρήνη). Macedonian (Tataki 305 no. 5). Daughter of Ptolemy I Soter and the courtesan Thaïs (no. 1103); sister of Leontiskos and Lagos. Like her brothers, she was probably born before the arrival at the Ptolemaic court of Antipatros' daughter, Eurydike (*c.*320). E. later became the wife of Eunostos (no. 344), king of Kyprian Soloi (Athen. 13.576e = Kleitarchos, *FGrH* 137 F11). Van Oppen de Ruiter 2015; Ager 2018.

ELAPTONIUS. See APHTHONIOS.

413 ENYLOS

(Ἔνυλος). Ainel on coinage: Hill 1910, 96. Phoinikian dynast of Byblos. In 333/2, upon learning of Alexander's capture of Byblos, E. defected (along with Gerostratos of Arados) from the Persian fleet of Autophradates (Arr. 2.20.1; cf. Curt. 4.1.15). His ships joined Alexander at Sidon and played no small part in the siege and capture of Tyre in 332. E., like many of the others who surrendered to Alexander, appears to have retained his position in Byblos (Arr. 2.20.3: τούτοις πᾶσιν ἔδωκεν Ἀλέξανδρος ἄδειαν τῶν πρόσθεν). Nothing further is known about him. Berve II 150 no. 299; cf. Hofstetter 56.

414 EPAINETOS

(Ἐπαινετός). Macedonian (Tataki 307 no. 14). If he is identical with the victor at the Lykaia in 308/7, his father's name was Silanos (*Syll*³ 314 = *IG* V 2, 550). *Nauarchos* of Ptolemy I, in 313 E. brought the fleet to Kyrene in support the army of Agis, which had been sent to suppress the rebellion there (Diod. 19.79.2). The expedition was successful. Hauben no 11; *PP* VI 17207.

415 EPHIALTES

(Ἐφιάλτης). Athenian politician (Kirchner 6156). Family background unknown. In 341/0 (Develin 335), E. was sent on an embassy to Artaxerxes III Ochos and received money with which he is said to have bribed both Demosthenes ([Plut.] *Mor.* 847f) and Hypereides ([Plut.] *Mor* 848e). Politically, E. was an opponent of Macedon and in 335 his name was on the list of orators and generals whose surrender was demanded by Alexander (Arr. 1.10.4, with Bosworth I 93–5; Plut. *Dem.* 23.4 = Idomeneus, *FGrH* 338 F11, and Douris, *FGrH* 76 F39; *Suda* A 2704). Although in the end Alexander insisted only on Charidemos, E. sailed away to Asia Minor (Din. 1.33; Diod. 17.25.6). He appears at Halikarnassos in 334 along with his fellow Athenian exile, Thrasyboulos, in the service of Memnon (Diod. 17.25.6). Taking with him 2,000 picked mercenaries, E. made a sortie out of Halikarnassos against the Macedonian siege-engines, which he put to the torch, and got the better of the fighting against the Macedonians (cf. Arr. 1.21.5); E. himself, being a man of some physical stature slew in hand-to-hand combat many of the enemy who opposed him (Diod. 17.26.1–7). But soon after E.'s initial success (which was followed by the arrival of reinforcements under Memnon) the Macedonians turned the tide of the battle and drove the Persian forces back into the city; in this reversal, he was killed (Diod. 17.27.1–4; cf. Din 1.33; Dem. *Epist.* 3.31). Berve II 160–1 no. 329; Bosworth I 93–5, 147; Hofstetter 57 no. 99; Seibert 1979, 149, 393, 501; Worthington 183–4.

416 EPHIALTES

(Ἐφιάλτης). A Greek who, together with Kissos, brought Alexander news of Harpalos' flight, only to be thrown into chains by the disbelieving King (Plut. *Alex.* 41.8). Presumably he was released once his report was verified. Berve II 161, 203 has argued that Alexander's disbelief suggests that it is Harpalos' first flight (333) that was reported by E. (cf. Hamilton 109; Heckel 1992, 219). But we cannot be certain. Nothing else is known about him. But, if Kissos is the Athenian actor Kittos (*IG* II² 2418; cf. Ghiron-Bistagne 1976, 72, 337), then E. might also have been an artist. Berve II 161 no. 330.

417 EPHIPPOS

(Ἔφιππος). Son of Chalkideus. Nothing else is known about E.'s background. He accompanied Alexander on the Asiatic campaign and, in 332/1, was left in Egypt as overseer (*episkopos*) of the mercenaries (Arr. 3.5.3) along with Aischylos. What became of him, we do not know. Tataki 136 identifies him, implausibly, with the author of the work *On the Deaths of Alexander and Hephaistion* (below). Berve II 161 no. 331.

418 EPHIPPOS

(Ἔφιππος). Olynthian (Gude no. 55; Tataki 136 no. 53), family background unknown. Born before 348 (in which year the city was destroyed by Philip II). Identification with the *episkopos* of mercenaries in Egypt depends upon the doubtful emendation of Arr. 3.5.3 to read "Ephippos the Chalkidian" (see Bosworth I 276; *contra* Berve II 161, Pearson 61) and is rendered unlikely by the fact that certain fragments of the Olynthian's history (or, rather, political pamphlet) suggest an eyewitness knowledge of events that the *episkopos* could not have seen. E. authored a work entitled *On the Deaths of Alexander and Hephaistion* (Jacoby, *FGrH* 126; cf. Athen. 3.1210e, 4.146c, 10.434a, 12.537d). The hostile nature of the work may have its origins in Alexander's treatment of E.'s compatriot, Kallisthenes. Berve's suggestion that it was published in Athens at the time of the Lamian War (II 161) is pure speculation. Berve II 161 no. 331; Pearson 61–8; Spawforth 2012; Müller, *LexAM* 224–5.

419 EPHOROS

("Εφορος). (c.405–330). Historian from Kyme (for the surviving fragments of his work see Jacoby, *FGrH* 70). A contemporary of Theopompos and, with him, a student of Isokrates, E. composed a *History* in 30 books, which extended from the earliest times to 340. Nothing is known about Ephoros' connections with Alexander except for the claim that he declined the King's request that he join his expedition, presumably as official historian (Plut. *Mor.* 1043). The truth of this claim cannot be determined. Schwartz, *RE* VI.1 (1907) 1–16 no. 1; Berve II 162 no. 332. Barber 1935; Brown 1973, 107–15; cf. Fornara 1983, 42–6; Pownall 2004.

420 EPIKOUROS

('Επίκουρος). Athenian (Kirchner 4854). One of Phokion's accusers. E. and Demophilos were hunted down and apparently killed by Phokion's son, Phokos (Plut. *Phoc.* 38.2).

421 EPIKYDES

('Επικύδης). Olynthian (Gude 42 no. 41). Perhaps identical with the son of Asklepiodoros and grandson of Thrason (*IG* II² 10019) and thus buried in Athens (Gude no. 41). Thibron after his successes and failures was captured by some Libyans and turned over to E., whom Ophellas had made ruler of Teuchira. He subjected Thibron to torture (Arr. *Succ.* 1.17) and then sent him to Kyrene, where he was crucified (Arr. *Succ.* 1.18). Diodorus does not mention him in his account of the affairs of Kyrene. *PP* no. 15062; Kirchner, *RE* VI (1907) 155 no. 2.

422 EPIMACHOS

('Επίμαχος). Athenian (Kirchner 4929). Architect and engineer in the service of the Antigonids. E. is credited with the creation of the *helepolis* or "city-taker" (Vitruv. 10.164; Athen. Mech. 27.2; cf. Plut. *Demetr.* 21.1; Diod. 20.91.2–8; Kern 1999, 243–4). Fabricius, *RE* VI.1 (1907) 160 no. 3; Billows 384 no. 37.

423 EPIMENES

('Επιμένης). Macedonian (Tataki 308 no. 18). The son of Arseas (Arr. 4.13.4, 7 has Arsaios; for the spelling of the patronymic see Hoffmann 180) and party to the "conspiracy of the Pages" (Curt. 8.6.9), he appears to have undergone a change of heart (Curt. 8.6.20) and revealed the plot either to his lover, Charikles (Arr. 4.13.7), who in turn informed E.'s brother, Eurylochos, or to Eurylochos himself (Curt. 8.6.22), who brought the matter to Alexander's attention (Curt. 8.6.22; Arr. 4.13.7). E. was spared for his role in alerting Alexander to the danger (Curt. 8.6.26). Nothing else is known about his career. Berve II 150 no. 300; Heckel 1992, 291; Hoffmann 180; cf. Carney 1980–1, 228–9.

424 EPOKILLOS

(Ἐπόκιλλος). Macedonian (Tataki 308 no. 20). Son of Polyeides. E. appears only as an officer in charge of transporting troops to and from Alexander's camp. In 330 he escorted the discharged allied cavalry to the coast, leading his own squadron of cavalrymen, presumably mercenaries (Arr. 3.19.6). He rejoined the King at Zariaspa (Baktra) at the end of winter 329/8, accompanied by Ptolemy and Menidas (Arr. 4.7.2, reading "Melamnidas"; Curt. 7.10.11, "Maenidas", emended by Hedicke to "Melanidas"; but cf. Hamilton 1955, 217). With the latter and the ilarch Sopolis, E. left Baktria in the winter of 328/7 to fetch reinforcements from Macedonia (Arr. 4.18.3). What became of him, we are not told. Only Menidas is known to have rejoined Alexander (Arr. 7.23.1; 7.26.2). Berve II 150–1 no. 301; Kirchner, *RE* VI (1907) 228; Hamilton 1955, 217; Heckel 1992, 364–5; Hoffmann 195–6.

ERICES. See **APHRIKES.**

425 ERIGYIOS

(Ἐρίγυιος). Son of Larichos and brother of Laomedon (no. 645; Arr. 3.6.5, 11.10). A Mytilenean by birth (Diod. 17.57.3), E. was a naturalized Macedonia (Tataki 51 no. 50), having been granted property in Amphipolis. An *hetairos* of Alexander, E. is wrongly characterized as a "boyhood friend": Curt. 7.4.34 describes him as "white haired" and *gravis aetate* in 330, it appears that he was born no later than 380 and had been appointed by Philip as an adviser of the young Alexander. He was banished in spring 336 for his role in the Pixodaros affair (Arr. 3.6.5; Plut. *Alex.* 10.4) but returned soon after Philip's death (Arr. 3.6.6). Diod. 17.17.4 claims that E. commanded 600 Greek allied cavalry since the beginning of the campaign; but it appears that E. was not appointed hipparch until Alexander Lynkestes (no. 45) was deposed as commander of the Thessalians in the winter of 334/3 and replaced by Philip son of Menelaos (Arr. 3.11.10; Diod. 17.57.4; Curt. 4.13.29); the Peloponnesian allies were then assigned to E. (Arr. 3.6.6). Thus he commanded the allied horse at Issos (Arr. 2.8.9; Curt. 3.9.8), and at Gaugamela (Arr. 3.11.10; Diod. 17.57.3). At Issos the Peloponnesians are mentioned but their commander is not named; Curt. 4.13.29 wrongly assigns Erigyios' command at Gaugamela to Krateros (cf. Atkinson I 425). Between these two battles, from winter 333/2 until spring 331, E. appears to have remained with Menon son of Kerdimmas (no. 722) in Koile-Syria, protecting the area with the allied cavalry (Arr. 2.13.7; cf. Berve II 151).

In 330 E. followed the King in his pursuit of Dareios III, at least as far as the Caspian Gates (Arr. 3.20.1). He is next attested leading the baggage train through Parthiene (Curt. 6.4.3) and rejoining the King at Arvai (Curt. 6.4.23) or Zadrakarta (Arr. 3.23.6). At Phrada he participated in the King's council concerning the action to be taken against Philotas (Curt. 6.8.17). Soon afterwards, he was sent against the rebel Satibarzanes (no. 1037; Curt. 7.3.2; Arr. 3.28.2), whom he slew in single combat (Curt. 7.4.32–8; Arr. 3.28.3). Thereafter he appears only as an adviser of the King at the Iaxartes, urging him not to campaign against the Skythians beyond the river (Curt. 7.7.21ff.). In winter 328/7, E. died in Sogdiana, apparently of illness, and was buried with suitable honors (Curt. 8.2.40). Berve II 151–2 no. 302; Kirchner, *RE* VI (1907) 452; Heckel, *Marshals*² 315–16; Lehmann-Haupt in Papastavru 1936, 85–6 no. 35.

426 ESIONEUS

('Ησιονεύς). Son of Alketas II of Epeiros (no. 62), and brother of Nisos (no. 803); they appear to have had a different mother from that of Teukros and Alexander; hence also nephew of Aiakides (Paus. 1.11.5), though Alketas and Aiakides were probably born to different mothers. He perished (probably in 307), when the Epeirots, in retaliation for Alketas' harsh rule, murdered the father along with E. and Nisos (Diod. 19.89.3). He could not have been born long before 320 at the earliest, since Diodorus says that both Alketas' sons were still children when they died. Heckel 2021. **Stemma IIa.**

427 ETEOKLES

('Ετεοκλῆς). Spartan (Poralla no. 282). Ephor in 331/0. At the conclusion of the war of Agis III, E. refused Antipatros' demand for 50 Spartan boys to be given as hostages, offering instead double the number of old men or women. (Plut. *Mor.* 235b–c). He is also credited with the remark that Sparta could not abide two Lysandroses (Ael. *VH* 11.7; cf. Athen. 12.535d). Niese, *RE* VI.1 (1907) 709 no. 3; Berve II 153 no. 306.

428 EUAGORAS

(Εὐαγόρας). Son of Eukleon of Korinth. In 326 he was appointed *grammateus* of Alexander's Hydaspes fleet (Arr. *Ind.* 18.9). Nothing else is known about him. Whether he was the later satrap of Aria is uncertain (Diod. 19.48.2). Identification with Euagoras the hunchback (no. 430 below) is unlikely (Athen. 6.244f). Berve II 153 no. 307; Billows 384–5 no. 38.

429 EUAGORAS

(Εὐαγόρας). Perhaps Kyprian, like Stasanor (no. 1076) and Stasandros (no. 1075). After his victory at Gabiene, Antigonos replaced Eumenes' supporter Stasandros as satrap of Aria by Euitos (no. 438). But Euitos died soon afterwards and was replaced by E., a man of courage and shrewdness (Diod. 19.48.2). Despite the similarity of the names, there is no compelling reason to assume (with Geer, *Diodorus* X 83 n.1 and Billows 385) that he is identical with Euagros (no. 432), satrap of the Persians (Diod. 19.92.4). What became of him when Seleukos made his triumphal anabasis to the East is unknown. Billows 384–5 no. 39. Willrich, *RE* VI.1 (1907) 828 no. 10

430 EUAGORAS

(Εὐαγόρας). Hunchback. Parasite of Demetrios Poliorketes (Athen. 6.244f). Willrich, *RE* VI.1 (1907) 828 no. 11.

431 EUAGROS

(Εὔαγρος). Called satrap of the Persians, E. was a supporter of the Median satrap Nikanor in his struggle against Seleukos in 312/11. E. was killed in a military engagement with Seleukos (Diod. 19.92.4). Willrich, *RE* VI.1 (1907) 834 no. 3.

432 EUDAMIDAS

(Εὐδαμίδας). Spartan (Poralla no. 161; Bradford 161 no. 1). Eudamidas I of Sparta (Bradford 161 no. 1). Eurypontid (*regn.* c.330 to before 294). Son of Archidamos III and brother of Agis III (no. 27) and Agesilaos (no. 24). Husband of Archidamia, by whom he had Archidamos IV (Polyb. 4.35.13). E. became king of Sparta after the death of Agis III (Plut. *Agis* 3.3). Little of historical value can be gleaned from his *apophthegmata* (Plut. *Mor.* 192a-b, 220d-221a) except that he was a younger contemporary of Xenokrates (no. 1162), that he was king at the time of Alexander's Exiles' Decree, and that he had a realistic view of Macedonian power. Niese, *RE* VI (1907) 892 no. 4; Berve II 154 no. 309. **Stemma XVIIIb.**

433 EUDAMOS

(Εὔδαμος). Macedonian (Tataki 198 no. 2). Brother of Peithon (no. 867), hence presumbably son of Krateuas, from Alkomenai (Diod. 19.14.1; Arr. *Ind.* 18.6). He may have participated in Alexander's conquest of Asia but his role is unattested in the Alexander historians. In 318/7, while Peithon was satrap of Media, he put to death the satrap of Parthia, Philip (Diod. 19.14.1 wrongly calls him Philotas), and replaced him with Eudamos. The move was clearly part of Peithon's bid to increase his power by treating his position as *strategos* of the Upper Satrapies as a continuing, rather than temporary, office. About E. himself Diodorus says nothing further. Willrich, *RE* VI (1907) 893 no. 4; Berve II 154 no. 310.

434 EUDAMOS

(Εὔδαμος, Εὔδημος). Probably Macedonian (Tataki 311-12 no. 36). Family background unknown. General of the Thrakians, E. had apparently been left in Taxiles' territory with the satrap Philip son of Machatas (no. 908). He was responsible for the murder of Poros (no. 987), perhaps in collusion with Taxiles (cf. Diod. 19.14.8). When the eastern satraps opposed Peithon son of Krateuas, E. came from India with 500 cavalry, 300 infantry and 120 elephants (Diod. 19.14.8) to join the forces of Eumenes. Eumenes paid him 200 talents from the treasury at Sousa, ostensibly for maintenance of the elephants but also as a bribe (Diod. 19.15.5). At Paraitakene (Diod. 19.27.2, 30.3, 9-10). Along with Phaidimos (no. 886), E. warned Eumenes of a plot against him by the commanders of the Silver Shields, but Plutarch alleges (*Eum.* 16.3) that their real concern was recovering the money that Eumenes owed them. He was executed by Antigonos after the battle of Gabiene (Diod. 19.44.1). Willrich, *RE* VI (1907) 893 no. 5; Berve II 154 no. 311; Heckel 1992, 333-4.

435 EUETION

(Εὐετίων). Athenian admiral (Kirchner 5461; possibly identical with Euetion son of Autokles, 4653), defeated in two naval battles by White Kleitos (no. 596; Diod. 18.15.9; *Syll*[3] 346 = *IG* II[2] 505); one of these appears to have been at Amorgos (*Marm. Par. FGrH* 239 B9). If Diodorus' reference to the Echinades refers to a sea battle in western waters (*Barr. Atl.* 54 D5), as Bosworth 2003b has argued (cf. Wrightson 2014; Meeus 2013, 94), this engagement must have occurred after the conclusion of the Lamian War and in conjunction with or in preparation for the Macedonian war on the Aitolians (Diod. 18.24-5). Hauben 33-4 no 12; Kirchner, *RE* VI (1907) 983 no. 2; Heckel, *Marshals*[2] 298-304.

436 EUGNOSTOS

(Εὔγνωστος). Son of Xenophantes. *Hetairos* of Alexander, hence apparently Macedonian (cf. Tataki 311 no. 35). Hoffmann does not include E. in his list of Macedonians, and Berve

II 154 suggests that he may be a prominent Greek who was enrolled in the *hetairoi*. In 332/1, Alexander appointed E. as secretary (*grammateus*) of the mercenaries in Egypt under Lykidas (no. 660) the Aitolian (Arr. 3.5.3). Bosworth I 275–6 sees the "mercenaries" as military settlers from the Persian period. He may be right in suggesting that E. received the position because Lykidas, an Aitolian, might not have been regarded as entirely trustworthy. Nothing else is known about him. Berve II 154 no. 308.

437 EUIOS

(Εὔιος). Flute player (Pollux 4.79) from Euboian Chalkis. He performed at the mass marriage ceremony in Sousa in 324 (Chares, *FGrH* 125 F4 = Athen. 12.538f). It was on this occasion that E. was billeted by Hephaistion into a home previously assigned to Eumenes of Kardia (no. 443), a move which further aggravated the unpleasant relationship between Hephaistion and the latter (Plut. *Eum.* 2.1–3). E. was said to have been the lover of Python (no. 1024; Plut. *Mor.* 180f). He is named in the choregic Thrasyllos monument of 320/19 (*Syll³* 1092). Berve II 155–6 no. 315; Graf, *RE* VI (1907) 993–4 no. 3.

438 EUITOS

(Εὔιτος). In 316 Antigonos defeated Eumenes in Gabiene and dealt with his supporters; E. was appointed by Antigonos as satrap of Aria—replacing Stasandros (no. 1075), a supporter of Eumenes—but E. died soon after and was, in turn, replaced by Euagoras (Diod. 19.48.2). Willrich, *RE* VI.1 (1907) 995; Billows 385 no. 39.

439 EUKLES

(Εὐ[κλῆς]). Greek or Macedonian. Perhaps an officer (almost certainly a supporter) of Polyperchon (no. 983), who requested that E. and Sonikos (no. 1058) be granted Athenian citizenship for their good services. This was done through the agency of Ktesias son of Chionides, who moved the decree (*IG* II² 387; *Syll³* 315; cf. Paschidis 72). Both E. and Sonikos are otherwise unknown. Paschidis 72 s.v. Ktesias son of Chionides A15.

440 EUKRATES

(Εὐκράτης). Known by the pseudonym Κόρυδος "the Lark," a notorious parasite of the age of the Diadochoi (cf. Athen. 6.240f). He was the object of ridicule in Timokles' *Epichairekakos* (6.241a), in Alexis' *Demetrios or Philetairos* (6.241b) and in Kratinos' *Titans* (6.241c); Alexis, in the *Poets*, shows that Korydos was an Athenian (6.241d); he was thought to be a male prostitute (6.241e: ὃς ἐδόκει πεπορνεῦσθαι). Lynkeus of Samos gives his real name as Eukrates (Lynkeus *ap.* Athen. 6.241d; cf. Machon *ap.* Athen. 6.242a). Eukrates appears to have made his way to Alexandria, where he became one of Ptolemy I's parasites (Athen. 6.242a–b, 245e). Some of his witticisms are collected by Athenaeus (6.245d–f).

441 EUKTEMON

(Εὐκτήμων). One of the spokesmen of the mutilated Greeks (cf. Theaitetos no. 1105) who encountered Alexander's army between the Araxes River and Persepolis. His name survives only in Curtius, but that is not to say that Curtius invented him: since Diod. 17.69.5–8 preserves the same general arguments, it is likely that the story was told in greater detail by Kleitarchos (Pearson 239; cf. Hammond 1983, 56). E. makes the case that they should not accept Alexander's offer of repatriation but instead remain together as a group in Asia. This group and its leaders are doubtless fictitious, the speeches of E. and Theaitetos little more than rhetorical exercises. See Atkinson II 107, citing Helmreich 1927, 82–7. Some have accepted the mutilated Greeks as historical (e.g. Radet 1927, 6–8); for a brief discussion of the problem see Yardley and Heckel 173–5; Heckel 149; Berve II 156 no. 316.

442 EUMELOS

(Εὔμηλος). Son of Pairisades and, most likely, Komosarye (no. 615). Brother of Satyros and Prytanis (Diod. 20.22.2); apparently also brother of Gorgippos (no. 484). Father of Spartokos (Diod. 20.100.7, "Spartakos"; IG II² 653, l.33). When Pairisades died c.311/10 after a 38-year reign, E. challenged Satyros' right to the throne. Allying himself with the king of the Sirakes, Aripharnes (who brought 42,000 troops: Diod. 20.22.4), E. was defeated near the Thates River (on which see s.v. Ariphanes no. 184) and besieged in Aripharnes' capital by Satyros (Diod. 20.22.5–23.1). But, although the latter died of a spear wound to the upper arm during the siege (Diod. 20.23.7), E. had yet to secure the throne for himself. Prytanis, who had received Satyros' corpse in Pantikapaion, conducted a funeral and buried his brother in the royal tombs, after which he hurried to Gargaza to take control of Satyros' army and claim the kingdom. E. attempted to negotiate a division of the kingdom, but Prytanis garrisoned Gargaza and returned to Pantikapaion to secure his position (Diod.20.24.1). E. nevertheless defeated his brother in battle and forced him to surrender his troops and relinquish his kingdom. But Prytanis rebelled soon afterwards, only to be defeated and forced to flee to Kepoi, where he was killed (Diod. 20.24.2). To secure his kingdom against rivals, E. put to death the friends of Satyros and Prytanis, as well as their wives and children. Only Pairisades (no. 838) son of Satyros escaped, taking refuge with the Skythian king, Agaros (probably the ruler of the Agaroi). E. won the goodwill of the people of Pantikapaion by returning their traditional political system and issuing tax exemptions (Diod. 20.24.4–5). When Lysimachos besieged the town of Kallatis (Barr. Atl. 22 F5), E. resettled 1,000 of its citizens, who were suffering from hunger, on farmland at Psoa. He cleared the Black Sea of pirates and annexed many of the adjacent territories to his realm (Diod. 20.25.1–2). E. ruled five years and five months before he died in a freak accident: he jumped from a runaway four-horse wagon but caught his sword in the wheels and was dragged to his death (Diod. 20.25.3–4; Diod. 20.100.7 says he died in the sixth year of his reign in 304/3) and was succeeded by his son Spartakos, who ruled for 20 years. A prophecy concerning his death and that of his brother Satyros (Diod. 20.26.1–2). Willrich, RE VI.1 (1907) 1079–80 no. 11; Volkmann, Kl. Pauly II 424 no. 4; Werner 416–18.

443 EUMENES

(Εὐμένης). [All references in **boldface** are to Plutarch's Life of Eumenes.] A Greek from Kardia (**1.1**; Nepos, Eum. 1.1), son of Hieronymos (Arr. Ind. 18.7) and clearly a member of a prominent Kardian family; apparently a kinsman of the famous historian, Hieronymos. E. was born in 362/1 and died in 316/15 at the age of forty-five (Nepos, Eum. 13.1) Grammateus of the Macedonian kings, beginning with Philip II in 342/1 and continuing for thirteen years under Alexander (Nepos, Eum. 13.1; 1.4: archigrammateus; or scriba, Nepos, Eum. 1.5–6; Arr. 5.24.6; on the importance of the position see Anson 39–42).

Author of the *Ephemerides* (*FGrH* 117 T1; others ascribed the work to Diodotos of Erythrai; cf. Anson 1996 and Anson 46). An exile from his homeland, where Hekataios had established a tyranny (Plut. *Sertorius* 1.11; Antipatros' support of Hekataios caused or exacerbated hatred between the regent and E.: 3.6–8, 5.6–7), E. became a *xenos* of Philip II, upon whom he made a favorable impression on account of his looks and intelligence (Douris of Samos, *FGrH* 76 F53; 1.2–3; Nepos, *Eum.* 1.4), though later scandal made him the son of a poor waggoner (1.1) or a funeral musician (Ael. *VH* 12.43: τυμβαύλης). E.'s first military service under Alexander came after the fall of Sangala: he was sent with three hundred cavalry to two Kathaian towns that had rebelled in concert with Sangala (Arr. 5.24.6; Curt. 9.1.19), but the inhabitants of these cities fled upon the news of Sangala's fall. E. served as a *trierarch* of the Hydaspes fleet (Arr. *Ind.* 18.7). Arrian's failure to say anything further about his military career is probably due to Ptolemy's bias against a supporter of Perdikkas. But it is clear that E. must have been one of the hipparchs of the cavalry before Alexander's death; for he led Perdikkas' hipparchy, when the latter was placed in charge of "Hephaistion's Chiliarchy" (1.5; Nepos, *Eum.* 1.6, wrongly saying he commanded one of *two* units of the Companions). At Sousa in 324, he married Artonis (no. 227), sister of Barsine, (1.7; Arr. 7.4.6; cf. Arr. *ap.* Phot. *Bibl.* 68b; perhaps the wife mentioned by Nepos, *Eum.* 13.2 who was residing in Kappadokia). In the same year, he quarreled with Hephaistion over the assignment of accommodations (2.1–3: Arr. 7.13.1; see no. 437; 2.8–10), and E., after his rival's death in Ekbatana, was careful to avoid the impression that he welcomed it (2.9–10; Arr. 7.14.9). The *Last Days and Testament* claims that he was present at Medeios' drinking party, where Alexander was allegedly poisoned, but that E. was not part of the conspiracy (Ps.-Call. 3.31.9; *LM* 98; for the pamphlet and its date see Ausfeld 1895, 1901; Heckel 1988; Bosworth 2000).

In the strife that followed the King's death, E. acted as peacemaker (3.1–2: cf. Curt. 10.8.15, for other Greeks involved in the process; cf. Atkinson and Yardley 199), though clearly serving the interests of Perdikkas (Nepos, *Eum.* 2.3 says Perdikkas actively sought his support; but see the comments of Rathmann 36). Arr. *Succ.* 1.2 names him as one of the officers of second rank (after Perdikkas, Ptolemy, and Leonnatos) at the time of the King's death. In the settlement, he received Kappadokia and Paphlagonia as his satrapy (3.3; Arr. *Succ.* 1.5; Nepos, *Eum.* 2.2; Diod. 18.3.1; Curt. 10.10.3; Justin 13.4.16; cf. App. *Syr.* 53, *Mithr* 8; cf. Diod. 31.19.4–5; Dexippos, *FGrH* 100 F8 §2; *LM* 116). Perdikkas gave him authority over other commanders whose task it was to secure Armenia and Kappadokia, but as a Greek he had difficulty winning the support of the arrogant Macedonians, including Perdikkas' brother Alketas (Diod. 18.29.2), Antigonos (Diod. 18.23.34; Arr. *Succ.* 1.20; 3.4–5) and Neoptolemos (1.6: the *archihypaspistes* derided E. as *archigrammateus*). Leonnatos cooperated with E., but only briefly, answering Antipatros' appeal for help, but secretly planning to marry Kleopatra and upstage the regent; he attempted to enlist E. in his scheme but the latter refused (3.5–12; Nepos, *Eum.* 2.4). Whether there is any truth to the rumor that Leonnatos attempted to kill E. (Nepos, *Eum.* 2.5) is unclear. E. decamped and reported Leonnatos' scheme to Perdikkas, who came in person to help him secure Kappadokia (3.12; Diod. 18.16.1–3, 22.1; Arr. *Succ.* 1.11). Thereafter he was sent to put Kappadokia in order and deal with Neoptolemos, who had created chaos in Armenia (4.1; see also Anson 1990; Kaerst 1085 calls him satrap, but he was almost certainly *strategos*), here he learned first hand the arrogance and insubordination of Neoptolemos (4.2–4).

E. encouraged Perdikkas to seek the hand of Kleopatra (no. 608), and thus win the support of Olympias, but Alketas argued that his brother should keep faith with Antipatros by marrying Nikaia (no. 775; Arr. *Succ.* 1.21; **5.3** shows that Alketas was favorably disposed toward Antipatros; but E. regarded him as a personal enemy, **5.7**: παλαιὸς ὢν ἐχθρός). Although Alketas' advice won out, it was not long before Perdikkas turned his attention to Kleopatra (for the deception see Diod. 18.23.1–3), using E. as a go-between (Arr. *Succ.* 1.26; cf. *Succ.* 25 §2). When Perdikkas turned his attention to Ptolemy in Egypt, he left E. to protect the Hellespontine region against Antipatros and Krateros (Diod. 18.25.6, 29.1; Nepos, *Eum.* 3.2; cf. Justin 13.6.14: Perdikkas entrusted all Asia west of the Tauros to him), ordering Alketas and Neoptolemos to support him (Diod. 18.29.2; Bengtson I 171–6). Alketas bluntly refused, saying his Macedonians would be ashamed to oppose Antipatros and were willing to side with Krateros (**5.3**); for the defection of Neoptolemos see **5.4**. E. took his forces to the Hellespont and augmented them with a large body of cavalry enlisted in his own satrapy; his army was previously deficient in cavalry (Diod. 18.29.3; for E.'s reliance on cavalry, Nepos, *Eum.* 3.6). When Antipatros and Krateros sought to lure him away from supporting Perdikkas, they failed (Arr. *Succ.* 1.26); for Antipatros was a longtime enemy (**5.6–7**). But E., allegedly, offered to broker a fair and just reconciliation between Krateros and Perdikkas (**5.8**). Neoptolemos, however, betrayed E. and, after an unsuccessful skirmish with his forces, fled with three hundred horsemen to join Antipatros (Diod. 18.29.4–6; Justin 13.8.3–5; **5.5–6**; Arr. *Succ.* 1.27; cf. *PSI* XII 1284; Bosworth 1978; Briant 1973, 223–4 n.13). Antipatros took a portion of the army to move against Perdikkas (Diod. 18.29.6), leaving Krateros to confront E. (Nepos, *Eum.* 3.4–5, E. feared desertion if his troops learned against whom they were fighting, **6.1–7**); his army comprised 20,000 infantry and 5,000 cavalry (Diod. 18.30.5; **4.4** says that earlier he had recruited 6,300 horsemen). In the battle that ensued E. was victorious— though he suffered several wounds (Nepos, *Eum.* 4.2; **7.11–12**), killing Neoptolemos with his own hand (Diod. 18.31.1–32.1; Arr. *Succ.* 1.27; Justin 13.8.6–8; Nepos, *Eum.* 4.2; **7.7–12**) and learning of the death of Krateros (Diod. 18.30.5–6; Arr. *Succ.* 1.27; Nepos, *Eum.* 4.1–3; **7.5–6**) on the battlefield (for the battle: Diod. 18.30–2; Justin 13.8.7 mistakenly substitutes Polyperchon: see Yardley–Wheatley–Heckel 159). News of the victory did not reach Perdikkas in time to affect the outcome of his campaign in Egypt (Diod. 18.37.1; 18.33.1 need not be contradictory and may refer to E.'s earlier battle with Neoptolemos: thus Anson 106–7 n.104). The story that Eumenes found Krateros still alive and tried to save his life is utter fiction (Nepos, *Eum.* 4.4); Nepos' claim that he gave Krateros a proper funeral and sent his ashes to his widow may be true but somewhat misrepresented, since it was not until Ariston, who had been entrusted with Krateros' ashes, was captured by Antigonos after the battle of Gabiene that the remains were sent to Phila (Diod. 19.59.3).

The defeat and death of Perdikkas in Egypt resulted in a realignment of power. E. and the remainder of the Perdikkans were outlawed, spontaneously (on the news of Krateros' death) by the army at the Nile and again, perhaps formally, at Triparadeisos (**8.3**; Nepos, *Eum.* 5.1; Diod. 18.37.1–2, cf. 19.12.2; Arr. *Succ.* 1.30, 39; Justin 13.8.10, cf. 14.1.1; App. *Syr.* 53.266, *Mithr.* 8; see also Granier 1931, 71–72; Engel 1974; Anson 114 n.132). At Triparadeisos, Antigonos was appointed *strategos* of Asia (App. *Syr.* 53.266 calls him *episkopos*) for the purpose of disposing of E. and the outlawed faction (Arr. *Succ.* 1.38; Diod. 18.39.7, 40.1; cf. Justin 13.8.10, out of context). E.'s satrapy was reassigned to Nikanor (Diod. 18.39.6; Arr. *Succ.* 1.37). The news reached E. before he led his army into

Aiolia (Justin 14.1.1–6) and, from there, to Sardis, where Kleopatra was now residing. He made the decision of the assembled Macedonians known to his men in order to test their loyalty, offering any who wished to leave the opportunity of doing so (Justin 14.1.1–4). But his decision to join Kleopatra in Sardis was intended to shore up the support of his men through her influence (Justin 14.1.7). Indeed, E.'s authority was frequently challenged, largely on the grounds of his Greek origins (see below). On the approach of Antipatros Kleopatra urged E. to depart, lest she incur the wrath of the Macedonians for her connections with him; that precaution was in vain (Arr. *Succ.* 1.40). E. attempted to summon Alketas and Attalos son of Andromenes to his aid, but they declined (Arr. *Succ.* 1.41).

In 319, E. was back in Kappadokia, where Antigonos, who had collected his troops from winter quarters, sought him out (Diod. 18.40.1; Nepos, *Eum.* 5.2–3). The weakness of E.'s position resulted in defection: a certain Perdikkas, with 3,000 infantry and 500 cavalry, deserted, but E. sent against them Phoinix of Tenedos, who fell upon them unexpectedly, capturing their leaders and the bulk of the deserters (Diod. 18.40.2–3). E. put Perdikkas and the other leaders to death but was reconciled with the deserters themselves, although he took the precaution of distributing them among the troops (Diod. 18.40.3–4). In the subsequent battle of Orkynia (Diod. 18.40.5–8; **9.1–5**; Engel 1971), although E. had a numerical advantage (20,000 infantry and 5,000 cavalry to Antigonos' 10,000 foot and 2,000 horse), he occupied the low ground, and Antigonos was victorious, largely through the (pre-arranged) treachery of Apollonides (no. 149), who deserted and turned the tide of battle (Diod. 18.40.5, 8). An attempt by Antigonos to win E. over to his cause failed primarily because he would not be reinstated in his satrapy or have the death sentence against himself rescinded (Diod. 18.41.6–7). E. was, at any rate, unwilling to entrust himself to the fortunes of others, which had been the case also with Leonnatos (**3.10**). Having lost 8,000 men (Diod. 18.40.8), E. resolved to flee to Armenia but, under pressure from his pursuer, he sought refuge in a fortress called Nora (Diod. 18.41.1; Nepos, *Eum.* 5.3; Justin 14.2.2–3; Strabo 12.2.6 C537, who says the place was called Neroassos in his time; cf. App. *Syr.* 53.266), where he held out with 600 men (Diod. 18.41.3, but see Diod. 18.53.7: 500 men; cf. **10.2**); the small numbers reflect E.'s concern for the food supply (Justin 14.2.3). E. took exceptional measures to keep his horses fit in a place that did not allow for proper exercise (**11.4–8**; Nepos, *Eum.* 5.4–6; Front. 4.7.34). For the date of E.'s confinement in Nora (winter of 319/18) see Diod. 18.58.1, who says that in the archonship of Archippos (318/7), E. had only recently escaped from Nora. Furthermore, Diod. 18.44.1 (cf. 18.50.1) says that in the archonship of Apollodoros (319/18) Antigonos had already defeated E. (Ἀντίγονος καταπεπολεμηκὼς τοὺς περὶ τὸν Εὐμενῆ) and was moving against Alketas and Attalos. Diod. 18.53.5 says that the siege lasted a year, and since E. escaped (or negotiated his freedom) from Nora in spring 318 (Nepos, *Eum.* 5.7), he must have sought refuge there in the preceding spring (which seems to be corroborated by the observation that Antigonos, before the battle of Orkynioi (or Orkynia), had summoned his troops from winter quarters: Diod. 18.40.1; for the chronology see Anson 131 n.53). According to Nepos, *Eum.* 5.7, E. remained in Nora until the winter ended and then made his escape. Justin 14.2.4 says that he received reinforcements from Antipatros, which caused Antigonos to abandon the siege. But Antipatros had died in the autumn of 319. E. had indeed sent Hieronymos to negotiate with Antipatros (Diod. 18.42.1), but he would have arrived in Macedonia to find him dead and Polyperchon ruling in his place (on these problems see Yardley–Wheatley–Heckel 174–5). Justin (or Trogus) may have substituted the name Antipatros for Arrhidaios (the satrap of Hellespontine Phrygia who did in fact aid E.: Diod. 18.52.4 says that Arrhidaios (no. 214), now under pressure from Antigonos, sent a force under an unnamed general to E.'s aid, while the latter was still at Nora. But E.'s "escape" from the fortress appears to have been the result of negotiation: Hieronymos was sent by Antigonos to E. with an offer of alliance (Diod. 18.50.4–5; **12.2**)—how he came to be in Antigonos' entourage is a matter of debate. For the negotiations and Eumenes' revision of the oath that Antigonos had required him to swear—Eumenes swore *philia* not to Antigonos alone but to Olympias and the "Kings" as well—see **12.3–7**.

If there is any truth to the story that Olympias wrote to E., asking whether she should remain in Epeiros or return to Macedonia to claim the throne (Nepos, *Eum.* 6.1; Diod. 18.58.2), this must have occurred after Polyperchon wrote to her and offered her the *epimeleia* of Alexander IV (Diod. 18.57.2) and sought E. as an ally (Diod. 18.57.3–4), with the promise of compensation for his previous losses. Nepos, *Eum.* 6.2 says that Eumenes urged Olympias not to act with severity towards anyone (i.e. her enemies). This is surely an invention after the fact; for Eumenes could not have known how Olympias would act (cf. Nepos, *Eum.* 6.3). It was, in fact, the struggle for power between Polyperchon and Kassandros, who allied himself with Antigonos, that led to E.'s rehabilitation and new role as champion of the "Kings" (for E.'s devotion to the royal house: **3.14**; Diod. 18.57.4, 58.2, 4; Nepos, *Eum.* 6.5, and 13.2–3 for his role in maintaining the royal house). Polyperchon placed him in charge of affairs in Asia (στρατηγὸς τῆς ὅλης Ἀσίας αὐτοκράτωρ), thus challenging Antigonos' authority, and told him to enlist the services of the Argyraspids (Diod. 18.58.1; cf. Justin 14.2.6–10). Thus began a campaign that would lead to a stormy relationship with the commanders of the Silver Shields and the ultimate downfall of E. himself. He moved from Kappadokia to Kilikia, where he was met by the commanders of the Argyraspids, Antigenes and Teutamos (Diod. 18.59.1–4); despite their initial enthusiasm, E. attempted to secure their loyalty by establishing the pretense that his orders were being directed by Alexander the Great himself (Diod. 18.60.1–61.3; Nepos, *Eum.* 7.2–3; Polyaenus 4.8.2). Sending out his *philoi* as recruiting agents in Asia Minor and the Levant, he soon levied an army of 10,000 infantry and 2,000 cavalry, to which he would add the 3,000-strong Argyraspids (Diod. 18.61.4–5). Nevertheless, his authority over the Argyraspids was called into question: Ptolemy failed to detach them, but Antigonos' agent, Philotas, bribed one of the commanders, Teutamos, though he failed to win over Antigenes (Diod. 18.62–3). It was, however, an omen of things to come. Failing in his endeavor to detach the Argyraspids from E., Antigonos prepared to march against him in Kilikia with 20,000 light infantry and 4,000 cavalry (Diod. 18.73.1), but E. moved on to Phoinikia and Koile-Syria before turning to Mesopotamia, where he overcame resistance from Seleukos (Diod. 18.73.2–3) and finally arrived in Persia with a force of 15,000 infantry and 3,300 cavalry, and summoned the satraps of the region to join him (Diod. 18.73.4). From winter quarters in the so-called villages of the Karians, E. attempted to enlist the services of Seleukos and Peithon, but these declined to serve a man outlawed by the assembled Macedonians (Diod. 19.12), and they attempted to undermine the loyalty of the Argyraspids (Diod. 19.13.1–2). Failing to do so they impeded E.'s progress by diverting the waters of the Tigris and flooding the region (Diod. 19.13.3–5), but E. reached Sousiana, where he hoped to assemble the forces of the satraps who were loyal to him (Diod. 19.13.6–7). These satraps had, in fact, already marshalled their forces in order to deal with the ambitions of Peithon (Diod. 19.14), and they numbered, in all, 18,700 infantry and 4600 cavalry (thus Diod. 19.14.8; but see Anson 164 n.51).

Despite the position granted him by Polyperchon, E. found that, once the armies had assembled in Sousiana, squabbles broke out over who should exercise command. Peukestas and Antigenes were particularly difficult, and it was finally agreed to create the impression that leadership was by committee, with meetings in a royal tent (as if Alexander were presiding) (Diod. 19.15.1–4; cf. the measures taken earlier in Kilikia: Diod. 18.60.1–61.3; Nepos, *Eum.* 7.2.3). E. won the goodwill of the Macedonians by giving them six months' pay, and he gave Eudamos two hundred talents for the maintenance of the elephants (Diod. 19.15.5); the enlargement of his forces caused Antigonos to give greater attention to his own preparations for war (Diod. 19.15.6). The *phrourarchos* of Sousa, Xenophilos, was instructed not to communicate with or give money to Antigonos (Diod. 19.17.3; cf. 19.18.1 for the Antigonos' siege of the citadel). From Sousa he moved to the Tigris, which he used as a line of defense against Antigonos, instructing Peukestas to summon 10,000 Persian archers from his satrapy to guard the position (Diod. 19.17.3–7). When Antigonos advanced to the Koprates River and began moving his troops across, they were roughly handled and driven back by E.'s forces (Diod. 19.18.3–7). Soon afterward, E., Antigenes and some other generals wished to take the army back to the West (ἐπὶ θάλατταν) but were pressured by the satraps of Central Asia to remain in the East; for they feared reprisals from Antigonos (Diod. 19.21.1–2). Hence they moved to Persepolis, where Peukestas set about trying to win the goodwill of the troops (Diod. 19.21.2–3), but the machinations of the satrap of Persia were undermined by a false letter produced by E., claiming to give news of Polyperchon's victory in Europe and the death of Kassandros (Diod. 19.22.1–3; Polyaenus 4.8.3). In order to cow Peukestas even further, E. brought charges against the satrap's friend, Sibyrtios, who escaped to Arachosia (Diod. 19.22.4) and was later an ally of Antigonos (Diod. 19.48.3; Polyaenus 4.6.15).

The battle of Paraitakene was an indecisive engagement that pro-Eumenes propaganda depicted as a victory of sorts: Diod. 19.27–31 and 19.25–6 for the preliminaries; cf. Devine 1985a; but see Anson 180–1 n.97. The battle is passed over briefly in 15.1–3, again suggesting that the event was inconsequential (cf. Nepos, *Eum.* 8.1). The troops went into winter quarters (Nepos, *Eum.* 8.3–5; Diod. 19.34.7–8), but the following spring saw the decisive battle of Gabene or Gabiene (16; Nepos, *Eum.* 10.1–2; Diod. 19.40.1–43.6, and 19.39 for preliminary skirmishing; cf. Devine 1985b; Justin 14.3.1–3, omitting a great deal of what came before), in which Antigonos captured the baggage of the Argyraspids and induced them to surrender E. to him (16.11–18.5; Diod. 19.43.7–9; Nepos, *Eum.* 10.2 calls it a victory for E.; Justin 14.3.3–4.16). Rightly or wrongly, they are held responsible for his death and castigated by the historians, and indeed some were punished by the victor (19.3; Diod. 19.44.1, 48.4; Polyaenus 4.6.15). The formal apprehension of E. was done through the agency of a certain Nikanor (17.5). Antigonos kept E. under guard for a while but, realizing that no meaningful agreement could be reached with him and fearing his popularity with the troops, had him put to death (19.1; Diod. 19.44.1; Nepos, *Eum.* 12 says he referred the matter to a council, who resolved to let E. die of starvation, though in the end he was strangled *insciente Antigono*—two forms of exculpation; Justin 14.4.21 does not report his death in context; see also Yardley–Wheatley–Heckel 189–91). The mockery of E. by Onomarchos is intended to discredit his captors (Nepos, *Eum.* 11.3–5). Although Demetrios and Nearchos were said to have asked Antigonos to spare his life, their pleas fell on deaf ears (**18.6**). For E.'s death see App. *Syr.* 53.267, *Mithr.* 8; Diod. 19.44.2–3; **19.1–3**; cf. Justin 15.1.1; Diod. 19.50.8). Antigonos sent his body to his relatives in Kappadokia for burial (Nepos, *Eum.* 13.4). Some former supporters of E. continued to resist Antigonos (Diod. 19.47.1), and the other leading Successors complained of Antigonos' failure to share the spoils from his defeat of E. with them (Diod. 19.57.1, 85.3).

For E. as a clever military tactician see Polyaenus 4.4.3 and 4.8.4–5; Nepos, *Eum.* 8.7–9.6; Diod. 19.39.1 cf. 18.53.2 for the success of his armies and his reputation for good fortune (εὐτυχία). But Polyaenus 4.6.9–13, 19 gives examples of E.'s being outmaneuvered by Antigonos. Despite his flashes of brilliance, he was defeated, captured and killed. Nevertheless, Paus. 1.6.7 believed that the lengthy campaign against E. played no small part in weakening Antigonos and led to his defeat at Ipsos. His disadvantages as a Greek in the Macedonian army (Nepos, *Eum.* 1.2–3, 7.1), his military skills (above), his former "friendship" with Antigonos (Diod. 18.41.6: τὴν προϋπάρχουσαν φιλίαν ἀνανεωσάμενος), his relations with Peukestas (Polyaenus 4.8.3; Diod. 19.15.1, 17.5; 19.22–3, 37.6–38.2) and the Argyraspids (discussed in detail above). For his alleged avarice, which led indirectly to the burning of the official records in his tent, see **2.4–7**; but a pro-Eumenid source, probably Hieronymos, depicted his indebtedness as a clever scheme to protect his life; for his creditors were concerned about recouping their money (**16.3–4**; see s.v. Phaidimos no. 886). Kaerst, *RE* VI (1907) 1083–90 no. 4; Vezin 1907; Volkmann, *Kl. Pauly* II 424–5 no. 1; Berve II 156–8 no. 317; Anson 2004 (2nd edn, 2015) and *LexAM* 227–8; Schäfer 2002; Billows 70–104; Bosworth 1992; Heckel 1992, 346–7.

444 EUNOSTOS

(Εὔνοστος). King of Soloi on Kypros. Probably the son of Pasikrates (no. 852) and brother of Nikokles, a trierarch of Alexander's Hydaspes fleet. E. married Eirene, daughter of Ptolemy I and Thaïs (Athen. 13.576e); probably not before 307 (but see Hill I 165 n.2). Since Alexander's conquest of Phoinikia, the Kypriot kings had been in a state of vassalage to the Macedonian rulers, and after 315 much of the island was subject to Ptolemy I. What became of E. is unknown. Schiff, *RE* VI.1 (1907) 1138–9 no. 4; Kiechle, *Kl. Pauly* II 429.

445 EUPHILETOS

(Εὐφίλητος). Athenian (Kirchner 6069). Euphiletos son of Aristeides Kephisieus had been an intimate friend of Phokion. Upon meeting Phokion as he was being led to death, he said: "What unmerited indignity you are suffering, Phokion," to which Phokion replied that nearly all distinguished Athenians had met such an end (Nepos *Phoc.* 4.3). Kirchner, *RE* VI.1 (1907) 1170 no. 3.

446 EUPHRANOR

(Εὐφράνωρ). Korinthian sculptor and painter (Quint 12.10.6). Born *c.*400 (his floruit was in the 360s, Pliny, *HN* 34.50; cf. 35.128). E. produced statues of Alexander and Philip in four-horse chariots (Pliny, *HN* 34.78), which Berve II 160 assumes were produced when Philip constituted the League of Korinth in 337. For his work see Palagia 1980. Robert, *RE* VI.1 (1907) 1191–4 no. 8; Berve II 160 no. 327.

447 EUPHRON

(Εὔφρων). Son of Adeas and grandson of Euphron (on whom see Xen. *HG* 7.1.43–4). Sikyonian (*IG* II² 448). He had been in exile since perhaps 331, when a pro-Macedonian tyranny was installed in the city. E. drove out the Macedonian garrison in Sikyon after the death of Alexander and joined the Hellenic alliance that opposed Antipatros in the Lamian War (cf. Diod. 18.11.2; Paus. 1.25.4; Justin 13.5.10). He was honored by the Athenians in 323/2, but his privileges were revoked by the oligarchic regime that dominated Athens after the war (cf. Habicht 1997, 45). In 318/17 the rights of E. and his descendants were reaffirmed on a motion by Hagnonides (no. 490) and both the original decree and the new one were inscribed on a single stele (*IG* II² 448). After the defeat of the Greek forces in the Lamian War, E. died at the hands of his enemies (lines 53–5). Swoboda, *RE* VI.1 (1907) 1218 no. 2; Berve II 160 no. 328; Skalet 1928, 193–4 no. 136; Wallace 2014; Schwenk no. 83; Harding no. 123A; Griffin 1982, 76; F. Kiechle, *Kl. Pauly* II 436.

448 EUPHRONIOS

(Εὐφρόνιος). Son of Hegemon. Akarnanian. Honored by the Ephesians in 302/1 for negotiating with Prepelaos (no. 993), who installed a garrison in the city. For his *eunoia* and service to the city and the temple he was awarded citizenship for himself and his descendants (*Syll³* 353). Lund 126; Picard 1951.

449 EUPOLEMOS

(Εὐπόλεμος). Macedonian (Tataki 314 no. 49). Son of Potalos (Robert, *Coll. Froehner* I no. 52, line 5; on the patronymic see Tataki 425; the name appears on sling bullets found at Olynthos dating from the time of Philip II: Hoffmann 229). Billows 1989, a brilliant discussion of E.'s career, has established beyond doubt that he was *dynastes* in Karia in the third century. For our purposes, only his career up to the year of Ipsos need be considered. E. is first attested in 314/13 as an officer of Kassandros, who sent him to Karia (presumably in the company of Prepelaos no. 993) to aid Asandros, who had defected from Antigonos (Diod. 19.68.5; cf. 19.68.2). Since Antigonos' general Polemaios had sent his army to separate winter quarters, Prepelaos and Asandros sent E. to ambush his forces at Kaprima (Diod. 19.68.5), but E. was defeated and captured (Diod. 19.68.7). Although Diodorus does not explicitly say so, it is a reasonable inference that E. was paroled and sent back to Kassandros in Greece. Certainly, Kassandros continued to value him as a military leader, even though both he and Prepelaos had rather dismal records before 302. E. is next found in 312/11 as Kassandros' *strategos* of Greece (στρατηγὸς ἐπὶ τῆς Ἑλλάδος: Diod. 19.77.6; Bengtson I 132–4), pitting him once more against Polemaios, but the series of successes by the latter in Euboia and Boiotia appear to have come with little or no resistance from E. (Diod. 19.78.2–4). E. was doubtless working with limited manpower and Billows 1989, 176 suggests that Kassandros may have hoped for nothing more than "delaying action" in the lead up to the peace negotiations of 311. After this, E. vanishes from Diodorus' history altogether. His name does, however, appear on a lead curse tablet found near the Athenian Dipylon Gate. On this E. is linked with Pleistarchos (who had commanded the garrison in Chalkis, persumably under E.'s authority: Diod. 19.77.6), Kassandros, and Demetrios of Phaleron; a fifth name is only partially preserved (Braun 1970). It probably dates to the time of the Four Years War (cf. Paus. 1.15.2 for an Athenian victory over

Pleistarchos near the Dipylon Gate; Burstein 1977b, refuted by Billows 1989, 178). E. was thus involved in Kassandros' unsuccessful effort to retake Athens and reinstate the government of Demetrios of Phaleron (who was at the time in exile in Thebes; see no. 363). It appears that E., like Prepelaos, was involved in the military action against Antigonos in 302/1, though probably as part of a supplementary force led by Pleistarchos (Diod. 20.112). Following the death of Antigonos at Ipsos, E. seems to have been Pleistarchos' general and, probably, his successor in the mid-to-late 290s. For his *dynasteia* see Billows 1989, 190–201, with epigraphic evidence on pp. 204–5. His coinage (Akarca 1959, 101–2) also belongs to the period after Ipsos (*contra* Buraselis 19–20, and Mørkholm 1991, 59 Pl. 68, who attributes the Alexander issues from Mylasa to E., Pl. 67). Willrich, *RE* VI.1 (1907) 1227 no. 8; Launey 1177; Buraselis 11–22.

450 EUPOLIS

(Εὔπολις). Officer in the service of Demetrios (probably in his campaigns in Greece: 304–302). Honored in 303, on the motion of Stratokles (no. 1082), with Athenian citizenship in 303 (*IG* II2 486). Otherwise unknown. Schoch, *RE* Supplbd. IV (1924) 450 no. 2a; Osborne, *Naturalization* no. D45; Billows 385–6 no. 40.

451 EUROPA

(Εὐρώπη). The daughter of Philip II and his seventh wife, Kleopatra-Eurydike (Athen. 13.557e = Satyros, *FHG* III 161 frg. 5), E. was born only a few days before Philip's death in mid-summer 336 (Diod. 17.2.3). The theory that E. was born in 337, and that Karanos (no. 576), was her younger brother (Green 1991, 95–6, 141), must be rejected and Karanos with it (Heckel 1979). She was murdered in her mother's arms by Olympias (Justin 9.7.12; according to Paus. 8.7.7 mother and *son* (τοῦτον τὸν παῖδα) were dragged onto a brazen oven) during Alexander's absence and without his approval (Plut. *Alex.* 10.8; cf. Burstein 1982b, 161). Berve II 160 no. 326; Beloch III² 2.71–2; Heckel 1979; Hoffmann 218.

452 EURYBOTADAS

(Εὐρυβωτάδας). Son of Tallos. One of twenty-four cavalrymen from Orchomenos, who served with Alexander's allied cavalry until the expedition reached Ekbatana in 330. There he and his compatriots were discharged. On their return (*c.*329), they made a dedication to Zeus Soter in Orchomenos (*IG* VII 3206). Berve II 158 no. 319.

453 EURYBOTAS

(Εὐρυβώτας). Kretan of unknown family. Leader of the Kretan archers (*toxarches*), a position to which he may have been summoned already by Philip II, when he planned his Asiatic campaign. He was killed, along with 70 of his men, in the attack on Thebes in 335 (Arr. 1.8.4). His successor appears to have been Ombrion (no. 812). Kirchner, *RE* VI.1 (1907) 1821; Berve II 158 no. 320; Launey 1162; Bosworth I 82–3.

454 EURYDIKE

(Εὐρυδίκη). Macedonian (Tataki 315 no. 53). A daughter (perhaps the youngest) of Antipatros and thus sister of Phila (no. 897), Nikaia (no. 775), and the anonymous woman who married Alexander Lynkestes (A18). Her brothers were Kassandros, Philip, Iolaos, Perilaos, Pleistarchos, Alexarchos, and Nikanor (**Stemma V**). She was offered as a bride to Ptolemy, though originally intended for Leonnatos (Diod. 18.12.1; 18.25.4, where the *koinopragia* must have included an offer of marriage). She could not have reached Egypt any earlier than 320, accompanied by her cousin and later rival, Berenike (no. 293); for the marriage see Paus. 1.6.8). Soon after her marriage she bore Ptolemy, surnamed Keraunos (App. *Syr.* 62.330; Porphyr. Tyr. *FGrH* 260 F3 §9), and at a later point Ptolemais (Plut. *Demetr.* 46.5). Her children appear to have included Lysandra, who became the wife of Agathokles son of Lysimachos (Paus. 1.9.6), and a son (whose name has not been preserved) who was killed by his half brother Ptolemy II Philadelphos (Paus. 1.7.1), perhaps identical with Meleagros (Porphyr. Tyr. *FGrH* 260 F3 §10; Diod. 22.4); Argaios was probably also her son. After the death of her sister, Phila, Demetrios' widow, she brought her daughter Ptolemais to the Besieger in Miletos. Ptolemais and Demetrios had been betrothed (through the efforts of Seleukos) for some time. When Demetrios married her, E. gave away the bride (Plut. *Demetr.* 46.5; cf. Heinen 14–15). Keraunos had allotted the city of Kassandreia (significantly, her sister Phila had committed suicide there) to his mother E., now in exile from the Ptolemaic court (cf. Walbank, *HMac* III 257). She granted freedom to the Kassandreians, for which she was honored, by Apollodoros, with a festival called the Eurydikeia (Polyaenus 6.7.2); though Apollodoros soon followed this up with the establishment of a tyranny. Berve II 158 no. 321; Willrich, *RE* VI (1907) 1326–7 no. 16; Macurdy 102–4; Beloch IV² 2. 178–9; Seibert 1967, 16–19; Heckel 1989, 32–3; Ogden 68–72; Aulbach §5.1.3 (6.2.1.3); Ager 2018. **Stemma V.**

455 EURYDIKE

(Εὐρυδίκη). Daughter of Lysimachos (Justin 16.2.4) and, to judge by her name, Nikaia (no. 775). Hence also the sister of Agathokles and Arsinoë (later Arsinoë I of Egypt). She was given in marriage to Kassandros' son Antipatros (no. 128), at some point after the death of Kassandros in 297. Eusebius (*Chron.* 1.232) states that the marriage dates to the time after Antipatros murdered his own mother Thessalonike, but Justin 16.1.7 suggests that the union was forged earlier (Seibert 1967, 96–7: between 297 and 294); for Antipatros probably expected a favorable reception in Lysimacheia on account of his marriage to E. (see also Carney 159). Lysimachos himself supplanted and murdered Antipatros in 287, after imprisoning his own daughter E. for assisting her husband in his complaints (Justin 16.2.4). What became of her is not recorded, but she may have become the pawn in another political marriage; cf Beloch IV² 2.130). The fact that Ptolemy Keraunos did not base any claims to Thrake and Macedonia by marrying her suggests that she was already dead (or, otherwise unavailable) in 281/0. Volkmann, *Kl. Pauly* II 452 no. 4; Beloch IV² 2.130; Seibert 1967, 96–7; Carney 159–60. **Stemma IX.**

EURYDIKE. Illyrian. See **AUDATA.**

EURYDIKE. Wife of Philip III Arrhidaios. See **ADEA.**

EURYDIKE. Wife of Philip II. See **KLEOPATRA.**

EURYDIKE (widow of Ophellas, wife of Demetrios Poliorketes). See **EUTHYDIKE.**

456 EURYLOCHOS

(Εὐρύλοχος). Prominent Macedonian (Tataki 315 no. 54). E. served Philip II as an ambassador with Parmenion (no. 848) and Antipatros (no. 127) in 346 (Theopompos, *FGrH* 115 F165; Hypothesis to Dem. 19 §5) and as a mercenary commander on Euboia in 342 (Dem. 9.58). Perhaps identical with the *hieromnemon* at Delphi in 342/1 (*Syll*³ 242 B6; but the text is uncertain). E. must have belonged to a political group or family that was hostile to Alexander: he was executed at the beginning of the new King's reign (Justin 12.6.14). Kirchner, *RE* VI.1 (1907) 1332–3 no. 6; Berve II 159 no. 323.

457 EURYLOCHOS

(Εὐρύλοχος). Macedonian (Tataki 316 no. 55). Brother of Epimenes (no. 423; Arr. 4.13.7; Curt. 8.6.20) and presumably a son of Arseas (Arr. 4.13.4). Curt. 8.6.20 claims that Epimenes had wished to keep Eurylochos out of the Hermolaos conspiracy, suggesting that E. was also one of the *paides basilikoi* (if we assume that the plot was restricted to this group). Whether E. learned of the conspiracy directly from Epimenes or through Charikles, he brought the matter to Alexander's attention through the agency of Ptolemy (Arr. 4.13.7) and Leonnatos (Curt. 8.6.22). He was rewarded by the King, who gave him fifty talents, as well as the estate of a certain Tiridates, and spared Epimenes (Curt. 8.6.26). Berve II 159 no. 322; Hoffmann 180; Heckel 1992, 291.

458 EURYLOCHOS

(Εὐρύλοχος). Macedonian from Aigai. Lover of the *hetaira* Telesippa (no. 1099), E. had himself fraudulently enrolled amongst the veterans and the infirm (νοσοῦντας) destined for discharge in 324 in order to accompany her back to Greece. Alexander learned of the deception and the affair and, instead of punishing him, urged E. to persuade Telesippa to stay with words or gifts (Plut. *Alex.* 41.9–10; cf. Hamilton 109 for the textual problem; see also Plut. *Mor.* 181a and 339c–d, where the same story is told of Antigenes of Pellene). Identification with the former *pais basilikos* (no. 457) seems unlikely. Berve II 159 no. 324.

459 EURYSILAOS

(Εὐρυσίλαος, Curt. Ersilaus). Greek from Eresos on the island of Lesbos (Curt. 4.8.11 wrongly says he was from Methymna). Installed, along with Agonippos (no. 30), as tyrant when Memnon recaptured most of Lesbos in 333 (Arr. 2.1.1; Diod. 17.29.2). The previous tyranny of Apollodoros and his brothers had been expelled in 334 (thus Lott 1996; Wallace 2016; but see R&O 417), probably through the efforts of Alkimachos son of Agathokles, whom Alexander had sent to establish democracies in the area (Arr. 1.18.1–2; cf. [Dem.] 17.7). E. and Agonippos exercised the tyranny in a most cruel fashion (*OGIS* 8a, b = Tod II 191). They were, however, overthrown by Hegelochos in 332 and taken to Alexander in Egypt (Arr. 3.2.6; cf. Curt. 4.8.11), who sent them back to Eresos to stand trial (Arr. 3.2.7; cf. *OGIS* 8a, lines 13–15). There they were convicted and executed (*OGIS* 8b, lines 60–9). Kirchner, *RE* VI.1 (1907) 1352; Berve II 159–60 no. 325; Baumbach 33ff., 79; Habicht² 15; Berve, *Tyrannis* I 338; II 691; Hofstetter 68 no. 115; Heisserer 39ff.; Harding no. 112 A and F; Lott 1996; R&O no. 83.

460 EUTELES

(Εὐτελής). Seleukos' governor of Sousiana. Patrokles (no. 854), who was in charge of Babylonia, sent some of the civilians from Babylon to E., who is described as being near the Persian Gulf (πρὸς Εὐτελῆ καὶ τὴν Ἐρυθρὰν θάλατταν: for the satrapy see Jacobs 204) when Demetrios attacked the city in 311 (Diod. 19.100.5). E. appears to be Seleukos' appointee, in which case he must have replaced whomever Antigonos installed as successor to Antigenes. He is otherwise unknown. Grainger, *SPG* 90.

461 EUTHYDIKE

(Εὐθυδίκη). Athenian (Kirchner 5547); her name appears in *IG* II² 1469 lines 30–1 Εὐθυδίκη Μιλτιάδου θυγάτηρ; cf *IG* II² 1466 lines 6–8; for her son by Ophellas Μιλτιάδης Ὀφέλου Λακιάδης see *IG* II² 6630 (Davies *APF* 309). E. had married Ophellas of Kyrene (no. 817), and his marriage to her was one thing that helped induce Athenians to come to his aid in 308; she was the daughter of a Miltiades who traced his descent back to the general of Marathon (Diod. 20.40.5). After Ophellas' death, E. moved back to Athens. It was during the months between Demetrios' capture of Athens in 307 and his departure to the naval battle at Salamis that Demetrios married her; the Athenians regarded the marriage as a mark of special favor and honor (Plut. *Demetr.* 14.1–2). E. bore him a son named Korrhagos (Plut. *Demetr.* 53.9). Nothing else is known about her. Gude 43 no. 49; Aulbach §8.2.1.2 ("Eurydike").

462 EUTHYKLES

(Εὐθυκλῆς). Spartan (Poralla no. 302), presumably a relative of the ambassador of the same name sent to the Persian court in 367 (Xen. *HG* 7.1.33; Poralla no. 301; thus Berve II 155; Badian 1967, 174 n.1; Hofstetter 69). Sent as ambassador to the Persian king, perhaps in connection with the early activities of Agis III (Beloch III² 1.646), and captured by Parmenion at Damaskos after the battle of Issos in late 333 (Arr. 2.15.2; for Curtius' confused list of Spartan captives see Bosworth I 233–4; Atkinson I 261–2). E. may be the unnamed Spartan ambassador (held in honorary detention by Alexander), whose quip is preserved by Plut. *Alex.* 40.4 in the context of (apparently) the Syrian lion hunt (cf. Willrich 1899a, 231; Hamilton 107). Alexander was at first hostile to him (on account of the political posture of his homeland) but later released him (Arr. 2.15.5), probably after the complete failure of Agis III and the Macedonian victory at Gaugamela. Niese, *RE* VI.1 (1907) 1506–7 no. 5; Berve II 155 no. 312; Hofstetter 69 no. 118.

463 EUTHYKRATES

(Εὐθυκράτης). From Sikyon (Paus. 6.2.7). Sculptor. One of three sons of Lysippos (no. 675) who were also his students and sculptors; his brothers were Laippos and Boëdas (Pliny, *HN* 34.66). E. produced the statue of Alexander the Hunter at Thespiai (*HN* 34.66) and the statue of Tyche in Antioch (Paus. 6.2.7). Teisikrates (no. 1097) was his student (Pliny, *HN* 34.67), who depicted Demetrios and also Peukestas. Robert, *RE* VI.1 (1907) 1507–8 no. 6; A. Rumpf, *Kl. Pauly* II 467 no. 2. Pollitt 108–9 for *testimonia*; Griffin 1982, 142–5; Berve II 155 no. 313.

464 EUTROPION

(Εὐτροπίων). Greek. Officer of Antigonos the One-Eyed, who according to Plutarch was also the King's chief cook or butcher (*archimageiros*). He invited Theokritos (no. 1112) to come to Antigonos to engage in learned discussion, but Theokritos resisted repeated invitations, saying to E. that he knew that he merely wished to serve him up raw to the Kyklops (a derogatory way of referring to the King: Plut. *Mor.* 11b–c). Nothing else is known about him. Billows 386 no. 42; Willrich, *RE* VI.1 (1907) 1520.

465 EUXENIPPOS

(Εὐξένιππος). The MSS of Curtius have *excipinon*. Hoffmann 180–1, following Foss, calls him Elpinikos. Macedonian. A young man who rivaled Hephaistion for his good looks but somewhat effeminate (Curt. 7.9.19). In 329 he was sent on a mission to the Sakai. Hoffmann 180 lists him as one of the *paides basilikoi*, but the mission clearly required a more mature individual. Nothing further is known about him. Berve II 158 no. 318.

466 EXEKESTOS

(Ἐξήκεστος). Rhodian admiral (*nauarchos*). In the second half of 305, when Demetrios was bringing his siege engines into the Rhodian harbor and destroying the ships there in order to disrupt the grain supply to the city (Diod. 20.88.1), the Rhodian *prytaneis* ordered three ships to be manned by the select crews. These ships, under the command of E., were to attempt to sink the ships that carried the Besieger's towers. Although they accomplished most of what they intended—destroying two of the three ships that carried towers—they became overconfident and reckless (Diod. 22.88.2–6). In the engagement E. was wounded and captured, as was the captain of his ship (the distinction shows that E. was in charge of all three ships) and several others (Diod. 20.88.6). The other two ships made their escape. What became of E. is not recorded. Hauben 34–6 no. 13; Berthold 71.

G

467 GERGITHIOS

(Γεργίθιος). Quintessential flatterer of Alexander. G. inspired Klearchos of Soloi to write a work on flattery called *Gergithios or Kolokeia* (Athen. 6.255c–d). Nothing else is known about him. Berve II 111 no. 224. Berve, *RE* Supplbd IV (1924) 686 no. 2.

468 GEROSTRATOS

(Γηρόστρατος, Gir-astart: "client of Astarte"). Phoinikian, King of Arados and the neighboring regions (including Marathos, Sigon, and Mariamne); father of Straton, who surrendered himself and the above-mentioned territories to Alexander in 333/2 (Arr. 2.13.7; Curt. 4.1.5–6). G. himself, like the other kings of Kypros and Phoinikia, was serving with the fleet of Autophradates (Arr. 2.13.7). Perhaps encouraged by the treatment his son had received (or by the result of the battle of Issos, cf. Berve II 111), G. deserted the fleet and, together with Enylos (Ainel) of Byblos, surrendered to Alexander at Sidon at the time of the siege of Tyre (Arr. 2.20.1); presumably he took part in the final assault on the city. Alexander reinstated him as king of Arados (Arr. 2.30.3), though we do not know how long he continued to rule. The coin of Straton (Head, *HN²* 788) is more convincingly dated by Bosworth I 226 to the period of Straton's regency than to the period after 323. For the coinage of G. see Betlyon 1982, 91–2. Berve II 111 no. 225; Hill 1910, xiv, xl; cf. Hofstetter 69; Grainger 1991, 33–4.

469 GLAUKETAS

(Γλαυκέτης, thus *Syll³* 409, lines 10–11). Greek of unknown origin (possibly from Aitolia, where the name is attested, Grainger, *APS* 176). G. appears to have been a pirate leader—he commanded πλοῖα (see Ormerod 28) and his defeat ensured "safety for those sailing the sea": ἀσφάλειαν τοῖς πλέουσι τὴν θάλατταν—who had captured Kythnos but was defeated and taken by Thymochares (no. 1135) in the archonship of Praxiboulos (315/14; *Syll³* 409 = *IG* II² 682). G. may have been a privateer in the service of Antigonos (Ormerod 124 n.3; Niese I 284 n.3; but an official relationship is rejected by Hauben 40; he is not listed in Billows). G. is not heard of again. Schoch, *RE* Supplbd. IV (1924) 709; Hauben 36–40 no. 14; Ormerod 116, 124.

470 GLAUKIAS

(Γλαυκίας). King of the Taulantians, an Illyrian tribe of the western region near Epidamnos (Arr. 1.5.1; Justin 17.3.18–20; Plut. *Pyrrh.* 3.1–2). Husband of the Epeirot Beroa (no. 294), one of the Aiakidai (Justin 17.3.19). In 335 he joined the Dardanian chieftain Kleitos (no. 594) in an uprising against Alexander (Arr. 1.5.1; for the campaign see Hammond 1974; Fuller 223–6; Heckel 32–5). He arrived when Alexander was blockading Kleitos in Pellion and occupied the high ground (Arr. 1.5.9–11), but was defeated by the Macedonians and fled to the mountains (Arr. 1.6.1–10); Kleitos who then set fire to Pellion took refuge with him (Arr. 1.6.11). The traditional enmity between Illyria and Macedon continued after Alexander's death. G. conducted several wars against Kassandros (Diod. 19.67–78); took in the infant Pyrrhos in 317 (Plut. *Pyrrh.* 3.1–3) and raised him with his own children (Plut. *Pyrrh.* 3.4–5) and even adopted him, presumably after the death of Aiakides in 313/12. He refused to surrender him to Kassandros, even when offered 200 talents. In 314, when Kassandros' general captured Apollonia, G. met him near the Hebros River only to be defeated and forced to make peace (Diod. 19.67.5–7). When Kassandros turned his attention to the east, G. besieged Apollonia but was compelled to come to terms with its inhabitants by the Spartan Akrotatos (no. 39), who had been driven there with his forces by bad weather in the Adriatic (Diod. 19.70.7). In the following year the Kerkyreans intervened and removed Kassandros' garrison from Apollonia but allowed G. to have possession of Epidamnos (Diod. 19.78.1). He restored Pyrrhos, now twelve years old, to his kingdom in 307 (Plut. *Pyrrh.* 3.5). But the young king attended the wedding of G.'s son in 303/2 and was driven out in his absence (Plut. *Pyrrh.* 4.1–2). Monunios may have been G.'s successor (cf. Niese II 10 n.4). Hammond 1966, 246; id. 1974; Staehelin, *RE* VII (1912) 1398–9 no. 7; Berve II 111–12 no. 227; Wirth, *Kl. Pauly* II 807 no. 2; Sandberger 104–7 no. 34; Papazoglou 1965, 159ff.

471 GLAUKIAS

(Γλαυκίας). Macedonian (Tataki 286 no. 6). Commander of an *ile* of the Companion Cavalry at Gaugamela, where his squadron was positioned between that of Kleitos (*ile basilike*) and Ariston (Arr. 3.11.8). He is otherwise unattested in the Alexander historians but may be identical with the Glaukias (no. 473) who, on Kassandros' orders, murdered Alexander IV and Rhoxane in 310 (Diod. 19.52.4, 105.2–3). Berve II 111 no. 226; Heckel 1992, 348.

472 GLAUKIAS

(Γλαυκίας, Plut. Γλαῦκος). Physician of unknown origin, presumably Greek (but Tataki 286 no. 7 believes he may have been Macedonian). G. attended Hephaistion (no. 513) during his final illness and was executed (by crucifixion) on Alexander's orders (Arr. 7.14.4; Plut. *Alex.* 72.2–3). Even if the charge was unfounded—since Hephaistion clearly disregarded his medical advice—the fact of the physician's execution need not be discounted as fiction created by the tradition hostile to Alexander. Arrian, as Berve II 112 suggests, may preserve the official version which excused Alexander's behavior by charging G. with giving Hephaistion "bad medicine." Berve II 112 no. 228; Gossen, *RE* VII (1912) 1399–1400 no. 9.

473 GLAUKIAS

(Γλαυκίας). One of the most trusted agents of Kassandros and apparently the *phrourarchos* of Amphipolis, where Rhoxane and Alexander IV were kept under guard (Diod. 19.52.4). G. was ordered to murder them, conceal their bodies and tell no one what happened (Diod. 19.105.2–3). Possibly identical with the Glaukias who appears at the battle of Gaugamela (thus Berve II 111 no. 226; Wirth, *Kl. Pauly* II 809 no. 1).

474 GLAUKIPPOS

(Γλαύκιππος). Prominent Milesian and presumably one of the city elders. He may be the father of the magistrates Leukippos and Chrysippos named in *I.Milet* 122 II 75, 78; thus Bosworth I 138. Sent in 334 by his fellow citizens and the mercenary occupation force as an envoy to Alexander who was then besieging the city. He offered to open the city and its harbors to both Macedonians and Persians. Alexander rejected his proposal and sent him back (Arr. 1.19.1–2). Nothing further is known about him. Berve II 112 no. 229.

475 GLAUKIPPOS

(Γλαύκιππος). Athenian (Kirchner 2987). Son of Hypereides from the deme Kollyte. G. was named for his paternal grandfather ([Plut.] *Mor.* 848d). Little is known of his personal life. His father is supposed to have turned him out of the house to make room for his courtesan Myrrhine (no. 760; Athen. 13.590c = Idomeneus, *FGrH* 338 F14a; [Plut.] *Mor.* 849d). G. was active in politics but a mere shadow of his famous father; he composed a speech that ran down Phokion's character (Plut. *Phoc.* 4.2). After his father's death— Hypereides had been captured by Archias of Thourioi, who took him to Macedonia, where he bit off his tongue before he died (thus [Plut.] *Mor.* 849b)—G. (according to one version) was given his bones by a doctor named Philopeithes (no. 936), who had prepared them for burial, and brought them back to Athens, despite a law prohibiting this; others said it was Hypereides' cousin, Alphinous (or Alphinos, on whom see Roisman and Worthington 255), who received the remains ([Plut.] *Mor.* 849c; *Suda* Υ 294 does not mention the intermediary role of Philopeithes).

476 GLAUKIPPOS

(Γλαύκιππος). Macedonian (cf. Tataki 286). Son of Dionysios, from Antigoneia. *IG* XII.9, 210; cf. Diod. 20.110.2. One of three brothers (see s.vv. Apollonios, Hippodamas) who served Demetrios in 304–302. Honored by the Eretrians for favors to their compatriots serving with Demetrios' fleet. Launey 1264; Billows 386 no. 43.

GLAUKOS. Physician. See **472 GLAUKIAS**.

477 GLAUKOS

(Γλαῦκος). Aitolian (Grainger, *APS* 177 no. 1). Greek mercenary leader who remained with Dareios III and some 2,000 men (Arr. 3.16.2; Curt. 5.12.4 says there were 4,000) after the disaster at Gaugamela (cf. Curt. 5.9.15, substituting Patron). In Curtius' highly dramatized account, G.'s fellow commander, Patron, warns Dareios of Bessos' treachery (5.11; cf. 5.12.7), but the Great King refuses to abandon his countrymen. Although Dareios did not avail himself of the mercenaries' protection, some of them may have put up an unsuccessful fight or deserted. After the King's death, 1,500 (presumably including G.) agreed through messengers to surrender unconditionally to Alexander's agent, Andronikos (no. 104) son of Agerros (Arr. 3.23.8–9). Kirchner, *RE* VII (1912) 1417 no. 29; Berve II 112 no. 230; Seibt 117–18; Hofstetter 70 no. 121.

478 GLYKERA

(Γλυκέρα). Athenian courtesan. Daughter of Thalassis, if she is identical with the courtesan named by Hypereides in his speech *Against Mantitheus* (Athen. 13.586b). G. was summoned by Harpalos (no. 494) after the death of his favorite, Pythionike (no. 1020). According to Theopompos (*FGrH* 115 F254a–b = Athen. 13.586c, 595d–e), whose comments are not only grossly exaggerated but also given far too much credence by modern scholars, she resided in the palace of Tarsos, where she received *proskynesis* and was addressed as queen (*basilissa*), as well as receiving a crown whenever one was dedicated to Harpalos. A bronze statue of her was set up at Rhossos in Syria. This was "corroborated" by Kleitarchos (*FGrH* 137 F30), although all that survives in the extant Alexander historians is a brief reference in Diod. 17.108.6. G. was mentioned in a satyr play attributed to Python of Katana (no. 1023), but the production date of the work is problematic (Athen. 13.586d; 13.595e–596b). Athen. 13.595e says that the play was produced at the Hydaspes River and *after* Harpalos' flight from Babylonia to the West. Now, if both statements are true we must assume either that Harpalos' flight occurred sometime in 327/6 or that the Hydaspes River is not the one in India. Droysen I² 244 n.101 suggests that the text should read "Choaspes" rather than "Hydaspes"; Beloch IV² 2.434–6 considers it the Medus Hydaspes (cf. Virgil, *Georgics* 4.211); Goukowsky II 77 and Bosworth 1988, 149–50 also believe the play was produced in the West, in this case in Karmania in 324. Whether G. came farther east than Tarsos (time would also have been a factor) is unclear. Diod. 17.108.6 speaks of her being kept in luxury by Harpalos before he mentions Alexander's return from India and Harpalos' flight. It may be possible, that Harpalos, in anticipation of the King's return had already taken up residence in Kilikia. G. returned to Athens with Harpalos in 324 (for her alleged gift of grain to the Athenians see Athen. 13. 586d; cf. Kingsley 1986, 168–9), but nothing is known for certain of her life thereafter. Menandros' character Glykera in the *Perikeiromene* may have been inspired by the famous courtesan, but stories of a love relationship between Menandros and a certain Glykera are inferences from the text and of little value (see Lefkowitz 1981, 113–14). For the numerous complex implications of Harpalos' alleged treatment of G.—and for the significance of such behavior for Alexander and his image—see Müller 2006. Over the years, I have become inclined to regard the details of Harpalos' misdeeds in Asia in the mid-320s as of limited historical worth. What can be attributed with any certainty to Theopompos must form part of a consistently hostile picture of the Macedonians and the decadent and near farcial nature of their army and court (cf. Müller 2006, 93: Th. "schildert den Hof in Pella als einen Sündenpfuhl und Philipp II. in dessen Zentrum als den großen Verderber seiner Besucher, die er zu Alkoholismus und orgiastischen Ausschweifungen genötigt habe"). Berve II 112–13 no. 231; Müller 2006; Stähelin, *RE* Supplbd. III (1918) 791 no. 3; *PAA* 277495.

479 GOBARES

(Γωβάρης). Justi 117 no. 2; Dareios' *phrourarchos* at Pasargadai (Curt. calls him *praefectus*); he surrendered to Alexander in 330. The treasure taken there amounted to 6,000 talents (Curt. 5.6.10). Nothing else is known about him. Berve II 115 no. 238; Shayegan 108 no. 50.

GOBARES (Cobares: Curt. 7.4.8). See **BAGODARAS**.

480 GORGATAS

The name occurs only in Curtius (Hedicke's emendation *Gorgidas* is plausible; cf. Tataki 287 no. 13). Macedonian. G. was a favorite of the Queen Mother, Olympias, and taken against her wishes from the court to Asia by Amyntas son of Andromenes (Curt. 7.1.38–9). He was probably one of the fifty Pages (*paides basilikoi*) brought to Alexander in 331 (cf. Curt. 5.1.42; Diod. 17.65.1). Berve II 113 no. 232; Hoffmann 205; Heckel 1992, 292.

481 GORGIAS

(Γοργίας). Macedonian (Tataki 287 no. 14). *Hetairos* of Alexander. G. commanded a battalion of discharged veterans in 324, but this need not mean that he himself was born *c*.380, as Berve II 113 maintains. G. is first attested as a phalanx commander in 328, commanding Krateros' former battalion in Baktria and in the company of Polyperchon and Attalos son of Andromenes (Arr. 4.16.1; cf. 4.17.1; Krateros appears to have had the supreme command on this mission). In India, G.'s battalion, along with that of Meleagros and White Kleitos, accompanied Perdikkas and Hephaistion as an advance force to the Indos (Arr. 4.22.7). At the Hydaspes he occupied a position upstream on the western bank of the river with Meleagros and Attalos, and thus did not participate in the actual battle (Arr. 5.12.1). Nothing further is known of his military career except that in 324 he was discharged along with Krateros and Polyperchon and led the veterans from Opis to Macedonia, via Kilikia (Justin 12.12.8). Kirchner, *RE* VII (1912) 1597 no. 30; Berve II 113 no. 233; Heckel 1992, 326–7.

482 GORGIAS

(Γοργίας). A young Macedonian (Tataki 287 no. 15), G. was a favorite of the Queen Mother, Olympias, and taken against her wishes from the court to Asia by Amyntas son of Andromenes (Curt. 7.1.38–9). He was probably one of the fifty Pages (*paides basilikoi*) brought to Alexander in 331 (cf. Curt. 5.1.42; Diod. 17.65.1). Identification with the officer of Eumenes who recognized the body of the fallen Krateros (Plut. *Eum.* 7.6) must be ruled out on the grounds of age (thus Berve II 114). Berve II 114 no. 234; Hoffmann 205; Heckel 1992, 292.

483 GORGIAS

(Γοργίας). Macedonian (Tataki 288 no. 16). An officer in the army of Eumenes in 321/0. He is said to have recognized the body of the fallen Krateros (Plut. *Eum.* 7.6). He appears too old to have been identical with the former Page and favorite of Olympias (thus Berve II 114). Berve II 114 no. 234; Berve, *RE* Supplbd IV (1924) 710 no. 32; Hoffmann 205.

484 GORGIPPOS

(Γόργιππος). Honored by the Athenians (perhaps in the early 320s) with a statue along with Pairisades I and Satyros II, rulers of the Kimmerian Bosporos (Din. 1.43). G. may have been a son of Pairisades (thus Worthington 206; Burstein 1978, 433; cautiously Beloch III² 2.93–4; but rejected by Werner 440: "Für einen zweiten Gorgippos . . . ist daher kein Platz") and thus a son of Komosarye (no. 615), the daughter of that Gorgippos who was the brother of Leukon (Polyaenus 8.55: son of Satyros I and brother also of Metrodoros). He appears to have been the second born of at least four children of Pairisades (no. 837), though it is not clear if all were sons of Komosarye. Born, in all likelihood, in the 340s (since he was associated with his father in the kingship, as was customary in this dynasty, no later than the early 320s: Din. 1.43). If the man who was honored with a statue was a son, and not the uncle and father-in-law of Pairisades, he must have died before 311/10, the year of Pairisades' death. Beloch III² 2.93–4; Werner 439–40. **Stemma XVII.**

485 GORGOS

(Γόργος). Greek from Iasos. Son of Theodotos and brother of Minnion (*Syll³* 307). *Hoplophylax* of Alexander. G. was apparently also a shameless flatterer; for in Ekbatana in 324 he honored (see *LSJ* s.v. στεφανόω Med. 3) the King, whom he addressed as "son of Amun," with a golden crown worth three thousand pieces of gold. He also promised to supply armor and equipment, in the event of a siege of Athens (Athen. 12.538b = Ephippos, *FGrH* 126 F5). G. is honored by the Iasians for his help in getting Alexander to award the city a disputed waterway (perhaps formerly belonging to Mylasa; see Heisserer 177) called the "little sea." The date of this service is, however, uncertain. A second inscription, this one from Samos (*Syll³* 312), honors him and his brother Minnion (no. 736) for their help in restoring the Samian exiles living in Iasos, and this is clearly in connection with Alexander's Exiles' Decree (and the subsequent actions of Perdikkas). For the chronology of these events see Heisserer 187–91. Certainly, the services of G. cannot be connected with his crowning of the King at Ekbatana, which must have occurred later in 324. Two fragmentary inscriptions from Epidauros suggest that G. had also helped the Epidaurians obtain what they sought from Alexander (cf. Diod. 17.113.3–4), and appear to confirm the title of *hoplophylax* or something similar (*IG* IV.2, 616 and 617, the latter preserving the letters ὁπλοφορ). What became of G., we do not know. Berve II 114 no. 236; Heisserer 169–203; Kirchner, *RE* VII (1912) 1660 no. 4.

486 GORGOS

(Γόργος). Apparently Greek. Tataki 288 no. 17 identifies him as Macedonian. A mining expert (*metalleutes*) in Alexander's entourage, G. reported that there were gold and silver mines in the territory of the Indian ruler, Sopeithes (Strabo 15.1.30 C700). The Indians were said to have had no expertise in mining, and there is no indication that the mines were exploited by the Macedonians. Nothing else is known about him. Berve II 115 regards identification with G. the *hoplophylax* as "unmöglich," but that man was clearly wealthy and may have made his fortune in the mining business. Berve II 114–15 no. 237.

487 GRYLLION

(Γρυλλίων). Athenian (Kirchner 3093). A member of the Areiopagos council. He was a fop and a parasite, living off the resources of both the satrap Menandros (Lynkeus *ap.* Athen. 6.245a; hence no later than 321) and the courtesan Phryne (Athen. 13.591d). He reportedly wore a purple-bordered robe. Whether Lynkeus knew of him from Menandros' court in Sardis or, on a later occasion, at the court of Antigonos or Demetrios—Menandros, after failing to regain his satrapy at Triparadeisos, was a *philos* of Antigonos—is unclear. The presence of Silanos the Athenian suggests that this encounter, like others that Lynkeus witnessed, occurred in Athens in the period 307–301. Willrich, *RE* VII.2 (1912) 1898 no. 1; *PAA* 281930.

H

488 HABREAS

(Ἀβρέας). Macedonian soldier of unknown background (Tataki 217 no. 3); a *dimoirites* (Arr. 6.9.3, 10.1, 11.7), a soldier with double pay (for this rank cf. Arr. 7.23.3), H. may have been one of the hypaspists, as Berve II 5 suggests; or perhaps a soldier from Perdikkas' battalion (cf. Arr. 6.9.2). Late in 326, he accompanied Alexander into the town of the Mallians (Arr. 6.9.3), along with Leonnatos, Peukestas and a certain Limnaios, and was killed when struck in the face by an arrow (Arr. 6.10.1). H.'s role in the battle was not recorded by the Vulgate authors, and perhaps by only one of Arrian's chief sources (cf. Arr. 6.11.7). Berve II 5–6 no. 6; Hoffmann 222; Sundwall, *RE* VII (1912) 2154.

489 HAGNON

(Ἄγνων). Son of Kaballas (Andron son of Kabeleus: Arr. *Ind.* 18.8), from Teos. The patronymic is confirmed by the Ephesian inscription published by Keil 1913, II*p*. It might be argued that Nearchos, the source of Arr. *Ind.* 18 (cf. *FGrH* 133 F1), ought to have known the correct name of the trierarch, but the list contains other errors that are doubtless scribal errors. These could be attributed to Arrian himself, if not to a later scribe. This would rule out the identification of the trierarch with the *archipeirates* of Polyaenus 5.19 (cf. Front. 3.3.7: Mandron; cf. Berve II 40). H. was one of Alexander's Greek *hetairoi*, but noted for his extravagance (Phylarchos, *FGrH* 81 F41 = Athen. 12.539c; Plut. *Alex.* 40.1; Ael. *VH* 9.3) and flattery (Plut. *Mor.* 65d), as well as his hostility towards Kallisthenes (Plut. *Alex.* 55.2). He was, in short, "an influential courtier whose wealth and power excited envy" (thus Billows 387). Plut. *Alex.* 22.3 claims that Alexander was angry with H. because he offered to buy a beautiful boy named Krobylos (no. 632) as a present for him. Andron, the trierarch of the Hydaspes fleet (Arr. *Ind.* 18.8), is almost certainly the same man. In 321/0 H. is attested as well disposed towards the Ephesians who supported Krateros (see Keil 1913, 242), and he appears soon to have joined Antigonos (perhaps through the influence of Nearchos?); for at some point between 317 and 315 he was defeated and captured off Kypros by the Athenian Thymochares (no. 1135) of Sphettos (*IG* II² 682 = *Syll³* 409; no. 1135). The date of H.'s defeat by Thymochares is uncertain. It was originally thought that H. was a supporter of Perdikkas and defeated in the Kypriot campaign of 321/0 (now revived by Paschidis 74 with n.7), but this appears to be refuted by H.'s support of the pro-Krateros party in Ephesos. Others have dated the battle to the archonship of Praxiboulos (315/14), which is mentioned in *Syll³* 409, line 9 (thus Hauben) but the inscription appears to make a distinction between the time of the naval battle and the archonship of Praxiboulos, implying that the battle took place before 315/14. Billows 387 is right to dismiss connections between the sea battle and the events described in Diod. 19.59.1, 62.3–6. The coins minted by the Tean magistrat H. (Poole, *BMC Ionia*, 312, nos. 24, 25) are presumably his. What became of H. is unknown. Berve II 9–10 no. 17; Sundwall, *RE* VII (1912) 2209 no. 3; Billows 386–8 no. 44; Keil 1913, 242 nn.30–1; Hauben 40–1 no. 15 and 1974, 62–4; Habicht 1957, 162 n.26; H. Callies, *Kl. Pauly* II 917 no. 2.

490 HAGNONIDES

('Αγνωνίδης, incorrectly Hagnon: Nepos, *Phoc.* 3.4). Athenian (Kirchner 176) from Pergase (*IG* II² 1629a), son of Nikoxenos. Apart from appearing in an Athenian naval list of 325/4, H. is attested in the lifetime of Alexander only as one of those accused of accepting bribes from Harpalos (Dion. Hal. *Din.* 10.654; Hyper. 5.40; Roisman and Worthington 231). A member of the anti-Macedonian party, he had apparently been exiled by Antipatros, but Phokion succeeded in persuading the regent to permit him to live in the Peloponnese rather than in the remote areas beyond the Keraunian Mountains or Cape Tainaron (Plut. *Phoc.* 29.4). Nevertheless, H. repaid the favor after Antipatros' death by denouncing Phokion (no. 952) and his supporters for betraying Peiraieus to Kassandros (Plut. *Phoc.* 33.4; cf. Diod. 18.65.6) and by supporting a motion by Archestratos to send a delegation to Polyperchon (Plut. *Phoc.* 33.6). Although H. ridiculed the proceedings, which had degenerated into farce (Plut. *Phoc.* 33.9), he eventually attained his purpose and Phokion was returned to Athens for trial and execution in spring 318 (Nepos, *Phoc.* 3.4; Plut. *Phoc.* 34.9, 35.2, H.'s greatest hostility was directed towards Kallimedon no. 568). In 317, with the return of Demetrios of Phaleron, the Athenians, in typical fashion, soon regretted the decision to execute Phokion and they condemned H. to death (Plut. *Phoc.* 38.2). H.'s chief supporters were Epikouros and Demophilos, who were hunted down and punished by Phokion's son (Plut. *Phoc.* 38.3). Berve II 10 no. 18; Sundwall *RE* VII.2 (1912) 2209; Berve II 10 no 18; K. Wickert, *Kl. Pauly* II 917.

491 HAGNOTHEMIS

('Αγνόθεμις). Plut. *Alex.* 77.2 reports that H. repeated a story, which he claims to have heard from Antigonos, that Aristotle had urged Antipatros to poison Alexander and had himself supplied the means to do so. The story of the poisoning is almost certainly a fiction, invented in the early years of the Successors. No other writings of H. are recorded and he too may be fictitious. Billows 445–6 no. 131.

492 HALKYONEUS

('Αλκυονεύς). Son of Antigonos II Gonatas and Demo, his mistress (Ptolemy son of Agesarchos *ap.* Athen. 13.578a = *FGrH* 161 F4). Born perhaps before 290, and at some point a student of the stoic philosopher Persaios (Arnim, *SVF* I 441). Hence, if Demo (no. 364) had actually been the mistress of Gonatas' father, Demetrios Poliorketes, her relationship with Antigonos must have begun during Demetrios' lifetime. Whether he was regarded as Antigonos' heir is uncertain (but see Ogden 178; also Tarn, *AG* 247–8, with n.92; Macurdy 70; Carney 181–2). In 272, in Argos, H. brought the head of Pyrrhos to his father, only to be rudely scolded by him (Plut. *Pyrrh.* 34.7–8); later he gave shelter to Pyrrhos' son, Helenos, yet even now his father was slightly critical of him, since he had allowed Pyrrhos' son to remain in rags (Plut. *Pyrrh.* 34.10). H. died in battle (Ael. *VH* 3.5), though the place and date are unspecified (Tarn, *AG* 301 believes it was the battle of Korinth in 264, in which the Spartan king Areus was killed). Although Antigonos was said to have been relatively unmoved by the news of his death (Ael. *VH* 3.5; cf. Plut. *Mor.*

119c), Diogenes Laertius (4.41–2) mentions an Athenian festival in honor of H.'s memory, presided over by the philosopher Hieronymos of Rhodes, who Ferguson 233 believes may have been a friend of the deceased. Sandberger no. 9; Tataki 233 no. 93; W. Kroll, *RE* VII.2 (1912) 2273 no. 1; Tarn, *AG* 232, 247–8, 273–4, 301, 335–6; Ogden 178–9; Carney 181–2.

493 HAMILCAR

Carthaginian, surnamed Rhodanus (Rhodinus, Front. 1.2.3). He was allegedly a crafty and eloquent man and, for that reason, was sent by his government to Alexander in 331 to discern the intentions of the Macedonians, whose capture of Tyre and establishment of Alexandria in Egypt had given them cause for concern (not to be confused with the Carthaginian embassy to Babylon in 324/3: Diod. 17.113.2). Hamilcar gained access to Alexander through Parmenion and, claiming to be an exile, joined the Macedonian army as a common soldier (presumably a mercenary). He kept detailed records on wooden tablets covered with fresh wax, but on his return to Carthage was executed on the charge of planning to betray the city (Justin 21.6.1–7; Oros. 4.6.21; Front. 1.2.3). The story is plausible but appears not to come from a well-known primary historian of Alexander. All three versions go back to Pompeius Trogus, but since the information comes from a section that does not deal with Alexander it appears to have been taken from an anecdotal passage by a non-Alexander historian. Lenschau, *RE* VII.2 (1912) 2300 no. 3; Berve II 25 no. 52.

494 HARPALOS

(Ἅρπαλος). Macedonian from Elimeia (Tataki 194 no. 3). Son of Machatas (Arr. 3.6.4), in all probability the nephew of Philip's Elimeiot wife Phila (Satyros *ap.* Athen. 13.557c). Tauron and Philip (Arr. 6.27.2; Curt. 10.1.20; Plut. *Alex.* 60.16) were probably H.'s brothers; Kalas son of H. may have been a cousin (Arr. 1.14.3; Diod. 17.17.4), as was perhaps Derdas, whom Alexander sent as ambassador to the Skythians beyond the Iaxartes (Curt. 7.6.12; 8.1.7). But we know little about the family, most of whose members vanish without a trace. Even Phila remains an enigma, though she was Philip's (second?) wife. The royal house of Elimeiotis, which enjoyed considerable prestige during Philip's reign and saw many of its members promoted by Alexander (but see the salutary remarks of Kuzmin 2013, 129), lapses into obscurity after H.'s disgrace and Alexander's death. The family may, however, have had connections with the house of Antigonos the One-Eyed. Tauron may have been in the service of Antigonos (*IG* XII 9 197, 4), and in the 2nd century we find a prominent Beroian named H. son of Polemaios (Tataki, *PB* no. 230; Kuzmin 2013); Polemaios was, of course, the name of Monophthalmos' nephew (and, apparently, his brother; cf. Billows 16–17). H. was physically unfit for military service (Arr. 3.6.6), but the nature of his ailment is unknown (cf. Müller 2006, 74–6). In 336, he was one of Alexander's advisers and banished for encouraging the prince to interfere in the negotiations with Pixodaros (Plut. *Alex.* 10.4; cf. Arr. 3.6.5). No doubt he returned as soon as Alexander came to the throne. H. accompanied the King to Asia and was appointed Imperial Treasurer, but he fled from the camp just before the battle of Issos, together with a scoundrel named Tauriskos who may have encouraged him to abscond with some of the King's money (Arr. 3.6.4–7). He remained for a time in the Megarid, having sent Tauriskos to Alexander of Epeiros in Italy; Tauriskos died there. Jaschinski

12–18 believes that H. returned to Europe in order to encourage Alexander of Epeiros to press his claims to the Macedonian throne; for he was married to Alexander's sister, Kleopatra, and would have had the support of the Queen Mother, Olympias. This strikes me as highly implausible. For a different interpretation of H.'s activities in Greece see Kingsley 1986; cf. Garnsey 1988, 158–62.

In 331 H. rejoined Alexander in Phoinikia and was reinstated as treasurer (Arr. 3.6.4). In the following year, he was left in Ekbatana, with 6,000 Macedonian troops, some cavalry and lightly armed infantry, Menidas, Sitalkes, Kleandros and, for a time, Parmenion (Arr. 3.19.7; cf. Curt. 10.1.1ff.). He thus became Alexander's link with the West. Perhaps while he wintered in Baktria-Sogdiana, Alexander received from H. a shipment of books (Plut. *Alex.* 8.3; cf. Hamilton 21). Earlier, it appears, he must have connived in the liquidation of Parmenion (thus Badian 1961, 22–3). At some point, he shifted the seat of his power to Babylon, almost certainly on Alexander's instructions, and was entrusted with the royal treasure and the collected revenues (Diod. 17.108.4). H. also enjoyed an extravagant lifestyle (Diod. 17.108.4; Plut. *Mor.* 648c–d; Plut. *Alex.* 35.15; for his attempts to transplant ivy from Media to Babylon see Theophrastos, *Hist Plant* 4.4.1; Pliny, *HN* 16.144). In 326, seven thousand infantrymen reached India from Babylon, bearing twenty-five thousand suits of exquisite armor (Curt. 9.3.21) sent by H., but they brought also tales of debauchery: H. had used the imperial treasures to buy and bring to Babylon the Athenian courtesan Pythionike (no. 1020), whom he pampered with gifts while she lived (Diod. 17.108.5) and worshipped as Pythionike Aphrodite after her death (Theopompos, *FGrH* 115 F253 = Athen. 13.595c, *Letter to Alexander*). From the resources of the empire, H. erected two great monuments to harlotry: a temple in Babylon and, on the Sacred Way to Eleusis, a tomb, which Dikaiarchos deemed "worthy of Perikles or Miltiades or Kimon" (Dikaiarchos *ap.* Athen. 13.594f). The tomb in Attika, impressive still in Pausanias' day (Paus. 1.37.4), cost thirty talents, according to Plutarch; Theopompos claimed that both buildings were erected at an expense of 200 talents (cf. Plut. *Phoc.* 22.1–2). And the cause of this extravagance, wrote Theopompos, a woman who was "thrice a slave and thrice a harlot" (*ap.* Athen. 13.595a–c = *FGrH* 115 F253: *Letter to Alexander*). Still H.'s passion for courtesans continued unabated: he summoned Glykera (no. 478) from Athens (Theopompos, *FGrH* 115 F254; Diod. 17.108.6), and ordered her to be revered as a queen in Tarsos; he even erected a statue to her in Syrian Rhossos.

The Alexander who emerged from Gedrosia was not the same man who had forgiven, or even laughed off, H.'s earlier indiscretions. Disappointed at the Hyphasis, he had suffered a serious wound in the town of the Mallians, where the lethargy of his troops had left him exposed to enemy fire. The incident fuelled rumors of his death and, with them, defection in the northeastern satrapies. And, even when reports of his demise proved false, few gave much consideration to the possibility, much less the consequences, of his return. H.'s crimes, it turned out, could be viewed as part of larger, more sinister, activities, done in concert with Kleandros, Sitalkes, Agathon, and others. His dealings with native women transgressed both law and acceptable behavior (Diod. 17.108.4; cf. Curt. 10.1.1–5, for similar atrocities by the generals who had remained with him), and they brought shame upon the new Great King.

Nevertheless, we are told that, when Kissos (no. 586) and Ephialtes (no. 416) brought the news of H.'s flight, Alexander was so struck with disbelief that he ordered them placed in chains: for he believed that they were surely slandering and falsely accusing him (Plut. *Alex.* 41.8). He did not yet know the enormity of H.'s crime. But patterns of maladministration soon became evident, and nothing short of a purge would restore order and security to the heart of the empire. H. himself had anticipated these measures and fled to Kilikia, whence he would make his way to Attika.

At this juncture, in 324, before H. had made the decision to sail for Athens, the King retained a certain macabre sense of humor and allowed the production in the Macedonian camp of a satyr play entitled *Agen* (cf. Bosworth 1988, 149; but Worthington 1986a, 64, follows Beloch IV² 2.434–6 in dating the production of the play to October 324, at Ekbatana. See also Snell 1964, 99–138; Sutton 1980a; Sutton 1980b, 75–81). The author was Python, a Byzantine (or possibly from Katane), though it was alleged—quite implausibly—in antiquity that Alexander himself wrote the play. This work, which depicted H. in the character of "Pallides," mocked his relationships with Pythionike and Glykera, and predicted that Agen (Alexander) would soon punish him for his crimes. For the troops, H.'s sex life served as a useful diversion after the hard campaigning in Baktria and India, and the deprivations of the Gedrosian march. And the view, held by many scholars, that Alexander would not have allowed such political lampooning, fails to take into account the poem of Pranichos or Pierion, which purportedly raised the ire of Kleitos in Marakanda (Plut. *Alex.* 50.8). Athen. 13.595e claims that the play was first performed at the Hydaspes; which Snell 109ff. takes to mean in India, in 326. Droysen I³ 406 n.101, suggests Choaspes instead of Hydaspes; Beloch IV² 2.434–6 argues that the Medus Hydaspes (Virgil, *Georgics* 4.211, explained by Servius as fluvius Mediae; possibly the Carcheh?) is meant. Goukowsky II 77 thinks it was the Iranian Hydaspes (Halil-rud), and that the *Agen* was produced at Salmous in Karmania. Cf. Bosworth 1988, 149–50. The truthfulness of historians (even—or, perhaps especially, those who were contemporaries) has always been difficult to ascertain; far less trustworthy is the evidence of orators and comic poets. However, Alexander allowed his former friend to be depicted on a stage that must have resembled USO venues during the Vietnam War, this was a far cry from what was later reported by Theopompos and others—indeed, Alexander hardly needed Theopompos to confirm the nature of H.'s behavior. One must assume that the "literary" tradition about Harpalos/Pallides was in fact a gross distortion of reality that aimed to depict the buffoonery of the self-important treasurer and possibly even the ineptitude of the Macedonian administrative system.

While the troops roared at Pallides, a more earnest H. set out for Attika with thirty ships (Curt. 10.2.1), bringing 6,000 mercenaries and 5,000 talents from the Babylonian treasury (Diod. 17.108.6). A general uprising, led by Athens, seemed the only way to avoid punishment (Arr. *Succ.* 16). But the Athenians were uncertain about how to deal with H.'s arrival (Ashton 1983, 56–7), and at first rebuffed him. Taking the fleet and his mercenaries to Tainaron in the Peloponnese, he soon returned to Athens as a suppliant (Plut. *Dem.* 25.3), bringing with him 700 talents. Demosthenes who had originally urged that he not be admitted to the city, now accepted a generous bribe (Justin 13.5.9. [Plut.] *Mor.* 846a (1,000 darics), 846c (30 talents); Plut. *Dem.* 25, a golden drinking cup and 20 talents), for which he was later indicted by Hypereides, Pytheas, Menesaichmos, Himeraios, and Stratokles ([Plut.] *Mor.* 846c, 848f; another opponent of H. and those who accepted his money was Deinarchos: *Mor.* 850c–d), convicted and forced to go into exile ([Plut.] *Mor.* 846c; Paus. 2.33.3 claims that Demosthenes did not take any money; for his exile cf. Diod. 18.13.6). H. himself was imprisoned and his money confiscated, but he escaped ([Plut.] *Mor.* 846b) to Megara (Justin 13.5.9); eventually he went to Tainaron and Krete ([Plut.] *Mor.* 846b). Plutarch details Phokion's involvement with H. The latter attempted to bribe Phokion with 700 talents; Phokion rejected his bribes, though others accepted (Plut. *Phoc.* 21.3–4). H. befriended Phokion's son-in-law, Charikles (Plut. *Phoc.* 21.5), who was put on trial for his dealings with H. (22.4). After H.'s death, his daughter (by Pythionike) was raised by Charikles and Phokion (22.3). The Athenians, though enticed by H.'s bribes, were frightened by the appearance of Alexander's admiral, Philoxenos (Plut. *Mor.* 531a; Hyper. *Dem.* col. 8; Paus. 2.33.4; Plut. *Mor.* 531a). Olympias and Antipatros had also demanded H.'s extradition (Diod. 17.108.7; on the chronological problems see Worthington 1986a; for the political and legal activities in Athens: Will 1983, 113ff.). Ultimately, his money helped finance the Lamian War (Diod. 18.9.1); for the Athenians sent some of it to Leosthenes (Diod. 18.9.4). But, by this time, it was too late for H. Disappointed by the Athenians, he sailed away, perhaps intending to go Kyrene, where his forces went after his death. On Krete, he was killed by one of his friends (Diod. 17.108.8; Curt. 10.2.3), namely Thibron (Diod. 18.19.2; Arr. *Succ.* 1.16; cf. Strabo 17.3.21 C837)—though others say he was killed by a servant or by a certain Macedonian named Pausanias (Paus. 2.33.4–5). Staehelin, *RE* VII (1912) 2397–401 no. 2; Berve II 75–80 no. 143; Badian 1961; Heckel, *Marshals*² 218–27; Blackwell 1999; Worthington 1986a–b, and *LexAM* 249–51. First Flight: Badian 1960b; Bosworth I 284; Carney 1982; Green 1991, 222–3; Heckel 1977c; Jaschinski, 10–18; Kingsley 1986; Worthington 1984; Müller 2006. **Stemma XIII.**

495 HAUSTANES

(Αὐστάνης). For the name: Justi 52. A local dynast in Paraitakene (Sogdiana) who supported the uprising of Spitamenes in 329; in 327 he and Katanes were arrested by Krateros who brought them to Alexander, who presumably executed them (Curt. 8.5.2; Arr. 4.22.1). Berve II 95 no. 186.

496 HEGELOCHOS

(Ἡγέλοχος). Macedonian (Tataki 319 no. 1). Son of Hippostratos (Arr. 3.11.8) and, apparently, the nephew of Philip II's last wife Kleopatra (Satyros *ap.* Athen. 13.557d; Heckel 1982a). H. survived the disgrace of his relative, Attalos, who was murdered on Alexander's instructions in 336/5, but his military functions may have been somewhat curtailed. In the events leading up to the battle at the Granikos, he commanded a portion of the *hippeis prodromoi*, also called *sarissophoroi* (Arr. 1.12.7), though clearly as a subordinate of Amyntas son of Arrhabaios (Arr. 1.31.1, with Bosworth I 114; cf. Arr. 1.14.1). The treasonous activities of Amyntas' kinsman, Alexander Lynkestes, over the winter of 334/3 may have caused the King to keep an eye on H. Hence, he was appointed as a joint commander, this time in tandem with the trustworthy Amphoteros, of the Macedonian fleet, which had been reconstituted in 333 (Curt. 3.1.19; cf. Arr. 3.2.6). Hauben 1972a, 57 argues on the basis of Curt. 3.1.19 that H. commanded the marines, while Amphoteros acted as admiral, but Arr. 3.2.6 speaks of H. sending Amphoteros to Kos in 332, suggesting that the latter was a subordinate (cf. Berve II 164). A lower rank for Amphoteros does not rule out the likelihood that his task was to keep an eye on Hegelochos' activities. H. effectively recaptured the Aegean states—Tenedos, Chios, Mytilene and the rest of Lesbos, and Kos (through the efforts of Amphoteros)—that had defected from Alexander as a consequence of the activities of Memnon the Rhodian (Arr. 3.2.3–7). He captured Pharnabazos (who later escaped), along with Aristonikos of Methymna, Apollonides, Phesinos, and Megareus, all of whom he brought to Alexander in Egypt (Arr. 3.2.4–5; cf. Curt. 4.5.14–22). In Egypt 332/1 (Arr. 3.2.3, 7), H. rejoined the land army and it was at this time that he is alleged to have urged Parmenion to conspire against Alexander (Curt. 6.11.22–9). Many of the army's senior officers were offended by Alexander's apparent rejection of Philip II when he accepted Amun as his divine father, and H. may also have reacted negatively to the chastising of Philotas, whose derogatory comments about the King had been reported to Alexander. The "conspiracy" came to naught and was not brought to light until 330, long after H.'s death. When the army moved out of Egypt, H. assumed command of an *ile* of the Companions. As such he fought and died at Gaugamela in 331 (Curt. 6.11.22; Arr. 3.11.8). Berve II 164–5 no. 341; Baumbach 49ff.; Heckel 1982a and *Marshals*² 12–18. **Stemma XIV.**

497 HEGEMON

('Ηγέμων). Athenian politician (Kirchner 6290). Family background unknown. H. is attested as a leader of the pro-Macedonian party in Athens in the time of Philip II and Alexander (Dem. 18.285; cf. Harpocration s.v. 'Ηγέμων) and is apparently identical with the supporter of Phokion, who in 318 met Polyperchon near Pharygai in Phokis and was nearly impaled on the spear of the enraged Philip III Arrhidaios (Plut. *Phoc.* 33.7, 10–12). He and his supporters were escorted by White Kleitos to Athens, where they were tried and executed (Plut. *Phoc.* 34–5). Berve II 166 no. 324.

498 HEGESIAS

('Ηγησίας). Presumably a native of Ephesos. H. established himself as tyrant of the city at some point during Alexander's Asiatic expedition with the support of the Macedonians. This can be deduced from the fact that Philoxenos demanded the surrender of H.'s murderers and imprisoned them in Sardis (cf. Julien 67). Perhaps around 324, he was murdered by the sons of Echeanax: Kodros, Anaxagoras, and Diodoros (Polyaenus 6.49). We have no firm dates. Polyaenus says that they had been imprisoned "for a long time" in Sardis before making their escape. One of them was crippled in the attempt and sent to Alexander in Babylon. Berve II 166 no. 343; Baumbach 22; Julien 67; cf. Berve, *Tyrannis* I 335–6.

499 HEGESIAS

('Ηγησίας). Sent with Aristodemos and Aischylos by Antigonos to receive pledges from Ptolemy, in the lead-up to the "Peace of the Dynasts" in 311 (*OGIS* 5, line 48; Welles, *RC* 1). H. is otherwise unknown. Billows 388 no. 45.

500 HEGESIMACHUS

The name occurs only in its Latin form. Macedonian (Tataki 320 no. 6). Apparently a member of the *hypaspistai basilikoi*. H. (along with Nikanor) led a band of young men in an unsuccessful attack on an island in the Hydaspes River (Curt. 8.13.13) and perished in the attempt (8.13.15). Berve II 166 no. 344; cf. Hoffmann 215 Σύμμαχος; Heckel 1992, 296.

501 HEGESIPPOS

(Ἡγήσιππος). Son of Onymon. Together with Philon and Ptolemy son of Lagos, H. made a dedication to Apollo at Miletos (probably in 334, but certainly before 306 (Rehm, *I.Miletos* no. 244). Nothing else is known about him, but he may have been an officer in Alexander's army. Berve II 166 no. 345.

502 HEGESIPPOS

(Ἡγήσιππος). Macedonian (Tataki 119 no. 1). Patronymic unknown. From Mekyberna in Chalkidike (*Barr. Atl.* 51 A 4). Historian of the second half of the fourth century (Jacoby, *FGrH* 491), author of a history of Pallene (Παλληνιακά and possibly *Milesiaka*). There are no details about his personal life or of connections with Alexander or the Successors, but the possibility remains that he was involved either politically or military in the events of this age.

503 HEGESIPPOS

(Ἡγήσιππος). From Halikarnassos. Antigonid fleet commander, stationed on the right wing with Pleistias of Kos at Salamis in 306 (Diod. 20.50.4). Sundwall, *RE* Supplbd. IV (1924) s.v. no. 2; Hauben 42, 119; Billows 388 no. 46.

504 HEGESISTRATOS

(Ἡγησίστρατος). Greek (perhaps Milesian), entrusted by Dareios III with the garrison of Miletos. H. had agreed by letter to surrender Miletos to Alexander in 334, but then, encouraged by the proximity of the Persian fleet, chose instead to defend the city against the Macedonian attack (Arr. 1.18.4). Arrian tells us nothing further about his role in the defense of the city or his fate. He may have perished during the resistance, but neither his death nor his possible pardon (cf. Arr. 1.19.6) is mentioned. Berve II 166–7 no. 346; Hofstetter 76 no. 135; Sundwall, *RE* VII.2 (1912) 2613 no. 4.

505 HEGETOR

(Ἡγέτωρ). From Byzantion. Engineer in the service of the Antigonids. H. constructed "tortoises" of great size for the siege of Rhodes (described in detail by Vitruv. 10.15.2–6; cf. Athen. Mech. 21–6; Anonymous of Byzantion). H. was clearly inspired by the work of Diades (Whitehead and Blyth 124), but there is no evidence that connects the two men personally. How long H. was in Antigonid service is unknown, but one assumes that, in the light of Demetrios' interest in siegecraft, H. was a fixture in his military camp. Billows 388–9 no. 47; Kroll, *RE* Supplbd. VI (1935) 104 no. 2.

506 HEKATAIOS

(Ἑκαταῖος). Probably Macedonian (Tataki 305 no. 7). Agent (and *hetairos*) of Alexander, sent in 336 to Parmenion in Asia to arrange the arrest or death of Attalos (Diod. 17.2.5–6), and soon thereafter murdered Attalos (Diod. 17.5.2), undoubtedly with Parmenion's approval. Wrongly identified by Heckel 2006, 131 with Hekataios of Kardia (cf. Berve II 148: "Gleichsetzung ... mit dem Tyrannen von Kardia ... entbehrt jeder Begründung"); his namesake, the favorite of Olympias, may however have been a relative. Berve II 148 no. 292.

507 HEKATAIOS

('Εκαταῖος). A young Macedonian (Tataki 305 no. 6) and a favorite of the Queen Mother Olympias (Curt. 7.1.38–9), H. was taken to Asia against her wishes by Amyntas son of Andromenes when he brought some fifty Pages (*paides basilikoi*) to Alexander in 331 (Curt. 5.1.42; Diod. 17.65.1). Nothing else is known about him. Berve II 149 no. 293; Hoffmann 205; Heckel 1992, 292.

508 HEKATAIOS

('Εκαταῖος). Kardian, a mortal enemy of Eumenes. Greek tyrant of Kardia. He was presumably supported by Philip II and continued to serve Antipatros, who in 323/2 sent him to Leonnatos to request his aid in Europe (Plut. *Eum.* 3.6–8). Although Leonnatos answered the call, Eumenes, who had in the past urged Alexander to terminate H.'s tyranny, slipped away (Diod. 18.14.4). Berve II 149 no 294 and *Tyrannis* I 314.

509 HEKTOR

('Εκτωρ). Macedonian (Tataki 306 no. 10). Son of Parmenion (Curt. 4.8.7; 6.9.27), brother of Philotas and Nikanor. H. was apparently the youngest of Parmenion's attested sons (Curt. 4.8.7 calls him *eximio aetatis flore* at the time of his death) and probably held no military office. Berve's estimate (II 149) that he was born *c.*360 is thus too high; *c.*350 is more likely. H. drowned in the Nile in 332/1 (Curt. 4.8.7–8, cf. also 6.9.27; Plut. *Alex.* 49.13) and was buried with great honors, befitting a son of Alexander's great marshal (Curt. 4.8.9). Julian, *Epistle* 82 (446a) claims that there was a second, almost certainly incorrect, version that the accident occurred at the Euphrates. Berve II 434 rightly rejects the suggestion by Domaszewski 1925/6, 8, that Curtius intended to foreshadow the death of Hadrian's favorite Antinous, on the grounds of uncertainty over Curtius' date (for which the reigns of Claudius or Vespasian command the most scholarly support). Hoffmann 207; Berve II 149 no. 295 and *RE* Supplbd IV (1924) 716 no. 10a; Tataki 306 n.10. **Stemma VII.**

510 HELEN

('Ελένη). A Greek woman, the daughter of Timon, H. lived in Egypt and painted the battle of Issos (Ptolemy Chennos *ap.* Phot. p. 248 Hoesch = Stewart 1993 T84; cf. Pollitt 174–5), a painting which Berve II 149 thinks may have been the model for the Alexander mosaic of Pompeii. The original was said by Ptolemy to have been housed in the *Templum Pacis* of Vespasian. Winter 1909, 8, regards Philoxenos of Eretria's painting (Pliny, *HN* 35.110; Pollitt 169) as the inspiration for the Alexander mosaic. Berve II 149–50 no. 297; Pollitt 174–5; Winter 1909; Stewart 1993 T84.

511 HELENOS

('Ελενος). Youngest of Pyrrhos' sons; his mother was the Illyrian, Birkenna (no. 299; Plut. *Pyrrh.* 9.3; Justin 23.3.3 appears to have confused him with Alexander and says his mother was Agathokles' daughter); the name reflects mythical ties of the Molossian royal house with Andromache and her brother Helenos (cf. Heckel 1981d). H. was born *c.*293/2. When Pyrrhos crossed over to Italy he left the 15-year-old Ptolemy, his son by Antigone, in charge of Epeiros, but took H. and Alexander with him (Justin 18.1.3). When he crossed to Sicily, he left H. in Locri (Justin 18.2.12: confusing him with Alexander who, as the grandson of Agathokles, was part of the Pyrrhos' Sicilian plans). When he returned from Italy, having failed in his campaigns in the West, Pyrrhos left H. in Tarentum along with his friend Milon (Justin 25.3.4), but he soon recalled him to Epeiros (Justin 25.3.6); he had marked out Italy as his future kingdom (and Sicily as that of Alexander: Justin 23.3.3, again incorrectly reversing the facts), but when Pyrrhos' campaigns in the West failed, he took both his sons back to Epeiros. H. joined him for the campaign against Sparta and Argos. At Argos H. led a force into the city (Plut. *Pyrrh.* 33.1, though the assault ended in defeat and his father's death. H. was taken prisoner and brought to Antigonos Gonatas by the latter's son Halkyoneus (Plut. *Pyrrh.* 34.10). He was released and given the ashes of his father to take back to his brother Alexander in Epeiros (Plut. *Pyrrh.* 34.11; Justin 25.5.2). If, and how, he served his brother at home is unknown. Nor do we know what became of him. Sandberger 107–9 no. 35; Ziegler, *RE* Supplbd. III (1918) 894 no. 5a.

512 HELLANIKOS

(Ἑλλάνικος). Macedonian (Tataki 306 no. 12; Hoffmann 195). Apparently a hypaspist, H. and Philotas (probably no. 939, *pace* Bosworth I 147) saved some of the siege equipment from destruction at Halikarnassos (334) when the defenders sallied forth from the city (Arr. 1.21.5; Diod. 17.27.1–2; cf. also Curt. 8.1.36). What office he held at this time is uncertain, though clearly it was a minor one; in 330, in the contests held in Sittakene, H. received the eighth prize and a pentakosiarchy of the hypaspists (Curt. 5.2.5; see literature s.v. Atarrhias no. 250). Berve II 150 no. 298; Hoffmann 195; Bosworth I 146–7; Heckel 1992, 306.

513 HEPHAISTION

(Ἡφαιστίων). Macedonian from Pella (Tataki 155 no. 48), son of Amyntor (Arr. 6.28.4; Arr. *Ind.* 18.3). A childhood friend and *syntrophos* of Alexander (Curt. 3.12.16; cf. Ps.-Call. 1.18.5; Jul. Valer. 1.10). Born *c.*356, H. entered the ranks of the Pages *c.*343 and heard at Mieza the lectures of Aristotle (cf. Diog. Laert. 5.27). Their friendship endured a lifetime (Diod. 17.114.1, 3; Lucian, *Dial. Mort.* 12.4 and *Pro Lapsu* 8; Plut. *Alex.* 28.5, 39.8; Plut. *Mor.* 180d, 332f–333a; Curt. 3.12.16; Plut. *Alex.* 47.9–10, *Mor.* 180d; Diod. 17.114.1–3; cf. Arr. 1.12.1; Ael. *VH* 12.7; cf. Bosworth I 103–4; Lucian, *Dial. Mort.* 12.4); but the story that H. crowned Patroklos' tomb at Troy, while Alexander honored that of Achilles, may be a literary fiction (Arr. 1.12.1; cf. Ael. *VH* 12.7). Choirilos of Iasos depicted Alexander as Achilles in his third-rate epic poem (Constantius Porphyrogenitus = *FGrH* 153 F10a), but it appears that most stories of Alexander's imitation of Achilles arose after H.'s death (see Perrin 1895; Heckel 2015). The story that Alexander and H. went to Olympia together (Ps.-Call. 1.18.5; Jul. Valer. 1.10) is pure fiction. Nevertheless, a close bond between the two existed: when the captive Persian Queen Mother, Sisygambis, mistook H. for the King and did obeisance to him, Alexander publicly acknowledged him as his *alter ego* (Arr. 2.12.6–7; Diod. 17.37.5–6, cf. 114.2; Curt. 3.12.15ff.; Val. Max. 4.7 ext. 2; *Itiner. Al.* 37; *Suda* H 660). In December 333 or January 332, Alexander permitted H. to choose a king for the Sidonians (Curt. 4.1.15–26; Plut. *Mor.* 340c–d; Diod. 17.46.6–47.6). Later, H. conveyed the fleet and the siege equipment from Tyre to Gaza (Curt. 4.5.10). In 331, he received a young Samian (or Plataian, so Diyllos, *FGrH* 73 F2) named Aristion (Marsyas, *FGrH* 135/6 F2 = Harpocration, s.v. "Aristion"), whom Demosthenes had sent in an effort to bring about a reconciliation with Alexander (cf. Aesch. 3.160, 162). Aristion's presence at the court is dated by an Athenian embassy, which found him there in 331. Goldstein 1968, 42–3 n.33, correctly rejects Badian's suggestion that H. was Demosthenes' "powerful protector at the Court" (1961, 34). *IG* II² 405, a decree of Demades granting Athenian citizenship to Amyntor son of Demetrios and his descendants in 334 may refer to H.'s father (Heckel 1991), which may explain why Demosthenes (and Aristion) sought H. out. It is interesting to note that the ships which conducted the siege equipment were probably those 20 Athenian vessels retained by Alexander at Miletos (Diod. 17.22.5).

Wounded at Gaugamela (Arr. 3.15.2; Diod. 17.61.3; Curt. 4.16.32) while "commanding the *somatophylakes*" (Diod. 17.61.3), H. was probably the leader of the Royal Hypaspists (*somatophylakes basilikoi*). He may have been the successor of Admetos who was killed at Tyre (Arr. 2.23.5; Diod. 17.45.6). At what point he became one of the Seven is unclear; possibly he replaced Ptolemy, the *somatophylax basilikos* killed at Halikarnassos (Arr. 1.22.4). Polyaenus 4.3.27 claims that H. and Philotas commanded the forces directly opposed to Phrasaortes [*sic*], while Alexander led the encircling forces at the Persian Gates (late 331). But both Arr. 3.18.4, 7–8 and Curt. 5.4.14–15, 29 assign this role to Krateros, and correctly identify the Persian satrap as Ariobarzanes (see Howe 2015b).

In autumn 330, H. was part of the King's *consilium*, which met to decide the fate of Philotas, who was implicated in the conspiracy of Demetrios (no. 358) the Bodyguard. H. no doubt influenced Alexander's views in their private conversations. He was of a particularly quarrelsome nature (Plut. *Alex.* 47.11–12; Plut. *Mor.* 337a; Plut. *Eum.* 2.1–3; Arr. 7.13.1; 7.14.9; cf. Berve II 173) and not above maligning others to Alexander (Plut. *Alex.* 55.1). It is hard to believe Plut. *Mor.* 339f that he and Alexander did not discuss the matter of Philotas. His name heads the list of those who came to Alexander's tent during the second watch on the night of Philotas' arrest (Curt. 6.8.17), and he appears as the foremost of Philotas' tormentors, recommending that he be tortured to gain a confession (Curt. 6.11.10; Plut. *Alex.* 49.12; cf. Heckel 1977b; Reames 2008). H. received, as his reward, command of one-half of the Companion Cavalry, a blatant case of nepotism. Given H.'s military inexperience, Alexander entrusted the other half to Black Kleitos (Arr. 3.27.4). In 329, H. is named as one of the King's advisers before the attack on the Skythians beyond the Iaxartes River (Curt. 7.7.9). In the spring of 328, when the army was divided into five parts, H. commanded one contingent (Arr. 4.16.2; cf. Curt. 8.1.1, 10) in a mission that appears to have done little more than recapture some small rebel fortresses. When the columns reunited at Marakanda in the summer of 328, H.'s role was adapted to suit his talents. A man of no extraordinary leadership skills, as his undistinguished military record shows, he provided useful service as Alexander's "utility-man." His first mission in Sogdiana was to synoecize local settlements (Arr. 4.16.3), an assignment that was to guarantee the loyalty of the native population by means of the establishment of garrisons, while it provided Alexander with a network of communications in the region. Alexander used him regularly for non-military operations: founding cities, building bridges, and securing lines of communication. Milns 1968, 112 claims Hephaistion bridged the Euphrates River (in two places) at Thapsakos, which is interesting in view of his later activities but undocumented by the ancient sources (cf. Arr. 3.7.1; Curt. 4.9.12). Ten days after the Kleitos affair, he was sent to collect provisions for the winter of 328/7 (Curt. 8.2.13). Aëtion's painting of the *Marriage of Alexander and Rhoxane* included him (Lucian *Aëtion* 5; Pollitt 175–6).

In spring 327, H. and Perdikkas were sent ahead into India with a substantial force to act as an advance guard, subdue the area around Peukelaotis, and build a boat-bridge on the Indos (Arr. 4.22.7–8; 4.23.1; 4.30.9; 5.3.5; Curt. 8.10.2–3; 8.12.4; Metz Epit. 48). It appears that, nominally at least, H. had supreme command, for Curtius' account of the dealings with Omphis, son of Taxiles, makes no mention of Perdikkas, who must certainly have been present. Perdikkas' participation in the mission may be attributable both to the need for a competent military man to accompany the relatively inexperienced H., and to their apparent personal compatibility. In the late stages of the campaigns, both men developed strong personal ties with Alexander, and it is not surprising that Perdikkas replaced the dead H. as Alexander's most trusted general and friend. The two generals followed the Kabul River valley, subduing some natives who resisted and winning over others by negotiation and show of force. At Peukelaotis they found that the local ruler, Astis, had rebelled (Arr. 4.22.8). He had perhaps been among the Indian hyparchs who had submitted to Alexander along with Omphis (Taxiles) (Arr. 4.22.6, so Anspach I 13), and his rebellion may have been caused not by anti-Macedonian sentiment but fear of his rival Sangaios, who had now allied himself with Omphis. Only after thirty days of siege did H. and Perdikkas take the city, handing it over to Sangaios, who later made an official surrender to Alexander; Astis himself was killed in the defense of his city. By the time that Alexander reached the Indos, H. had built the boat-bridge and acquired provisions, chiefly from Omphis, for the bulk of the army (Arr. 5.3.5; Curt. 8.10.2–3; 12.4,6, 15; Metz Epit. 48; Fuller 126–7).

In the battle with Poros at the Hydaspes, H. commanded cavalry and was directly under Alexander's control on the left wing (Arr. 5.12.2; Curt. 8.14.15). In concert with the hipparch Demetrios son of Althaimenes, he led a smaller force into the kingdom of the so-called cowardly (or bad) Poros, a cousin of the recently defeated king, who had fled eastward to the Gandaridai (Diod. 17.91.1–2; cf. Arr. 5.21.3–4). Alexander pursued him as far as the Hydraotes (Ravi) River, whence he sent H. into the defector's kingdom in order to hand it over to the friendly Poros (Arr. 5.21.5; cf. Diod. 17.91.2). H.'s mission was primarily organizational—to oversee the transfer of the kingdom and establish a Macedonian outpost on the Akesines (cf. Arr. 5.29.3)—and hardly a war of conquest despite the exuberant praise of Diod. 17.93.1. He rejoined the King after the Sangala campaign—a particularly bloody undertaking (Arr. 5.24.5) he was lucky to avoid—and before the expedition reached the Hyphasis (Diod. 17.93.1; Curt. 9.1.35). His duties in India continued to be primarily non-military. With Perdikkas he had founded the city of Orobatis (Arr. 4.28.5) *en route* to the Indos (which he bridged), and gathered provisions from Omphis. After transferring the territories of "bad" Poros to his namesake, he established a fortified site near the Akesines (Arr. 5.29.3); later he founded settlements at Patala and in the land of the Oreitai (Arr. 6.21.5). The latter, named Alexandria, may in fact have been the synoecism of Rhambakia, which Leonnatos completed (see Hamilton 1972).

H. is named as a trierarch of the Hydaspes fleet (Nearchos, *FGrH* 133 F1 = Arr. *Ind.* 18.3). In the actual descent of the Indos River system, Alexander divided the bulk of his land forces into two parts, with H. taking the larger portion, including two hundred elephants, down the eastern bank, while Krateros with the smaller force descended on the west (Arr. 6.2.2; Arr. *Ind.* 19.1–3; Diod. 17.96.1). The separation of the two commanders had become a virtual necessity: friction between them had erupted during the Indian campaign into open hand-to-hand combat, with the troops ready to come to the aid of their respective leaders (Plut. *Alex.* 47.11–12; cf. Diod. 17.114.1–2). The rivals were to proceed downstream, on opposite sides of the river, and to await the fleet, which would join them three days' sail from the point of departure (Arr. *Ind.* 19.3; Arr. 6.4.1; cf. Milns 1968, 227). Two days after Alexander's arrival at the predestined location, H. continued south toward the junction of the Hydaspes and Akesines, toward the territory of the peoples allied to the Mallians (Arr. 6.4.1). By the time he arrived, Alexander (who had sailed ahead) had subdued the tribes of that region and was preparing to march against the Mallians themselves. In the ancient accounts of that campaign—which saw the destruction of the Mallian town (near modern Multan: Wood 1997, 199–200) and the near-fatal injury to Alexander—there is no mention of H.

The army continued southward, with both H. and Krateros now occupying the eastern bank, since the terrain on the western side proved too difficult for Krateros' troops (Arr. 6.15.4). But Krateros was soon dispatched westward via the Bolan Pass to police the regions of Arachosia and Drangiana (Arr. 6.17.3; on the error at 6.15.5 see Bosworth 1976, 127–29; see also s.v. Krateros no. 622). Krateros' departure left H. as Alexander's second-in-command, but in fact the King continued to assign him organizational tasks. At Patala, in the delta, he built city walls while Alexander sailed down the western arm of the Indos (Arr. 6.18.1). On his return, the King found this task completed and instructed H. to fortify the harbor and build dockyards; he himself followed the river's eastern branch to the Ocean (Arr. 6.20.1). H. appears to have completed this work by the time of Alexander's return, although it is possible that Patala harbor, which became the base for Nearchos' Ocean fleet, was set in final order by Nearchos himself (Arr. 6.21.3).

Returning west, Alexander left H. with the main force at the Arabios River, while he, Leonnatos and Ptolemy ravaged the land of the Oreitai in three columns (Arr. 6.21.3; Curt. 9.10.6); the forces reunited at the borders of the Oreitai (Arr. 6.21.5). H. began the synoecism of Rhambakia in the land of the Oreitai, but was soon was replaced by Leonnatos and rejoined Alexander, who embarked on his march through the Gedrosian desert (Arr. 6.21.5, 22.3). After the army's rest in Karmania, he led the slower troops and the baggage train into Persia along the coastal route and rejoined Alexander—who took the lighter troops to Pasargadai and then through the Persian Gates (Arr. 6.28.7–29.1)—on the road to Sousa.

His unlikeable personality is well attested. He quarreled with, and was critical of, Kallisthenes in 327. Perhaps he objected to his brusqueness and austerity; for Kallisthenes himself was not an endearing person (Arr. 4.10; Plut. *Alex.* 53). H. enthusiastically espoused Alexander's orientalism and extravagance. Plut. *Alex.* 47.9 says that Alexander would employ H. in his dealings with the Persians, and this may have earned him the disfavor of both Macedonians and Greeks—though, as the beneficiary of Alexander's favoritism, he must have incurred resentment. Whether any of his contemporaries encouraged rumors that H. was Alexander's minion, cannot be determined (Ael. *VH* 12.7; Justin 12.12.11; Lucian, *Dial. Mort.* 12.4 (397); Diod. 17.114.3; cf. Tarn II 319–326, Appendix 18: "Alexander's Attitude to Sex," esp. 321). That he organized the unpopular *proskynesis* affair (Droysen I³ 312; Berve II 171; Schachermeyr 383; Hamilton 153; Wilcken 169; Green 1991, 375–6, though Chares of Mytilene, whom Schachermeyr regards as Alexander's "Chef der Kanzlei," would be a more suitable candidate for such work: Schachermeyr 1970, 17–18, 34) is not certain. H. was to claim that Kallisthenes had promised to do *proskynesis* and gone back on his word. He wasted no time in maligning Kallisthenes, once the sycophant, Demetrios son of Pythonax (Arr. 4.12.5), had drawn the man's misconduct to the attention of Alexander and his courtiers (Plut. *Alex.* 55.1). H. also quarreled with Eumenes: once over the assignment of living quarters (Plut. *Eum.* 2.2; see s.v. Euios no. 437), the second time on account of a gift or a prize (*Eum.* 2.8). Alexander was at first angry with H., but soon came to resent Eumenes. Fortunately for Eumenes, the animosity and H. were both short-lived; nevertheless, Eumenes was careful to avert any suspicion that he rejoiced at H.'s death by proposing that honors be granted to him posthumously (Arr. 7.14.9; cf. Diod. 17.115.1). Then there is the matter of his relationship with Krateros. We are told (Plut. *Alex.* 47.11) that Alexander rode up and openly reproached H., calling him a madman if he did not know that "without Alexander he would be nothing." Alexander noted that H. was *philalexandros* and Krateros *philobasileus* (Plut. *Alex.* 47.10; Plut. *Mor.* 181d; Diod. 17.114.2). With Krateros' departure in 324, H. emerged as the army's foremost officer, commanding the first hipparchy ("chiliarchy") of the Companions (Arr. 7.14.10).

At Sousa H. received a golden crown (Arr. 7.5.6) and was awarded Drypetis, sister of Alexander's own bride Stateira, as his wife; for Alexander wished their children to be first cousins (Arr. 7.4.5; cf. Diod. 17.107.6; cf. Curt. 10.5.20). From Sousa, H. led the bulk of the infantry to the Persian Gulf, while Alexander sailed down the Eulaios River to the coast (Arr. 7.7.1), and from here he followed the Tigris upstream where the army and fleet reunited (Arr. 7.7.6). Together they proceeded to Opis, and thence to Ekbatana (autumn 324). There, Alexander offered sacrifices and celebrated athletic and literary contests. Plut. *Alex.* 72.1 says that some 3,000 artists had arrived from Greece; cf. Arr. 7.14.1; Diod. 17.110.7–8 (dramatic contests only). Shortly thereafter H. fell ill with a fever, though the details of the ailment are vague (Plut. *Alex.* 72.2). Invariably, H.'s death is linked with heavy drinking: Arrian implies that the drinking bouts were the cause of his illness, Diodorus is more explicit, but Plutarch does not specify the cause of H.'s fever, only that immoderate eating and drinking were the proximate cause of his death. For accounts of his death see Arr. 7.14.1ff.; Diod. 17.110.8; Polyaenus 4.3.31 (incorrectly, it happened at Babylon!); Justin 12.12.11; Arr. 7.18.2–3; Epictetus 2.22.17; Plut. *Alex.* 72; Plut. *Pel.* 34.2; Nepos, *Eum.* 2.2; App. *B. Civ.* 2.152. Ephippos of Olynthos (*FGrH* 126), in his scandalous pamphlet *On the Deaths of Alexander and of Hephaistion*, will have attributed it solely to barbaric drinking habits. At any rate, it was on the seventh day of his illness that H. died (so Arr. 7.14.1). The only other details are supplied by Plutarch, according to whom, H. disregarded the strict diet imposed by his doctor Glaukos (Plut. *Alex.* 72.2; Glaukias in Arr. 7.14.4), who had gone off to the theater. After eating a boiled fowl and drinking a great quantity of wine, H.'s fever heightened and he died (Plut. *Alex.* 72.2); news of his deteriorating condition reached Alexander at the stadium, where he was watching the boys' races, but he returned too late and found H. already dead (Arr. 7.14.1). The King's grief was excessive: see Arr. 7.14.2; for different attitudes towards the display of emotion, Arr. 7.14.3. The emulation of Achilles: Arr. 7.14.4 (he also cut his own hair); Ael. *VH* 7.8; Plut. *Pelop.* 34.2 (horses' manes, demolished walls). For his refusal of food and drink, Arr. 7.14.8. Cf. Alexander's behavior after Kleitos' death, Arr. 4.9.1ff.; Plut. *Alex.* 51.10–52.1; Curt. 8.2.1ff.

Magnificent, indeed ostentatious, were the funeral arrangements, some of which were later cancelled at the instigation of Perdikkas, who conveyed H.'s body to Babylon.

The cost of his funeral pyre was estimated at 12,000 talents (Justin 12.12.12; Diod. 17.115.5; cf. Arr. 7.14.8, 10,000; cf. Hamilton 1984, 14; McKechnie 1995). In his role as Great King, Alexander ordered that the sacred fire of Persia be extinguished (Diod. 17.114.4; see also Schachermeyr 1970, 38–48, esp. 47) until such time as H.'s last rites had been completed. Not surprisingly, history was quick to discover prophecies of H.'s death (Arr. 7.18.2 = Aristoboulos, *FGrH* 139 F54). The seer Peithagoras foretold the deaths of both Alexander and H. (cf. App. *B. Civ.* 2.152). Alexander sent envoys of Siwah to inquire if H. should be worshipped as a god; the prudent oracle replied that he should be revered as a hero (Arr. 7.14.7: envoys are sent to Ammon. Arr. 7.23.6: the response comes that he should be revered as a hero; cf. Plut. *Alex.* 72.3, but incorrectly that he should be deified Diod. 17.115.6; Justin 12.12.12; Lucian, *Cal.* 17). The hero-cult of H. is alluded to by Hyper. 6.21; cf. Treves 1939 (the cult was in place already in April/May 323); Bickerman 1963; Habicht² 28–36. See also Hamilton 200–1, where these views are summarized; the notion that Alexander sought to introduce his own deification by means of H.'s hero cult antedates Habicht, see Kornemann 1901, 65. Arr. 7.23.6–8 relates that Alexander was willing to forgive Kleomenes his crimes in Egypt if he saw to a hero's shrine there. For small likenesses of H. made by the *hetairoi* see Diod. 17.115.1. The lion of Hamadan—3.56 m long and of brown sandstone (similar in size and style to the lions of Chaironeia and Amphipolis)—may be the one surviving monument of H. For this statue, and its history, see Luschey 1968: esp. 121–2; cf. Lane Fox 435. Hoffmann 170–1; Berve II 169–75 no. 357. Cf. Schachermeyr 511–15 and *passim*; Schachermeyr 1970, 31–7; Heckel, *Marshals*² 75–100; Reames-Zimmerman 1998; Reames 2010; Müller 2011, 2012a, 2018; Müller, *LexAM* 253–5.

514 HERAIOS

('Ηραῖος). Brother of Hermon and Apollodoros. Tyrant of Eresos (with his brothers) between 338 and 334 (so Lott 1996; confirmed by Wallace 2016). *OGIS* 8 = Tod no. 191. Hofstetter 77–8 no. 139; Berve, *Tyrannis* I 337–8, II 691 (see also literature listed under Apollodoros no. 145).

515 HERAKLEIDES

('Ηρακλείδης). Macedonian (Tataki 193 no. 2). Son of Antiochos (Arr. 3.11.8). Herakleides commanded the Bottiaian squadron of Companion Cavalry against the Triballians (Arr. 1.2.5) and remained an ilarch until at least the Gaugamela campaign (Arr. 3.11.8). After that he disappears from our sources. Sundwall, *RE* VIII (1912) 459 no. 17; Berve II 167 no. 347; Heckel 1992, 348–9.

516 HERAKLEIDES

('Ηρακλείδης). Possibly Macedonian (Tataki 321 no. 15). Son of Argaios. Early in 323 (that is, after the winter campaign against the Kossaians), Alexander commissioned H. to take some shipbuilders to Hyrkania and construct a fleet of warships with which to explore the Caspian Sea and its connecting rivers (Arr. 7.16.1–2). Since these formed part of Alexander's "Final Plans," Berve II 167 rightly questions whether the task was ever undertaken or completed. Nothing else is known about him, unless he can be identified with Herakleides the Thrakian, which is unlikely. Berve II 167 no. 348.

517 HERAKLEIDES

('Ηρακλείδης). Thrakian (Ps.-Call. 3.31.8; *LM* 97), presumably of high standing in Alexander's entourage. According to the *Liber de Morte*, H. attended Medeios' dinner party, at which Alexander became fatally ill. The Pamphlet alleges that Alexander was poisoned, and that H. was aware of the plot (Ps.-Call. 3.31.8–9; *LM* 97–8). Identification with Herakleides son of Argaios is unlikely, since the latter, on the basis of his patronymic, appears not to have been a Thrakian. Berve II 167 no. 350; Heckel 1988, 44.

518 HERAKLEIDES

('Ηρακλείδης). Family origin unknown; a Greek from Chalkedon, he was found in 330 with Dareios III as an ambassador of his state; Alexander released him and allowed him to return to his homeland (Arr. 3.24.5). Sundwall, *RE* VIII.2 (1912) 459; Berve II 167 no. 349; Hofstetter 79 no. 141.

519 HERAKLEIDES

('Ηρακλείδης, possibly, 'Ηρακλείτος). Greek from Erythrai (*IG* II² 1492B; the name is restored in lines 106, 116). One of two Antigonid officers in Athens (see also Polykleitos no. 980) named in the disbursement of funds in 306/5 from the 140 talent gift from Antigonos. H. was part of a contingent of troops left by Demetrios for the defense of Athens against Kassandros. The fact that he and Polykleitos are named separately from the *strategoi* suggests that they were military overseers. Hence, H. appears to be the man whom Demetrios left in charge of the forces in Athens when he left for Lydia in 295 (Polyaenus 5.17). His mercenary commander, Hierokles, warned him of a plot to betray the city. Nothing else is known about him. Billows 389 no. 498.

520 HERAKLEITOS

('Ηράκλειτος). Juggler (*thaumatopoios*) from Mytilene in Alexander's entourage (Athen. 1.20a), H. performed at the mass marriage ceremonies at Sousa in 324 (Chares, *FGrH* 125 F4 = Athen. 12.538e). Berve II 167–8 no. 351.

521 HERAKLEITOS

('Ηράκλειτος). Harpist (cf. Diog. Laert. 9.17) from Tarentum; performed at the mass marriage ceremony in Sousa in 324 (Chares, *FGrH* 125 F4 = Athen. 12.538e). He later became a jester (*spoudogeloios*), according to Diog. Laert. 9.17. Berve II 168 no. 352.

522 HERAKLES

('Ηρακλῆς). Son of Alexander the Great and Barsine (no. 287), the daughter of Artabazos (Diod. 20.20.1, 28.1; Justin 11.10.3; Plut. *Eum.* 1.7; cf. Justin 13.2.7; 15.2.3; Paus. 9.7.2; Curt. 10.6.11, 13; cf. App. *Syr.* 52.261, 54.275; Porphyr. Tyr. *FGrH* 260 F3 §2). Born in 327/6 or 325/4: according to Diod. 20.20.1 and Justin 15.2.3 respectively, he was seventeen or fifteen years old in 310/09. Most of his life was spent at Pergamon, which had belonged to the former satrapal territory of Barsine's father's family (Diod. 20.20.1; Justin 13.2.7). His claim to his father's throne was advocated by Nearchos (Curt. 10.6.10–12), but rudely rejected by the Macedonian cavalry officers (cf. Curt. 10.6.13); in 310/09, Polyperchon, recognizing the boy's potential had him (and his mother) brought to Europe, with the intention of installing him as King of Macedon. This move was, however, pre-empted by Kassandros, who bought off Polyperchon with promises of lands in Macedonia and the generalship of the Peloponnese, thereby inducing him to kill H. (Diod. 20.28; cf. Justin 15.2.3; by poison, according to Paus. 9.7.2). Justin 14.6.2 confuses H. with Alexander IV. In a later passage, Demetrios' claim that Antigonos had been guardian of Alexander's children (Justin 16.1.13) can refer only to the brief period in 320 when he was guardian of Alexander IV (and Philip III Arrhidaios); cf. Arr. *Succ.* 1.38. H.'s death must have occurred in late 309 or early 308 (Wheatley 1998a); see also Yardley-Wheatley-Heckel 233–8. Tarn 1921 (cf. II 330–7) expressed doubts about his paternity, which are now echoed by Müller 2019, 110–11. Nevertheless, his existence as a historical player in the age of the Diadochoi is virtually certain. Berve II 168 no. 353; Schoch, *RE* Supplbd. IV (1924) 731–2 no. 2; Tataki 322 no. 22; Tarn 1921; Brunt 1975; Wheatley 1998a; Landucci, *LexAM* 256. **Stemmata I and IV.**

523 HERAKON

(Ἡράκων). Macedonian officer (Tataki 323 no. 23). In 330, H. remained in Ekbatana with Parmenion, whom he, along with Kleandros (no. 589), Agathon (no. 21) and Sitalkes (no. 1053), later murdered on Alexander's orders (Curt. 10.1.1; rejected by Berve II 168 on the basis of Arr. 3.26.3). H. may have commanded mercenaries, though nothing specific is recorded about his unit. Little else is known about his career except that he had apparently been shifted to an administrative post in Sousa—perhaps when Harpalos moved from Ekbatana to Babylon. H. and his colleagues were summoned to Karmania in 324 and there charged with maladministration and temple robbery (Curt. 10.1.1–4; Arr. 6.27.3–4). Though Kleandros and Sitalkes were found guilty and executed, H. was acquitted, only to be indicted by the natives in Sousa on similar charges and this time required to pay the ultimate penalty (Arr. 6.27.5). Berve II 168–9 no. 354; Heckel 1992, 341.

524 HERMAIOS

(Ἑρμαῖος). Son of Nikias. One of twenty-four cavalrymen from Orchomenos, who served with Alexander's allied cavalry until the expedition reached Ekbatana in 330. There he and his compatriots were discharged. On their return (*c.*329), they made a dedication to Zeus Soter in Orchomenos (*IG* VII 3206). Berve II 152 no. 303.

525 HERMOGENES

(Ἑρμογένης). One of two slaves (the other was Kombaphes) who were present when Alexander dictated his last will and testament (Ps.-Call. 3.32.9; *LM* 103). This document was clearly a forgery produced in the early years of the Diadochoi (Heckel 1988; Bosworth 2000), but most individuals named therein were historical. Hence H. *may* have been a slave at Alexander's court. Berve II 152 no. 304.

526 HERMOLAOS

(Ἑρμόλαος). Macedonian (Tataki 309–10 no. 27). Son of Sopolis (almost certainly the ilarch). *Pais basilikos* and student of Kallisthenes (Arr. 4.13.2; Curt. 8.7.2–3), though the latter relationship was unduly emphasized in order to implicate Kallisthenes (no. 570), who was probably responsible for the education of all the Pages (but see Pownall, *LexAM* 292) and was most likely innocent of involvement in the Pages' conspiracy (Plut. *Alex.*

55.6; Curt. 8.7.10; 8.8.21; Justin 12.7.2). After he had been flogged for anticipating the King by striking a boar during the hunt (Arr. 4.13.2; Curt. 8.6.7), H. conspired with several other Pages to murder Alexander while he slept (Arr. 4.13.3; Curt. 8.6.8–10). In Curtius' version (8.6.8), it was H.'s lover Sostratos (no. 1065) who persuaded him to join a plot against the King. Whether there is any truth to the story of the boar hunt, we cannot say. But there were clearly political overtones (Arr. 4.14.2; Curt. 8.7), and the "conspiracy of the Pages" was symptomatic of the friction between Alexander (and his faithful clique) and the more conservative elements in the Macedonian aristocracy. Betrayed by some of his accomplices and denounced by his own father (Curt. 8.7.2), H. was arrested, tried (Curt. 8.6.24–8.18; Arr. 4.13.7–14.2), and condemned to death by stoning (Arr. 4.14.3; Plut. *Alex.* 55.7; Curt. 8.8.20 says that the Pages themselves put H. and his accomplices to death). Plaumann, *RE* VIII (1912) 890–1 no. 1; Hoffmann 179; Berve II 152–3 no. 305; Carney 1980–1; Heckel 1992, 292–3; Heckel 217–20.

527 HERODAS

('Ηρῴδας). Son of Tertikon from Eresos. Grandson of the tyrant Heraios, who, along with his brothers Hermos and Apollodoros, controlled the city before Alexander's invasion. He was banished when Eresos went over to the Macedonians. H., together with Agesimenes, surrendered and accompanied Hegelochos in 332/1 to Alexander in order to plead for a trial, leading to their restoration. But Alexander left the matter in the hands of Eresian *demos*, which chose to uphold the banishment along with that of the unnamed sons of Apollodoros (*OGIS* 8; Harding no. 112; Heisserer 36–45). Berve II 169 no. 356; see text in Heisserer 39, 45.

528 HEROMENES

('Ηρομένης). Macedonian from Lynkestis (Tataki 202 no. 10), son of Aëropos and brother of Arrhabaios (no. 213) and Alexander (no. 45; Arr. 1.25.1). H. and Arrhabaios were accused of conspiring with Pausanias of Orestis to assassinate Philip II in October 336, and executed by Alexander (Arr. 1.25.1; cf. Justin 11.2.1). The charges were apparently false—unless the Lynkestians had hopes of placing Amyntas Perdikka on the throne— and their elimination had more to do with their threat to Alexander than to conspiracy against Philip. Berve II 169 no. 355; Bosworth 1971a; Heckel 22–3. **Stemma XV.**

529 HIERON

('Ιέρων). Greek from Soloi on Kypros. In 324/3 he was sent by Alexander in a *triakontoros* to circumnavigate the Arabian peninsula. H. travelled a considerable distance—farther than either Archias or Androsthenes—but was forced to turn back by the desolate nature of the coastline (Arr. 7.20.7; cf. Arr. *Ind.* 43.8–9). Although he is not named in Arrian's *Indica*, it is likely that he participated in Nearchos' voyage—his designation as *kybernetes* may point to his role in the enterprise—from the Indos delta to the Persian Gulf. Nothing else is known about him. Berve II 183 no. 382.

530 HIERON

('Ιέρων). One of three officers (see also Machaon no. 676, and Sopolis no. 1063) of the garrison stationed at Iasos by Polemaios, the nephew of Antigonos (cf. Diod. 19.75.1–6). An inscription (*I.Iasos* I no. 2), dating in all likelihood to 309/8, when Polemaios defected to Ptolemy (Diod.20.27.1–3), shows that they and the city came to terms with Ptolemy I. Billows 390 no. 50; Bagnall 89–91.

531 HIERONYMOS

('Ἱερώνυμος). Greek from Kardia (*Suda* I 201) and, perhaps, a kinsman of Eumenes (cf. Diod. 18.50.4). Agatharchides (*FGrH* 86 F4 = [Lucian] *Macrob.* 22) says that he lived to the age of 104, and since Hieronymos recorded the death of Pyrrhos in 272 (*FGrH* 154 F15), it appears that Hieronymos' life ran from roughly mid fourth to mid-third century. Hence it is conjectured (and it is nothing more than conjecture) that he lived from *c.*364 to 260 (Reuss 1876, 1 suggests a birthdate of 361, assuming that he was close in age to Eumenes). But, since Eumenes was forty-five at the time of his death in 317/16 (Nepos, *Eum.* 13.1) and there is a possibility that Eumenes was Hieronymos' uncle, a birthdate in the late 350s may be preferable (cf. Hornblower, *Hieronymus* 6). Of his life we know little. In 320/19 he was sent to negotiate an agreement between Eumenes (who was besieged at Nora) and Antipatros (Diod. 18.42.1), and after Antipatros' death he acted as a go-between for Antigonos and Eumenes (Plut. *Eum.* 12.2; Diod. 18.50.4). He appears to have served with Eumenes in the war with Antigonos and become a prisoner-of-war after the defeat at Gabiene, but was later held in a position of trust by the Antigonids (Diod. 19.44.3). In 312, he was instructed to collect bitumen from the Dead Sea (Diod. 19.100.1–2) but the project was thwarted by the Arabs. He was present at Antigonos' death at Ipsos in 301 ([Lucian] *Macrob.* 22). In 293, Demetrios left him as governor (*epimeletes kai harmostes*) of Thebes (Plut. *Demetr.* 39.3–7), and it appears that from this point on he developed closer links with Antigonos Gonatas, son of Demetrios Poliorketes and Phila. Whether he was with Antigonos Gonatas in 272 when Pyrrhos died is unclear. Paus. 1.9.8 says he was biased against all Successors except Antigonos. When he said Lysimachos destroyed the Epeirot royal tombs he was lying; perhaps he hated Lysimachos because he destroyed Kardia and replaced it with Lysimacheia (Paus. 1.9.8). But see Lund 13–18, who remarks that "if Lysimachos was the target of negative bias on the part of Hieronymos of Kardia, this seems to manifest itself mainly in understatement." Reuss 1876; Hornblower, *Hieronymus*; Sandberger 113–14 no. 38; Billows 390–2 no. 51; Jacoby, *FGrH* 154; id., *RE* VIII.2 (1913) 1540–60 no. 10; Brown 1947; Olshausen nos. 1, 69.

532 HIMERAIOS

('Ἱμεραῖος). Son of Phanostratos, brother of Demetrios of Phaleron. Anti-Macedonian politician and supporter of Hypereides, he was nevertheless a prosecutor of Demosthenes in the Harpalos case ([Plut.] *Mor.* 846c; cf. Roisman and Worthington 230; Worthington 52–4 for H. and Deinarchus' *Against Demosthenes*; Tritle 1988, 120–1 for supposed political affiliations). H. fled Athens and went first to Aigina after the Lamian War; he was sentenced to death *in absentia* by the Athenians on Demades' proposal. Antipatros sent Archias of Thourioi to hunt him down (Arr. *Succ.* 1.13–14; cf. Karystios of Pergamon *ap.* Athen. 12.542e). Kirchner 7578; Berve II 184 no. 385. Berve-Schoch, *RE* Supplbd. IV (1924) 743.

533 HIPPARCHOS

('Ἵππαρχος). Son of Heniochos of Kyrene. Honored for aiding the Samian exiles before 322 and for his treatment of Samians under his command, presumably in the period 306–

301 (*IG* XII 6, 31, a decree moved by Aspasios son of Theupropos; revised by Paschidis 390 to shortly after Ipsos). Official in the service of Demetrios and Antigonos. Otherwise unknown. Billows 392 no. 52; Paschidis 389–90.

534 HIPPIAS

(Ἱππίας). Greek, presumably Spartan (Poralla 67 no. 388). An agent of the Spartan king Agis III, H. was sent in 333/2 to the King's brother, Agesilaos, conveying to Tainaron ten triremes and thirty talents of silver, which Agis had secured from Pharnabazos at Siphnos. He brought also Agis' instructions that Agesilaos should pay the crews and sail to Krete in order to prepare it as a safe retreat for the Persian fleet (Arr. 2.13.6; cf. Bosworth I 224). What became of him is unknown. Berve II 184–5 no. 388; Hofstetter 89 no. 156.

535 HIPPIAS

(Ἱππίας). Epeirot (Molossian, Hammond, *Epirus* 805), possibly identical with the Ambrakiot who was honored at Delphi (J. Bousquet, *BCH* 64/65 (1940/41) 83; Hammond, *Epirus* 805 lists them separately). H. was a supporter of Aiakides and his family. When Aiakides was driven from the throne, H., with Androkleion (no. 98) and Neandros (no. 764), fled with the young prince, Pyrrhos, to Megara in Macedonia, while their pursuers were held off and finally routed by Androkleides (no. 97) and Angelos (no. 107; Plut. *Pyrrh.* 2.2; for a full and dramatic account of the escape see Plut. *Pyrrh.* 2.3–8). The party came eventually to the court of the Illyrian king, Glaukias, whose wife was Aiakid by blood (Justin 17.3.18–19, see s.v. Beroa). Sandberger 114–15 no. 39.

536 HIPPODAMAS

(Ἱπποδάμας). Son of Dionysios. Brother of Apollonios (no. 153) and Glaukippos (no. 476), from Antigoneia. Honored along with his two brothers by the Eretrians for favors to their compatriots serving with Demetrios' fleet (*IG* XII.9, 210 = *Syll*³ 348; cf. Wilhelm, *AE* 1892, 119–25). They served Demetrios in Greece in 304–302. Cf. Diod. 20.110.2. Launey 1264; Billows 392–3 no. 53.

537 HIPPOKRATES

(Ἱπποκράτης). Doctor from Kos. Son of Drakon, the personal physician of Rhoxane. H. appears to have succeeded his father in this position and was killed along with Rhoxane in 310 at Amphipolis (cf. Diod. 19.105.2–3). He was also the author of a work entitled *Iatrika* (*Suda* I 567). Berve II 185 no. 389. Sherwin-White 468

538 HIPPOSTRATOS

(Ἱππόστρατος). The name appears to be Macedonian, but it was also the name of the father of Oxythemis of Larisa, who was honored by the Athenians in 307/6 for service to the city and support of Antigonos and Demetrios (*Syll*³ 343). Hence, Billows 393 follows Dittenberger in identifying him as a brother of Medeios, the uncle of the honorand (cf. Bengtson I 180 n.2). But an identification of the father of Oxythemis with Antigonos' *strategos* is anything but certain, nor does Diodorus says anything about the man's ethnicity or his fate. Although both Medeios and Oxythemis are attested as supporters of Antigonos, H. may well have been a Macedonian and unrelated to his Thessalian namesake. After the defection of Peithon son of Krateuas, H. was sent by Antigonos to support Orontobates, to whom the satrapy of Media was entrusted, with a force of 3,000 mercenary infantry and five hundred cavalrymen (Diod. 19.46.5). This separation of the functions of satrap and *strategos* represents a continuation of Alexander's practice in the former Achaimenid heartland (thus, rightly, Beloch IV² 1.116) and the somewhat larger number of troops at H.'s disposal reflect the need to suppress a rebellion by Peithon's followers and not that Antigonos had revived for H. Peithon's erstwhile position as *strategos* of the Upper Satrapies (cf. Diod. 19.14.1); for if the latter had been the case, H. would undoubtedly have been given satrapal authority, which would have allowed him to draw on the regional troops of Media. For the time being, H.'s role was to support the newly installed native satrap. As the two were on their march, they were attacked at night by the supporters of Peithon (Diod. 19.47.2), who enjoyed only limited success and were eventually overcome by the forces of H. and Orontobates, who trapped them in a gorge and killed in a last stand Peithon's friend Meleagros (no. 697) and Okranes the Mede (Diod. 19.47.3–4). It is, however, possible that H. was killed in the fighting (Beloch IV² 1.117 n.5). Nothing else is recorded about him, but if he did survive he was apparently not a man of great consequence. He was soon replaced by Nikanor, who exercised greater powers. Such a demotion (which Billows 393 supposes occurred "quite shortly after his appointment") would appear to rule out H.'s identity as a brother of Medeios of Larisa. Otto, *RE* VIII.2 (1913) no. 5; Billows 393 no. 54; Bengtson I 181–3.

539 HIPPOSTRATOS

(Ἱππόστρατος). Thessalian from Larisa. Father of Oxythemis and brother of Medeios (*Syll*³ 343). Since both were active supporters of the Antigonids, it is a fair assumption that H. was as well. Unless he is identical with no. 538 above, which does not seem very likely, he is otherwise unattested.

540 HOLKIAS

(Ὁλκίας). Perhaps Illyrian, though Berve II 283 identifies him as Macedonian (cf. Hoffmann 211–12; Tataki 391 no. 1). This enigmatic figure, who plays such an important role in the events described by the political pamphlet on *The Last Days and Testament of Alexander the Great* (*LM* 97–8, 103, 106, 109, 111–12, 114, 116, 122; Ps.-Call. 3.31–3) and who may be the author of the tract, is attested only once outside the work: as a commander of infantry, he led an uprising of some three thousand troops against Antigonos in 319. There was some concern that the rebels might make their way to the outlawed faction under Alketas, and Antigonos captured H.'s men through the agency and trickery of Leonidas. Their lives were spared on the condition that they would return to Macedonia and remain inactive (Polyaenus 4.6.6). In the Pamphlet, H. is depicted as intimate with the King, and his sister Kleodike (or Kleonice) was considered a worthy bride for Leonnatos. His importance is almost certainly exaggerated, but it is possible that he was a member of a prominent Illyrian family—H. is awarded Illyria in the Testament: *LM* 122; Ps.-Call. 3.33.23—who was educated at the court of Philip II and thus a *syntrophos* of Alexander (see further Heckel 1988). It appears that Holkias served with Alexander at some point in the Asiatic campaign (334–323), perhaps as a junior infantry officer; from 323 to 320, he belonged to the Royal Army of Perdikkas, and after his leader's death made his way to Triparadeisos. There he was assigned to Antigonos, to whom Antipatros had assigned the extirpation of Eumenes and the Perdikkan party. H.'s sympathies, however, lay with the latter, whom he attempted to join at the beginning of 319. After his capture by Leonidas he was paroled to Macedonia, but after Antipatros' death, H. became a supporter of Polyperchon, for whom he may have composed the *Last Days and Testament* as part of the propaganda war against Kassandros (for different views of the pamphlet's date and purpose see Ausfeld 1895, 1901; Merkelbach 1954; and Bosworth 2000). Berve II 283 no. 580; Launey 1182; Billows 412–13 no. 83; Heckel 1988, 79–81. See also Ausfeld 1895, 1901 for more detailed discussion; Merkelbach 1954, 121–51, 220–51; Bosworth 2000.

541 HORISMOS

(Ὁρισμός). Son of Damistratos. From Elaia in Aiolis. Honored by the Samians for help during their exile. The decree (*IG* XII 6, 23) shows that at some point after 306, H. was in service of Demetrios Poliorketes. Schoch, *RE* Supplbd. IV (1924) 761; Billows 393–4 no. 55; Paschidis 386 s.v. Melouchos son of Myon (the mover of the decree).

542 HYDARNES

(Ὑδάρνης). Prominent Persian. H. had apparently served with the fleet of Pharnabazos, which recaptured Miletos in 333 (cf. Curt. 4.1.37). H. was placed in command of the Persian forces there but was defeated in 333/2 by Balakros (Curt. 4.5.13). What became of him is unknown. Berve II 376 no. 759; Shayegan 109 no. 51.

543 HYDARNES

(Ὑδάρνης). Son of Mazaios (Arr. 7.6.4). He may have surrendered to Alexander along with his father at Babylon (Curt. 5.1.17). H., along with his brother, Artiboles, was enrolled in the Companion Cavalry in 324 (Arr. 7.6.4). There is no compelling reason to identify him (as Berve II 376 and Shayegan 109 no. 51 do) with the man who served on the Aegean coast with Pharnabazos. Berve II 376 no. 759.

544 HYDRAKES

(Ὑδράκης). Gedrosian. H. acted as pilot for Nearchos, promising to take the fleet from the harbor of Mosarna to Karmania (Arr. *Ind.* 27.1). Nothing else is known about him. Berve II 376 no. 760; Shayegan 109 no. 52.

547 HYPERBOLOS

(Ὑπέρβολος). Flute player from Kyzikos. H. performed at the mass marriage ceremony in Sousa in 324 (Athen. 12.538f = Chares, *FGrH* 125 F4). Berve II 376 no. 760.

546 HYPEREIDES

(Ὑπερείδης). Athenian (Kirchner 13912). Son of Glaukippos. Born 390. He is said to have been a student of Plato and Isokrates (Athen. 8.342c). Father of Glaukippos (Plut. *Phoc.* 4.2). He began his career as a *logographos* (speech writer for others). His political stance was anti-Macedonian, and he was an opponent of Phokion (Plut. *Phoc.* 23.3; but unlike him, H. was not a general and man of action: *Phoc.* 7.5), and Demades (cf. his remark about the mother of Demeas: Athen. 13.591f). H. made a name for himself with his prosecution of Aristophon in 362 and of Philokrates in 343. He opposed the surrender of those generals and rhetors whose extradition was demanded by Alexander after the fall of Thebes in 335 ([Plut.] *Mor.* 848e), and his name appears (perhaps incorrectly) on three lists of those named by Alexander (Arr. 1.10.4; *Suda* A 2704; Plut. *Phoc.* 17.2; see Plut. *Dem.* 23.4 and Bosworth I 94). In 323 he went on a mission to the Peloponnese to encourage rebellion against Macedon (Justin 13.5.10) and, after the death of Leosthenes in the Lamian War, he was chosen to deliver the funeral oration for the Athenian dead, because he was foremost in both his eloquence and his hostility to Macedon (Diod. 18.13.5). When Athens suffered defeat in the Lamian War, H. fled the city (Plut. *Phoc.* 26.2). Antipatros demanded that he and Demosthenes be delivered up (Plut. *Phoc.* 27.5). He was hunted down by Archias of Thourioi, who found Hypereides and Himeraios, the brother of Demetrios of Phaleron, in Aigina and dragged them from the sanctuary of Aiakos. Archias sent them to Antipatros at Kleonai, where H.'s tongue was cut out before he was killed (Plut. *Dem.* 28.4; Arr. *Succ.* 1.13; cf. Plut. *Phoc.* 29.1). His body was repatriated and buried against an Athenian prohibition [Plut.] *Mor.* 849c; *Suda* Υ 294; see Glaukippos no. 475; Philopeithes no. 936). For a brief account of his life see [Plut.] *Mor.* 848d–850b. Berve II 376–8 no. 762; Roisman and Worthington 246–61; Cooper, *LexAM* 269–70.

547 HYPSIDES

The name appears only in its Latin form. Macedonian (Tataki 443 no. 1). Probably a lower-ranking officer, H. was a friend of Menedemos. In the Polytimetos battle he remained by the side of his mortally wounded friend although Menedemos urged him to take his horse and save himself. H. instead charged into the enemy and gained a glorious death (Curt. 7.7.36–7). That the story was invented for dramatic effect is doubted by Atkinson, *Curzio* II 472. H. is otherwise unattested. Berve II 378–9 no. 764.

548 HYSTASPES

('Υστάσπης). High-ranking Persian, kinsman of Dareios III and the husband of an unnamed granddaughter of Artaxerxes III Ochos (see A49). H. was captured in 330 after the death of Dareios (Curt. 6.2.7). Curtius adds that H. had been one of Dareios' military commanders, and we may suppose that he was one of the many unnamed commanders of regional troops at Gaugamela. It seems highly likely that he is identical with Hystaspes "the Baktrian," who commanded the new oriental cavalry squadron (Arr. 7.6.5); Berve's suggestion that he was a descendant of Hystaspes son of Xerxes (Diod. 11.69.2) is rightly questioned by Briant 1033. Berve II 378 no. 763; Shayegan 109 no. 53.

I

549 IDOMENEUS

('Ιδομενεύς). Family background unknown; probably Greek. Agent of Antigonos Monophthalmos. In 315—when Antigonos was organizing his opposition to Ptolemy, Lysimachos, and Kassandros—I. and Moschion were sent to confirm the support of the Rhodians (Diod. 19.57.4). The mission was apparently successful: according to Diodorus, Antigonos was soon having ships built there using imported timber (19.58.5). Sundwall, *RE* IX.1 (1914) 909 no. 3; Olshausen 93 no. 70; Billows 394 no. 56.

550 ILIONEUS

Youngest son of Artabazos (no. 223), probably by a wife (A37) other than the sister of Mentor and Memnon (cf. Diod. 16.52.4). The name is attested only in Curtius, but suits the family's interests in the Hellespontine region. I. was captured by Parmenion at Damaskos in 333/2 (Curt. 3.13.13). What became of him, we do not know. Berve II 183–4 no. 384; Shayegan 109 no. 54. **Stemma IV.**

551 IOLAOS

('Ιόλαος, Ἰόλλας). The youngest son of Antipatros and, along with his brother Philip, probably a Page (*pais basilikos*) of Alexander during the latter portion of the Asiatic campaign (Justin 12.14.9: *Philippus et Iollas praegustare ac temperare potum regis soliti*). I. is given the title οἰνοχόος or "wine pourer" (Plut. *Alex.* 74.2; cf. Arr. 7.27.2: οἰνοχόος βασιλικός), but it is likely that he held this position as one of the Pages (cf. Aretis the *anaboleus*, also identified as a Page). Except for rumors that he was the *eromenos* of Medeios of Larisa (Arr. 7.27.2) and responsible for poisoning the King (Arr. 7.27.1–3; Justin 12.13.6–10, 12.14.6–9; Curt. 10.10.14–19; Plut. *Alex.* 77.2–3; *LM* 89, 96–100; cf. Pliny, *HN* 30.149; Paus. 8.18.6), nothing else is known of his career under Alexander. In 323/2, he acted as an intermediary for his father and Perdikkas, bringing to Asia in the following year his sister Nikaia, the latter's intended bride (Arr. *Succ.* 1.21). Thereafter, he appears to have returned to his father's court in Macedonia. By 317/6, he was already dead: Olympias, as an act of vengeance against her son's "murderers," overturned his grave (Diod. 19.11.8; cf. 19.35.1). [Plut.] *Mor.* 849f claims that Hypereides proposed a decree honoring the assassins of Alexander; but Oikonomides' attempt (1987) to link this statement with *IG* II² 561 fails on that grounds that the decree was moved by Stratokles, and the Iolaos in question (see below) was still alive in the late 300s. Berve II 184 no. 386; Heckel 1992, 293. **Stemma V.**

552 IOLAOS

('Ιόλαος, Ἰόλλας). Prominent Macedonian; family background unknown. I. was a member of the conspiracy of Demetrios (no. 358) the Bodyguard in 330, whose name was given by Dimnos (no. 377) to Nikomachos (Curt. 6.7.15) and eventually reported to Alexander (cf. Curt. 6.8.2). He and his accomplices were found guilty by the Macedonian army and stoned to death (Curt. 6.11.38). The names of the conspirators are found only in Curtius, but there is no good reason to assume they were invented. Berve II 184 no. 387; Heckel 1977b, 21.

553 IOLAOS

('Ιόλαος, 'Ιόλλας). Macedonian. Family background unknown. An inscription from Athens (*IG* II² 561) honors him, Philip and, perhaps, a third individual as supporters of Demetrios and Antigonos and former *somatophylakes* of a certain King Alexander. I. may have been appointed Somatophylax of Alexander IV at Triparadeisos. Apart from his continued support for the Antigonids and his *eunoia* towards the Athenians, nothing else is known about him. Billows 394–5 no. 57; *IG* II² 561; cf. Heckel 1980b, 1981a; Burstein 1977a; Habicht 1973, 373 n.35; Schoch, *RE* Supplbd. IV (1924) s.v. no. 5a.

554 IPHIKRATES

('Ιφικράτης). Athenian from Rhamnous (Kirchner 7736). Son of the famous general Iphikrates and a sister of the Thrakian dynast Kotys, and thus born *c*.370 (Hofstetter 95 n.2; Davies 249). Sent by the Athenians on an embassy to Dareios, I. was captured, along with Euthykles the Spartiate and Thessaliskos and Dionysodoros the Thebans, in late 333 by Parmenion at Damaskos (Arr. 2.15.2; cf. Curt. 3.13.15). Curtius adds the Athenians, Aristogeiton and Dropides, and names, instead of Euthykles, Pasippos, Onomastorides, Onomas, and Kallikratidas. But this appears to confuse those captured at Damaskos with those taken after Dareios' death in 330 (cf. Atkinson I 464–5). I. received kind treatment from Alexander, who respected both Athens and his father's fame, but he died of illness soon after his capture; Alexander sent his remains to his relatives in Athens (Arr. 2.15.4). Berve II 186 no. 393; Davies 251; Hofstetter 95 no. 165; Hofstetter 1972, 99.

555 ISOKRATES

('Ισοκράτης). (436–338). Athenian (Kirchner 7716). Son of Theodoros. Famous rhetor and teacher. He studied under, among others, the sophist Gorgias, and in 403 he spoke in favor of Theramenes, whom the Thirty sentenced to death. He was best known as a pamphleteer who promoted Panhellenism, urging the Greeks to unite under leader states or individuals (Athens, Sparta, Alexander of Pherai, Philip II) and wage war on Persia. In 342/1 he wrote a *Letter to Alexander* (*Ep.* 5), which accompanied a letter to Philip. The letter is extremely short and comments on Alexander's education, praising him for not paying excessive attention to *eristic* (i.e. argument for its own sake) and for devoting himself to acquiring the kind of wisdom that will benefit a statesman. Although the authenticity of the *Letter* was once challenged, it is now generally regarded as genuine. We have no clear idea, however, to what extent Isokrates' ideas of Panhellenism and unity in the face of the common enemy (i.e. Persia) influenced Alexander's thinking (on which see Flower 2000). I. died in 338, the year of Chaironeia. Berve II 185–6 no. 391; Blaß II² 327–8; Münscher, *RE* IX.2 (1916) 2146ff.; Heinrichs, *LexAM* 376–7 s.v. "Panhellenism."

556 ITANES

(Ἰτάνης, Istanes = Wistana preferred by Marquart II 162 n.1). Son of Oxyartes; brother of Rhoxane. He was probably in Alexander's entourage since early 327, when the King married his sister. Curt. 8.4.22, however, refers to the sons of Chorienes (Sisimithres; the MSS have *cohortandus*, almost certainly a corruption of Chorienes. Alde's emendation to Oxyartes is implausible; cf. Heckel 1986, 225). In 324 he was enrolled in the *agema* of the Companions, along with other orientals (Arr. 7.6.5). What became of him after the King's death, we do not know. Berve II 186 no. 392; Shayegan 109 no. 55.

K

557 KADMEIA

(Καδμεία). Sister of Neoptolemos II. Her name suggests that she may have been the daughter of Kleopatra (daughter of Olympias and Philip II) and Alexander I of Epeiros. This couple married in October 336, and a birthdate in the summer of 335 (Berve II 186: "im August 335") would coincide with Alexander the Great's victory over the Thebans (cf. Heckel 1981d, 82, with n.18, a conclusion I would now withdraw). But this identification clouds the picture of the Molossian dynasty, since it requires us to accept that Neoptolemos II was a son of Alexander I; and this is rendered unlikely for various reasons, including the fact that the inscriptional evidence does not identify Neoptolemos' father Alexander as *basileus*. Nor is it certain that the name Kadmeia commemorated a historical event; possibly there are mythical connections. She could have been the daughter of Alexander son of Alketas II. It was in K.'s home that her brother Neoptolemos boasted that he would eliminate Pyrrhos—a remark overheard by a certain Phainarete, who reported it to Pyrrhos' wife Antigone (Plut. *Pyrrh.* 5.11). What became of her, we do not know: she may have perished with her brother. Berve II 186; Klotzsch 84; Hammond, *Epirus* 560 n.1; Sandberger 115 no. 40; Garoufalias 191–2; Heckel 2021. **Stemma IIa–b.**

558 KALANOS

(Κάλανος, Diod. Κάρανος) Indian philosopher, better known by the nickname Kalanos for his habit of addressing Greeks and Macedonians with the word καλέ (instead of χαῖρε), according to Onesikritos (*FGrH* 134 F17b = Plut. *Alex.* 65.5, who says his real name was Sphines). This appears to be a false etymology and Kalanos may in fact be a Graecism of the Indian Kalyāna. K. was born in 397 (Strabo 15.1.68 C717; Diod. 17.107.2) and was among those philosophers summoned to Alexander at Taxila. A hostile tradition arose which contrasted the actions of Dandamis (Mandanis), who rejected Alexander's claims to divinity and was swayed neither by the promise of gifts nor the threat of punishment, and K. who is depicted as lacking self-control and a slave to Alexander's dinner table (Strabo 15.1.68 C718). Lysimachos, who is elsewhere reported to have had an interest in philosophy, was said to have been one of his students, and it was to him that he presented his Nesaian horse (Arr. 7.3.4). K. accompanied Alexander as far as Pasargadai, where he became ill for the first time in his life (Diod. 17.107.2). On the borders of Sousiana he mounted his own funeral pyre and was consumed by the flames. For the various accounts of his death see Arr. 7.3.1–6; Diod. 17.107.1–6; Val. Max. 1.8 ext. 10; Strabo 15.1.68 C717–18, cf. 15.1.4 C686. He was reported to have said to Alexander as he mounted his own funeral pyre, "I shall see you shortly," thus alluding to Alexander's imminent death in Babylon (Val. Max. 1.8 ext. 10). Kroll, *RE* X.2 (1919) 1544–6 no. 2; Berve II 187–8 no. 396; Bosworth 2013, 76–7; Stoneman 2019, 312–19.

KALANOS. See KARANOS.

559 KALAS

(Κάλας). Son of Harpalos (Arr. 1.14.3; Diod. 17.17.4), probably a kinsman (possibly a cousin) of Harpalos the Treasurer, hence a member of the Elimeiot royal house. K. crossed into Asia Minor with Parmenion, Attalos, and Amyntas (presumably the son of Arrhabaios) in spring 336 (Justin 9.5.8–9; cf. Diod. 16.91.2), unless, as Berve II 188 conjectures, K. was Attalos' successor and was not sent to Asia until later. K.'s conduct of the war in the Troad was far from successful: he nearly lost Kyzikos to Memnon (Diod. 17.7.3–8; Polyaenus 5.44.5) and was driven back into Rhoiteion (Diod. 17.7.10; cf. McCoy 1989, 423–4; Judeich 305–6). When Alexander crossed in 334, K. was appointed hipparch of the Thessalian cavalry (Diod. 17.17.4), which he commanded at the Granikos (Arr. 1.14.3), though he and the other officers on the left were subordinated to Parmenion (Arr. 1.14.1). But he was soon assigned the satrapy of Hellespontine Phrygia and took up residence in Daskyleion, which Parmenion occupied (Arr. 1.17.1–2). Together with Lynkestian Alexander, who now commanded the Thessalian horse, K. gained control of "Memnon's Land" (Arr. 1.17.8; cf. Polyaenus 4.3.15). In 333, Paphlagonia was annexed to Hellespontine Phrygia (Arr. 2.4.2; Curt. 3.1.24), and K. helped Antigonos the One-Eyed and Balakros son of Nikanor in suppressing Persian resistance to Macedonian authority in Asia Minor (Curt. 4.5.13; cf. Billows 43–5). Memnon of Herakleia (*FGrH* 434 F12 §4) records a defeat at the hands of a Bithynian dynast named Bas no later than 328/7 (cf. Bosworth I 127, with further literature). This need not have been the occasion of K.'s death, nor is it likely, as Billows suggests (45, with n.85), that the campaign against Bas, and K.'s death, occurred in the late 330s. Alexander appointed Demarchos satrap of Hellespontine Phrygia, probably late in the campaign (Arr. *Succ.* 1.6). Badian's suggestion (1961, 18) that K. was removed from office in the aftermath of Harpalos' misconduct is mere speculation. Berve II 188 no. 397 and *RE* Supplbd. IV (1924) 854 no. 1; Baumbach 29, 43, 56; Billows 38–40, 44–5; Heckel 1992, 355–7 and *Marshals*² 217–18; Tataki 195 no. 11. **Stemma XIII.**

560 KALLAS

(Κάλλας). Macedonian (Tataki 335 no. 8). For the name see Hoffmann 196. General of Kassandros, and thus perhaps an officer in the forces that Alexander left behind with Antipatros when he set out on the Asiatic campaign; for, in his struggle with Polyperchon, Kassandros relied on *hetairoi* who were personally loyal to himself (cf. Diod. 18.49.2). In 317, after Olympias had defeated Adea-Eurydike and moved on to Pydna, Kassandros sent K. against Polyperchon's army in Perrhaibia (Diod. 19.35.3). Here K. managed to persuade the bulk of Polyperchon's army to defect, leaving their commander helpless and thus contributing to the collapse of Olympias' cause (Diod. 19.36.6). Nothing else is known about him. Hoffmann 196; Schoch, *RE* Supplbd. IV (1924) 854–5 no. 3 s.v. "Kalas."

561 KALLIAS

(Καλλίας). Son of Mnesarchos, from Chalkis (Aesch. 3.85), brother of Taurosthenes (Hyper. 5.20). K. was politically active in Euboia during the 340s, and was falsely accused of betraying the island to Philip. He gained Athenian citizenship through the efforts of Demosthenes (Din. 1.44), who in 332/1 appears to have sent him on a mission to Olympias (no. 808)—apparently at the same time as Aristion's mission to Hephaistion (Hyper.

5.20; cf. Aesch. 3.162). Aesch. 3.85 says Demosthenes accepted bribes for this service; cf. 3.103–4. Swoboda, *RE* X.2 (1919) 1624–6 no. 14; Berve II 189 no. 399; Schaefer III² 195 n.5.

562 KALLIKLES

(Καλλικλῆς). Athenian (Kirchner 7934). Son of Arrheneides, of the deme Paiania (Plut. *Dem.* 25.7; *IG* II² 1632). K. was one of the politicians implicated in the Harpalos affair in 334 but, when the Athenians conducted a search of the houses of those suspected of taking Harpalos' money, they avoided his because he was newly married and his wife was in the house (Theopompos, *FGrH* 115 F330 = Plut. *Dem.* 25.7–8). He was trierach in Athens in 322 (*IG* II² 1632). Kroll, *RE* X.2 (1919) 1635 no. 2; Berve II 189 no. 400; Davies 68.

563 KALLIKRATES

(Καλλικράτης). Unknown background, perhaps Greek. Accompanied Alexander on the Asiatic expedition and was placed in charge of the treasures at Sousa in late 331 (Curt. 5.2.17). Identification with the *philos* of Ptolemy (Diod. 20.21.2–3) is possible but highly doubtful.

Berve II 189 no. 401.

564 KALLIKRATES

(Καλλικράτης). Macedonian (Tataki 336 no. 14; *IG* XI.2 203B l. 78). *Philos* of Ptolemy Soter, who in 310 sent him with Argaios (Seibert 1969, 185 calls it a "Sonderauftrag") to put Nikokles, king of Paphos, to death because he had formed a secret alliance with Antigonos (Diod. 20.21.2–3). At Paphos K. received soldiers from Menelaos (Ptolemy's brother and general: cf. Diod. 19.62.4) and ordered Nikokles (on confusion with Nikokreon see Gesche 1974) to commit suicide; this he did and his whole family followed suit (cf. Polyaenus 8.48; see s.v. Axiothea no. 273). K. made two dedications of crowns at Delos (full epigraphic references in Hauben 1970, 26 and Tataki 336) probably in 308 (Hauben 1970, 31) and in the company of Ptolemy and Leonidas (no. 652). Euphantos of Olynthos *ap.* Athen. 6.251d (= *FGrH* 74 F1; cf. Jacoby 1934) says that K. was a *kolax* of Ptolemy, who advertised his guile by wearing an image of Odysseus on his ring (on the nature of his flattery of Ptolemy see Jacoby 1934); the same source adds that he named his children Telegonos and Antikleia. It was common for *philoi* and officials of dynasts and kings to be depicted as flatterers and parasites, and perhaps a man noted for his skill at deception was an appropriate agent for Ptolemy's dealings with the Kypriot defectors. Identification with the man who was honored at Ephesos is rightly rejected by Hauben 1972b, 58. What became of K. is unknown. Hauben 1970, 21–32; Hauben 42–3 no. 17; *PP* VI no. 14606; cf. Gesche 1974.

565 KALLIKRATES

(Καλλικράτης). Honored with *proxenia* at Ephesos (Keil, *JÖAI* 16 (1913) 240 no. 1g) at some point between 306 and 294 (thus Hauben 1970, 20). Identification with the *philos* of Ptolemy is rejected by Hauben 1970, 20–1 and 1972b, 58. He may have been in the service of the Antigonids or possibly Lysimachos. K. is otherwise unknown. Hauben 1970, 16–21; Billows 446 no. 132.

566 KALLIKRATIDAS

(Καλλικρατίδας). Eminent Spartan (Poralla no. 409), ambassador (along with Pausippos, Monimos and Onomastoridas) to Dareios III. According to Curt. 3.13.15, he was captured by Parmenion at Damaskos in late 333, but Arr. 3.24.4 places his capture after the death of Dareios, in which case his embassy was probably linked with Agis III's efforts in Europe (thus Hofstetter 99). Schoch, *RE* Supplbd IV s.v. "Kallikratidas (1a)"; Berve II 189–90 no. 402; Hofstetter 99 no. 171; Bosworth I 233–4.

567 KALLIKRON

(Καλλικρῶν). Son of Euryphaon. One of twenty-four cavalrymen from Orchomenos, who served with Alexander's allied cavalry until the expedition reached Ekbatana in 330. There he and his compatriots were discharged. On their return (*c.*329), they made a dedication to Zeus Soter in Orchomenos (*IG* VII 3206). Berve II 190 no. 403.

568 KALLIMEDON

(Καλλιμέδων). Athenian politician (Kirchner 8032), surnamed *Karabos* (Plut. *Dem.* 27.2), "the Crab." Son of Kallikrates, from Kottylos (*IG* II² 653, 7), and probably a kinsman of Kallistratos of Aphidna (Davies 279). Pro-Macedonian and an adherent of Phokion—hence an opponent of Demosthenes (cf. Din. 1.94, with Worthington 264–5). He was the butt of comic poets' jokes (Athen. 3.100c–e, 104c–d; Lucian, *Encom.* 46, 48), perhaps already in the 340s, but he is best known for activities between 322 and 318. Soon after Alexander's death, he went first to Antipatros in Macedonia and then accompanied Antipatros' "friends and ambassadors" (*philoi kai presbeis*) as they travelled around Greece urging states not to join the Athenians in the Lamian War (Plut. *Dem.* 27.2). K. was, however, not a mere sycophant and opposed, unsuccessfully, Antipatros' plan to install a garrison in Mounychia (Plut. *Phoc.* 27.9). He is attested as a lessee of a mine at Thorikos (*IG* II² 1587, 12), probably around 320/19 (for the date see Crosby 1950, 280–81). After the proclamation of Polyperchon's *diagramma* on the Freedom of the Greeks, when Hagnonides denounced Phokion and his party, K. was among those who fled (Plut. *Phoc.* 33.4), probably to the safety of Nikanor in Peiraieus. He was condemned to death *in absentia* (Plut. *Phoc.* 35.5; Hagnonides is said to have favored that K. be tortured before he was put to death: Plut. *Phoc.* 35.2), but may have survived to return to Athens in the time of Demetrios of Phaleron (Ferguson 33). Swoboda, *RE* X.2 (1919) 1647–8 no. 1; Berve II 190 no. 404; Davies 279; Tritle 1988, 107, 124–5; Paschidis 67–8 A6.

569 KALLINES

(Καλλίνης). Macedonian (Tataki 337 no. 16) of unknown family. He appears only in Arrian's account of the Opis mutiny (324), where he is described as an officer of the Companions, distinguished in age and rank. He acted as a spokesman for the Macedonians, indicating that they were hurt by the King's apparent preference for the Persians (namely that he allowed the Persians to kiss him but did not extend the privilege to Macedonians: a strange reversal of the *proskynesis* episode). K. then came forward and kissed Alexander, and others followed suit (Arr. 7.11.6–7; cf. Roisman 2003, 300). Berve II, 190 no. 405

570 KALLISTHENES

(Καλλισθένης). Olynthian (Arr. 4.10.1). Son of Demotimos (*Syll*³ 275; *Suda* K 240, although according to the *Suda* it was thought that K.'s father was also named Kallisthenes) and Hero, who may have been a niece of Aristotle (Plut. *Alex*. 55.8; cf. 52.3). "Official" historian of Alexander's campaign (Arr. 4.10.1; Plut. *Sulla* 36). K. was a student of Aristotle (Arr. 4.10.1; Justin 12.6.17; Cic. *de Or*. 2.58; *Suda*), with whom he resided, and and he may have joined Alexander's expedition on Aristotle's recommendation (*Suda*; Diog. Laert. 5.4); cf. Simplicius, on Aristotle, *de coelo* 2.12 = *FGrH* 124 T3. K. and Aristotle were both honored with crowns at Delphi at some point between 337 and 327 (*Syll*³ 275; R&O no. 80) for drawing up the lists of the victors in the Pythian Games. K. had already written a Greek history (*Hellenica*). Aristotle is said to have recognized early the potential danger of K.'s tendency to speak too freely in the presence of Alexander (Diog. Laert. 5.4–5). K. is wrongly depicted as one of Alexander's tutors (Strabo 13.1.27; Dio Chrys. 64.20; Solinus 9.18, p. 66). Although he accompanied Alexander from the beginning of the campaign, little is known of his personal relationship with Alexander until the last year of his life. It is certain, however, that although he wrote accounts that were favorable to the King (cf. Polyb. 12.12b, which must refer to his writings), in his personal speech he was brusque and critical, to the point of annoying and offending Alexander (Diog. Laert. 5.4–5; Plut. *Alex*. 52.7; Seneca, *Suas*. 1.5, confused; Cic. *Tusc*. 3.21). He was, indeed, the victim of envious members of Alexander's entourage (Plut. *Alex*. 53.1–2); his manner and his lack of social graces—to say nothing of a perceived anti-Macedonian bias—contributed in no small way to his fall (Plut. *Alex*. 53–4; Arr. 4.10.1; Curt. 8.5.13, 6.1). On the morning after Alexander's murder of Kleitos, K. attempted to console the King with gentle words and circumlocutions, but he found himself trumped by his rival Anaxarchos, who resorted to flattery and insinuated himself with the King at K.'s expense (Plut. *Alex*. 52.3–7; cf. Arr. 4.9.7–9). For the rivalry see Plut. *Alex*. 52.8–9; Arr. 4.9.7–11.9; Arr. 4.9.9 names both Agis and Anaxarchos. Curt. 8.5.8–20 mentions Agis and Kleon in place of Anaxarchos. Justin 12.6.17 describes K.'s consolation as having the desired effect and says nothing about Anaxarchos (see also Borza 1981). Furthermore, he incurred the hatred of Hephaistion and Hagnon (Plut. *Alex*. 55.1–2). He opposed the introduction of *proskynesis* in spring 327 (Plut. *Alex*. 54.4–6; Arr. 4.12.3–5; Justin 12.7.2; Curt. 8.5.13–20) and, because he was most likely the tutor of the Pages (*paides basilikoi*), was accused of participating in some way in the Hermolaos conspiracy and arrested (Plut. *Alex*. 55.3–5; Arr. 4.12.7, 14.2; 8.6.24–5, 27), though not one of the Pages denounced Kallisthenes. The place of his arrest was Kariatai in Baktria (Strabo 11.11.4 C517); but Arr. 4.22.2 says it occurred in Baktra (Zariaspa), where the Pages had earlier been left behind (Arr. 4.16.6; Bosworth II 141 suggests that Strabo's Kariatai may be a corruption of Zariaspa). There is no agreement on the manner of K.'s death (Plut. *Alex*. 55.9; Arr. 4.14.3): Chares, *FGrH* 125 F15, says that he died of obesity and a disease of lice (cf. Plut. *Sulla* 36.5; *Suda* K 240), which appears to be supported by Aristoboulos, 139 F33 = Arr. 4.14.3, claims that he was imprisoned and thereafter died of illness (Justin 15.3.4–6). This gives some credence to the view that Alexander intended to have K. tried by the League of Korinth for treason (Plut. *Alex*. 55.9). Ptolemy, 138 F17 = Arr. 4.14.3, says that he was killed by hanging (cf. Plut. *Alex*. 55.9, crucifixion; Curt. 8.8.21 says he died under torture—both accounts may go back to Ptolemy). A statue of K. by Amphistratos was located in Pliny's time in the Gardens of Servilius (Pliny, *HN* 36.36). Berve II 191–9 no. 408; Gude no. 74; Pownall, *LexAM* 287–91. K. as historian: Prentice 1923; Brown 1949; Pearson 22–49; Jacoby, *FGrH* 124 TT1–36 (translated into English in Robinson I 45–56); Bosworth 1970; Golan 1988; Devine 1994; Zahrnt 2013; Heckel 2020; Pownall, *LexAM* 287–91. To the literature on *proskynesis* we may now add Bowden 2013; Matarese 2013.

571 KALLISTHENES

(Καλλισθένης). Son of Menandros. One of twenty-four cavalrymen from Orchomenos, who served with Alexander's allied cavalry until the expedition reached Ekbatana in 330. There he and his compatriots were discharged. On their return (*c.*329), they made a dedication to Zeus Soter in Orchomenos (*IG* VII 3206). Berve II 199 no. 409.

572 KALLISTHENES

(Καλλισθένης). Athenian politician (Kirchner 8090) with anti-Macedonian leanings, K. is probably identical with the mover of a decree urging the Athenians to accept an alliance with the Thrakian Ketriporis, Lyppeios the Paionian, and Grabos the Illyrian in 356/5 (*Syll*³ 196 = R&O no. 53; cf. Kirchner 8090), and apparently also the man involved in securing grain from Leukon, king of the Bosporos (Dem. 20.33). After the Peace of Philokrates, K. proposed a decree to secure Peiraieus and bring people in from the countryside (Dem. 18.37–8, cf. 19.125; Aesch. 2.139, 3.80). In 335 Alexander demanded his extradition along with other prominent enemies of Macedon (Plut. *Dem.* 23.4). That he was implicated in the Harpalos affair, we know only from a comic fragment of Timokles (Athen. 8.341e–f) which, like the source of Plutarch's *Demosthenes*, links K. with Demon. Both are absent from the other two lists of politicians whose extradition was demanded after the sack of Thebes (Arr. 1.10.4; *Suda* A 2704; Plut. *Phoc.* 17.2). K. is also ridiculed in a fragment of Antiphanes (Athen. 8.338f). Berve II 199 no. 410.

573 KALLIXEINA

(Καλλίξεινα). An exceptionally attractive Thessalian *hetaira*, who at the request of Philip and Olympias (who were worried about their son's indifference to women), slept with Alexander and was reputed to be the first woman to do so (Hieronymos, *Epistles*, frg. 10 [Hiller] = Athen. 10.435a, quoting Theophrastos); Olympias frequently asked her son to have sex with K. Ael. *VH* 12.34 calls Pankaste (said to have been from Larisa) the first woman Alexander slept with, but he appears to have confused her with K. The historicity of Hieronymos' story is suspect, coming from a hostile Peripatetic tradition. In Athenaeus, Alexander's lack of interest in sex is connected with his love of drinking, which cannot have been a serious factor in his youth. There is no good reason, however, to question the existence of K. herself. Berve II 190–1 no. 406; Ogden 2011, 144–6.

574 KAPHISIAS

(Καφισίας). Greek. Renowned flute player and presumably a rival of Python (Plut. *Pyrrh.* 8.7, *Mor.* 184c, the anecdote demonstrates that Kaphisias was still alive in the late 4th/ early 3rd century), K. performed at the mass marriage ceremonies in Sousa, along with Diophantos, Timotheos, Euios, and Phrynichos (Chares *ap.* Athen. 12.538f = *FGrH* 125 F4; cf. Athen. 14.629a–b; Diog. Laert. 7.21 for an anecdote relating to his interaction with one of his music students). Sandberger 116 no. 41; Berve II 202–3 no. 416; id., *RE* Supplbd. IV (1924) 875 no. 2.

575 KAPHISODOROS

(Καφισόδωρος). Son of Arxillos. One of twenty-four cavalrymen from Orchomenos, who served with Alexander's allied cavalry until the expedition reached Ekbatana in 330. There he and his compatriots were discharged. On their return (*c*.329), they made a dedication to Zeus Soter in Orchomenos (*IG* VII 3206). Berve II 203 no. 417.

576 KARANOS

(Κάρανος). Macedonian (Tataki 338 no. 22). Allegedly a son of Philip II (Justin 11.2.3). Although many scholars have accepted K. as a son of Philip II and a half-brother and rival of Alexander, he is most likely fictitious (Tarn II 260–2; Heckel 1979; but see Unz 1985; Ogden 26, 39 nn.161–2; Meeus 2013, 92). Named only by Justin in his abbreviation of the *Philippic History* of Pompeius Trogus, K. is clearly nothing more than the son who, Alexander feared, might have fulfilled Attalos' wish that his niece Kleopatra (no. 607) would produce a legitimate heir to the Macedonian throne (Justin 11.2.3 picks up the wording of 9.7.3). Since Kleopatra's child turned out to be a daughter, Europa, and there was no time for a second child to be born before Kleopatra's murder in 336, K. must be dismissed as an invention (thus Beloch III² 2.72, who adds "Karanos mag der Name eines der Bastarde Philipps gewesen sein." This cannot be ruled out entirely, but one wonders why his murder is treated as a matter of importance). Paus. 8.7.7 is thought to be a reference to K. but since Justin 9.7.12 says that Europa (no. 451) was murdered in her mother's arms (*in gremio eius prius filia interfecta*), and this preceded the murder of Kleopatra (*finire vitam suspendio coëgit*), we cannot have a second mother-and-child murder (this time involving a son). I see no merit in the view that Phila (no. 895) was K.'s mother (Berve II 200; Milns 1968, 18). Berve II 199–200 no. 411; Heckel 1979; Yardley and Heckel 82–3; Müller, *LexAM* 292–3.

577 KARANOS

(Κάρανος). Macedonian (Tataki 337 no. 21). Commander of the allied infantry from 331 to 330. Karanos assumed the command when his predecessor, Balakros son of Amyntas was appointed *strategos* of Egypt (Arr. 3.5.6, "Kalanos") and retained it until the allied infantry were dismissed in 330 at Ekbatana. He may be identical with Berve's no. 412 and also with Arrian's Koiranos (Arr. 3.12.4; Berve II 219 no. 442), both of whom commanded allied cavalry (cf. Brunt II 262 n.1). "Kalanos," as a proper name or nickname, is simply not Macedonian (but see Hoffmann 196–7). Understanding the infantry commander's fate depends, in part, on what we make of this name. It was unusual enough to prompt Plutarch to explain how it came to be applied to the Indian philosopher Sphines (Plut. *Alex.* 65.5). I suspect that we are dealing with a textual error in which Karanos was corrupted into *Kalanos* by a scribe influenced by the repetition of the name *Balakros* in the same passage (see Heckel 1981e, 64, 69–70). Berve II 186–7 no. 395 and II 200–1 no. 412.

KARANOS (Arr. 3.28.2-3). See **613 KOIRANOS**.

578 KASSANDROS

(Κάσσανδρος). Macedonian (Tataki 338 no. 25). Apparently, the son of Iolaos and from Palioura. Brother of Antipatros and father of Antigone; thus grandfather of Ptolemy Soter's wife Berenike (Schol. Theocr. 17.61). Nothing else is known about him. Beloch IV² 2.180; Grainger 2019, 53. **Stemma V.**

579 KASSANDROS

(Κάσσανδρος). Macedonian (Tataki 338 no. 27). Son of Antipatros (Diod. 18.39.7; 21.1.4; Arr. *Succ.* 1.14; Justin 13.4.18; *LM* 96; Val. Max. 1.7 ext. 2; App. *Syr.* 53) and hence brother of Nikanor, Iolaos, Philip, Pleistarchos (Plut. *Demetr.* 31.6, 32.4), Alexarchos, Eurydike, Nikaia and Phila. Married Thessalonike (no. 1122) in 315 and produced three sons: Philip, Antipatros and Alexander (Paus. 1.10.1). K. must have been born no later than 354, if we accept the claim of Hegesandros (*ap.* Athen. 1.18a) that he continued to sit up at meals with his father at the age of 35 because he had not earned the right of reclining at dinner by killing a boar without a hunting net. He may have been a frail youth, and it appears that, at least later in life, he suffered from a lingering fatal illness, probably tuberculosis. The evidence is late: Euseb. 1.231; Syncellus 265a 504. Bonn. Paus. 9.7.2 says he died of a disease of worms: see Africa 1982; for tuberculosis (*phthisis*) see Carney 1999.

When Alexander crossed into Asia in 334, K. appears to have remained in Macedonia with his father. The text of Diod. 17.17.4, assigning 900 Thrakian and Paionian *prodromoi* to K., is probably corrupt: their commander was either Asandros son of Philotas or Asandros son of Agathon. In 324, he was sent by Antipatros to Alexander in Babylon to answer charges against his father; rumors that he brought poison and formed a conspiracy to kill the King are the product of the propaganda wars of the successors (Val. Max. 1.7 ext. 2; *LM* 89, 96, 100; see Heckel 1988). Although the charge of poisoning appears to be false, there is evidence of bad feeling between Alexander and K. (Plut. *Mor.* 180f; Plut. *Alex.* 74.2–6). After Alexander's death, he appears to have been designated commander of the Royal Hypaspists (thus Justin 13.4.16: *stipatoribus regiis satellitibusque Kassandros, filius Antipatros, praeficitur*) in place of Seleukos, who was promoted to chiliarch. If so, he did not take up the position but returned to Macedonia, perhaps bearing news that Perdikkas was prepared to cooperate with the old regent. But Perdikkas' duplicity soon became apparent (see s.vv. Kleopatra no. 608, Nikaia no. 775). He accompanied his father as far as Triparadeisos in 320 and there was appointed *chiliarchos* of the cavalry and Antigonos' second-in-command, for Antipatros was distrustful of Antigonos' ambition (Diod. 18.39.7; Arr. *Succ.* 1.38; cf. Heid. Epit. 1.4). His suspicions were soon confirmed by K., who quarreled with Antigonos and urged his father to remove the "Kings" from the latter's custody (Arr. *Succ.* 1.42). After his return from Asia, and during his father's illness, K. accused Demades of writing to Perdikkas and urging him to save the Greeks who were fastened by "an ancient and rotting thread," meaning Antipatros; he killed Demades and his son, who had been taken to Macedonia (Arr. *Succ.* 1.14; Plut. *Phoc.* 30.9–10). But K. was disappointed when his father, on his deathbed entrusted the guardianship of the Kings to Polyperchon—which K. regarded as a birthright (Diod. 18.49.1)—and appointed him, for a second time, *chiliarchos* (Diod. 18.48.4–5). Going into the country, using a hunting trip as a pretext (Diod. 18.49.3), K. met with his Friends and plotted rebellion (Diod. 18.49.1–2; cf. 18.54.1–2; Plut. *Eum.* 12.1; Plut. *Phoc.* 31.1, 32.1). He sent to Ptolemy asking to renew the alliance (Diod. 18.49.3), which had been sealed by his marriage to K.'s sister Eurydike, and urged him to send ships from Phoinikia to the Hellespont. Later, he crossed to Asia and renewed the Antipatrid alliance with Antigonos, who promised (Diod. 18.54.3) and delivered (Diod. 18.68.1) both 35 ships and 4,000 infantry. Polyperchon countered with a declaration of the "Freedom of the Greeks" in the name of King Philip III (Diod. 18.56; see esp. Poddighe 2013), thus attempting to destroy the base of K.'s power, the garrisons and oligarchic governments in Greece, which were faithful to the house of Antipatros (Diod. 18.55.2–4). He hoped to secure the exile or execution of the pro-Antipatrid leader (Diod. 18.57.1), and at first there was general support for Polyperchon in the Peloponnese, except in Megalopolis (Diod. 18.69.3–4). K. had in effect been driven out of Macedonia (Nepos, *Phoc.* 3.2). But, through the services of Damis (no. 334), K. managed to retain Megalopolis and gradually restore control over the Greek cities, which perceived Polyperchon as weak (Diod. 18.74.1, 75.2; cf. Paus.1.4.1). Athens was secured for K. by Nikanor (no. 782) and eventually entrusted to Demetrios of Phaleron (Diod. 18.74.2–3; cf. Athen. 12.542f); but Nikanor, who had won a naval victory over White Kleitos (Diod. 18.72.3–8), incurred the suspicions of K., who had him killed (Diod. 18.75.1; Polyaenus 4.11.2; for K.'s dealings with Athens see also Diod. 18.64; Nepos, *Phoc.* 2.4–5, 3.1). With ships sent by Antigonos, K. seized Aigina and besieged Salamis, but Polyperchon forced him to abandon the latter and to return to Peiraieus (Diod. 18.69.1–2; cf. Polyaenus 4.11.1, perhaps the same campaign). K.'s control of Athens lasted until its "liberation" by Demetrios Poliorketes (Plut. *Demetr.* 8.1, 4; cf. 23.1–3 for K.'s failed attempt to recover Attika in 304 during the so-called Four Years War), who also removed K.'s garrison from Megara (Plut. *Demetr.* 9.4–8).

In his struggle with Olympias (no. 808), whose hostility towards Antipatros extended also to his son (Diod. 18.57.2; cf. Paus.1.11.3), he was aided by Adea-Eurydike (no. 10), who had turned over the guardianship of Philip III to him (Justin 14.5.1–4); she soon summoned him back to Macedonia (Diod. 19.11.1; Justin 14.5.5). But Olympias was victorious over Eurydike and Philip III and also killed a hundred of the most distinguished of K.'s friends, as well as executing one brother, Nikanor (no. 777), and overturning the grave of another, Iolaos (Diod. 19.11.8). K., learning of these events, made peace with the Tegeans and marched north (Justin 14.5.8), using barges to by-pass Thermopylai and land in Thessaly (Diod. 19.35.1–2). Keeping Polyperchon's forces in check, through the efforts of two generals, Kallas and Deinias (Diod. 19.35.3–4), K. besieged Olympias and her entourage in Pydna (Diod. 19.35.5–36.1; 19.49.1–50.5; Justin 14.6.2–5). Atarrhias was sent to prevent Aiakides of Epeiros from bringing aid, and the action resulted in the deposing of the Epeirot king (Paus. 1.11.4) and the installation of K.'s agent Lykiskos (no. 661) as *epimeletes* and *strategos* of Epeiros (Diod. 19.36.2–5); for K.'s hostility to Aiakides and his family see Plut. *Pyrrh.* 3.2; Paus. 1.11.4–5. Kassandros is said to have offered Glaukias (no. 470) 200 talents to hand over the child Pyrrhos, but Glaukias refused (Plut. *Pyrrh.* 3.5; cf. Justin 17.3.20). Kallas meanwhile caused large numbers of Polyperchon's soldiers to defect (Diod. 19.36.6). Having forced Olympias to surrender (Polyaenus 4.11.3), K. secured her murder (Paus. 9.7.2; Justin 14.6.9–12; Diod. 19.51.3–5), which he sanctioned by a vote of the Macedonian army (Justin 14.6.6–8; Diod. 19.51.1–2). K. also eliminated Monimos (no. 753) of Pella and Aristonous, who was guarding Amphipolis (Diod. 19.50.7–51.1). K. razed a number of cities on the Thermaic Gulf and transferred their populations to his new metropolis, Thessalonike (Strabo 7, frag. 21, 24). Potideia was restored and named Kassandreia (Diod. 19.52.2–3; Strabo 7, frag. 25; Livy 44.11). In order to please K., Lysippos allegedly designed a new vessel for Mendean wine, which was exported from Kassandreia (Athen. 11.784c). K. gained control of Rhoxane and her son, Alexander IV, whom he sent to Amphipolis (Justin 14.6.13; Diod. 19.52.4), and married Thessalonike (Diod. 19.52.1; Paus.9.7.3; 8.7.7; Justin 14.6.13; cf. Plut. *Demetr.* 36.1; Plut. *Pyrrh.* 6.3; Diod. 19.61.2, according to Antigonos, this was against the woman's will), who was captured at Pydna, and restored the city of Thebes (Diod. 19.53.2; Paus. 7.6.9; 9.7.1, 4; Plut. *Mor.* 814b), having first obtained the permission of the Boiotians to do so (Diod. 19.54.1; cf. Paus. 10.18.7: K.'s attack on Elateia may belong to this period). These were clear gestures that K. had chosen to link himself with the tradition of Philip II, abandoning all connections with Alexander the Great, whom he had personal reasons to hate (Plut. *Mor.* 180f, *Alex.* 74.2–6. *Demetr.* 37.3; cf. Justin 16.1.15, 16.2.5; Errington 1976; but see Meeus 2009). The first child from his marriage with Thessalonike was named Philip (Paus. 9.7.3), and K. also gave royal burials to Adea-Eurydike and Philip III as well as to Adea's mother, Kynnane (Athen. 4.155a = Diyllos *FGrH* 73 F1; Diod. 19.52.5). Perhaps too much is made of this. The youngest son was called Alexander, but, by the time of his birth K.'s own position will have changed dramatically. The suggestion by Palagia 2008 that Philip IV was the son of Kynnane (whom she identifies as a daughter of the famous Kynnane) is unconvincing (Heckel 2013b). For K.'s attempts to control the western regions, where he was opposed at various times by the Aitolians, Epeirots, and the Illyrians under Glaukias see Diod. 19.35.2–3 (see Deinias no. 346), 19.67.3–68.1, 19.74.3–6, 19.78.1, 19.88.1–89.1; see also Grainger 2019, 166, 171.

K. was responsible for the murder of Alexander IV and his mother and, in the following year, persuaded Polyperchon to kill the illegitimate Herakles in return for a measure of power in the Peloponnese (Paus. 9.7.2; Justin 15.2.3–5, confused). The elimination of the last of Alexander's male relatives paved the way for K.'s assumption of the kingship after the initial step had been taken by the Antigonids after their victory at Salamis (Justin 15.2.10–12), and thus he was one of those considered responsible for the dismemberment of Alexander's empire (Nepos, *Eum.* 13.3). Athen. 4.144e says that Theophrastos wrote a treatise *On Monarchy* for K., although some claim it was the work of Sosibios. Plut. *Demetr.* 18.4 claims that K. did not use the title king in his letters, but this merely reflects Macedonian royal style. During his reign he remained on good terms with Lysimachos (Paus.1.10.1), who was married to his sister Nikaia, and who joined him, as well as Ptolemy and Seleukos, in coalitions against Antigonos (App. *Syr.* 53. 270–3; Diod. 19.56.3; Justin 15.1.2, 15.2.15–17; cf. Diod. 21.1.4[b]; Paus. 1.6.4). The first coalition against the Antigonids came after the defeat of Eumenes and the expulsion of Seleukos from Babylon (Diod. 19.56.3, 57.2); Antigonos' counter-arguments to K. were ineffective (Diod. 19.56.4). Instead the coalition demanded concessions, including that Kappadokia and Lykia be handed over to K. (Diod. 19.57.1). K. sent Asklepiodoros (no. 241) to invade Kappadokia, and Antigonos sent his nephew Polemaios (no. 968) against him (Diod. 19.57.4; 19.60.2). Polemaios also overcame Eupolemos (no. 449) in Karia (Diod. 19.68), who had been sent by Asandros, who had briefly joined the opponents of Antigonos. For his part, Antigonos accused K. of murdering Olympias, mistreating Alexander IV and his mother, marrying Thessalonike by force and rebuilding Thebes (Diod. 19.61.1–2) and urged that the Macedonians condemn him as an outlaw (Diod. 19.61.3). The establishment of Kassandreia was also criticized, since it brought together Olynthians who were traditionally hostile to Macedon. The years after 315 saw K. struggling with Polyperchon and his son Alexander for control of the Greek cities (Diod. 19.63–4), a problem which was partially overcome by K.'s ability to detach Alexander from his father (Diod. 19.64.4). This was followed by further campaigns in the northwestern regions of Greece, from Patrai in the south to Epeiros in the north (Diod. 19.66–7; 19.74.2–6; 19.88–9) as well as in Euboia (Diod. 19.75.6–8, 77.5–6; cf. 19.78.2–3, 5), after an abortive attempt by Antigonos to make peace (Diod. 19.75.6). In 310, K. took the bold step of ordering Glaukias to kill Alexander IV and his mother in Amphipolis (Diod. 19.105.2), a move that was in fact welcomed by all the Successors who aspired to the kingship (Diod. 19.105.3). But, when Polyperchon attempted to use Alexander's illegitimate son, Herakles (no. 522), as a means of gaining power (Diod. 20.20), K. induced him to murder the boy in exchange for a subordinate role as *strategos* of the Peloponnese (Diod. 20.28.1–3). Although K. came to terms with Antigonos' nephew, Polemaios, in 308 (Diod. 20.37.1–2), he soon lost Athens to Demetrios (Diod. 20.45.1–5). After the assumption of the kingship, K. renewed his alliance with Lysimachos, Ptolemy, and Seleukos (Diod. 20.76.7); he responded to an appeal by the Rhodians (Diod. 20.84.1) with a shipment of 10,000 medimnoi of barley (Diod. 20.96.3), in return for which the Rhodians set up a statue of him (Diod. 20.100.2). Demetrios Poliorketes, however, countered by waging war on K. and Polyperchon in Greece (20.100.6; 20.102–3; 20.105.1–106.1), forcing K. to seek peace with Antigonos (Diod. 20.106.2). But Antigonos' excessive demands merely resulted in a renewal of the alliance with Ptolemy, Lysimachos, and Seleukos (Diod. 20.106.2–5), which led eventually to the battle of Ipsos. K. attempted to divert Demetrios' attention in Thessaly, but with no military success (Diod. 20.110), and was forced to negotiate a truce that allowed Demetrios to cross to Asia in support of his father (Diod. 20.111.1–2). But K. too had sent a substantial force under Prepelaos (no. 993) to serve with Lysimachos in Asia (Diod. 20.107.1), and after recovering Thessaly in Demetrios' absence, he sent further forces with his brother Pleistarchos (Diod. 20.112.1). K. benefited from the Antigonid defeat at Ipsos in 301, although he was not himself present (Justin 15.2.17; App. *Syr.* 55; Paus.1.6.7). We know also of an attack on Kerkyra (in 299/8), in which K.'s ships were burned by Agathokles of Syracuse, but the latter failed to follow up his victory and K.'s forces escaped destruction (Diod. 21.2.1–3). K. died in 297, perhaps of consumption, and he was succeeded by his son Philip IV (Justin 15.4.24, 16.1.1; Plut. *Demetr.* 36.1). Stähelin, *RE* X.2 (1919) 2293–2313 no. 2; Berve II 201–2 no. 414; Sandberger 116–19 no. 42; Landucci 2003; Fortina 1965; Adams 1984, 1993; Grainger 2019, 129–202; Landucci, *LexAM* 295. See also Africa 1982; Carney 1999. **Stemma V.**

580 KATANES

(Κάτανης). Perhaps Persian, though possibly a local dynast of Sogdianian Paraitakene (Arr. 4.22.1). Although K. was a trusted follower of Bessos (no. 295; Curt. 7.5.21), he conspired with Spitamenes (no. 1072) and Dataphernes (no. 342) to arrest him and hand him over to Alexander in chains (Curt. 7.5.21–6; Metz Epit. 5–6). Because of his skill in archery, he was assigned the task of keeping the birds off Bessos' crucified body (Curt. 7.5.41–2). He persisted in his opposition to Alexander (Curt. 7.6.14–15), however, until the spring of 327 when Krateros led a punitive expedition into Paraitakene against K. and his supporter Haustanes; the latter was captured but K. fell on the battlefield (Curt. 8.5.2; cf. Arr. 4.22.2, who estimates the barbarian casualties at 120 cavalry, 1,500 infantry); Metz

Epit. 23 curiously says that the Dahai arrested K. and Dataphernes and turned them over to Alexander in order to pre-empt an attack upon them. Schoch, *RE* Supplbd IV (1924) s.v.; Berve II 202 no. 415; Shayegan 109–10 no. 56.

581 KEBALINOS

(Κεβαλῖνος). Greek or Macedonian (Tataki 339 no. 30) of obscure background. K. was the brother of Dimnos' lover, Nikomachos (Plut. *Alex.* 49.4; Diod. 17.79.2; Curt. 6.7.16); the charge that Nikomachos was a male prostitute may be nothing more than slander (Curt. 6.7.2); certainly, it was not used by Philotas to impugn his testimony when he spoke in his own defense. K. learned of the conspiracy of Demetrios the Bodyguard (on the background to the conspiracy see Heckel 203–8) from Nikomachos, to whom Dimnos, one of the *hetairoi*, had given the details in an attempt to enlist him in the plot (Diod. 17.79.2). K. then sought to pass the information on to Alexander through Philotas (no. 940) son of Parmenion (Curt. 6.7.18–22), whom he happened upon on his way to the King (noted by Adams 2003, 118; but Plut. *Alex.* 49.4 and Diod. 17.79.3 imply that he sought Philotas out). Philotas' failure to convey this information to the King (Curt. 6.7.17–18; Plut. *Alex.* 49.5–6; Diod. 17.79.4), led K. to approach a royal page, Metron, who arranged for the King to hear the full story (Curt. 6.7.23; Diod. 17.79.4). For K. there was considerable risk, since Alexander was slow to believe that he was telling the truth about Philotas' negligence (Curt. 6.7.31–2). Ultimately, K.'s testimony played no small part in the arrest, conviction, and execution of Philotas. What became of him is unknown. Kroll, *RE* XI (1921) 101; Berve II 203 no. 418; Adams 2003.

KELBANOS. Launey 1179; Tataki 339 no. 32. See **KEPHALON**.

582 KEPHALON

(Κεφάλων). Greek. K. came with the contingent of Arachosians who joined Eumenes in 317. At Paraitakene, he commanded the Arachosians, after their commander Sibyrtios (no. 1044) fled from Eumenes' camp (Diod. 19.27.4). It appears that he was captured at Gabiene and executed by Antigonos (Diod. 19.44.1, where the reference to the otherwise unknown Kelbanos must be a scribal error for Kephalon: Heckel 1980c; certainly, identification with Kebalinos no. 581 above (see Bizière, Budé *Diodore de Sicile* XIX, *ad loc.*) is unlikely and unnecessary).

583 KEPHISOPHON

(Κεφισόφων). Athenian politician who, along with Demosthenes and Demades, had been investigated by the Areiopagos for six months on the matter of having taken money from Harpalos (Din 1.45). The identity of Kephisophon is unclear. Berve II 203 assumed that he was the son of Kallibios (thus also Kirchner 8417). But he may have been dead by mid-century (Davies 149). Worthington 210 argues instead for Kephisophon son of Lysiphon Cholargeus (Kirchner 8419), but there can be no certainty. Kroll, *RE* XI.1 (1921) 240 no. 4; Berve II 203 no. 419; Kirchner 8417; Davies 149; Worthington 210.

584 KETEUS

(Κητεύς). Indian commander in the army of Eumenes. K. died fighting valiantly in the battle of Paraitakene in 317 (Diod. 19.33.1). His fate may have gone unnoticed by the Greek historians but for the fact that his two wives vied for the honor of committing *sati* (or *suttee*), that is, dying on the funeral pyre of the husband (for the practice, McCrindle 369–70; see also Diod. 17.91.3; Onesikritos, *FGrH* 134 F20 = Strabo 15.1.30 C700 is skeptical; but Strabo 15.1.62 C714 expresses no doubts when he cites Aristoboulos, *FGrH* 139 F42). The cases of the two wives were heard and it was decided that, since the older one (**A104**) was pregnant, the younger (**A105**) would be allowed to accompany her husband into the afterlife (Diod. 19.34; see also Yardley and Heckel 1981; cf. Bosworth 2013, 78). Launey 1251.

585 KILLES

(Κίλλης). Macedonian (Tataki 340 no. 37). *Strategos* and *philos* of Ptolemy I Soter (Plut. *Demetr.* 6.2; Diod.19.93.1), who sent him against Demetrios Poliorketes soon after the latter's defeat at Gaza in 312. Demetrios, however, caught Killes unprepared in his camp at Myus (Diod.19.93.2) and inflicted a defeat on him (Plut. *Demetr.* 6; Diod.19.93.2). Killes and the other *philoi* of Ptolemy were returned to their leader, along with their possessions (Plut. *Demetr.* 6.5). Hoffmann 209; Schoch, *RE* Supplbd. IV (1924) 902–3; *PP* II no. 2164; VI 14609; Launey 1179; Tataki 340 no. 37.

586 KISSOS

(Κίσσος, Κίττος). A Greek who, together with Ephialtes, brought Alexander news of Harpalos' flight, only to be thrown into chains by the disbelieving King (Plut. *Alex.* 41.8). Presumably he was released once his report was verified. Berve II 161, 203 has argued that Alexander's disbelief suggests that it is Harpalos' first flight (333) that was reported by K. (cf. Hamilton 109). But we cannot be certain. K. is otherwise unknown, unless he is to be identified with the Athenian actor Kittos (*IG* II² 2418). Berve II 203 no. 420; Ghiron-Bistagne 72, 337.

587 KLEAINETOS

(Κλεαίνετος). Athenian of unknown family. K., Xenokles (no. 1160), and Chionides (no. 327) appear at the head of an embassy to Antigonos the One-Eyed in 305 (II² 1492B). The embassy was perhaps instigated by Stratokles and resulted in a donation of 140 talents of silver and timber, as well as the restoration of Lemnos to the Athenians (thus Paschidis 107). He is otherwise unattested. Identification with K. son of Kleomedon is impossible: this K. was too old to be an *eromenos* of the Besieger (Plut. *Demetr.* 24.6–7). Paschidis 109 A32.

588 KLEAINETOS

(Κλεαίνετος). Athenian (Kirchner 8461). Son of Kleomedon. At some point between 307/6 and 302/1, K. petitioned Demetrios Poliorketes to excuse his father from paying a 50 talent fine. Demetrios did so but the Athenians passed a decree preventing any citizen from making a similar appeal to the King, and this incurred his anger and had serious political consequences, such as death and exile for those who moved and supported the decree (Plut. *Demetr.* 24.6).

589 KLEANDROS

(Κλέανδρος). Macedonian (Tataki 195–6 no. 12). Son of Polemokrates (Arr. 1.24.2) and, in all probability, the brother of Koinos (no. 610). He served Alexander since at least the beginning of the Asiatic campaign and, in late 334, was sent to recruit mercenaries from the Peloponnese (Arr. 1.24.2; Curt. 3.1.1: on the date see Heckel 1991). He rejoined Alexander at Sidon in early 332, bringing with him 4,000 mercenaries (Arr. 2.20.5; cf. Curt. 4.3.11). In 331 K. replaced Menandros (no. 706) as commander of the *archaioi xenoi* (mercenaries); Arr. 3.6.8 writes "Klearchos" in place of Kleandros and the text should be emended (Bosworth I 285; Brunt I 240 n.8; Heckel 1981e, 65). K. is securely attested as commander of the mercenaries at Gaugamela (Arr. 3.12.2). In the following year, Kleandros remained with Parmenion in Ekbatana and, on the instructions brought by Polydamas, orchestrated the old general's murder (Arr. 3.26.3; cf. Curt. 7.2.19–32). In 324, he was summoned to Karmania, along with Herakon (no. 523), Sitalkes (no. 1053), and Agathon (no. 21), and executed on charges of maladministration and crimes against the native population (Arr. 6.27.4; Curt. 10.1.1–7, who does not mention K.'s own death but adds (10.1.8) that 600 common soldiers, who carried out the orders of K. and his fellow officers, were executed *en masse*). The allegation that K. raped a virgin of the native aristocracy and gave her to his slave as a concubine (Curt. 10.1.5) may go back to Kleitarchos (for similar charges against Harpalos, cf. Diod. 17.108.4). Kroll, *RE* XI (1921) 558 no. 6; Schoch, *RE* Supplbd. IV (1924) 908 no. 7a; Berve II 204 no. 422; Badian 1961, 21–3; Heckel 1992, 340.

590 KLEANDROS

(Κλέανδρος). Macedonian (Tataki 341 no. 42). Commander of archers (*strategos* of *toxotai* or *toxarches*). K. replaced Klearchos who was killed at Halikarnassos in 334 (Arr. 1.22.7). K. was killed in the Pisidian campaign (334/3: Arr. 1.28.8). His successor was Antiochos. Kroll, *RE* XI (1921) 558 no. 5; Berve II 205 no. 423.

591 KLEARCHOS

(Κλέανδρος). Macedonian (Tataki 342 no. 45). Commander of archers, perhaps the successor of Eurybotas, who died at Thebes in 335 (Arr. 1.8.4); thus Berve II 205, but this implies that Macedonian and Kretan commanders were employed interchangeably. K. was killed at Halikarnassos in 334 and replaced by Kleandros (Arr. 1.22.7). Berve II 205 no. 424.

592 KLEARCHOS

(Κλέανδρος). Athenian (Kirchner 8480). Son of Nausikles (on whom see Kirchner 10552; Davies 396–8). Born before 356 into his father's adoptive deme, Aigilieus, though Nausikles transferred back into Oe. Trierarch and syntrierarch in 334 (*IG* II² 1628, lines 71–2, 100–1), *hieropoios* to Delphi in 326/5 (*Syll*³ 296, line 7). One of three Athenians (the others were Phokion and Konon son of Timotheos) sent in 318 to Nikanor, who occupied Mounychia, asking him to restore autonomy to the Athenians in accordance with Philip III's *diagramma* (Diod. 18.64.5). The mission was unsuccessful. Nothing else is known about him. Davies 397; Paschidis 68–9 A9.

593 KLEARCHOS

(Κλέανδρος). Son of Amastris (no. 67) and Dionysios of Herakleia Pontika (no. 386). Brother of the younger Amastris and Oxathres (Memnon 4.7; Diod. 20.77.1). Born *c.*321, K. was about sixteen when his father died and was briefly under the guardianship of his mother. When he was old enough to rule (he shared power with his brother Oxathres; Diod. 20.77.1), K. fought as an ally of Lysimachos, who was for a short time his stepfather, against the Getai, who captured both leaders. When Lysimachos was released from captivity, he gained K.'s freedom soon afterward (Memnon 5.1). K. and his brother were harsh rulers, who not only mistreated their subjects but, around 284, devised and executed a plan to drown their mother in the Black Sea (Memnon 5.2). The brothers were killed by Lysimachos, who exacted revenge for the death of his former wife (Memnon 5.3). As a consequence, Herakleia was restored to democratic rule. Burstein, *Outpost* 83–5.

KLEARCHOS (Arr. 3.6.8). See KLEANDROS.

594 KLEITOS

(Κλεῖτος). Son of Bardylis (Arr. 1.5.1); Illyrian, perhaps king of the southern Dardanians (Hammond 1966, 245). Together with Glaukias, king of the Taulantians, K. rebelled against Alexander in 335 (Arr. 1.5.1). Alexander attacked and hemmed him in at Pellion before Glaukias' arrival (Arr. 1.5.8). After Glaukias was defeated and routed (Arr. 1.6.10), K. put Pellion to the torch and fled to the mountains to join the Taulantians (Arr. 1.6.11). He appears to have been the grandfather of Birkenna, daughter of Bardylis, who later married Pyrrhos, king of Epeiros (Plut. *Pyrrh.* 9.2; neither Nederlof 45 nor Sandberger 62 attempts to identify Bardylis). Stähelin, *RE* XI.1 (1921) 668 no. 11; Berve II 205–6 no. 426; Hammond 1966; Hammond 1974.

595 KLEITOS

(Κλεῖτος). Macedonian (Tataki 342–3 no. 48). Son of Dropidas (Arr. 1.15.8; 3.11.8, 27.4; cf. 4.9.3), was surnamed Melas ("the Black": Diod. 17.20.7, 57.1; Plut. Alex. 16.11) in order to distinguish him from his namesake, the taxiarch and later hipparch, White Kleitos (Athen. 12.539c). Although we are reasonably well informed about his family, nothing is recorded about his place of birth or residence. Lanike, his sister, was Alexander's nurse (Arr. 4.9.3; Curt. 8.1.21 (Hellanike); cf. 8.2.8–9, and Justin 12.6.10): born *c.*375, she was apparently still alive in 328 and had at least three sons who served Alexander during the Asiatic expedition, two of whom died at Miletos in 334 (Curt. 8.2.8; cf. Arr. 4.9.4), while a third son, Proteas (no. 998)—*syntrophos* and drinking companion of Alexander (Ael. *VH* 12.26; cf. Athen. 4.129a and 10.434a)—was very likely the admiral who defeated Datames at Siphnos, hence the son of Andronikos (Berve II 328–9 no. 664 = no. 665; thus Carney 1981, 152–3). If the identification is correct, Andronikos—almost certainly the son of Agerros (so Carney 1981, 153)—would have been Lanike's husband and K.'s brother-in-law. Theodoros (Berve II 176 no. 362), identified merely as a "brother of Proteas" but on intimate terms with Alexander (Plut. *Mor.* 760c), may also have been Lanike's son (cf. Carney 152, with n.10). K. commanded the Royal Squadron (*ile basilike*) since at least the beginning of the expedition; in what capacity he had served under Philip II (Curt. 8.1.20), we do not know. At the Granikos, he saved Alexander's life, killing either

Rhoisakes or Spithridates, who was on the point of striking the King (Arr. 1.15.8; Plut. *Alex.* 16.11; Diod. 17.20.7; cf. Curt. 8.1.20). Arrian and Plutarch relate that K. severed Spithridates' arm just as he was about to strike the King; Diodorus, however, records that this man was Rhoisakes, Spithridates' brother. The confusion is inexplicable, the truth indeterminable. The episode may have been the inspiration for the Apelles' portrait of K. on horseback (Pliny, *HN* 35.93; Pollitt 162; cf. Berve II 206. White Kleitos had also been a hipparch and the identity of Apelles' *Kleitos* is not certain). At Gaugamela he continued to command the *ile basilike*, as he must have done at Issos, though he is not named in any account of the battle (Arr. 3.11.8; Diod. 17.57.1; Curt. 4.13.26, the cavalry *agema*). When the King left Sousa at the end of 331, K. remained behind on account of illness. In the following spring, he proceeded to Ekbatana, taking from there those Macedonians who had been responsible for protecting the treasures that had been conveyed from Persepolis to Ekbatana and rejoining the King somewhere in Parthyaia (Arr. 3.19.8). After the fall of Philotas, K. shared the command of the Companions with Hephaistion (Arr. 3.27.4). We know nothing of K.'s participation in the campaigns of 330–328. Carney 1981, 151 suggests that Alexander "granted Clitus the honor of his position ... then ... prevented him from acquiring much glory through it." Arr. 4.8.1–9.9 and Plut. *Alex.* 50.1–52.4 report K.'s death out of chronological context, which may explain their failure to mention him again. There may also have been further changes in the way the Companions were used; for we hear virtually nothing of Hephaistion as hipparch (see no. 513). Schachermeyr 364 suggests that K.'s appointment as satrap may be linked with the restructuring of the cavalry commands. Krateros, Koinos, Perdikkas, and others had all joined Hephaistion as hipparchs, and they now may have contributed to K.'s demise. Shortly before he was killed in Marakanda (autumn 328), K. had been designated satrap of Baktria and Sogdiana, which Artabazos had relinquished on account of age (Curt. 8.1.19). Alexander had gradually replaced Philip's officers with men of his own generation, men who very often shared his vision of the empire or, even if they did not, were content to say that they did. The quarrel which precipitated the murder involved the clash of generations and ideologies: Philip against Alexander (Arr. 4.8.4ff.; Curt. 8.1.23ff.; Plut. *Alex.* 50.11; Justin 12.6.2–3); the Macedonian kingdom versus the new empire (Plut. *Alex.* 51.2–3, 5). K.'s anger at the drinking party in Marakanda has been attributed to offensive verses, mocking a Macedonian defeat (Plut. *Alex.* 50.8ff.), the excesses of Alexander's flatterers (Arr. 4.8.2–3), the wrath of Dionysos (Arr. 4.8.1–2, 9. 5; or neglected sacrifices, Plut. *Alex.* 50.7) or K.'s own belligerence (Arr. 4.8.6–9; Curt. 8.1.49ff.; Plut. *Arr.* 51.8ff.). Certainly K. objected publicly to Alexander's personal and political transformation. The King, though restrained by his Somatophylakes (Curt. 8.1.45ff.; Plut. *Alex.* 51.6), grabbed a spear from a guard in the tent and killed K. (Arr. 4.8.8–9.1; Curt. 8.1.49–52; Plut. *Alex.* 51.9–11; Justin 12.6.3) in a drunken rage. There is no reason to doubt that Alexander experienced genuine remorse (Arr. 4.9.2ff.; Curt. 8.2.1ff.; Plut. *Alex.* 52.1–2; Justin 12.6.7–11). Kroll, *RE* XI.1 (1921) 666 no. 9; Berve II 206–8 no. 427; Carney 1981; Heckel 1992, 34–7; Hoffmann 183; Müller, *LexAM* 299–300. **Stemma VIII.**

596 KLEITOS

(Κλεῖτος). Prominent Macedonian (Tataki 342 no. 47), family background unknown. K. was nicknamed "the White" (Athen. 12.539c) to distinguish him from "Black" Kleitos, the son of Dropides. He first appears as taxiarch in 327, at the beginning of the Indian campaign: his battalion, along with those of Gorgias and Meleagros, accompanied Perdikkas and Hephaistion to the Indos River (Arr. 4.22.7). In the Hydaspes battle, K. and Koinos made the river crossing with the King (Arr. 5.12.2), while the other five battalions remained on the western bank. But when Kleitos next appears, it is as hipparch in the Sangala campaign (Arr. 5.22.6), a position which he held also in the Mallian campaign (Arr. 6.6.4). Who assumed control of Kleitos' battalion and what became of it, we do not know. K. himself was dismissed with the veterans at Opis and accompanied Krateros as far as Kilikia (Justin 12.12 8; cf. Arr. 7.12.4). There Krateros appears to have entrusted him with the task of building a fleet which would secure the Hellespont crossing (cf. Schoch, *RE* XI 666; Beloch IV² 1.72). K.'s responsibility was undoubtedly to secure the crossing of the Hellespont by Krateros himself, not by Leonnatos, as some have maintained. The latter's crossing into Europe was clearly facilitated by the fleet of Antipatros, some 110 ships sent in 324/3 by Alexander which defeated the Athenians near Abydos at the beginning of spring 322 (*IG* II² 398; II² 493, neither of which names K.). Krateros, at any rate, was likely to have awaited the outcome of Leonnatos' battle with the Greeks in Thessaly. The death of Leonnatos and Antipatros' deficiency in cavalry made it necessary for Krateros to leave Kilikia, probably in early June. The Athenian admiral Euetion, having been unable to prevent reinforcements from reaching Antipatros from Hellespontine Phrygia, now moved south to intercept K.'s fleet as it entered the Aegean. Near the island of Amorgos, K. defeated the Athenian fleet in the last major naval engagement of the year of Kephisodoros (323/2; *Marm. Par. FGrH* 239 B9; Bengtson 1987, 25, suggests "Herbst 322," which is much too late). At this point, K.'s fleet could not have numbered much more than 130 ships, a force which the Athenians, defeated at the Hellespont and forced to keep ships in reserve in the Malian Gulf, would have difficulty matching. After his victory near Amorgos, K. added the Hellespontine fleet to his own and sailed to the Malian Gulf, where he caught the remainder of the Athenian fleet either off the Lichades Islands (Cape Echinos) or at the Echinades, near Oiniadai, in western waters (Bosworth, 2003: 16–19 Wrightson 2014). With some justification, K. could now play the part of Poseidon and carry the trident (Plut. *Mor.* 338a); Phylarchos and Agatharchides go so far as to claim that he conducted business while walking on purple robes (Athen. 12.539b–c = *FGrH* 86 F3). But where K.'s showmanship ended and their malice begins is impossible to say. Justin 13.6.16 claims that K. commanded Perdikkas' fleet just before Perdikkas invaded Egypt, and it is tempting to emend the text to read *Attalo cura classis traditur* instead of *Clito cura classis traditur* (cf. Schoch, *RE* X (1922) 667). But a decree from Ephesos, dating to the period before the death of Krateros and granting citizenship to K. and Alketas, shows that the two were still cooperating in the year 322/1 (Keil, *JÖAI* 16 (1913) 235 no. II*n*; commentary on 241). When Antipatros and Krateros prepared to cross to Asia to confront Perdikkas, K. defected to the old regent and helped secure the crossing of the Hellespont (Arr. *Succ.* 1.26: τοὺς τὸν πόρον φυλάσσοντας διὰ πρεσβείας ὑπαγόμενοι) and he appears to have aided Antigonos against the Perdikkan fleet near Kypros (*OGIS* 4 14–15). For this change of allegiance he received the satrapy of Lydia in the settlement at Triparadeisos (Diod. 18.39.6; Arr. *Succ.* 1.37), replacing Antigonos' friend Menandros, who had ruled there since 331 (Arr. 3.6.7). Antipatros' intention appears to have been to limit the ambitions of Antigonos the One-Eyed, by entrusting Hellespontine Phrygia to Arrhidaios, Kilikia to Philoxenos and Lydia to K.; all these territories bordered on Antigonos' enlarged satrapy of Phrygia. Antigonos, however, moved against Arrhidaios and K. soon after Antipatros' death. Kleitos himself fled to Macedonia and brought charges against Antigonos (Diod. 18.52.5–8). He served Polyperchon briefly and took the Athenians arrested in Phokis, including Phokion, to Athens for execution (Plut. *Phoc.* 34.2–4, 35.2). As admiral of Polyperchon's fleet he won an initial victory over Nikanor in the Propontis (Diod. 18.72.2–4), but his ships were attacked while they were at anchor by light-armed troops sent by Antigonos. The disorganized fleet then put out to sea and was destroyed by Nikanor (Diod. 18.72.5–8; Polyaenus 4.6.8; cf. Engel 1973). K. himself escaped to the Thrakian shore only to be killed by Lysimachos' men (Diod. 18.72.9). Berve II 209 no. 428; Schoch, *RE* XI.1 (1921) 666–8 no. 10; Hauben 43–51 no. 18; Heckel 1992, 185–7 and *Marshals*² 298–304. Also Ashton 1977; Bosworth 2003b; Engel, 1973; Morrison 1987; Walek 1924; Wrightson 2014.

597 KLEOCHARES

(Κλεοχάρης). Probably Macedonian. Sent by Alexander in 326 as an envoy to Poros, telling him that he must pay tribute and present himself to the King at the entrance to his realm (Curt. 8.13.2). Metz Epit. 55–6 claims that Poros had K. whipped and sent an arrogant letter to Alexander. The letter is almost certainly a fabrication and a later addition. Hence the story of K.'s mistreatment may also be false. Identification with the son of Pytheas (below) is speculative at best. Berve II 214 no. 436; Launey 1169.

598 KLEOCHARES

(Κλεοχάρης). The son of Pytheas, from Amphipolis (Tataki 54 no. 72). Honored by the Eretrians (*IG* XII.9 199; *IG* II² 559 + *IG* XII suppl., p. 178) in a decree attesting to his connections with the kings (Antigonos and Demetrios). Probably participated in the Demetrios campaigns of 303–302. Billows 395 no. 58; Paschidis 450–1.

599 KLEODIKE

(Κλεοδίκη). Sister of Holkias. K. is known only from the propaganda pamphlet on the *Last Days and Testament of Alexander*, a product of the early age of the Successors. According to this document K. was to marry Leonnatos (*LM* 119; Jul. Valer. 3.58 [94]; Ps.-Call. 3.33.14). Although the testament of Alexander is a forgery, the individuals named therein are historical and we have no reason to doubt K.'s existence. Berve II 209–10 no. 429; Heckel 1988, 80.

KLEOMANTIS (Plut. *Alex.* 50.5). See **KLEOMENES**.

600 KLEOMEDON

(Κλεομέδων). Father of Kleainetos. He had been fined 50 talents by the Athenians, but his son performed favors for Demetrios in order to get him to write a letter ordering the Athenians to drop the charges. The issue was a disgrace for Kleainetos and an outrage to the Athenians, although they did rescind the fine (Plut. *Demetr.* 24.6–7).

601 KLEOMENES

(Κλεομένης). Greek. Possibly identical with "Kleomantis the Lakedaimonian" of Plut. *Alex.* 50.5, which appears to be a corruption of a text that originally read "the seers, Aristandros and Kleomenes the Lakedaimonian"; Berve II 212, for different reasons, concluded that K. must have been a seer or priest and accepts him as historical; cf. Poralla no. 431. For the textual problem see Ziegler 1935, 379; for the identification of Kleomantis with this Kleomenes see Hamilton 140. K. was thus a seer in Alexander's entourage in 328 who interpreted an unfavorable omen for the King at the time of the Kleitos affair (Plut. *Alex.* 50.4–5). K. was one of several men who slept in the temple of Serapis at the time of Alexander's fatal illness (Arr. 7.26.2). Identification with K. of Naukratis seems impossible (Alexander had written to him from Babylon shortly before his illness: Arr. 7.23.6–8). The entire episode has, however, been called into question as has the existence of a temple of Serapis in Babylon at this time. Berve II 211–12 no. 432; cf. Poralla no. 431.

602 KLEOMENES

(Κλεομένης). Greek from Naukratis. Ptolemy's hyparch in Egypt (Justin 13.4.11; Arr. *Succ.* 1. 5; Dexippos, *FGrH* 100 F8 §2). Allegedly the man who built (*aedificaverat*) Alexandria (Justin 13.4.11). K. had been appointed by Alexander in 331 as governor of the Arabian portion of Egypt, i.e., east of the Delta (Arr. 3.5.4), to which was added responsibility for Egyptian finances (Arr. 3.5.4; cf. Curt. 4.8.5; for the position of *arabarchos* see Dittenberger, *OGIS* 570, pp. 256–8), which, in the opinion of Seibert 1969, 50), he handled with skill. Arr. 7.23.6, 8, speaks of "wrongdoings," but this may reflect Egyptian complaints about overzealous tax collection or tight-fisted financial management; Diod. 18.14.1 says that Ptolemy found 8,000 talents in the Egyptian treasury. For the vexed question of whether K. ever became satrap in Alexander's lifetime, possibly after Hephaistion's death (Paus. 1.6.3 and [Arist.] 2.2.33, 1352a 16 call him "satrap"; [Dem.] 56.7 is ambiguous). In all likelihood, Alexander (like Augustus and his successors) thought it wise not to entrust Egypt to a single official, a practice which may explain the decision of the marshals in Babylon to assign K. to Ptolemy as *hyparchos*; in effect, he continued in the functions originally assigned him by Alexander (cf. Julien 24: "Obersteuereinnehmer"). Killed by Ptolemy, who considered him friendly towards Perdikkas and therefore unfaithful to himself (Paus. 1.6.3). Berve II 210–11 no. 431; Stähelin, *RE* XI.1 (1921) 710 no. 8; Bosworth I 277; Vogt 1971; *contra* Seibert 1969 and 1972; Baynham 2015; Müller, *LexAM* 300.

603 KLEOMENES

(Κλεομένης). Spartan (Poralla 77 no. 437) Kleomenes II, Agiad king (*regn.* 370–309/8). Son of Kleombrotos I and brother of Agesipolis II; father of Akrotatos and Kleonymos, and grandfather of Areus, who acceded to the throne in 309/8 (Plut. *Agis* 3.6; Paus. 1.13.4–5; 3.6.2). Although he succeeded Agesipolis in 370 and ruled until his death in 309 (Diod. 20.29.1: he reigned for 60 years and 10 months; but Diod.15.60.4 wrongly gives him 34 years), K. did not attract the attention of the Alexander historians. He was apparently married to the daughter of Gyrtias (Athen. 4.142b–f; Diod. 19.70.4, Plut. *Mor.* 53e). Berve II 8 no. 13 includes Agesipolis II in his prosopography and assumes that (a) Diodorus mistakenly reported his death, when he was merely deposed, and (b) K. surrendered his brother to Antipatros as a hostage after Agis' war (Plut. *Mor.* 215b). But Agesipolis' death is reported also by Paus. 1.13.4. Cartledge 1989, 16 rightly calls K. a "prodigious nonentity." **Stemma XVIIIa.**

604 KLEON

(Κλέων). Greek from Syracuse. Named by Curt. 8.5.8 as one of the King's flatterers (*kolakes*) who advocated the public acknowledgement of Alexander's divinity (Curt. 8.5.10). He may be identical with the author of a work *On Harbors* (also a Syracusan named Kleon from the fourth century) and thus one of Alexander's "technical" experts. I see no evidence for Pearson's view (78) that Kleon was a poet. Nothing else is known about him. Jacoby, *RE* XI.1 (1921) 718–19 no. 8; Berve II 215 no. 437; Müller, *FHG* IV 365.

605 KLEON

(Κλέων). Son of Kleon from Erythrai. Honored with a proxeny by the Megarians. An officer of Demetrios in the period 304–302 (*IG* VII 5). Billows 395 no. 59.

KLEONIDAS. See LEONIDAS.

606 KLEONYMOS

(Κλεώνυμος). Spartan (Bradford 246–7 no. 1). Eurypontid (c.340–c.272). Younger son of Kleomenes II, younger brother of Akrotatos (Paus. 3.6.2; but Paus. 3.24.1 wrongly calls him grandson of Agesipolis, whose nephew he was). Father of Leonidas (Plut. *Agis* 3.8). Late in life he married Leotychidas' daughter, Chilonis (Parthenius 23), who committed adultery with Areus' son Akrotatos (Plut. *Pyrrh.* 26.17–18). When Kleomenes II died in 309/8, the *gerousia* decided that the kingship should go to K.'s nephew Areus (Paus. 1.13.5; 3.6.2; Polyaenus 2.29.1 calls K. "King of the Lakedaimonians" in error). In order to placate K., the Spartans made him general of their forces, in the hope that he would direct his anger over the lost throne against their enemies rather than the state (Paus. 1.13.5; 3.6.3). Hence, in 303, he set out on an Italian campaign in defense of the Tarentines against the Lucanians (Diod. 20.104.1–2, 105.2–3; Livy 10.2; Athen. 13.605e, he took women as hostages from Metapontum rather than men; cf. Diod. 20.104. 3; Plut. *Mor.* 233a–b belongs in the context of this campaign; cf. Strabo 6.3.4 C280; Trogus, *Prol.* 15 discussed "the exploits of K. in Kerkyra, Illyricum and Italy and his loss of Kerkyra"). K. recruited 5,000 mercenaries at Tainaron, still a depot for such troops, and an equal number in Tarentum; from the citizen population he added 20,000 infantry and 2,000 cavalry (Diod. 20.104.2). In short order he brought the Lucanians and the Metapontines to heel (20.104.3). After his initial successes he gave himself over to debauchery and luxurious living, proving himself unworthy of his homeland (20.104.4). Although he contemplated a campaign against Agathokles, he went instead to Kerkyra, taking the city and installing a garrison. Diodorus says nothing more about his activities there. In 293/2, he invaded Boiotia and, with the help of Peisis of Thespiai, attempted to recover the region from Demetrios Poliorketes. But, although the Thebans came over to him, K. took fright at Demetrios' arrival and fled, leaving the Thebans to surrender to Demetrios (*Demetr.* 39.2–4). In 279, "K. and the Lakedaimonians" were alleged to have denied the Messenians a truce so that they could fight the Gallic invaders (Paus. 4.28.3), though it is not clear on what authority K. did so. He depopulated the town of Zarax (*Barr. Atl.* 58 E4), near Epidauros Limera (Paus. 3.24.1). K. also took Troizen by trickery (277/6), firing "propaganda" arrows into the city. These were inscribed with a message that he had come to liberate the city. When the commander of the city, Eudamidas, turned to suppress insurrection within, K. scaled the walls and took the city, establishing a Spartiate as *harmostes* (Polyaenus 2.29.1; Front. 3.6.7). At an unspecified time he mediated in Krete, establishing a truce between the Polyrhenians and Phalosarnians (*I.Cret.* II 11.1). Defeated the Macedonians at Edessa by neutralizing the effectiveness of the *sarissa* (Polyaenus 2.29.2, although P. does not say, presumably the city was taken; 273). But K. eventually induced Pyrrhos to invade Lakonia (Paus. 1.13.4; 3.6.3; Plut. *Pyrrh.* 26–7), who clearly planned to use him as his puppet in Sparta (Plut. *Mor.* 219f). Sandberger 130–2 no. 44; Lenschau, *RE* XI.1 (1921) 730–2 no. 3; Launey 1120. **Stemma XVIIIb.**

607 KLEOPATRA

(Κλεοπάτρα). Macedonian (Tataki 343 no. 52). Arr. 3.6.5 calls her "Eurydike," which, if not an error, must be the name she assumed at marriage (Heckel 1978a; Bosworth I 283; *contra* Badian 1982; Ogden 22–4). Sister of Hippostratos and niece of Attalos (wrongly the sister of Attalos: Diod. 17.2.3; Justin 9.5.9), K. was Philip's seventh and last wife (Diod. 17.2.3; Satyros *ap.* Athen. 13.557d–e; cf. Athen. 13.560c), and possibly the aunt of the ilarch and admiral, Hegelochos (no. 496). She had borne Philip a daughter named Europa (Satyros *ap.* Athen. 13.557e; cf. Justin 9.7.12) only a few days before the King's death (Diod. 17.2.3). But this child was soon murdered along with her mother by Olympias (Justin 9.7.12; Paus. 8.7.7 speaks of a male child). Palagia 2010 argues that she is the "Eurydike" of the statue group in the Philippeion (*contra* Carney 2007, 49–60 and *King and Court* 89–90). Stähelin, *RE* XI.1 (1921) 734–5 no. 12; Badian 1982; Berve II 213 no. 434; Tarn II 260–2; Heckel 1978a and 1979; Prestianni-Giallombardo 1981; Whitehorne 1994, 30–42. **Stemma XIV.**

608 KLEOPATRA

(Κλεοπάτρα). Macedonian (Tataki 343 no. 51). Daughter of Philip II and Olympias (Satyros *ap.* Athen.13.557c; Diod. 16.91.4–6), sister of Alexander the Great (Justin 13.6.4; 14.1.7). K. was born, in all likelihood, between 355 and 353. Plut. *Alex.* 3.2 may suggest that shortly before losing his eye at Methone, Philip had ceased to have sexual relations with Olympias. Heidelberg Epit. 4 wrongly says that the mother of K. had the same name. In 336 she married her uncle, Alexander I of Epeiros (no. 43), in Aigai; it was during the celebrations associated with this wedding that Philip was assassinated (Diod. 16.91.4–6; Justin 9.6.1–3, 7.7). Whether the union produced any children is uncertain. It is tempting to identify Kadmeia (no. 557) as K.'s daughter, but this is based on the assumption that the girl was named for Alexander the Great's sack of Thebes in 335. If this is true, then Neoptolemos II (no. 773) would have been K.'s child as well, since he is identified as Kadmeia's brother (Plut. *Pyrrh.* 5.11; cf. Sandberger 115 no. 40). But there are other historical arguments that appear to favor the view that Kadmeia and Neoptolemos were grandchildren of Alketas II. After the departure of Alexander I from Epeiros, K. appears to have exercised power as regent (cf. Carney 89). After the death of Alexander I (Aesch. 3.242 mentions an Athenian delegation that brought condolences; cf. Livy 8.24.14–17 for the return his remains), Olympias returned to her native Epeiros and sent K. back to Macedonia. She sent a shipment of grain via Leukas to Korinth in 333/2 (Lyc. 1.26); acted as *thearodochos* in 330 (*SEG* XXIII 198) and is named as a recipient of grain from Kyrene (*SEG* IX 2; cf. Kingsley 1986, 169–70). K. also intervened with her brother on behalf of Dionysios of Herakleia (no. 386) who was threatened by those who had been exiled by the

Herakleiot tyranny (Memnon 4.1; cf. Burstein, *Outpost* 74). In the years after her brother's death K. became the political tool of others with regal aspirations, though she herself appears to have made an offer to marry Leonnatos (Plut. *Eum.* 3.9) along with the promise of supreme power. But Leonnatos died before the promise could be fulfilled (Diod. 18.15.3–4) and K. entered into negotiations with Perdikkas. These were, however, complicated by Perdikkas' previous commitment to marry Nikaia the daughter of Antipatros (Justin 13.6.4, 7; Diod. 18.23.1–3), an arrangement that Alketas urged his brother to honor (Arr. *Succ.* 1.21); Eumenes at the same time acted as Perdikkas' go-between with K., who had now taken up residence in Sardis (Arr. *Succ.* 1.26). Perdikkas' intrigues were reported by Antigonos to Antipatros (Diod. 18.25.3). After Perdikkas' death and the outlawing of his party, Eumenes came to Sardis in order to shore up his own authority as the defender of the royal cause through K.'s support (Justin 14.1.7) but K. was afraid of compromising her position with Antipatros, and Eumenes departed (Plut. *Eum.* 8.6–7). Some indication of her earlier support for Eumenes and the Perdikkan party can be found in the fragmentary text of Arr. *Succ.* 25, in which we learn also that Perdikkas had taken control of Lydia away from Menandros and given it to K. (25.2). When Antipatros himself reached Sardis, there was a heated exchange in which K. gave as good as she got (Arr. *Succ.* 1.40). Between 320 and 308, K. remained in Sardis until Ptolemy made an offer of marriage, in connection with his only serious bid for greater power (Diod. 20.37.3; Heidelberg Epit. 4). Bosworth 2000 puts the *Last Will and Testament of Alexander*, which offers Kleopatra as bride to Ptolemy (*LM* 117), into this historical context. Diod. 20.37.4 claims that Antigonos, Kassandros, and Lysimachos had all at one point sought her hand in marriage. Antigonos, however, sensing the danger of such an alliance had her killed (Diod. 20.37.5–6). Stähelin, *RE* XI.1 (1921) 735–8 no. 13; Berve II 212–13 no. 433; Macurdy 22–48; Whitehorne 1994, 57–69; Carney 75–6, 89–90, 123–8, *LexAM* 301–2; Aulbach §6.2.1.5. **Stemma I.**

609 KODROS

(Κόδρος). Ephesian, son of Echeanax. Together with his brothers Anaxagoras (no. 91) and Diodoros (no. 378), he murdered Hegesias, tyrant of Ephesos. Philoxenos, acting on behalf of Alexander the Great, forced the Ephesians to surrender K. and his brothers and imprisoned them for some time in Sardis. From here K. and Anaxagoras escaped to Athens, but Diodoros was injured in the escape and recaptured. After Alexander's death, when Perdikkas sent Diodoros back to Ephesos to be tried, K. and Anaxagoras returned to save him (Polyaenus 6.49). Berve II 215 no. 438.

610 KOINOS

(Κοῖνος). Macedonian (Tataki 196 no. 13). Son of Polemokrates (Arr. 1.14.2; cf. *Syll*³ 332, 7–8) and apparently the brother of Kleandros (Arr. 1.24.2). The father had been allotted estates in Chalkidike, and Koinos too received additional land in Philip's reign, all of which his son Perdikkas (no. 873) inherited (*Syll*³ 332 = Hatzopoulos II no. 20). Born no later than 366: it is doubtful that he would have defended his right to speak out at the Hyphasis with reference to his age (δίκαιος δέ εἰμι καθ' ἡλικίαν), had he not been at least forty in 326 (Arr. 5.27.3). In the campaign against the Taulantians near Pellion in 335, he commanded a phalanx battalion (Arr. 1.6.9), presumably the Eleimiotai. He married, perhaps in late 335, Parmenion's daughter (Curt. 6.9.30; cf. Arr. 1.24.1, 29.4: K. was one of the "newlyweds" (*neogamoi*) sent home in the winter of 334/3), probably Attalos' widow. The couple's son, Perdikkas, was born no later than the end of 333 (see above).

At the Granikos, K. was stationed on the right, between Perdikkas and Amyntas son of Andromenes (Arr. 1.14.2). At Issos (Arr. 2.8.3; Curt. 3.9.7) and Gaugamela (Arr. 3.11.9; Diod. 17.57.2; Curt. 4.13.28, wrongly claiming that Koinos' troops stood in reserve: cf. Atkinson I 422), he had displaced Perdikkas in the position closest to the hypaspists. During the winter 334/3 K. was sent on a recruiting mission from Karia to Macedonia (Arr. 1.24.1–2); he rejoined Alexander at Gordion with 3,000 infantry and 300 cavalry from Macedonia, 200 Thessalian horse and 150 Eleian cavalry (Arr. 1.29.4; cf. Curt. 3.1.24). Griffith believes that the shift of K.'s unit to the right at Issos recognized its performance, the term *asthetairoi* denoting "Best Companions" (Griffith, *HMac* II 712; but see Bosworth 1973; Hammond 1989, 129–31; Heckel and Jones 2006, 31–2; Heckel 2009; English 2009, 25–7; Anson 2010; Sekunda 2010, 456–7). In the final assault on Tyre, K.'s battalion (or rather a portion of it) boarded a ship suitable for landing troops, and once inside the city walls distinguished itself in a particularly bloody engagement (Arr. 2.23.2, 24.3). At Gaugamela he was wounded by an arrow in the heavy fighting (Curt. 4.16.32; Diod. 17.61.3; Arr. 3.15.2; but cf. Bosworth I 311).

At the Persian Gates (late 331), K.'s battalion formed part of the force that circumvented the position of the Persian defender, Ariobarzanes: Koinos, Amyntas, Polyperchon, and Philotas son of Parmenion were detached from this encircling force in order to begin the bridging of the Araxes River (Curt. 5.4.20, 30; Arr. 3.18.6). From Persepolis, he marched with Alexander from Awan-i-Kif, through the Caspian Gates—usually identified with Sar-i-Darreh (Seibert 1985, 112; cf. Bosworth I 340, with map opposite)—and gathered provisions in the region of Choarene (mod. Khar) with a force of cavalry and a few infantry (Arr. 3.20.4). But news of Dareios' arrest caused Alexander to push ahead without awaiting K.'s return (Arr. 3.21.2); the latter rejoined Krateros, who followed the King at a slower pace. In the campaigns against the Mardians (Arr. 3.24.1–3) and Satibarzanes near Artakoana (Arr. 3.25.6), K. was again directly under the King's command.

Charges that Philotas was involved in the conspiracy of Demetrios the Bodyguard (no. 358) placed K. in danger on account of their familial relationship (Curt. 6.9.30). K., however, belonged to the *consilium*, which met with the King to discuss the matter (Curt. 6.8.17). He denounced Philotas as a parricide and a traitor to his country (Curt. 6.9.30), in an effort to deflect any charge of complicity. Curtius' claim that there was a Macedonian law that relatives of those who plotted against the King be put to death may reflect what was practiced on occasion, but not an iron-clad rule. Nevertheless K.'s attitude towards his wife's brother and his demand that Philotas be tortured, was first and foremost an act of self-preservation (Curt. 6.9.30–1; 6.11.10–11). A brief hiatus in our knowledge of K.'s activities between 330 and 328 may be due to the sources, which are confused and uneven at this point, rather than fallout from Philotas' misdeeds. Indeed, his prominence in the years 328–326 suggests that he was not tarnished by the Philotas affair. In 328, he led one of five mobile units in a sweep-campaign in Sogdiana (Arr. 4.16.2–3). Hephaistion, Perdikkas, Ptolemy, K. (with Artabazos) and the King each led one contingent; Curt. 8.1.1 mentions only three divisions, led by Alexander, Hephaistion, and K. The heavy infantry (at least four battalions) remained with Krateros in Baktria (Arr. 4.16.1; 4.17.1). K. and Artabazos (at that time the satrap of the region) moved toward Skythia, whither Spitamenes had fled (Arr. 4.16.3). But Spitamenes eluded them and crossed the Oxos to attack Baktra (Zariaspa), only to be driven out again by Krateros (Arr. 4.16.4–17.2). In late summer or early autumn, K. rejoined Alexander at Marakanda where Kleitos was murdered by the King. As winter approached, K. remained in Sogdiana with the new satrap, Amyntas son of Nikolaos, two battalions of *pezhetairoi*, 400 Companion Cavalry and the *hippakontistai* with orders to guard the territory against Spitamenes and the Massagetai (Arr. 4.17.3). He retained his own battalion (perhaps already led by Peithon son of Agenor) and that of Meleagros. The 400 Companions may represent what were to become K.'s hipparchy (cf. Arr. 5.16.3). He inflicted heavy casualties (Arr. 4.17.5–6: 800 casualties), and brought the Massagetai to terms: they soon showed their good faith by sending Spitamenes' head to Alexander (Arr. 4.17.7; a much different story in the Vulgate: Curt. 8.3.1–15; Metz Epit. 20–3). K. rejoined the King at Nautaka before the end of winter (Arr. 4.18.1).

Effective campaigning in Sogdiana led to more independent roles during the Swat campaign (cf. Fuller 245ff.; Seibert 1985, 150–4). Against the Aspasian hyparch, he remained with Alexander (Arr. 4.24.1) and also against the Gouraians and Assakenians as far as Massaga (Arr. 4.25.6); from Massaga he was sent against Bazeira (= Bir-Kot: Stein 46–8; Eggermont 184; Arr. 4.27.5, 7–8; Curt. 8.10.22 calls it Beira; *Itiner. Al.* 107.), where he inflicted heavy losses on the natives while Alexander took the nearby town of Ora ('Ude-gram; Stein 1929, 58–60; cf. Seibert 1985, 152, with n.40; Karten 25–6). Arr. 4.27.5 names Attalos, Alketas, and Demetrios the hipparch as the commanders in charge of the siege; Curt. 8.11.1 names Polyperchon and credits him with the capture of the town. Arr. 4.27.7, 9 gives Alexander the honor of taking Ora. The natives of Bazeira fled to Aornos (Pir-Sar), to which the King advanced via Embolima, taking Koinos and some more nimble troops (Arr. 4.28.8); in addition to K.'s battalions, Alexander took the archers, the Agrianes, select troops from the phalanx, 200 Companion Cavalry and 100 mounted archers. On his return from Aornos, Alexander learned that Aphrikes was preparing to blockade his path, and he left K. to bring up the slower troops while he advanced to meet the enemy (Diod. 17.86.2; Curt. 8.12.1).

By the time the Macedonians reached the Hydaspes (Jhelum), K. had effectively become hipparch. His former battalion still retained his name, though its commander was in all probability Peithon son of Agenor (Tarn II 190 implausibly assigns it to Antigenes). Before the battle with Poros, he was sent back to the Indos to dismantle the ships and transport them overland to the Hydaspes (Arr. 5.8.4). In the actual engagement, K.'s battalion and hipparchy crossed the river upstream along with the King and took part in the initial assault on Poros (Arr. 5.12.2; Curt. 8.14.15, 17; Plut. *Alex.* 60): he and Demetrios son of Althaimenes attacked the cavalry (about 2,000 in number) on the Indian right, pursuing them as they transferred their position to the left, where Poros' horsemen were outnumbered by Alexander's (Arr. 5.16.3; 5.17.1; Curt. 8.14.15 must be emended to make sense of K.'s activities).

At the Akesines (Chenab) K. was left behind to oversee the crossing by the bulk of the army and to forage for supplies; a similar task was given also to Krateros (Arr. 5.21.1, 4). He rejoined Alexander at or near the Hyphasis (Beas) after the bloody Sangala campaign. Here, when the troops were stubborn in their refusal to continue eastward, K. put the soldiers' case to the King during a council of war, reminding him of their sufferings and losses and their desire to see their homeland and loved ones (Arr. 5.27.2–9; Curt. 9.3.3–15). Curtius adds an appeal to the poor state of the soldiers' equipment, a point which may well be true, but which contributes to the general irony of the situation: K., who spoke so passionately in favor of returning to Macedonia, died soon afterwards (Curt. 9.3.20), and there arrived shortly after his death 25,000 splendid suits of armor (9.3.21). For doubts concerning Alexander's plans to advance to the Ganges see Spann 1999, Heckel 2003b; *contra* Anson 2015. Whatever suspicions his death at the Hydaspes arouses (Arr. 6.1.1, 2.1; cf. 5.59.5; Curt. 9.3.20 puts it at the Akesines; for the confusion see Hammond 1983, 152–3), coming as it did so soon after his opposition to Alexander, there is no good reason to assume that it was not caused by illness (Holt 2000; Müller 2003, 93 n.504). Honigmann, *RE* XI.1 (1921) 1055–7 no. 1; Berve II 215–18 no. 439; Heckel *Marshals*[2] 67–74; Hatzopoulos II 43–5 no. 20.

611 KOINOS

(Κοῖνος). If not the product of textual error, Koinos was apparently Macedonian, though nothing further is known of his background. K. arrived in Persia in 324 with mercenaries and reports of the political situation in Europe (Curt. 10.1.43). He ruled Sousiana in 323 (Justin 13.4.14) after the brief rule of Oropios (Dexippos, *FGrH* 100 F8 §6; perhaps "Argaios of Oropos," thus Berve II 57 no. 107; cf. *LM* 121), who had replaced Aboulites. Sousiana was awarded to Antigenes at Triparadeisos. What became of K. is unknown. Berve II 218 no. 440; Honigmann, *RE* XI.1 (1921) 1057 no. 2; Lehmann-Haupt 154.

612 KOIRANOS

(Κοίρανος). Macedonian from Beroia (Arr. 3.16.9; Tataki, *PB* 205 no. 750). K. appears to have been with Alexander since the beginning of the Asiatic expedition. Before the battle of Issos, when Harpalos fled to Greece (Arr. 3.6.7), Alexander divided the control of the treasury between K. and Philoxenos. Upon Harpalos' return to favor, K. was appointed the finance officer for Phoinikia, Kilikia, and Koile-Syria (Arr. 3.6.4). Bosworth I 279–80 rejects the view that he was overseer of all these areas and limits him to Phoinikia, but just such a division of power is implied by Arrian's remark that Philoxenos was given charge of the area on the other side of the Tauros (τῆς Ἀσίας τὰ ἐπὶ τάδε τοῦ Ταύρου), and Phoinikia must be used by Arrian in a general (broader) sense. In 331, Alexander sent Menes son of Dionysios with 3,000 talents of silver to become *hyparchos* of this region (Arr. 3.16.9–10). It does not follow (*pace* Berve II 219) that he replaced K. as finance officer (see Brunt I 278 n.11). Berve II 219 no. 441; Tataki, *PB* no. 750.

613 KOIRANOS

(Κοίρανος). Macedonian (Tataki 345 no. 67). Family and geographic background unknown. Arr. 3.12.4 calls the commander of the allied horse Koiranos. Possibly this is an error for Karanos (thus Roos emends the text; cf. Brunt I 262 n.1; Heckel 1981e, 70) but Bosworth I 303, argues for retaining Koiranos. He may be identical with Karanos (no. 577), who commanded allied infantry (Arr. 3.5.6: "Kalanos"), but this is far from certain. Koiranos is not heard of again; Karanos, on the other hand, is found commanding similar troops later in the campaign. Together with Erigyios, and with Artabazos as a guide, K. was sent against the rebellious satrap of Aria, Satibarzanes (Arr. 3.28.2); his role in the campaign is overshadowed by Erigyios, who is said to have killed Satibarzanes in hand-to-hand combat (Arr. 3.28.3; cf. Curt. 7.4.33–40). In 329, at the Polytimetos (Zeravshan) River, where he was ambushed and killed by Spitamenes (Arr. 4.3.7, 5.7, 6.2),

K.'s troops are 800 *misthophoroi hippeis*, but it may be that the allied horse continued to serve Alexander as mercenaries. Schoch, *RE* Supplbd IV s.v. "Koiranos (9)"; Berve II 219 no. 442; (Koiranos); Berve II 200–1 no. 412 (Karanos); Brunt I 262 n.1; Heckel 1981e, 70; Bosworth I 303.

614 KOMBAPHES

(Κομβάφης). Apparently a barbarian (for the name see Justi 165 s.v. Kombaphis). Slave of Alexander. According to the *Liber de Morte*, he and a fellow slave, Hermogenes, were summoned to the King's deathbed, where one copied out his testament (which the King dictated) while the other held the lamp (*LM* 103). Alexander's testament itself is fictitious, but the *Liber de Morte* in other cases refers to historical individuals, and K. and Hermogenes may, in fact, have been actual slaves of the King. Berve II 219 no. 443; Heckel 1988.

615 KOMOSARYE

(Κομοσαρύη). In the next generations the name appears as Καμασαρύη (*IPE* II 19; cf. *Syll*³ 439, Pairisades II also had a queen named Kamasarye; Werner 424–5). Daughter of Gorgippos (on whom see Polyaenus 8.55), the brother of Leukon and son of Satyros I, K. married her cousin Pairisades I (though, unlike the wife of Pairisades II, she is not attested with the title *basilissa*). Known only from a dedication (R&O no. 65 D = *Syll*³ 216) found near Phanagoria (on the eastern side of the Kimmerian Bosoporos). Mother of Gorgippos (no. 484), named for the maternal grandfather, and thus (as is often the case) the second of her sons (thus Beloch III2 2.93, tentatively; Burstein 1978, 433; Worthington 206; but rejected by Werner 440: "Für einen zweiten Gorgippos . . . ist daher kein Platz"). Satyros II was then also her son, and it is likely that Prytanis and Eumelos were too. Nothing else is known about her. Beloch III² 2.93. **Stemma XVII.**

616 KONON

(Κόνων). Athenian (Kirchner 8708). Son of Timotheos ([Dem.] 40.39) of Anaphlystos, hence grandson of the famous K., the victor of Knidos. For the inscriptional evidence for his liturgies in Athens see Kirchner 8708; also Davies 511. After his father's death in 354/3, the fine of 100 talents imposed upon the family was reduced from 100 to 10 talents, which K. was required to pay for the repair of the Athenian walls (Nepos, *Timoth.* 4.1). His only direct involvement with Macedonian affairs came in 318, when he was sent by the Athenians, along with Phokion and Klearchos son of Nausikles, to Nikanor, who controlled Mounychia, asking him to restore autonomy to the Athenians in accordance with the Decree (*Diagramma*) issued by Philip III (Diod. 18.64.5). The mission was unsuccessful. It has been argued that in 318, despite his previous connections with Phokion, he received a golden crown from the Athenians (*IG* II² 1479 A18–21; cf Habicht 1997, 49; Bayliss 114). But Paschidis 68 n.2 voices strenuous objections and notes that the name Konon is too common to allow such an identification without patronymic or ethnic. The date and circumstances of his death are unknown and the family appears to have died out in the third century. Kirchner 8708; Davies no. 13700 for the family, and pp. 511–12 for K. in particular; Paschidis 68 A8.

617 KOPHAIOS

(Κωφαῖος). Indian dynast of the upper Kophen (Kabul) region (Lassen II² 147–8), but Bosworth II 185 more plausibly places him near the confluence of the Kophen and the Indos. K. surrendered to Alexander upon his arrival and retained the position of *hyparchos* of his country. Together with Assagetes, K. appears to have brought a contingent to Alexander at Peukelaotis and helped with the assault on Aornos (Arr. 4.28.6). Nothing else is known of his career. Wecker, *RE* XI.1 (1921) 1361–2; Berve II 229 no. 458; Lassen II² 147–8.

618 KOPHEN

(Κώφην, Κώφης). Son of Artabazos (Arr. 2.15.1), and one of the eleven sons of the same mother, the sister of Memnon and Mentor the Rhodians (Dem. 23.154, 157), who may have joined their father in exile at the court of Philip II. They were summoned to the court of Artaxerxes III, when he pardoned their father (Diod. 16.52.4, under the year 349/8, but the chronology is hopelessly confused; cf. Judeich 219–20); hence also the brother of Alexander's mistress, Barsine. Before the battle of Issos, K. was ordered to convey the royal treasures and the family members of the most prominent Persians to Damaskos for safekeeping (Arr. 2.15.1; cf. 2.11.9; Diod. 17.32.3; Curt. 3.8.12). Damaskos was, however, captured by Parmenion (Arr. 2.15.1; Curt. 3.13). K. himself appears either to have rejoined Dareios at Issos, whence he escaped with the King, or to have escaped capture at Damaskos (identification with Curtius' prefect of Damaskos (3.13.2–3, 17) is impossible, since that man was murdered). In 330, after the arrest of Dareios III by Bessos and his supporters, K. (with his father and brothers) surrendered to Alexander (Arr. 3.23.7), who later sent him to the Sogdianian rebel Ariamazes to negotiate his surrender (Curt. 7.11.5, 22–3; Metz Epit. 17 calls this man Dares). What became of him we do not know. Willrich 1899a sees K. as the intended occupant of the Alexander sarcophagus of Sidon. Although Willrich is right to suggest a Persian "Grabherr," K. himself is an unlikely candidate. See s.v. Mazaios no. 685; Heckel 2006. Willrich 1899a; Berve II 230 no. 459; Shayegan 110 no. 57.

619 KORRHAGOS

(Κόρραγος). Macedonian (Tataki 346 no. 72). Served as Antipatros' *strategos* in the Peloponnese during Alexander's absence. In summer 331 his forces suffered a stunning defeat at the hands of Agis III and his allies (Aesch. 3.165). Whether he himself survived the battle is unknown. Identification with the father of Stratonike, the mother of Demetrios Poliorketes (Plut. *Demetr.* 2.1), is possible but cannot be proved. Schoch, *RE* Supplbd IV (1924) 1036 no. 1; Berve II 219–20 no. 444.

620 KORRHAGOS

(Κόρραγος). Prominent Macedonian (Tataki 346 no. 73) and apparently one of Alexander's *hetairoi*. At a drinking party in India (326/5), he challenged the wrestler Dioxippos to single combat. K., in full armor, was defeated by Dioxippos who fought without body armor and carried a club (Curt. 9.7.16–26; Diod. 17.100.1–101.6). Ael. *VH* 10.22 says that he was killed in the duel, an incorrect inference. Nothing further is known about him. Schoch, *RE* Supplbd IV (1924) 1037 no. 5; Berve II 220 no. 445.

621 KORRHAGOS

(Κόρραγος). Macedonian. Son of Menoitas. One of the *hetairoi*. Participated in Alexander's Balkan campaign. Possibly identical with the man who fought the duel with Dioxippos. Clarysse and Sheppens 1985; Hammond 1987; Whitby 2004.

622 KRATEROS

(Κρατερός). Macedonian from Orestis (Tataki 205–6 no. 9). Son of Alexander (Arr. *Ind.* 18.5; Arr. 1.25.9; cf. Perdrizet 1899, 274) and Aristopatra (Strabo 15.1.35 C702 = *FGrH* 153 F2, although the letter appears to be spurious); Amphoteros was his brother (Arr. 1.25.9). Born perhaps *c.*370. Wounds (Plut. *Alex.* 41.5; Arr. 4.3.3) and illness (Arr. 7.12.4; Plut. *Alex.* 41.6–7) took their toll and hard campaigning may have aged him prematurely. In 334 K. commanded a battalion of *pezhetairoi* on the left at the Granikos (Arr. 1.14.2, 3; cf. Bosworth 1976, 126); he commanded the entire infantry on the left at Issos (333), though subordinate to Parmenion (Arr. 2.8.4; Curt. 3.9.8). Early in 332, K. and Perdikkas directed the siege of Tyre in Alexander's absence (Curt. 4.3.1) and K.'s troops effectively countered a Tyrian sortie (Polyaenus 4.13). Alexander placed him in charge of the left wing, along with Pnytagoras of Salamis, in the naval assault on Tyre (Arr. 2.20.6; Curt. 4.3.11). At Gaugamela (331), he led the infantry-battalions on the left wing, again under Parmenion's general command (Arr. 3.11.10; Diod. 17.57.3; but Curt. 4.13.29 is corrupt). His first independent mission was in the Ouxian campaign, where his troops occupied the heights, to which the enemy fled to escape Alexander's forces, only to be butchered in large numbers by K.'s men (Arr. 3.17.4–5; cf., in general, Diod. 17.67 and Curt. 5.3.1–16; Bosworth I 321–2 assumes that Arrian refers to a different engagement from that mentioned by Diodorus and Curtius; see also Fuller 226–8; Olmstead 519; Stein 1938: 313ff.; Strabo 11.13.6 C524, 15.3.6 C729). Henceforth, Alexander regularly entrusted the larger, less mobile, forces to K. For K.'s independent commands see Metz Epit. 35, 59, 60; Polyaenus 4.13; Curt. 4.3.1; Arr. 3.17.4–5, 18.4–8; Curt. 5.4.14–16, 29, 34; 5.6.11; Arr. 3.21.2; Curt. 6.4.2, 23–4; Arr. 3.25.6, 8; Curt. 6.6.25, 33; Arr. 4.2.2; Curt. 7.6.16, 19; 7.9.20–2; Arr. 4.17.1; Curt. 8.1.6, 5.2; Arr. 4.18.1, 22.1–2, 23.5; Curt. 8.10.4; Arr. 4.24.6–7, 28.7; 5.12.1, 18.1, 21.4; Diod. 17.96.1; Arr. 6.2.2, 4.1, 5.5, 7; Arr. *Ind* 19.1, 3; Curt. 9.8.3, 10.19; Arr. 6.15.5, 7; 6.17.3, 27.3; 7.12.3–4. At the Persian Gates, only days later, Alexander led a select force to Ariobarzanes' rear, leaving the rest of his troops at the foot of the "Gates" under the direction of K. (Arr. 3.18.4–8; Curt. 5.4.14–34; Polyaenus 4.3.27 wrongly places Hephaistion and Philotas in charge of the main camp).

Soon after the fall of Persepolis, Alexander conducted a thirty-day campaign into the interior of Persia, while the bulk of the army remained behind with Parmenion and K. (Curt. 5.6.11, probably to coordinate the removal of the treasures). It is doubtful that K. took part in the actual transporting of the treasures to Ekbatana, even though some units of pezhetairoi did remain to guard the treasure (Arr. 3.20.1); that task was given to Parmenion (Arr. 3.19.7, though Berve II 221 assumes that K. helped Parmenion). When Alexander hurried after Dareios and his captors, K. led the slower forces eastward from the Caspian Gates and awaited the return of Koinos and his foraging party (Arr. 3.20.4, 21.2). In Hyrkania, K. commanded one-third of the army, taking his own battalion and that of Amyntas son of Andromenes, the archers and some cavalry against the Tapourians (Arr. 3.23.2; cf. Curt. 6.4.2). Curt. 6.4.2 claims that K. was left behind to guard Parthiene against invaders, though his mission was to patrol, round up fugitive mercenaries (Arr. 3.23.6), and restore order to the satrapy. He rejoined Alexander at Zadrakarta in Hyrkania, along with Autophradates, the Tapourian satrap (Arr. 3.23.6; Curt. 6.4.23–4: "Phradates"). When Satibarzanes defected, K. was left to besiege a rocky outcrop some thirty-two stades in circumference (about 3.5 miles) to which some 13,000 Arians had fled (Curt. 6.6.23). Satibarzanes himself eluded Alexander, and the King returned to conduct the siege in person; his informants may have told him that Satibarzanes had moved to Artakoana (usually identified as Herat and equated with Alexandria in Aria), and perhaps he sent K. ahead to Artakoana, which he besieged in the King's absence, but allowed him the honor of taking it (Curt. 6.6.33). In Arrian's version, Alexander breaks off his march to Baktra, leaving K. with the rest of the army, while he himself rushed to Artakoana; no satisfactory account of the town's surrender is given. Some time later, when Alexander had already made administrative changes in the satrapy, K. and the remainder of the army joined him (Arr. 3.25.6–8).

In the autumn of 330, at Phrada (mod. Farah), K. took a leading role in the prosecution of his rival Philotas. Earlier, in Egypt (331), upon learning of "treasonous" remarks uttered by Philotas to his mistress, Antigone (no. 112; Plut. *Alex.* 48.6; Plut. *Mor.* 339e–f), K. brought this news, and Antigone herself, to the King. And, although Alexander forgave Philotas, K. remained suspicious and kept him under surveillance (Plut. *Alex.* 48.7–49.1). How long this "prolonged espionage" (Badian 1960, 331) lasted is unknown; Antigone's information cannot have revealed much that was not already known about Philotas. But in 331, when the opportunity presented itself in Phrada, K. once again worked against his rival. Alexander at first made no firm decision on how he would deal with what amounted to a case of negligence, the only offence of which Philotas was clearly guilty (cf. Curt. 6.7.34). For Philotas himself admitted that he had failed to pass on the news of a conspiracy involving some lesser-known Macedonians. Philotas' fate was, in fact, decided at a council of the *hetairoi*. K. spoke first and most effectively, for he was dear to Alexander and exceedingly hostile to Philotas (Arr. 7.12.3; Plut. *Alex.* 47.9–10; Diod. 17.114.1–2; Curt. 6.8.2). Whether or not K. was attempting to disguise his ill will towards Philotas with a show of piety, as Curt. 6.8.2, 4 claims, is debatable. He had already gained in power and importance as a result of Parmenion's relegation to Ekbatana. He earnestly desired to protect Alexander from the insidious, and he sought to ruin Philotas for personal reasons: he argued that Alexander could not go on excusing Philotas forever, nor would Philotas cease to conspire. Nor could they ignore the threat from Parmenion, who would not endure his son's execution (Curt. 6.8.7). But K. was only one of a clique of younger commanders who, united against a common enemy, denounced Philotas, first to Alexander and then the army, until even his relatives and friends saw fit to abandon him (see s.v. Philotas no. 940).

In Baktria-Sogdiana, as earlier in Hyrkania and Aria, K. had supreme authority over the army while Alexander led detachments on special missions. Thus, while Alexander subdued the rebellious outposts along the Iaxartes River (Syr-Darya), K. supervised the siegework (Arr. 4.2.2; Curt. 7.6.16) at the largest of these, Kyroupolis (Kurkath), which was then taken under the King's leadership (Arr. 4.3.1–4; Curt. 7.6.19–21)—though both Alexander and K. were wounded (Arr. 4.3.3; Plut. *Mor.* 341b, incorrectly placing it in Hyrkania; Curt. 7.6.22, saying the wound occurred at the town of the Memaceni, after the fall of Kyroupolis). We know nothing of his role in the brief skirmish with the Skythians who lived beyond the Iaxartes. Curtius (7.7.9–10) says that he, along with Erigyios and Hephaistion, attended the council held in Alexander's tent before the battle, but no source records his participation in the actual fighting (Arr. 4.4.1–9; Curt. 7.8.6–9.17 is quite different; cf. Fuller 237–41 for analysis). It seems likely that he retained the bulk of the army on the south bank of the river when Alexander crossed with a select force to attack the Skythians.

Learning of the disaster at the Polytimetos River (Arr. 4.3.6–7, 4.5.2–6.2; Curt. 7.7.30–9; cf. 7.6.24), Alexander hurried south, leaving K. to follow with the main body at a more restrained pace (Curt. 7.9.20; for Alexander's relief of Marakanda: Arr. 4.5.3–6.5; Curt. 7.9.20–21; *Itiner. Al.* 39; Metz Epit. 13; for K.'s arrival: Curt. 7.9.22.). In the spring of 328, Alexander moved out of winter quarters at Baktra (Balkh) and re-crossed the Oxos River, leaving behind the battalions of Polyperchon, Attalos, Gorgias, and Meleagros, all under the command of K. (Arr. 4.16.1 does not mention K., though his position is clear from 4.17.1 and corroborated by Curt. 8.1.6.). Their instructions were to prevent further defection in Baktria and to crush the insurrection (Arr. 4.16.1). But, while Alexander and the mobile troops conducted a sweep-campaign in Sogdiana, the rebel Spitamenes, supported by horsemen of the Massagetai, attacked the smaller Macedonian garrisons in Baktria. K. drove the Massagetai to the edge of the desert, where he defeated them in a bitter struggle—killing 150 of 1,000 horsemen—only to be forced by the desert to abandon his pursuit (thus Arr. 4.17.1–2; Curt. 8.1.6 claims that the Massagetai fled but that K. slew 1,000 Dahai, perhaps confusing this battle with the one fought by Koinos: Arr. 4.17.6–7). By driving Spitamenes out of Baktria, K. inadvertently took some of the luster off his own victory; for Koinos, who had been left in Sogdiana at the beginning of winter 328/7, won a more decisive battle, as a consequence of which the Massagetai delivered Spitamenes' head to Alexander (Arr. 4.17.3–7; cf. Curt. 8.3.1–15 and Metz Epit. 20–3). Both Koinos and K. rejoined the main force at Nautaka for the remainder of that winter (Arr. 4.18.1–2; Curt. 8.4.1 says that when Alexander moved out of winter quarters in spring 327—cf. Arr. 4.18.4—he had stayed there just over two months: *tertio mense ex hibernis movit exercitum*. Cf. Beloch III² 2.319).

K. was not present in Marakanda when Alexander murdered Kleitos (no. 595) in a drunken brawl, and we can only guess at what his reaction might have been. Like Kleitos, K. espoused the traditional values of Macedon (Plut. *Alex.* 47.9) and rejected the King's orientalism (Plut. *Eum.* 6.3), but his objections appear to have been tactful and restrained; for he retained the love and respect of Alexander. When the King moved south into Baktria, K. remained in Sogdiana with the battalions of Polyperchon, Attalos, and Alketas, capturing the rebel Haustanes and killing Katanes (Arr. 4.22.2; Curt. 8.5.2). It was perhaps no coincidence that Alexander's attempt to introduce the Persian practice of *proskynesis* at his own court was made during K.'s absence. But, even without him, the stubborn opposition of the Macedonian *hetairoi* forced Alexander to abandon the attempt. Details of the conspiracy of the Pages, which occurred soon afterwards, were reported to K. by letter (Plut. *Alex.* 55.6). Some time later, K. rejoined Alexander in Baktria, whence the army set out for India.

In early summer 327, Alexander moved towards India (Arr. 4.22.3–6). While Perdikkas and Hephaistion led the advance force to the Indos, K. at first remained with Alexander, following the course of the Choes. But the heavy infantry and siege equipment crossed the river with great difficulty and made slow progress through the mountains

(Arr. 4.23.2), and Alexander left them behind to follow at their own speed, presumably under K.'s command (for the division of the forces cf. Curt. 8.10.4: *Cratero cum phalange iusso sequi* refers to a time before Alexander's arrival at Andaka). Probably they did not reunite with Alexander until they reached Andaka (Arr. 4.23.5; Curt. 8.10.5), where K. was left with instructions to subdue those neighboring cities that had not submitted voluntarily. The composition of his force is not specified, but it can have included not more than two phalanx battalions (Polyperchon, Alketas), since the battalions of Attalos and Koinos were with the King and those of Kleitos, Meleagros, and Gorgias (formerly K.'s own) had accompanied Hephaistion and Perdikkas to the Indos (Arr. 4.24.1, cf. 22.7). From Andaka, he advanced to Arigaeum, where Alexander again left him behind with instructions to fortify the main wall, to settle in the city those of the neighboring peoples who so wished, and to leave behind such Macedonians as were unfit for service (Arr. 4.24.6–7). Next, K. led his troops and the siege equipment into the land of the Assakenians, where he rejoined the King (Arr. 4.25.5). From here he moved with the main army to Embolima, where he gathered provisions for the army's operations against Aornos (Arr. 4.28.7). From Aornos, where K. is unattested, the main force advanced to the Indos, which had been bridged by Hephaistion and Perdikkas, and thence to the Hydaspes. Here Poros awaited the Macedonians with a sizable force. In the ensuing battle—Alexander's last major engagement—K.'s role was similar to that at the Persian Gates. He held the attention of the enemy while Alexander conducted an encircling manoeuvre. When Poros turned to deal with Alexander, K. crossed the river in order to attack him from the rear (Arr. 5.12.1, 18.1). But the battle appears to have been decided before K.'s troops could play a significant part.

K. had perhaps advanced militarily as far as Alexander would allow. After the Hydaspes battle we hear of the fortification of Nikaia and Boukephala (Arr. 5.20.2), of a foraging expedition conducted with Koinos near the Hydraotes River (Arr. 5.21.4). In India he came into open conflict with Hephaistion (Plut. *Alex.* 47.11–12; Plut. *Mor.* 337a), forcing Alexander to intervene in person. For the remainder of the campaign, the Indos served to separate the foes and their armies, but the advantage shifted to Hephaistion, who, initially, commanded the larger force (Arr. 6.2.2; Arr. *Ind.* 19.1) as they descended the River in stages (Arr. 6.2.2, 4.1, 5.5, 5.7; Arr. *Ind.* 19.1, 3; Diod. 17.96.1). After Alexander was critically wounded in the Mallian campaign, K. acted as the spokesman for the *hetairoi*, begging him not to risk his life unnecessarily (Curt. 9.6.6–14). From the junction of the Indos and Akesines rivers, K. led the greater part of the army and the elephants along the left (east) bank of the Indos, arriving at Mousikanos' capital (near Rohri and ancient Alor) after Alexander's fleet (end of spring 325). K. was ordered to garrison and fortify the town. It was his last major operation—and one that he completed while Alexander himself was present (Arr. 6.15.7)—before being sent westward through Arachosia and Drangiana with orders to rejoin Alexander in Karmania. Arrian records K.'s departure twice (6.15.5, 17.3), first from Mousikanos' kingdom, then from Sind (for textual problems see Bosworth 1976, 127–9). K. had continued south with his troops, not much beyond Pardabathra—he appears not to have participated in the campaign against Oxikanos— where he appears to have remained with the main force while Alexander dealt with Sambos, the defecting satrap of the hill-country to the west of the Indos (Arr. 6.16.3–5; Curt. 9.8.13ff.; Diod. 17.102.6–7). Soon it was learned that Mousikanos had rebelled— perhaps massacring the Macedonian garrison. Reprisals were conducted by Alexander, and Peithon son of Agenor (the new satrap of the region) soon brought Mousikanos prisoner to Sind, where he was executed (Arr. 6.17.2; Curt. 9.8.16). At this point, K. was sent back to Rohri-Alor to restore order there—in the absence of Peithon, who continued south with Alexander—and also in Arachosia and Drangiana.

Thus K., with the battalions of Attalos, Meleagros, Antigenes, and Polyperchon, some of the archers, all the elephants and the *apomachoi*, moved westward, policing Arachosia and Drangiana and arresting the rebel leaders (Arr. 6.27.3: Ordanes; Curt. 9.10.19: Ozines and Zariaspes), whom he brought in chains to Alexander in Karmania (Arr. 6.27.3; cf. Strabo 15.2.11 C725; Stasanor, satrap of Aria and Drangiana, may very well have been summoned to Karmania by K. on the march; see Arr. 6.27.3; Arr. 6.29.1 says that he was sent home shortly afterward; cf. Bosworth 1971b: 123 n.3). Arr. 6.17.3 omits Polyperchon, but see Justin 12.10.1. Polyperchon had accompanied K. in the past (Arr. 4.16.1; 4.17.1; cf. Curt. 8.5.2) and was to do so again in 324 (Arr. 7.12.4; Justin 12.12.8–9, cf. Bosworth 1976, 129 n. 65). On the other hand, Justin substitutes the name Polyperchon for K. on a number of occasions (13.8.5, 8.7; 15.1.1). In Sousa (324) K. married the daughter of Oxathres, Amastris (no. 67; Arr. 7.4.5), whom he later repudiated and gave to Dionysios of Herakleia (Memnon, *FGrH* 434 F1 §4.4; Strabo 12.3.10). Soon afterwards he was ordered to lead some 10,000 veterans back to Macedonia, where he was to replace Antipatros as regent and overseer of Greek affairs (Arr. 7.12.4). Cf. Justin 12.12.8–9 (K. was accompanied by Kleitos, Gorgias, Polydamas, and Antigenes). See Curt. 10.10.15: *credebant etiam Craterum cum veterum militum manu ad interficiendum eum missum*, where *eum* refers to Antipatros (wrongly "Alexander" in J. C. Rolfe's Loeb translation, II 557). According to Plut. *Phoc.* 18.7, K. was to offer Phokion the revenues from one of four Asian towns. K., however, made slow progress and had not advanced beyond Kilikia when Alexander died in June 323. His progress was impeded initially by his own ill health (Arr. 7.12.4) and, later, by the conditions in Kilikia itself: the satrap Balakros (no. 283) had recently been killed in a campaign against the Pisidians (Diod. 18.22.1) and Harpalos (no. 494) had passed through Tarsos before K.'s arrival and created further disruptions. That K. deliberately disobeyed the King's orders is unlikely. See, however, Badian 1961, 34ff.; Green 1991, 460 suspects that Krateros was involved in a conspiracy with Kassandros, who was on his way to Babylon. Griffith 1965, 12–17 argues that K. was waiting for the new recruits to leave Macedonia before marching on.

When Alexander died, the orders to replace Antipatros were still in effect, at least until the army voted to cancel Alexander's "final plans" (Badian 1967b, 201–4), and soon the feuding marshals in Babylon designated him guardian (*prostates*) of Arrhidaios (Arr. *Succ.* 1.3; Dexippos, *FGrH* 100 F8 §4; cf. Justin 13.4.5). But Antipatros was urgently summoning reinforcements to help him in the Lamian War (Diod. 18.12.1). In fact, K. remained cautious and did not leave Kilikia until it became clear that Leonnatos' help would prove insufficient. Plut. *Phoc.* 26.1 says that the battle of Krannon was fought a short time afterwards, but, since it is dated to 7 Metageitnion (probably 5 August; cf. Beloch IV² 1.74), K. will not have reached the Hellespont until late June or early July 322. At that point, patriotism won out over personal ambition and K. brought a force of about 12,500 to Macedonia (Diod. 18.16.4). Over the winter he supplemented his forces; for he had decided to leave Antigenes and the three thousand Argyraspids in Kilikia for security, and other troops were given to Kleitos, who was preparing a fleet with which he would sail to the Hellespont. K. therefore recruited fresh troops, perhaps from the satrapies of Asia Minor. Diod. 18.16.4 is instructive: ἦγε δὲ πεζοὺς μὲν τῶν εἰς Ἀσίαν Ἀλεξάνδρῳ συνδιαβεβηκότων ἑξακισχιλίους, τῶν δὲ ἐν παρόδῳ προσειλημμένων τετρακισχιλίους ... This has been taken to mean that K.'s infantrymen were divided into two units: 6,000 who had campaigned with Alexander since 334 (who had crossed the Hellespont with him at that time), and another 4,000 who had joined Alexander's in the course of his campaigns (e.g., Brunt II, 489; and now Bosworth 2002, 73 n.31). But this is a curious distinction for the historian to make, and ἐν παρόδῳ probably refers to K.'s own march. The 1,000 Persian archers and slingers, as well as the 1,500 horse, were part of the original force that left Opis (Diod. 18.16.4). Antipatros' appeal included, in all probability, an offer of marriage to his eldest daughter Phila, widow of the satrap Balakros. K. probably found her residing in Tarsos in 324 and now escorted her to Macedonia. It was at this time, too, that K. offered Amastris to Dionysios of Herakleia Pontika. The choice of a new husband must have been linked with Dionysios' ability to help secure the crossing of the Hellespont, which was still threatened by the Athenian fleet. By the time K. reached the Hellespont, White Kleitos had already won control of the sea, but in the early stages this was far from predictable.

K.'s arrival greatly augmented the Macedonian fighting force, but he willingly yielded the supreme command to Antipatros (Diod. 18.16.5). Including the remnants of Leonnatos' army (Diod. 18.14.4–5), their forces numbered 40,000 infantry, 5,000 cavalry and 3,000 archers and slingers (Diod. 18.16.5). Victory at Krannon was decisive (Arr. *Succ.* 1.12; Plut. *Dem.* 28.2, *Phoc.* 26.1; Diod. 18.17), as the Thessalian cities were brought to terms one by one and the Hellenic alliance crumbled. When the Macedonian army reached Boiotia, K. favored an invasion of Attika (Pllut. *Phoc.* 26.6), but Antipatros, for Phokion's sake, overruled him and the Athenians saved themselves through negotiation and accepted a garrison in Mounychia on the twentieth day of Boëdromion (17 September 322; cf. Beloch IV² 1.76: Plut. *Phoc.* 28.2–3, *Dem.* 28.1, *Cam.* 19.10; cf. Schaefer III³ 391: 16 Sept.; also Berve II 259 and Diod. 18.18.5).

Once back in Macedonia, Antipatros celebrated the marriage of K. to Phila, heaping honors and gifts upon the groom and preparing for his "return to Asia" (Diod. 18.18.7). But first it was necessary to deal with the Aitolians, the only Greeks who remained unsubdued (Diod. 18.24–5). K. may have directed the campaign (Diod. 18.25); undoubtedly, he employed his experience gained in the East with Alexander to his advantage. It was now the height of winter, and K. built shelters for his troops, forcing the Aitolians, who had forsaken their cities for the highlands, to hold out against the elements and a shortage of food; for it appears that K. controlled the lines of communication (Diod. 18.25.1). But events in Asia were to extricate the Aitolians from this grave situation and lead K. to his doom.

Perdikkas, in the meantime, had wasted little time usurping the regency (cf. Diod. 18.23.2), and in winter 321/0 Antigonos the One-Eyed arrived with news of Perdikkas' aspirations and duplicity. K. and Antipatros now made peace with the Aitolians and prepared to confront Perdikkas in Asia (Diod. 18.25.5; Justin 13.6.9 wrongly speaks of peace with the *Athenians*, adding that Polyperchon was left in charge of Europe; he dealt effectively with the Aitolians, Diod. 18.38. For the decision to go to war with Perdikkas see Arr. *Succ.* 1.24; also an alliance was made with Ptolemy (Diod. 18.25.4; cf. 18.14.2). For K.'s aims in Asia see Völcker-Janssen 1993, 123-4; Paspalas 2000, 2015–16; cf. Voutiras 1984, 61. Cf. Seibert 1969, 96ff. K. departed from Macedonia for the last time in the spring of 320, leaving behind Phila and an infant son. Perdikkas, for his part, had left Eumenes to deal with Antipatros and K. while he himself marched on Egypt. Neoptolemos abandoned Eumenes (Diod. 18.29.1–30.3; Plut. *Eum.* 5; Arr. *Succ.* 1.26 says that he was lured away). K.'s popularity with the Macedonian troops was also a concern, but Eumenes had no intention of revealing his opponent's identity to his own men (Nepos, *Eum.* 3.5–6; Plut. *Eum.* 6.7; Arr. *Succ.* 1.27). In the ensuing battle K. was thrown from his horse, felled by a Thrakian or Paphlagonian, or as some said, trampled by his own horse's hoofs (Plut. *Eum.* 7.5–6; Arr. *Succ.* 1.27; Nepos, *Eum.* 4.3–4; Diod. 18.30.5); Plut. *Eum.* 7.6 relates that a certain Gorgias, one of Eumenes' generals recognized the fallen K. That Eumenes himself found him as he gasped out his life defies credulity, particularly if we are meant to believe that Eumenes had only shortly before overcome his arch-rival Neoptolemos in a bloody hand-to-hand encounter (Nepos, *Eum.* 4.2; cf. Justin 13.8.8; Plut. *Eum.* 7.7–12; Diod. 18.31). Justin 13.8.5, 7 writes Polyperchon where K. is clearly meant (cf. Trogus, *Prol.* 13). Eumenes was almost certainly remorseful and treated K.'s body with respect (Plut. *Eum.* 7.13; Arr. *Succ.* 26; Nepos, *Eum.* 4.4; Diod. 19.59.3 states that Eumenes kept the bones of K. and only when he himself was on the point of dying gave them to Ariston to convey to Phila in 315). Geyer, *RE* Supplbd IV s.v. "Krateros (1a)"; Berve II 220–7 no. 446; Heckel, *Marshals*² 122–52; Ashton 1993 and 2015; Pitt and Richardson 2017; Müller, *LexAM* 304–6.

623 KRATEROS

(Κρατερός). Macedonian (Tataki 349 no. 93). Son of the famous Krateros son of Alexander and Phila. Thus a half-brother of Antigonos Gonatas, with whom he was on good terms (Plut. *Mor.* 486a; cf. Phlegon, *Mir.* 32). Born no later than early 320. The parents were married in the winter of 322/1 (Diod. 18.18.7) and the father died in battle in spring 320. If the inscription that accompanied the lion hunt monument of Krateros can be taken literally, the younger K. was a child when his father crossed over to Asia for the last time (for the date of that dedication see Dunn and Wheatley 2012; cf. Heckel, *Marshals*² 147–8, with a summary of literature on 148 n.158). K. was in all likelihood the compiler of decrees (Ψηφισμάτων Συναγωγή or Περὶ Ψηφισμάτων, *FGH* 342), sharing with his uncle Marsyas (no. 683) an interest in historical research. K. was not militarily or politically active until the third century, though as a youth he must have spent a considerable time in the military camp of his stepfather Demetrios Poliorketes. Whether he fought at Ipsos, when he was about nineteen or twenty years old, is unclear. Billows 396–7 no. 60; Schoch, *RE* XI (1922) 1617–22 no. 1; Jacoby, *FGrH* IIIb 62–77; Tarn, *AG passim*; Homolle 1897; Dunn and Wheatley 2012. **Stemma V.**

624 KRATES

(Κράτης). Greek from Chalkis. K. was a mining engineer (μεταλλευτής) entrusted with draining Lake Kopais in Boiotia, which was in flood and threatening neighboring towns. He wrote to Alexander concerning his activities and their disruption by civil strife in Boiotia (Strabo 9.2.18 C407; cf. Steph. Byz. s.v. "Athenai"). Diog. Laert. 4.23 mentions a miner named Krates who accompanied Alexander on his expedition and Ps.-Call. 1.31 speaks of a certain Karteros (or Krateros), an Olynthian, whom Alexander consulted on the construction of Alexandria in Egypt (cf. Jul. Valer. 1.26). It appears that K. may have been an Olynthian who settled in the Euboian mother-city, Chalkis, after the destruction of Olynthos in 348 by Philip II. Fabricius, *RE* XI.2 (1922) 1642 no. 21; Berve II 227 no. 448.

625 KRATES

(Κράτης). Son of Askondas. [All reference in **boldface** to Diogenes Laertius.] Theban philosopher (**6.85–93**) who, for a Cynic, was relatively engaged in public life. He was a wealthy man who sold his property for about 200 talents, which he distributed to his fellow citizens (**6.87**). Alexander was said to have stayed in his home (**6.88** with textual problems), which (if true; Berve does not include him in his prosopography) may have occurred in 336, at the time of the abortive first uprising of the Thebans (Diod. 17.4.4). After Thebes' destruction, Alexander purportedly asked K. if he would like his city rebuilt, to which the philosopher replied: "What's the use, some other Alexander will just destroy it again" (**6.93**). Plut. *Demetr.* 46.3 mentions a philosopher named K. who, in 287/6, participated in negotiations between Demetrios Poliorketes and Ptolemy's agent Sostratos on behalf of the Athenians, with the aim of raising the siege by Poliorketes (Plut. *Demetr.* 46.3–4). The talks were primarily between Demetrios and Ptolemy, which preceded the Besieger's return to Asia, but K. was present to protect Athenian interests. K. is generally identified as the son of Antigenes of Thria (Kirchner 8745), on whom see **4.21–23**; we know from **4.23** that the Athenian philosopher had acted as an ambassador (*pace* Rose 2015, 320); K.'s collected works included λόγους ... πρεσβευτικούς. But Paschidis 151 argues that a man who was described as "not a friend of the people," ought not to have presented a case in favor of democratic Athens (*contra* Shear 1978, 77 n.212; Sonnabend 1996, 314). Hence, Paschidis 151–2 (followed by Rose 2015, 320–1) proposes K. son of Askondas of Thebes as the envoy in question. There can be no certainty. Paschidis 150–2 A48; Rose 2015, 320–1.

626 KRATESIPOLIS

(Κρατησίπολις). Macedonian (Tataki 350 no. 200). Wife of Alexander son of Polyperchon (Plut. *Demetr.* 9.5). After the death of her husband, the Sikyonians despising a mere woman leading an army, rose in revolt. She defeated them with great slaughter and crucified thirty men whom she had captured. K. maintained a firm hold on Sikyon and governed it with many soldiers who were ready for any emergency (Diod. 19.67.1–2). Her behavior elicits from Diodorus (and thus probably his source) the remark that she conducted herself in a manner "beyond what was typical of a woman" (Diod. 19.67.2: μείζων ἢ κατὰ γυναῖκα). She possessed both Korinth and Sikyon but in 308 handed them over to Ptolemy (Diod. 20.37.1; cf. Niese II 308–9) and even helped him secure Akrokorinth against the wishes of her own garrison (Polyaenus 8.58). Her motive appears to be concern about Polyperchon's alliance with Kassandros (thus Niese II 309; for the background see Griffin 1982, 76–8). Plutarch's account (*Demetr.* 9.5–7) of her secret meeting with Demetrios, which almost resulted in the latter's capture, has been accepted by most scholars on its face value. But, as Wheatley 2004 points out (cf. Rose 2015, 159–60), the account is rife with historical problems: if the event occurred around the time of the Besieger's attack on Megara, then perhaps Plutarch or his source meant to write Pagai instead of Patrai, since the former was a port of Megara and the latter some 150 km distant. If Patrai is correct, the liaison must belong to another time—perhaps 303 or 302, or possibly even 294—although, despite the fact that Demetrios had a fondness for older women, it is doubtful that K.

was in 294 still the celebrated beauty that she had been in 312. Plutarch treats it as a mere sexual encounter, but K. may have intended to entrap Demetrios or perhaps increase her political power by use of her charms. What became of her is unknown. Concerning her name, Hoffmann 219 writes "Fast scheint es, als habe die Schwiegertochter Polyperchons ihren Namen Κρατησίπολις erst dadurch erhalten, dass sie nach dem Tode ihres Gatten Alexander (314 v. Chr.) sich tatkräftig und glücklich bis zum Jahre 309 als Herrscherin in den Städten Sikyon und Korinth zu behaupten wusste ..." But this is rightly denied by Macurdy 1929, who points to the occurrence of the name in a Macedonian tomb on Euboia, probably from the late fourth century. Macurdy 1929; Stähelin, *RE* XI.2 (1922) 1643 no. 2; Wheatley 2004. **Stemma XII.**

627 KRATEUAS

(Κρατεύας). Macedonian (Tataki 349 no. 96; Hoffmann 155). *Strategos* of Kassandros; K. had been defeated in battle by Aristonous (no. 207) at the time that Kassandros was waging war on Olympias and her supporters. K. himself had fled with 2,000 men to Bedyndia in Bisaltia and was invested there by Aristonous, who captured him and dismissed him after he surrendered his arms (Diod. 19.50.7). K.'s kinsmen subsequently slew Aristonous (Diod. 19.51.1). Perhaps K. was a relative of the Somatophylax Peithon (no. 867). It appears that Aristonous and Peithon went separate ways in the wars of the Diadochoi. Schoch, *RE* XI.2 (1922) 1644 no. 1.

628 KRATINOS

(Κρατῖνος). Methymnean lyre player (*psilokitharistes*) of unknown family, K. performed at the mass marriage ceremony in Sousa in 324 (Chares, *FGrH* 125 F4 = Athen. 12.538e). Berve II 227 no. 449 and *RE* Supplbd. IV (1924) 1048 no. 6.

629 KRETHEUS

(Κρηθεύς). A Greek, patronymic unknown, from the Milesian colony of Kallatis (*Barr. Atl.* 22 F5) on the Black Sea coast of Thrake, he may have joined Alexander during the Danubian campaign of 335 and remained for the duration of the Asian campaign. During the Gedrosian march of 325, when the army came to a region of the satrapy where supplies were plentiful, he was instructed to gather provisions for Nearchos' fleet and convey them to a depot where they could avail the fleet (Arr. 6.23.5). Nothing else is known about him. Schoch, *RE* Supplbd IV (1924) 1060 no. 1a; Berve II 228 no. 450.

630 KRISON

(Κρίσων). A runner from Himera on Sicily, K. once raced Alexander but lost deliberately, much to the King's annoyance (Plut. *Mor.* 58f, 471e). He is otherwise unattested. Berve II 228 no. 451.

631 KRITOBOULOS

(Κριτόβουλος). A physician (Curt. 9.5.25) from Kos, K. was one of the trierarchs of the Hydaspes fleet (Arr. *Ind.* 18.7). Since the trierarchs were responsible for the expenses of fitting out the ships and not actually the commanders of the vessels themselves, there is no obstacle to identifying the trierarch and the physician. During the descent of the Indos river system, K. treated the near-fatal wound sustained by Alexander in the town of the

Mallians (Curt. 9.5.25). Arr. 6.11.1 calls the physician Kritodemos, but Curtius' version preserves the name of the man who is credited with extracting the arrow from Philip II's eye at Methone some 28 years earlier (Pliny, *HN* 7.37). I do not regard the length of time between K.'s service at Methone and his treatment of Alexander in India as an argument against identification. Lengthy service, both in the military and in other spheres, is well attested in this period. Leonidas, Lysimachos the tutor, Philip the physician and Aristandros the seer were all well advanced in years, and in the army we may point not only to veteran officers like Parmenion and Antipatros but to the soldiers who were to form the Argyraspids. Furthermore, it is likely that Alexander's medical staff included men of proven ability. Kind, *RE* XI.1 (1922) 1927–8; Berve II 228 no. 452; cf. Heckel 1981f; Sherwin-White 479–80.

KRITODEMOS. Berve II 228 no. 453. See **KRITOBOULOS**.

632 KROBYLOS

(Κρώβυλος). Slave boy renowned in Korinth for his beauty. Hagnon of Teos was reported to have wished to buy him for Alexander, only to be rebuked for the offer (Plut. *Alex.* 22.3). He is otherwise unknown. Berve II 228 no. 454.

633 KTESIPHON

(Κτησίφων). Athenian of the deme Anaphlystos (Kirchner 8894); son of Leosthenes (Dem. 18.54, 118). Introduced a motion to crown Demosthenes in 336, which was the basis of the charges brought by Aischines in 330 (Aesch. 3 and Demosth. 18). K.'s personal link with Alexander came in 331/0, when he was sent as an ambassador to Alexander's sister, Kleopatra, offering her the condolences of the Athenians for the death of her husband, Alexander I of Epeiros (Aesch. 3.242). Honigmann, *RE* XI.1 (1922) 2079 no. 2; Berve II 228–9 no. 455; Schaefer III² 83, 86, 221, 292.

634 KYNNANE

(Κυννάνη, Κύνα, Κύννα), [Κ]υννάνα appears on two inscriptions from Beroia (*SEG* XXIV 503, XXXI 625; see Tataki, *PB* nos. 780–1, with literature; cf. also Palagia 2008). The name is Greek (thus Bartels 2015) and appears to mean "radiant" ("leuchten," or "glänzen," Hoffmann 220); Mayor 2014, 474 n.16, deriving the name from κύων ("dog" or "bitch") is misguided. Macedonian (Tataki 351 no. 103). Daughter of Philip II and Audata-Eurydike, the daughter of the Illyrian king Bardylis (Satyros *ap.* Athen. 13.557b–c; Arr. *Succ.* 1.22). Born 358/7, K. accompanied her father on an Illyrian campaign in the mid-340s in which she is said to have slain with her own hand an Illyrian queen (Polyaenus 8.60; the supposed name of this queen, Caeria, that has found its way into some modern scholarship is the result of mistranslation of καιρίαν ἐς αὐχένα πλήξασα "striking a mortal blow to the neck"). If the repetition of the story in modern scholarship implies acceptance of its details, this must be a mistaken view; for the single combat between the royal women belongs to K.'s legend, probably fashioned by Douris of Samos (cf. Heckel 1983–4). Soon thereafter she married Amyntas Perdikka (no. 76) and bore him a daughter, Adea (Arr. *Succ.* 1.22). When Amyntas was executed by Alexander in 336/5 (Arr. *Succ.* 1.22), the widowed K. was offered as a bride to Langaros, king of the Agrianes (Arr. 1.5.4); but he died of illness before he could come to Pella to receive his bride (Arr.

1.5.5). She remained unmarried in Macedonia, raising her daughter, whom she trained in the Illyrian arts of war (Douris, *FGrH* 76 F52 = Athen. 13.560f). After Alexander's death, she crossed the Strymon in spite of Antipatros' attempt to prevent her journey and took her daughter to Asia, where she planned to arrange her marriage to Philip III Arrhidaios (Bosworth 2002, 12 n.26 argues that this was *not* her intention, but it is hard to see for what other reason she came to Asia Minor). She was, however, met by Alketas, the brother of Perdikkas, who sought to turn her back in the vicinity of Ephesos. Defiant, she was murdered by Alketas (Polyaenus 8. 60; Arr. *Succ.* 1.22; cf. 1.24 for the news of her death in Europe). Her murder helped to accomplish her goal; for the army of Alketas mutinied and demanded that Adea be taken to Philip III in order that K.'s death might not be in vain (Polyaenus 8.60; Arr. *Succ.* 1.23). She was later buried at Aigai, near the tomb of her daughter and son-in-law (Diyllos, *FGrH* 73 F1 = Athen. 4.155a; Diod. 19.52.5). According to Diyllos the funeral games included four of Kassandros' soldiers matched in single combat (see Alsono 2009, 287–8; Landucci 2010). Hoffmann 220; Berve II 229 no. 456; Fluss, *RE* Supplbd. VI (1935) 209–11; Heckel 1983–4; Carney 69–70, 129–31, and 1988, 385–404; Ogden 16–26. **Stemma I.**

635 KYRSILOS

(Κύρσιλος). Thessalian from Pharsalos, patronymic unknown. Accompanied Alexander on his expedition—perhaps as one of his Thessalian *hetairoi*, possibly as member of the Thessalian cavalry—and appears to have written, together with Medeios of Larisa, an early history (*archaeologia*) of Armenia, claiming that the region was named for the Thessalian Armenos, who accompanied Jason on the *Argo* (Strabo 11.14.12 C530). Kroll, *RE* XI.1 (1922) 204; Berve II 229 no. 457; Jacoby, *FGrH* 130; Pearson 69.

L

636 LACHES

(Λάχης). Son of Melanopos, Athenian from the deme Aixone (Kirchner 9020). Imprisoned in Athens (at some undetermined point in Alexander's reign) for inability or failure to pay a fine but was freed as a result of a letter from Alexander (Dem. *Ep.* 3.24, 26). Berve II 232 no. 465.

637 LAGOS

(Λάγος). Macedonian (Tataki 352 no. 3). Son of Ptolemy and his mistress, the Athenian courtesan Thais; brother of Leontiskos and Eirene (Athen. 13.576e). L. must have been born during Alexander's campaign (i.e. before 323): *Syll.*³ 314 names him as a winner in the chariot race in the Lykaian games in Arkadia in 308/7. Stähelin, *RE* XII.1 (1924) 464 no. 2; *PP* VI no. 14527; Ogden 68, 232–3. **Stemma X.**

638 LAMACHOS

(Λάμαχος). Sophist from Myrrhine on Lesbos (or possibly from Tereina, unless the text of [Plut.] *Mor.* 845c is corrupt), L. wrote a panegyric on Philip II and Alexander which was read out at Olympia and drew an angry response from Demosthenes. L. was forced to leave the festival out of shame and fear for his safety (Plut. *Dem.* 9.1; [Plut.] *Mor.* 845c; cf. Roisman and Worthington 224). Berve II 231 no. 461.

639 LAMIA

(Λάμια). Athenian flute girl (prostitute), daughter of the Athenian Kleanor (Athen. 13.577c), L. was an exceptional flute player (Athen. 3.101e; 4.128b; Plut. *Demetr.* 16.5). Anecdotal evidence shows that she was no longer young—at least, by the standards of courtesans (Mania is supposed to have referred to her as γραῦς, an old woman, surely an exaggeration: Plut. *Demetr.* 27.7–10)—and she seems to have been born in the 340s. Diog. Laert. 5.76 cites Favorinus and claims that L. was the mistress of Demetrios of Phaleron, which, despite the possibility that he confused the two men of the same name (thus Wheatley 2003, 31, with n.9; Rose 2015, 188; O'Sullivan 2009, 9 n.1), is not entirely unlikely. She may have encountered Ptolemy Soter in 309 or 308 and accompanied him to Egypt. L. was captured by Demetrios among the spoils of his victory at Salamis in 306 (Put. *Demetr.* 16.5), though it is not at all clear whether she had been a mistress of Ptolemy (as Ogden 177 assumes). Nor is it clear if she remained with Demetrios—she had clearly become his mistress very soon after her capture—or was sent back to Athens to await his return in 304. It was there that her relationship with the Besieger gained notoriety (cf. Plut. *Demetr.* 24.1); even Antigonos could not resist a joke at his son's expense, saying that he greeted him with kiss "as if he were kissing Lamia" (Plut. *Demetr.* 19.6). The bulk of what we know about her comes from the period 304–302, when Demetrios consorted openly with her, and it creates perhaps a false impression of a long-lasting and intense relationship (Plut. *Demetr.* 16.6; Wheatley 2003, 30 calls her "the love of his life"; Aelian, *VH* 12.17; Athen. 6.253b; Plut. *Demetr.* 27.8: τοσοῦτον ἤρα χρόνον). The story that Demetrios defended L. against slanders by Lysimachos by saying that "his whore was more chaste than Lysimachos' Penelope" (Athen. 14.614f–615a; Plut. *Demetr.* 25.9: τὴν ἑαυτοῦ πόρνην σωφρονεστέραν εἶναι τῆς ἐκείνου Πηνελόπης) has been taken by some to be a comparison of L. and Arsinoë, thus dating the remark to the 290s (Lund 16; Carney 2013, 39); but Bosworth 2002, 272–3 (cf. Rose 2015, 232) rightly notes that in the context it probably is a reference to Nikaia (Phila's sister). Demetrios' relationship with L. doubtless cooled, if only to keep up appearances, when the Besieger married Deidameia (no. 343) in 303 and lived with her Athens (cf. Plut. *Demetr.* 30.3). L. bore him an illegitimate daughter named Phila (Athen. 13.577c). When Demetrios captured Sikyon in 303/2 and resettled her citizens (Diod. 20.102.2–4) Lamia was responsible for the building of the Painted Stoa (Athen. 13.577c). Her influence with Demetrios was such that both the Athenians and the Thebans were said to have set up temples to "Aphrodite Lamia" (Demochares *ap.* Athen. 6.252f–253a = *Histories,* Bk 20, *FHG* II 449; Polemon, *On the Painted Porch in Sikyon ap.* Athen. 6.253b; cf. Plut. *Demetr.* 27; Athen. 3.101e, 4.128b; Alciphr 4. 16 sch.; Ael. *VH* 13. 9), though Demetrios was allegedly disgusted by the gestures. Several stories are told about her as a result of a dinner party given by her for Demetrios, which was attended and described by Lynkeus of Samos, a brother of the historian Douris (Athen. 3.101e, 4. 128b). She was slighted by the flute player Theodoros, who when invited (summoned) to L.'s house ignored the invitation (Aelian, *VH* 12.17). Her relationship with Demetrios is discussed at length by Plutarch (*Demetr.* 19.6; 24.1; 25.9; 27). Geyer, *RE* XII.1 (1924) 546–7 no. 5; *PP* VI no. 14727; Gow, *Machon* 93–5; Ogden, 177; Wheatley 2003; Yardley-Wheatley-Heckel 240, 260; Aulbach §8.2.2.4.

640 LANASSA

(Λάνασσα). Syracusan. Daughter of the tyrant Agathokles of Sicily and his second wife, Alkia (Sandberger 132; cf. Beloch IV² 2. 255–6; see s.v. Alkia no. 63); hence also sister of the younger Agathokles (Diod. 21.15; 21.16.3). That the mythical Neoptolemos (also known as Pyrrhos) was married to Lanassa, daughter of Kleodaios (Plut. *Pyrrh.* 1.2; Schol. ad Eur. *Androm.* 24; cf. Justin 17.3.4) may be a later invention by Proxenos, reflecting the historical relationship of the 3rd century (cf. Sandberger 132). Born, most likely, *c.*310, L. was offered as bride to Pyrrhos, whose wife Antigone had died in 295/4; she brought as a dowry Kerkyra, which Agathokles had captured (Plut. *Pyrrh.* 9.2), as well as Leukas (Demochares *ap.* Athen. 6.253b; Plut. *Mor.* 176, 557c; cf. Seibert 1969, 101 n.7). In 294/3, she bore Pyrrhos a son, Alexander (Plut. *Pyrrh.* 9.3; Diod. 22.8.2; but Justin 23.3.3 mistakenly says Helenos was her son). The birthdate of Antigone's son Ptolemy (Justin 18.1.3: he was 15 when Pyrrhos left for Italy, thus born 295/4) provides another indicator for the date of the marriage. She soon quarreled with her husband, who preferred, at least in his private life, his barbarian wives. In 291, L. withdrew to Kerkyra and offered herself in marriage to Demetrios Poliorketes, who, as she knew, was favorably disposed to such matches, offering to turn Kerkyra over to him (Plut. *Pyrrh.* 10.6–7). What role her father, Agathokles, played in this is unclear, but there was a political shift away from support for Pyrrhos to Demetrios. The latter availed himself of the relationship and seized control of the island in 291/0 (Plut. *Pyrrh.* 10.7; L. is not mentioned in Plutarch's *Demetrios*). The liaison with Demetrios was no more enduring than that with Pyrrhos, and L. appears to have been the political tool of her father and both husbands. A fragment of Diodorus (21.4.1) shows that Agathokles himself used a faked message that he was escorting his daughter to Epeiros, as a means of catching Kroton off guard and taking that city. What became of L. is unknown. Sandberger 132–6 no. 45; Stähelin, *RE* XII 617–18 no. 2; Seibert 1967, 30, 100, 107–8; Carney 169–71; Volkmann, *Kl. Pauly* III 474 no. 2; Aulbach §8.2.1.4. **Stemma IIb.**

641 LANGAROS

(Λάγγαρος). King of the Agrianes, a tribe of the Paionians, who lived on the upper Strymon towards the Axios River. Their contingent later formed an important element in Alexander's expeditionary force. L. had developed close personal ties with Alexander already in Philip's lifetime, and had come to him personally on an embassy (Arr. 1.5.2), perhaps while Alexander ruled in Philip's absence in 340 or 338/7. In 336/5, when Alexander was contemplating a campaign against the Autariatai (Mócsy 1966, 104; Tomaschek, *RE* II.2 (1896) 2593; Hammond 1966, 249), L. arrived with his best-equipped hypaspists, deriding the Autariatai as the least warlike of the tribes in that region (Strabo 7.5.11 C317–18 says they were once powerful) and offered to conduct the campaign against them in person. This he did successfully, leaving Alexander free to deal with the Illyrians and Taulantians under Kleitos and Glaukias (Arr. 1.5.2–3). For his efforts he was handsomely rewarded by Alexander and summoned to Pella to marry the King's half-sister Kynnane (no. 634; now the widow of Amyntas son of Perdikkas III). L., however, died of illness on his return from the campaign against the Autariatai (Arr. 1.5.5). Berve II 230 no. 460.

642 LANIKE

(Λανίκη, Hellanice and Alacrinis). Macedonian (Tataki 352 no. 5). Daughter of Dropidas and sister of "Black" Kleitos. She was born, most likely, shortly after 380; for she is named as the mother of Proteas (Hippolochos *ap*. Athen. 4.129a; Ael. *VH* 12.26) and two other sons who died in battle at Miletos in 334 (Curt. 8.2.8; cf. Arr. 4.9.4). L. had been Alexander's nurse (Curt. 8.1.21, 2.8–9; cf. Arr. 4.9.3; Ael. *VH* 12.26; Athen. 4.129a; Ps.-Call. 1.13; Jul. Valer. 1.17), a circumstance which only heightened the grief which Alexander felt for his murder of Kleitos. Her husband may have been Andronikos, though not the Olynthian (Berve's comments at II 39 and 231 are contradictory; see Carney 1981, 153, with n.11). Berve II 231 no. 462; Stähelin, *RE* XII.1 (1924) 688. See also Samuel 1986, 430 n.8; Alonso 2007. **Stemma VIII.**

643 LAODIKE

(Λαοδίκη). A woman of the Macedonian aristocracy (Tataki 352 no. 6), but of unknown family background, L. married Antiochos (perhaps a member of the Orestian nobility, cf. Hoffmann 153). Mother of Seleukos Nikator (no. 1041). The story that she slept with Apollo and conceived Seleukos (Justin 15.4.3–6) is later invention, imitating Olympias' alleged liaison with Zeus-Amun (Justin 15.4.3–6; Grainger 1990a, 2–3; Hadley 1969, 152, dating it to after Ipsos). The story is connected in some way with that of the ring, engraved with the device of an anchor, which L. gave to her son (App. *Syr.* 56. 284–7). Seleukos is said to have founded five cities named in her honor (App. *Syr.* 57. 295; Strabo 16.2.4 C749–750; Steph. Byz. s.v. Λαοδίκεια; cf. Grainger 1990b, 48–50; Ogden 2017, 169–70).

The existence of a daughter of Seleukos named Laodike may be the creation of Eustathius 915, who believes that Laodikeia was named for Antiochos I's *sister* (Grainger, *SPG* 50 no. 17). Berve II 231 no. 463; Volkmann, *Kl. Pauly* III 479 no. 1; Bevan, *Seleucus* II 275–6; Hoffmann 220; Hadley 1969; Grainger, *SPG* 50 no. 14; Ogden 2017, 23–6, 169–70. **Stemma XI.**

644 LAODIKE

(Λαοδίκη). Macedonian (Tataki 353 no. 7). Daughter of Seleukos and Apama (Malalas 8.198, 202–3). L. was the sister of Apama. Their existence is doubted by Grainger and Beloch, but Eustathius 915 mentions L. Since three different sources speak of multiple children of Seleukos and his first wife (App. *Syr.* 61; Justin 15.4.9; *OGIS* 213 = Burstein no. 2), we may assume that not all the children were male; certainly the names Laodike and Apama are those of the paternal grandmother and the mother respectively. Malalas 8.202–3 is wrong in claiming that the cities Laodikeia and Apamea were named after them (in the case of the former, cf. Steph. Byz. s.v. Ἀντιόχεια, where L. is identified as A.'s sister), but this need not mean that the girls did not exist (cf. Ogden 2017, 170). Stähelin, *RE* XII.1 (1924) 700–1 no. 13; Ogden 120; Grainger, *SPG* 50 no. 17 (treated as fictitious); Beloch IV² 2.198. **Stemma XI.**

645 LAOMEDON

(Λαομέδων). Naturalized Macedonian (Tataki 55 no. 75). Son of Larichos (Arr. 3.6.5; Arr. *Ind.* 18.4) and younger brother of Erigyios. Mytilenean by birth (Arr. *Succ.* 1.34; Diod. 18.3.1, 39.6; Justin 13.4.12; App. *Syr.* 52. 263; cf. Diod. 17.57.3), he settled in Amphipolis (Arr. *Ind.* 18.4). Possibly father of that Larichos honored at Priene (*OGIS* 215, 13). An *hetairos* of Alexander, L. was almost certainly not coeval with the King, but already mature when he settled in Amphipolis in the 350s or early 340s. Born perhaps in the late 370s. L. was exiled by Philip in the spring of 336 (along with Erigyios, Harpalos, Nearchos, and Ptolemy) for his part in the Pixodaros affair (Arr. 3.6.5; cf. Plut. *Alex.* 10.4, naming Erigyios but omitting L.), but recalled after Philip's death (Arr. 3.6.6). He accompanied Alexander to Asia and was given charge of the Persian prisoners after Issos because he was bilingual (Arr. 3.6.6). Hence, it is curious that Alexander is said to have sent Leonnatos to the captive Persian queens, and not L. (Curt. 3.12.6–7), and it is possible that the original source of this information (accidentally or deliberately?) substituted the name of Leonnatos for Laomedon. Curtius notes that the man whom Alexander intended to send, Mithrenes, was a Persian speaker (Heckel 1981b). He was one of the trierarchs of the Hydapses fleet in 326 (Arr. *Ind.* 18.4). Nothing else is known of his career under Alexander. After the King's death in June 323, L. received the satrapy of Koile-Syria (Arr. *Succ.* 1.5; Dexippos, *FGrH* 100 F8 §2; Diod. 18.3.1; Curt. 10.10.2; Justin 13.4.12; App. *Syr.* 52; in the forged will of Alexander, this territory was assigned to Meleagros: Jul. Valer. 3.58; Leo 33; Ps.-Call. 3.33.15; *LM* 117; cf. Heckel 1988, 67; cf. Lehmann-Haupt §26; cf. §§129ff.); perhaps he aided his old friend Ptolemy in diverting Alexander's funeral carriage to Egypt (Arr. *Succ.* 1.25). At Triparadeisos in summer 320, his position as satrap was confirmed (Arr. *Succ.* 1.34; Diod. 18.39.6; App. *Syr.* 52.263); L. rejected Ptolemy's offer to purchase the territory from him in 319 (App. *Syr.* 52. 264). Not long after Antipatros' return to Europe, Ptolemy sent his general Nikanor (otherwise unknown) to capture L. and occupy the satrapy (Diod. 18.43.2; cf. Paus. 1.6.4; cf. App. *Mithr.* 9.27, incorrectly saying that Antigonos expelled him). L. bribed his guards and escaped to Alketas in Karia (App. *Syr.* 52.265). What became of him, we do not know. He may have perished along with many of Alketas' supporters at Kretopolis. Judeich's view (1895) that Laomedon was the occupant of the Alexander Sarcophagus is incompatible with both the artistic and historical evidence. Berve II 231–2 no. 464; Judeich 1895; Stähelin, *RE* XII.1 (1924) 755 no. 6; Bux, *RE* XII 756 no. 7; Hoffmann 118 n.2; Lehmann-Haupt in Papastavru 1936, 88–92 no. 50; Launey 1148; Heckel 1992, 211–12; Heckel 1981b.

646 LEAINE

(Λεαίνη, Λεαίνα). Nickname ("lioness" was apparently the same one used by the mistress of Harmodios and Aristogeiton, the tyrannicides: Polyaenus 8.45) of an Athenian prostitute, mistress of Demetrios Poliorketes (Athen. 6.253b; 13.577c–d). Demochares in Book 20 of his *Histories* claims that the Athenians flattered Demetrios by setting up temples to Aphrodite Leaine and Lamia, but that Demetrios himself was disgusted by the gesture (Athen. 6.252f–253a = *FHG* II 449). Aulbach §8.2.2.5.

647 LEOCHARES

(Λεωχάρης). Greek sculptor, apparently Athenian. Born *c.*390—a letter attributed to Plato calls him a young man in 366 ([Plato] *Ep.* 13.361a; cf. Pliny, *HN* 34.50)—and died *c.*310. The statues of the royal family (Philip, Alexander, Amyntas III, Eurydike, and Olympias) in the *Philippeum* at Olympias, produced soon after Chaironeia, were the work of Leochares (Paus. 5.20.10; Stewart 1993, T97–8). L. also worked with Lysippos on the lion hunt scene that included Alexander and Krateros at Delphi (Plut. *Alex.* 40.5; cf. Perdrizet 1899). See Pollitt 90–1 for *testimonia*; Richter 1950, 284ff. Berve II 237 no. 472.

648 LEON

(Λέων). Son of Leon, from Byzantion (*Suda* Λ 265). Author of several historical works including *Events concerning Philip and Byzantion* and *On the Sacred War*, as well as an Alexander history. He was perhaps a student of Aristotle (Jacoby IID 444), but the *Suda* confuses him with the student of Plato (Plut. *Phoc.* 14.7; Philostratos, *VS* 1.2; cf. Nikas of Nikaia *ap.* Athen. 11.506c; Diog. Laert. 3.62) who led the Byzantine opposition to Philip II. Pearson 254 is perhaps right to comment: "It is useless to spend time on these shadowy figures." The one authentic fragment of the Alexander history adds nothing to our knowledge (*FGrH* 132 F1 = Athen. 12.550f). Berve II 235 no. 468; Jacoby, *FGrH* 132.

649 LEONIDAS

(Λεωνίδας, Leukonides; Leuconides: Ps.-Call. 1.13.4; Jul. Valer. 1.7). Epeirot, kinsman of Olympias and tutor of Alexander (Diogenes of Babylon *ap.* Quint. 1.1.9; Jerome, *Letters* 57; Pliny, *HN* 12.62), noted for his austere nature (Plut. *Alex.* 5.7; 22; 25; cf. Ps.-Call. 1.13; Jul. Valer. 1.7) and laconic discipline (illustrated in two anecdotes by Plut. *Alex.* 22.9–10). L. was said to have shunned luxury and preached frugality to the extent of scolding Alexander for wasting incense: the King later sent L. one hundred talents of frankincense and cassia (Pliny, *HN* 12.62; Plut. *Mor.* 179e–f; Plut. *Alex.* 25.6–8: 500 talents of frankincense and 100 of myrrh). Nothing else is known about him. Berve II 235–6 no. 469; Tataki 355 no. 27 implausibly listing him as Macedonian.

650 LEONIDAS

(Λεωνίδας). Background unknown, presumably Macedonian. Commander of the *ataktoi*, or "Disciplinary Unit" (but see Welles 351 n.3), formed by Alexander after the Philotas affair (330), L. is said to have been a friend of Parmenion (Curt. 7.2.35; rejected by Berve II 236 n.2 as "Erfindung"). Arrian does not mention the unit, but both the creation of the office (Curt. 7.2.35–38; Justin 12.5.8; Diod. 17.80.4), and the individual (named only by Curtius) may be historical. L., the agent of Antigonos Monophthalmos who captured by trickery Holkias and his 3,000 rebellious troops in Kappadokia and escorted them back to Macedonia (Polyaenus 4.6.6), *may* have been the same man (Berve II 236; Heckel 1988, 79; Billows no. 61). Identification with Ptolemy's *strategos* is less likely. Stähelin, *RE* XII.2 (1925) 2019 nos. 5–6; Berve II 236 no. 470; Billows 397 no. 61; Heckel 1988, 79.

651 LEONIDAS

(Λεωνίδας). Apparently Macedonian (Tataki 355 no. 28). L. appears in 320/19 as an agent of Antigonos Monophthalmos; he captured by trickery Holkias and his 3,000 rebellious troops in Kappadokia and escorted them back to Macedonia (Polyaenus 4.6.6). Possibly, he was identical with the commander of the *ataktoi* (above). Identification with Ptolemy's *strategos*, sent against the Antigonid cities of Kilikia Tracheia in 310 (Diod. 20.19.4; cf. *IG* XI 4, 161b, l. 77), is less likely: although many officers did change sides during the wars of the Successors, L., if he truly was a friend of Parmenion and one of the "old guard," may have been too old for such activity in 310. Stähelin, *RE* XII.2 (1925) 2019 nos. 5–6; Berve II 236; Heckel 1988, 79; Billows no. 61.

652 LEONIDAS

(Λεωνίδας). Macedonian officer in the service of Ptolemy. He was sent against the Antigonid cities of so-called Rough Kilikia in 310, which he "liberated" (Diod. 20.19.4). He appears to have been sent to control Korinth and Sikyon in 308 or 307 (*Suda* Δ 431), which he held even though Demetrios offered him a bribe to abandon them (Plut. *Demetr.* 15.1–2, calling him Kleonides). L. made an offering at Delos at an unspecified time (*IG* XI 2, 161b). Hauben no. 19; Launey 1180; Bagnall 112, 114.

653 LEONNATOS

(Λεοννάτος). Macedonian (Tataki 40 no. 10). Son of Antipatros, from Aigai (Arr. *Ind.* 18.6), Leonnatos' father is otherwise unknown. About Leonnatos himself we know only that he was one of the trierarchs of the Hydaspes fleet in autumn 326 (Arr. *Ind.* 18.6), hence a man of means. How long he had been in Alexander's entourage, and what became of him, we do not know. Berve II 235 (followed tentatively by Bosworth II 87) implausibly identifies him with the man who ridiculed *proskynesis* in 327 (Arr. 4.12.2). Geyer, *RE* XII.2 (1925) 2038 no. 2; Berve II 235 no. 467.

654 LEONNATOS

(Λεοννάτος). Macedonian (Tataki 156 no. 55). Son of Anteas, L. was related to Eurydike, mother of Philip II (Arr. *Succ.* 12 = *Suda* Λ 249; cf. Curt. 10.7.8), hence a member of the Lynkestian royal house (cf. Macurdy 17; Bosworth 1971a, 99–101). A *syntrophos* of Alexander, L. was raised at the Court (Arr. 6.28.4; Arr. *Ind.* 18.3). Whether he is the same man mentioned in an inscription concerning Philippi (Vatin 1984, 259–70; Missitzis 1985, 3–14; Hammond 1988a, 382–91) cannot be determined. The son of Anteas is first mentioned in the literary sources as one of the *somatophylakes* (i.e. the Royal Hypaspists; Hammond 1990, 172–3 does not understand that this was a junior position) who pursued and killed Philip II's assassin Pausanias son of Kerastos in October 336; in this he was joined by Perdikkas and Attalos (Diod. 16.94.4). It is reported that L. was sent to console the captive Persian queens, who wrongly believed that Dareios III had been killed at Issos (Arr. 2.12.4–5; Curt. 3.12.4ff.; Diod. 17.37.3; Plut. *Alex.* 21.1–2). Curt. 3.12.6–12 claims that Alexander had intended to send Mithrenes, former satrap of Sardis and a Persian speaker (§§6–7), but sent instead L., despite L.'s lack of the linguistic skills; for Arr. 6.30.3 says that Peukestas was the only Macedonian to learn the Persian language. Arrian does note (3.6.6) that the King placed Laomedon in charge of the captive Persians precisely because he was bilingual (*diglossos*). Perhaps Curtius was following Ptolemy who, in his *History*, may have substituted Leonnatos for Laomedon, a former friend whom he later drove out of Koile-Syria (cf. Heckel 1981b, 272–4). Hegesias (*FGrH* 142 F5) claims that L. and Philotas son of Parmenion brought Batis, the garrison commander of Gaza (Arr. 2.25.4; cf. *Itiner. Al.* 45), in chains to Alexander (late 332). In 332/1 L. was appointed Somatophylax, replacing Arybbas, who died of illness in Egypt (Arr. 3.5.5). He acted as a member of the King's council in 330 at the time of the Philotas affair (Curt. 6.8.17; cf. Arr. 1.25.4). What role he played in Philotas' downfall is uncertain: certainly he was not an obvious beneficiary (Heckel 1977b; cf. Badian 1960). L. is not heard of again until 328 when he attempted to disarm the King during the Kleitos affair (Curt. 8.1.46). In 327, he incurred the King's wrath by ridiculing *proskynesis* (Arr. 4.12.2). But Alexander's anger was short-lived. L. and Ptolemy son of Lagos learned of the conspiracy of the Pages from Eurylochos (thus Curt. 8.6.22, but Arr. 4.13.7 mentions only Ptolemy's role; cf. Seibert 1969, 18–19; Strasburger 1934, 40). L.'s first military command came in 328/7, conducting nighttime operations in the siege of the Rock of Cho? rienes in rotation with his fellow Somatophylakes Perdikkas and Ptolemy (Arr. 4.21.4). When the army left Baktria for India, L. and Ptolemy emerged as prominent officers under Alexander's personal leadership. Both were wounded in the territory around the Choes (Kunar) River (Arr. 4.23.3), though not seriously, for each commanded one-third of Alexander's forces in the Aspasian campaign; L.'s forces included the *taxeis* of Attalos son of Andromenes and Balakros (Arr. 4.24.10). L. proved his military competence, driving the Aspasians from their positions in the hills and defeating them (Arr. 4.25.3).

At the Hydaspes, L. appears together with Antigenes and Tauron (Curt. 8.14.15), crossing the Hydaspes some distance upstream from the main camp that faced Poros' army. They appear to have commanded lightly armed troops and hypaspists, and it is possible that L. is named by mistake in place of Seleukos (Arr. 5.13.1, 4; Berve II 233). As Somatophylax, L. ought to have remained close to Alexander when he crossed the Hydaspes and fought among the troops that were directly under Alexander's control (Arr. 5.16; Curt. 8.14.15). Presumably L.'s activities were similar to those of Ptolemy, with whom he shared the rank of Somatophylax and whose earlier military career was somewhat similar (for Ptolemy and Leonnatos together see Curt. 8.1.45–6; Arr. 4.21.4; Curt. 8.6.22; Arr. 4.23.3, 24.10, 25.2–4; Curt. 8.14.15; Plut. *Mor.* 344d; Arr. 6.28.4). But this is of little help, for we know only that the Somatophylakes, Perdikkas, Ptolemy, and Lysimachos, crossed the Hydaspes in the same triakontor as Alexander (Arr. 5.13.1; but cf. Berve II 172 n.1); of the other Somatophylakes Arrian says nothing, though Hephaistion, as hipparch, certainly crossed the river at the same time. Curtius, for his part, exaggerates the role of Ptolemy (Curt. 8.13.17–27). L. next appears as one of about thirty trierarchs of the Hydaspes fleet some three or four months after the battle with Poros (Arr. *Ind.* 18.3–10 = Nearchos, *FGrH* 133 F1). Since he was among the forces that habitually accompanied the King, he very likely sailed downriver with him as far as the confluence of the Hydaspes and the Akesines (Chenab) and later accompanied him by land in the campaign against the Mallians living between the Akesines and Hydraotes (Arr. 6.4.3; Curt. 9.3.24). At the town of the Mallians, L. and Peukestas were foremost in protecting the seriously wounded King from certain death (for the episode see Arr. 6.8.4–13.5; cf. Curt. 9.4.26–5.30; Diod. 17.98.1–100.1; Plut. *Alex.* 63; see also Plut. *Mor.* 327b; 341c; 343d; 344c–d; Strabo 15.1.33 C701; Justin 12.9.3–13; Oros. 3.19.6–10; *Itiner. Al.* 115–16; Metz Epit. 76–7; cf. Ps.-Call. 3.4.12–15; Zonaras 4.13; p.299, 16). There is confusion in the sources over the identities of Alexander's "protectors." One is certain: Peukestas, who was later appointed an eighth Somatophylax for his part in saving the King's life (Arr. 6.28.3–4). The rest are problematic. Aristonous and Ptolemy are named, the former only by Curtius; Ptolemy himself (in conflict with the testimony of Kleitarchos) said that he was not present at the battle (Curt. 9.5.21; cf. Arr. 6.11.8; 6.5.6–7). Three others are mentioned by various sources: Habreas and Limnaios (= Timaios), both killed in the skirmish, and Leonnatos, who for his heroism was crowned at Sousa by Alexander (Arr. *Ind.* 23.6; Arr. 7.5.5): see Curt. 9.5.15, 17 (Leonnatos, Peukestas, Aristonous, Timaios); Plut. *Mor.* 344d (Leonnatos, Ptolemy, Limnaios), but Plut. *Mor.* 327b names only Ptolemy and Limnaios; Arr. *Ind.* 19.8 = Nearchos, *FGrH* 133 F1 (Leonnatos, Peukestas); Arr. 6.9.3, 10.1–2 (Leonnatos, Peukestas, Habreas); Arr. 6.11.7 says Leonnatos' role is not attested by all sources). From the Mallians to the junction of the Akesines and Hydraotes, and thence to Patala, L. accompanied Alexander by ship both because he was wounded and because of his duties as Somatophylax (cf. Curt. 9.8.3). At Patala, L. led a force of one thousand cavalry and eight thousand hoplites and lightly armed troops along the shore of the island in the Indos Delta, while Alexander took the fleet to the Ocean via the river's western arm (Arr. 6.18.3). When Alexander returned upstream, L. retraced his steps to Patala. From there he accompanied the King, by land, along the eastern arm of the river as far as a great lake, where he remained in charge of his own troops and those ships with their crews that Alexander left behind as he took a smaller fleet to the Ocean (Arr. 6.20.3). On Alexander's return, it seems, L. led the land forces back to Patala.

Alexander now prepared to lead his army to the West. He sent L. ahead to dig wells along the route that the army was to follow (Curt. 9.10.2). When he had completed this task (late summer 324: Beloch III² 2.320), L. awaited Alexander on the borders of the land of the Oreitai. At the Arabios River, Alexander left the bulk of the army under the command of Hephaistion. The remainder he divided into three contingents, led by Ptolemy, L., and himself, and moved south of the Arabios into the territory of the Oreitai. These forces ravaged the land, subduing those of the Oreitai who resisted (Curt. 9.10.6–7; Diod. 17.104.5–6). Ptolemy and L. reunited first with Alexander and then with Hephaistion's troops. In one body they proceeded to Rhambakia, whence Alexander took a force to the Gedrosian border, where the remainder of the Oreitai and the Gedrosians were preparing to resist (Arr. 6.21.5–22.2). When these had been overcome, Alexander sent L., together with Apollophanes, whom he had appointed satrap of the area, to Rhambakia. L., with the Agrianes, some archers and cavalry, and a force of mercenary cavalry and infantry, was ordered to remain in the Oreitan land with instructions "to await the fleet until it sailed past this region, to synoecize the city which had been established by Hephaistion (Arr. 6.21.5) and to settle affairs among the Oreitai" (Arr. 6.22.3; cf. Hamilton 1972, 605–6). The Alexandria founded by L. (Pliny, *HN* 6.97 = Onesikritos, *FGrH* 134 F28) is apparently that amongst the Oreitai (cf. Fraser 165 n.115). L. won an impressive victory over the Oreitai, who had risen against him, killing 6,000 of them, and all their leaders (Arr. *Ind.* 23.5 = Nearchos, *FGrH* 133 F1; cf. Curt. 9.10.19). Of his own forces only fifteen cavalrymen and a handful of infantry were lost; Apollophanes the satrap fell in the battle. When Nearchos arrived at the shore near Rhambakia (Arr. 6.22.3; cf. Arr. *Ind.* 23), L. had prepared provisions for his Ocean voyage. He also exchanged troops with Nearchos, taking with him those men who, on account of their laziness, had caused or might cause disciplinary problems in the fleet (Arr. *Ind.* 23.8). Then, L. put everything in order among the Oreitai (as he had been instructed) and set out for Gedrosia by land. The news of his exploits had already reached Alexander by letter (Curt. 9.10.19), but it is uncertain where L. himself rejoined Alexander; perhaps it was in Karmania, though possibly only at Sousa. There (324), L. was awarded a golden crown in honor of his courage in India and his victory over the Oreitai (Arr. 7.5.5–6; Arr. *Ind.* 23.6, 42.9). Presumably he took a Persian bride in the marriage ceremony, though we have no record of her or her fate. When Alexander died, L. emerged as one of the leading men of the succession crisis: together with Perdikkas and Ptolemy, he belonged to the *megistoi*, as opposed to those lesser lights (Arr. *Succ.* 1.2). In the debate that followed, in which the supporters of Perdikkas proposed that Rhoxane's child (if male) should inherit the kingdom, it was suggested by Peithon, one of the Bodyguards, that L. share with Perdikkas the guardianship of the child, on the grounds that both were of royal stock (Curt. 10.7.8; cf. Justin 13.2.13–14). But when the common soldiery declared for the feeble Arrhidaios, whom they hailed as King under the title Philip III, L. led the cavalry outside the city of Babylon, while Perdikkas himself remained within the city. Perdikkas' stay was brief, owing to the hostility of Meleagros, who induced Arrhidaios to order his assassination, and he soon rejoined L. and the cavalry (Curt. 10.7.20, 8.4). L.'s support for Perdikkas' regency was due in part to his opposition to Meleagros and Philip Arrhidaios.

At Babylon (323), L. received the satrapy of Hellespontine Phrygia, which, despite its strategic location, must have disappointed him (Arr. *Succ.* 1.6; Dexippos, *FGrH* 100 F8 §2; Curt. 10.10.2; Diod. 18.3.1, cf. 18.12.1, wrongly "Philotas"; Justin 13.4.16). He intrigued against Perdikkas; for he had been contacted—perhaps at Olympias' instigation— by Kleopatra, the sister of Alexander, through whom he hoped to gain power. Such a marriage carried with it a serious—possibly "legitimate"—claim to the throne of Macedon (Plut. *Eum.* 3.9). When he received orders to aid Eumenes in Kappadokia (Plut. *Eum.* 3.4–5), he had already formulated his plan to overthrow Perdikkas. Renewed turmoil in Greece offered L. a pretext for crossing the Hellespont and seeking the throne; for Antipatros, blockaded at Lamia in Thessaly by the allied Greek forces, sent Hekataios of Kardia to summon him to Greece (Plut. *Eum.* 3.6; Diod. 18.12.1, 14.4–5; Justin 13.5.14). L. attempted to persuade Eumenes to cross into Europe with him. He revealed to Eumenes his dealings with Kleopatra. But Eumenes, fearing his old enemy Hekataios (Plut. *Eum.* 3.8–10), slipped away with his troops, bringing the news of L.'s designs to Perdikkas (Plut. *Eum.* 3.10; Nepos, *Eum.* 2.4–5, claiming L. planned to kill Eumenes when he could not persuade him). L. crossed into Europe with his satrapal army, which he augmented in Macedonia before pushing south towards Lamia with a force of more than 20,000 foot and 1,500 cavalry. The Athenian general Antiphilos engaged him before he could reach Lamia; Diod. 18.15.5 tells us that Antipatros joined L.'s army on the day after the battle. L., with less than half the enemy's number of cavalry, found himself cut off in a marshy region where he was overcome by wounds and carried from the battlefield (Diod. 18.15.3; Justin 13.5.14; cf. Plut. *Phoc.* 25.5; Strabo 9.5.10 C434; see also Sprawski 2008). Antipatros may indeed, as Justin 13.5.15 claims, have welcomed his death: not only had the engagement removed a dangerous rival (cf. Arr. *Succ.* 1.9) but it had lifted the siege of Lamia and added to Antipatros' 13,600 forces an additional 20,000 foot and 1,500 horse. In his arrogance, his fondness for Persian luxury (Arr. *Succ.* 12)—evinced by his dress and the decoration of his arms, even the gilded bridles of his Nesaian horses—and in the style of his hair, L. was clearly emulous of his kinsman Alexander and jealously eager to exercise at least some of his power. He was also passionately fond of wrestling and gymnastics (Plut. *Alex.* 40.1; Pliny, *HN* 35.168) or hunting (Athen. 12.539d = Phylarchos, *FGrH* 81 F41 and/or Agatharchides of Knidos, 86 F3; Ael. *VH* 9.3). Berve II 232–5 no. 466; Heckel, *Marshals*² 107–21 and *LexAM* 313–15; Sprawski 2008. **Stemma I.**

655 LEONTISKOS

(Λεοντίσκος). Sicilian. Wrestler and Olympic victor from Messene on Sicily (ἀπὸ τῆς ἐν τῷ πορθμῷ Μεσσήνης; cf. *Suda* A 1023), who had his statue set up in Olympia (Paus. 6.4.3). Pausanias says that L. did not know how to throw his opponent but won by bending back his fingers (cf. *Suda* A 1023). Paus. 6.2.10 says that the only Messenians to win Olympic victories were L. and Symmachos, and these were not of Messenian blood but of indigenous Zanklean origin. He was a rival of another athlete, the pankratiast Antenor, for the affections of the courtesan, Mania (no. 681): she claimed that she wanted to see what two Olympic athletes could do, blow for blow, in one night (Athen. 13.578f–579a = Machon, frag. XV; cf. commentary by Gow, *Machon* 101–2). *RE* XII.2 (1925) 2051; Ogden 233–4.

656 LEONTISKOS

(Λεοντίσκος). Macedonian (Tataki 354 no. 22). Apparently the younger son of Ptolemy I and the courtesan Thaïs; his brother, Lagos, was named for the paternal grandfather and probably older; his sister, Eirene, married Eunostos of Soloi (Athen. 13.576e). Of L.'s life little is known. He served as an officer in an unspecified capacity at the naval battle at Salamis. Defeated and was captured by Demetrios Poliorketes, L. and his uncle Menelaos were released and allowed to retain their possessions by the magnanimous victor (Justin 15.2.7–8). Despite the relatively low status of his mother, Athen. 13.576e = Kleitarchos, *FGrH* 137 F11 says that she was actually married to Ptolemy (Πτολεμαίῳ ἐγαμήθη). Even if this is not strictly accurate, L.'s career, the name of his brother, and his sister's high-status marriage, suggest that Ptolemy treated Thaïs and her children with respect. Stähelin, *RE* XII (1925) 2051 no. 1; Ogden 69; Ager 2018, 39–40. **Stemma X.**

657 LEOSTHENES

(Λεωσθένης). (For the name see *LGPN* II 284 no. 6). Athenian (Kirchner 9142 = 9144). Son of Leosthenes (who had been exiled by the Athenians after 362/1 and took up residence at the court of Philip II) of Kephale, born *c.*350 (Plut. *Phoc.* 23; Hieron. adv.

Jovin. 1. 41, p. 307). Athenian *strategos* in 323/2 (Develin 408; he had held the generalship in 324/3 as well; for an earlier trierarchy see II² 1529. 500, 606, 682, with discussion in Davies 342–3) and commander of the Greek forces in the Lamian War (Arr. *Succ.* 1.9); noted for his military skill (Paus. 1.25.5; Diod. 17.111.3), but thought by Phokion to lack caution (Plut. *Phoc.* 23). Phokion likened L.'s words to the cypress tree: beautiful and tall, but bearing no fruit (Plut. *Mor.* 188d). L.'s initial success was a good victory in the "short race" but Phokion said he feared the "long-distance race of the war." (Plut. *Mor.* 803a–b). L. was praised for being more than a mere public speaker but one who turned his words into action (Plut. *Mor.* 486d). Before the news of Alexander's death was known, the Athenians authorized Leosthenes to recruit the mercenaries (Diod. 17.111.3; he was given 50 talents; cf. Diod. 18.9.1) at Tainaron—some 8,000 had recently been dismissed (Paus. 8.52.5 gives the unrealistic figure of 50,000 mercenaries serving with L.; see also Diod. 17.106.3, 111.1; 18.9.1; cf. Paus. 1.25.5 for the demobilization of mercenaries in Asia)—but to do so as if for his own private purpose, so that Antipatros should not become suspicious of Athenian intentions (Diod. 18.9.2–3). Certain news of the King's death precipitated the Lamian War and Leosthenes was given money that had been brought to Athens by Harpalos and ordered to win further allies (Diod. 18.9.4–5); he was elected commander-in-chief of the Greek forces (Paus. 1.25.5). He marched north, defeated the Boiotians and occupied Thermopylai (Diod. 18.11.4–5), anticipating Antipatros who was moving down from the north. A full list of the anti-Macedonian allies is given by Diod. 18.11.1–2; Strabo 9.5.10 C434; cf. Justin 13.5.10, where it is wrongly stated that Korinth was persuaded to join. The defection of Thessaly was a serious setback for Antipatros (cf. the role of Menon no. 725: Plut. *Pyrrh.* 1.6), and L. managed to defeat his troops and besiege Antipatros in Lamia during the winter of 323/2 (hence the name of the war; Diod. 18.12.3–13.3; Plut. *Dem.* 27.1). In the course of the siege, he must have offered Antipatros harsh conditions for surrender, for the Macedonian regent threw these terms back at the Athenians when the war ended (Plut. *Phoc.* 26.7). But while his troops were investing the city (Lamia) Antipatros' soldiers made an attack on those who were digging a moat; L. coming to their aid was hit on the head by a stone (or some missile: Justin 13.5.12; Diod. 18.13.5; Strabo 9.5.10 C434; Paus. 1.25.5). He swooned and was carried back to camp; on the third day he died. He was buried with honors of a hero (Diod. 18.13.5; cf. *Suda* Λ 276; Plut. *Phoc.* 24.1) and in the absence of Demosthenes, who had been exiled on account of the Harpalos scandal, the funeral oration was delivered by Hypereides (Diod. 18.13.5; Hyper. 6; [Plut.] *Mor.* 849f). His successor was Antiphilos. In Peiraieus, in a precinct of Zeus and Athena (or at least in a long portico near a marketplace for those who live by the sea), there was a portrait of L. by Arkesilaos (Paus. 1.1.3; cf. Paus. 3.6.1, who puts him in the same class as Kleombrotos, who died at Leuktra, and Hippokrates, who fell at Delion; cf. Paus. 1.29.13, 8.52.5). Berve II 236–7 no. 471; Geyer, *RE* XII.2 (1925) 2060–2 no. 2; Davies 342ff.; Develin 408; cf. Lepore 1955.

LETODOROS. See LIPODOROS.

658 LIMNAIOS

(Λιμναῖος, Curtius: Timaeus). The form Limnaios (Plut. *Alex.* 63.7–8; Plut. *Mor.* 327b, 344d) is apparently correct. A Limnaios son of Harpalos appears in an inscription from Kassandreia (cf. Henry 1990, 179–80); at Beroia (Tataki, *PB* 215 nos. 812–14, and p. 423);

and at the court of Philip V (cf. Polyb. 18.34.4). One of the Royal Hypaspists (Plut. *Alex.* 63.5), L. accompanied Alexander into the town of the Mallians (near mod. Multan), where he was killed defending the King, who was himself seriously wounded (Plut. *Alex.* 63.8; Plut. *Mor.* 327b, 344d; Curt. 9.5.15–16). Arr. 6.9.3, 10.1–2 omits him; there was some disagreement about who defended Alexander on this occasion (Arr. 6.11.7). Arrian names Habreas where the Vulgate sources refer to L. (Berve II 237 wrongly assumes a confusion of Limnaios and Leonnatos). Berve II 237 no. 474; Heckel 1992, 296; Hoffmann 147.

659 LIPODOROS

(Λιπόδωρος MSS; emended by Dittenberger to Λητόδωρος but rejected by Holt 2005, 117 and Waterfield 2019, 531). Greek mercenary leader of unknown family and origin, possibly Ainianian. L. had been left behind in Baktria in 327 when Alexander marched into India. He took an active part in the uprising after the King's death, as is clear from the fact that he commanded 3,000 of the rebels, and may have had a role in the earlier disturbance of 326/5 (cf. Curt. 9.7.1–11; see s.vv. Boxus, Biton). Peithon son of Krateuas, who had been sent by Perdikkas to put down the rebellion in 323, suborned L. through the agency of a certain Ainianian. During the battle L. and his 3,000 men fled, thus giving Peithon complete victory (Diod. 18.7.5–6). Despite Diodorus' (18.7.8–9) claim that the Macedonians murdered the Greek rebels—doubtless anti-Perdikkan propanda—it is likely that L. and his supporters were rewarded by Peithon. What became of him is unknown. Berve II 237 no. 473 (Letodoros); Holt 1988, 87–91; Iliakis 2013, 190–2.

660 LYKIDAS

(Λυκίδας). Aitolian of unknown family. L.'s position before 332/1, when he was appointed commander of the *xenoi* at Memphis (Arr. 3.5.3), is unclear. Berve II 237 assumed that he had been a commander of Alexander's mercenaries since the beginning of the Asiatic campaign. But Tarn I 44 (cf. Schachermeyr 238 n.263) regards the *xenoi* in Egypt as "military settlers" from the time of the Persian occupation (i.e., precursors of the Hellenistic *katoikoi*), and Bosworth I 275 goes so far as to suggest that L. "was an Egyptian resident who had served in the invasion of 343." Nothing else is known of Lykidas' career. Berve II 237–8 no. 475; Launey 1135; Grainger, *APS* 217 no. 1.

661 LYKISKOS

(Λύκισκος). Macedonian (Tataki 357 no. 40). Family background unknown. L. appears for the first time as Kassandros' *epimeletes kai strategos*, that is, as civil and military overseer of Epeiros in 316, after the expulsion of Aiakides by the *koinon* of the Epeirots (Diod. 19.36.4–5; cf. Plut. *Pyrrh.* 2.1). The measure appears to have been temporary, since in 314 we find L. commanding Kassandros' forces in Akarnania, which the latter had brought into an alliance when Antigonos sided with the Aitolians (Diod. 19.67.5). From this base L. later (312) attacked Epeiros, which upon the death of Aiakides (who had been restored to power some time earlier) had taken a hostile stance against Kassandros and placed Alketas II on the throne (Diod. 19.88). L. defeated the army of Alketas (no. 62) at Kassope (*Barr. Atl.* 54 C3) and besieged him at Eurymenai; although Alketas' son Alexander (no. 44) arrived with reinforcements and inflicted heavy casualties (among the dead was Lysandros (no. 669) the governor of Leukas), L. was in turn relieved by Deinias and captured and razed the city of Eurymenai (Diod. 19.88.4, 6; Eurymenai is apparently

Kastritsa, northwest of Dodona; Hammond 174–5 and Map 16; also Plan 15; *Barr. Atl.* 54 C2). Nevertheless, Kassandros reached agreement with Alketas, which allowed him to retain the kingship of the Molossians (Diod. 19.89.1). In this position Alketas remained, as it seems, until 307. Nothing else is known about L. himself, although we may assume that he returned to Akarnania. Since L. is unattested in the Alexander sources, his high rank under Kassandros suggests that he had gained his military experience serving with Antipatros, perhaps participating in the war against Agis and the Aitolian campaign that followed the Lamian War. Schoch, *RE* XIII (1927) 2295–6 no. 6; Volkmann, *Kl. Pauly* III 811–12 no. 4; Bengtson I 92, 139ff.

662 LYKISKOS

(Λύκισκος). A decree of Statokles (306/5) honors friends or relatives of L. for their service to the city while in the employ of Antigonos and Demetrios (*IG* II² 471). Another fragmentary decree (published by Schweigert in *Hesperia* 7 (1938) 303–5 and creatively restored by A.M. Woodward, *ABSA* 51 (1956) 6–8 no. 9) may refer to this L. and the sea battle at the Hellespont during the Lamian War (cf. *IG* II² 493). The beginning of the decree appears to date it to 320/19 (R. Stroud, *Hesperia* 40 (1971) 174–8 no. 25). But I would, nevertheless, hesitate to place so much faith in so little firm evidence. Billows 397–8 no. 62.

663 LYKOMEDES

(Λυκομήδης). Rhodian. L. had probably served as a mercenary captain with his compatriot Memnon. But the latter died in 333 (Arr. 2.1.3), and L. remained with Pharnabazos and Autophradates, who installed him as garrison commander of Mytilene in support of the tyrant Diogenes, a Mytilenean exile (Arr. 2.1.5). L. himself is not mentioned again, but we are told that Chares, who came either to support or replace him, was expelled (or captured?) by Hegelochos (Arr. 3.2.6; Curt. 4.5.22). Berve II 238 no. 476; Olmstead 502; Hofstetter 117–18 no. 200; Bosworth I 183; Atkinson I 331–2.

664 LYKON

(Λύκων). A comic actor from Skarpheia in Lokris (Plut. *Alex.* 29.6), L. was twice victorious at the Lenaian festival *c.*350 (*IG* II² 670 [x]). He appears to have joined Alexander in 332/1 in Egypt (Arr. 3.1.4), and, while performing in Phoinikia in early 331, inserted a line asking Alexander for a gift of ten talents, which the King good-naturedly provided (Plut. *Alex.* 29.6; cf. Plut. *Mor.* 334e). L. was among the notable comic actors who performed at the mass marriage ceremony at Sousa in 324 (Chares, *FGrH* 125 F4 *ap.* Athen. 12.539a), and appears to have headed his own troupe of actors (Plut. *Mor.* 334e). We know nothing about his activities between 331 and 324, or afterwards. Antiphanes may have named his *Lykon* after him. Berve II 239 no. 478; O'Connor 114 no. 319.

665 LYKON

(Λύκων). When Lysimachos was besieging Kallatis (*Barr. Atl.* 22 F5) in 313/12, Antigonos sent forces to aid the city: a naval force under L. (there are no details about the size of his force) and a land army under Pausanias (Diod. 19.73.6). Lysimachos managed to overcome his enemy on land, defeating first the Thrakians under Seuthes and then Pausanias (Diod. 19.73.7–10). What became of Kallatis is not recorded, and we may assume that L. soon returned to Antigonos to report the failure of the relief force. Identification of L. with the Lykos (*sic*) of Polyaenus 5.19, who was in the service of Lysimachos almost 20 years later (cf. Hauben 57), is virtually impossible given the variant forms, the frequency of both names, as well as the historical circumstances. Billows 398 no. 63; Hauben 56–9 no. 21.

666 LYKOURGOS

(Λυκοῦργος). [All references in **boldface** are to [Plut.] *Vit. X Or.*]. Son of Lykophron, Athenian from the deme Boutadai, from the family of the Eteoboutadai. Born *c.*390. According to Libanius, *ad Dem* 23.768, he was older than Demosthenes. L. is said to have been a student of Plato (Polemon *ap.* Diog. Laert. 3.46; **841b**) and Isokrates (cf. Zosimus, *Life of Isocrates*). Married Kallisto, the daughter of Habron, and by her had three sons: Lykourgos, Lykophron, and Habron (**842f–843a**). L. gained prominence after Chaironeia as organizer and overseer of Athenian finances from 338 to 327 (**852b**). Diod. 16.88.1 is mistaken when he says that L. had already managed the city's finances for twelve years at the time of his prosecution of Lysikles. Strongly anti-Macedonian (*Syll*³ 326 = *IG* II² 457), and thus an opponent of Phokion (no. 952) and Demades (no. 349; Plut. *Phoc.* 9.10). In 343 he is said to have accompanied Demosthenes and Polyeuktos to the Peloponnese and some other cities to garner support against Philip II (**841f**). In 338/7, he prosecuted Lysikles for his generalship at Chaironeia (Diod. 16.88.1; Hamel 1998, 156 no. 62) and secured the death sentence. He was one of a number of politicians whose extradition was sought by Alexander after the sack of Thebes in 335 (Arr. 1.10.4; Plut. *Phoc.* 17.2; Plut. *Dem.* 23.4; *Suda* A 2704; *IG* II² 457.17–18). But Alexander later relented (Arr. 1.10.6). L. died in 324 and was thus untouched by the Harpalos scandal. Berve's assertion (II 238–9) that **842d**, mentioning his prosecution of Demades, relates to that orator's support of Alexander's apotheosis, is virtually impossible on chronological grounds (cf. Roisman and Worthington 207). Of his fifteen speeches (**843c**), only the one *Against Leocrates* is extant. For his life see [Plut.] *Vit. X Or.* 7 = *Mor.* **841a–844a** (commentary and extensive bibliography in Roisman and Worthington 189–211). Kirchner 9251; Berve II 238–9 no. 477; Davies 350–1; *LGPN* II, 288 no. 4; Schwenk 1984.

667 LYNKEUS

(Λυγκεύς). Samian, brother of the historian Douris. Friend and student of Theophrastos of Eressos (Athen. 3.100e–f, 4. 128a–b), Lynkeus is our source for much gossip from the age of the Diadochoi, for he attended and described banquets hosted by Ptolemy I Soter and by the courtesan, Lamia, on behalf of Demetrios Poliorketes. Athenaeus preserves details from Lynkeus about the sorts of dishes served (indeed, Lynkeus and Hippolochos the Makedonian agreed to describe any sumptuous banquet they attended, Athen. 4.128a–b. Plutarch's description of the, not altogether worthless, dinner chatter derives also derives from Lynkeus' writings (Plut. *Demetr.* 27.3; cf. s.v. Lamia no. 639). Author of a comedy entitled *The Centaur*, and works *On Menandros, Apophthegmata* and *Apomnemoneumata*, which included the above-mentioned gossip and trivia. W. Kraus, *Kl. Pauly* III 828 no. 4.

668 LYSANDRA

(Λυσάνδρα). Daughter of Ptolemy I and Eurydike (cf. Paus. 1.10.3) and Eurydike; sister of Ptolemy Keraunos (Paus. 1.16.2). Born perhaps after 316 (I see no evidence for the view of

Macurdy 57, that she was older than Arsinoë II; Soter continued to have children with Eurydike after he entered into a relationship with—or even married—Berenike; see also Greenwalt 1988 for normal marriageable age). She had earlier been married to Alexander V of Macedon (Porphyr. Tyr. *FGrH* 260 F3 §5; Euseb. *Chron.* 1.232), the son of Kassandros and Thessalonike, whom Demetrios Poliorketes killed in 294 (Paus. 9.7.3; Diod. 21.7; Justin 16.1.8; Plut. *Demetr.* 36; Lund 94). Soon thereafter she married Agathokles (Paus. 1.10.3, though mistaken about the date of the marriage; cf. 1.9.6 dating it to after the disaster against Dromichaites). Pausanias' claim (1.10.3) that by the time Lysimachos married Arsinoë (300/299) Agathokles already had children by L. must be rejected— as must the improbable theory that Ptolemy had two daughters named Lysandra (Volkmann, *RE* XXIII.2 (1959) 1625)—even though Plut. *Demetr.* 31.5 appears to indicate an earlier date for the marriage of L. and Agathokles. She became a rival of her half-sister Arsinoë (II), who married Lysimachos and was, according to rumor, responsible for the death of Agathokles (Paus. 1.10.3–4). L. and her children, accompanied by her "brothers" (τοὺς ἀδελφοὺς τοὺς αὐτῆς), fled to the court of Seleukos (Paus. 1.10.4). Since Pausanias adds that she was joined by her brother-in-law Alexander separately, the use of the plural is rhetorical—since those "brothers" were with Ptolemy Keraunos, this appears to be a reference to Meleagros (no. 698). It is said that after Lysimachos' death at Koroupedion, L. was reluctant to hand over his body for burial to his son Alexander, though she finally relented (Paus. 1.10.5; App. *Syr.* 64.341 says that Alexander buried his father but fails to mention L.). What became of L. and her children is unknown. H. Volkmann, *Kl. Pauly* III 830 no. 1; Beloch IV² 2.179; Grainger, *SPG* 655; Geyer, *RE* XIII.2 (1927) 2501–2 no. 1; Macurdy 55–8; Seibert 1967, 75–6; Ogden 1999, 59–60; Carney 2000, 160–1. **Stemma IX and X.**

669 LYSANDROS

(Λύσανδρος). An Athenian (Kirchner 9281) who had been placed in charge of Leukas by Kassandros (cf. Diod. 19.67.5); defeated and killed in battle at Eurymenai in 312 by Alexander (no. 44) son of Alketas II (Diod. 19.88.5). Launey 1126; Dobesch, *Kl. Pauly* III 831 no. 2.

670 LYSANIAS

(Λυσανίας). Macedonian (Tataki 358 no. 44). In spring 335, L. and a certain Philotas conveyed the booty taken from the "independent" Thrakians to the coastal cities of Macedonia (Arr. 1.2.1). Otherwise unattested during Alexander's reign, he may not have accompanied the King to Asia. Identification with the cavalry officer of the same name who served with Antigonos the One-Eyed in 316 (Diod. 19.29.2) is remotely possible (thus Billows 398). Berve II 239 no. 479.

671 LYSANIAS

(Λυσανίας). Macedonian (Tataki 358 no. 44, possibly). In 317, he commanded 400 horsemen armed with the *xyston* in the army of Antigonos at Paraitakene (Diod. 19.29.2). He is otherwise unattested, unless he is identical with the cavalry officer who served with Alexander in the Thrakian campaign in 336/5 (Arr. 1.2.1). Billows 398 no. 64.

672 LYSIMACHOS

(Λυσίμαχος). Akarnanian. Though somewhat uncultivated (Plut. *Alex.* 5.8), L. served as tutor of Alexander and endeared himself to the young prince by referring to himself as Phoinix while calling his pupil Achilles and Philip II Peleus (Plut. *Alex.* 5.8; cf. 24.10). Plutarch mentions him after Leonidas, a strict disciplinarian and kinsman of Olympias, it is likely that L. educated Alexander at an earlier stage of life, as the playful references to Achilles suggest. As an educator he occupied a middle ground between the keen intellect of Aristotle and the laconic austerity of Leonidas. That Akarnanians found employment at Philip's court (cf. Philip, who was Alexander's physician; Curt. 3.6.1) may be due to the influence of Olympias, who came from neighboring Epeiros; certainly the allusions to the Aiakids will have found favor with her (cf. Heckel 1981d, 80–2). L. accompanied the King to Asia. During an expedition against the Arabs of Antilebanon, he failed, on account of his old age, to keep up with the Macedonian forces who had dismounted. Chares (*FGrH* 125 F7 = Plut. *Alex.* 24.10–14) faults him for his foolishness, which endangered the mission and the life of Alexander, who refused to abandon him. Nothing else is known about his career, except that a reference to his opposition to Kallisthenes of Olynthos (Plut. *Alex.* 55.2) may indicate that he was still alive in 327. What became of him, we do not know. Berve II 241 no. 481.

673 LYSIMACHOS

(Λυσίμαχος). Son of Agathokles (Arr. 6.28.4, *Ind.* 18.3, *Succ.* 1.2; Strabo 13.4.1 C623), a Thessalian from Krannon (Porphyry of Tyre *ap.* Euseb. Arm. = *FGrH* 260 F3 §8) whom Theopompos (*ap.* Athen. 6.259f–260a = *FGrH* 115 F81) describes as a flatterer of Philip II (Geyer, *RE* XIV.1, *contra* Berve II 239; Hünerwadel 1910, 13; Merker 1979; accepted by Lund 2; Landucci, *Lisimaco* 73–6). His origins were presumably not as humble as Theopompos claims (cf. Beloch IV2 2.129). The father was granted Macedonian citizenship (Justin 15.3.1; Paus. 1.9.5 says of L. γένος ἦν Μακεδών, and Plut. *Demetr.* 44.6 calls him *homophylos* with Demetrios Poliorketes) and at least three of his sons were born in Macedonia. L. was educated at the Court in Pella (Arr. 6.18.4; *Ind.* 18.3; though Westlake 1935, 195 is probably wrong in assuming that Agathokles was given land in Pella). The assertion by [Lucian] *Macrob.* 11, based on Hieronymos of Kardia (*FGrH* 154 F10, who perhaps confused him with Antigonos Monophthalmos), that L. was eighty when he died at Koroupedion should probably be discounted. I would now rescind my earlier view (Heckel 1978d, 228; 1982b, 375; 1992, 274) that L. was appointed Somatophylax by Philip II. Justin's claim that he was seventy-four at the time of his death (17.1.10) appears more realistic, although it may be an attempt to make L. coeval with Alexander. If the award of citizenship to Agathokles belongs to the time of his intervention in Perrhaibia (*FGrH* 115 F81), probably in 353 or 352 (thus Landucci, *Lisimaco* 75), then App. *Syr.* 64.339 may be correct in assigning L.'s year of birth to 352/1. This would mean that, if L. accompanied Alexander from the beginning of the expedition, he did so at the age of 17 or 18 as a *pais basilikos* or a member of the Royal Hypaspists. L. is first attested as participating in a lion hunt in the forests of Bazeira in Sogdiana in 328 (Curt. 8.1.13–17); presumably in his capacity as Somatophylax (Paus. 1.9.5 calls him *doryphoros*) he tried to protect the King from a charging lion. Alexander, however, ordered him aside and killed the beast with his own spear, reminding L. of the lion hunt in Syria, where he had been seriously injured by a lion of great size (Curt. 8.1.15). Justin 15.3.6 alleges that L. had been deliberately caged with a lion as punishment for giving poison to Kallisthenes, whose "student" L. had been (*audire Callisthenen et praecepta ab eo virtutis accipere solitus*), in order to relieve his suffering. L. allegedly cultivated the philosophers—Onesikritos, a pupil of Diogenes, was present at L.'s court (Plut. *Alex.* 46.4)—and already in 324 he had been given the funerary horse of the Indian philosopher Kalanos, whose student he had been (Arr. 7.3.4). L., a man of prodigious strength, overcame the lion and killed it by tearing out its tongue (Justin 15.3.7–8) and the King in admiration forgave him his offence and the two were reconciled (Justin 15.3.9–10; for this story see also Lucian, *Dial. Mort.* 14.43 (397); Seneca, *de Clem.* 1.25.1; *de Ira* 3.17.2; 3.23.1; Val. Max. 9.3 ext. 1; Plin. *HN* 8.21.54; Paus. 1.9.6; cf Tatian, *ad Gr.* 2, p.2; Curt. 8.1.17; Heckel 1992, 268–71; Yardley–Wheatley–Heckel 259–61). But L. was himself charged with similar cruelty (conduct befitting a tyrant), sometime after 300, when allegedly he mutilated and caged Telesphoros the Rhodian, merely because he made a tasteless joke about L.'s wife, Arsinoë (Athen. 14.616c; Seneca, *de Ira* 3.17.3–4). Hence, the lion story establishes a precedent for L.'s treatment of Telesphoros and is itself explained in terms of Alexander's cruelty to Kallisthenes. Plut. *Demetr.* 27.3 gives the lion story a humorous context, and compares L.'s scars, sustained while he was caged with a lion, with the bites on Demetrios' neck, inflicted by the flute girl Lamia. Immediately preceding this anecdote is a reference to Lynkeus of Samos, who attended and described in detail a dinner party given by Lamia in honor of Demetrios (Plut. *Demetr.* 27.2; cf. Athen. 3.101e; 4.128a–b). Lynkeus, will have been the source of, and the inspiration for, much of the gossip concerning the Diadochoi, and especially the stories about Demetrios, Lamia and L. (cf. Athen. 6.246e, 261b; 14.614f–615a; Plut. *Demetr.* 27.3).

The L. of Plutarch's version of the Kallisthenes' opposition to *proskynesis* (*Alex.* 55.2) is not the son of Agathokles: Berve (II 241 no. 481; cf. Hamilton 14, 153–4; Pearson 57) correctly recognized that this is Alexander's Akarnanian tutor, the victim of Chares' hostility. It is puzzling, however, that Berve (II 240) does not credit L.'s participation in the Kleitos episode. There is no good reason to disbelieve Curtius (8.1.46). For the political issues that lay behind Kleitos' confrontation with Alexander, Curtius' version demonstrates a sober approach to the affair. Nor does Plutarch's account, which claims that Aristophanes (read "Aristonous") disarmed the King, vitiate that of Curtius, for the former concerns the removal of Alexander's own sword (which was the first weapon that he might be expected to reach for, if he carried it on his person), while the latter involves a spear, which Alexander had taken from a bystander (Curt. 8.1.45). Plut. *Alex.* 51.11 implies that all the Somatophylakes were present at the banquet, as we should expect. Presumably they did not stand idly by while Aristonous alone attempted to restrain the King. Very likely each one attempted, in his own way, to avert the disaster. L., who appears in the company of Leonnatos, Perdikkas, and Ptolemy (all of whom were already Somatophylakes), undoubtedly held the same rank. Not long after Kleitos' death, L.'s younger brother, Philip, a Royal Hypaspist, accompanied the King some five hundred stades on foot, refusing to mount the horse of L., who rode nearby. Remaining ever by the King's side, both in the pursuit of the supporters of Sisimithres and in the skirmish that followed, Philip finally collapsed from exhaustion and expired in the King's arms. This story is told only by Curtius (8.2.35–9) and Justin (15.3.12). It is preceded in Justin 15.3.10–11 by a similar story, in which L. remains at the side of Alexander in India when all others have fallen behind. This story is surely a doublet (cf. Berve II 240 n.4), with further complications. App. *Syr.* 64 and Justin 15.3.13–14 relate that L.—here a hypaspist, which in the Indian campaign is impossible—was wounded by Alexander's spear as Alexander leapt from his horse. He began to bleed profusely and the King, for want of proper bandages, placed his diadem on L.'s head in an attempt to stop the bleeding (Justin 15.3.13). That Aristandros (who vanished from the accounts of Alexander, probably with the end of Kallisthenes' historical work) or any other seer prophesied that this act signified that L. would himself be King defies all credulity. A similar story regarding Alexander's diadem is told of Seleukos by Arrian 7.22.5, a variant on the version given by Aristoboulos (*FGrH* 139 F53). This tale of L.'s wound is a later invention, as is Aristoboulos' claim (*FGrH* 139 F54 = Arr. 7.18.5) that the seer Peithagoras predicted L.'s victory over Antigonos at Ipsos. Near Sangala in India some 1,200 of Alexander's troops were wounded, among them L. the Somatophylax (Arr. 5.24.5). He had earlier boarded a thirty-oared vessel at the Hydaspes (in the company of two other Somatophylakes), before the battle with Poros, though his role in the actual battle is not attested (Arr. 5.13.1); presumably he fought in the immediate vicinity of Alexander himself. When Alexander decided to sail down the Indos river system to the Ocean, L. was one of those from Pella charged with a trierarchy in the Attic fashion (Arr. *Ind.* 18.3 = Nearchos, *FGrH* 133 F1). He is named by Arrian in the only complete list of the Somatophylakes (Arr. 6.28.4). At Sousa in spring 324, L. and the rest of the Somatophylakes were crowned by Alexander, though unlike Leonnatos, L. appears to have earned no special distinction (Arr. 7.5.6). Very likely, he took a Persian bride: her name is not recorded, nor her fate. She may have been repudiated after Alexander's death, although it is worthy of note that in 302 L. married (albeit for only a brief time) Amastris, whom Krateros had married at Sousa but put aside in favor of Antipatros' daughter, Phila. This should dispel the notion that the Macedonians put racial prejudice ahead of political advantage.

According to Ps.-Call. 3.32, L., Ptolemy and Perdikkas (*LM* 103 includes the enigmatic Holkias) were summoned to Alexander's deathbed. This may be true, but the claim that Alexander assigned Thrake to L. (*LM* 111), because he was best qualified to subdue and rule it (Justin 15.3.15), is fabrication. Similarly, the charge that Alexander envied him his abilities as a commander (so Ael. *VH* 12.16; 14.47a) must be rejected: rumors circulated in the years that followed Alexander's death that various Successors had, at one time or another, fallen out of favor with Alexander. Such stories reflected, either favorably or unfavorably, upon the individuals in question and were generated by the propaganda mills of this turbulent age. In 323 L. was assigned control of Thrake (Curt. 10.10.4; Diod. 18.3.2, Thrake and the tribes on the Pontic Sea; Arr. *Succ.* 1.7; Dexippos, *FGrH* 100 F8 §3, Thrake and the Chersonese; Justin 13.4.16; cf. Paus. 1.9.5; *LM* 111; Ps.-Call. 3.33.13; App. *Syr.* 53.270), and was probably *strategos* rather than satrap (Lund 54 considers L. a satrap but "officially subordinate to Antipatros, the *strategos* of Europe"). The subordinate position of *strategos* may account for the failure of the sources to mention L. in the settlement of Triparadeisos; his brother Autodikos was, however, named as a Somatophylax of Philip III at that time (Arr. *Succ.* 1.38). A campaign against Seuthes, in which the Thrakian forces greatly outnumbered those of L., ended in an indecisive battle (Diod. 18.14.2–4; Arr. *Succ.* 1.10). The sequel to this is unrecorded but Seuthes may have become a reluctant ally. L. married Antipatros' daughter Nikaia, who had been jilted by Perdikkas (Seibert 1967, 13–16), and as an ally of Kassandros and Antigonos, he ordered his men to kill Kleitos the White, who had fled to his territory after his defeat at the Hellespont in 318

(Diod. 18.72.9). Since Antigonos' ambitions soon alienated the other dynasts (Ptolemy, Kassandros and Seleukos), L. was easily convinced to lend his support to their coalition in 316 (Diod. 19.56.3–4; 19.57.1–2; Justin 15.1.2–4; Paus. 1.6.4; cf. Nepos, *Eum*. 10.3) and on later occasions (Diod. 20.19.4, 76.7, 84.1; Justin 15.2.15–17). His campaign in 313 against the rebels of Kallatis (who had expelled his garrison) brought him into conflict once more with Seuthes, as well as the Skythians and forces sent by Antigonos; L. appears to have prevailed (Diod. 19.73; cf. 20.25.1, the siege of Kallatis was clearly protracted). Soon afterwards L. managed to prevent Byzantion from supporting Antigonos (Diod. 19.77.7). In 311 he and the other Successors made an agreement with Antigonos which would see Kassandros as *strategos* of Europe, until Alexander IV came of age, and L. as ruler of Thrake, but the death of the young king (carried out by Kassandros' agent Glaukias; Nepos, *Eum*. 13.3 holds all the Successors responsible for the destruction of the Argead line) led the dynasts, including L., to aspire to royal power (Diod. 19.105; Justin 15.2.10–14; for L.'s assumption of the kingship see Diod. 20.53.4). In 306 or 305, he assumed the title of "King" (Plut. *Demetr*. 18.3; App. *Syr*. 1.3, 54.277, 55.279; cf. Ael. *NA* 15.2).

The Antigonid victory at Salamis, following on the heels of Demetrios' liberation of Athens, as well as the attack on Rhodes, made it clear to the other Diadochoi that a coalition against them of the sort that preceded the Peace of the Dynasts was vital to preservation of their own powers. There followed the so-called Four Years War, highlighted by Kassandros' activities in Boiotia and Attika; L. for his part was content to let his rival in Macedonia expend his resources. In response to Rhodian appeals, L. sent 40,000 medimnoi of wheat and an equal amount of barley (Diod. 20.96.3), for which the Rhodians, after Demetrios abandoned the siege, set up statues to both L. and Kassandros (Diod. 20.100.2). But L. did not become personally engaged in the war against the Antigonids until 302, in the events that would lead up to the battle of Ipsos in 301 (Diod. 20.106.2, 107.1; Paus. 1.6.7). With his forces augmented by those of Kassandros, under the general Prepelaos (Diod. 20.107.1, 111.3), L. crossed the Hellespont, winning over Lampsakos and Parion (by negotiation) and Sigeion (by force), and pressing the war against Antigonos and Demetrios in western Asia Minor (Diod. 20.107–9). It was in the context of his push into Asia Minor that L. married Amastris (no. 67), the widow of Dionysios of Herakleia Pontika (Diod. 20.109.7; Memnon 4.9; Polyaenus 6.12); the union brought with it political influence in Herakleia, and L. was able, in 289/8(?), to secure greater control by punishing Amastris' son for her murder (Memnon 5.3; for the date see, however, Lund 98). Kassandros sent additional forces to L. under the command of his brother Pleistarchos (Diod. 20.112). Kassandros himself did not participate in the war against Antigonos, nor did Ptolemy, who returned to Egypt (from Sidon) after being fooled by a false report that L. and Seleukos had suffered defeat at Antigonos' hands (Diod. 20.113.1–2); but there was at least some truth to the matter: some of L.'s soldiers did in fact desert to Antigonos, leaving winter quarters and complaining about unpaid wages (Diod. 20.113.3). Diodorus' narrative, which at any rate rarely dealt with the affairs of L., breaks off before the battle of Ipsos and the remainder of L.'s career must be reconstructed from fragments in the historical (and biographical) literature, as well as from epigraphic evidence. Even more than Seleukos, whose activities in the East drew only limited attention, L.'s career, except when it overlapped in the West with the activities of Ptolemy, Kassandros, Demetrios, and (to a lesser extent) Pyrrhos, remains largely hidden from us. Much of what survives comes from hostile sources and we get snapshots of scenes in which his role is generally unflattering (for discussion of sources see esp. Landucci, *Lisimaco* 11–72).

The death of Antigonos at Ipsos, offered L. his first serious opportunity to enlarge his kingdom in areas other than the barbarian lands of Thrake and the Pontic regions, although it should be noted that until Ipsos, L. had been content with his Thrakian realm. The death of Antigonos created, in effect, a vortex that drew L. into the complex political relationships of Asia Minor (for L.'s eastern territories, see Hünerwadel 110–28; Lund 80–5, 113–15; Landucci, *Lisimaco* 231–43). But it was the events that followed the deaths of Kassandros and his son Philip IV in 297 that had the greater impact, disrupting the stable relationship between Macedon and Thrake that had prevailed during Kassandros' reign. When Philip IV died, Macedonia was ruled jointly by the two younger sons, Antipatros and Alexander, with their mother acting as regent (no doubt with a regency council). Thessalonike may have played a role in arranging the marriage of Antipatros to L.'s daughter Eurydike (no. 455; Justin 16.1.7, 19; 16.2.4; Porphyr. Tyr. *FGrH* 260 F3 §5). But, if the mother had proposed the union, it was to no avail; for Antipatros, who had been sharing the kingship with Alexander, murdered his mother on the grounds that she was favoring his brother, and sought the throne for himself. Antipatros was forced to flee to his father-in-law when Alexander summoned both Pyrrhos and Demetrios to his aid. L. was preoccupied with the Getai and their king, Dromichaites (for the Getic campaign, Diod. 21.11; Plut. *Demetr.* 39.6; 52.6; Justin 16.1.19; Paus. 1.9.6; Delev 2000), and content to seek a diplomatic solution through the agency of Pyrrhos (Plut. *Pyrrh.* 6; Justin 16.1.7). If an agreement was reached, there was no time for the settlement to go into effect (Plut. *Pyrrh.* 6.9 shows that it was ill fated). Demetrios arrived after Pyrrhos' departure and killed Alexander, seizing the kingship in the autumn of 294 (Plut. *Pyrrh.* 7.1–2; *Demetr.* 36.3–37.4; Justin 16.1.8–18). For the time being, L. was content to cede Antipatros' share to Demetrios—indeed, the latter had used the charge that Antipatros was a matricide (having killed a daughter of Philip II and a half-sister of Alexander the Great). Once free of Dromichaites (literally: Dromichaites had captured him), L. was left with the option of attempting to restore Antipatros to his throne militarily or to take the throne for himself; not surprisingly he opted for the latter. In 288, Pyrrhos and L. drove Demetrios out of Macedonia and, although they divided the country initially (probably along the line of the Axios), L., as a Macedonian (and doubtless he encouraged reports of his service under Alexander), managed to depict Pyrrhos as a foreigner and win the hearts of both the Macedonian troops and the people (Plut. *Pyrrh.* 12). He now added the Macedonian homeland to his territories, disinheriting his son-in-law. L. imprisoned his own daughter, who was agitating on her husband's behalf (Justin 16.2.4), and put Antipatros to death. By 285, he had made himself sole ruler of Macedon. But the advantages of the Macedonian throne were outweighed by a succession struggle in Lysimacheia. These were exacerbated by Arsinoë, the daughter of Ptolemy I, whom L. had married *c.*300/299 and by whom he had three sons, who was now pitting her husband against his heir Agathokles, the son of Nikaia. Whether he approved of the deed officially or was to weak to prevent it, L. stood by as Agathokles was poisoned by Ptolemy (not Keraunos, as Memnon 5.6 claims, but almost certainly Arsinoë's son; thus Heinen 3–17; discussion s.vv. Arsinoë no. 221 and Ptolemy no. 1011). This precipitated the flight of Lysandra and her children, Alexander, and many of Agathokles' supporters to the court of Seleukos. In the end, war broke out between L. and Seleukos, culminating in L.'s death at Koroupedion in 282/1 (App. *Syr.*

55.279, 64.339; Plut. *Mor.* 970c; Ael. *NA* 6.25; Douris *ap.* Pliny, *HN* 8.143 Hieronymos *ap.* [Lucian] *Macrob.* 11), killed by a spear thrown by a certain Malakon of Herakleia Pontika (Memnon 5.6).

Lysimachos' Family. For full discussion see particularly Beloch IV^2 2.179–80; Seibert 1967, 93–9; Ogden 57–62. The son of Agathokles (on the question of his Thessalian origins see Merker 1979, Heckel 1992, 267), L. had two firmly attested brothers, Philip (Curt. 8.2.35) and Autodikos (Arr. *Succ.* 1.38; *Syll*^{3} 373); a third brother, Alkimachos (Arr. 1.18,1–2; cf. *IG* II^2 239) is not positively identified as such. His mother's name, to judge from that of one of his daughters, may have been Arsinoë. Whether L. left behind a wife in Macedonia is unknown; nor do we know the name of the Persian bride he was undoubtedly given at Sousa (Arr. 7.4.6). His first named wife was Nikaia, daughter of Antipatros, whom he married after she had been jilted by Perdikkas (details s.v. Nikaia no. 775). Although L. may have flirted with the idea of marrying Kleopatra for political advantage (Diod. 20.37.4), he did not make another significant marriage until 302, when he took Amastris (no. 67), the widow of Dionysios of Herakleia (Memnon 4.9), whom he abandoned after the battle of Ipsos in favor of Arsinoë (Plut. *Demetr.* 31.5; Memnon 4.9; see no. 221), the daughter of Ptolemy I and Berenike. Justin says that before his death at Koroupedion, L. had lost fifteen children from various causes (Justin 17.2.1). Most of these are not known by name. Nikaia was the mother of Agathokles, Arsinoë (the later Arsinoë I, who married Ptolemy II and was the mother of Ptolemy III Euergetes), and Eurydike (wife of Kassandros' son Antipatros no. 128). Alexander was the son of an Odrysian concubine (**A99**; Paus. 1.10.4), though he is mistakenly identified as a son of Amastris (Polyaenus 6.12; accepted by Macurdy 113). By Arsinoë (II) he had three sons: Ptolemy, Lysimachos and Philip, the last two of whom were murdered by Ptolemy Keraunos in 280 (Justin 24.3.7). His fateful marriage to Arsinoë II (Paus. 1.10.3; cf. Polyaenus 8.57) played no small part in the extirpation of his line and the collapse of his kingdom (Paus. 1.10.2– 3; cf. Heinen 3–20). Hünerwadel 1910; Hoffmann 171–72; Geyer, *RE* s.v. "Lysimachos (1)"; Berve II 239–42 no. 480; Merker 1979; Heckel 1982b; Heckel 1992, 267–75; Lund; Landucci, *Lisimaco* and *LexAM* 320–1. **Stemma IX.**

674 LYSIMACHOS

(Λυσίμαχος). Son of Lysimachos and Arsinoë (no. 221), brother of Ptolemy (no. 1013) and Philip (no. 922), born in 297 or 296 (Justin 24.3.5; he was sixteen at the time of his death; Philip was three years younger: Justin 24.3.5; cf. Beloch IV^2 2.130). Ptolemy Keraunos, who had recently married Arsinoë, killed L., along with Philip in Kassandreia, despite the efforts of their mother to defend them (Justin 24.3.5–7; cf. Memnon, *FGrH* 434 F1 8.7). A third brother, Ptolemy, was not present in Kassandreia and survived. Müller, *Königspaar* 81–2; Carney 2013, 59–64; Longega 1968, 59–67. **Stemma IX.**

675 LYSIPPOS

(Λύσιππος). Greek bronze sculptor, from Sikyon (Tzetz. *Chil.* 8.200, 417; Douris, *FGrH* 76 F32 = Pliny, *HN* 34.61, who adds that he was not the student of any artist, but originally a coppersmith). His work spanned the middle years of the fourth century (c.370–315) and he was noted for his innovation and his exclusive use of bronze. He had three sons, who were his pupils: Laippos, Boëdas, and Euthykrates (Pliny, *HN* 34.66); Lysistratos was his brother. The most prolific of all sculptors (some 1,500 works: Pliny, *NH*

34.37; for other works see the *testimonia* in Pollitt 98–104), he was famous, among other things, for his depictions of Alexander, whom he knew before his accession to the throne: he sculpted a youthful Alexander (Pliny, *HN* 34.63) as well as his friend Hephaistion (34.64), though we do not know the date of this work. It was L. who gave Alexander the famous tilt of the head (Tzetz. *Chil.* 11.368, 97–108; Plut. *Mor.* 335a–b) and was the only sculptor permitted to make representations of him (Plut. *Alex.* 4.1–2; for the so-called edict concerning the depiction of Alexander see Stewart 1993, TT51–8). It was also L. who made the bronze equestrian statues of the *hetairoi* who fell at the Granikos (Arr. 1.16.4; Plut. *Alex.* 16.16; Velleius 1.11.3; Justin 11.6.13; Pliny, *HN* 34.64; Kosta 1974). He and Leochares were responsible for the lion hunt group set up by Krateros at Delphi (Plut. *Alex.* 40.5; discussion and further literature in Heckel, *Marshals*² 147–8). He is said to have made special vessels for Kassandros for his Mendean wine from Kassandreia, using earthenware models but apparently producing them in bronze (Athen. 11.784c). Berve II 241–43 no. 482. W. H. Groß, *Kl. Pauly* III 843–4 no. 2; Pollitt 98–104 and Pollitt 1986, 47–54; Johnson 1927; Salis 1956; Moreno 1973, 1974; Schwarzenberg 1976, 249–53; Stewart, *OCD*³ s.v. "Lysippos."

M

676 MACHAON

(Μαχάων). One of three officers (see also Hieron no. 530, and Sopolis no. 1063) of the garrison stationed at Iasos by Polemaios, the nephew of Antigonos (cf. Diod. 19.75.1–6). An inscription (*I.Iasos* I no. 2), dating in all likelihood to 309/8, when Polemaios defected to Ptolemy (Diod.20.27.1–3), shows that they and the city came to terms with Ptolemy I. Billows 398–9 no. 65; Bagnall 89–91.

677 MADATES

(Μαδάτης). A relative of Dareios III (Diod. 17.67.4), M. had married the daughter (**A49**) of Sisygambis' sister (**A50**; Curt. 5.3.12) and was satrap of the Ouxians who lived in the mountains east of the Pasitigris River (Curt. 5.3.1–4; cf. Diod. 17.67.1–4). He opposed, unsuccessfully, Alexander's entry into his territory and was soon defeated and besieged (Curt. 5.3.5–11; cf. Diod. 17.67.4–5; but the details are difficult to reconcile with Arr. 3.17; see Bosworth I 321–4), so that in the end Sisygambis was forced to intercede on behalf of his people and for the sake of M.'s life (Curt. 5.3.12–14). M. himself was pardoned (Curt. 5.3.16), but his territory was assigned to Sousiana and its satrap, Aboulites. Nothing else is known of his career. As for the Ouxians, Curt. 5.3.13 claims that Alexander not only spared the Ouxians but granted them immunity from taxation. This was, however, merely recognition of the fact that the natives could not be subdued (cf. Cook 1983, 185; Heckel 144 n.46). Indeed, we find the Ouxians creating difficulties for Antigonos in 317 (Diod. 19.19.3–4, 8). See also Briant 728–9; 1022. Berve II 243 no. 483; Speck 2002, 22–37; Shayegan 110 no. 58.

678 MAGAS

(Μάγας). Macedonian (Tataki 360 no. 1). Father of Berenike (no. 293). Husband of Antigone (no. 113), a daughter of Antipatros' brother, Kassandros. The MS reading of Schol. Theocr. 17.63 is Λάγου, which is rightly emended to Μάγα. Hence Berenike's son (no. 679 below) is named for the maternal grandfather. The view that Berenike's husband was her half-brother is as unnecessary as it is misguided. Geyer, *RE* XIV (1928) 292–3 no. 1.

679 MAGAS

(Μάγας). Macedonian (Tataki 360 no. 2). Son of Berenike and an otherwise unknown Philip; brother of Antigone, wife of Pyrrhos. M. was born before 320 and became ruler of Kyrene (Paus. 1.7.1 says it was given to him by his mother, which must mean that he obtained the position through Berenike's influence), but Paus. 1.6.8 indicates that he took the city in the fifth year of its rebellion, and that this rebellion came after the death of Antigonos I (ἀποθανόντος δὲ Ἀντιγόνου), thus after 301. This may explain Diodorus' failure to mention the event, since we have only fragments of his history covering the events after Ipsos (Chamoux 1956, 21). M. did not style himself "King" during his stepfather's lifetime—Paus. 1.7.2 implies that he was *epitropos*—but rather after 283 (though his kingdom was referred to as an *eparchia*: Bagnall 33): his kingship is attested on inscriptions (*SEG* IX 112; XVII 817; *Inscr. Cret.* II 211–12), as well as later coinage (*BMC Cyrenaica* CLVIII; coins bearing the legend ΒΑΣΙΛΙΣΣΗΣ ΒΕΡΕΝΙΚΗΣ and a monogram indicating Magas: see Bagnall 185). At some point between 279 and 274, M. married the Seleukid princess, Apama (Paus. 1.7.3; Justin 26.3.3, 7 wrongly calls her Arsinoë; Seibert 1967, 51–3 for the circumstances; see also McAuley 2016). Father of Berenike, who later became wife of Ptolemy III Euergetes. According to Agatharchides, in the sixteenth book of *European History* (*FGrH* 86 F7), Magas ruled Kyrene for 50 years (Athen. 12.550b–c), that is, from 301/0 to 251/0 (Beloch IV² 2.186–8; Chamoux 1956, 24; Will 2003, 243–6); Eusebius' dates must be rejected, since he places Magas' death after that of Demetrios the Fair, even though the latter came to Kyrene at the invitation of M.'s widow (Justin 26.3). See full discussion in Beloch IV² 2.186–90; Chamoux 1956. Of his military activities little is known, which lends credence to Agatharchides' claim that his reign was one without war (ἀπολέμητος): Polyaenus 2.28.1 records a stratagem which has no specific historical value, but a campaign in the 260s around Paraitonion and Chi is attested in 2.28.2. Paus. 1.7.2 speaks of a revolt against Ptolemy Philadelphos (*c*.275), in which both sides were distracted by problems closer to home: in M.'s case there was a revolt of the Libyan Marmaridai, while Ptolemy was distrustful of the Gallic mercenaries in his army. Like many of the dynasts of this period M. was an object of ridicule by an "intellectual," in this case Philemon, whom he repaid with a warning that he could have executed him but chose not to (Plut. *Mor.* 449e–f, 458a). In keeping with this display of restraint, M. also gave refuge to the abrasive and outspoken Theodoros (Diog. Laert. 2.103; cf. Cic. *Tusc.* 1.102). M. died in 250, having lived a life of luxury and become excessively corpulent (*FGrH* 86 F7). Geyer, *RE* XIV (1928) 293–7 no. 2; H. Volkmann, *Kl. Pauly* III 871–2 no. 2; Chamoux 1956; Sandberger 154 no. 51; Bagnall 26–7, 185–7. **Stemma X.**

680 MAIANDROS

(Μαίανδρος). Greek from Magnesia. Son of Mandrogenes. M. served as a trierarch of the Hydaspes fleet in 326 (Arr. *Ind.* 18.7). Otherwise unknown. Berve II 246–7 no. 488.

681 MANIA

(Μανία). A native of Attika. A good-looking prostitute of less than average height, Mania's real name was Melitta (Athen. 13.578c = Machon 196 Gow; for the origins of her nickname: Athen. 13.578c–e; Plut. *Demetr.* 27.9 is probably in error when he claims that her true name was Demo: the latter was the mistress of Antigonos Gonatas; see also Ogden 247–8). Mistress of Demetrios Poliorketes (Ptolemy son of Agesarchos *ap.* Athen. 13.577f–578a = *FGrH* 161 F4), M. was noted for her wit (Athen. 13.579a–d; cf. Plut. *Demetr.* 27.9–10 for jokes made at the expense of her rival Lamia, whom M. dismissed as "old": γραῦς). M. had many lovers as well, some insignificant, others celebrated for their achievements. She became the lover of two pankratiasts (Antenor no. 108; Leontiskos no. 655), saying that she wanted to compare the men "blow for blow" (Athen. 13.578f, Machon fr. 15 Gow). Volkmann, *Kl. Pauly* III 957 no. 5; Gow, *Machon* 97ff.

682 MANTIAS

(Μαντίας). Officer of Demetrios Poliorketes. Together with Alkimos (no. 66), M. led a select force of 1,500 in a disastrous night attack on Rhodes in 304. Both Alkimos and M. were killed and most of the men lost (Diod. 20.98.9). Billows 399 no. 66.

683 MARSYAS

(Μαρσύας). Macedonian (Tataki 147 no. 59). Son of Periandros. Raised in Pella as *syntrophos* of Alexander (*Suda* M 227). Half-brother (by the same mother) of Antigonos Monophthalmos (Plut. *Mor.* 182c; *Suda*). Author of *Macedonika* (*FGrH* 135/136; cf. Heckel 1980d; Howe, *BNJ*), which focused primarily on the reign of Philip II; the account of Alexander appears not to have been carried beyond the description of the campaign in Asia Minor. Born *c.*356, M. appears to have accompanied Alexander to Asia but probably remained with Antigonos in Phrygia in 333. In 307/6 he participated as a navarch in Demetrios' victory over Ptolemaic forces in the battle of Salamis (Diod. 20.50.4). Nothing else is known about him except that he was involved in a legal dispute at an unspecified time, though certainly after 333, and possibly after Antigonos assumed the title of "King" in 306 (Plut. *Mor.* 182c). Laqueur, *RE* XIV (1930) 1995–8 no. 8; Berve II 247–8 no. 489; Billows 399–400 no. 67; Heckel 1980d; Hauben 59–60 no. 22, and p. 119; Hornblower, *Hieronymus* 130; Howe, *BNJ* s.v.; Pownall, *LexAM* 336–7. **Stemma VI.**

684 MAUAKES

(Μαυάκης). Commander of the Sakai mounted archers (*hippotoxotai*) at Gaugamela (Arr. 3.8.3). He appears to have brought his troops to Dareios in the company of Bessos and the Baktrians and Sogdianians, but his independence (on which Arr. 3.8.3 remarks) is supported by the fact that he served on the opposite wing of the Persian force, under the general command of Mazaios (Arr. 3.11.4). What became of M. is unknown. Berve II 248 no. 490; Shayegan 110 no. 59.

685 MAZAIOS

(Μαζαῖος). Prominent Persian (Curt. 5.1.18; Diod. 17.55.1 calls him a *philos* of Dareios III; cf. Plut. *Alex.* 39.9). Born no later than 380 (he died of natural causes in 328: Arr. 4.18.3; Curt. 8.3.17); father of several sons, at least some by a Babylonian mother (Briant 783), though there seems to be some confusion in the names of Antibelos, Artiboles (no. 226) and Brochubelus (no. 311). Satrap of Kilikia since no later than 350 (Diod. 16.42.1; Head, *HN*² 731ff.; Leuze 1935, 231), and—after the fall of Sidon and the demise (for reasons unknown) of Belesys—satrap of Syria (Curt. 5.13.11, emending the text to read *praetoris*) and Mesopotamia (cf. Arr. 3.8.6, 11.4). At some point around 351/o, M., then satrap of Kilikia, and Belesys of Syria attempted to put down the Phoinikian revolt led by Tennes of Sidon; they were, however, defeated by a force of 4,000 Greek mercenaries from Egypt led by Mentor the Rhodian (Diod. 16.42.1–2). But in 346/5, Sidon surrendered through the treachery of Tennes and M. appears as satrap of both Kilikia and Abarnahara (Trans-Euphrates) in the reign of Artaxerxes III (Head *HN*² 732). The date for the fall of Sidon can be estimated from Isoc. *Phil.* 102, which speaks of the revolt as still going on in 347, and a Babylonian inscription (*ABC* no. 9) mentioning Sidonian prisoners in Babylon in 345. The date of M.'s assumption of the satrapy of Kilikia is often given as 361, after the Satraps' Revolt (Berve II 244; Head, *HN²* 731), but there is no solid evidence for his holding of the office until 351/0 (Diod. 16.42.1), and even here the date is not certain. In 331, he had been ordered by Dareios to prevent Alexander's crossing of the Euphrates at Thapsakos, but he had insufficient numbers to do much more than prevent the completion of the bridges. Upon Alexander's arrival M. withdrew (Arr. 3.7.1) and joined Dareios, who was following the Tigris northward. Diod. 17.55.1 claims that M. had been ordered to guard the Tigris crossing, a task which had perhaps been assigned to Satropates; Curt. 4.9.7–25 conflates two sources (Ptolemy and Kleitarchos?) in a clumsy way that obscures the operations of both M. and Satropates (on the problem of the rivers see Stronk 316 n.162). Diod. 17.55.2 claims that Mazaios neglected his duty here, because he considered the Tigris uncrossable, and turned to laying waste the countryside. At Gaugamela M. commanded the Persian cavalry on the right wing (Diod. 17.59.5, 60.5) and led a charge of dense squadrons together with the scythe-chariots (Diod. 17.58.2; for the success of these vehicles in this stage of the battle see Heckel, Willekes, and Wrightson 2010; Heckel 137–8), where he inflicted heavy casualties and sent a Skythian squadron to capture the Macedonian camp (Diod. 17.59.5–8). Soon he exerted pressure on Parmenion and the Thessalian cavalry on the Macedonian left (Diod. 17.60.5–7)—Parmenion sent a force to summon Alexander to his aid, but they returned without having contacted him (Diod. 17.60.7)—but was eventually overcome by the tenacity of the Thessalians and the flight of Dareios (Diod. 17.60.8). M. fled from the battlefield to Babylon (Curt. 4.16.7; cf. 5.1.17), which he later surrendered to Alexander (Curt. 5.1.17–19; cf. Diod. 17.64.4; Arr. 3.16.3), only to be installed as its satrap, the first Persian to be so honored by Alexander (Arr. 3.16.4; Curt. 5.1.44; cf. Diod. 17.64.5–6). M. was not satrap of Babylon before Gaugamela, where the Babylonians were commanded by Boupares (Arr. 3.8.5). Briant 846, 848 refers to a Babylonian tablet (*ADRTB* no. –330), which suggests that there had been some communication between Alexander and Babylon after the battle of Gaugamela, either with Mazaios or with the Babylonians themselves. For the "ritual surrender" of the city see Kuhrt 1987, 48–9. M. held this office until his death in late 328, whereupon he was replaced by Stamenes (Arr. 4.18.3; cf. Curt. 8.3.17 "Ditamenes"). He was perhaps the intended occupant of the so-called Alexander Sarcophagus in Sidon, if the details of sculptures relate to the life of the man who commissioned it (Heckel 2006; Heckel 142 n.37; but see discussion s.v. Abdalonymos no. 1). Berve II 243–5 no. 484; Leuze 1935 (*passim*); Briant 848–9; Shayegan 110–11 no. 60.

686 MAZAKES

(Μαζάκης). Persian. Appointed satrap of Egypt by Dareios (Arr. 3.1.2; Curt. 4.7.4: *praetor Darei*) after the death of the previous satrap Sabakes (Arr. 2.11.8; no. 1029) at Issos (Curt. 3.11.10; 4.1.28) and in the months that Alexander was occupied with the affairs of Phoinikia. M., making a sortie from Memphis, defeated and killed all the invading forces of Amyntas (no. 77) son of Antiochos, including their leader (Curt. 4.1.32–3). In 332 he surrendered Memphis and its treasure to Alexander (Curt. 4.7.4; Arr. 3.1.2). He may have been retained in the King's entourage. Berve II 245–6 no. 485; Shayegan 111 no. 61.

687 MAZAROS

(Μάζαρος). According to Arr. 3.16.9, one of Alexander's *hetairoi* and *phrourarchos* of Sousa (331). The name sounds suspiciously Iranian and it is likely that the text is corrupt;

possibly Arrian meant to record that Xenophilos (no. 1165) replaced M. as *phrourarchos* (see Curt. 5.2.16; Bosworth I 319; Heckel 2002) rather than that M. was a Macedonian *phrourarchos* who was later replaced by Xenophilos (thus Brunt I 278 n.10). Berve II 246 no. 486.

688 MAZENES

(Μαζήνης). Persian *hyparchos*; governor of the island of Oarakta, which may have belonged to the satrapy of Karmania (thus Berve II 246; cf. Tomaschek 47–8). Nearchos discovered him in 325/4 along with Mithropastes, who had fled there (Arr. *Ind.* 37.2; cf. Strabo 16.3.7 C767 = Nearchos, *FGrH* 133 F28). He accompanied Nearchos as far as Sousa where he appears to have submitted to the King in person. Berve II 246 no. 487; Shayegan III no. 62.

689 MEDA

(Μήδα). Thrakian princess. Daughter of Kothelas. Philip II married her at some point after his marriage to Olympias (Athen. 13.557d: γήμας δὲ ταύτην ἐπεισήγαγεν τῇ Ὀλυμπιάδι), most likely in 342 (Ellis 1976, 166–7). She appears to have borne no children and her fate is unknown. The view that she is the woman in the antechamber of Tomb II in Vergina (Lane Fox 2011a, 32), and that she committed *suttee* (Hammond 1994, 182) is implausible. The Thrakian means of following the husband into the afterlife involved strangulation (Hdt. 4.71.4: ἀποπνίξαντες), not cremation on the same pyre, as in the Indian custom. It would be odd if the Macedonians allowed Meda to follow her Thrakian practice in one respect and then cremated her contrary to custom. Ellis 1976, 166–7, 211–12; Carney 68; Ogden 18–19.

690 MEDEIOS

(Μήδειος, Μήδιος). Son of Oxythemis (Arr. *Ind.* 18.7; Strabo 11.14.12 C530 = *FGrH* 129 T1, F1), from Larisa, where the grandfather, also named Medeios, is attested as *dynastes* in 395 and an enemy of Lycophron of Pherai (Diod. 14.82.5; cf. Westlake 1935, 59–66). A Thessalian *hetairos* of Alexander (cf. Arr. 7.24.4; Diod. 17.117.1), M. appears to have accompanied the King from the beginning of the campaign (Strabo 11.14.12–14 C531 = *FGrH* 129 T1, F1 suggests that he was with Alexander in the late 330s, but in no known military capacity; he is first attested as a trierarch of the Hydaspes fleet in 326 (Arr. *Ind.* 18.7). Billows 400 assumes, plausibly, that M. was a commander of Thessalian cavalry in the period 334–330, but I do not accept his view that after 326 he "becam[e] one of the *hetairoi*." As a member of the Aleuadai, his status as one of the Macedonian king's *hetairoi* will have predated 334. Otherwise, he is described as a flatterer of Alexander (Plut. *Mor.* 65c) and the *erastes* of Iolaos son of Antipatros (Arr. 7.27.2). He gained notoriety as a result of the political pamphlet on *The Last Days and Testament of Alexander*, which alleged that it was at a drinking party in the residence of M. in Babylon (cf. Arr. 7.25.1 = *FGrH* 117 F3a; Plut. *Alex.* 76 = *FGrH* 117 F3b) that the King was poisoned (*LM* 97–8; Ps.-Call. 3.31; cf. Arr. 7.27.2; Plut. *Alex.* 75.4–6; Heckel 1988, 37–8). After the King's death, he was briefly a supporter of Perdikkas and served the admiral Sosigenes and the *strategos* Aristonous as commander of the mercenaries (*xenagos*) sent to Kypros in 321/0 (Arr. *Succ.* 24.6). M. entered Antigonos' service, either after the defeat of Sosigenes' expedition or upon the news of Perdikkas' death (whichever came first). Later he is found as an admiral of the Antigonid fleet (Hauben no. 23), defeating Kassandros' ships as he sailed from Phoinikia to Karia in 313 (Diod. 19.69.3) and, in the following year, continuing to serve in the Aegean and at the Hellespont (Diod. 19.75.3–4, 7–8, 19.77.2–5). At Salamis (306) M. commanded ships on the left wing of Demetrios' fleet (Diod. 20.50.3). Afterwards, he participated in the unsuccessful move on Egypt (Plut. *Demetr.* 19.1–2). An Athenian inscription, dated 303/2, honors M. for some unspecified service to the state in the period before 307/6 and mentions his role in attempting to liberate Greece (*Syll*³ 342 = *IG* II² 498), probably in 308/7. Bayliss 2002, 91 suggests that M.'s earlier service to Athens had to do with Athenian sailors under his command at Salamis in 306; but such service is often spelled out in honorary decrees, and unless it is mentioned elsewhere presents a problem, the arguments of Bayliss, based on Herman 1981 notwithstanding. M. was the uncle of Oxythemis son of Hippostratos, who was for a while a favorite at the Antigonid court but later executed by Antigonos Gonatas (Athen. 13.578a–b; see also Billows 414 no. 86), and he himself appears to have remained a faithful supporter of Demetrios towards the end of his life (Habicht² 265–9, 266 n.4). For his historical work see Jacoby, *FGrH* 129; Pearson 68–70. Geyer, *RE* XV.1 (1932) 103–4 no. 2; Berve II 261–2 no. 521; Launey 1141; Volkmann, *Kl. Pauly* III 1133 no. 2; Billows 400–1 no. 68; Hauben 60–9 no. 23; Hornblower, *Hieronymus* 126–30; Bayliss 2002.

691 MEDON

(Μέδων). The father's name is only partially preserved (—ρας). Honored by the Athenians in 304/3 in a decree published by Matthaiou, *Horos* 4 (1986) 19–23. M. was sent by Demetrios to report the capture of the border forts from Kassandros and Pleistarchos (lines 18–22; cf. Plut. *Demetr.* 23.1–3). Nothing else is known about him. Billows 401–2 no. 69.

692 MEGABYXOS

(Μεγάβυξος, but Greek literary texts have Μεγάβυζος). The form Megabyxos has both epigraphic and etymological support (Persian: *Bagabuksha*, which may mean "servant of the god" or "giving joy to the god"; thus Burkert 2004, 106). *Syll*³ 282.1 calls him "Megabyxos son of Megabyxos, *neokoros* of Artemis of Ephesos" (cf. Xen. *Anab.* 5.3.6), that is the priest of Artemis (cf. Pliny, *HN* 35.93, 131–2), but the name appears rather to be a title and the priests themselves were eunuchs (*Suda* s.v. βαβαὶ Μύξος and Strabo 14.1.23 C641). The inscription shows the people of Priene honoring the Megabyxos with a crown and a bronze statue in 333 for his support of the rebuilding of the temple of Athena in their city; and they granted him *proxenia* and recognized him as a benefactor (lines 8–10). Apelles painted a *Procession of the Megabyxos* (Pliny, *HN* 35.93; for M.'s association with Apelles Plut. *Mor.* 58d, 471f–472a; Ael. *VH* 2.2). Alexander wrote to him, presumably in 324/3 (after the appointment of Antimenes of Rhodes as treasurer; see no. 122), regarding a runaway slave who had taken refuge in the sanctuary of Artemis (Plut. *Alex.* 42.1), asking him to recapture the slave but not violate the sanctity of the temple. Berve II 248 no. 491; Burkert 2004, 105–7.

693 MEGAREUS

(Μεγαρεύς). A Chian of unknown family background, M. was a leader of the pro-Persian oligarchy at Chios (see also Apollonides and Phesinos), which had been brought to power in the summer of 333 with the support of Pharnabazos' fleet. In 332 M. and his colleagues were captured by Hegelochos and brought to Alexander in Egypt (Arr. 3.2.5); the latter sent them to Elephantine to be imprisoned (Arr. 3.2.7), apparently countermanding thereby his own edict to Chios (Tod II 192; see Bosworth I 268 for discussion). Berve II 248 no. 492; Berve, *Tyrannis* I 339, II 691; Hofstetter 124 no. 211

694 MEGASTHENES

(Μεγασθένης), Greek of unknown origin, though apparently an Ionian. He is said to have resided with Sibyrtios, the satrap of Arachosia (Arr. 5.6.2), and it may be that he was a friend and compatriot of that man. From Arachosia he was sent as an envoy to Sandrokottos (Strabo 2.1.9 C70; Arr. 5.6.2; cf. Pliny, *HN* 6.21.58) and Poros (Arr. *Ind.* 5.3), and if he visited both on the same mission, this must date to the period 322–317. Clement of Alexandria 1.72.5 says he lived in the time of Seleukos Nikator, which is technically correct, but it need not imply that his mission to Sandrokottos occurred late in the fourth century (but see Olshausen 174); nor need Arr. 5.6.2 mean that he made several trips, though this cannot be ruled out: πολλάκις δὲ λέγει ἀφικέσθαι παρὰ Σανδράκοττον should be translated "he often speaks of visiting Sandrokottos" and not "he says he often visited Sandrokottos" (Bosworth II 244; cf. Olshausen 172, who speaks of a single visit). He was the author of an *Indica* (see Jacoby, *FGrH* 715 for the fragments; cf. Brown 1955). Stein, *RE* XV.1 (1931) 230 no. 2; Grainger, *SPG* 103; Olshausen no. 127; Bosworth 1996b.

MELAMNIDAS. See MENIDAS.

695 MELEAGROS

(Μελέαγρος). Macedonian (Tataki 378 no. 8). Son of Neoptolemos (Arr. 1.24.1, 29.4). His regional origins are unknown, but the father's name suggests the western highlands, the only attested examples in Alexander's reign coming from Epeiros and Lynkestis (Justin 7.6.10; 17.3.14; Plut. *Pyrrh.* 5.2, *Eum.* 1.6; Arr. 1.20.10; Diod. 17.25.5; cf. Hoffmann 202 n. 119). M.'s birthdate is unknown, but the fact that he was not dismissed with the veterans in 324 suggests that he may have been one of the younger marshals. Furthermore, he had only recently married in 334 (Arr. 1.24.1), which implies (though it does not prove) a birthdate perhaps in the 360s (cf. Berve II 249). In 335 M. and a certain Philip (possibly the son of Balakros) conveyed back to the Macedonian base the booty taken from the Getai beyond the Danube (Arr. 1.4.5); the association with Philip suggests that he was already a taxiarch. At the Granikos (334) M. was stationed on the left, between Philip and Krateros (Arr. 1.14.3), and at Halikarnassos he joined Perdikkas and Amyntas, as Alexander led three battalions of infantry in an unsuccessful attack on Myndos (Arr. 1.20.5). In winter 334/3 he was one of the leaders of the *neogamoi* (newlyweds) together with Koinos son of Polemokrates and Ptolemy son of Seleukos. These men spent the winter in Macedonia and secured new recruits for the expedition (Arr. 1.24.1). He rejoined the King at Gordion in the spring of 333, bringing 3,000 infantry and 300 cavalry from Macedonia, along with 200 Thessalian horse, and 150 Eleians under the command of Alkias (no. 64; Arr. 1.29.4). Of his participation in the battles at Issos and Gaugamela, nothing is known beyond his position in the battle line (Issos: Curt. 3.9.7; Arr. 2.8.4. Gaugamela: Diod. 17.57.2; Arr. 3.11.9; but M. has dropped out of the battle order at Curt. 4.13.28). At the Persian Gates, at the end of 331, M. and his battalion remained with Krateros, holding the attention of Ariobarzanes, while Alexander conducted the encircling maneuver (Arr. 3.18.4; Curt. 5.4.14).

In 329, at the Iaxartes, M. and Perdikkas besieged the Memaceni (Curt. 7.6.17ff., the name occurs only in Curt.), who were said to have killed some 50 Macedonian horsemen by treachery (Curt. 7.6.17–18). The honor of taking the city was left to Alexander, who sustained a serious wound to the neck in the assault on the walls (Curt. 7.6.22–3; Arr. 4.3.3 claims that this injury occurred at Kyroupolis). In spring 328, when the main force returned to Sogdiana, M. remained with Polyperchon, Attalos, and Gorgias in Baktria (Arr. 4.16.1). Berve II 249 thinks each phalanx commander operated independently in a separate part of Baktria, but there is no good evidence for this. The cavalry units were active in Sogdiana, and it seems unlikely that individual battalions would have operated in Baktria without cavalry support. M. soon joined Koinos, with whom he spent the remainder of the campaigning season and the winter of 328/7 in Sogdiana (Arr. 4.17.3). In 327, his battalion, along with those of White Kleitos and Gorgias, accompanied Perdikkas and Hephaistion to the Indos, subduing the local dynast Astis *en route* (Arr. 4. 22. 7; cf. Curt. 8. 10. 2). Sometime later, when Alexander gave Omphis (Taxiles) 1,000 talents at a banquet, M. remarked to his King that "at least in India he had found a man worth one thousand talents" (Curt. 8.12.17–18; cf. Strabo 15.1.28 C698; Plut. *Alex.* 59.5). Whether this reflects M.'s personal dislike of Omphis, or his opposition to Alexander's favorable treatment of orientals, or perhaps his own pettiness, we cannot say. Curtius claims that Alexander suppressed his anger at M.'s outspokenness (Curt. 8.12.18). Some modern scholars have seen in this episode, or perhaps in M.'s personality in general, the reason for his failure to be promoted to hipparch (cf. Green 1991, 388); he was the only surviving taxiarch of those who held the office in 334 who was not promoted. Furthermore, he appears never to have exercised an independent command. Of his personality, little else is known, except that his conservative attitudes led him to reject the kingship of Alexander IV or of Herakles son of Barsine and to espouse the cause of the incompetent Arrhidaios. His fondness for wrestling is attested by Pliny, who claims that he imported powdery dust from the Nile region for this very purpose (*HN* 35.167–8; unless Pliny has confused him with Menelaos). But he was clearly not a man of learning, nor politically astute (cf. Berve II 250). At the Hydaspes, M., Attalos, and Gorgias occupied the camp at the halfway point between Krateros' position (opposite Poros) and Alexander's crossing-point (Arr. 5.12.1). These three taxiarchs were placed in command of the mercenary cavalry and infantry, almost certainly in addition to their own battalions (Berve II 249, following Anspach II 7 n.134; *contra* Bosworth 1973, 247 n.2, who thinks they commanded *only* mercenaries). They crossed the Hydaspes, once Alexander's forces had successfully diverted Poros' attention, and helped to secure the Macedonian victory (Arr. 5.18.1). In 325 M. returned from India via Arachosia and Drangiana along with Attalos and Antigenes, all under the leadership of Krateros (Arr. 6.17.3).

In 323, M. supported the cause of the conservative phalanx (Diod. 18.2.2; Arr. *Succ.* 1.2 lists him as the only infantry officer amongst the *megistoi*) and opposed the claims of Alexander's half-barbarian sons (Justin 12.2.6–8; Curt. 10.6.20–1). Instead he championed the cause of the common soldier and those veteran commanders who disdained Alexander's orientalism. M. espoused the hereditary claims of Arrhidaios to the Macedonian kingship. Whether he took his cue from an *ignotus*, as Curtius (10.7.1–3, 6–7) says, is impossible to determine. Justin 13.3.2 and Diod. 18.2.2–3 (probably from

Hieronymos) say that M. was sent by the cavalry to negotiate with the infantry but betrayed the former group. Curtius, however, appears to derive from Kleitarchos (who used eyewitnesses; so Schachermeyr 1970, 85), and the story that M. betrayed the cavalry may have been a later invention intended to justify his execution. The aristocratic faction, stunned by the unexpected turn of events and cowed by the surging mob, withdrew from the phalanx, eventually leaving Babylon altogether (Curt. 10.7.10–21). The victory was temporary and hollow: agents sent to assassinate Perdikkas (Curt. 10.8.1–3; but Justin 13.3.6–8 names Attalos as the instigator), were unwilling to do so, placing little confidence in the authority of M. or his puppet Arrhidaios; Attalos son of Andromenes was easily detached by the prospect of alliance with Perdikkas, who offered his sister Atalante in marriage (Diod. 18.37.2; cf. Heckel 1978c, 381–4). The phalanx in general soon repented and called for M.'s head and reconciliation with the cavalry (Curt. 10.8.5ff.); M. alleged that the order to murder Perdikkas had come from Philip Arrhidaios himself. The cavalry, however, demanded that the leaders of the sedition be handed over, and the fact that the infantry made an exception of M., whom they wanted as a third leader (along with Perdikkas and Krateros), shows that at this time he still had considerable support (Curt. 10.8.14–22). The agreement, which ended the discord, recognized the kingship of Arrhidaios, but transferred the guardianship (*prostasia*) to Krateros, an arrangement much more appealing to the common soldier. M., although recognized as *tertius dux* (Curt. 10.8.22–3; Arr. *Succ.* 1.3 makes M. Perdikkas' *hyparch*os; Justin 13.4.5 treats them as equals), was now isolated and soon abandoned by the infantry, who saw his death as a necessary sacrifice for the well-being of the empire (Curt. 10.9.1). Disguising his intentions (Justin 13.4.7; cf. Curt. 10.9.20), Perdikkas arranged with M. himself a lustration of the Macedonian army, officially on the instructions of the new King (Curt. 10.9.7–11). But, at the head of the cavalry and the elephants, Perdikkas suddenly called for the surrender of the authors of the discord. Some three hundred were handed over for punishment and trampled beneath the feet of the elephants (Curt. 10.9.11–18). M., their leader, sought refuge in a nearby temple, only to be murdered there (Curt. 10.9.20–1; cf. Arr. *Succ.* 1.4; Justin 13.4.7–8 does not name M., but it is clear that he was among those who were executed). The pamphlet on *The Last Days and Testament of Alexander the Great* names Meleagros as one of some fourteen guests at Medeios' dinner party who were involved in the plot against Alexander, and the forged Testament contained in the pamphlet awards him the satrapy of Koile-Syria and Phoinikia (*LM* 117; Jul. Val. 3.58; Leo 33; Ps.-Call. 3.33.15); this satrapy was, in fact, assigned to Laomedon. Diod. 18.4.7 says that Perdikkas used a personal quarrel and the charge that Meleagros was plotting against him in order to eliminate him. Berve II 249–50 no. 494; Geyer, *RE* XV.1, 478–9 no. 2; Hoffmann 146–7, 187; Heckel, *Marshals*² 101–6.

696 MELEAGROS

(Μελέαγρος). Macedonian (Tataki 364 no. 22) of aristocratic family. M. led a squadron of the Companion Cavalry at Gaugamela (Arr. 3.11.8; Curt. 4.13.27) and may have served as ilarch since at least 334. Perhaps identical with the supporter of Peithon (below). Berve II 250 no. 495; Hoffmann 183; Heckel 1988, 40; Heckel 1992, 349.

697 MELEAGROS

(Μελέαγρος). Macedonian (Tataki 364 no. 23) cavalry commander, supporter of Peithon son of Krateuas (no. 867), the former Somatophylax, who since 323 was the satrap of Media. After the death of Eumenes (316), when Peithon was executed for plotting to rebel against the authority of Antigonos (Diod. 19.46.1–4), M. continued to resist and foment rebellion in Media, where Antigonos had appointed Orontobates as satrap (Diod. 19.46.5). M. and Menoitas gathered the remnants of Eumenes' and Peithon's supporters, assembling about 800 horsemen, with whom they attacked the camp of Orontobates and his *strategos* Hippostratos with only limited success; eventually his troops were hemmed in by the terrain and overcome. M., Okranes and some other notable officers were killed (Diod. 19.47). M. may have been identical with the ilarch of the Companion Cavalry at Gaugamela (Arr. 3.11.8; Curt. 4.13.27), a position he appears to have held since at least 334. Berve II 250 no. 495; Geyer, *RE* XV 480 no. 5 (= no. 6); Hoffmann 183; Heckel 1988, 40; Heckel 1992, 349.

698 MELEAGROS

(Μελέαγρος). Macedonian (Tataki 364 no. 24). Brother of Ptolemy Keraunos and Lysandra, and thus son of Ptolemy I Soter and Eurydike (Porphyr. Tyr. *FGrH* 260 F3 §10; cf. Diod. 22.4, who wrongly calls him a *brother* of Ptolemy son of Lagos). He may have left the court in Alexandria along with his brother (Paus. 1.10.4). The details are unclear, but he found himself eventually (after the death of Agathokles) accompanying Lysandra to the court of Seleukos. After the death of Keraunos in 279, M. became king but ruled for only two months (Porphyr. Tyr. *FGrH* 260 F3 §10; but Diod. 22.4 says a few *days* ὀλίγας ἡμέρας δυναστεύσας) before being deposed by the Macedonians on the grounds that he was unworthy. Beloch IV² 2.121 dates his reign to May–July, 279. He was replaced by Antipatros (no. 129) son of Philip (no. 910), a nephew of Kassandros, whose reign was similarly brief, though he lasted 45 days. Pausanias 1.7.1 says that Ptolemy II Philadelphos put to death an unnamed half-brother (a son of Eurydike) for fomenting rebellion in Kypros. He is generally treated as a separate individual, but Geyer identifies him with M., who (in his opinion) returned to the Egyptian kingdom after being rejected by the Macedonians. Geyer, *RE* XV (1931) 479 no. 3. **Stemma X.**

699 MELESIPPOS

(Μελήσιππος). Son of Bakchios. Boiotian from Plataiai. *I.Ephesos* VI 2003; Robert, *Hellenica* II 17 n.1. Honored with citizenship by the Ephesians for his good services while at the court of Phila, wife of Demetrios Poliorketes. Hence M. was in Phila's employ, perhaps between 306 and 301 in Asia Minor (thus Billows 402). Cf. Demarchos (Billows no. 28). Billows 402 no. 70.

700 MELON

(Μέλων). Greek of unknown family background, Melon served for an unspecified time as interpreter for Dareios III (Curt. 5.13.7). Curtius 5.11.4 says, implausibly but for dramatic effect (Heckel 1994a, 72–3), that Dareios understood some Greek. Left behind, on account of illness, at the Parthian town of Thara (where Dareios was arrested by Bessos and Nabarzanes) in 330, he fell into Alexander's hands (Curt. 5.13.7). What became of him is unknown, though it is likely that, if he survived his illness, Alexander made use of his linguistic skills. Berve II 250 no. 496; Hofstetter 125 no. 214.

701 MEMNON

(Μέμνων). Rhodian (Diod. 17.7.2). Brother of Mentor and brother-in-law of Artabazos (Diod. 16.52.3–4; Dem. 23.157), a relationship which accounts for his influence with Dareios III (Seibt 106). Born, perhaps, soon after 390: Dem. 23.157 describes both M. and his brother as young men (νέοι) in 360, but both were fighting as mercenaries for Artabazos in 366/5. Married Barsine, the widow of his brother Mentor and daughter of Artabazos (Arr. 7.4.6; Plut. *Alex.* 21.8); the only known offspring of this marriage was captured, while still a child, at Damaskos in late 333 together with his mother (Curt. 3.13.14). Artabazos awarded M. and Mentor lands in the Troad, which included the cities of Skepsis, Kebren and Ilion (cf. Polyaenus 4.3.15), although it is unclear whether this constituted what Arr. 1.17.8 calls τὴν χώραν τὴν Μέμνονος (Heckel 1994b and Strabo 13.1.11 C587). M. fought against Autophradates, joined forces with Charidemos, and shared Artabazos' exile in Macedon (Demosthenes 23; Athen. 6.256d–e). The recall of Artabazos and M. was facilitated by Mentor (Diod. 16.5.3–4). After the death of Philip II, Dareios sent M. with a force of 5,000 mercenaries to traverse Mt. Ida and gain possession of Kyzikos (Diod. 17.7.2), a task which M. failed to accomplish (Diod. 17.7.8); he did, however, prevent Parmenion and the Macedonian forces from capturing Pitane, compelling them to break off their siege (Diod. 17.7.9). When Alexander crossed into Asia, M. advocated a scorched earth policy, advice rejected by the Persian commanders (Diod. 17.18.2–3). At the River Granikos, M. and Arsames held the left wing (each with his own cavalry: Diod. 17.19.4; but earlier we heard only that M. had 5,000 Greek mercenaries, presumably infantry). Nothing else is recorded about his role in the battle; after the defeat, he and the Persian survivors fell back on Miletos (Diod. 17.22). Arr.1.18.4 appears to suggest that Memnon had not entered the city when it was besieged by Alexander. If he was in the city, there is no mention in Diodorus or Arrian of his escape. After the fall of Miletos, M. and his supporters withdrew to Halikarnassos (Diod. 17.23.4). Around this time, he also sent his wife and children to Dareios, both for their safety and as a token of good faith; for he hoped to be given supreme command of the forces in Asia Minor (Diod. 17.23.5). And this actually came about (Diod. 17.23.6; cf. Arr. 1.20.3). At Halikarnassos, M. conducted a gallant defense (Diod. 17.24.3–27.4), but in the end was forced to withdraw to Kos, leaving behind his best men to defend the acropolis of Halikarnassos (Diod. 17.27.5). In spite of these setbacks, Dareios appointed M. commander-in-chief of operations in Asia Minor and sent him money to hire mercenaries and man ships (Diod. 17.29.1–2). M. captured Chios and the Lesbian towns of Antissa, Methymna, Pyrrha, and Eresos; as well as Mytilene, with heavy losses on his own side (Diod. 17.29.2: Arr. 2.1.1–2 places the fall of Mytilene *after* Memnon's death). But, just when M. was threatening to turn the war back on Greece (Diod. 17.29.3; Arr. 2.1.1; cf. Diod. 17.30.1)—he had distributed bribes there—by sailing to Euboia, he died of illness (Diod. 17.29.3–4; Arr. 2.1.3; cf. Curt. 3.1.21; 3.2.1). His successor was his brother-in-law Pharnabazos (Curt. 3.3.1; Arr. 2.1.3). Berve II 250–3 no. 497; Seibt 1977, 99–107; Hofstetter 125–7 no. 215 (with further bibliography); Müller, *LexAM* 337–9; Badian, *Encyclopaedia Iranica* s.v. "Mentor and Memnon." **Stemma IV.**

702 MEMNON

(Μέμνων). Descendant of the great satrap Pharnabazos and his son Artabazos. M. was honored in Athens in 327/6 (*IG* II² 356 = Tod II no. 199). There is no patronymic on the surviving portion of the inscription, but a reference to the euergetism of his ancestors, Pharnabazos and Artabazos, follows eleven illegible lines of text which must have given the family details. A subsequent comment (lines 30–1) on "Mentor, the father of Thymondas," makes it virtually certain that Thymondas was his father and that his mother was either a daughter (thus Hofstetter 127) or granddaughter of Artabazos. That he was the son of the famous M. and Barsine (perhaps the child captured with his mother at Damaskos in 333 (Curt. 3.13.14) is far less likely; for it would be pointless to identify Mentor, the elder Memnon's brother, as the father of Thymondas. That is, by identifying Mentor as Thymondas' father, the decree makes clear that there was a close relationship between the honorand and Thymondas himself. It has been suggested that the younger Memnon must have been an adult and have done some service for the Athenians (R&O 508; cf. Schwenk 294), but the Athenians may have taken in the young son of Thymondas just as they had earlier sheltered Tharyps the Molossian (Justin 17.3.9–11; cf. Hammond, *Epirus* 507). If we are dealing with a relative of Barsine, the year is significant, since it was in 327 that Barsine was sent back to coastal Asia Minor, where she bore Alexander's son, Herakles. Athens was almost certainly attempting to curry favor with Alexander by means of the decree for M. (thus Hofstetter 127). Identification with the *strategos* of Thrake (thus Badian 1967a, 179–80) is rightly rejected by Bosworth 1988, 201 n.15; Heckel 126 n.126 for the weakness of the argument. Berve II 253–4 no. 498; Hofstetter 127–8 no. 216; R&O 506–9 no. 98. **Stemma IV.**

703 MEMNON

(Μέμνων). *Strategos* of Thrake. According to Diod. 17.62.4–5, he rose in rebellion against Alexander and was defeated by Antipatros. Both the essence and the chronological context of the report are incorrect. Justin relates in this chronological context the defeat of M.'s predecessor Zopyrion (no. 1174 for details) at the hands of the Getai (12.1.4, 2.16–17; cf. Curt. 10.1.44). The correct form of his name may be Menon. M. was clearly Zopyrion's successor and appointed in 331/0. He reached Alexander at the Hydaspes with reinforcements from Thrace in 326/5 (Curt. 9.3.21). Berve II 254 no. 499; Badian 1967a; I no longer hold the view expressed in Yardley and Heckel 196–9.

704 MEMPSIS

(Μέμψις). Barbarian ruler of one of the cities of Hellespontine Phrygia attacked by Arrhidaios (who had received the satrapy at Triparadeisos in 320). He brought his townspeople (including women and children), along with their possessions, outside the city and deterred the Macedonian satrap, who feared that they would fight to the death (Polyaenus 7.30). The episode dates to 319, and Arrhidaios' actions served as an excuse for Antigonos the One-Eyed to attack him. What became of M. is unknown.

705 MENANDROS

(Μένανδρος). Macedonian (Tataki 366 no. 32). *Hetairos* of Alexander. At some time *c.*329–327, he was left behind as the commander of a small fortress in Baktria-Sogdiana or perhaps in the territory bordering on India. He did not wish to remain there and rebelled against the King, who had him put to death (Plut. *Alex.* 57.3). Whether he had anything to do with the uprising of Orsodates is not clear. Geyer, *RE* XV (1931) 707 no. 6; Berve II 255 no. 502.

706 MENANDROS

(Μένανδρος). Macedonian (Tataki 365–6 no. 31) *hetairos* of Alexander (Arr. 3.6.7) and father of the Page Charikles (Arr. 4.13.7), M. commanded mercenary infantry from perhaps 334 until the spring of 331. In the spring of 331, he relinquished the command of the *xenoi* to Kleandros (Arr. 3.6.8; Κλέαρχος in the MSS should probably read Κλέανδρος, cf. Brunt I 240 n.8; Bosworth I 285; Arr. 3.12.2) in order to become satrap of Lydia (Arr. 3.6.7; cf. 7.23.1; *Syll*³ 302, 4–5). As satrap he appears to have been responsible for sending some 2,600 Lydian infantry and 300 cavalrymen, who reached Alexander near Artakoana in 330 (Curt. 6.6.35; it had perhaps been one of M.'s first tasks, upon taking charge of the satrapy, to secure these reinforcements for the King). M. commissioned a painting of himself by Apelles, apparently during Alexander's lifetime (Pliny, *HN* 35.93, wrongly "King of the Karians," unless Pliny confuses him with Asandros son of Agathon; cf. Pollitt, p. 162). His satrapal court was lavish enough to attract parasites such as Gryllion, though there is no evidence of the types of excesses that characterized Harpalos' "court." We know the name of one of his officials in Lydia, Krateuas. In 323, M. brought fresh troops to Alexander in Babylon (7.23.1) and attended the dinner party given by Medeios, at which the King became fatally ill. It is alleged in the pamphlet on the *Last Days and Testament of Alexander* that M. was guilty of complicity in the plot to poison the King (Ps. –Call. 3.31.8; *LM* 97–8), but this appears to be hostile propaganda spread by the Polyperchon faction (Heckel 1988; but see Bosworth 2000). M. was confirmed as satrap of Lydia in the settlement at Babylon (Arr. *Succ.* 1.6, cf. 1. 26; Dexippos, *FGrH* 100 F8 §2; Curt. 10.10.2; Diod. 18.3.1; Justin 13.4.15), but he was humiliated by Perdikkas, who assigned control of the satrapy to Kleopatra, the sister of Alexander the Great, leaving M. in charge of the army (Arr. *Succ.* 25.2). He soon defected to Antigonos, who had returned from Europe, having incited Antipatros and Krateros to war with Perdikkas. In the settlement of Triparadeisos, M. was relieved of his satrapy, which was assigned instead to White Kleitos. M., for his part, took refuge with Antigonos, who appears to have promised to restore Lydia to him. M. served Antigonos faithfully, especially in the events following the battle of Orkynia (Plut. *Eum.* 9.8–12; cf. Diod. 18.59.1–2), but there is no clear indication that Antigonos kept his word. Nor can we say what became of M. I cannot understand why Berve II 255 says that M. died in 321. Billows 403, thinks that Antigonos left M. behind as *strategos* of Kappadokia, where he may have died *c.*317/6. Berve II 255 no. 501; Geyer, *RE* XV. 706–7 no. 5; G. Wirth, *Kl. Pauly* III 1198 no. 2; Heckel 1988, 39–40; Heckel 1992, 339–40; Billows 402–3 no. 71.

707 MENEDEMOS

(Μενέδημος). Family and regional origins unknown; Hoffmann omits M., but the name is attested in Macedonia (*IG* II² 1335, 35; Tataki 367 no. 37 accepts him as Macedonian). He is mentioned by the sources only in connection with the campaign in which he was killed, that at the Polytimetos (Zeravshan) against Spitamenes (329). Here M. led 1,500 mercenary infantry, as we may deduce from Arrian's description (4.3.7): Andromachos led 60 Companions, Karanos 800 mercenary cavalry; the Lykian Pharnouches was (allegedly) in charge of the entire expedition. Hence M. must have been the commander of the mercenary infantry. But Curtius, who names only M. in his account (7.6.24; 7.7.31–9; 7.9.21; cf. Metz Epit. 13), gives him 3,000 foot in addition to 800 horse (7.6.24), a figure rejected by Berve (II 256) without good reason. Whether Andronikos son of Agerros served under M. cannot be determined. The mercenaries, through the ineptitude of the Macedonian commanders, were lured into an ambush and defeated by Spitamenes (Arr. 4.6.2, forty cavalry and 300 infantrymen escaped). M. perished in the engagement and was duly buried by Alexander when he returned from the Iaxartes (Curt. 7.9.21; Metz Epit. 13). Berve II 256 no. 504; Heckel 1992, 343.

708 MENEDEMOS

(Μενέδημος). Rhodian. In 305/4, during the siege of Rhodes, M. commanded three ships and took an Antigonid warship at Patara in Lykia, virtually empty and at anchor, while the men crew dined on shore. This he burned, and he captured the supply ships it was accompanying. He also captured, en route from Kilikia, a quadrireme which carried the royal robes and other clothes sent by Phila to her husband Demetrios Poliorketes. The clothing was sent to Ptolemy in Egypt, the crews of the captured ships sold (Diod. 20.93.3). Paschidis 357 sees the gift of the captured royal clothes as both gratitude for Ptolemaic benefactions and recognition of Ptolemy's recently assumed royal title. Hauben 69–70 no. 24; Fiehn, *RE* XV 787 no. 3; H. Volkmann, *Kl. Pauly* III 1205 no. 1; Paschidis 357–8 D3.

709 MENEDEMOS

(Μενέδημος). [All references in **boldface** are to his biography in Diogenes Laertius.] Eretrian. Son of Kleisthenes (**2.125**). Father of three daughters by a wife from Oropos (**2.138**). Philosopher of the school of Phaidon (the Eleian school); he was a poor man trained either as a builder or a scene painter (**2.125**). He served in the garrison at Megara (Paschidis 452 supposes this was during the Lamian War) and visited Plato in Athens (though he later grew to despise the Academy). M. later lived in Megara and attended the lectures of Stilpon before going to Elis. Noted for his arrogance, for which Krates and Timon ridiculed him (**2.126–9**, with further examples of his behavior); he even insulted Nikokreon of Kypros (**2.129**), dangerous in light of Nikokreon's treatment of Anaxarchos (no. 92). For his political life M. was criticized by Krates, whose arrest he ordered (**2.131**). Though he associated with numerous intellectuals, he was generally critical of others whose views he did not share (**2.133–4, 136**). But his devotion to his friend Asklepiades was exemplary (**2.137–8** for their relationship). His reputation with the Eretrians was poor, but they soon used him in their dealings with Ptolemy I and Lysimachos (in the 280s, Paschidis 453 n.3; cf. Knoepfler 1991, 197 nn. 69–70, though he identifies Ptolemy as Philadelphos and places the embassy in 279/8); indeed, he was accused of conspiring to hand his city over to Ptolemy (**2.140**). Ambassador to Demetrios (probably in 304, thus Paschidis 453, with n.1) with respect to the question of Oropos (**2.141**). He praised Antigonos Gonatas (**2.141–2**), but was accused of betraying his city to Demetrios (allegedly in an attempt to prevent the establishment of tyranny (**2.143**). It was probably in 304, when Demetrios "liberated" Eretria from Kassandros, that M. came to know the young Antigonos, their relationship perhaps encouraged by Stilpon (cf. Paschidis 453).

He left Eretria and eventually came to Gonatas' court with his wife and daughters. There he died of of a "broken heart" (*athymia*: **2.142**, but another version says he died at the age of 73 after a hunger strike because he could not persuade Gonatas, who was apparently under the influence of Persaios, to free Eretria: **2.143–4**; cf. Tarn, *AG* 233, 286–7; Gabbert 1997, 38–9). Giannantoni I 164–78; Knoepfler 1991; Paschidis 452–6.

710 MENELAOS

(Μενέλαος). Macedonian (Tataki 268 no. 48). Son of Lagos and brother of Ptolemy I Soter (Diod. 19.62.4), hence presumably from Eordaia. M. is said to have been an avid hunter and, together with Leonnatos, carried with him curtains that measured 100 stades, with which to close off a hunting area (Phylarchos, *FGrH* 81 F41 = Athen. 12.539d; cf. Ael. *VH* 9.3). Nothing further is known about him until Ptolemy gained control of Kypros in 315 and sent M. to join forces with the exiled Seleukos and Nikokreon of Salamis (Diod. 19.62.4). It was probably at this time that M. was established as his *strategos* there (Diod. 20.47.3, *strategos* of the island; 20.52.5, *strategos* in Salamis; Paus. 1.6.6 calls him satrap; cf. Polyaenus 4.7.7: Πτολεμαίου στρατηγός). After the death of Nikokreon, and until his expulsion from Kypros, Menelaos is styled BA (that is, *basileus*) on coinage (see Bagnall 41). In 310 he supplied troops to Ptolemy's agents, Argaios and Kallikrates, who used them to surround the palace of Nikokles of Paphos and force his surrender and the noble deaths of his family (Diod. 20.21.1–3; cf. Polyaenus 8.48; see also Gesche 1974). In 306, Demetrios Poliorketes sailed to Kypros and defeated M. in a land battle (Diod. 20.47.1– 4). M., having lost many men withdrew into the city of Salamis, sent to Ptolemy for aid (Diod. 20.47.7–8), and took what action he could against Demetrios' siege equipment (Diod. 20.48.6). Ptolemy soon arrived with a larger fleet (Plut. *Demetr.* 15.2; Paus. 1.6.6), and summoned from M. the sixty ships that lay at anchor in the harbor of Salamis. These, however, were blockaded by Demetrios' ships (Diod. 20.49.3–6; cf. Plut. *Demetr.* 16.1–2, confused; cf. also Polyaenus 4.7.7). Nevertheless, in the ensuing battle, M. assigned these ships to Menoitios, who, although they routed Demetrios guard ships, could not join Ptolemy's fleet in time to make a difference (Diod. 20.52.5). Polyaenus says that M., "who put out from Salamis in order to bring aid, joined Ptolemy in flight." I see no reason to doubt Justin's (Trogus') claim that M. surrendered to Demetrios and was released by him. It is tempting to assume that Polyaenus has confused Menelaos with Menoitios, but the latter also returned to Salamis after the battle (Diod. 20.52.5). Soon after the naval defeat of his brother M. surrendered Salamis (Plut. *Demetr.* 16.7). After his capture, he was allowed by Demetrios to return, along with Ptolemy's son by Thaïs, Leontiskos, to Egypt (Justin 15.2.7; cf. Plut. *Demetr.* 17.1). The Menelaite Nome by the Canobic canal near Alexandria is named for Ptolemy's brother (Strabo 17.1.18 C801). He is attested as eponymous priest of Alexander in 284/3 (year 40 of Ptolemy Soter: *PEleph* 2). Berve II 256 no. 505; Volkmann, *Kl. Pauly* III 1210 no. 4; *PP* no. 5196; Bagnall 40–2; Markou 2013. **Stemma X.**

711 MENELAOS

(Μενέλαος). Macedonian (Tataki 368 no. 44). Listed along with Peukestas and Oxythemis as a courtier of Demetrios (Athen. 14.614f). Identification with Ptolemy I Soter's brother is impossible. Nothing else is known about M., unless he is the hunting companion of Leonnatos (Tataki 368 no. 43; Phylarchos, *FGrH* 81 F41 = Athen. 12.539d; cf. Ael. *VH*

9.3); but this man is probably the son of Lagos (no. 710). Perhaps Menelaos in this passage should read Menandros, a supporter of the Antigonids.

712 MENES

(Μένης). Macedonian (Tataki 157 no. 61). Son of Dionysios, from Pella (Diod. 17.64.5), M. was appointed Somatophylax to replace Balakros son of Nikanor, whom Alexander had designated satrap of Kilikia in late 333 (Arr. 2.12.2). As Somatophylax he did nothing worthy of record, nor did he hold the office long: towards the end of 331, he was sent out from Sousa as hyparch of Phoinikia, Syria, and Kilikia (Arr. 3.16.9; cf. Diod. 17.64.5; Curt. 5.1.43), probably as temporary overseer of the area and of the existing satraps and financial officers. M.'s position is not clear and no explanation is entirely satisfactory. Berve's assumption that he controlled finances, replacing Koiranos of Beroia, is rejected for want of evidence by Brunt I 278 n.11. Bosworth thinks M. replaced Balakros as satrap of Kilikia, assuming control of Syria and Phoinikia as well (I.319; cf. Bosworth 1974, 59–60), but this would place Balakros' death in 332 or 331 and make M.'s disappearance more difficult to explain. As Bosworth II 148 notes, the term *hyparchos* refers to someone who ruled *under* the King, but although the terms *hyparchos* and *satrapes* are used synonymously, they are not always the same, and I see no reason why hyparchs cannot have satraps who are in some way subordinate to them. Thus the Vulgate refers to M. and Apollodoros as "*strategoi* of Babylon and of the satrapies as far as Kilikia" (Diod. 17.64.5; cf. Curt. 5.1.43, as emended by Shackleton-Bailey 1981, 176). Considering the political situation in Europe and the need to press eastwards against Dareios, Alexander entrusted the coastal region to a single individual. Hence he sent M. to the coast with 3,000 talents (Arr. 3.16.9; Curt. 5.1.43 says 1,000), which were to be transported to Antipatros for use in the war with Agis III. It was also his responsibility to see that the discharged Greek veterans (brought from Ekbatana by Epokillos son of Polyeides) found their way back to Europe (Arr. 3.19.5–6). Coins minted in the region bearing the mark M will also belong to the time of M.'s coordination of affairs in this region (see Berve II 257). M.'s disappearance from the sources, with no indication of his successor, suggests that his position was intended to be temporary. Berve II 257 no. 507; Julien 62 n.2; Lehmann-Haupt 157–8; Brunt I 278–9 n.11; Bosworth 1974, 59–60; Bosworth I 319; Shackleton-Bailey 1981, 176; Heckel 1992, 262–3.

713 MENESAICHMOS

(Μενέσαιχμος). Athenian orator and politician. Family background unknown. Lykourgos had once brought a charge against him ([Plut.] *Mor.* 843d; Dion. Hal. *de Din.* 11; cf. [Plut.] *Mor.* 842e–f for their enmity). His connection with Alexander is only marginal: M. was one of those who brought charges against Demosthenes for accepting money from Harpalos in 324 ([Plut.] *Mor.* 846c). Kirchner 9983; Berve II 255–6 no. 503; Develin 405.

714 MENESTHEUS

(Μενέσθευς). Athenian from Rhamnous. Born *c.*381. Son of Iphikrates and Thressa, the daughter of the Thrakian king Kotys (Nepos, *Iphic.* 3.4). In 362 (Davies 251) M. married a daughter of Timotheos (Nepos. *Timoth.* 3.2; [Dem.] 49.66). He was appointed commander of a fleet of 100 triremes hastily organized by the Athenians in response to Hegelochos' seizure of the grain ships from the Hellespontine region ([Dem.] 17.20). M.

died before 325/4: in that year a debt was paid on his behalf by his heirs (*IG* II² 1629.486–7; cf. [Dem.] *Ep.* 3.31). For his trierarchies: *IG* II² 1622.199–200, 721–22, 729–30; II² 1623.47; II² 1629.486–7, and Davies 250–1. Berve II 256–7 no. 506; Kirchner 9988; Schaefer III² 175; Davies 250–1.

715 MENIDAS

(Μενίδας). Macedonian (Tataki 369 no. 54). M. appears in all extant texts without patronymic. Arr. 3.5.1 records that, in the winter of 332/1, Menoitas son of Hegesandros brought 400 mercenaries to Alexander in Memphis. *Menoitas* may, however, be an error for *Menidas* (so Hamilton 1955, 217–18; *contra* Bosworth I 275) and, if so, M. will have been the son of Hegesandros and commander of 400 mercenary cavalry from 332/1 onwards. It is not specified whether these are cavalry or infantry, but Hamilton 1955, 217–18 comments: "Four hundred seems to me too small a number and certainly in no other case is so small a number of infantry reinforcements recorded." Identification of the son of Hegesandros with Menoitas, the supporter of Peithon (no. 867), remains a possibility (Diod. 19.47.1). At Gaugamela, Alexander positioned the mercenary horse on the right tip of his angled line, followed by the *prodromoi* and Paionians, with the Agrianes, archers and Kleandros' mercenary infantry in reserve (Arr. 3.12.2–3). M. had been instructed to attack the enemy cavalry, should they attempt to outflank the Macedonians (Arr. 3.12.4). This is precisely what happened, but his force proved inadequate (Arr. 3.13.3), on account of their small numbers, and had to be supported by the *prodromoi*, Paionians and the mercenary infantrymen, which managed to break the Persian formation (Arr. 3.13.3–4). Curtius (4.15.12) depicts M.'s skirmish with the enemy as an, apparently unauthorized, attempt to save the baggage. But his efforts were half-hearted, and he abandoned the endeavor. In the end, Alexander, reluctantly, sent the *prodromoi* under Aretes to repulse the Skythians who were plundering the camp (Curt. 4.15.13–18). Curtius' source may have attempted to vindicate Parmenion and, in the process, depicted M.—arguably one of the heroes of Gaugamela who was wounded in action (Arr. 3.15.2; Diod. 17.61.3; Curt. 4.16.32)—as cowardly and inept (Atkinson I 440–1; cf. Devine 1986, 91); he was destined to become one of Parmenion's assassins (Arr. 3.26.3–4). In 330, M. remained in Ekbatana with Parmenion's forces (Arr. 3.26.3), and must have played a role in the old general's execution (Arr. 3.26.4; cf. Berve II 258). The mercenary cavalry were assigned to Philip son of Menelaos, who brought them to Alexander in Aria (Arr. 3.25.4; cf. Curt. 6.6.35). M. rejoined Alexander at Zariaspa (Baktra) over the winter of 329/8, in the company of Ptolemy (commander of the Thrakians) and Epokillos (Arr. 4.7.2: Μελαμνίδας should be emended to read Μενίδας, so Hamilton 1955, 217; Curt. 7.10.11 says he and Ptolemy brought 5,000 mercenaries: 4,000 infantry and 1,000 cavalry). In the following year, M. was sent out from Nautaka, together with Epokillos and the ilarch Sopolis to recruit new forces in Macedonia (Arr. 4.18.3). It appears that these reinforcements did not reach Alexander until his return to Babylon (Arr. 7.23.1: the cavalry which M. led were probably new recruits). Menidas is last attested sleeping in the temple of Sarapis in Babylon when the King had become fatally ill (Arr. 7.26.2: but see the comments of Grainger 1990a, 218–19). I do not see why Berve II 258, with n.4, following Ausfeld, thinks that Dardanos in the Armenian version of Ps.-Call. 3.31 is Menidas. Berve II 257–8 no. 508; Hamilton 1955, 217–18; Heckel 1992, 362–3.

716 MENISKOS

(Μενίσκος). Greek of unknown family in the service of Dareios III. In 332, after the capture of Dareios' family at Issos, M. was sent along with Arsimas to deliver a letter from the Great King to Alexander. Thereafter he returned to Dareios with Thersippos, who carried Alexander's response (Arr. 2.14.1, 3; cf. Curt. 4.1.7–14; Plut. *Alex.* 29.7–9). Berve II 258 no. 509; Hofstetter 128 no. 218; Schachermeyr 222–3.

717 MENISKOS

(Μενίσκος). Greek mercenary captain in the service of Satyros son of Pairisades (no. 1040; who ruled the Kimmerian Bosporos for 9 months in 311/0–310/09: Werner 430). He led some 2,000 Greek mercenaries (Diod. 20.22.4) in the battle fought by Satyros against Eumelos (no. 442) and Aripharnes (no. 184) near the Thates river. In the siege of Aripharnes' capital, on that river, M. distinguished himself with his military sense and daring (συνέσει καὶ τόλμῃ διαφέρων), but when he met stubborn resistance and Satyros came to his aid the latter was mortally wounded (Diod. 20.23.6–7). M. conveyed Satyros' corpse first to Gargaza (Gerousa? Ptol. *Geog.* 5.8.2) and then to the King's brother, Prytanis, at Pantikapaion (Diod. 20.23.8). At that point M. vanishes from our records. Niese I 413–14.

718 MENOITAS

(Μενοίτας). Macedonian (Tataki 371 no. 59). Son of Hegesandros. In 332/1 M. brought 400 mercenary infantrymen to Alexander at Memphis in 332/1 (Arr. 3.5.1), unless this man's name is a corruption of *Menidas* (thus Hamilton 1955, 217–18; *contra* Bosworth I 275). See s.v. Menidas (no. 715).

719 MENOITAS

(Μενοίτας). Macedonian (Tataki 370 no. 58). Cavalry officer who supported Peithon son of Krateuas after Antigonos' defeat of Eumenes of Kardia. He had perhaps been among those who served in the satrapal forces of Peithon since 323. In 316 he joined in Peithon's attempt to raise a rebellion in Media. Although Peithon was tricked and captured by Antigonos, who executed him, M. and a certain Meleagros collected a force of 800 men, some of whom had served with Eumenes. With these he attacked Antigonos' newly appointed satrap, Orontobates (no. 822), and his general Hippostratos (no. 538; Diod. 19.46.5–47.2). After some initial success, the rebels, who were vastly outnumbered, especially with regard to infantry, were cut off and defeated. Diod. 19.47.3–4 says that some were killed and others captured, and, since he names only Meleagros (no. 697) and Okranes (no. 807) as notable amongst the dead, we may assume that M. either escaped or was captured. Perhaps he made his peace with the Antigonid officers and continued to serve in the East—though Antigonos' opponents did not fare well after defeat. Possibly identical with the son of Hegesandros who, in 332/1 brought 400 mercenary infantrymen to Alexander at Memphis in 332/1 (Arr. 3.5.1), unless this man's name is a corruption of "Menidas" (thus Hamilton 1955, 217–18; *contra* Bosworth I 275). Berve II 258–9 no. 510.

720 MENOITIOS

(Μενοίτιος). Origin unknown. Apparently Macedonian (Hoffmann 211; cf. Diod. 19.47 for the name). Berve II 259 considers him "anscheinend Grieche aus Ilion," for which there is no support. Instinsky's suggestion (71 n.1), that *kybernetes* is the corruption of an ethnic, is unnecessary and unhelpful. M. was apparently helmsman of Alexander's ship (cf. Bosworth I 103), with which he crossed the Hellespont. He presented the King with a golden crown at Troy (Arr. 1.12.1). Nothing else is known about him. Identification with Menoitios, the *nauarchos* of Menelaos (son of Lagos) at Salamis in 306 (Diod. 20.52.5), is possible but cannot be proved. Berve II 259 no. 511; Instinsky 1949, 71 n.1; Bosworth I 102–3.

721 MENOITIOS

(Μενοίτιος). When Kyprian Salamis was besieged by Demetrios and a sea battle was about to take place, Demetrios placed a guard of ten ships at the entrance to the Salaminian harbor, under the command of Antisthenes (no. 137; Diod. 20.50.1; cf. Plut. *Demetr.* 16.1). Menelaos, who was in charge of the city assigned control of the fleet of 60 Salaminian ships to Menoitios, who managed to break the blockade, but arriving too late to affect the outcome of the battle returned to the city (Diod. 20.52.5). Hauben 70–1 no. 25.

722 MENON

(Μένων). Macedonian (Tataki 372 no. 65). Son of Kerdimmas. Given charge of Koile-Syria in late 333 (Arr. 2.13.7). Curt. 4.8.11 says that, after the Samaritans murdered the Syrian satrap, Andromachos (apparently the ruler of Palestine), Alexander appointed *Memnon* in his place. This must be a reference to M. son of Kerdimmas. Arr. 3.6.8 says that Alexander, on his way to Thapsakos in 331, replaced *Arimmas* with Asklepiodoros. This creates a virtually insoluble set of problems concerning the administrative divisions of Syria and the various satraps (see Leuze 1935, 413–25; Bosworth I 224–5, reiterating the arguments of Bosworth 1974; cf. Brunt I 240 n.9). Some have argued that Arimmas was M.'s successor in northern Syria when M. replaced Andromachos. Arrian's *Arimmas* may be a scribal error for Kerdimmas, in which case Asklepiodoros replaced M. son of Kerdimmas in 331. Is it mere coincidence that neither M. nor Arimmas is heard of again? Berve II 259 no. 514.

723 MENON

(Μένων). Macedonian (Tataki 371 no. 63). Patronymic unknown. M. was appointed satrap of Arachosia in 330 and left with 4,000 infantry and 600 cavalry (Curt. 7.3.5; Arr. 3.28.1). He died of illness in 325 and was replaced by Sibyrtios (Curt. 9.10.20). Berve II 259 no. 515; Julien 39; Lehmann-Haupt 146.

724 MENON

(Μένων). Perhaps Macedonian (Tataki 371 no. 64). M. was sent by Alexander to gold mines at Syspiritis (Hyspiritis) near Kaballa in Armenia (*Barr. Atl.* 87 G4). He may have perished in the attempt at the hands of the natives (Strabo 11.14.9 C529). Berve II 260 believes that M. and his troops may have accompanied Mithrenes (no. 739) into

Armenia in 331 (cf. Arr. 3.16.5; Diod. 17.64.6; Curt. 5.1.44). The incident may shed light on Mithrenes' disappearance from our records. Berve II 260 no. 516.

725 MENON

(Μένων). Thessalian from Pharsalos and most likely descended from the general of the same name who served the younger Kyros at Cunaxa (Xen. *Anab.* 2.6.21, for an unfavorable portrait; see also Brown 1986). That Menon was alleged to have been the lover of Tharypas (Arybbas) the Molossian (Xen. *Anab.* 2.6.28), and it is, in part, a reflection of the two families' close ties that the daughter of the younger M., Phthia (no. 960), married Aiakides (no. 31), the son of the younger Arybbas and Troas, of the Molossian royal house; their children were Pyrrhos, Troas, and Deidameia (Plut. *Pyrrh.* 1.6; cf. Heckel 1981d, 81 n.11; **Stemma IIb**). During the Lamian War, when the Thessalians defected from Antipatros, M. commanded the Thessalian cavalry and served with Leosthenes (Plut. *Phoc.* 25.5; cf. Diod. 18.12.3, not naming M.); he commanded the cavalry in the battle against Leonnatos, in which Antiphilos (no. 136) led the infantry (Plut. *Phoc.* 25.5; Diod. 18.15.4). Defeated by Antipatros and Krateros at Krannon (Diod. 18.17.1–5), Antiphilos and M. were forced to accept unconditional surrender (Diod. 18.17.6). In 321/0, Alexander of Aitolia invaded Thessaly and encouraged Thessalians to revolt from Antipatros (in response to an appeal from Perdikkas); but the Aitolians were called back home by invasion from Akarnania (Diod. 18.38.1–4). M. and the Thessalians, who numbered about 13,000 infantry and 1,100 horse (subtracting 12,000 and 400 Aitolians (18.38.1) from the total of 25,000 and 1,500 (18.38.3, 5), were defeated by Polyperchon; M. himself was killed in battle (Diod. 18.38.6). Most of his army was cut to pieces. Berve II 260 no. 517.

726 MENTOR

(Μέντωρ). Greek. Family background unknown. He was apparently a friend and supporter of Eumenes. When, on the return march from India, Hephaistion had assigned quarters prepared for Eumenes to the flute player Euios, M. joined Eumenes in lodging a complaint with Alexander (Plut. *Eum.* 2.2). Although Alexander reproached Hephaistion, the incident created ill will towards Eumenes (Plut. *Eum.* 2.3), and perhaps M. as well. Berve II 259 is probably right in believing that M.'s participation in the appeal to Alexander is an indicator of higher standing. Nothing else is known about him. Berve II 259 no. 512.

727 MENYLLOS

(Μένυλλος). Macedonian (Tataki 371 no. 62). Friend of Phokion (Plut. *Phoc.* 28.1), M. was installed as *phrourarchos* of Mounychia after the Athenian surrender in the Lamian War. The purpose of this garrison was to prevent political change (νεωτερισμός) in Athens (Diod. 18.18.5; cf. Plut. *Phoc.* 28.1; Plut. *Dem.* 28.1). M. saw to it that the garrison did not harm Athenian citizens (Plut. *Phoc.* 28.7). He attempted to bribe Phokion, who resisted, just as he had earlier refused to take money from Alexander (Plut. *Phoc.* 30.1–2, *Mor* 188f). After Antipatros' death in 319, M. was replaced by Nikanor (Plut. *Phoc.* 31.1). What became of him is unknown. H. Volkmann, *Kl. Pauly* III 1228 no. 1; Berve II, 259 no. 513.

728 MEROES

(Μερόης). Indian of unknown background. He was a longtime friend of Poros (φίλον
ἐκ παλαιοῦ τῷ Πώρῳ) who had either defected to Alexander before the battle at the
Hydaspes or surrendered during the course of it. The King sent him to Poros, who had
suffered serious wounds, to urge him to surrender and to guarantee his safety (Arr. 5.18.7).
Nothing else is known about him. Schwarz 1968, 225 suggested that Meroes was a form
of Maurya and equated Poros' friend with Chandragupta (Sandrokottos). This is rejected
on linguistic grounds by Karttunen 259 and is historically impossible since Plut. *Alex.* 53.9
says Chandragupta was a youth (*meirakion*) when he saw Alexander, and thus could not
have been Poros' friend ἐκ παλαιοῦ. Berve II 260 no. 518.

729 METRON

(Μέτρων). Son of Epicharmos. Macedonian from Pydna (Tataki 171 no. 11). M. was a
trierarch of the Hydaspes fleet in 326 (Arr. *Ind.* 18.5) and one of the King's *hetairoi*. He
may be identical with the Page of the same name. Berve II 260 no. 519; Berve, *RE* XV
(1932) 1484–5 no. 1; Heckel 1992, 293–4.

730 METRON

(Μέτρων). Macedonian, perhaps identical with the son of Epicharmos from Pydna
(Arr. *Ind.* 18.5), unless this identification is rejected on the grounds of age (thus Berve
II 260 no. 519; but we may have a parallel case of rapid promotion if Aretis is identical
with Aretes). When Kebalinos had no success in bringing the news of Dimnos' plot to
the King's attention through Philotas, he informed M., one of the Pages (Curt. 6.7.22:
*nobili iuveni—Metron erat ei nomen—super armamentarium posito, quod scelus pararetur
indicat*. Diod. 17.79.4 speaks of "one of the *paides basilikoi*" but does not name M. For
his identification as a Page see Berve II 260; Heckel 1992, 293–4). M. promptly reported
Dimnos' conspiracy and Philotas' suspicious behavior (Curt. 6.7.22–3; Diod. 17.79.5; cf.
Plut. *Alex.* 49.6; Hamilton 136). As a Page, he undoubtedly came from a good aristocratic
family, and Alexander may have further enriched him for his part in bringing the
Dimnos/Philotas affair to his attention. Hence a trierarchy in 326 is not entirely out of
the question. Berve II 260–1 no. 520; Heckel 1992, 293–4.

731 MIKION

(Μικίων). Macedonian, perhaps *nauarchos*. Tataki 374 no. 76 rightly identifies him as
Macedonian (cf. Hoffmann 211), against the doubts of Berve II 264 no. 529. If M. was not
a fleet commander but simply the leader of the troops who landed at Rhamnous, we must
ask who Antipatros' admiral was in 323. M. led a force of Macedonians and mercenaries
that landed at Rhamnous in Attika in 323/2. He was, however, met by the Athenians under
Phokion, defeated and killed (Plut. *Phoc.* 25.1–4, this occurred just before Leonnatos
reinforced Antipatros in Thessaly; cf. Plut. *Mor.* 188e). If this chronology is correct, M.
may have been the admiral who secured the Hellespont in preparation for Leonnatos'
crossing and thus commander of Antipatros' fleet, which was deployed before the arrival
of White Kleitos in the Aegean. Bosworth 2003b, 21 with nn. 62–3 believes that M.'s raid
came at the end of the sailing season in 323, perhaps launched from Chalkis in Euboia.
There is, at any rate, no justification for Ferguson's view (18) that the raid occurred after

the battle of Amorgos and that M. was a lieutenant of White Kleitos. About his earlier service under Antipatros nothing is recorded. Berve II 264 no. 529; Hauben 71–2 no. 26; H. Volkmann, *Kl. Pauly* III 1292 no. 1; Berve, *RE* XV (1932) 1554 no. 1.

732 MIKKALOS

(Μίκκαλος). Greek from Klazomenai. In 323 he was sent with five hundred talents to Phoinikia and Syria in order to recruit experienced sailors for Alexander's planned colonization of the coast of the Persian Gulf (Arr. 7.19.5). The project was part of Alexander's so-called Final Plans, which were cancelled after his death. What became of M. we do not know. Berve II 264 no. 530.

733 MIKYTHOS

(Μίκυθος). Macedonian (Tataki 374 no. 77). An officer of Lykiskos (no. 661; hence also of Kasandros), killed in battle with Alexander (no. 44) son of Alketas before Eurymenai (Diod. 19.88.5). Bechler, *RE* XV (1932) 1563 no. 3.

734 MILTIADES

(Μιλτιάδης). Athenian (Kirchner 10210; Davies 309) from Lakiadai; patronymic unknown. Son of Kimon, who was an ambassador to Philip II in 346 (Aesch. 2.21; Dem. 19 hyp. 2.4; cf. Schaefer II² 240 n.1 and 275 n.1), M. traced his descent back to the Miltiades who fought at Marathon (Diod. 20.40.5; cf. Plut. *Demetr.* 14.1). M. was the *oikistes* of a colony sent to the Adriatic in 324 (*IG* II² 1629 = Tod 200 = R&O no. 100, with discussion on pp. 523–6); father of Euthydike (see s.v.), who married first Ophelas and then Demetrios Poliorketes (Plut. *Demetr.* 14.1–2); thus also grandfather of Korrhagos (Plut. *Demetr.* 53.9). Kinzl, *Kl. Pauly* III 1306 no. 3.

735 MILTIADES

(Μιλτιάδης). Son of Ophellas and Euthydike (Kirchner 5547, with stemma), born no later than 308/7 (Kirchner 10211). Hence also stepson of Demetrios Poliorketes (Plut. *Demetr.* 14.1) and half-brother of Korrhagos (Plut. *Demetr.* 53.9).

736 MINNION

(Μιννίων). Greek from Iasos. Son of Theodotos, brother of Gorgos (no. 485) the *hoplophylax*. Like his brother, M. appears to have served with Alexander, although we do not know in what capacity. He was honored, together with Gorgos, by both the Iasians and Samians for securing benefactions from Alexander (*Syll*³ 307, 312; cf. Heisserer 169–203). Berve II 264 no. 531.

737 MITHRACENES

(Also Mithrazenes). The name appears only in the Latin form (Curt. 5.13.9). Justi 214. Persian of unknown origin. He and a certain Orsilos had apparently been with Dareios III since, at least, the battle of Gaugamela. Both abandoned Bessos and the other conspirators who had taken the King prisoner, and, falling in with Alexander, reported that the conspirators were some 500 stades distant and offered to point out a shorter route (Curt. 5.13.9). M. is otherwise unknown. Berve II 262 no. 522; Justi 214; Shayegan 111 no. 63.

738 MITHRAUSTES

(Μιθραύστης). Persian noble of unknown family background. Together with the satrap Orontes, M. led the Armenian troops at Gaugamela in 331 (Arr. 3.8.5; cf. 3.11.7); Berve II 262 may be correct in assigning to him command of the infantry (cf. Bosworth I 291). What became of him is unknown. If he was not killed or captured in the battle, he may have returned to Armenia with Orontes. Berve II 262 no. 523; Bosworth I 291; Justi 217; Shayegan III no. 64.

739 MITHRENES

(Μιθρήνης). Persian noble of unknown family background, M. was citadel commander of Sardis under Dareios III (Arr. 1.17.3; cf. Dio Chrys. 73.2; cf. Diod. 17.21.7 calls him "satrap," which may be an error, unless M. became interim satrap of Ionia after the death of Spithridates at the Granikos). In 334 he surrendered the city and its treasures to Alexander without resistance (Diod. 17.21.7; cf. Curt. 3.12.6; Plut. *Alex.* 17.1), meeting the King when he was still seventy stades from the city (Arr. 1.17.3). He remained with Alexander (Arr. 1.17.4), who later decided against sending him to the captive Persian queens with news about Dareios III, lest the sight of a traitor should cause them further grief (Curt. 3.12.6–7). This depiction of M. as a traitor to Dareios (3.12.7; 5.8.12) is perhaps Curtius' own invention (cf. Atkinson I 247). In late 331, Alexander appointed him satrap of Armenia (Arr. 3.16.5; Diod. 17.64.6; Curt. 5.1.44), an unconquered satrapy which he appears to have been unable to win (cf. Julien 28). M. is not heard of again, and he may have perished in an unsuccessful attempt to wrest the territory from Orontes; for the latter is found in command of the Armenians at Gaugamela (Arr. 3.8.5) and again in 317 in charge of Armenia (Diod. 19.23.3; Polyaenus 4.8.3). See further s.v. Orontes no. 819. Badian 1965, 175 n.1; Berve II 262–3 no. 524; Bosworth I 315; Julien 27–8; Justi 217; Shayegan III–12 no. 6.

740 MITHRIDATES

(Μιθριδάτης). Noble Persian, son-in-law of Dareios III (Arr. 1.15.7, 16.3). Diod. 17.20.2 names Dareios' son-in-law Spithrobates (thus conflating Spithridates and M.); the satrap of Ionia may also have married a daughter of Dareios, but it is more likely that Diodorus confused the two men, since there is no mention of M. in either his account of the battle or his casualty list. Berve II 263 assumes that M. was from the area of Kappadokia-Pontos, and that he was married to the daughter of Dareios III (A20) and the sister of Pharnakes, a relative of M. (as were also Ariobarzanes and Artabazos). But this is highly speculative. Alexander killed M. in hand-to-hand combat at the Granikos River (334), when he thrust his lance into his face (Arr. 1.15.7; cf. 1.16.3; Plut. *Mor.* 326f). Berve II 263 no. 525; Shayegan 112 no. 66. **Stemma III.**

741 MITHRIDATES

(Μιθριδάτης). Mithridates II of Kios. The son of Ariobarzanes, a descendant of the Seven Persians (Diod. 19.40.2; cf. App. *Mithr.* 9.27); presumably from the ruling family of Hellespontine Phrygia (cf. Billows 403). Ariobarzanes died in 337/6 having ruled for 26 years; he was succeeded by M. who ruled for 35 (Diod. 16.90.2). He is almost certainly the M. who fought in the army of Eumenes at Gabiene, where he was placed, with his satrapal cavalry on the left wing, opposite the best horsemen on Antigonos' right; Diodorus praises the military training and martial prowess of M. (Diod. 19.40.2; 20.111.4). After Eumenes' defeat he appears to have made his peace with Antigonos Monophthalmos, probably giving his (adopted?) son, also named Mithridates, as a hostage (thus McGing 1986b, 250; Plut. *Demetr.* 4.1–4, *Mor.* 183a mistakenly calls this Mithridates "son of Ariobarzanes"; Reinach 1895, 6 n.1 observes that several authors "verwechseln . . . Mithradates dem Vater mit seinem Sohn"; but Mithridates III may have been adopted by his uncle). He was killed in Kios in Mysia in 302/1, when he was on the verge of abandoning Antigonos to join Kassandros (20.111.4; he was succeeded by his son who ruled for 36 years). Justin 16.4.6–9; McGing 1986a–b. But others identify the man who served with Eumenes as Mithridates III (= Mithridates Ktistes) and thus as a nephew of Mithridates II. Billows 403–4 no. 72; Geyer, *RE* XV.2 (1932) 2158 no. 6; Hornblower, *Hieronymus* 243–5; Bosworth and Wheatley 1999; Rose 134.

742 MITHRIDATES

(Μιθριδάτης). Mithridates III (*Ktistes*, that is, the founder) = Mithridates I of Pontos (*regn.* 302–266). Called the son of Ariobarzanes (Plut. *Demetr.* 4.1), which is either a case of confusion with the elder Mithridates (no. 741) or, if correct, an indication that he was that man's nephew and perhaps adopted son. Billows 404 no. 73 regards him as the M. who fought for Eumenes of Kardia (Diod. 19.40.2); if he was roughly coeval with Demetrios Poliorketes, it is doubtful that by 317/16 he had already earned a great renown for prowess in battle (but see also Ballesteros Pastor 2013, 186). And, if the ruler of Kios led his army to battle against Antigonos (instead of sending his less experienced son), it appears more likely that the heir would remain at the Antigonid court as a hostage than that the elder M. would be kept from the territory he ruled. The danger to his person, of which Demetrios warned him in a secret message (Plut. *Demetr.* 4.1–4; *Mor.* 183a; App. *Mithr.* 9; [Lucian], *Macrob.* 13), was probably connected with Antigonos' suspicions about the loyalty of the elder M. and thus his flight must date to *c.*302 (see no. 741 above). Although he was recognized as his father's successor, his position was not secure until after Ipsos. M. escaped to Kimiata at the foot of Olgassys in Kappadokia (Strabo 12.3.41 C562; cf. App. *Mith.* 9.28; *Barr. Atl.* 86 D3). He maintained and increased his power until his death in 266 (Diod. 20.111.4, who says nothing about M.'s paternity, *pace* McGing 1986a, 15 n.15). Whether he played any role in the battle of Ipsos or the events leading up to it is unknown (for his later career see McGing 1986a, 15–19). Geyer, *RE* SV.2 (1932) 2158–60 no. 7; Hornblower, *Hieronymus* 123, 243–5; Olshausen, *RE* Supplbd. XV (1974) s.v. "Pontos."

743 MITHROBAIOS

(Μιθροβαῖος). Prominent Persian, brother of Autobares (or Aigobares); their father is not named. Both were enrolled in the *agema* of the Companion Cavalry in 324 at Sousa (Arr. 7.6.5). Berve II 263 no. 526. Justi 208; Shayegan 112 no. 67.

744 MITHROBOUZANES

(Μιθροβουζάνης). Persian noble and ruler of Kappadokia near the Tauros (Arr. 1.16.3; for the division of Kappadokia, Strabo 12.1.4 C534; Julien 18–19), M. commanded the satrapal contingent at the Granikos (334), where he lost his life (Diod. 17.21.3; Arr.

1.16.3). Alexander installed Sabiktas in his place (Arr. 2.4.2; Curt. 3.4.1 incorrectly "Abistamenes"). Berve II 263 no. 527; Justi 209; Julien 18–19; Shayegan 112 no. 68.

745 MITHROPASTES

(Μιθροπάστης). Son of Arsites (satrap of Hellespontine Phrygia). At some point, M. took refuge with Mazenes on the island of Oarakta in the Persian Gulf (Tomaschek 47–8), where Nearchos encountered him in 325/4. He accompanied Nearchos on the remainder of his journey as guide familiar with the voyage (Nearchos, FGrH 133 F28 – Strabo 16.3.7 C767). There is no further record of him. Berve II 263 speculates that M.'s flight may in some way be connected with the Granikos fiasco or his father's subsequent suicide. It is more likely that he fought at Gaugamela and sought refuge on Oarakta in the hope of avoiding the Macedonians. Berve II 263–4 no. 528; Justi 216; Shayegan 112 no. 69.

746 MNASIDIKOS

(Μνασίδικος). Son of Athanodoros. One of twenty-four cavalrymen from Orchomenos, who served with Alexander's allied cavalry until the expedition reached Ekbatana in 330. There he and his compatriots were discharged. On their return (c.329), they made a dedication to Zeus Soter in Orchomenos (IG VII 3206). Berve II 264 no. 532.

747 MNASIKLES

(Μνασικλῆς). Kretan mercenary captain. M. accompanied Thibron (no. 1124) from Kydonia on Krete to Kyrene (cf. Arr. Succ. 1.16), but quarreled with him over the distribution of spoils after Thibron had captured the Kyrenean harbor and extracted concessions (Diod. 18.20.1). Hence, M. deserted and denounced Thibron to the Kyreneans, who, perhaps at M.'s instigation, attacked the Barkaians and the Hesperitai, allies of Thibron. When the latter went to their aid, M. recaptured the port of Kyrene, restoring what was left of the captured cargo to the merchants (Diod. 18.20.1–5). On his advice, the Kyreneans contributed only 60 of their promised 500 talents to Thibron's cause; Kyrene held out against Thibron. What became of M. is not recorded. If he survived the fighting in Libya, he may have been taken into the service of Ptolemy's *strategos*, Ophellas (no. 817). Nor is it known if M. was recruited by Thibron on Krete or had been one of the mercenaries brought by Harpalos from Asia in 324 (Diod. 17.108.6; 18.19.2). Berve II 264–5 no. 533; Launey 1164.

748 MNASON

(Μνάσων). Greek, son of Mnaseas (Arist. Pol. 5.3.4 1304a). Tyrant of Elateia in Phokis during the reign of Alexander. Student of Aristotle (Ael. VH 3.19; Timaios, FGrH 566 F11a = cf. Athen. 6.264d, a companion of Aristotle). Man of considerable wealth (Athen. 6.264d, 6.272b = FGrH 566 F11b), who owned more than 1,000 slaves. M. is said to have purchased from Aristeides his painting of one of Alexander's battles with the Persians for an exorbitant price: since the picture contained more than 100 human figures, M. paid ten minae per figure, that is, over one thousand (Pliny, HN 35.99; cf. 35.107 for another expensive purchase). Whether he had any personal contact with Alexander is unknown. Berve II 265 no. 534 and Tyrannis I 298–9; Schaefer III² 39 n.3.

749 MNESITHEOS

(Μνησίθεος). Athenian dancer. The name is uncertain but restored by Blass (Μνησ]ίθεον τὸν χορευτήν). Demosthenes is said to have sent him to determine the amount of money Harpalos had brought with him to be deposited on the Acropolis. The answer was 700 talents (Hyper. 5, col. 9 [Burtt]). He is perhaps identical with M. of Myrrhinoussa (Aesch. 1.98), in which case he is the son of Tachyboulos (Kirchner 10297). Berve II 265 no. 535.

750 MOERIS

The name occurs only in its Latin form; (Lassen II² 189 n.2 emends the name to Soeris, for which there is no support in the MSS). Named only by Curt. 9.8.28. Indian dynast in the Patala region of the Indos Delta (Arr. 6.17.2: ὁ τῶν Πατάλων τῆς χώρας ἄρχων). Marched north upon Alexander's approach and surrendered to the King. Alexander sent him back to his realm and ordered him to prepare everything for the Macedonian fleet (Arr. 6.17.2–3). This M. appears to have failed to do, and he and most of his people fled to the hills at the news of Alexander's approach (Arr. 6.17.5–6; Curt. 9.8.28–29); Curtius says Alexander plundered the city, but Arrian claims that many of the citizens returned in response to Alexander's appeal. M., however, was not among them, nor is he heard of again. According to Diod. 17.104.2 Patala was ruled by a dyarchy similar to that of Sparta; but Arrian and Curtius clearly treat M. as sole ruler. Eggermont's suggestion that M. may be Sandrokottos (1976, 27) is geographically and chronologically implausible (cf. Karttunen 260 n.40). Berve II 265 no. 536.

751 MOIROKLES

(Μοιροκλῆς). Athenian from Salamis (Kirchner 10400); family background unknown (*Suda* M 1447; Harpocration). Convicted earlier in his career of extorting money from the lessees of the silver mines (Dem. 19.293), M. was one of the anti-Macedonian politicians whose extradition Alexander demanded after the sack of Thebes in 335 (Arr. 1.10.4; Plut. *Dem.* 23.4; *Suda* A 2704 has "Patrokles"; Will 1983, 44 n.303). In the end, Alexander relented and insisted only upon the surrender of Charidemos. M. is accused by the comic poet, Timokles, in a fragment of his *Delos* (Athen. 8.341f), of accepting money from Harpalos. Berve II 266 no. 537; cf. Schaefer III² 137 n.2, 321 n.2, 349 n.3; Sealey 204.

752 MONIMOS

(Μόνιμος). Spartan (Poralla no. 540) ambassador to Persia, probably sent out in connection with the activities of Agis III; captured by Alexander after the death of Dareios in 330 (Arr. 3.24.4). Curt. 3.13.15 dates his capture to 333, at Damaskos: here the MS reading *omaio*, emended to *Onomas*, could be rendered *Monimus*. But the name Monimos is not otherwise attested in Sparta. Berve II 266 no. 538; Hofstetter 135 no. 226; Schachermeyr 308.

753 MONIMOS

(Μόνιμος). Son of Pythion, sought (and won) the hand of Pantika (no. 845) of Kypros, who lived at Olympias' court. She was a beautiful woman of ill repute. Olympias said he was marrying with his eyes not with his mind (Phylarchos *ap.* Athen. 13.609c = *FGrH* 81 F21). Plut. *Mor.* 141c–d tells the same story, naming neither M. or Pantika and calling the former a young man of the court (αὐλικοῦ τινος νεανίσκου), an indication that the marriage occurred perhaps before Alexander's death. M. probably belonged to the group of favorites at the Queen Mother's court that included Gorgatas, Gorgias and Hekataios; these three were summoned to Asia to serve as *paides basilikoi* in 331. Though he need not have been strictly coeval, M. was most likely born between 350 and 345. By 317, when Olympias was being besieged at Pydna by Kassandros, M., who remained loyal to her, ruled Pella (Diod. 19.50.3), but surrendered the city when he learned of Olympias' fate (Diod. 19.50.7). What became of him is unknown.

754 MOSCHION

(Μοσχίων). Elean who served with Alexander in Asia; father of two distinguished boxers named Hippomachos and Theotimos (Paus. 6.12.6, 17.5). Nothing specific is known about M.'s participation in the campaign, though he may have been a member of the Elean cavalry contingent led by Alkias that joined Alexander at Gordion (Arr. 1.29.4). He was thus probably dismissed with the remainder of the allied troops at Ekbatana in 330. Berve II 266 no. 539.

755 MOSCHION

(Μοσχίων). Son of Moirichos, from Thera. Agent of Antigonos Monophthalmos. In 315 M. was sent with Idomeneus to confirm the support of the Rhodians (Diod. 19.57.4). The mission was apparently successful. The honor of citizenship bestowed upon him some years later by the Kalymnaians, on the testimony of Nikostratos son of Nikophantos (*TitCal* 17), shows that he was in charge of the Kalymnian troops at the Antigonid garrison at Pogla, south of Kretopolis in Asia Minor, and thus both a diplomat and military leader. Seibert 1969, 227, W. Kroll *RE* XVI 345 no. 2; Olshausen 93 no. 71; Segrè, *TC* no. 8. Billows 406 no. 75; Berthold 61; Paschidis 381.

756 MOUSIKANOS

(Μουσικανός). Indian dynast of southwestern Sogdia; ruler of the Mushika. M.'s bountiful kingdom (Aristoboulos *ap.* Strabo 15.1.22; Arr. 6.15.5) lay to the east of the Indos, opposite that of his enemy Sambos (Arr. 6.16.3), to the north of the realm of Oxikanos and south of the confluences of the various rivers of the Punjab. The capital of this region was probably Alor, and M.'s rival, Sambos (Arr. 6.16.3), presumably controlled the Kandahar to Alor trade route (Eggermont 5–9). Alexander arrived in M.'s kingdom before the news of the Macedonian advance—though apparently he had expected envoys offering friendship—but M. quickly made his submission (Arr. 6.15.6) and thus gained a pardon. He was allowed to retain his kingdom, although his capital was fortified and garrisoned by the Macedonians under Krateros' supervision (Arr. 6.15.7; cf. Curt. 9.8.10). But, when Alexander turned his attention toward M.'s neighbors, the ruler, not content with what Berve II 267 calls his "Scheinherrschaft" and incited by the Brahmins, rebelled. He was captured by Peithon (Arr. 6.17.1) and brought in chains to Alexander, who had him hanged or crucified along with his Brahmin accomplices (Arr. 6.17.2; Curt. 9.8.16). Berve II 266–7 no. 540; Jacobs 247 and 245 Abb. 4.

757 MYLLEAS

(Μυλλέας). Son of Zoïlos. Macedonian from Beroia (see Tataki, *PB* 231 no. 909). Possibly father of a certain Alexander (*IG* II² 710: Ἀλέξανδρον Μυλλ[έου]), who was honored with citizenship by the Athenians at some point between 295/4 and 276/5 for his services to the state. How long M. served with Alexander in Asia is unknown, but in 326 he was assigned a trierarchy of the Hydaspes fleet (Arr. *Ind.* 18.6). Berve II 267 no. 541; Tataki, *PB* 231 no. 909.

758 MYLLENAS

(Μυλλένας). Curt. "Mullinus." Apparently Macedonian. Described as *scriba regis* (the king's secretary: γραμματεύς). Placed in charge of the light-armed troops at Aornos (Curt. 8.11.5); this mission is not at odds with his role as secretary, as the case of Eumenes demonstrates (Plut. *Eum.* 1.6). He may be identical with Myllenas son of Asandros (identified as Makedon), who is honored by a decree of the Eretrians along with Tauron son of Machatas (*IG* XII 9, 197; cf. Tataki, *PB* 231–2 no. 910, but his Beroian origin is uncertain). Berve II 267–8 no. 542; Paschidis 446–7.

759 MYRMIDON

(Μυρμιδών). Athenian (Kirchner 10479) *strategos* in the service of Ptolemy, who sent him with 10,000 soldiers, together with the *nauarchos* Polykleitos, to Kypros in 315/14. All were under the command of Menelaos (Diod. 19.62.4). From Kypros, M. was sent to Karia to help him in his struggle against Antigonos' general Polemaios (Diod. 19.62. 5). M. is described as leading mercenaries, hence probably a portion of the 10,000: some of them were sent with Polykleitos to the Peloponnese, while others remained in Kypros with Menelaos (Diod. 19.62.5; cf., however, Billows 119, who thinks all 10,000 went to Karia; *contra* Wheatley 1998b, 270 n.71). It appears that M. and his mercenaries accomplished little in Karia; for in the following year Asandros had returned from Athens (*IG* II² 450) and Prepelaos and Eupolemos were soundly defeated by Polemaios (Diod. 19.68.5, 75.1–2). Of M.'s role in these and later events nothing is reported. Launey 1126; Billows 119.

760 MYRRHINE

(Μυρρίνη). Samian courtesan who resided in Athens. M. had been the mistress of Hypereides, who kept her in his home, even though he confessed his love for Phryne (Idomeneus *ap.* Athen. 13.590c), after he had evicted his own son (Athen. 13.590d; [Plut.] *Mor.* 849d). She later became a favorite of Demetrios Poliorketes who, according to Nikolaos of Damaskos (Athen. 13.593a = *FGrH* 90 F90) did not give the crown to M. the courtesan, but she shared his kingdom. Roisman and Worthington 256–7.

761 MYS

(Μῦς). Son of Proteas, from Eresos. Honored with *proxenia* by the Megarians (*IG* VII 4). He appears to have been in the service of Demetrios. Billows 406 no. 76.

N

762 NABARZANES

(Ναβαρζάνης). Chiliarch of Dareios III (Arr. 3.21.1, 23.4; his seal was on the letter carried by Sisines, Curt. 3.7.12–15). Commanded the cavalry and 20,000 slingers and archers on the Persian right at Issos (Curt. 3.9.1). Together with Bessos, he plotted the arrest and murder of Dareios (Arr. 3.21.1; Curt 5.9.2–8; 5.9–12; cf. 6.4.8). Fled to Hyrkania (Curt. 6.3.9) and eventually surrendered to Alexander along with Bagoas, who intervened on his behalf (Curt. 6.5.22–3; Arr. 3.23.4). He is probably identical with "Barzanes" (Arr. 4.7.1; cf. 4.18.1; Heckel 1981e, 66–69. His career can be reconstructed as follows: after the death of Dareios, Bessos assigned Hyrkania and Parthyaia to N. (assuming Arr. 4.7.1 meant to write <Na>barzanes; the two satrapies were linked administratively: Strabo 11.9.1–2 C514; cf. Julien 34–6). Curt. 5.13.18 (cf. 6.3.9) says he went to Hyrkania, replacing Phrataphernes who had remained loyal to Dareios and fled (cf. Curt. 6.4.23). When Alexander approached, N. surrendered, but only after cautious diplomatic exchanges (Curt. 6.4.12–14; 5.22–3; the affair is compressed by Arr. 3.23.4). Through the agency of Bagoas, N. was pardoned (Curt. 6.5.23), but he received no further honors from Alexander. He soon returned to Hyrkania but was arrested by Phrataphernes and delivered to Alexander (Arr. 4.7.1, 18.1; with Heckel 1981e and 2018b, 102–4), who presumably had him executed. Berve II 268–9 no. 543; Shayegan 112–13 no. 70; Heckel 2018b.

763 NEAIOS

(Νεαῖος). Greek of unknown origin. N. was honored by the Athenians c.304/3. He was awarded a golden crown as well as citizenship for benefactions to the city (*IG* II² 553), probably in the service of Demetrios Poliorketes. Billows 447 no. 134.

764 NEANDROS

(Νέανδρος). Epeirot, supporter of the house of Aiakides. When the latter was driven from the throne, N., together with Androkleion and Hippias (see s.vv.) hurried on to Megara in Macedonia with the young prince, Pyrrhos, while Androkleides and Angelos held off and finally routed the pursuers (Plut. *Pyrrh.* 2.2; for a full and dramatic account of the escape see Plut. *Pyrrh.* 2.3–8). The party came eventually to the court of the Illyrian king, Glaukias, whose wife was Aiakid by blood (Justin 17.3.18–19, see s.v. Beroa no. 294). Sandberger 164 no. 57; Pape-Benseler II 982; Hammond, *Epirus* 809.

765 NEARCHOS

(Νέαρχος). Son of Androtimos (Arr. 3.6.5; Arr. *Ind.* 18.4, 10; *Syll*³ 266, 1–2). Kretan by birth (Diod. 19.69.1; Polyaenus 5.35; Arr. *Ind.* 18.10), apparently from Lato (Steph. Byz. s.v. Λήτη, thought he came from Lete in Macedonia), but settled in Amphipolis during the reign of Philip II (Arr. *Ind.* 18.4, 10). His birthdate is unknown, though most scholars consider him coeval with the King and thus born *c.*360 (so Berve II 269). But the Crown Prince's *hetairoi*, to which number N. belonged in 336 (Arr. 3.6.5; Plut. *Alex.* 10.4) should not be confused with Alexander's "boyhood friends": the latter were his *syntrophoi.* Alexander's *hetairoi* in 336 were, for the most part, older advisers of the Prince (cf. Diod. 19.69.1, for the case of Demetrios Poliorketes; see Heckel 1992, 205–8). For his part in Alexander's dealings with Pixodaros, N. was exiled along with his colleagues (Arr. 3.6.5; Plut. *Alex.* 10.4) but promptly recalled after Philip's death. A grant of *proxenia* from the Delphians (*Syll*³ 266) may date to this period (Tod II 239 no. 182; Berve II 269; but Wirth 1988, 258, with n.85, argues for the late 290s). One wonders, however, why similar honors were not extended to the other exiled *hetairoi.* But *Syll*³ 268, another proxeny decree from Delphi, honors Euainetos of Amphipolis: it may be that the city of origin is the common denominator.

In 334/3, Alexander installed him as satrap of Lykia and Pamphylia (Arr. 3.6.6; cf. 1.24.3–4; cf. Justin 13.4.15), and it was perhaps in the period 334–330 that N. developed ties with Antigonos the One-Eyed, with whom he is closely associated in the age of the Successors. During his time as satrap of Lykia, N. may have founded the city of Kretopolis in Pisidia (Sekunda 1997; for the city and its location see Mitchell 1994). Since Alexander's campaign in the area involved extensive use of *psiloi* (particularly archers, many of whom were of Kretan origin), the original settlers may have included a fair number of *apomachoi* from the ranks of the Kretan archers. Probably from Ekbatana, Alexander summoned N., who rejoined him at Baktra (Zariaspa) in the spring of 328, bringing mercenaries (Arr. 4.7.2; cf. Curt. 7.10.12: 4,000 infantry, 500 cavalry) in the company of Asandros son of Philotas. Curt. 7.10.12 names only Asandros, who brought the troops from Lykia. Badian 1975, 150 assumes that Nearchos was recalled from his satrapy because he "had not proved up to expectation in his arduous assignment." I see no evidence for the view that Nearchos himself recruited troops in Greece (Berve II 269). Near Dyrta in the land of the Assakenians, Nearchos led a reconnaissance force of Agrianes and three chiliarchies of hypaspists under Antiochos (Arr. 4.30.5–6); the results of the mission are not known. Against the view that N. himself was a hypaspist commander (Berve II 269 with n.2; Billows 407) see Badian 1975, 150–1. Bosworth II 195, following Hoffmann 191, distinguishes between this N., a hypaspist commander, and the son of Androtimos. But Diod. 19.19.4–5 mentions a Nearchos, almost certainly the Kretan, serving in a similar role under Antigonos Monophthalmos.

In 326, Alexander ordered a fleet to be built at the Hydaspes (Jhelum), and Nearchos was designated its admiral (Arr. 6.2.3; Arr. *Ind.* 18.10). This, at least, is N.'s own assertion. His trierarchy (Arr. *Ind.* 18.4) was, however, a financial responsibility, in the Attic fashion of public service (cf. Put. *Eum.* 2.4–7 for Alexander's shortage of money). The voyage began in the autumn of that year (so Strabo 15.1.17 C691; cf. 15.1.18 C692), reaching the confluence of the Hydaspes and Akesines (Chenab) on the ninth or tenth day (thus Arr. 6.4.1–4; but cf. Brunt II 109 n.1). Here the fleet suffered considerable damage in the eddies and on the riverbanks where the ships ran aground (Arr. 6.4.4–5.4; cf. Curt. 9.4.9–14; Diod. 17.97); N. was entrusted with the repair of the vessels and ordered to sail to the borders of the Mallian territory and meet Alexander, who advanced by land. Arr. 6.5.4 places the repair of the ships before Alexander's departure, but Berve II 270 may be right in seeing the refitting of the fleet as Nearchos' responsibility. Badian 1975, 152–3, sees the damage to the fleet as a sign of Nearchos' incompetence and suggests that Alexander did not allow the fleet to proceed to the junction of the Akesines and Hydraotes "until his own pilot Onesikritos could take charge of the actual navigation" (153). But Alexander's ship fared no better at the confluence of the Akesines and Hydaspes (Diod. 17.97; Curt. 9.4.9–14), and I see no good reason why, in this instance, Alexander should prefer Onesikritos to Nearchos.

The fleet awaited the land forces at the junction of the Hydraotes and the Akesines (Arr. 6.13.1), where N. encountered Alexander who was recovering from his wounds at the Mallian town (Arr. 6.13.4–5). Of N.'s activities from this point, until the fleet reached Patala, nothing is recorded. The descent of the river took, according to Aristoboulos (*FGrH* 139 F35 = Strabo 15.1.17 C692), ten months. Calculations based on Aristoboulos' own dates for the departure of the fleet and its arrival at Patala result in a voyage of almost 9 months. Plut. *Alex.* 66.1 says seven months, Pliny, *HN* 6.60, only five. But it is not entirely clear what Plutarch and Pliny regard as the starting point of the voyage; they could be counting from Alexander's departure from the junction of the Akesines and the Indos (cf. Hamilton 1969: 181–2). For the chronology in general see Beloch III² 2.305–7, 320–1.

From the Indos delta (perhaps from Xylinepolis, on the island of Killouta: Plut. *Alex.* 66.1, "Psiltoukis"; Pliny, *HN* 6.26.96; cf. Arr. 6.19.3), N. and Onesikritos were ordered to sail to the Ocean and in the direction of the Euphrates (Curt. 9.10.3; Diod. 17.104.3; Plut. *Alex.* 66.3; Arr. 6.19.5; Arr. *Ind.* 20ff.; Strabo 15.2.4 C721). Despite N.'s attempts to make it seem otherwise (esp. Arr. *Ind.* 20), the actual naval responsibilities for the expedition were given to Onesikritos. N. was commander-in-chief of the expedition (Plut. *Alex.* 66.3; Badian 1975, 153–60), and his protestations about Onesikritos' mendacity appear to have been aimed at depriving the man of any credit for the undertaking. *Suda* N 117 claims that it was N. who lied about being admiral, when he was in fact a steersman. Onesikritos is sometimes termed *archikybernetes* (Strabo 15.1.28 C698; 15.2.4 C721; Plut. *Mor.* 331e: ἄρχων τῶν κυβερνητῶν), although Pliny too makes him "leader" of the fleet (Pliny, *HN* 2.185: *dux*; 6.81: *classis praefectus*). For office of *archikybernetes* see Hauben 1987b.

The expedition is described in passionate detail by both N. (Arr. *Ind.* 20.1–42.10, contained in *FGrH* 133 F1) and Onesikritos (*ap.* Pliny, *HN* 6.96–100 = *FGrH* 134 F28) themselves. Attacks on the fleet by the natives, who were emboldened by Alexander's departure, forced N. to set out on 21 September (20 Boëdromion: Arr. *Ind.* 21.1; cf. Strabo 15.2.5 C721) 325; but the fleet made slow progress, being forced by high winds to put in at a place which N. named "Alexander's Harbor," (Near Gujo; hence east of modern Karachi, if the latter is the Morontobara of Arr. *Ind.* 22.4. So Brunt II 371 n.1; Seibert 1985, 182, identifies "Alexander's Harbor' with Karachi, but see Eggermont 33–4) where the island of Bibakta, two stades offshore, gave shelter for 35 days (Arr. *Ind.* 21.10–13). When the winds subsided (late October/early November), N. led the expedition westward, establishing a camp at Kokala in Oreitan territory, where he received supplies for ten days from Leonnatos (Arr. *Ind.* 23.4–7); Capelle speaks of a "Rast von zehn Tagen" (*RE* XVI.2, 2133). We do not know how long N.'s men remained at Kokala. Malnutrition and poor morale plagued the maritime expedition. Those who had posed disciplinary problems were left with Leonnatos; new sailors were recruited from the army (Arr. *Ind.* 23.8).

With fresh recruits N. advanced to the Tomeros River (Hingol), about three hundred stades east of what N. called the last settlement of the Oreitai at Malana (Arr. *Ind.* 25.1; mod. Ras Malan). It was at the Tomeros River that he demonstrated his true talents, which reflect the nature of his training before he came to Macedonia from Krete. He had earlier been used by Alexander as a commander of light infantry (cf. Arr.4.30.5–6), and would be employed in a similar capacity by Antigonos in 317/6 (Diod. 19.19.4–5). At this time, he led lightly armed troops, supported by archers on the ships anchored offshore, against the natives, who carried heavy wooden spears (with points hardened by fire), and easily routed them (Arr. *Ind.* 24). N.'s force must have included a sizable contingent of Kretan archers (cf. Arr. *Ind.* 28.3, 5), and, although little is known about him, Archias son of Anaxidotos of Pella appears to have been placed on Nearchos' staff by Alexander for his military expertise.

The journey along the Makran coast and the villages of the Ichthyophagoi (or "Fish Eaters") was marked by a scarcity of provisions, though date palms grew in places (Arr. *Ind.* 27.2; 29.1, 5) and plundering raids yielded little in the way of grain and a few animals (cf. Arr. *Ind.* 27.6–28.9, 29.5). At Mosarna (mod. Pasni; cf. Brunt II 384 n.1; Seibert 1985, 183), they took on board a Gedrosian guide, Hydrakes, who led them as far as Karmania (Arr. *Ind.* 26.1–27.1). Rounding the Ras-al-Kuh headland, the fleet began to sail northwest into the Strait of Hormuz (cf. Arr. *Ind.* 32.3). Maketa (Ras Musandam, the promontory of Oman) became visible (cf. Strabo 15.2.14 C726; Pliny, *HN* 6.98), and Nearchos rejected Onesikritos' suggestion that they abandon the Karmanian coast and make for it instead (Arr. *Ind.* 32.7, 9–13). In December 325 (Beloch III² 2.321), N. rejoined Alexander (Curt. 10.1.10–15). Diodorus 17.106.4 mentions a coastal town named Salmous (Curt. 10.1.10 and Strabo 15.2.11 C725 are vague, but appear to be following the same source as Diodorus); Plut. *Alex.* 67.7 speaks of the "capital of Gedrosia" (read "Karmania"? Thus Badian 1958, 151; cf. Hamilton 186), which could be identical with Salmous. They anchored at the mouth of the River Anamis (Arr. *Ind.* 33.2; cf. Arr. 6.28.5, on an uninhabited shore of Karmania) in the district of Harmozeia; the King's camp was five days' march inland (Arr. *Ind.* 33.7), and we are treated in Nearchos' own account to the hazards of the journey. Alexander was allegedly reluctant to send him back to the coast and subject him to further risks (see Badian 1975, 160–5, rightly sceptical). In fact, it is hard to imagine that Alexander had any other plans for N. than for him to sail on to the mouth of the Euphrates (Curt. 10.1.16; Diod. 17.107.1; cf. Plut. *Alex.* 68.6), whereafter he was to sail up the Pasitigris (Eulaios) to Sousa (Arr. 6.28.6; Arr. *Ind.* 36.4–9; Pliny, *HN* 6.99). The last leg of the voyage was considerably easier, and N.'s expedition proceeded to the mouth of the Euphrates and sailed as far as Diridotis, a village of Babylonia (Arr. *Ind.* 41.6; for the voyage see Arr. *Ind.* 37–41; cf. Strabo 16.3.5–7 C766–7; cf. also s.v. Mazenes no. 688). There it was learned that Alexander was not far from Sousa (Arr. *Ind.* 42.1), and N. sailed back to the Pasitigris, eventually coming to a pontoon bridge, which Alexander's advance force had prepared for the King's crossing to Sousa (Arr. *Ind.* 42.7). The reuniting of the forces occurred in March 324.

N. continued to Sousa, witnessing on the way the self-immolation of Kalanos (Arr. 7.3.6 = *FGrH* 133 F4). At Sousa, he was wedded to the daughter of Barsine and Mentor (Arr. 7.4.6)—a fact which explains both N.'s support of Barsine's son, Herakles, as Alexander's successor (Curt. 10.6.10–12) and his friendship with Eumenes (Plut. *Eum* 18.6), who had married Artonis, a sister of Barsine (Plut. *Eum.* 1.7)—and crowned for his valorous achievements on the Ocean voyage (Arr. 7.5.6; Arr. *Ind.* 42.9 gives the impression that N. and Leonnatos were crowned when the fleet and army were reunited; rejected by Badian 1975, 166). From Sousa, N. took Alexander by ship to the mouth of the Eulaios (Arr. 7.7.1), but thereafter the King sailed up the Tigris to rejoin Hephaistion at Opis (Arr. 7.7.6), while N. conducted the fleet up the Euphrates to Babylon (Arr. 7.19.3). Here he was said to have brought the warnings of the Chaldaian astrologers to the King's attention (Diod. 17.112.3–4; Plut. *Alex.* 73.1, with Hamilton 202–3). Alexander designated him admiral of his planned Arabian fleet (Arr. 7.25.4; cf. Plut. *Alex.* 68.1, with Hamilton 187–9), a project cut short by the King's sudden death in Babylon. For it was after a banquet, which he had given in N.'s honor (Plut. *Alex.* 75.4), that Alexander went to the drinking party in the home of Medeios, at which he became fatally ill. N.'s part in the plot to poison Alexander is a fabrication of the Polyperchan camp (*LM* 97–8; Ps.-Call.3.31.8–9; cf. Heckel 1988, 36; for a later date and a pro-Ptolemaic bias see Bosworth 2000).

Justin 13.4.15 says that N. was assigned Lykia and Pamphylia in the division at Babylon, generally dismissed as an error influenced by his earlier administration of the satrapy. But it is doubtful that the ultimate source for this information remembered that N. had once been satrap of the region. N. clearly returned to Asia Minor and Antigonos' entourage, in whose service he captured Telmissos, where Antipatrides, an old friend of his (Polyaenus 5.35; I see no reason for dating this to the period 333–331), had been installed, most likely by Attalos and Alketas in 320/19 (cf. Billows 408). In 317/6 Antigonos sent him with a lightly armed force into Kossaian territory in order to seize passes of strategic importance to Eumenes (Diod. 19.19.4–5). He accompanied Antigonos to Gabiene, and is said to have been one of the officers who begged him, unsuccessfully, to spare the life of the captive Eumenes (Plut. *Eum.* 18.6). N. is last mentioned as one of four advisers (along with Andronikos, Peithon son of Agenor and Philip) left by Antigonos with Demetrios Poliorketes in Syria in 313/2 (Diod. 19.69.1; for the chronology: Errington, 1977, 498–500). Soon afterwards, he may have retired into private life, turning his attention to the publication of his historical account, an earlier version of which he had read to Alexander in the last days of his life (Plut. *Alex.* 76.3; but see Hamilton 211; according to Arr. 7. 25. 4, Alexander was briefing Nearchos on the details of the upcoming naval expedition to Arabia). It is perhaps significant that N., a supporter of Antigonos and Demetrios, is not mentioned in connection with the naval battle of Salamis in 306. Berve II 269–72 no. 544; Capelle, *RE* s.v. "Nearchos (3)"; Lehmann-Haupt in Papastavru 97–137 no. 61; Launey 1156; Tataki 57 no. 93; Wirth 1972 and 1988; Badian 1975; Pédech 1984, 162–3; Billows 406–8 no. 77; Heckel 1992, 228–34; Sekunda 1997; Bucciantini, *LexAM* 349–52. For his *History* see Jacoby *FGrH* 133; Pearson 112–49.

766 NEARCHOS

(Νέαρχος). Tragedian and friend of Kallisthenes, in the entourage of Alexander, who executed him, presumably in the aftermath of the Pages' conspiracy (*Suda* K 240). But the *Suda* N 218 calls this man Neophron the Sikyonian (see below).

767 NEILOXENOS

(Νειλόξενος). Macedonian (Tataki 377 no. 2). Son of Satyros. One of the *hetairoi*. In winter 330/29 he was installed as *episkopos* of the troops left in Alexandria-in-the-Kaukasos, along with the satrap Proexes (Arr. 3.28.4). In 327, he was replaced by Nikanor, another *hetairos* (Arr. 4.22.5). He was, in all likelihood, the delinquent *hyparchos*, who was deposed ὅτι οὐ καλῶς ἐξηγεῖσθαι ἔδοξε (*pace* Bosworth II 145; Julien 42 appear to suggest that this phrase refers to Proexes). Arrian uses the terms *episkopos* and *hyparchos* interchangeably, in this case referring to an individual who acted as *strategos* (cf. Archelaos in Sousa: Arr. 3.16.9; Julien 56). Since it was N.'s role to oversee the activities of the satrap Proexes, a Persian who was replaced in 327 by Tyriespis (Arr.4.22.5: both Proexes and Tyriespis are designated *satrapes*), N. may have been held responsible for Proexes' administrative delinquencies. On the other hand, since Nikanor was entrusted with bringing order to the city (τὴν πόλιν αὐτὴν κοσμεῖν), which received an infusion of new settlers, Alexander's dissatisfaction may have to do with the state of his new foundation. In any case, both the "overseer" and the satrap were cashiered. Berve II 272–3 no. 545.

768 NEON

(Νέων). Greek from Messenia. Son of Philiades. Leader of the pro-Macedonian party (Dem. 18.295; Theopompos, *FGrH* 115 F41 = Harpocration s.v. Νέων and *Suda* N 231). N. and his brother Thrasylochos were exiled in 336/5, in the turmoil that followed Philip's death (Schaefer III² 115 n.2) but reinstated as tyrants of Messenia soon afterwards on Alexander's orders ([Dem.] 17.4, 7), probably in 333; but see Polyb. 18.14.3 and Berve, *Tyrannis* I 308. Berve II 274 no. 550.

769 NEON

(Νέων). Greek in the service of Demetrios Poliorketes in 306. After the battle of Salamis, Neon and Bourichos (no. 309) were sent with the transports to pick up the survivors of the battle (Diod. 20.52.4). The use of the word διώκειν ("to pursue") suggests that they were collecting prisoners as well as their own men. Billows 409 no. 78; Schoch, *RE* s.v. no. 4; Hauben 114–15.

770 NEOPHRON

(Νεόφρων. Perhaps Νεόφων). Sikyonian tragedian and friend of Kallisthenes of Olynthos, N. accompanied Alexander on his campaign and, for allegedly plotting against the King, was tortured and killed along with Kallisthenes (*Suda* N 218). *Suda* K 240, discussing Kallisthenes, wrongly gives the man's name as Nearchos, but adds that he was supposed to have been imprisoned in an iron cage because, together with Kallisthenes, he advised Alexander not to demand of the Athenians the title "Lord" (*despotes*). The *hypothesis* of Eur. *Medea* claims that Euripides reworked the *Medea* of Neophron (see A.L. Brown, *OCD*³ 1034); if this is correct, the tragedian and the friend of Kallisthenes must have been different people. Berve II 273–4 no. 549.

771 NEOPTOLEMOS

(Νεοπτόλεμος). Son of Arrhabaios and brother of Amyntas (Arr. 1.20.10). Arrian adds that he was one of those who deserted to the Persians, leaving little doubt that he was a grandson of Aëropos, and that he fled Macedonia after the arrest and execution of his father (cf. Arr. 1.25.1). He perished in a skirmish at the gates of Halikarnassos (Arr. 1.20.10; but Diod. 17.25.5 places him on the Macedonian side, which is probably the result of carelessness). Welles 188 n.1 argues that Diodorus' version is correct, a view taken up also by Bosworth I 145. But the argument that Alexander would not have trusted Amyntas son of Arrhabaios if his brother had been a deserter and his father a suspected regicide is all but negated by the case of Alexander Lynkestes, who was actually promoted during the first year of the campaign. If the King had concerns about Amyntas' loyalty, he will not have acted upon them until after the arrest of his uncle. I am inclined to believe that Diodorus, or his source, recognizing Neoptolemos as a prominent Macedonian, wrongly assumed that he was fighting on Alexander's side. The details provided by Arrian put the matter of Neoptolemos' identity beyond doubt. Bosworth's rejection of it forces him to conclude that "[t]he note about his desertion must then be Arrian's own addition." Berve II 273 no. 547; Hofstetter 136 no. 230; Tataki 203 no. 12. **Stemma XV.**

772 NEOPTOLEMOS

(Νεοπτόλεμος). N.'s patronymic is unknown but he is described as one of the Aiakidai (Arr. 2.27.6); hence he was a scion of the Molossian royal house (Beloch IV² 2.145) and perhaps a relative of Arybbas the Somatophylax (cf. Arr. 3.5.5). First attested at Gaza (late 332), where he was the first to scale the wall (Arr. 2.27.6). This act of courage did not go unnoticed: he succeeded Nikanor son of Parmenion, who died of illness in 330, as *archihypaspistes* (Plut. *Eum.* 1.6), that is, as commander of the regular hypaspists (cf. Berve II 273). Bosworth 1988, 104, thinks that N.'s relationship with Alexander (though somewhat distant) may account for his command of the entire hypaspist corps at a time when the King was eliminating larger commands (e.g., the command of the Companion Cavalry was divided between Hephaistion and Black Kleitos after Philotas' death). N. may have been awarded the satrapy of Armenia in the settlement of 323, but the doctored text of Dexippos (*FGrH* 100 F8 §6) is suspect: Νεοπτολέμου Καρμανία is emended by Ausfeld to Νεοπτολέμου <Ἀρμενία, Τλεπολέμου> Καρμανία (see discussion in Anson 1990). This does violence to the geographical sequence (i.e. it is doubtful that any source would have placed the administrators of Armenia and Karmania back to back. Furthermore, it is much easier simply to emend Νεοπτολέμου to Τλεπολέμου. Briant 152 n.8 is probably correct to regard him as *strategos* rather than satrap (cf. Plut. *Eum.* 4.1; 5.2). Diod. 19.14.1, however, calls Philotas (sc. Philip; cf. Billows 90 n.17) *strategos*, although he was clearly satrap of Parthia (Diod. 18.39.6; Arr. *Succ.* 1.35). The satrapy was assigned by Alexander to Mithrenes in 331 (Curt. 5.1.44); but Orontes, who commanded the Armenians at Gaugamela (Arr. 3.8.5), is found ruling it in 317. He may have regained his ancestral territory at Triparadeisos, perhaps through the influence of his friend Peukestas. That N. managed only to create havoc in Armenia (Plut. *Eum.* 4.1) suggests that he was not cooperating with any existing satrap.

When it became clear that war with Krateros and Antipatros was imminent, Perdikkas assigned Kappadokia and Armenia to Eumenes and instructed both his brother Alketas and N. to obey the Greek commander (Plut. *Eum.* 5.2; Diod. 18.29.2; Justin 13.6.15). Alketas refused to serve, arguing that his Macedonians would be ashamed to fight against Krateros (Plut. *Eum.* 5.3). N. remained with Eumenes but soon intrigued with Antipatros (Arr. *Succ.* 1.26) and plotted betrayal (Plut. *Eum.* 5.4), presumably intending to defect with his forces to the enemy once the engagement had begun. Schubert 163 imagines a more important role for N.: that he would keep Eumenes in check in Asia Minor while Krateros and Antipatros proceeded to Egypt. Eumenes, discovering the plot, brought him to battle and defeated him (Plut. *Eum.* 5.5; Diod. 18.29.4–5; Arr. *Succ.* 1.27; cf. *PSI* 12.1284, with Bosworth 1978); N., however, escaped with some 300 horsemen (Diod. 18.29.6; cf. Plut. *Eum.* 5.6; Arr. *Succ.* 1.27; Justin 13.8.5). Taking refuge with Krateros, he persuaded him that the Macedonians in Eumenes' service would receive him favorably (Plut. *Eum.* 6.1–2); for the mere sight of Krateros would be sufficient to turn the tide of battle. But, when Eumenes learned that N. was stationed on the left (Diod. 18.30.3, 31.1), he placed his Macedonian troops opposite him and deployed his barbarians on his own left, facing Krateros (Plut. *Eum.* 6.7; 7.3). The stratagem worked, and Krateros, uttering curses against N. (Plut. *Eum.* 7.4), found the enemy stubborn in its resistance. As fate would have it, he perished in the engagement. The final struggle between Eumenes and Neoptolemos (it occurred ten days after the initial engagement (Plut. *Eum.* 8.1), as reported by Plut. *Eum.* 7.7–12, Diod. 18.31 Nepos, *Eum.* 4.1–2), derives from a single primary source— Hieronymos (Schubert 178–9), who emphasized the long-standing hatred between the two men. That Neoptolemos, who had berated Eumenes as the King's secretary (Plut. *Eum.* 1.6), found himself overcome in a bitter hand-to-hand struggle (Arr. *Succ.* 1.27), is perhaps Douris' coloring (cf. Hornblower, *Hieronymus* 196). Felled by his adversary, and prevented by a wound to the knee from rising from the ground, N. directed a feeble blow to Eumenes' groin as the Greek was already stripping the armor from his body, a heroic scene which does for Eumenes what Kallisthenes had intended for Alexander in his description of the Granikos battle. One final thrust to the neck ended N.'s life (Diod. 18.31.5; Justin 13.8.8). Since Krateros had already fallen, and with the right wing in disarray, Neoptolemos' death signalled total defeat (Diod. 18.32.1; cf. 18.37.1). Eumenes' attitude to his defeated adversaries was mixed: he regarded Krateros with honor, N. with contempt (Plut. *Eum.* 7.13). But to have overcome both opponents greatly enhanced his reputation (Diod. 18.53.3). N. was a man of great pride and warlike spirit (Arr. *Succ.* 1.27). At some point after 330 he, or perhaps his family, commissioned Apelles to depict him on horseback, fighting the Persians (Pliny, *HN* 35.96; Pollitt 162). It is remotely possible that N. was the grandfather of Neoptolemos II, in which case we must postulate a son named Alexander (see Heckel 2021). Anson 1990; Beloch IV² 2.145–6; Berve II 273 no. 548; Bosworth 1978; Heckel, *Marshals*² 305–7; Wirth 1965.

773 NEOPTOLEMOS

(Νεοπτόλεμος). Neoptolemos II of Epeiros (*regn.* 302–297). Brother of Kadmeia (Plut. *Pyrrh.* 5.11) and son of a certain Alexander. The father was most likely Alexander son of Alketas II, though he may have been a grandson of Neoptolemos the *archihypaspistes* (no. 772). Others have identified him as the son of Alexander I, who ruled from 342–331, and Kleopatra (e.g. Hammond, *Epirus* 558–68). In the latter case, N. would have been born no later than 333, since Alexander I left for Italy in the previous campaigning season. But Plutarch's reference to τοὺς Νεοπτολέμου παῖδας (*Pyrrh.* 2.1) need not refer to a son of Alexander I; and, indeed, in the context of the affairs of 317/16 this identification appears less likely. Plutarch says the Epeirots brought in (ἐπηγάγοντο) the sons (or descendants) of Neoptolemos, and it is hard to imagine that N. son of Alexander I (if he, in fact, existed) was anywhere but with Olympias until her surrender and death at Pydna (for the remainder of Olympias' entourage see Diod. 19.35.5; Justin 14.6.2–3, aptly calling it a *speciosus magis quam utilis grex*) and thus a captive of Kassandros. Cross 1932, App. III 106–8, sees N. as a grandson of Alketas II (who also had a son Alexander). If Plutarch is correct, N. ruled Epeiros after the expulsion of the two-year-old Pyrrhos, but not one ancient source mentions him by name, speaks of him as the co-ruler with any king before 297, or suggests what he might have been up to in those chaotic years from 317/16 to 303/2. The confusion about N.'s identity and the years of his reign is based, in all likelihood on a mistake in Plut. *Pyrrh.* 2.1, which anticipates the events described at 4.1. It is virtually certain that he replaced Pyrrhos, when he was driven from Epeiros a second time in 302 (Plut. *Pyrrh.* 4.1); for he later shared the kingship with Pyrrhos, when Ptolemy secured his return. N. was soon accused of plotting against his co-ruler (Plut. *Pyrrh.* 5.2–13)—we have no way of knowing whether the charge was warranted or fabricated by Pyrrhos himself. He was invited to dinner and killed (Plut. *Pyrrh.* 5.14). Sandberger 164–70 no. 58; Berve, *RE* XVI 2463–4 no. 4; Berve II 273 no. 546; Lévêque 1957, 103ff., 117ff.; Heckel 2021. Stemma IIa–b.

774 NIKAGORAS

(Νικάγορας). Tyrant of Zeleia (Athen. 7.289c). Aristos of Salamis (*FGrH* 143 F4) claims that he lived in the time of Alexander and both dressed and had himself addressed as Hermes. This he did on the instructions of a delusional physician, Menekrates of Syracuse (on whom see Tarn II 433–4), who may have treated him for epilepsy (Baton of Sinope, *FGrH* 268 F2 = Athen. 7.289b–c). Supporter of Dareios III (that is, his regime was supported by the Persians). After the battle of the Granikos, Alexander pardoned the Zeleians since they had opposed him under pressure from N. (Arr. 1.17.2), but in the city a democracy was instituted in 334/3 (*Syll*[3] 279) and N. was probably banished, if not put to death. Berve II 274 no. 551; Berve, *Tyrannis* I 314, II 679; Hofstetter 136 no. 231.

775 NIKAIA

(Νικαία). Daughter of Antipatros (Strabo 12.4.7 C565; Diod. 18.23.3; Arr. *Succ.* 1.21; Steph. Byz. s.v. Νικαία), N. had at least three sisters (see s.vv. Phila, Eurydike; the name of the third sister is unknown) and seven brothers (Kassandros, Philip, Iolaos, Nikanor, Pleistarchos, Perilaos, Alexarchos). In 322 she was brought to Asia (perhaps to Pisidia, thus Rathmann, *Perdikkas* 61) by her brother Iolaos and a certain Archias to marry Perdikkas (Arr. *Succ.* 1.21), who by the time of her arrival was contemplating marriage to Alexander's sister, Kleopatra. Eumenes recommended the latter union, but Alketas favored N. and Perdikkas decided at least temporarily to marry her (Arr. *Succ.* 1.21); for he had sought N.'s hand in order to seal a pact (κοινοπραγία) with Antipatros (Diod. 18.23.1). When Kleopatra presented herself as a valuable political bride, Perdikkas disguised his plans by marrying N. first, while continuing to woo Alexander's sister (Diod. 18.23.2–3; Justin 13.6.5–6; Arr. *Succ.* 1.26). Antipatros, learning of the deception, made war on Perdikkas (Justin 13.6.7; Arr. *Succ.* 1.24, 26). After Perdikkas' death, N. was married to Lysimachos, who later founded Nikaia the metropolis of Bithynia (Steph. Byz. s.v. Νικαία; Strabo 12.4.7 C565). It was originally founded by Antigonos Monophthalmos as Antigoneia but refounded by Lysimachos and named for his wife. The date of N.'s marriage to Lysimachos is unclear. She may have returned to Europe in 320/19 with her father, who may have arranged the union when he crossed the Hellespont (cf. Landucci, *Lisimaco* 105). By Lysimachos she appears to have had at least three children: Agathokles, Eurydike, and Arsinoë (I), who later married Ptolemy II Philadelphos (Ogden 58 thinks that the woman (A100) given in marriage to Dromichaites was also N.'s daughter: Paus. 1.9.6). Whether N. was still alive when Lysimachos married Amastris, and later Arsinoë (II), is unknown. Seibert 1967, 95–6 believes that the Thrakian king was not polygamous but practiced serial monogamy, though this appears to be contradicted by Plut. *Comp. of Demetrios and Antony* 4 (cf. Landucci, *Lisimaco* 122–3; Ogden 57). Berve II 274 no. 552; Beloch IV² 2.127; Seibert 1967, 16, 93; Ogden 57–8; Rathmann 59–64; Aulbach §5.1.2.

776 NIKANOR

(Νικάνωρ). Macedonian (Tataki 383 no. 44). Apparently the second of Parmenion's attested sons (Arr. 1.14.2; 2.8.3; 3.11.9; Diod. 17.57.2; Curt. 3.9.7; 4.13.27; *Suda* N 376), N. was the brother of Philotas and Hektor. Philotas was roughly coeval with Amyntas son of Perdikkas and born *c.*365; N. can scarcely have been born much later. The prominence of these brothers already in 335/4 may be seen as a reward for Parmenion's help in eliminating Alexander's rival Attalos (Diod. 17.2.4–6, 5.2; Curt. 7.1.3), his own son-in-law (Curt. 6.9.17). Hence N., presumably as commander of the hypaspists, was given charge of the phalanx in the Getic campaign of 335 (Arr. 1.4.2; cf. Berve II 275). Arrian's account of the battle at the Granikos River, provides the first explicit mention of N. as the hypaspist commander, holding a position to the right of center on the Macedonian line, between the Companions and the units of the pezhetairoi (Arr. 1.14.2). This pattern was repeated at Issos (Arr. 2.8.3; Curt. 3.9.7) and again at Gaugamela (Arr. 3.11.9; cf. Curt. 4.13.27); for the hypaspists acted as a hinge between the cavalry and the heavy infantry. Of N.'s personal participation in these battles nothing is known. Alexander took with him, in his final pursuit of Dareios in 330, the most mobile of the infantry, N.'s hypaspists, and the Agrianes. But, when it became necessary to proceed only on horseback, he substituted some 500 mounted infantrymen for cavalry and pushed ahead with these *dimachae*, as they were called (Pollux 1.132; Curt. 5.13.8 says they were 300 strong; cf. Hesychius 1, p. 997). N. and Attalos (the commander of the Agrianes) were ordered to follow with the remaining troops (Arr. 3.21.8; cf. Curt. 5.13.19). Although the *archihypaspistes* (Arrian does not use the term but calls him τῶν ὑπασπιστῶν ἡγεμών) would seem to be the superior officer, Arrian (3.21.8) treats N. and Attalos as equals—perhaps Attalos was considerably senior, perhaps the special position of the Agrianes in Alexander's army was a factor. Not long afterwards, N. died of illness in Aria (Arr. 3.25.4; Curt. 6.6.18). The army lamented his death; whether the King's grief was genuine is debatable, given his stormy relationship with the family of Parmenion (Curt. 6.6.18–19). Philotas remained to perform the funeral rites, retaining 2,600 men while Alexander himself continued in pursuit of the rebel Bessos (Curt. 6.6.19). N.'s successor appears to have been Neoptolemos. Berve II 275 no. 554; Heckel 1992, 299–300.

777 NIKANOR

(Νικάνωρ). Macedonian (Tataki 382 no. 40). Son of Antipatros, brother of Kassandros (Diod. 19.11.8), and thus apparently from Palioura (Tataki 146). Berve II 274 assumes that he was born *c.*350 and spent Alexander's reign at the Court of his father (cf. Beloch III² 2.84). N. appears to have accompanied his father to Asia in 320, where, at Triparadeisos, he was made the satrap of Kappadokia (Diod. 18.39.6; Arr. *Succ.* 1.37; cf. App. *Mithr.* 8), from which territory, with the help of Antigonos, he would have to drive out the forces of Eumenes. But Kassandros, who was also attached to Antigonos' army as χιλιάρχης τῆς ἵππου, suspected that Antigonos had ambitions to place all Asia under his control and returned with the "Kings" to his father's army; at that time N. must have rejoined Antipatros as well and thus never occupied Kappadokia. N. returned to Europe where, after the deaths of Philip III Arrhidaios and Adea-Eurydike, he was put to death by Olympias, who claimed to be avenging her son's death (Diod. 19.11.8). Kassandros did not relinquish the family's claim to Kappadokia (cf. Diod. 19.57.1) and sent his general

Asklepiodoros to the satrapy, where he was defeated by Polemaios when he was besieging Amisos (Diod. 19.57.4, 60.2; but see Buraselis 8–9; *Barr. Atl.* 87 B3). Billows 409 no. 79 considers the N. who was awarded Kappadokia a different individual, perhaps the later general of Media (see below). Berve II 274 no. 553. **Stemma V.**

778 NIKANOR

(Νικάνωρ). Macedonian (Tataki 383 no. 42), son of Balakros, known only from a reference in the lexicographers (*Suda* N 376, Harpocration). Since the other two men listed in this entry are both from the time of Alexander, we may assume that N. son of Balakros also belongs to this period. He could be a son of Alexander's *Somatophylax* (no. 283) by a wife other than Phila, a brother of Philip son of Balakros (no. 906), or possibly both (see the stemma in Heckel 2007b). On the other hand, it is remotely possible that the Balakros who campaigned in Asia Minor in 333/2 was not the former *Somatophylax* and satrap of Kilikia, and that N. was the son of that man. Bosworth 1994; Heckel 2007b.

779 NIKANOR

(Νικάνωρ). Macedonian (Tataki 380 no. 26). Officer, and presumably *philos* of Antigonos the One-Eyed, who negotiated the surrender of Eumenes after the battle of Gabiene (Plut. *Eum.* 17.5). He is probably the same man whom Antigonos installed as satrap of Media in 315, assigning him the *strategia* of the Upper Satrapies (Diod. 19.92.1–5, 100.3; App. *Syr.* 55.278, 57.292–3; cf. Schober 1981, 97–103; Bengtson I 183–5). Billows (409) believes N. is the same man who was assigned Kappadokia at Triparadeisos but then claims, without good reason, that Antigonos "did not install Nikanor in Kappadokia, preferring to send Menandros there as general." It is more likely that the putative satrap of Kappadokia was Antipatros' son (see above). Identification of the satrap of Media with N. son of Balakros cannot be ruled out. Berve, *RE* XVII (1936) 269–70 no. 72; Billows 409–10 no. 79.

780 NIKANOR

(Νικάνωρ). Macedonian from Stageira (*Suda* N 376, Harpocration s.v. Νικάνωρ; Tataki 175 no. 5) and thus a compatriot of Aristotle, whose daughter he was later to marry, by the terms of Aristotle's will (Diog. Laert. 5.12). The N. described by Steph. Byz. s.v. Μίεζα as *Miezaios* ("from Mieza") seems to be the same man. Educated with Alexander at Mieza and thus a contemporary, he appears to have accompanied the King on his Asiatic expedition (thus Berve II 276, based on the reference to N.'s absence in Diog. Laert. 5.12). N. was sent to proclaim the "Exiles' Decree" in 324 (Diod. 18.8.3–4; Din. 1.169; 1.175; Diod. 17.109.1; Curt. 10.2; Justin 13.5.3–4; Hyper. 5, col. 18). Ferguson 1911, 28 n.4 identifies him with the garrison commander at Mounychia, but this rests on the flimsiest evidence and has been called into question (see Bosworth 1994; Heckel 2007b). Berve II 276–7 no. 557.

781 NIKANOR

(Νικάνωρ). Macedonian of unknown family (Tataki 380 no. 23). Born, in all likelihood, before 360. Commander of the "Hellenic fleet" in 334, which anchored at Lade and then moved into the harbor of Miletos to complete the blockade of the city (Arr. 1.18.4–5, 19.3–11). But Alexander soon disbanded this fleet (Arr. 1.20.1) and N. found himself without a command, unless he oversaw the actions of the transports (Diod. 17.22.5; cf. Curt.

4.5.10). The reconstituted Aegean fleet was entrusted to Hegelochos and Amphoteros. Identification with the son of Balakros (*Suda* N 376, Harpocration) is remotely possible. But, in that case, his mother was not Antipatros' daughter, Phila (who cannot have been born earlier than 360), and it is less likely that his father was Alexander's *Somatophylax*. Given his naval experience it is tempting to identify him as Kassandros' lieutenant in Mounychia (no. 782), the man who defeated White Kleitos in the Propontis. Berve II 275 no. 555; Bosworth I 137; Hauben 1972a, 55–6; Bosworth 1994 and Heckel 2007b.

782 NIKANOR

(Νικάνωρ). Macedonian. *Phrourarchos* of Mounychia, installed in 319/18 (Plut. *Phoc.* 31.1–2). N. was encouraged by Phokion to act as *agonothetes* and put on games in Athens (Plut. *Phoc.* 31.3). When he heard that Polyperchon was on his way to Attika—while Kassandros had gone to Antigonos—he tried to persuade the Athenians to remain loyal to Kassandros, stalling for time and secretly introducing more troops until he had sufficient troops to withstand a siege (Diod. 18.64.1–2); furthermore, he captured Peiraieus as well (Diod. 18.64.3–4; Nepos, *Phoc.* 2.4–5; cf. 3.4; Plut. *Phoc.* 32). The Athenians sent Phokion, Konon son of Timotheos, and Klearchos son of Nausikles to negotiate autonomy for Athens, but N. said he could do nothing without Kassandros' approval (Diod. 18.64.5–6). Olympias also wrote to N. demanding that he restore Mounychia and Peiraieus, but Nikanor put off doing so. In Athens, N. had the support of Phokion and the pro-Antipatros politicians, and he also entered into negotiations with Alexander son of Polyperchon (Diod. 18.65.3–5; Plut. *Phoc.* 33.1, 3), thus making it clear that neither party was interested in the good of the Athenians. According to Karystios of Pergamon, in the 3rd book of his *Hypomnemata*, when Antipatros had Himeraios put to death, Demetrios of Phaleron (his brother) went to live with N. (Athen. 12.543e). When Kassandros arrived from Asia, N. had firm control of Mounychia and Peiraieus (18.68.1–2). In 317, N. was sent by Kassandros with the entire fleet to oppose Kleitos in the Hellespont and Propontis (18.72.3–8; Polyaenus 4.6.8). After an initial setback, he defeated Kleitos in the Propontis and sailed into Peiraieus, his fleet ornamented with the beaks of Kleitos' ships (Diod. 18.75.1). His success went to his head and his arrogance (as well as the fact that he was garrisoning Mounychia with his own troops, τὴν Μουνυχίαν διὰ τῶν ἑαυτοῦ στρατιωτῶν φρουροῦντα) incurred the suspicions of Kassandros, who had him assassinated (Diod. 18.75.1; Polyaenus 4.11.2); Dionysios may have replaced him. The long-accepted view that he is identical with the Stageirite, a nephew of Aristotle (Ferguson 1911, 28, with n.4) is based on no good evidence, and the suggestion that he was the son of Balakros (Bosworth 1994) presents other problems (discussed by Heckel 2007b). There is a strong likelihood that the *phrourarchos* is the same man as Alexander's fleet commander (no. 781, above). Berve II 276–7 no. 557; Bosworth 1994; Habicht 1997, 47–53; Hauben 72–7 no. 27; Heckel 2007b.

783 NIKANOR

(Νικάνωρ). Macedonian. *Hetairos* of Alexander. In 327, N. was left to set in order the affairs of Alexandria-in-the-Kaukasos in tandem with the new satrap of Parapamisadai, Tyriespis (Arr. 4.22.5). N. replaced Neiloxenos, who had been appointed in 330/29 (Arr. 3.28.4) and was apparently the *hyparchos* of the city deposed in 327 (Arr. 4.22.4; *contra* Bosworth II 145). Arrian's terminology is imprecise and misleading: *hyparchos* and *episkopos* are probably both the rough equivalents (in this case) of *strategos*; this does not imply that Neiloxenos and N. were *phrourarchoi* (for the distinction see Mazaros and Archelaos at Sousa [Arr. 3.16.9]). N. is apparently the same man who was made satrap of the region to the west of the Indos (Arr. 4.28.6), hence apparently also the *hyparchos* who was killed by the Assakenians in 326 (Arr. 5.20.7). Berve II 275–6 no. 556.

784 NIKANOR

(Νικάνωρ). Macedonian of unknown family (Tataki 380 no. 25). He was implicated in the so-called Dimnos conspiracy of 330 (Curt. 6.7.15), denounced and executed by stoning (Curt. 6.11.38). Berve II 277 no. 558.

785 NIKANOR

(Νικάνωρ). Prominent young Macedonian (*nobilis iuvenis*), probably a member of the *hypaspistai basilikoi*. N. (along with Hegesimachos) led a band of young men in an unsuccessful attack on an island in the Hydaspes River and perished, through his own recklessness, in the attempt (Curt. 8.13.13–16). Berve II 277 no. 560; Heckel 1992, 297.

786 NIKANOR

(Νικάνωρ). Macedonian (Tataki 381 no. 28), *philos* of Ptolemy I Soter. At some point in 320/19 he took an adequate force into Koile-Syria, capturing the territory and its satrap Laomedon; N. placed garrisons in Phoinikia and returned to Egypt after a "short and effective campaign" (Diod. 18.43.2). Nothing else is known about him, but Berve II 277 reasonably assumes that he held some higher office already under Alexander. Berve II 277 no 559.

787 NIKARCHIDES

(Νικαρχίδης). Apparently Macedonian (Tataki 384 no. 49); family background unknown. In 331/0 he was appointed *phrourarchos* of Persepolis and placed in charge of a garrison of 3,000 men (Curt. 5.6.11). Identification with the trierarch of the Hydaspes fleet (below), though unlikely, is not impossible. Berve II 278 no. 563.

788 NIKARCHIDES

(Νικαρχίδης). Macedonian from Pydna (Tataki 171 no. 12). Son of Simos. In 326 he was appointed a trierarch of the Hydaspes fleet (Arr. *Ind.* 18.5). Nothing else is known about him. Berve II 278 no. 562.

789 NIKESIAS

(Νικεσίας). Flatterer in Alexander's entourage. Apparently a Greek, though his family background is unknown. He was one of the flatterers (*kolakes*) who encouraged Alexander's belief in his own divinity (Phylarchos *ap.* Athen. 6.251c = *FGrH* 81 F11; Hegesandros *ap.* Athen. 6.249d–e = Müller, *FHG* IV 414, frg. 6). Müller implausibly identifies the Alexander of this passage as *Epiri rex*. Berve II 278 no. 564.

790 NIKESIPOLIS

(Νικησίπολις). Thessalian (Athen. 13.557d; cf. Paus. 8.7.7). Niece of Jason of Pherai (Steph. Byz. s.v. Θεσσαλονίκη), a relationship which seems to rule out the suggestion (Green 1982,

143–4; against which see Ogden 18–19) that she was a mere concubine. Married Philip II (Paus. 9.7.3) in 352 or 346, as the name of her daughter suggests. Since Thessalonike did not marry until 315, the latter date is far more likely. Green 1982, 143 puts her liaison with Philip in 352; Carney 60–1 suggests, implausibly, that Philip may have married both Philine and N. before Olympias (in 357). The age of Thessalonike at the time of her marriage to Kassandros in 315 must be a determining factor. N.'s beauty won the admiration of even her rival Olympias (Plut. *Mor.* 141b–c). Mother of Thessalonike (Satyros *ap.* Athen. 13.557d; Paus. 9.7.3). She died on the twentieth day after giving birth to her daughter (Steph. Byz. s.v. Θεσσαλονίκη). Carney 60–1; Ogden 18–19. **Stemma I.**

791 NIKIAS

(Νικίας). Family background and place of origin unknown; apparently a Greek in Alexander's entourage. N. was placed in charge of the assessment and collection of tribute in Lydia in 334. He was probably subordinate to the newly appointed satrap, Asandros son of Philotas (Arr. 1.17.7). Berve II 278 n.1 notes that there is no attested Macedonian bearer of the name. Tataki 57 nos. 95–6 and 140 no. 88 includes an Amphipolitan and Olynthian of that name. These (or their children) may have become naturalized Makedones. N. with the ethnic Makedon is first attested in the 2nd century (Tataki 385 nos. 54–5, cf. 491 no. 177, first cent. BC). Berve II 278 no. 565.

792 NIKODEMOS

(Νικόδημος). Messenian. Accused by Plutarch of changing his support to the winning side (*Demosthenes* 13.4: ἀεὶ γὰρ εἶναι συμφέρον ἀκροᾶσθαι τῶν κρατούντων). It appears that in 303, he shifted his support from Kassandros to Demetrios Poliorketes (for the date see Paschidis 269–70, who rules out the alternative date, 295, since Kassandros was already dead and "Nikodemos' turnabout would be perfectly justified"). He may be the son of Nikarchides honored at Delphi in 323/2 (*Syll*³ 325 = *FD* III 4, 7). Nothing else is known about him. Billows 410–11 no. 81; Paschidis 269–70 B29.

793 NIKOKLES

(Νικοκλῆς). Son of Pasikrates of Soloi (Arr. *Ind.* 18.8), possibly brother of Eunostos. He accompanied Alexander since 331, if not already in 332, and is named as one of the trierarchs of the Hydaspes fleet; hence N. may be counted among Alexander's non-Macedonian *hetairoi*. Identification with the envoy sent to Abisares in 326 is a strong possibility. Berve II 278–9 no. 566; Berve, *RE* XVII.1 (1936) 352 no. 4.

794 NIKOKLES

(Νικοκλῆς). Apparently the son of Timarchos (cf. Pliny, *HN* 11.167). Dynast of Paphos on Kypros and husband of Axiothea (Diod. 20.21.2; Polyaenus 8.48). N. was the successor of [Cha]ridamus, attested on the coinage of the mid-fourth century (see Head *HN*² 741; cf. Hill 1904: LXXVI). Berve II 406 no. 822 thinks he is the ruling member of the Kinyradai whom Alexander deposed (Plut. *Mor.* 340d). Since Plutarch gives a garbled version of the story of Straton and Abdalonymos, his comments may have no value for the affairs of Paphos. N. was a rival of Straton of Sidon (Ael. *VH* 7.2). In 321/0 he sided with Ptolemy against Perdikkas (Arr. *Succ.* 24.6). In 310, however, when it was discovered that he had secretly formed an alliance with Antigonos the One-Eyed, Menelaos, the brother of

Ptolemy, sent Argaios and Kallikrates against him. These ordered him to commit suicide, which he did; his wife Axiothea (no. 273) slew their daughters and committed suicide as well (Diod. 20.21.1–3; cf. Polyaenus 8.48). For the confusion of N. and Nikokreon see Gesche 1974. Stähelin, *RE* XVII.1 (1936) 351 no. 3; Berve II 279 no. 567; Bagnall 40–2.

795 NIKOKLES

(Νικοκλῆς). Greek. Sent by Alexander in 326 to negotiate the submission of the Indian dynast Abisares (Metz Epit. 55; cf. Diod. 17.90.4 and Curt. 9.1.7–8, neither of whom names N.). Nikokles appears to have rejoined Alexander on the way to the Hyphasis (thus Metz Epit. 65) or at the Akesines, when Alexander had returned from the Hyphasis (Arr. 5.29.4–5). Berve identifies him with the son of Pasikrates. Berve II 278–9 no. 566.

796 NIKOKLES

(Νικοκλῆς). Athenian (Kirchner 10892). Close friend of Phokion (Plut. *Phoc.* 17.3). N. was condemned to death by the Athenians on a charge of treason (in effect, anti-Macedonian activity) along with Phokion, Thoudippos, Hegemon and Pythokles (Plut. *Phoc.* 35.5: Demetrios of Phaleron, Kallimedon and Charikles were among those condemned *in absentia*). N. asked Phokion for the privilege of being the first to drink the hemlock prepared by the executioner (Plut. *Phoc.* 36.5).

797 NIKOKREON

(Νικοκρέων). Son and successor of Pnytagoras as king of Kypriot Salamis. Pnytagoras had defected to Alexander after Issos and served with his ships at Tyre (Arr. 2.22.2). In 332/1, when Alexander returned from Egypt to Phoinikia, N. is already attested as king of Salamis, he and Pasikrates of Soloi served as *choregoi* for dramatic competitions: N. supported Thessalos (Alexander's favorite, who was defeated in the contest) and Pasikrates, Athenodoros (Plut. *Alex.* 29.2–4). He was also insulted by Anaxarchos, whom he later captured and put to death (Diog. Laert. 9.58–9; cf. Plut. *Alex.* 28.4; Val. Max. 3.3 ext. 4; Plut. *Mor.* 449e; cf. Cic. *Nat. D.* 3.82 and *Tusc.* 2.52). He supported Ptolemy against Perdikkas in 321/0 (Arr. *Succ.* 24.6), and remained a supporter of Ptolemy (Diod. 19.59.1, 62.5), who made him *strategos* of Kypros (Diod. 19.79.5), until his death in 311/10 (*Marmor Parium, FGrH* 239 F17). N. issued coins with the legends BA NI and BA NK (ΒΑΣΙΛΕΩΣ ΝΙΚΟΚΡΕΟΝΤΟΣ). He was honored at Argos (*IG* IV 583) and made offerings at Delos during his reign (see Bagnall 39 with n.4). He is wrongly identified by Machon *ap.* Athen. 8.349e as the husband of Axiothea (no. 273; see the long but misguided discussion in Hill I 161 n.1 and a useful corrective by Gesche 1974). Berve II 279 no. 568; *PP* no. 15059; Bagnall 39–40.

798 NIKOMACHOS

(Νικόμαχος). Brother of Kebalinos and lover of Dimnos (Diod. 17.79.1–2; Curt. 6.7.2, 16; Plut. *Alex.* 49.3–4) of Chalaistra, whose conspiracy set the stage for the so-called Philotas affair. N. was low born—Curtius calls him *exoletus* (6.7.2, 8) and *scortum* (6.7.33), that is, a male prostitute—but despite his station in life, he retained a modicum of decency (Curt. 6.7.13). Dimnos attempted to involve him in the plot and revealed the identities of the conspirators. N. would have no part in it and reported all the details to his brother (Curt. 6.7.2–16; Plut. *Alex.* 49.4). N. remained in his tent while Kebalinos attempted to bring the matter to the King's attention (Curt. 6.7.16); two days later he was summoned by the King and corroborated Kebalinos' information (Curt. 6.8.1–2). N. later gave testimony before the Macedonian assembly (Curt. 6.9.7; cf. Diod. 17.79.6), to which Philotas later responded, questioning N.'s reliability (Curt. 6.10.5–7, 16). But ultimately, Philotas, and those named by N.—as well as Calis, who had not been named but confessed—were executed (Curt. 6.11.37–8). It appears that N. himself escaped punishment. Berve II 279–80 no. 569.

799 NIKOMEDES

(Νικομήδης). Son of Aristandros, from Kos. Brother of Kleumachos. An important official at Antigonos' court (as is clear from the fact that twenty-six foreign states voted him honors: *I. di Cos* ED 71a–g; 162; 203; Paschidis 361 n.3 for details), though he clearly acted as a diplomat rather than a military officer (thus Paschidis 87 n.4, rejecting Billow's view (411) that he participated in Demetrios' campaign of 307). The inscription on the base of his mother's statue (Paton and Hicks no. 227) tells us that her name was Olympias. The honors for N. fail to mention Demetrios, and it appears that he was not part of the Besieger's entourage. N. clearly facilitated good relations between the various cities and Antigonos (cf. Sherwin-White 87). Chionides proposed a decree honoring him with citizenship and a golden crown in the aftermath of Chionides' embassy to Antigonos in 305, and probably for service related to that embassy (cf. *IG* II² 1492B; *Syll*³ 334; Paschidis 87 n.1). Billows 411–12 no. 82 with earlier literature; Sherwin-White 86–8, 122 n.217; Osborne, *Naturalization* no. D51; Paschidis 361–5 D8.

800 NIKON

(Νίκων). Runaway slave of Krateros, N. was recaptured, presumably in Persia, by Peukestas, who received written praise from Alexander (Plut. *Alex.* 42.1). The episode seems to have occurred in 324, after Peukestas' appointment as satrap and before Krateros left Opis with the discharged veterans. N.'s capture and return to his master was apparently an example of the implementation and effectiveness of the slave insurance scheme of Antimenes of Rhodes, who had replaced Harpalos as financial overseer (Pseudo-Aristotle, *Oecon.* 2.2.34b; Garlan 1988, 194–5). What punishment was meted out to N. is not stated, though it was doubtless severe. Berve II 280 no. 571.

801 NIKOSTRATOS

(Νικόστρατος). Son of Nikophantos. Probably from Kalymna (*Barr. Atl.* 61 D/E3/4). Testified in support of honors voted for the Antigonid official Moschion (no. 755), late fourth century (*TitCal* 17). Since Moschion was honored for his treatment of Kalymnian troops stationed at Pogla (south of Kretopolis in Asia Minor), N. was probably a Kalymnian in Moschion's service. He is otherwise unknown.
Paschidis 381 D21.

NIKOSTRATOS. See SOSTRATOS.

802 NIPHATES

(Νιφάτης). For the name see Justi 229. Prominent Persian. N. was one of the commanders at the Granikos (Arr. 1.12.8); he was killed in the engagement (Arr. 1.16.3). Berve II 280 no. 573; Shayegan 113 no. 71.

803 NISOS

(Νίσος). Son of Alketas II (no. 62) and brother of Esioneus (no. 426). When Alketas was murdered (probably in 307) because his rule was too harsh, the Epeirots put to death N. and Esioneus, who were still children (Diod. 19.89.3; cf. Paus. 1.11.5). Two other children of Alketas, Teukros and Alexander were already grown up and probably not borne by the same mother. **Stemma IIa**.

804 NITHAPHON

(Νιθάφων). Kypriot. Son of King Pnytagoras of Salamis. In 332 or 331 he appears to have joined Alexander's entourage, along with his younger brother Nikokreon, perhaps as hostages. He is attested in India as a trierarch of the Hydaspes fleet (Arr. *Ind.* 18.8). Nothing else is known of his career. Berve II 280 no. 572.

805 NYSA

(Νύσα). According to Steph. Byz. s.v. Ἀντιόχεια, N. was a wife of Antiochos I, who named a city in Margiana after her. She is otherwise unattested, but it is possible that she was Antiochos' first wife—he was at least thirty when he married his stepmother, Stratonike—and perhaps of Indian descent. Strabo (15.2.9 C724) and Appian (*Syr.* 55.282) mention a treaty between Seleukos and Sandrokottos (Chandragupta) which seems to have been sealed by political marriage (κῆδος, ἐπιγαμία). Although this has been interpreted by scholars as involving the marriage of a daughter of Sandrokottos to Seleukos (hence Macurdy 77: "a marriage of Seleucus with the daughter of the Hindoo king") or the latter's daughter to the Indian ruler. N. may have been the Mauryan king's daughter and she became Antiochos' wife in 304/3. N. would thus have been a sister of Amitrochates (Bindusara), and this might explain the contacts between him and Antiochos (Strabo 2.1.9 C70; Athen. 14.652f). Grainger, *SPG* 52 no. 2 (treating her as unhistorical); Ogden 120 (somewhat convoluted); Bouché-Leclercq, *Séleucides* 73, 542; Aulbach §7.2.1.2. **Stemma XI**.

O

806 OCHOS

(Ὦχος). Son of Dareios III and Stateira, his name occurs only in Curtius (4.11.6, 14.22) and the *Fragmentum Sabbaiticum* (*FGrH* 151 F1 §5). Born in 339/8 (he was in his sixth year at the end of 333: Curt. 3.11.24; Diod. 17.38.2). O. accompanied his father to Issos, where he was captured, along with his mother, sisters and grandmother (Diod. 17.36.2, 37.3–38.3; Curt. 3.11.24–12.26; cf. 4.14.22; Arr. 2.11.9). Alexander and Hephaistion admired his courage, which they deemed greater than that of his father (Diod. 17.38.2; cf. Curt. 3.12.26). Justin neither mentions his capture nor includes him in the terms of the diplomatic negotiations that occurred between the winter of 333/2 and summer 331 (cf. Curt. 4.11.6, where Dareios proposes that Alexander retain O. as a hostage in exchange for a peace settlement); but the omission of O. can be attributed to imprecise abbreviation of Trogus. O. was left behind in Sousa in 330, with his grandmother and sisters (Diod. 17.67.1; Curt. 5.2.17). What became of him we do not know. If he did not die of natural causes before 324/3, he may have been murdered shortly before, or soon after, Alexander's death: certainly, the political motives behind the murder of Stateira and her sister by Rhoxane and Perdikkas (Plut. *Alex.* 77.6) must have pertained to O. as well. Berve II 409–10 no. 833. **Stemma III**; Shayegan 113 no. 72.

807 OKRANES

(Ὀκράνης). For the name see Justi 232. One of the commanders of the rebellious Medes, and thus probably a former officer of Peithon, whom Antigonos had put to death in 316 and replaced with Orontobates (19.46.4–5). O. and Meleagros and Menoitas led the revolt in Media; at first they harassed Orontobates and his general Hippostratos (19.47.2) but finally they were cornered in difficult terrain and defeated. O. and Meleagros were killed (Diod. 19.47.4).

OLKIAS. See HOLKIAS.

808 OLYMPIAS

(Ὀλυμπιάς). Epeirot princess. Daughter of Neoptolemos; sister of Troas (Justin 7.6.10–11) and Alexander I of Epeiros (Justin 8.6.4–5; 12.2.1; 9.7.5, 7; cf. Diod. 16.72.1; 17.3.14–16; 19.51.6; Livy 8.24.17); niece and sister-in-law of Arybbas (Justin 7.6.10–11; Diod. 16.72.1). Born sometime after 375 (Carney 2006, 12). Descended from Pyrrhos son of Achilles and, on her mother's side, from the Trojan prince Helenos (Tzetzes, *ad Lycophr.* 1439 = Theopompos, *FGrH* 115 F355); hence one of the Aiakidai. Favorinus *ap.* Jul. Valer. 1.7 (frg. 49) says O.'s mother was called Anasatia (for the Aiakidai see Paus. 1.9.8, 1.11.1; Justin 12.16.3; Plut. *Alex.* 2; Plut. *Pyrrh.* 1; Hesychius s.v. Πυρριάδαι; Diod. 17.1.1). Leonidas, Alexander the Great's tutor, was also a kinsman (Plut. *Alex.* 5.7). As a child she was called Polyxena and then, at marriage, Myrtale; later in life she was also known as O.

and Stratonike (Plut. *Mor.* 401a–b; Justin 9.7.13; for the origin and order of the names see Heckel 1981d). In 357 she married Philip II, whom she had met as a child on Samothrake (Plut. *Alex.* 2.2; cf. Curt. 8.1.26; Himerius *ap.* Phot. p.367a [ed. Bekker]; Justin 7.6.10–11; Satyros *ap.* Athen. 13.557c; on the background see Greenwalt 2008), to whom she bore first Alexander on 20 July 356 (Plut. *Alex.* 3.5 with Hamilton 7. See also Plut. *Mor.* 105a–b; Satyros *ap.* Athen. 13.557c; Arr. 4.10.2; Justin 9.5.9, 9.7.1–2, 11.11.3–5, 12.14.3, 13.6.12, 14.5.8–10; Plut. *Alex.* 3.4–5; Gell. *NA* 6.1.1, 13.4.1–3; Athen. 14.659f–660a; Paus. 4.14.7; Lucian, *Alexander* 7; Ael. *VH* 12.64, 13.30; Arr. *Succ.* 1.21; Curt. 5.2.22; 9.6.26; 10.5.30; Metz Epit. 115–16) and later Kleopatra (Diod. 16.91.4; Satyros *ap.* Athen. 13.557c); App. *Syr.* 54.275 wrongly calls Arrhidaios O.'s son. Since the news of Alexander's birth coincided with that of Philip's Olympic victory, it may be at this point and for this reason that Myrtale's name was changed to Olympias (Plut. *Alex.* 3.8; cf. Plut. *Mor.* 105a–b; Justin 12.16.6; Macurdy 24). Her pedigree is celebrated in an anonymous epigram (Plut. *Mor.* 747f–748a; cf. Diod. 19.51.6). Stories that she slept with Zeus (= Amun), who disguised himself as a snake, were doubtless fabricated after Alexander's visit to Siwah (Plut. *Alex.* 3.3–4; cf. Gell. *NA* 13.4.13; Arr. 4.10.2; cf. Cic. *de divin* 2.135; see also Ogden 2011, 29–56). She allegedly told Alexander before his departure for Asia about τὸ περὶ τὴν τέκνωσιν ἀπόρρητον. But she was said to have publicly denied stories of a liaison with the god in order to avert Hera's jealousy (Plut. *Alex.* 3.3–4). That she was a devotee of exotic cults and maenadism (Plut. *Alex.* 2.8–9; Athen. 14.659f–660a; cf. Douris, *FGrH* 76 F52 = Athen. 13.560f) is probably true. She is described as high-minded (Plut. *Mor.* 243d), jealous and brooding (Plut. *Alex.* 9.5: δύσζηλος καὶ βαρύθυμος). As a mother she was domineering and interfering, yet she retained her son's love until the end (cf. Plut. *Alex.* 39.13; Curt. 5.2.22; 9.2.26; 10.5.30) and corresponded with him during his absence (Athen. 14.659f–660a; Arr. 6.1.4–5; Metz Epit. 87; Plut. *Alex.* 39.7–8; cf. her complaints about Antipatros, below; also Plut. *Mor.* 180d; for her correspondence, Zumetikos 1894). Her concern about her son's apparent lack of interest in women caused her (in consultation with Philip) to encourage him to have sexual relationships with the courtesan Kallixeina (Hieronymos of Rhodes, citing Theophrastos *ap.* Athen. 10.435a). Philip's letters to O. were intercepted but unopened by the Athenians (Plut. *Mor.* 799e; Plut. *Demetr.* 22.2); and the fact that in 341 Anaxinus of Oreos was making purchases for O. in Athens (Dem. 18.137; cf. Aesch. 3.223) shows that her relationship with Philip endured well beyond the births of their two children.

Although jealous of Philip's other wives, she appears to have been complimentary about the charms of Nikesipolis (Plut. *Mor.* 141b–c). Her rivalry with Kleopatra, the niece of Attalos, will have had to do with her concerns about Alexander's rights of inheritance (Arr. 3.6.5; Athen. 13.557d–e; Plut. *Alex.* 9.6–10), but the story that she was "divorced" on the grounds of adultery (*stuprum*) is a fabrication (Justin 9.5.9), as is the claim that she corrupted the mind of young Arrhidaios (Philip's son by Philine) by giving him drugs (Plut. *Alex.* 77.8). Nevertheless, Arr. 3.6.5, speaking of the dishonoring of O., may well refer to Kleopatra's recognition as Philip's "Queen" (Heckel 1978a). After the quarrel of Alexander and Attalos on the occasion of Philip's wedding to Kleopatra (Athen. 13.557d; Plut. *Alex.* 9.6–10; Justin 9.7.3–4), O. took refuge with her brother Alexander I of Epeiros, whom she tried unsuccessfully to incite to war against her husband (Justin 9.7.5, 7; Plut. *Alex.* 9.11). But Philip's decision to marry his (and O.'s) daughter, Kleopatra, to Alexander I was intended not, as some scholars have claimed, to drive a wedge between brother and sister but rather to effect a reconciliation with his Epeirot family. The view that O. did not return for her daughter's wedding, and that the marriage of Alexander I and Kleopatra was directed against her, is perverse. Plut. *Mor.* 179c is certainly right when he claims that Philip was reconciled with both the son and his mother (διηλλάγη πρὸς αὐτούς). Nevertheless, O. was not fully reconciled with her husband and encouraged Alexander to believe that his father meant to cut him out of the succession; for thus she appears to have depicted Philip's plans to marry Arrhidaios to the daughter of Pixodaros (Plut. *Alex.* 10.1). She was also believed to have incited the assassin Pausanias, who had been humiliated by Attalos (Justin 9.7.2). That she favored and perhaps encouraged Philip's assassination is credible but there can be no proof (Justin 9.7.1–2, 8; Plut. *Alex.* 10.5); accounts that she openly acknowledged her role are doubtless false (Justin 9.7.10–14). On the other hand, it is quite plausible that she brought about the murder of Kleopatra and her young child (Plut. *Alex.* 10.7; Justin 9.7.12; Paus. 8.7.7). Alexander was distressed by this action, if not for personal, then certainly for political reasons (Plut. *Alex.* 10.8; cf. Burstein 1982b; also Howe 2015a).

Of her activities in Macedonia during her son's absence we know little: she is said to have sent to her son the cook Pelignas (Athen. 14.659f), to have sent him a written warning against Alexander Lynkestes (Diod. 17.32.1; cf. Curt. 7.1.6; Abramenko 1992 implausibly argues that the "mother of the King" is Ada); she made a dedication to Hygeia in Athens in 333 (Hyper. *Eux.* 19); and, in 332/1, she objected to the recruitment by Amyntas son of Andromenes of some youths from her court (Curt. 7.1.37–8). She may already have been in Epeiros when she made the dedication of spoils from Gaugamela at Delphi in 331/0 (*Syll*³ 252: thus Dittenberger 447 n.3 *Matrem Epiri morantem has coronas . . . dedicavisse*). Certainly it was around this time that she quarreled with Antipatros (perhaps after his return from the Peloponnese) and withdrew to Epeiros, sending Kleopatra back to Macedonia at some point after 330 (*LM* 87–8; 96–7; Diod. 18.49.4; Paus. 1.11.3; Plut. *Alex.* 68.4–5; cf. 77.2; Arr. 7.12.6–7; Justin 12.14.3; Hyper. *Eux.* 25; cf. Livy 8.24.27). Alexander in India was said to have hoped that O. would be given divine honors after her death (Curt. 9.6.26).

After her son's death (for her grief see Ael. *VH* 13.30), she could not refrain from meddling in the affairs of the Successors: after inducing Kleopatra to offer herself in marriage to Leonnatos (who promptly met his death in the Lamian War), she sent her to Perdikkas (Arr. *Succ.* 1.21; Justin 13.6.4–5, 11–13). Although this scheme also came to naught, she soon received an appeal from Polyperchon that she return to Macedonia and assume the *epimeleia* and *prostasia* of Alexander IV (Diod. 18.49.4, 57.2; hence also her favorable treatment in the *Last Days and Testament*: *LM* 115–16, 122; cf. Heckel 1988, 52; cf. Baynham 1998b); if Polyperchon imagined that O. would be content to act as a mere figurehead, he was mistaken. O. wrote first to Eumenes for his advice (Diod. 18.58.2–3; cf. 18.62.2) and received a reply that urged caution and suggested that she remain in Epeiros for the time being (Diod. 18.58.4; but cf. Eumenes' stratagem at Polyaenus 4.83). O. did, however, play a role in the struggle between Polyperchon and Kassandros, writing a letter to Nikanor, the commander of Mounychia, ordering him to restore the fort and Peiraieus to the Athenians (Diod. 18.65.1–2), but her orders were disregarded (Diod. 18.74.1). With the help of her nephew Aiakides, she prepared to return to Macedonia, and met her opponent Adea-Eurydike at Euia (Paus. 1.11.3–4; Douris *ap.* Athen. 13.560f = *FGrH* 76 F52; Justin 14.5.1–10; Diod. 19.11.1–8; Ael. *VH* 13.36; Plut. *Alex.* 77.2); her very presence induced the Macedonians to desert, but she followed up the victory by putting to death

Philip III Arrhidaios (Justin 14.5.10; Diod. 19.11.4–5) and Adea-Eurydike (Justin 14.5.10; Diod. 19.11.6–7; Ael. *VH* 13.36: Diodorus and Aelian both mention the story that O. sent Adea a dagger, a rope and some poison and told her to choose the instrument of her death; she decided to hang herself with her own girdle), and taking vengeance on her political enemies (Diod. 19.11.8–9, 35.1; cf. Paus. 1.11.4). But the tide soon turned against Polyperchon and his supporters (Aristonous and Monimos), and O. and her entourage, which included Thessalonike, Rhoxane, Alexander IV, and his betrothed, Deidameia (Diod. 19.35.5; Justin 14.6.2–3), were besieged at Pydna (Diod. 19.36.1–2; Justin 14.6.4), waiting in vain for help from Aiakides and Polyperchon (Diod. 19.36.2, 5–6). An escape attempt apparently miscarried (Polyaenus 4.11.3; Diod. 19.50.4) and, on the point of starvation (Diod. 19.49.1–50.2), O. surrendered to Kassandros on the promise of her own personal safety (Diod. 19.50.5; Justin 14.6.5). This was, however, disregarded and Kassandros, after first gaining approval for the act from the assembled Macedonians, had her put to death by relatives of her victims (Diod. 19.51; Justin 14.6.6–12). For O. on "coinage," see Dahmen 2007, Pl. 23, 26.4–5, 28.1, 28.4. Berve II 283–8 no. 581; Strasburger, *RE* s.v. "Olympias (5)"; Macurdy 22–44; Carney 2006 and 1987a, 1993; O'Neil 1999; Carney 62–7, 85–8, 119–23 and *LexAM* 354–9; Aulbach §4.1. For alleged role in Philip's death see Develin 1981, Heckel 1981c, Willrich 1899b, and Heckel, Howe and Müller 2017. Stemmata I, IIa–b.

809 OLYMPIAS

(Ὀλυμπιάς). Daughter of Pyrrhos and Antigone, sister of Ptolemy (Justin 28.1.1; Beloch IV² 2.148), for whom one of her sons was named. According to Justin (28.1.1), she married her brother Alexander (the son of Lanassa; *germano fratre* need not mean "full brother," but "her own brother") and bore two sons, Pyrrhos and Ptolemy. A daughter named Phthia married Demetrios II of Macedon in 239/8 (Justin 28.1.2; cf. Beloch IV² 2.149; Seibert 1967, 37–8; D'Agostini 2019, 13–16, 20–2) and became the mother of Philip V (Walbank, *Philip V* 9–10). Corradi 1912; Sandberger 174 no. 62.

810 OLYMPIODOROS

(Ὀλυμπιόδωρος). Prominent Athenian (Kirchner 11388), who makes his first appearance in the late fourth century but whose most notable services belong to the period after Ipsos. Most of what we know about him comes from Pausanias. In 306 he was sent by sea as an ambassador to Aitolia, where he won their support against Kassandros, and he soon repelled a Macedonian attack on Eleusis (Paus. 1.26.3; Paschidis 133 dates this to 306/5; but see Habicht 1997, 75 with n.26). As general, he brought military aid which allowed the Elateians to withstand Kassandros' siege (Paus. 10.18.7; 1.26.3, the Elateians set up a bronze statue to O. at Delphi), but the date is again disputed and the episode may date to the period between 301 and 297. Habicht has now argued that Pausanias' claim that O. "saved" Peiraieus (1.26.3) belongs to a point before 295 (and not 287, as some have thought); he did not free the port but rather saved it when the Macedonians tried to capture it (Habicht 1985, 101; full discussion in Habicht 1979, 95–112) O. was a leader of the democratic party, clearly trusted by Demetrios, who in 294/3 and 293/2 must have been behind his illegal second election to the archonship (Habicht 1997, 96 calls him Demetrios' "righthand man"). He was honored with a statues on the acropolis and in the prytaneion, as well as a with a portrait at Eleusis (Paus. 1.26.3–4). *LGPN* II s.v. Ὀλυμπιόδωρος no. 17; Ferguson 114–57; Habicht 1997, 75, 90–6; Paschidis 133–9 A44.

811 OMARES

(Ὠμάρης). Persian. Commander of 20,000 mercenaries at the Granikos River (Arr. 1.14.4; cf. 1.16.3). The figures are problematic. It is hard to imagine that 18,000 Greeks could have been slaughtered with miniscule losses on the Macedonian side (see Parke 1933, 180–1; cf. Grote 1913, 18 with n.1). O. died in the battle (Arr. 1.16.3). Berve II 409 no. 832; Shayegan 113 no. 73.

812 OMBRION

(Ὀμβρίων). Kretan. O. was appointed toxarches by Alexander in Egypt in 331 (Arr. 3.5.6) to replace the Macedonian Antiochos. At Gaugamela we find the Macedonian archers commanded by a certain Brison (Arr. 3.12.2). Neither toxarches is heard of again and Bosworth I 302 suspects a textual problem in Arr. 3.12.2 and that ὧν Βρίσων is a corruption of ὧν <Ὀμ>βρίων. The emendation is ingenious, and, although the Kretan origin of O. would seem to weigh against this view, it was in fact another Macedonian whom O. had earlier replaced. Berve II 288 no. 582; Launey 1164.

813 ONESIKRITOS

(Ὀνησίκριτος). Greek from Aigina or Astypalaia (Arr. *Ind.* 18.9; Ael. *NA* 16.39; Diog. Laert. 6.84). Son of Philiskos (Arr. *Ind.* 18.9), father of the younger Philiskos and Androsthenes The elder Philiskos (no. 925) was said to have been a teacher (*grammatodidaskalos*) of Alexander (*Suda* Φ 359), but this may be an invention based on the fact that O. wrote a work on the education of Alexander. O. is said to have sent first one, then the other, of his sons to Diogenes of Sinope; both fell under the philosopher's spell. Finally, O. too became a student of Diogenes (Diog. Laert. 6.75–6, Ὀνησίκριτόν τινα is an odd way of designating the famous historian; cf. Plut. *Alex.* 65.2; Plut. *Mor.* 331e; Strabo 15.1.65 C716). The story, if it is true, means that O. must have been around forty in the mid-330s and in his fifties when he participated in Alexander's naval expedition down the Indos and on to Mesopotamia. What O. did in the years before the Indian campaign is unknown, although it seems he was with the expedition from the start (Diog. Laert. 6.84). At Taxila, he was sent to Kalanos and Dandamis (Onesikritos, *FGrH* 134 F17a = Strabo 15.1.63–5; cf. F17b = Plut. *Alex.* 65.3). When the Hydaspes fleet was formed, he was appointed helmsman of Alexander's ship (Arr. 7.5.6, 20.9; Arr. *Ind.* 18.9; and, perhaps, by virtue of this position, *archikybernetes* or "chief helmsman"; Strabo 15.1.28, 2.4; Plut. *Alex.* 66.3; cf. Pliny, *HN* 9.7; Arr. 6.2.3 criticizes O. for falsely claiming to be *nauarchos*; see Hauben 1987b). It appears that O. had the naval (technical) expertise that Nearchos lacked, and once the ocean voyage began Nearchos was in charge of the direction of the expedition and the command of the forces, whereas O. was responsible for the safety of the ships (the disagreement at Maketa is one of policy: Arr. *Ind.* 32.9–13). Pliny, *HN* 6.81 calls him *classis praefectus*; cf. *HN* 2.185: *dux*. These are, then, only slight exaggerations of O.'s role. Pliny, *HN* 9.6 refers to *Alexandri Magni classium praefecti*, clearly referring to Nearchos and O. See also Curt. 9.10.3; 10.1.10. In 324, O. and Nearchos each received a golden crown for their achievements (Arr. 7.5.6; Arr. *Ind.* 42.9, which derives from Nearchos, makes no mention of O.). Very soon after Alexander's death, he wrote that the King had been poisoned—perhaps his aim was to discredit his political enemies—though he did not name the perpetrators of the crime for fear of reprisals; but he no doubt thought that most contemporaries were familiar with the names of those who attended Medeios' dinner party, at which the King became ill (*LM* 97). How long O. lived is uncertain: Plut. *Alex.* 46.4 speaks of O. reading his *History* to Lysimachos, "who was already king," which implies that he was still alive in 306. O.'s connections with Lysimachos reflect a shared interest in philosophy (cf. Lund 8–10, who also cautions that "Justin's emphasis on philosophy as a guiding force in [Lysimachos'] life is at least exaggerated," 10). As an historian (see Jacoby, *FGrH* 134; Brown, *Onesicritus*; Pearson 83–111), O. modeled himself on Xenophon, writing an *Education of Alexander* to rival Xenophon's *Cyropaedia*, though his style was said to have been inferior (Diog. Laert. 6.84); he was noted for his flattery (Lucian, *How to Write History* 40) but not for his veracity (Plut. *Alex.* 46.4; Strabo 15.1.28; cf. 11.1.9; Gell. *NA* 9.4.1–3; Arr. *Ind* 3.6, 6.8). Xen. *Cyr.* 8.7 includes what amounts to the Testament of Kyros, which was no doubt read by O., who is known to have recorded the last days of Alexander (*LM* 97 = *FGrH* 134 F37). It may be that the political pamphlet on the *Last Days and Testament* was inspired by O.'s imitation of Xenophon (Heckel 2007c). Berve II 288–90 no. 583; Brown, *Onesicritus*; Pearson 83–111; Winiarczyk 2007, with extensive literature; Müller, *LexAM* 364–5.

814 ONOMARCHOS

('Ονόμαρχος). Officer or henchman of Antigonos the One-Eyed, O. was probably of Greek origin. He was in charge of those who kept watch on Eumenes in his final days—after the battle of Gabiene—and treated Eumenes' query about his impending fate with derision and condescension (Plut. *Eum* 18.7–9; Nepos, *Eum.* 11. 3–4). Nothing else is known about him. Billows 413 no. 84.

815 ONOMASTORIDAS

('Ονομαστορίδας). Spartan ambassador to Dareios III, sent out in all likelihood in connection with the activities of Agis III in Greece. He was captured, along with Kallikratidas, Monimos, and Pausippos, soon after the death of Dareios in 330 (Arr. 3.24.4). Curt. 3.13.15 mistakenly places his capture at Damaskos in 333. Berve II 290–1 no. 584; Poralla no. 580; Hofstetter 140 no. 240.

816 OPHELLAS

('Οφέλλας). Olynthian of unknown family. O. is attested only once, in [Arist.] *Oecon.* 2.35 p. 1353a, who reports that he was guilty of extortion in Athribis in the southern Nile Delta, perhaps in the period shortly before Alexander's death when Kleomenes was supposed to have been guilty of financial mismanagement. Identification with O. son of Seilenos is impossible. Nothing else is known about him. Berve II 297 no. 599; Wilcken 1901, 195–6.

817 OPHELLAS

('Οφέλλας). For the name see Hoffmann 199. Son of Seilenus; Macedonian from Pella (Arr. *Ind.* 18.3, Arr. *Succ.* 1.17). Of his career under Alexander, we know virtually nothing, except for his role as trierarch in 326 (cf. Diod. 20.40.1 for his service under Alexander). He appears to have gone to Egypt with Ptolemy in 323. When Thibron (no. 1124) made his bid to control Kyrene, some of the well-to-do exiles appealed to Ptolemy, who sent O.

as *strategos* to the aid of the city with a large force of infantry and ships (Diod. 18.21.7; Arr. *Succ* 1.17); he defeated the Kyreneans and captured Thibron, whom he handed over to the people of Teucheira to torture (Diod. 18.21.8–9; Arr. *Succ.* 1.18). Kyrene became part of the Ptolemaic kingdom, probably with O. as its governor. But we hear nothing about him until 309/8, when Agathokles of Syracuse sent Orthon to Kyrene to urge O. to join in the subjugation of the Carthaginians. The alliance appealed to Thibron, who aspired to greater power, especially since Agathokles relinquished any claims to Libya (Diod. 20.40.1–4; Justin 22.7.5, saying that O. initiated the alliance). O. recruited mercenaries from the Athenians—he had married Euthydike (no. 461), daughter of Miltiades, a descendant of the famous general (Diod. 20.40.5; Plut. *Demetr.* 14.1; see Davies 309), by whom he had a son named Miltiades (*IG* II² 6630; Kirchner 10211)—and other Greek states (Diod. 20.40.6–7). With a large army he marched westward (Diod. 20.41.1–2), suffering great hardships along the way and finally linking up with Agathokles' forces (Diod. 20.42.1–2). But Agathokles betrayed O. and, claiming that he was plotting against him, attacked the Kyrenean force, killed O. and took over his army (Diod. 20.42.3–5; cf. 20.43.3–4, 70.3–4; cf. Justin 22.7.5–6; *Suda* O 994; cf. *Suda* Δ 431). There is a story that O. was infatuated with Agathokles' son, Herakleides, whom Agathokles had sent to him as hostage and a distraction, knowing that he was fond of boys (Polyaenus 5.3.4; Justin 22.7.6 says he adopted the boy). Thus caught off guard, O. was attacked by Agathokles. His death occurred in 308. Berve II 296 no. 598; Gude no. 102 (confused); *PP* no. 15062; Launey 1171; Hauben 77–8 no. 28; Bagnall 25–6.

818 ORDANES

('Ορδάνης. Justi 351, "Wardan (1)"; Curt. calls him Ozines). Persian leader who had incited rebellion in Drangiana or Arachosia. He was captured and brought to Alexander by Krateros, who had returned from India via the Bolan pass. The King learned of the arrest of O. (and Zariaspes) while he was in Gedrosia; Krateros and his captives rejoined Alexander in Karmania (Arr. 6.27.3; Curt. 9.10.19; 10.1.9), where O. and Zariaspes were executed. Berve II 293–4 no. 590; Shayegan 114 no. 74, also 116 no. 84.

819 ORONTES

('Ορόντης). A Persian noble, descended from Hydarnes, one of the Seven (thus Strabo 11.14.15 C531). The family ruled Armenia from at least the time of Artaxerxes II (Xen. *Anab.* 3.4.17; cf. 4.3.4; Lehmann-Haupt 127) until Antiochos III. Hence O. is probably to be identified as the satrap of Armenia under Dareios III (he may, in fact, have succeeded Dareios in this position; Justin 10.3.4; cf. Osborne 1973, 520), commanding the satrapal contingent at Gaugamela (Arr. 3.8.5; Mithraustes, who is named with him, appears to have led the infantry; cf. Berve II 295). It appears that, after the battle, he escaped to his satrapy, which Alexander assigned to Mithrenes, the former citadel commander of Sardis (Arr. 3.16.5; Diod. 17.64.6; Curt. 5.1.44). But the latter is not heard of again, and may have perished in an unsuccessful attempt to wrest the territory from O., who is found again in charge of Armenia in 317 (Diod. 19.23.3; Polyaenus 4.8.3). Bosworth I 315–16 thinks that he may have surrendered to Alexander soon after Gaugamela, and that the friendship between Peukestas and O. (Polyaenus 4.8.3) developed in the years 331–324, when O. was at the Court of Alexander. But it seems not unlikely that Peukestas, satrap of Persis, came to know the most important members of the Persian aristocracy. In all likelihood,

Armenia, which was bypassed by the Macedonian army, was never part of Alexander's empire. The possible awarding of the satrapy to Neoptolemos in 323 (Dexippos, *FGrH* 100 F8 §6; cf. Plut. *Eum.* 4.1; 5.2; Briant 1973, 152 n. 8, thinks he was *strategos* rather than *satrapes*) may have been contingent upon his ability to conquer the territory (cf. Plut. *Eum.* 4.1; 5.2). Neoptolemos created havoc in the satrapy (Plut. *Eum.* 4.1), but O. appears to have regained his position after the former's death in 320 BC. Nothing further is known about him. Berve wrongly asserts that he married the daughter of Artaxerxes II, Rhodogune (Plut. *Artox.* 27.4; cf. Xen. *Anab.* 2.4.8), who may, however, have been his mother (cf. Beloch III² 2.141, dating O.'s birth *c.*386) or grandmother (Judeich 225). Beloch argues that Artaxerxes II (born *c.*428–426; cf. III² 2.131) could not have had a daughter of marriageable age before about 390; on the other hand, Deinon, *FGrH* 690 F20a–b, gives Artaxerxes' age at the time of his death (359/8) as 94 (*ap.* [Lucian], *Macrob.* 15) or 86 (*ap.* Plut. *Artox.* 30.9). Berve II 295 no. 593; Justi 235 no. 7; Osborne 1973; Bosworth I 315–16; Shayegan 114 no. 75.

820 ORONTOBATES

(Ὀροντοβάτης, Ὀροντοπάτης). The name appears in Arrian and Curtius as Orontobates, but coin-legends from Karia preserve the form Ῥοοντοπάτης, that is, Orontopates (*BMC Caria* LXXXIV; Head, *HN*² 630). A prominent Persian, O. was a son-in-law of Pixodaros (no. 963), who had usurped the satrapy of Karia (Arr. 1.23.8); he was thus the husband of the younger Ada, who had at one point been offered to Arrhidaios. O. was given charge of the satrapy, probably as joint ruler with Pixodaros (Krumbholz 1883, 83) by Dareios III until the death of Pixodaros in 335, and he defended it, and its chief city, Halikarnassos, with the help of Memnon, even after Alexander had returned Karia to Ada (Arr. 1.23.8; cf. Diod. 17.24.2). After a spirited but unsuccessful defense of Halikarnassos, O. was bottled up in the island citadel of the city. He retained control of this fortress, Myndos, Kaunos, Thera, Kallipolis, Kos, and Triopium, but he was defeated in a pitched battle by Ptolemy and Asandros, losing 700 infantry and 50 cavalry, along with 1,000 men who were captured (Arr. 2.5.7). Most of his territories were recaptured as a result of the battle (Curt. 3.7.4), but the Persians retained Halikarnassos and Kos. Possibly, O. joined Dareios after the collapse of the Persian counter-offensive in the Aegean, but the commander attested at Gaugamela (Arr. 3.8.5; Curt. 4.12.7) need not be the same man; *contra* Berve II 296 nn.1–2. Berve II 295–6 no. 594; Shayegan 114 no. 76.

821 ORONTOBATES

(Ὀροντοβάτης, Ὀροντοπάτης). Prominent Persian or Mede. O. appears as one of three commanders of the forces from the lands that bordered on the Red Sea (i.e., the Persian Gulf); the other two were Ariobarzanes and Orxines (Arr. 3.8.5; but Curt. 4.12.7–8 says O. and Ariobarzanes commanded the Persians, Mardians and Sogdianoi, all under the supreme command of Orxines). Atkinson I 404 believes that Curtius refers to the "Persian Mardians" and not those of the Caspian area, but this does not explain the presence of Sogdianian troops in the contingent of troops of the three commanders, two of whom (Orxines and Ariobarzanes) are explicitly associated with Persis. Bosworth (I 290–1) assumes that something has dropped out of Arrian's text, but even this does not solve all the problems. Berve's identification (II 295–6 no. 594) of O. with the son-in-law of Pixodaros, who thus returned to Persia after the failures in Asia Minor, is mere speculation. If he commanded Mardians from the Caspian area, he may be identical with Antigonos' satrap of Media (no. 822).

822 ORONTOBATES

('Ορον τοβάτης, 'Ορον τοπάτης). A Mede (Diod. 19.46.5: 'Ορον τοβάτην Μῆδον), found in the service of Antigonos in 316; he was probably one of the Medes in Peithon's contingent who remained loyal to Antigonos. O. may be identical with the commander attested at Gaugamela (Arr. 3.8.5; Curt. 4.12.7); for it is doubtful that Antigonos placed his faith in an untried leader. Berve II 296 n.2 rejects the identification on the grounds that O. was a Mede, but he may have commanded the Mardian contingent from the Caspian region. Antigonos sent O. back to Media as satrap, accompanied by Hippostratos, who was to serve as his *strategos* (with a force of, at least, 3,500 men) to secure the satrapy against those who had rebelled after Peithon's elimination (Diod. 19.46.5). Although they were ambushed by the rebels, O. and Hippostratos overcame them, hemming in their force in a gorge, killing some and taking others alive. Meleagros and Okranes were among the dead (Diod. 19.47.2–4). Nikanor, who is described as *strategos* of Media (Diod. 19.92.1) and *strategos* of Media and the Upper Satrapies (Diod. 19.100.3) in 312/11, appears to have been Hippostratos' replacement, but not necessarily the new satrap of Media. If O. remained as satrap, he was probably replaced by Seleukos, when he overcame Nikanor (App. *Syr.* 57.293). Billows 413–14 no. 85, Schober 85, 89–90.

823 OROPHERNES

('Οροφέρνης. 'Ολοφέρνης). Son of Ariamnes, brother of Ariarathes I, who was exceedingly fond of him. Father of Ariarathes II and Arsyes (Diod. 31.19.2–4). In 343, O. had been sent to campaign with Ochos in Egypt, where he distinguished himself and was greatly honored by the King; he died in Kappadokia some time later (Diod. 31.19.3); his son Ariarathes was adopted by his uncle and thus became heir to the kingdom. Nothing else is known about him. Shayegan 114 no. 77.

824 OROPIOS

('Ορώπιος). The name is uncertain and looks more like an ethnic, but it could be a corruption of an Iranian name. Dexippos makes the curious comment that O. ruled Sousiana "not by ancestral right" (οὐ πάτριον ἔχων ἀρχήν) but as an appointee of Alexander (Dexippos, *FGrH* 100 F8 §6). Such a remark would not have been made about a Graeco-Macedonian official. Berve II 57 no. 107 wishes to identify him with Argaios of Oropos (cf. *LM* 121). But there is no indication that Argaios came from Oropos and a greater likelihood that Argaios is a corruption of, or error for, Oropios. O. was undoubtedly appointed to replace Aboulites, who was executed in 324 for failure to supply Alexander during the Gedrosian campaign. Charged with inciting rebellion, Oropios was deposed, fled and perished. His successor was Koinos (Dexippos, *FGrH* 100 F8 §6; cf. *LM* 121; Justin 13.4.14). Berve II 57 no. 107 ('Αργαῖος); B. A. Müller, *RE* Supplbd. I 127 no. 7b; Beloch III² 2. 242; Ausfeld 1901, 538.

825 ORSILOS

The form of the name is attested only in Curtius; cf. Atkinson II 159. Berve II 296 has *Orsillus*; this may be a familiar form of the name Orsines/Orxines but there is no compelling reason to identify him with the descendant of the Seven. Prominent Persian. O. surrendered to Alexander, along with Mithracenes, in 330 after Dareios' arrest by Bessos and the conspirators (Curt. 5.13.9). Nothing else is known about him. Berve II 296 no. 595; Justi 236.

826 ORSODATES

('Ορσοδάτης, Justi 236). A barbarian rebel, O. was reportedly killed by Alexander himself (Plut. *Alex.* 57.3). The context of the incident is unknown. Berve II 296 assumes that this occurred in Baktria-Sogdiana between 329 and 327, which is possible and perhaps supported by an earlier reference to Alexander's punishment of the disobedient *phrourarchos* Menandros. Numerous garrisons were planted in that area and many served unwillingly. The verb κατατοξεύω ("to shoot with an arrow") is unusual since the bow was the weapon of choice of the Persian rather than the Macedonian King. It is possible that the story is a doublet of the one told by Plut. *Alex.* 68.7 that Aboulites' son was killed by Alexander's own hand; in that case, Orsodates may be corruption of the name Oxathres (Oxyathres); Hyland 2013, 128 believes Orsodates is a mistake for Oxydates (no. 835), which is possible in the context of 327. But Plutarch seems to link O. with local uprisings (hence Berve II 296: "beteiligte sich an den großen Aufständen in seiner Heimat"), during which Menandros' conduct was also unsatisfactory. He does not speak of O. as "the rebel" but rather as "one of the barbarian rebels" (τῶν ἀποστάντων βαρβάρων 'Ορσοδάτην). Berve II 296 no. 596; Shayegan 114 no. 78.

827 ORTHAGORAS

('Ορθαγόρας). Author of a work called *Indikoi Logoi*, mentioned together with both Nearchos and Onesikritos. O. confirmed Onesikritos' observation concerning the size of sea monsters of the coast of Gedrosia (Ael. *NA* 17.6), agreeing also with Nearchos on the distance between the mainland and the island of Ogyris (Strabo 16.3.5 C766). Berve believes he was a contemporary and companion of the two writers. The connection is tenuous at best; O. may simply have used both authors as sources. He is cited also by Ael. *NA* 16.35; Philostratus, *Life of Apollonius* 2.53 p.137; Phot. *Bibl.* 241 p.327b. Jacoby, *FGrH* IID, p.479 believes that Philostratus may have used Onesikritos "vermittelt und verdorben durch Orthagoras"; cf. Brown, *Onesicritus* 119. Berve II 294 no. 591.

828 ORXINES

('Ορξίνης). Persian. Justi 234 no. 1. Descended from one of the Seven and also from Kyros the Great (Curt. 4.12.8; 10.1.23); commanded the Persians, Mardians, and Sogdianoi at Gaugamela (Curt. 4.12.8; less accurately, Arr. 3.8.5) and later governed Persia (without Alexander's approval) since the death of Phrasaortes, which occurred while Alexander was in India (Arr. 6.29.2, 30.1). Alexander executed him in 324 on charges of plundering temples and royal tombs and putting innocent Persians to death; he was hanged (impaled) by those to whom the task was assigned (Arr. 6.30.2); Peukestas was his successor. Curtius ascribes O.'s death to the machinations of the eunuch Bagoas (Curt. 10.1.22–38). Berve II 294 no. 592; Shayegan 114–15 no. 79.

829 OSTANES

('Οστάνης, Justi 52, the name is the same as Austanes/Haustanes). A magus who, on Alexander's order, accompanied the King from Persis onward (Pliny, *HN* 30.3, 11; Apul. *Apol.* 1.326; Euseb 1.43; Syncellus 198; Tatian, *ad Gr.* 75 Schw.). Nothing else is known about him. Berve II 296 no. 597.

830 OXATHRES

('Οξάθρης, 'Οξυάθρης). Perhaps more correctly Oxyathres (cf. below no. 834); Plut. *Alex.* 68.7 has *Oxyartes*. Son of Aboulites, satrap of Sousiana, O. commanded at Gaugamela the Ouxians and Susians (Arr. 3.8.5), who were positioned on the left side towards the center (Arr. 3.11.3); he was thus acting as military leader on behalf of his father, who may have been unfit for such service. The fact that O. appears to have acted as the agent in Aboulites' surrender to Alexander may support this view (Arr. 3.16.6). Alexander appointed O. satrap of Paraitakene (Arr. 3.19.2), which he appears to have governed until 324, when he was executed along with his father for maladministration (Arr. 7.4.1; cf. Plut. *Alex.* 68.7, who says that Aboulites had failed to send supplies in accordance with Alexander's instructions, apparently during the Gedrosian campaign, and that Alexander felled O. with his lance). Berve II 291 no. 585; Justi 232 no. 4; Shayegan 115 no. 80.

831 OXATHRES

('Οξάθρης. 'Οξάθρας). Son of Dionysios of Herakleia Pontika (Diod. 20.77.1). Born soon after 320, in all likelihood. In 305, on the death of their father, he and his brother, Klearchos succeeded to the tyranny (20.77.1). Little is known about his life. O. and his brother were harsh rulers, who not only mistreated their subjects but, around 284, devised and executed a plan to drown their mother in the Black Sea (Memnon 5.2). The brothers were killed by Lysimachos, who exacted revenge for the death of his former wife (Memnon 5.3). As a consequence, Herakleia was restored to democratic rule. Burstein, *Outpost* 83–5.

832 OXIKANOS

('Οξικανός). The form Oxykanos (given by Berve no. 587) is unattested in the MSS. Indian dynast, *nomarches* of a region of Sind, perhaps based at the city of Azeika (Ptol. *Geog.* 7.1.57; Eggermont 12). He did not submit to Alexander, who sailed down the Indos from Alor (Mousikanos' realm; summer 325) and took two of his cities by assault, capturing O. in the second (Arr. 6.16.1–2). His fate is not recorded, but it is likely that Alexander had him executed. Berve II 293 identifies him with Portikanos (Strabo 15.1.33 C701; Curt. 9.8.11–12; Diod. 17.102.5; cf. Jacobs 247, 251), but the names and the details concerning them are sufficiently different—even though both Diod. 17.102.5 and Arr. 6.16.2 place the "capture" of Porti/Oxikanos in the second city—that we may suspect conflation of two successive incidents. See further s.v. Portikanos no. 988. O.'s designation as *nomarches* (Arr. 6.16.1) suggests that he may have been a subordinate of Portikanos, whom Curt. 9.8.11 calls *rex*. Anspach III 33 n.374; Berve II 293 no. 589; Eggermont 9–15.

833 OXYARTES

('Οξυάρτης). Baktrian or Sogdianian noble (Curt. 8.4.21–4, but the text is corrupt); father of Rhoxane, father-in-law of Alexander (Diod. 18.3.3, 39.6; Plut. *Mor.* 332e; Paus. 1.6.3; Arr. 6.15.3; cf. Curt. 10.3.11; *LM* 118, 121; Arr. *ap.* Phot. *Bibl.* 68a; Curt. 8.4.21–7, for the details of the marriage see Rhoxane no. 1028). His role in the early resistance to Alexander (i.e. from Gaugamela on) is unclear, as are his associations with Bessos and Spitamenes. Arr. 4. 28.9 does not necessarily imply that he was with Bessos when he murdered Dareios, only that he joined him in Sogdiana. O. was one of those nobles of Baktria-Sogdiana who continued to resist Alexander after the execution of Bessos, but it appears that he submitted to Alexander at the time of the Macedonian siege of the Rock of Sisimithres, where he had left his family for safe-keeping, and acted as a go-between for Alexander and Sisimithres (Curt. 8.2.25–31; cf. Arr. 4.21.6). He is also known to have had a son named Itanes, but the three sons ascribed to him by Curt. 8.4.21 appear to belong to Chorienes (Sisimithres). Arr. 4.18–19 claims that O.'s wife and daughter were captured at the so-called Rock of Sogdiana in spring 327. But this Rock is clearly the fortress of Ariamazes, whom Alexander crucified along with many of his followers, selling the remainder into slavery (Bosworth II 131 suggests, less plausibly, that Rhoxane was captured on Ariamazes' Rock but not married to Alexander until he enjoyed the hospitality of Chorienes in 327). Rhoxane may have influenced her husband's decision to give O. the satrapy of the Parapamisadai (or Paropanisadai) in 325 in place of Tyriespis (Arr. 6.15.3); Curt. 9.8.9 calls the governor of Parapamisos Terioltes and says that he was tried for greed and tyrannical acts and executed; he adds that O., *praetor Bactrianorum*, was acquitted and given a more extensive territory (9.8.10), but Curtius appears to have forgotten at this point that O. was Rhoxane's father; he mistakenly reports that he was put on trial; and wrongly calls him the governor of Baktria. That O. shared the satrapy with Peithon son of Agenor is highly unlikely and editors are right to emend the text of Arr. 6.15.4: Arr. 6.15.3 calls O.'s satrapy "Parapamisadai"; perhaps this was extended in a southeasterly direction to the confluence of the Indos and Akesines (Chenab) and was thus adjacent to Peithon's. He retained Paropanisadai in the settlement of 323 (Dexippos, *FGrH* 100 F8 §5; Diod. 18.3.3; Justin 13.4.21; cf. *LM* 121), and again at Triparadeisos (Diod. 18.39.6). Although he gave aid to Eumenes in 317, he did not come in person but rather sent troops under the command of Androbazos (Diod. 19.14.6). After the battle of Gabiene, Antigonos allowed O. to retain his satrapy, considering it too difficult to dislodge him from there (Diod. 19.48.2). What became of him, we do not know. Berve II 292–3 no. 587; Shayegan 115 no. 81.

834 OXYATHRES

('Οξυάθρης). Son of Arsanes and Sisygambis. Brother of Dareios III (Diod. 17.34.2; Curt. 3.11.8; 6.2.9; Arr. 7.4.5; Strabo 12.3.10 C544; Ps.-Call. 2.7.5) and of Stateira, who had given him Timosa, a beautiful captive sent by the king of Egypt, as a concubine (Athen. 13.609a–b). He was younger—we do not know by how much—than Dareios who was born *c*.380 (Arr. 3.22.6). Fought with distinction in defense of his brother at Issos (Diod. 17.34.2–3; Curt. 3.11.8; for his merits see also Curt. 6.2.9). After his brother's death he was among some 1,000 noble Persian captives (Curt. 6.2.9) and later enrolled in Alexander's *hetairoi* (Plut. Alex. 43.7; Curt. 6.2.11) and as one of his bodyguards (Diod. 17.77.4; Curt. 7.5.40; Metz Epit. 2). The captive regicide Bessos was handed over to O. for punishment

(Curt. 7.5.40–1; Justin 12.5.11). O. was the father of Amastris, who married Krateros in 324 at Sousa (Arr. 7.4.5; Strabo 12.3.10 C544; Memnon 4.4), and perhaps a second daughter, captured at Damaskos in 333 (Curt. 3.13.13). He was apparently still alive in 323 (assuming that the remark in Curt. 10.5.23 that only one of Sisygambis' seven children remained alive refers to Oxyathres). What became of him is unknown, although it may be speculated that all of the immediate relatives of Dareios III were quietly eliminated after Alexander's death. Berve II 291–2 no. 586; Shayegan 115–16 no. 82. **Stemma III.**

835 OXYDATES

('Οξυδάτης). For the name, see Justi 233 (cf. Marquart 26, *Waxsu-data*; also Hyland 2013, 125 n.19). A prominent Persian (his family background is unknown) who had been arrested by Dareios III and imprisoned in Sousa (we do not know the charge against him or the historical context, but Curt. 6.2.11 says that he had been condemned to death). O. was released by Alexander, whom he accompanied as far as Rhagai (Rey), where, in 330, he was appointed satrap of Media; as a victim of Dareios, he was considered trustworthy (Arr. 3.20.3; cf. Curt. 6.2.11, who postpones his appointment until after Dareios' death). In late 328, however, O. was charged with misconduct (ἐθελοκακεῖν). If Arrian uses ἐθελοκακεῖν in the Herodotean sense, the word means "to do badly in battle on purpose" (Powell, *Lexicon to Herodotus* s.v.); cf. Bosworth 1981, 21, who assumes that O. did not aid Phrataphernes against the rebel Arsakes (cf. Arr. 4.7.1). Hyland 2013, 124–8 shows that O.'s resources were limited (especially if, as Olbrycht 2011, 73–5 notes, he sent elite troops to Alexander) and that his position may have been undermined by the local aristocracy. He was replaced by Atropates (no. 261; Arr. 4.18.3; Curt. 8.3.17, wrongly calls Atropates Arsakes). It is hard to imagine that Atropates was not instructed to arrest (if not execute) him. If O. fled at Atropates' approach, there is no record of him afterwards. Nor is it clear if he had anything to do with the rebels who were later taken to Alexander at Pasargadai (Arr. 6.29.3; see s.v. Baryaxes no. 288). Curt. 8.3.17 suggests that O. simply went elsewhere: *ut Oxydates inde discederet. LM* 121 says that he was still ruling Media in 323: *ex †teis† imperiis omnibus excedat Oxydates, et pro eo Medis imperator sit Craterus* [sc. *Pitho Crateua*]. But the forged *Testamentum Alexandri Magni* contains numerous errors, and it may be best to dismiss this as one of them. Hyland 2013, 128 suspects that Plutarch's report of Alexander's execution of a rebel named Orsodates (*Alex.* 57.3) may be a reference to Oxydates. But see s.v. Orsodates (no. 826). Berve II 293 no. 588; Bosworth 1981, 21; Shayegan 116 no. 83; Hyland 2013.

836 OXYTHEMIS

('Οξύθεμις). Thessalian. Son of Hippostratos, from Larisa (*Syll³* 343), and thus, probably, a member of the Aleuadai and a nephew of Medeios (Billows 414). O. appears in the entourage of Demetrios Poliorketes in the last decade of the fourth century (Athen. 6.253a; 14.614f = Phylarchos, *FGrH* 81 F12). He was honored by the Athenians in 303/2 with a golden crown and citizenship for service to the city on behalf of the Antigonids (*Syll³* 343); hence, he was with Demetrios during his time in Athens, though there is no specific mention of military service. According to the twentieth book of Demochares' *Histories* (*FGrH* 75 F1), he was a flatterer of Demetrios and the Athenians poured libations and sang paeans to O. and others of his ilk; Demetrios was said to be disgusted by this and commented that there was no decent Athenian left (Athen. 6.252f–253a). In

289, O. was sent by Demetrios on an embassy to Agathokles of Syracuse, a mission that served as a cover for espionage (Diod. 21.15; 21.16.5; see s.v. Agathokles no. 20). He was still in Syracuse when Agathokles died and was said, implausibly, to have placed his still living body on the funeral pyre (see no. 19; Diod. 21.16.5). Herakleides Lembos, in the thirty-sixth book of his *History* (Athen. 13.578a–b = *FHG* III 168–9) says that Antigonos "the father of Demetrios" put O. to death for various misdeeds including the maidservants of Demo (no. 364). This is clearly an error for Antigonos Gonatas. As Billows 414 notes, this must have occurred after Demetrios' death. Billows 414 no. 86; Lenschau, *RE* XVIII.2 (1942) 2046; Olshausen no. 77; Habicht[2] 55–8; Wehrli 1968, 124–5; Osborne, *Naturalization* no. D47.

P

837 PAIRISADES

(Παιρισάδης, Παιρυσάδης, Polyaenus; Παρυσάδης Diodorus). P. styled himself both *archon* of the Bosporos and Theodosia and *basileus* of the Sindoi, Maïtai and Thateis (R&O no. 65A–F; see Hind, *CAH* VI² 496 for discussion of the titles), though the Greeks often referred to the Spartokids as *tyrannoi* (cf. Din. 1.43). Son of Leukon, who ruled the Kimmerian Bosporos (geography and historical background in Niese I 408–12; Werner) from 389/8 to 349/8 (Diod. 16.31.6 incorrectly places his death in 354/3 and names Spartokos as his sole successor). But Tod I 163 (a reduction of export duties for the Milesians in the name of Λεύκων καὶ οἱ παῖδες α[ὐτοῦ]) shows that Leukon and his sons ruled jointly in 350. P. had two brothers; Spartokos, who (according to Diod. 16.31.6, ruled for five years after his father's death; hence jointly with P. from 349/8 to 344/3), and Apollonios. An Athenian decree of 347/6 honors all three sons of Leukon (*Syll³* 206 = *IG* II² 212+; translation in Harding no. 82; R&O no. 64), though Apollonios appears in a supplemental motion, perhaps *honoris causa* (Werner 416 n.3). P. was also the nephew of Gorgippos, whose daughter Komosarye (no. 615) he married (*Syll³* 216 = R&O no. 65D). P. ruled from 349/8 to 311/10 (Diod. 20.22.1: thirty-eight years) His sons were Satyros (no. 1040), who ruled for nine months (Diod. 20.22.2, 23.7), Prytanis (no. 1003; *regn.* 311/10), and Eumelos (no. 442; *regn.* 310/309–304/3: Diod. 20.100.7); if P. had a son named Gorgippos (honored in Athens with a statue alongside P. and Satyros (Din. 1.43 with Worthington 206; cf. Burstein 1978, 433), he must have died before 311/10. In the period after the death of Spartokos II, P. appears to have taken a somewhat less favorable attitude towards the Athenians, who as *IG* II² 212 shows, had for a long time been exempt from export duties. Burstein 1978 shows that this relationship was restored in 327 through the diplomacy of Demosthenes. Though he clearly engaged in war with his neighbors (Polyaenus 7.37 tells us he had a different outfit for ordering his troops, going into battle, and flight: he wished to be conspicuous to his troops in preparation for battle, unrecognized by the enemy in battle, and in flight he wanted to be to be recognized by neither friend nor foe!), the details and outcomes of these campaigns are unknown. Although he had left the throne to Satyros (Diod. 20.22.1–2), the eldest son, the kingdom was thrown into turmoil by the ambitions of Eumelos (Diod. 20.22.2–26.2). See also s.vv. Eumelos (no. 442), Pairisades (no. 838), Satyros (no. 1040). Niese I 408–16; Werner; Burstein 1978; Worthington 205–7; Hind, *CAH* VI² 476–511, esp. 495–502. **Stemma XVII.**

838 PAIRISADES

(Παιρισάδης. Παρυσάδης, Diodorus). Pairisades II (*regn.* 284/3–c.245). Son of Satyros II (Diod. 20.24.3, who ruled for nine months in 311/310; thus Werner, 430; Diod. 20.22.2, 23.7), grandson of Pairisades I (above). He fled his uncle Eumelos and took refuge with

Agaros (no. 16), king of the Skythians (Diod. 20.24.3), and was thus the only surviving son of Satyros. After the death of Spartokos in 284/3, he gained the throne and ruled with his queen Kamasarye (clearly, a variation on his grandmother's name; *Syll*³ 439). He is last attested in 250 on a Delian inscription (*IG* XI 287 B126; Werner 421). He appears to have had at least two sons: Leukon and Spartokos (Werner 422, with references). **Stemma XVII.**

839 PANKASTE

(Παγκάστη. Pliny, *HN* 35.86: Pancaspe; Lucian 43.7: Πακάτη); Ael. *VH* 12.34 says she was from Larisa and that she was the first woman with whom Alexander was intimate (confusing her with Kallixeina the Thessalian courtesan; Athen. 10.435a). Alexander commissioned a nude painting of her by Apelles, and, when the latter fell in love with his subject, Alexander presented her to him as a gift (Pliny, *HN* 35.86); she was rumored to be the model for his Aphrodite Anadyomene (Pliny, *HN* 35.87). Berve II 297 no. 600; Pollitt 160.

840 PANEGOROS

(Πανήγορος). Macedonian (Tataki 395 no. 4). Son of Lykagoros. *Hetairos* of Alexander. Left behind with an unspecified force to occupy Priapos (Arr. 1.12.7), which surrendered to Alexander as he advanced to the Granikos in 334. Nothing else is known about him. Berve II 297 no. 602; Hoffmann 197.

841 PANKLES

(Πανκλῆς). Son of Dorotheos. One of twenty-four cavalrymen from Orchomenos, who served with Alexander's allied cavalry until the expedition reached Ekbatana in 330. There he and his compatriots were discharged. On their return (*c*.329), they made a dedication to Zeus Soter in Orchomenos (*IG* VII 3206). Berve II 297 no. 601.

842 PANTALEON

(Πανταλέων). Macedonian *hetairos* from Pydna (Tataki 171 no. 13). Appointed *phrourarchos* of Memphis in Egypt in 332/1 (Arr. 3.5.3). P. is otherwise unknown. Berve II 297 no. 603.

843 PANTAUCHOS

(Πάνταυχος). Macedonian (Tataki 44 no. 3). Son of Nikolaos, from Aloros. Born no later than the 350s, P. was a trierarch of the Hydaspes fleet in 326 (Arr. *Ind.* 18.6). Berve II 298 no. 604.

844 PANTAUCHOS

(Πάνταυχος). Officer of Demetrios Poliorketes, perhaps already in the fourth century. In 289, when Demetrios invaded Epeiros, he left Pantauchos behind in Aitolia. There he encountered the army of Pyrrhos, who was moving to meet Demetrios by a different route, and engaged in single combat with Pyrrhos. Pantauchos, although he inflicted one wound on Pyrrhos, was struck in the thigh and the neck and saved by the intervention of his friends; the success of Pyrrhos nevertheless inspired the Epeirotes to rout Pantauchos' forces with heavy casualties (Plut. *Pyrrh.* 7.4–10; cf. *Demetr.* 41.2–3). Identification with

Pantauchos son of Nikolaos, who was trierarch at the Hydaspes in 326 (Arr. *Ind.* 18.6; cf. Berve II 298 no. 604), is possible but unlikely, given the lengthy interval. Sandberger 175–7 no. 64; Berve, *RE* XVIII.2 (1949) 694 no. 2; Schoch 108–9.

845 PANTIKA

(Παντίκα). A beautiful woman of ill repute from Kypros who lived at the court of Olympias. Monimos (no. 752) son of Pythion is said to have sought her in marriage, to which Olympias commented that he was marrying "with his eyes instead of his mind" (Phylarchos *ap.* Athen. 13.609c = *FGrHist* 81 F21; Plut. *Mor.* 141c–d).

846 PANTORDANOS

(Παντόρδανος). Macedonian (Tataki 119 no. 2). Son of Kleandros (Arr. 2.9.3). Whether he was the son of Kleandros (no. 589) son of Polemokrates is impossible to determine given the name's frequent occurrence in Macedonia. P. commanded the so-called Leugaian squadron. Leugaia is probably not a toponym (though Tataki 119 treats it as one; but see Bosworth I 211). In the battle of Issos, P. was positioned at first on the left wing but then transferred (along with the squadron of Peroidas) to the right, just as the battle began (Arr. 2.9.3). He is not heard of again, and the battle order at Gaugamela (Arr. 3.11.8) shows that he had been replaced. Arr. 2.10.7 says that some 120 Macedonians of note died at Issos, but names only Ptolemy son of Seleukos. It is not impossible that P. was killed at Issos, but, since Arrian drew attention to his maneuver at the beginning of the battle, it would be unusual for him to omit his death, had it occurred. Berve II 298 no. 605; Hoffmann 183–4; Heckel 1992, 349–50.

847 PARIS

(Πάρις). Origin unknown. Courtier of Lysimachos. According to Phylarchos *ap.* Athen. 14.614f (= *FGrH* 81 F12), Demetrios compared the court of Lysimachos with the comic stage, which featured characters with disyllabic names: Bithys (no. 301) and Paris. Lund believes P. may be Phrygian. The anecdote belongs in the context of Demetrios' sojourn in Athens with Lamia. Otherwise unknown. Lund 180–1.

848 PARMENION

(Παρμενίων). Macedonian (Tataki 397 no. 17). Son of Philotas (Arr. 3.11.10; but not a brother of Asandros (no. 232) son of Philotas: Heckel 1977a; Bosworth I 130). P. may have come from Upper Macedonian (Ellis 1976, 253 n.7; Worthington 2008, 34 calls him "one of the Paeonian chieftains" but provides no evidence; he was certainly not the king of the Pelagonians: *IG* II² 190, 5–6). Macedon's foremost general in the years leading up to Alexander's accession (Curt. 4.13.4; Justin 12.5.3; cf. Plut. *Alex.* 49.13; Plut. *Mor.* 177c) and no less influential at the Court (Plut. *Mor.* 179b). Together with Antipatros and Eurylochos, P. negotiated the Peace of 346 (Dem. 19.69; Aesch. 3.72; Din. 1.28; cf. Theopompos *FGrH* 115 F165). Born *c.*400 (Curt. 6.11.32; cf. 7.2.33.), he was already a dominant force in Pella in the first years of Philip II, on whose orders he arrested and killed at Oreos Euphraios, an adherent of Perdikkas III (Karystios *ap.* Athen. 11.508e). In 356 he campaigned successfully against Grabos the Illyrian (Plut. *Alex.* 3.8), and the value of his generalship is summed up in Philip's remark that whereas the Athenians elected ten generals every year, he himself had found only one general in many years—Parmenion

(Plut. *Mor.* 177c). P. had three attested sons: Philotas (no. 940), Nikanor (no. 776) and Hektor (no. 509); an unnamed daughter (**A27** probably identical with **A26**) is known to have married Attalos, the uncle of Kleopatra (Curt. 6.9.18). The family may have had estates in the highlands: Philotas commanded in the Triballian campaign the cavalry from Upper Macedonia (Arr. 1.2.5) and his friends included the sons of Andromenes from Tymphaia (Curt. 7.1.11); P. himself normally commanded the infantry, on the left, where at least four of six taxiarchs were from Upper Macedonia; he was also associated with Polyperchon of Tymphaia (Curt. 4.13.7ff.) and the sons of Polemokrates (Elimeia), one of whom, Koinos, appears to have married P.'s daughter after Attalos' death (Curt. 6.9.30; cf. Arr. 1.24.1, 29.4).

Sent ahead with Attalos and Amyntas to prepare for Philip's invasion (Diod. 16.91.2; 17.2.4; Justin 9.5.8; cf. Trogus, *Prol.* 9), P. enjoyed mixed success in Asia Minor: Polyaenus 5.44.4 provides a vague account of a defeat at Magnesia on Sipylos (Heckel 15–16) inflicted by Memnon the Rhodian. Polyaenus' account, and the figure of 10,000 Macedonian troops (accepted by McCoy 1989, 424), must be treated with caution (cf. Niese I 59 n.2). In 336/5, on Alexander's orders, he eliminated Attalos (Diod. 17.2.4–6, 5.2). Some time later, he captured Gryneion and sold its inhabitants into slavery; Memnon, however, forced him to abandon the siege of Pitane (Diod. 17.7.9) and drove his accomplice, Kalas son of Harpalos, back to Rhoiteion (*Barr. Atl.* 57 E1; Diod. 17.7.10). The campaign had not been an overwhelming success, but P. had only limited resources with which to secure a beachhead in Asia. In winter of 335/4, he rejoined Alexander in Europe, where he and Antipatros urged the King, without success, to postpone the expedition until he had produced an heir (Diod. 17.16.2). In the spring, P. transported most of the infantry and cavalry from Sestos to Abydos; in Asia Minor, he commanded the infantry—12,000 Macedonians, 7,000 allies and 5,000 mercenaries (Arr. 1.11.6; Diod. 17.17.3). At the Granikos, P. counselled Alexander not to attack late in the day, advice rejected by the King (Arr. 1.13.2–7; Plut. *Alex.* 16.3). Diod. 17.19.3, says that Alexander attacked at dawn, thus giving the impression that he was following P.'s advice. Diodorus may, however, be basing his account on a corrective (pro-Parmenion) version—he does not mention P.'s advice, or Alexander's rejection of it—or he may simply have mistakenly translated P.'s proposal into action. Beloch IV² 2. 296–7 accepts Diodorus' version as correct (cf. Berve II 300; also Bosworth I 114–16; Green 1991, 489–512). In the battle P. commanded the left, including the Thessalian cavalry (Arr. 1.14.1), who acquitted themselves well in the engagement (Diod. 17.19.6). After the battle, P. captured and garrisoned Daskyleion (*Barr. Atl.* 52 D4) Arr. 1.17.2), ensuring that Kalas son of Harpalos, Alexander's newly appointed satrap of Hellespontine Phrygia, was securely established there. Both P. and Kalas were familiar with the region, having campaigned there in 336 and 335 (Diod. 17.7.10). It appears that P. took with him to Daskyleion the Thessalian horse, which he left there for the time to help Kalas recover the Troad (Arr. 1.17.8). Arrian curiously separates the appointment of Kalas and P.'s mission (1.17.1–2) from the instructions given to Kalas and Alexander son of Aëropos concerning "Memnon's land" (1.17.8; did they set out from Sardis?) It would be odd if Alexander made the appointment and then took Kalas to Sardis, only to send him back into his satrapy from Ionia. Kalas replaced Arsites (Arr. 1.12.8; 1.17.1); for previous rulers of the satrapy see Krumbholz 1883, 93.

Upon his return, P. secured Magnesia and Tralles (which had surrendered) with 2,500 infantry, an equal number of Macedonians and 200 of the Companions (Arr.

1.18.1). He rejoined the King at Miletos, where he advised against disbanding the fleet. P. drew attention to an omen, an eagle perched on the shore behind Alexander's ships. If the Macedonians won a naval engagement at the beginning of the campaign it would be beneficial to their cause, but a setback would not harm them, since the Persians were already dominant at sea (Arr. 1.18.6). But Alexander responded that he would not fight against a force superior in numbers—400 Persians (Arr. 1.18.5) to 160 Macedonians under Nikanor (1.18.4)—and in training, and risk good lives to an uncertain element; that a loss would harm Macedonian prestige at a crucial point in the campaign; and that the omen showed that the Macedonians should fight on land, for that was where the eagle was situated, not at sea (Arr. 1.18.7–9). From Miletos, P. accompanied the King into Karia. With winter approaching, P. moved to Sardis, taking a hipparchy of Companions, the Thessalian horse, the allies, and the wagons, from there to march into Phrygia and await the King (Arr. 1.24.3; cf. 1.29.3). There he apprehended Dareios' agent, Sisines, who had been sent to induce Alexander Lynkestes to murder the Macedonian King. Sisines was sent in chains to Alexander (now at Phaselis) and interrogated. On the basis of his testimony, Alexander sent Amphoteros back to Parmenion with orders to arrest the Lynkestian (Arr. 1.25.4–10; a different version in Diod. 17.32.1–2; cf. Curt. 7.1.6, and 3.7.11–15, for the arrest and death of Sisines). In spring 333, Parmenion rejoined the remainder of the army at Gordion (Arr. 1.29.3–4). When the expedition moved out of Kappadokia to Kilikia, P. remained at the so-called Camp of Kyros with the heavy infantry while Alexander took the hypaspists, archers, and Agrianes in order to occupy the Kilikian Gates (Arr. 2.4.3). These had been abandoned by Arsames' guards, who were frightened by the King's approach and alarmed by Arsames' scorched earth policy; and Alexander, fearing lest the satrap should destroy Tarsos, sent P. ahead to capture the city. This, at least, is Curtius' version; Arrian says nothing about his contribution (Curt. 3.4.14–15; Arr. 2.4.5–6). It was near Tarsos that Alexander fell ill, and Justin's claim that P. wrote to Alexander from Kappadokia, warning the King to beware of Philip, the Akarnanian physician, may reflect his (or rather Trogus') belief that P. had remained in Kappadokia while Alexander rushed ahead to Tarsos. Bosworth I 190 points out that from the Gates to Tarsos it is only about "55 km, a manageable day's stint for the advance column." And it appears more likely that Alexander himself (or possibly Philotas) advanced with the more mobile troops and that P. remained at the Gates, awaiting further instructions from the King. P. had in fact passed through the Gates (Arr. 2.4.4; cf. Atkinson I 155), but this does not rule out the possibility that he stayed behind or followed at a slower pace. A letter from him might be thought to have come from the direction of Kappadokia. Diod. 17.31.4–6 knows nothing about any warning concerning Philip and follows his account of Alexander's illness with the arrest of Alexander Lynkestes (17.32.1–2). It is precisely in this context that the Vulgate discusses the arrest of Alexander Lynkestes, who, like the doctor Philip, had allegedly been bribed by the Persian king. On this occasion, as on others, P.'s advice was disregarded and proved to be wrong.

From Tarsos, P. advanced to the "other" or Syrian Gates (Arr. 2.5.1; Diod. 17.32.2), which he secured before rejoining the King at Kastabalon (Curt. 3.7.5; cf. Arr. 2.6.1–2, with Bosworth I 199); thereafter he took Issos and advised Alexander to fight Dareios in the narrows where the numerical supremacy of the Persians could be negated. The advice was accepted (Curt. 3.7.6–10)! At Issos, P. acted as commander-in-chief of the forces on the left, and was told to extend his line to the sea (Curt. 3.9.8–10; Arr. 2.8.4, 9–10). To his contingent Alexander added the Thessalian cavalry (Arr. 2.8.9; Curt. 3.11.3), who again fought with distinction (Curt. 3.11.13–15). After the battle, P. captured without difficulty the treasures at Damaskos (Curt. 3.12.27; Arr. 2.11.10; Plut. *Alex.* 24.1). Dareios had sent most of his baggage and the Persian women (except those of his immediate family) to Damaskos before he reached Issos (Arr. 2.11.9; Diod. 17.32.3; Curt. 3.8.12). For P.'s capture of the city see Arr. 2.15.1; Curt. 3.13.1ff. is heavily dramatized; cf. Polyaenus 4.5.1. Athen. 13.607f–608a quotes from what is purportedly a letter of P. to Alexander itemizing the captured spoils, among them 329 of the Great King's concubines. This letter (if genuine) appears to have reached Alexander at Marathos. Alexander instructed him to send on only the captive Greek envoys and to take the remaining spoils back to Damaskos (Arr. 2.15.1–2). The captives included Barsine, the widow of both Mentor and Memnon the Rhodians and allegedly the first woman with whom Alexander was intimate. P., it is said, urged him to take up this relationship (Diod. 17.16.2; Baynham 1998a; for Alexander and Barsine: Justin 11.10.2–3); she may have been brought to the King at Marathos. P. himself became military overseer of Koile-Syria (Curt. 4.1.4; cf. Bosworth 1974, 47–8): it is tempting to see Par*menion* as a corruption of Menon (son of Kerdimmas), on whom see Arr. 2.13.7. But Justin 11.10.4–5, seems to corroborate some kind of independent command for P., though *Parmeniona ad occupandam Persicam classem* is clearly corrupt, unless it implies that P. was to secure the coast of Koile-Syria. See also Bosworth I 225. This was a temporary command: the satrapy was soon assigned to Andromachos, whom the Samaritans later put to death (Curt. 4.5.9; cf. 4.8.9–11). Curtius places the appointment of Andromachos and P.'s reunion with Alexander after the fall of Tyre, when the army prepared to move south towards Gaza, the logical time for such an administrative change. Polyaenus 4.3.4 gives P. charge of the army at Tyre, while Alexander conducted his Arabian campaign; but Curtius claims that the siege had been entrusted to Krateros and Perdikkas (Curt. 4.3.1; cf. Polyaenus 4.13). The story that P., hard-pressed by the Tyrians, had to summon Alexander from Arabia sounds like another attempt to discredit the old general. From Gaza, P. accompanied the King to Egypt. There he used his influence to pacify Hegelochos (Curt. 6.11.27–29), and his mere presence in the camp sufficed to save Philotas from charges of treason (Arr. 3.26.1). Still his sojourn in Egypt was not free of tragedy: his youngest son Hektor drowned in the Nile (Curt. 4.8.7ff.; 6.9.27; cf. Plut. *Alex.* 49.13).

P. exercised a role in the army that is close to that of a modern general. He was not tied to one particular unit, nor was he one of the Somatophylakes, as Berve II 299 has noted. He normally held the defensive position (the anvil for Alexander's hammer), and this perhaps contributed to the view of the man as cautious, or even uninspired, an attitude reflected in the numerous stories that pit P.'s opinion (or advice) against that of his King. Whatever the historicity of these accounts, Alexander undoubtedly sought to free himself from P.'s influence and the belief that his military victories were owed to the old general (cf. Curt. 7.2.33). But it is difficult to determine what role Alexander played in blackening P.'s memory or if this was even done in the King's lifetime. Certainly, we have a collection of stories that put him in a bad light: he urges acceptance of Dareios' peace offer (Plut. *Alex.* 29.7–9 and *Mor.* 180b: 10,000 talents; cf. Arr. 2.25.1, in a different chronological context; Diod. 17.54; Curt. 4.11.1–14 and Justin 11.12.1–10: 30,000 talents), which Alexander arrogantly rejects; the old general's advice that they attack the Persians by night at Gaugamela is dismissed as a plan to "steal victory" (Curt. 4.13.4, 8–9; Arr. 3.10.1–2; Plut. *Alex.* 31.11–12); P.'s anxiety before the battle is contrasted with Alexander's confidence in the face of danger (Diod. 17.56.2; Curt. 4.13.17ff., Plut. *Alex.* 32.1–4); and, in the actual battle, he is depicted as incompetent and tarnishing the King's victory over Dareios (Plut. *Alex.* 33.10). But in some cases, for the Alexander historians, P. was simply a convenient foil for Alexander (Plut. *Mor.* 180b). It is difficult to imagine that these episodes could have been written in P.'s lifetime, or even in the King's, when too many influential commanders—to say nothing of the common soldiers—knew the truth of what had happened. Lysimachos' rejection of Onesikritos' story about the Amazon queen shows that fiction was instantly recognizable as such (Plut. *Alex.* 46.4–5); and Kleitos' outrage at the negative portrayal of Macedonian officers demonstrates the kind of hostility that could be generated by such falsehoods (Plut. *Alex.* 50.9). The only thing we can be certain about is that the hostile portrait of P. originated with one of the first Alexander historians. A more positive tradition can be found in Curtius, who in P.'s obituary notice says: *multa sine rege prospere, rex sine illo nihil magnae rei gesserat* (7.2.33). Beloch IV² 2.295–6 argues that Philotas was essentially speaking the truth to his mistress when "he declared that the greatest deeds were those accomplished by himself and by his father, and he called Alexander a stripling who reaped on their account the fame of empire" (Plut. *Alex.* 48.5). Passages favorable to P. thus appear to be later inventions: his advice that the army fight in the narrows at Issos (Curt. 3.7.8–10) and that Alexander not read to his soldiers letters from Dareios urging them to murder their leader (Curt. 4.10.16–17) is accepted in each case. Curtius himself regards the criticism of P. excessive and directs against Polyperchon Alexander's rejection of the night attack at Gaugamela (4.13.4, 7–10; cf. also 4.12.21).

P. commanded the Macedonian left at Gaugamela (Arr. 3.11.10; cf. 3.15) and soon found himself hard-pressed by the Persian cavalry under Mazaios (Diod. 17.60.5–7); Skythian horsemen had, furthermore, broken through Macedonian lines and begun to plunder the camp (Curt. 4.15.2ff.). A detachment sent to recall Alexander failed to make contact with the King and returned with its mission unfulfilled (Diod. 17.60.7). Arr. 3.15.1 claims that Alexander responded and came to the rescue. Fuller 178 accepts the story; it is rejected by Bosworth 1988, 82–3; cf. Bosworth I 310; cf. Devine 1975, 381. P., with the Thessalian cavalry, managed to hold Mazaios until Dareios' flight signalled the collapse of the Persian effort (Diod. 17.60.8). He had thus fulfilled his role in the battle by holding the enemy in check on the left while Alexander turned the tide of battle on the right. Despite later claims that his performance was lackluster (Plut. *Alex.* 33.10 = Kallisthenes, *FGrH* 124 F37), his contribution should not be diminished. Once the Persians were routed, and Alexander had established his camp beyond the Lykos River, P. occupied the Persian camp, capturing the baggage, the camels, and the elephants (Arr. 3.15.4). From Sousa to Persepolis, P. led the slower troops and the baggage train along the wagon road into Persis (Arr. 3.18.1), while Alexander took an unencumbered force through the Persian Gates. At Persepolis he advised Alexander not to destroy the palace; for it was unwise to destroy one's own property (Arr. 3.18.11). Alexander may have wished to accept P.'s advice for once, but he had little choice: constrained by his own claims to be the *ultor Graeciae*, he was forced to make at least a symbolic gesture at Persepolis. From Persepolis the King sent him to Ekbatana with the accumulated treasure (Justin 12.1.3; Arr. 3.19.7), details of which are again provided in a letter from P. to Alexander (Athen. 11.781f–782a). When Alexander continued his pursuit of Dareios in 330, he left P. in Ekbatana, presumably as (temporary) *strategos* of Media. P.'s instructions to invade the land of the Kadousians and Hyrkania (Arr. 3.19.7) were apparently cancelled (cf. Bosworth I 337; Seibert 1985, 110–11; cf. Brunt I 529, Appendix 13.5). The matter is academic, since Alexander's decision to execute Philotas sealed the old man's fate. Polydamas was sent in disguise to deliver the order for P.'s execution (Arr. 3.26.3; Curt. 7.2.11ff.). In Media, Kleandros, Agathon, Sitalkes, and Menidas carried out the sentence (Arr. 3.26.3; cf. Curt. 7.2.19ff.; Curt. 10.1.1 adds Herakon), as the old man learned of this conviction and of the charges (cf. Curt. 6.9.13–24, 11.21ff.) against him (Arr. 3.26.3–4; Plut. *Alex.* 49.13; Diod. 17.80.3; Justin 12.5.3; Curt. 7.2.11–32, with a eulogy at 7.2.33–4). Beloch IV² 2.290–306, Abschn. XV; Berve II 298–306 no. 606; Robinson 1945; Heckel, *Marshals*² 44–51; Carney 2000, 264–73; Müller, *LexAM* 377–82. **Stemma VII.**

849 PARYSATIS

(Παρύσατις). The youngest of the daughters of Artaxerxes III Ochos (Arr. 7.4.4), P. and her two older sisters were captured at Damaskos by Parmenion in 333 (Curt 3.13.12). From that point, she remained in Alexander's camp until late 331 and, presumably, was left behind at Sousa in 331 with Dareios III's womenfolk, when Alexander the Great continued on to Persepolis (cf. Curt. 5.2.17; Diod. 17.67.1). There, in 324, she married Alexander (Arr. 7.4.4). What became of her or whether she was treated with suspicion by Rhoxane after Alexander's death and eliminated (cf. Stateira and Drypetis; Plut. *Alex.* 77.6), we do not know. Berve II 306 no 607; Brosius 77; Shayegan 116 no. 85; Aulbach §4.2.3. **Stemmata I and III.**

850 PASAS

(Πάσας). Thessalian. Family background unknown. P. appears, along with Damis (Amissus) and Perillos, as an intermediary in the dispute between the cavalry and infantry factions after the death of Alexander in Babylon (Curt. 10.8.15). It is impossible to determine the precise nature of his service under Alexander or how long he had participated in the campaign. Berve II 306–7 no. 608; Atkinson and Yardley 199.

851 PASIKRATES

(Πασικράτης). Ruler of Kourion. Son of Aristokrates and brother of Themistagoras (Bosworth I 250, citing Miller 1979, 78–9: an inscription from Nemea supports the emendation of Arr. 2.22.2 from Θουριέως to Κουριέως and disproves the theory of Beloch III² 2.322 that Arrian refers to the ruler of Soloi). P., like the other kings of Kypros, joined the Aegean fleet of Pharnabazos and Autophradates in 334, only to defect after the battle of Issos and submit to Alexander at Sidon in 332 (Arr. 2.20.3). The Kyprian fleet played an important role in the final assault on Tyre, though P.'s own quinquereme (along with those of Pnytagoras of Salamis and Androkles of Amathos) was destroyed by a Tyrian counterattack as it lay at anchor in the harbor (Arr. 2.22.2). Nothing else is known of his career. Berve II 307 no. 609.

852 PASIKRATES

(Πασικράτης). Ruler of Kypriot Soloi (Plut. *Alex.* 29.3). Father of Nikokles (Arr. *Ind.* 18.8) and, probably, Eunostos (Athen. 13.576e; Beloch III² 2.322). He appears to have defected to Alexander along with the other Kypriot kings soon after Issos. In early 331, when Alexander conducted dramatic contests in Phoinikia and enlisted the Kypriot kings as *choregoi*, there was particularly keen competition between P. and Nikokreon of Salamis (Plut. *Alex.* 29.3). But Pasikrates' actor Athenodoros defeated Thessalos, a favorite of Alexander's who had been assigned to Nikokreon (Plut. *Alex.* 29.1–4). In the first war of the Diadochoi, P. and other rulers of Kypros made an alliance with Ptolemy (Arr. *Succ.* 24.6); Perdikkan forces sent against him were unsuccessful. He remained an ally of Ptolemy and resisted Antigonos' overtures in 315 (Diod. 19.59.1; cf. Olshausen 87 no. 62). His successor was Eunostos (Athen. 13.576e). Berve II 307 no. 610.

853 PATRAOS

(Πάτραος). Ruler of the Paionians (Tataki 210 no. 18; Head, *Catalogue of Greek Coins, Macedonia* 1879, p. LI and Head, *HN*² 236). He must have supplied the Paionian horsemen who served with Alexander (Diod. 17.17.4). These were commanded by his relative (Berve II 307: "vielleicht eines Bruders des P."), Ariston. P. minted silver tetradrachms depicting what appears to be Ariston's victory in a duel with the Persian Satropates (Merker 1965, 44–5 and 55 no. 4). P. succeeded Lyppeios (Lykpeios, Lykkeios) as ruler of the Paionians and was followed (no later than 310) by his son Audoleon, the father of Ariston. Nevertheless, any attempt to reconstruct a family tree must be speculative. Berve II 307 no. 611; Merker 1965.

854 PATROKLES

(Πατροκλῆς). Macedonian (Tataki 398 no. 23). Friend of Seleukos, established as *strategos* of Babylonia in 312, which he was unable to defend against the large army brought by Demetrios. Instead he shadowed and harassed the enemy after evacuating the population and appealing to Seleukos in Media for help (Diod. 19.100.5–6). At the direction of Seleukos and Antiochos I, P. conducted an exploration of the Caspian Sea and adjacent areas (Pliny, *HN* 6.58; Strabo 11.7.1, 3; 11.11.5; *FGrH* 712), probably in the 290s (Grainger 1990a, 153). He is not heard of again until 286, when he advised Seleukos to capture Demetrios Poliorketes when he was in Kilikia (Plut. *Demetr.* 47. 4). He is last heard of serving Antiochos in his struggle with Herakleia (Memnon 9.1). Grainger, *SPG* 111; Gisinger, *RE* XVIII (1949) 2263–73 no. 5.

855 PATRON

(Πάτρων). Phokian. Mercenary in the service of Dareios III; P. commanded those Greek mercenaries who remained with the Great King after the disaster at Gaugamela (Curt. 5.9.15). Curt. 5.12.4 says there were 4,000 mercenaries; Arr. 3.16.2 says only 2,000, adding Glaukos the Aitolian as joint commander. In Curtius' highly dramatized account, he makes an effort to warn Dareios of Bessos' treachery (5.11; cf. 5.12.7), speaking Greek to the King in the very presence of the unilingual conspirator. Although Dareios did not avail himself of the mercenaries' protection, some of them may have put up an unsuccessful fight or deserted. After the King's death, 1,500 (presumably including P.) agreed through messengers to surrender unconditionally to Alexander's agent, Andronikos son of Agerros (Arr. 3.23.8–9). Berve II 307–8 no. 612; Seibt 117–18; Hofstetter 142–3 no. 245.

856 PAUSANIAS

(Παυσανίας). Prominent Macedonian (Tataki 399 no. 31). *Hetairos* of Alexander. In 334 P. was appointed commandant (*epimeletes*, in effect, as *phrourarchos*) of the citadel of

Sardis (Arr. 1.17.7). As such he was presumably responsible to the newly appointed satrap of Lydia, Asandros son of Philotas. Nothing else is known about him, unless he can be identified with the officer of Antigonos (Diod. 19.73; Billows 414–15 no. 87; Lund 41). Berve II 308 no. 613; Fiehn, *RE* XVIII (1949) 2401 no. 7.

857 PAUSANIAS

(Παυσανίας). Macedonian (Tataki 400 no. 34). Identified merely as a lover of Philip II and friend of Attalos (Diod. 16.93.4–5), P. was apparently close in age to his namesake from Orestis, whose rival he had become for Philip's favor. Their homosexual relations with the King had presumably begun during their terms as Pages at the Court. The Orestian is described as *somatophylax* (Diod. 16.93.3), and the fact that P. died fighting on foot at the side of Philip II suggests that he too was a Royal Hypaspist, that is, a member of the *agema*. His death occurred in a battle with the Illyrians (Diod. 16.93.6), presumably in early 336 (Heckel 1981c, 56). Fears 1975; cf. also Ogden 1996, 120–1.

858 PAUSANIAS

(Παυσανίας). Son of Kerastos (Joseph. *AJ* 11.8.1 [304]), Macedonian (Tataki 206 no. 11) from Orestis (Diod. 16.93.3). P. was born in the mid-350s: as a Page (*pais basilikos*) he appears to have become an *eromenos* of Philip II, but as he approached manhood he found himself replaced by another young man, also named Pausanias, as Philip's favorite (Diod. 16.93.3–4). The rival was abused by P. as effeminate and sought to prove his manliness by dying on the battlefield (presumably in an Illryian campaign in 337/6) in defense of Philip II (Diod. 16.93.5–6). Attalos, who was a friend of the dead Pausanias, invited P. of Orestis to a drinking party where he was allegedly gang-raped by muleteers at Attalos' instigation (Justin 9.6.5–6; Diod. 16.93.7–8; Arist. *Pol.* 5.10 1311[b]; Plut. Alex. 10.5 includes Attalos' niece Kleopatra as an instigator; Hatzopoulos 2005 is pure fantasy; see Heckel, *Marshals*[2] 10–11 and Heckel, Howe and Müller 2017, 100 n.32). P. sought redress from Philip, who failed to take action because the culprit was a kinsman and would soon be sent to Asia Minor with the advance force (Diod. 16.93.9). Hence P. directed his hostility against the King and murdered him as he entered the theater in Aigai (Diod. 16.94.3; Justin 9.6.4; Plut. *Alex.* 10.5–6; Joseph. *AJ* 11.8.1 [304]; 19.1.13 [95]; Arist. *Pol.* 5.10 1311[b]; cf. Ael. *VH* 3.45; Val. Max. 1.8 ext. 9; Cic. *de Fat.* 3.5). At the time of Philip's death Pausanias was a *somatophylax*, that is, a Royal Hypaspist (John of Antioch frg. 40; Plut. *Mor.* 170e-f calls him *doryphoros*; cf. Justin 9.6.4, *nobilis ex Macedonibus adulescens*; Joseph. *AJ* 19.1.13 [95], calls him one of Philip's *hetairoi*). It was alleged that he was incited by Olympias, or even Alexander, to kill Philip (Justin 9.7.1ff.; Plut. *Alex.* 10.5); Diod. 16.94.1–2 claims he was inspired by the sophist Hermokrates. P. was killed by other Royal Hypaspists, as he tried to escape (Diod. 16. 94. 4; cf. Justin 9.7.9, where the reference to "getaway horses" suggests that Justin is compressing a similar story), and his body crucified (Justin 9.7.10; 11.2.1; cf. *P.Oxy.* 1798). The Athenians, upon the news of Philip's death, voted a crown for P., possibly at the urging of Demosthenes (Plut. *Dem.* 22.2). Berve II 308–9 no. 614; Bosworth 1971a; Fears 1975; Heckel 1992, 297–8; Heckel, Howe, and Müller 2017; Hoffmann 212; Müller, *LexAM* 388–9.

859 PAUSANIAS

(Παυσανίας). Macedonian (Tataki 399 no. 32). P. accompanied Harpalos to Athens in 324 and then Krete, where he murdered him (Paus. 2.33.4), perhaps on the orders of Thibron (Diod. 17.108; Strabo 17 C837; Arr. *Succ.* 1.16). Nothing else is known about him. Berve II 309 no. 615.

860 PAUSANIAS

(Παυσανίας). Apparently Macedonian. Physician who treated Krateros at some point (perhaps in 324) and received a letter from Alexander concerning the use of hellebore (Plut. *Alex.* 41.7). Nothing else is known about him. Berve II 309 no. 616.

861 PAUSANIAS

(Παυσανίας). Macedonian (Tataki 400 no. 35). When Lysimachos was besieging Kallatis (*Barr. Atl.* 22 F5) in 313/12, Antigonos sent P. with an army of unspecified size to the relief of the city, sending also a naval force under Lykon (Diod. 19.73.6). Lysimachos acted quickly and, after attacking and defeating the Thrakian king, Seuthes (Diod. 19.73.8–9), turned to deal with the forces of P. whom he also defeated: P. himself was killed in the engagement (Diod. 19.73.10). The survivors from his force were either ransomed or enrolled in Lysimachos' army. See also s.v. Lykon no. 665. Billows 414–15 no. 87; Lenschau, *RE* XVIII (1949) 2401 no. 8.

862 PAUSIPPOS

(Παύσιππος). Spartan (Poralla no. 598). Sent as ambassador to Dareios III, perhaps in the period leading up to Agis' war, along with Kallikratidas, Monimos, and Onomastoridas. All were captured by Alexander after Dareios' death in 330 (Arr. 3.24.4). But Curt. 3.13.15 places their capture at Damaskos (333/2), in which context Arr. 2.15.2 names Euthykles (partially corroborated by Plut. *Alex.* 40.4; full discussion in Bosworth I 233–4; Atkinson I 261). Berve II 310 no. 617; Hofstetter 145 no. 247.

863 PEISIS

(Πεῖσις). Son of Charias from Thespiai. P. was foremost in reputation and power among the Boiotians (Plut. *Demetr.* 39.2). He was honored with a statue by the Oropians (*I.Orop.* 366), probably after the expulsion of Kassandros' garrisons from Thebes and Oropos in 312 (Paschidis 312). Praised in a Delphic epigram (*CEG* II 789) as a Boiotian cavalry leader, who helped to drive out the garrison in Lokrian Opous (cf. Gullath 1982, 159). In 292, P. urged the Boiotians to revolt against Demetrios Poliorketes with the help of Kleonymos the Spartan (Plut. *Demetr.* 39.2). But, on Demetrios' arrival before Thebes with his siege engines, Kleonymos fled and the Boiotians surrendered (Plut. *Demetr.* 39.4). Demetrios showed kindness to P., whom he made *polemarchos* of Thespiai. Boiotia rebelled again soon afterwards (on the chronology of the two revolts see Paschidis 312 n.4; cf. Niese I 367; Wheatley and Dunn 2020, 450) and so it appears that Demetrios' trust in P. was misplaced (Plut. *Demetr.* 39.5–6). What became of him is unknown. Paschidis 312–15 C15.

864 PEITHAGORAS

(Πειθαγόρας, also Πυθαγόρας). Seer. Macedonian from Amphipolis (Tataki 59 no. 108), brother of Apollodoros (Plut. *Alex.* 73.3–4). He appears to have accompanied his brother to Asia—though we do not know when they left Macedonia—and remained in Babylon with Apollodoros in 331/0 (Arr. 3.16.4). P. is said to have predicted the deaths of Hephaistion and Alexander as well as those of Perdikkas and Antigonos (Arr. 7.18.1–5 = Aristoboulos, *FGrH* 139 F54; App. *BCiv.* 2.152). Hence, he must have lived until at least 301. Berve II 310 no. 618. Billows 447–8 no.135.

865 PEITHON

(Πείθων, Πίθων). Macedonian (Tataki 402 no. 44). Son of Antigenes. According to Nearchos (ap. Arr. *Ind.* 15.10), P. captured a snake of considerable length in India. That he was a man of some importance is suggested by the use of both the name and patronymic, as Berve observed, but that need not require us to identify him with the only attested Peithon without a patronymic, namely the taxiarch, who is probably to be equated with the son of Agenor. Whether this Peithon's father is identifiable with the commander of the Argyraspids (or Antigenes of Pallene, if this was a separate or historical individual) is impossible to determine. Berve II 311 no. 620.

866 PEITHON

(Πείθων, Πίθων). Macedonian (Tataki 402 no. 45). Son of Sosikles. P. was placed in charge of the Royal Pages, who had been left in Zariaspa-Baktra in 328, in which place there were also some mercenary cavalry and several of the *hetairoi* who were suffering from illness. When the town was attacked by the Massagetai, a force of 80 mercenaries, a few Companions, Pages and P., along with the harpist Aristonikos, rode out and defeated them. On their return, however, they were ambushed by Spitamenes and a force of Skythians: some 60 mercenaries, seven Companions and Aristonikos were all killed. P. was wounded and captured alive; he was undoubtedly killed later (Arr. 4.16.6–7). Arrian says that he was responsible for the Pages (i.e. the *therapeia basilike*); cf. *Itiner. Al.* [43] 98: *aulico ministerio.* And we need not assume that he was more than the equivalent of a "cadet instructor"; this is surely the point of Arrian's comment that the force was without a leader (4.16.7). Berve II 311–12 no. 622.

867 PEITHON

(Πείθων, Πίθων). Macedonian (Tataki 199 no. 9). Son of Krateuas from Eordaia (Arr. 6.28.4, *Succ.* 1.2, *Ind.* 18.6) or Alkomenai in Deuriopos (Strabo 7 C326; Arr. *Ind.* 18.6; Justin 13.4.13; 13.8.10 calls him Illyrian, perhaps because his source confused his place of origin with Alkomenai in Illyria: so Berve II 311 n.3); perhaps a relative of Kassandros' general Krateuas (Diod. 19.50–51). Although he first appears as a trierarch of the Hydaspes fleet in 326 (Arr. *Ind.* 18.6), P. had been a Somatophylax for an unspecified time (Arr. 6.28.4), perhaps since at least 336. He received a golden crown at Sousa in 324 (Arr. 7.5.6), but we are not told of any distinguished contribution; nor do we know the name of his Persian bride at the Sousan mass marriage. At the time of Alexander's fatal illness in Babylon, P., along with Seleukos and others, slept in the temple of Sarapis (Arr. 7.26.2; doubted by Grainger 1990a, 218–19). P. opposed the kingship of Arrhidaios and supported Perdikkas: his proposed joint guardianship of Rhoxane's child by Perdikkas and Leonnatos, leaving the direction of European affairs to Antipatros and Krateros (Curt. 10. 7. 8–9) was intended to prevent the complete erosion of Perdikkas' authority. (Curt. 10.7.4–5). In return for his support, P. received the satrapy of Media Maior (Justin 13.4.13; Curt. 10.10.4; Diod. 18.3.1; Arr. *Succ.* 1.5; Dexippos, *FGrH* 100 F8 §2; cf. *LM* 117, with Heckel 1988, 66–7), and also the task of suppressing the Greek rebellion in the Upper Satrapies (Diod. 18.4.8; 18.7.3–9). For this purpose, he received special powers, perhaps as "*strategos* of the Upper Satrapies" (cf. Diod. 19.14.1), to levy troops from the neighboring satraps and to act as commander-in-chief of the expedition. P. took 3,000 infantry and 800 horse from Babylon, as well as written orders to the satraps to supply a further 10,000 infantry and 8,000 cavalry for the expedition. This command fueled P.'s ambitions, and he planned to come to terms with the insurgents and translate his *strategia* into greater powers in the Upper Satrapies (Diod. 18.7.4). But Perdikkas, suspecting his designs, gave instructions that the rebels be slaughtered upon their surrender. Despite P.'s intrigues and the cooperation of Lipodoros the Ainianian, the troops were moved more by the expectation of plunder than by compassion and carried out Perdikkas' orders (Diod. 18.7.3–9) This action discredits Perdikkas and eliminated a much-needed supply of mercenaries in the area. For these reasons, it is doubtful that there was slaughter on such a scale (but see Iliakis 2013, 193). Rejoining Perdikkas, probably in time to participate in the expedition against Ariarathes of Kappadokia, P. later accompanied him to Egypt, where he was foremost of the mutineers who killed him near Memphis (Diod. 18.36.5). With Ptolemy's approval, he and Arrhidaios become *epimeletai* of the Kings (Diod. 18.36.6–7; Justin 13.8.10 wrongly says he was outlawed by the army), but Ptolemy left them with the dregs of the Royal Army and problems of back-pay. At Triparadeisos in Syria, P. and his colleague found themselves upstaged by Adea-Eurydike, who courted the troops. P. and Arrhidaios thus resigned the *epimeleia* and the office was given to Antipatros (Diod. 18.39.1–2); it was enough, for the time, to be reaffirmed as satrap of Media (Diod. 18.39.6; Arr. *Succ.* 1.35).

In the turmoil that followed Antipatros' death in 319 P. revived for himself the title of *strategos* of the Upper Satrapies and he expelled the Parthian satrap Philip (Diod. 19.14.1 calls him Philotas, but in the division of satrapies at Triparadeisos he is listed as Philip: Diod. 18.39.6; Arr. *Succ.* 1.35), installing in his place his own brother Eudamos. But the neighboring satraps joined Peukestas in driving P. (and Eudamos) out of Parthia (Diod. 19.14.2). When Eumenes asked him to support the Kings, he was already intriguing with Seleukos, now satrap of Babylonia (Diod. 19.14.3). The two joined forces against Eumenes (Diod. 19.12.1–2, 5; cf. Diod. 19.17.2), but Seleukos chose to recognize the authority of Antigonos. P. joined Antigonos as well (Diod. 19.19.4), giving him useful advice, which Antigonos rejected at his own peril (Diod. 19.19.8). Before the battle of Paraitakene, P. was sent by Antigonos to bring reinforcements and pack animals from Media (Diod. 19.20.2), which he supplied in large numbers (Diod. 19.20.3; cf. 19.27.1). That Antigonos had complete trust in him is doubtful, though he valued his generalship and assigned to him the less mobile forces while he pursued the enemy with his cavalry (Diod. 19.26.7). In Paraitakene P. commanded the cavalry on the left (Diod. 19.29.2–3), but his force was routed (Diod. 19.30.1–4). While the army was in P.'s satrapy (Diod. 19.32.4), it was important for Antigonos to keep his goodwill, and we find P. closely associated with his commander until the final defeat of Eumenes at Gabiene (Diod. 19.38.4, 40.1, 43.4). Soon, however, P. was suspected of plotting rebellion. Antigonos pretended that he was about to hand over troops to him and to leave him as *strategos* of the Upper Satrapies. Catching him off guard, he arrested and executed him (Diod. 19.46.1, 3; Polyaenus 4.6.14). In P.'s place, Antigonos appointed Orontobates (no. 822; Billows 413–14 no. 85), a native of the region, who was supervised by Hippostratos (no. 538). Hieronymos may have given P. bad press since P. had failed to cooperate with Eumenes and was plotting to betray Antigonos. But Champion 2014, 70 rightly calls P. "one of the most active intriguers and perennial losers of the era of the Successors." Berve II 311 no. 621; Bengtson I 178ff., Schober 1981, 15–26, 88, 91–6, 158–60; Heckel 1988 38–9, 66–7, 74–5; Heckel 1992, 276–9; Billows 415–16 no. 88.

868 PEITHON

(Πείθων, Πίθων). Macedonian (Tataki 401 nos. 42–3). Son of Agenor (Arr. 6.17.1; Justin 13.4.21). P. assumed command of Koinos' battalion of *asthetairoi*, perhaps as early as the Hydaspes battle (326). He accompanied Alexander against the Mallians (Arr. 6.6.1), capturing and enslaving those who had fled to a neighboring fortress (Arr. 6.7.2–3). Together with Demetrios the hipparch, he led further reprisals against the Mallians (Arr. 6.8.2–3). Perhaps P. led one of the two battalions of infantry that accompanied Hephaistion and Demetrios into the territory of the "cowardly Poros" (Arr. 5.21.5). It appears that, as a reward for his efforts and because of his experience in this region, Alexander appointed the son of Agenor satrap of India from the confluence of the Indos and Akesines Rivers to the Indian Ocean (Arr. 6.15.4)—that is, the west bank of the Indos, down to the sea and including Patala. After the appointment of Agenor's son as satrap, P. the taxiarch is not heard of again. Consequently, I do not understand why Berve II 312 n.2 believes that the taxiarch was the son of Krateuas, an identification that Bosworth 1988, 275 considers "highly probable." Nor does Billows 415 no. 88 identify the son of Agenor with the taxiarch. That P. shared the satrapy with Oxyartes is highly unlikely and editors are right to emend the text of Arr. 6.15.4: Oxyartes' satrapy is described above (Arr. 6.15.3) as Parapamisadai; perhaps this was extended in a southeasterly direction to the confluence of the Indos and Akesines (Chenab) and was thus adjacent to P.'s. As satrap, he brought the rebellious Mousikanos captive to Alexander, who crucified him (Curt. 9.8.16; Arr. 6.17.1–2). Although Justin 13.4.21 implies that P. retained this satrapy after Alexander's death (cf. Curt. 10.10.4), it appears that, probably after the death of Philip son of Machatas, he was transferred to the Kophen satrapy (Gandhara), between Parapamisos and the Indos (so Diod. 18.3.3; Dexippos, *FGrH* 100 F8; cf. Bosworth 1983, esp. 39ff.). At Triparadeisos (320) his position was confirmed (Diod. 18.39.6; Arr. *Succ.* 1.36; Justin 13.4.21).

Nothing further is heard of P. until 315, when Antigonos appointed him satrap of Babylonia in place of Seleukos, who had fled to Egypt (Diod. 19.56.4). It is not possible to determine whether he took part in the battle of Gabiene or if he had, perhaps, been recalled from India when Antigonos reformed the administration of the East (Diod. 19.48.1–2). P.'s support of Antigonos raises some interesting questions. Did he join him before the battle of Paraitakene? If so, he could have brought with him only a small force of elephants; for Antigonos had a significant number of the beasts at Kretopolis (Diod. 18.45.1; no specific figure is given, but they were clearly a sizable force) and deployed 65 of them at Paraitakene (Diod. 19.27.1) and Gabiene (19.40.1), far short of the 120 brought to Eumenes by Eudamos (cf. Diod. 19.14.8, 15.5, 27.2; cf. Plut. *Eum.* 16.3). Furthermore, it will be difficult to explain why P. joined Antigonos at this point, when the eastern satraps had uniformly aligned themselves with Eumenes. They had, in fact, assembled to oppose Peithon son of Krateuas (Diod. 19.14.1). Of course, P. may have been motivated by strong personal friendship with Antigonos or by fear of Eudamos, who had murdered Poros in the adjacent satrapy (Diod. 19.14.8), but neither of these can be documented. Against the view that he fought with Eumenes and surrendered to Antigonos are both the silence of the sources and the fact that Antigonos dealt harshly with the prominent subordinates of Eumenes (Diod. 19.44.1). Since he was not in a position to remove P. from India—for he could not even exert his authority over Tlepolemos, Stasanor, and Oxyartes (Diod. 19.48.1–2)—it seems likely that he left his satrapy soon after Gabiene, because of the instability there (Tarn 1951, 168; cf. Billows 415.); perhaps he arrived at the same time as, if not together with, Sibyrtios, whom Antigonos reinstated as governor of Arachosia (Diod. 19.48.3). Antigonos appointed P. satrap of Babylonia (Diod. 19.56.4), but he soon summoned him to Syria in 314/3 (Diod. 19.69.1)—though not necessarily relieving him of his satrapy, since no successor is named in the sources. Possibly on account of his experience in India with elephants, he became an adviser of Demetrios Poliorketes (Diod. 19.69.1) and joint commander of his forces (cf. Diod. 19.82.1). In 313, Demetrios left him with the elephants and heavily armed troops to hold Koile-Syria while he tried in vain to deal with the enemy in Kilikia (Diod. 19.80.1). When Demetrios returned and engaged Ptolemy at Gaza, Peithon fought on Demetrios' left wing, sharing the command (Diod. 19.82.1); in this engagement, he fell and his body was recovered under truce (Diod. 19.85.2). Berve II 310 no. 619; Billows 415–16 no. 88; Bosworth 1983, 39ff.; Heckel 1992, 323–6.

869 PELAGON

(Πελάγων). Ephesian; son of Syrphax, a leader of the pro-Persian oligarchy in Ephesos. After the restoration of the democracy, P. and Syrphax had taken refuge in the temple (of Artemis), from which they were dragged out and stoned to death (Arr. 1.17.12). Their fate was shared also by Syrphax's nephews. Berve II 312 no. 624; Berve, *Tyrannis* I 335–6, II 690; Hofstetter 146 no. 249.

870 PELIGNAS

(Πελίγνας). A cook purchased by Olympias and sent to Alexander at some point during the campaign in Asia Minor (Athen. 14.659f–660a). He is otherwise unknown. Berve II 312 no. 625.

871 PERDIKKAS

(Περδίκκας). Macedonian (Tataki 206–7 no. 12). Son of Orontes (Arr. 3.11.9; 6.28.4; Arr. *Ind.* 18.5) from Orestis (Arr. 6.28.4; Diod. 17.57.2), a member of that canton's royal house and possibly even of Argead descent (Curt. 10.7.8). Born c.360 (cf. Berve II 313). Brother of Alketas (Arr. *Succ.* 1.21) and Atalante (Diod. 18.37.2), who later married Attalos son of Andromenes. A steadfast supporter of Alexander, P. declined Alexander's gifts in 334, preferring to share the King's fortune (Plut. *Alex.* 15.4–5; cf. Plut. *Mor.* 342d–e). A member of the Royal Hypaspists at the time of Philip II's assassination in October 336, P. pursued and killed the regicide Pausanias (Diod. 16.94.4). In 335, he commanded the *taxis* of Orestians and Lynkestians (Diod. 17.57.2) in the campaign against Kleitos and Glaukias

(Arr. 1.6.9). Arr. 1.8.1–3 claims that P.'s troops acted without orders from Alexander when they attacked Thebes (but this is refuted by Diod. 17.12.3) and that he was wounded in the engagement. At the Granikos River he was stationed between the hypaspists of Nikanor and Koinos' battalion (Arr. 1.14.2), roughly the same position that he occupied at Issos and Gaugamela (Arr. 2.8.3; Curt. 3.9.7 (Issos); Arr. 3.11.9; Curt. 4.13.28). In an abortive attempt on Myndos Alexander took with him the *taxeis* of P., Amyntas, and Meleagros (Arr. 1.20.5; cf. Fuller 202); a second reference to P. at Halikarnassos is less creditable: two of his men, motivated by drunkenness and *philotimia,* led an unauthorized assault on the city walls that ended in failure (thus Arr. 1.21.1–3; the poor discipline of P.'s troops is corroborated by Diod. 17.25.5; Fuller 200–6; cf. Welles 189 n. 2). In 332, P. and Krateros shared the command over the besieging forces at Tyre, while Alexander raided the neighboring Arabs (Curt. 4.3.1; Krateros' role is corroborated by Polyaenus 4.13, but Arrian says nothing of joint command; cf. Errington 1969, 237; Fuller 206–16).

Not one to lead from the rear, P. was wounded at Gaugamela (Curt. 4.16.32; Diod. 17.61.3; omitted by Arr. 3.15.2). At the Persian Gates, he joined Alexander's force which encircled Ariobarzanes (Arr. 3.18.5). What part he played in the Philotas affair can be determined only from Curtius: P. came to Alexander's tent on the night of Philotas' arrest, accompanied by Hephaistion, Krateros, Koinos, Erigyios, and Leonnatos, to discuss the crisis (Curt. 6.8.17). Probably, he belonged to the *consilium amicorum*, which had met with Alexander earlier that day and urged that Philotas be punished: in short, he was party to the conspiracy *against* Philotas (Curt. 6.8.1ff.). What P. gained from Philotas' fall is less clear; for he was already well advanced in the Macedonian chain of command. He appears to have replaced Menes as Somatophylax (Curt. 6.8.16 designates Perdikkas as *ex armigeris*; cf. Arr. 3.16.9 for Menes' reassignment) but served as both taxiarch and Somatophylax from late 331 to early 329. In Sogdiana, Meleagros and P., functioning as taxiarchs, besieged one of the seven fortresses along the Iaxartes (Syr-Darya) (Curt. 7.6.19, 21; cf. Holt 54–5). In 328 P. was promoted to hipparch and led one of five divisions that swept Sogdiana (Arr. 4.16.2); the pezhetairoi of Orestis and Lynkestis were now entrusted to his younger brother, Alketas (cf. Arr. 4.22.1). As Somatophylax, on the other hand, he occupied a seat near the King at the fateful banquet in Marakanda (late summer 328), and joined Ptolemy in trying to restrain the King, who was incensed by Kleitos' outspokenness (Curt. 8.1.45, 48). Three Somatophylakes—Ptolemy, Leonnatos, P.—conducted the night operations against the Rock of Chorienes (Koh-i-nor) early in the following spring (Arr. 4.21.4).

With Hephaistion, P. led the advance force to the Indos, which they were to bridge (Arr. 4.22.7; cf. Curt. 8.10.2), subduing on the way Peukelaotis, whose ruler Astis (no. 246) offered stubborn resistance (Arr. 4.22.8). By the time Alexander reached the Indos, P. and Hephaistion had brought the natives under Alexander's sway, gathered provisions from Taxiles (Curt. 8.12.6, 15; Metz Epit. 48), and bridged the river by means of what clearly was a boat-bridge (Curt. 8.10.2; cf. Arr. 5.7.1–2). On their way they had also fortified a city called Orobatis, in which they left an armed guard (Arr. 4.28.5). At the Hydaspes (Jhelum), P. crossed the river in the same triakonter as Alexander, Lysimachos, Ptolemy, and Seleukos (Arr. 5.13.1) and, in the actual battle, commanded one of the hipparchies directly under Alexander's control, the main striking force against Poros (Arr. 5.12.2; cf. 5.13.1; Curt. 8.14.15; Fuller 180–99, esp. 186–7). In the Sangala campaign, P. led his own hipparchy and the infantry battalions on the left (Arr. 5.22.6); but Arrian describes in detail only the action on the right. After the battle P. was sent to ravage the region around Sangala with a light-armed force (Curt. 9.1.19). During the descent of the Indos river system in 326, P. took a special force against one of the Mallian towns, which he captured, killing those inhabitants who did not manage to escape into the marshes (Arr. 6.6.4, 6). Reunited with Alexander for the assault on the main Mallian stronghold, he commanded a portion of the army, which Arrian (Ptolemy) implies was, through its sluggishness, responsible for Alexander's critical wounding there (Arr. 6.9.1–2). According to at least one (unnamed) source, it was P. who cut the arrow from Alexander's body (Arr. 6.11.1; others attribute the surgery to Kritoboulos, a doctor from Kos (Curt. 9.5.25). Arr. 6.11.1 calls this man Kritodemos). While Alexander convalesced, P. completed the subjugation of the region before rejoining the main force (Arr. 6.15.1; he subdued the Abastani).

At Sousa in 324 he married the daughter (**A88**) of Atropates (Arr. 7.4.5; cf, Justin 13.4.13) and was crowned, along with the other Somatophylakes (Arr. 7.5.6). Later in 324 he conveyed Hephaistion's corpse from Ekbatana to Babylon for burial (Diod. 17.110.8) and received Hephaistion's (the first) hipparchy or chiliarchy of the Companion Cavalry—though the unit, out of respect for the dead Hephaistion, retained the name of its original commander (Arr. 7.14.10); in effect, he was Alexander's second-in-command (when Seleukos held the office after P., he is called by Justin 13.4.17 *summus castrorum tribunatus*). P. was thus the most influential of the marshals in Babylon at the time of Alexander's death (Nepos, *Eum.* 2.2), indeed, it was reported that the King, on his deathbed and in the presence of the other generals, handed P. his signet ring (Curt. 10.5.4, 6.4–5; Justin 12.15.12; Diod. 17.117.3; 18.2.4; Nepos, *Eum.* 2.1; *LM* 112). Alexander may also have entrusted to him his wife, Rhoxane, with instructions that he should marry her (*LM* 112, 118), a reasonable move in view of the fact that she was carrying Alexander's child (Curt. 10.6.9; Justin 13.2.5; cf. 12.15.9; Arr. *Succ.* 1.1; Dexippos, *FGrH* 100 F8 §1). Despite early support from Aristonous (Curt. 10.6.16–18) and Peithon (Curt. 10.7.4–8), his position was soon undermined by the unexpected proclamation of Arrhidaios, who was renamed Philip (no. 903). A compromise saw Krateros appointed *prostates* of the mentally deficient King, while P. retained his rank of *chiliarchos*, which was further restricted by the appointment of Meleagros as *hyparchos* (Arr. *Succ.* 1.3). P., however, worked to eliminate his rival and encouraged rumors that Meleagros was plotting against him (Diod. 18.4.7; cf. Curt. 10.9.7ff.) and then conducted a lustration of the army, using the opportunity to round up and execute the ringleaders of the uprising (Curt. 10.9.11ff.; Justin 13.4.7; cf. Diod. 18.4.7) and Meleagros himself (Curt. 10.9.20–1; Arr. *Succ.* 1.4–5; Justin 13.4.7–8; cf. Diod. 18.4.7).

In the name of the King, P. assigned some satrapies to the leading men in Babylon while retaining some of the existing satraps (Diod. 18.3.1–3; Justin 13.4.10–23; Curt. 10.10.1–4; Arr. *Succ.* 1.5–7; Dexippos, *FGrH* 100 F8 §§2–7). He also arranged the murder of Stateira and her sister Drypetis (Plut. *Alex.* 77.6); what Plutarch depicts as an act of jealousy on Rhoxane's part, was meant to secure the interests of her unborn child and eliminate the Achaimenid princesses as political tools for the ambitions of others. P. also held an assembly of the Macedonian troops and cancelled Alexander's plans, as they were set out in the *Hypomnemata*, thereby, protecting himself against any possible future charge of having failed to carry out the King's instructions and cancelling Krateros' orders to replace Antipatros as regent of Macedonia (Diod. 18.4.1–6; Badian 1967b, 201–4). In this scheme he may have had the support of Eumenes who, as Royal Secretary, had prepared the *Hypomnemata*. P.'s motive must have been to secure the goodwill and support of the old Regent, and at this time he must have entered into negotiations for the hand of his daughter, Nikaia. P. entered into negotiations with Antipatros when his own position was not yet secure, before he had taken control of the "royal armies and the guardianship (*prostasia*) of the kings" (thus Diod. 18.23.2). Now the reference to the "royal armies" cannot be accurate, for it is certain that P. commanded them from the start by virtue of his *chiliarchia* (Curt. 10.10.4; Justin 13.4.5; Diod. 18.3.1). As chief commander he conducted the lustration of the army (Justin 13.4.7ff.; Arr. *Succ.* 1.4; Curt. 10.9.11ff.). But the *prostasia* may well—and very likely does—refer to the time of the birth of Alexander IV, Rhoxane's son; for Diodorus speaks of the *prostasia* of the Kings, not just of Arrhidaios, with whom alone the enigmatic *prostasia* of Krateros is linked. At that point in time P. was formidable: he was *epimeletes* for Philip Arrhidaios, *prostates* (or guardian) for Alexander IV, and *strategos* of the imperial forces in Asia. But Krateros' position had become weak indeed. Before the birth of Alexander's son, however, P. had isolated Krateros in Kilikia and was himself in a precarious state, having incurred the suspicion of the Macedonians in Babylon through his treacherous elimination of Meleagros (Arr. *Succ.* 1.5). But Antipatros too was prepared to deal: there was the matter of the Lamian War, and he wanted Krateros in Europe. Thus he recognized P.'s claim to a share of the supremacy in Asia and bound him to a political alliance by promising his daughter Nikaia. In return P. acknowledged Antipatros' sole authority in Europe. The negotiations must belong to the period of instability at Babylon. One of those who brought Nikaia to P. in the following year was Iolaos (Arr. *Succ.* 1.21), the girl's brother, who had been present at Alexander's death.

In the upper satrapies, where Alexander had settled the Greek mercenaries, there was rebellion, a direct consequence of Alexander's death (Diod. 18.4.8, 7.1). Accordingly, P. sent out Peithon (Diod. 18.7.3), formerly one of the Somatophylakes, who had been allotted Media and now showed the first signs of seditious intent. His army, augmented by contributions from the other satraps (in accordance with P.'s instructions), overcame the Greek force partly by deceit (Diod. 18.7.5–7). Whether the ensuing slaughter of the Greeks who had surrendered was indeed ordered by P. at the outset of the campaign is difficult to determine (Diod. 18.7.5, 8–9). In view of P.'s growing dependence on Eumenes, the annihilation of the Greek force was scarcely good politics. It is possible, however, that Peithon's troops got out of control and that the blame for the slaughter devolved upon P.

In the west, Antigonos and Leonnatos had been instructed to aid Eumenes in conquering his satrapy of Kappadokia, which had been bypassed by Alexander (Plut. *Eum.* 3.4). Antigonos defected from the Perdikkan cause and refused aid to Eumenes; but Leonnatos joined him in the spring (Plut. *Eum.* 3.5). At that point, however, Hekataios, tyrant of Kardia, arrived with an urgent appeal from Antipatros, asking Leonnatos to come with all haste to Europe (Diod. 18.14.4–5; Plut. *Eum.* 3.6); for he was besieged in Lamia by the Hellenic forces under Leosthenes. For Leonnatos it was the perfect opportunity for seeking the throne. He had already had communications with Olympias, the unyielding foe of Antipatros, and had received from her daughter Kleopatra, Alexander's sister, a promise of marriage (Plut. *Eum* 3.9; cf. Macurdy 37–8; Seibert 1967, 20; see no. 608). So much he confided to Eumenes, with whose support he hoped to gain the throne. But Eumenes, whether wary of Leonnatos' impetuosity or sincerely devoted to the Perdikkan cause, rejected the appeal on the ground that he feared that Antipatros would betray him to his arch-enemy Hekataios (Plut. *Eum.* 3.8). Therefore, he slipped away from Leonnatos' camp during the night, leaving Leonnatos to take his chances in Europe (Plut. *Eum.* 3.10; cf. Nepos, *Eum.* 2.4–5, who claims that Leonnatos planned to kill Eumenes when he failed to win his support).

P. came to regard Kleopatra as a means of gaining supreme power. Eumenes, deserted by Antigonos and Leonnatos, appealed to P. for help and divulged the details of Leonnatos' intrigues. P. moved to join Eumenes for an invasion of Kappadokia; it was late spring or early summer 322 (cf. Anson 1986, 214). In the Kappadokian campaign, P. continued the conquest of Alexander's empire and punished Ariarathes for his refusal to submit; he defeated him in two decisive engagements (Arr. *Succ.* 1.11; cf. Diod. 18.16.1–3, 22.1; App. *Mithr.* 8 = Hieronymos, *FGrH* 154 F3; Justin 13.6.1–3; [Lucian], *Macrob* 13 = *FGrH* 154 F4; Hornblower, *Hieronymus* 239–43). In a single campaigning season, he had extended the boundaries of Alexander's empire and taken a barbarian king captive. But the victory was tarnished by his cruel treatment of Ariarathes, who was impaled (Arr. *Succ.* 1.11) along with his relatives (Diod. 18.16.3; Plut. *Eum.* 3.13 says only that he was captured; Diod. 31, frag. 19.3–5, from a different source, says Ariarathes fell in battle). Thereafter, he instructed Eumenes to settle affairs in Armenia, which had been thrown into confusion by Neoptolemos (Plut. *Eum.* 4.1), while he himself directed his attention to Pisidia (Diod. 18.22.1). Here the Isaurians and Larandians had risen against and killed Alexander's satrap Balakros son of Nikanor (Diod. 18.22.1). These cities P. took without great difficulty, and they proved a source of plunder for his men. Victorious in the field and offering lucrative rewards to his soldiers, P. now enjoyed his greatest success (Diod. 18.22.2–8; Justin 13.6.1–3; but Justin and Diodorus disagree on the question of booty).

It was at this time that Antipatros' daughter Nikaia was brought to Asia by Iolaos and Archias (Diod. 18.23.1; Arr. *Succ.* 1.21; Justin 13. 6. 4–6). But P., who had found a marriage alliance with Antipatros' family desirable in 323, now had second thoughts. To make matters worse, Kleopatra, Alexander's sister, had arrived in Sardis, having been sent out (no doubt) at the instigation of Olympias (Arr. *Succ.* 1.21; cf. Justin 13.6.4). Eumenes may have had a hand in the affair: Leonnatos had opened his eyes to Kleopatra's potential, and Eumenes, who urged P. to marry her in place of Nikaia, may have corresponded with the scheming Olympias, encouraging her to send out her daughter. For his part, P. had begun to formulate a new policy, one that he hoped would win for him the throne. With the Kings securely in his possession and the army favorably disposed towards him on account of his recent successes in Kappadokia and Pisidia, P. was prepared to take two final steps to the kingship: union with Kleopatra and the ceremonious return of Alexander's body to Macedonia. What army would oppose the man returning to Macedonia with the son of Philip II, the wife, son and sister—indeed, the very body—of Alexander himself?

The almost contemporaneous arrivals of Nikaia and Kleopatra were most inopportune. In fact, Nikaia's very presence was an indication of changing events: the Macedonians had been victorious in the Lamian War, Antipatros' power restored. And he meant to achieve stability by wedding Phila to Krateros, Nikaia to P. By rejecting Nikaia now, P. would certainly invite civil war. Diod. 18.23.3; the sentiment at least is expressed by Justin 13.6.5; see also Macurdy 37–8; Vezin 39; cf. Beloch IV² 1.83. But there was also the matter of the rebellious Antigonos, satrap of Phrygia and friend of Antipatros. What P. needed was time enough to settle affairs in Asia to his satisfaction. To this time belongs the restoration of the Samian exiles, a matter referred by Antipatros to the Kings and carried out by P. in the name of Philip Arrhidaios; Diod. 18.18.6, 9 (see Habicht 1957, 1974, and 1996a; Errington 1975b). Perhaps P. received news of this from Iolaos and Archias, when they brought out Nikaia.

P. now called Antigonos to account, planning to remove him under the guise of legality (Diod. 18.23.3–4). But Antigonos, who understood P.'s intention—and, indeed, would use similar methods in the future—made no attempt to clear himself of the charges brought against him: guilty of insubordination, he now fled from his satrapy (Diod. 18.23.4, 25.3; Justin 13.6.7–9; Arr. *Succ.* 1.24) and joined Krateros and Antipatros, revealing P.'s ambitions and duplicity in his dealings with Nikaia; he also reported Alketas' murder of Kynnane (Arr. *Succ.* 1.24), which must have been committed without P.'s approval (contrary to the views of Droysen II³ 61; Niese I 214; Vezin 36; Beloch IV² 1.83 wrongly says that Perdikkas himself killed her). At any rate, the army mutinied and demanded that Kynnane's purpose be fulfilled, that Adea be taken to Arrhidaios (Polyaenus 8. 60; Arr. *Succ.* 1.22–4). Antigonos thus sought refuge with Antipatros and Krateros, warning them of P.'s intention to march on Macedonia (Diod. 18.23.4, 25.3–4; Justin 13.6.7–9; Arr. *Succ.* 1.24; cf. Vezin 37; Kaerst II² 21). Ptolemy, who had long feared Perdikkan intervention in Egypt (Diod. 18.14.2, 25.4), made an alliance with the *strategoi* in Europe, who now abandoned their Aitolian war in mid-winter 321/0 and prepared to cross into Asia (Diod. 18.25.5; Justin 13.6.9). Polyperchon held Europe (Justin 13.6.9).

P. abandoned Nikaia and openly courted Kleopatra, sending Eumenes with gifts to Sardis, where she had taken up residence (Arr. *Succ.* 1.26). Antigonos' defection had been followed by that of Asandros, the Karian satrap, and now Menandros of Lydia also took flight (Arr. *Succ* 1.26; 25.2; cf. Engel 1972: 215–19). P. knew that a confrontation with Antipatros and his allies was inevitable, and he meant to bolster his position by marrying Kleopatra before he took to the field and marched on Macedonia. But at this point the bottom fell out of P.'s carefully conceived scheme: Arrhidaios had completed the funeral car in Babylon and had begun to transport the King's body to Egypt. This had clearly been the King's intention, but Arrhidaios (no. 214), who spent almost two years overseeing the funeral arrangements, was surely instructed by P. that there would be a change in plans: Alexander's body would be taken to Macedonia, not Egypt (Diod. 18.3.5; Justin 12.15.7; 13.4.6; Curt. 10.5.4). Paus. 1.6.3 does say that the body was destined for Aigai, but this was in accordance with P.'s change of policy; there is no mention of Alexander's wishes here. Cf. Arr. *Succ.* 1.25, where Arrhidaios acts against Perdikkas' wishes. Seibert 1969, 110–11, also supposes that there is a contradiction between Pausanias' account and the version given by Diodorus, Justin and Curtius. For Perdikkas' change of policy see Droysen II³ 67 n.2, placing Pausanias' testimony in the proper light. The most thorough discussion is that of Schubert 180–9; see also Badian 1967b, 185–9; Errington 1970, 64–5; Beloch IV² 1.86–7. Tarn II 355–6, predictably, disbelieves Alexander's wish to be buried at Siwah, ascribing these reports to Ptolemy's propaganda. We can only assume, as P. himself did, that there had been collusion between Ptolemy and the satrap of Babylonia, Archon; it was symptomatic of widespread disaffection among the officials of the empire (Arr. *Succ.* 24.3). Word came to P. that Arrhidaios had turned southward and was making for Egypt. A contingent headed by the sons of Andromenes (Arr. *Succ.* 1.25; 24.1), sent out to retrieve Alexander's body, proved inadequate; for Ptolemy had marched out in full force to meet Arrhidaios' procession and escort it to Egypt (Diod. 18.28.2ff.; Arr. *Succ.* 1.25; Paus. 1.6.4; cf. Curt. 10.10.20). News of the "body-snatching" emphasized the need to secure Asia first

(Diod. 18.25.6; Justin 13.6.10–13; Arr. *Succ.* 24.1; Seibert 110–17). P. had other grievances against Ptolemy: his execution of the hyparch Kleomenes and his expansionist war against Kyrene. Making what arrangements he felt necessary for the security of Asia Minor, P. began his assault on Egypt, where Ptolemy had spent the two years after the settlement at Babylon fortifying his satrapy and winning the loyalty of his followers (Diod. 18.33.3–4). P., if indeed he did try to win support among his generals through gifts and promises (so Diod. 18.33.5), was less successful; for he seems not to have been well liked by the army or its officers (Justin 13.8.2; Arr. *Succ.* 1.28; *Suda* Π 1040; Memnon 4.3; cf. Beloch IV² 1.88). Failing to take Kamelon Teichos, by storm, P. broke camp on the following night and marched upstream to an island that lay opposite Memphis. But in the attempt to reach the island, he lost many men in the river, which was unexpectedly swift and deep. Once across, P. recognized that he had too few men for an assault on Memphis and was forced to re-cross the treacherous river. In all, according to Diod. 18.36.1, some 2,000 men were lost, including some prominent officers, though none of these is named. It was as much as the army was willing to endure from P., whom they held responsible for their present miseries. He had failed for the last time. The foremost of his generals, including Peithon and Seleukos, conspired against him during the night and murdered him in his tent. For P.'s campaign against Ptolemy see Diod. 18.33–7 (the only extensive account); also Arr. *Succ.* 1.28; Pllut. *Eum.* 8.2–3; Justin 13.8.1–2; see Seibert 118–28 for an analysis of the accounts. For his death: Arr. 7.18.5 (it was prophesied by the seer Peithagoras); Nepos, *Eum.* 5.1; Justin 13.8.10; 14.1.1, 4.11; 15.1.1; Diod. 18.36.5; Paus. 1.6.3; *Suda* Π 1040; Heidelberg Epit. 1. See also Molina Marín 2018: interesting but unconvincing. Hoffmann 153, 168; Berve II 313–16 no. 627; Geyer, *RE* XIX (1937) 604–14 no. 4; *PP* no. 16088; Wirth 1967; Heckel, *Marshals*² 153–84 and *LexAM* 406–7; Rathmann. **Stemma XII**.

872 PERDIKKAS

(Περδίκκας). Macedonian (Tataki 403 no. 48); family background unknown. P. first appears (spring 320) as a prominent officer in the army of Eumenes (τις τῶν ἐπιφανῶν ἡγεμόνων), whom he deserted in Kappadokia with 3,000 infantry and 500 horse (Diod. 18.40.2). The cause of his falling out with Eumenes is unknown (cf. Anson 255), but there is no mention of any earlier contacts with Antigonos' camp. Schäfer 2002, 111, with n.59, believes P. may have commanded Eumenes' rearguard, but his separation of the main army (he was encamped three days distant from Eumenes' forces: Diod. 18.40.2) can be explained by the withdrawal of the mutineers. Eumenes sent Phoinix with 4,000 foot and 1,000 horse against the mutineers and fell upon them as they slept. The mutinous contingent was captured, together with its leaders, who were executed by Eumenes (Plut. *Eum.* 9.3 speaking of the crucifixion of a traitor probably refers to P.: see also the discussion s.v. Apollonides no. 149); the common soldiers were, however, spared (Diod. 18.40.2–4). Nothing is known of his earlier career, but his association with Eumenes, who was outlawed at Triparadeisos with the other leaders of the Perdikkan party and who received no reinforcements from Europe between 323 and 320, suggests that he had served under Alexander the Great (thus also Berve II 317). Berve II 317 no. 628; Geyer, *RE* XIX.1 (1937) 614 no. 6.

873 PERDIKKAS

(Περδίκκας). Macedonian (Tataki 107 no. 17). Son of Alexander's general, Koinos, and grandson of Polemokrates. His mother was perhaps the unnamed daughter of Parmenion (Curt. 6.9.30), who had formerly been married to Attalos (Curt. 6.9.17). If so, he can have been born no later than 333, since Koinos' last sojourn in Macedonia occurred in the winter of 334/3 (Arr. 1.24.1, 29.4); he may, however, have been a newborn when his father returned from Asia Minor. His possession of ancestral lands was confirmed by Kassandros at some point between 306 and 297 (*Syll*³ 332 = Hatzopoulos II 43–5 no. 20). In light of his father's "traditional" Macedonian sentiments, it is likely that Perdikkas remained a supporter of Antipatros and his son. Geyer, *RE* XIX.1, 614 no. 7; Berve II 312–13 no. 626.

874 PERILAOS

(Περίλαος, Πέριλλος). Macedonian (Tataki 405 no. 63). *Hetairos* of Alexander. Perilaos asked Alexander for a dowry for his daughters and received fifty talents (Plut. *Mor.* 179f). The story itself is one of many illustrating the generosity of kings, and we may place no faith in the figures given. If this anecdote did, in fact, have its roots in some historical event, then we must suppose that it dates to after 331/0—after Alexander's capture of the Persian treasures—and that Perilaos, who had daughters of marriageable age at that time was born not later than the mid-360s. Berve II 317 no. 630.

875 PERILAOS

(Περίλαος, Πέριλλος). One of three men who acted as negotiators for the Macedonian cavalry and infantry in Babylon immediately after Alexander's death (Curt. 10.8.15). Since the other two, Damis (Amissus) of Megalopolis and Pasas the Thessalian, were Greeks (as was Eumenes, Plut. *Eum.* 3.1), P. may also have been Greek and thus considered neutral (for the frequency of the name outside Macedonia see Pape-Benseler s.v.; but see Atkinson and Yardley 199). He is perhaps identical with the Perilaos who served Antigonos in 315/14 and/or with the *hetairos* of Alexander (Plut. *Mor.* 179f, see no. 877). Berve II 317 no. 630.

876 PERILAOS

(Περίλαος, Πέριλλος). Macedonian (Tataki 405 no. 61). Son of Antipatros and younger brother of Kassandros, Perilaos supported his brother's military and political affairs (Plut. *Mor.* 486a); he seems to have remained in Pella with his father during the period 334–323. Billows 1989, 188 n.43 suggests that Perilaos is an error for Prepelaos. Berve II 317 no. 629. **Stemma V.**

877 PERILAOS

(Περίλαος, Πέριλλος). Officer in the service of Antigonos, P. led land forces, in concert with the fleet of Antigonos' *nauarchos* Theodotos, to Patara in Lykia, in 315/14. He was ambushed and captured by Polykleitos, Ptolemy's admiral. P. was soon ransomed by Antigonos (Diod. 19.64.5–8), an indication of his importance. Possibly identical with the man who mediated the dispute between the cavalry and infantry factions in Babylon in 323 (Curt. 10.8.15) or with Perillos, the *hetairos* of Alexander (Plut. *Mor.* 179f). Identification with Antipatros' son (above) is highly unlikely, since Kassandros and Antigonos were at war in 315/14 and Diodorus (Hieronymos) would no doubt have commented on the relationship, if Perilaos had defected to Antigonos. Billows 416 no. 89.

878 PEROIDAS

(Περοίδας). Macedonian (Tataki 64 no. 2). Son of Menestheus. Commander of the *ile* of Companions from Anthemos, The troops appear to have been recruited from the Chalcidic peninsula and to have held land they received at the hands of Philip II (see Bosworth I 211). P. appears to have accompanied Alexander from the beginning of the campaign. At Issos, his squadron was transferred, along with that of Pantordanos, from the left to the right wing before the battle began (Arr. 2.9.3). Nothing further is known of his role in that engagement. Like Pantordanos, he was no longer an ilarch at Gaugamela. Who his replacement was is unclear: Ariston, Demetrios, Glaukias, Hegelochos, and Meleagros all appear for the first time at Gaugamela, though two of them may well have been ilarchs at Issos. Hegelochos was not an ilarch at Issos and is thus the most likely one to have replaced either Pantordanos or Peroidas. Berve II 317 no. 631; Heckel 1992, 350; Hoffmann 184–5.

879 PETENES

(Πετήνης). A high-ranking Persian commander at the Granikos battle (Arr. 1.12.8), who was killed during the cavalry engagement (Arr. 1.16.3; Diod. 17.21.3 appears to have confused Petenes with Atizyes, whom he records a second time at Issos: 17.34.5). Berve II 317 no. 632 (Πετίνης Justi 251); Shayegan 116 no. 86.

880 PETISIS

(Πέτισις). Egyptian. In 331, Alexander appointed Petisis and Doloaspis (another Egyptian) as nomarchs of Egypt; they must have been overseers of the lesser nomarchs of Upper and Lower Egypt, although we cannot say which of the two regions was assigned to Petisis. At any rate, Petisis declined the position for unspecified reasons and the offices were combined under Doloaspis (Arr. 3.5.2). Berve II 317–18 no. 633.

881 PEUKESTAS

(Πευκέστας). Macedonian (Tataki 406–7 no. 69). Son of Makartatos; *strategos* in Egypt together with Theramenes (Arr. 3.5.5; Curt. 4.8.4, naming only Peukestas and numbering his force at 4,000). Lehmann-Haupt 152, suggests that Upper and Lower Egypt were divided between Peukestas and Theramenes, though we do not know who received which. Bosworth I 277 thinks Curtius' figure of 4,000 troops "may be the army of Upper Egypt only"; but for comparable numbers of occupation troops see Atkinson I 366. Berve II 319 no. 635.

882 PEUKESTAS

(Πευκέστας). Macedonian (Tataki 123 no. 6). Son of Alexander, from Mieza (Arr. *Ind.* 18.6; cf. Arr. *Succ.* 1.38). Born no later than *c*.355; Amyntas, a Somatophylax of Philip III Arrhidaios in 320, was his brother. Peukestas is first mentioned as a trierarch of the Hydaspes fleet (Arr. *Ind.* 18.6), an indication of his high standing and financial status. Not much later, in the Mallian campaign, he was seriously wounded in an attempt to save the King's life (Curt. 9.5.14–18; Arr. 6.9.3, 10.1–2, 11.7–8; 6.28.4; Arr. *Ind.* 19.8; Diod. 17.99.4;

Plut. *Alex.* 63.5; cf. Ps.-Call. 3.4.14–15; *Itiner. Al.* 115; cf. Diod. 19.14.15). In his account of the Mallian campaign, Diodorus calls P. εἷς τῶν ὑπασπιστῶν (17.99.4), which must mean that he was one of the Royal Hypaspists, also known as *somatophylakes basilikoi*. Plut. *Alex.* 63.5, 8 agrees with Diodorus (17.99.4) in calling Peukestas a hypaspist; Arr. 6.9.3 claims he carried the Sacred Shield from Ilion, having stated earlier (1.11.7–8) that the arms taken by the Macedonians from the Temple of Athena at Troy were "carried before them by the hypaspists." As a reward for his bravery, Alexander made P. an exceptional eighth Bodyguard (Arr. 6.28.4; cf. 7.5.4: he was also awarded a golden crown at Sousa in 324) and very soon thereafter assigned him the satrapy of Persis (Arr. 6.30.2), which P. administered with such zeal that he adopted Persian dress and became the first Macedonian of record to learn the Persian language (Arr. 6.30.3). This conduct, though pleasing to Alexander himself, earned the disapproval of his countrymen (Arr. 7.6.3; cf. 7.23.3). Diod. 19.14.5, however, says that, on account of his heroism, P. alone received Alexander's *permission* to adopt Persian dress. P. was in Babylon at the time of Alexander's death in June 323, having brought recruits from the Kossaians and Tapourians (Arr. 7.23.1; cf. Diod. 17.110.2: 20,000 Persian archers and slingers). And he is said to have attended the drinking party hosted by Medeios of Larisa, at which the King became fatally ill; indeed, it is alleged that he was involved in a conspiracy to poison the King (Ps.-Call. 3.31.8; cf. Heckel 1988, 38–9; 74–5). Along with Attalos, Peithon, Seleukos and others, P. spent the night in the temple of Sarapis, inquiring about the health of Alexander (Arr. 7.26.2). Little is known about P. in the years between Alexander's death and the settlement of Triparadeisos, where his brother, Amyntas, was appointed Somatophylax of Philip III in 320 (Arr. *Succ.* 1.38). He himself was confirmed as satrap of Persis (at Babylon: Diod. 18.3.3; Justin 13.4.23; Dexippos, *FGrH* 100 F8 §6; cf. *LM* 121; at Triparadeisos: Diod. 18.39.6; Arr. *Succ.* 1.35).

P.'s immense popularity in the East and the importance of his satrapy made him a natural leader of the resistance to Peithon, who in 317 tried to revive for himself the position of *strategos* of the Upper Satrapies, which he had held temporarily under Perdikkas in 323/2 (Diod. 19.14.1–4). And he had gathered, in addition to his own forces (10,000 Persian archers and slingers; 3,000 Macedonian-style infantrymen; and 400 Persian horsemen: Diod. 19.14.6–8), contingents led by the satraps Tlepolemos, Stasandros, and Sibyrtios. Oxyartes had sent troops under the command of Androbazos, and Eudamos had come from India (Diod. 19.14.6–8). It was this army, assembled to oppose Peithon, that Eumenes sought to bring under his own control in Sousiana (Diod. 19.15.1; Plut. *Eum.* 13.9). But the question of leadership went beyond the rivalry of the respective commanders (Nepos, *Eum.* 7.1); the division of sentiment appears to have followed racial lines (Diod. 19.15.1; cf. Plut. *Eum.* 14.8ff.). P., it appears, did not formally acknowledge Eumenes' leadership, but accepted for the time, a joint command in the name of Alexander the Great, a face-saving proposal. Fear of Antigonos induced P. to throw in his lot with Eumenes (Diod. 19.17.5). Reluctantly, he summoned 10,000 archers from Persia (Diod. 19.17.4–6). But, upon reaching his home province, P. attempted to gain the supreme command through an extravagant show of pomp (Diod. 19.21.2–23.1; cf. Plut. *Eum.* 14.5), which might have succeeded, had not Eumenes resorted to deception in order to win back the troops (Diod. 19.23.2–3; Polyaenus 4.8.3; Olbrycht 2013, 165–6). Rivalry between Eumenes and P. was intense (Nepos, *Eum.* 7.1), despite their friendship in Alexander's lifetime (Plut. *Eum.* 13.9): Eumenes further undermined P.'s authority by bringing charges against the latter's friend Sibyrtios (Diod. 19.23.4), and, when he fled,

Eumenes led P. on with idle promises (Diod. 19.24.1). In Paraitakene, P.'s subordinate position may be seen in the fact that Eumenes had an *agema* of horsemen (300 strong), whereas a corresponding *agema* was shared by P. and Antigenes (Diod. 19.28.3). Perhaps disillusionment affected his performance. P. appears now to have been seeking a pretext for breaking with Eumenes and his ally Antigenes. The dispersal of the troops in winter quarters in Media might have facilitated a withdrawal. But the army of Antigonos had sought to catch the enemy disunited, only to be forced by the weather to make its size and presence known. Natives on dromedaries, sent out on a spying mission (Diod. 19.37.6), brought news of Antigonos' army which prompted P. to consider flight (Plut. *Eum.* 15.7–8). The accounts, deriving from Hieronymos (Hornblower, *Hieronymus* 151), are hostile to Peukestas and depict him as overcome by fear (Plut. *Eum.* 15.8; cf. Diod. 19.38.1); the defeat at Gabiene is attributed to his poor showing in the cavalry engagement (Plut. *Eum.* 16.9; Diod. 19.42.4, 43.2–3 and esp. 19.43.5). After the battle, P. and his Persian force abandoned Eumenes, though only after the desertion of the Argyraspids had sealed his fate (Polyaenus 4.6.13). That P. betrayed his allies during the battle is almost certainly not the case (though Olbrycht 2013, 166 believes he had every reason to do so), for the hostile sources would not have failed to bring this charge. Perhaps the intervention of Sibyrtios helped him escape the fate of the other prominent officers who had surrendered (Diod. 19.44.1). Antigonos removed him from his satrapy but kept him in his entourage until he returned to Asia Minor, where P. resurfaces on an inscription from Karian Theangela (*Staatsv.* III 249; Momigliano 1931, 245–6; Buraselis 21 n. 70; Billows 1989, 185–86 dates P.'s activities in Karia to 312–310). P. was at Demetrios' court in the last decade of the fourth century, as we know from the caustic exchanges between the Besieger and Lysimachos (Phylarchos *ap.* Athen. 14.614f = *FGrH* 81 F12). Berve II 318–19 no. 634; Billows 417–18 no. 90; Billows 1989, 180, 185; Buraselis 21 n.70; Momigliano 1931; Hornblower, *Hieronymus passim*; Milns 1982; Olbrycht 2013.

883 PEUKOLAOS

(Πευκόλαος). Macedonian (Tataki 407 no. 71) of unknown origin. One of the fellow conspirators of Dimnos in 330 (Curt. 6.7.15, 9.5); his name was given by Dimnos to Nikomachos and came eventually to Alexander's attention. He was arrested and executed at Phrada for his part in the plot (Curt. 6.11.38). Berve II 319–20 no. 637.

884 PEUKOLAOS

(Πευκόλαος). Macedonian (Tataki 407 no. 70). P. was left with 3,000 men in Sogdiana, when Alexander returned to Zariaspa-Baktra for the winter of 329/8 (Curt. 7.10.10). The small number of men and the relative obscurity of P. suggest that he was left as *phrourarchos* of a fortified place. Nothing further is known about him or the fate of his garrison. Berve II 319 no. 636.

885 PEUKOLAOS

(Πευκόλαος). A Macedonian (Tataki 407 no. 72) of humble origins, P. is alleged to have made a tearful speech to Alexander as he lay on his deathbed and to have elicited a grateful response from the dying King (*LM* 105–106; Ps.-Call. 3.32.14–15). Whether he is a historical figure or a fiction is impossible to determine. Berve II 320 no. 638.

886 PHAIDIMOS

(Φαίδιμος). Probably Greek. Commander in Eumenes' army. When, shortly before the battle of Gabiene, the commanders of the Argyraspids and other officers plotted to kill Eumenes (but only after he had proved useful in the battle), Ph. and Eudamos, the commander of the elephants brought news of these plans to Eumenes (Plut. *Eum.* 16.3). Ph. was, allegedly, one of his creditors, whose concern for Eumenes' well-being amounted to protecting his financial interests (cf. Plut. *Eum.* 13.12; Diod. 19.24.2–3). He may have shared the fate of many of Eumenes staunch supporters after the defeat at Gabiene; it is certainly not surprising that he is not heard of again. Anson 185 with n.114; Schäfer 2002, 158 n.124.

887 PHARASMENES

(Φαρασμένης, Justi 91 no. 1). Ruler of the Chorasmians, who lived on the lower Oxos in the region beyond Bokhara (Arr. 4.15.4; Curt. 8.1.8, wrongly Phrataphernes). Bessos had hoped in vain for his support (Curt. 7.4.6), as did Spitamenes (Strabo 11.8.8 C513), but Ph. wisely refrained from joining the resistance to Alexander. In 328 he came to Zariaspa (Baktra) to make submission and to offer his services in a campaign against the Amazons and Kolchians (Arr. 4.15.4; cf. Curt. 8.1.8; for the land of the Kolchians see *Barr. Atl.* 88 A2). Ph.'s activities were apparently monitored by Artabazos, satrap of Baktria (Arr. 4.15.5), and, although Alexander declined his offer at that time, he suggests that he might avail himself of it on a later occasion (Arr. 4.15.6). Ph. is not heard of again. Berve II 379 no. 765; Shayegan 116 no. 87.

888 PHARISMENES

(Φαρισμένης). Son of Phrataphernes the satrap of Hyrkania and Parthyaia. Sent to Karmania by his father with supplies for Alexander, who had finished the Gedrosian march (Arr. 6.27.3, 6; there is no need to assume that Phrataphernes himself was present). He may be the same man who is elsewhere referred to as Phradasmenes (Arr. 7.6.4; cf. Berve II 400 no. 812; Bosworth II 105), but the identification is far from certain. Shayegan 117 no. 90.

889 PHARNABAZOS

(Φαρνάβαζος). Persian (Justin 92 no. 4). Son of Artabazos (Plut. *Eum.* 7.1) and a Rhodian woman; hence also nephew of Memnon and Mentor. Named for his paternal grandfather, the famous satrap of Hellespontine Phrygia. When Memnon died in 333 he entrusted the affairs of the Aegean littoral to Ph., along with the fleet commander Autophradates, pending Dareios III's approval (Arr. 2.1.3). Ph. and Autophradates secured Mytilene, which they forced to abandon its alliance with Alexander and exacted monies from the citizens (Arr. 2.1.4–5); the city was garrisoned, with Lykomedes the Rhodian as *phrourarchos*, and entrusted to the tyrant Diogenes (Arr. 2.1.5). From Lesbos Ph. sailed to Lykia, where he was met by Thymondas son of Mentor, who brought news that Ph.'s position as Memnon's successor had been confirmed but took from him the mercenary troops to lead back to the Great King (Arr. 2.2.1; Curt. 3.3.1). Ph. now joined Autophradates, in concert with whom he captured Tenedos (Arr. 2.2.2–3) and Chios (Arr. 2.13.4); some ships were sent to Kos and Halikarnassos. At Siphnos Ph. met Agis III of Sparta and received from the East news of the disaster at Issos. Leaving Autophradates to deal with Agis, Ph. sailed to Chios to prevent its defection (Arr. 2.13.5). But he soon lost Chios and, although he was captured in the process by Hegelochos (Arr. 3.2.3–4; Curt. 4.5.15–18), he managed to escape at Kos (Arr. 3.2.7). He reappears in 321/0, after a long absence, as a supporter of Eumenes, who had married his sister, Artonis. When Eumenes fought Krateros in Hellespontine Phrygia, he did not set Macedonians opposite him—for he was afraid of the general's popularity with the Macedonian troops; instead he assigned the task to two commanders of mercenary cavalry: Ph. and Phoinix of Tenedos (no. 950). They were ordered to attack quickly and prevent Krateros from sending a herald to induce the troops to defect (Plut. *Eum.* 7.10). What became of Ph. is unknown. Berve II 379–80 no. 766; Shayegan 116–17 no. 88.

890 PHARNAKES

(Φαρνάκης, Justi 93 no. 8). The brother of an earlier wife of Dareios III, his name and that of his nephew, Ariobarzanes, suggest that Ph. belonged to the aristocracy of Kappadokia-Pontos (thus Berve II 380) or that he was related to the family of Artabazos (cf. Bosworth II 125). Certainly, his presence as one of the Persian leaders in the Granikos battle, where he perished (Arr. 1.16.3; Diod. 17.21.3), supports the assumption that he came from Asia Minor. Berve II 380 no. 767; Shayegan 117 no. 89.

891 PHARNOUCHES

(Φαρνούχης, Justi 94 no. 4). Lykian by birth, but the name is distinctly Persian. An expert in the languages of Baktria and Sogdiana. Ph. had probably entered Alexander's entourage after the death of Dareios, unless he was found in one of the Persian capitals. Berve II 380 thinks he accompanied Alexander since 334/3 (cf. Bosworth II 24) but this strikes me as less plausible. It is more likely that Ph. was an Iranian of Lykian origin who had been settled in the Persian heartland. Identification with the unnamed Lykian who led Alexander around the Persian Gates is also unlikely (on this person see Zahrnt 1999). In 329 Ph., along with Menedemos, Karanos, and Andromachos, was sent against the rebel Spitamenes (Arr. 4.3.7). Their force was ambushed at the Polytimetos River and annihilated (Arr. 4.5.3–9 = Ptolemy, *FGrH* 138 F34). In Aristoboulos' version, Ph. attempted to resign his command but found no one willing to accept it (Arr. 4.6.1–2 = *FGrH* 139 F27). Clearly, Ph. was intended to be the scapegoat for the disaster. Ph. was almost certainly the father of Bagoas the trierarch (Arr. *Ind.* 18.8). If Bagoas was the famous eunuch, it is less surprising that Ph. should be blamed for the disaster. Berve II 380–1 no. 768.

892 PHASIMELOS

(Φασίμηλος). Harpist of unknown origin who performed at the mass marriage ceremony in Sousa in 324 (Chares, *FGrH* 125 F4 = Athen. 12.539a). He is otherwise unknown. Berve II 381 no. 769.

893 PHEGEUS

(Φηγεύς). Perhaps more correctly *Phegalas* (Sanskrit *Bhagala*, thus McCrindle 401). Indian ruler, who lived east of the kingdom of Sophytes and near the Hyphasis. His name appears to reflect the region he ruled, that is, the Begas River area (Anspach II 38 n.245). Ph. submitted to Alexander (who made him subordinate to Poros), bearing gifts and reporting the existence, extent and power of the Nanda kingdom to the east (Diod. 17.93.1–2; Curt. 9.1.36–2.4). Berve II 381 no. 770.

894 PHESINOS

(Φησῖνος). Chian rebel and member of the oligarchic pro-Persian party. Captured when Hegelochos took the city, and brought by him to Alexander in Egypt (332/1). Ph., Apollonides, Megareus, and a few others (Curt. 4.5.17 adds Athenagoras) were imprisoned in Elephantine (Arr. 3.2.5, 7). Berve II 381–2 no. 771; Baumbach 35ff.; Berve, *Tyrannis* I 339, II 691; Hofstetter 149 no. 254.

895 PHILA

(Φίλα). Macedonian (Tataki 197 no. 21). Sister of Derdas and Machatas (Athen. 13.557c), a woman of the Elimeiot royal house (Carney 59 regards her as a daughter of Derdas II; cf. Beloch III² 2.75) and thus probably a relative of Alexander's treasurer, Harpalos. Born soon after 375, in all likelihood. She was apparently the first or second wife of Philip II, but Satyros' list as preserved in Athenaeus is not in chronological order. She appears to have remained childless; the view that she was the mother of Karanos (Berve II 200; Milns 1968, 18) is unsupported by the evidence. Carney 59–60.

896 PHILA

(Φίλα). Theban girl, enslaved after Alexander's sack of the city in 335, ransomed for 20 minas by Hypereides, who kept her at his estate in Eleusis ([Plut.] *Mor.* 849d; cf. Idomeneus, *FGrH* 338 F14 = Athen. 13.590d). Berve II 382 no. 773.

897 PHILA

(Φίλα). Macedonian (Tataki 444 no. 5). Eldest of at least four daughters of Antipatros, son of Iolaos (Diod. 18.18.7; Plut. *Demetr.* 14.2); her sisters were Nikaia, Eurydike (Plut. *Demetr.* 46.5) and a third, whose name is unknown and who married Alexander Lynkestes (Justin 12.14.1; Curt. 7.1.6–7). Born shortly before 350, she married Balakros, son of Nikanor, in the mid-330s and bore him a son, Antipatros (no. 130; *IG* xi. 2 161b, line 85; xi. 2 287b, line 57); Balagros (no. 281) and Thraseas (no. 1132) were apparently also her sons, or stepsons (Reger 1991). She appears to have remained with her father in Macedonia— Antonius Diogenes ap. Phot. *Bibl.* 111a–b mentions a letter written by Balakros to Ph. at some time after the fall of Tyre in August 332; the details of the letter need not be believed, but there is little reason to doubt the biographical information—until at least 331 or 330; she may have been escorted to Kilikia, where her husband was now satrap, by Amyntas son of Andromenes (but this is merely speculation). Her son, Antipatros, if he was not born in the mid-330s, will have been born at some time between 330/29 and 324; for in 324 Balakros was killed in a skirmish with the Pisidians. Ph. appears to have returned to Macedonia with Krateros, whom she married in 322/1 (Memnon, *FGrH* 434 F1 §4.4; Plut. *Demetr.* 14.2; Diod. 18.18.7). To him she bore a son of the same name (*FD* 3.42 no. 137; cf. Perdrizet 1899; Dunn and Wheatley 2012), but she was soon widowed a second time; for Krateros died in the battle with Eumenes (his remains were entrusted by Eumenes to Ariston, who returned them to Ph. for burial in 316 or 315; Diod. 19.59.3). Soon after the settlement at Triparadeisos in 320, Ph. married Demetrios Poliorketes although she was considerably older than he (Plut. *Demetr.* 14.2–4, 27.8), to whom she bore Antigonos Gonatas (cf. Plut. *Demetr.* 37.4) and a daughter, Stratonike (Plut. *Demetr.* 31.5, 53.8). It is perhaps an indication of the kind of abuse Demetrios subjected her to that he named his daughter by Lamia the prostitute Phila, Athen. 13.577c. In contrast, flatterers of Demetrios, among them Adeimantos, set up statues of Ph. Aphrodite in Thria, and they called the place where they stood the *Philaion* (Athen. 6.255c; cf. 6.254a). Ph. accompanied her husband to Rhossos in Syria, where her daughter Stratonike married Seleukos (Plut. *Demetr.* 32.2) and soon thereafter was sent to her brother Kassandros to defend Demetrios' actions in Kilikia (Plut. *Demetr.* 32.4). After Demetrios was driven out of Macedonia in 288, she could no longer bear her husband's misfortunes and committed suicide by poison in Kassandreia (Plut. *Demetr.* 45.1). Her exceptional personal qualities are spelled out by Diodorus, who notes that she was capable of dealing with troublemakers in the camp, arranged marriages for sisters and daughters of the poor at her own expense, and saw to it that men unfairly charged received justice; even her father, Antipatros, was said to have valued her advice (Diod. 19.59.3–5). A regal outfit and other items that she had sent to Demetrios were intercepted during the siege of Rhodes and sent to Egypt (Diod. 20.93.4; Plut. *Demetr.* 22.1). Her dedication to her husband and her brother anticipates, as Tarn, *AG* 17–18 has noted, the behavior of Octavia. Berve II 382 no. 772; Macurdy 58–69; Wehrli 1964; Seibert 1967, 12–13; Heckel 1987; Carney 165–9; Aulbach §§5.1.1 and 8.2.1.1.

898 PHILA

(Φίλα). Daughter of Demetrios and Lamia, (Athen. 13.577c), the daughter of Kleanor the Athenian (Athen. 13.577c). The choice of this name must have been considered an insult by his wife of the same name, the daughter of Antipatros (see above).

899 PHILA

(Φίλα). Macedonian (Tataki 443 no. 4). Daughter of Seleukos I and Stratonike, hence also the granddaughter of Demetrios. Ph. married her uncle, Antigonos Gonatas (*OGIS* 216; *I.Didyma* 114). Grainger, *SPG* 52.

900 PHILETAIROS

(Φιλέταιρος). Son of Attalos (*OGIS* 748). From Tieion, near Paphlagonia (*Barr. Atl.* 86 C2; though Pausanias calls him a Paphlagonian), he was a eunuch (Strabo 13.4.1 C623 states implausibly that his nurse, who was holding him at a crowded public event, squeezed him too tightly) in the service of Dokimos (no. 400), the Macedonian *strategos* (Paus. 1.8.1). Strabo 12.3.8 C543 says that Tieion's only claim to fame was that it was the birthplace of the founder of the Attalid dynasty. Karystios (*FHG* IV 358 frag. 12) claimed that Ph.'s mother was a courtesan named Boa, a flute player of Paphlagonian origin (Athen. 13.577b). Eumenes I refers to Ph. as his father (Welles, *RC* 23), but this is by adoption. [Lucian] *Macrob.* 12 says he died at the age of eighty; hence we may establish 343/2 as the year of his birth (for his death in 263/2: Strabo 13 C624; cf. Polyb. 18.41.8). Of Ph.'s earlier military or administrative service nothing is known. He appears in the company of Dokimos in 302 shortly before Dokimos defected to Lysimachos (Paus. 1.8.1); Ph. thus continued in Lysimachos' service, though he later abandoned him in favor of Seleukos (Paus. 1.10.4; Strabo 13.4.1 C623 says he had been slandered by Lysimachos' wife Arsinoë). He bought Seleukos' body from Keraunos for a large sum, cremated it and sent the remains to Antiochos (App. *Syr.* 63.335). For his later career and the Attalid kingdom which he established see Hansen 1971 and Allen 1983. Billows 418–19 no. 91; W. Hoffmann, *RE* XIX.2 (1938) 2336 no. 1; Hansen 1971, 12–21, 26–30, 36–8; Grainger, *SPG* 112.

901 PHILINE

(Φιλίνη). From Larisa. Wife of Philip II and mother of Arrhidaios (Satyros *ap.* Athen. 13.557c; Arr. *Succ.* 1.1). Philip appears to have married her in 358 and her son was born before Alexander but showed early signs of mental impairment (see no. 903). Stories that she was a dancing-girl (*saltatrix*) and a harlot are, as Carney 61 notes, later inventions meant to discredit Philip III and his guardians (ὀρχηστρίς, Athen. 13.577f–578a = Ptolemy son of Agesarchos of Megalopolis *FGrH* 161 F4; Justin 9.8.2; 13.2.11). Since the marriage was meant to strengthen the bond between Philip and his Larisan allies, it is likely that Ph. belonged to the aristocracy, probably to the Aleuadai. The doubts of Green 1982, 142–4, esp. 143 n.39 concerning the status of Ph. and the nature of Philip's unions with the two Thessalians (cf. Westlake 1935, 168) are unfounded. Ptolemy son of Agesarchos is hardly an unimpeachable source and the language of Satyros is at best ambiguous. The verb ἐπαιδοποιήσατο need not be significant. It lends some variation and it emphasizes the fact that not all Philip's wives produced children. Furthermore, the word *gyne* (like the German *Frau* or the French *femme*) can mean "wife" as well as "woman." See Ogden 18–19. That she was the mother of Amphimachos by another marriage is highly unlikely (see Arr. *Succ.* 1.35 with Jacoby IID p. 563; Beloch IV² 2.316): the suggestion is based on a misunderstanding on the part of Arrian's source, possibly Douris of Samos. Bosworth 2002, 113, with n.61, accepts Amphimachos as Ph.'s son. But Beloch's criticism of Niese I 225 n.3 is to the point: "ich weiß nicht, ob es möglich ist, den Buchstabenkultus weiter zu treiben." Carney 61–62; Ogden 17–27. **Stemma I.**

902 PHILIP

(Φίλιππος). (Tataki 445 no. 13). Philip II of Macedon. (*regn.* 360/59–336). Born in 383/2, Ph. was the third son of Amyntas III (*regn.* 393–369) and Eurydike (Diod. 16.1.3) and the brother of Alexander II, Perdikkas III, and Eurynoë (Justin 7.4.5). Hostage in Thebes, probably during the reign of Alexander II, and briefly during the regency of Ptolemy Alorites (Justin 7.5.2–3; Diod. 15.67.4; Plut. *Mor.* 178c); he may earlier have been a hostage of the Illyrians (Diod. 16.2.2; Justin 7.5.1). On the death of Perdikkas III in battle against the Illyrians, Ph. ruled either as regent (Justin 7.5.9–10; Satyros *ap.* Athen. 13.557b) for his nephew Amyntas (no. 76), or as King in his place (Diod. 16.1.3, 2.1; cf. Griffith, *HMac* II 208–9, 702–4). If he served as regent, he assumed the kingship very soon afterwards. Ph. took the reins of power at a critical time: over 4,000 Macedonians had been killed in the Illyrian disaster and the confidence of those who survived was badly shaken (Diod. 16.2.5); and, in addition to numerous external enemies, he had to overcome challenges from his three half-brothers, the sons of Gygaia (Justin 7.4.5; 8.3.10), at least one of whom, Archelaos, was probably executed in 359 (Justin 7.6.3; cf. Ellis 1973; Griffith, *HMac* II 699–701). Immediately, Ph. placed the Macedonian army on a stronger footing by improving discipline, training, and equipment (Diod. 16.3.1–2). His introduction of the *sarissa* revolutionized Greek warfare and provided the basis of Macedonian military power. In the first year of his rule, he was challenged by Argaios, who claimed the throne with Athenian support but was defeated by Ph.'s general, Mantias; the Paionians were for the time being bought off. With his reformed army he defeated the Illyrian king, Bardylis, in 358 (Justin 7.6.7; Diod. 16.4.3–7, 8.1) and cemented the peace by marrying his daughter Audata, who later bore him a daughter named Kynnane (Athen. 13.557c). In 358 he intervened in the affairs of northern Thessaly (Justin 7.6.8–9; Diod. 16.14.1–2) and took another political wife, Philine of Larisa, who, in 357, gave birth to Arrhidaios (Athen. 13.557c; Justin 9.8.2, 13.2.11). His alliance with Epeiros was accompanied by marriage to the princess Olympias: their children were Alexander the Great and Kleopatra (Athen. 13.557d). Ph. later took Alexander, Olympias' brother and the heir to the Epeirot throne, to Macedonia as a hostage (Justin 7.6.10–12; 8.6.4–8). When Alexander reached maturity in 342, Ph. installed him as king of Epeiros, driving out the incumbent, Arybbas (Diod. 16.72.1; cf. *IG* II² 226 = R&O no. 70, with commentary on 352–4; see no. 228).

Ph. exploited the Athenians' troubles in the Social War (357–355) to gain control of Amphipolis and Pydna (357) and Potidaia (356). On the day Potidaia fell, he learned of the birth of a son, Alexander, of Parmenion's victory over the Illyrians, and of the success of his chariot team at Olympia (Plut. *Alex.* 3.8). In 354 he captured Methone but lost his right eye to a defender's arrow (Justin 7.6.14–15; Plut. *Alex.* 3.2). Ph. soon became involved in the Sacred War against the Phokians who had violated the sanctuary of Delphi; he posed as champion of the Greeks and, in the process, secured control of the remainder of Thessaly. After two military setbacks in 353, in at least one of which the Phokians used artillery to great advantage (Polyaenus 2.38.2; Diod. 16.35.2), Ph. defeated the enemy in the battle of the Crocus Field in 352 (Justin 8.2.1–4; Dod 16.35.4–5, 38.1). A final reckoning with the Phokians was thwarted when they occupied Thermopylai against him. Pherai now fell into his hands and with it control of the Thessalian League, which elected him as its *archon*. Again he strengthened his position by political marriage, this time to Nikesipolis of Pherai, who bore him another daughter; Ellis (1976, 212, with n.10) puts the marriage in 352 but a date of 346/5 is also possible (Athen. 13.557c; see no. 1122 for details). The steady growth of Ph.'s power created great anxiety in Athens, which was only increased when he attacked and destroyed Olynthos, which was harboring his political rivals (Justin 8.3.10–11); despite Demosthenes' impassioned *Olynthiac* orations, the Athenians were slow to respond to the threat. In 346, an agreement with the Greeks left Ph. free to fortify Thermopylai, dismantle Phokian power (Diod. 16.59–60; Justin 8.4–5), and pursue his interests in the northeast.

It may be that he had already conceived a plan to attack the Persian Empire (thus Diod. 16.60.5); and it is at this time that Isokrates wrote his *Philippus*, urging Ph. to do just that. Artabazos, the rebellious satrap of Hellespontine Phrygia, had been received as a suppliant in Pella along with his large family around 353/2 (thus Ellis 1976, 92), and Diod. 16.52.3 speaks of them as still resident there in 349. Furthermore, Ph. may have had an "agent" in Asia Minor in Aristotle, son of the former court physician Nikomachos (see Guthrie 35–6; cf. Ellis 1976, 97–8), who would soon be invited to Macedonia to become tutor of the young Alexander (Plut. *Alex.* 7.2–4; see no. 210 for further details). That Ph. seriously considered an expedition against Persia before bringing the Greek states under his control is doubtful. But it does not follow that, because he initiated the Persian war only after the creation of the League of Korinth, he could not have launched such an expedition without the subjugation of the Greeks. Access to Greece via Thermopylai was, however, important, and Ph. also held out hope of Athenian cooperation. But this was not forthcoming. His activities in the north in the years that followed 346 may indeed have been intended to pressure the Athenians, who had agreed to the Peace of Philokrates reluctantly. The anti-Macedonian faction, led by Demosthenes and Hegesippos ([Dem.] 7, *On Halonnesus*, is apparently his speech) incited the Athenians against Ph. Although the Macedonian king made sincere attempts to reach an agreement, the terms were clearly intended to work in his favor. For the Athenians, opposition to Macedon was an attempt to salvage lost pride, a futile and dangerous undertaking. Ph.'s subsequent activities in Thrake and Illyria were essential to Macedonian security. But Perinthos and Byzantion, against which he moved in 340 (Diod. 16.74.2–76.4; Justin 9.1.1–7), lay on Athens' economic lifeline, as did the Thrakian Chersonese, and the aim was clearly to force a showdown with the Athenians.

In 338, Ph. defeated a coalition of Thebans and Athenians at Chaironeia (Diod. 16.85.2–86.4; Polyaenus 4.2.2, 7; Justin 9.3.4–11), in a battle that saw the 18-year-old Alexander commanding the Macedonian left, where the vaunted Sacred Band of the Thebans were annihilated (Plut. *Alex*. 9.2). The victory brought Boiotia into Ph.'s power and cowed the Athenians into submission. Ph. took no punitive action against the Athenians (Justin 9.4.1–3; Plut. *Mor*. 177e–f)—indeed, he had taken to heart the rebuke of Demades who, when Ph. celebrated his victory in a drunken stupor, charged him with "playing the part of Thersites, when history had cast him in the role of Agamemnon" (Diod. 16.87.1–2). They in turn accepted Macedonian hegemony (albeit reluctantly) and joined the League of Korinth, which the King convened in the spring of 337 (Justin 9.5.1; Diod. 16.89.1–3; *IG* II² 236 = Harding no. 99 = R&O no. 76). The winter of 338/7 appears to have been spent imposing a Macedonian settlement on the Peloponnese (see Roebuck 1948). The Spartans, however, remained aloof, militarily impotent but politically obstinate.

Domestic (i.e., matrimonial) problems would prove to be Ph.'s undoing. He had married six times before becoming master of Greece, beginning perhaps with a member of the Upper Macedonian aristocracy, Phila, the sister of Derdas and Machatas (Athen. 13.557c; for the family see s.v. Harpalos), and ending with a Thrakian princess (Athen. 13.557d; see s.v. Meda); he considered adoption by the Skythian king, Ateas, no doubt for want of a suitable bride (Justin 9.2.1–3; *contra* Hammond 1994, 182). But his decision to marry Kleopatra, a niece of the Macedonian nobleman, Attalos (no. 262), threw the household into a state of confusion (Athen. 13.560c; Plut. *Alex*. 9.5). It was not the marriage itself that caused the rift between Ph. and Alexander (cf. Köhler 1892), for Alexander was present at the wedding feast, and his mother, Olympias, was still in Pella. Instead, a tactless prayer by the bride's guardian, that the marriage might produce *legitimate* heirs, was interpreted by Alexander as a challenge and an insult (Plut. *Alex*. 9.7–10; Satyros *ap*. Athen. 13.557d; cf. Justin 9.7.3–4). The resulting feud between father and son was ended through the intervention of Demaratos of Korinth (Plut. *Mor*. 179c) and the arranged marriage of Alexander's sister Kleopatra to her uncle, Alexander I of Epeiros (Justin 9.7.7; Diod. 16.91.4). The reconciliation was genuine but the young prince came to question the motives of Ph.'s every action, and his insecurity was exploited by the jealous Queen Mother, who felt herself dishonored by the new bride and her family (Heckel 1978a, 1981c). Hence, Ph.'s plans to marry Arrhidaios to Ada, a daughter of Pixodaros of Karia, were misinterpreted by Alexander and his advisers (Plut. *Alex*. 10.1–5; Arr. 3.6.5). Furthermore, Alexander's flight to Illyria in late 337 (Plut. *Alex*. 9.11; Justin 9.7.5) necessitated a punitive campaign on the western marches of the kingdom (Diod. 16.93.6; often confused with the campaign of 344/3: Diod. 16.69.7). In October 336, after celebrating the nuptials of Kleopatra and Alexander I, Ph. was assassinated as he entered the theater in Aigai (modern Vergina) by a member of the Royal Hypaspists (Diod. 16.91.2–94.4; Justin 9.7; see no. 858).

Justin 9.8.1 says that Ph. was 47 years old at the time of his death, having ruled twenty-five years, but these numbers should perhaps be taken as ordinals: he died in his 47th year of life and the 25th year of his reign (Diod. 16.1.3, 95.1; 17.1.1 says he ruled for twenty-four years; Hammond 1992, 361–4 explains the discrepancy in terms of calculation by Athenian and Macedonian years). Despite his injuries (Marsyas, *FGrH* 135/6 F17)—broken collarbone (Plut. *Mor.* 177f; cf. 178a); an eye lost at Methone (Justin 7.6.14; Douris, *FGrH* 76 F36; Theopompos, *FGrH* 115 F52); and a wound to the thigh in the Triballian campaign (Justin 9.3.2, the weapon passed through his leg and killed his horse)—Ph. remained for the most part a vigorous and charming man. His fondness for drink was legendary (*FGrH* 115 F282), but Theopompos saw heavy drinking as a Macedonian trait (FF 163, 236) and depicted the *pezhetairoi* as male-sodomizers (F225b). Ph. himself was both a womanizer and an admirer of boys (Justin 8.6.5–8; Diod. 16.93.3–4); excesses in both cases played no small part in his death. His relationship with Alexander, despite the unfortunate break in 337, was close and cordial. Indeed, after the victory at Chaironeia, Ph. is supposed to have been fond of hearing his troops remark that "Ph. was their general and Alexander their King" (Plut. *Alex.* 9.4). Although Justin 9.8 contrasts the characters and actions of the two men, their methods and manners were in many respects the same, and Alexander could truly be seen as Ph.'s son—except perhaps for Alexander's apparent rejection of pederasty (Plut. *Alex.* 22.1). Not merely for the splendid Macedonian army and the forcible unification of the Greek states was Alexander indebted to his father; he appears to have learned a great deal about the power of propaganda and political expediency. Alexander's use of political marriage and his elevation of the conquered nobility to positions amongst the *hetairoi* and administrators, as well as the use of foreign, specialist troops, were all learned in his youth from his brilliant and dynamic father.

Ph. so dominated his times that he was the central subject of Theopompos of Chios' historical work, *Philippica*, in fifty-eight books (on which see Jacoby, *FGrH* 115; Shrimpton 1991, 58–126; Flower 1994, 98–135); the major portion of the *Macedonica* of Marsyas of Pella (no. 683) also recounted the affairs of Ph. (*FGrH* 135/6; Heckel 1980d; Howe, *BNJ* s.v.); many of the political speeches of Demosthenes deal with Ph., especially the *Olynthiacs, On the Peace,* and *On the Crown,* as do the three extant speeches of Aeschines and Isocrates' *Philippus*. For a collection of readings with commentary see Ellis and Milns 1970 and Phillips 2004, 67–106. For a brief discussion of Tomb II at Vergina, often identified as that of Ph., see Borza 1999, 68–74; for discussions of the physical remains, a reconstruction of the skull from Tomb II, and two possible representations of Ph., see Prag, Musgrave, and Neave 1984; Xirotiris and Langenscheidt 1981; Riginos 1994. Ellis 1976; Cawkwell 1978; Wirth 1985; Griffith, *HMac* II 203–726; Errington 1990, 35–102; Borza 1990, 198–230, and 1999, 51–74; Hammond 1994; Worthington 2008; Gabriel 2010; Wirth, *LexAM* 415–20. Philip's assassination: Heckel, Howe, and Müller 2017, 92 n.3 for earlier bibliography; also Antela-Bernárdez 2012; Lindholmer 2016. **Stemma I.**

903 PHILIP

(Φίλιππος Ἀρριδαῖος). Philip III of Macedon *regn.* 323–317). Son of Philip II (Satyros, *ap.* Athen. 13.557c; Justin 9.8.2; 13.2.11; App. *Syr.* 54.275, mistakenly, a son of Olympias; Justin 14.6.13, incorrectly, the father of Thessalonike) and Philine of Larisa, in all probability a woman of the Aleuadai (cf. Ellis 1976, 61) and not a harlot, as the tradition records (Justin 13.2.11; Ptolemy son of Agesarchos of Megalopolis, *ap.* Athen. 13.577f–578a = *FGrH* 161 F4; Plut. *Alex.* 77.1). He was born in 358 or 357 and given the name Arrhidaios. That Amphimachos, the satrap of Mesopotamia in 320, was his half-brother is unlikely; Arr. *Succ.* 1.35 or his source confused Arrhidaios the satrap with the King (thus Jacoby, *FGrH* IID, "Kommentar" 563; but Bosworth 2002, 113 with n.60 accepts Amphimachos no. 901 as a son of Philine; cf. Meeus 2013, 91–2). He was of marriageable age in 337/6, when Philip II considered an alliance with Pixodaros (Plut. *Alex.* 10.1), but afflicted since childhood with an incurable mental illness (Plut. *Alex.* 10.2; App. *Syr.* 52; Justin 13.2.11; 14.5.2; Diod. 18.2.2; Plut. *Mor.* 337d; Porphyr. Tyr., *FGrH* 260 F2; Heid. Epit. 1 calls him "epileptic"), which Plutarch alleges was induced by mind-destroying drugs given to him by Olympias (Plut. *Alex.* 77.8). The marriage to Ada, daughter of Pixodaros, was pre-empted by the intervention of Alexander, who appears to have revealed to the Karian dynast what he did not know, that his half-brother was mentally unstable (Plut. *Alex.* 10.2). Nothing else is known about him during Alexander's lifetime. When the King died in 323, Arrhidaios was already in Babylon (Justin 13.2.8; Curt. 10.7.2 ff.; but see Martin 1983; Sharples 1994); there is no indication as to how long he had been there. Paradoxically, he was declared King by the army under the name of Philip (Curt. 10.7.1–7; Diod. 18.2.2, 4; Justin 13.2.6–8, 3.1, 4.2; Arr. *Succ.* 1.1; Paus. 1.6.2; App. *Syr.* 52.261; Porphyr. Tyr., *FGrH* 260 F2; cf. *LM* 115), and it was in his name that Perdikkas allotted the satrapies (Arr. *Succ.* 1.5; App. *Syr.* 52.262; cf. Diod. 18.2.4), for Ph. was never anything more than a puppet (Plut. *Mor.* 791e). Although, by the terms of the compromise settlement in Babylon, Krateros had been designated Ph.'s guardian (*prostates*), Ph. remained in Perdikkas' custody and accompanied him first into Kappadokia (Diod. 18.22.1; cf. Justin 13.6.10: when Justin writes that Ph. and Alexander IV were "removed to Kappadokia" he must be in error: they were taken from Kappadokia into Pisidia; thus Diod. 18.22.1, 25.6) and then to Egypt (Paus. 1.6.3). At some point in between—perhaps in Pisidia—Ph. was married to Adea, the daughter of Kynnane (Arr. *Succ.* 1.23; cf. Polyaenus 8.60). After Perdikkas' murder in Egypt, Peithon and Arrhidaios (no. 214) assumed the guardianship of the kings (Diod. 18.36.6–7; Arr. *Succ.* 1.30), but they soon found Adea-Eurydike impossible to deal with (Arr. *Succ.* 1.31–3) and surrendered this office to Antipatros at Triparadeisos (Diod. 18.39.1–2). Ph. was then left briefly with Antigonos (Arr. *Succ.* 1.38), before returning to Macedonia with Antipatros (Arr. *Succ.* 1.45). Diod. 18.39.7 omits the intermediate stage, in which Antipatros assigned the Kings to Antigonos and then removed them from his possession. This could either be the result of abbreviation or a deliberate omission on the part of Hieronymos of Kardia. Upon Antipatros' death in 319, the guardianship passed to Polyperchon (Diod. 18.48.4), who in 318 issued a decree proclaiming the "Freedom of the Greeks" in the name of Philip III Arrhidaios (Diod. 18.56). Together with Polyperchon, and enthroned beneath a golden canopy, Ph. received Phokion and his party in Phokis (Nepos, *Phoc.* 3.3; Plut. *Phoc.* 33.8), and in an outburst of anger nearly impaled Hegemon with a spear (Plut. *Phoc.* 33.11–12). Threatened by Polyperchon's summoning of Olympias to Macedonia, Adea-Eurydike transferred custody of Ph. to Kassandros (Justin 14.5.1–4). An attempt was made to block the forces of Olympias and her kinsman Aiakides at Euia (Justin 14.5.9), but the troops deserted to Alexander's mother, who murdered Ph. soon afterwards (Diod. 19.11.2–5; Paus. 1.11.3–4; 8.7.7; Justin 14.5.10); he was stabbed by his Thrakian guards after a reign of six years and four months (Diod. 19.11.5; cf. Justin 14.5.10, "six years"). Kassandros learned of Ph.'s death when he returned from the Peloponnese (Diod. 19.35.1); cf. App. *Syr.* 54.275 for another reference to his death. Kassandros later buried him and Adea-Eurydike, along with Kynnane, at Aigai (Diyllos, *FGrH* 73 F1 = Athen. 4.155a; Diod. 19.52.5). For the vexed question of whether Ph. and Adea-Eurydike are the occupants of Tomb II in Vergina see Borza-Palagia 2007 and Lane Fox 2011a. Kaerst, *RE* II.1 (1895) 1248–9 no. 4; Berve II 385–6 no. 781; Greenwalt 1984; Ogden 17–27; Carney 2001. Also Borza and Palagia 2007; Lane Fox 2011a; Müller, *LexAM* 114–15. **Stemma I.**

904 PHILIP

(Φίλιππος). (Tataki 445 no. 15). Philip IV of Macedon. Son of Kassandros and Thessalonike; brother of Antipatros and Alexander (Porphyr. Tyr. *FGrH* 260 F3 §5). Succeeded Kassandros (Justin 15.4.24) but died soon after his father's death (Justin 16.1.1; Porphyr. Tyr. *FGrH* 260 F3 §5, says he died in Elateia) of a wasting disease (Paus. 9.7.3), thought to be tuberculosis and apparently the same one that killed his father (Porphyr. Tyr. *FGrH* 260 F3 §4). Geyer, *RE* XIX (1938) 2303 no. 9; Oikonomides 1989a; Grainger 2019, 196–8. **Stemmata I and V.**

905 PHILIP

(Φίλιππος). Macedonian (Tataki 449 no. 36). Arr. 1.14.2 mentions a Ph. son of Amyntas in the Macedonian line at the Granikos. There are, however, some textual difficulties and Ph.'s patronymic may have been corrupted by the proximity of the name Amyntas (i.e. the son of Andromenes) in the preceding line. Berve II 383 no. 775 treats him as a separate individual (cf. Bosworth I 118), and, although I am inclined to regard this Ph. as the son of Balakros, I cannot with certainty deny the existence of a phalanx commander named Ph. son of Amyntas.

906 PHILIP

(Φίλιππος). Macedonian (Tataki 449 no. 40). Son of Balakros (Diod. 17.57.3; Curt. 4.13.28) and possibly a brother of Nikanor. Phalanx commander. Together with Meleagros he was responsible for conveying the booty taken from the Getai in 335 back to the Macedonian base (Arr. 1.4.5, without patronymic). Ph.'s association with the battalion commander Meleagros son of Neoptolemos suggests that he is identical with the Ph. of equal rank attested at the Granikos (Arr. 1.14.2–3). On the assumption that the patronymikon Ἀμύντου is an error (following the name Amyntas son of Andromenes), Ph. is perhaps the son of Balakros, named as a phalanx commander at Gaugamela in the Vulgate. At Gaugamela he commanded the battalion of Amyntas son of Andromenes during the latter's absence (thus Diod. 17.57.3; Curt. 4.13.28; but Arr. 3.11.9 assigns this battalion to Amyntas' younger brother Simmias). Nothing else is known about him unless he can be identified with the friend of Demetrios, honored together with a certain Iolaos in Athens in 307 (*IG* II² 561). Billows 422 believes that the letter following the name Ph. in this inscription is B, i.e., the beginning of the patronymic Balakrou. I believe this letter is M, if not the first letter of the patronymic then what remains of the ethnic "Makedon" (Heckel 1981a; Heckel 1988, 43). Berve II 383–4 no. 778; Billows 421–3 no. 93; Wheatley 1997b.

907 PHILIP

(Φίλιππος). Macedonian (Tataki 450 no. 43). Son of Menelaos. He is first attested as hipparch of the allied cavalry (from the Peloponnese) at the Granikos (Arr. 1.14.3), a unit which he appears to have led from the very beginning of the Asiatic expedition. He next reappears at Gaugamela, where he leads the Thessalian cavalry (Arr. 3.11.10; Diod. 17.57.4; Curt. 4.13.29). It appears that Ph. was promoted to hipparch of the Thessalians in the winter of 334/3, after the arrest of Alexander Lynkestes (Arr. 1.25), or at the latest in the spring of 333 at Gordion; at that time Erigyios (no. 425) was assigned the allied cavalry. After the battle of Issos, Ph. and the Thessalians were taken by Parmenion to Damaskos, where they captured the Persian treasures and many relatives of Persian notables (Plut. *Alex.* 24.1–3). Probably, like Erigyios, Ph. remained with Menon son of Kerdimmas in Koile-Syria between early 332 and spring 331 (Arr. 2.13.7). At Ekbatana, however, Alexander dismissed the Thessalian cavalry, and Ph. was reassigned to the command of the mercenary horse (Arr. 3.25.4; cf. Berve II 384), replacing Menidas, who remained in Media with Parmenion. Ph. remained for some time in Ekbatana and rejoined the King in Aria ("on the way to Baktra," Arr. 3.25.4), bringing the mercenary cavalry, the *xenoi* of Andromachos (no. 101), and those of the Thessalians who had volunteered to continue serving Alexander (Arr. 3.25.4; Curt. 6.6.35 says the Thessalians numbered 130). The son of Menelaos is not heard of again. He may, however, have been identical with the later satrap of Baktria and Sogdiana, whom Alexander appointed after the death of Amyntas (no. 85) son of Nikolaos, or possibly the friend of Antigonos the One-Eyed and adviser and general of Demetrios Poliorketes. Berve II 384 no. 779; Heckel 1992, 358–9; Wheatley 1997b.

908 PHILIP

(Φίλιππος). Macedonian from Elimeia (Tataki 198 no. 23). Son of Machatas (Arr. 5.8.3) and probably brother of Harpalos and Tauron. Although Ph. is attested with patronymic only once in the Alexander historians, his career can be reconstructed with a measure of certainty. He first appears in the Aspasian campaign of 327/6, leading a battalion of light infantry under the command of Ptolemy son of Lagos (Arr. 4.24.10). At Taxila, Ph. was ordered to govern the newly formed satrapy east of the Indos (Arr. 5.8.3), and on the death of Nikanor (Arr. 5.20.7) his province was extended to include Gandhara (Arr. 6.2.3), where he restored order with the help of Tyriespis, satrap of the Parapamisadai. The Ph. who was installed as *phrourarchos* of Peukelaotis (= Charsada), under the general supervision of Nikanor (no. 783), who ruled the Kophen (Gandhara) satrapy (Arr. 4.28.6), is unlikely to have been the son of Machatas. As the Macedonian conquests continued, he received additional territory between the rivers Akesines and Indos as far south as their confluence (Arr. 6.14.3, 15.2; cf. Plut. *Alex.* 60.16), regions which he had himself helped to subdue (Arr. 6.2.3, 4.1; cf. Arr. *Ind.* 19.4). When Alexander moved south towards Sogdia and the kingdom of Mousikanos (with its capital at Alor; cf. Eggermont 5–9), Ph. remained in the enlarged satrapy, supported by all the Thrakians (under Eudamos' command) and a force of mercenaries, with instructions to found a city at the junction of the rivers and build dockyards (Arr. 6.15.2). The city may be the one described by Diod. 17.102.4 and Curt. 9.8.8 (so Welles 413 n.2); Brunt II 144 n.3 thinks Curt. 9.8.8 could refer to the city founded by Alexander near Sogdia (Arr. 6.15.4; cf. Tarn II 237). In 325 Ph. was assassinated by mercenaries, some of whom were killed in the act by the satrap's Bodyguard, others were arrested and executed. Alexander, who learned of Ph.'s death as he marched from Gedrosia to Karmania, appointed Eudamos as his replacement (Arr. 6.27.2; Curt. 10.1.20–1). Berve II 384–5 no. 780, and II 386–7 no. 784; Bosworth 1973, 252–3; Heckel 1992, 331–2. **Stemma XIII.**

<h2 style="text-align:center">909 PHILIP</h2>

(Φίλιππος). Physician from Akarnania (Diod. 17.31.5; Curt. 3.6.1; Arr. 2.4.8; Plut. *Alex.* 19.4), he had been Alexander's most trusted physician since the King's boyhood (Curt. 3.6.1). When Alexander became ill in Kilikia, he used an untried potion to treat him and thereby saved his life (Diod. 17.31.5–6)—although, for a time, it looked as if the treatment might fail. Alexander subsequently treated him as one of his most loyal friends (Diod. 17.31.6). Whether the term *philos* is used in a technical sense here is unclear. Curt. 3.6.1 says that Ph. was a companion (*comes*) of the young Alexander, and at the time of Alexander's illness he is already described as φίλατος Ἀλεξάνδρῳ ἰατρός (Ps.-Call. 2.8.4; cf. Arr. 2.4.8). Val. Max. 3.8 ext. 6 calls him *amicus et comes*. It is interesting to note that Alexander's tutor, Lysimachos, was also an Akarnanian. There is, however, a tradition that Parmenion sent Alexander a letter warning him that Ph. had been bribed by the Great King to administer poison (Arr. 2.4.9–10; Plut. *Alex.* 19.5–10; Val. Max. 3.8 ext. 6; Curt. 3.6.4–17; Sen. *de Ira* 2.23.2; Justin 11.8.5–8; cf. Ps.-Call. 2.8.5; Jul. Valer. 2.24), a story which appears to have been confused in some way with the alleged conspiracy of Alexander the Lynkestian. Later, at Gaza (332), Ph. treated an arrow wound to Alexander's shoulder (Curt. 4.6.17). But from that point onwards nothing else is recorded about him, unless he is to be identified with Ph. the physician, named in the *Last Days and Testament* (Ps.-Call. 3.31.8). His name may have been added to the list of conspirators because of the earlier charge of attempted poisoning. Berve II 388–9 no. 788.

<h2 style="text-align:center">910 PHILIP</h2>

(Φίλιππος). Macedonian (Tataki 449 no. 38). Son of Antipatros (Justin 12.14.6, 9), brother of Iolaos, Kassandros, and others (**Stemma V**). Ph. and Iolaos were apparently Pages (παῖδες βασιλικοί, described by Justin as *praegustare ac temperare potum regis soliti*; cf. Heckel 1992, 294) of Alexander at the time of his death in Babylon and implicated in the alleged plot to poison the King (Justin 12.14.6–9). It appears that, after the death of Alexander and the settlement of affairs in Babylon, Ph. returned to Macedonia with his brother Iolaos. In 313/12, Ph. was sent by his brother Kassandros to wage war on the Aitolians: setting out from his base in Akarnania he plundered their territory, but he soon learned that Aiakides (no. 31), who had been returned to the Epeirot throne, was nearby with an army. Ph. attacked and defeated Aiakides before he could join forces with his Aitolian allies. He took many prisoners, including some fifty men who had helped restore Aiakides; these Ph. sent to Kassandros, clearly as traitors to his cause (Diod. 19.74.3–4). When Aiakides regrouped and joined forces with the Aitolians, Ph. defeated him again, killing the Epeirot king and totally disheartening the Aitolians (Diod. 19.74.5). Nothing else is known about Ph. personally. His son Antipatros (no. 129) ruled Macedonia for forty-five days in 279 (Porphyry, *FGrH* 260 F3 §10; for the date see Beloch IV² 2.109–10, 121), following the death of Ptolemy Keraunos and the brief reign of the latter's brother, Meleagros (no. 698; cf. Walbank, *HMac* III 253). Identification with the Ph. of *IG* II² 561, as suggested by Oikonomedes 1987, is impossible for at least three reasons: (1) the decree was almost certainly moved by Stratokles in 307, by which time Iolaos son of Antipatros was already dead, and not by Hypereides in 323/2 ([Plut.] *Mor.* 849f); (2) Ph. and Iolaos on this inscription appear to have different patronymics; and (3) both were supporters of Demetrios in the years up to and including 307, which would most likely not have been true of Kassandros' brothers. Berve II 383 no. 777; Sandberger 19; Heckel 1992, 294–5.

911 PHILIP

(Φίλιππος). Macedonian (Tataki 446 no. 24). Patronymic unknown. Ph. appears to have replaced Amyntas son of Nikolaos as satrap of Baktria and Sogdiana. He retained his satrapy in the settlement of 323 (Diod. 18.3.3; Dexippos, *FGrH* 100 F8 §6; *LM* 121; Jul. Valer. 3.59; Ps.-Call. 3.33.22 makes him satrap of Sousiana; cf. Justin 13.4.19, 23 with Yardley-Wheatley-Heckel 114) but was shuffled to Parthia in 320 in the reorganization at Triparadeisos (Diod. 18.39.6; Arr. *Succ.* 1.35). Ph. may have been held responsible for not quelling the uprising in the Upper Satrapies after Alexander's death. Some three years later, Peithon son of Krateuas deposed and killed a *strategos* of Parthyaia named Philotas and installed his own brother Eudamos as satrap of the region (Diod. 19.14.1). It is generally assumed that Diodorus wrote Philotas instead of Philip (Wheatley 1997b, 62; Billows 90 n.17). But Schäfer 2002, 159 (without comment) identifies the Ph. who served Eumenes at Gabiene as the former satrap of Parthyaia, and it may be that Peithon had deposed and killed, in Ph.'s absence, his subordinate, the *strategos* Philotas. It is more likely, however, that Diodorus' text is corrupt, especially since the virtually certain restoration of Ph. in *PSI* xii 1284, line 14 increases the likelihood that the Ph. who served Eumenes at Gabiene was already with him in 320 (cf. Hornblower, *Hieronymus* 123–4). Schäfer does not comment on the problem in Diod. 19.14.1 (Πίθων ... Φιλώταν μὲν τὸν προϋπάρχοντα Παρθυαίας στρατηγὸν ἀπέκτεινε), but since Diodorus claims that Peithon's actions in Parthia resulted in a coalition of satraps against him (19.14.2), it is unlikely that Philip had already left his satrapy to join forces with Eumenes, leaving Philotas behind as *strategos*. But it would be a desperate solution to assume that Diodorus was wrong about the name (Philotas) of the official, his rank (*strategos* instead of *satrapes*) and his fate (that he was killed rather than driven out). The problem of the ruler of Parthia is explored also by Bosworth 2002, 105–6, who notes (106 n.32) that "Philotas is surely the *lectio difficilior*." This is undoubtedly true, but it helps establish only the authentic reading of the MSS not the historical correctness of Diodorus' claim. Berve II 387 no. 785; Treves, *RE* XIX (1938) 2548–9 no. 62.

912 PHILIP

(Φίλιππος). Macedonian (Tataki 446 no. 22). Ph. was appointed *phrourarchos* of Peukelaotis in 326 (Arr. 4.28.6). Bosworth II 185 tentatively identified him with the son of Machatas (no. 908), but the office of *phrourarchos* is generally allotted to men of lower rank, and Ph., who is not named as one of the *hetairoi*, is also named without patronymic. Berve II 386 no. 783.

913 PHILIP

(Φίλιππος). Macedonian (Tataki 161 no. 89). Born c.350. Brother of Lysimachos (Curt. 8.2.35; Justin 15.3.12), hence also a son of Agathokles (Arr. 6.28.4, *Ind.* 18.3, *Succ.* 1.2), and brother of Autodikos (no. 270) and, perhaps, Alkimachos (no. 65). On a campaign in Sogdiana, Ph. accompanied on foot the King (who rode; hence Ph. was functioning as *hamippos*), declining to take Lysimachos' horse (Curt. 8.2.35–6). Later, after fighting by Alexander's side, he fainted and died in his arms (Curt. 8.2.37–40; cf. Justin 15.3.12). The wording of Curt. 8.2.35 implies that Ph. was a member of the Royal Hypaspists at the time of his death (cf. Heckel 2012). Berve II 382–3 no. 774; Lund 3; Heckel 1992, 298. **Stemma IX.**

914 PHILIP

(Φίλιππος). Macedonian (Tataki 447 no. 25). A senior officer who had campaigned with Alexander (Diod. 19.69.1). He was probably the officer of Eumenes, who is named in *PSI* xi 1284, line 14, and thus already with Eumenes in 321/0. He is later found in Eumenes' service, as commander of elephants and cavalry, at Gabiene (Diod. 19.40.4, 42.7). Presumably, he survived the battle and surrendered to Antigonos, who in 314 appointed him, together with Nearchos (no. 765), Peithon (no. 868) son of Agenor and Andronikos of Olynthos (no. 104), as an adviser of young Demetrios Poliorketes in 314 (Diod. 19.69.1; cf. Wheatley 1997b). He is not actually named in the account of the battle of Gaza, though Peithon and Andronikos play prominent roles. Whether he is identical with the friend of Antigonos who occupied the acropolis of Sardis in 302 is unclear (Diod. 20.107.5). To identify him with any of the known officers of Alexander is nothing more than guesswork and hardly worth the effort: he may be the son of Menelaos, the son of Balakros, Ph. mechanikos. Possibly, he is the man honored with Iolaos in Athens in the period 307–301 (*IG* II² 561; but Billows 421–3 no. 93 identifies the adviser of Demetrios, the commander of Sardis and the honorand of *IG* II² 561 with Ph. son of Balakros). Berve II 387 no. 786; Launey 1185; Treves, *RE* XIX (1938) 2335 no. 16; Billows 421–3 no. 93; Wheatley 1997b.

915 PHILIP

(Φίλιππος). Macedonian (Tataki 446 no. 21). One of Alexander's friends, Ph. had been sent to the oracle of Ammon at Siwah to inquire if the recently deceased Hephaistion (no. 513) should be honored as a god. The oracle answered in the affirmative (Diod. 17.115.6). But this is at odds with other sources who claim that he should be revered as a hero. Berve identifies him with the Ph. of *LM* 92–4. Berve II 386 no. 782; Treves, *RE* XIX (1938) 2552 no. 67.

916 PHILIP

(Φίλιππος). Macedonian (Tataki 447 no. 27). Engineer (*mechanikos*) of unknown ethnic and family background. Ph. was one of the guests at Medeios' dinner party, and allegedly one of the poisoners of Alexander (Ps.-Call. 3.31; *LM* 97). Berve II 389 no. 789; Heckel 1988, 42–3.

917 PHILIP

(Φίλιππος). Macedonian (Tataki 449 no. 41). Patronymic unknown (for the difficulties associated with the restoration of the patronymic see Heckel 1981a; Billows 422; Wheatley 1997b, 66). Ph. was honored in Athens at some point between 307 and 301, on a motion by Stratokles, a strong supporter of Demetrios Poliorketes (*IG* II² 561). He and a certain Iolaos are described as former *somatophylakes* of King Alexander, which presumably means that they were two of the three Somatophylakes assigned to Alexander IV at Triparadeisos in 320 (Arr. *Succ.* 1.38 names four for Philip III, and it follows that the infant Alexander received three to bring the total to the traditional seven). At some point, perhaps after the capture of Alexander IV at Pydna, Ph. entered the service of Antigonos and Demetrios. What became of him after Ipsos, we do not know. Berve II 420 includes Ph.'s colleague Iolaos amongst individuals who are wrongly associated with Alexander (Abschnitt 2 no. 31) but does not list Ph. Burstein 1977a; Heckel 1980b, 1981f; Billows 421–3 no. 93; Wheatley 1997b.

918 PHILIP

(Φίλιππος). Macedonian (Tataki 449 no. 37). Son of Antigonos and Stratonike; younger brother of Demetrios Poliorketes (Plut. *Demetr.* 2.1–2, 3.4, 23.6; Plut. *Mor.* 182b). Billows 420, dates his birth to 334, cf. Wheatley and Dunn 11, he was conceived before Antigonos' departure for Asia). Demetrios was twenty-two in 314/13 (Diod. 19.69.1; App. *Syr.* 54.272; Plut. *Demetr.* 5.2; full discussion in Wheatley 1997b) and Ph. was a few years younger (Plut. *Demetr.* 2.2: Φίλιππον οὐ πολλοῖς ἔτεσι τοῦ Δημητρίου νεώτερον ὄντα συνέβη). Hence it is likely that he was born in Kelainai *c.*332/1 at the latest. Ph. took the name of his paternal grandfather, although he was the second son; Demetrios was named for his uncle, who probably died before his nephew's birth (Plut. *Demetr.* 2.1–2). A story that Antigonos arranged with one of his officers to have Ph. removed from a house, occupied by three girls, has little historical value but, if true, may illustrate Antigonos' concern for his son's upbringing (Plut. *Demetr.* 23.6; see also Plut. *Mor.* 182b, 506c; Cicero, *De officiis* 2.48; Front. 4.1.10.). Like his brother, he was voted a crown by the Skepsians, when they honored Antigonos in 311 (*OGIS* 6 lines 28–9 = Austin² no. 39). In 310, Ph. was sent with an army to the Hellespontine region to make war on Phoinix of Tenedos, whom Antigonos' rebellious nephew Polemaios had left to garrison the cities (Diod. 20.19.5). Diodorus says nothing further about the success or failure of Ph.'s mission. The brief mention of the victories of Demetrios, who was simultaneously sent to Kilikia, may indicate general success of Antigonid ventures in Asia Minor (Diod. 20.19.5). He died in 306 and was buried with royal honors (Diod. 20.73.1, wrongly calling him Phoinix). Berve II 383 no. 776; Billows 419–21 no. 92; Treves, *RE* XIX (1938) 2333–4 no. 14. **Stemma VI.**

919 PHILIP

(Φίλιππος). Macedonian (Tataki 447 no. 26) of low birth; first husband of Berenike and father of Magas (Paus. 1.7.1) and Antigone (Plut. *Pyrrh.* 4.7). That marriage dates to the time before Berenike married Ptolemy I (*Plut. Pyrrh.* 4.7); hence Ph. was probably already dead *c.*320. Berve II no. 787; Treves, *RE* XIX (1938) 2334–5 no. 15.

920 PHILIP

(Φίλιππος). Macedonian (Tataki 447 no. 25). *Philos* of Antigonos Monophthalmos and *phrourarchos* of the citadel of Sardis, which he refused to surrender to Lysimachos' forces in 302 (Diod. 20.107.5). Identification with Philip the advisor of young Demetrios Poliorketes (Diod. 19.69.1) is possible but not compelling. Treves, *RE* (1938) 2335 no. 16.

921 PHILIP

(Φίλιππος). Macedonian (Tataki 447 no. 29). Appointed as *phrourarchos* of Sikyon by Ptolemy. He lost the city to Demetrios in 303/2. Described as ἐπιφανέστατος στρατηγός (Diod. 20.102.2), which suggests that he may have served with Alexander, but not clearly identifiable with any other known Philip. Launey 1185; Treves, *RE* XIX (1938) 2335–6 no. 19; Billows 421–3 no. 93 (highly speculative).

922 PHILIP

(Φίλιππος). Macedonian (Tataki 450 no. 42). Son of Lysimachos and Arsinoë; brother of Ptolemy and Lysimachos. Born in 294 or 293 (he was thirteen at the time of his death in 280: Justin 24.3.5; cf. Beloch IV² 2.130) He was murdered by his stepfather Ptolemy Keraunos in Kassandreia after the latter married his mother (Justin 24.3.5). The third son, Ptolemy, was not present at the time and survived. Beloch IV² 2.130; Treves, *RE* XIX (1938) 2336 no. 20. **Stemma IX.**

923 PHILIPPIDES

(Φιλιππίδης). Athenian (Kirchner 14356). Son of Philokles of Kephale. Comic poet, author of 45 plays. Born in the mid-fourth century (*Suda* Φ 345; for the date see Paschidis 116 n.2; cf. Gell. *NA* 3.15.2). Ph. was an opponent of Stratokles (Plut. *Demetr.* 12.6–9; 26.5; *Mor.* 750f), whom he maligned in verse, and a friend of Lysimachos (Plut. *Mor.* 183e). Thus Lysimachos granted the Athenians many favors (Plut. *Demetr.* 12.6–9, comparing him favorably with Stratokles). The Athenians honored him in 283/2 on a motion by Nikeratos son of Phileas (*IG* II² 657 = *Syll*³ 374 = Burstein no. 11; cf. Shear 1978 no. 11), a decree that provides most of the details concerning Ph.'s career. He went away to live at the court of Lysimachos, a self-imposed exile (Landucci, *Lisimaco* 140; cf. Bayliss 126), probably in 303 (Paschidis 117) and in 299/8 he secured a gift of 10,000 medimnoi of grain for the Athenians from the Thrakian king (lines 13–14); he also secured the yardarm and mast for the *peplos* of Athena (lines 14–15). Ph. saw to the burial of Athenians who had fallen at Ipsos and to the release of prisoners, including some 300 Athenians, who were allowed to go wherever they wished (lines 16–29) Paschidis 120 n.4 suggests that many of these were mercenaries, but it appears that with the change in Antigonid fortunes some of his supporters had no desire to return to Athens. Ph. also sought assistance for the removal of Macedonian garrisons in Peiraieus and elsewhere, though this met with only limited success, since Athens soon came under the control of the tyrant Lachares and then a second domination by Demetrios Poliorketes (295–287). Ph.'s efforts to secure the freedom of the *demos* were probably concentrated on the period 287–285, when the Athenians sought support wherever they could find it (for diplomatic activities see Pachidis 122 n.3). The date of his return from exile (Lund 181 dates it to 301–286) is not explicitly stated, but we are told that he served as *agonothetes* in 284/3, at which time he established from his own resources contests in Eleusis to commemorate the liberation of the *demos* (lines 38–45; Shear 1978, 84–6; Paschidis 117). For the most part, Ph. was honored because of his benefactions to the Athenians, but also because he had served as a useful conduit to King Lysimachos. Paschidis 116–25 A4; Davies 541–2; Philipp 1973; Landucci, *Lisimaco* 139–40, 258–9; Lund 86–7.

924 PHILIPPIDES

(Φιλιππίδης). Athenian (Kirchner 14361). Son of Philomelos of Paiania. Born into a wealthy family (for his trierarchies down to 322, see Paschidis 113 n.5 and Kirchner p. 360; see, e.g., Dem. 21.208, 215) no later than 379 (Davies 549), he was about ninety when he was honored by the Athenians in spring 292 (*IG* II² 649), a decree that recounts his long public service (albeit in a rather general terms) and his concern for the welfare of the city. That the decree was moved by Stratokles is in itself an indication of his political leanings, and Paschidis 114 notes that he held no elected office in the pro-Antipatrid regimes of 322–318 and 317–307. But Paschidis 114 n.3 identifies him with Kirchner 1435, the famously emaciated politician mocked by the comic poets (Athen. 6.230c, 6.238c, 11.502f–503a, and especially 12.552d–e) and the man attacked by Hypereides for his pro-Macedonian stance in 336/5 for his positive attitude towards Philip II after the victory at Chaironeia (Hyp. 2), when he proposed to crown those who introduced an illegal motion to honor Macedonians (Bayliss 241 n.11 treats the identification as certain, speaking of "Hypereides' speech against Philippides of Paiania"). In autumn 299, Ph. moved a decree honoring Poseidippos for his role in an embassy to Kassandros (*IG* II² 641; *Syll*³ 362), an embassy that he himself may have participated in. It is thus rather odd that Stratokles would propose honors for a man who did not share his political views (or, at least, not many of them). Paschidis 105 believes that Stratokles was trying to "regain some political standing" by honoring "a respected adversary" (but see Bayliss 184). Paschidis 113–15 A38.

925 PHILISKOS

(Φίλισκος). Greek from Aigina and apparently father of Onesikritos. Diog. Laert. 6.75–76 speaks of an Onesikritos of Aigina, who had two sons named Androsthenes and Philiskos, who became students of Diogenes the Cynic; later Onesikritos himself studied under him. *Suda* Φ 359 claims that he was a teacher of the young Alexander (*grammatodidaskalos*), and Ael. *VH* 14.11 preserves some advice given by Ph. to Alexander on statecraft. Onesikritos may have been introduced to the King by his father and inspired to write a work on Alexander's education along the lines of Xenophon's *Cyropaedia* (see no. 813). Nothing else is known about Ph. and there is, of course, the risk that the few "biographical" observations that survive were invented. Berve II 389 no. 790.

926 PHILISTIDES

(Φιλιστίδης). A juggler from Syracuse in Alexander's entourage (Athen. 1.20a), Philistides performed at the mass marriage ceremonies at Sousa in 324 (Chares, *FGrH* 125 F4 = Athen. 12.538e). See also Herakleitos and Skymnos. Berve II 389 no. 791.

927 PHILOKLES

(Φιλοκλῆς). Athenian (Kirchner 14521). Possibly the son of Phormion of Eroiadai (Worthington 1986a, 71–2 rejects the identification of the *strategos* with the *kosmetes* of the Ephebes; accepted by Davies 540). *Strategos* in 325/4 (Develin 402). He was in charge of Mounychia and ordered to refuse Harpalos admission into Peiraieus (Din. 3.1). This he did when he first appeared (cf. Plut. *Dem.* 25.3, 7; [Plut.] *Mor.* 846a), but he later admitted Harpalos and was accused of having accepted a bribe from him (Din. 3 repeats the charge but is short on details). He was convicted and apparently fined (Dem. *Ep.* 3.32), although Din. 3.2 claims that he proposed a decree "against himself" that he should be put to death if found guilty. Berve II 389 no. 792; Davies 539–41; Worthington 315–16.

928 PHILOKLES

(Φιλοκλῆς). Son of Apollodoros. Born *c.*350, Ph. became king of Sidon at an unspecified time, probably instead of (or possibly after) Abdalonymos' son Diotimos, who appears only on one document and without the title *basileus* (see no. 397); whether he belonged to a collateral branch of Sidonian royal house is unclear. The Ph. who is attested as a generous donor in Thebes *c.*310 (*Syll*³ 337 = *IG* VII 2419) and on a later occasion, appears to be the son of Apollodoros, but both the view that he was already king of the Sidonians (or at least claiming to be) and his identification as the son of Apollodoros, are based solely on different restorations of line 27 (Merker 1970, 144). It would, however, be difficult to find another individual of that name who would have had the resources to make such donations. He appears as the *strategos* of Ptolemy I (Polyaenus 3.16) who captured Kaunos; for the view that this occurred in 309 and that Ph. was in Ptolemy's entourage between 310 and 308 see Hauben 2004 (reiterating and refining views express in 1987). Seibert 1970 has argued that Ph.'s career belongs to the third century and that the evidence pointing to the fourth is inconclusive at best is not without its merits. Speculation concerning whether he was ever in Demetrios' camp is best avoided. If Philokles made his first appearance in the Ptolemaic camp at the end of the fourth century, the strongest evidence comes from the Theban list of donations; the chronology of the Kaunos expedition is uncertain (we may note that most of the stratagems concerning Ptolemy, Seleukos, and Lysimachos belong to the third century). For a full account of Ph.'s career see Hauben 1987c, 2004. *PP* VI no. 15085; Moser 1914; Tarn *AG* 105; Seibert 1970; Paschidis 439–40.

929 PHILOMELOS

(Φιλόμηλος). Athenian from Lamptrai (Kirchner 14666). In 318 he urged the Athenians to take up arms and support Phokion (Plut. *Phoc.* 32.10), only to be disappointed by him. Otherwise unknown. Bayliss 143.

930 PHILON

(Φίλων). Son of Antipatros (though not the famous regent). Sculptor (Pliny, *HN* 34.91). Ph. produced a statue of Hephaistion (Tatian, *Or. ad Gr.* 55 p. 121 Worth), either early in Alexander's reign or perhaps in Alexandria, after Hephaistion's death, when the latter's hero cult had been established there (for Hephaistion's hero cult see Arr. 7.14.7, 23.6; Diod. 17.115.6; Lucian, *Cal.* 17). Berve II 391–2 no. 797.

931 PHILON

(Φίλων). Ainianian mercenary leader in the Upper Satrapies, Ph. was elected *strategos* by the rebellious mercenaries, whose force numbered 20,000 foot, 3,000 horse (Diod. 18.7.2). These were defeated and killed—or at least in large number—by Peithon (no. 867), whom

Perdikkas had sent to quell the rebellion (Diod. 18.7.5–9). The unnamed Ainianian, who persuaded the mercenary officer Lipodoros (no. 659) to defect (Diod. 18.7.5) and thus secure the victory for Peithon, may have had a personal grudge against Philon, who (in all likelihood) was killed either in battle or in the massacre that followed the mercenaries' surrender (Diod. 18.7.8). His role in 323/2 suggests that he had served as a mercenary (probably as an officer) in Alexander's lifetime and, like many others, been relegated to garrison duty in a remote part of the empire. Philon thus played an unattested role in the upheavals of 325, which followed the false report of Alexander's death in India (Curt. 9.7.1–11). Berve II 392 no. 798; Launey 1134.

932 PHILON

(Φίλων). Son of Kleon, of Erythrai. Brother of Kleon (no. 605). The brothers were in the service of Demetrios Poliorketes (304–302) and honored with *proxenia* by the Megarians (*IG* VII 6). Nothing else is known about Ph. or his brother. Billows 423 no. 94.

933 PHILON

(Φίλων). Athenian (Kirchner 14806). Student of Aristotle (Athen. 13.610f). In 306 Ph. prosecuted Sophokles son of Amphikleides for passing an unconstitutional law against the philosophical schools (Pollux 9.42). Despite a vigorous defense by Demochares (Athen. 11.508f), Sophokles was found guilty and fined five talents (Diog. Laert. 5.38). Nothing else is known about him. Ferguson 106–7.

934 PHILONEIKOS

(Φιλόνεικος). Thessalian (from Pharsalos: Pliny, *HN* 8.154). According to Plut. *Alex.* 6.1, Ph. was the man who brought Boukephalas to Macedonia and offered to sell him for thirteen talents (cf. Gell. *NA* 5.2 = Chares, *FGrH* 125 F18; but Pliny, *HN* 8.154 says XVI). Diod. 17.76.6 says the horse came from Demaratos of Korinth, and it may be (as Hamilton 15 suggests) that Demaratos purchased the horse from Ph. as a gift for Philip. The remainder of the story of how Alexander tamed what was judged to be an unruly horse is one of the most famous anecdotes about the King (Plut. *Alex.* 6.2–8).

935 PHILONIDES

(Φιλωνίδης). Kretan from Chersonessos (*Syll*³ 303 = Harding no. 110; Paus. 6.16.5). The son of Zoitos, Philonides was a *hemerodromos* ("courier") of Alexander and a bematist of the Asia expedition. He is said to have covered the distance from Sikyon to Elis, 1200 stades, in nine hours, though the return trip took him longer (Pliny, *HN* 2.181; 7.84). For his work, which must have resembled that of Diognetos, see Pliny, *HN* 1.4, 5.129; Jacoby, *FGrH* 121. Nothing else is known about him. Berve II 392 no. 800; Launey 1158.

936 PHILOPEITHES

(Φιλοπείθης). Perhaps Athenian. Physician who recovered the remains of the orator Hypereides, who had been killed by Archias the exile-hunter, and brought them back to Athens despite a legal prohibition to Hypereides' cousin or to his son Glaukippos ([Plut.] *Mor.* 849c; *Suda* Υ 294 does not mention his role).

937 PHILOTAS

(Φιλώτας). Macedonian (Tataki 455 no. 72) of unknown family. *Phrourarchos* of the Kadmeia in 335 (Diod. 17.8.7), a position which he may have held since 338. Besieged by the Thebans (Diod. 17.8.3–7), he held out until the arrival of the King, who demanded that the Thebans surrender Phoinix (no. 949) and Prothytes (no. 999); in an absurd counter demand, the Thebans asked for Ph. and Antipatros (Plut. *Alex.* 11.8). Bosworth I 79 believes the Thebans were referring to the son of Parmenion (since he is paired with Antipatros). What became of Ph. after the destruction of Thebes is unknown. Identification with the commandant of Tyre (332) is remotely possible (Curt. 4.5.9), although it does not follow that a man who was once a *phrourarchos* would always remain in such a position. Berve II 399 no. 808; Hamilton 30.

938 PHILOTAS

(Φιλώτας). Macedonian (Tataki 455 no. 71). of unknown family. In spring 335, along with Lysanias, he conveyed the booty acquired from the "independent" Thrakians to the coastal cities of Macedonia to be sold (Arr. 1.2.1). Identification with Ph. the taxiarch is possible but cannot be proved. Berve II 398 no. 805.

939 PHILOTAS

(Φιλώτας). Macedonian (Tataki 7 no. 1). Ph. Augaeus (Curt. 5.2.5); possibly from Augaia in Chalkidike (thus Berve II 398; but *Augaeus* might be easily emended to *Aegaeus*, i.e. "from Aigai." We know of two other individuals from that city: Leonnatos son of Antipatros and Eurylochos). In the contest of valor, held in Sittakene in late 331, Ph. took third place and thus became a chiliarch of the hypaspists (Curt. 5.2.5; see literature s.v. Atarrhias no. 250). He may be the same Ph. who, along with Hellanikos, distinguished himself during the siege of Halikarnassos (Arr. 1.21.5). Note that Atarrhias (like Ph. and Hellanikos, a victor in Sittakene) was also conspicuous at Halikarnassos (Curt. 8.1.36). Nothing else is known about about him. If he survived Alexander and participated in the wars of the Successors, it was most likely as one of the Argyraspids. Berve II 398–9 no. 807; Heckel 1992, 304–5; Heckel and Jones 2006, 43–4.

940 PHILOTAS

(Φιλώτας). Macedonian (Tataki 456 no. 80). Son of Parmenion; brother of Nikanor the *archihypaspistes*, Hektor and at least one unnamed sister, who in 336 had married Attalos, the guardian of Kleopatra-Eurydike (Curt. 6.9.17). Born probably in the late 360s, Ph. appears to have been a *syntrophos* of Amyntas son of Perdikkas (see Amyntas no. 76); the sons of Andromenes (Curt. 7.1.10–11; cf. Arr. 1.27.1) and, perhaps, also Amyntas son of Antiochos were personal friends. An early friendship with Alexander may be implied by Plut. *Alex.* 10.3, who records that in 336, Philip had brought Ph. with him "as a witness" (so Hamilton 26) when he reproached his son for his dealings with Pixodaros. Whether this means that Ph. had informed against the prince or, what seems more likely, Philip was using Ph. as a paradigm of good behavior, the incident cannot have endeared him to Alexander. Ph. is first attested as a commander of cavalry (from Upper Macedonia) in the Triballian campaign (Arr. 1.2.5; cf. also Hammond 1987, 340, lines 32–3). In the following year, during the attack on Pellion, Alexander sent Ph. with sufficient horsemen to protect a foraging party. These, however, were surrounded by Glaukias and the Taulantians, who had come to Kleitos' aid, and had to be rescued by the King (Arr. 1.5.9–11). By the beginning of the Asiatic expedition, he commanded the entire Companion Cavalry (Diod. 17.17.4; cf. Curt. 6.9.21), perhaps as a reward for his father's elimination of Attalos (see s.v. Parmenion no. 848).

At the Granikos, Ph.'s cavalry were drawn up on the right, alongside the archers and the Agrianes (Arr. 1.14.1; there is no evidence, *pace* Berve II 393, that these other units were under Ph.'s command). Nothing else is known of his role in the battle. When the army moved to Miletos, Ph. was sent with the cavalry and three battalions of infantry to Mykale to prevent the Persian fleet from disembarking and obtaining water and supplies (Arr. 1.19.7–8). In the Halikarnassos campaign, he participated in the abortive attempt on Myndos (Arr. 1.20.5–7). It appears that he spent the winter of 334/3 with Alexander in Pamphylia and Lykia. Berve II 393 thinks Ph. accompanied his father to Gordion. Arr. 1.24.3 gives Parmenion a "hipparchy" of Companions. At best, Arrian can be referring to only a few *ilai*, though possibly the term "hipparchy" is wrongly and anachronistically used as a substitute for *ile* (cf. Bosworth I 155; Brunt 1963, 29; Brunt I lxxv §60; Griffith 1963, 70). When the reunited army moved from Gordion to Tarsos, the Companion Cavalry accompanied Alexander and were probably instrumental in capturing Tarsos before it could be put to the torch by the satrap Arsames. After Alexander's recovery from his illness at the Kydnos, Ph. accompanied him to Soloi and via Anchiale to the Aleian plain. Here Alexander turned south to the coastal town of Magarsus, sending Ph. across the plain to Mallos, where the army was later reunited (Arr. 2.5.5–9). Of his role in the battle of Issos, nothing is recorded except his position in the battle line: on the right wing with the King (Arr. 2.8.3). Hegesias (*FGrH* 142 F5 = Dion. Hal. *de comp. verb.* 18 p. 123–6R) claims that during the capture of Gaza Ph. and Leonnatos brought the eunuch (Arr. 2.25.4; *Itiner. Al.* 45) Batis, whom Dareios had entrusted with the defense of the city, to Alexander as a captive. Whatever the truth concerning the nature of Batis' death, there is no good reason for doubting Ph.'s involvement in his arrest. Nor does Alexander's treatment of Batis, if it is indeed historical, reflect badly on Ph. But Alexander's adoption by Amun-Re (winter 332/1), marked a turning point in the relationship between Ph. and the King. The "friendship," of which some writers (ancient and modern) speak, may never have been warm. In Egypt, Ph. made his true feelings about the King known to his mistress, Antigone (no. 112), who had been with him since her capture at Damaskos in late 333: he told her that Alexander's achievements were due to the efforts of his father, Parmenion, and complained about the King's pretensions to be the son of Amun. But these comments were carelessly passed on to others, who reported the matter to Krateros, and through him they came to Alexander's attention. These disloyal rumblings constituted Ph.'s so-called Egyptian conspiracy (Arr. 3.26.1; cf. Plut. *Alex.* 48.4–49.2), and Alexander rightly took no action against him. Nor was he aware of Ph.'s conversations with Hegelochos (no. 496), whose treasonous remarks did not come to light until 330 (Curt. 6.11.22–9).

At Gaugamela, Ph. commanded the Companions (Arr. 3.11.8; Curt. 4.13.26; Diod. 17.57.1), probably in the immediate vicinity of the King and followed him in his pursuit of the fleeing Persians, which, rumor held, was cut short by Parmenion's request for help. At Sousa, he is said to have treated with disdain the laments of those Persians who saw Alexander sitting on the throne and resting his feet on the table from which Dareios used to eat (Curt. 5.2.13–15; Diod. 17.66.3–7). At the Persian Gates, Ph. was sent with the infantry battalions of Koinos, Amyntas, and Polyperchon (Curt. 5.4.20, 30; Arr. 3.18.6) to circumvent the forces of Ariobarzanes and perhaps begin the bridging of the Araxes River (thus Arr. 3.18.6; but Curt. 5.4.30 has Ph. and the taxiarchs participating in the attack on Ariobarzanes, with the bridging of the Araxes taking place later under Alexander's direction (5.5.3–4); Polyaenus 4.3.27 wrongly assigns command of the main camp to Ph. and Hephaistion; cf. Heckel 1980a, 169–71; Howe 2015b, 177–8). Nothing else is recorded about Ph. until the death of his brother Nikanor in the autumn of 330. He remained behind in Aria for several days to see to his brother's funeral.

Ph. rejoined the army in Phrada (modern Farah?), the capital of Drangiana (Diod. 17.78.4), later renamed Prophthasia ("Anticipation"; cf. Steph. Byz. s.v. Φράδα) for the events which would unfold. There Ph. was implicated in a plot to kill the King, though it is clear that he could not have been a member of the conspiracy. The ancient sources focus on Dimnos, one of the *hetairoi*, but the truly dangerous member of the plot was Demetrios the Somatophylax (Heckel 203–8), who doubtless objected to the introduction of Persian practices at Alexander's court after Dareios' death. Curtius alone names the other conspirators (6.7.15): Peukolaos, Aphobetos, Theoxenos, Archepolis, Nikanor, Iolaos, Amyntas, Demetrios (cf. Arr. 3.26.3, without names). Dimnos is wrongly said to have planned the deed (Plut. *Alex.* 49.3); more plausibly to have been party to Demetrios' conspiracy (Curt. 6.7.6 does not say that Dimnos himself planned it: cf. 6.11.37, where a certain "Calis"—unnamed by Curt. 6.7.15—confesses that he and Demetrios planned the crime). Dimnos was betrayed by his lover Nikomachos, who revealed everything to his own brother Kebalinos. Kebalinos reported the matter to Ph., who failed to act on the information (Badian's bizarre theory (1960) that Alexander set Ph. up to fail is disproved in part by the fact that Kebalinos encountered Ph. by accident rather than seeking him out in order to make the report: noted by Adams 2003, 118, following Curt. 6.7.17–18: *ipse Cebalinus ante uestibulum regiae—neque enim propius aditus ei patebat—consistit opperiens aliquem ex prima cohorte amicorum, <a> quo introduceretur ad regem. forte ceteris dimissis unus Philotas, Parmenionis filius—incertum quam ob causam—substiterat in regia. huic Cebalinus ore confuso magnae perturbationis notas prae se ferens aperit, quae ex fratre compererat, et sine dilatione nuntiari regi iubet*). When Ph. did not act as expected, Kebalinos approached the Royal Page, Metron, who reported the matter to the King. Those sent to arrest Dimnos could not take him alive, and thus the uncertainty concerning Ph.'s role increased. Nothing could be asserted with confidence, however, either by the prosecution or the King's historians, except that Ph. had been negligent. But a conspiracy involving one of the King's own Bodyguards could not be taken lightly (cf. MacLean Rogers 2004, 147), and Ph.'s negligence may well show that he hoped the plot would succeed. With Alexander dead, the army would almost certainly turn back, and Parmenion in Ekbatana would be the logical man to assume control of affairs until a new king could be selected. Indeed, Alexander Lynkestes, a candidate for the throne, was at the time accompanying the army in chains. Nor should Parmenion's position be underestimated: the old general controlled Alexander's lifeline to Macedonia.

Ph. owed much to his father's influence. But he was arrogant and outspoken (Plut. *Alex.* 48.1–3; cf. Them. *Or.* 19.229c–d), and his prestigious command was coveted by the younger commanders, who through their connections with Alexander hoped for greater power. He had foolishly disregarded Parmenion's advice to "make less of himself" (Plut. *Alex.* 48.3), and his arrogance and general unpopularity contributed to his fall. Through his inaction, Ph. afforded his enemies the perfect opportunity for seeking his elimination (Curt. 6.8.4). What we know from the detailed but highly dramatized account of Curtius is that several of the younger *hetairoi* of Alexander—Krateros, Hephaistion, Koinos, Leonnatos, Perdikkas (Curt. 6.8.17, adding Erigyios)—took leading roles in securing his condemnation. Krateros renewed his prosecution of an old enemy. Alexander was told to guard himself against the enemy within (Curt. 6.8.4), a warning that masked their personal enmity and ambitions. If Alexander himself desired Ph.'s removal from office, there were several who supported such a move, if they did not in fact initiate it. Certainly they took an active part in torturing the prisoner (Curt. 6.8.15) and Ph. was right to remark that the bitterness of his enemies had overcome Alexander's goodwill (Curt. 6.8.22). They had all hated Ph. for a long time (Plut. *Alex.* 49.8), particularly Hephaistion and Krateros. The latter had already monitored his activities in Egypt, and the former was feared by many for his influence with the King. Koinos, Ph.'s brother-in-law, was his most outspoken prosecutor (Curt. 6.9.30), perhaps as an act of self-preservation. Similarly, Amyntas son of Andromenes, averted danger by repudiating his friendship with Ph. (Curt. 7.1.18ff.). For a full but dramatic account see Curt. 6.7–11; cf. Diod. 17.79; Plut. *Alex.* 49.3–12; Arr. 3.26.1–2; Justin 12.5.1–3. Convicted by the Macedonian assembly he was killed by stoning (Curt. 6.11.10; cf. Diod. 17.80.2) or with javelins (Arr. 3.26.3). For his death see also Plut. *Alex.* 49.13; Justin 12.5.3; Curt. 7.1.1. Later references to his death, which provoked outrage in some sectors of the army and command: Arr. 4.14.2; Curt. 8.1.33, 38, 52; 8.7.4–5; 8.8.5; Justin 12.6.14. Berve II 393–7 no. 802; Heckel, *Marshals*² 52–9. For his conspiracy, see Badian 1960, 2000a; Heckel 27–33; cf. Heckel 203–8 and 2003a; Cauer 1894, 8–38; Hamilton 132–8; Rubinsohn 1977; Bosworth I 359–63; Goukowsky I 38ff.; II 118–34; Adams 2003; MacLean Rogers 2004, 142–9; Reames 2008; Müller, *LexAM* 426–8. **Stemma VII.**

941 PHILOTAS

(Φιλώτας). Son of Karsis (Arr. 4.13.4), a Thrakian who may have married the daughter of a Macedonian aristocrat named Ph. (thus Hoffmann 180; Tataki 456 no. 79 lists him as Macedonian, despite his Thrakian father). Ph.'s birth must be dated to between 345 and 340, since he is named as one of the Pages involved in Hermolaos' conpiracy of 327 (Curt. 8.6.9; Arr. 4.13.4). He is not mentioned again by name, but it is virtually certain that he was executed by stoning (Arr. 4.14.3) for his part in the conspiracy, after first being tortured (Arr. 4.13.7; Plut. *Alex.* 55.6; cf. Curt. 8.6.20). Hoffmann 180; Berve II 392 no. 801; Heckel 1992, 295.

942 PHILOTAS

(Φιλώτας). Macedonian (Tataki 455 no. 73). Family background unknown. A battalion commander and later satrap of Kilikia, Ph.'s early career is entirely obscure. It is tempting to identify him with the officer who, in the company of Lysanias, conveyed the Thrakian booty to Amphipolis in 335 (Arr. 1.2.1), an identification made more attractive by the possibility that Lysanias is the cavalry commander of Antigonos the One-Eyed (Diod. 19.29.2; cf. Billows 398 no. 64). Hence, both would have found their way eventually into Antigonos' service. Otherwise, Ph. is attested as the commander of an infantry battalion sent with Ptolemy son of Lagos to arrest the regicide Bessos (Arr. 3.29.7) and again in the Aspasian campaign of 327/6 (Arr. 4.24.10). The view of Milns 1966 that the Ph. at the Persian Gates (Curt. 5.4.20, 30; Arr. 3.18.6) commanded a seventh *taxis* of pezhetairoi is not compelling. This Ph. was almost certainly the son of Parmenion and thus a cavalry officer. But the Ph. who accompanied Lysanias in 336/5 could easily have been a commander of *psiloi* rather than pezhetairoi. Four battalions are mentioned in the Aspasian campaign (327/6)—those of Ph., Attalos, Balakros, and Philip—of which only Attalos' can have comprised *pezhetairoi*. Perdikkas and Hephaistion, *en route* to the Indos, had taken Gorgias, Kleitos, and Meleagros (Arr. 4.22.7). Krateros retained the battalions of Polyperchon and Alketas, as can be deduced from Arr. 4.23.1, 5; 4.24.1, 25.5–6. Gorgias' battalion was formerly Krateros'; Kleitos' was a new (seventh) unit. Hence Alexander was left with only Koinos and Attalos. Balakros' men are undoubtedly light infantry (*psiloi*), and it is highly likely that Philip (probably the son of Machatas) and Ph. led similar troops (cf. Bosworth II 154–5 and Bosworth 1973, 252–3).

In 323 Ph. resurfaces as satrap of Kilikia (Diod. 18.3.1; Justin 13.4.12; Arr. *Succ.* 1.5; Dexippos, *FGrH* 100 F8 §2; cf. Justin 13.6.16; Diod. 18.12.1 confuses him with Leonnatos), an appointment which was perhaps made by Alexander himself; for the previous satrap, Balakros son of Nikanor had been killed by the Pisidians while Alexander was still alive (Diod. 18.22.1). He appears to be the Ph. named as one of the King's poisoners (Ps.-Call. 3.31.8–9); the charge was almost certainly fabricated but suggests nevertheless that he was still in Babylon in May/June 323 (Heckel 1988, 36–7, though I would now withdraw the tentative identification with Ph. Augaeus, Curt. 5.2.5). Perdikkas removed him from his satrapy in 321/0, perceiving that he was loyal to Krateros (Arr. *Succ.* 24.2; Justin 13.6.16; cf. Boerma 1979, 185). Ph. may now have joined the forces of Antipatros, if he did not go directly to Antigonos. If Ph. had been a *philos* of Antigonos before the settlement at Triparadeisos, Antipatros may have failed to reinstate him as satrap of Kilikia in 320 for this very reason, allowing Philoxenos to remain in office (Arr. *Succ.* 1.34; Diod. 18.39.6; Philoxenos was Perdikkas' appointee, and we must assume that he remained in office because he had defected to Antipatros after Krateros' defeat at the Hellespont in 320). Antipatros may have used the argument that Ph. had been unable to hold Kilikia and, therefore, did not deserve to be restored (cf. Menandros, who abandoned Lydia and was replaced by Kleitos in 320), but his real purpose must have been to offset Antigonos' power in Asia by leaving Kilikia and Lydia in the hands of men more loyal to himself; Diod. 18.50.5 shows that Antigonos wanted to reinstate *his* men in Asia Minor (cf. also 18.62.6–7). See also Heckel 2002, 90–1. In 318, Ph. was sent with thirty other Macedonians to seduce the Argyraspids away from their allegiance to Eumenes. For this purpose, he bore a letter from Antigonos himself (Diod. 18.62.4). Ph. suborned Teutamos to approach Antigenes in an effort to bring about his defection, but instead the latter succeeded in bringing Teutamos back into Eumenes' camp (Diod. 18.62.5–7). Although he read out to the Argyraspids Antigonos' letter, urging them to arrest Eumenes, whom the Macedonians had outlawed at Triparadeisos, he met with no success and returned to Antigonos (Diod. 18.63.1–5). Nothing else is known about him. I can find no support for Billows' suggestion (103 n.27) that Antigenes may have been killed because "he had caused the execution of Antigonos' friend Philotas." Berve II 397–8, nos. 803–4; Billows 423–4 no. 95; Heckel 1992, 328–30.

943 PHILOTAS

(Φιλώτας). Macedonian (Tataki 455 no. 75). Commandant (*phrourarchos*) of Tyre in 332 (Curt. 4.5.9). Nothing else is known about him, unless he is identical with the man captured at Kretopolis (no. 944). Berve II 398 no. 806.

944 PHILOTAS

(Φιλώτας). Macedonian (Tataki 455–6 no. 76). One of Alketas' commanders, captured at Kretopolis along with Attalos (no. 265), Polemon (no. 971), Dokimos (no. 400) and Antipatros (no. 132; Diod. 19.16.1). There is a strong likelihood that he had seen service with Alexander, but there is no compelling evidence for identification with any known Ph. from that period.

945 PHILOTAS

(Φιλώτας). Macedonian (Tataki 455 no. 74). *Strategos* of Parthyaia in 317; killed by Peithon son of Krateuas (Diod. 19.14.1, unless this is an error for Philip no. 918 above). Although his existence has been doubted on the grounds that Diodorus was either mistaken or his text is corrupt, we cannot definitively dismiss his existence.

946 PHILOTERA

(Φιλοτέρα). A daughter of Ptolemy I Soter and Berenike (sister of Ptolemy II, Pliny, *HN* 6.33.168). A city in the Troglodytic country, founded by Satyros, bears her name (Strabo 16.4.5 C769). Carney 2013, 98 and Ager 2018, 49 suggest that Philotera's failure to marry and her apparent early death (*P. Berlin* 13417; Macurdy 127) may point to some type of disability. Beloch IV² 2.180; Carney 2013, 98; Ager 2018, 43, 49; *PP* VI 14574; Regner, *RE* XX.1 (1941) 1285.

947 PHILOXENOS

(Φιλόξενος). Macedonian (Tataki 453 no. 61). Family background unknown. In late 333, after the flight of Harpalos, he was appointed financial officer in charge of tax collection in Asia west of the Tauros mountains (Arr. 3.6.4). Plut. *Alex.* 22.1 calls him *strategos* of the forces on the coast, and he seems to have exercised, in addition to his functions as a financial officer, the role of satrap or *hyparchos* (cf. Polyaenus 6.49, speaking of the *hyparchos* of Ionia; cf. Plut. *Mor.* 333a: *hyparchos* of the coastal region: ὕπαρχος τῆς παραλίας); his residence was probably Sardis, where he imprisoned the murderers of Hegesias of Ephesos (Polyaenus 6.49). In fact, Philoxenos appears to have had an overarching authority, reminiscent of the younger Kyros' powers as *karanos* in the late fifth century (Xen. *Hell.* 1.4.3; cf. Briant 600). According to Plut. *Alex.* 22.1–2 (cf. Plut. *Mor.* 333a; Athen. 1.22d) he wanted to send Alexander some good-looking slave boys, but Alexander indignantly declined the offer. The date of this offer is not given, and it could belong to the 330s. The official who demanded the extradition of Harpalos, arrested the steward of Harpalos' money and reported to the Athenians the names of those who had received bribes (Paus. 2.33.4–5; cf. Hyp. 1.8) could just as easily have been the satrap of Karia. Even if the *hyparchos* can be identified with the satrap of Karia (see below), as Bosworth I 280–2 suggests—but not the later satrap of Kilikia—, Philoxenos plays no role in the history of the Successors, and he may have died or returned to Macedonia, perhaps with Krateros in 322. His special command appears to have ended with the death of Alexander. Berve II 389–90 no. 793; Bengtson 1937.

948 PHILOXENOS

(Φιλόξενος). Macedonian of obscure origins and undistinguished military service (Arr. *Succ.* 24.2), Philoxenos was installed as satrap of Kilikia by Perdikkas in place of Philotas, who was known to a friend of Krateros (Arr. *Succ.* 24.2; Justin 13.6.16). Philoxenos, despite his appointment by Perdikkas, must have cooperated with Antipatros and was consequently confirmed as satrap of Kilikia at Triparadeisos (Diod. 18.39.6; Arr. *Succ.* 1.34). It appears that he is identical with the Philoxenos who was, after the death of Ada, satrap of Karia ([Aristotle], *Oecon.* 2.31, 1351; but see Bosworth I 280–2). Φιλόξενός τις Μακεδών is hardly how one would describe the *hyparchos* who had exercised power in the coastal region for almost ten years. In 323, he brought troops from the coast to Alexander in Babylon (Arr. 7.23.1, 24.1), but he was overlooked in the settlement of 323. His sojourn in Babylon may, however, explain how he came to be in Perdikkas' camp in 321/0. But Arrian's comments (ἕνα τῶν ἀφανῶν Μακεδόνων, οἷα δὴ ἐν ἡμιολίῳ μισθοφορᾷ ὑπ' Ἀλεξάνδρῳ ἐστρατευμένον) may reflect a bias against Philoxenos on the part of Hieronymos. What became of him is unknown. Berve II 390–1 no. 794.

PHILOXENOS. Berve II 391 no. 795. Tataki 453 no. 60. Arr. 3.16.6. See **XENOPHILOS**.

949 PHOINIX

(Φοῖνιξ). Theban. A leader of the anti-Macedonian faction. In 335, Alexander demanded that the Thebans surrender him and Prothytes in return for amnesty; but the Thebans arrogantly demanded the surrender of Philotas and Antipatros (Plut. *Alex.* 11.7–8). This can easily be reconciled with the admittedly apologetic version of Arr. 1.7.10–11, which shows that there was in Thebes a party willing to negotiate, but that their efforts were undermined by the anti-Macedonian faction (cf. Diod. 17.9.4). Berve II 399 no. 809.

950 PHOINIX

(Φοῖνιξ). Greek from Tenedos. Whether Phoinix had served with Alexander or had been recruited by Eumenes in northwestern Asia Minor is unclear. In the battle with Krateros at the Hellespont (321), Phoinix and Pharnabazos commanded the mercenary cavalry, with orders to attack quickly before a herald from Krateros' army could come persuade Eumenes' forces to defect (Plut. *Eum.* 7.1). After Triparadeisos he remained true to Eumenes and, when 3,000 infantry and 500 cavalry led by a certain Perdikkas deserted Eumenes in Kappadokia, Phoinix pursued them with 4,000 infantry and 1,000 cavalry, catching the deserters in their camp during the second watch and bringing them back to Eumenes for punishment (Diod. 18.40.2–4). After Eumenes' defeat at Gabiene, Phoinix joined Antigonos, serving his nephew Polemaios. When that man rebelled against his uncle (310), he left Phoinix in charge of Hellespontine Phrygia, where he was subsequently attacked by Philip son of Antigonos (Diod. 20.19.2, 5). We are not told the outcome of events in the Hellespont but, since Polemaios was murdered by Ptolemy on Kos in 309, it may be that Phoinix was reconciled with Antigonos, only to betray him a second time by handing over Sardis to Lysimachos in 302 (Diod. 20.107.5). Phoinix is designated *strategos*.

The citadel, however, remained in the hands of Philip, who stayed true to Antigonos. Nothing else is known about Phoinix. Billows 424 no. 96; W. Hoffmann, *RE* XX (1941) 425 nos. 8 and 9; Schoch, *RE* no. 10; Launey 1151; Hornblower, *Hieronymus* 130 n.105.

PHOINIX. Diod. 20.73.1. See PHILIP.

951 PHOINIX

(Φοῖνιξ). Antigonid *strategos* of Sardis in 302 (Diod. 20.107.5). Possibly identical with Phoinix of Tenedos (see above). But Billows 424–5 no. 97 and Hoffmann, *RE* XX (1941) no. 9 treat him as a separate individual.

952 PHOKION

(Φωκίων). [All references in boldface are to Plutarch's *Life of Phocion*.] Athenian. Son of Phokos (Kirchner 15076). He had two wives: the first was the sister of Kephisodotos the sculptor and the second known only for her modesty and character (**19**). It was presumably the second wife who was the mother of Phokos (Davies 559), a son whose lifestyle did not imitate that of his father (**20.1–3; 38.3–4**), as well as a daughter who married Charikles (**21.5**). Born 402/1 (**24.5**; Nepos, *Phoc.* 2.1). Student of Plato and friend of Xenokrates (**4.2; 14.7**; Plut. *Mor.* 1126c). In his early years he served with Chabrias (**6–7**; Plut. *Mor.* 791a), but he died in 357. Ph. took Chabrias' son Ktesippos under his wing after the father's death but found him to be stupid and troublesome (**7.3–4**). Ph. held the *strategia* forty-five times, more than any other Athenian, and is first attested in a military capacity in 349/8 on Euboia (Aesch. 3.86–8; Dem. 21.162ff.; **12.1–14.2**), unless his command of mercenaries on Kypros is correctly dated by Diod. 16.42.7ff. to 351/0. It is more likely, however, that this campaign in the service of Idrieus of Karia and in conjunction with Euagoras II belongs to 344/3. In 343/2 he supported Aischines in the *parapresbeia* trial and in 341/0 he defeated Kleitarchos of Eretria, whom Philip II had installed as tyrant there (Diod. 16.74.1; cf. Gehrke 1976, 45 n.29; Dem. 18.71, 295). His intervention in Byzantion in 340/39, made possible by the trust its citizens placed in him and on account of his friendship with Leon (**14.7**; the Byzantines had refused to accept help from Chares, whom they distrusted, **14.3–4**), kept the city out of Philip's hands. Hence, although he can be called a conservative, with leanings towards the policies of Euboulos, he was prepared to act in the interests of the state and thus appears on these occasions to be following a Demosthenic policy. But Ph.'s actions were dictated by principle rather than party politics, and the charge that Demosthenes had often defended Ph. only to be betrayed by him (Nepos, *Phoc.* 2.2–3) fails to take account of the complexities of Athenian politics and Ph.'s adherence to his own beliefs. Demosthenes had also supported Ph. against his political opponent Chares. For Chares' opposition to Ph. see **5.1–2**. He did not join Demosthenes in ridiculing the youth of Alexander (**17.1**) or opposing his request for ships (**21.1**; Plut. *Mor.* 188c). Certainly, Ph. regarded Alexander's demand for the extradition of the most bellicose orators and generals after the sack of Thebes perfectly reasonable (**9.10**, although it not clear whether Ph.'s advice that the men be surrendered was made in earnest). Although he argued that Athens should surrender the mischief-makers rather than go to war with Alexander, he later used his influence to persuade the King to relent (**17.3–6**). During Alexander's lifetime Ph. steered a course between the ardent opponents of Macedon and the dangers of the King's friendship. For his political rivals see **4.2, 10.6**

(Glaukippos and Hypereides); **5.4**, **9–10**; **16.3** (Demosthenes); **9.8** (Demosthenes; but Plut. *Mor.* 811a tells the same story about Demades); **10.3–5, 9** (Aristogeiton; cf. Plut. *Mor.* 188b); **17.2–3** (Demosthenes, Hypereides, Charidemos); **20.6** (Demades). For his sayings, many of them concerning Athenian politics and politicians see Plut. *Mor.* 187f–189b. In fact, his lifestyle was simple and frugal (Ael. *VH* 2.43, 7.9; Nepos, *Phoc.* 1.1)—though stories of his low origins must be rejected (Ael. *VH* 12.43; Idomeneus, *FGrH* 338 F15 = **4.2**)—and he is said to have rejected gifts of money from various Macedonian leaders (Nepos, *Phoc.* 1.3–4; Ael. *VH* 1.25, 11.9; **18.1–4**, 7–8; 30.1–4; Plut. *Mor.* 188c, 188f; for Ph.'s remark to Antipatros that he could not be both flatterer and friend, see Plut. *Agis* 2.2; Plut. *Mor.* 64c, 142b–c, 532f–533a). Instead of accepting bribes from Alexander—for thus his gifts would be perceived—Ph. secured the release of political prisoners from Sardis (**18.6**), and it said that Alexander used the polite form of address (*chairein*) only in his letters to Antipatros and Ph. (**17.9–10** = Douris, *FGrH* 76 F1 and Chares, *FGrH* 125 F10). In 324 he also resisted attempts by Harpalos to buy his favor (**21.3–4**), only to find that his son-in-law, Charikles, had become a confidant of the deserter, to his own detriment (**21.5–22.4**). In fact, when Charikles was charged by the Athenians for his dealings with Harpalos, Ph. would not speak in his defense (**22.4**). Nor did Ph. support Leosthenes and those who favored war after Alexander's death; for he felt that Athenian chances in the long run were not very good (Plut. *Mor.* 803a–b; **23**). There may be some truth that he was deliberately passed over for supreme command when Leosthenes was killed (**24.1–2**). Nevertheless, he did serve his country in the Lamian War, when he led out forces to Rhamnous to defeat and kill Mikion, who had invaded Attika (**25**).

But Ph.'s policy of avoiding war with Macedon, and his friendship with Macedonian leaders, brought him grief when he supported Demades in turning over the city to Antipatros (**30.8**) and later allowed Nikanor to control both Mounychia and Peiraieus (Nepos, *Phoc.* 2.4–5; **31.2–3**, **32.4–10**; Diod. 18.64.5); together with Demetrios of Phaleron he was the outspoken voice of the aristocratic party that sided with Kassandros (Nepos, *Phoc.* 3.1). Although he resisted Athenian appeals that he intervene with Antipatros for removal of the Macedonian garrison, Ph. did secure a delay in the payment of the fine imposed after the Lamian War (**30.8**). But when Polyperchon gained temporary supremacy in Macedon, the democratic party expelled Ph. and his supporters (Nepos, *Phoc.* 3.2; Diod. 18.65.6); indeed, Polyperchon had sparse hopes of achieving his purpose as long as Ph. remained influential in Athens (**32.2**). When he went to Polyperchon, now at Pharygai in Phokis, to plead his case—ostensibly before Philip III Arrhidaios—he was shouted down by the regent and charged with betraying Peiraieus (Nepos, *Phoc.* 3.3; **33.4–12**; cf. Ael. *VH* 3.47; 12.49; Diod. 18.66.3). Ph. was sent to Athens for trial (Nepos, *Phoc* 3.4; Diod. 18.66.4), but had to be taken to court by carriage since he was too old to walk. Nevertheless, although the crowd pitied him, the Athenians' anger over his betrayal of Peiraieus was so great (cf. Plut. *Mor.* 189a) that they would not even allow him to speak in his own defense (Diod. 18.66.5–67.2). Hence, he was condemned—some even wanted to subject him to torture (**35.1**)—and handed over to the Eleven for execution (Nepos, *Phoc.* 4.1–2; cf. Plut. *Mor.* 189a–b; Diod. 18.67.5–6; **35–36**; executed with Ph. were Nikokles, Thoudippos, Hegemon, and Pythokles; Demetrios of Phaleron, Kallimedon and Charikles were sentenced to death *in absentia*: **5.4**). His fate was lamented by a close friend, Euphiletos (Nepos, *Phoc.* 4.3). As a final insult, his enemies decreed that he should not have a proper burial within the limits of Attika (**37.3**). His funeral rites were conducted in private by a servant and his wife (Nepos, *Phoc.* 4.3–4; **37.3–5**), though later the Athenians regretted their actions and gave him a public funeral and statue (**38.1**). At his death, he was 83 or 84 years old (cf. Plut. *Mor.* 791e–f; Polyaenus 3.12). The Athenians condemned Hagnonides to death, and Ph.'s son, Phokos, tracked down and punished Demophilos and Epikouros (**38.2**). Kirchner 15076; Berve II 402–3 no. 816; Lenschau, *RE* XX.1 (1941) 458–74 no. 2; Davies 559–60; Gehrke 1976; Bearzot 1985; Tritle 1988.

953 PHOKOS

(Φῶκος). Athenian (Kirchner 15081). [References in **boldface** are to Plutarch's *Life of Phocion.*] Son of Phokion and named for the paternal grandfather. He was fond of drink and unruly (**20.1**: φιλοπότης καὶ ἄτακτος), and his father encouraged him to engage in sport—he actually won the horse race at the Panathenaic games—(not for the sake of glory but to change his lifestyle; cf. also **30.1–2**); the father even took him to Sparta to be trained in their rigorous regime (**20**), which brought criticism down on Phokion himself. Despite the advice which his father gave when he was facing execution, that he should not hold a grudge against the Athenians (**36.4**), Ph. took an active part in punishing his father's accusers (**38.2**). Most of what we know about Ph. involves his poor judgment and dissolute life (Athen. 4.168e–169a; **20.1–3**, **38.3–4**). He was notorious for squandering his inheritance and was universally loathed in Athens. The profligacy of Ph. was, at least, a testament to his father's wealth (Tritle 1988, 42). Lenschau, *RE* XX.1 (1941) 502 no. 8.

954 PHORMION

(Φορμίων). Greek. Phormion was among the notable comic actors who performed at the mass marriage ceremonies at Sousa in 324 (Chares, *FGrH* 125 F4 = Athen. 12.539a; possibly a Lenaian victor *c.*350 (*IG* II² 670 [x], but the name is restored and far from secure). Berve II 399 no. 811; O'Connor 138 no. 498.

955 PHORMION

(Φορμίων). Parasite of Seleukos I (Athen. 6.244f). Otherwise unknown. Grainger, *SPG* 114.

956 PHRADASMANES

(Φραδασμάνης). Son of Phrataphernes. Ph. was enrolled, along with this brother Sisines, in the *agema* of the cavalry (Arr. 7.6.4). Nothing further is known about him, unless he is identical with Pharismenes son of Phrataphernes. Berve II 400 no. 812; Shayegan 117–18 no. 90.

957 PHRASAORTES

(Φρασαόρτης). Persian. Son of Rheomithres. Appointed by Alexander as satrap of Persis (Arr. 3.18.11) after the flight and (apparent) death of Ariobarzanes (no. 87). Polyaenus 4.3.27 mistakenly names Phrasaortes as defender of the Persian Gates instead of Ariobarzanes (see Howe 2015b). Phrasaortes died of illness while Alexander was in India (Arr. 6.29.2). His position was taken, without the King's permission, by Orxines (Arr. 6. 30.1). Berve II 400 no. 813; Shayegan 118 no. 91.

958 PHRATAPHERNES

(Φραταφέρνης). Persian. Justi 104 no. 1. Father of Sisines, Pharismanes and Phradasmenes (unless Pharismenes is a scribal error for Phradasmenes or vice versa and the two forms refer to the same individual). In the reign of Dareios III Ph. was satrap of Parthyaia and Hyrkania and commanded the regional troops at Gaugamela (Arr. 3.8.4; cf. Curt. 4.12.9, 11). He remained faithful to Dareios until the king's death and when he surrendered to Alexander, he may have been restored to the satrapy of Parthyaia (Arr. 3.23.4, 28.2); but Arr. 3.22.1 says that both Hyrkania and Parthyaia were given to Amminapes (no. 71). In 330 he was ordered to accompany Erigyios and Karanos, who were sent to subdue Aria. Later he met Alexander in Zariaspa (Arr. 4.7.1) or Nautaka (Arr. 4.18.1), bringing Arsakes captive. Alexander made him satrap of Hyrkania, adding control of the Mardians and Tapourians, and ordering him to arrest Autophradates, who was guilty of misrule (Curt. 8.3.17). Arrian refers to Ph. as satrap of Parthyaia only (Arr. 3.23.2; 4.7.1; 4.18.1). Only at Arr. 5.20.7 is he called satrap of Parthyaia and Hyrkania. In India he returns to Alexander the Thrakians who had been assigned to him for this purpose (Arr. 5.20.7). Alexander appealed to him for supplies during his Gedrosian march (Curt. 9.10.17) and these were brought to him in Karmania by Ph.'s son Pharismenes (Arr. 6.27.3, 6). Two of Ph.'s sons—Phradasmenes (no. 956) and Sisines (no. 1051)—were enrolled in the *agema* of the cavalry in 324 (Arr. 7.6.4). In the settlement that followed Alexander's death in Babylon Ph. retained his satrapy (Diod. 18.3.3; cf. *LM* 121; Justin 13.4.23 gives only Hyrkania, assigning the Parthians to Philip, but this looks ahead to 320). He is not named in the satrapal reorganization at Triparadeisos. Bosworth 2002, 105–6 speculates that Ph. may have been removed from office by Philip, perhaps for supporting the Perdikkan faction. Given the location of Ph.'s satrapy and the fact that Perdikkas was active in the West this seems unlikely, unless he supplied troops for Perdikkas' Kappadokian campaign. Ph. may simply have died of natural causes, although it is worth noting that he was not the only Iranian replaced at Triparadeisos (cf. Atropates). Berve II 400–1 no. 814; Berve, *RE* XX.1 (1941) 744; Shayegan 118 no. 92.

959 PHRYNICHOS

(Φρύνιχος). Flutist, apparently of Greek origin. Ph. performed at the mass marriage ceremony in Sousa in 324 (Chares, *FGrH* 125 F4 = Athen. 12.538f). Berve II 401 no. 815.

960 PHTHIA

(Φθία). Daughter of the Thessalian Menon, who fought with distinction with Leosthenes in the losing cause of the Lamian War; married Aiakides (no. 31), probably c.323 (though Aiakides, for all we know, did not participate in the Lamian War). Her children were Pyrrhos, Troas and Deidameia (Plut. *Pyrrh.* 1.6–7); the name is later borne by a great-granddaughter, the mother of Philip V (Justin 28.1.2). About her personal life nothing is known. Sandberger 178–9 no. 66; Ziegler, *RE* XX.1 (1941) 961 no. 10.

961 PIERION

(Πιερίων). Greek poet in Alexander's entourage, whose verses at a dinner party in Marakanda in 328 ridiculed a recent Macedonian defeat and prompted Kleitos to the outburst that resulted in his death at Alexander's hands (Plut. *Alex.* 50.8). Plutarch tells us that some sources reported the poet's name as Pranichos. Whether this means that only the form of the name is disputed or that both Pranichos and P. were known to have been in Alexander's camp is uncertain (Berve II 320 assumes the latter). Berve II 320 no. 639.

962 PIGRES

(Πίγρης). Paphlagonian (or possibly Kappadokian) who served with Neoptolemos in 322/1, possibly a descendant to that Pigres who served with the younger Kyros in 402/1 (Xen. *Anab.* 1.2.17, 5.7, 8.12), although the name itself is too common for certainty. That Pigres was a herald and thus probably bilingual, since he was sent by Kyros to the Greek generals (*Anab.* 1.2.17). If the commander who fought against Eumenes is a descendant of his it is more likely that he was of Paphlagonian than Kappadokian descent, given Paphlagonia's proximity to the Greek settlements in Asia Minor. Plutarch (*Eum.* 6.7) says that, fearing that his troops might be reluctant to fight against Krateros, Eumenes informed them that they were confronted by Neoptolemos and P., with a force of Paphlagonian and Kappadokian cavalry. The story may have been false, but it is likely that P.'s presence in the region is historical.

963 PIXODAROS

(Πιξώδαρος, Πιζώδαρος, Πιξώταρος). Son of Hekatomnos (Diod. 16.74.2; *SEG* XXVII 942, line 2), younger brother of Mausolos and Idrieus, Artemisia and Ada, from whom he seized the rule of Karia in 341/0 (Diod. 16.74.2; cf. 16.69.2; Arr. 1.23.7–8). Unlike his older brothers, who ruled in conjunction with their sisters, P. does not appear to have had a sister-consort. Instead, his wife was a Kappadokian woman named Aphneis (Strabo 14.2.17 C656–7). The trilingual inscription from the Letoon at Xanthos shows that he was also satrap of Lykia in 337, Year 1 of Artaxerxes IV Arses (*SEG* XXVII 942 = Hornblower, *Mausolus* M9). He appointed Hieron and Apollodotos as *archontes* of the satrapy, and Artemelis as *epimeletes* of Xanthos. Diod. 16.74.2 assigns him a reign in Karia of five years, which indicates that he died no later than 335; certainly, he had already been replaced by Orontobates, his son-in-law, by the time Alexander crossed into Asia. In the spring of 336, he sent Aristokritos to Pella in order to seek a marriage alliance; Philip II responded by proposing the marriage of P.'s daughter, the younger Ada, to Arrhidaios (Plut. *Alex.* 10.1), but these plans were disrupted by Alexander, who sent Thessalos to Karia and offered himself in Arrhidaios' place (Plut. *Alex.* 10.2). The alliance came to naught, and P. gave his daughter to a Persian named Orontobates. When Alexander reached Halikarnassos, P. had already died and Dareios had entrusted the rule of Karia to Orontobates (Arr. 1.23.8; cf. Diod. 16.74.2). Berve II 320–1 no. 640; Judeich 251ff.; Ruzicka 1992, 120–34; 2010; Hornblower 1982; Hatzopoulos 1982 (exaggerating the threat to P. from Philip's expeditionary force); French and Dixon 1986a–b. **Stemma XVI.**

964 PLEISTARCHOS

(Πλείσταρχος). Macedonian (Tataki 408 no. 76). One of at least seven sons of Antipatros. Younger brother of Kassandros (Beloch IV² 2.126; Paus. 1.15.1; Plut. *Demetr.* 31.6: Κασσάνδρου ἀδελφός). Born no later than 340 (cf. Hülden 2000, 385), he did not participate in Alexander's Asiatic expedition. P. first appears as garrison commander of Chalkis in Euboia in 312/11 (Diod. 19.77.6), where he was unable to hold the city against Polemaios (no. 968; Diod. 19.78.2). Whether he fled either to Macedonia or to Athens, which was at the time held by Kassandros' man, Demetrios of Phaleron (thus Gregory 1995, 13), or was captured and paroled is uncertain. Some years later, it was with great enthusiasm and relief that the Athenians in 304/3 honored a certain Medon (no. 691), an officer to the "Kings" (namely, Antigonos and Demetrios), who announced to the *demos* that Kassandros and P. had been driven out of the border forts of Attika (that is, he brought good news ὑπέρ τε τῶν χωρίω[ν ἃ κατέλαβεν Κάσσαν]δρος καὶ Πλείσ[ταρχος). Hence we know that P. had been militarily active around Attika and Boiotia. His name appears on a lead curse tablet from Athens, found near the Dipylon Gate. It is accompanied by the names of Kassandros, Eupolemos, and Demetrios (of Phaleron) as well a few surviving letters of a fifth name (Braun 1970, 197–8; Jordan 1980, 234). This appears to belong to the time of the Four Years War, when Kassandros attempted to reinstall Demetrios, who had been driven out of Athens by Poliorketes (cf. Habicht, *Pausanias* 79–80; cf. Habicht 1997, 75). The attack by P. (in 304) breached the walls but his force was driven back by the Athenian cavalry (Paus. 1.15.1). Burstein 1977b, 129 links the memorial to a victory in the Peloponnese (on which see Ferguson 1948, 114–36), but Billows 1989, 178 and Habicht 1985, 80 rightly note that trophies were normally erected at the site of the battle. The curse tablet, on the other hand, indicates ongoing concern on the part of the Athenians that Kassandros and his forces might recover the city and reinstall Demetrios of Phaleron. In 303, P. was active in the Peloponnese, where an inscription from Argos (see Gregory 1995 18 n.32, who quotes the text) celebrates the expulsion (during the night: νύκ[τ]ωρ) of P. from the city, which religious piety attributed to the god Apollo (Moretti *ISE* 89–91 no. 39; cf. Wheatley and Dunn 219–20). In 302, P. was sent to join Lysimachos and Prepelaos in Asia in an attempt to carry the war to the Antigonid heartland; he brought 12,000 infantry and 500 cavalry (Diod. 20.112.1), but misfortune continued to dog him. Demetrios had blockaded the Hellespont, forcing P. to march his troops to the Black Sea coast to Odessos (*Barr. Atl.* 22 E5). From here, on account of a shortage of ships, he ferried his troops to Herakleia (*Barr. Atl.* 86 B2). One third reached their destination safely, another third was captured by the enemy, and P. himself encountered a storm and lost most of his ships and men (Diod. 20.112.2–3). His own ship (a *hexareme*) sank, taking with it all but thirty-three of the 500 men aboard; P. saved himself by clinging to the wreckage and, after recovering in Herakleia, he joined Lysimachos' troops in winter quarters (Diod. 20.112.4). He must certainly have participated in the victory over the Antigonids at Ipsos, although there is no mention of him. The main narrative of Diodorus breaks off just before the battle and this will account for the lack of information, not only about P. but concerning other commanders as well. In the aftermath of the victory, P. stood to gain from the collapse of Antigonid fortunes, and he set about carving out territory for himself in Asia Minor; for P. this meant primarily Kilikia. But P. became a casualty of the grander schemes of Seleukos and Demetrios, in which his sister Phila (no. 897) played no small part. After Seleukos' alliance with Demetrios (which saw him marry Stratonike no. 1086; *c*.299/8), Demetrios expelled P. from Kilikia; P. urged Seleukos not to have dealings with Demetrios (Plut. *Demetr.* 31.6.7). Failing to win Seleukos' support, P. went to Macedonia to argue his case before Kassandros, accompanied by his sister, who defended her husband's actions (Plut. *Demetr.* 32.4). It appears that P. had little choice other than to pin his hopes on Karia, where his rule lasted at least into the seventh year (Robert 1945, 55 no. 44, ll. 1–2); his rule in the area was ended or at least severely restricted in 294/3 or 290. P. appears to have functioned with the support of his eventual successor Eupolemos. For this stage in his career and the chronology see Gregory 1995, 20–7; Hülden 2000, 387–91; Billows 1989, 192–3; also Beloch IV² 2.317–19. Berve II 321 no. 641; Beloch IV² 2.317–19; Schaefer, *RE* XXI.2 (1951) 196–9; Ferguson 1948; Gregory 1995; Hülden 2000, 185–91.

965 PLEISTIAS

(Πλειστίας). From Kos. P. was one of Antigonos' chief naval officers, and served as chief pilot (*archikybernetes*) of Demetrios' fleet at Salamis in 306, stationed on the right wing with Hegesippos of Halikarnassos (Diod. 20.50.4). Honored at Samos in a decree proposed by Epikouros son of Zoilos, otherwise unknown (*IG* XII 6, 48), but the portion of the text giving the reasons for the honors has been lost (Paschidis 384–5 s.v. Epikouros). Billows 425 no. 98; Lenschau, *RE* XXI.1 (1951) 205; Hauben 78, 117–19.

966 PNYTAGORAS

(Πνυτάγορας). King of Salamis on Kypros from *c*.351 to 332/1, P. was a relative of Euagoras I, although the relationship is not clearly spelled out. He was apparently the son of the elder Pnytagoras, who perished in 374/3, together with his father Euagoras I, under bizarre circumstances (Theopompos, *FGrH* 115 F103; cf. Diod. 15.47.8; Arist. *Pol.* 5.1331¹ᵇ). Beloch III² 2.99–101 suggests, not implausibly, that the younger Pnytagoras was the son of Nikokreon's daughter (that Pnytagoras the elder was in fact married to the woman with whom Euagoras was having an affair). Nikokreon son of Pnytagoras thus bears the name of the maternal great-grandfather; see also Hill I 143 n.3; for the elder Pnytagoras, Isoc. 9.62; Diod. 15.4.3. If he was, in fact, the son of the elder Pnytagoras, he could have been born no later than 373/2. In 351, he drove out Euagoras II (who had succeeded Nikokles) and joined the other kings of Kypros in their revolt from Artaxerxes III (Olmstead 434–5); Euagoras II had the temporary support of Artaxerxes and Phokion, but lost this advantage through the slanders of P., who appears to have won the Great King's recognition in return for his promise of loyalty to Persia after the submission of the Phoinikians in 345/4 (Diod.16.46.2; cf. Beloch III² 2.287 for the date). P. and the other kings of Kypros joined the Aegean fleet of Pharnabazos and Autophradates in 334, but, after Dareios' defeat at Issos, they defected to Alexander at Sidon in 332 (Arr. 2.20.3). P. played no small part in the final assault on Tyre (July/August 332): together with Krateros, he commanded the ships on the left wing of the assault force (Arr. 2.20.6; Curt. 4.3.11), and, when the Tyrians would not engage in a sea battle, since they were outnumbered, he and the other Kyprians blockaded the harbor that looked towards Sidon (Arr. 2.20.10). Pnytagoras' own quinquereme (along with those of Androkles of Amathos and Pasikrates of Kourion) was sunk in a Tyrian counterattack as it lay at anchor (Arr. 2.22.2).

For his services, he was richly rewarded: Tamasos in the territory of Kition, which had formerly belonged to Pymiathon's realm (Douris, *FGrH* 76 F4 = Athen. 4.167c; *CIS* i.10–11; Hill 150). P. appears not to have lived long to enjoy his reward, for in spring 331 we find his son Nikokreon (no. 797) ruling in Salamis (Plut. *Alex.* 29.3; cf. Diog. Laert. 9.58). A second son, Nithaphon (no. 804), is named as one of the trierarchs of Alexander's Hydaspes fleet (Arr. *Ind.* 18.8). For *proxenia* and dedications at Delos see Hill 1 150 n.4 with references. Berve II 321 no. 642; Hill I 146–50. For the coins of P. see Hill, *Catalogue of the Greek Coins of Cyprus*, p. CXff.; Head, *HN*² 744; Babelon, *Les Perses Achéménides* CXXV nos. 627–33.

967 POLEMAIOS

(Πολεμαῖος, Πτολεμαῖος). Macedonian (Tataki 409–10 no. 82). Son of Philip (Arr. 1.14.6). *I.Iasos* I no. 2 identifies P. as the father of that Polemaios who was a nephew of Antigonos. Since Antigonos was the son of Philip, it appears that P. was his brother (see Billows 425 no. 99). In 334, P. led, in a special but unspecified capacity, a battalion of infantry and a squadron of Companions—that of Sokrates—at the River Granikos and conducted the initial assault on the Persian position (Arr. 1.14.6; cf. 1.15.1, 16.1). The infantry battalion (τῶν πεζῶν μίαν τάξιν) appears to have comprised hypaspists (cf. Berve II 336), who were located next to Sokrates' squadron (Arr. 1. 14. 6). Alexander left P. behind as *strategos* of Karia (Arrian calls him *hegemon*, but the term is used loosely), in support of the reinstated queen Ada, with 3,000 mercenary infantry and 200 horse (Arr. 1.23.6). Together with Asandros, the satrap of Lydia, he eventually defeated those who were holding the citadel of Halikarnassos, driving out Orontobates and killing some 700 infantry and 50 cavalry, while taking 1,000 prisoners. Hence he gained control also of Myndos, Kaunos, Thera, Kallipolis, Kos, and Triopion (Arr. 2.5.7; cf. Curt. 3.7.4). He appears to have remained in Asia Minor, possibly at the court of Antigonos, the satrap of Phrygia, or else giving military support (and oversight) to Ada. There is no mention of him in the sources until his death in 313 (Diod. 19.68.5). Billows' suggestion (426) that P. received land at Spartolos from Alexander (*Syll*³ 332: Πτολεμαίωι τῶι πατρὶ Πτολεμαίου) is speculation at best. Berve II 337 nos. 672, 674; Volkmann, *RE* XXIII (1959) 1594 no. 5, 1595 no. 10; Billows 425–6 no. 99; s.v. "Polemaios I"; Heckel 1992, 259.

968 POLEMAIOS

(Πολεμαῖος, Πτολεμαῖος). Macedonian (Tataki 409 no. 81). Nephew of Antigonos (Diod. 19.57.4, 62.5; 20.27.3) and perhaps the son of Ptolemy son of Philip (see Billows). When Eumenes had retreated to Nora, he would not come out to meet Antigonos unless the latter sent a hostage into Eumenes' camp; Antigonos sent his nephew P. (Plut. *Eum.* 10. 5). With the exception of this passage in Plutarch and one reference in Memnon, everything we know about P. in the literary sources comes from Diodorus. In 315, P. was sent with an army to Kappadokia to raise the siege of Amisos and to drive Kassandros' men out of the satrapy; he was also ordered to take up a position in the Hellespont to prevent any attempt by Kassandros to cross from Europe into Asia (Diod. 19.57.4); P. proceeded to Kappadokia and saved Amisos, which Asklepiodoros, Kassandros' general, was besieging. He sent Asklepiodoros and his men away under truce and recovered the satrapy of Kappadokia (Diod. 19.60.2). Thereafter, he moved through Bithynia and found Zibytes, the Bithynian king, besieging "the city of the Astakenians and Chalkedonians"; P. forced him to abandon the siege, made alliances with these cities and with Zibytes, and took hostages. At this time, he appears to have reached an agreement with Dionysios of Herakleia Pontika, which was sealed by P.'s marriage to Dionysios' daughter (**A92**; Memnon 4.6). P. moved to Ionia on Antigonos' orders and he found Seleukos besieging Erythrai, but the latter abandoned the attempt when he heard of P.'s approach (Diod. 19.60.2–4). In 314, when he is designated Antigonos' *strategos*, P. attacked Asandros, satrap of Karia, who had allied himself with Ptolemy of Egypt and received aid from Myrmidon and a mercenary army (Diod. 19.62.5). P. divided his army for winter (314/13) and was himself busy with the funeral rites of his father. Asandros' commander, Eupolemos (on whom see Billows 1989), along with Prepelaos set an ambush for him near Kaprima in Karia with 8,000 infantry and 200 horse (Diod. 19.68.5). P. learned of Eupolemos' plan from deserters and gathered together from those troops who were wintering nearby some 8,300 foot soldiers and 600 cavalry. P. fell upon Eupolemos' fortified camp around midnight, catching the troops off guard and asleep. He captured Eupolemos alive and forced his army to surrender (Diod. 19.68.6–7).

In 312/11, Antigonos sent P. with 5,000 infantry and 500 cavalry to Greece, along with a fleet of 150 ships under Medeios, in order to "free" the Greeks (Diod. 19.77.2). He began his campaign by landing in Boiotia, where he collected 2,000 foot and 1,300 horse, and then moved to Euboia, which was under Kassandros' control (19.77.4). With Kassandros distracted by the actions of Antigonos, who had moved an army to the Propontis, P. captured Chalkis, which he did not garrison as a sign of Antigonos' good intentions. With further successes in Boiotia and Euboia, P. invaded Attika, where Demetrios of Phaleron was prepared to negotiate (Diod. 19.78.2–4). P. continued his successful campaign by liberating Thebes and then marching into Phokis and Lokris (Diod. 19.78.5). That he is not the Ptolemaios of OGIS 5 ll. 9–10 has been convincingly demonstrated by Hauben 1987a, 31–3. Antigonos' reliance on his nephews as generals led to rivalry; for the old man seemed to favor P., whereas Telesphoros had to content himself with the role of admiral of the fleet based at Korinth. Hence the latter sold the ships and recruited an army in the hope of personal gain (Diod. 19.87.1). He moved to capture Elis, plundered Olympia, and hired more mercenaries (Diod. 19.87.2–3). P. responded by recovering Elis, dismantling Telesphoros' fortifications, and repaying the god at Olympia; furthermore, he persuaded Telesphoros to turn over Kyllene, which he promptly returned to the Eleans (Diod. 19.87.3). But, in 310, although he commanded Antigonos' army in the Peloponnesus, P. took offense because he was not accorded proper honors. Now he too rebelled and made an alliance with Kassandros. P. also established Phoinix (one of his most trusted friends) as satrap of Hellespontine Phrygia, telling him to garrison the cities and not obey Antigonos (Diod. 20.19.2). This measure gave Ptolemy son of Lagos an excuse to wage war on Antigonos, claiming to be defending the "freedom of the Greeks" (Diod. 20.19.3). In 309, P. was in open revolt against his uncle and made a pact with Ptolemy Soter, from Chalkis to Kos. Soter at first was favorable but when he discovered that P. was trying to win people over to his private cause, he arrested him and forced him to drink hemlock (Diod. 20.27.3).

Like Billows, I have retained the form Polemaios for clarity in the narrative and because I believe this was the form used by both father and son. Billows plausibly identifies P.'s father as Ptolemy son of Philip, arguing that Ptolemy was a brother of Antigonos, Philip being the name of Antigonos' father and of his second son. The patriarch would thus have had at least three sons: Demetrios, Antigonos, and Ptolemy. Demetrios the Besieger and Polemaios would thus have been cousins and grandsons of the elder Philip. Berve II 321–2 no. 643; Volkmann, RE XXIII (1959) 1595–6 no. 11; Billows 426–30 no. 100. **Stemma VI.**

969 POLEMON

(Πολέμων). Macedonian (Tataki 158 no. 74) *hetairos*. Son of Megakles, from Pella. In 332/1 he was appointed *phrourarchos* of Pelousion in Egypt (Arr. 3.5.3). Nothing else is known about him. Berve II 322 no. 645.

970 POLEMON

(Πολέμων). Macedonian (Tataki 410 no. 86). Son of Theramenes. Left in Egypt as admiral of the fleet in 331 (Arr. 3.5.5); he was given thirty triremes with which to protect the mouths of the Nile (Curt. 4.8.4). Nothing else is known about him. Berve II 322 no. 646.

971 POLEMON

(Πολέμων). Macedonian (Tataki 212–13 no. 5). Youngest of the attested sons of Andromenes, brother of Amyntas, Simmias, and Attalos. Born not long after 350, P. appears to have been in his late teens—and thus a member of either the *paides basilikoi* or the *somatophylakes basilikoi*—when Amyntas was implicated in the Philotas affair (Curt. 7.2.4). His flight from the camp at that time heightened suspicions that Amyntas and his brothers had been in some way involved in the Philotas affair (Arr. 3.27.1–2; Curt. 7.1.10). But P. was persuaded by Amyntas to return and, in the subsequent trial, acquitted (Arr. 3.27.3; cf. Curt. 7.2.1–10 for a different version). Curt. 7.2.4, plausibly, adds that P. was carried away by the panic amongst the cavalrymen who had served Philotas: he was not the only one to flee from the camp. He is not heard of again during Alexander's lifetime. The marriage of Attalos to Perdikkas' sister Atalante brought the sons of Andromenes into the Perdikkan camp. In 321/20 P. (Arr. *Succ.* 1.25) and Attalos (Arr. *Succ.* 24.1) were sent to stop the funeral carriage of Alexander from continuing south to Egypt. Their force was, however, repulsed and they returned to Perdikkas empty-handed. Whether P. served with the land army that approached Memphis or remained with his brother and the fleet, we cannot say. He is found with Attalos and Alketas (cf. Plut. *Eum* 8.8) after Perdikkas' death: at Kretopolis (319) P., Attalos, Dokimos, Antipatros, and Philotas were captured by Antigonos (Diod. 18.45.3; 19.16.1). Imprisoned in a fortress not far from Kelainai, he and his fellow captives made a desperate bid for freedom, only to be hemmed in and besieged for one year and four months (Diod. 19.16). He was probably executed upon his surrender (cf. Billows 383 s.v. "Dokimos"; Simpson 1957, 504–5). Berve II 322 no. 644; Hoffmann 157; Heckel 1992, 183–4 and *Marshals*² 199.

972 POLYAINETOS

(Πολυαίνετος). Megalopolitan, exiled for treason (perhaps in the context of Agis' war in 331/0), P.'s restoration is specifically denied in the *diagramma* on Greek Freedom issued by Polyperchon in the name of Philip III in 319 (Diod. 18.56.5). Cf. Schmitt, *Staatsv.* III no. 403 (III), p. 11.

973 POLYARCHOS

(Πολύαρχος). Greek or Macedonian. P. had been placed in command of some 1,000 garrison troops in an unnamed part of Babylonia, either by Seleukos, when he assumed the satrapy, or by Antigonos, when he drove Seleukos out in 315. On Seleukos' return in 312/11 he went over to him, although many other officers remained loyal to Antigonos (Diod. 19.91.3). Although he is not mentioned again, it is reasonable to assume that he remained in Seleukos' service. Billows 430 no. 101; Lenschau, *RE* XXI.2 (1952) 1439 no. 1; Grainger, *SPG* 114.

974 POLYDAMAS

(Πολυδάμας). *Hetairos* (Arr. 3.26.3), possibly Macedonian (thus Hoffmann 200, followed by Berve II 322, who tentatively identifies him with the son of Antaios from Arethousa, *Syll³* 269K; cf. Tataki 70 no. 13) but, more likely, one of the Thessalian *hetairoi* (cf. Ariston of Pharsalos and Medeios of Larisa). He was perhaps related to the great Polydamas of the second quarter of the fourth century, or indeed one of that man's children, whom Jason of Pherai held hostage (Xen. *HG* 6.1.18). Arr. 3.11.10 describes Parmenion leading the left, accompanied by the Pharsalian horse, and P. may have been included in Parmenion's guard. During the battle he was sent by Parmenion to seek help from Alexander, when Parmenion's troops were hard-pressed on the left (Curt. 4.15.6–7). Ironically, he was later sent (in Arab dress) by Alexander to Kleandros with the orders that Parmenion be put to death (Arr. 3.26.3; Curt. 7.2.11–33; Strabo 15.2.10 C724; Diod. 17.80.3) and was nearly lynched by Parmenion's troops after the order was carried out (Curt. 7.2.29). Nothing else is known of his career, except that he was dismissed with the veterans at Opis and returned to Macedonia with Krateros (Justin 12.12.8). Nothing else is known about him. Berve II 322–3 no. 648; Heckel 359–61; Scherling, *RE* XXI (1952) 1602 no. 7.

975 POLYDOROS

(Πολύδωρος). A physician from Teos, who dined with Antipatros (Karystios of Pergamon, *Hypomnemata*, quoting Kephisodoros of Thebes, *ap.* Athen. 12.548e). He may have been Antipatros' personal physician. Metz, *LM* 97 names *polydorus* as one of the poisoners of Alexander at Medeios' dinner party in 323. P. is not attested in either Ps.-Call. or the Armenian version of the Alexander Romance, where the name Ariston of Pharsalos occurs. Possibly, Polydoros was the name of Ariston's father (the name is common in Thessaly) and the text should read *Aristo Polydori*. Many of the alleged conspirators had connections with Antigonos and/or Antipatros. The fact that P. dined with Antipatros does not mean that he remained in Macedonia for the entire duration of Alexander's campaign. But the identification is highly speculative. Berve II 429 no. 68; Heckel 1988, 44–5.

976 POLYEIDOS

(Πολύειδος). Thessalian. Engineer in the service of Philip (Athen. Mech. 10.7–9; Vitruv. 10.13.3). Whether he belongs to the era of Philip or Alexander and his Successors, or even both, is uncertain. P. is linked with the siege of Byzantion in 340 but also Rhodes, which can only refer to the siege of 305/4 (discussion in Whitehead 2015, 79–80). He is credited with the *helepolis* and the *tetrakyklos* ("four-wheeler"). Vitruv. 8.14 says he wrote on siege engines. Diades was his student (Vitruv. 10.13.3) and successor in Alexander's army. Marsden 1977, 218–20; Whitehead 2015, 79–80.

977 POLYEUKTOS

(Πολύευκτος). Athenian (Kirchner 11950) orator and politician from Sphettos (Plut. *Phoc.* 5.5; Plut. *Dem.* 10.3). Son of Sostratos (the patronymic can be determined from the combined evidence of *IG* II² 350, 363 and 368; Schweigert 1939; Paschidis 73–4). One of the anti-Macedonian politicians (Plut. *Phoc.* 9.9), in 343/2 he had gone to the Peloponnese with Demosthenes, Hegesippos, and others to stir up hostilities against Philip (Dem.

9.72; cf. [Plut.] *Mor.* 841e). His surrender was demanded by Alexander in 335, after the fall of Thebes (Arr. 1.10.4; Plut. *Dem.* 23.4; *Suda* A 2704). Phokion criticized him for being fat and out of breath, a man who would advocate war with Philip but be unfit to fight one (Plut. *Phoc.* 9.9). A supporter of Demosthenes, P. may have been charged with accepting bribes from Harpalos in 324 and acquitted, though the evidence is flimsy (Din. 1.100; cf. Worthington 55–6; 270–1). P. was an opponent of Demades. At least, he and Lykourgos opposed honors for Demades introduced by Kephisodotos in 335 (Din. 1.101; [Plut.] *Mor.* 820f), despite the fact that both men benefited from Demades' actions (see Will 58–9). Before the outbreak of the Lamian War, P. was sent to the Arkadians but failed to persuade them to break with Antipatros until he had the aid of the exiled Demosthenes ([Plut.] *Mor.* 846c–d). Plutarch, on three different occasions, quotes P. as saying that Demosthenes was the best orator but Phokion the most effective speaker (*Phoc.* 5.5; *Dem.* 10.3; *Mor.* 803e). *IG* II² 350 is the last recorded public action by P., honoring two individuals from western Greece, one from Apollonia, the other from Epidamnos, in 318/17. It appears that in desperate times the staunchly democratic P. was prepared to cooperate with Olympias (who had written to demand that Nikanor relinquish control of Peiraieus) and Polyperchon. Berve II 323–4 no. 650; Paschidis 73–4.

978 POLYKLEITOS

(Πολύκλειτος). Thessalian from Larisa. P. wrote what appears to have been an eyewitness account of Alexander's expedition in at least eight books (Athen. 12.539a, the reference to Alexander's extended drinking bouts probably refers to the last years of his life). Fragments of his work deal with geography, Persian antiquities and gossip; for example, P. (MSS Polykritos; the Polykritos named by Strabo 15.3.21 C735, describing Persian practices, is probably Polykritos of Mende) is cited by Plut. *Alex.* 46.1 as one of those who credited the story of the visit of the Amazon queen. Nevertheless, for a work of its size, P.'s book does not seem to have attracted much attention, and it appears to have more a collection of stories than a serious history (see Pearson 70–7). On the identity of the man and his career, little can be said with certainty. He may have belonged to a prominent Thessalian family and it is likely that he was a friend or acquaintance of his compatriot Medeios. Two other prominent men named P. come to mind: a Polykleitos of Larisa whose daughter, Olympias, was the wife of Demetrios the Fair and mother of Antigonos Doson; and the admiral of Ptolemy I Soter (Diod. 19.62.4). Despite Berve II 324, there is, however, no compelling reason to identify the historian with either of these men. Demetrios' father-in-law is mentioned in the Armenian version of Eusebius' *Chronicle* (see Jacoby, *FGrH* 128 T1) but Olympias, if she was the mother of Antigonos Doson, must have been born *c.*280, almost certainly too late to be daughter of the Alexander historian. If Eusebius' information is correct, we are dealing with a different Polykleitos. On the other hand, he may have confused the details concerning Phthia, daughter of Olympias II of Epeiros, who married both Demetrios II and Antigonos Doson; Olympias II was the great-granddaughter of Menon of Pharsalos. Berve II 324 no. 651; Jacoby, *FGrH* 128; Pearson 70–7.

979 POLYKLEITOS

(Πολύκλειτος). Greek in the service of Ptolemy I. In 315 or 314, he was sent to Kypros with 100 ships (Diod. 19.62.4); here they they met Seleukos' fleet and it was decided that P. take

50 ships to the Peloponnese to fight Aristodemos, Polyperchon, and Alexander (Diod. 19.62.5). P. advanced to Kenchreai but learned that Polyperchon's son Alexander had gone over to Kassandros (Diod. 19.64.3) and, since there was no enemy to deal with, sailed back to Pamphylia (Diod. 19.64.4); from there he moved to Aphrodisias in Kilikia, where he learned that Antigonos' naval commander Theodotos was sailing to Patara in Lykia and Perilaos was leading the army there overland. P. set an ambush by land and defeated and captured Perilaos. He also won a naval battle and captured Theodotos (Diod. 19.64.5–7). After his victory over Perilaos and Theodotos, P. sailed to Kypros and then to Pelousion. Ptolemy praised him for his victory and gave him gifts. P. released Perilaos and other captives and went in person to confer with Antigonos at Ekregma—the negotiations were apparently initiated by Antigonos (thus Billows 118)—but the latter would not agree to his demands (Diod. 19.64.8). His dedication of a golden laurel wreath is recorded in the inventories of Delos (see the table, with references, in Hauben 79). Lenschau, *RE* XXI (1952) 1699 no. 3; *PP* V 13784; Hauben 79–83 no. 30.

980 POLYKLEITOS

(Πολύκλειτος). Athenian (Kirchner 11971). One of two Antigonid officers in Athens (see also Herakleides no. 519) named in the disbursals of funds in 306/5 from the 140 talent gift from Antigonos. P. was part of a contingent of troops left by Demetrios for the defense of Athens against Kassandros (*IG* II² 1492B). The fact that he and Herakleides are named separately from the *strategoi* suggests that they were military overseers. Billows 430–1 no. 102.

981 POLYKLES

(Πολυκλῆς). Macedonian (Tataki 411–12 no. 93). General of Antipatros in 321/0. After Antipatros left for Asia, the Aitolians, true to their compact with Perdikkas, attacked Thessaly in order to divert Antipatros; they had 12,000 foot and 4,000 horse under Alexander the Aitolian and besieged the city of the Amphissan Lokrians, overran their country and captured neighboring towns; they defeated and killed P. (Diod. 18.38.1–2). If he, like Polyperchon, had returned to Europe with Krateros, he may have served with Alexander in Asia. Berve II 324–5 no. 652; Ziegler, *RE* XXI (1952) 1723 no. 4.

982 POLYKLES

(Πολυκλῆς). Macedonian. Perhaps one of the *hetairoi* of Kassandros. Adviser of Adea-Eurydike in 317. After the defeat of Eurydike and Philip III at Euia, the latter was captured, but Eurydike and P. attempted to escape to Amphipolis. They were captured as they fled. To judge from Eurydike's fate and Olympias' treatment of Eurydike's and Kassandros' friends, P. was probably executed (Diod. 19.11.3).

983 POLYPERCHON

(Πολυπέρχων). The form *Polysperchon* found in some literary sources (Plut. *Mor.* 184c; Ael. *VH* 12.43; Athen. 4.155c) is etymologically sound (Pape-Benseler 1230), but the epigraphic and papyrological evidence supports the form Polyperchon, as found in the Latin sources (cf. Polypercon): *IG* II² 387 (an Athenian decree of 319/8), line 8; *OGIS* 4, line 24 (with n. 14) and 5, line 39. Macedonian (Tataki 213 no. 6). Son of Simmias (Arr. 2.12.2; 3.11.9) from Tymphaia (Tzetz. *ad Lycophron* 802; cf. Diod. 17.57.2; 20.28.10), hence perhaps a kinsman of Andromenes. Identification of Polyperchon with the mercenary of the same name, who served Kallippos at Rhegion and took part in his murder in 351/0 (*PDion* 58.6), should be rejected as implausible. It is unlikely that a member of the Upper Macedonian aristocracy served as a mercenary. Aelian's story (*VH* 12.43) that the son of Simmias was formerly a brigand derives from the propaganda wars of the Successors (Heckel 2007a; cf. Ael. *VH* 12.16, 14.47a; cf. Justin 15.3.3–10). The same will be true for the story that he angered Alexander by supporting Parmenion's call for a night attack at Gaugamela (Curt. 4.13.7–10) and that he mocked *proskynesis* (Curt. 8.5.22–6.1). Born between 390 and 380 BC, P. was among the prominent veterans sent home in 324 from Opis (Justin 12.12.8); his son, Alexander, was born probably in the late 340s (see Alexander no. 46). P. replaced Ptolemy son of Seleukos, who died at Issos (Arr. 2.12.2), as taxiarch of the Tymphaian battalion of pezhetairoi; thus at Gaugamela, P. and his *taxis* of "so-called Stymphaians" (Diod. 17.57.2: τῶν ὀνομαζομένων Στυμφαίων), are found between Meleagros and Amyntas (Arr. 3.11.9; cf. Diod. 17.57.2–3 and Curt. 4.13.28). At the Persian Gates (winter 331/0), P., Amyntas, and Koinos, along with some cavalry under Philotas' command, were sent ahead to bridge the Araxes River, while Alexander dealt with Ariobarzanes (Curt. 5.4.20, 30; but Arr. 3.18.6 omits him). P. is next attested in 328, when he is left at Baktra with Meleagros, Attalos, and Gorgias, with instructions to protect the area against the incursions of rebels like Spitamenes (Arr. 4.16.1). Hence, Curt. 8.5.22–6.1 must be wrong when he claims that P. mocked *proskynesis* in 327; this is refuted by Arr. 4.12.2, who names Leonnatos instead, and by the fact that P. was absent when the alleged episode took place (Heckel 1978b). Arr. 4.22.1 says that in 327 Polyperchon, Attalos, and Alketas were in Sogdiana, under the command of Krateros, completing the subjugation of Paraitakene, while Alexander returned to Baktria. Curt. 8.5.2 records Polyperchon's mission before the introduction of *proskynesis* at Baktra (8.5.5ff.), and Plut. *Alex.* 55.6 (cf. Hamilton 155) shows that Krateros and his force were still in Sogdiana when the Hermolaos conspiracy was uncovered; for we are told that Alexander informed them of it by letter; Plutarch's failure to mention Polyperchon indicates merely that he was absent from Krateros' camp, probably on a separate mission into the region of Bubacene (Curt. 8.5.2). The story is accepted by Bosworth II 86–7.

At the beginning of the Indian campaign (327), P. accompanied Krateros, whom Alexander left in the vicinity of Andaka to subdue the neighboring towns (Arr. 4.23.5; since Alexander left Andaka with only Koinos and Attalos [Arr. 4.24.1], Alketas and Polyperchon must have remained with Krateros) and rejoined Alexander briefly at Arigaeum, only to be left there again with Krateros to restore and fortify the city (Arr. 4.24.6–7). He reunited with Alexander a second time to attack the Assakenians (Arr. 4.25.6) and fight at Massaga (Arr. 4.26.1–27.4; Curt. 8.11.1 says that it was Polyperchon who was sent to attack Ora; Arr. 4.27.5 names only Attalos, Alketas, and Demetrios the hipparch). For the remainder of the Indian campaign, P. is regularly found with Krateros. At the Hydaspes, his battalion, and that of Alketas, remained with Krateros in the main camp, opposite Poros, and thus played only a secondary role in the defeat of Alexander's most formidable Indian adversary (Arr. 5.11.3; cf. 5.15.3ff.). In the descent of the Indos River system, he served briefly under Hephaistion, but was soon transferred to the west bank, thus rejoining Krateros (Arr. 6.5.5). Whether Polyperchon left India with Krateros or continued with Alexander through Gedrosia is uncertain. Justin 12.10.1 mentions his departure for Babylonia just before Alexander's Gedrosian march. But Justin regularly substitutes the name of Polyperchon for Krateros (cf. 13.8.5, 7; 15.1.1). It was shortly before Alexander reached the mouth of the Indos that he sent Krateros to Karmania via Arachosia and Drangiana: according to Arrian (6.17.3), Krateros took with him the battalions of Attalos, Meleagros, Antigenes, as well as those hetairoi and other Makedones who were unfit for military service. Polyperchon does resurface in the company of Krateros, at Opis in 324, but, unless Arrian has failed to mention him (deliberately or by accident), there is no good reason for preferring the evidence of Justin, who appears once more to have confused the two marshals (Boerma 1979, 199). In 324, when Krateros was sent from Opis, with some 10,000 discharged veterans, to replace Antipatros as regent of Macedonia, P. was designated his second-in-command (Arr. 7.12.4; cf. Justin 12.12.8).

When Alexander died (June 323), P., Krateros and the veterans had not advanced beyond Kilikia, where they now remained for a second winter. In 322, they answered Antipatros' call and returned to Macedonia and Thessaly. Augmenting the Macedonian forces, they contributed in no small way to the defeat of Antiphilos at Krannon (Diod. 18.16.4ff.). And, when Krateros and Antipatros made a truce with the Aitolians in the winter of 321/0, in order to give themselves a free hand to deal with Perdikkas (Diod. 18.25.4–5), P. was entrusted with the defense of Macedonia in their absence (Justin 13.6.9). P. may, in fact, have replaced Sippas as *strategos* in Macedonia upon his return from Europe, although there is no explicit statement to that effect. The Aitolians, however, had made a secret pact with Perdikkas to invade Thessaly in order to distract Antipatros. Quickly they attacked Amphissa, defeating and killing the Macedonian general, Polykles (no. 981), who had been left behind in Lokris, and moved into Thessaly where they incited rebellion and threatened Macedon with a force of 25,000 infantry and 1,500 horse; Alexander the Aitolian had brought 12,000 infantry and 400 cavalry, which are surely included in this number (Diod. 18.38.1, 3). But the danger was lessened by the sudden departure of the Aitolians themselves—in response to an attack by the Akarnanians—and P. won a decisive victory over the Thessalians and Menon of Pharsalos (Diod. 18.38.5–6).

Antipatros, on his deathbed (319), named P. *epimeletes* of the Kings, with Kassandros as his chiliarch (Diod. 18.49.1–3; cf. Plut. *Phoc.* 31.1; Heidelberg Epit. 1.4 = *FGrH* 155 F1). Thus he inherited the political and military leadership of Macedonia (Diod. 18.47.4, 48.4; cf. Plut. *Phoc.* 31.1). The decision was doubtless made in consultation with Antipatros' *consilium* (cf. Hammond, *HMac* III 130, with n.3) and not, as Lenschau (*RE* XXI.2, 1800) suggests, by the terms of Antipatros' testament. But Kassandros, who had served as Antigonos' chiliarch in 320 (Arr. *Succ.* 1.38; Diod. 18.39.7), did not welcome the subordinate role, and P. sought to strengthen his own position by offering the guardianship of Alexander IV to Olympias and by proclaiming the "Freedom of the Greeks," which was, to some extent at least, an anti-Antipatrid measure (Diod. 18.55.2–57.1; Plut. *Phoc.* 32.1; see esp. Poddighe 2013; Grainger 2019, 135–7). At first, there seems to have been considerable support for P. in Macedonia (Diod. 18.54.2), and he was joined by White Kleitos, whom Antigonos had driven from Asia (Diod. 18.52.6); Olympias took a more cautious approach. Diod. 18.57.2 does not imply a second invitation. 18.49.4 records the original decision of P. and his Council, 18.57.2 the issuing of the invitation to the Queen Mother. For her reluctance to come immediately see 18.58.3–4. For all his efforts, P. found the threat from Kassandros greater than he may have imagined. After a long absence in the East, he may not have had a strong following among the Macedonians who had remained at home and were faithful to the house of Antipatros; perhaps his highland origins also worked against him. P. extended an amnesty to Eumenes and the outlaws, if they supported the cause of the Kings, promising also to come in person to Asia with an army to oppose Antigonos (Diod. 18.57.3–4). Indeed, he wrote to the Argyraspids, now in Kyinda (Diod. 18.58.1), instructing them to cooperate with Eumenes. Athens in February 318 made public its enthusiasm for P. (*Syll*³ 315 = *IG* II² 387; cf. Nepos, *Phoc.* 3.1). But the March deadline for the implementation of Philip III's decree passed, with Nikanor still firmly entrenched in Mounychia (Diod. 18.56.5; Ferguson 30–2; but see Williams 1984). A force led by P.'s son Alexander advanced to Attika (Diod. 18.65.3ff.), bringing with it many of the exiles and putting pressure on Nikanor, who had seized and fortified Peiraieus and was ignoring orders from Olympias to withdraw his garrison (Diod. 18.65.1). But P.'s duplicity soon became evident: Alexander entered into frequent and secret negotiations with Nikanor, perhaps even through the agency of Phokion, who thought to ingratiate himself with the Polyperchan party and to protect himself at home if he could persuade Nikanor to turn over Mounychia and Peiraieus to Alexander (Diod. 18.65.3–5; but Plut. *Phoc.* 33 omits Phokion's role; cf. Gehrke 115 n. 39).

P., meanwhile, held the bulk of the Macedonian army in reserve in Phokis, that is, inside Thermopylai, where he was met by delegations of the Athenians (Diod. 18.68.2; Plut. *Phoc.* 33.4–12; cf. Nepos, *Phoc.* 3.3). One of these was headed by Phokion, whose crimes included collaborating with Nikanor in his seizure of Peiraieus and whose favorable stance towards the house of Iolaos now placed him in jeopardy; nevertheless, his recent negotiations with Alexander must have caused him to hope for a better reception from P. (cf. Gehrke 115 n. 39). The latter made a great show of ceremony—with Philip III enthroned beneath a golden canopy—but the process quickly degenerated into a shouting match, and P. was forced to restrain the enraged King, who nearly transfixed Phokion's comrade, Hegemon, with his spear (Plut. *Phoc.* 33.7–12). In the end, White Kleitos was instructed to take the opponents of the new regime under guard to Athens, where they were denounced and executed (Plut. *Phoc.* 34–5).

Unable to win Athens for himself (though he did manage to send relief to Salamis, which was being besieged by Kassandros' forces: Diod. 18.69.2), P. left behind a small force under Alexander, and proceeded against Megalopolis, which had mustered some 15,000 men and prepared to withstand a siege (Diod. 18.70.1–3). Elsewhere in the Peloponnese, his envoys called upon the cities to overthrow the oligarchies of Antipatros and even to put the latter's supporters to death, and in this P. was generally successful (Diod. 18.69.3–4). The Megalopolitans, however, held out under the leadership of Damis, a veteran of Alexander's campaigns (Diod. 18.70–1; cf. Polyaenus 4. 14), and P. soon withdrew to tackle more pressing matters (Diod. 18.72.1). It appears that he returned to Macedonia to guard against an invasion by Kassandros. But, having taken precautions there, he moved south to Epeiros—in order to prepare for Olympias' return to Macedonia, which he entrusted to his ally, and Olympias' own nephew, Aiakides (Diod. 19.11.1–2)—and, from there, perhaps to the Aitolians, whose friendship he cultivated (cf. Mendels 1984, 158ff.). In his absence, Adea-Eurydike, transferred the guardianship of her husband, Philip III, to Kassandros (cf. Justin 14.5.1–3).

This move, perhaps instigated by Kassandros himself during his first return to Macedonia (probably in spring 317; so Hammond, *HMac* III 137; Diod. 18.75.2; cf. 19.35.7 and Polyaenus 4.11.2), severely damaged P.'s prestige. The failure at Megalopolis also had devastating effects in the south: contemptuous of P. (Polyaenus 4.11.2), some Greek cities went over to Kassandros (Diod. 18.74.1 exaggerates Kassandros' popularity; cf. Beloch IV² 2.440–1), who had pursued his goals with great energy and through the formidable alliances secured by his father in the first years that followed Alexander's death. To counter the most dangerous of these alliances—that with Antigonos, who had supplied Kassandros with thirty-five ships to secure Nikanor's position in Peiraieus—P. sent out Kleitos with the Macedonian fleet. This man had a score to settle with Antigonos, who had driven him from Lydia soon after Antipatros' death. But his initial success near Byzantion, in which he destroyed or captured about half Nikanor's fleet, was followed by an overwhelming disaster; for Antigonos, with a large contingent of lightly armed troops, fell upon Kleitos' sailors after they had disembarked for the night. Those who managed to board ship and make for open water fell in with the remnants of Nikanor's fleet and were annihilated. Kleitos himself fled to shore and attempted to reach Macedonia by land, only to fall in with Lysimachos' troops, who put him to death (Diod. 18.72.2–9; Polyaenus 4.6.8; cf. Engel 1973, 141–5; Beloch IV² 1.103–4; Billows 86–8). Lysimachos was, as a result of his marriage to Nikaia, an ally of Kassandros. But I see no strong evidence for Engel's characterization of him as "Polyperchons persönlicher Feind" (Engel 98 n.166). Cf. Will, commenting on Polyperchon's appointment as *epimeletes*: "The illegality of the procedure was not what shocked the new masters of the empire, however, but the fact that the succession to Antipatros aroused secret ambitions in some of them. Lysimachos, Macedon's immediate neighbor, would certainly not have disdained the idea of one day restoring for his advantage the union of Macedon and Thrake..." (*CAH* VII² 1.41).

In contrast to the lethargy and ineffectiveness of P.'s party, Kassandros had shown himself a force to be reckoned with. Now the return of Nikanor's fleet, sailing into Peiraieus with the beaks of Kleitos' warships, spelled the end of P.'s hopes in Athens (Diod. 18.75.1). The Athenians, having flirted briefly with democratic revolution, came to terms with Antipatros' son and Greece in general reverted to a pro-Antipatrid stance. P. could do little but concentrate his efforts on driving Kassandros and his supporters from Macedonia, while hoping that his son Alexander could keep in check the dissension in the Peloponnese.

In the northwest, Olympias and Aiakides brought their forces to Euia, on the Macedonian-Epeirot border (Hammond, *HMac* III 140, with n.2), where they confronted Philip III and Eurydike. Douris' description of the battle as one fought between women, with Olympias in Bacchic attire and Eurydike in Macedonian armor, is surely a later embellishment (Douris *ap.* Athen. 13.560f = *FGrH* 76 F52; cf. Heckel 1981d, 83–4; Carney 1987b, 496ff., esp. 500). At first, the benefits of alliance with Olympias became clear: overawed by the prestige of the Queen Mother, the troops of Philip and Eurydike deserted, leaving their "King" to fall into enemy hands and his bride to make a desperate bid at escape (Diod. 19.11.1–7). She was captured as she made her way to Amphipolis with her adviser, Polykles (Diod. 19.11.3), perhaps a relative of the general who had been killed by the Aitolians in 321/o (Diod. 18.38.2). But P. would have been wise to curtail Olympias' power: her reprisals against personal enemies, and those of her family, soon turned the reverence of the Macedonians into disgust, and this feeling for the woman was extended also to the man who had summoned her (Diod. 19.11.4–9).

Kassandros was, at the time, besieging Tegea, and P. occupied Perrhaibia, while his son Alexander threatened the Peloponnese; the Aitolians, meanwhile, blocked

Kassandros' advance at Thermopylai (Diod. 19.35.1–2). But Kassandros ferried his men around the pass, landing them in southern Thessaly, and sent one of his officers, Kallas, to hold P. in check. A second general, Deinias, secured the entrances to Macedonia before Olympias' forces could seize them (Diod. 19.35.3), and the Queen Mother took refuge in Pydna (Diod. 19.35.5–7; Justin 14.6.1–4), entrusting the campaign against Kassandros to Aristonous (Diod. 19.35.4). Besieged at Azoros (or Azorios, Diod. 19.52.6), P. watched his troops desert to Kallas (Diod. 19.36.6), and was forced to sit idle as Kassandros starved Olympias and the remnants of the royal family into submission ((Diod. 19.35.5; cf. Justin 14.6.2–3. A rescue attempt may have misfired (Polyaenus 4.11.3); nor was Polyperchon able to bring much-needed relief to Monimos in Pella or Aristonous, both of whom remained loyal to the house of Alexander (Diod. 19.50.7–8). Indeed, it was only with difficulty that he escaped to Aitolia (Diod. 19.52.6). Little remained of his former power, except perhaps those cities of the Peloponnese that retained their allegiance thanks to the presence of Alexander (Diod. 19.35.1, 53.1)—and even he was hard-pressed by Kassandros. Alexander had blocked the Isthmus, but Kassandros was able to land his troops in the Argolid and capture Argos. From there he marched across to Messenia and won over all the towns of the region except Ithome. On his return to the north, he left 2,000 troops with Molykkos at the passes between Megara and the Korinthiad (Diod. 19.54.3–4).

A rift between Kassandros and Antigonos offered P. some hope of recouping his losses. In 315, Antigonos sent his agent Aristodemos to secure a pact with P. and his son, whereby P. was recognized as *strategos* in the Peloponnese. Oaths were exchanged by Aristodemos and P.; Alexander sailed to Asia to complete negotiations with Antigonos (Diod. 19.57.5, 60.1, 61.1; cf. 62.5). But P. had clearly accepted a subordinate role in return for Antigonid support in Greece (Diod. 19.61.3; cf. Billows 114, with n. 41); for Aristodemos brought to his new allies some 8,000 mercenaries recruited in the Peloponnese (Diod. 19.60.1). Kassandros meanwhile secured Orchomenos in Arkadia but failed to make further gains in Messenia and prepared to return to the north, stopping first to celebrate the Nemean games (Diod. 19.64.1). It was presumably during this brief respite that he tried, in vain, to persuade P. to abandon Monophthalmos (Diod. 19.63.3). On his return to Macedonia, Kassandros sent Prepelaos to Alexander (Diod. 19.64.3–5), offering him the title of general of the Peloponnese—the very office which the father exercised for Antigonos—and inducing him to defect. Thus Kassandros did even greater harm to P.'s credibility. Antigonos meanwhile sent his nephew Telesphoros to liberate the cities in which Alexander (and Kassandros) had placed garrisons. Soon only Sikyon and Korinth held out against Antigonos (Diod. 19.74.2). It appears also that the willingness of the Aitolians to join Aristodemos—they had formerly been allies of P.—was prompted by an alliance between P. and Kassandros, and Beloch IV² 2.443 suggests, plausibly, that Alexander served as Kassandros' *strategos* because P. could not bring himself to serve the younger man. Now seventy years old, P. may have relinquished control of affairs to his son, allowing him to make his best deal, which, in this case involved abandoning Antigonos in favor of his father's bitter enemy. P.'s "retirement" thus paved the way for *rapprochement*. But Alexander was quickly swept aside by Aristodemos, and his alliance with Kassandros was perhaps the cause of his assassination and the uprising in Sikyon in 314 (Diod. 19.66–7). These events drew P. out of retirement to pursue an independent policy. Hence, in the Peace of 311, P. plays no part, and Antigonos' letter to Skepsis (*OGIS* 5 = Welles, *RC* 1) shows that Antigonos at least was anxious to deprive him of allies.

P. made one last bid for power, bringing Herakles, son of Alexander and Barsine, from Pergamon to Greece. The claims of this child to the throne had been rejected in 323 (Curt. 10 6.11–12; cf. Justin 13.2.7), but at that time the marshals were already divided on the question of Rhoxane's unborn child. In 310, Kassandros laid that problem to rest by ordering the murder of Alexander IV and his mother in Amphipolis (Diod. 19.105.1–2; Paus. 9.7.2; Justin 15.2.5). Herakles, now seventeen or eighteen, could be exploited for political gain (Diod. 20.20). P. brought him to his native Tymphaia in Upper Macedonia, at the head of an army of 20,000 infantry and 1,000 horse, and seriously threatened Kassandros. But Kassandros understood P.'s nature and the limits of his ambitions, and persuaded the old man to murder the boy in exchange for a share of power, which amounted, in fact, to little more than the theoretical *strategia* of the Peloponnese (Diod. 20.28.2). Since P.'s support came primarily from the Aitolians, Mendels 1984, 176 reasonably infers that the agreement may have included territorial concessions for the Aitolians as well. The murder of Alexander's son cost P. what little remained of his credibility. Satisfied that he had obtained as much as he could from the exercise, he attempted to return to the south, only to be forced by a coalition of Peloponnesians and Boiotians to winter in Lokris (Diod. 20.28.4; Trogus, *Prol.* 15). Kassandros had given him 4,000 Macedonian infantry and 500 Thessalian horse (Diod. 20.28.3). Kratesipolis, holding Korinth and Sikyon in his absence, was forced to turn the cities over to Ptolemy Soter (Diod. 20. 37. 1), who in 308 made his only serious bid for power in Europe and revived the old slogan of "Greek Liberty." Paschidis 2008, 246–8 argues that P. died in 308, since there are only two other general references to him thereafter (Diod. 20.100.6, 103.6) and these need not imply that he was still alive. But, even though Diod. 20.103.6 (Στρόμβιχον τὸν ὑπὸ Πολυπέρχοντος κατεσταμένον φρούραρχον) indicates that Strombichos was appointed before the events described, the following sentence reads "since there was no aid coming from Kassandros, Prepelaos, and Polyperchon" (τῶν μὲν περὶ Κάσανδρον καὶ Πρεπέλαον καὶ Πολυπέρχοντα μὴ βοηθούντων). Even if [οἱ] περὶ Πολυπέρχοντα means "Polyperchon's men" (and the Greek does not require this) it is clearly unlikely (given that Kassandros and Prepelaos were still alive) that Strombichos was looking for help from, among others, a man who was no longer alive. Why include Polyperchon in this list when he was long dead and no longer relevant? And, if Diodorus refers to officers appointed previously by Kassandros, Prepelaos, and Polyperchon, there is a more precise and effective way of saying so. P. continued to wreak havoc in the Peloponnese in the years between Ptolemy's defeat at Salamis and the battle of Ipsos in 301. In 304/3, Demetrios was still intent on liberating the Greek cities from Kassandros and P., and indeed he captured and crucified the latter's garrison commander in Arkadian Orchomenos (Diod. 20.100.6, 103.5–7). What became of P. himself is unknown. Demetrios' campaign against Messene in 295 (Plut. *Demetr.* 13.3–4) may have been directed against him, though he was by now nearly 90 years old! For the possible tomb of Polyperchon see Palagia 1998, 28 and 2000, 202–6, with figs. 15–18. Berve II 325–6 no. 654; Hoffmann 156; Beloch IV² 1.97ff.; Lenschau, *RE* s.v. "Polyperchon (1)"; Sandberger 179 no. 67; Heckel, *Marshals*² 200–16; Paschidis 2008; Poddighe 2013; Carney 2014; Grainger 2019, 131–91, *passim*; Pownall, *LexAM* 432–3. **Stemma XII.**

984 POLYSTRATOS

(Πολύστρατος). Macedonian (Tataki 412 no. 96) soldier said to have found Dareios when he had been left by his assassins to die (Plut. *Alex.* 43; Curt. 5.13.24). The story that he found the Persian king still alive and received his dying words (cf. Justin 11.15.5–14, referring only to "one of Alexander's men") is undoubtedly a fiction. Whether P. was a historical figure, perhaps even the first man to come across upon the dead Persian king, cannot be determined. Berve II 326 no. 655; Ziegler, *RE* XXI (1952) 1807.

985 POLYXENOS

(Πολύξενος). Son of Xenotimos. One of twenty-four cavalrymen from Orchomenos, who served with Alexander's allied cavalry until the expedition reached Ekbatana in 330. There he and his compatriots were discharged. On their return (*c.*329), they made a dedication to Zeus Soter in Orchomenos (*IG* VII 3206). Berve II 322 no. 647.

986 POROS

(Πῶρος). Indian dynast, ruler of the Paurava. Poros was thus his official, rather than personal name; the latter is unrecorded. He was physically imposing (Justin 12.8.1; Arr. 5.19.1; Curt. 8.13.7, 14.13; cf. *Itiner. Al.* 111; Metz Epit. 54; *Suda* Π 2180), with a height of at least five cubits (Arr. 5.19.1; Diod. 17.88.4; Plut. *Alex.* 60.12), which contrasted with the shortness of Alexander (cf. Ps.-Call. 3.4.3; Jul. Valer. 3.7). See the comments of Bosworth II 233, 308–9. The estimates of P.'s height may be somewhat exaggerated, but there is no reason to reject the view that he was exceptionally tall. Nor does this reference (or the rubbish at Arr. 5.4.4) lend support to the view (Tarn II 169–71) that there was a "short Macedonian cubit," which I wrongly accepted in Yardley and Heckel 245. An enemy of Taxiles, P. had an ally in Abisares, with whom he had previously campaigned against the Sydrakai (Arr. 5.22.2), and even on his own was perhaps the most powerful of the rulers of the Punjab (cf. Curt. 8.12.13); certainly his kingdom lay beyond the limits of the Persian Empire. Not surprisingly, he rejected the demand for tribute brought by Alexander's envoy, Kleochares (Curt. 8.13.2; Metz Epit. 56–7 says that P. had Kleochares whipped and sent Alexander an arrogant letter; cf. Ps.-Call. 3.2).

Instead P. moved to prevent Alexander's crossing of Hydaspes (Jhelum) in April 326 (Arr. 5.9.1; Plut. *Alex.* 60), occupying a position that proved unassailable, and forcing Alexander to resort to various feints (Arr. 5.10; Curt. 8.13.18–19; Plut. *Alex.* 60; Polyaenus 4.3.9) in an attempt to confuse him. Eventually, Alexander under the cover of heavy rain and thunder effected a crossing of the river some 28 km upstream after leaving Krateros to watch the main river crossing (Arr. 5.11.3–4). Once P.'s position had been turned, a major engagement followed, in which his troops were routed. Wounded and defeated, P. nevertheless refused to treat with Taxiles, whom Alexander had sent to urge his surrender; instead he attempted to kill him with a javelin, which Taxiles evaded (Arr. 5.18.6–7; Curt. 8.14.35–6 says that it was Taxiles' brother who was sent to P., and that P. killed him). His surrender was negotiated by another Indian, Meroes (Arr. 5.18.7). Poros' haughty demeanor is perhaps somewhat exaggerated by the sources, but Alexander respected him as a worthy opponent and a valuable ally (Plut. *Alex.* 60.14–15; Plut. *Mor.* 181e, 332e, 458b; Arr. 5.19.2–3; Themistius *Or.* 7.89d; Curt. 8.14.41–5). Alexander arranged an alliance between Taxiles and P. (Curt. 9.3.22). News sent by P. and Taxiles in 324 that Abisares had died (Curt. 10.1.20) suggests that the alliance was still in existence. After Alexander's death, Perdikkas did not disturb the organization of the eastern satrapies and allowed P. to retain his kingdom (Diod. 18.3.2; Dexippos, *FGrH* 100 F8 §5a; cf. *LM* 121). This right was reaffirmed at Triparadeisos in 320; for neither he nor Taxiles could be removed from power without a royal army and an outstanding general (Diod. 18.39.6; Arr. *Succ* 1.36). But in 318/17 he was treacherously killed by Eudamos, who subsequently joined Eumenes with 120 elephants taken from the region (Diod. 19.14.8). P.'s kingdom was soon absorbed into the empire of Sandrokottos (Chandragupta Maurya). Berve II 340–5 no. 683; Howe 2020.

987 POROS

(Πῶρος). Indian dynast. Distinguished from his cousin (Diod. 17.91.1; Strabo 15.1.30 C699) and namesake by the epithet *kakos* ("bad" or "cowardly"). His official name, like that of most Indian dynasts, derives from the people he ruled, in this case those of the Paurava who lived east of Akesines River (cf. Arr. 5.21.4–5). Arr. 5.20.6 calls him *hyparchos* of the Indians; Diod. 17.91.1 calls him *basileus* (king). In Arrian the term *hyparchos* has a variety of meanings; most often it is used as the equivalent of satrap (cf. Bosworth I 112). The "term" is discussed at length by Bosworth II 147–9, and I am persuaded by his argument that Alexander and/or his historians regarded the Indian rulers as subjects of the Achaimenid kings. It is, however, unlikely that the word indicates that the second Poros was subordinate to his famous namesake, as Berve II 345 suggests. He sent envoys to Alexander offering to surrender (Arr. 5.20.6), apparently in the hope of gaining power and territory at the expense of his kinsman who was actively opposing the Macedonians. But when Alexander treated that man favorably, P. (*kakos*) fled to the Gandaridai (Diod. 17.91.1; Strabo 15.1.30 C699 says that P. ruled an area called Gandaris, perhaps, as Bosworth II 325 suggests, confusing the region to which he fled with the area he ruled) with a number of warlike tribesmen (Arr. 5.21.2–3). His initial contact with Alexander was doubtless regarded as submission to Macedonian authority, and Alexander, who now regarded him as a defector, sent Hephaistion and Demetrios son of Althaimenes (along with two battalions of *pezhetairoi*) into his territory; they were to hand his territory over to the good Poros (Arr. 5.21.5; Diod. 17.91.2), a mission which was successfully carried out (Diod. 17.93.1). That he was later an agitator at the court of Chandragupta (no. 1035), as Bosworth II 325 suggests, is plausible but little more than speculation. What became of the second P. is unknown. Berve II 345 no. 684; Anspach II 25–6, with nn. 197, 199; Bosworth II 320, 325; Howe 2020.

988 PORTIKANOS

(Πορτικανός). Indian dynast (Strabo 15.1.33 C701), ruler of the Praistoi (Curt. 9.8.11; cf. Lassen II² 186). Eggermont 11–12 would make him ruler of Pardabathra (Ptol. *Geog.* 7.1.58); hence we should distinguish him from Oxikanos (Arr. 6.16.1–2), who ruled Azeika (Axika; Ptol. *Geog.* 7.1.57). Indeed the details are sufficiently different to argue against identification of the two (*pace* Berve II 293 no. 587 and McCrindle 399, 401). P. was killed in the citadel (of Pardabathra?) on the third day, after Alexander had destroyed two of the city's towers and before P. could send envoys to negotiate his surrender (Curt. 9.8.11–12; summer 325). Diod. 17.102.5, however, adds that Alexander had taken two of P.'s cities, and that the Indian died fighting in the third. The two cities that were taken earlier may well have been those of Oxikanos, who was captured in the second (Arr. 6.16.2). Berve II 293 no. 589 (Ὀξυκανός); Eggermont 9–15; Jacobs 247, 251.

989 POSEIDONIOS

(Ποσειδώνιος). Macedonian (Tataki 413 no. 99) engineer in Alexander's army who designed the *helepolis* ("city taker"). Biton (52.1 Wescher = 4.1 Rehm-Schramm; on Biton see also Lewis 1999) records that he built a particularly effective siege engine, but the historical context is not known (cf. Kern 1999, 210). One suspects that this was done in the context of the sieges of either Tyre or Gaza, though Whitehead 2015, 81 notes its use at Mazaga (Arr. 4.26.5). Wescher 1867, 52.1; Berve II 327 no. 656; Whitehead 2015, 80–1.

990 POULAMACHOS

(Πουλάμαχος). Macedonian (Tataki 159 no. 75). For the name see Hoffmann 212–13; Berve II 339. A prominent Macedonian from Pella, P. was left behind in Persis in 330. At an unspecified time, he plundered the tomb of Kyros the Great and, on Alexander's return in 324, was convicted and executed (Plut. *Alex.* 69.3–4). Berve II 339 no. 679; Hoffmann 212–13.

991 PRANICHOS

(Πράνιχος). Poet in Alexander's entourage (apparently Greek), who in 328 sang verses ridiculing a recent Macedonian defeat and thus angered Kleitos sufficiently to begin quarreling with Alexander (Plut. *Alex.* 50.8). Plutarch tells us that some sources reported the poet's name as Pierion. Whether this means that only the form of the name is disputed or that both Pranichos and Pierion were known to have been in Alexander's camp is uncertain. Berve II 327 no. 657.

992 PRAXIPPOS

(Πράξιππος). Last independent king of Lapethos, on the north coast of Kypros. The name may indicate Lakonian ancestry (cf. Strabo 14 C682). He played no attested role in the history of Alexander the Great (but for bronze coinage in the time of Alexander see Bagnall 187; *BMC Cyprus*, pp. liii–lv). Persuaded by Agesilaos to ally himself with Antigonos Monophthalmos in 315 (Diod. 19.57.4, 59.1), he changed his allegiance when Lapethos was besieged by Seleukos (Diod. 19.62.6). In 312, he was, however, suspected of treasonous dealings with Antigonos and arrested (Diod. 19.79 4; cf. Hill 1949: I 158–60). He does not resurface in historical accounts. Hill I 158–60; Meyer, *Kl. Pauly* III 489 s.v. "Lapethos."

993 PREPELAOS

(Πρεπέλαος). Macedonian (Tataki 414 no. 106). If he is identical with the P. honored at Delphi in 287 (*Syll³* 379), his father's name began with the letter N. But there is no compelling reason to assume that this is the same man; the ethnic Makedon is pure conjecture. Billows 1989, 188 n.43 considers P. a brother of Kassandros (assuming that Plut. *Mor.* 486a mistakenly calls P. Perilaos), but by equating him with the honorand at Delphi he is forced to conclude that P. is a uterine half-brother. Now a relationship between Kassandros and Prepelaos would perhaps help to explain the latter's readiness to serve Lysimachos, who would thus have been the husband of P.'s sister Nikaia. But the identification with the honorand of *Syll*³ 379 is made less likely by the fact that, as a uterine half-brother, P. must have been born before Kassandros and his siblings, probably no later than 360. It would, of course, involve a relationship similar to that of the younger Krateros to Antigonos Gonatas (also named in Plut. *Mor.* 486a). This is speculation at best. Rathmann 2006 believes the general of Lysimachos is a different person, seeing non-existent problems in Diodorus' account.

General of Kassandros. In 315/14 P. was sent to Alexander son of Polyperchon, who was now cooperating with Aristodemos, urging him to defect (Diod. 19.64.3). Alexander was won over and made *strategos* of the Peloponnese (Diod. 19.64.4). In the following year P. joined with Asandros to fight Antigonid forces in Karia (Diod. 19.68.5). He was subsequently involved in the negotiations that led to the "Peace of the Dynasts" (*OGIS* 5 = *RC* 1), when he represented the interests of Kassandros and Lysimachos (the significance of which is noted by Hauben 1987a, 34). Although P. falls out of our historical accounts for several years, he resurfaces in 303/2 in Korinth, where he was in charge of Kassandros' garrison (Diod. 20.103.1) at a time when Demetrios set out win over the Peloponnese (Diod. 20.102.1). When Demetrios' troops gained access to Korinth through treachery (Polyaenus 4.7.8: Κόρινθον προδιδομένην), P.'s forces withdrew to the Sisypheion, and eventually to Akrokorinth; but even from here they were dislodged (Diod. 20.103.1–3; for virtual lack of resistance see Plut. *Demetr.* 25.1, who says the garrison was bought off with 100 talents). P., for his part, retreated to join Kassandros in the north (Diod. 20.103.4), and neither P. nor his superiors (Kassandros and Polyperchon) contested Demetrios in the Peloponnese (Diod. 20.103.7). Instead, in 302/1, P. accompanied Lysimachos to Asia Minor, where he took 6,000 infantry and 1,000 cavalry against the cities of Aiolis and Ionia (Diod. 20.107.2); he took Adramyttion and forced Ephesos to surrender, releasing the hundred Rhodian hostages that were held there and returning their freedom to the Ephesians, but only after burning the ships in their harbor (Diod. 20.107.4) and leaving a garrison in the city (Diod. 20.111.3; cf. *Syll*³ 353; Rogers 2013, 72–4), which was later dismissed under truce when Demetrios recaptured Ephesos. From there, after winning over Teos and Kolophon, P. failed to capture Erythrai and Klazomenai, which were reinforced by sea. He moved towards Sardis, where he induced Antigonos' general, Phoinix (no. 951), to defect and thus captured the city; but since Philip (no. 920) remained faithful to Antigonos he could not take the citadel (Diod. 20.107.5). Nothing else is known about P. If Koehler 1901, 1062 n.1 is correct in assuming that P. did not outlive Ipsos, this may perhaps explain his disappearance from our records, but it would also rule out identification with the Delphic honorand (*Syll*³ 379). Köhler 1901; Ziegler *RE* XXII (1954) 1836–8; Badian, *DNP* X (2001) 1127; Schoch 121; Olshausen 9–11 no 4; Rathmann 2006 (unconvincing).

994 PROEXES

(Προέξης). Prominent Persian (Justi 225) in Alexander's entourage, though it is unclear when he surrendered to the Macedonians. Appointed satrap of Parapamisadai in 330/29, apparently residing in the new settlement of Alexandria-in-the-Kaukasos (Arr. 3.28.4); his activities were curtailed by an *episkopos*, Neiloxenos son of Satyros, with an unspecified number of troops. In 327, P. was replaced as satrap by Tyriespis; for it appears that the performance of both the *episkopos* and the satrap was unsatisfactory (Arr. 4.22.4–5). Berve II 327 no. 658; Shayegan 118–19 no. 93.

995 PROKLES

(Προκλῆς). Athenian (Kirchner 12208). One of the accusers of Demosthenes in the Harpalos proceedings in 324/3 ([Plut.] *Mor.* 846c; Phot. *Bibl.* 494a, 38). Possibly identical with the P. named by Demosthenes himself in 348 (Dem. 37.48). Berve II 327 no. 659; Schaefer III² 329 n. 1.

996 PROMACHOS

(Πρόμαχος). Macedonian (Tataki 414 no. 107). Perhaps a common soldier in Alexander's army. In 324 at Sousa, when a drinking contest was held in connection with the funeral of the Indian Kalanos, P. drank the equivalent of thirteen liters of unmixed wine and won the first prize of a talent (or possibly a golden crown worth a talent). He died three days later from the after-effects of the drinking (Chares, *FGrH* 124 F19a = Athen. 10.437b; F19b = Plut. *Alex.* 70.1–2; cf. Ael. *VH* 2.41). Forty-one other contestants allegedly died of alcohol poisoning. Berve II 327 no. 660; Zwicker, *RE* XXIII (1957) 645–6 no. 17.

997 PROPPEI

(Πρόππει). Son of Thiogiton. One of twenty-four cavalrymen from Orchomenos, who served with Alexander's allied cavalry until the expedition reached Ekbatana in 330. There he and his compatriots were discharged. On their return (*c.*329), they made a dedication to Zeus Soter in Orchomenos (*IG* VII 3206). Berve II 328 no. 663.

998 PROTEAS

(Πρωτέας). Macedonian (Tataki 415 nos. 111–12). Son of Andronikos and, in all likelihood, of Lanike, Alexander's nurse (Athen. 4.129a; cf. Arr. 4.9.3; see Carney 1981, 152); hence also the nephew of Black Kleitos and brother of two men killed near Miletos in 334 (Curt. 8.2.8). A *syntrophos* of Alexander, P. was born in the mid-350s (Ael. *VH* 12.26). He had been sent with fifteen ships by Antipatros to protect the islands and the Greek mainland against Persian attack. Putting in at Chalkis on Euboia he advanced to Kythnos and then caught the Persian admiral Datames at Siphnos at dawn, capturing eight of his ten ships (Arr. 2.2.4–5); there is no mention of Macedonian losses. P. came with a fifty-oared ship from Macedon to join Alexander at Sidon (Arr. 2.20.2). Whether he came on official state business—hence the reference to the single *pentekontoros*—or if he participated in the naval action around Tyre is unclear. Nor is it clear if he had anything to do with the Rhodian contingent of nine ships and the submission of that island to Alexander. Hauben 1977, 308 n.7 rightly sees the dating of Rhodes' surrender after the siege of Tyre (thus Justin 12.11.1; Curt. 4.5.9) as incorrect and due to the fact that the siege of Tyre was already underway when the delegation and the ships came to Sidon. Possibly, P. stopped at Rhodes on the way to the Levant. It is difficult to argue that the ten ships represent only the pro-Macedonian faction: the inclusion in this number of the state trireme seems to weigh against this (Arr. 2.20.2: ἡ περίπολος καλουμένη). On the status of Rhodes at this time see Bosworth I 242–3. Like Hegelochos, who served with the fleet, P. soon joined Alexander's expedition and accompanied him by land from at least Egypt (cf. Berve II 328). Of his military actions nothing further is known. He was a notorious drinking companion of Alexander (Hippolochos *ap.* Athen. 4.129a; Ael. *VH* 12.26), and the King on one occasion gave him five talents to prove that he was no longer angry with him (Plut. *Alex.* 39.6). How he reacted to the death of his uncle in 328 is unknown, but Ephippos may have implied some form of poetic justice when he claimed that Alexander became ill and died as a result of a drinking contest with Proteas (*FGrH* 126 F3 = Athen. 10.434a–b). Berve II 328 no. 664; II 328–9 no. 665; Ziegler, *RE* XXIII (1957) 929 nos. 2–3; Carney 1981, 152; cf. Wirth 1989, 1–4. **Stemma VIII.**

999 PROTHYTES

(Προθύτης). Theban. A leader of the anti-Macedonian faction. In 335 Alexander demanded that the Thebans surrender P. and Phoinix in return for amnesty; but the Thebans arrogantly demanded the surrender of Philotas and Antipatros (Plut. *Alex.* 11.7–8). This can easily be reconciled with the admittedly apologetic version of Arr. 1.7.10–11, which shows that there was in Thebes a party willing to negotiate, but that their efforts were undermined by the anti-Macedonian faction (cf. Diod. 17.9.4). Cf. also the discussion in Bosworth I 78–9. Berve II 328 no. 661.

1000 PROTOGENES

(Πρωτογένης). Greek from Kaunos (Pliny, *HN* 35.101; Plut. *Demetr.* 22.4; Paus. 1.3.5). Born perhaps in the 370s: Pliny claims that he was a ship painter (*naves pinxisse*) until he was fifty, which must mean that he painted them on canvas, not that he applied paint to the actual ships. Famous painter and sculptor; friend of Apelles (Pliny, *HN* 35.81–3, 87–8). P. appears to have spent some time in Athens, where he painted numerous famous individuals, including writers, athletes, the mother of Aristotle, Antigonos the One-Eyed, and Alexander himself (Pliny, *HN* 35.106). He also painted the state triremes Paralos and Ammonias, but his masterpiece appears to have been the *Ialysos*, which had been commissioned by the Rhodians and which the artist was in the process of completing in the suburbs of Rhodes when the city was besieged by Demetrios Poliorketes. Demetrios spared the painter and his work, thus winning great renown (Plut. *Demetr.* 22.4–7; Pliny, *HN* 35.104–5; Plut. *Mor.* 183a–b). P. was noted for the laborious care and accuracy he put into his work (Quint. 12.10.6)—his *Ialysos* was already seven years in the making when Demetrios attacked Rhodes (Plut. *Demetr.* 22.5)—and was counted amongst the greatest of painters (Cic. *Brutus* 70). Berve II 329 no. 666; Pollitt 171–3.

1001 PROTOMACHOS

(Πρωτόμαχος). A Macedonian of unknown family background, P. is once attested: at Issos, he commanded the *prodromoi* (Arr. 2.9.2). He replaced Amyntas son of Arrhabaios in this office, perhaps, as Berve II 329 suggests, at Gordion in spring 333. But by the time of the Gaugamela campaign (summer 331) he had himself been replaced by Aretes. He did not hold this position, as Berve suggests, "als Nachfolger des Hegelochos." Hegelochos may have held a special command over the *prodromoi* and 500 lightly armed troops (Arr. 1.13.1), but this office, reported between Amyntas' scouting mission (Arr. 1.12.7) and the latter's command of the *prodromoi* at the Granikos (1.14.1, 6) looks suspiciously like an error on Arrian's part, ascribable perhaps to the conflicting reports of Ptolemy and Aristoboulos (cf. Bosworth I 114). That Hegelochos ever commanded the four squadrons of *prodromoi*, only to be demoted at Gaugamela (Arr. 3.11.8), is highly unlikely. What became of P. is unknown. Berve II 329 no. 667; Heckel 1992, 353.

1002 PROXENOS

(Πρόξενος). Macedonian (Tataki 415 no. 109) or Greek of unknown background. P. is found in Alexander's entourage as the man in charge of the household equipment (*stromatophylax*). As he was pitching the King's tent at the River Oxos in 329, he discovered petroleum. The discovery was reported by Alexander in a letter to Antipatros (Plut. *Alex.* 57.5–8; cf. Athen. 2.42f). Berve II 328 no. 662; Ziegler, *RE* XIII (1957) 1033 no. 9; Müller 2014.

1003 PRYTANIS

(Πρύτανις). Son of Pairisades I, king of the Kimmerian Bosporos (Diod. 20.22.1) and probably Komosarye (no. 615). Brother of Satyros, Eumelos, and (apparently) Gorgippos (no. 484). When his father died, he designated Satyros as his heir, but the latter's right to rule was challenged by Eumelos, who allied himself with Aripharnes, the king of the Sirakes (Diod. 20.22.4–23.6). P., it appears, remained in Pantikapaion to protect his brother's interests; for it was there that Meniskos, the mercenary captain, brought the corpse of Satyros (Diod. 20.23.8). P. celebrated Satyros' rites and buried him in the royal tomb (Diod. 20.24.1; cf. Strabo 11.2.7 C494), then he took over the army and garrisoned Gargaza, refusing Eumelos' offer to share the kingdom, before returning to Pantikapaion to assert his kingship (Diod. 20.24.1). In a subsequent battle with Eumelos, he was defeated, forced to surrender his army and renounce the kingdom. But P. made an attempt to recover the throne and was driven off; he sought refuge in an area called Kepoi (on the Apatourian Gulf on the Asian side of the Bosporos), where he was killed (Diod. 20.24.1–2). His friends, wife and children were all murdered by Eumelos, as were those of his brother, with the exception of Pairisades (no. 838), who escaped (Diod. 20.24.3). Niese I 414; Hind, *CAH* VI² 501–2.

1004 PSAMMON

(Ψάμμων). Egyptian philosopher of unknown family, though Hamilton 73, suggests plausibly that Ps. is merely a variation of Ammon (cf. Plut. *Mor.* 180d). While in Egypt, Alexander listened with approval to his lectures on the nature of the divine (Plut. *Alex.* 27.10–11). Nothing else is known about him. Berve II 409 no. 831; Hamilton 73.

1005 PTOLEMAIS

(Πτολεμαΐς). Macedonian (Tataki 423 no. 171). Daughter of Ptolemy I Soter and Eurydike (Plut. *Demetr.* 23.5, 46.5; Beloch IV² 2.179), and thus sister of Ptolemy Keraunos and Lysandra. After Deidameia's death (300/299), when through the agency of Seleukos Demetrios was reconciled with Ptolemy, he agreed to marry Ptolemais, a marriage alliance arranged by Seleukos (Plut. *Demetr.* 32.6); but the girl was very young and the union did not take place until many years later (Ager 2018, 49). In 286/5 (for the date, Shear 1978, 82) when Demetrios, who had been driven out of Macedonia (after which his wife Phila committed suicide) and was now shut out of Athens as well, had returned to Asia, Eurydike arrived in Miletos with Ptolemais in tow (Plut. *Demetr.* 46.5). Miletos may have changed hands, from Lysimachos to Demetrios, something that Ptolemy I may have welcomed; at any rate, by the mid-280s the children of Eurydike were becoming declining political assets, and the marriage was clearly not the social event of the season (cf. Wheatley and Dunn 410, also n.7), though each partner gained from it. Ptolemais bore Demetrios a son, also named Demetrios ("the Fair"), who later ruled Kyrene (Plut. *Demetr.* 53.8). Ogden 176; Aulbach §8.2.1.5. **Stemma X.**

1006 PTOLEMY

(Πτολεμαῖος). Prominent Macedonian (Tataki 418 no. 134). *Somatophylax basilikos.* Led two *taxeis* of hypaspists (those of Adaios and Timandros) and some light-armed infantry (*psiloi*) in the skirmish against defenders who made a sortie from the Tripylon at Halikarnassos (Arr. 1.22.4). Pt. himself was killed in that engagement (Arr. 1.22.7). Although Arrian is careless in his use of terminology, *somatophylax basilikos* can only refer to a member of the "Royal Hypaspists" (the young adults of aristocratic descent) or one of the Seven. In light of his military responsibilities, he must have been one of the Seven, and thus the first of the Seven with an attested special military command (Heckel 1992, 259–60). He may have been the father of the Ptolemy who was appointed Somatophylax of Philip III Arrhidaios in 320 (Arr. *Succ.* 1.38; see below) and/or the man who was granted land in the vicinity of Spartolos in 335/4 (*Syll³* 332, 25). Berve II 337 no. 672.

1007 PTOLEMY

(Πτολεμαῖος). Son of Seleukos, probably from Tymphaia (so Berve II 335) or from Orestis and a relative of Seleukos son of Antiochos (Hoffmann 174). Arr. 1.24.1 calls him "one of the royal bodyguard" (ἕνα τῶν σωματοφυλάκων τῶν βασιλικῶν), which must mean that he was one of the Royal Hypaspists. In late 334 Ptolemy led the newlyweds back to Macedonia for the winter (Arr. 1.24.1), returning to Gordion in the spring of 333 with these men and 3,000 infantry and 300 horse from Macedonia, 200 Thessalian cavalry, and 150 Eleians under Alkias (Arr. 1.29.4; cf. Curt. 3.1.24). He was probably in line for the command of one of the two Tymphaian phalanx battalions, replacing Philip son of Amyntas (or Balakros?) who led the unit at the Granikos. At Issos we find Pt. exercising that command. He died on the battlefield of Issos—perhaps as a result of his youthful daring—and his battalion was assigned to the Tymphaian Polyperchon (Arr. 2.12.2). Berve II 335–6 no. 670; Hoffmann 174; Beloch III² 2.327; Heckel 1992, 286.

1008 PTOLEMY

(Πτολεμαῖος). Macedonian (Tataki 418 no. 133). Commander of the Thrakians (Arr. 4.7.2), Pt. was apparently the Macedonian officer in charge of all Thrakian infantry, except the Agrianes, during the first half of the expedition. Of the native commanders, only Sitalkes is known to us. In 329/8, Pt. returned from the coast of Phoinikia and Kilikia to Alexander in Zariaspa (Arr. 4.7.2; cf. Curt. 7.10.11: he returned with 5,000 mercenaries; Arr. 4.7.2 says he was accompanied by Epokillos and Melamnidas; Curt. 7.10.11 mentions only "Maenidas"), having been sent there in the winter of 331/0 to accompany Menes the hyparch and the discharged Thessalian cavalrymen (cf. Arr. 3.16.9). On his departure for the coast, he was replaced by Eudamos. What became of Pt. after his return to Baktria is unknown. Berve II 337 no. 673; Heckel 1992, 333.

1009 PTOLEMY

(Πτολεμαῖος). Chosen Somatophylax of Philip Arrhidaios at Triparadeisos (Arr. *Succ.* 1.38); apparently the son of Ptolemy the Somatophylax of Alexander, who died at Halikarnassos. Billows 427 identifies him with Polemaios son of Polemaios but the Somatophylax of Philip Arrhidaios was almost certainly in Macedonia with the new king when Polemaios is attested as a hostage of Eumenes in 320/19. Certainly, in light of the frequent occurrence of the name Ptolemaeus/Polemaios, there is nothing odd about two different men named after their fathers (cf. Launey 1183 for two other cases of Πτολεμαῖος Πτολεμαίου). Berve II 355 no. 669.

1010 PTOLEMY

(Πτολεμαῖος). Macedonian (Tataki 200 no. 10). Son of Lagos (Arr. 2.11.8; 3.6.5 etc.; cf. *P. Eleph.* 2; *Syll*[3] 2.588, 181; on Lagos see also Plut. *Mor.* 458a–b; as Bevan 127, 20 n.4 notes, it is primarily French scholars who refer to the dynasty as the Lagids) and Arsinoë (Porphyry *ap.* Euseb. Arm. *Chron.* p. 74, 19ff. = *FGrH* 260 F2 §2), purportedly a member of a lesser branch of the Macedonian royal house (Satyros, frg. 21 = *FHG* 3.165; Theocr. 17.26, with Gow II 331; Curt. 9.8.22; *OGIS* 1.54, line 6). Pt. came from Eordaia (Arr. 6.28.4; Arr. *Ind.* 18.5; Steph. Byz. s.v. "Orestia" says he came from Orestis) and may have been brought up at the Court in Pella. Rumors that he was an illegitimate son of Philip II (Paus. 1.6.2; Curt. 9.8.22; Ael. frg 285; *Suda* Λ 25; Collins 1997; Ogden 67–8; Van Oppen 2013) appear to have originated in the early years of the Diadochoi, when blood relationship with the house of Philip had tremendous propaganda value (cf. Errington 1976, 155–6). The only source for Pt.'s birthdate is [Lucian], *Macrob.* 12, placing it in 367/6, a date wrongly rejected because it conflicts with the popularly accepted view that Pt. was coeval with Alexander (but see Heckel 1992, 205, 207 and 2018a, 5–6). The view espoused by Bouché-Leclercq 1903, 1.3, and accepted by Bevan 1927, 21, that he was raised as a *pais basilikos* has no support in the sources.

Banished by Philip II in spring 336 for his role in the Pixodaros affair—Pt., along with Erigyios, Laomedon, Nearchos, and Harpalos had induced the Crown Prince to conduct private negotiations with the Karian dynast—he appears not to have returned to Macedonia until after Philip's death (Plut. *Alex.* 10.4; Arr. 3.6.5). Although he crossed into Asia with Alexander in 334, nothing is known about his participation in the campaign in the early years. Volkmann (*RE* XXIII 1607) speculates that, at this time, Pt. may have been appointed *edeatros* (the equivalent of the Roman *praegustator*) or "King's Taster" (Athen. 4.171b = Chares, *FGrH* 125 F1). Not only would Alexander not risk the life of a Somatophylax for this purpose, but Justin 12.14.9 indicates that there were others appointed to do this job: the sons of Antipatros (who were Pages of Alexander) are described as *praegustare ac temperare potum regis soliti* (but see Collins 2012a and Hesychius s.v. ἐδέατρος). He appears to have joined in the pursuit of the Persians who fled from the battlefield of Issos, though he embellished his account with images of the Persians crossing a ravine on the bodies of their own dead (Arr. 2.11.8; cf. Bosworth I 216–17, with earlier literature). There is no mention of an independent command until late 331, at the Persian Gates. Here Arrian (3.18.9)—probably drawing on Pt.'s own *History*—assigns to him the command of 3,000 troops guarding one of Ariobarzanes' possible escape routes. But the Vulgate authors say nothing about Pt.'s role, and we may be justified in questioning the veracity of Arrian's account (but see Howe 2015b, 184; Heckel 2018a, 8). Kleitarchos certainly had no reason to diminish Pt.'s contributions; for there are two later episodes in which the Vulgate clearly invents stories that enhance Pt.'s reputation (Curt. 9.5.21, 8.22–7; Diod. 17.103.6–8). Certainly, Pt.'s lack of achievement up to this point, combined with the conspicuous silence of the Vulgate, raises suspicions about the man's sudden prominence in an account based, most likely, on his own record of events. Bosworth I 328 may be correct in suggesting that "he cast himself for the role played by Philotas."

In autumn 330, after Demetrios had been deposed (and presumably executed) on charges of conspiring against the King, Alexander appointed Pt. Somatophylax (Arr. 3.27.5; cf. 6.28.4 = Aristoboulos, *FGrH* 139 F50; cf. Curt. 9.8.22). Arr. 3.6.6 anticipates the appointment and regards it as a reward for Pt.'s loyalty to the King in the past, especially in 337/6. When Justin 13.4.10 writes that he had been "promoted from the ranks (*ex gregario milite*) on account of his *virtus*," he is merely indicating that Pt., up to this point, had had no unit under his command. It was at about this time that Alexander began to make greater use of his Somatophylakes on an *ad hoc* basis. This is almost certainly because the composition of the unit had changed significantly and its members were all younger men whom the King felt he could trust. Thus, in 329, we find Pt. assigned the task of bringing in the regicide Bessos, whom Spitamenes and Dataphernes had arrested and were prepared to extradite, presumably in exchange for immunity (Arr. 3.29.6–30.5; cf Seibert 1969, 10–16). Here again, Arrian, when he follows Pt. (*FGrH* 138 F14), shows signs of embellishment; for other accounts of Bessos' arrest see Arr. 3.30.5 = Aristoboulos, *FGrH* 139 F24; Diod. 17.83.7–9; Curt. 7.5.19–26, 38–43; Justin 12.5.10–11; *Itiner. Al.* 34; Heckel 2018a, 9–10. But, from his account, we do gain a sense of how delicate the extradition process was and how great the fear of betrayal. Spitamenes and Dataphernes had asked that only a small force be sent to them; Pt.'s contingent probably exceeded 5,000 men. Three hipparchies of Companions; the battalion of Philotas; one chiliarchy of hypaspists, all the Agrianes and half the archers. Seibert 11 n. 33, following Berve, puts the figure at *c*.5,000. But the calculation of 300 men per hipparchy (*ile*) is probably incorrect, since the hipparchies had by this time been reformed (cf. Bosworth I 375–6), and the strength of a battalion of *psiloi* (i.e. Philotas' battalion) was not necessarily equal to that of its counterpart in the pezhetairoi. Alexander had clearly not forgotten Satibarzanes' treachery and the death of Anaxippos (Arr. 3.25.2, 5).

In 328, Pt. commanded one of five columns that swept through Sogdiana (Arr. 4.16.2–3; cf. Holt 1988, 60–6; Curt. 8.1.1, 10, however, mentions only three contingents). His claim to have reported the discovery of oil at the Oxos (Arr. 4.15.7–8) is contradicted by Plut. *Alex.* 57.5ff. and Curt. 7.10.14 (cf. Seibert 16–17). For the story and its meaning see Müller 2014a, 83, and 2014b). In late summer or autumn of that year, he attended the banquet in Marakanda where Alexander killed Kleitos. Although it is generally agreed that he made some attempt to restrain Kleitos (Arr. 4.8.9 = Aristoboulos, *FGrH* 139 F29) or Alexander himself (Curt. 8.1.45, 48), it could be argued that he had failed to prevent the murder, and it is difficult to determine what, if anything, Pt. said about the episode in his *History*. Over the winter, when the Macedonian forces besieged the fortress of Sisimithres (the Rock of Chorienes), Pt. and his fellow Somatophylakes, Perdikkas and Leonnatos, conducted the night operations in shifts (Arr. 4.21.4).

In the spring of 327, after Alexander's marriage to Rhoxane and before the departure for India, Pt. played a major role in bringing the conspiracy of Hermolaos and the Pages to Alexander's attention. The details of the plot had been divulged to him by Eurylochos, and, in Arrian's version (4.13.7), Pt. alone informed Alexander. Curtius (8.6.22) says that Pt. *and Leonnatos* were approached by Eurylochos, and it appears that, in his own *History*, Pt. took full credit by suppressing Leonnatos' contribution (Errington 1969, 234; cf. Arr. 4.25.3). During the Swat campaign, Pt. was wounded in a skirmish with the Aspasians near the Choes River (Arr. 4.23.3). The wound could not have been serious, for Pt. soon afterwards pursued the Indian hyparch up a hill and killed him in single combat, the account of which almost certainly comes from Pt.'s own pen (Arr. 4.24.3–4; Jacoby rightly includes Pt.'s *aristeia* in F18; cf. Brunt I 421 n.3; and Seibert 1969, 19, with n.54.). Once the Macedonians had advanced beyond Arigaion, Pt. was again sent ahead to reconnoiter, and he reported large numbers of enemy campfires (4.24.8). In the attack on this concentration of Indian forces, Alexander divided his troops into three contingents, assigning the command of one third to Pt., to whom he assigned the light-armed battalions of Philotas and Philip, as well as one-third of the hypaspists (Arr. 4.24.10). While Alexander dealt with the Indians who had rushed down onto the plain, Pt. successfully dislodged those who occupied the hills (Arr. 4.25.2–3). And Pt. himself reported that in the engagement more than 40,000 Indians and 230,000 oxen were captured by the Macedonians (Arr. 4.25.4 = *FGrH* 138 F18). But, despite Pt.'s tendency to focus in his *History* on his own achievements, there is little to support Curtius' remark that "Pt. took the most cities, but Alexander captured the greatest ones" (8.10.21). Not surprisingly, Pt. also played a key role in the assault on Aornos in Arrian's version (4.29.1–6). The Vulgate knows nothing of it, and Curtius in particular (8.11.5) ascribes a similar command to Myllinas (probably the son of Asandros, a Beroian; cf. Tataki, *PB* no. 910). When Alexander was wounded by the Mallians, Pt. (like Krateros) advised the King not to risk his life, and set limits on his pursuit of glory (Curt. 9.6.15), but Arrian's failure to mention this suggests that Pt. himself did not wish to appear critical of Alexander.

The Vulgate preserves a story that Pt. was one of many Macedonians wounded at Harmatelia, a town of Brahmins—located by Diodorus and Curtius in the kingdom of Sambos, but placed by Strabo (15.2.7 C723, followed by Eggermont 125ff.) in the land of the Oreitai. These Indians smeared the tips of their weapons with poison extracted from snakes, thus causing the wounded to die in excruciating pain (Diod. 17.103.3–6; Curt. 9.8.20; Strabo 15.2.7 C723). In addition to the implausible tale that Alexander saw in a dream a serpent carrying in its mouth the plant which was the antidote to the poison, it is clear that the whole story is a fiction invented to glorify Pt. Like the false report that Pt. saved Alexander's life in the town of the Mallians (Curt. 9.5.21; Paus. 1.6.2; cf. Plut. *Mor.* 327b, 344d), which is disproved by Pt.'s own *History* (Arr. 6.11.8), this story contains late elements which render it even more suspect. Diodorus (17.103.6–7; cf. Curt. 9.8.23–24) emphasizes the character and popularity of the later ruler of Egypt; Curtius (9.8.22; cf. Paus. 1.6.2) adds that Pt. was thought to be an illegitimate son of Philip II. The snake itself is thought by some to be connected with the cult of Sarapis (see Eggermont 112–14, with earlier literature; cf. also Bosworth 1988, 167–70; Fraser 1967, 23–45), instituted in Egypt by Pt. He commanded light-armed troops against the Oreitai of the maritime region (Curt. 9.10.6–7; Diod. 17.104.5–6; cf. Arr. 6.21.3, naming only Hephaistion, who appears to have had supreme command).

He was responsible for building the funeral pyre, on which the famed Indian philosopher Kalanos committed suicide amidst the flames shortly before the army reached Sousa (Arr. 7.3.2). At Sousa in 324, Pt. married Artakama, a daughter of Artabazos (Arr. 7.4.6; cf. Arr *ap* Phot *Bibl* 68b; Plut. *Eum.* 1.7, who calls her Apama)—hence a sister of Alexander's mistress Barsine—and, along with his fellow Somatophylakes, was awarded a golden crown (Arr. 7.5.6). There is no evidence that Pt. had been previously married. The Athenian courtesan Thaïs, who had accompanied the expedition, became Pt.'s mistress (Plut. *Alex.* 38.2; Hamilton 100)—possibly she joined the expedition in that capacity— and bore him two sons (Lagos and Leontiskos) and a daughter, Eirene, who later married Eunostos, King of Kypriot Soloi (Athen. 13.576e).

Pt.'s last commission under Alexander came against the Kossaians, whose territory the King invaded in the winter of 324/3. Here he seems to have been Alexander's second-in-command, but Arrian's narrative (undoubtedly based on Pt.'s own account: Strasburger 1934, 47), though vague and abbreviated (7.15.1–3), suffices to depict Pt. as a full partner in the undertaking and, consequently, equally responsible for its success (Seibert 1969: 25–6). His prominence in this undertaking can also be explained by the absence of Krateros, who had taken some 10,000 veterans from Opis to Kilikia (cf. Arr. 7.12.1–4) and the death of Hephaistion (Arr. 7.14; Plut. *Alex.* 72); Perdikkas had been given the task of conveying Hephaistion's corpse to Babylon (Diod. 17.110.8). The forty-day campaign, which served to divert Alexander's attention away from the recent loss of Hephaistion (cf. Plut. *Alex.* 72. 4), was not as successful as Diod. 17.111.5–6 claims, as Antigonos discovered in 317 (Diod. 19.19.3–8; Billows 1990, 92–3; cf. Bosworth 1988, 165).

When Alexander died in 323, Pt.—described as one of the *megistoi* amongst the cavalry officers (Arr. *Succ.* 2)—was among the first to reject the legitimacy of the inept candidates for the throne—the half-witted Arrhidaios, the illegitimate Herakles, and the half-barbarian and as-yet-unborn Alexander IV—proposing instead a ruling junta of officers (Curt. 10.6.13–16; Justin 13.2.11). In the propaganda pamphlet (*Liber de Morte*), Pt. is named as one of those who was ignorant of the plot to murder the King, and in Alexander's forged testament he is offered the hand of the King's sister Kleopatra (*LM* 98, 103, 111, 117, 119, 122); hence, Bosworth 2000 believes that the testament was written for Pt.'s benefit (but see Heckel 1988). When an agreement was reached in Babylon, he was given Egypt as his satrapy (Curt. 10.10.1; Diod. 18.3.1; Justin 13.4.10; *P. Eleph.* 1, noting that he was in his fourteenth year as satrap in 311); some have suggested that the distribution of satrapies was Pt.'s idea, and this led in no small way to the disintegration of the empire (cf. Curt. 10.6.15; Justin 13.2.12; Paus. 1.6.2; but see Seibert 1969, 32). Kleomenes was named as his *hyparchos*, doubtless because Perdikkas distrusted Pt. (Arr. *Succ.* 1.5; Dexippos, *FGrH* 100 F8 §2; Justin 13.4.11). Nevertheless, he assumed control of the satrapy, treating the inhabitants with kindness, and attracting many supporters on account of his fairness (Diod. 18.14.1; Justin 13.6.18–19; Ael. *VH* 13.13; on his cleverness, and Alexander's alleged resentment, see Ael. *VH* 12.16; 14.47a; cf. Diod. 17.103.6–7 for his popularity; further references to the positive portrayal of Pt. in Anson 2018 22 n.2); he found 8,000 talents in the treasury, which he used to recruit mercenaries.

Pt. soon eliminated Kleomenes (Paus. 1.6.3), whose record of corruption in Alexander's lifetime provided a convenient pretext (Arr. 7.23.6, 8), and began to forge closer ties (κοινοπραγία) with Antipatros (Diod. 18.14.2, 25.4). Sending a force to Syria in 321/0, he made sure that Alexander's funeral carriage would come to Egypt (Arr. *Succ.* 1.25; 24.1;

Diod. 18.28.2–3; Paus. 1.6.3; cf. Ael. *VH* 12.64, with the implausible story that Ptolemy created a likeness [εἴδωλον] of Alexander's body in order to deceive Perdikkas), as the King had originally intended, though Perdikkas had instead hoped to bring it back to Europe. Thus Arr. *Succ.* 1.25: παρὰ γνώμην . . . Περδίκκου. See also no. 871. (For Pt.'s later transfer of Alexander's body to Alexandria and the benefit to his reputation see Diod. 18.28.3–6). The hijacking of the King's corpse drew Perdikkas' forces to Egypt (Diod. 18.25.6, 29.1; cf. Nepos, *Eum.* 3.2), but Pt. had prepared for this eventuality (Justin 13.6.18–19, 8.1) and after a disastrous campaign at Kamelon Teichos Perdikkas was killed by his own men (Arr. *Succ.* 1.28; Diod. 18.33–6; Justin 13.8.10; cf. Polyaenus 4.19 [18]; Front. 4.7.20). Pt.'s victory over Perdikkas was said to have been prophesied by Peithagoras (Arr. 7.18.5 = Aristoboulos, *FGrH* 139 F54). Pt. treated the remnants of the Perdikkan army and its mutinous commanders with respect (Diod. 18.36.1–2, 6) and, after selecting the best troops for his own service, he sent the remainder under the leadership of Peithon and Arrhidaios to northern Syria (Diod. 18.36.6, 39.1; Arr. *Succ.* 1.30). There the empire was divided up anew, and Pt. retained Egypt (Diod. 18.39.5; Arr. *Succ.* 1.34), to which he could add Libyan Kyrene, whither he had sent his general Ophellas (no. 817) to suppress the army of Thibron (no. 1124; Diod. 18.19–21; Arr. *Succ.* 1.16–19; Justin 13.6.20). Later he would send his stepson, Magas, to administer the area.

At some point in 320/19 (probably winter; for the chronological problem see Wheatley 1995; also Seibert 1969: 129–31. *Marm. Par. BNJ* 239 B12 dates the annexation of Syria to 319/18, but this appears to be refuted by the fact that Alketas was still alive and actively opposing Antigonos when he was joined by Laomedon), Pt. sailed to Laomedon and offered to purchase Syria from him because it was valuable for the defense of Egypt and attack on Kypros. Thus App. *Syr.* 52.264, and if the story is true we may assume that there was at least an implicit threat of force; but Diod. 18.43.2 makes no mention of an offer of compensation, and it may be that this was a later invention to exculpate Pt. Diod. 18.73.2 says that Phoinikia was unjustly (ἀδίκως) annexed by Pt., as noted by Worthington 2015, 103 n.72; but this may exclude the taking of Koile-Syria or represent Antigonos' interpretation of Pt.'s actions. When Laomedon turned down his offer Pt.'s general Nikanor defeated and imprisoned him (App. *Syr.* 52.264–5; cf. App. *Mithr.* 9.27; Paus. 1.6.4; Diod. 18.43.2). Laomedon escaped and joined Alketas in Karia. Pt. held Syria for some time, leaving garrisons in the cities, and sailed back to Egypt (App. *Syr.* 52.265); for his alleged seizure of Jerusalem on the Sabbath see Joseph. *AJ* 12.7, 8–9.

Pt.'s opposition to the "Kings" continued after the death of Antipatros, and he sided with Kassandros against the old regent's appointee, Polyperchon (Diod. 18.49.3; cf. 18.54.3, 55.2), who asked him to send a fleet from Phoinikia to the Hellespont. An effort to detach the Argyraspids, who were guarding the treasures of Kyinda (Kilikia), from Eumenes and Polyperchon met with no success (Diod. 18.62). But Eumenes' plan to recover Phoinikia for the "Kings" was abandoned when Pt.'s ally Antigonos threatened to win control of Asia Minor (Diod. 18.73.2). Indeed, Pt. soon had reason to regret his alliance with Monophthalmos, although the latter's campaigns against Eumenes on the Iranian plateau gave him a welcome opportunity to concentrate on the affairs of Egypt (for friction between Pt. and Antigonos, Nepos, *Eum.* 10.3).

In 316/15, he gave refuge to Seleukos, who fled from Antigonos (App. *Syr.* 53.268; Diod. 19.55.5, 56.1); it was allegedly Seleukos who urged Pt. to ally himself with Lysimachos and Kassandros in 315. They sent ambassadors to Antigonos demanding that he share his newly won land and wealth with them and those Macedonians who had lost their satrapies; for they were envious and feared the growing power of Antigonos (App. *Syr.* 53.270; Paus. 1.6.4; Diod 19.56.3–4; cf. Justin 15.1; for Ptolemy's ineffective support of Asandros see no. 233). When Antigonos rejected the demands of the "allies" (cf. Diod. 19. 57.1–2) they made war on him and he, in turn, drove Pt.'s garrisons out of Syria and stripped him of Phoinikia and Koile-Syria (App. *Syr.* 53.271; cf. Diod. 19.58–9). For Pt.'s victory over the twenty-two-year-old Demetrios at Gaza, (Paus. 1.6.5; for the battle Devine 1989); although Pt.'s general Killes suffered a defeat at Demetrios' hands soon afterward. The victory at Gaza was followed by Seleukos' return to Babylon with 1,000 infantry and 300 horse supplied by Pt. (App. *Syr.* 54.272–3; Diod. 19.90.1, 800 inf. and 200 horse). Seleukos reported his success in a letter to Pt. (Diod. 19.92.5). Meanwhile, in 315, Antigonos had sent Agesilaos (no. 25) to win over the kings of Kypros, of whom the rulers of Kition, Lapithos, Marion, and Keryneia were persuaded, though Nikokreon (no. 797) remained loyal to Pt. (Diod. 19.57.4, 59.1). Pt. responded by sending a force under the command of his brother Menelaos—10,000 soldiers led by Myrmidon (no. 759) and 100 ships under Polykleitos (no. 979)—which joined the ships of Seleukos, who arrived from the Aegean (Diod. 19.62.3–4). Keryneia and Lapithos were captured; Sasioikos returned to the fold; and the ruler of Amathous was compelled to give hostages (Diod. 19.62.6). Things were, however, far from secure and Pt., who had just suppressed an uprising in Kyrenes (Diod. 19.79.1–3; see also Agis no. 29 and Epainetos no. 414), came in person in 312. He found that Pymiathon had been secretly negotiating with Antigonos, and put him to death; he also arrested Stasioikos, who had been equally duplicitous, and demolished Marion (Diod. 19.79.4: calling Pymiathon Pygmalion). Nikokreon was left in charge of affairs on Kypros (Diod. 19.79.5; see Bagnall 39–40). The death of Nikokreon in 311/10, recorded in the *Marmor Parium (FGrH* 239 F17), led to the elevation of Menelaos to the position of *strategos* of the island (cf. Diod. 20.47.3, 52.5). The defection of Nikokles of Paphos in 310 was suppressed by Pt.'s agents Argaios (no. 174) and Kallikrates (no. 564), who forced the family to commit suicide (Diod. 20.21.1; see also s.v. Axiothea no. 273). In 306, Pt. was defeated near Salamis on Kypros in a sea battle by the ships of Antigonos under Demetrios' command (App. *Syr.* 54.275; Paus. 1.6.6; Diod. 20.47.3–52.6, with details s.v. Menelaos no. 710); among the captives were Pt.'s son Leontiskos and his brother Menelaos, who along with their property were returned without ransom by Demetrios (Justin 15.2.6–8). When Antigonos' troops subsequently hailed him and his son kings, Pt.'s troops followed suit and declared him king as well, lest he be thought inferior on account of his defeat (App. *Syr.* 54.276; Justin 15.2.11; Diod. 20.53.2; cf. 21.1.4b; Plut. *Demetr.* 18.2). Demetrios was, however, said to have encouraged his courtiers to toast him as "King," while giving his opponents lesser, derogatory, titles—in Pt.'s case (in reference to his defeat at Salamis), the title of ναύαρχος, admiral (Phylarchos *ap.* Athen 4.261b; Plut. *Demetr.* 25.6–9, *Mor.* 823c–d; also Hauben 1974; Yardley, Wheatley, and Heckel 243). Pt. had also entered into an alliance with Rhodes—their failure to campaign with the Antigonids against Egypt (Diod. 20.73–6, for the details of which see s.v. Demetrios no. 360) was a pretext for Demetrios' siege of the city in 305/4—and his support of the city during this crisis (Diod. 20.82–99; for Ptolemaic aid see 20.88.9, 98.1) was said to have earned him the *epiklesis* Soter ("Savior"), though it was not applied to him during his lifetime (see Hazzard 2000, 3–24).

He again formed a coalition with Seleukos, Kassandros, and Lysimachos (Justin 15.2.15–17), which led to the confrontation with Antigonos and Demetrios at Ipsos in 301 (Diod. 21.1.2; 21.1.4b). The defeat and death of Antigonos at Ipsos in 301, led to an increase in territory for Pt. and his allies (App. *Syr.* 55.280; cf. Polyb. 5.67.6–7 for the dispute over Koile-Syria; for the ambitions of the most powerful Successors see Nepos, *Eum.* 13.4; cf. Justin 13.1.15). Pt. complained that he had been given no share of Antigonos' kingdom, but Seleukos responded by pointing to Pt.'s failure participate in the battle itself; nevertheless, Seleukos did not try to take Koile-Syria by force because of his friendship (φιλία) towards Pt., saying he would consider how to deal with the matter in the future (Diod. 21.1.5). Victory at Ipsos, and the death of Antigonos, saw Seleukos ally himself with Demetrios, while Pt. found an ally in Lysimachos (Justin 15.4.23–4; cf. 16.2.1 for further problems with Demetrios). But as the fortunes of these houses changed, Pt. made a final marriage alliance (or, rather, put into effect an earlier agreement), sending Eurydike to Miletos with her daughter Ptolemais to marry Demetrios in 286/5. He used the opportunity to remove from court his jilted wife: Berenike had now supplanted her, and her son (the future Philadelphos) was recognized as co-ruler and heir in place of Eurydike's son before the year was out. He died in 283, at the age of 84 ([Lucian], *Macrob.* 12); but the story that he was murdered by his own son (Philadelphos) is almost certainly a fiction (Nepos, *De Regibus* 3.4) and at odds with Justin 16.2.7–9. In the period after Ipsos he scarcely ventured outside Egypt and, by the standards of the Diadochoi, he was militarily inactive.

Family and dynastic considerations. In 322/1, once Krateros and Antipatros were preparing to cross to Asia, Pt. made an alliance (περὶ κοινοπραγίας) with Antipatros, sealed by marriage to Eurydike (Diod. 18.25.4), whose cousin, Berenike, accompanied her and later became his mistress (Paus. 1.6.8). Earlier he had kept Thaïs (no. 1103) as his mistress and, probably, his wife, by whom he had three children: Lagos, Leontiskos, and Eirene (Athen. 13.576e). That he took his Persian bride Artakama to Egypt with him has been doubted, but there is no explicit evidence that he repudiated the marriage. By Eurydike (Paus. 1.6.8, 7.1, 9.7) he produced Ptolemy (later known as Keraunos; App. *Syr.* 62.330), Lysandra (Paus. 1.9.6), Ptolemais (Plut. *Demetr.* 46.3), Meleagros and, apparently, Argaios; Berenike's children were Arsinoë, Ptolemy (Ptolemy II: Paus. 1.1.1, 6.8; Theocr., *Id.* 17), and probably Philotera (see Ogden 68–73; Beloch IV² 2.186). For the origins of Theoxene see no. 1117. His dealings with Kratesipolis (no. 626) were political rather than personal (Diod. 20.37.1; Polyaenus 8.58). The kingship which he established in Egypt, officially in 306 or 305, devolved in 285 upon his son by Berenike, Ptolemy II (known as Philadelphos after his marriage to his sister Arsinoë). It appears that in the period of co-rule with Philadelphos (285–283), Pt. composed his *History of Alexander*, which was used extensively by Arrian (*Prooem.* 2), and to a lesser extent by Curtius; Errington 1969, however, proposes a much earlier date for the composition of the work. Berve II 329–35 no. 668; Volkmann, *RE* XXIII (1959) 1603–45 no. 18; Seibert 1969; Heckel 1992, 222–7; 2018a; and *Marshals*² 230–9; Bengtson 1975, 10–35; Pédech 1984, 215–22; Landucci, *Lisimaco* 1987. Collins 1997; Meeus 2014; Worthington 2016; Ager 2018 and 2020; Anson 2018; Lorber 2018; Howe 2008, 2013a–b; 2014, 2015b; and Howe (ed.) 2018; Müller, *LexAM* 448–53. For his historical work see Jacoby, *FGrH* 138; Strasburger 1934; Kornemann 1935; Pearson 188–211; Errington 1969; Roisman 1984. **Stemma X.**

1011 PTOLEMY

(Πτολεμαῖος). Macedonian (Tataki 421 no. 154). Nicknamed Keraunos (Paus. 1.16.2; Memnon 5.6: ἐπώνυμον διὰ τὴν σκαιότητα καὶ ἀπόνοιαν τὸν Κεραυνὸν ἔφερεν). Son of Ptolemy I Soter and Eurydike (App. *Syr.* 62.330). Born *c.*320/19. His siblings (from the same mother) were Lysandra (Paus. 1.16.2), Ptolemais, and Meleagros (whom Diod. 22.4 wrongly calls a *brother* of Ptolemy Soter) and possibly Theoxene (no. 1117; see Beloch IV² 2.178–9; but Ogden 70 thinks she was a daughter of Berenike and her first husband Philip). Pt. was for some time the putative heir to the Ptolemaic throne but left Egypt out of fear because Ptolemy I Soter was going to leave the kingdom to the younger Ptolemy (the future Philadelphos), son of Berenike (App. *Syr.* 62.330); if we take Appian literally, this occurred before (though perhaps not by much) the formal joint rule of Soter and Philadelphos in 285 (Prophyr. Tyr. *FGrH* 260 F2 §3). Although there is no explicit statement to this effect, Pt. may have left Egypt when his mother escorted Ptolemais to Miletos to marry Demetrios Poliorketes (now dated to 286/5; see no. 1005). Nep. *De Regibus* 3.4 is probably wrong in claiming that he was exiled (*a patre expulsum Alexandrea*). The standard view, combining the evidence of Memnon and Pausanias, is that Pt. went to the court of Lysimachos, looking for the support of Agathokles and Lysandra, and later killed Agathokles (in collusion with Arsinoë); subsequently (indeed, consequently) he fled to Seleukos. But App. *Syr.* 62.330 implies that he went directly to Seleukos, who took him in "as the unfortunate son of a friend" (echoed by Memnon 8.2, but in the wrong historical context), which despite the evidence of Paus. 1.16.2 that he went there from the court of Lysimachos (παρὰ Λυσιμάχου παρ' αὐτὸν [sc. Σέλευκον] πεφευγώς) and Memnon's assertion that he was the murderer of Agathokles (see below), ought not to be taken seriously. It is highly improbable that Pt. went to Lysimachos' court thinking he would find support for his claim to the Egyptian throne directly or indirectly from Lysandra and her husband Agathokles. And, if he did, why then conspire with the full sister of his rival Philadelphos (Memnon calls it an *epiboule*) and murder Agathokles? What need then to escape to the court of Seleukos with the very sister whose husband he had allegedly murdered? The instigator of the crime was Arsinoë—if Lysimachos himself was responsible for the death of his son (App. *Syr.* 64.341), it must have been at Arsinoë's urging—and, although Memnon attributes the act to Keraunos, the Ptolemy who committed the crime may have been Arsinoë's eldest son (thus Heinen 3–17). For the initial attempt to murder Agathokles by poison (Memnon 5.6: φαρμάκῳ), Arsinoë had no need of either her son or her half-brother to carry out the crime. One would be forced to conclude that Keraunos arrived in Lysimacheia only to discover that, as in Alexandria, the offspring of Berenike prevailed (on which see Heckel 1989). Pt. found himself once more without support and in rather grave danger. No extant source actually says that he fled from Lysimachos' court *with* Lysandra and others of her "faction" to Seleukos in 283/2; Paus. 1.10.4 speaks of Lysandra's brothers (the plural need not be taken literally) "who were taking refuge with Ptolemy." This appears to be a garbled version of events. Perhaps it refers to only Meleagros (no. 698) and the probability that he left Egypt at the same time as Keraunos (possibly, she found him in Miletos with their mother). In truth, it is more likely that Pt. went directly to the man who was most able (and probably most inclined) to help him depose his rival after Soter's death (cf. Memnon 8.2, anachronistic but otherwise accurate); indeed, Seleukos (and his son Antiochos) will have met Keraunos during the years of exile (315-312). App. *Syr.* 62.330 says Seleukos cared for Pt. at his court, unwittingly housing the man who would murder him. After Koroupedion, Pt. repaid his benefactor by stabbing him in the back and killing him not far from Lysimacheia (App. *Syr.* 62; Nepos, *De Regibus* 3.4). Hence, he won a throne despite a series of setbacks. He ransomed Seleukos' body to Philetairos of Pergamon (App. *Syr.* 63.335). In 281/0, Pt. entered into negotiations with Arsinoë, offering to make her queen and to protect her sons if she married him. For these events and Pt.'s murder of two of Arsinoë's sons in Kassandreia see Justin 24.2.6–3.9; also s.v. Arsinoë (no. 221); Carney 49–64. He refused to negotiate with the Gauls and rashly engaged them, not waiting for reinforcements, and thus was defeated and killed (Diod. 22.3, attributing this to Pt.'s youth, but he was about 40 at the time; Plut. *Pyrrh.* 22.2). Volkmann, *RE* XXIII.2 (1959) 1597–9 no. 15; Sandberger 195–8 no. 71; Heinen 3–94. **Stemma X.**

1012 PTOLEMY

(Πτολεμαῖος). Macedonian (Tataki 416 no. 116). Son of Ptolemy I Soter and Berenike (Paus. 1.6.8). Ruled jointly with his father from 285 to 283 and was later known, as a result of his marriage to his full sister, Arsinoë II (Strabo 10.2.22 C460), as Philadelphos (*regn.* 283–245). Born in 309/8 on the island of Kos (*Marm. Par.* B§19; Theocr. 17.58; Callimachus, *Hymn to Delos* 182–8), he was some eight years younger than his sister Arsinoë; two other siblings are known: Philotera and Theoxene (see s.vv.). His designation as Soter's heir appears to have been delayed until he neared or reached adulthood; for when, soon after Kassandros' death in 297, Demetrios of Phaleron came to Alexandria, he (unwisely, as it turned out) urged Soter to favor the elder Ptolemy (later known as Keraunos) as his heir. Although Pt. ruled together with his father for almost two years, there was a report, clearly false, that he murdered him (Nepos, *De Regibus* 3.4; *contra* Justin 16.2.7–9). Probably at the beginning of their joint regency (285), Pt. married Arsinoë, the daughter of Lysimachos, who bore him three children—Lysimachos (cf. Polyb. 15.25.2, with Walbank, *HCP* 481), Berenike and the later Ptolemy III Euergetes (schol. Theocr. 17.128)—before she was banished for conspiring against her husband in the early 270s (Schol. Theocr. 17.128). As sole ruler, Pt. was content to engage in political intrigue, preferring negotiation to war; certainly, he did not personally lead armies against his opponents. Bouché-Leclercq, *Lagides* I 141–243; Bevan, *Ptolemaic Dynasty* 56–78; McKechnie and Guillaume 2008. **Stemma X.**

1013 PTOLEMY

(Πτολεμαῖος). Macedonian (Tataki 421 no. 155). Son of Lysimachos and Arsinoë (later Arsinoë II Philadelphos); eldest of three sons, of whom the younger ones were Lysimachos and Philip. He was born, in all likelihood in 299 or 298 (see Beloch IV² 2.130). Since the children of Arsinoë now rivaled those of Nikaia for the succession, it has been argued plausibly by Heinen 10–12 that Memnon 5.6 mistakenly attributes the murder of Agathokles to Ptolemy Keraunos (or, at least, that the reference to Keraunos was not in the original work of Nymphis of Heraclea), when it is most likely that Arsinoë's son enacted the crime, doubtless at his mother's urging. In 280 he openly and vociferously opposed his mother's decision to marry her half-brother, Ptolemy Keraunos (Justin 24.2.10). He was thus not present in Kassandreia and escaped death at the hands of his new stepfather (cf. Justin 24.3.5–9). He appears to have sought refuge with Monunios the Illyrian at the time of the Gallic invasion (Tarn, *AG* 135) and perhaps held the kingship of Macedon briefly after Sosthenes (Diod. 22.4). For Ptolemy son of Lysimachos at Telmessos see (*OGIS* 55 = Austin² no. 270). Volkmann, *RE* XXIII (1959) 1596–7 no. 13; Carney, *Arsinoë* 125; Heinen 1972. **Stemma IX.**

1014 PTOLEMY

(Πτολεμαῖος). Son of Pyrrhos and Antigone, named in honor of Antigone's stepfather Ptolemy Soter (Plut. *Pyrrh.* 6.1; 9.3), and thus a departure from the naming practices of the Aiakids (cf. Nilsson 1909, 8). Born in 296/5 (Justin 18.1.3 says he was fifteen in 280), he was older than his brothers Alexander II and Helenos (cf. Plut. *Pyrrh.* 9.3). The father had emphasized the military arts, and it appears that the sons were educated accordingly (Plut. *Pyrrh.* 9.4–6; cf. *Mor.* 184c), and thus Pt. with only 60 men captured Kerkyra, having also seized a quinquireme, which he boarded with only seven men (Justin 25.4.8); these exploits appear to belong to the same campaign, and have been dated, on the evidence that the Tarentines had given Pyrrhos naval support against Kerkyra (Paus. 1.12.1), to 281 (thus Lévêque 1957, 175–6; cf. Sandberger 199 n.1). But Niese II 54 more plausibly suggests that this occurred during Pt.'s regency in his father's absence (280–275, see below). When his father crossed into Italy in 280, taking his younger brothers with him, Pt. was left behind as *custos regni* (Justin 18.1.3); the earlier claim that Ptolemy Keraunos was to be *vindex regni* (Justin 17.2.15) probably means that he was to act as an external protector of the kingdom that Pt. was managing. I see no need to assume that Justin, who also mentions a marriage bond between Keraunos' daughter and Pyrrhos, is mistaken (thus Sandberger 199 n.3; cf. Hammond 1988b, who believes in the confusion of three different Ptolemies). Nothing is known of his activities in his father's absence, but the argument from silence suggests (rightly or wrongly) that affairs in northwestern Greece were relatively stable in that time. Soon after Pyrrhos' return from Italy, he waged war with Antigonos Gonatas, whom he drove out of his kingdom (Justin 25.3.5–7); when Gonatas returned with an army, he was decisively defeated by Pt. (probably in 273; Justin 25.3.8). In 272, Pt. accompanied Pyrrhos to Sparta (Plut. *Pyrrh.* 28.2; 30.5); the kingdom was at that time assigned to Alexander II. In the attack on Spartan defenses, Pt., with 2,000 Galatians and a picked force of Chaonians, attempted to move around the trench which the defenders had fortified with carts, buried up to their axles in the earth; unable to dig them out and attacked by a force led by Akrotatos, Pt.'s troops were forced to withdraw (Plut. *Pyrrh.* 28.1–4). Like his father (Plut. *Pyrrh.* 8.4), he was reckless in the face of danger: Justin 25.4.9 says that he burst into the center of Sparta, only to be overwhelmed and killed (possibly confusing the circumstances of his father's death in Argos); but Plutarch places his death at the time when Pyrrhos' rearguard was being harassed by Spartan ambushes on the road to Argos. Pyrrhos sent Pt. back to help out. But Pt.'s troops were attacked by a force led by Eualkos the Spartan, and Oroissos the Kretan killed Pt. with his spear (Plut. *Pyrrh.* 30.5–6). Justin 25.3.10 aptly remarks that Pyrrhos said Pt.'s death came later than both he himself had feared or his recklessness demanded. His death and that of his father soon afterwards placed Alexander II securely on the Molossian throne. Sandberger 198–201 no. 72; Volkmann, *RE* XXIII.2 (1959) 1599–1600 no. 16; Hammond 1988b. **Stemma IIb.**

PYGMALION. See PYMIATHON.

1015 PYMIATHON

(Πυμιάθων). King of Kition; apparently the son and successor of Melekiaton (for the form Pymiathon, see Head, *HN*² 788; Athen. 4.167c has πυμάτωνι, emended by Kaibel to Πυγμαλίωνι; cf. Diod. 19.79.4, incorrectly Pygmalion). Born at least by the late 380s, he acceded to the throne *c*.362/1. Among his possessions was Tamassos, an area rich in copper, which he had purchased for fifty talents from its bankrupt king, (otherwise unknown), who subsequently retired into private life in Amathos (Douris *ap.* Athen. 4.167c = *FGrH* 76 F4). That the territory in question was Tamassos seems to be confirmed by *CIS* I 10–11 (cf. Hill 1949, 150 n.2; *CIS* I 10 dates to the twenty-first year of P.'s reign (342/1) and mentions it as one of his possessions; *CIS* I 11, from the thirty-seventh year (326/5), no longer includes Tamassos). P. appears not to have given Alexander his whole-hearted support (perhaps he did not report to Alexander at Sidon as the other Kyprian kings had done; cf. Arr. 2.20.3), but sought instead to buy the King's favor by sending him a splendid sword (Plut. *Alex.* 32.10). Alexander allowed him to retain his throne, although P. did not mint coins independently until after Alexander's death (Head, *HN*² 788; cf. Bagnall 1976, 187–8), but gave Tamassos as a gift to Pnytagoras (Douris, *FGrH* 76 F4). P. remained in power in Kition until 312. In 315 he entered into negotiations with Antigonos Monophthalmos through the agency of Agesilaos (Diod. 19.57.4; cf. Olshausen 1974, 87 no. 62) and agreed to an alliance (Diod. 19.59.1). When Ptolemy counterattacked in 312, the Kypriot rulers who had gone over to Antigonos came to terms, but P., who held out, was put to death (Diod. 19.79.4; cf. also Hill 1949, 159 n.5). Berve II 339–40 no. 680; Hill I 151–2, 158–9; Bosworth I 243–4.

1016 PYRGOTELES

(Πυργοτέλης). Greek engraver. His depictions of Alexander were regarded as so authentic that he was allegedly the only artist whom the King allowed to portray him in this medium (Pliny, *HN* 7.125, 37.8; Apul. *Flor.* 7; Stewart 1993, T54 and 154). He may have been responsible for the Alexander with "horns of Amun" images on the Lysimachos coinage and the Ashmolean quartz ringstone of the same type (Pollitt 1986, 26), but this is speculation at best. Except for Alexander's favor, Pyrgoteles is virtually unknown otherwise (Stewart 1993, 35–6). Berve II 340 no. 681 (inaccurate); Pollitt 217–18.

1017 PYRRHON

(Πύρρων). Son of Pleistarchos. Philosopher from Elis (Strabo 9.1.8 C393) and founder of Scepticism. His life spanned the years *c*.365–275, and his career is summarized by Diog. Laert. 9.61–108, followed by *Suda* Π 3238. P. was originally a painter but then studied philosophy under Bryson. He went on Alexander's expedition in the company of Anaxarchos of Abdera. As a result of his travels he was influenced by the Gymnosophists (Diog. Laert. 9.61, 63) and the Magi. Alexander gave him ten thousand pieces of gold the first time he met him (Plut. *Mor.* 331e, a passage that illustrates Alexander's fondness for philosophers). On the confused stories concerning intellectuals and artists in Alexander's entourage see Berve II 340. Berve II 340 no. 682; Long 1974, 79–80; *OCD*³ 1283 s.v. "Pyrrhon." On Pyrrhon and Pyrrhonism see Long and Sedley I 13–24.

1018 PYRRHOS

(Πύρρος). [All references in **boldface** are to Plutarch's *Life of Pyrrhos*.] King of Epeiros. Son of Aiakides (*Syll*³ 369; Paus. 3.6.3) and Phthia (daughter of Menon of Pharsalos), grandson of Arybbas (whose death is probably misdated by Diod. 16.72.1) and thus also a kinsman of Olympias, Alexander the Great and Alexander I of Epeiros (**1.5–6**; cf. Justin 17.3.14; Paus. 1.9.8, 11.1; cf. Gellius *NA* 10.16.16); he had two sisters, Troas and Deidameia (**1.7**). He married Antigone (no. 114), daughter of Berenike and her first husband Philip, shortly before his return to power in Epeiros in 297 (**4.7**), who bore him Ptolemaios (**6.1**, **9.3**) and Olympias (Justin 28.1.1); after Antigone's death, P. married Agathokles' daughter Lanassa (no. 640), who was the mother of Alexander (**9.3**; Athen. 3.73b); two further marriages to Illyrian women—Birkenna (no. 299), daughter of Bardylis and mother of Helenos, and the daughter of Autoleon (**9.3**). Unless Justin 17.2.15 confuses Ptolemy I and Ptolemy Keraunos, it appears that P. also married a daughter of the latter in 280.

Born in 318, P. narrowly escaped from Epeiros when his father was driven from power in 317/16; he was taken to Megara in Macedonia by men loyal to Aiakides (**2.1–8**: see s.vv. Androkleion, Hippias, and Neandros). The story that a man named Achilleus carried him across a swollen river into Macedonia (**2.8**) is probably fiction based on the fact that the Pyrrhos of legend was the son of Achilles (Schubert, *Pyrrhos* 27, 111). From Megara he was taken to Glaukias, king of the Illyrians, where he impressed both the king and his wife (her name was Beroa, or possibly Beroia, and she was an Aiakid: Justin 17.3.19) and was brought up in their household together with their own children (**3.1–5**; Justin 17.3.19–20), despite the fact that Kassandros offered him 200 talents to give the boy up (**3.5**; cf. Paus. 1.11.5). Even after suffering a defeat at Kassandros' hands, Glaukias did not give the boy up (Diod. 19.67.6) and it appears that he adopted him after Aiakides' death (Justin 17.3.20). Glaukias helped restore P. to his ancestral throne in 306, when he was in his twelfth year (Justin 17.3.21). P. ruled Epeiros until 302/1, when at the age of seventeen he attended the wedding of one of Glaukias' sons, and it was on that occasion that the Epeirots expelled him and put Neoptolemos II on the throne (**4.1–2**). P. now attached himself to Demetrios Poliorketes, who had married his sister Deidameia (**4.3**; their wedding took place in Argos in 303: Plut. *Demetr.* 25.2), and accompanied Demetrios to Ipsos. Here he fought with distinction, routing those forces directly opposed to him (**4.4**). After the battle, P. kept the cities of Greece which Demetrios had garrisoned loyal to him (**4.5**; cf. Plut. *Demetr.* 31.2).

When Demetrios finally came to terms with Ptolemy (298?), P. was sent to Egypt as a hostage, impressing Ptolemy with his skill at hunting and his physical prowess and charming his wife, Berenike (**4.5–6**). Eventually, he married Antigone, Berenike's daughter by her previous husband (**4.7**), although it is clear that the marriage had more to do with politics and Ptolemy's interests in Greece than Berenike's attachment to the young man. Soon after the marriage, P. regained Epeiros with Ptolemy's help (**5.1**; Paus. 1.6.8, 11.5), and he later founded the city of Berenicis on the Epeirot Chersonese (near modern Preveza; for the location see Hammond, *Epirus* 578–9) in honor of his mother-in-law and named his first born son Ptolemy (**6.1**; cf. **9.3**).

Returning to Epeiros, P. at first agreed to share the throne with Neoptolemos II. Later (perhaps in 296) P. met him at Passaron in Molossian territory (**5.1**), for by now Neoptolemos had made himself unpopular with the Epeirots and P. feared that they would call in one of the other "kings" (5.2–3). During the sojourn in Passaron, P. uncovered a conspiracy against him which was used to justify the murder of Neoptolemos at a dinner party (5.4–14). The alleged conspiracy may, in fact, have been fabricated after the fact to exculpate P. Once firmly re-established in his kingdom, P. began to interfere in Macedonian affairs. The death of Antigone presented P. with the opportunity of consolidating his power in the Adriatic by marrying Lanassa, who brought as her dowry Kerkyra, from which her father Agathokles had expelled Kassandros (9.2; Diod. 21.4; cf. Diod. 21.2.1–3 for Agathokles' campaign). At about this time, P. gained control of much of the coastline, including southern Illyria (App. *Illyr.* 7; cf. Hammond, *Epirus* 586–7). The marriage to Lanassa was, however, of short duration and she soon abandoned P. in favor of Demetrios, to whom she now offered control of Kerkyra. P. responded by attacking the island and securing it against his rival (Paus. 1.11.6)

When Antipatros, the son of Kassandros and Thessalonike, killed his mother and drove his brother Alexander into exile, Alexander appealed to P., although he had already summoned Demetrios Poliorketes (6.3; Plut. *Demetr.* 36.1). P. came to his aid but demanded (and obtained) in compensation Tymphaia and Parauaia, along with Ambrakia, Akarnania, and Amphilocheia (6.4); these were garrisoned by P., who went on to deprive Antipatros of his share of Macedonia (6.5). Lysimachos supported Antipatros and tried to make peace with P., after allegedly attempting to deceive him with a forged letter from Ptolemy. But P. was warned by the seer Theodotos, who saw an ill omen in the religious sacrifices that accompanied the ceremony, and declined to make peace with Lysimachos and Antipatros (6.6–9). At an unspecified point, apparently after the death of Deidameia, P. took control of Thessaly, an act that caused enmity between him and Demetrios Poliorketes (7.3). Although Plutarch implies that this preceded Demetrios' intervention in Macedonia, it probably follows his recognition as king there. P. took advantage of a report that Demetrios was ill and marched into Macedonia, but although he met with little opposition, he lost the goodwill of the Macedonians by allowing his troops to plunder (10.2–5). Since Demetrios was anxious to return to Asia to recover his father's kingdom, he made an agreement with P. But P. was encouraged by the other kings to abandon Demetrios. And, when Lysimachos invaded Upper Macedonia and Demetrios turned to deal with him, P. marched to Beroia and favorable reports about him and his leadership caused Demetrios' forces to defect (11; Justin 16.2.1–3 says this happened when Demetrios left for Asia and says that P. bribed the forces of his enemy). P. formed an alliance with Lysimachos, Ptolemy and Seleukos, and when Demetrios took his forces to Asia, he used the opportunity to bribe Demetrios' forces and seize the kingdom of Macedon (Justin 16.2.1–3). But after Demetrios' defeat in Asia, Lysimachos did not remain idle; for he killed Antipatros (Justin 16.2.4) and drove P. out of Macedonia (Justin 16.3.1–2). Under pressure from Lysimachos, P. divided the kingdom of Macedon. P. went to Athens and visited the acropolis; while he was there he advised the Athenians not to allow any of the kings into their city (according to Paus. 1.11.1, the Athenians erected a statue of him). Lysimachos, however, attacked P. and drove him out of Macedonia. Soon after he returned to Epeiros, Lysimachos was killed at Koroupedion, and not long after that his conqueror, Seleukos, fell victim to Ptolemy Keraunos. By this time, P. was lured into new undertakings by the Tarentines. Antigonos Gonatas, Keraunos, and Antiochos, fighting over the inheritance were happy to see him go: they offered support in the form of money, troops, and ships. Keraunos was even said to have proposed a marriage alliance, which saw P. wed his daughter (A101; Justin 17.2.11–15; Heinen 71–2 with nn. 273–4; also Manni 1949, 107–8, 112; I see no merit in Hammond 1988b, a convoluted and unoriginal solution to a non-problem). For his campaigns in Italy and Sicily see **13.4–26.1**; also Kent 2020, with additional ancient sources and modern literature.

When he returned from the West in 274, P. did not remain idle for long. He was invited by Kleonymos to invade Sparta (**26.15**; Paus. 3.6.3; cf. Plut. *Mor.* 219f, for his encounter with the Spartan envoy, Derkylidas). P. pretended friendship with the Spartans before attacking them (Polyaenus 6.6.2; cf. 6.6.3, he regularly used non-military means to supplement warfare; for the campaign see **27–30**). The Spartans were inspired by the bravery of their women (Polyaenus 8.49). As P. set out for Argos by night, an owl landed on his spear and would not leave him; it was an ill omen; P. died an inglorious death in Argos (Ael. *NA* 10.37); killed by a roof tile thrown by an Argive woman (Polyaenus 8.68); for the Argos campaign see **31.1–34.6**). According to Pausanias, there was a memorial to P. in the city of Argos, showing the battles of the king and his elephants; but P.'s bones were buried in the sanctuary of Demeter, near which he died, where there is a bronze shield of P. hung over the door (Paus. 2.21.5). A story is told that P.'s eagle was consumed on his funeral pyre, see Pollux 5.42, Pliny *NH* 10.18, 8.144 (Plut. *Mor* 970c). His ashes in a golden urn were given by Antigonos Gonatas to Helenos to take to his brother Alexander II in Epeiros (Val. Max. 5.1 ext. 4).

Personal aspects. Plutarch comments on P.'s physical features (**3.6–9**): his teeth appeared to be defined as if notches had been cut into a single bone; and he had special powers in his big toe to heal diseases of the spleen—indeed, when he was cremated that toe did not burn (**3.9**; Pliny *HN* 7.2 [20] says it was preserved in a chest and stored in a temple; cf. Val. Max. Nepotiani Epit. 9.24). He was mild and considerate when it came to his friends (**8.8–9**) and lenient towards his political opponents or those who spoke candidly about him (**8.10–11**); as a result, his charm won the affection of Berenike of Egypt (**4.5–7, 6.1**) and the approval of Ptolemy Soter, who of course employed him against his enemies. His personal valor was undisputed and often on display on the battlefield (at Ipsos, **4.4**; against Pantauchos, **7.4–9**; in the early stages of the battle of Heraclea, **16.10–11**), to the point that he disregarded danger (**16.12**), and also in other situations (during a storm on the Adriatic, **15.3–7**, reminiscent of Alexander's alleged battle with the Indos). He delighted in being called and compared to the eagle (**10.1**; Plut. *Mor.* 184d, 975b; cf. Ael. *NA* 7.45 [iii]; Plut. *Aristeides* 6.2) and even had a pet eagle, which abstained from food after the king's death and thus followed him to the afterlife (Ael. *NA* 2.40). Frequently compared with his kinsman, Alexander (**8.2**), especially for his recklessness and conduct in battle, P. was ranked by Antigonos Gonatas and Hannibal among the greatest of generals (**8.4–6**). He regarded military ability as superior to other arts (**8.6–7**). His character is illuminated by the *apophthegmata* attributed to him (Plut. *Mor.* 184c–d; cf. Val. Max. 5.1 ext. 3a). The numerous stories about P. that involve animals tell us very little of importance about the king. Ael. *NA* 2.40; 7.10, 41; Pliny, *HN* 8.142; Plut. *Mor.* 969c–d. Billows 431 no. 103; Kienast, *RE* XXIV (1963) 108–65 no. 13; Bengtson 1975, 91–109; Lévêque 1957; Garoufalias; Champion 2009; Heckel, *LexAM* 454. **Stemma IIb.**

1019 PYTHEAS

(Πυθέας). Athenian orator and demagogue (Kirchner no 12342); hence not surprisingly depicted as of low origin (*Suda* Π 3125) and of unscrupulous character (Ael. *VH* 14.28;

Plut. *Phoc.* 21.2; Dem. *Ep.* 3.30). Born perhaps *c.*360, he was a supporter of Antipatros, with whom he had on at least two occasions taken refuge (*Suda* Π 3125; Plut. *Dem.* 27.2), and, perhaps for that reason, opposed to the granting of divine honors to Alexander (Plut. *Mor.* 804b); he was thus also an opponent of Demosthenes and Demades (Athen. 2.44e–f). At some point before 324, he and Lykourgos prosecuted a certain Simmias, who was defended by Hypereides (Hyper. frg. 62 [Burtt], cited by Harpocration); Deinarchos composed a speech against him *Concerning the Affairs of the Marketplace* (Περὶ τῶν κατὰ τὸ ἐμπόριον. Din. frg. 3 [Burtt]). In 324, he was one of those who brought charges against Demosthenes in the Harpalos bribery scandal ([Plut.] *Mor.* 846c; Dem. *Ep.* 3.29). P. was supposed to have been criticized for being too young to speak on the issue of Alexander's deification, but pointed out that he was older than the man who was being honored ([Plut.] *Mor.* 804b; cf. [Plut.] *Mor.* 784c and Plut. *Phoc.* 21.2 for P.'s relative youth). In 323/2 he was entrusted by the city with the traditional sacrifices at Delphi (Dem. *Ep.* 3.30). After Alexander's death he belonged to the *philoi kai presbeis* who went round the Peloponnese urging states to remain loyal to Macedon and not join a Greek uprising (Plut. *Dem.* 27.2), and in Arkadia he openly debated with Demosthenes, without success, it appears (Plut. *Dem.* 27.4–5; cf. Phylarchos, *FGrH* 81 F75). Berve II 337–8 no 675.

1020 PYTHIONIKE

(Πυθιονίκη). P.'s family background is unknown. She was, according to Theopompos (*FGrH* 115 F253 = Athen. 13.595a), a slave of the *hetaira* Bacchis and became a courtesan first in Korinth and then Athens (Paus. 1.37.5); reputedly the most glamorous *hetaira* of her time (Diod. 17.108.5). Her name comes up in the comedies of Antiphanes (Athen. 8.339a), Alexis (Athen. 8.339c–d), who says that the sons of Chairephilos the fish seller were among her lovers, and Timokles (Athen. 8.339d), adding that Anytos also enjoyed her favors. She may have met Harpalos in 333/2, during his first flight from Alexander's camp (cf. Arr. 3.6.7), at which time Harpalos spent some time in the Megarid. At some point after 330, when Harpalos was securely in charge of the imperial treasures, she joined him in Babylon, where Alexander's treasurer lavished gifts upon her and treated her like a queen, and after death erected a magnificent tomb for her of the Attic type (Diod. 17.108.5) and a similar monument near Eleusis (Paus. 1.37.5; Athen. 13.595b; cf. Dikaiarchos *ap.* Athen. 13.594f; mentioned also by Plut. *Phoc* 22.2, who says that it does not merit the 30 talents that Charikles charged Harpalos for the project); according to Theopompos (*FGrH* 115 F 253 = Athen. 13.595c), he also set up a shrine where she was worshipped as Pythionike Aphrodite. She bore him a daughter (Plut. *Phoc.* 22.1), who after Harpalos' death was raised in the home of Charikles, a kinsman of Phokion (Plut. *Phoc.* 22.3). P. and Harpalos were the subjects of a satyr play performed in front of the army in Asia (see Python no. 1023 below). Berve II 338 no. 676: Müller 2006; *PAA* 793690.

1021 PYTHODOROS

(Πυθόδωρος). Athenian. Torchbearer (i.e. priest) of the Mysteries of Eleusis, P. was the only one to oppose Demetrios Poliorketes' request to be initiated into all the stages of the mysteries. His objections were to no avail (Plut. *Demetr.* 26.3).

1022 PYTHOKLES

(Πυθοκλῆς). Son of Pythodoros (Kirchner 12444). Condemned to death along with Phokion in 318 (Plut. *Phoc.* 35.5).

1023 PYTHON

(Πύθων). Greek poet from Katane or Byzantion (Athen. 2.50f, 13.595e), allegedly the author of the satyr play *Agen*, which satirized the activities of Harpalos in Babylon (Kleitarchos, *FGrH* 137 F30 = Athen. 13.586c–d; cf. Theopompos, *FGrH* 115 F254) and, according to Athenaeus, was produced at the Hydaspes River. It seems virtually impossible the performance could have taken place in India (although this is accepted by Snell 1964, 113–17), since the play speaks of Harpalos' affair with Pythionike, who was by this time dead, of Harpalos' treatment of Glykera in Tarsos and Rhossos (see Glykera no. 478), and his dealings with the Athenians. This makes it likely that the play was written after Harpalos' flight: indeed, it would perhaps not have been safe to criticize Alexander's *hetairos* before that time. Droysen I³ 406 n. 101 suggested the Choaspes River, and Goukowsky II, 77 and Bosworth 1988, 149 believe it was produced in Karmania in 324. But Beloch IV² 2.434–6 thinks of the Medus Hydaspes (Virgil, *Georgics* 4.211), possibly the Carcheh is meant. Identification of the poet with Python of Byzantion, the highly regarded orator in the service of Philip II (Aesch. 2.125; cf. *Suda* Π 3139), is unlikely. Berve II 338–9 no. 677; Snell 1964, 99–138, for the *Agen*.

1024 PYTHON

(Πτολεμαῖος). Greek. As a young man, P. was the *eromenos* of the flute player Euios. Kassandros is said to have kissed P. against his wishes and thus incurred Alexander's displeasure (Plut. *Mor.* 180f). The story appears to have been set in the last year of Alexander's life, probably in Babylon, and belongs to a set of anecdotes that illustrate the king's hostility towards Kassandros, who did not participate in the Asiatic campaign but joined Alexander in 323. Euios too is not attested before 324. Berve II 339 is probably correct in identifying him with the famous flute player of Pyrrhos' time, apparently a rival of Kaphisias (Plut. *Mor.* 184c; *Pyrrh.* 8.7). Berve II 339 no. 678; Sandberger 201–2 no. 73.

R

RHADAPHERNES. See s.v. **PHRATAPHERNES.**

1025 RHEBOULAS

('Ρηβούλας). Son of Seuthes III, younger brother of Kotys (*IG* II² 349; Schwenk no. 45). Rh. and Kotys had both been honored earlier with citizenship (Dem. 23.118). Rh. was sent to Athens in 330, in the archonship of Aristophanes, by his father, perhaps in the context of the unrest in Thrake (see s.vv. Memnon no. 703; Zopyrion no. 1174), although it is difficult to see a clear connection with the later Odrysian uprising (Curt. 10.1.45). Berve II 346 no. 686; Beloch III² 2. 89–91.

1026 RHEOMITHRES

('Ρεομίθρης). For the name ("to whom Mithra is friendly") see Justi 260. Noble Persian, father of Phrasaortes—who was appointed satrap of Persis in 330 (Arr. 3.18.11)—and other children, who along with their mother were left as hostages with the Egyptian ruler Tachos, whom Rh. betrayed in 362 during the Satraps' Revolt (Xen. *Cyr.* 8.8.4; Diod. 15.92.1ff.). This identification was rejected by Leuze (1935, 403 n.1; cf. Atkinson I 231) without compelling chronological arguments; a birthdate for Rh. in the mid-380s is perfectly compatible with all the other evidence (Justi 260; cf. Bosworth I 111). He commanded 2,000 cavalry on the right wing (between 1,000 Medes and 2,000 Baktrians) at the Granikos River (Diod. 17.19.4; cf. Arr. 1.12.8); after that battle he joined Dareios III and fought at Issos, where he lost his life (Arr. 2.11.8; Curt. 3.11.10; Diod. 17.34.5). Judeich 205–6; Berve II 346 no. 685; Briant 663–4, 674; Shayegan 119 no. 94.

1027 RHOISAKES

('Ροισάκης, 'Ρωσάκης). Persian nobleman and brother of Spithridates (Diod. 17.20.6), satrap of Lydia and Ionia under Dareios III (Arr. 1.12.8; cf. Diod. 17.20.2), Rh. was descended from the "Seven" Persians (Diod. 16.47.2). The Spithridates (*fl.* 400) of Xenophon (*HG* 3.4.10; 4.1.3, 20, 26–7), who was active in Hellespontine Phrygia and Paphlagonia, may have belonged to the same family; possibly he was Rh.'s grandfather. Berve's view (II 346; accepted by Hamilton 40) that he held the satrapy around 344/3 (Diod. 16.47.1– 2) assumes that Rh. was deposed, for an unspecified reason, and yet fought gallantly at the side of his brother, who had replaced him. Beloch's assumption (III² 2.137; followed by Bosworth I 111–12), that the satrap of 344/3 was the father of both Spithridates and the younger Rh. is preferable. If these assumptions about the family are correct, we may postulate a birthdate *c.*370 for the younger Rh. In the battle at the Granikos, Rh. struck Alexander on the helmet but was himself killed by the King (Arr. 1.16.7, by a lance; Plut. *Alex.* 16.8, 11, by Alexander's sword, with Spithridates striking the King's helmet); Kleitos cut off the arm of his brother, as he intended to deal Alexander a fatal blow (Arr. 1.16.8; Plut. *Alex.* 16.8–11; Curt. 8.1.20 and Diod. 17.20.1–7 have reversed things somewhat, with

Rh. losing his arm and life to Kleitos, though he nevertheless strikes Alexander's helmet; according to Diod. 17.20.6, he splits the King's helmet and inflicts a scalp wound). Berve II 346 no. 687; Justi 262; Shayegan 119 no. 95.

1028 RHOXANE

('Ρωξάνη. Roshanak: "Little Star," so Rawlinson 1912, 46 n.2). The daughter of Oxyartes, a Sogdianian noble (Arr. *ap.* Phot. Bibl. 68b; Dexippos, *FGrH* 100 F8 §5; Metz Epit. 118, 121; Diod. 18.3.3; 19.48.2; Paus. 1.6.3; Curt. 10.3.11; Strabo 11.11.4 C517); wrongly identified as daughter of Dareios III in the *Alexander Romance* (Ps.-Call. 2.20.11, 22.3; cf. also Malalas 8.194). Rh. was born not long before 342; for she was of marriageable age in late 328, when she took refuge, together with her mother and sisters, at the fortress of Sisimithres (Strabo 11.11.4 C517; Schwarz 83), whose surrender was negotiated by Oxyartes himself (Curt. 8.2.25–31, "Oxartes"). After his campaign against the Sakai, Alexander was entertained by Sisimithres (Chorienes, Metz Epit. 28; Curt. 8.4.19 MSS *cohortandus*) and on that occasion (spring 327; cf. Niese I 122 n.1; Beloch IV² 1.25) he met Rhoxane, who was among 30 maidens introduced at the banquet (Curt. 8.4.23; cf. Metz Epit. 28–9; Arr. 4.18.4, 19.4–5 wrongly places her capture on the Rock of Ariamazes, which was taken by Alexander in the spring of 328). Arrian calls it the "Sogdian Rock" and dates its capture to the spring of 327; Curt. 7.11 puts the capture of Ariamazes in its proper context, sometime before the summer in which Kleitos was murdered. In Kleitos' criticisms of Alexander there is no mention of the marriage to Rh.—which suggests that the marriage had not yet occurred in mid-328. Different is the interpretation of Bosworth 1981, 31 n.98, who thinks that Rh. was captured on the Rock of Ariamazes and married on that of Chorienes. But Bosworth rejects the identification of Chorienes and Sisimithres. According to the romantic tradition Alexander was so impressed by her beauty—she was reputed to be the most beautiful woman in Asia after the wife of Dareios (Arr. 4.19.5; cf. Curt. 8.4.25)— that he married her (Plut. *Alex.* 47.7–8; Plut. *Mor.* 332e, 338d; Curt. 8.2.26–9; Metz Epit. 29–31; the wedding was painted by Apelles: see Lucian, *Imag.* 7; *Herodotus* 4–6; cf. Pollitt 175–6; also Schwarz 82; Renard and Servais 1955). But the chief motive will have been political: the marriage helped to end the opposition to him in the northeast (Hamilton 129–30; cf. Curt. 10.3.11); Curtius compares her with Briseis for literary effect (8.4.26). Rhoxane bore a son (A87), who appears to have been stillborn or to have died within days of his birth at the Akesines River in autumn 326 (Metz Epit. 70); the silence of the other extant sources carries little weight. Otherwise we know nothing of Rhoxane during the campaign until the last days of Alexander's life. She may have influenced her husband's decision to give Oxyartes the satrapy of the Parapamisadai (or Paropanisadai) in 325 (Arr. 6.15.3; cf. Curt. 9.8.9–10, confused).

Rh.'s political value was undoubtedly diminished when Alexander married Stateira, daughter of Dareios III, and Parysatis, daughter of Ochos (Arr. 7.4.4 = Aristoboulos, *FGrH* 139 F52, calling Stateira "Barsine") at Sousa in 324; but in October (Justin 13.2.5) or December (Curt. 10.6.9) she became pregnant with Alexander's child, whose birthright she sought to protect by murdering Stateira and her sister, Drypetis, soon after Alexander's death in early June 323 (Plut. *Alex.* 77.6); whether she had a role in Parysatis' death (assuming, as many scholars do, that she was also killed at this time) is unclear. The tender scenes of Rh. and Alexander during his final days are romanticized by the author of the *Liber de Morte* and perhaps exaggerated in the interests of the claims of

Alexander IV (*LM* 101–2; 110; 112; Ps.-Call. 3.32.4–7; cf. Arr. 7.27.3), but there is no good reason to deny that the two felt genuine love for each other; and, if Curtius' date for Rh.'s conception is correct (10.6.9), then Alexander may have turned to her for consolation, as Green 1991, 467 notes, when Hephaistion died in October of 324.

The status of Rh.'s child became a matter of great contention, both because of uncertainty about the unborn child's sex and Rh.'s "Persian" origin (Justin 13.2.5–6, 9; Curt. 10.6.9, 13–14); but a compromise was reached, whereby Rh.'s child, if male, should become *symbasileus* with Philip III Arrhidaios (Arr. *Succ.* 1.1, 1.8; Dexippos 1, 5; somewhat different is App. *Syr.* 52.261; Heid. Epit. 1), a fact supported by the epigraphic evidence (*OGIS* 1.4) but denied by the author of the *Liber de'Morte* (*LM* 115; Ps.-Call. 3.33.13). For the son see s.v. Alexander no. 41. *P. Eleph.* 1 dates Alexander IV's reign from the time of Philip III's death.

She and her son accompanied Perdikkas to Egypt, in the campaign against Ptolemy (Paus. 1.6.3), and after Perdikkas' death was taken to Macedonia by Antipatros (Arr. *Succ.* 1.44; Diod. 18.39.7; Heid. Epit. 2), although she was briefly in the camp of Antigonos Monophthalmos (Arr. *Succ.* 1.38, 42–3). Rh. and her son took refuge with Olympias at Pydna over the winter 317/6, where they were subsequently captured (Diod. 19.35.5; Justin 14.6.2, confusing her son with Herakles, son of Barsine; Justin 15.1.3). She and Alexander IV were imprisoned at Amphipolis by Kassandros (Diod. 19.52.4; cf. 19.61.1, 3; Justin 14.6.13) and later murdered by Glaukias, a henchman of Kassandros (Diod. 19.105.1–2; Justin 15.2.2–5; Paus. 9.7.2; Trogus, *Prol.* 15). Against the view, prevalent in much modern scholarship (see, most recently, Hammond, *HMac* III 139), that Alexander IV and Rh. were left for some time in Epeiros, see Macurdy 1932. At some point she made a dedication to Athena Polias (*IG* II² 1492, A, lines 45–57). The dedication is discussed at length by Kosmetatou 2004, but the date remains uncertain, except that we can say with relative certainty that it is unlikely that Rh. would have been able to make such a gesture while she was a prisoner in Amphipolis (316–310). Berve II 346–7 no. 688; Justi 262 no. 3; Stähelin, *RE* IA (1920) 1155–6 no. 5; Shayegan 119–20 no. 97; Schachermeyr 1920; Macurdy 1932; Renard and Servais 1955; Schoder 1982; Kosmetatou 2004; Aulbach §4.2.1; Carney, *LexAM* 457–8. **Stemma I.**

S

1029 SABAKES

(Σαβάκης, Σαυάκης; also Satakes, Tasiakes or Stasiakes in Diodorus). Satrap of Egypt (Curt. 3.11.10, 4.1.28: *praetor Aegypti*) under Dareios III, in late 333 S. led the Egyptian contingent to Issos where he fell on the battlefield (Arr. 2.11.8; Diod. 17.34.5; Curt. 3.11.10; 4.1.28). Dareios replaced him with Mazakes (Arr. 3.1.2) soon after the defeat at Issos. Berve II 348 no. 689; Justi, p. 268; Shayegan 121 no. 102.

SABBAS (Σάββας). See SAMBOS.

1030 SABIKTAS

(Σαβίκτας). Possibly a high-ranking Persian—or perhaps a native Kappadokian—S. was appointed satrap of Kappadokia-Tauros (cf. Baumbach 59; Julien 18–19; Strabo 12.1.4 C534) by Alexander in the summer of 333 (Arr. 2.4.2; cf. Curt. 3.4.1, "Abistamenes"). Berve suggests that Abistamenes was S.'s successor (II 348; rejected by Bosworth I 189), but it is more likely that we are dealing here with a corruption of the name Sabiktas. Hedicke writes *Sabistamenes*; cf. Schachermeyr 194 n. 206: "Vielleicht hat schon Kleitarch irrtümlich Sabiktamenes statt Sabiktas geschrieben, wie er ja auch einen Arsamenes bot (Diod. 17,19,4) anstelle des korrekten Arsames." He may have been tasked with the conquest of Kappadokia-Pontos, but if so he had only native troops for this purpose. How long he remained in office—or if he was involved in any way with the Persians who fled into Kappadokia after Issos (Curt. 4.1.34–35)—we do not know. Berve II 348 no. 690; Justi 269; Baumbach 59 n. 2; Julien 18–19; Shayegan 120 no. 98.

1031 SAMAXOS

Ruler (*regulus*) of an Indian region adjacent to Arachosia. He had apparently served with Barsaentes at Gaugamela (see Arr. 3.8.4, with Eggermont 18) and had given refuge to the regicide. After the deaths of Satibarzanes and Bessos, S. joined in a rebellion with Barsaentes, but both men were captured and brought in chains to Alexander at the Hydaspes (Curt. 8.13.3–4). Barsaentes was executed by Alexander (Arr. 3.25.8); but we cannot be certain what became of S. Eggermont 16–21 plausibly suggests that Samaxos is identical with Sambos, since both appear to have ruled the territory controlling the Khojak and Bolan passes. *Samaxos* may be little more than a corruption of the name Sambos, perhaps brought on by the confusion of another Indian *hyparchos*, Doraxes, who met Alexander near the Hydaspes in the presence of ambassadors from Abisares (Arr. 5.8.3; cf. Curt. 8.13.1 for Abisares' ambassadors). It appears that the original source may have mentioned both Sambos and Doraxes, which Curtius conflated into a single individual named Samaxos (hence Hedicke's curious emendation of the name to *Damaraxus*). If this is the case, the remainder of his career can be found s.v. Sambos below. If S. is indeed a separate individual, he may have been executed along with Barsaentes. Berve II 348 no. 692; Eggermont 16–21.

1032 SAMBOS

(Σάμβος). Justin 12. 10. 2, the MSS have *ambiregi regis* and *ambigeri regis*, which can easily be emended to *Ambi regis*); "Ambira" (Oros), that is *Sambi regis*, "of King Sambos." Ruler of the Indian region centered on Sindimana (traditionally identified with Sehwan, but Eggermont 22 suggests that it lay somewhere west of Alor on the road to Kandahar). Alexander had himself appointed S. satrap of the area (Arr. 6.16.3), which suggests an earlier meeting (perhaps at the Hydaspes: see Samaxos above; Curt. 9.8.17 speaks of S.'s recent surrender). Eggermont 19–20, notes that Barsaentes and Samaxos came to Alexander with 30 elephants (Curt. 8.13.3); S. later fled, when he heard of Alexander's favorable treatment of Mousikanos, with 30 elephants (Diod. 17.102.7). The case for identifying Samaxos and Sambos is strengthened by the fact that Curtius and Diodorus were almost certainly following the same source (Kleitarchos). He is said to have fled when Alexander reinstated his enemy Mousikanos in the adjacent region; his relatives opened the gates of Sindimana and explained that S.'s flight was due to fear of Mousikanos (Arr. 6.16.3–4). Curt. 9.8.13–20 gives a completely different picture of resistance within the territory of Sambos, but it should be noted that S. himself is not mentioned. Diod. 17.102.6–103.3 gives a compressed account that shares some details of both Curtius and Arrian, but Diodorus makes it clear that S. had fled soon after Alexander's arrival. The real instigators of the rebellion against Alexander were those of the Brahmin class (*Pap. Berolin.* 13044 = *FGrH* 153 F9; Plut. *Alex.* 64.1; cf. Curt. 9.8.15 and Diod. 17.102.7, both from Kleitarchos, for the death of 80,000 Brahmins), but the details of the conflict are hopelessly confused. What happened to S. is unknown. Berve II 348–9 no. 693; Eggermont *passim*; Jacobs 246–7.

1033 SAMBOS

(Σάμβος). Indian commander, who during the defense of the Mallian town was transfixed by a 3-ft catapult dart (Metz Epit. 75). The author of the Metz Epitome may have confused the name of this commander with that of the more famous king, whom he otherwise appears not to know; but the name may have been common in the region. We are clearly dealing with two separate individuals. Berve II 349 no. 694.

1034 SANBALLAT

(Σαναβαλλέτης). A Horonite. Dareios III's satrap in Samaria (Joseph. *AJ* 11.302), S. was already an old man at the time of Alexander's invasion (Joseph. *AJ* 11.311). He was the father of Nikaso and father-in-law of Manasses, the brother of the high priest of Jerusalem, Iaddus (Joseph. *AJ* 11.302–3; but *Nehemiah* 13:28 says that S.'s son-in-law was son of the high priest Eliashib and grandson of Jehoiada; Berve II 349 tentatively identifies Josephus' Sanaballetes as grandson of Nehemiah's Sanballat). The mixed marriage was frowned upon and S. planned to make Manasses high priest of a new temple he was to found on Mt. Gerizim (Joseph. *AJ* 11.310). But the war between Alexander and Dareios intervened, and after the battle of Issos S. abandoned Dareios and brought 8,000 men to Alexander at Tyre (Joseph. *AJ* 11.321), thus retaining his position and gaining permission for the construction of the temple on Mt. Gerizim. At this point the classical sources speak of the appointment of Andromachos in Koile-Syria, presumably as *strategos* (Curt. 4.5.9). S. died before Alexander had completed the siege of Gaza (Joseph. *AJ* 11.322–5). The remainder of Josephus' story, which has Alexander coming to Jerusalem and revering the Hebrew god is dismissed by many scholars as fiction (Bickerman 1988, 5). The story includes another of those famous exchanges between Parmenion and Alexander (Joseph. *AJ* 11.331ff.), in which Parmenion assumes that Alexander is doing *proskynesis* before the Jewish high priest. For this problem see Schäfer 2003, 1–7; Marcus 1926, 512–32; Bickerman 1988, 3–12. The value of the details of S.'s administration of Samaria and submission to Alexander is also uncertain (cf. Briant 1048). Berve II 349 no. 695.

1035 SANDROKOTTOS

(Σανδρόκοττος). Chandragupta Maurya. Ἀνδράκοττος (Plut. *Alex.* 62.4; *Mor.* 542d; Strabo 2.70; App. *Syr.* 55; Arr. *Ind.* 9.9 MS., Ἀνδρόκοττος). Σανδρόκυπτος in the Aldine. King of Magadha and founder of the Mauryan dynasty. There is no firm evidence of any personal connection between S. and Alexander. Plut. *Alex.* 62.9 says that when he was still a youth he saw Alexander, presumably when his army reached the limits of the Punjab. But this appears to be a later embellishment. But S. clearly exploited the weakness of the Nanda dynasty that is reported by King Phegeus (and verified by Poros) to Alexander at the Hyphasis (Curt. 9.2.5–7; Diod. 17.93.2–3). Justin 15.4.13–19 gives us a "rags to riches" story of the allegedly lowborn S., who fled into exile, fearing the wrath of Nandrus (apparently Mahapadma Nanda). Smith 1914, 117 assumes that this occurred before Alexander's advance and that it was during this exile that S. saw Alexander. According to Buddhist tradition, he overthrew the Nanda king in 322 and established himself at Pataliputra (Palimbothra, Strabo 2.1.9 C70; Palibothra, Strabo 15.1.36 C702; mod. Patna) on the Ganges. The Greek sources say nothing about the pivotal role played by Kautilya in S.'s rise to power (see Burrow 1968). Soon after gaining the throne of Magadha, Sandrokottos expelled Macedonian garrisons from the Punjab (Justin 15.4.12, 19). The historian Megasthenes appears to have been sent on an embassy to S. by Sibyrtios, satrap of Arachosia (Arr. 5.6.2; cf. Strabo 2.1.9 C70, 15.1.36 C702; 15.1.57 C711) at some point between S.'s accession and the death of Poros (cf. Bosworth 1996b, 121). After the death of Poros (318/17) S. extended his empire into the Indos region, and he came into conflict with Seleukos *c*.304. Impressed by S.'s army of 400,000 (Megasthenes *ap.* Strabo 15.1.53 C709; Pliny, *HN* 6.68 has 600,000 infantry and 9,000 elephants), Seleukos made peace with him, ceding the territories adjacent to the Indos (Parapamisadai, Arachosia, Gedrosia) in return for a large number of elephants (cf. Plut. *Alex.* 62.4) and a marriage alliance (Justin 15.4.21; App. *Syr.* 55.282; Strabo 15.2.9 C724). The treaty between S. and Seleukos involved some type of marriage agreement (κῆδος: App. *Syr.* 55; ἐπιγαμία: Strabo 15.2.9 C724), possibly the union of Antiochos I with S.'s daughter (see Nysa no. 805). Phylarchos *ap.* Athen. 1.18d–e says that S. gave Seleukos presents including aphrodisiacs. Appian's story of Seleukos' waging war against Sandrokottos east of the Indos is face-saving propaganda. S. ruled for 24 years, dying *c*.298. Plaumann, *RE* IA, 2269; Berve II 349–50 no. 696; Smith[3] 113–20; Hamilton 172ff.; Bosworth 1996b; Yardley–Wheatley–Heckel 275–97; Wheatley 2014a.

1036 SANGAIOS

(Σαγγαῖος. Sangaja: "Victory," so Lassen II² 135 n.3; Anspach I 13 n.35). An Indian leader and, apparently, a subordinate of Astis—if not a neighboring chieftain whose territory was threatened by Astis—who fled to the army of Perdikkas and Hephaistion, which was at that time advancing to the Indos. After the defeat of Astis, S. was made ruler of Peukelaotis in the territory of Gandhara (Arr. 4.22.8; cf. Bosworth *ad loc.*). By the terms of Alexander's settlement of the area, he was responsible to the Macedonian satrap (Philip son of Machatas and, later, Peithon son of Agenor). Nothing else is known about him. Berve II 348 no. 691; Lassen II² 135. n. 3; Anspach I 13 n.35.

1037 SATIBARZANES

(Σατιβαρζάνης). Noble Persian. Satrap of the Arians, a contingent of whom he brought to Gaugamela (Arr. 3.8.4). He is otherwise unattested in the battle. Arr. 3.21.10 calls S. a regicide, which Schmieder wanted to emend to Nabarzanes (cf. Heckel 1981e; but Bosworth I 344 notes that Σατιβαρζάνης is the *lectio difficilior*; but the correctness of the text does not imply historical accuracy). On the other hand, S. may very well have participated in the plot against Dareios (cf. Metz Epit. 3, where *Ario*barzanes should read *Sati*barzanes). S. surrendered to Alexander at Susia (Tūs) in Aria, and was confirmed in his satrapy (Arr. 3.25.1; Curt. 6.6.20; he brought news that Bessos had assumed the tiara and the name Artaxerxes and was mobilizing the Skythians, Curt. 6.6.13). But S. murdered Anaxippos and the forty javelin-men whom Alexander had sent with him (Arr. 3.25.2), butchering them once Alexander had set out for Baktria and then gathering the rebellious Arians at Artakoana, the satrapal capital (Arr. 3.25.5; Curt. 6.6.20–24; Diod. 17.78.1 calls it Chortakana; for the location see Engels 1978a, 89–90; *contra* Atkinson II 207–8; Heckel 1992, 379–80; also Fraser 110–15). Within two days of receiving the news of S.'s treachery, Alexander arrived at Artakoana, from which the satrap fled to Baktria with 2,000 horsemen (Curt. 6.6.22; cf. Arr. 3.25.6–7). In his place Alexander appointed a Persian, Arsakes (Arr. 3.25.7), but S. soon returned to his satrapy to incite rebellion (Curt. 7.3.2; Arr. 3.28.2; Diod. 17.81.3), whereupon he was killed in single combat by Erigyios (Arr. 3.28.3; Curt. 7.4.33–7; Diod. 17.83.4–6), who returned to Alexander with the barbarian's head (Curt. 7.4.40). Berve II 350–1 no. 697; Justi 291; Shayegan 120 no. 99.

1038 SATRAKES

(Σατράκης). One of the commanders of the Skythians (apparently in the force led by Carthasis, brother of their king), who confronted Alexander on the north bank of the Iaxartes River (Syr-Darya) in 329. S. died in the battle that ensued (Arr. 4.4.8). See also Curt. 7.7.1 and Metz Epit. 8 for the campaign of Carthasis. Berve II 351 no. 698; Shayegan 120–1 no. 100.

1039 SATROPATES

(Σατροπάτης. Perhaps Ἀτροπάτης). A Persian cavalry officer, sent by Dareios with 1,000 picked horsemen to prevent Alexander's crossing of the Tigris shortly before the eclipse of 20 September 331 (Curt. 4.9.7). Curtius' account is, however, unclear: S. is given 1,000 men and sent ahead by Dareios to patrol the east side of the Tigris, while Mazaios with 6,000 is ordered to prevent Alexander's crossing *the river*—clearly the Euphrates; Curt. 4.9.12

(Atkinson I 379). Yet at Curt. 4.9.2 we find only 1,000 horsemen sent by Mazaios against Alexander at the *Tigris*, and in the ensuing battle S. is killed by the Paionian Ariston, who brings his head to Alexander (Curt. 4.9.25; cf. Plut. *Alex.* 39.2). Arr. 3.7.7–8.2 appears to be referring to the same battle, which he dates to four days after the eclipse. Either Mazaios had nothing to do with the battle near the Tigris (and Curtius has conflated the missions of S. and Mazaios), or Mazaios, after withdrawing from Thapsakos, joined forces with Satropates (cf. also Berve II 244–5). S.'s death may be depicted on the coinage of the Paionian king, Patraos, who appears to have been Ariston's brother (Merker 1965, 44–5; Atkinson I 384–5). Berve II 351 no. 699; Marsden 1964, 31; Shayegan 121 no. 101.

1040 SATYROS

(Σάτυρος). Son of Pairisades (*regn.* 349/8–311/0), brother of Prytanis and Eumelos, father of the younger Pairisades (Diod. 20.22.1; 20.24.3); probably also a brother of Gorgippos (no. 484) and thus a son of Komosarye (no. 615). He was the rightful heir to the kingdom (Diod. 20.22.2). He and Gorgippos were associated with their father's rule already in the 320s (Din. 1.43), but it is clear that Gorgippos died before his father. S. was challenged in 311/0 by Eumelos, who had allied himself with Aripharnes, king of the Sirakes (Diod. 20.22.2–4). S. collected an army of 2,000 Greek mercenaries, an equal number of Thrakians, and about 30,000 Skythians: 20,000 infantry and 10,000 cavalry (Diod. 20.22.4). In a hard-fought battle at the Thates River, he defeated Aripharnes in the center of the line and then turned his attention to Eumelos who had up to this point enjoyed success on the right wing. Defeating Eumelos, he besieged him at Aripharnes' capital on the Thates (Diod. 20.22.4–23.1; for the Thates see s.v. Aripharnes no. 184). After a siege of several days, S. was wounded by a spear in the upper arm, when he came up in support of the mercenary leader, Meniskos; he was taken to the camp and died that night of the wound, presumably from the loss of blood or blood poisoning (Diod. 20.23.2–7). He had ruled for nine months after the death of his father Pairisades (Diod. 20.23.7). The nature of his death is said to have fulfilled the prophecy "beware of the μῦς" (which he mistook to mean "mouse" rather than "muscle," thus Diod. 20.26.1). His corpse was taken by the mercenary captain, Meniskos, to Prytanis at Pantikapaion (Diod. 20.23.8). According to Strabo 11.2.7 C494 there was a mound to S., whom he calls "one of the notable dynasts of the Bosporos," 90 stades from Parthenion (*Barr. Atl.* 87 L2). Niese I 413–14; Werner 416–18; Hind, *CAH* VI² 501–2.

SAUAKES. See SABAKES.

1041 SELEUKOS

Σέλευκος. Chapters IX–X in the Loeb edition of Appian's *Syriaka* constitute a biography of sorts of Seleukos Nikator. This work is cited using the more precise numbering of the Teubner edition. Son of Antiochos (*OGIS* I, 413; Justin 13.4.17; 15.4.3, 8; Arr. *Succ.* 1.2; also Strabo 16.2.4 C749; App. *Syr.* 57.295; Oros. 3.23.10; Libanius, *Or.* 11.93), a prominent officer of Philip II (Justin 15.4.3: *claro inter Philippi duces viro*), and Laodike (Justin 15.4.3; Strabo 16.2.4 C750; App. *Syr.* 57.295; Steph. Byz. s.v. Λαοδίκεια). He appears to have been born in Europos (Steph. Byz. s.v. Ὠροπός, cf. App. *Syr.* 57.298) in Lower Macedonia, but the family may have been given lands in the area. Relationship to Ptolemy son of S., apparently from Tymphaia, is therefore not impossible. The existence of a sister, named

Didymeia, is uncertain (rejected by Grainger, *SPG* 44; see no. 376). Stories of Laodike's liaisons with Apollo are creations of the Diadochic era and influenced in part by Olympias' alleged affair with Ammon, who visited her in the form of a snake (for stories of Olympias and Ammon see Plut. *Alex.* 2.6; 3.1–2; Justin 11.11.3; 12.16.2; Gell. *NA* 13.4.1–3; Ogden 2009 and 2011, 29–56; cf. also Mehl 5–6; Grainger 1990a, 2–3; Hadley 1969, 144, 152). For S.'s background and omens of his future greatness see esp. Justin 15.4.1–9 and App. *Syr.* 56.283–5. Libanius, *Or.* 11.56, 91, traces S.'s ancestry back to Herakles (full discussion in Mehl 6–12), which of course implied kinship with Alexander the Great.

According to Eusebius Arm. (*ap.* Porphyry of Tyre, *FGrH* 260 F32 §4), he was 75 years old when he died in 281/0. But this dating is suspicious, since it represents the middle ground between the dates of Appian and Justin, and makes S. an exact contemporary of Alexander the Great (cf. Grainger 1990a, 1). App. *Syr.* 63.331, 64.342 claims that he was 73 years old at the time of his death, having ruled for 42 years; Justin 17.1.10 (cf. Oros. 3.23.59) makes him 77 at Koroupedion, seven months before he was assassinated by Ptolemy Keraunos (Justin 17.2.4). Appian's evidence would date S.'s birth to 354, which helps to explain why we hear nothing of his military career before 326. But both Appian and Justin compare S.'s age with that of Lysimachos (Appian: S. 73; Lysimachos 70; Justin: S. 77; Lysimachos 74), and the matter is confounded by [Lucian], *Macrob.* 11, who gives Lysimachos' age at his death as 80 and cites Hieronymos of Kardia as his source. Appian and Justin agree on one point: S. was three years older than Lysimachos (see no. 673).

S. came to Pella in the mid-to-late 340s as a Page of Philip II and slightly older *syntrophos* of the Crown Prince. Hence Malalas (p. 203 Bonn) names Pella as S.'s birthplace, and Paus.1.16.1 says that he set out from Pella on the Asiatic expedition. App. *Syr.* 56.284 mentions Macedonia in general. Appian's claim that S. began the campaign as a common soldier (στρατιώτης) is hostile propaganda (Mehl 5, comments "daß man über Seleukos' Abstammung nichts Negatives erfährt" and treats his low standing in the army in the early years as factual), just like Justin's remark about Ptolemy Soter (13.4.10: *quem ex gregario milite Alexander virtutis causa provexerat*). It appears that he set out for Asia with Alexander in 334; for it is reported that he consulted the oracle at Didyma about his return to Macedonia in that year (App. *Syr.* 56.283). A member of Alexander's *hetairoi*, his aristocratic standing is virtually proved by his promotion—probably in 330—to the command of the Royal Hypaspists (*pace* Mehl 3, with n.9, and 13). Hephaistion held this office at Gaugamela and must surely have relinquished it when he was appointed hipparch in 330, upon the death of Philotas (Arr. 3.27.4). When S. appears as commander of the Royal Hypaspists at the Hydaspes (Arr. 5.13.1, 4), he may have held the office for almost four years. Certainly the fact that S. coordinated the infantry (i.e. hypaspists, archers) against Poros (Arr. 5.16.3; Curt. 8.14.15 incorrectly substitutes Leonnatos for S. in his account of the Hydaspes battle) suggests that by this time he had acquired considerable experience in command—primarily in the campaigns of Baktria and Sogdiana. Mehl's comment (13) that appointment to this high office marked a great step forward ("Nun hat er…einen gewaltigen Sprung nach vorn gemacht") ignores the fact that a common soldier did not rise to command the Royal Hypaspists, who were recruited from the aristocracy (see Heckel, *Marshals*[2] 251–8). The Hydaspes is S.'s only attested military action during Alexander's lifetime, but it taught him the value of war elephants, which he put to good use in his later career. He must have acquitted himself well in the engagement; for Aelian,

VH 12.16 (whatever the value of the passage) claims that Alexander resented S. for his bravery (cf. *VH* 14.47a).

At Sousa in 324 he received as his bride Apama, the daughter of Spitamenes (Arr. 7.4.6; cf. Arr. *ap.* Phot. *Bibl.* 68b; Plut. *Demetr.* 31.5; App. *Syr.* 57.295–6; Strabo 12.8.15 C578 calls her daughter of Artabazos; cf. 16.2.4 C750; Pliny, *HN* 6.132); she was to become the mother of Antiochos I Soter (Justin 17.2.10), and S. later named at least three cities for her (App. *Syr.* 57.295; Livy 38.13.5 calls Apama "sister" of S.; Steph. Byz. s.v. "Apamea"; cf. Strabo 16.2.4 C750). That Apama was the only bride from the Northeast, besides Alexander's wife Rhoxane (as Mehl 18 points out), cannot be determined. At any rate, we do not know the names of all the brides of prominent *hetairoi*; there may have been others from Baktria and Sogdiana. Whether the marriage hints at Alexander's plans for the administration of the Northeast is also unclear.

S. is named in connection with perhaps three episodes in Babylonia associated with the King's death: a sailing trip on the marshes near Babylon (Arr. 7.22.5; App. *Syr.* 56.288–9); the dinner party of Medeios the Thessalian (Ps.-Call. 3.31.8: if "Europios" is a reference to him); and the visit to the temple of Sarapis (Arr. 7.26.2; Plut. *Alex.* 76.9). In the first of these episodes, S. recovered Alexander's diadem, which had been blown off his head and had settled on some reeds near the tombs of Assyrian kings. In order to keep it dry, he placed the diadem on his head while he swam back to the King's ship. The actions were regarded as ominous: the diadem, landing near the tombs, foretold the King's death; placed on S.'s head, it presaged the kingship of the bearer (App. *Syr.* 56.287–91; Arr. 7.22.5); some say a sailor swam after it and put it on his head to keep it from getting wet. Alexander rewarded him with a silver talent (App. *Syr.* 56.290–1; cf. Arr. 7.22.5). But, according to Aristoboulos (*FGrH* 139 F55 = Arr. 7.22.5), it was a Phoinikian sailor and not S. who recovered the diadem, and Justin 15.3.13–14 tells a similar story about Lysimachos' future kingship. Such stories circulated in the Diadochic age, almost certainly after 307/6, to support the regal pretensions of one Successor or another. We may place very little faith in their historicity (cf. Hadley 1969).

That S. attended the dinner party of Medeios, at which Alexander became fatally ill, may be true. That he was involved in a plot to poison the King is, however, unlikely. The story that S. (along with Peithon, Attalos, Menidas, Demophon, Peukestas, and Kleomenes) slept in the temple of Sarapis in Babylon in the hope that Alexander's health might improve (Arr. 7.26.2; Plut. *Alex.* 76.9) has also been challenged by scholars, since the cult of Sarapis is generally thought to have been instituted by Ptolemy I in Egypt (discussion in Hamilton 212–13). Grainger 1990a, 218–19 may be right in assigning this story to the propaganda wars of the Diadochoi as well.

In the factional strife that broke out after Alexander's death in June 323, S. is scarcely mentioned. He is referred to once as a marshal of the second rank: the most powerful cavalry leaders in Babylon were Perdikkas, Leonnatos, and Ptolemy; with them, but clearly of lesser importance, were Lysimachos, Aristonous, Peithon, S. and Eumenes (Arr. *Succ.* 1.2). S. was, however, a man whom Perdikkas trusted—perhaps wrongly, as events would show. When Perdikkas had eliminated his rival Meleagros and distributed the satrapies, he took steps to secure for himself the guardianship of (first) Philip III Arrhidaios and (later) Alexander IV. Hence he named S. his second-in-command (at least in the military sphere: *summus castrorum tribunatus,* Justin 13.4.17), assigning to him "the hipparchy of the Companions, which was the most distinguished" (Diod.

18.3.4), namely the "first hipparchy" or "Hephaistion's chiliarchy" (Arr. 7.14.10), which Perdikkas himself had once commanded (cf. App. *Syr.* 57.292). Arr. *Succ.* 1.2 shows that S. was a cavalry officer *before* the division of power after Alexander's death. Diod. 18.3.4 calls Hephaistion's hipparchy the most distinguished (ἐπιφανεστάτη), and names the men who held it in succession; Plut. *Eum.* 1.5 shows that cavalry officers were advanced from a hipparchy of lower status to a higher one. Hence, when Perdikkas relinquished Hephaistion's hipparchy/chiliarchy and Eumenes was assigned a satrapy, S. moved up at least two ranks to replace Perdikkas, thus leap-frogging the second hipparchy held first by Perdikkas and then Eumenes. [The pamphlet on *The Last Days and Testament of Alexander*, which was composed no later than fifteen years after the King's death (for the possible dates see Ausfeld 1895, 1901; Merkelbach 1977; Heckel 1988; Bosworth 2000) and which displays a surprising amount of historical accuracy calls S. *hoplophoros* (Ps.-Call. 3.33.15) or *armiger* (*LM* 117). Which suggests that he would have been best known to his contemporaries as the commander of Royal Hypaspists. But their role as *hamippoi* may explain his connections with the cavalry.] As such, he was, in theory, second only to Perdikkas who exercised power in the name of the Kings. It is reasonable to assume that he participated in all Perdikkas' military campaigns between 323 and 321/0 (see Perdikkas no. 871). But S.'s power depended on Perdikkas' ability to preserve the integrity of Alexander's empire and to impose the decisions of the Kings on the satraps and the *strategos* of Europe. In this endeavor, Perdikkas failed miserably, only to be confronted by a mutiny of his officers—among them Antigenes, Peithon and S.—who murdered him in his tent as the Royal Army was encamped near Memphis (Nepos, *Eum.* 5.1; cf. Arr. *Succ.* 1.28, 35; Diod. 18.33.2ff.; Paus. 1.6.3; Strabo 17.1.8 C794; *Diadochoi Chronicle*, BM 34660, col. 4).

At Triparadeisos, he was rewarded for his betrayal of Perdikkas—and for coming to Antipatros' aid (Arr. *Succ.* 1.33)—with the satrapy of Babylonia (Diod. 18.39.6; Arr. *Succ.* 1.35; Heidelberg Epit. 1.4 = *FGrH* 155 F1 §1.4; cf. App. *Syr.* 1; cf. Diod. 19.12.2). Whether S. chose the satrapy of Babylonia at Triparadeisos or merely accepted what was awarded is unclear (cf. Mehl 39, with n.36). By accident or design, the satrapies of the heartland were firmly in the hands of men who had openly opposed Perdikkas—Peithon, S., Antigenes, and Amphimachos (brother of Arrhidaios). In what state S. found the satrapy is unclear: Perdikkas had sent Dokimos to depose the satrap, Archon (no. 169), who died in battle against the Perdikkan forces (Arr. *Succ.* 24.3–5). There is, however, no clear evidence of Dokimos opposing S. in 320, unless a reference in the *Diadochoi Chronicle* to burning implies a military struggle (Grainger 1990a, 30). Dokimos may have rejoined Perdikkas in Egypt or fled to Asia Minor either when he learned that the Perdikkans had been outlawed by the Macedonians or after he saw the futility of opposing S. (see no. 400). A Babylonian text speaks only of S.'s entry into the city, but the circumstances are obscure (*Diadochoi Chronicle*, BM 34660, col. 5; for a summary of chronological questions see Anson 2014, 59). The same chronicle implies that S.'s first actions in Babylon were intended to strengthen his rule and conciliate the priest class. His arrival in Babylon was certainly not greeted with overwhelming enthusiasm (for anti-Macedonian sentiment see Sherwin-White and Kuhrt 1993, 8–10, with earlier literature; but see also the full discussion in Sherwin-White 1987). There is little to illuminate his career until he became embroiled in the conflict between Antigonos and Eumenes, or indeed, initially, in a dispute between the eastern satraps and the ambitious Peithon (on whom see Bevan, *Seleucus* I 40–1).

He continued to support the decision of the assembly at Triparadeisos, which had outlawed the Perdikkan party, and he attempted to impede Eumenes' progress eastward (Diod. 18.73.3–4; cf. 19.12.1–2, 5). After a fruitless struggle to keep Eumenes from crossing the Tigris, he negotiated a truce (19.13.5) under which Eumenes would leave the satrapy (Diod. 19.12–13). But S. also urged Antigonos to come with his army to deal with Eumenes (Diod. 19.13.5; Nepos, *Eum.* 10.3 saying that in the time leading up to Eumenes' death Antigonos was already threatened by the power of S. looks ahead to the period after 315). Meanwhile, Peithon son of Krateuas was also making a bid for power in the Upper Satrapies and trying to enlist S. in his cause, but the satrap of Babylon remained non-committal (Diod. 19.14.3). S. did cooperate with Antigonos and supplied troops (Diod. 18.17.2), thus accepting his authority. Antigonos assigned Sousiana, and the task of bringing Xenophilos to heel, to S. (Diod. 19.18.1) and, although we hear of reinforcements from S. and Peithon at Paraitakene (Diod. 19.27.1), it appears that only Peithon fought in Antigonos' forces at Paraitakene (Diod. 19.29.3) and Gabiene (Diod. 19.38.4). S. meanwhile came to terms with Xenophilos, who greeted the returning Antigonos at the Pasitigris River (Diod. 19.48.6), and prepared to entertain Antigonos in Babylon (Diod. 19.55.2; App. *Syr.* 53.267). But Antigonos sought to relieve S. of his satrapy by demanding an audit of his accounts—a similar trick had been used by Perdikkas against Antigonos himself, and he was quick to learn the lesson—and charging him with taking actions against a subordinate without his authority (Diod. 19.55.3–4; App. *Syr.* 53.268; Antigonos in turn deposed S.'s appointee Blitor: App. *Syr.* 53.269). S., alert to the danger and mindful of Peithon's fate (no. 867), fled to Ptolemy (Diod. 19.55.5–6; Paus. 1.6.4). Diodorus' claim that S. was a friend (ἀνὴρ φίλος) of Antigonos (19.55.6) shows yet again how little friendship mattered to the ambitious Monophthalmos. Diod. 19.55.7–9 says that Antigonos was disturbed by a Chaldaian prophecy that if S. escaped his grasp he would return to become master of Asia (cf. Diod. 21.3). S.'s flight also prompted Antigonos to depose Blitor from Mesopotamia (App. *Syr.* 53.269); in fact, it may have been S.'s decision to replace the absent Amphimachos, who had allied himself with Eumenes, with Blitor that formed one of the charges against him. Revealing to Ptolemy the details of Antigonos' actions and ambitions, he persuaded him to form a coalition with Lysimachos and Kassandros (Diod. 19.56.1–4; App. *Syr.* 53.270; cf. Paus. 1.6.5; Diod. 21.2). Consequently, envoys sent to Antigonos demanded, *inter alia*, that S. be reinstated as satrap of Babylonia (Diod. 19.57.1; Justin 15.1.4; cf. App. *Syr.* 53.271 for the ultimatum).

In 315, Ptolemy gave S. a fleet of one hundred ships, with which he sailed past the Antigonids who were besieging Tyre, taunting the enemy (Diod. 19.58.5). From there he sailed to Asia Minor and besieged Erythrai, despite the arrival of Polemaios, who had insufficient force to oppose him (Diod. 19.60.3–4). Reinforced by Menelaos, S. now sailed to Kypros, winning a good portion of the island for Ptolemy (Diod. 19.62.4–6), and sending Polykleitos to Kenchreai to negotiate with Alexander son of Polyperchon (Diod. 19.64.4–5). In 314, S. answered the call of Aristoteles (who had been sent to Lemnos on Kassandros' orders) in order to help win the island from Antigonos (Diod. 19.68.3), but when he took his fleet to Kos, Dioskourides drove Aristoteles away and secured the island (Diod. 19.68.4). S.'s importance as a partner in Ptolemaic ventures is clear from Diodorus (19.68.2, 75.2, 81.5, 83.1, 85.3; cf. Bosworth 2002, 215, with n.25), and although he is undoubtedly the junior partner, their joint ventures show that Ptolemy recognized S.'s talent for both the planning and execution. He knew also that it was in his interests to restore the power of S., who in turn induced his patron to make an incursion into Koile-Syria (Diod. 19.80.3). The decisive engagement came at Gaza, where S. is again involved in Ptolemy's tactical decisions (Diod. 19.83.1) and their execution (Diod. 19.83.4). The Ptolemaic forces defeated the young Demetrios Poliorketes in 312, and after the battle S., with 1,000 infantry and 300 cavalry (but Diod. 19.90.1 says 800 foot and 200 horse) given to him by Ptolemy, rushed to Babylon (App. *Syr.* 54.273; cf. Diod. 19.86.4), where he was received enthusiastically by its citizens (App. *Syr.* 54.274; for the campaign see Diod. 19.90–1). With the exception of a few hiccups, the relationship between Ptolemy and S. remained a good one (cf. Diod. 20.76.7). The recovery of Babylonia was, of course, a turning point in S.'s career and, in retrospect, prophecies of his future greatness were easily found. As he was setting out for Babylon, he stumbled over a rock, which when dug up turned out to be an anchor. Ptolemy, who was with him, countered the soothsayers who said it was an omen of delay, by calling it a sign rather of safety, and for this reason S., as king, engraved the anchor on his signet ring (App. *Syr.* 56.286–7). For full discussion of the legends concerning S. see Ogden 2017.

Once established in Babylon, S. overcame Nikanor, whom Antigonos had left in charge of Media, winning in part because of the defection of the Persian troops, whose satrap Euagros had fallen in battle (Diod. 19.92; see also Appian's confused version *Syr.* 57.293 and 55.278; Justin 15.4.10–11). In response to a letter from Nikanor (Diod. 19.100.3), Antigonos sent Demetrios to Babylon, where he captured one of the citadels of the city, which had been abandoned by S.'s general, Patroklos. Demetrios left Archelaos to continue the besieging of the city and returned to the coast (Diod. 19.100.5–7; Plut. *Demetr.*7.2–4). But the Antigonid efforts to regain the territory were ultimately thwarted (cf. Polyaenus 4.9.1). S. turned his attention to consolidating his power in the East and Central Asia, and as a result, during this period, he is seldom mentioned in the historical narratives (his return from the East to Kappadokia is reported in the penultimate paragraph of Diodorus' twentieth book: 20.113.4; cf. App. *Syriaka* for similar brevity).

After the Antigonids assumed the kingship in 306, S., Ptolemy, Lysimachos, and Kassandros followed suit (cf. App. *Syr.* 54.277; Plut. *Demetr.* 18.3; Diod. 20.53.4), but were mocked by Demetrios (Athen. 6.261b; Plut. *Demetr.* 25.7, cf. *Mor.* 823c–d), whose flatterers referred to S. as the *elephantarchos*, because he had ceded territory in Asia to Chandragupta in exchange for a large number of elephants (App. *Syr.* 55.282 and Justin 15.4.12–21 for the Indian campaign; cf. Hauben 1974). Nepos, *Eum.* 13.3 names S. along with Antigonos, Lysimachos, Ptolemy, and Kassandros as responsible for the extirpation of the Macedonian royal house. Antigonos founded the city of Antigoneia on the Orontes, designed to keep a watch on affairs in Babylon, but S. soon dismantled it and founded Antioch (Antiocheia; Diod. 20. 47.6 wrongly calls it Seleukeia) nearby. In 302 there was a renewal of the coalition of Kassandros, Lysimachos, Ptolemy, and S. against Antigonos (Diod. 20.106.2–5), and Lysimachos decided to await the arrival of S. from the East before meeting their enemy on the battlefield in Asia Minor (Diod. 20.108.5, 109.5). Ptolemy, now in Phoinikia, was forestalled by a false report brought to Ptolemy that Antigonos had defeated Lysimachos and S. in the vicinity of Herakleia (Diod. 20.113.1–2). But in 301, Lysimachos and S. defeated and killed Antigonos at Ipsos (Nepos, *de Regibus* 3.1–2; Justin 15.4.22; cf. App. *Syr.* 55.279; Paus. 1.6.7; Diod. 21.4a–b). S. greatly expanded his kingdom. As part of the division of spoils after Ipsos, S. was awarded Syria from the Euphrates to the sea and inland Phrygia (App. *Syr.* 55.280), but the agreement was not upheld and this led to conflict among the former allies (Justin 15.4.23–4; Diod. 21.5). At the height of his power, S. had 72 satraps under him, and he transferred most of them to his son, Antiochos, but ruled the lands between the Euphrates and the sea (App. *Syr.* 62.328; cf. *Syr.* 55.281: he was acquisitive and ruled a greater empire than anyone after Alexander).

In the last half of the 280s, S. was instrumental in bringing down both Demetrios Poliorketes (he had crossed back into Asia Minor in 286/5), whom he captured in the Tauros region and kept in honorable detention in the Syrian Chersonese (for Demetrios' death see Plut. *Demetr.* 47–51), and Lysimachos, whom he defeated and killed at Koroupedion (App. *Syr.* 55.279, 64.339; Memnon 5.6). But the support that he gave to Agathokles' widow Lysandra and her brother Ptolemy Keraunos (references svv. Agathokles no. 18, Arsinoë no. 221, Lysandra no. 668, and Ptolemy no. 1011), which helped him win Lysimachos' territories in Asia Minor and cross to Europe with his army, proved to be his undoing. For Keraunos murdered him on the road to Lysimacheia and claimed the kingship for himself (App. *Syr.* 62; Nepos, *De Regibus* 3.4; Justin 17.2.4–5; full discussion in Heinen 50–63). His body was ransomed from Keraunos by Philetairos (no. 900). For omens of his death see Ogden 2017, 247–69.

His character, his person, and family. His bravery (Ael. *VH* 12.16, 14.47a) was matched by sheer physical strength. Once in Babylon, when Alexander was about to sacrifice, he subdued a bull that had broken from his bonds by holding the beast by the horns with his bare hands (App. *Syr.* 57.294), and consequently his statues were ornamented with horns. Since he was not the subject of an ancient biography, there are few anecdotes that illuminate his character. But he was clearly a man of principle who was not willing to challenge Ptolemy I in Koile-Syria since the man had taken him in in 315 and helped him recover his satrapy in 312. Similarly, he did not entertain an offer of a large sum of money from Lysimachos (a man he distrusted anyway) to kill Demetrios (Plut. *Demetr.* 51.3–4, contrasting the good nature of S. with the savagery of Lysimachos: ὁ δ' ἐκεῖνον μὲν ἄλλως προβαλλόμενος, ἔτι μᾶλλον ἐπὶ τούτῳ μιαρὸν καὶ βάρβαρον). His willingness to allow his son Antiochos to marry Stratonike had more to do with politics than curing him of lovesickness (Plut. *Demetr.* 38; App. *Syr.* 59–61; Diod. 21.20). S. had only two attested wives: Apama (no. 138) and Stratonike (no. 1086, with modern literature; Nepos, *De regibus* 3.3; Plut. *Demetr.* 31.5–6). By the first he had a son Antiochos (no. 125), named for the paternal grandfather, and at least another unnamed son (Justin 15.4.9 mentions *filii* of Seleukos; *OGIS* 213, lines 3, 26 calls him the oldest of Seleukos' sons); Apama (no. 139) and Laodike (no. 644) are attested by Malalas (8.198, 203) as sisters, though some scholars have doubted their existence. Stratonike bore him a daughter Phila (no. 899) who later married Antigonos Gonatas (no. 116). That he married a daughter of Sandrokottos (Chandragupta) is doubtful (see s.v. Nysa no. 805).

The cities founded by Seleukos: he built cities throughout his realm: sixteen were named Antioch for his father Antiochos; five Laodikeia for his mother; nine Seleukeia after himself; three for his wife Apama; and one for his other wife Stratonike. He named others after cities in Greece or Macedonia, or Alexander's exploits: Beroia, Edessa, Perinthos, Maronea, Kallipolis, Achaia, Pella, Oropos, Amphipolis, Arethusa, Astakos, Tegea, Chalkis, Larisa, Herea, Apollonia. In Parthia there was Sotera, Kalliope, Charis, Hekatompylos, Achaia, Alexandropolis in India, Alexandreschata in Skythia. Also Nikophorion in Mesopotamia, Nikopolis in Kappadokia near Armenia (App. *Syr.* 57;

cf. Strabo 12.8.15 C578). For Seleukeia by the sea and Seleukeia on the Tigris see App. *Syr.* 58; the reference to Seleukeia in Diod. 21.6 appears to be an error for Antiocheia (cf. Diod. 20.47.6). Pliny, *HN* 6.17.43 says that S. founded Ekbatana, but this was probably a reorganization of the Achaimenid city (Grainger, *SPG* 713); Strabo 11.13.6 C524 says that Rhagai was founded by Nikator (cf. Grainger, *SPG* 719 s.v. "Europos [1]"). For full discussion of Seleukid foundations see Cohen 1978 and the gazetteer in Grainger, *SPG*. References to geography, exploration, and foundations relating to S. are confused and often inaccurate (Plin. *HN* 2. 67 (167); 6. 18 (49); 6. 21 (58); 6. 59 (135). Berve II 351–2 no. 700; Stähelin, *RE* IIA (1921) 1208–34 no. 2; Bevan, *Seleucus* I 28–73; Hadley 1969; Mehl 1–28; Grainger 1990a, 1–23 and *SPG* 53–60; cf. Heckel 1992, 253–7; Sandberger 203 no. 75; Hauben 83–90 no. 31; *PP* VI no. 14625 (also 16094, 16130; V, 13789); Van der Spek 2014; Ogden 2017 and *LexAM* 468–9. **Stemma XI.**

1042 SERAPION

(Σεραπίων). Youth in Alexander's entourage with whom the King used to play ball (Plut. *Alex.* 39.5), to whom the King, allegedly, did not give gifts because he did not ask for them. The boy's name (and thus his existence) has been called into question because it implies that the cult of Serapis existed before the time of Ptolemy I (see Hamilton 103 and 212–13, with bibliography). The anecdote is inane and the identity of the individual is of no consequence. Possibly, in its original form, the story mentioned a servant (θεράπων or the participial form θεραπεύων), and this was corrupted into Σεραπίων. Berve II 352–3 no. 701; Hamilton 103.

1043 SEUTHES

(Σεύθης). Besevliev 1970, 2–3; Tomaschek, *SB Wien* 131, 42. King of the Odrysian Thrakians (Strabo 7, frag. 47), Seuthes III (*regn. c.*330–*c.*300/295) was apparently the son of Kotys and brother of Kersobleptes (thus Beloch III² 2.90–1) and is attested as the father of Rheboulas and Kotys (*IG* II² 349 = Tod II 193). The Odrysians were reluctant allies of Macedon (cf. Arr. 3.12.4 for Odrysian cavalry in Alexander's service), and S.'s position was doubtless one of vassalage. In June 330 he sent his son Rheboulas to Athens to forge an alliance, probably in the aftermath of the expedition by the Macedonian *strategos* of Thrake, Zopyrion (for the problem of the identity of the Macedonian *strategos* see s.vv. Zopyrion no. 1174 and Memnon no. 703). The Athenians appear to have done little more than renew old ties with Thrake and honor Rheboulas with citizenship (*IG* II² 349 = Tod II 193); after the failure of Agis' war, they could scarcely do more. The disastrous campaign of Zopyrion led S. into open rebellion (Curt. 10.1.45; cf. Beloch IV² 1.44–5 for the traditional view). Sometime before 323, he founded Seuthopolis (on which see Danoff, *RE* Supplbd IX 1370–8; id., *Kl. Pauly* V. 152; Dimitrov and Cicikova 1978; Lund 22–3, 26–7). In 323/2, when Thrake was awarded to Lysimachos, the latter invaded S.'s territory (from "the middle and upper reaches of the Tonsus, extending west perhaps as far as the Strymon River and east to the Sasliyka," Lund 24) with a force of 4,000 foot and 2,000 horse, against which the Thrakian king mustered 20,000 infantry and 8,000 cavalry (Diod. 18.14.2). In the stubborn ensuing battle, Lysimachos claimed a doubtful victory (ἀμφίδοξον ἔχων τὴν νίκην), and killed large numbers of S.'s men. But the outcome was clearly indecisive (Diod. 18.14.3–4; Arr. *Succ.* 1.10 incorrectly says that Lysimachos was killed in the engagement). On the other hand, S.'s lack of further action suggests that he entered into some kind of alliance with Lysimachos until 313 (Diod. 19.73.8; Polyaenus 7.25). For his coinage see Mørkholm 1991, 83 (pl. 192), who notes that many of S. III's coins "are overstruck on Macedonian ones, especially on bronze issues of Kassandros." Berve II 353 no. 702; Hoeck, *Hermes* 26, 89ff.; Swoboda, *RE* IIA, 2022–3 no. 4; Badian 1967a; Besevliev 1970, 1 (with stemma), 8. Cf. Lund 19ff.; Atkinson and Yardley 104–6.

1044 SIBYRTIOS

(Σιβύρτιος). Macedonian (Tataki 429 no. 15; Hoffmann 201: "der Name [ist] allerdings schwerlich echtgriechisch"). We do not know how long he had been in Alexander's entourage before his appointment as satrap of Arachosia in 325. Arr. 6.27.1 gives a garbled and implausible account of the administrative changes, particularly with regard to S.'s position (Heckel 2017a for the view that he was never satrap of Karmania). He omits all reference to the deposing of Astaspes, which occurred after Alexander reached Karmania (Curt. 9.10.21, 29; cf. Arr. *Ind.* 36.8) and thus after S.'s designation as satrap of Arachosia. It appears that Alexander appointed Thoas when he reached Gedrosia, after receiving news of Apollophanes' death. Whether he had intended to recall Apollophanes (Arr. 6.27.1) is a moot point. Learning of Menon's death (Curt. 9.10.20), the King sent S. to replace him. On the news of Thoas' death Gedrosia was assigned to S. in addition to Arachosia; he retained both regions in the subsequent distribution of satrapies at Babylon in 323 (Diod. 18.3.3; Justin 13.4.22; Dexippos, *FGrH* 100 F8 §6; cf. Metz, *LM* 121) and at Triparadeisos in 320 (Arr. *Succ.* 1.36; cf. Arr. 5.6.2). In 317 he appears to have joined the coalition of "Upper Satraps" against Peithon son of Krateuas; we find him in command of 1,000 infantry and 610 cavalry in 316, directly under the authority of Peukestas (Diod. 19.14.6), who was a personal friend. S. fled the camp after being called to account by Eumenes (Diod. 19.23.4); his troops are assigned to Kephalon (Diod. 19.27.4, see no. 582). He appears to have joined Antigonos Monophthalmos (though there is no record of military command in 316/15), who restored him to his satrapy and assigned some 1,000 Argyraspids to him with orders that he should wear them out with service (Polyaenus 4.6.15; Plut. *Eum.* 19; Diod. 19.48.3). Nothing else is known about his career except that he retained his position under Seleukos I Nikator, whose agent to India, Megasthenes, visited him on his way to Sandrokottos (Arr. 5.6.2). Berve II 353 no. 703; Billows 432–3 no. 106; Heckel 2017a; Grainger, *SPG* 644 s.v. "Chandragupta"; see also Scharfe 1971.

1045 SIMMIAS

(Σιμμίας). Macedonian from Tymphaia (cf. Arr. *Ind.* 18.6). Apparently the second oldest of the sons of Andromenes (Arr. 3.11.9), perhaps named after the maternal grandfather. Brother of Amyntas, Attalos, and Polemon (Curt. 7.1.10), and like them he appears to have accompanied Alexander since the beginning of the Asiatic expedition. Since Attalos appears to have been coeval with Alexander (cf. Diod. 16.94.4), S. must have been born c.360. In 331, in the absence of Amyntas, who was sent to Macedonia on a recruiting mission, S. exercised at least nominal command of his brother's battalion (Arr. 3.11.9; although Diod. 17.57.3 names Philip son of Balakros in this context; cf. Curt. 4.13.28: *philagros* in the MSS appears to be a corruption of Philip son of Balagros); the gap which developed in the line of the phalanx may have been due to his inexperience (Arr. 3.14.4; Bosworth

1976, 14 argues that the Vulgate, assigning the command to Philip, is more likely to be correct, and that Ptolemy substituted S. "so that he could lay at his door, by implication at least, the break of the Macedonian line and the attack upon the base camp"). S., Amyntas, and Attalos were placed in jeopardy by the flight of the youngest brother, Polemon, at the time of Philotas' disgrace (Curt. 7.1.10). But Amyntas spoke convincingly in their defense, saving the family (Arr. 3.27.1–3; Curt. 7.1.18–40, embellished). After Amyntas' death, S. was passed over as phalanx commander in favor of his younger brother, Attalos. Whether this was due to his associations with Philotas and Amyntas Perdikka or to his poor showing at Gaugamela (or both) is unclear. On the other hand, we cannot rule out the possibility that S. may have left the army in 330 or died of illness. Berve II 353–4 no. 704; Bosworth I 300–1; Bosworth 1976, 125 and 1976b, 9–14; Heckel, *Marshals*[2] 191–2; Tataki 214 no. 9. **Stemma III.**

1046 SIMMIAS

(Σιμμίας). Son of Phaiyllus. One of twenty-four cavalrymen from Orchomenos, who served with Alexander's allied cavalry until the expedition reached Ekbatana in 330. There he and his compatriots were discharged. On their return (*c*.329), they made a dedication to Zeus Soter in Orchomenos (*IG* VII 3206). Berve II 354 no. 705.

1047 SIPPAS

(Σίππας). Macedonian (Tataki 430 no. 21). Hoffmann 214 suggests the name in the text may be a corruption of Simmias or Sirrhas. One of the group of capable officers who remained with Antipatros during Alexander's absence (see also s.vv. Deinias, Lykiskos) and thus out of the limelight of the historical accounts. When Antipatros left Macedonia for Thessaly at the outbreak of the Lamian War, he left S. as *strategos* of Macedon, giving him sufficient troops to defend the country and ordering him to enlist additional forces (Diod. 18.12.2; for the limited number of citizen soldiers in Macedonia at the time see Adams 1985; Bosworth 1986). Nothing else is known about him. Berve II 354 no. 706; Hoffmann 214.

1048 SISIKOTTOS

(Σισίκοττος. Sanskrit "Sasigupta," Prakrit "Sasigutta" Eggermont 185). Native dynast, and originally a supporter of Bessos. He went over to Alexander, who appointed him ruler of the Assakenians (Udyana) after the capture of Aornos (Arr. 4.30.4; Curt. 8.11.25), though clearly under the watchful eye of the satrap Nikanor. In 326 messengers from S. reported to Alexander that the Assakenians had risen in revolt and killed their *hyparchos* Nikanor (Arr. 5.20.7; Heckel 233 with n.40). Anspach I 28, 81; II 27, 200; Berve II 354 no. 707; Eggermont 185, 188; Bosworth II 192–3, 321–2; Shayegan 121 no. 103.

1049 SISIMITHRES

(Σισιμίθρης). A local chieftain of eastern Sogdiana (Paraitakene), apparently also known as Chorienes (Arr. 4.21.6–10; cf. Metz Epit. 28), which may be an official name taken from the territory he ruled. According to native custom, he had married his own mother (Curt. 8.2.19, 28), on whom he fathered at least two sons, who had reached military age in 328/7 (Curt. 8.2.19; 8.4.21 gives Chorienes three sons), and three daughters (Metz Epit. 19). Thus he could not have been born much later than 370 (cf. Berve II 354: "vor 365"). In late autumn 328, S. took refuge, along with the other hyparchs of the region, on the so-called Rock of Chorienes (Koh-i-nor, Kaerst I³ 440 n.3, following Schwarz 83ff.), which was said to be 20 stades high and 60 stades in circumference (Arr. 4.21.2; cf. Strabo 11.11.4 C517, who says it was 15 stades in height with a circuit of 80) and was surrounded by a deep ravine. This ravine Alexander filled with rocks and trees in order to facilitate the approach of the army (Curt. 8.2.23–4; Arr. 4.21.3–4; the work was supervised in shifts during the night by Perdikkas, Ptolemy, and Leonnatos, whereas Alexander himself conducted the assault by day). Alexander sent to S. Oxyartes (Curt. 8.2.25ff. has *Oxartes*; Arr. 4.21.6 says that Chorienes asked that Oxyartes be sent to him), who induced him to surrender (Arr. 4.21.6–8; Curt. 8.2.27–31). This voluntary surrender probably saved S.'s life (cf. the punishment of Ariamazes), and he was allowed to retain his territory, which was perhaps around Gazaba (Curt. 8.4.1; cf. Metz Epit. 28, Gazabes), although his two sons were retained as hostages in Alexander's army (Curt. 8.2.33). Not much can be inferred from Plutarch's claim (Plut. *Alex.* 58.4) that Oxyartes told Alexander that S. was the greatest coward in the world, although this opinion is echoed by Curt. 8.2.28, where S.'s mother shows more courage than her son. Plut. *Mor.* 181c probably refers to S. but wrongly makes him the commander of Aornos. Alexander found that S. had surrendered after consuming only one-tenth of his provisions, which supported the view that he had capitulated out of goodwill rather than necessity (Arr. 4.21.10). S. was later (early 327) able to supply Alexander's army (Arr. 4.21.10, supplies for two months; Curt. 8.4.19, "a large number of pack animals, 2,000 camels, and flocks of sheep and herds of cattle"), which had suffered from adverse weather in the region (Arr. 4.21.10 says that they experienced heavy snowfall *during the siege*; Curt. 8.4.2–18 and Metz Epit. 24–7 claim the privations occurred after the capture of the Rock). Not to be outdone in generosity, Alexander plundered the territory of the Sakai and returned to S. with a gift of 30,000 head of cattle (Curt. 8.4.20). This was almost certainly the occasion of the banquet given by Chorienes (*cohortandus* in Curt. 8.4.21, with textual difficulties), at which Rhoxane was introduced to Alexander, along with the host's own unmarried daughters, and Alexander took his first oriental bride (Curt. 8.4.22–30; Metz Epit. 28–31; Strabo 11.11.4 C517; but Arr. 4.19.4ff. places the marriage after the capture of the Rock of Sogdiana; see further s.v. Rhoxane no. 1028). Curt. 8.4.21–3 has, however, badly conflated Chorienes (MS *cohortandus*) and Oxyartes. The sons taken into Alexander's service are those of Chorienes (Sisimithres; cf. 8.2.33), and the thirty maidens introduced at the banquet included Chorienes' own daughters (perhaps all three mentioned by Metz Epit. 19) and Rhoxane, the daughter of Oxyartes. Because both Sisimithres and Chorienes appear in Metz Epit. 19, 28, and because Sisimithres corresponds to Chorienes in Arr. 4.21.1, it is clearly not a case of Curtius' use of Kleitarchos for the name Sisimithres and Ptolemy for Chorienes (*pace* Schachermeyr 353 n. 425). Rather, the failure to reconcile the names Sisimithres and Chorienes probably goes back to Kleitarchos himself, who may have found Chorienes (the father of three sons) in a written source (Onesikritos?) and failed to recognize that he was identical with Sisimithres. Curtius then compressed the episode in such a way that he made it appear that Rhoxane was Chorienes' daughter: *filia ipsius* = *filia Oxyartis* only if *cohortandus* in 8.2.21 is wrongly emended (as by Alde) to "Oxyartes." But, if Alde's emendation stands, then Curtius is guilty of introducing Oxyartes twice (once under the name Oxartes, a compatriot of S., and again as an illustrious satrap), which would in itself not be particularly disconcerting, except that *cohortandus* in 8.2.21

must be the Choriones of Metz Epit. 28–31. Bosworth argues (1981, 32) that Choriones and Sisimithres are different individuals. Otherwise, S. is not heard of again. Berve II 354–5 no. 708; Bosworth 1981; Heckel 1986; Heckel 199 n.104; Vacante 2012; Shayegan 121 no. 104.

1050 SISINES

(Σισίνης. Also Σισήνης). Prominent Persian, but of unknown family background. According to Curtius (3.7.11) he had been sent to Philip's court by the ruler of Egypt. There is considerable confusion about S.'s role, though it is clear that he acted as an agent of some sort. Arrian reports that he was sent to corrupt Alexander Lynkestes but was arrested by Parmenion and sent to Alexander for interrogation. See Curt. 3.7.11–15 and Arr. 1.25.3–10 with the commentaries of Atkinson and Bosworth. Implausibly, Badian 2000a, 56–60 believes that S.'s testimony was manipulated (i.e. deliberately mistranslated) in order to "frame" the Lynkestian (see Heckel 2003a, 212–13). If there is any truth to Curtius' version, S. may have been killed (secretly) before the battle of Issos. Berve II 356 no. 710; Shayegan 121–2 no. 106.

1051 SISINES

(Σισίνης). Son of Phrataphernes (Arr. 7.6.4; Arr. *Succ.* 3), satrap of Hyrkania and Parthia, and brother of Phradasmenes. Both S. and his brother were enrolled in the cavalry *agema* in 324 at Sousa (Arr. 7.6.4). Whether they had been in Alexander's entourage since Phrataphernes' surrender to the King in 330 (as Berve II 355 assumes) is unclear. Arr. *Succ.* 3 shows that he played some part in the early history of the Successors, but says only that his name was mentioned in the first two books of Arrian's *Events after Alexander*. See further s.v. Phrataphernes no. 958. Berve II 355 no. 709; Shayegan 121 no. 105.

1052 SISYGAMBIS

(Σισύγαμβις. Σισύγγαμβρις, Diod. 17.37.3, 59.7, 118.3; the *Alexander Romance* calls her Rhodogune). Mother of Dareios III, Oxyathres and (possibly) Stateira (Brosius 68 notes that the sources do not attest a mother-daughter relationship) and four other children (Curt. 10.5.23). If she was both sister and wife of Arsanes, then her father was Ostanes, a son of Dareios II and brother of Artaxerxes II (thus Neuhaus 1902, followed by Berve II 356; Hamilton 78; Brosius 67; Briant 772–3; but see Bosworth I 218). She could have been one of the few surviving relatives of Artaxerxes III (Val. Max 9.2 ext. 7; Justin 10.3.1). S., her daughter, and three grandchildren accompanied Dareios to Issos (Curt. 3.3.22; Diod. 17.31.2), where they were captured (Arr. 2.11.9; Curt. 3.11.24; Diod. 17.36.2), and received a false report that Dareios had been killed (Plut. *Alex.* 21.1; Diod. 17.37.3; Curt. 13.12.3–5). The truth was reported to them by Leonnatos (Diod. 17.37.3; Curt. 3.12.6–12; Plut. *Alex.* 21.2), and his visit was followed by another by Alexander himself; there followed the famous episode in which S. mistook Hephaistion for Alexander (Curt. 3.12.13–17; Justin 11.9.12; *Suda* H660; Diod. 17.114.2; Val. Max. 4.7 ext. 2; Diod. 17.37.4–6; Arr. 2.12.6–7; Plut. *Mor.* 522a implies he visited S. on other occasions; *Fragmentum Sabbaiticum* §5 = *FGrH* 151 F1; *Itiner. Al.* 37). The scene is depicted in a painting by Paolo Veronese, now in the National Gallery, London. At Gaugamela, she and the other captives were kept in the baggage camp (Curt. 4.13.35), where she allegedly refused to celebrate a Persian victory prematurely when the Skythians broke through (Diod. 17.59.7; Curt. 4.15.10–11).

Left behind at Sousa, with tutors to teach her Greek (Diod. 17.67.1; Curt. 5.2.18–22 has a different story; on which see Briant 2015, 3331–4), she appears to have intervened on behalf of the Ouxians and their satrap Madates (her niece's husband: Curt. 5.3.12) by writing a letter to Alexander (Curt. 5.3.12–15; confirmed to some extent by Ptolemy, *FGrH* 138 F12 = Arr. 3.17.6; but see Bosworth I 321–4). In 330, Alexander sent her Dareios' corpse for burial (Plut. *Alex.* 43.7). Whether she made the arduous journey to Ekbatana to witness the punishment and execution of Bessos (Arr. 4.7.3; Curt. 7.10.10) is unknown. Also uncertain is whether Sisygambis attended the mass marriage ceremony in Sousa in 324, which saw Alexander marry Stateira and Hephaistion Drypetis. When she learned of Alexander's death in June 323, S. refused food and died five days later (Curt. 10.5.19–25; Diod. 17.118.3; Justin 13.1.5). This, at least, is the romanticized version of events; for in the Vulgate sources she is depicted as a second mother to Alexander (Curt. 3.12.17; 5.2.22; Justin 13.1.5; Plut. *Mor.* 522a; Brosius 21). Niese I 191 n.2 speculates that her death might be related to that of her granddaughter (incorrectly, "ihrer Tochter") Stateira. Berve II 356–7 no. 711; Neuhaus 1902; Brosius 21, 67–8; Briant 1996, 752–3; Shayegan 122 no. 107. **Stemma III.**

1053 SITALKES

(Σιτάλκης). Apparently a prince of the Odrysian royal house (Hoffmann 182; Bosworth I 171), possibly even the son of Kersobleptes, S. commanded the Thrakian javelin-men (*akontistai*) since at least the beginning of the Asiatic campaign, and in this capacity served also as a hostage for the good conduct of his father; according to Front. *Strat.* 2.11.3 (cf. Justin 11.5.3), Alexander took the sons of Thrakian kings with him in order to ensure the loyalty of their fathers at home (cf. Ariston no. 201). S. first appears in the Pisidian campaign, in the attack on Sagalassos (334/3). Here the natives had occupied a hill-fort near the city and could only be dislodged by an attack of the lightly armed troops—the archers and Agrianes on the right, S.'s javelin-men on the left (Arr. 1.28.4). Doubtless, the latter played an important role in defeating the enemy, though Arrian's account concentrates on the activities of the right wing, where Alexander himself was present (1.28.5–8). In late 333, S. accompanied Parmenion, when he occupied the "other" Gates that led from Kilikia to Syria (Arr. 2.5.1; for their location see Bosworth I 192–93). And, at Issos (Arr. 2.9.3), as at Gaugamela (Arr. 3.12.4), he was stationed on the left wing. In 330, he remained with Parmenion at Ekbatana and later received, through the agency of Polydamas, orders to kill the old general (Arr. 3.26.3–4). But, when Alexander returned from India, S. like his colleagues, Kleandros, Herakon, and Agathon, who had participated in the murder of Parmenion, was found guilty of maladministration and executed (Arr. 6.27.4; cf. Curt. 10.1.1). Berve II 357 no. 712; Hoffmann 182; Heckel 1992, 334.

1054 SKYMNOS

(Σκύμνος). A magician or juggler (*thaumastopoios*) from Tarentum in Alexander's entourage (Athen. 1.20a), S. performed at the mass marriage ceremonies at Sousa in 324 (Chares, *FGrH* 125 F4 = Athen. 12.538e). See also Herakleitos and Philistides. Berve II 357 no. 713.

1055 SOKRATES

(Σωκράτης). Macedonian (Tataki 67 no. 10). Son of Sathon (Arr. 1.12.7), commanded the squadron from Apollonia since at least the beginning of the Asiatic expedition. In 334, he joined Amyntas son of Arrhabaios and the four squadrons of *prodromoi* in a scouting mission from Hermotos in the direction of the River Granikos (Arr. 1.12.7). At the river, he was again stationed next to Amyntas on the right wing (Arr. 1.14.1), and their units, along with an infantry battalion led by Ptolemy son of Philip, inititated the fighting by being the first to cross to the opposite bank (Arr. 1.14.6–15.1). Arrian does not name S. again. No full list is provided for the battle of Issos (late 333), but S. is no longer amongst the ilarchs at Gaugamela (Arr. 3.11.8). If Curtius (4.5.9) is not mistaken, S. took over, temporarily, the governorship of Kilikia; for Balakros, whom Alexander had appointed after the battle of Issos (Arr. 2.12.2), is soon found campaigning at, and capturing, Miletos (Curt. 4.5.13). Berve assumes that the Platon, who brought reinforcements from Kilikia to Alexander in 331/0 (Curt. 5.7.12), is actually Sokrates—with the Vulgate or Curtius himself confused by the names of two prominent philosophers (II 367; cf. II 429, Abschn. II no. 67; rejected by Bosworth 1974, 59 n.1). Curtius, however, calls Platon "an Athenian" and, if Berve's theory is correct, we have a confusion of both the man's name and his nationality. What became of S. the ilarch we do not know. Berve II 367 no. 732; Bosworth 1974; Bosworth I 120; Heckel 1992, 350–1; Hoffmann 186.

1056 SOLON

(Σόλων). Plataian, a metic (Paschidis 69 A11) and friend of Phokion (Plut. *Phoc.* 33.5). S. accompanied Phokion and Deinarchos of Korinth on a mission to Polyperchon in 319/18, which had disastrous consequences for the embassy (Plut. *Phoc.* 33–4). Those individuals who were subsequently put to death appear to have been Athenians. What became of S. is unclear. He may, like many others, have gone into hiding. Paschidis 69 A11.

1057 SOLON

(Σόλων). Son of Straton from Bargylia in Karia. He was honored by the Athenians for promoting their cause while campaigning with Demetrios Poliorketes in 304–302. (*IG* II² 496 + 507 = *Syll³* 347). He is otherwise unknown. Billows 433–4 no. 107; Osborne, *Naturalization* no. D61.

1058 SONIKOS

(Σώνικος). Greek or Macedonian. Perhaps an officer (almost certainly a supporter) of Polyperchon, who requested that he and Eukles be granted Athenian citizenship for their good services. This was done through the agency of Ktesias son of Chionides, who moved the decree (*IG* II² 387; *Syll³* 315; cf. Paschidis 72). Both S. and Eukles are otherwise unknown.

1059 SOPATROS

(Σώπατρος). Greek of unknown origin, though it is remotely possible that he is identical with the poet from Paphos who lived from the time of Alexander the Great to that of Ptolemy II Philadelphos (Athen. 2.71a). S. was said to have given the hoof of a Skythian donkey to Alexander; this was subsequently dedicated by the King to Delphi (Ael. *NA*

10.40; cf also Stobaeus, *Eclog.* 1.62, p. 421, 15 Wachsmuth). The truth of the story and the historicity of S. cannot be known. Whether the story has any bearing on that of Alexander's alleged poisoning, where the poisonous waters of the Arkadian Styx were transported to Babylon in an ass' hoof (Plut. *Alex.* 77; cf. Curt. 10.10.16; Arr. 7.27.1; Ps.-Call.3.31; Paus. 8.18.6; Justin 12.14.7), cannot be determined. Berve II 367 no. 733.

SOPEITHES. See SOPHYTES.

1060 SOPHOKLES

(Σοφοκλῆς). Athenian (Kirchner 12835). Sophokles son of Amphikleides Sounieus (Pollux 9.42). In 307/6, after the restoration of the democracy by Demetrios Poliorketes, S. sponsored a law making it illegal—on penalty of death—to run a philosophical school without the permission of the Athenian *boule* and *demos* (Diog. Laert. 5.38; Pollux 9.42; Athen. 13.610e–f). The measure induced Theophrastos to flee the city. But Philon prosecuted S. for introducing a law that was unconstitutional and, despite a vigorous defense by Demochares, S. was condemned and fined five talents (Diog. Laert. 5.38). The immediate effect of this court battle was that Theophrastos returned from his self-imposed exile (Diog. Laert. 5.38) and Epikouros soon came from Lampsakos to establish a third school of philosophy in Athens. Ferguson 104–7; Habicht 1997, 73–4.

1061 SOPHYTES

(Σωπείθης, Σωφύτης). Although we are dealing with Graecisms of an Indian name (perhaps Saubhūti), the form Sophytes appears on coin legends of the early third century (ΣΩΦΥΤΟΥ; see Mørkholm 73; cf. Holt 96–7). The dynast who issued the coinage was clearly not the same individual who encountered Alexander. The form Sophites occurs in Curtius, but is restored from *cufites* or *cofites* in Justin 12.8.10; Oros 3.19.5 has *cufides*. Indian king, whose realm was situated between the Hyarotis (or Hydraotis) and Hyphasis, and between that of the Adrestai and Kathaians (Diod. 17.91.2–4) and of Phegeus (Curt. 9.1.35–6). Sophytes surrendered voluntarily to Alexander (Curt. 9.1.28–30), together with his sons and was allowed to retain his kingdom (Diod. 17.91.7)—though probably as a vassal of Poros—which was reputed for its good institutions and the beauty of its inhabitants (Diod. 17.91.4–7; Curt. 9.1.24–6; Metz Epit. 66–8), and the Alexander historians comment on the good looks of the king himself. It was in Sophytes' kingdom that Alexander was treated to a demonstration of the courage and tenacity of Indian dogs (Diod. 17.92; Curt. 9.1.31–3; Metz Epit. 66–7; Strabo 15.1.31). Arrian, who does not mention Sophytes or Phegeus, says that when the fleet began its descent of the Hydaspes, Hephaistion, whose forces marched along the eastern bank of the river, was to hurry to the capital city of King Sopeithes (Arr. 6.2.2). Sophytes' kingdom cannot have extended in that direction, and we must assume that either there were two men named Sophytes or Sopeithes (certainly there were two rulers named Poros, but their territories were at least adjacent and they were different groups of the Pauravas) or Arrian's source is mistaken about the location of Sophytes' kingdom; Bosworth II 328 distinguishes between an "eastern" and "western" Sopeithes. The latter seems likely; for Strabo 15.1.30 C699 mentions just such a discrepancy in the sources and then tells the story of the king's hunting dogs (Strabo 15.1.31 C700). Strabo takes his information from Onesikritos (*FGrH* 134 F21), whose account was probably followed by Kleitarchos (and then Diodorus,

Curtius and Justin). The hunting dogs were discussed also by Aristoboulos (*FGrH* 139 F40). Berve II 367–8 nos. 734–5.

1062 SOPOLIS

(Σώπολις). Macedonian (Tataki 426 no. 56). Son of Hermodoros (Arr. 3.11.8), commanded the Amphipolitan squadron of Companion Cavalry since at least the Triballian campaign of 335 (Arr. 1.2.5), in which he appears together with Herakleides son of Antiochos, who led the Bottiaians. At Gaugamela, S.'s squadron was stationed between those of Ariston and Herakleides (Arr. 3.11.8). That he belonged to the Macedonian aristocracy is indicated not only by his important cavalry command but also by the fact that his son, Hermolaos, served as one of Alexander's Pages in 327. In the winter of 328/7 S. was sent from Nautaka, in the company of Menidas and Epokillos, to bring new recruits from Macedonia (Arr. 4.18.3). There is no record of his return to Alexander's camp, and we may assume that, after the disgrace of his son in 327, he did not think it wise to do so. Alexander may have sent orders that he be arrested and, perhaps, executed. But this is far from certain. It appears that Asklepiodoros, father of Hermolaos' fellow conspirator, Antipatros, lived on to become a trierarch of the Hydaspes fleet (Arr. *Ind.* 18.3, with Jacoby's emendation). Berve II 368–9 no. 736; Hoffmann 186; Heckel 1992, 351.

1063 SOPOLIS

(Σώπολις). One of three officers (see also Hieron no. 530, and Machaon no. 676) of the garrison stationed at Iasos by Polemaios, the nephew of Antigonos (cf. Diod. 19.75.1–6). An inscription (*I.Iasos* I no. 2), dating in all likelihood to 309/8, when Polemaios defected to Ptolemy (Diod.20.27.1–3), shows that they and the city came to terms with Ptolemy I. Billows 343 no. 108; Bagnall 89–91.

1064 SOSIGENES

(Σωσιγένης). Rhodian. Sosigenes is not mentioned by the Alexander historians, but he served as *nauarchos* of the fleet of about 200 ships sent by Perdikkas against the pro-Ptolemaic forces in Kypros in 321/0 (Arr. *Succ.* 24.6), very soon after the King's death. Although the expedition achieved little—in part, because of the efforts of Antigonos the One-Eyed, but also because of Perdikkas' defeat and death in Egypt—Sosigenes and his fleet appear to have remained with Eumenes. In 317/16, S. sailed with money from Eumenes from Phoinikia and put in at Kilikia. There he was met by victorious ships from Antigonos' victory at the Hellespont. The appearance of these caused S.'s men to defect with the treasure while the admiral, who was on shore surveying the tides was helpless to stop them (Polyaenus 4.6.9). S. may, if not at that point then later (I do not see on what evidence Billows 87 asserts that S. "managed to get away to sea"), have gone over to Antigonos. In that case, he may be identical with the friend of Demetrios who was with him at the time of capture by Seleukos (Plut. *Demetr.* 49.7). Berve II 369 no. 737; Hauben 91–3 no. 32.

1065 SOSTRATOS

(Σώστρατος). Son of Amyntas, lover of Hermolaos (Arr. 4.13.3; Curt. 8.6.8). S. joined (Arr.) or instigated (Curt.) the "conspiracy of the Pages" on account of the outrage done to Hermolaos. For his part he was arrested, tortured and executed (Arr. 4.13.7–14.2; Curt.

8.8.20; Plut. *Alex.* 55.6; Justin 12.7.2). Curt. 8.6.9 lists a conspirator named Nikostratos (Berve II 280 no. 570; Hoffmann 180); this is probably a corruption of the name Sostratos. Berve II 369 no. 738; Hoffmann 179; Heckel 1992, 295.

1066 SOSTRATOS

(Σώστρατος). Son of Ste(phanos?). Honored by the Ephesians citizenship for his actions while serving Demetrios. (*I.Ephesos* V no. 1440). It is not clear whether this refers to activities before or after the battle of Ipsos. Billows 434 no. 109

1067 SOTIMOS

(Σώτιμος). Honored in 304/3 by the Athenians at Demetrios' request for benefactions to the city while serving Poliorketes (Koumanoudes, *Horos* 4 (1986) 11–18). He is otherwise unknown. Billows 434 no. 110

1068 SPARTOKOS

(Σπάρτοκος). Spartokos II. Brother of Pairisades I, with whom he shared the kingship. First the brothers were co-rulers with their father, Leukon (Tod. I 163 dating to 350), and then with each other. S. was honored by the Athenians, along with his two brothers, Pairisades and Apollonios in 347/6 (*IG* II² 212; Harding no. 82; *Syll³* 206). He and his immediate ancestors extended favorable trade privileges to the Athenians (details in Tuplin 1982). S. died in 344/3. No sons are attested. Full discussion in Werner; Burstein 1978; Tuplin 1982.

1069 SPARTOKOS

(Σπάρτοκος). Spartokos III (*regn.* 304/3–284/3: Werner 430). Son of Eumelos (no. 442) son of Pairisades I. His father ruled the Kimmerian Bosporos from 310/09 to 304/3 after overcoming his brothers. Since his father had killed all potential rivals, except for Pairisades son of Satyros, who fled to the Skythians (Diod. 20.24.3), S. gained the throne on Eumelos' death and ruled for 20 years (Diod. 20.100.7). He was honored in Athens in 289/8 (*IG* II² 653, on which see Burstein 1978).

1070 SPARTON

(Σπάρτων). Rhodian, patronymikon unknown, brother of Demaratos. He and his brother were arrested at Sardis by Alexander but freed through the efforts of Phokion (Plut. *Phoc.* 18.6; Ael. *VH* 1.25). The reason for his arrest is unknown; nor do we know anything about his personal or political connections with Phokion. It is possible that he and his brother belonged to the anti-Macedonian faction in Rhodes, which reasserted itself in 323. S. himself is not heard of again, but Demaratos reappears in 320 as a Rhodian nauarch, defeating the forces of Attalos, son of Andromenes (Arr. *Succ.* 1.39). Berve II 358 no. 714; Obst, *RE* IIIA. 2 (1929) 1543; Hofstetter 167 no. 295.

1071 SPITAKES

(Σπιτάκης, also Πιτακκός). Arr. 6.18.2 speaks of an Indian nomarch named Spitakes who was killed in the battle at the Hydaspes. He does not, however, identify him as a relative of Poros, but instead mentions also two sons of Poros who were killed in the same battle. Hence, it is unlikely that Arrian regarded S. as one of Poros' relatives. Polyaenus 4.3.21

corrupts the name Spitakes into Pittakos and calls him a nephew of the Indian ruler (cf. Curt. 8.14.2 who speaks of a brother of Poros). The confusion of ἀδελφός and ἀδελφιδοῦς is easy enough, as is the corruption of the genitive Σπιτάκου into Πιττάκου. The problem is, however, that Arr. 5.18.2; cf. 5.14.3–15.2 makes a distinction between S. and the sons of Poros, saying that it was one of Poros' sons who led the force assigned by Curt. 8.14.2 to Poros' brother. To add to the confusion the text of Curtius reads *praemisit Hages* which has been emended to *praemisit Spitaces*. The emendation is compelling, but it does not solve the basic problem that the lost sources appear to have distinguished between the nomarch S. and a relative (son, nephew, brother) of Poros. Polyaenus' story clearly refers to an incident before the Hydaspes battle, an attempt to ambush Alexander en route to the Hydaspes (cf. Stein 1937, 11, with n.7). Thus it seems that after the unsuccessful ambush, S. withdrew to Poros' main force and then was sent with 100 chariots and 4,000 cavalry to oppose Alexander's crossing to the north of Poros' main camp (Curt. 8.14.2). S. was apparently killed in the skirmish that followed (Curt. 8.14.2–8; Arr. 5.18.2). It appears that the primary sources were confused about the identity of S. and his role in the battle. It is clear that the command attributed by some to a son of Poros was ascribed by others to S. I find it difficult to accept Bosworth's suggestion (II 303–4) that Pittakos was a nephew of the so-called Bad Poros. The sources speak of no resistance by the other Poros (or his relatives) and the campaign against him was conducted by Hephaistion. Berve II 358 no. 716.

1072 SPITAMENES

(Σπιταμένης). Prominent Baktrian or Sogdianian, perhaps of Iranian ancestry. Supporter and close friend of Bessos (Curt. 7.5.19), S. accompanied him across the Oxos River into Sogdiana when Alexander invaded Baktria (Arr. 3.28.10) but soon plotted to arrest Bessos and hand him over to the Macedonians (Arr. 3.29.6, 30.1; Curt. 7.5.19–26). Whether he surrendered Bessos in person (Curt. 7.5.36–8; Arr. 3.30.5 = Aristoboulos, *FGrH* 139 F24) or left him in chains to be picked up by Ptolemy son of Lagos (Arr. 3.30.2–4) is unclear. Certainly, S. did not trust Alexander, for in 329 he refused to attend a conference at Zariaspa-Baktra (Arr. 4.1.5) and soon continued to resist the Macedonians. S. besieged the Macedonian garrison at Marakanda when Alexander advanced to the Iaxartes (Arr. 4.3.6, 5.2–3). When the King sent Andromachos, Menedemos, Karanos, and Pharnouches against him (Arr. 4.3.7), S., with the aid of some 600 Skythian horsemen ambushed the Macedonian force at the Polytimetos River (Arr. 4.5.4–9; a slightly different version in Aristoboulos: Arr. 4.6.1–2 = *FGrH* 139 F27) and then withdrew at the news of Alexander's advance, perhaps to the vicinity of Bokhara (Arr. 4.6.3–4; cf. Brunt I 505). In the following year S. attacked Baktra, which was lightly defended, killing several, including Aristonikos the harpist, and taking Peithon son of Sosikles prisoner (Arr. 4.16.4–7). His incursions were checked by Krateros and Koinos (Arr. 4.17), and soon S. was betrayed by his Massagetan allies, who sent his head to Alexander (Arr. 4.17.7; Strabo 11.11.6 C518). Curt. 8.3.1–10 and Metz Epit. 20–1 have a different version of S.'s death, reporting that he was murdered by his own wife, who brought his head into the Macedonian camp. (Burstein 1999 believes that the story of Judith may have been influenced by Kleitarchos' account of the death of S.) His daughter Apama married Seleukos at the mass marriage in Sousa in 324 (Arr. 7.4.6; Plut. *Demetr.* 31.5; see also s.v. Apama no. 138 and Grainger, *SPG* 67). Berve II 359–61 no. 717; Shayegan 122–3 no. 108; Heckel 190–6.

1073 SPITHRIDATES

(Σπιθριδάτης, Σπιθροβάτης, Diod. 17.20.2; Spinther: Ps.-Call. 1.39, 2.10; Jul Val 1.41, 2.18). A Persian noble descended from the Seven (cf. Diod. 16.47.2)—perhaps a relative of that Spithridates who was active in the Hellespontine region and Paphlagonia at the beginning of the fourth century (Xen. *HG* 3.4.10; 4.1.3, 20, 26–7) and apparently the son of Rhoisakes, the satrap of Ionia *c.*344/3 (Diod. 16.47.1–2)—S. was a son-in-law of Dareios III (unless Diodorus confuses him with Mithridates, Arr. 1.16.3; cf. Berve II 358 n.2) and satrap of Ionia in 334 (Diod. 17.20.2; Arr. 1.12.8, Lydia and Ionia); the younger Rhoisakes (no. 1027) was his brother (Diod. 17.20.6, Rhosakes). S. led some 40 of the Persian Kinsmen (*syngeneis*) against the Macedonian line at the Granikos River (Diod. 17.20.2), and, according to Diod. 17.20.3–5 (cf. Curt. 8.1.20), he engaged in single combat with Alexander only to be killed by him. Arr. 1.16.7–8 and Plut. *Alex.* 16.8–11 reverse the roles of the brothers, but S.'s death in the battle is certain (Arr. 1.16.3; Plut. *Mor.* 326f). Berve II 358 no. 715; Krumbholz 70; Shayegan 119 no. 96, also 123–4 no. 109.

1074 STAMENES

(Σταμένης, Ditamenes: Curt. 8.3.17). Iranian, but both forms of the name may be corrupt. In the winter of 328/7, at Nautaka, Alexander appointed S. satrap of Babylonia, to replace Mazaios, who had recently died (Arr. 4.18.3; cf. Curt. 8.3.17; Arrian says he was sent to Babylon, apparently from Nautaka). How long S. remained in office is unclear. In the settlement that followed Alexander's death, Archon of Pella was appointed satrap of Babylonia, but it is not clear whether this was a new appointment or the confirmation of one made by Alexander himself after the death or removal from office of S. The latter seems more likely. Nothing else is known about him. Berve II 361 no. 718; Shayegan 124 no. 110.

1075 STASANDROS

(Στάσανδρος). Kypriot Greek, possibly a relative or friend of Stasanor of Soloi (see below). He is not mentioned by the Alexander historians but may have spent the mid-320s in Aria-Drangiana with Stasanor, whom he replaced in the settlement at Triparadeisos in 320 (Diod. 18.39.6), when Stasanor was assigned Baktria-Sogdiana. In the war against Antigonos in 318–317, S. supported Eumenes, bringing with him a contingent of Baktrians (Diod. 19.14.7, 27.3). He is not heard of again after the battle of Gabiene. Perhaps he was one of those leaders in Eumenes' army whose deaths are alluded to in Diod. 19.44.1. Unlike Stasanor and Tlepolemos, of whom the former was not present and the latter appears to have fled, S. was replaced as satrap (Diod. 19.48.2). This suggests that he did not return to his satrapy. It is possible of course that he died in the battle of Gabiene and that the fact went unrecorded, though he may have taken refuge with Stasanor, whose satrapy was left untouched by Antigonos. Aria-Drangiana was assigned by Antigonos to Evitos, who died soon afterwards and was replaced by Euagoras, possibly another Kypriot (Diod. 19.48.2; Klinkott 2000, 75). Launey 1229; Fiehn, *RE* IIIA.2 (1929) 2152.

1076 STASANOR

(Στασάνωρ). Kypriot Greek from Soloi, probably a member of the ruling house, S. accompanied Alexander since 332/1 as one of his *hetairoi* (Strabo 14.6.3 C683; Arr. 3.29.5). Berve II 361 suggests that he may have been a younger brother of Pasikrates. Although this is far from certain—indeed, it is curious that Nikokles is identified as a son of Pasikrates but no mention is made of S.'s family background—there were several members of Kypriot ruling houses enrolled as *hetairoi* of the King. Stasandros may have been a relative. In 330/29 he was assigned the task of arresting and replacing the rebellious satrap of Aria, Arsakes (Arr. 3.29.5). In winter 328/7 he brought Arsakes in chains to Alexander at Nautaka (Arr. 4.18.1) and had his satrapy enlarged to include Drangiana (Arr. 4.18.3). Cf. Bosworth II 38–9. Arr. 4.7.1 says he returned in 329/8 to Alexander in Zariaspa. This is unlikely, and it appears that we are dealing with a failure on Arrian's part to reconcile the information of his sources. Diod. 17.81.3 says that S. and Erigyios were sent to deal with the rebel Satibarzanes. Arr. 3.28.3 and Curt. 7.3.2, 4.32 name Karanos as Erigyios' colleague. Diodorus may have compressed the information about the crushing of Satibarzanes' rebellion and the later appointment of Stasanor. Curt. 8.3.17 muddles things as well, saying that S. replaced "Arsames" (but see s.v. Arsames no. 218) and confusing Atropates with Arsakes. When Alexander reached Karmania, Stasanor joined him with Phrataphernes' son Pharismenes (Arr. 6.27.3), bringing a large number of pack animals and camels (Arr. 6.27.6). Alexander again sent him back to his satrapy (Arr. 6.29.1) but he appears to have rejoined the King in Sousa, bringing barbarian troops to serve in his army (Arr. 7.6.1, 3). According to the Pamphlet on the *Last Days and Testament of Alexander*, S. was present at the dinner party given by Medeios of Larisa, at which the King was poisoned; S. is named as one of the conspirators (*LM* 97–8; Ps.-Call. 3.31.8–9). In the settlement at Babylon, he was confirmed as satrap of Aria and Drangiana (Diod. 18.3.3; Justin 13.4.22–3, "Staganor," and 41.4.1, mistakenly assigning him Parthia; Dexippos, *FGrH* 100 F8 §4; cf. *LM* 121). In 320, at Triparadeisos, he was reassigned to Baktria-Sogdiana (Diod. 18.39.6; Arr. *Succ.* 1.36). He appears to have sent troops to aid Eumenes but did not come in person (Diod. 19.14.7; these were led by Stasandros). Antigonos did not attempt to dislodge him from his satrapy after Gabiene because of the remoteness of the area and the difficulty involved (Diod. 19.48.1). Billows 449, on the basis of Diod. 19.56.5, 61.4, assumes that S. and the other "inner Asian" satraps recognized Antigonos' authority. S. later made himself unpopular in his satrapy (Porphyr. *de abstin.* 4.21) and may not have remained in power for long. At the latest, he may have been ousted by Seleukos (thus Billows 449, though I do not accept the view that he had earlier assumed control of Parthia). Berve II 361–2 no. 719; Julien 38; Lehmann-Haupt, *Satrap* 158; Launey 1228. Badian 1961, 18; cf. Briant 1973, 94 n.5; Billows 448–9 no. 136; Mendoza Sanahuja 2017.

1077 STASIOIKOS

(Στασίοικος). Stasioikos II. Kypriot. King of Marion (330?–313). Put to death by Ptolemy in 313/12 for siding with Antigonos (Diod. 19.79.4). The town was destroyed and its inhabitants moved to Paphos. Catling, *OCD*³ 924–5 s.v. "Marium-Arsinoë."

1078 STATEIRA

(Στάτειρα). Her name is given only by Plut. *Alex.* 30.5, 8. The wife and sister of Dareios III (Plut. *Alex.* 30.3; Arr. 2.11.9; Justin 11.9.12; Gell. *NA* 7.8.3), S. need not, however, have been the daughter of Sisygambis. The sources describe the latter as "mother of Dareios" and "grandmother of Dareios' children" but never as S.'s mother (cf. Brosius 68). She may thus have been the daughter of Arsanes (Diod. 17.5.5) by another wife or concubine (cf. the brother-sister relationship of Dareios II and Parysatis, who were children of Artaxerxes I by different Babylonian concubines, if Ktesias, *FGrH* 688 F15 §47, is to be believed). Born perhaps between 370 and 365, S. married Dareios not much later than 350; for their daughters, Stateira (below) and Drypetis, are described as *adultae virgines* in late 333 (Curt. 3.12.25). A son, Ochos, was born in 339 (Diod. 17.38.2; Curt. 3.11.24). According to the romantic tradition, she was the most beautiful woman in Asia (Arr. 4.19.5–6; Plut. *Alex.* 21.6; Curt. 3.11.24, 12.22; 4.10.24), a claim which serves to emphasize Alexander's restraint. In 333 S., together with her mother and children, accompanied Dareios to Issos, where, after his flight from the battlefield they were captured by Alexander (Curt. 3.11.24ff.; Plut. *Alex.* 21; Diod. 17.36.2–4, 37.3, 38.2; Arr. 2.11.9). Alexander's moderation and respectful treatment of the Persian queens, and his famous visit to their tent, became well-worn themes of the Alexander-Vulgate (Plut. *Alex.* 21; Curt. 3.11.24–5, 12.1–26; Diod. 17.36.3–5; Justin 11.9.12–16; Arr. 2.12.3–8; cf. Val. Max. 4.7 ext. 2). But Alexander must have given serious consideration to the value of the King's wife and daughters as hostages (cf. their importance in the diplomatic exchanges: Arr. 2.25.1; Curt. 4.1.8; cf. 4.5.1ff.; Diod. 17.54.1–5) or for their political impact (cf. Bosworth I 221). Ptolemy and Aristoboulos (*FGrH* 138 F6, 139 F10 = Arr. 2.12.3–6) imply that Alexander never saw S. (cf. Plut. *Mor.* 338e, 522a; Gell. *NA* 7.8.3: he would not even hear about her beauty). Yet, the date and circumstances of her death cloud the issue considerably: the Vulgate is consistent in dating S.'s death to shortly before the battle of Gaugamela (Justin 11.12.6; Curt. 4.10.18ff.; Diod. 17.54.7; Plut. *Alex.* 30.1) and Justin agrees with Plutarch that she died in childbirth (miscarriage). Berve (II 363; cf. Hamilton 78) places her death in 332, which cannot be inferred from Arr. 4.20.1–2 (conflating the eunuch who escaped after Issos with Teireos. Note that Dareios learns that his wife and children are alive). Either pregnancy played no part in S.'s death or she was not carrying Dareios' child (cf. Bradford Welles 275 n. 3; Bosworth I 221). On the other hand, it was certainly not the aim of the Vulgate to suggest (even in the most subtle way) that S. was pregnant with Alexander's child, since the same tradition reiterates that Alexander had seen her only once (Curt. 4.10.24), in late 333. Furthermore, the eunuch Teireos brings the news of her death, and of Alexander's grief and honorable conduct, to Dareios (Plut. *Alex.* 30.2ff.; Curt. 4.10.25–34, with dramatic embellishment, calling the eunuch Tyriotes). Why her death would have been recorded in the wrong historical context (Atkinson I 392) is difficult to understand; but the diplomatic negotiations of 331, admittedly, make no further reference to Dareios' wife (Curt. 4.5.1ff.; Diod. 17.54.1–5). Alexander ordered a sumptuous funeral, in keeping with the woman's former station (Curt. 4.10.23; Diod. 17.54.7; Plut. *Alex.* 30.1; Plut. *Mor.* 338e). Berve II 362–3 no. 721; Shayegan 124 no. 111. **Stemma III.**

1079 STATEIRA

(Στάτειρα). Daughter of Dareios III, she is named by Curt. 4.5.1; Diod. 17.107.6; Justin 12.10.9; Plut. *Alex.* 70.3, 77.6; cf. *Fragmentum Sabbaiticum* = *FGrH* 151 F1 §5; Aristoboulos calls her Barsine (Arr. 7.4.4 = *FGrH* 139 F52; Arr. *ap.* Phot. Bibl. 68b §7 has Ἀρσινόη, an easy corruption of Βαρσίνη). S. was apparently the elder of the known daughters of Dareios III and Stateira, an assumption based on the fact that Alexander married her instead of Drypetis but otherwise unsubstantiated. Granddaughter of Sisygambis (cf. Curt. 3.11.25; 4.10.19, 21); sister of Drypetis and Ochos; cousin of Amastris (Memnon 4.4 *ap.* Phot. *Bibl.* 224 = *FGrH* 434 F1). She and her mother, grandmother, and siblings accompanied Dareios III to Issos, where, after Dareios' flight, they were captured by Alexander (Curt. 3.11.25; Diod. 17.36.2; Arr. 2.11.9, cf. Arr. *ap.* Phot. *Bibl.* 67b; Justin 11.9.12; Plut. *Alex.* 21.1) and visited by both Leonnatos (Plut. *Alex.* 21.1–4; Curt. 3.12.7–12) and the King himself (Curt. 3.12.13–26). Alexander treated her with respect (Curt. 3.12.21; 4.11.3, respecting her royal status) and said he would see to their dowries better than even Dareios would have (Diod. 17.38.1). Although Dareios wrote Alexander, shortly before the battle at Gaugamela (Arr. 2.25.1 places it in the preceding year, during the siege of Tyre; cf. Curt. 4.5.1; see also Bosworth I 256–7; Atkinson I 320–1), offering to pay a ransom—of 10,000 talents each—for the members of his family (Curt. 4.11.6, 12; Plut. *Alex.* 29.7; Diod. 17.54.2; Justin 11.12.10) and to give one of his daughters (Curt. 4.5.1 names S. in an earlier context) to Alexander as his wife (Curt. 4.11.5–6, the return of *duas virgines filias* demanded by Dareios in §6 does not rule out that S. was the intended bride in §5; Diod. 17.54.2; Justin 11.12.3), the offers—favored by Parmenion (Curt. 4.11.12)—were rejected (Curt. 4.11.15; Justin 11.12.2). Left behind at Sousa at the very end of 331 (Curt. 5.2.17)—she was given instruction in the Greek language (Diod. 17.67.1; Curt. 5.2.18ff. has an implausible story about "wool-working"; cf. Briant 2015, 331–4)—where she remained until Alexander's return in 324, when she became (along with Parysatis, daughter of Ochos) one of his royal brides (Diod. 17.107.6; Justin 12.10.9; Plut. *Alex.* 70.3; Aristoboulos, *FGrH* 139 F52 = Arr. 7.4.4: Brosius 77 n.68 believes her name was changed from Barsine to Stateira for political reasons, to emphasize Alexander's legitimacy; cf. Curt. 10.3.12; Memnon 4.4 *ap.* Phot. *Bibl.* 224 = *FGrH* 434 F1); her sister Drypetis married Hephaistion (Arr. 7.4.5; Diod. 17.107.6). Soon after the marriage, however, Alexander died, leaving his first wife, Rhoxane, pregnant; the latter concerned for the birthright of her child, summoned S. and her sister to her, murdered them both and threw them into a well (Plut. *Alex.* 77.6); the fact that she was aided in this by Perdikkas underscores the political background to S.'s murder. Berve II 363 no. 722; Kaerst, *RE* III 29 s.v. "Barsine (1)"; Shayegan 124–5 no. 112; Aulbach §4.2.2. **Stemma III.**

1080 STEPHANOS

(Στέφανος). Greek youth in Alexander's entourage and, because of his ugliness, the object of ridicule. He was nearly killed as a result of a cruel joke played by an Athenian named Athenophanes, who smeared naphtha on the boy's face and set it on fire (Plut. *Alex.* 35.5–9). Strabo 16.1.15 C743 attributes this act of cruelty to Alexander himself, an unlikely story. Nevertheless, the King appears to have condoned the mockery, at least in its early stages (Tarn II 300, predictably, rejects the story in its entirety). Berve II 15 no. 31; Kirchner 285.

1081 STILPON

(Στίλπων). References in **boldface** are to Diogenes Laertius. Megarian philosopher. About his personal life very little is known, and most of that trivial. Though he was married with a spendthrift daughter (who married Simmias of Syracuse), S. had a mistress named Nikarete (**2.114**). In 308, Ptolemy offered him a large sum of money and wanted him to accompany him to Egypt. S. accepted only a small amount and declined to visit Ptolemy's court, going instead to Aigina until Ptolemy sailed away from Megara (**2.115**). When Demetrios Poliorketes captured Megara in 307, he met with Stilpon and asked him if he had lost anything, but the philosopher simply replied that, to his knowledge, no one had stolen any knowledge (Plut. *Demetr.* 9.9; cf. Plut. *Mor.* 5f). Furthermore, Stilpon commented on Demetrios' remark that he left Megara a city of free men that this was true because the Antigonid forces had carried off all the slaves (Plut. *Demetr.* 9.10). The besieger and the philosopher may, indeed, have met, but the nature of their verbal exchange is strongly reminiscent of Alexander's meeting with Diogenes in Korinth and therefore suspect. His fame was such that he attracted crowds when he came to Athens, probably after its "liberation" by Demetrios (**2.119**). S. died a very old man (probably in the early third century), having consumed wine to hasten his death (**2.120**). Praechter, *RE* III A.2 (1929) 2525; Sedley, *OCD*³ 1444.

1082 STRATOKLES

(Στρατοκλῆς). Athenian (Kirchner 12938; *LGPN* II no. 22) from a wealthy family (Davies 494–5). Son of Euthydemos of Diomeia. Orator and flatterer of Demetrios. Plut. *Mor.* 798e–f censures Stratokles and Dromokleides and their supporters for seeking profit from the *bema* (cf. Plut. *Mor.* 799f–800a for his shameless behavior; cf. also Plut. *Demetr.* 11). S. began his political career, as far as we know, as one of the prosecutors of Demosthenes, and although his speech is not preserved we are told that he held Demosthenes responsible for the fate of Thebes in 335 (Phot. *Bibl.* 447a). After his false report of an Athenian victory at Amorgos (Plut. *Demetr.* 11.4–5; Bayliss sees this as a ploy to encourage the Athenians; but Plutarch's view that it demonstrated his buffoonery was probably shared by many of S.'s contemporaries, and not just his enemies), he was absent from political life (not surprising in the time of Demetrios of Phaleron) until the restoration of the democracy in 307. S. proposed honors for Antigonos and Demetrios that included golden statues and crowns, and also altars that recognized them as Saviors. Two tribes were named after them, as were a pair of state triremes, and their images were displayed on the *peplos* of Athena (Plut. *Demetr.* 10.3–11; 12.1; 13.1; Diod. 20.46.2; Philochoros, *FGrH* 328 FF48, 165–6; Polemon *ap.* Harpocration s.v. ἔνη καὶ νέα). This flattery had the desired effect of eliciting benefactions from the Antigonids. Some twenty-eight decrees survive that attest to his activities under the restored democracy (see Paschidis 80, with nn.2–11 for details, references and literature), many of them honoring friends of the Antigonids (for *eunoia* towards the city and for aid against its enemies: *IG* II² 469, 471, 486, 492, 495, 496, 503, 507). Paschidis gives a nuanced picture of S.'s career, suggesting that his actions and acts of 307–304 were more for the benefit of the city than has usually been thought, but that in 303–302 he was more concerned with his own political power, in the face of increased opposition to Demetrios (2008, 105–6). Certainly, S. was, and portrayed himself as, the intermediary between the city and the King. But his final known decree, honoring the oligarch Philippides in 294 (Paschidis 105 rightly notes that it represents a "reconciliaton between two former opponents") indicates that without Demetrios, S.'s influence in the city was negligible. Berve II 364 no. 724; Paschidis 78–106 A19; Bayliss 152–86 for a revisionist view of Stratokles.

1083 STRATON

(Στράτων). A Graecism of the Phoinikian Abd-astart ("servant of Astarte"). The son of Gerostratos, S. ruled the island Arados (also Marathos, Sigon and Mariamme) in the absence of his father (Curt. 4.1.6 calls him *rex eius insulae*; but Gerostratos' kingship is clear from Arr. 2.13.7), who served with the Persian fleet under Autophradates. On Alexander's entry into Phoinikia, S. met him (near Marathos), surrendered himself and his territories, and presented the King with a golden crown (Arr. 2.13.7–8; 4.1.5–6). Grainger 1991, 34 suggests plausibly that Arados, as an island, could have attempted to hold out against Alexander, especially if Gerostratos had returned with the fleet (but see Droysen I³ 180). The impact of Issos must have been a deciding factor. It appears that Gerostratos was reinstated as ruler of Arados upon his own surrender (Arr. 2.20.1); the coin issued in S.'s name (Head, *HN*² 788) probably belongs to the period of S.'s regency in 333/2 (cf. Bosworth I 226). Aside from this coin, of disputed date, we have no further record of him. Berve II 365 no. 727; Grainger 1991, 33–5.

1084 STRATON

(Στράτων, Abd-astart; for the name see above). Phoinikian, King of Sidon. Although he was the successor of Tennes, or Tabnit II (Head, *HN*² 796), who had rebelled against Artaxerxes III in 351 and later sought to save himself by betraying the city to the Great King in 345 (Diod. 16.43.1–45.4; for the date see Smith, *BHT* 148ff.; also Judeich 148–9), he appears to have been unrelated to him (thus Grainger 1991, 28). Tabnit's treachery did not save him, and he was executed on Ochos' instructions once Sidon had fallen into Persian hands (Diod. 16.45.4). If it was his own father whom Straton succeeded in 345/4, he was both the son of a traitor and a Persian appointee (presumably he remained under the watchful eye of Mazaios, to whose satrapy of Kilikia-Syria had been added; cf. Olmstead 437) and thus an object of suspicion. It appears, however, that Straton II was either the son or grandson of Straton I, the luxury-loving Sidonian king, mentioned by Anaximenes and Theopompos as a rival of the Kypriot ruler, Nikokles, and honored by the Athenians *c.*367 (Tod II no. 139; but R&O 88–91 no. 21 propose a date for the decree a decade earlier), or he may have been the grandfather. S.'s extravagant lifestyle is described at length by Theopompos (*FGrH* 115 F114; cf. Shrimpton 1991, 74, 148; Flower 1994, 68) and Anaximenes, *FGrH* 72 F18. See Judeich 209. Athen. 12.531d–e (= Anaximenes, *FGrH* 72 F18, though perhaps ultimately from Theopompos; see Flower 1994, 195) speaks of a violent death. Straton I may have been overthrown by Tennes. After Tennes' death the kingship may have returned to the house of Straton. The numismatic evidence suggests two rulers by the name of Straton (Abd-astart) between 345 and 333. That family appears to have remained loyal to Persia, and, even after the Persian defeat at Issos, S. continued to side with Dareios III, and he was consequently deposed by Alexander upon his arrival in Sidon (Curt. 4.1.16; Diod. 17.47.1). His pro-Persian stance was not popular with the Sidonians themselves, who appear to have forced S. into submitting to the King (Arr. 2.15.6; cf. Curt. 4.1.16). On the basis of Curt. 4.1.24, Berve II 3 sees the opponents of

Abdalonymos as the supporters of S. and the wealthy nobility ("Geldadel"). If Sidon was, in fact, destroyed on the scale depicted by Diod. 16.45 (questioned by Beloch III² 1.535 n.2), then S. must have taken important measures to revive the city, ones which doubtless benefited the business class. Straton was perhaps executed, or turned over to the Sidonians for punishment. The extant Alexander historians do not speak of him as present in Sidon when the Macedonians arrived, and Niese I 78 n.5 assumes that he was with the fleet at the time that the city surrendered (cf. Rawlinson 216). For his coinage see Betlyon 1982, 29–2. Hill LX–LXV; Bosworth I 235; Betlyon 1976; Cawkwell 1963, 136–8; Beloch III² 1.535; Olmstead 437; Babelon 1891, 311–13; Berve II 365–6 no. 728.

1085 STRATONIKE

(Στρατονίκη). Macedonian (Tataki 433 no. 42). Daughter of Korrhagos and wife of Antigonos Monophthalmos (Plut. *Demetr.* 2.1); she was the mother of Demetrios and Philip (Diod. 21.1.4b), though Plutarch reports a rumor that she was previously married to Antigonos' brother Demetrios, who was thought by some to be the father of Poliorketes. She followed her husband to Asia Minor and resided in or near Kelainai—at least, not far from where Dokimos and Attalos son of Andromenes were imprisoned. She appears to have intrigued with the former to secure his escape and his subsequent loyalty to the Antigonids (Diod. 19.16.4, also indicating that Stratonike had a personal guard). At the time of the battle of Ipsos (301) she remained in Kilikia with all her possessions, and after the battle and Antigonos' death, she was taken by Demetrios to Salamis on Kypros, an Antigonid possession (Diod. 21.1.4b). In 297, however, Salamis was taken by Ptolemy, and S. and Demetrios' young children were captured but soon released (Plut. *Demetr.* 35.5; 38.1). Macurdy 62, 64–6; Ogden 172; Aulbach §8.1.1. **Stemma XI.**

1086 STRATONIKE

(Στρατονίκη). Macedonian (Tataki 433 no. 40). Daughter of Demetrios Poliorketes and Phila, the daughter of Antipatros (Plut. *Demetr.* 31.5); sister of Antigonos Gonatas (Plut. *Demetr.* 53. 8). Married Seleukos I Nikator (Nepos, *De regibus* 3.3; Plut. *Demetr.* 31.5–6) in Syria, soon after the battle of Ipsos. Phila joined Demetrios and S. en route to Rhossos, where the marriage was celebrated with great festivity; thereafter S. accompanied her new husband to Antioch (Plut. *Demetr.* 32.2–3). Bore Seleukos a daughter named Phila, who later married Antigonos Gonatas. But S. soon captivated the young Antiochos I (Soter) and, on the advice of the physician Erasistratos, married him with Seleukos' approval (Plut. *Demetr.* 38; App. *Syr.* 59.308–12, 61.327). Seleukos named the city Stratonikeia after her (App. *Syr.* 57.295). After the second marriage, S. went with Antiochos I to Upper Asia (App. *Syr.* 61.327) and disappointed her father Demetrios, who had been captured in Kilikia and imprisoned in Syria, by not interceding on his behalf (Plut. *Demetr.* 50.9, 51.4). The couple had four children: Antiochos II (App. *Syr.* 65), Seleukos and Apama (Euseb. 1.250), and another Stratonike (Porph. Tyr. F32.5). Her death in 253 is recorded in Babylon (Sachs and Hunger, *Astronomical Diaries* –253). Grainger, *SPG* 67–8; Macurdy 78–82; Broderson 1985; Aulbach §7.1.1.3 (7.2.1.1). **Stemma XI.**

1087 STRATTIS

(Στράττις). Olynthian of unknown family. Born before the destruction of the city by Philip in 348, S. may have accompanied Alexander on the expedition, possibly as a member of the chancellery (thus Berve II 365). Of his actual activities nothing is known, but he is named as an author of a work *On Rivers, Springs and Lakes*, as well as what appears to have been a commentary in five books of the *Ephemerides* (*Suda* Σ 1179). Nothing that is recorded about him or his works can be taken as certain. Berve II 365 no. 726; Bosworth 1988, 180–2; Gude no. 112; Jacoby, *FGrH* 118; omitted by Pearson.

1088 STROIBOS

(Στροῖβος). Greek slave who used to read aloud to Kallisthenes. S. had apparently accompanied his master from the beginning of the campaign. He gave a written account to Aristotle of Kallisthenes' quarrel with Alexander, which Plutarch used via Hermippos (Plut. *Alex.* 54.1). Nothing else is known about him. Berve II 366 no. 729; Hamilton 149.

1089 STROMBICHOS

(Στρόμβιχος). Macedonian (Tataki 434 no. 47). Polyperchon's *phrourarchos* of Arkadian Orchomenos. In 302, he refused to surrender to Demetrios Poliorketes, and went so far as to abuse him verbally. When Demetrios captured the citadel, he crucified S. in front of the town, along with 80 of the most hostile defenders; the rest of the mercenary force— some 2,000—he incorporated in his army (Diod. 20.103.5–6). In this episode Demetrios practiced a brutality that was more typical of his father.

1090 SYRMOS

(Σύρμος, also Σύρμιος). King of the Triballians (Arr. 1.2.2; Plut. *Alex.* 11.5). Learning of Alexander's approach in spring 335, he sent the women and children to the island of Peuke on the Danube, where he himself took refuge, joining the Thrakians who had also fled there (Arr. 1.2.2–3; Strabo 7.3.8 C301). A large number of Triballian fighting-men doubled back to the River Lyginos, where they were defeated, with 3,000 dead (Arr. 1.2.4–7; cf. Plut. *Alex.* 11.5 says Alexander "defeated Syrmos in a great battle" but this need not mean that S. was at the Lyginos in person). An attempt to take the island by means of ships that sailed up the Danube from the Black Sea failed because the defenders controlled the banks of the island and because of the small number of ships (Arr. 1.3.3–4; cf. Strabo 7.3.8). After Alexander's success against the Getai, S. sent ambassadors to make peace (Arr. 1.4.6; Strabo 7.3.8). Whether the peace terms included a requirement to contribute troops is unclear: Diod. 17.17.4 mentions 7,000 Odrysians, Illyrians, and Triballians at the beginning of the Asiatic campaign. Berve II 366 no. 730; Fuller 221–3; Bosworth I 57–64.

1091 SYRPHAX

(Σύρφαξ). Ephesian, patronymikon unknown. A leader of the pro-Persian oligarchy (in practice, a tyranny: "faktisch, die Tyrannis einer oder mehrer Hetairen": Berve, *Tyrannis* I 336) in Ephesos. After the restoration of the democracy, S., together with his son, Pelagon, and his nephews, had taken refuge in the temple (of Artemis), from which they were dragged out and stoned to death (Arr. 1.17.12). Alexander put an end to further reprisals which would destabilize the city. Berve II 366 no. 731 and *Tyrannis* I 335–6, II 690; Hofstetter 169–70 no. 302; Baumbach 12, 22; Judeich 303 n. 1.

T

1092 TAURISKOS

(Ταύρισκος). Man of unknown family, apparently a Greek (cf. Pape-Benseler 1495). Since he first appears in the context of Issos, Tauriskos could be an ethnic; but the name is also attested in Aitolia (Grainger, *APS* 7, 314). Perhaps a member of Alexander's army or entourage, he befriended Harpalos, whom he persuaded to flee from Alexander's camp shortly before the battle of Issos. Little is known about the man or the circumstances of his flight with Harpalos. Arrian, our only source for the episode, calls him an "evil man" (ἀνὴρ κακός), and it appears that he had some mischief in mind when he befriended Alexander's treasurer. That their crime was theft or embezzlement seems likely, given Harpalos' position, but it cannot be proved. T. accompanied Harpalos to Greece and thence to Alexander of Epeiros in Italy, where he met his end (Arr. 3.6.7). Berve II 371 no. 740; Heckel 1977c; Carney 1982; Worthington 1984; cf. Heckel, *Marshals*² 223.

1093 TAURON

(Ταύρων). Son of Machatas (*IG* IX.9, 197), hence a brother of Philip and Harpalos and a member of the royal house of Elimeia, T. first appears in late 331. Alexander, intending to attack a town of the Ouxians, sent him with a force of 1,500 mercenary archers and 1,000 Agrianes to occupy the heights above that town (Curt. 5.3.6; cf. Diod. 17.67.4–5). Arr. 3.17.4 assigns to Krateros the command of this force, which in his version was intended to cut down the Ouxians who fled to the heights. It may be that T. commanded only the archers, with the supreme command belonging to Krateros. But Bosworth (I 321ff.) argues persuasively for two different engagements fought on the journey from Sousa to the Persian Gates. T.'s maneuver was carried out successfully and the appearance of the archers and Agrianes disheartened the Ouxians who were now under attack by Alexander (Curt. 5.3.10). T. is not mentioned again until 326, this time with the title *toxarches*, in the battle with Poros (Arr. 5.14.1). Along with Seleukos and Antigenes, he commanded infantrymen who were clearly not pezhetairoi (Arr. 5.16.3; cf. Curt. 8.14.15, wrongly substituting Leonnatos for Seleukos). According to Diodorus (17.88.5) the archers were used to make a direct attack on Poros himself. His career undoubtedly suffered on account of his relationship to Harpalos, whose flight to Greece in 324 was an overt act of rebellion. He reappears in the late 4th century, honored at Eretria together with Myllenas son of Asandros (*IG* XII.9, 197), a *grammateus* of Alexander. Since most of the honorific decrees of Eretria in this period concern men in the service of Antigonos and his son, it appears that T. too became an Antigonid supporter (Billows 450, "Taurion"; Paschidis 446–7). It is tempting to postulate a family connection between the Antigonids and the royal house of Elimeia: a certain Harpalos appears, perhaps as governor of Beroia, in the mid-third century (Tataki, *PB* 116 no. 228) in the service of Antigonos Gonatas; a later Harpalos son of Polemaios (Tataki, *PB* 116–117 no. 230; on this family see Kuzmin 2013) was Perseus' ambassador to Rome in 172. Polemaios was, of course, the name of Antigonos the One-Eyed's nephew (cf. Tataki, *PB* 255 no. 1082). Furthermore, T. is honored along with Myllenas son of Asandros (possibly another Beroian; cf. Tataki, *PB* 231–2 no. 910); Asandros son of Agathon, satrap of Karia, is described by Arr. *Succ.* 25.1 as welcoming Antigonos, who was κατὰ γένος ἐπιτήδειος. Berve II 371–2 no. 741; Hoffmann 201; cf. Billows 450 no. 139; Heckel 1992, 338. **Stemma XIII.**

1094 TAXILES

(Ταξίλης). Indian dynast, ruler of Taxila at the time of Alexander's invasion of the Upper Satrapies. T. appears to have died around the time the King was in Sogdiana (Diod. 17.86.4), and his son Omphis (Mophis) had contacted him at that time to offer his obedience, if Alexander would support him against his enemies. Although the date of his death is not specified, it is certain that T. was dead by the time Alexander crossed the Indos (Diod. 17.86.4). Omphis replaced him, taking on the royal name Taxiles (Curt. 8.12.5–6, 14).

1095 TAXILES

(Ταξίλης). Indian dynast, ruler of Taxila, which can be located in the vicinity of Rawalpindi (for the city see Arr. 5.3.6 and Strabo 15.1.28 C698, located between the Indos and the Hydaspes; Arr. 5.8.3; Plut. *Alex.* 59; see also Marshall 1921 and 1951; Dani 1986; Karttunen 1990; cf. Wheeler 1968: 103–6, and Wheeler 1976: 23, 25). His personal name was Omphis (Curt. 8.12.5; Sanskrit Ambhi) or Mophis (Diod. 17.86.4; Metz Epit. 49–52), but in the fashion of that region he later took the official name Taxiles (Curt. 8.12.14). While Alexander was still in Sogdiana (Diod. 17.86.4), Omphis induced his father, Taxiles, to offer submission. But the elder Taxiles died very soon thereafter and Omphis awaited Alexander's approval before assuming the kingship (Curt. 8.12.5–6). He communicated with the advance forces of Hephaistion and Perdikkas, sending them supplies for the army, but would not make formal submission to anyone but Alexander himself (Curt. 8.12.6; Arr. 4.22.6 says that Alexander summoned Taxiles—he does not say whether this was the father or the son—when he reached Parapamisadai). His motive was clearly to win Macedonian support against his neighbors, Abisares and Poros. But when Omphis came out to meet Alexander at the head of his army, the gesture was mistakenly interpreted as a hostile move and military action narrowly averted (Curt. 8.12.7–11; Diod. 17.86.5–6; cf. Arr. 5.3.5–6, 8.2, without the drama). Omphis was now given lavish gifts by Alexander, to the extent that the Macedonians resented Alexander's generosity (Curt. 8.12.15–17; cf. Strabo 15.1.28 C698; see s.v. Meleagros no. 695; cf. also Plut. *Mor.* 181c). He took the name of his father and his kingdom (Curt. 8.12.14; Diod. 17.86.7) and Alexander turned over to him the thirty elephants captured with Barsaentes (Curt. 8.13.3–5). Taxiles accompanied Alexander to the Hydaspes with 5,000 troops (Arr. 5.8.5). As it became clear that Poros was defeated, Alexander sent Taxiles to urge his enemy to surrender and accept terms. Poros, however, attempted to kill him with a javelin but Taxiles evaded him (Arr. 5.18.6–7; this story is transformed by Curtius, who says that Taxiles' brother was sent to urge Poros to surrender, only to be killed by him: Curt. 8.14.35–6). Alexander arranged an alliance between Taxiles and Poros (Curt. 9.3.22). Nothing else is known about Taxiles in Alexander's lifetime except that in 324 he reported the death of Abisares (Curt. 10.1.20; the fact that the report came from Taxiles *and* Poros suggests that the alliance still held).

After the King's death, he retained control of his kingdom (Diod. 18.3.2; Dexippos, *FGrH* 100 F8 §5; Justin 13.4.20; cf. *LM* 121); this was confirmed at Triparadeisos in 320 (Diod. 18.39.6; Arr. *Succ.* 1.36), for neither he nor Poros could be removed without a royal army and an outstanding general. Berve II 369–71 no. 739.

1096 TEIREOS

(Τείρεως, Justi 325: Τιραῖος. Curtius: Tyriotes). Eunuch of the Persian queen, Stateira, he had been captured at Issos (333) along with the family of Dareios. In 331 he escaped from Alexander's camp to Dareios, bringing the news that the queen had died (perhaps in childbirth, Plut. *Alex.* 30.1; Justin 11.12.6; but see no. 1078 for the date and circumstances) and that Alexander had ordered a sumptuous burial for her (cf. Diod. 17.54.7; Plut. *Mor.* 338e). Alexander's grief over Stateira's death led Dareios to suspect that the conqueror had been intimate with her (Curt. 4.10.31), but T. testified that Alexander's treatment of the queen had always been honorable (Curt. 4.10.25–34; Plut. *Alex.* 30.2–6; for Alexander's alleged restraint see Arr. 4.20.1–2). The story, and T. himself, may very well have been invented, though the fact that T. does not appear elsewhere is not, in itself, proof that he is fictitious. Berve II 372 no. 742; Shayegan 125 no. 113.

1097 TEISIKRATES

(Τεισικράτης). Sikyonian sculptor. A student of Euthykrates, who was in turn the son and student of Lysippos (Paus. 6.2.7). T. produced a statue of Demetrios Poliorketes and also one of Peukestas (Pliny, *HN* 34.67). Pollitt 108–9.

1098 TELEPHOS

(Τήλεφος). Macedonian (Tataki 440 no. 11). One of Alexander's *hetairoi*, hence apparently a prominent Macedonian. During the Gedrosian campaign, T. was ordered to convey a small quantity of ground corn to an unnamed location, where it could be used by Nearchos' fleet (Arr. 6.23.6). Nothing else is known about him. Berve II 372 no. 745.

1099 TELESIPPA

(Τελεσίππα). Greek *hetaira*. Telesippa had among her lovers a certain Eurylochos of Aigai, who, upon hearing of her planned return to Greece in 324, tried to have himself declared unfit for battle in order to return with her. The matter was brought to the attention of Alexander, who ordered Eurylochos to attempt to persuade Telesippa to remain, but not to force her (Plut. *Alex.* 41.9–10; Plut. *Mor.* 181a). The same story is told, implausibly, of Antigenes, who was in fact discharged in 324 (Plut. *Mor.* 339c–d). Berve II 372 no. 743.

1100 TELESPHOROS

(Τελέσφορος). Macedonian (Tataki 439 no. 8). A nephew of Antigonos Monophthalmos but, as Billows 435 notes, clearly not a brother of Polemaios. Sent in 313/12 with fifty ships to the Peloponnese, where he freed the cities, except Sikyon and Korinth, from Polyperchon's control (Diod. 19.74.1–2, adding that Polyperchon had his headquarters in Sikyon and Korinth); it seems that Polyperchon had sheltered all his troops here and left the other cities virtually undefended. T. followed this up by bringing 20 ships and a thousand soldiers (aided by Medeios with 100 ships) to Oreos, which Kassandros was besieging (Diod. 19.75.7). Although T. and Medeios burnt four of Kassandros' ships and nearly destroyed them all, the latter received reinforcements from Athens and managed to drive them off and even the score by sinking one of the Antigonid ships and capturing three others (Diod. 19.75.8). Diod. 19.87.1 says that T. kept his fleet at Korinth, which appears to contradict his earlier remarks about it being Polyperchon's stronghold, though perhaps it indicates once again Polyperchon's characteristic timidity or lethargy. Niese I 291 n.1 remarks that this shows "daß sich Antigonos in gutem Einvernehmen mit Polyperchon und Kratesipolis befand." But I see no evidence that Antigonos and Polyperchon had reached an accommodation. The latter probably held Akrokorinth, but at least one of the harbors of Korinth must have fallen into Antigonid hands. In 311, T. betrayed Antigonos because he felt that he was favoring Polemaios. He sold his ships, recruited additional troops and marched to Elis, which he captured. Thereafter, he plundered the treasury of Olympia, using the money to hire more mercenaries, and garrisoned Kyllene. Polemaios, however, recaptured Elis and entered into negotiations with his cousin, persuading him to end his hostilities (Diod. 19.87.1, 3). The episode was a lesson in management that Antigonos clearly did not take to heart; for not long afterwards Polemaios himself defected (see no. 968) Diog. Laert. 5.79 says that T., whom Diogenes calls "a cousin (ἀνεψιός) of Demetrios," intervened to protect the comic poet Menander from prosecution on account of friendship with Demetrios of Phaleron. If this is correct, it demonstrates that T. had returned to favor and was present when the Besieger liberated Athens in 307. Identification with the officer of Lysimachos is impossible, since that man was a Rhodian. What became of him is unknown. Billows 435–6 no. 111; Hauben 93–8; Bengtson I 149–53; Berve, *RE* V.A (1934) 390 no. 2. **Stemma VI.**

1101 TEUKROS

(Τεῦκρος). Son of King Alketas II of Epeiros. Brother of Alexander and two younger brothers (possibly half-brothers), Nisos and Esioneus. In 312/11, when Lykiskos invaded Epeiros, T. and Alexander were sent to the cities to levy an army for Alketas against Lykiskos; they were to join Alketas with their forces—Alketas had already taken the field with the army he had and gone to meet Lykiskos at Kassope (Diod. 19.88.3). T. and his brother were defeated in a second battle at Eurymenai when Deinias brought reinforcements to Lykiskos, forcing T. to flee to a fortified place with his brother and his father (Diod. 19.88.6). Alketas eventually secured the throne, from which he was ousted in 307/6 (Diod. 19.89.3, the date is established by the reinstatement of Pyrrhos as king: Plut. *Pyrrh.* 3.5; Paus. 1.11.5). T.'s younger brothers were killed by the Epeirots. Nothing more is reported about T. and Alexander. Berve, *RE* VA.1 (1934) 1131 no. 3; Cross 1930, 47–8; Hammond, *Epirus* 567–8. **Stemma IIa.**

1102 TEUTAMOS

(Τεύταμος). Macedonian (Tataki 440 no. 9). Unattested in the Alexander historians, but possibly a member of the hypaspists (Argyraspids) during the King's lifetime (Berve II 372); he may, however, have been appointed by Antipatros at Triparadeisos to keep a watchful eye on his colleague, Antigenes. The two are regularly spoken of as commanders of the Silver Shields, but T. was clearly the junior colleague. Diod. 18.62.6–7 says that both men were satraps, and if this is correct T.'s satrapy must have been a minor one, perhaps Paraitakene (thus Bosworth 1992, 66–7). In 318, Polyperchon, writing in the name of the Kings, instructed T. and Antigenes to support Eumenes who had been appointed General of Asia (Diod. 18.58.1); they joined forces with Eumenes (Plut. *Eum.* 13.2–4), whom they congratulated on his escape from Nora (Diod. 18.59.3) but served with some reluctance on account of his ethnic origins. T. was willing to accept the theoretical leadership of Alexander (Plut. *Eum.* 13.7–8; Polyaenus 4.8.2). He appears to have resisted the appeals of Ptolemy, who had landed at Zephyrion in Kilikia and urged the Argyraspid commanders to abandon Eumenes (Diod. 18.62.1); but a second embassy, by Antigonos' agent Philotas, would have persuaded T., had not Antigenes intervened to keep him loyal (Diod. 18.62.4–6). Billows 85 n.8 suggests that T. may have commanded Eumenes' hypaspists, also 3,000 strong (Diod. 19.28.1, cf. 40.3); for Diod. 19.28.1 says that Antigenes and T. commanded both the Argyraspids and the hypaspists. But T. is regularly described as a commander of the Argyraspids (Diod. 18.59.3, 62.4, 5; cf. 18.58.1 and 62.1; Plut. *Eum.* 13.3, 7; 16.2; Polyaenus 4.8.2), and Diodorus' references to Antigenes alone constitute a kind of shorthand that can be explained in terms of Antigenes' seniority (Diod. 19.12.1–2, 13.2, 15.2, 21.1, 41.1, 44.1). Eumenes' hypaspists have no early connection with T., who in 318 and in 315 is still linked with the Argyraspids. Hammond 1978, 135 thinks the hypaspists in Eumenes' army were the "new hypaspists," the successors and "descendants of the hypaspists"; these had failed at Kamelon Teichos, mutinied against Perdikkas, and were assigned by Antipatros to Antigenes, in addition to the Argyraspids, at Triparadeisos; see, however, Anson 1988, 131–3. T. commanded the Argyraspids at Paraitakene (Diod. 19.28.1), but soon he plotted with some of the other commanders to make use of Eumenes in the coming battle in Media and then to eliminate him (Plut. *Eum.* 16.2). The conspiracy was, however, reported to Eumenes by Eudamos and Phaidimos. When the Macedonian baggage was captured at Gabiene, T. took the lead in negotiating with Antigonos, who promised to return the property of the Silver Shields in exchange for Eumenes (Plut. *Eum.* 17.1–2). Justin 14.3.11 says the Silver Shields sent a deputation *ignaris ducibus,* which must mean that they did so without the knowledge of Antigenes and other officers in the army, but T. was clearly not ignorant of the proceedings. What became of T., we are not told. It appears that he avoided Antigenes' fate by initiating the arrest and betrayal of Eumenes (Plut. *Eum.* 17.1). There is no indication that he served under Antigonos—perhaps he was dismissed on account of his age. It is possible that he commanded the remnants of the Silver Shields, whom Antigonos entrusted to Sibyrtios and thus consigned to difficult service and obscurity. Polyaenus 4.6.15; Plut. *Eum.* 19.3; Diod. 19.48.3–4 says that the Argyraspids who went with Sibyrtios to Arachosia included "those who had betrayed Eumenes." It would be in character for Antigonos to "double-cross" T.; cf. his treatment of Seleukos (Diod. 19.55.2ff.). Stähelin, *RE* V.A (1934) 1152–3 no. 3; Berve II 372 no. 744; Launey 1184; Billows 85 n.8; Heckel 1992, 316–19.

1103 THAÏS

(Θαΐς). Athenian courtesan. Thaïs may have accompanied Alexander from the beginning of the campaign—or perhaps since Alexander's sojourn in Egypt. She was present when Persepolis was destroyed (Athen. 13.576d–e), perhaps already as the mistress of Ptolemy son of Lagos. The Vulgate depicts her as the person who induced Alexander to burn the royal palaces in a drunken revel (Diod. 17.72; Curt 5.7.3–7; Plut. *Alex.* 38.2), but Arr. 3.18.11–12 and Strabo 15.3.6 C730 both record the destruction of Persepolis without reference to Thaïs. This has been taken to mean that Ptolemy, in his *History*, suppressed her role for personal reasons (see Heckel 2018a, 8 with n.43; Ager 2018, 39–40). She bore Ptolemy three children (Lagos, Leontiskos, Eirene)—perhaps all before she accompanied him to Egypt in 323 BC—and at some point actually married him (Athen. 13.576e; Berve II 175 n.4 ascribes only *two* children to her: Leontiskos and Eirene). Kleitarchos' observation that she was married to Ptolemy *after* Alexander's death (*FGrH* 137 F11 = Plut. *Alex*. 38.2: μετὰ τὸν Ἀλεξάνδρου θάνατον καὶ Πτολεμαίῳ ἐγαμήθη) need not be taken to mean that she was Alexander's mistress during his lifetime. What became of her we do not know. Berve II 175 no. 359; Tarn II 324 n.7; Ogden 68–9, 241; Hamilton 100; Aulbach §§4.3.1 and 6.2.1.1.

1104 THALESTRIS

(Θάληστρις, Θάλληστρις, also Minythyia). Fictitious Amazon Queen encountered by Alexander in 330 (full accounts in Curt. 6.5.24–32; Justin 12.3.5–7; Diod. 17.77.1–3); Plut. *Alex*. 46.2 dismisses the story as fictitious but records the names of writers who either accepted or rejected the tale. Those who reported it as historical were Kleitarchos, Polykleitos, Onesikritos, Antigenes, and Ister; those who rejected it were Ptolemy, Aristoboulos, Chares, Antikleides, Philon, Philip of Theangela, Hekataios of Eretria, Philip the Chalkidian, and Douris of Samos. The story may have been inspired by the (probably factual) offer of the Skythian king (perhaps Carthasis) to give Alexander his daughter in marriage (Plut. *Alex*. 46.3; Arr. 4.15.2–3, 5). There is no reason to believe that the Skythian woman actually came to Alexander's camp for a tryst with the King (but see Bosworth II 102–3; Lane Fox 276). Those writers who sought to compare Alexander with Achilles may have included the story in order to call to mind Penthesilea. According to Justin 2.4.33 and 12.3.5 (cf. Oros 3.18.5) she was also known as Minythyia. Th. allegedly came to Alexander in Hyrkania from her home on the plains of Themiskyra near the River Thermodon (Curt. 6.5.24) travelling for 35 days (Justin 12.3.5; Strabo 11.5.4 C505, calling her Θαληστρία, claims that the distance was 6,000 stades) and arrived at Alexander's camp with 300 women, having left the remainder of her army at the borders of Hyrkania (Curt. 6.5.26; Diod. 17.77.1). Her purpose was to have a child by Alexander (Curt. 6.5.30), believing that two superior beings would produce a remarkable child (Diod. 17.77.3). After thirteen days of sexual relations with the King, in which she showed herself to be the more enthusiastic partner, she departed convinced that she had conceived (Curt. 6.5.32; Diod. 17.77.3; Justin 12.3.5–7). Justin 2.4.33, however, says that she died soon after returning to her homeland and "with her died the Amazon name" (*reversa in regnum brevi tempore cum omni Amazonum nomine intercidit*). Berve II 419, Abschn. II no. 26; Baynham 2001; Chugg 2006, 155–61; Mayor 2014, 319–38.

1105 THEAITETOS

(Θεαίτητος). Allegedly Athenian (Curt. 5.5.17). One of the spokesmen of the mutilated Greeks who encountered Alexander's army between the Araxes River and Persepolis. His name survives only in Curtius, but that is not to say that Curt. invented him: since Diod. 17.69.5–8 preserves the same general arguments, it is likely that the story was told in greater detail by Kleitarchos (Pearson 239; cf. Hammond 1983, 56). Th. makes the case that they should accept Alexander's offer of repatriation (Curt. 5.5.17–20). This group and its leaders are doubtless fictitious, the speeches of Th. and Euktemon little more than rhetorical exercises (see no. 441). Berve II 175–6 no. 360.

1106 THEMISON

(Θεμίσων). Samian. Naval commander in the service of the Antigonids. In 314, Th. brought forty ships from the Hellespontine region to Antigonos at Tyre (Diod. 19.62.7; Billows 436 speculates that Th. made have served in the fleet that defeated Kleitos at the Hellespont in 317). Antigonos placed one portion of his fleet under the command of Dioskourides and sent a part to the Peloponnese (Diod. 19.62.9). Whether Th. participated in either campaign or possibly even commanded the ships sent to the Peloponnese is unclear. In 306, Th. and Marsyas (no. 683) commanded the lightest ships in the center of Demetrios' line at Salamis (Diod. 20.50.4); the joint command may have been intended to compensate for Marsyas' lack of experience, especially in naval affairs. Nothing else is known about him. Schachermeyr, *RE* V.A (1934) 1631 no. 1; Bengtson I 149–53; Hauben 93–8; Billows 436 no. 112.

1107 THEODOROS

(Θεόδωρος). Macedonian (Tataki 325 no. 7). Brother of Proteas and thus probably son of Lanike (the sister of Black Kleitos and Alexander's former nurse) and Andronikos son of Agerros. He is known only from Plut. *Mor.* 760c, who records correspondence between the King and Theodoros concerning a *hetaira*/musician. Berve believes he may have been Philip II's *hieromnemon* in 341–340 (*Syll*³ I 230 pp. 314–15; cf. Ellis 1976, 132, Table 3) but the identification is at best tentative. Berve II 176 no. 362.

1108 THEODOROS

(Θεόδωρος). Greek. Dancer from Tarentum. At an unspecified time in Alexander's campaign, Theodoros was with Philoxenos in Asia Minor and in possession of two slave boys whom he was trying to sell. Philoxenos offered to buy these for Alexander, whose letter in response to the offer was a stinging rebuke of Philoxenos and a general condemnation of Theodoros (Plut. *Alex.* 22.1–2; cf. Athen. 1.22d). Berve II 176 no. 363.

1109 THEODOROS

(Θεόδωρος). [All references in **boldface** are to Diog. Laert.] Greek philosopher from Kyrene (Val. Max. 6.2 ext. 3), Th. was notorious for his atheism (*Suda* A3908; **2.97**; he wrote a book on the gods, Περὶ θεῶν, which influenced the work of Epikouros; but **1.16** says he left behind no writings). Various anecdotes depict him as arrogant and disdainful, showing indifference to Lysimachos' thinly veiled threat that he could easily suffer the fate of Telesphoros (see s.v.), whom he had mutilated and caged (Plut. *Mor.* 606b). A student of Annikeris and Dionysios the dialectician (**2.98**), also of Aristippos, Zenon, and Pyrrhon (*Suda* Θ150). Born *c.*340, Th. was banished from Kyrene early in his life and came to Athens. It was during his stay in Greece that, according to Diog. Laert., he encountered both Stilpon in Megara (**2.100**) and Metrokles the Cynic in Korinth (**2.102**). His comments on the Mysteries of Demeter, made to the *hierophantes* Eurykleides, were so offensive that he narrowly escaped punishment on a charge of *asebeia* only through the intervention of Demetrios of Phaleron (hence at some point between 317 and 307; see O'Sullivan 2009, 153–4, 213; Filonik 2013, 75–6); allegedly he had been condemned to drink hemlock (**2.101**, citing Amphikrates of Athens, *On Famous Men*, says he drank the hemlock: κώνειον αὐτὸν πιεῖν καταδικασθέντα). He was sent as an ambassador to

Lysimachos by Ptolemy I Soter (perhaps Th. was in Egypt at the same time as Demetrios of Phaleron) and enraged the Thrakian King (and his finance minister Mithras) by his rudeness (2.102). Th. was at Lysimachos' court, having been exiled by the Kyreneans. Allegedly, he so enraged Lysimachos that he ordered him to be crucified (Val. Max. 6.2 ext. 3; Cic. *Tusc.* 1.43; Sen. *Tranq.* 14.3), but this seems to be a corruption of the story of Antigonos Monophthalmos and Theokritos (no. 1112). At any rate, having eluded death on at least two occasions, Th. went to live in Kyrene with Magas and, one may assume, died there (2.103, who speaks of what must have been an earlier exile). It is tempting to identify him with the Th. who was at the court of Antigonos (apparently, Gonatas) who was derided as a water drinker (ὑδροπότης); on so-called water drinkers see Tarn, *AG* 207 n.127. But Athen. 2.44b (= Phylarchos, *FGrH* 81 F64) says this man was from Larisa. Full discussion in Winiarczyk 1981. K. von Fritz, *RE* VIA (1934); Filonik 2013; O'Sullivan 2009, 153–4, 213.

1110 THEODOTOS

(Θεόδοτος). Macedonian (Tataki 324 no. 5). Th. was awarded seventh place in the contest of valor in Sittakene (331); hence he became a pentakosiarch of the hypaspists (Curt. 5.2.5; see literature s.v. Atarrhias no. 250). He is otherwise unknown. Age would seem to rule out identification with Lysimachos' *thesaurophylax* of the late 280s (Polyaenus 4.9.4); for the hypaspists were already well advanced in years during the first Diadochic wars, whereas the relatively low status of the commanders of regular hypaspists makes it unlikely that he was the *nauarchos* of Antigonos the One-Eyed. Berve II 176 no. 361; Heckel 1992, 305.

1111 THEODOTOS

(Θεόδοτος). Admiral of Antigonos the One-Eyed. In 315, Th. commanded a fleet of Rhodian ships (cf. Diod. 19.58.5) with Karian crews and made his way eastward from Patara in Lykia, accompanied by an army under Perilaos. He was ambushed by Polykleitos near Aphrodisias in Kilikia, when he went to the aid of Perilaos' forces who had been defeated by troops disembarked from Polykleitos' fleet. Th. lost all his ships (Diod. 19.64.5–7) and died of his wounds a few days later (Diod. 19.64.7). Hauben 100–1 no. 35; Geyer, *RE* VA (1934) 1954 no. 8; Billows 436 no. 113.

1112 THEOKRITOS

(Θεόκριτος). Greek from Chios. Theokritos was an orator and poet (the author of *Chreai*, as well as a *History of Libya*) who had studied with Metrodoros, a student of Isokrates (*Suda* Θ 166); he was an enemy of Theopompos the historian, also a Chian (Strabo 14.1.35 C645; *FGrH* 115 F252), as well as Anaximenes (Athen. 1.21c). A man of low origins, he was later prone to extravagance (Athen. 6.230f). Nevertheless he is supposed to have criticized Aristotle for developing a taste for life at the Macedonian court (Plut. *Mor.* 603c; cf. Diog. Laert. 5.11). He made light of Alexander's request for purple dye from the Chians, with which to adorn the garments of his *hetairoi* (Athen. 12.540a; Plut. *Mor.* 11a–b). Famous for his witticisms, one of which allegedly sealed his doom. He was put to death at some point after 306, as is clear from the reference to King Antigonos, for making a tasteless joke about Monophthalmos (Plut. *Mor.* 11b–c, 633c; see also s.v. Eutropion no. 464). Stobaeus, *Sermon* 36.217; Macrobius, *Satires* 7.3. See also Stobaeus, *Anthologion* 46 and

123; and Macrobius, *Saturnalia* 7.3.12. Laqueur, *RE* V.A2 (1934) 2025 no. 2; Berve II 176–7 no. 364; Billows 436–7 no. 114; Teodorsson 1990; Weber 1995, 294 with n.51.

1113 THEOPHILOS

(Θεόφιλος). Greek or possibly Macedonian craftsman who made the polished iron helmet that Alexander wore at Gaugamela (Plut. *Alex.* 32.9). Presumably, Th. made several helmets for the King. We know of one iron helmet that was split during the battle of the Granikos (Diod. 17.20.6). Nothing else is known about him. Berve II 178 no. 366.

1114 THEOPHRASTOS

(Θεόφραστος). References in **boldface** are to Diogenes Laertius' biography, much of which is summarized by *Suda* Θ 199. (*c*.371–287, though Pliny, *HN* 15.1.1 gives 314 as his *floruit*). Son of Melantas from Eresos (**5.36**). Philosopher, like his countryman Phanias, Th. was a student of Aristotle. His own numerous students (some 2,000, **5.37**) included Lynkeus and Douris of Samos (Athen. 4.128a; but see Pownall, *LexAM* 210; Athen. 3.100e; *Suda* Λ 776), the comic poet Menander (**5.36**), and Deinarchos ([Plut.] *Mor.* 850c). According to Strabo 13.2.4 C618 (cf. **5.38**) his real name Tyrtamos was changed by Aristotle (*Suda* Θ 199 claims Aristotle's first name for him was Euphrastos), who considered him the most eloquent of his students. Aristotle left his school (**5.36**) and library to Th.; later on Neleus, who had been a pupil of both, inherited the combined library of Aristotle and Th. (Strabo 13.1.54 C608–9; Athen. 1.3a–b, the books were sold by Neleus to Ptolemy Philadelphos). He is supposed to have commented on Harpalos' vain attempt to grow ivy in Media (Pliny, *HN* 16.62.144). Th. was probably in Macedonia with Aristotle; later he is said to have twice saved Eresos from tyranny with the help of Alexander (Plut. *Mor.* 1097b, 1126f), though this is probably an attempt to show that he, like Aristotle and Anaximenes, had elicited benefactions for his countrymen through their connections with the King. In 318, Hagnonides unsuccessfully prosecuted him on a charge of *asebeia* (**5.37**). Th. left Athens when Sophokles (no. 1060) introduced a law regulating the philosophical schools and returned only when the law was rescinded (**5.38**). Kassandros entertained him (**5.37**; cf. Plut. *Mor.* 633b), and it was for him that he wrote a treatise on monarchy (**5.47**, Athen. 4.144e, though some attributed this to Sosibios; Landucci, *Lisimaco* 2003, 114–15 n.139); Ptolemy, as he had done with Stilpon, attempted to lure him to Egypt (**5.37**). In a rare political act, in 292/1, he persuaded Demetrios Poliorketes to recall some of the oligarchs, including Deinarchos (no. 344) who had been banished in 307 (Dion. Hal. *Din.* 3, 9 = Philochoros, *FGrH* 328 F167; [Plut.] *Mor.* 850d). Th. died at the age of eighty-five (**5.40**). He was a prolific writer, composing 232,808 lines altogether: a list of his works is given at **5.42–50**. Among these was one entitled *Kallisthenes or On Bereavement* (Καλλισθένης ἢ περὶ πένθους), which contributed to the negative image of Alexander on the part of the Peripatetics. Berve II 178–9 no. 367; Paschidis 139–40 A45.

1115 THEOPOMPOS

(Θεόπομπος). Son of Damasistratos, from Chios (Strabo 14.1.35 C645; Paus. 2.9.5, 6.18.5; *Suda* Θ 172). Born in 377/6 (we are told that when he returned to Chios in 332 from exile he was 45 years old: Photius' *Life of Theopompos*, Westermann, *Vitarum Scriptores* 204–6). Rhetor and historian, Theopompos was a student of Isokrates and fellow student of Ephoros (Cic. *De Oratore* 2.13, 22–3; 3.9 = Quint. 2.8.11). He had left Chios as a child in the company of his exiled "Spartanizing" father, and Memnon's capture of Chios in 333 (Arr. 2.1.1; Diod. 17.29.2) will have prevented any plans to return. He was, however, recalled as a result of Alexander's decree in 332 (*Syll*³ 283), but Heisserer 83–95 makes a good case for the issuing of this decree in 334. At any rate, Theopompos is unlikely to have returned until 332. As an opponent of the oligarchic party, he was an enemy of Theokritos (see s.v.) and a supporter of Alexander (Strabo 14.1.35 C645; Athen. 6.230f; Berve II 177 rightly sees the quarrel between Theopompos and Theokritos as political rather than academic: cf. Flower 1994, 23–4). The author of an *Epitome of Herodotus' Histories, Hellenica* and *Philippica*, Theopompos wrote only *Letters* to Alexander (of which we have five fragments: *FGrH* 115 FF250–254), primarily itemizing the misdeeds of Harpalos, and an *Encomium* (F257; there is, however, also a reference to a *Censure of Alexander* (F258); he also wrote an *Encomium of Philip*), but there are references to Alexander's expedition in the *Philippica*. For his historical work see Jacoby, *FGrH* 115; cf. Shrimpton 1991, 196–274 for *testimonia* and fragments). At some point after Alexander's death, Theopompos was again exiled from Chios. He sailed to Egypt but did not find a good reception from Ptolemy, possibly for his negative comments about Harpalos (Phot. *Life of Theopompos*). Berve II 177–8 no. 365; Shrimpton 1991; Flower 1994; Pownall, *LexAM* 487–8.

1116 THEOTIMIDES

(Θεοτιμίδης). Son of Theophilos, Makedonian. Honored at Samos in a decree moved by Naniskos son of Epigenes (*IG* XII 6, 25; the decree antedates 306, since Antigonos is not given the royal title) for helping Samians in exile. Th. was thus a *philos* of Antigonos before 322/1 and while Monophthalmos was satrap of Greater Phrygia. Billows 438 speculates that he may have been among those *philoi* of Antigonos who accompanied him in flight in 321 (Diod. 18.23.3–4). Billows 437–8 no. 115; Paschidis 382.

1117 THEOXENE

(Θεοξένη). Daughter of Ptolemy I Soter, possibly by Eurydike (but Ogden 70 thinks she is a daughter of Berenike and her first husband Philip no. 919), and wife of Agathokles of Sicily, whom she bore two children (Justin 23.2.6; the fact that they were described as *parvuli* at the time of their father's death indicates that the year of the marriage was no earlier than 300). Agathokles, as he sensed that he was dying, sent her and the children back to Egypt, although Theoxene did not wish to abandon her husband (Justin 23.2.6–12). What became of Th. and her children is unknown. Beloch IV² 2.179, 255–6; Ogden 70 (a daughter of Berenike and Philip); Ager 2018, 49–50. **Stemma X.**

1118 THEOXENOS

(Θεόξενος). Possibly Dioxenos (thus Tataki 302 no. 76); the name appears only in Curtius, in its Latin form. Macedonian of unknown family, Theoxenos conspired with Dimnos against Alexander at Phrada in 330 (Curt. 6.7.15). On the evidence of Nikomachos (or his brother Kebalinos) he was arrested and executed (Curt. 6.11.38). Berve II 146 no. 280 (s.v. Διόξενος).

1119 THERSIPPOS

(Θέρσιππος). Greek from Nesos (*Barr. Atl.* 56 D3). Envoy of Alexander. In the diplomatic negotiations of 332, which followed Alexander's victory at Issos and the capture of

Dareios' family, Thersippos was sent from Marathos to Dareios with the Persian envoys (see Arsimas no. 219; Meniskos no. 716) and a letter that rejected the Great King's offers and charged him with crimes against Macedon (Arr. 2.14.4; Curt. 4.1.14; for the contents of Alexander's letter see Arr. 2.14.4–9; Curt. 4.1.7–14). He is honored by his countrymen for his services to the state during the reigns of Philip III and Alexander IV and during the regencies of Antipatros and Polyperchon (*OGIS* 4), an inscription that attests to his high standing with the Macedonian kings and generals. Th. secured for Nesos exemption or mitigation of contributions to the war chests of Antipatros and Kleitos, the latter case for the Kyprian campaign (lines 9–16). He also kept the city on friendly terms with Polyperchon and Arrhabaios (*sic*), probably Arrhidaios, satrap of Hellespontine Phrygia. Paschidis 411 believes that the *polemos* for which Antipatros exacted *eisphora* was for the war against Eumenes, declared at Triparadeisos. Hence if the decree recounts events in chronological sequence Kleitos' Kypriot campaign would have to belong to 320/19 by Paschidis' reckoning (cf. Billows 67 n.29). For problems associated with an expedition to Asia by Polyperchon (based on the interpretation of lines 23–4) see Heckel, *Marshals*² 210–11 n.61; cf. Anson 2014, 99; see also Paschidis 2008. The decree appears to indicate that Th. kept Nesos in alliance with Polyperchon and Arrhidaios against Kassandros and Antigonos. Berve II 179 no. 368; Hofstetter 179 no. 312; Poddighe 2001; Paschidis 408–13 D49.

1120 THESPIOS

(Θέσπιος). The name in this form is not Iranian. Perhaps a Graecism of Teispes. Leading Persian and supporter of the Macedonian satrap, Peukestas. When the latter was deposed (316/5), Th. declared openly that the Persians would obey no one but Peukestas. Antigonos put him to death (Diod. 19.48.5).

1121 THESSALISKOS

(Θεσσαλίσκος). Theban. Son of Ismenias (Aristotle, *Rhet.* 2.1398b.3ff.). He was sent on an embassy to Dareios at some point before the destruction of his city in 335 and was captured at Damaskos, together with Dionysodoros, by Parmenion after the battle of Issos (Arr. 2.15.2). Alexander released both prisoners, in part because he regretted the severity of the action he had taken against Thebes (cf. Plut. *Alex.* 13.5; Plut. *Mor.* 181b), and in Th.'s case out of respect for his lineage (Arr. 2.15.4). Berve II 179 no. 369; Hofstetter 99, 179 no. 313.

1122 THESSALONIKE

(Θεσσαλονίκη, Θετταλονίκη: Athen. 13.557c). Macedonian (Tataki 327–8 no. 24). Daughter of Nikesipolis of Pherai and Philip II (Satyros *ap.* Athen. 13.557c; Paus. 9.7.3; cf. 8.7.7; Justin 14.6.13, wrongly calls her the daughter of Philip Arrhidaios!; Heid. Epit. 2; Diod. 19.35.5, 52.1); a niece of Jason of Pherai (Steph. Byz. s.v. Θεσσαλονίκη). Thessalonike was born in all likelihood *c.*345/4, for Philip will have married Nikesipolis soon after he gained possession of Pherai in 346. Nothing is known of her life before 316/5, when she was found with Olympias during the siege of Pydna (Justin 14.6.13; Diod. 19.35.5). Olympias appears to have acted as her guardian (Landucci, *Lisimaco* 2009, 262 is surely right in claiming that "Thessalonike's long spinsterhood depended on the refusal of Olympias ... to open the Argead clan to new male members to avoid further dynastic disputes"), since Nikesipolis died twenty days after the girl's birth (Steph. Byz., citing

Lucius of Tarrah, says that Philip gave his daughter to a woman named Nike to raise, hence the name Thessalonike. But this is surely a false etymology and we need not credit the existence of Nike). In 315 she was allegedly compelled to marry Kassandros (Diod. 19.52.1, 61.2; cf. Paus. 8.7.7; Justin 14.6.13; Porphyr. Tyr. *FGrH* 260 F3 §4; the coercion may be nothing more than hostile propaganda), to whom she bore three sons: Philip, Alexander and Antipatros (Plut. *Demetr.* 36.1–2; Porphyr. §5; cf. Plut. *Pyrrh.* 6.3; Plut. *Demetr.* 36.1). He founded the city of Thessalonike in her honor (Strabo 7. frgs. 21, 24; Heid. Epit. 2, ascribing the foundation to Thessalonike herself). She was killed in 294 by her own son, Antipatros (Plut. *Demetr.* 36.1; Plut. *Pyrrh.* 6.3; Diod. 21.7.1; Porphyr. Tyr. §5), because she favored his younger brother, Alexander (Justin 16.1.1–4; Paus. 9.7.3). The forged Testament of Alexander claims it was the King's wish that she marry Lysimachos (Ps.-Call. 3.33.13; this provision is not in the *Liber de Morte* from Metz; see Heckel 1988, 55–7 for discussion.). Beloch III² 2.69; IV² 2.127–8; Berve II 179–80 no. 370; Macurdy 52–5; Carney 1988; Carney 155–8; Aulbach §5.2. **Stemma I.**

1123 THESSALOS

(Θέσσαλος). Tragic actor; victor in the Dionysiac festival in 347 and 341 (*IG* II² 2318, 2320) as well as the Lenaian (for the second time *c.*356, *IG* II² 2325). Th. acted as the envoy of Alexander to Pixodaros of Karia in 336, bringing about the failure of the proposed marriage of Arrhidaios to Ada and therefore Philip II ordered him to be arrested and imprisoned (Plut. *Alex.* 10.2). Th. appears to have come to no harm, perhaps because Philip II died before the orders to arrest him could be carried out. In 332/1 he was defeated by the actor Athenodoros, much to Alexander's dismay (Plut. *Alex.* 29.4; Plut. *Mor.* 334e–f; Arr. 3.1.4). Th. later performed, again in the company of Athenodoros, at the mass marriage ceremony in Sousa in 324 (Chares, *FGrH* 125 F4 = Athen. 12.538f). Berve II 180 no. 371; O'Connor 103 no. 239 (with numerous factual errors).

1124 THIBRON

(Θίβρων). Spartan (Poralla 65–6 no. 376; Arr. *Succ.* 1.16), family background unknown. Th. was amongst the friends of Harpalos who joined him in his flight to Athens in 324 (Diod. 18.19.2). Later he sailed with Harpalos to Kydonia on Krete, where he murdered him (Diod. 17.108.8; 18.19.2) or, possibly, instructed an agent to do so (Paus. 2.33.4; cf. Strabo 17.3.21 C837) and took control of the 6,000 or 7,000 mercenaries who had come with the disgraced treasurer from Asia (Diod. 17.108.6: 6,000; Diod. 18.19.2: 7,000. Arr. *Succ.* 1.16 says there were 6,000 mercenaries who accompanied Th. to Kyrene). After Alexander's death, Th. was induced by Kyrenean and Barkaian exiles to attack Kyrene, which at that point was independent of Macedonian rule, with an army of 6,000 (Arr. *Succ.* 1.16; Diod. 18.19.2; Strabo 17.3.21). After some initial successes on the battlefield, Th. besieged the harbor and extracted from the Kyreneans 500 talents of silver and a contribution of half their chariots to his army; furthermore, he plundered the merchant ships in the port in order to pay his troops (Diod. 18.19.3–5). But a quarrel soon arose with one of his commanders, the Kretan Mnasikles (no. 747), over the division of spoils, and Mnasikles defected to the Kyreneans and encouraged them to stop paying the indemnity, of which they had turned over only 60 talents to that point. Th. countered by seizing 80 Kyreneans in the port and marching on the city, but he accomplished little. Later he went to the aid of his allies, the Barkaians and Hesperitai, which were under attack from Kyrene, but in Th.'s absence Mnasikles recaptured the harbor (Diod. 18.20.1–5). For Th.'s fleet and its sailors, this created serious supply problems: many were killed or captured by the Libyans as they foraged, and the fleet was subsequently destroyed by bad weather (Diod. 18.20.6–7). Th. nevertheless took Taucheira (thus Diodorus and Strabo; Arr. *Succ.* 1.17–18 has Teucheira) by siege (Diod. 18.20.6) and continued his campaign after summoning 2,500 mercenaries from Tainaron (Diod. 18.21.1–3). Although he won a decisive victory against a larger force of Kyreneans, Th.'s fate was sealed when exiles from Kyrene summoned aid from Ptolemy in Egypt, who sent a force under Ophellas to deal with him (Diod. 18.21.4–7). Captured by the Libyans, Th. was taken in chains to Epikydes of Olynthos, whom Ophellas had placed in charge of Taucheira. He allowed the Taucheirans to torture Th. before sending him to Kyrene where he was crucified in the harbor (Arr. *Succ.* 1.17–18; cf. Diod. 18.21.7–9). Berve II 180 no. 372; Launey 1119.

1125 THIODEXILAS

(Θιοδεξίλας). Son of Mnasikles. One of twenty-four cavalrymen from Orchomenos, who served with Alexander's allied cavalry until the expedition reached Ekbatana in 330. There he and his compatriots were discharged. On their return (*c.*329), they made a dedication to Zeus Soter in Orchomenos (*IG* VII 3206). Berve II 180 no. 373.

1126 THIODOTOS

(Θιόδοτος). Patronymic lost. One of twenty-four cavalrymen from Orchomenos, who served with Alexander's allied cavalry until the expedition reached Ekbatana in 330. There he and his compatriots were discharged. On their return (*c.*329), they made a dedication to Zeus Soter in Orchomenos (*IG* VII 3206). Berve II 180–1 no. 374.

1127 THIOPOMPOS

(Θιόπομπος). Son of Olympiochos. One of twenty-four cavalrymen from Orchomenos, who served with Alexander's allied cavalry until the expedition reached Ekbatana in 330. There he and his compatriots were discharged. On their return (*c.*329), they made a dedication to Zeus Soter in Orchomenos (*IG* VII 3206). Berve II 181 no. 375.

1128 THOAS

(Θόας). Son of Mandrodoros from Magnesia-on-the-Maiandros (Arr. 6.23.2; Arr. *Ind.* 18.7 calls him son of Menodoros). He is first encountered as a trierarch of the Hydaspes fleet in 326 (Arr. *Ind.* 18.7). During the Gedrosian march he operated by land and secured landing places and water supplies for the fleet (Arr. 6.23.2). He replaced Apollophanes (no. 155), who had been killed in battle with the Oreitai, but soon died of illness and was in turn replaced by Sibyrtios (Arr. 6.27.1, incorrectly claiming that Apollophanes was deposed). Berve II 181 no. 376.

1129 THOINON

(Θοίνον). Son of Timogiton. One of twenty-four cavalrymen from Orchomenos, who served with Alexander's allied cavalry until the expedition reached Ekbatana in 330. There he and his compatriots were discharged. On their return (*c.*329), they made a dedication to Zeus Soter in Orchomenos (*IG* VII 3206). Berve II 181 no. 377.

1130 THORAX

(Θώραξ). Probably an Aleuad from Larisa; cf. Westlake and also Pindar *Pythian* X honoring an Aleuad Thorax in 498; Appian's claim (*Syr.* 64.341) that Th. was from Pharsalos is at any rate part of a variant story, disproved by Plut. *Demetr.* 29.8, who claims that Th. guarded the body of Antigonos in 301 (for his origins see Westlake 1935, 41); Appian claims it was Th. who found the body of *Lysimachos*, which had been guarded by his faithful dog (named Hyrkanos or possibly a Hyrkanian breed), but adds another story to the effect that Lysimachos' corpse was buried by his son Alexander. These stories must be rejected. Billows 438 suggests that Th. may have been a relative of Medeios, Hippostratos, and Oxythemis. Ogden 2017, 331–3 advances the interesting but implausible theory that Thorax was not the name of a man but of the dog who guarded the body. Nothing else is known about him. Billows 438–9 no. 116; Geyer, *RE* s.v. no. 7; Marasco 1982, 134–9.

1131 THOUDIPPOS

(Θούδιππος). Wealthy Athenian (Kirchner 7253), lampooned by Timokles *ap.* Athen. 9.407f. Th. opposed Polyperchon and was condemned to death by the Athenians, together with Phokion, Nikokles, Hegemon and Pythokles, on a motion by Hagnonides (Plut. *Phoc.* 35.5). Demetrios of Phaleron, Kallimedon and Charikles were sentenced to death *in absentia*. Th. died drinking hemlock (Plut. *Phoc.* 36.3; *Mor* 189a; cf. Ael. *VH* 9.41).

1132 THRASEAS

(Θρασέας). Son of Balagros, honored at Delos (*IG* XI 4, 585) as *agathos*, having done good service for the shrine and the *polis*. Nothing is known about the nature of this service. Reger 1991 identifies him as a brother of Antipatros (no. 130) and Balagros (no. 281)— both attested at Delos (see Paschidis 438 n.3)—and thus a son of Balakros (no. 283) son of Nikanor and Phila (no. 897); stemma in Reger 1991, 154. He was thus a stepson of Demetrios Poliorketes and solidly in the Antigonid camp. Nothing else is known about him. Reger 1991; Paschidis 383–4 s.v. Tharsynon son of Choirylos D80.

1133 THRASYBOULOS

(Θρασύβουλος). Athenian (Kirchner 7304). Son of Thrason. Born no later than 375; he appears in a naval list of 353/2 (*IG* II² 1613.270); he served with Chares at the Hellespont. He is named as one of the Athenian generals and politicians whose extradition was demanded by Alexander after the sack of Thebes in 335 (*Suda* A 2704), but the list given by the *Suda* may not be reliable. Certainly, Thrasybulos fled from Athens, probably in the company of Ephialtes, soon after the sack of Thebes and served with Memnon of Rhodes at Halikarnassos (Diod. 17.25.6). Ephialtes was killed during the siege (Diod. 17.27.3) but Thrasybulos escaped from the city with Memnon (cf. Diod. 17.27.5). In 326/5 he reappears in Athens as *strategos* (*IG* II² 1628.40–1; cf. Develin 400) and makes a dedication at Eleusis (*IG* II² 2969). Berve II 181–2 no. 378; Davies 239; Seibt 105 n.3; Hofstetter 181 no. 317.

1134 THRASYLOCHOS

(Θρασύλοχος). Greek from Messenia. Son of Philiades. Leader of the pro-Macedonian party (Dem. 18.295). Thrasylochos and his brother Neon were exiled in 336/5, in the turmoil that followed Philip's death, but reinstated as tyrants of Messenia soon afterwards on Alexander's orders ([Dem.] 17.4, 7). Berve II 182 no. 379.

1135 THYMOCHARES

(Θυμοχάρης). Athenian (Kirchner 7412). Son of Phaidros of Sphettos, father of that Phaidros who was honored by the Athenians c.275/4 (*Syll³* 409 = *IG* II² 682). The text of this decree is our only source for Th.'s military career. Member of a wealthy family, Th. served the state in the oversight of the games of the Amphiaraon in Oropos in 329/8. At some point before the archonship of Praxiboulos (315/14; see Billows 387), he was elected *strategos* and took a contingent of Athenian ships that sailed with the Macedonian fleet (of Kassandros) to Kypros, where he captured Hagnon of Teios and his ships. The capture of Hagnon shows that the decree does not refer to the 321/0 campaign (Paschidis 2008, 74; *contra* Ferguson 21) against the Perdikkan forces (details no. 489). In 315/14, in what was clearly a different campaign, Th. liberated Kythnos and captured Glauketas (no. 469). Later, in 313, as a successor to Aristoteles, he was involved in the attack on Oreos, but the nature of his participation is not entirely clear: he appears to have come late, while Kassandros was besieging the city and thus gained exemption for the Athenians from the siegework (lines 16–18: ὥστε [τ]ῶν συμμάχων μόνους Ἀθηναίους ἀλειτουργήτους εἶναι τῶν ἔργων τῶν πρὸς τὴν πολιορκίαν). The campaign itself was unsuccessful, but Th. was praised for positive action in an otherwise failed undertaking. See the discussion in Paschidis 75–6, who notes that these events demonstrate the extent to which Athenian actions were dictated by Kassandros. Nothing else is known of Th.'s career. Ferguson 21, 51; Paschidis 7–6; Billows 387; Bayliss 91, 221;

1136 THYMONDAS

(Θυμώνδας. Curt. Thimodes). Son of Mentor the Rhodian (Curt. 3.3.1; Arr. 2.13.2), Thymondas was born c.355, as we may gather from his father's age (Dem 23.157) and Curtius' description of him as *impiger iuvenis* in 334/3 (Curt. 3.3.1). He had perhaps spent the time before the death of his uncle Memnon at the court of the Great King; then he was sent out to confirm Pharnabazos as Memnon's successor (Arr. 2.2.1; Curt. 3.3.1). Thymondas joined Dareios at Sochoi and in the battle of Issos commanded 30,000 infantry on the right wing (Curt. 3.9.2; cf. Arr. 2.13.2). After the Persian defeat, he and other mercenary captains (Amyntas son of Antiochos, Bianor, and Aristomedes) fled to Tripolis in Syria and from there took ships to Kypros. Although Amyntas went on to Egypt with 4,000 mercenaries, all of whom perished there, there is no evidence that Thymondas accompanied him. What happened to him, we do not know. He appears to have been the father of Memnon, honored by the Athenians in 327/6 (*IG* II² 356). Berve II 182 no. 380; Seibt 110–13; Hofstetter 182 no. 319. **Stemma IV.**

1137 TIMANDROS

(Τίμανδρος). Macedonian (Tataki 160 no. 87). Commander of a battalion (*taxis*) of hypaspists. He is attested at Halikarnassos, together with Adaios, under the command of the Somatophylax Ptolemy (Arr. 1.22.4). Identification with Timandros, father of Asklepiodoros, is doubtful (*pace* Tataki 160). The name Timandros may be the result of a textual error in Arr. *Ind.* 18.3 (Jacoby, *FGrH* IIB, p.450). If the text is correct, it is unlikely that an officer of relatively low standing would have been the father of one of the Hydaspes trierarchs. What became of Timandros is unknown. Berve II 373 no. 746; Heckel 303.

1138 TIMANTHES

(Τιμάνθης). Son of Pantiades, a Macedonian from Pella (Tataki 160 no. 88). One of the trierarchs of the Hydaspes fleet in 326 (Arr. *Ind.* 18.3 = Nearchos, *FGrH* 133 F1). Nothing else is known about him or his father. Berve II 373 no. 747.

1139 TIMARCHOS

(Τίμαρχος). Son of Nikokles (Pliny, *HN* 11.167) and grandson of Euagoras I ([Plut.] *Mor.* 838a). Very little is known about him, most of that trivial: Pliny comments on his teeth, that he had two rows of maxillaries (*HN* 11.167). He was the father of that Nikokles who ruled Paphos from at least 321. The exact relationship of Timarchos to [Cha]ridamus (Berve no. 822) is uncertain, though it appears that Timarchos replaced [Cha]ridamus at some point in Alexander's reign. Berve II 373 no. 748.

1140 TIMOKLEIA

(Τιμόκλεια). Theban woman; sister of Theagenes who died on the Greek side at Chaironeia (Plut. *Mor.* 259d; cf. Din. 1.74). Raped by Thrakians during the sack of Thebes (335), she killed their leader (see no. 47) by tricking him into thinking that she had hidden her gold and silver in a well. When he climbed down to see, T. (aided by her maid-servants) threw rocks down upon him and killed him. She was brought to Alexander, who acquitted her (Polyaenus 8.40). See also Plut. *Mor.* 259d–260d; Plut. *Alex.* 12; Zonaras 4.9; also Plut. *Mor.* 1093c = Aristoboulos, *FGrH* 139 F2, and Plut. *Mor.* 145e. It is important to note that Alexander did not acquit T. on account of the justice of her case (as a victim of rape) but because of her lineage and her noble bearing. Berve II 374 no. 751; Hamilton 31–2. Stadter 1965, 112–15; Heckel and McLeod 2015, 256–8.

1141 TIMOKLES

(Τιμοκλῆς). Comic poet of the late fourth century (*Suda* T 623). Timokles' comedies touched on contemporary events like the Harpalos scandal (Athen. 8.341e); his play, *The Icarians* featured Pythionike, who was later Harpalos' mistress (Athen. 8.339d). Berve II 374 no. 753.

1142 TIMOKLES

(Τιμοκλῆς). Pirate commander (*archipeirates*) in the service of Demetrios Poliorketes. Captured off the coast of Karia, during the famous siege of 305–304, by the Rhodian navarch Amyntas (Diod. 20.97.5–6). Billows 439 no. 117; Ziegler, *RE* VI.A (1937) 1260 no. 2; Hauben 106; Ormerod 123.

1143 TIMOLAOS

(Τιμόλαος). Theban, leader of the pro-Macedonian party, described by Theopompos (*FGrH* 115 F210 = Athen. 10.436b) as one of the most dissolute public figures. Demosthenes, in the *de Corona*, depicts him as a traitor to his country (18.48, 295; cf. Polyb. 18.14.4, citing Demosthenes). He was among those supporters of Macedon (Din. 1.74 says he took bribes from Philip II) who resided on the Kadmeia and in 335 he and Amyntas (Anemoitas) were caught off guard and murdered by Theban exiles who had slipped into the city (Arr. 1.7.1). Timolaos' death was followed by rebellion, which ultimately led to the city's destruction. Berve II 374 no. 752.

1144 TIMOSTHENES

(Τιμοσθένης). Son of Demophanes, from Eretria. T. was honored by the Athenians in 306/5 (*IG* II² 467; Harding no. 123B) for service to the city both in the time of the Lamian War (323/2) and when Kassandros invaded Attika in late summer 306 (cf. Ferguson 114). He was voted a golden crown, apparently worth 1,000 drachmas (the number is restored by the editor). Nothing else is known about him. Paschidis 197.

1145 TIMOTHEOS

(Τιμόθεος). Macedonian (Tataki 441 no. 13) common soldier under the command of Parmenion (apparently in Syria, as the context of Plutarch's account suggests). He and Damon were charged with seducing the "wives" (γύναια) of certain Greek mercenaries. Alexander instructed Parmenion to investigate and execute Timotheos and Damon if they were guilty (Plut. *Alex.* 22.4). The outcome of the proceedings is unknown. Berve II 373–4 no. 750.

1146 TIMOTHEOS

(Τιμόθεος). Son of Lysanias. Macedonian (Tataki 441 no. 15). Honored by the Eretrians, on a motion by Elpinikos son of Stilbos (Paschidis D90), in the late fourth century with a golden crown worth a thousand drachms and a bronze equestrian statue (*IG* XII 9 196). The cavalry officer Lysanias, who served Antigonos in 316 (Diod. 19.29.2; see no. 671), may be a relative, possibly even the father of T. The date of the honors for T. cannot be determined with certainty, although the possibilities range from 322 to *c.*304. Knoepfler 2001, 184 n.497; Paschidis 446–8.

1147 TIMOTHEOS

(Τιμόθεος). Son of Oiniades (Didymos col. 12.61–2; Gibson 2002, 97). Flutist (*auletes*) noted for his long beard (Athen. 13.565a). He performed at the Court of Philip II and gave martial inspiration to young Alexander (Dio Chrys. 1.1). Seneca, *de Ira* 2.2 confuses him with Xenophantos (Berve II 282 no. 577). A similar story is told by Plut. *Mor.* 335a of Antigenides, who was no longer alive in Alexander's time (see Berve II 415 no. 8). Timotheos joined Alexander in Memphis, where he took part in the musical competitions (*Suda*; Arr. 3.1.4); he also performed at the mass marriage ceremony in Sousa in 324 (Chares, *FGrH* 125 F4 = Athen. 12.538f; see also Phrynichos, Kaphisias, Diophantos, and Euios). Berve II 373 no. 749.

1148 TIRIDATES

(Τιριδάτης). Persian, possibly a eunuch (Achaimenid rulers regularly employed eunuchs as *gazophylakes*. Ael. *VH* 12.1 mentions a different eunuch of that name in the time of Artaxerxes II). Royal treasurer (*gazophylax*) at Persepolis (Curt. 5.5.2; Diod. 17.69.1 describes him vaguely as "the man in charge of the city"), T. offered to betray the city to Alexander (Diod. 17.69.1; Curt. 5.2.2) and was probably instrumental in shutting the city's gates to the defeated satrap Ariobarzanes (Curt. 5.4.34; cf. Bosworth I 329; Briant

467). Alexander thus secured a treasure of 120,000 talents of silver (Diod. 17.71.1; Curt. 5.6.9) before it could be plundered by the Persian garrison (Arr. 3.18.10). T. was retained as treasurer, but with a Macedonian garrison and Nikarchides as *phrourarchos* (Curt. 5.6.11) and Phrasaortes as satrap of Persis (Arr. 3.18.11). His tenure appears to have been brief, for the treasures were transferred from Persepolis to Ekbatana and placed in the charge of Alexander's Imperial Treasurer, Harpalos (Arr. 3.19.7). What became of him we do not know. Berve II 374–5 no. 754; Shayegan 125 no. 114.

1149 TIRIDATES

(Τιριδάτης). Persian or possibly a native of the region around Lake Sistan. According to Diod. 17.81.2, Alexander appointed T. to the *strategia* of the Gedrosians and Ariaspians. Curt. 7.3.4, however, says that Amedines, the former secretary of Dareios III (*scriba regis*), was made satrap of the Ariaspians (Euergetai); perhaps Amedines was T.'s subordinate. It is remotely possible (*pace* Berve) that T. is the same man who surrendered Persepolis; cf. the case of Mithrenes, who surrendered Sardis and then became satrap of Armenia. Berve II 375 no. 755; Shayegan 125 no. 115.

1150 TIRIDATES

(Τιριδάτης). Prominent Persian. His estates in an unspecified area (perhaps Baktria) were given to Eurylochos as a reward for bringing the Hermolaos conspiracy to Alexander's attention (Curt. 8.6.26). One may conclude that T. had been an enemy of the King and that his property had thus been confiscated. Berve II 375 no. 756; Shayegan 125 no. 116.

1151 TLEPOLEMOS

(Τληπόλεμος). Macedonian (Tataki 442 no. 18; cf. Hoffmann 201). Son of Pythophanes (Arr. 3.22.1; 6.27.1); *hetairos* of Alexander (Arr. 3.22.1). T. first appears in 330 as the *episkopos* in Parthia-Hyrkania (cf. Anaxippos and Neiloxenos), that is, the military watchdog of the Amminapes, the native satrap (Arr. 3.22.1; cf. Bosworth I 346). He continued in that capacity when Amminapes was replaced by Phrataphernes, sometime between 330 and 326 (cf. Brunt I 301 n.2). In 325/4 T. was appointed satrap of Karmania, replacing Astaspes (Arr. 6.27.1; cf. Curt. 9.10.21, 29, without reference to T.) but he had not succeeded in establishing order there when Nearchos arrived (Arr. *Ind.* 36.8; for changes in Karmania and surrounding satrapies see Heckel 2017a). T. was recognized as satrap of Karmania in 323 (Justin 13.4.23; Diod. 18.3.3; Dexippos, *FGrH* 100 F8 §6 makes "Neoptolemos" satrap of Karmania. This is clearly a scribal error and the emendation that makes Neoptolemos satrap of Armenia and T. ruler of Karmania is unlikely to represent the original text. He also received the satrapy in the forged will of Alexander: *LM* 121; Ps.-Call. 3.33.22.), and his position was confirmed at Triparadeisos (Diod. 18.39.6; Arr. *Succ.* 1.35). In the war between Eumenes and Antigonos, T. supported the former (Diod. 19.28.3); Antigonos' failure to depose him after Gabiene may reflect the fact that he fled to his satrapy after the battle (cf. Heckel 1980c 44 with n.6) as much as his popularity with the Karmanians, whom he had governed well (Diod. 19.48.1). Berve II 375–6 no. 757; Lehmann-Haupt 145–6 §118; Billows 449 no. 137.

1152 TROAS

(Τρωάς). Epeirot. Daughter and eldest surviving child of Neoptolemos the Molossian; sister of Olympias and Alexander I (Justin 7.6.10–11; cf. 8.6.4), and thus an aunt of Alexander the Great. T. was born perhaps *c.375*. After the death of her father, she married her uncle, Arybbas son of Alketas, to whom she bore a son, Aiakides (Plut. *Pyrrh.* 1.5); she was, in all likelihood, not Arybbas' first wife and thus probably not the mother of Alketas II. Nothing else is known about her life. **Stemma IIa–b.**

1153 TROAS

(Τρωάς). Epeirot. Daughter of Aiakides and Phthia, and sister of Deidameia and Pyrrhos (Plut. *Pyrrh.* 1.7). Plutarch's list is no secure guide to the birth-order of Aiakides' children, though T., named after the paternal grandmother (see above), is mentioned as the second of Pyrrhos' two sisters. In light of the prominence of Deidameia, it appears that T. was younger (*contra* Lévêque 1957, 83 n.1, who suggests a birthdate of *c.321*). Nothing else is recorded about her life, but she, like her sister, may have been in Olympias' entourage when she was captured by Kassandros. If so, she probably returned to Epeiros at some point between 307 and 303. Sandberger 210–11 no. 82; Hammond, *Epirus* 815. **Stemma IIb.**

1154 TYRIESPIS

(Τυρίεσπις, Curt. Terioltes). Iranian (Justi 330). Installed as satrap of Parapamisadai in 327, replacing Proëxes, while Nikanor, one of the *hetairoi*, was entrusted with the administration of Alexandria-in-the-Kaukasos, where the neighboring population (*perioikoi*) and the *apomachoi* were settled (Arr. 4.22.5). When Nikanor was moved to the satrapy to the west of the Indos and killed by an uprising of the Assakenians, T. and Philip son of Machatas were sent to put down the revolt (Arr. 5.20.7). T.'s administration of Parapamasadai was marked by cases of improper behavior and he was removed in 325 and replaced by Oxyartes (Arr. 6.15.3). T. was put on trial and executed (Curt. 9.8.9). Berve II 376 no. 758; Shayegan 125–6 no. 117.

W–Z

1155 WANAXION

Son of Saondas. One of twenty-four cavalrymen from Orchomenos, who served with Alexander's allied cavalry until the expedition reached Ekbatana in 330. There he and his compatriots were discharged. On their return (c.329), they made a dedication to Zeus Soter in Orchomenos (*IG* VII 3206). Berve II 162 no. 334.

1156 XANDRAMES

(Ξανδράμης. Aggrammes; Sanskrit Chandramas = "Moon god," so McCrindle 409; Nandrus: Justin 15.4.16). Ruler of the Prasioi and Gandaridai, X. commanded an army of 200,000 infantry, 20,000 cavalry and 2,000 chariots (Diod. 17.93.2; Curt. 9.2.3; Metz Epit. 68) as well as a substantial number of elephants (Metz Epit. 68 has 180; Curt. 9.2.3 gives 3,000 and Diod. 17.93.2 says 4,000). He is Mahapadma Nanda, last king of the Nanda dynasty, which ruled the Magadha kingdom on the Ganges in the mid-fourth century. Alexander learned about him from Phegeus (no. 893) at the Hyphasis (Beas) River in 326. According to the report, X. was the son of the king's barber, who killed his master and married the queen (Curt. 9.2.6–7; Diod. 17.93.2–3 claims that it was the queen herself who killed her husband). Plut. *Alex.* 62.9 says that Chandragupta (Sandrokottos) sneered at the base origins of Xandrames. Chandragupta himself deposed and killed X. and established the Mauryan dynasty not long after Alexander's departure from India (c.322 according to Buddhist tradition). Berve II 281 no. 574.

1157 XANTHIPPOS

(Ξάνθιππος). Son of Ampharetos. Phokian, probably from Elateia. Honored by the Elateians for twice liberating the city: once from Kassandros in 304, and then again from Lysimachos (285–281). For his status as a local hero see Paus. 10.4.10. Paschidis 323–6 C24 with epigraphic sources.

1158 XENNIAS

(Ξεννίας). Macedonian (Tataki 389 no. 2). It does not follow from the Greek (ἄνδρα μακεδονίζοντα τῇ φ[ω]νῇ) that Xennias was not himself a Macedonian. The author is trying to make the point that the communication took place in the Macedonian tongue. Who better to transmit a message in this language than a Macedonian himself. Indeed, had he not been Macedonian one might expect a comment to that effect (see also Anson 208–9.) X. served in some capacity, and perhaps not solely as a herald, in the army of Eumenes of Kardia. Since he is found with Eumenes in the campaign against Neoptolemos (thus Bosworth 1978) in early 320, it is virtually certain that he had served in Asia during Alexander's lifetime. Eumenes sent him, because he was a Macedonian speaker (*PSI* XII 1284, 6) to address the Macedonian nucleus of Neoptolemos' force and gain a truce by threatening to cut off Neoptolemos' forces from their supplies. Nothing else is known about X. Bosworth 1978.

1159 XENODOCHOS

(Ξενόδοχος). Greek from Kardia. X. and Artemios of Kolophon had traveled from the coast and reached Sogdiana in the summer of 328. X. was present at the banquet at which Kleitos was murdered (Plut. *Alex.* 51.4). Nothing else is known about him, but the mere fact of his presence at the King's banquet suggests that he was a man of some importance. Berve II 281 no. 575.

1160 XENOKLES

(Ξενοκλῆς). Athenian democrat (Kirchner 11234). Son of Xeinis of Sphettos. Born *c.*375. Active in the time of Lykourgos. X. and Kleainetos (no. 587) appear at the head of an embassy to Antigonos the One-Eyed in 305 (II² 1492B). The embassy was perhaps instigated by Stratokles and resulted in a donation of 140 talents of silver and timber, as well as the restoration of Lemnos to the Athenians (thus Paschidis 107). X. was lampooned by Matron (Athen. 4.134e = *SH* 534). Paschidis 107–9 A31.

1161 XENOKLES

(Ξενοκλῆς). Described by Strabo 2.1.6 C69 simply as *gazophylax*, a term that is used of a man in charge of the treasures in a specific place. X. is supposed to have been presented with an accurate description of the Asian countryside. Perhaps Xenokles is an error for Xenophilos, who was *phrourarchos* (also *thesaurophylax*) of Sousa (see below).

1162 XENOKRATES

(Ξενοκράτης). Son of Agathenor. Born *c.*395 (Diog. Laert. 4.14). Greek philosopher from Chalkedon (Strabo 12.4.9 C566), X. was a student and successor of Speusippos (*Suda* s.v.), heading the Academy from 339 to his death in 314 (Plut. *Phoc.* 4.2 says he was a teacher of Phokion). He was associated with both Plato and Aristotle, accompanying the former to Sicily and spending time with the latter at Assos, where he went at the invitation of Hermias of Atarneus; when Memnon of Rhodes arrested Hermias and sent him to the Great King to be executed, X. and Aristotle escaped from the area (Strabo 13.1.57 C610). X.'s connections with Alexander are slight: when the King sent X. a gift of 50 talents, he returned it saying that money was for kings, not philosophers (Plut. *Mor.* 181e, 331e, 333b; Val. Max. 4.3 ext. 3b; *Suda* s.v.; for his integrity in general see Val. Max. 2.10 ext. 2). Val. Max. 4.3 ext. 3a relates how the courtesan Phryne, for all her beauty, had been unable to seduce X. at an all-night drinking party. He dedicated a work *On Kingship* in four books to Alexander (cf. Plut. *Mor.* 1126d), as well as works for Arybbas (whether this was the Somatophylax of Alexander or Olympias' uncle is unclear) and Hephaistion (Diog. Laert. 4.14). In 322, after their defeat in the Lamian War, the Athenians sent him as one of their ambassadors to Antipatros, but X.'s tone was defiant and Antipatros' treatment of him cool (Plut. *Phoc.* 27.1–3, 6; but Diog. Laert. 4.9 paints a different picture); his relationship with Polyperchon appears to have been better (Plut. *Mor.* 533c). Soon afterwards he was offered, but declined, citizenship by the pro-Macedonian Athenian regime (Plut. *Phoc.* 29.6). An account of his career is given by Diog. Laert. 4.6–16. Berve II 281–2 no. 576; Paschidis 68–9.

1163 XENOPEITHES

(Ξενοπείθης). Greek. *Phrourarchos* of the fortress in which Antigonos Monophthalmos had imprisoned Attalos, Polemon, and Dokimos. During the escape of the prisoners he was thrown from the walls to his death six hundred feet below (Diod. 19.16.1). Billows 439 no. 118.

1164 XENOPHANTOS

(Ξενόφαντος). Greek flute player, the most celebrated of his time. He performed the funeral hymn for Demetrios Poliorketes (Plut. *Demetr.* 53.5). Seneca, *de Ira* 2.2 appears to have confused him with Timotheos, and Berve's suggestion (II 282) that he may have been in Alexander's entourage some forty years earlier is not impossible but highly unlikely. Berve II 282 no. 577.

1165 XENOPHILOS

(Ξενόφιλος). Macedonian. In 330, X. was installed as *phrourarchos* in Sousa with 1,000 veterans (Curt. 5.2.16), a position he retained until 317/16 (the city itself was under the control of the *strategos* Archelaos son of Theodoros). Arr. 3.16.9 says that the garrison commander at Sousa was one of the *hetairoi*, a man named Mazaros. This is almost certainly an error: Mazaros was probably the Persian whom X. replaced. Furthermore, there is a strong likelihood that the man who arranged the surrender of Sousa after Gaugamela, Philoxenos, is actually Xenophilos (the two parts of the name have been transposed: see Heckel 2002). X. served as *phrourarchos* under the satrap Aboulites, then Oropios and Koinos, and eventually Antigenes; the *gazophylax* Xenokles, named by Strabo 2.1.6 C69, may in fact be X., whom Diod. 19.18.1 calls *thesaurophylax*. During the war between Antigonos and Eumenes, he defended Sousa against the forces of Seleukos (Diod. 19.17.3, 18.1), and after Eumenes' death and that of Antigenes, he entered into "friendship" with Antigonos. Diod. 19.48.6 makes it clear, however, that Antigonos merely pretended friendship (τοῦτον μὲν οὖν προσδεξάμενος προσεποιεῖτο τιμᾶν ἐν τοῖς μεγίστοις τῶν φίλων, εὐλαβούμενος μὴ μετανοήσας πάλιν αὐτὸν ἀποκλείσῃ). Billows 440, is less suspicious: "Antigonos received him honorably and enrolled him among his *philoi* (i.e., personal staff) . . . X. presumably remained thenceforth in Antigonos' service." What became of him is unknown, but it is likely that Antigonos either kept him in honorable detention (cf. Peukestas) or eliminated him. Sousiana was entrusted to neither Seleukos nor X., but rather to the native Aspeisas (Diod. 19.55.1), on whom see no. 242 and Billows 376–7 no. 21. Berve II 282 no. 578; Billows 440–1 no. 119; Heckel 2002.

1166 ZARIASPES

(Ζαριάσπης). Noble Persian rebel. Z. was defeated and captured, along with Ozines (see Ordanes no. 818), by Krateros in 325 (Curt. 9.10.19). He was brought to Alexander in Karmania in 324 and executed there (Curt. 10.1.9). Berve II 162–3 no. 335; Shayegan 126 no. 118.

1167 ZENODOTOS

(Ζηνόδοτος). Son of Baukideus. Hicks 1881 makes a strong case for regarding Z. as a citizen of Halikarnassos possibly with family connections to Troizen, played a leading role in the liberation of Troizen from Kassandros' control and the removal of the garrison (ἐξαγωγὴν τῆς φρουρᾶς suggests that they left under truce). He was therefore honored by the Troizens; the inscription itself was set up in Halikarnassos (Michel, *RIG* no. 252; Hicks 1881), the pride of the Halikarnassians appears to be expressed by the claim that he acted ἀξίως τῆς πατρίδος. Z. was clearly in Demetrios' service during his campaign in the Peloponnese in 303. Hicks 1881, 98–101; Billows 440 no. 120.

1168 ZEPHYROS

(Ζέφυρος). Macedonian (Tataki 318 no. 2). A common soldier, Z. is named only in the apocryphal *Letter to Aristotle* 14 as the man who brought Alexander a helmet full of water when the army was suffering greatly from privations in the desert. The famous story of how Alexander poured the water into the ground in front of the army is told by a number of sources, although there is no agreement on the location of the episode: see Arr. 6.26.1–3 (Gedrosia or Parapamisadai); cf. Plut. *Alex.* 42.7–10 (pursuit of Dareios); Curt. 7.5.10–12 (Baktria); Front. 1.7.7 (Africa: i.e., Egypt); Polyaenus 4.3.25 (desert). Curtius and Plutarch say that Alexander did not pour out the water but returned it to the men who had brought it, telling them to give it to their sons, for whom they had procured the water in the first place. The story itself may contain an element of truth, but the name Z. may have been invented. Berve II 163 no. 337.

1169 ZIPOITES

(Ζιποίτης, Ζειποίτης, Ζιβύτης). Bithynian, son of Bas and father of Nikomedes I (Arr. *Bithynica* F63 = Tzetzes, *Chil.* 3.950). Born *c*.356, he succeeded his father in 328/7 but did not take the royal title until 297. His attempt to capture Astakos (*Barr. Atl.* 52 F3) and Chalkedon in 314 was thwarted by Antigonos' general, Polemaios; Z. abandoned his sieges, became an ally of Antigonos, and gave hostages (Diod. 19.60.3; Plut. *Mor.* 302e–303a probably refers to a different campaign). Z. was an opponent of Lysimachos and Seleukos, both of whom were regarded as a threat to his kingdom. After Lysimachos' death, Z. attacked Herakleia Pontika, laying waste the territory but suffering heavy casualties in the process (Memnon 6.3). He maintained the independence of Bithynia against the Macedonians, resisting incursions by two of Lysimachos' generals, one of whom fell in battle and the other was driven out; he also defeated the forces of Antiochos I (Memnon 12.5–6). Z. founded a city at the foot of Mt. Lyparos, which he named for himself (cf. Steph. Byz. s.v. Zipoition; Paus. 5.21.7 says that Astakos was renamed Nikomedeia by Nikomedes but that it was originally founded by Zypoites, whom Pausanias identifies as a Thrakian: Ζυποίτης ἐγένετο οἰκιστής, Θρᾷξ γένος εἰκάζοντί γε ἀπὸ τοῦ ὀνόματος). From the death of his father, Z. ruled for forty-eight years and died in 280 (Memnon 12.4–5). He had four sons, of whom the eldest, Nikomedes I, succeeded him. Berve II 163 no. 338; Habicht, *RE* X.A (1972) 448–55 no. 121; Vitucci 1955, 11–21; Grainger, *SPG* 669; Billows 440–2 no. 121.

1170 ZOES

Officer of the Antigonids, honored in Athens between 307 and 301. The inscription of the honorific decree is too fragmentary to allow further comment (*Hesperia* 2 (1933) 402–3 no. 19). Billows 442 no. 122.

1171 ZOÏLOS

(Ζωΐλος). Boiotian. Son of Kelainos. Z. was the garrison commander of Aigosthena for Demetrios Poliorketes. Between 306 and 301, he was honored by the Megarians with a golden crown; he and his descendants were granted Megarian citizenship on account of good conduct and that of his garrison troops (*IG* VII 1 = *Syll*³ 331). Billows 442 no. 123.

1172 ZOÏLOS

(Ζωΐλος). Origins uncertain. Probably Macedonian and perhaps even the father of Mylleas of Beroia (cf. Arr. *Ind.* 18.6; Tataki 78 no. 27 and *PB* 151 no. 517). Z. met Alexander as he was moving on from Artakoana in 330, bringing 500 allied Greek horsemen (Curt. 6.6.35), part of a larger group that included 3,000 Illyrians sent by Antipatros; 130 Thessalian cavalrymen under Philip son of Menelaos; and 2,600 infantry and 300 cavalry from Lydia. Nothing else is known about him. Berve II 163–4 no. 339.

1173 ZOÏLOS

(Ζωΐλος). Greek armorer from Kypros (Plut. *Demetr.* 21.4). Sent two suits of lighter, but seemingly impenetrable, iron armor—they could withstand undamaged a catapult dart shot at 20 paces (Plut. *Demetr.* 21.5)—to Demetrios, who wore one and gave the other to Alkimos the Epeirot (Plut. *Demetr.* 21.5–6), though the latter perished in the fighting at Rhodes in 305/4 (cf. Diod. 20.98.9; Plut. *Demetr.* 21.6). In fairness to Z.'s reputation, we must assume that Alkimos' wounds were sustained where the armor could not avail him. Billows 442–3 no. 124.

1174 ZOPYRION

(Ζωπυρίων). Macedonian (Tataki 318 no. 4). Z. is generally (and incorrectly) thought to have succeeded as *strategos* of Thrake an otherwise unknown Memnon (Berve II 164 "Nachfolger Memnons"). Memnon, furthermore, according to the less-than-reliable testimony of Diod. 17.62.4–5, fomented rebellion among the Thrakians at the same time as Agis III (no. 27) was preparing his uprising in the south. The common view is that Memnon and Antipatros came to terms and that this same Memnon, after continuing in his office as *strategos*, eventually brought Thrakian reinforcements to Alexander in 326/5 and, if the *argumentum e silentio* is worth anything, suffered no consequences for his unruly behavior (see full discussion s.v. Memnon no. 703). Z. is thus regarded as his successor. In fact, Justin 12.2.16 calls Z. *praefectus Ponti ab Alexandro Magno relictus* (see Noethlichs 1987, 411; Heckel 127). The reference is clearly to the Thrakian area bordering on the Black Sea (cf. Arr. *Succ.* 1.7; Diod. 18.3.2). In 331/0 Z. conducted an expedition, allegedly totalling 30,000 (Justin 12.2.16; 37.3.2), against the Getai, marching to the Borysthenes and besieging Olbia (*Barr. Atl.* 23 E2; Curt. 10.1.44; cf. Justin 2.3.4; 12.2.17; cf. Macrob. *Sat.* 1.11.33; Beloch IV² 1.44–5 puts the campaign in 325 and regards Z. as Memnon's successor); this was either to suppress the rebellion by Seuthes or an event that prompted Seuthes' subsequent defection (Curt. 10.1.44; cf. Lund 22–4). The Macedonian force was annihilated, together with its leader, by a combination of the enemy and bad weather. The upheavals in this area forced Antipatros to take military action. He appears to have named Memnon (or, what is more likely, Menon) as Z.'s successor. Berve II 164 no. 340.

Anonymous Individuals
(Excluding Non-Entities)

A1 A woman of a prominent Rhodian family; sister of Memnon (no. 701) and Mentor (Demosth. 23.154, 157; Diod. 16.52.4), wife of Artabazos (no. 223). For her luxurious lifestyle (involving the use of *klimakides* or "human ladders") see Klearchos of Soloi *ap.* Athen. 6.256d. Sometime around 349/8 she accompanied Artabazos to the Court of Philip II with her eleven sons and ten daughters (Diod. 16.52.4). These sons seem to have been Pharnabazos (no. 889) and an *anonymus*, as well as Ariobarzanes (no. 183), Arsames, Kophen (no. 618), and six further *anonymi* who surrendered with their father to Alexander in Hyrkania in 330 (Curt. 6.5.4; cf. Arr. 3.23.7). Her daughters included Apame (Artakama), Artonis, and Barsine (no. 287); to whom we must add seven unnamed sisters. It is doubtful that she was the mother of Ilioneus, or that she is identical with the wife of Artabazos captured at Damaskos in 333. Brunt 1975; also Beloch III² 2.149–50.

A2–8 Seven daughters of Artabazos and his Rhodian wife. Diod. 16.52.4 says that they had ten daughters in 349/8, of whom we know the names of Barsine, Artonis, and Artakama or Apame.

A9–14 Six unnamed sons of Artabazos and the sister of Memnon and Mentor the Rhodians (see Brunt 1975 for the family); they surrendered to Alexander, along with their father and three other brothers, Ariobarzanes (but see Bosworth I 325), Arsames, and Kophen, in 330 (Arr. 3.23.7). They had earlier spent some time at the Court of Philip II (Diod. 16.52.4), and they now received good treatment at Alexander's hands. What became of them is unknown, although it is possible that we do not recognize one or more Persians in the later history of Alexander (or in the age of the Successors) as the son(s) of Artabazos.

A15 A seventh anonymous son of Artabazos (no. 223). Diod. 16.52.4 says that, in 349/8, Artabazos and the sister of Memnon and Mentor had eleven sons and ten daughters. Nine of the sons are accounted for above (**A9–14**, Ariobarzanes, Arsames, Kophen); we know the names of two others, Pharnabazos (no. 889) and Ilioneus, but the latter was most likely born to a different mother. Ilioneus was captured at Damaskos in late 333, apparently still a youth ("im Knabenalter," Berve II 183), and was presumably born after 349/8. That leaves one more *anonymus* to bring the total of Artabazos' sons by the Rhodian woman to eleven (possibly the Memnon of *IG* II² 356).

A16 An unnamed Illyrian queen, killed in single combat by the young princess Kynnane (no. 634), the daughter of Philip II and Audata-Eurydike (Polyaenus 8.60). Berve II 229 dates her death to *c.*344/3, i.e., before Alexander's accession. This seems somewhat early, since Kynnane was born *c.*357, and there is no reason to equate every skirmish with Illyrians with the famous battle of 344/3! But, since Polyaenus mentions Kynnane's exploits before her marriage to Amyntas son of Perdikkas (no. 76), the battle in question probably occurred late in Philip's reign.

A17 The champion of the Kadousians; he was killed in single combat in 341/0 (cf. Olmstead 488) by Dareios III (Diod. 17.6.1), and, on account of this, Dareios was promoted to satrap of the Armenians by Artaxerxes III (Justin 10. 3. 3–4).

A18 Daughter of Antipatros (no. 127; Diod. 17.80.2 wrongly "Antigonos"), wife of Alexander Lynkestes (no. 45; Justin 12.14.1; Curt. 7.1.6–7). First referred to in the discussion of events after Philip II's death in 336. If she was in fact the mother of Arrhabaios, the father of Kassandros (thus Habicht 1977a), then she is unlikely to have been identical with any of the known daughters of Antipatros: Eurydike, Nikaia, Phila.

A19 An earlier (Berve II 380 writes "erste," but we cannot know this) wife of Dareios III. She was the sister of Pharnakes (no. 890), who fell in battle at the River Granikos (Arr. 1.16.3; Diod. 17.21.3). On the basis of her brother's name, it appears that this wife of Dareios came from the Kappadokian-Pontic nobility. She is, in all probability, the mother of Ariobarzanes (no. 181), the son of Dareios who tried to betray his father and was executed (Aretades of Knidos *ap.* Plut. *Mor.* 11a = *FGrH* 285 F1).

A20 A daughter of Dareios III (we do not know by which wife; though her mother could very easily have been one of Dareios' concubines); wife of Mithridates (no. 740), who died at the Granikos, felled by Alexander's own lance (Arr. 1.15.7, 16.3).

A21 A daughter of Dareios III, she was the wife of Spithrobates (so Diod. 17.20.2, other sources call him Spithridates no. 1073), the satrap of Ionia. Diodorus' Spithrobates was killed in battle at the Granikos River by Alexander himself (17.20.5). Her existence is uncertain, however, since Diodorus may have conflated Spithridates and Mithridates, and transferred to the former the position of the King's son-in-law. On the other hand, it may indeed be true that the satrap of Ionia was also a son-in-law of Dareios III.

A22–3 At least two sons of Memnon the Rhodian; they fought in the battle at the Granikos River in 334 (Arr. 1.15.2; thus born before 352). Nothing more is known about them.

A24–5 Two sons of Lanike (no. 642), the sister of Black Kleitos; they died in battle at Miletos in 334 (Curt. 8.2.8; cf. Arr. 4.9.4). Their father's name is unknown, though Carney 1981, 153 speculates that he may have been Andronikos.

A26 A daughter of Parmenion (no. 848) (Curt. 6.9.30). She married Koinos (no. 610) son of Polemokrates, probably in 334 (Arr. 1.24.1, 29.4 lists him among the *neogamoi*), and bore him a son, Perdikkas (Dittenberger, *Syll*³ 332, 10). She may have been the widow of Attalos (no. 262).

A27 If not the same woman who married Koinos (above), then a second, older, daughter of Parmenion, who was married briefly to Attalos (Curt. 6. 9. 17), the uncle of Kleopatra-Eurydike (no. 607). But the fact that Koinos belonged to the newlyweds in 334/3 (Arr. 1.24.1, 29.4), i.e., shortly after Attalos' death, suggests that Parmenion merely found a new husband for Attalos' widow.

A28 Wife of Meleagros (no. 695) son of Neoptolemos. The marriage occurred in late 335 or early 334; Meleagros was sent home with other "newlyweds" (*neogamoi*) in the winter of 334/3 (Arr. 1.24.1, 29.4). Whether she had any children by him is unknown. She never saw her husband, who died in 323, again.

A29 Wife of Ptolemy (no. 1007) son of Seleukos. The marriage occurred in late 335 or early 334; Ptolemy was sent home with other "newlyweds" (*neogamoi*) in the winter of 334/3 (Arr. 1.24.1, 29.4). Whether she had any children by him is unknown. Ptolemy died at the battle of Issos (Arr. 2.12.2) in late 333, and their reunion almost a year earlier was their last meeting. What became of her is unknown.

A30 The governor of Damaskos (*praefectus:* Curt. 3.13.2), that is, probably the commander of the city or citadel. After the battle of Issos, he sent a certain Mardian to Parmenion (no. 848), telling him that he was prepared to betray the city and its treasures (Curt. 3.13.2); this he did by leading the Persians, whom Dareios III had left with him for safe-keeping, and the treasures outside the city walls (Curt. 3.13.5ff.). He has been wrongly identified (most recently by Atkinson I 257) with Kophen (no. 618), who had taken the treasures to Damaskos before the battle of Issos (Arr. 2.15.1). But this is impossible, since the governor of Damaskos was murdered by one of his own men and his head taken to Dareios (Curt. 3.13.17). Kophen lived on to surrender to Alexander in 330 and to serve him in Baktria-Sogdiana (cf. the comments of Berve II 230).

A31 A Mardian agent of the governor of Damaskos, sent by him to Parmenion to promise his planned betrayal of the city and its treasures.

A32 A confidant of the governor of Damaskos (above) and, possibly, also a high-ranking Persian; he murdered him and brought his head to Dareios (Curt. 3.13.17).

A33 The daughter of Oxyathres (no. 834), and thus niece of Dareios III; she was captured at Damaskos by Parmenion (Curt. 3.13.13). This may, of course, have been Amastris (no. 67), or an otherwise unknown sister of hers, but it is also possible that she was the daughter of Oxyathres, son of Dareios II (cf. Berve II 24 n.2: "Die in Damaskos genannte Tochter des Oxyathres kann freilich auch ein Kind des jüngsten Bruders Artaxerxes II., der ebenfalls Oxyathres hieß, gewesen sein . . ."). Justi 232; Neuhaus 1902, 619.

A34 The wife of Ochos (Artaxerxes III). She too was captured at Damaskos by Parmenion (Curt. 3.13.13). Berve, in his stemma (II 442), identifies her with the mother of Parysatis (no. 849) and of the three daughters of Ochos captured along with her (Curt. 3.13.12), one of these being, apparently, Parysatis herself (cf. Fiehn, *RE* XVIII (1949) 2052 no.2). Is this wife of Ochos the daughter of Atossa, the sister whom Ochos murdered after his accession (Val. Max. 9.2 ext. 7: *Apertior et taetrior alterius Ochi cognomine Artaxerxis crudelitas, qui Atossam sororem atque eandem socrum vivam capite defodit . . .*)? Justi 341, s.v. Wahuka, reads *Ocha* in Valerius Maximus, instead of Atossa, as proposed by Rumpf. This is rendered more likely by the claim that Atossa, Ochos' sister, contracted leprosy in the lifetime of Artaxerxes II (Plut. *Artox.* 23.4). Justi 232, and Neuhaus 1902, 619, think that Curt. 3.13.13 (*in eodem grege uxor eiusdem Ochi fuit Oxathrisque — frater hic erat Darei — filia*) refers to the same woman, a daughter of Oxathres, who married Ochos, but who is then not identical with the mother of two unnamed daughters and Parysatis, all captured at Damaskos. But this is not required by the Latin, which appears to indicate that the wife of Ochos and the daughter of Oxathres are two different women.

A35–6 Two daughters of Ochos (Artaxerxes III) and an unnamed wife. They were captured at Damaskos by Parmenion in 333 (Curt. 3.13.12), along with a third sister, probably Parysatis (no. 849), the youngest, who married Alexander in Sousa in 324 (Arr. 7.4.4). This last identification is, however, far from certain. What became of the other two we do not know.

A37 A wife of Artabazos; captured at Damaskos together with her son Ilioneus (no. 550) in 333 (Curt. 3.13.13). The fact that Ilioneus was taken at Damaskos with his mother suggests that he was still very young. If Artabazos' Rhodian wife had borne all eleven sons before 349/8, then none could have been younger than sixteen at the time of the battle of Issos, and it would appear that Ilioneus was a twelfth son of Artabazos by a younger wife. But everything depends on the date of Artabazos' flight to Macedonia (Diod. 16.52.4).

A38 Wife of Pharnabazos (no. 889); mother of his young son, together with whom she was captured at Damaskos in 333 (Curt. 3.13.14).

A39–41 Three daughters of Mentor the Rhodian (and of Barsine?); captured at Damaskos by Parmenion in late 333 (Curt. 3.13.14). One of these daughters married Nearchos at Sousa in 324 (Arr. 7.4 6).

A42 A young son of Pharnabazos (no. 889); he had been left with other Persians of note in Damaskos before the battle of Issos in late 333 (Diod. 17.32.3; cf. Curt. 3.8.12). Soon after the battle, he was captured, along with his mother, by Parmenion; Curt. 3.13.14. He is not mentioned again.

A43 The young son of Memnon (no. 701) and Barsine (no. 287); he had been left behind at Damaskos along with this mother and other notable Persians (Diod. 17.32.3; cf. Curt. 3.8.12). Here he was captured by Parmenion in late 333, soon after the battle of Issos (Curt. 3.13.14).

A44 Son of Azemilkos (no. 274), king of Tyre, who was with the Persian fleet of Autophradates. He ruled in his father's place and came with an unspecified number of noble Tyrians to submit to Alexander, who was at that time approaching the city (Arr. 2. 15. 6–7). When the Tyrians refused to admit Alexander into the city and were besieged by the Macedonians, Azemilkos was apparently recalled (cf. Arr. 2.24.5). Presumably, he was spared along with his father when the city was captured (Arr. 2.24.5).

A45 The leader of the Skythians who plundered the Macedonian baggage at Gaugamela (cf. Curt. 4.15.12ff.); he was killed by Aretes (Curt. 4.15.18).

A46 The leader of the Persian cavalry squadron encountered by Alexander after the battle of Gaugamela, once he had broken off his pursuit of Dareios (Curt. 4.16.23). Alexander killed him with his spear. As a leader of a cavalry squadron, he doubtless belonged to the Persian nobility. This episode is not mentioned elsewhere, and, since it is just one of a number of duels found in Curtius (cf. 4.6.15–16; 4.9.25; 4.15.18; 7.4.33–40; 8.14.35–6; 9.7.16–22), we cannot be certain about the historicity of the event.

A47 A Macedonian royal page, he placed a small table under Alexander's feet, when the latter sat on the throne of the Great King at Sousa and could not touch the ground (Curt. 5. 2. 13; Diod. 17. 66. 3).

A48 A Macedonian royal page; when burning incense fell onto his arm and seared his skin, he did not cry out with pain, lest he disturb Alexander's sacrifices (Val. Max. 3.3 ext. 1). If the story is not apocryphal, he may have gone on to serve in some military or administrative capacity.

A49 The wife of Madates (no. 677), who ruled the territory of the Ouxians and opposed Alexander at the end of 331. The woman herself was a daughter of the sister of Sisygambis, the mother of Dareios III (Curt. 5.3.12).

A50 Sister of Sisygambis (no. 1052); mother-in-law of Madates (Curt. 5.3.12). She was apparently the daughter of Ostanes, a brother of Artaxerxes II. Neuhaus 1902, 610ff.

A51 Wife of Hystaspes (no. 548); granddaughter of Ochos (Curt. 6.2.7). Berve II 378 identifies her as the daughter of Bisthanes (no. 300), but this is far from certain (cf. Berve's more cautious stemma, II 442). She was found among the Persian captives in 330, apparently taken at one of the royal residences. Alexander, upon learning her identity, had her reunited with her husband (Curt. 6.2.6–9). Berve II 378 for no good reason makes her a daughter of Bisthanes. Brosius 95 calls her Barsine and identifies her as a daughter of Arses. I do not see any evidence for her name, and the assumption that Arses was her father is based on the claim that he was the only one of Ochos' sons to survive (Diod. 17.5.4). But this ignores two facts: there were sons of concubines who survived (witness Bisthanes, Arr. 3.19.4 with Bosworth I 335) and Hystaspes' wife could have been born to one of the sons whom Bagoas later killed.

A52–3 At least two brothers of Polydamas (no. 974); they served as hostages while Polydamas went on his mission to secure the execution of Parmenion in 330 (Curt. 7.2.13–14; Berve II 323 prefers to read *filii* instead of *fratres* in Curtius). They may, of course, be fictitious, inserted by Curtius himself for dramatic effect.

A54 A Skythian princess (βασίλισσα); offered as a bride to Alexander in 329/8 (Arr. 4.15.2–3; Curt. 8.1.9; Plut. *Alex.* 46.3). This is possibly the daughter of Carthasis (no. 314), who had succeeded his dead brother (Arr. 4.15.1; cf. Curt. 7.7.1); Alexander declined the offer (Arr. 4.15.5).

A55 The wife of Spitamenes (no. 1072), and possibly the mother of Apama (no. 138), the mother of Antiochos I Soter and wife of Seleukos I Nikator (cf. Arr. 7.4.6; Plut. *Demetr.* 31.5); this Apama could have been one of the *tres adulti liberi* mentioned by Curt. 8.3.3, who, despite J.C. Rolfe's translation of *adulti* as "who had now reached manhood" (Loeb II 259), need not all have been male. The bizarre account of how, at the beginning of 327, Spitamenes' wife (with the aid of slave) murdered him in order to win Alexander's favor scarcely flatters Seleukos' mother-in-law (Curt. 8.3.1ff.; Metz Epit. 20–23). Although the woman is doubtless historical, what speaks against the story itself is not only the common folk-motif but also Arrian's report that Spitamenes was killed by the Massagetai, who *sent his head to Alexander* (Arr. 4.17.7; *Itiner. Alex.* 87). On the basis of the daughter's name,

Apama, it is tempting to regard her as an adherent of the Achaimenid house, but this seems to be ruled out by Metz Epit. 20, which calls her *quaedam Bactriana* Nothing else is known about her. Justi 310 (confused).

A56 The mother and wife of Sisimithres (no. 1049) (Curt. 8.2.19, 28–31; Metz Epit. 19), she bore Sisimithres two sons (Curt. 8.2.19; Metz Epit. 19 adds three daughters). In Curtius' version, she displays more courage than her son, but is finally persuaded to surrender to Alexander (in late autumn 328), who pardoned her and the rest of Sisimithres' family (Curt. 8.2.31).

A57–9 The three daughters of Sisimithres and his mother/wife (Metz Epit. 19). They surrendered to Alexander in late 328 and were pardoned by him (Curt. 8.2.31). Berve II 354 suggests plausibly that Chorienes was another name for Sisimithres (Brunt I 407 n.1 thinks it was an official title); if the two are identical, as appears to be the case (*pace* Bosworth 1981, 32ff.), then Sisimithres' three daughters will have been the ones introduced at the banquet where Alexander first met Rhoxane (Metz Epit. 28; they were among the thirty noble maidens mentioned by Curt. 8.4.23; *cohortandus* in 8.4.21 is almost certainly a corruption of Chorienes, but most editions wrongly follow Alde's correction to *Oxyartes*).

A60 The wife of Oxyartes (no. 833); mother of Rhoxane (no. 1028), and at least two other girls (**A61–2**), and a son named Itanes (no. 556). She took refuge with her family on the Sogdian Rock (thus, incorrectly, Arr. 4.18.4, 19.4), where she was captured.

A61–2 Two sisters of Rhoxane (no. 1028) and daughters of Oxyartes. They took refuge in a mountain fortress, either that of Sisimithes/Chorienes or of Ariamazes (thus Arr. 4.18.4, 19.4, implausibly) and were captured by Alexander. What became of them is unknown, but as sisters of the King's bride they too may have found Macedonian husbands (cf. Metz Epit. 31; Diod. 17 contents: ὡς Ἀλέξανδρος ἐρασθεὶς Ῥωξάνης τῆς Ὀξυάρτου ἔγημεν αὐτὴν καὶ τῶν φίλων πολλοὺς ἔπεισε γῆμαι τὰς τῶν ἐπισήμων βαρβάρων θυγατέρας).

A63–5 Three adult sons of Spitamenes (no. 1072) and the unnamed wife (**A55**) who, in the Vulgate tradition, murdered him (Curt. 8.3.3; cf. Metz Epit. 20–3, mentioning only the wife). Of course, these *adulti liberi* need not all have been male, and one of them might have been Apama, who later married Seleukos Nikator. What became of them, if they are not in fact fictitious, we do not know. As brothers of Seleukos' wife, they may have held higher offices in the Seleukid empire.

A66–8 Three sons of Chorienes (Curt. 8.4.21 mss. *cohortandus*, wrongly emended to "Oxyartes") = Sisimithres (no. 1049); Curt. 8.2.33 and Metz Epit. 19 say Sisimithres had two sons. When Chorienes surrendered to Alexander, he was required to give two of his three sons as hostages to serve in the Macedonian army (Curt. 8.4.21). Different primary sources knew the man by different names, and it is likely that one attributed to him three sons, another only two.

A69 The King of the European Skythians; brother of Carthasis (Curt. 7.7.1). He sent Carthasis to the Iaxartes to oppose Alexander (Curt. 7.7.1ff.; Metz Epit. 8; Arr. 4.5.1). The King himself appears to have died shortly afterwards (cf. Arr. 4.15.1).

A70 One of the Persian elders who performed *proskynesis* in front of Alexander in Baktria; his style was ridiculed by Leonnatos (Arr. 4.12.2; cf. Curt. 8.2.22–24: Polyperchon; Plut. *Alex.* 74.2–5: Kassandros, in Babylon; for the episode see Heckel 1978b).

A71 A divinely inspired Syrian woman who protected Alexander at the time of the Pages' conspiracy (Aristoboulos, *FGrH* 139 = Arr. 4.13.5–6; cf. Curt. 8.6.16).

A72 Son of Akouphis (no. 38), ruler of Nysa. In 327/6, he was required to serve with Alexander in India, presumably as a hostage for the good behavior of his father.

A73 Son of Akouphis' daughter; he had reached military age in 327/6 and served with Alexander in India, presumably as a hostage for the good behavior of his grandfather.

A74 The commander (*hegemon*) of Massaga; he was killed by a Macedonian catapult missile (Arr. 4.27.2). Certainly he could not have been Assakenos, who had died shortly before Alexander's arrival (Curt. 8.10.22; Metz Epit. 39); it is remotely possible, though there is no way of determining, that he is identical with Amminais, a brother of Assakenos, who was responsible for bringing 9,000 mercenaries into the city (Metz Epit. 39). Berve II 26 thinks that Amminais is the unnamed "brother of Assakenos" who opposed Alexander in the Buner region (Arr. 4.30.5), after the capture of Aornos, but this man appears more likely to have been Aphrikes (cf. Diod. 17.86.2; Curt. 8.12.1–3, Erices; Metz Epit. 43, Ariplex). See Anspach I 32; Eggermont 1975, 183–4; against Berve II 97–8.

A75 An Indian *hegemon* or *hyparchos* of the Aspasians, killed by Ptolemy son of Lagos in single combat in 327/6 (Arr. 4.24.3–4). Lassen II² 1.145 n.2, equates the Aspasians with the Assakenians and makes an argument (accepted by Berve II 89 no. 172) for the identification of this Indian chieftain with Assakenos, who had died shortly before Alexander reached Massaga. But Arrian, although he mentions Assakenos' brother (4.30.5), daughter (*sic*) and mother (4.27.4), is curiously silent about Assakenos himself, suggesting, what might be inferred from Curt. 8.10.22 and Metz Epit. 39, that he died of natural causes.

A76 The Indian *hyparchos* of the Assakenians, whose death at the hands of his rebellious subjects in late spring 326 was reported to Alexander by Sisikottos (no. 1048; Arr. 5.20.7). Berve II 354 identifies him with the Macedonian *hetairos*, Nikanor (cf. Arr. 4.28.6 and Brunt II 65 n.8; cf. Bosworth 1983, 38 n.6); but, despite Arrian's notoriously sloppy use of terminology, the *hyparchos* here appears to be a local dynast, perhaps Assagetes or Amminais, if the latter is not identical with **A74** above; possibly, an otherwise unknown tribal chieftain.

A77 A daughter of Assakenos (Arr. 4.27.4); she was captured by Alexander together with her grandmother, Cleophis (no. 332). Curt. 8.10.35 and Metz Epit. 39, 45 say the child was male.

A78 A son of the Indian dynast Assakenos; grandson of Cleophis. Arr. 4. 27. 4 makes this child female, but Curt. 8. 10. 35 and Metz Epit. 39, 45 agree that it was male. Curt. 8.10.35 says that he was Cleophis' own son. Perhaps the infant gave rise to the story that Alexander fathered on Cleophis a son bearing his name (Curt. 8.10.36; Justin 12.7.9–11).

A79 A son of Poros (no. 986), who, according to Aristoboulos, was sent by his father with 60 chariots to oppose Alexander's crossing of the Hydaspes. He could have prevented the crossing had he attacked, but instead he merely drove by with his chariots, only to be routed by Alexander's *hippotoxotai* (Arr. 5.14.3). Ptolemy records that this son was sent by Poros, but not with 60 chariots (Arr. 5.14.5); he gives the number as 120 chariots and 2,000 cavalry. When he arrived, Alexander had already crossed the river (Arr. 5.14.6), and in the ensuing battle some 400 Indian horsemen fell, including Poros' son (Arr. 5.15.2–3, Poros learns of his death; cf. 5.18.2 and Diod. 17.89.1). According to a third version, Poros' son gave battle, wounded Alexander himself and struck Boukephalas (Alexander's horse) a mortal blow (Arr. 5.14.4).

A80 A second son of the Indian King Poros (no. 986); he died in battle at the Hydaspes River in 326 (Diod. 17.89.1; Arr. 5.18.2).

A81–2 Two sons of the Indian King, Sopeithes (Sophytes no. 1061); they surrendered to Alexander along with their father (Curt. 9.1.28). Nothing else is known about them.

A83 A brother of Omphis/Taxiles. Alexander sent him to advise Poros to surrender (Curt. 8. 14. 35), but Poros responded by killing him with a javelin (Curt. 8.14.36).

A84 A brother of Abisares (no. 2), sent by the latter as a legate to Alexander in 326 (Arr. 5.8.3; 5.20.5, 29.4; Metz Epit. 55; cf. Curt. 8.13.1; 9.1.7, who speaks only of envoys in general terms).

A85 The mother of Xandrames (no. 1156), ruler of the Indians beyond the Ganges (Diod. 17.93.3; Curtius 9.2.3, *Aggrammes*); she had been the wife of the previous ruler, whose name is not preserved, but became the lover of Xandrames' father, a barber, who gained the throne when the queen murdered her husband (Curt. 9.2.6–7; Diod. 17.93.3; cf. Plut. *Alex.* 62).

A86 The father of Xandrames. He was allegedly a barber and lover of the queen. He gained the kingship when the queen (**A85**) murdered her husband (Curt. 9.2.6–7; Diod. 17.93.3; cf. Plut. *Alex.* 62).

A87 A son of Alexander the Great and Rhoxane (no. 1028); according to Metz Epit. 70, he died at the Akesines River in 326 If this report is true, then it is likely that he died at birth; for no other extant source mentions him. Berve II 347 accepts the information as historical but wrongly places the child's death "im Herbst 326 am Hydaspes" (followed by Hamilton 129).

A88 Daughter of Atropates (no. 261), she married Perdikkas (no. 871) at Sousa in 324 (Arr. 7.4.5; cf. Justin 13.4.13). Nothing else is known about her, but, in the light of Perdikkas' political marriages with Nikaia and Kleopatra, it is possible that she was repudiated soon after Alexander's death.

A89 The daughter of Harpalos (no. 494) and Pythionike (no. 1020). Her mother died *c*.326; the girl, still very young (θυγάτριον), came to Athens with her father in 324. After his death, she was taken in by Phokion and his son-in-law Charikles (no. 323), who saw to her upbringing (Plut. *Phoc.* 22.1, 3).

A90–1 The daughters of Attalos (presumably only two), captured with Olympias' party at Pydna in 316 (Diod. 19.35.5). In all likelihood, they were the daughters of Attalos (no. 265), son of Andromenes, and Atalante (no. 249), the sister of Perdikkas. They were born no earlier than 322 and may have been twins. Since both Atalante and her brother were killed in Egypt, and Attalos withdrew to Tyre, Atalante's children may have remained with Rhoxane and Alexander IV, with whom they came to Macedonia and, eventually, into the custody of Olympias. What became of them, we do not know.

A92 Daughter of Dionysios (no. 386) of Herakleia by an unnamed wife who preceded Amastris. Married Polemaios (no. 968), the nephew of Antigonos Monophthalmos (Memnon 4.6).

A93 Daughter of the Paionian king Audoleon (no. 268). She married Pyrrhos at some point after the death of Antigone and, probably, after the king had married Birkenna (Plut. *Pyrrh.* 9.3). Like the latter, she enjoyed the favor of her husband (who preferred his barbarian wives over Lanassa (no. 640): Plut. *Pyrrh.* 10.7). He appears to have produced no children, certainly no sons. What became of her is unknown.

A94–5 Daughters (at least two) of Perilaos (no. 874); since they were approaching marriageable age, their father asked Alexander for dowries for them and received 50 talents (Plut. *Apophth. Al.* 6 = *Mor.* 179f). The anecdote involves the standard *topos* about the generosity of kings, but the existence of Perilaos and his daughters need not be doubted. If Perilaos is identical with the man of the same name who acted as a mediator in Babylon (Curt. 10.8.15), then he was very likely a Greek *hetairos* of Alexander.

A96 Wife of Archelaos (possibly the son of Theodoros, so Berve II 85 no. 158), she was painted by Apelles together with her husband and daughter (Pliny, *HN* 35.96).

A97 Daughter of Archelaos (no. 159), she was painted together with her parents by Apelles (Pliny, *HN* 35.96).

A98 An Illyrian woman, either a wife or a concubine of Demetrios Poliorketes. Their son was known as Demetrios *Leptos* "the Thin" (Plut. *Demetr.* 53.8). Aulbach §8.2.1.6.

A99 An Odrysian woman, apparently a concubine of Lysimachos. Mother of Alexander (no. 52; Paus. 1.10.5).

A100 A daughter of Lysimachos (and perhaps Nikaia, thus Ogden 58), given in marriage to Dromichaites in the mid-290s (Paus. 1.9.6).

A101 A daughter of Ptolemy Keraunos, offered in 281/0 as a wife to Pyrrhos, who left him as a guardian of his kingdom (though the power was officially in the hands of Pyrrhos' son Ptolemy) during his Italian expedition (Justin 17.2.15; 24.1.8; see Niese II 10; Tarn, *AG* 134 n.47; Heinen 71–2; the objections of Hammond 1988b are unconvincing).

A102 A son of Aboulites of Sousa, apparently younger (cf. Plut. *Alex.* 68.7) than Oxathres (no. 830). Sent to Alexander to negotiate his father's surrender (Arr. 3.16.6; Curt. 5.2.8–9).

A103 Ruler of Keryneia on Kypros. When Agesilaos (no. 25) was sent to the island in 315, this man agreed to an alliance with Antigonos (Diod. 19.59.1).

A104 An older widow of the Indian leader, Keteus (no. 584). She vied with a younger wife for the honor of performing *sati*, i.e. accompanying her husband on the funeral pyre, but was denied because she was pregnant (Diod. 19.34.1–3).

A105 Younger widow of the Indian leader, Keteus (no. 584). She was given the honor of joining her husband on his funeral pyre, a task she performed with happiness and bravery (Diod. 19.34.1–5).

Stemmata

Stemma I: The Macedonian Royal House

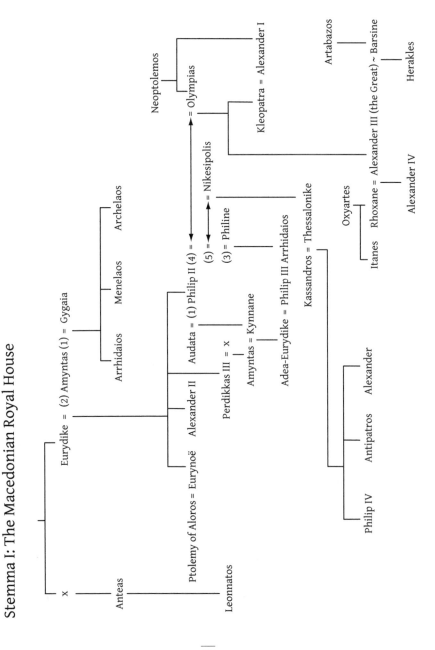

Stemma IIa: The Molossian Royal House to Neoptolemos II

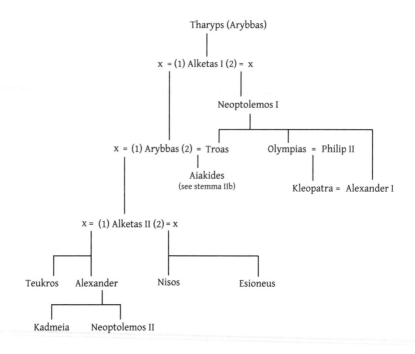

Stemma IIb: The Molossian Royal House to Alexander II

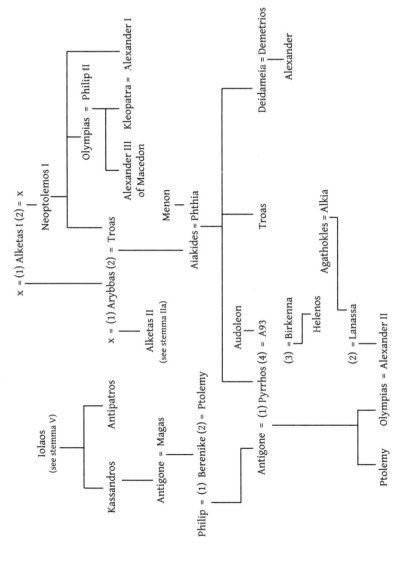

Stemma III: The Last Achaimenids

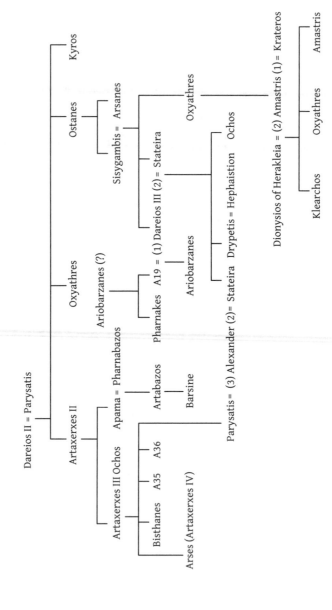

Stemma IV: The House of Pharnabazos

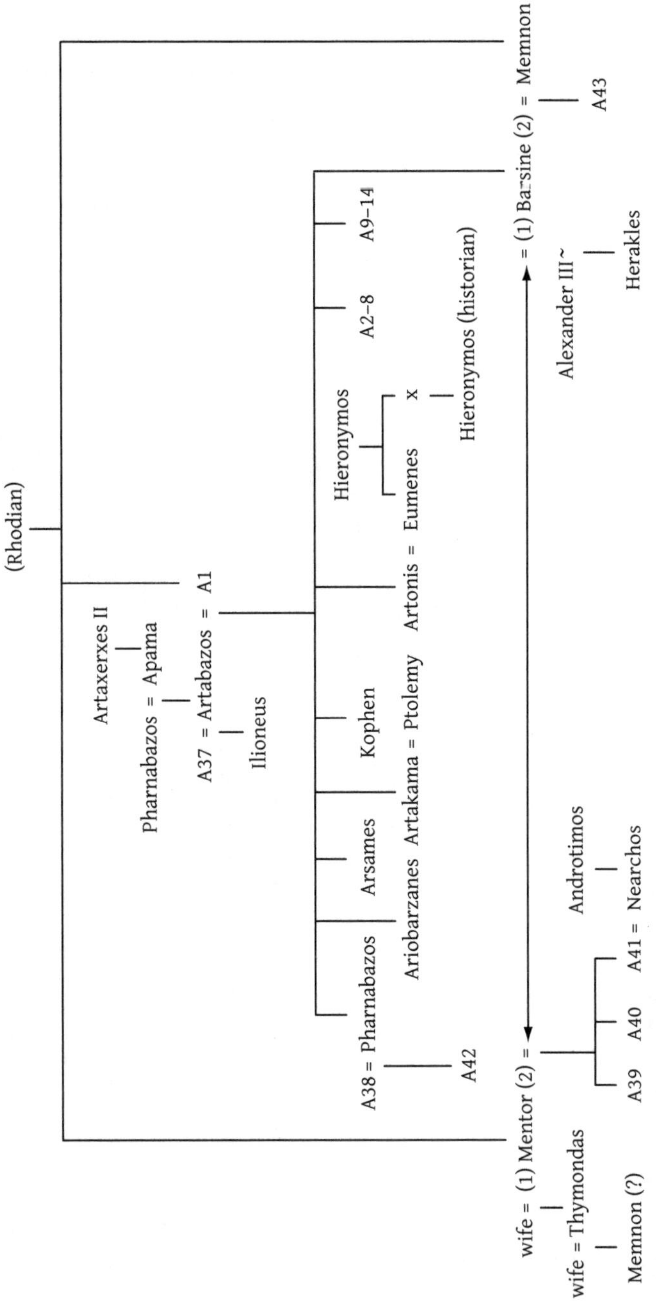

Stemma V: The House of Iolaos

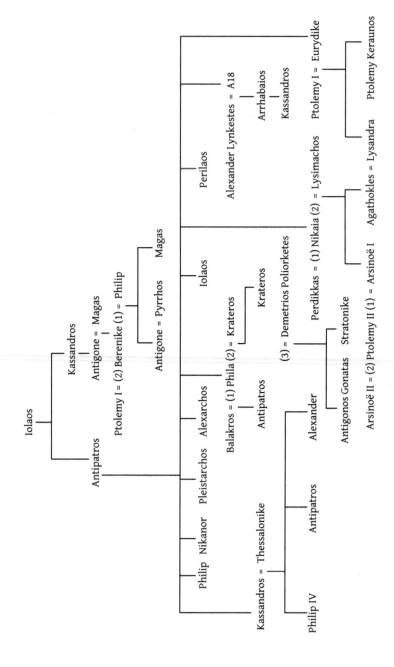

Stemma VI: The Family of Antigonos

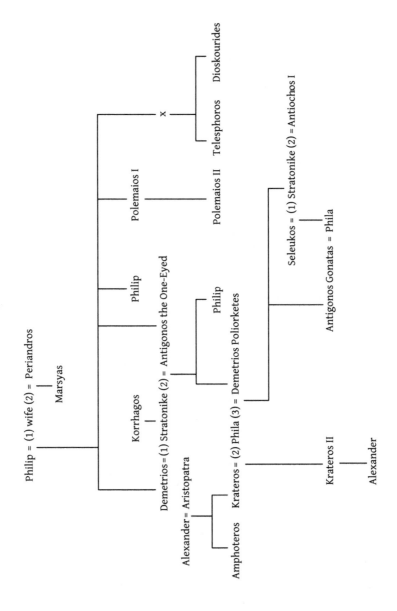

Stemma VII: The House of Parmenion

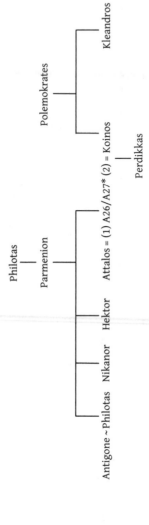

Philotas

Parmenion

Antigone ~ Philotas   Nikanor   Hektor   Attalos = (1) A26/A27* (2) = Koinos

Polemokrates

Kleandros

Perdikkas

* A26 and A27 may be the same daughter of Parmenion

Stemma VIII: The Family of Kleitos the Black

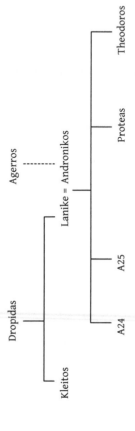

Dropidas

Kleitos

A24   A25   Lanike = Andronikos   Agerros

Proteas   Theodoros

Stemma IX: The House of Agathokles

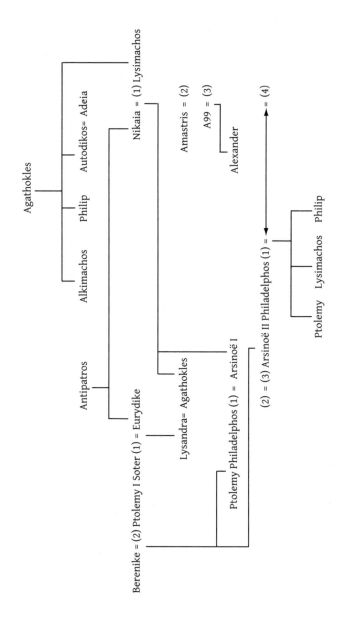

Stemma X: The House of Ptolemy

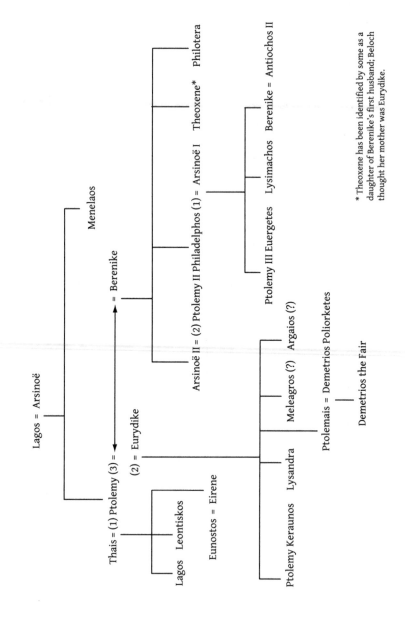

Lagos = Arsinoë

Menelaos

Thais = (1) Ptolemy (3) = Berenike

(2) = Eurydike

Lagos Leontiskos

Eunostos = Eirene

Arsinoë II = (2) Ptolemy II Philadelphos (1) = Arsinoë I   Theoxene*   Philotera

Ptolemy III Euergetes   Lysimachos   Berenike = Antiochos II

Ptolemy Keraunos   Lysandra

Meleagros (?)   Argaios (?)

Ptolemais = Demetrios Poliorketes

Demetrios the Fair

* Theoxene has been identified by some as a daughter of Berenike's first husband; Beloch thought her mother was Eurydike.

Stemma XI: The House of Seleukos

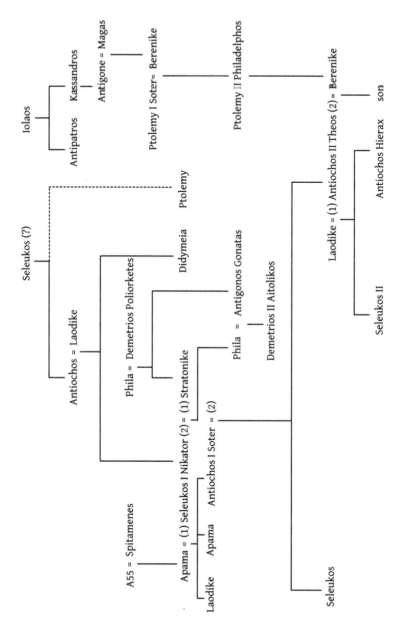

Stemma XII: The Relatives of Simmias and Andromenes of Tymphaia

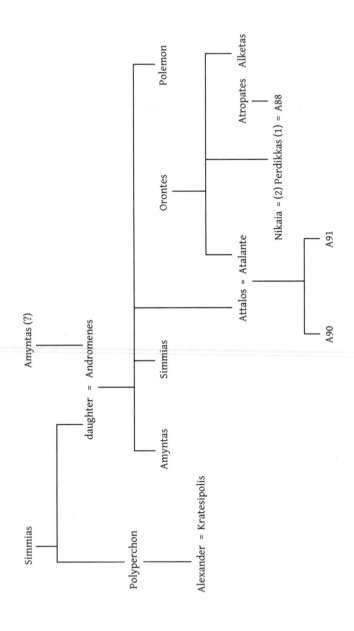

Stemma XIII: The Family of Harpalos of Elimeia

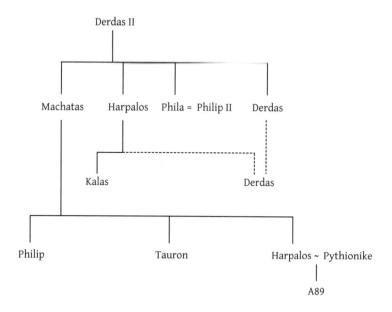

Stemma XIV: The House of Attalos

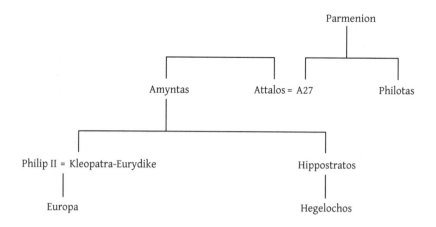

Stemma XV: The House of Aëropos of Lynkestis

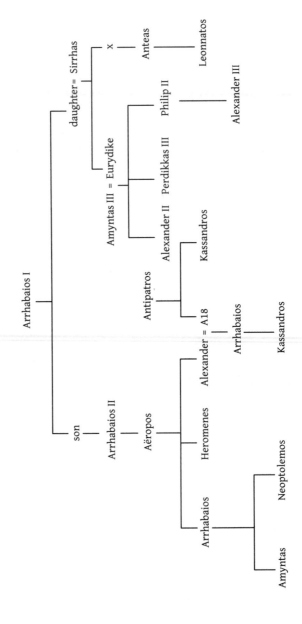

Stemma XVI: The Hekatomnids of Karia

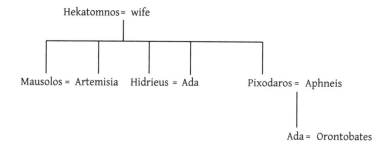

Stemma XVII: The Spartokid Rulers of the Kimmerian Bosporos

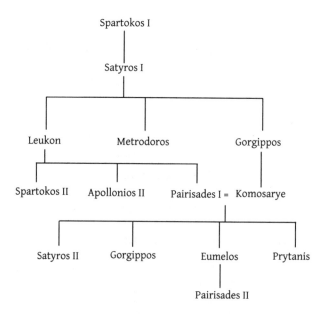

Stemma XVIIIa: The Agiad Royal Family of Sparta

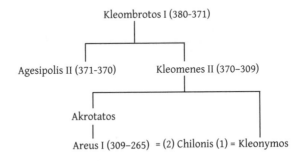

Kleombrotos I (380-371)

Agesipolis II (371-370)   Kleomenes II (370–309)

Akrotatos

Areus I (309–265) = (2) Chilonis (1) = Kleonymos

Stemma XVIIIb: The Eurypontid Royal Family of Sparta

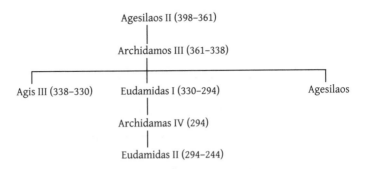

Agesilaos II (398–361)

Archidamos III (361–338)

Agis III (338–330)   Eudamidas I (330–294)   Agesilaos

Archidamas IV (294)

Eudamidas II (294–244)

Bibliography

Abramenko, Andrik. 1992. "Die Verschwörung des Alexander Lyncestes und die 'μήτηρ τοῦ βαυιλέως'. Zu Diodor XVII 32, 1." *Tyche* 7: 1–8.

——. 2000. "Der Fremde auf dem Thron. Die letzte Verschwörung gegen Alexander d. Gr." *Klio* 82: 361–78.

Adams, W. L. 1984. "Cassander and the Crossing of the Hellespont: Diodorus 17.17.4." *AncW* 2: 111–15.

——. 1985. "Antipater and Cassander: Generalship on Restricted Resources in the Fourth Century." *AncW* 10: 79–88.

——. 2003. "The Episode of Philotas: An Insight." In Heckel and Tritle, 113–26.

Adams, W. L., and E. N. Borza (eds.). 1982. *Philip II, Alexander the Great and the Macedonian Heritage*. Washington, DC.

Africa, Thomas. 1982. "Worms and the Death of Kings: A cautionary note on disease and history." *Classical Antiquity* 1: 1–17.

Ager, Sheila. 2005. "Familiarity breeds: incest and the Ptolemaic dynasty." *JHS* 125: 1–34.

——. 2018. "Building a Dynasty: The Families of Ptolemy I Stoter." In Howe, 36–59.

Akarca, A. 1959. *Les monnaies grecques de Mylasa*. Paris.

Allen, R. E. 1983. *The Attalid Kingdom. A Constitutional History*. Oxford.

Almagor, Eran. 2016. "Seleukid Love and Power: Stratonike I." In Coşkun and McAuley, 67–86.

Alonso Troncoso, Victor. 2007. "Alexander, Cleitus and Lanice: Upbringing and Maintenance." In Heckel, Tritle, and Wheatley, 109–23.

——. 2009. "Some Remarks on the Funerals of the Kings: From Philip II to the Diadochi." In Wheatley and Hannah, 276–98.

——. 2013. "The Diadochi and the Zoology of Kingship." In Alonso Troncoso and Anson, 254–70.

Alonso Troncoso, Victor, and Edward M. Anson (eds.). 2013. *After Alexander. The Time of the Diadochi (323–281 BC)*. Oxford: Oxbow.

Anson, E. M. 1988. "Antigonus, the Satrap of Phrygia." *Historia* 37: 471–7.

——. 1990. "Neoptolemus and Armenia." *AHB* 4: 125–8.

——. 1996. "The *Ephemerides* of Alexander the Great." *Historia* 45: 501–4.

——. 2014. *Alexander's Heirs. The Age of the Successors*. Oxford and Malden.

——. 2015. "Alexander at the Beas." In Wheatley and Baynham, 65–74.

——. 2018. "Ptolemy and the Destruction of the First Regency." In Howe, 20–35.

Antela-Bernárdez, B. 2012. "Philip and Pausanias: A Deadly Love in Macedonian Politics." *CQ* 62: 423–9.

Ashton, N. G. 1977. "The *Naumachia* near Amorgos in 322 BC." *ABSA* 72: 1–11.

——. 1983. "The Lamian War: A false start?" *Antichthon* 17: 47–63.

——. 1993. "Craterus from 323 to 321." *AM* 5: 1.125–31.

——. 2015. "Craterus Revisited." In Wheatley and Baynham, 107–16.

Atkinson, J. E. 1987. "The infantry commissions awarded by Alexander at the end of 331." In Will, I 413–35.

Aulock, H. von. 1964. "Die Prägung des Balakros in Kilikien." *JNG* 14: 79–82.

Ausfeld, A. 1895. "Über das angebliche Testament Alexanders des Großen." *RhM* 50: 357–66.

——. 1901. "Das angebliche Testament Alexanders des Großen." *RhM* 56: 517–42.

Badian, E. 1958. "The eunuch Bagoas: A study in method." *CQ* 8: 144–57.

——. 1960a. "The death of Parmenio." *TAPA* 91: 324–38.

——. 1960b. "The First Flight of Harpalus." *Historia* 9: 245–6.

——. 1961. "Harpalus." *JHS* 81: 16–43.

——. 1963. "The death of Philip II." *Phoenix* 17: 244–50.

——. 1965."The Administration of the Empire." *G&R* 12: 166–82.

——. 1967a. "Agis III." *Hermes* 95: 170–92.

——. 1967b. "A king's notebooks." *HSCPh* 72: 183–204.

——. 1975. "Nearchus the Cretan." *YCS* 24: 147–70.

——. 1981. "The deification of Alexander the Great." In Dell, 27–71.

——. 1982. "Eurydice." In Adams and Borza, 99–110.

——. 1987. "Alexander at Peucelaotis." *CQ* 37: 117–28.

——. 1988. "Two postscripts on the marriage of Phila and Balacrus." *ZPE* 73: 116–18.

——. 1994. "Agis III: Revisions and Reflections." In *Ventures into Greek History*, edited by I. Worthington, 258–82. Oxford.

——. 1996. "Alexander the Great between the two thrones and Heaven: Variations on an old theme." In *Subject and Ruler: The cult of the Ruling Power in Classical Antiquity*, edited by A. Small. *Journal of Roman Archaeology* supplement no. 17, 11–26. Ann Arbor.

——. 1999. "A Note on the *Alexander Mosaic.*" In Titchener and Moorton, Jr., 75–92.

——. 2000a. "Conspiracies." In Bosworth and Baynham, 50–95.

——. 2000b. "Darius III." *HSCP* 100: 241–68.

——. 2000c."The Road to Prominence." In I. Worthington (ed.). *Demosthenes, Statesman and Orator*. London: 9-44.

——. 2012. *Collected Papers on Alexander the Great*. London.

Badian, E., and T. R. Martin. 1985. "Athenians, Other Allies, and the Hellenes in the Athenian Honorary Decree for Adeimantos of Lampsakos." *ZPE* 61: 167–72.

Ballesteros Pastor, Luis. 2013. *"Nullis umquam nis domesticis regibus*: Cappadocia, Pontus and the Resistance to the Diadochi in Asia Minor." In Alonso and Anson, 183–98.

Barber, G. L. 1935. *The Historian Ephorus*. Cambridge.

Bartels, J. 2015. "Cynnane 'the Illyrian'? The Perils of Onomastics." *CQ* 65 384–7.

Bayliss, Andrew J. 2002. "A Decree Honouring Medeios of Larisa." *ZPE* 140: 89–92.

Baynham, E. J. 1998a. *Alexander the Great: The Unique History of Quintus Curtius*. Ann Arbor.

——. 1998b. "The Treatment of Olympias in the Liber de Morte—a Rhodian Retirement." In Will, 103–15.

——. 2001. "Alexander and the Amazons." *CQ* 51: 115–26.

——. 2015. "Cleomenes of Naucratis: Villain or Victim?" In Howe, Garvin and Wrightson, 127–34.

Bean, G. E. 1960. "Notes and Inscriptions from Pisidia, II." *Anatolian Studies* 10: 42–82.

Bearzot, C. 1985. *Focione tra storia e trasfigurazione ideale*. Milan.

Bengtson, H. 1937. "Philoxenos ho Makedon." *Philologus* 92: 126–55.

——. 1975. *Herrschergestalten des Hellenismus*. Munich.

Bennett, C. J. 2003. "Three Notes on Arsinoë I." In Eyma and Bennett, 64–70.

Benveniste, E. 1966. *Titres et noms propres en iranien ancien*. Paris.

Bernard, P. 1984. "Le philosophe Anaxarche et le roi Nicocréon de Salamine. "*JS*: 3–49.

Bernhardt, R. 1988. "Zu den Verhandlungen zwischen Dareios und Alexander nach der Schlacht bei Issus." *Chiron* 18: 181–98.

Berve, Helmut. 1938. "Die Verschmelzungspolitik Alexanders des Grossen." *Klio* 31: 135–68.

——. 1953. *Die Herrschaft des Agathokles*. SB Munich.

Besevliev, V. 1970. *Personennamen bei den Thrakern*. Amsterdam.

Betlyon, J. W. 1976. "A New Chronology for the Pre-Alexandrine Coinage of Sidon." *ANSMN* 21: 11–35.

——. 1982. *The Coinage and Mints of Phoenicia. The Pre-Alexandrine Period.* Chico, CA: Scholar's Press.

Bickerman, E. 1940. "La lettre d'Alexandre le Grand aux bannis grecs." *REA* 42: 25–35.

——. 1963. "Sur un passage d'Hypéride (Epitaphios, col. VIII)." *Athenaeum* 41: 70–85.

——. 1988. *The Jews in the Greek Age.* Cambridge, MA.

Bieber, M. 1964. *Alexander the Great in Greek and Roman Art.* Chicago.

Billows, R. 1989. "Anatolian dynasts: The case of the Macedonian Eupolemus in Karia." *CA* 8: 173–205.

Blackwell, C. 1999. *In the Absence of Alexander. Harpalus and the Failure of Macedonian Authority.* Bonn.

Blänsdorf, J. 1971. "Herodot bei Curtius Rufus." *Hermes* 99: 11–24.

Bloedow, Edmund F. 1995. "Diplomatic Negotiations between Darius and Alexander: Historical Implications of the First Phase at Marathus in Phoenicia in 333/332 BC." *AHB* 9: 93–110.

Boerma, R. N. H. 1979. *Justinus' Boeken over de Diadochen. Een historisch Commentaar. Boek 13–15, cap. 2.* Amsterdam.

Borza, E. N. 1981. "Anaxarchus and Callisthenes: Intrigue at Alexander's Court." In Dell, 73–86.

——. 1990. *In the Shadow of Olympus. The Emergence of Macedon.* Princeton.

——. 1999 *Before Alexander: Constructing Early Macedonia.* Claremont.1999.

Borza, E. N., and Olga Palagia. 2007. "The Chronology of the Macedonian Royal Tombs at Vergina." *JDAI* 122: 81–125.

Bosworth, A. B. 1970. "Aristotle and Callisthenes." *Historia* 19: 407–13.

——. 1971a. "Philip II and Upper Macedonia." *CQ* 21: 93–105.

——. 1971b. "The death of Alexander the Great: Rumour and propaganda." *CQ* 21: 112–36.

——. 1973. "ΑΣΘΕΤΑΙΡΟΙ," *CQ* 23: 245–53.

——. 1974. "The government of Syria under Alexander the Great." *CQ* 24: 46–64.

——. 1975. "The mission of Amphoterus and the outbreak of Agis' War." *Phoenix* 29: 27–43.

——. 1976. "Arrian and the Alexander Vulgate." In *Fondation Hardt, Entretiens* 22: 1–46. Geneva.

——. 1978. "Eumenes, Neoptolemus and *PSI* XII 1284." *GRBS* 19: 227–37.

——. 1980. "Alexander and the Iranians." *JHS* 100: 1–21.

——. 1981. "A missing year in the history of Alexander the Great." *JHS* 101: 17–39.

——. 1983. "The Indian satrapies under Alexander the Great." *Antichthon* 17: 37–46.

——. 1986. "Alexander the Great and the decline of Macedon." *JHS* 106: 1–12.

——. 1988. *Conquest and Empire. The Reign of Alexander the Great.* Cambridge.

——. 1992. "History and artifice in Plutarch's *Eumenes.*" In *Plutarch and the historical tradition*, ed. P. A. Stadter, 56–89. London.

——. 1993. "Perdiccas and the kings." *CQ* 43: 420–7.

——. 1994. "A New Macedonian Prince." *CQ* 44: 57–65.

——. 1996a. *Alexander and the East: The tragedy of triumph.* Oxford.

——. 1996b. "The historical setting of Megasthenes' *Indica.*" *CP* 91: 113–27.

——. 1996c. "The tumult and the shouting: Two interpretations of the Cleitus episode." *AHB* 10: 19–30.

——. 2000. "Ptolemy and the Will of Alexander." In Bosworth and Baynham, 207–41.

——. 2002. *The Legacy of Alexander. Politics, Warfare, and Propaganda under the Successors.* Oxford.

——. 2003a. *"Plus ça change . . .* Ancient Historians and their Sources." *CA* 22: 167–98.

——. 2003b. "Why Did Athens Lose the Lamian War?" In Palagia and Tracy, 14–22.

——. 2013. "Strabo, India and Barbequed Brahmans." In Alonso Troncoso and Anson, 71–83.

Bousquet, J. 1957. "Inscriptions de Delphes: Les Aitoliens à Delphes au IVᵉ siècle." *BCH* 81: 485–95.

Bowden, H. 2013. "On Kissing and making up: Court Protocol and Historiography in Alexander the Great's 'Experiment with *Proskynesis'*." *BICS* 56: 55–77.

Breebaart, A. B. 1967. "King Seleucus I, Antiochus, and Stratonice." *Mnemosyne* 20: 154–64.

Briant, Pierre. 1973. *Antigone le Borgne*. Paris.

——. 1999. "The Achaemenid Empire." In Raaflaub and Rosenstein, 105–28.

——. 2008. *Lettre ouverte à Alexandre le Grand*. Arles.

——. 2015. *Darius in the Shadow of Alexander*. Translated by Jane Marie Todd. Cambridge, MA.

Broderson, K. 1985. "Der liebeskranke Königssohn und die Seleukidische Herrschaftsauffassung." *Athenaeum*: 459–69.

Brown, T. S. 1947. "Hieronymus of Cardia." *AHR* 53: 684–96.

——. 1949. "Callisthenes and Alexander." *AJP* 70: 225–48.

——. 1950. "Clitarchus." *AJR* 71: 134–55.

——. 1955. "The Reliability of Megasthenes." *AJP* 76: 18–33.

——. 1973. *The Greek Historians*. Lexington.

——. 1986. "Menon of Thessaly." *Historia* 35: 387–404.

Brunt, P. A. 1963. "Alexander's Macedonian Cavalry." *JHS* 83: 27–46.

——. 1975. "Alexander, Barsine, and Heracles." *RFIC* 103: 22–34.

Buckler, J. 1989. *Philip II and the Sacred War*. Supplements to Mnemosyne 109. Leiden.

——. 2003. *Aegean Greece in the Fourth Century B.C*. Leiden.

Burkert, Walter. 2004. *Babylon, Memphis, Persepolis: Eastern Contexts of Greek Culture*. Cambridge, MA.

Burrow, T. 1968. "Canakya and Kautalya." *ABORI* 48/49: 17-31.

Burstein, S. M. 1977a."*IG* II² 561 and the court of Alexander IV." *ZPE* 24: 223–5.

——. 1977b. "The Date of the Athenian Victory over Pleistarchus. A Note on Pausanias 1.15.1." *CW* 71: 128–9.

——. 1978. "*IG* II² 653, Demosthenes and the Athenian Relations with Bosporus in the Fourth Century BC." *Historia* 27: 428–36.

——. 1980. "Bithys, Son of Cleon from Lysimacheia: A Reconsideration of the Date and Significance of *IG* II² 808." *CSCA* 12: 39–50.

——. 1982a. "Arsinoe II Philadelphos: A Revisionist View." In Adams and Borza, 197–212.

——. 1982b. "The tomb of Philip II and the Succession of Alexander the Great." *EMC* 26: 141–63.

——. 1999. "Cleitarchus in Jerusalem. A Note on the Book of Judith." In Titchener and Moorton, 105–12.

——. 2000. "Prelude to Alexander: The Reign of Khababash." *AHB* 14: 149–54.

——. 2007. "The Gardener Became a King, or Did He? The Case of Abdalonymus of Sidon." In Heckel, Tritle, and Wheatley, 139–49.

Campbell, Brian, and Lawrence A. Tritle (eds.). 2013. *The Oxford Handbook of Warfare in the Classical World*. Oxford.

Cannadine, David, and Simon Price (eds.). 1987. *Rituals of Royalty. Power and Ceremonial in Traditional Societies*. Cambridge.

Carney, E. D. 1980. "Alexander the Lyncestian: The disloyal opposition." *GRBS* 21: 23–33.

——. 1980–1981. "The conspiracy of Hermolaus." *CJ* 76: 223–31.

——. 1981. "The death of Clitus." *GRBS* 22: 149–60.

——. 1982. "The first flight of Harpalus again." *CJ* 77: 9–11.

——. 1987a. "The career of Adea-Eurydice." *Historia* 36: 496–502.

——. 1987b. "Olympias." *Anc. Soc.* 18: 35–62.

——. 1988. "The sisters of Alexander the Great: Royal relicts." *Historia* 37: 385–404.

——. 1999. "The Curious Death of the Antipatrid Dynasty." *AM* 6: 209–16.

——. 2000. "Artifice and Alexander History." In Bosworth and Baynham, 263–85.

——. 2001. "The Trouble with Philip Arrhidaeus." *AHB* 15: 63–89.

——. 2005. "Women and Dunasteia in Caria." *AJP* 126: 65–91.

——. 2006. *Olympias*. London.

——. 2007. "The Philippeum, Women and the Formation of a Dynastic Image." In Heckel, Tritle, and Wheatley, 27–60.

——. 2013. *Arsinoë of Egypt and Macedon. A Royal Life*. Oxford.

——. 2014. "Successful Mediocrity: The Career of Polyperchon." *Syll. Clas.* 25: 1–31.

Caroe, O. 1962. *The Pathans*. London.

Cartledge, P. 2004. *Alexander the Great. The Search for a New Past*. New York.

Cartledge, P., and A. Spawforth. 1989. *Hellenistic and Roman Sparta. A Tale of Two Cities*. London.

Cauer, F. 1894. "Philotas, Kleitos, Kallisthenes: Beiträge zur Alexandergeschichte." *Neue Jahrbücher für classische Philologie,* Supplbd 20.

Cawkwell, G. L. 1963. "Demosthenes' Policy after the Peace of Philocrates." *CQ* 13: 120–38, 200–13.

——. 1969. "The crowning of Demosthenes." *CQ* 19: 161–80.

——. 1978. *Philip of Macedon*. London.

Chambers, M. 1954. "The First Regnal Year of Antigonus Gonatas." *AJP* 75: 385–94.

Chamoux, F. 1956. "Le roi Magas." *Rev. Hist.* 216: 18–34.

Champion, J. 2009. *Pyrrhus of Epirus*. Barnsley.

——. 2014. *Antigonos the One-Eyed*. Barnsley.

Charbonneaux, J. 1952. "Antigone le Borgne et Démétrios Poliorcète sont-ils figurés sur le sarcophage d'Alexandre?" *Rev. des Arts* 2: 219–23.

Charles, M. B. 2012. "The Persian ΚΑΡΔΑΚΕΣ." *JHS* 132: 7–21.

Chroust, A. H. 1973 *Aristotle,* vol. 1. South Bend, Indiana.

Clarysse, W., and G. Schepens. 1985. "A Ptolemaic Fragment of an Alexander-History." *CE* 60: 30–47.

Clauss, Manfred. 1983. *Sparta. Eine Einführung in seine Geschichte und Zivilisation*. Munich.

Clayman, Dee L. 2014. *Berenice II and the Golden Age of Ptolemaic Egypt*. Oxford.

Cohen, G. M. 1978. *The Seleucid Colonies*. Wiesbaden.

Collins, A. W. 2001. "The Office of Chiliarch under Alexander and the Successors." *Phoenix* 55: 259–83.

——. 2012a. "Alexander the Great and the office of *edeatros*." *Historia* 61: 414–20.

Collins, N. I. 1997. "The Various Fathers of Ptolemy I." *Mnemosyne* 50: 436–76.

Cook, J. M. 1983. *The Persian Empire*. New York.

Cooper, C. 1993. "A Note on Antipater's Demand of Hyperides and Demosthenes." *AHB* 7: 130–5.

Corradi, G. 1912. *Gli ultimi Eacidi*. Turin.

Coşkun, Altay, and Alex McAuley (eds.). 2016. *Seleukid Royal Women. Creation, Representation and Distortion of Hellenistic Queenship in the Seleukid Empire*. Stuttgart.

Cross, G. N. 1932. *Epirus: A study in Greek constitutional development*. Cambridge.

D'Agostini, M. 2019. *The Rise of Philip V. Kingship and rule in the Hellenistic World*. Alessandria.

D'Agostini, M., E. M. Anson, and F. Pownall (eds.). 2021. *Affective Relations and Personal Bonds in Hellenistic Antiquity*. Oxford and Philadelphia.

Dahmen, Karsten. 2007. *The Legend of Alexander the Great on Greek and Roman Coinage*. London and New York.

Delev, P. 2000. "Lysimachus, the Getae, and Archaeology." *CQ* 50: 384–401.

Dell, H. J. (ed.). 1981. *Ancient Macedonian Studies in Honor of Charles P. Edson*. Thessaloniki.

Depuydt, L. 1997. "The Time of Death of Alexander the Great: 11 June 323 BC (–322), ca 4:00–5:00 P. M." *Die Welt des Orients* 28: 117–35.

Develin, R. 1981. "The murder of Philip II." *Antichthon* 15: 86–99.

Devine, A. M. 1975. "Grand tactics at Gaugamela." *Phoenix* 29: 374–85.

——. 1984. "Diodorus' Account of the Battle of Gaza." *AC* 27: 31–40.

——. 1985a. "Diodorus' account of the Battle of Paraitacene." *AncW* 12: 75–86.

——. 1985b. "Diodorus' account of the Battle of Gabiene." *AncW* 12: 87–96.

——. 1986. "The Battle of Gaugamela: A tactical and source-critical study." *AncW* 13: 87–116.

——. 1989. "The Generalship of Ptolemy I and Demetrius Poliorcetes at the Battle of Gaza (312 BC)." *AncW* 20: 29–38.

——. 1994. "Alexander's Propaganda Machine: Callisthenes as the ultimate source for Arrian." In Worthington, 89–102.

Dimitrov, D. P., and M. Cicikova. 1978. *The Thracian City of Seuthopolis*. Oxford.

Dmitriev, S. 2007. "The Last Marriage and the Death of Lysimachus." *GRBS* 47: 137–49.

Doherty, P. 2004. *The Death of Alexander the Great*. New York.

Domaszewski, A. von. 1925/6. *Die Phalangen Alexanders und Caesars Legionen*. Sitzungsber. Heidelberger Akad. d. Wiss. Abh. 1.

Drews, R. 1974. "Sargon, Cyrus, and Mesopotamian Folk History." *JNES* 33: 387–93.

Dunn, Charlotte, and Pat Wheatley. 2012. "Craterus and the Dedication Date of the Delphi Lion Monument." *AHB* 26: 39–48.

Düring, I. 1957. *Aristotle in the Ancient Biographical Tradition*. Göteborg.

Edson, C. P. 1934. "The Antigonids, Heracles and Beroea." *HSCP* 45: 213–46.

Eggermont, P. H. L. 1970. "Alexander's Campaign in Gandhara and Ptolemy's List of Indo-Scythian Towns." *OLP* 1: 63–123.

Eissfeldt, O. 1940–41. "Abdalonymus und 'LMN'." *ZAW* 58: 248–51.

Elkeles, Günter. 1911. *Demetrios der Städtebelagerer*. Breslau.

Ellis, J. R. 1971. "Amyntas Perdikka, Philip II, and Alexander the Great: A study in conspiracy." *JHS* 91: 15–24.

——. 1973. "The step-brothers of Philip II." *Historia* 22: 350–4.

——. 1976. *Philip II and Macedonian Imperialism*. London.

Ellis, J. R., and R. D. Milns. 1970. *The Spectre of Philip*. Sydney.

Elayi, Josette. 2013. *Histoire de la Phénicie*. Paris.

Engel, R. 1971. "Anmerkungen zur Schlacht bei Orkynia." *MusHelv.* 28: 227–31.

——. 1972. "Die Überlieferung der Schlacht bei Kretopolis." *Historia* 21: 501–7.

——. 1973. "Polyäns Stratagem IV 6, 8 zur 'Seeschlacht am Hellespont'." *Klio* 55: 41–5.

——. 1974. "Zwei Heeresversammlungen in Memphis." *Hermes* 102: 122–4.

——. 1976. *Untersuchungen zum Machtaufstieg des Antigonos I. Monophthalmos*. Kallmünz.

Engels, David, and Kyle Erickson. 2016. "Apama and Stratonike – Marriage and Legitimacy." In Coşkun and McAuley, 39–65.

Engels, D. W. 1978a. *Alexander the Great and the Logistics of the Macedonian Army*. Berkeley and Los Angeles.

——. 1978b. "A Note on Alexander's Death." *CP* 73: 224–8.

English, S. 2009. *The Sieges of Alexander the Great*. Barnsley.

Errington, R. M. 1969. "Bias in Ptolemy's history of Alexander." *CQ* 19: 233–42.

——. 1970. "From Babylon to Triparadeisos: 323–320 BC." *JHS* 90: 49–77.

——. 1974. "Macedonian 'royal style' and its historical significance." *JHS* 94: 20–37.

——. 1975a. "Arybbas the Molossian." *GRBS* 16: 41–50.

——. 1975b. "Samos and the Lamian War." *Chiron* 5: 51–7.

——. 1976. "Alexander in the Hellenistic world." In Badian, 137–79. Geneva.

——. 1977. "Diodorus Siculus and the Chronology of the Early Diadochoi: 320–311 BC." *Hermes* 105: 478–504.

——. 1990. *A History of Macedonia*. Berkeley and Los Angeles.

Erskine, Andrew (ed.). 2003. *A Companion to the Hellenistic World*. Oxford and Malden.

Eyma, A. K., and C. J. Bennett (eds.). 2003. *A Delta Man in Yebu*. No place of publication.

Faber, R. (ed.). 2020. *Celebrity, Fame, and Infamy in the Hellenistic World*. Toronto.

Fears, J. Rufus. 1975. "Pausanias, the assassin of Philip II." *Athenaeum* 53: 111–35.

Fedak, Janos. 1990. *Monumental Tombs of the Hellenistic Age: A Study of Selected Tombs from the Pre-Classical to the Early Imperial Era*. Toronto.

Ferguson, W. S. 1948. "Demetrius Poliorcetes and the Hellenic League." *Hesperia* 17: 112–36.

Flower, M. A. 1994. *Theopompus of Chios*. Oxford.

——. 2000. "Alexander the Great and Panhellenism." In Bosworth and Baynham, 96–135.

Fornara, C. W. 1983. *The Nature of History in Ancient Greece and Rome*. Berkeley and Los Angeles.

Forrest, W. G. 1969a. *A History of Sparta 950–192 BC*. New York.

——. 1969b. "Alexander's Second Letter to the Chians." *Klio* 51: 201–6.

Fortina, Marcello. 1965. *Cassandro, Re di Macedonia*. Turin.

Fraenkel, A. 1883. *Die Quellen der Alexanderhistoriker*. Breslau.

Fraser, P. M. 1967. "Current problems concerning the early history of the cult of Sarapis." *Opuscula Atheniensia* 7: 23–45.

French, Valerie, and Patricia Dixon. 1986a. "The Pixodaros affair: Another view." *AncW* 13: 73–86.

——. 1986b. "The source traditions for the Pixodaros affair." *AncW* 14: 25–40.

Gabbert, J. 1997. *Antigonus II Gonatas. A Political Biography*. London.

Garlan, Y. 1975. "Alliance entre iasiens et Ptolemee Ier." *ZPE* 18: 193–8.

——. 1988. *Slavery in Ancient Greece*. Translated from the French by Janet Lloyd. Ithaca.

Garnsey, P. 1988. *Famine and food supply in the Graeco-Roman world*. Cambridge.

Geer, R. M. 1947–1954. *Diodorus of Sicily*. Loeb Classical Library, vols. 9–10. Cambridge, MA.

Gehrke, Hans-Joachim. 1976. *Phokion. Studien zur Erfassung seiner historischen Gestalt*. Zetemata, Heft 64. Munich.

——. 1978. "Das Verhältnis von Politik und Philosophie im Wirken des Demetrios von Phaleron." *Chiron* 8: 149–93.

Gesche, H. 1974. "Nikokles von Paphos und Nikokreon von Salamis." *Chiron* 4: 103–25.

Ghiron-Bistagne, P. 1976. *Recherches sur les Acteurs dans la Grèce antique*. Paris.

Golan, D. 1988. "The fate of a court historian: Callisthenes." *Athenaeum* 66: 99–120.

Goldstein, J. A. 1968. *The Letters of Demosthenes*. New York.

Gow, A. S. F. 1965. *Theocritus*, 2 vols. Cambridge.

Graeve, V. von. 1970. *Der Alexandersarkophag und seiner Werkstatt*. Berlin.

Grainger, John D. 1990a. *Seleukos Nikator. Constructing a Hellenistic Kingdom*. London.

——. 1990b. *The Cities of Seleukid Syria*. Oxford.

——. 1991. *Hellenistic Phoenicia*. Oxford.

——. 2011. *Hellenistic and Roman Naval Wars, 336–31 BC*. Yorkshire and Philadelphia.

——. 2014. *The Rise of the Seleukid Empire (323–223 BC). Seleukos I to Seleukos III*. Barnsley.

——. 2019. *Antipater's Dynasty. Alexander the Great's Regent and his Successors*. Barnsley.

Granier, F. 1931. *Die makedonische Heeresversammlung. Ein Beitrag zum antiken Staatsrecht*. Munich.

Grayson, A. K. 1975. *Babylonian Historical-Literary Texts*. Toronto.

——. 1995. "Eunuchs in Power: Their Role in the Assyrian Bureaucracy." In M. Dietrich and O. Loretz (eds.). *Vom Alten Orient zum Alten Testament* (Neukirchen-Vluyn): 85–98.

Green, Peter. 1982. "The Royal Tombs at Vergina: A Historical Analysis." In Adams and Borza, 129–51.

——. 1990. *Alexander to Actium. The Historical Evolution of the Hellenistic Age.* Berkeley and Los Angeles.

——. 1991. *Alexander of Macedon.* Second edition. Berkeley and Los Angeles.

Greenwalt, W. S. 1982. "A Macedonian Mantis." *AncW* 5: 17–25.

——. 1984. "The search for Arrhidaeus." *AncW* 10: 69–77.

——. 1988. "The Age of Marriageabililty at the Argead Court." *CW* 82: 93–7.

——. 2008. "Philip II and Olympias on Samothrace: A Clue to Macedonian Politics during the 360s." In Howe and Reames, 79–106.

Gregory, Andrew Pearce. 1995. "A Macedonian ΔΥΝΑΣΤΗΣ: Evidence for the Life and Career of Pleistarchos Antipatrou." *Historia* 44: 11–28.

Griffin, A. 1982. *Sikyon.* Oxford.

Griffith, G. T. 1935. *The Mercenaries of the Hellenistic World.* Cambridge.

——. 1963. "A Note on the Hipparchies of Alexander." *JHS* 83: 68–74.

——. 1965. "Alexander and Antipater in 323 BC." *PACA* 8: 12–17.

——. 1968. "The letter of Darius at Arrian 2. 14." *PCPhS* 14: 33–48.

Grote, Karl. 1913. "Das griechische Söldnerwesen der hellenistischen Zeit." Diss., Jena, publ. Weida.

Gruen, E. S. 1985. "The coronation of the Diadochoi." In *The craft of the ancient historian: Essays in honor of Chester G. Starr,* edited by J. Eadie and J. Ober, 253–71. Lanham, Md.

Guthrie, W. K. C. 1981. *A history of Greek philosophy,* vol. 6. Cambridge.

Gutschmid, A. V. 1882. "Trogus und Timagenes." *RhM* 37: 548–55.

Habicht, Christian. 1957. "Samische Volksbeschlüsse der hellenistischer Zeit." *MDAI(A)* 72: 152ff.

——. 1973. "Literarische und epigraphische Überlieferung zur Geschichte Alexanders und seiner ersten Nachfolger." *Akten des VI. Intern. Kongr. für griechische und Lateinishe Epigraphik.* Munich: 367–77.

——. 1974. "*IG* II² 492 and the Siege of Athens in 304 BC." *ZPE* 124: 10.

——. 1975. "Der Beitrag Spartas zur Restitution von Samos während des Lamischen Krieges." *Chiron* 5: 45–50.

——. 1977a. "Zwei Angehörige des lynkestischen Königshauses." *AM* 2: 511–26.

——. 1977b. "Athenisches Ehrendekret vom Jahre des Koroibos (306/5) für einen königlichen Offizier." *AJAH* 2: 37–9.

——. 1979. *Untersuchungen zur politischen Geschichte Athens im 3. Jahrhundert v. Chr.* Munich.

——. 1985. *Pausanias' Guide to Ancient Greece.* Berkeley and Los Angeles.

——. 1993. "The Comic Poet Archedikos." *Hesperia* 62: 253–6.

——. 1996a. "Athens, Samos, and Alexander the Great." *PAPhS* 140: 397–405.

——. 1996b. "Neue Inscriften aus Kos." *ZPE* 112: 83–94.

——. 1997. *Athens from Alexander to Antony.* Translated by Deborah Lucas Schneider. Cambridge, MA.

Hadley, R. A. 1969. "Hieronymus of Cardia and early Seleucid mythology." *Historia* 18: 142–52.

——. 1974. "Royal propaganda of Seleucus I and Lysimachus." *JHS* 94: 50–65.

Hamel, D. 1998. *Athenian Generals. Military Authority in the Classical Period.* Leiden.

Hamilton, C. D., and P. Krentz (eds.). 1997. *Polis and Polemon. Essays on Politics, War, and History in Ancient Greece in Honor of Donald Kagan.* Claremont.

Hamilton, J. R. 1955. "Three passages in Arrian." *CQ* 5: 217–21.

——. 1965. "Alexander's early life." *G&R* 12: 116–25.

——. 1972. "Alexander among the Oreitae." *Historia* 21: 603–8.

——. 1984. "The Origins of Ruler-Cult." *Prudentia* 16: 3–16.

——. 1988. "Alexander's Iranian Policy." In Will and Heinrichs, II 467–86.

Hammond, N. G. L. 1966. "The Kingdoms in Illyria *circa* 400–167 BC." *ABSA* 61: 239–53.

——. 1974. "Alexander's campaign in Illyria." *JHS* 94: 66–87.

——. 1978. "A Cavalry Unit in the army of Antigonus Monophthalmus. *Asthippoi.*" *CQ* 28: 128–35.

——. 1980. "The Battle of the Granicus River." *JHS* 100: 73–88.

——. 1983. *Three Historians of Alexander the Great.* Cambridge.

——. 1984 "Alexander's veterans after his death." *GRBS* 25: 51–61.

——. 1985. "Some Macedonian offices: *c.*336–309 BC." *JHS* 105: 156–60.

——. 1987. "A papyrus commentary on Alexander's Balkan campaign." *GRBS* 28: 331–47.

——. 1988a. "The king and the land in the Macedonian kingdom." *CQ* 38: 382–91.

——. 1988b. "Which Ptolemy gave Troops and Stood as Protector of Pyrrhus' Kingdom?" *Historia* 37: 405–13.

——. 1989. "Casualties and reinforcements of citizen soldiers in Greece and Macedonia." *JHS* 109: 56–68.

——. 1990. "Inscriptions concerning Philippi and Calindoea in the reign of Alexander the Great." *ZPE* 82: 167–75.

——. 1992. "The Regnal Years of Philip and Alexander." *GRBS* 33: 355–73.

——. 1993. *Sources for Alexander the Great. An Analysis of Plutarch's* Life *and Arrian's* Anabasis Alexandrou. Cambridge.

——. 1994. *Philip of Macedon.* Baltimore.

Hansen, E. V. 1971. *The Attalids of Pergamum.* Second edition. Ithaca.

Harders, Ann-Cathrin. 2016. "The Making of a Queen – Seleukos Nikator and his Wives." In Coşkun and McAuley, 25–38.

Harle, K. W. 1997. "Alexander's Cavalry Battle at the Granicus." In Hamilton and Krentz, 303–26.

Harris, Edward M. 1988. "When was Aeschines Born?" *CP* 83: 211–14.

Hatzopoulos, M. B. 1982. "A Reconsideration of the Pixodaros Affair." *Studies in the History of Art.* Vol. 10. Symposium Series I: Macedonian and Greece in Late Classical and Early Hellenistic Times: 59–66.

——. 2005. "The Reliability of Diodorus' Account of Philip II's Assassination." In C. Bearzot and F. Landucci (eds.). *Diodoro e l'altra Grecia: Macedonia, Occidente e Hellenismo.* Milan: 43–65.

Hauben, Hans. 1970. *Callicrates of Samos. A Contribution to the Study of the Ptolemaic Admiralty.* Leuven.

——. 1972a. "The command structure in Alexander's Mediterranean fleets." *Anc. Soc.* 3: 55–65.

——. 1972b. "On Two Ephesian Citizenship Decrees from the Diadochian Period." *ZPE* 9: 57–8.

——. 1974. "A royal toast in 302 BC." *Anc. Soc.* 5: 105–19.

——. 1975–76. "Antigonos' Invasion Plan for his Attack on Egypt in 306 BC." *OLP* 6–7: 267–71.

——. 1976. "Fleet Strength at the Battle of Salamis, 306 BC." *Chiron* 6: 1–5.

——. 1977. "Rhodes, Alexander, and the Diadochi from 333/332 to 304 BC." *Historia* 26: 307–339.

——. 1987a. "Who is Who in Antigonus' Letter to the Scepsians (OGIS 5 = Welles, Royal Correspondence 1)." *Epigraphica Anatolica* 9: 29–36.

——. 1987b. "Onesicritus and the Hellenistic *archikybernesis.*" In Will and Heinrichs, I 569–93.

——. 1987c. "Philocles, King of the Sidonians and General of the Ptolemies." *Studia Phoenicia* 5: 413–27. Leuven.

——. 2004. "A Phoenician King in the Service of the Ptolemies: Philocles of Sidon Revisited." *Anc. Soc.* 34: 27–44.

Hauben, H., and A. Meeus (eds.). 2014. *The Age of the Successors and the Creation of the Hellenistic Kingdoms (323–276)*. Leuven.

Hazzard, R. A. 1999. *Imagination of a Monarchy: Studies in Ptolemaic Propaganda*. Toronto.

Heckel, W. 1975. "Amyntas, Son of Andromenes." *GRBS* 16: 393–8.

——. 1977a. "Asandros." *AJP* 98: 410–12.

——. 1977b. "The conspiracy *against* Philotas." *Phoenix* 31: 9–21.

——. 1977c. "The flight of Harpalos and Tauriskos." *CP* 72: 133–5.

——. 1978a. "Kleopatra or Eurydike?" *Phoenix* 32: 155–8.

——. 1978b. "Leonnatos, Polyperchon and the introduction of *proskynesis*." *AJP* 99: 459–61.

——. 1978c. "On Attalos and Atalante." *CQ* 28: 377–82.

——. 1978d. "The *somatophylakes* of Alexander the Great: Some thoughts." *Historia* 27: 224–8.

——. 1979. "Philip II, Kleopatra and Karanos." *RFIC* 107: 385–93.

——. 1980a. "Alexander at the Persian gates." *Athenaeum* 58: 168–74.

——. 1980b. "IG II² 561 and the status of Alexander IV." *ZPE* 40: 249–50.

——. 1980c. "Kelbanos, Kebalos or Kephalon?" *Beiträge zur Namenforschung* 15: 43–5.

——. 1980d. "Marsyas of Pella, historian of Macedon." *Hermes* 108: 444–62.

——. 1981a. "Honours for Philip and Iolaos: IG II² 561." *ZPE* 44: 75–7.

——. 1981b. "Leonnatos and the captive Persian queens: A case of mistaken identity." *SIFC* 53: 272–4.

——. 1981c. "Philip and Olympias (337/6 BC)." *Classical Contributions. Studies in Honour of Malcolm Francis McGregor,* edited by G. S. Shrimpton and D. J. McCargar, 51–7. Locust Valley, NY.

——. 1981d. "Polyxena, the mother of Alexander the Great." *Chiron* 11: 79–86.

——. 1981e. "Some speculations on the prosopography of the Alexanderreich." *LCM* 6: 63–70.

——. 1981f. "Two Doctors from Kos?" *Mnemosyne* 34: 396–8.

——. 1982a. "Who was Hegelochos?" *RhM* 125: 78–87.

——. 1982b. "The early career of Lysimachos." *Klio* 64: 373–381.

——. 1983. "Adea-Eurydike." *Glotta* 61: 40–2.

——. 1983–1984. "Kynnane the Illyrian." *RSA* 13–14: 193–200.

——. 1984. "Demetrios Poliorketes and the Diadochoi." *La Parola del Passato* 219: 438–40.

——. 1985. "The Macedonian veterans in Kilikia." *LCM* 10: 109–10.

——. 1986. "Chorienes and Sisimithres." *Athenaeum* 64: 223–6.

——. 1987. "A grandson of Antipatros at Delos." *ZPE* 70: 161–2.

——. 1988. *The Last Days and Testament of Alexander the Great. A Prosopographic Study.* Historia Einzelschriften 56. Stuttgart.

——. 1989. "The granddaughters of Iolaus." *Classicum* 15: 32–9.

——. 1991. "Q. Curtius Rufus and the date of Cleander's mission to the Peloponnese." *Hermes* 119: 124–5.

——. 1992. *The Marshals of Alexander's Empire*. London and New York.

——. 1994a. "Notes on Q. Curtius Rufus' *History of Alexander.*" *Acta Classica* 37: 67–78.

——. 1994b. "Kalas son of Harpalos and 'Memnon's Land'." *Mnemosyne* 47: 93–5.

——. 2002. "The Case of the Missing Phrourarch: Arr. 3.16.6–9." *AHB* 16: 57–60.

——. 2003a. "King and 'Companions': Observations on the nature of power in the reign of Alexander." In Roisman, 197–225.

——. 2003b. "Alexander the Great and the 'Limits of the Civilised World'." In Heckel and Tritle, 147–74.

——. 2006. "Mazaeus, Callisthenes and the Alexander Sarcophagus." *Historia* 55: 385–96.

——. 2007a. "Polyperchon as Brigand: Propaganda or Misunderstanding?" *Mnemosyne* 60: 123–6.

——. 2007b. "Nicanor son of Balacrus." *GRBS* 47: 401–12.

——. 2007c. "The Earliest Evidence for the Plot to Poison Alexander." In Heckel, Tritle, and Wheatley, 265–75.

——. 2008. *The Conquests of Alexander the Great.* Cambridge.

——. 2009. "A King and his Army." In Heckel and Tritle, 69–82.

——. 2012. "The Royal Hypaspists in Battle: Macedonian *hamippoi*." *AHB* 26: 15–20.

——. 2013a. "The Three Thousand: Alexander's Infantry Guard." In Campbell and Tritle, 162–78.

——. 2013b. "'The Sounds of Silence': A New Wife for Kassandros son of Antipatros." *Anabasis* 4: 53–62.

——. 2015. "Alexander, Heracles and Achilles: Between Myth and History." In Baynham and Wheatley, 21–33.

——. 2017a. "Was Sibyrtios ever Satrap of Karmania?" *Anabasis* 8: 36–41.

——. 2017b. "Darius III's military reforms before Gaugamela and the Alexander Mosaic: A Note." *AHB* 31: 65–9.

——. 2018a. "Ptolemy. A Man of his own Making." In Howe, 1–19.

——. 2018b. "Artabazos in the Lands beyond the Caspian." *Anabasis* 9: 93–109.

——. 2020. "Creating Alexander: The 'Official' History of Kallisthenes of Olynthos." In Faber, 199–216.

——. 2021. "The Limits of Brotherly Love: Neoptolemus II and Molossian Dynastic History." In D'Agostini, Anson, and Pownall, 63-77.

Heckel, W., Timothy Howe, and Sabine Müller. 2017. "'The giver of the bride, the bridegroom, and the bride': A study of the murder of Philip II and its aftermath." In Howe, Müller and Stoneman, 92–124.

Heckel, W., and Ryan Jones. 2006. *Macedonian Warrior. Alexander's Elite Infantryman.* Osprey: Oxford.

Heckel, W., and J. L. McLeod. 2015. "Alexander the Great and the Fate of the Enemy: Quantifying, Qualifying, and Categorizing Atrocities." In Heckel, Müller, and Wrightson, 233–67.

Heckel, W., C. Willekes, and G. Wrightson. 2010. "Scythed Chariots at Gaugamela: A Case Study." In Carney and Ogden, 103–9, 171–5.

Heckel, W., and J. C. Yardley. 1981. "Roman Writers and the Indian Practice of Suttee." *Philologus* 125: 305–11.

Heckel, W., Sabine Müller, and Graham Wrightson (eds.). 2015. *The Many Faces of War in the Ancient World.* Newcastle upon Tyne.

Heckel, W., and L. A. Tritle (eds.). 2003. *Crossroads of History. The Age of Alexander.* Claremont, CA.

Heckel, W., and L. A. Tritle (eds.). 2009. *Alexander the Great. A New History.* Oxford.

Heckel, W., L. A. Tritle, and Pat Wheatley (eds.). 2007. *Alexander's Empire. From Formulation to Decay.* Claremont, CA.

Heckel, W., and J. C. Yardley. 2003. *Alexander the Great. Historical Sources in Translation.* Oxford.

Helmreich, F. 1927. *Die Reden bei Curtius.* Paderborn.

Herman, G. 1981. "The 'Friends' of the Early Hellenistic Rulers: Servants or Officials?" *Talanta:* 103–35.

Higgins, W. E. 1980. "Aspects of Alexander's imperial administration: Some modern methods and views reviewed." *Athenaeum* 58: 129–52.

Hill, G. 1904. *Catalogue of Greek Coins in the British Museum. Cyprus.* London.

——. 1910. *Catalogue of Greek Coins in the British Museum. Phoenicia.* London.

Holt, F. L. 1988. *Alexander the Great and Bactria.* Mnemosyne Supplements 104. Leiden.

——. 2000. "The Death of Coenus: Another Study in Methodology." *AHB* 14: 49–55.

——. 2005. *Into the Land of Bones. Alexander the Great in Afghanistan*. Berkeley and Los Angeles.

Howe, Timothy. 2008. "Alexander in India: Ptolemy as Near Eastern Historiographer." In Howe and Reames, 215–33.

——. 2013a. "The Diadochi, Invented Tradition, and Alexander's Expedition to Siwah." In Alonso Troncoso and Anson, 57–70.

——. 2013b. "Athens, Alexander and the Politics of Resistance." *AncW* 44: 55–65.

——. 2014. "Founding Alexandria: Alexander the Great and the Politics of Memory." In Philip Bosman (ed.). *Alexander in Africa*. Acta Classica Supplementum V. Pretoria: 72–91.

——. 2015a. "Cleopatra–Eurydice, Olympias, and a 'Weak' Alexander." In Wheatley and Baynham, 133–46.

——. 2015b. "Introducing Ptolemy: Alexander and the Persian Gates." In Heckel, Müller, and Wrightson, 166–95.

—, ed. 2018. *Ptolemy I Soter. A Self-Made Man*. Oxford and Philadelphia.

——. 2020. "The 'Good' Poros and the 'Bad' Poros: Infamy and Honour in Alexander Historiography." In Faber, 156–71.

— 2021. "(Re)Taking Halikarnassos: Ada, Alexander the Great and Karian Queenship." In K. Droß-Krüpe and S. Fink (eds.) *Perception and (Self)Presentation of Powerful Women in the Ancient World*. Münster: 241–67.

Howe, Timothy, E. Edward Garvin and Graham Wrightson (eds.). 2015. *Greece, Macedon and Persia. Studies in Social, Political and Military History in Honour of Waldemar Heckel*. Oxford and Philadelphia.

Howe, Timothy, and Sabine Müller. 2012. "Mission Accomplished: Alexander at the Hyphasis." *AHB* 26: 21–38.

Howe, Timothy, Sabine Müller and Richard Stoneman (eds.). 2017. *Ancient Historiography on War and Empire*. Oxford and Philadelphia.

Howe, Timothy, and Frances Pownall (eds.). 2018. *Ancient Macedonians in the Greek and Roman Sources: From History to Historiography*. Swansea.

Howe, Timothy, and Jeanne Reames (eds.). 2008. *Macedonian Legacies. Studies in Ancient Macedonian History and Culture in Honor of Eugene N. Borza*. Claremont.

Hülden, O. 2000. "Pleistarchos und die Befestigungsanlagen von Herakleia am Latmos." *Klio* 82: 382–408.

Hünerwadel, W. 1910. "Forschungen zur Geschichte des Königs Lysimachos von Thrakien." Diss., Zürich.

Hyland, J. 2013. "Alexander's Satraps of Media." *JAH* 1: 119–44.

Iliakis, M. 2013. "Greek Mercenary Revolts in Bactria: A re-appraisal." *Historia* 62: 182–95.

Iliescu, Vladimir, Decebal Nedu, and Andreea-Raluca Barboş (eds.). 2014. *Graecia, Roma, Barbaricum. In memoria Vasile Lica*. Galați.

Instinsky, H. U. 1949. *Alexander der Große am Hellespont*. Godeberg.

Jacoby, F. 1934. "Die Schmeichelei des Kallikrates." *Hermes* 69: 214–17.

Jaschinski, S. 1981. *Alexander und Griechenland unter dem Eindruck der Flucht des Harpalos*. Bonn. 1981.

Johnson, Franklin P. 1927. *Lysippos*. Durham, North Carolina.

Judeich, W. 1895. "Der Grabherr des Alexandersarkophages." *Arch. Jahrb.* 10: 164ff.

Kahn, D., and O. Tammuz. 2009. "Egypt is difficult to enter (Strabo, Geography, 17.1.21): Invading Egypt—A Game Plan (7th–4th centuries BCE)." *JSSEA* 36: 37–66.

Kaiser, W. B. 1956. "Der Brief Alexanders des Grossen an Dareios nach der Schlacht bei Issos." Diss., Mainz.

Kanatsulis, D. 1942. *Antipatros: Ein Beitrag zur Geschichte Makedoniens in der Zeit Philipps, Alexanders und der Diadochen.* Thessaloniki.

——. 1958–1959. "Antipatros als Feldherr und Staatsmann in der Zeit Philipps und Alexanders des Grossen." *Hellenika* 16: 14–64.

——. 1968. "Antipatros als Feldherr und Staatsmann nach dem Tode Alexanders des Grossen." *Makedonika* 8: 121–84.

Karttunen, K. 1990. "Taxila: Indian city and a stronghold of Hellenism." *Arctos* 24: 85–96.

Kebric, R. B. 1977. *In the Shadow of Macedon: Duris of Samos.* Historia Einzelschriften, Heft 29. Wiesbaden.

Keil, J. 1913. "Ephesische Bürgerrechts – und Proxeniedekrete aus dem vierten und dritten Jahrhundert v. Chr." *JÖAI* 16: 231–48.

Kelly, D. H. 1990. "Charidemos's Citizenship: the Problem of *IG* II² 207." *ZPE* 83: 96–109.

Kent, P. A. 2020. *A History of the Pyrrhic War.* London and New York.

Kern, P. B. 1999. *Ancient Siege Warfare.* London.

Kingsley, B. 1986. "Harpalos in the Megarid (333–331 BC) and the grain shipments from Cyrene." *ZPE* 66: 165–77.

Kleiner, G. 1963. *Diadochen-Gräber.* Wiesbaden.

Klinkott, Hilmar. 2000. *Die Satrapienregister der Alexander- und Diadochenzeit.* Historia Einzelschriften, Heft 145. Stuttgart.

Knibbe, D., and B. Iplikcioglu. 1982. "Neue Inschriften aus Ephesos." *JÖAI* 53: 87–150.

Knoepfler, D. 1991. *La vie de Ménédème d'Erétrie de Diogène Laërce.* Basel.

——. 2001. *Décrets érétriens de proxénie et de citoyenneté.* Lausanne.

Köhler, Ulrich. 1890. "Über die Diadochengeschichte Arrians." *SB Berlin:* 557–8.

——. 1892. "Über das Verhältniss Alexanders des Grossen zu seinem Vater Philipp." *SB Berlin:* 497–514.

——. 1898. "Das asiatische Reich des Antigonos." *SDAW:* 824–43.

——. 1901. "Über die Correspondenz zwischen dem asiatischen Herrscher Antigonos und der Stadtgemeinde der Skepsier." *SB Berlin:* 1057–68.

Kornemann, E. 1901. "Zur Geschichte des antiken Herrscherkultes." *Klio* 1: 51–146.

——. 1935. *Die Alexandergeschichte des Königs Ptolemaios I. von Aegypten.* Leipzig.

Kosmetatou, Elizabeth. 2004. "Rhoxane's Dedication to Athena Polias." *ZPE* 146: 75–80.

Kuhrt, Amélie. 1987. "Usurpation, conquest and ceremonial: From Babylon to Persia." In Cannadine and Price, 20–55.

Kuhrt, Amélie, and Susan Sherwin-White (eds.). 1987. *Hellenism in the East.* Berkeley and Los Angeles.

Kuzmin, Yuri N. 2013. "The Macedonian Aristocratic Family of Harpaloi-Polemaioi from Beroea." In Mehl, Makhlayuk and Gabelko, 123–32.

Landucci Gattinoni, F. 1987. "La figura di Tolomeo nei libri XVIII–XX di Diodoro." *Aevum* 61: 37–42.

——. 1997. *Duride di Samo.* Rome.

——. 2003. *L'arte del potere: vita e opera di Cassandro di Macedonia.* Historia Einzelschriften 171. Stuttgart.

——. 2009. "Cassander's Wife and Heirs." In Wheatley and Hannah, 261–75.

——. 2010. "Cassander and the Legacy of Philip II and Alexander in Diodorus' *Library.*" In Carney and Ogden, 113–21.

——. 2013. "Seleucus vs. Antigonus: A Study on the Sources." In Alonso Troncoso and Anson, 30–42.

——. 2021. "Antipater and his Family: A Case Study." In D'Agostini, Anson, and Pownall, 97–109.

Lane Fox, Robin. 2011a. "Introduction: Dating the Royal Tombs at Vergina." In Lane Fox, 1–34.

———. 2011b. "Philip's and Alexander's Macedon." In Lane Fox, 367–91.

———. 2015. "King Ptolemy: Centre and Periphery." In Wheatley and Baynham, 163–95.

Lane Fox, Robin (ed.). 2011. *Brill's Companion to Ancient Macedon. Studies in the Archaeology and History of Macedon, 650 BC–300 AD.* Leiden.

Lefkowitz, M. 1981. *The Lives of the Greek Poets.* London.

Lenschau, T. 1940. "Alexander der Große und Chios." *Klio* 33: 207–14.

Lepore, E. 1955. "Leostene e le origini della guerra lamiaca." *PP* 10: 161ff.

Leuze, O. 1935. *Die Satrapieneinteilung in Syrien und im Zweistromlande von 520–320.* Halle.

Lévêque, P. 1957. *Pyrrhos.* Paris.

Lewis, M. J. T. 1999. "When was Biton?" *Mnemosyne* 52: 159–66.

Lica, Vasile (ed.). 2006. *Philia. Festschrift für Gerhard Wirth.* Galaţi.

Lindholmer, M. 2016. "The Assassination of Philip II: An elusive Mastermind." *Palamedes* 11: 77–110.

Litvinsky, B. A. 1968. "Archaeology in Tadzikistan under Soviet Rule." *East and West* 18: 134–5.

Lock, Robert. 1977. "The origins of the Argyraspids." *Historia* 26: 373–8.

Long, A. A. 1974. *Hellenistic Philosophy. Stoics, Epicureans, Sceptics.* London.

Longega, Gabriella. 1968. *Arsinoe II.* Rome.

Lorber, Catharine. 2018. "The Currency Reforms and Character of Ptolemy I Soter." In Howe, 60–87.

Lott, J. Bert. 1996. "Philip II, Alexander, and the Two Tyrannies at Eresos of *IG* XII.2.526." *Phoenix* 50: 26–40.

Luschey, Heinz. 1968. "Der Löwe von Ekbatana." *Archaeologische Mitteilungen aus Iran* 1: 115–122.

Maclean Rogers, Guy. 2004. *Alexander. The Ambiguity of Greatness.* New York.

Macurdy, Grace. 1929. "The political activities and the name of Cratesipolis." *AJP* 50: 273–8.

———. 1932. "Roxane and Alexander IV in Epirus." *JHS* 52: 256–61.

Mairs, Rachel. 2014. *The Hellenistic Far East. Archaeology, Language and Identity in Greek Central Asia.* Berkeley.

Manni, E. 1949. "Pirro e gli stati greci nel 281/0." *Athenaeum* 27: 102–21.

Marasco, G. 1982. *Appiano e la storia dei Seleucidi fino all'ascesa al trono di Antioco III.* Florence.

Markou, E. 2013. "Menelaos, king of Salamis." In D. Michaelides (ed.). *Epigraphy, Numismatics, Prosopography and History of Ancient Cyprus. Papers in Honor of Ino Nicolaou.* Uppsala: 3–8.

Marsden, E. W. 1964. *The Campaign of Gaugamela.* Liverpool.

———. 1977. "Macedonian Military Machinery and its Designers." *AM* 2: 211–23.

Martin, Thomas R. 1983. "Quintus Curtius' presentation of Philip Arrhidaeus and Josephus' accounts of the accession of Claudius." *AJAH* 8: 161–90.

Matarese, C. 2013. "Proskynesis and the Gesture of the Kiss at Alexander's Court: The Creation of a New Elite." *Palamedes* 8: 75–85.

Mayor, Adrienne. 2014. *Amazons. Lives and Legends of Warrior Women across the Ancient World.* Princeton.

McAuley, Alex. 2016. "Princess & Tigress: Apama of Kyrene." In Coşkun and McAuley, 175–89.

McCoy, W. J. 1989. "Memnon of Rhodes at the Granicus." *AJP* 110: 413–33.

McGing, B. C. 1986a. *The Foreign Policy of Mithridates VI Eupator King of Pontus.* Leiden.

———. 1986b. "The Kings of Pontus: Some Problems of Identity and Date." *RhM* 129:248–59.

McKechnie, P. 1995. "Diodorus Siculus and Hephaestion's Pyre." *CQ* 45: 45 418–32.

McKechnie, P., and Philippe Guillaume (eds.). 2008. *Ptolemy II Philadelphus and his World.* Leiden.

McQueen, E. I. 1978. "Some notes on the anti-Macedonian movement in the Peloponnese in 331 BC." *Historia* 27: 40–64.

Meeus, A. 2009. "Alexander's Image in the Age of the Successors." In Heckel and Tritle, 235–50.

——. 2013. "What we do not know about the Age of the Diadochi: The Methodological Consequences of the Gaps in the Evidence." In Alonso and Anson, 84–98.

——. 2014. "The Territorial Ambitions of Ptolemy I." In Hauben and Meeus, 263–306.

——. 2015. "The Career of Sostratos of Knidos: Politics, Diplomacy and the Alexandrian Building Programme in the Early Hellenistic Period." In Howe, Garvin, and Wrightson, 143–71.

Mehl, A. 1986. *Seleukos Nikator und sein Reich*. Leuven.

Mehl, A., A Makhlayuk, and O. Gabelko (eds.). 2013. *Ruthenia Classica Aetatis Novae. A Collection of Works by Russian Scholars in Ancient Greek and Roman History*. Stuttgart.

Mendels, D. 1984. "Aetolia 331–301: Frustration, political power and survival." *Historia* 33: 129–80.

Mendoza Sanahuja, M. 2017. "Stasanor of Soloi and the Government of Bactria during the Wars of the Successors." *Anabasis* 8: 44–70.

Merkelbach, R. 1977. *Die Quellen des griechischen Alexanderromans*. Zetemata, Heft 9. Munich 1954; 2nd edition, 1977.

Merker, I. L. 1965. "The ancient kingdom of Paeonia." In *Balkan Studies* 6: 35–55.

——. 1970. "The Ptolemaic Officials and the League of the Islanders." *Historia* 19: 141–60.

——. 1979. "Lysimachus—Thessalian or Macedonian?" *Chiron* 9: 31–6.

Meyer, Ed. 1879. *Geschichte des Königsreichs Pontos*. Leipzig.

Milns, R. D. 1966. "Alexander's seventh phalanx battalion." *GRBS* 7: 159–66.

——. 1968. *Alexander the Great*. London.

——. 1982. "A note on Diodorus and Macedonian military terminology in Book XVII." *Historia* 31: 123–6.

Missitzis, L. 1985. "A royal decree of Alexander the Great on the lands of Philippi." *AncW* 12: 3–14.

Mitchell, Stephen. 1994. "Three Cities in Pisidia." *Anatolian Studies* 44: 129–48.

Moloney, E. 2015. "Neither Agamemnon nor Thersites, Achilles nor Margites: The Heraclid Kings of Ancient Macedon." *Antichthon* 49: 50–72.

Momigliano, A. 1931. "Peucesta." *RFIC* 59: 245–6.

Moreno, P. 1973. *Testimonianze per la teoria artistica di Lisippo*. Treviso.

——. 1974. *Lisippo, I: Biografia. Iscrizioni. Fonti. Storia e civiltà*. Bari.

Moretti, L. 1975. *Iscrizioni storiche ellenistiche*. Vol. 2. Florence.

Moritani, Kimitoshi. 2014. *A Historical and Topographical Study of Alexander's Expedition in Iran*. Tokyo.

Mørkholm, O. 1991. *Early Hellenistic Coinage from the Accession of Alexander to the Peace of Apamea (336–186 BC)*. Cambridge.

Morrison, J. S. 1987. "Athenian sea-power in 323/2 BC: Dream and reality." *JHS* 107: 88–97.

Moser, G. 1914. "Untersuchungen über die Politik Ptolemaios' I. in Griechenland (323–285 a. Chr. n.)." Diss. Leipzig.

Mosley, D. J. 1971. "Greeks, Barbarians, Language and Contact." *Anc. Soc.* 2: 1–6.

——. 1973. *Envoys and Diplomacy in Ancient Greece*. Historia Einzelschriften 22. Wiesbaden.

Müller, O. 1973. *Antigonos Monophthalmos und "Das Jahr der Könige."* Bonn.

Müller, Sabine. 2003. *Maßnahmen der Herrschaftssicherung gegenüber der makedonischen Opposition bei Alexander dem Großen*. Bonn.

——. 2006. "Alexander, Harpalos und die Ehren für Pythionike und Glykera: Überlegungen zu den Repräsentationsformen des Schatzmeisters in Babylon und Tarsos." In Lica, 71–106.

——. 2009. *Das hellenistische Königspaar in der medialen Repräsentation. Ptolemaios I. und Arsinoë I*. Berlin.

——. 2011. "In Abhängigkeit von Alexander. Hephaistion bei den Alexanderhistoriographen." *Gymnasium* 118: 429–56.

——. 2012a. "Ptolemaios und die Erinnerung an Hephaistion." *Anabasis* 3: 75–91.

——. 2012b. "Stories of the Persian bride: Alexander and Roxane." In Stoneman et al., 111–25.

——. 2013. "The Female Element of the Political Self-fashioning of the Diadochi: Ptolemy, Seleucus, Lysimachus, and their Iranian Wives." In Alonso Troncoso and Anson, 199–214.

——. 2014a. *Makedonien und Persien*. Berlin.

——. 2014b. "Ptolemaios und das Ölwunder (Arr. an. 4, 15, 7–8)." In Iliescu, Nedu, and Barboş, 175–97.

——. 2018. "Hephaistion—A Reassessment of his Career." In Howe and Pownall, 77–102.

——. 2019. *Alexander der Große. Eroberung—Politik—Rezeption*. Stuttgart.

——. 2021. "Barsine, Antigone and the Macedonian War." In D'Agostini, Anson and Pownall, 81–96.

Murray, William M. 2012. *The Age of Titans. The Rise and Fall of the Great Hellenistic Navies*. Oxford.

Neuhaus, O. 1902. "Der Vater der Sisygambis (und das Verwandtschafts–verhältniss des Dareios III Kodomannos zu Artaxerxes II und III)." *RhM* 57: 610–23.

Nylander, C. 1993. "Darius III—the Coward King: Points and Counterpoints." In Carlsen et al., 145–59.

O'Brien, J. M. 1992. *Alexander the Great. The Invisible Enemy*. London.

Ogden, D. 1996. "Homosexuality and warfare in ancient Greece." In Lloyd: 107–68.

——. 2009. "Alexander's Snake Sire." In Wheatley and Hannah, 136–78.

——. 2011. *Alexander the Great. Myth, Genesis and Sexuality*. Exeter.

——. 2017. *The Legend of Seleucus*. Cambridge.

Oikonomides, A. 1987. "The decree of the Athenian orator Hyperides honoring the Macedonians Iolaos and Medios." *PRAKTIKA Bv*. Athens: 169–82.

——. 1989a. "Philip IV of Macedonia: A King for Four Months (296 BC)." *AncW* 19: 109–12.

——. 1989b. "The elusive portrait of Antigonos I, the 'One-Eyed' king of Macedonia." *AncW* 20: 17–20.

Olbrycht, J. M. 2013. "Iranians in the Diadochi Period." In Alonso and Anson, 159–82.

Osborne, M. J. 1973. "'Orontes." *Historia* 22: 515–51.

O'Sullivan, Lara. 1997. "Asander, Athens and *IG* II² 450: A New Interpretation." *ZPE* 119: 107–16.

——. 2009. *The Regime of Demetrius of Phalerum in Athens, 317–307 BCE. A Philosopher in Politics*. Leiden.

Palagia, Olga. 1980. *Euphranor*. Leiden.

——. 1998. "Alexander the Great as Lion Hunter." *Minerva* 9.4: 25–8.

——. 2000. "Hephaestion's Pyre and the Royal Hunt of Alexander." In Bosworth and Baynham, 167–206.

——. 2008. "The Grave Relief of Adea, Daughter of Cassander and Cynnana." In Howe and Reames, 195–214.

——. 2010. "Philip's Eurydice in the Philippeum at Olympia." In Carney and Ogden, 33–41.

——. 2017. "Alexander's Battles against Persians in the art of the Successors." In Howe, Müller and Stoneman, 177–87.

Palagia, Olga, and Stephen V. Tracey (eds.). 2003. *The Macedonians in Athens 322–229 BC*. Oxford.

Papastavru, J. 1936. *Amphipolis. Geschichte und Prosopographie*. Klio Beiheft 37. Leipzig.

Papazoglou, F. 1965. "Les origines et la destinée et l'état Illyrien: Illyrii proprie dicti." *Historia* 14: 143–79.

Parke, H. W. 1928. "When was Charidemus made an Athenian Citizen?" *CR* 42: 170.

——. 1933. *Greek Mercenary Soldiers from the Earliest Times to the Battle of Ipsus*. Oxford.

Paschidis, P. 2008. "Missing years in the biography of Polyperchon (318/7 and 308 BC onwards)." *Tekmeria* 9: 233–50.

——. 2013. "Agora XVI 107 and the Royal Title of Demetrius Poliorcetes." In Alonso and Anson, 121–41.

Paspalas, S. A. 2000. "The *Taurophonos Leon* and Craterus' Monument at Delphi." In Tsetskhladze, Prag, and Snodgrass, 211–19.

Pearson, Lionel. 1972. *Demosthenes. Six Private Speeches*. Norman.

——. 1987. *The Greek Historians of the West. Timaeus and his Predecessors*. Atlanta.

Pédech, P. 1984. *Historiens compagnons d'Alexandre*. Paris.

Perdrizet, Paul. 1899. "Venatio Alexandri." *JHS* 19: 273–9.

Pekridou, A, 1986. *Das Alketas-Grab in Termessos*. Tübingen.

Perrin, B. 1895. "Genesis and growth of an Alexander-myth." *TAPA* 26: 56–68.

Peters, C. 1941. "Zum Namen Abdalonymos." *OLZ* 44: 265ff.

Petrakos, B. 1993. "Anskaphes: Rhamnous." *Tὸ Ἔργον τῆς Ἀρχαιολογικῆς Ἑταιρείας* 40: 1–9.

Philipp, G. 1973. "Philippides, ein politischer Komiker in hellenistischer Zeit." *Gymnasium* 80: 493–509.

Picard, C. 1951. "Prépélaos et les courétes éphésiens." *Rev. Arch.* 37: 151–60.

——. 1964. "Sépultures des compagnons de guerre ou successeurs macédoniens d'Alexandre le Grand." *Journal des Savants*, 215–28.

Pitt, E. M., and W. P. Richardson. 2017. "Hostile Inaction? Antipater, Craterus and the Macedonian Regency." *CQ* 67: 77–87.

Poddighe, Elisabetta. 2001. "Il decreto dell'isola di Nesos in onore di Tersippo." *AHB* 15: 96–101.

——. 2002. *Nel segno di Antipatro. L'eclissi della democrazia ateniese dal 323/2 al 319/8 a.C.* Rome.

——. 2013. "Propaganda Strategies and Political Documents: Philip III's *Diagramma* and the Greeks in 319 BC." In Alonso and Anson, 225–40.

Pollitt, J. J. 1986. *Art in the Hellenistic Age*. Cambridge.

Potts, D. T. 1990. *The Arabian Gulf in Antiquity*. 2 vols. Oxford.

Pownall, Frances. 2004. *Lessons from the Past. The Moral Use of History in Fourth-Century Prose*. Ann Arbor.

——. 2013. "Duris of Samos and the Diadochi." In Alonso Troncoso and Anson, 43–56.

——. 2018. "Was Kallisthenes the Tutor of Alexander's Royal Pages?" In Howe and Pownall, 59–76.

Prandi, Luisa. 1996. *Fortuna e Realtà dell' Opera di Clitarcho*. Historia Einzelschriften 104. Stuttgart.

——. 1998. "A few remarks on the Amyntas 'conspiracy'." In Will, 91–101.

——. 2012. "New Evidence for the Dating of Cleitarchus (*POxy* LXXI. 4808)?" *Histos* 6: 15–26.

Prentice, W. K. 1923. "Callisthenes, the original historian of Alexander." *TAPA* 54: 74–85.

Prestianni-Giallombardo, A. M. 1973–74. "Aspetti giuridici e problemi cronologici della reggenza di Filippo II di Macedonia." *Helikon* 13–14: 191–204.

——. 1981. "Eurydike-Kleopatra. Nota ad Arr. *Anab.* 3, 6, 5." *ASNP* S. III, 11: 295–306.

Queyrel, F. 2011. "L'invention de l'histoire: Réflexions sur le 'Sarcophage d'Alexandre' de la nécropole royal de Sidon." *Mare Internum* 3: 35–45.

Raaflaub, Kurt, and Nathan Rosenstein (eds.). 1999. *War and Society in the Ancient and Medieval Worlds*. Cambridge, MA.

Ramsay, W. M. 1920. "Military operations on the north front of Mount Taurus, III: The imprisonment and escape of Dokimos (Diod. XIX 16)." *JHS* 40: 107–12.

——. 1923. "Military operations on the north front of Mount Taurus, IV: The campaigns of 320 and 319 BC." *JHS* 43: 1–10.

Ramsey, Gillian. 2016. "The Diplomacy of Seleukid Women: Apama and Stratonike." In Coşkun and McAuley, 87–104.

Rathmann, M. 2006. "Prepelaos bei Diodor: Ein Diener zweier Herren?" *Hermes* 134: 119–22.

Rawlinson, G. 1912. *Bactria*. London.

Reames, J. 2008. "Crisis and Opportunity: The Philotas Affair . . . Again." In Howe and Reames, 165–81.

——. 2010. "The Cult of Hephaestion." In Paul Cartledge and Fiona Rose Greenland (eds.). *Responses to Oliver Stone's* Alexander: *film, history and cultural studies*. Madison: 183–216.

Reames-Zimmerman, J. 1998. "Hephaistion Amyntoros: Eminence grise at the Court of Alexander the Great," Diss. Pennsylvania State University.

——. 1999. "An Atypical Affair: Alexander the Great, Hephaistion Amyntoros and the Nature of their Relationship." *AHB* 13: 81–96.

Reger, G. 1991. "The Family of Balakros son of Nikanor, the Makedonian, on Delos." *ZPE* 89: 151–4.

Renard, M., and Servais, J. 1955. "À propos du mariage d'Alexandre et de Roxane." *L'Antiquité Classique* 24: 29–50.

Reuss, F. 1876. *Hieronymos von Kardia*. Berlin.

——. 1881. "König Arybbas von Epeiros." *RhM* 36: 161–74.

Rice, E. E. 1993. "The glorious dead: Commemoration of the fallen and portrayal of victory in the late classical and Hellenistic world." In Rich and Shipley, 224–57.

Robinson, C. A., Jr. 1929. "The seer Aristander." *AJP* 50: 195–7.

——. 1945. "Alexander the Great and Parmenio." *AJA* 49: 422ff.

Robinson, C. A., Jr. (ed.). 1953. *The history of Alexander the Great*. Brown University Studies XVI, vol. 1. Providence, RI.

Roebuck, C. 1948. "The settlements of Philip II with the Greek states in 338 BC." *CP* 43: 73–92.

Rohde, E. 1914. *Der griechische Roman und seine Vorläufer*. 3rd edition. Leipzig.

Roisman, J. 1984. "Ptolemy and his rivals in his History of Alexander." *CQ* 34: 373–85.

——. 2003. "Honor in Alexander's Campaign." In Roisman, 279–321.

——, ed. 2003. *Brill's Companion to Alexander the Great*. Leiden: Brill.

——. 2010. "Hieronymus of Cardia: Causation and Bias from Alexander to the Successors." In Carney and Ogden, 135–48.

——. 2012. *Alexander's Veterans and the Early Wars of the Successors*. Austin.

Roisman, Joseph, and Ian Worthington (eds.). 2010. *A Companion to Ancient Macedonia*. Oxford: Wiley-Blackwell.

——. 2015. *Lives of the Attic Orators. Texts from Pseudo-Plutarch, Photius, and the* Suda. Translated by Robin Waterfield; commentary by Roisman and Worthington. Oxford.

Rose, T. C. 2015. "A historical commentary on Plutarch's Life of Demetrius." Diss. University of Iowa.

Rubinsohn, Z. 1977. "The 'Philotas Affair'—A reconsideration." *AM* 2: 409–20.

Rüegg, A. 1906. "Beiträge zur Erforschung der Quellenverhältnisse in der Alexandergeschichte des Curtius." Diss. Basel.

Ruzicka, S. 1992. *Politics of a Persian Dynasty. The Hecatomnids in the Fourth Century BC*. Norman.

——. 2010. "The 'Pixodarus Affair' Reconsidered again." In Carney and Ogden, 3–12.

Salis, A. von. 1956. *Löwenkampfbilder des Lysipp*. Berlin.

Schachermeyr, F. 1920. "Das Ende des Makedonischen Königshauses." *Klio* 16: 332–7.

——. 1970. *Alexander in Babylon und die Reichsordnung nach seinem Tode*. Vienna.

Schäfer, C. 2002. *Eumenes von Kardia und der Kampf um die Macht im Alexanderreich.* Frankfurt a. M.

Schäfer, P. 2003. *The History of the Jews in the Graeco-Roman World.* London.

Scharfe, H. 1971. "The Maurya dynasty and the Seleucids." *Zeitschrift für Vergleichende Sprachforschung* 85: 211–25.

Schober, L. 1981. *Untersuchungen zur Geschichte Babyloniens und der Oberen Satrapien von 323–303 v. Chr.* Frankfurt a. M.

Schoder, R. V. 1982. "Alexander's Son and Roxane in the Boscoreale Murals." *AncW* 5: 27–32.

Scholten, J. 2000. *The Politics of Plunder.* Berkeley and Los Angeles.

Schubert, R. 1894. *Geschichte des Pyrrhus.* Königsberg.

——. 1898. "Der Tod des Kleitos." *RhM* 53: 98–117.

——. 1901. "Die Porusschlacht." *RhM* 56: 543–62.

Schwarz, F. F. 1968. "Mauryas und Seleukiden. Probleme ihrer gegenseitigen Beziehungen." *Studien zur Sprachwissenschaft und Kulturkunde.* Innsbrucker Beiträge zur Kulturwissenschaft 14: 1.220–30.

Schwarzenberg, E. von. 1967. "Der lysippische Alexander." *Bonner Jahrb.* 167: 58–118.

——. 1976. "The Portraiture of Alexander." In Badian, 223–67.

Schweigert, E. 1938. "Inscriptions from the North Slope of the Acropolis." *Hesperia* 7: 264–310.

——. 1939. "Greek Inscriptions." *Hesperia* 8: 1–47.

Sears, Matthew A. 2014. "Alexander and Ada Reconsidered." *CP* 109: 211–21.

Seel, O. 1972. *Ein römische Weltgeschichte.* Nürnberg.

Seibert, Jakob. 1967. *Historische Beiträge zu den dynastischen Verbindungen in hellenistischer Zeit.* Historia Einzelschriften 10. Wiesbaden.

——. 1969. *Untersuchungen zur Geschichte Ptolemaios' I.* Münchener Beiträge zur Papyrusforschung und antiken Rechtsgeschichte. Heft 56. Munich.

——. 1970. "Philokles, Sohn des Apollodoros." *Historia* 19: 337–51.

——. 1979. *Die politischen Flüchtlinge und Verbannten in der griechischen Geschichte.* Darmstadt.

——. 1985. *Die Eroberung des Perserreiches durch Alexander den Großen auf kartographischer Grundlage.* TAVO. Wiesbaden.

——. 1987. "Dareios III." In Will and Heinrichs, I 437–56.

Sekunda, N. V. 1992. *The Persian Army 560–330 BC.* London.

——. 1997. "Nearchus the Cretan and the foundation of Kretopolis." *Anatolian Studies* 47: 217–23.

——. 2010. "The Macedonian Army." In Roisman and Worthington 445–71.

Servais, J. See Renard, M.

Shackleton-Bailey, D. R. 1981. "Curtiana." *CQ* 31: 175–80.

Shear, T. Leslie, Jr. 1978. *Kallias of Sphettos and the Revolt of Athens in 286 BC.* Princeton.

Sherwin-White, Susan. 1987. "Seleucid Babylonia: A case study for the installation and development of Greek rule." In Kuhrt and Sherwin-White, 1–31.

Sherwin-White, Susan, and Amélie Kuhrt. 1993. *From Samarkhand to Sardis. A new approach to the Seleucid empire.* Berkeley and Los Angeles.

Shoemaker, G. 1968. "Dinarchus: Traditions of his Life and Speeches." Diss. Columbia University.

Shrimpton, G. S. 1991. *The Historian Theopompus.* Montreal and Kingston.

Simpson, R. H. 1957. "A possible case of misrepresentation in Diodorus XIX." *Historia* 6: 504–5.

Skalet, Charles H. 1928. *Ancient Sikyon with a Prosopographia Sicyoonia.* Baltimore.

Smith, R. R. R. 1988. *Hellenistic Royal Portraits.* Oxford.

Smith, S. 1924. *Babylonian Historical Texts Relating to the Capture and Downfall of Babylon.* London.

Smith, V. 1914. *The Early History of India. From 600 BC to the Muhammadan Conquest, including the Invasion of Alexander the Great.* 3rd ed. Oxford.

Snell, B. 1964. *Scenes from Greek drama*. Berkeley and Los Angeles.

Sonnabend, H. 1996. *Die Freundschaften der Gelehrten und die zwischenstaatliche Politik im klassischen und hellenistischen Griechenland*. Altertumswissenschaftliche Texte und Studien no. 30. Hildesheim.

Spann, Philip O. 1999. "Alexander at the Beas. Fox in a Lion's Skin." In Titchener and Moorton, Jr., 62–74.

Spawforth, Antony J. S. 2012. "The Pamphleteer Ephippus, King Alexander and the Persian Royal Hunt." *Histos* 6: 169–213.

Speck, Henry. 2002. "Alexander at the Persian Gates: A Study in Historiography and Topography." *AJAH* n.s. 1: 1–234.

Spencer, D. 2002. *The Roman Alexander. Reading a Cultural Myth*. Exeter.

Sprawski, S. 2008. "Leonnatus' campaign of 322 BC." *Electrum* 14: 9–31.

Stein, Sir Aurel. 1929. *On Alexander's Track to the Indus*. London.

——. 1938. "An archaeological journey in western Iran." *GJ* 92: 313–342.

Stewart, Andrew. 2014. *Art in the Hellenistic World*. Cambridge.

Stoneman, R. 1994. "Who are the Brahmans?" *CQ* 44: 500–10.

——. 1995. "Naked Philosophers." *JHS* 115: 99–114.

——. 2019. *The Greek Experience of India from Alexander to the Indo-Greeks*. Princeton.

Stoneman, Richard, Kyle Erickson and Ian Netton (eds.). 2012. *The Alexander Romance in Persia and the East*. Groningen.

Strasburger, Hermann. 1934. *Ptolemaios und Alexander*. Leipzig.

Stylianou, P. J. 1998. *A Historical Commentary on Diodorus Siculus Book XV*. Oxford.

Sutton, D. F. 1980a. *The Greek satyr play*. Meisenheim am Glan.

——. 1980b. "Harpalus as Pallides." *RhM* 123: 96.

Tarn, W. W. 1921. "Heracles, son of Barsine." *JHS* 41: 18–28.

——. 1930. *Hellenistic Military and Naval Developments*. Cambridge.

——. 1951. *The Greeks in Bactria and India*. 3rd edition. Oxford.

Teodorsson, Sven-Tage. 1990. "Theocritus the Sophist, Antigonus the One-Eyed, and the limits of clemency." *Hermes* 118: 380–2.

Titchener, Frances B., and Richard F. Moorton, Jr. (eds.). 1999. *The Eye Expanded. Life and the Arts in Graeco-Roman Antiquity*. Berkeley.

Tomaschek, W. 1890. "Topographische Erläuterung der Küstenfahrt Nearchs vom Indus bis zum Euphrat." *SB Wien* 121, Abhandlung viii, 1–88.

Treves, P. 1939. "Hyperides and the cult of Hephaestion." *CR* 53: 56–7.

Tritle, L. 1988. *Phocion the Good*. London.

——, ed. 1997. *The Greek World in the Fourth Century. From the fall of the Athenian Empire to the successors of Alexander*. London.

——. 2003. "Alexander and the Killing of Cleitus the Black." In Heckel and Tritle, 127–46.

Tuplin, C. 1982. "Satyros and Athens: IG ii² 212 and Isokrates 17.57." *ZPE* 49: 121–8.

Unz, R. 1985. "Alexander's Brothers." *JHS* 105: 171–4.

Vacante, Salvatore. 2012. "Alexander the Great and the 'Defeat' of the Sogdianian Revolt." *AHB* 26: 87–130.

Van der Spek, R. J. 2014. "Seleukos, Self-Appointed General (*Strategos*) of Asia (311–305 B.C.), and the Satrapy of Babylonia." In Hauben and Meeus, 323–42.

Van Oppen de Ruiter, B. F. 2015. "The Marriage of Eirene and Eunostus of Soli. An episode in the Age of the Successors." *Athenaeum* 103: 458–76.

Vatin, C. 1984. "Lettre adressée à la cité de Philippes par les ambassadeurs auprès d'Alexandre." In *PRAKTIKA*, 259–70. Athens.

Vezin, A. 1907. *Eumenes von Kardia*. Tübingen.

Vitucci, A. 1955. *Il Regno di Bitinia*. Rome.

Vogelsang, W. 1985. "Early historical Arachosia in south-east Afghanistan." *Iranica Antiqua* 20: 55–99.

Völcker-Janssen, W. 1993. *Kunst und Gesellschaft an dem Höfen Alexanders d. Gr. und seiner Nachfolger*. Munich.

Voutiras, E. 1984. "Zur historischen Bedeutung des Krateros-Weihgeschenkes in Delphi." *Würzburger Jahrbücher* 10: 57–62.

Walek, T. 1924. "Les opérations navales pendant la guerre lamiaque." *RP* 48: 23–30.

Wallace, Shane. 2013. "Adeimantus of Lampsacus and the Development of the Early Hellenistic *Philos*." In Alonso and Anson, 142–57.

——. 2014. "History and Hindsight. The Importance of Euphron of Sikyon for the Athenian Democracy in 318/7." In Hauben and Meeus, 599–629.

——. 2016. "The Rescript of Philip III Arrhidaios and the Two Tyrannies at Eresos." *Tyche* 31: 239–59.

Weber, G. 1995. "Herrscher, Hof und Dichter. Aspekte der Legitimierung und Repräsentation hellenistischer Könige am Beispiel der ersten drei Antigoniden." *Historia* 44: 283–316.

Wehrli, C. 1964. "Phila, fille d'Antipater et épouse de Démétrius, roi des Macédoniens." *Historia* 13: 140–6.

——. 1968. *Antigone et Démétrios*. Geneva.

Welles, C. Bradford. 1970. *Alexander and the Hellenistic World*. Toronto.

Werner, R. 1987. "Alexander der Molosser in Italien." In Will and Heinrichs, 335–90.

Wescher, C. 1867. *Poliorcétique des Grecs*. Paris.

Westlake, H. D. 1935. *Thessaly in the Fourth Century BC*. London.

Wheatley, P. V. 1995. "Ptolemy Soter's Annexation of Syria in 320 BC." *CQ* 45: 433–40.

——. 1997a. "Problems in analysing source documents in Ancient History: The case of Philip, adviser to Demetrius Poliorcetes, 314–312 BC, and IG II² 561." *Limina* 3: 61–70.

——. 1997b. "The Lifespan of Demetrius Poliorcetes." *Historia* 46: 19–27.

——. 1998. "The Date of Polyperchon's Invasion of Macedonia and the Murder of Heracles." *Antichthon* 32: 12–23.

——. 1999. "Young Demetrius Poliorcetes." *AHB* 13: 1–13.

——. 2001. "Three Missing Years in the Life of Demetrius the Besieger: 310–308 BC." *Journal of Ancient Civilizations* 16: 9–19.

——. 2003. "Lamia and the Besieger: an Athenian hetaera and a Macedonian king." In Palagia and Tracey, 30–6.

——. 2004. "Poliorcetes and Cratesipolis: A Note on Plutarch, *Demetr.* 9.5–7." *Antichthon* 38: 1–9.

——. 2014a. "Seleukos and Chandragupta in Justin XV 4." In Hauben and Meeus, 501–15.

——. 2014b. "Demetrius the Besieger on the Nile." *Acta Classica Supplementum* 5: 92–108.

——. 2015. "Diadoch Chronology after Philip Arrhidaeus." In Wheatley and Baynham, 241–58.

——. 2020. "The Implications of 'Poliorcetes': Was Demetrius the Besieger's Nickname Ironic?" *Histos* 14: 152–84.

Wheatley, P., and Elizabeth Baynham (eds.). 2015. *East and West in the World Empire of Alexander. Essays in Honour of Brian Bosworth*. Oxford.

Wheatley, P., and Robert Hannah (eds.). 2009. *Alexander and his Successors. Essays from the Antipodes*. Claremont, CA.

Whitehead, David. 2015. "Alexander the Great and the *Mechanici*." In Wheatley and Baynham, 75–91.

Whitehorne, J. 1994. *Cleopatras*. London.

Will, Ed. 2003. *Histoire politique du monde hellénistique (323–30 av. J.C.)*. Paris. Originally published in Nancy. 1966–7.

Will, W. 1983. *Athen und Alexander. Untersuchungen zur Geschichte der Stadt von 338 bis 322 v. Chr.* Münchener Beiträge zur Papyrusforschung und antiken Rechtsgeschichte, Heft 77. Munich.

Will, W., and J. Heinrichs (eds.). *Zu Alexander d. Gr. Festschrift für Gerhard Wirth*. 2 vols. Amsterdam. 1987–88.

Williams, J. M. 1984. "A note on Athenian chronology, 319/8–318/7 BC." *Hermes* 112: 300–5.

——. 1989. "Demades' last years, 323/2–319/8 BC: A 'revisionist' interpretation." *AncW* 19: 19–30.

Willrich, H. 1899a. "Krateros und der Grabherr des Alexandersarkophags von Sidon." *Hermes* 34: 231–50.

——. 1899b. "Wer liess König Philipp von Makedonien ermorden?" *Hermes* 34: 174–82.

Winiarczyk, Marek. 1981. "Theodorus Ο ΑΘΕΟΣ." *Philologus* 125: 64-94.

——. 2007. "Das Werk *Die Erziehung Alexanders* des Onesikritos von Astypalaea (FGrHist 134 F1–39). Forschungsstand (1832–2005) und Interpretationsversuch." *Eos* 94: 197–50.

Winter, F. 1909. *Das Alexandermosaik*. Strassburg.

Wirth, Gerhard. 1965. "Zur grossen Schlacht des Eumenes 322 (PSI 1284)." *Klio* 46: 283–8.

——. 1967. "Zur Politik des Perdikkas 323." *Helikon* 7: 281–322.

——. 1971. "Alexander zwischen Gaugamela und Persepolis." *Historia* 20: 617–32 = *Studien* 76ff.

——. 1972. "Nearchos, der Flottenchef." *Acta Conventus XI, "Eirene."* Warsaw: 615–39.

——. 1985. *Philip II. Geschichte Makedoniens*. Band 1. Stuttgart.

——. 1988. "Nearch, Alexander und die Diadochen: Spekulationen über einen Zusammenhang." *Tyche* 3: 241–59.

——. 1989. *Der Kampfverband des Proteas. Spekulationen zu den Begleitumstände der Laufbahn Alexanders*. Amsterdam.

Worthington, I. 1984. "The first flight of Harpalus reconsidered." *G&R* 31: 161–9.

——. 1986a. "The chronology of the Harpalus affair." *SO* 61: 63–76.

——. 1986b. "*IG* II² 1631, 1632 and Harpalus' ships." *ZPE* 65: 222–4.

——, ed. 1994. *Ventures into Greek History*. Oxford.

——. 2003. "Alexander's Destruction of Thebes." In Heckel and Tritle, 65–86.

——. 2008. *Philip II of Macedonia*. New Haven.

——. 2015. "From East to West: Alexander and the Exiles Decree." In Wheatley and Baynham, 93–106.

——. 2016. *Ptolemy I. King and Pharaoh of Egypt*. Oxford.

——. 2021. *Athens after Empire. A History from Alexander the Great to the Emperor Hadrian*. Oxford.

Wrightson, G. 2014. "The naval battles of 322 BCE." In Hauben and Meeus, 517–35.

Yardley, J. C., trans. 1984. *Quintus Curtius Rufus: The History of Alexander,* with introduction, notes and appendices by Waldemar Heckel. Penguin Classics: Harmondsworth.

—, trans. 1994. *Justin: Epitome of the* Philippic History *of Pompeius Trogus*, with introduction and notes by Robert Develin (Atlanta, 1994).

Zahrnt, M. 1999. "Alexander der Grosse und der lykische Hirt. Bemerkungen zur Propaganda während des Rachekrieges (334–330 v. Chr.)." *AM* 6.2: 1381–7.

——. 2013. "Kallisthenes von Olynth—ein verkannter Oppositioneller?" *Hermes* 141: 491–96.

Ziegler, K. 1935 "Plutarchstudien." *RhM* 84: 369–90.

Zumetikos, Alexander M. 1894. *De Alexandri Olympiadisque Epistularum fontibus et reliquiis*. Berlin.

Concordance

This concordance lists only those names that appeared in their Latin forms in the 2006 edition of this *Who's Who* and gives their entry numbers in the current edition. Entries marked — appeared in the previous edition but are not included in this one.

Abdalonymus 1
Abisares [1] 2
Abisares [2] 3
Abulites 4
Achilles 5
Acuphis 38
Ada [1] 7
Ada [2] 8
Adaeus 9
Adea 10
Admetus 13
Aeacides 31
Aëropus 15
Aeschines 34
Aeschrion 35
Aeschylus 36
Agathocles 17
Agathon [1] 21
Agathon [2] 22
Agesilaus 24
Agesimenes 26
Agis [1] 27
Agis [2] 28
Agonippus 30
Alcetas 61
Alkias 64
Alcimachus [1] 65
Alcimachus [2] 65
Alexander [1] 43
Alexander [2] 40
Alexander [3] 41
Alexander [4] 45
Alexander [5] 48
Alexander [6] 46
Alexander [7] 49
Alexander [8] 47
Alexippus 57
Alexis 58
Amastris 67
Amedines 69

Amminais 70
Amminapes 71
Amphimachus 72
Amphistratus 74
Amphoterus 75
Amyntas [1] 76
Amyntas [2] 77
Amyntas [3] 78
Amyntas [4] 79
Amyntas [5] 80
Amyntas [6] 81
Amyntas [7] 82
Amyntas [8] 84
Amyntas [9] 85
Amyntas [10] 86
Amyntas [11] 87
Anaxagoras 91
Anaxarchus 92
Anaximenes 93
Anaxippus 95
Androcles 99
Androcydes 100
Andromachus [1] 101
Andromachus [2] 102
Andromachus [3] 103
Andronicus [1] 104
Andronicus [2] 105
Androsthenes 106
Antibelus 311
Anticles 120
Antigenes [1a] 109
Antigenes [1b] 110
Antigenidas 111
Antigone 112
Antigonus [1] 115
Antigonus [2] 117
Antigonus [3] 118
Antimenes 122
Antiochus [1] 123
Antiochus [2] 124

Antipater [1] 127
Antipater [2] 132
Antipatrides 126
Antiphanes [1] 133
Antiphanes [2] 134
Antiphilus 135
Apame [1] 138
Apame [2] 224
Apelles 141
Aphobetus 142
Aphrices 143
Aphthonius 144
Apollodorus [1] 146
Apollodorus [2] 147
Apollonides [1] 148
Apollonides [2] 149
Apollonius 152
Apollophanes 155
Arbupales 156
Arcesilaus 211
Archelaus [1] 158
Archelaus [2] 159
Archelaus [3] 160
Archepolis 163
Archias [1] 166
Archias [2] 168
Archon 169
Aretes 171
Aretis 172
Argilias 176
Ariaces 177
Ariamaze 178
Ariarathes 179
Arimmas —
Ariobarzanes [1] 181
Ariobarzanes [2] 182
Ariobarzanes [3] 183
Aristander 185
Aristarchus 186
Aristeides 187

Aristion 188
Aristobulus 189
Aristocrates 194
Aristocritus 195
Aristogeiton [1] 192
Aristogeiton [2] 193
Aristomedes 196
Aristomenes [1] 197
Aristomenes [2] —
Ariston [1] 198
Ariston [2] 199
Ariston [3] 201
Ariston [4] 202
Aristonicus [1] 203
Aristonicus [2] 204
Aristonicus [3] 205
Aristonicus [4] 206
Aristonus 207
Aristonymus 208
Aristotle 210
Arrhabaeus 213
Arrhidaeus [1] 902
Arrhidaeus [2] 214
Arsaces [1] 215
Arsaces [2] 216
Arsames [1] 217
Arsames [2] 218
Arsimas 219
Arsites 222
Artabazus 223
Artacama 224
Artemius 225
Artiboles 226
Artonis 227
Arybbas [1] 228
Arybbas [2] 229
Asander [1] 232
Asander [2] 233
Asclepiades 234
Asclepiodorus [1] no. 237
Asclepiodorus [2] no. 238
Asclepiodorus [3] no. 239
Asclepiodorus [4] no. 240
Assacenus 244
Assagetes 243
Astaspes 245
Astis 246
Astycratidas 247
Astylus 248
Atalante 249
Atarrhias 250

Athenagoras 252
Athenodorus [1] 255
Athenodorus [2] 256
Athenodorus [3] 257
Athenodorus [4] 258
Athenophanes 259
Atizyes 260
Atropates 261
Attalus [1] 262
Attalus [2] 263
Attalus [3] 265
Attalus [4] 264
Attinas 266
Audata 267
Autodicus 270
Autophradates [1] no. 271
Autophradates [2] no. 272
Azemilcus 274

Baeton 280
Bagisthanes 275
Bagoas [1] 276
Bagoas [2a] 277
Bagoas [2b] 277
Bagodaras 278
Bagophanes 279
Balacrus [1] 282
Balacrus [2] 283
Balacrus [3] 284
Barsaentes 286
Barsine 287
Baryaxes 288
Barzanes 289
Bas 290
Batis 291
Belephantes 292
Berenice 293
Bessus 295
Bianor 296
Bion 298
Bisthanes 300
Biton 302
Bolon 305
Boxus 310
Brochubelus 311
Bubaces [1] 306
Bubaces [2] 307
Bupares 308

Cadmeia 557
Calanus 558

Calas 559
Calis 313
Callias 561
Callicles 562
Callicrates 563
Callicratidas 566
Callicron 567
Callimedon 568
Callines 569
Callisthenes [1] 570
Callisthenes [2] 571
Callisthenes [3] 572
Callixeina 573
Caphisias 574
Caphisodorus 575
Caranus [1] 576
Caranus [2] 577
Carthasis 314
Cassander 579
Catanes 580
Cebalinus 581
Cephisophon 583
Chaereas 315
Chaeron [1] 316
Chaeron [2] 317
Chares [1] 318
Chares [2] 319
Charias 320
Charicles [1] 322
Charicles [2] 323
Charidemus 321
Charon 324
Charus 325
Choerilus 328
Chrysippus 329
Cissus 585
Cleadas 331
Cleander [1] 589
Cleander [2] 590
Clearchus 591
Cleitarchus —
Cleitus [1] 594
Cleitus [2] 595
Cleitus [3] 596
Cleochares 597
Cleodice 599
Cleomenes [1] 602
Cleomenes [2] 601
Cleomenes [3] 603
Cleon 604
Cleopatra [1] 607

Herodas 527
Heromenes 528
Hieron 529
Hieronymus 531
Himeraeus 532
Hippias 534
Hippocrates 537
Holcias 540
Hydarnes 543
Hydraces 544
Hyperbolus 545
Hypereides 546
Hypsides 547
Hystaspes 548

Ilioneus 549
Iolaus [1] 551
Iolaus [2] 552
Iolaus [3] 553
Iphicrates 554
Isocrates 555
Itanes 556

Laches 636
Lamachus 638
Langarus 641
Lanice 642
Laodice 643
Laomedon 645
Leochares 647
Leon 648
Leonidas [1] 649
Leonidas [2] 650
Leonnatus [1] 653
Leonnatus [2] 654
Leosthenes 657
Letodorus 659
Limnaeus 658
Lycidas 660
Lycomedes 663
Lycon 664
Lycurgus 666
Lysanias 670
Lysimachus [1] 672
Lysimachus [2] 673
Lysippus 675

Madates 677
Maeander 680
Marsyas 683
Mauaces 684

Mazaces 686
Mazaeus 685
Mazarus 687
Mazenes 688
Meda 689
Medius 690
Megabyxus 692
Megareus 693
Megasthenes 694
Meleager [1] 695
Meleager [2] 696
Melon 700
Memnon [1] 701
Memnon [2] 702
Memnon [3] 703
Menander [1] 706
Menander [2] 705
Menedemus 707
Menelaus 710
Menes 712
Menesaechmus 713
Menestheus 714
Menidas 715
Meniscus 716
Menoetas 719
Menoetius 720
Menon [1] 722
Menon [2] 723
Menon [3] 724
Menon [4] 725
Mentor 726
Meroes 728
Metron [1] 729
Metron [2] 730
Miccalus 732
Micion 731
Minnion 736
Mithraustes 738
Mithrazenes 737
Mithrenes 739
Mithridates 741
Mithrobaeus 743
Mithrobuzanes 744
Mithropastes 745
Mnasicles 747
Mnasidicus 746
Mnason 748
Mnesitheus 749
Moeris 750
Moerocles 751
Monimus 752

Moschion 754
Musicanus 756
Mylleas 757
Myllenas 758

Nabarzanes 762
Nearchus 765
Neiloxenus 767
Neon 769
Neophron 770
Neoptolemus [1] 771
Neoptolemus [2] 772
Neoptolemus [3] 773
Nicaea 775
Nicagoras 774
Nikanor [1] 776
Nikanor [2] 781
Nikanor [3] 777
Nikanor [4] 778
Nikanor [5] 780
Nikanor [6] 783
Nikanor [7] 784
Nikanor [8] 785
Nikanor [9] 782
Nikanor [10] 779
Nikanor [11] 786
Nikanor [12] 779
Nicarchides [1] 787
Nicarchides [2] 788
Nicesias 789
Nicesipolis 790
Nicias 791
Nicocles [1] 793
Nicocles [2] 794
Nicocles [3] 795
Nicocreon 797
Nicomachus 798
Nicon 800
Niphates 802
Nithaphon 804

Ochus 806
Olympias 808
Omares 811
Ombrion 812
Onesicritus 813
Onomastoridas 815
Ophellas [1] 816
Ophellas [2] 817
Ordanes 818
Orontes 819

Sabictas 1030
Samaxus 1031
Sambus [1] 1032
Sambus [2] 1033
Sanballat 1034
Sandrocottus 1035
Sangaeus 1036
Satibarzanes 1037
Satraces 1038
Satropates 1039
Sauaces 1029
Scymnus 1054
Seleucus 1041
Serapion 1042
Seuthes 1043
Sibyrtius 1044
Simmias [1] 1045
Simmias [2] 1046
Sippas 1047
Sisicottus 1048
Sisimithres 1049
Sisines [1] 1050
Sisines [2] 1051
Sisygambis 1052
Sitalces 1053
Socrates 1055
Sopater 1059
Sophytes 1061
Sopolis 1062
Sosigenes 1064
Sostratus 1065
Sparton 1070
Spitaces 1071
Spitamenes 1072
Spithidates 1073
Stamenes 1074

Stasander 1075
Stasanor 1076
Stateira [1] 1078
Stateira [2] 1079
Stephanus 1080
Straton [1] 1083
Straton [2] 1084
Stratonice 1085
Strattis 1087
Stroebus 1088
Syrmus 1090
Syrphax 1091

Tauriscus 1092
Tauron 1093
Taxiles 1095
Teireus 1096
Telephus 1098
Telesippa 1099
Teutamus 1102
Thais 1103
Thalestris 1104
Theaetetus 1105
Theocritus 1112
Theodorus [1] 1107
Theodorus [2] 1108
Theodotus 1110
Theophilus 1113
Theopompus 1115
Theoxenus 1118
Thersippus 1119
Thessaliscus 1121
Thessalonice 1122
Thessalus 1123
Thibron 1124
Thiodexilas 1125

Thiodotos 1126
Thiopompus 1127
Thoas 1128
Thoenon 1129
Thrasybulus 1133
Thrasylochus 1134
Thymondas 1136
Timander 1137
Timanthes 1138
Timocleia 1140
Timocles 1141
Timotheus [1] 1145
Timotheus [2] 1146
Tiridates [1] 1148
Tiridates [2] 1149
Tiridates [3] 1150
Tlepolemus 1151
Troas 1152
Tyriespis 1154

Wanaxion 1155

Xandrames 1156
Xennias 1158
Xenocrates 1162
Xenodochus 1159
Xenophantus 1164
Xenophilus 1165

Zariaspes 1166
Zephyrus 1168
Zipoetes 1169
Zoilus 1172
Zopyrion 1174